Instrument Rating

2023 Test Prep

Study and prepare for your pilot FAA Knowledge Exam

AVIATION SUPPLIES & ACADEMICS, INC.
NEWCASTLE, WASHINGTON

The FAA Knowledge Exam Questions can change throughout the year. Stay current with test changes; sign up for ASA's free email update service at **asa2fly.com/testupdate**

Instrument Rating Test Prep
2023 Edition

Aviation Supplies & Academics, Inc.
7005 132nd Place SE
Newcastle, Washington 98059
asa@asa2fly.com | 425.235.1500 | asa2fly.com

Visit **asa2fly.com/TPI** for additional information and resources related to this book.

Sample Federal Aviation Administration (FAA) questions herein contain information as of: September 2022. Stay informed of changes since the book was printed: **asa2fly.com/testupdate**

Cover photo: mark_gusev/stock.adobe.com

ASA-TP-I-23
ISBN 978-1-64425-245-1

Additional format available:
eBook PDF ISBN 978-1-64425-246-8

Also sold as *Instrument Rating Test Prep Plus*, which includes this book plus Prepware software.
ASA-TPP-I-23, ISBN 978-1-64425-257-4

Printed in the United States of America

2023 2022 5 4 3 2 1

About the Contributors

Jackie Spanitz
General Manager
Aviation Supplies & Academics, Inc.

As ASA General Manager, Jackie Spanitz oversees maintenance and development of more than 1,000 titles and pilot supplies in the ASA product line. Ms. Spanitz has worked with airman training and testing for more than 25 years, including participation in the Airman Certification Standards (ACS) development committees. Jackie holds a Bachelor of Science in Aviation Technology from Western Michigan University, a Master of Science from Embry-Riddle Aeronautical University, and Instructor and Commercial Pilot certificates. She is the author of *Guide to the Flight Review*, and the technical editor for ASA's Test Prep and FAR/AIM series.

James Johnson
Director of Aviation Training
Aviation Supplies & Academics, Inc.

James Johnson holds a Bachelor of Science in Aeronautics and minors in Aviation Safety and Airport Management from Embry-Riddle Aeronautical University. He has worked as a flight and ground instructor with both Part 141 and 61 flight schools and as a pilot for corporate flight departments and media outlets covering breaking news and traffic. As Director of Aviation Training, James provides ongoing product research, development, and support of aviation training curriculum and pilot supplies. He is a regular contributor to ASA's Learn To Fly Blog and part of the editorial team for the *Pilot's Manual* textbook series. James holds a Commercial Pilot Certificate with Instrument rating and Advanced and Instrument Ground Instructor Certificates.

Aviation Supplies & Academics, Inc. (ASA) is an industry leader in the development and sale of aviation supplies and publications for pilots, flight instructors, aviation maintenance technicians, aircraft dispatchers, air traffic controllers, flight attendants, and drone operators. We manufacture and publish more than 1,000 products and have been providing trusted and reliable training materials to the aviation industry for over 80 years. Visit **asa2fly.com** to learn more.

Stay informed with ASA online resources.

Website

asa2fly.com

Updates

asa2fly.com/testupdate

Follow, like, share.

twitter.com/asa2fly
instagram.com/asa2fly
facebook.com/asa2fly
youtube.com/asa2fly
linkedin.com/company/asa2fly

Contents

Instructions

Chapter 1 **Weather**

Chapter 2 **Weather Services**

Chapter 3 **Flight Instruments**

Chapter 4 **Navigation**

Chapter 5 **Regulations and Procedures**

Chapter 6 **Departure**

Chapter 7 **En Route**

Chapter 8 **Arrival and Approach**

Cross References

FAA Figures

Airman Knowledge Testing Supplement for Instrument Rating (FAA-CT-8080-3F)

Updates and Practice Tests

Free Test Updates for the One-Year Life Cycle of Test Prep Books

The FAA modifies tests as needed throughout the year. ASA keeps abreast of changes to the tests and posts free Test Updates on the ASA website. Before taking your test, be certain you have the most current information by visiting the ASA Test Updates webpage: **asa2fly.com/testupdate**. Additionally, sign up for free email notifications, which are sent when new Test Updates are available.

We Invite Your Feedback

After you take your FAA exam, let us know how you did. Were you prepared? Did ASA's products meet your needs and exceed your expectations? We want to continue to improve these products to ensure applicants are prepared and become safe aviators. Send your feedback to: **cfi@asa2fly.com**.

Introduction

Welcome to the Aviation Supplies & Academics, Inc., (ASA) Test Prep Series. This series has been helping pilots prepare for the FAA Knowledge Tests for more than 60 years with great success. We are confident that with proper use of this book you will score very well on your Instrument Rating test.

Begin your studies with a classroom or home-study ground school course, which will involve reading a comprehensive textbook. Visit the Reader Resources for this Test Prep (**asa2fly.com/TPI**) and become familiar with the FAA guidance materials available for this certification exam. Then use this Test Prep to prepare for your exam: read the question, select your choice for the correct answer, and then read the explanation. Use the references that conclude each explanation to identify additional resources for further study of a subject. Upon completion of your studies, take practice tests at **prepware.com** (see inside the front cover for your activation code).

The questions in this book have been arranged into chapters based on subject matter to promote better understanding, aid recall, and provide a more efficient study guide. Place emphasis on questions most likely to be included in your test (identified by the aircraft category above each question). For example, a pilot preparing for the Instrument Airplane test would focus on the questions marked "ALL" and "AIR," and a pilot preparing for the Instrument Helicopter test would focus on the questions marked "ALL" and "RTC." Applicants who are preparing for the Instrument Ground Instructor need to study all the questions. See the Description of the Tests section for more on planning your studies.

Prior to taking an FAA Airman Knowledge Test, all applicants must establish an FAA Tracking Number (FTN) by creating a profile in the Integrated Airman Certification and Rating Application (IACRA) system at **iacra.faa.gov**. Then visit **faa.psiexams.com** to register for your exam and take FAA-created practice tests to become familiar with the computer testing platform.

It is important to answer every question assigned on your FAA Knowledge Test. If in their ongoing review, the FAA decides a question has no correct answer, is no longer applicable, or is otherwise defective, your answer will be marked correct no matter which one you chose. However, you will not be given the automatic credit if you have not marked an answer. Unlike some other exams you may have taken, there is no penalty for guessing in this instance.

The FAA exams are "closed tests" which means the exact database of questions is not available to the public. The question and answer choices in this book are based on our extensive history and experience with the FAA testing and airman certification process. You might see similarly worded questions on your official FAA exam, or answer stems might be rearranged from the order you see in this book. Therefore, be sure to fully understand the intent of each question and corresponding answer while studying, rather than memorizing the letter associated with the correct response. You may be asked a question that has unfamiliar wording; studying and understanding the information in this book and the associated references will give you the tools to answer question variations with confidence.

If your study leads you to question an answer choice, we recommend you seek the assistance of a local instructor. We welcome your questions, recommendations, and concerns—send them to:

Aviation Supplies & Academics, Inc.
7005 132nd Place SE
Newcastle, WA 98059-3153
Voice: 425.235.1500 Fax: 425.235.0128
Email: cfi@asa2fly.com Website: asa2fly.com

The FAA appreciates testing experience feedback. You can contact them at:

Federal Aviation Administration
AFS-630, Airman Testing Standards Branch
PO Box 25082
Oklahoma City, OK 73125
Email: afs630comments@faa.gov

Description of the Tests

The FAA Knowledge Exam is an objective, multiple choice test. Each question can be answered by one of the three choices. Each test question is independent of the others—a correct response to one question does not depend on the correct response to another. You must score at least 70 percent to pass the test.

A significant number of the questions are "category-specific" and appear only on the airplane test or the helicopter test. The 20 question "added rating" tests are composed mostly of these category-specific questions. A 20 question "added rating" test is administered to an instrument instructor applicant (CFII) who already holds an instrument instructor rating in one category (airplane or helicopter) and wishes to meet the knowledge requirements for the other category. The category-specific questions pertain to such knowledge areas as recency of experience and weather minimums.

If you are pursuing a Powered Lift Instrument Rating, you may take either the Airplane or the Helicopter Knowledge Test. You are not required to take an additional knowledge test when you already hold an Instrument Rating.

The same questions are used for the Instrument Rating (airplane/helicopter) on the CFII (Instrument Flight Instructor) and IGI (Instrument Ground Instructor) Knowledge Tests. For those persons planning to acquire all three of these ratings within a two-year span, we recommend preparing for all three exams at the same time to save study time. However, the FAA does require all three tests be taken separately; one test session cannot be applied to all three tests.

The table below lists the number of questions and the allotted time for each test. Each question in this book is preceded by a category. Use these categories to study the content that may appear on your test. Study all the questions first, then refer to the following table, placing emphasis on those questions most likely to be included on your test (identified by the test prep category above each question number).

Test Code	Test Name	Test Prep Study	Number of Questions	Min. Age	Allotted Time (hrs)
IRA	Instrument Rating—Airplane	ALL, AIR	60	15	2.5
IRH	Instrument Rating—Helicopter	ALL, RTC	60	15	2.5
IFP	Instrument Rating—Foreign Pilot	ALL & AIR or RTC	50	N/A	2.5
FII	Instrument Flight Instructor—Airplane	ALL, AIR	50	16	2.5
FIH	Instrument Flight Instructor—Helicopter	ALL, RTC	50	16	2.5
IGI	Instrument Ground Instructor	All questions	50	16	2.5
AIF	Instrument Flight Instructor—Airplane (Added Rating)	ALL, AIR	20	16	1.0
HIF	Instrument Flight Instructor—Helicopter (Added Rating)	ALL, RTC	20	16	1.0
ICP	Airplane Instrument Rating, Canadian Conversion*	ALL, AIR	40	15	2.0
ICH	Instrument Rating Helicopter, Canadian Conversion*	ALL, RTC	40	15	2.0
IEP	Instrument Rating Airplane EU Part–FCL Conversion*	ALL, AIR	40	16	2.0

* This test focuses on U.S. regulations, airspace, ATC services and practices, communications, and emergency procedures.

Knowledge Test Registration

The FAA testing provider authorizes hundreds of test center locations that offer a full range of airman knowledge tests. For information on authorized testing centers and to register for the knowledge test, visit **faa.psiexams.com**.

When you contact a knowledge testing center, be prepared to select a test date and make payment. You may register for test(s) several weeks in advance online or by phone, and you may cancel in accordance with the testing center's cancellation policy.

Regardless of your registration method, you will need an FAA Tracking Number (FTN) prior to registering for the FAA Airman Knowledge Test. This FTN will follow you throughout your aviation career. You will obtain your FTN as part of the test registration process, by creating a profile in the Integrated Airman Certificate and Rating Application (IACRA) system at **iacra.faa.gov/IACRA**. This FTN will be printed on your Airman Knowledge Test Report (AKTR).

The test registration process includes collection of this information: name, FTN, physical address, date of birth, email address, photo identification, phone number, test authorization (credentials of the individual such as an instructor endorsement), and previous number of test attempts.

Step 1: Create a profile using the IACRA system and login to obtain your FTN.
Step 2: Register for your knowledge test with PSI by phone or online.

For more information, contact:
PSI Services LLC
844-704-1487 or examschedule@psionline.com
faa.psiexams.com

Knowledge Test Eligibility

When you take your FAA Knowledge Test, you will be required to show proper identification and have certification of your preparation for the examination, endorsed by an appropriately certified flight or ground instructor.

Ground schools will issue an endorsement when you complete their course. If you choose to home-study, you can either get an endorsement from your instructor or submit your home-study materials to an FAA Office for review and approval prior to taking the test.

Complete two Prepware practice tests with scores of 80% or higher to get your knowledge test endorsement for any pilot rating directly from ASA. Visit **asa2fly.com/prepware** or **prepware.com** for more details.

If you are taking the test again, you must present the unsatisfactory AKTR (if failed) or register after 30 days (if seeking a higher passing score). See Retesting Procedures for more details.

If a flight or ground instructor is providing your endorsement, they may adapt the following statement:

Instrument Rating Endorsement

Endorsement for aeronautical knowledge: 14 CFR §61.65(b)

I certify that *(First name, MI, Last name)* ______________________ has received the training of 14 CFR §61.65(b). I have determined he/she is prepared for the *(Test name; e.g., Instrument Rating – Airplane)* ______________________ knowledge test.

Signed ______________________ Date ____________

CFI Number ______________________ Expires ____________

FIH, FII, ICH, ICP, IEP, IFP, and IGI

Requires no instructor endorsements or other form of written authorization.

AIF and HIF

Written statement or logbook endorsement from an authorized ground or flight instructor certifying that the applicant completed an applicable ground training or home study course (14 CFR §61.185(a)(3)).

IRA and IRH

You will be required to show proper identification and the following:

1. Certificate of graduation or a statement of accomplishment certifying the satisfactory completion of the ground school portion of a course from an FAA certified pilot school within 60 days from the date of graduation. (14 CFR §61.71(a))
2. Written statement or logbook endorsement from an FAA authorized ground or flight instructor certifying that the applicant is prepared to take the required knowledge test. (14 CFR §61.65(a)(4))

Acceptable Materials

The applicant may use the following aids, reference materials, and test materials during the test, as long as the material does not include actual test questions or answers.

Acceptable Materials	Unacceptable Materials	Notes
Supplement book provided by proctor.	Written materials that are handwritten, printed, or electronic.	Testing centers may provide calculators and/or deny the use of personal calculators.
All models of aviation-oriented calculators or small electronic calculators that perform only arithmetic functions.	Electronic calculators incorporating permanent or continuous type memory circuits without erasure capability.	Test proctor may prohibit the use of your calculator if he or she is unable to determine the calculator's erasure capability.
Calculators with simple programmable memories, which allow addition to, subtraction from, or retrieval of one number from the memory; or simple functions, such as square root and percentages.	Magnetic cards, magnetic tapes, modules, computer chips, or any other device upon which pre-written programs or information related to the test can be stored and retrieved.	Printouts of data must be surrendered at the completion of the test if the calculator incorporates this design feature.
Scales, straight-edges, protractors, plotters, navigation computers, blank log sheets, holding pattern entry aids, and electronic or mechanical calculators that are directly related to the test.	Dictionaries.	Before, and upon completion of the test, while in the presence of the test proctor, actuate the ON/OFF switch or RESET button, and perform any other function that ensures erasure of any data stored in memory circuits.
Manufacturer's permanently inscribed instructions on the front and back of such aids, such as formulas, conversions, regulations, signals, weather data, holding pattern diagrams, frequencies, weight and balance formulas, and ATC procedures.	Any booklet or manual containing instructions related to use of test aids.	Test proctor makes the final determination regarding aids, reference materials, and test materials.

Testing Procedures for Applicants Requesting Special Accommodations

If you are an applicant with a learning or reading disability, you may request approval from the local FAA office to take an airman knowledge test, using the special accommodations procedures outlined in the most current version of FAA Order 8080.6 Conduct of Airman Knowledge Tests.

Prior to approval of any option, the FAA Aviation Safety Inspector must advise you of the regulatory certification requirement of being able to read, write, speak, and understand the English language.

Test Reports

Your test will be graded immediately upon completion and your score will display on the computer screen. You will receive your Airman Knowledge Test Report (AKTR), which will state your score. See sample AKTR on next page.

Visit **faa.psiexams.com** to request a duplicate or replacement AKTR due to loss or destruction.

Airman Knowledge Test Reports are valid for 24 calendar months preceding the month you complete the practical test. If the AKTR expires before completion of the practical test, you must retake the knowledge test.

The AKTR lists the Airman Certification Standard (ACS) code (if an Airman Certification Standard is available for the certificate and rating specific to the test) or Learning Statement Code (LSC) (if a Practical Test Standard is in effect for the certificate and rating specific to the test) for questions answered incorrectly. The total number of ASCs/LSCs shown on the AKTR is not necessarily an indication of the total number of questions answered incorrectly. Study these knowledge areas to improve your understanding of the subject matter. See Cross-Reference B in the back of this book for a listing of ASCs/LSCs and their associated questions.

Your instructor is required to provide instruction on each of the knowledge areas listed on your AKTR and to complete an endorsement of this instruction. You must present this to the examiner prior to taking the practical test. During the oral portion of the practical test, the examiner is required to evaluate the noted areas of deficiency.

Retesting Procedures

Applicants retesting ***after failure*** are required to submit the applicable AKTR indicating failure, along with an endorsement (on the test report) from an authorized instructor, who gave the applicant the additional training, certifying the applicant is competent to pass the test. The original failed AKTR and retest endorsement presented as authorization shall be retained by the proctor and attached to the applicable sign-in/out log. The latest test taken will reflect the official score.

Applicants retesting ***in an attempt to achieve a higher passing score*** may retake the same test for a better grade after 30 days. The latest test taken will reflect the official score. Applicants are required to submit the original applicable AKTR indicating previous passing score to the testing center prior to testing. Testing center personnel must collect and destroy this report prior to issuing the new test report.

Cheating or Other Unauthorized Conduct

Computer testing centers must follow strict security procedures to avoid test compromise. These procedures are established by the FAA and are covered in FAA Order 8080.6 Conduct of Airman Knowledge Tests. The FAA has directed testing centers to terminate a test at any time a test proctor suspects a cheating incident has occurred. An FAA investigation will then be conducted. If the investigation determines that cheating or unauthorized conduct has occurred, then any airman certificate or rating that you hold may be revoked, and you will be prohibited for one year from applying for or taking any test for a certificate or rating under 14 CFR Part 61.

U.S. DEPARTMENT OF TRANSPORTATION
Federal Aviation Administration
Airman Knowledge Test Report

NAME: TAYLOR SMITH

FAA TRACKING NUMBER (FTN): C1234567 **EXAM ID:** 98765432109876543

EXAM: Instrument Rating – Airplane (IRA)

EXAM DATE: 09/15/2022 **EXAM SITE:** ABC12345

SCORE: 88% **GRADE:** Pass **TAKE:** 1

The Airman Certification Standards (ACS) codes listed below represent incorrectly answered questions. These ACS codes and their associated Areas of Operation/Tasks/Elements may be found in the appropriate ACS document at http://www.faa.gov/training_testing/testing/acs.

A single code may represent more than one incorrect response.

IR.I.B.K2 IR.I.C.K2 IR.I.C.K3a IR.II.B.K1a IR.II.B.R1 IR.IV.A.K1 IR.VI.E.K1 IR.VII.A.K1

EXPIRATION DATE: 09/30/2024

DO NOT LOSE THIS REPORT

- -

AUTHORIZED INSTRUCTOR'S STATEMENT: (if applicable)

On __________ (date) I gave the above named applicant _____ hours of additional instruction, covering each subject area shown to be deficient, and consider the applicant competent to pass the knowledge test.

Name ____

Cert. No. ____ *(print clearly)*

Type of instructor certificate ____

Signature ____

FRAUDULENT ALTERATION OF THIS FORM BY ANY PERSON IS A BASIS FOR SUSPENSION OR REVOCATION OF ANY CERTIFICATES OR RATINGS HELD BY THAT PERSON.
ISSUED BY: PSI Services LLC
FEDERAL AVIATION ADMINISTRATION

THIS INFORMATION IS PROTECTED BY THE PRIVACY ACT. FOR OFFICIAL USE ONLY.

Sample Airman Knowledge Test Report

Test-Taking Tips

Prior to launching the actual test, the test proctor's testing software will provide you with an opportunity to practice navigating through the test. This practice (or tutorial) session may include a "sample" question(s). These sample questions have no relation to the content of the test, but are meant to familiarize you with the look and feel of the system screens, including selecting an answer, marking a question for later review, time remaining for the test, and other features of the testing software.

Follow these time-proven tips, which will help you develop a skillful, smooth approach to test-taking:

- Visit **faa.psiexams.com** to take a small sample test to become familiar with the latest PSI exam interface you will see on your actual FAA knowledge test.
- Be careful to fully understand the intent of each question and corresponding answer while studying, rather than memorize the A, B, C answer choice—answer stems may appear in a different order than you studied and have some wording differences.
- Remember to bring a sign-off from an instructor, photo I.D., the testing fee, calculator, flight computer (ASA's E6-B or CX-3 Flight Computer), plotter, magnifying glass, and a sharp pointer, such as a safety pin.
- Your first action when you sit down should be to write any formulas and information you can remember from your study on the scratch paper they will provide. Remember, some of the formulas may be on your E6-B.
- Read each question carefully before looking at the possible answers. You should clearly understand the problem before attempting to solve it.
- After formulating an answer, determine which answer choice corresponds the closest with your answer. The answer chosen should completely resolve the problem.
- From the answer choices given, it may appear that there is more than one possible answer. However, there is only one answer that is correct and complete. The other answers are either incomplete, erroneous, or represent popular misconceptions.
- Answer each question in accordance with the latest regulations and guidance publications.
- If a certain question is difficult for you, tag it for REVIEW and proceed to the other questions. After you answer the less difficult questions, return to those which you tagged and answer them. Be sure to untag these questions once you have answered them. The review marking procedure will be explained to you prior to starting the test. Although the computer should alert you to unanswered questions, make sure every question has an answer recorded. This will allow you to use the available time to your maximum advantage.
- Perform each math calculation twice to confirm your answer. If adding or subtracting a column of numbers, reverse your direction the second time to reduce the possibility of error.
- When solving a calculation problem, select the answer nearest to your solution.
- Remember that information is provided in the Legends and Figures contained within the Airman Knowledge Testing Supplement (FAA-CT-8080 document) you'll be using during the test.
- Remember to answer every question, even the ones with no completely correct answer, to ensure the FAA gives you credit for a bad question.
- Take your time and be thorough but relaxed. Take a minute off every half-hour or so to relax your brain and body. Get a drink of water halfway through the test.

Instrument Rating Eligibility Requirements

If you are pursuing an Instrument Rating, you should review 14 CFR §61.23 "Medical Certificates: Requirement and Duration," §61.35 "Knowledge Test: Prerequisites and Passing Grades," and §61.65 "Instrument rating requirements."

To be eligible for an Instrument Rating in the Airplane category, a pilot must:

- Hold at least a current Private Pilot Certificate with an aircraft rating appropriate to the Instrument rating sought.
- Be able to read, speak, write, and understand the English language.
- Score at least 70 percent on the FAA Knowledge Test on the appropriate subjects.
- Pass an oral and flight check on the subjects and maneuvers outlined in the Instrument Airman Certification Standards (#ASA-ACS-8).
- Have a total of 50 hours cross-country flight time as pilot-in-command, of which at least 10 hours must be in airplanes for an airplane instrument rating (each flight must have a landing at least 50 NM from the departure point).
- Have 40 hours of simulated or actual instrument time (no more than 30 hours may be instruction in a ground trainer if following a Part 142 program, and no more than 20 hours if not following a Part 142 program).
- Have 15 hours instrument flight instruction by an authorized flight instructor.
- Must have received ground instruction or logged home-study pertaining to IFR regulations, procedures, various methods of navigation, weather report procurement and use, and the *Aeronautical Information Manual*, among others. A complete list of requirements can be found in 14 CFR §61.65.

Knowledge Exam References

The FAA references the following documents to write the FAA Knowledge Exam questions. You should be familiar with all of these as part of your ground school studies, which you should complete before starting test preparation.

FAA-H-8083-1 *Aircraft Weight and Balance Handbook*

FAA-H-8083-2 *Risk Management Handbook*

FAA-H-8083-3 *Airplane Flying Handbook*

FAA-H-8083-13 *Glider Flying Handbook*

FAA-H-8083-15 *Instrument Flying Handbook*

FAA-H-8083-16 *Instrument Procedures Handbook*

FAA-H-8083-21 *Helicopter Flying Handbook*

FAA-H-8083-25 *Pilot's Handbook of Aeronautical Knowledge*

FAA-S-ACS-8 *Instrument Rating Airman Certification Standards, Airplane*

FAA-S-8081-4 *Instrument Rating Practical Test Standards, Helicopter Powered Lift*

FAA-S-8081-9 *Instrument Flight Instructor Practical Test Standards*

AC 00-6 *Aviation Weather*

AC 00-45 *Aviation Weather Services*

AC 00-54 *Pilot Wind Shear Guide*

AC 60-28 *English Language Skill Standard for an FAA Certificate Issued Under 14 CFR Parts 61, 63, 65, and 107*

AC 91-74 *Pilot Guide: Flight in Icing Conditions*

Chart Supplements U.S.

Low Altitude Enroute Chart

U.S. Terminal Procedures

Aeronautical Information Manual (AIM)

14 CFR Parts 1, 61, 68, 91, 97

49 CFR Part 830 (NTSB)

Visit **asa2fly.com** for these and many more titles and pilot supplies for your aviation endeavors.
Visit **asa2fly.com/TPI** for reader resources useful to instrument pilots.

Acronyms

For reference, acronyms appearing in this book are defined below.

AC	Convective Outlook
ADS-B	Automatic Dependent Surveillance–Broadcast
AGL	above ground level
AHRS	attitude and heading reference system
AIM	Aeronautical Information Manual
AIRMET	airman's meteorological information
ALD	available landing distance
AOA	angle of attack
ASR	airport surveillance radar
ATC	air traffic control
AWC	Aviation Weather Center
CAS	calibrated airspeed
CAT	clear air turbulence
CDI	course deviation indicator
CONUS	continental United States
COP	changeover point
DA	decision altitude
DH	decision height
DME	distance measuring equipment
DP	departure procedure
EAC	expect approach clearance
EAS	equivalent airspeed
EFC	expect further clearance
ELT	emergency locator transmitter
ETA	estimated time of arrival
FA	area forecast
FAF	final approach fix
FAP	final approach point
FAR	Federal Aviation Regulations
FB	winds and temperatures aloft forecast
FL	flight level
FSDO	Flight Standards District Office
FSS	Flight Service Station
GFA	Graphical Forecast for Aviation
GPS	Global Positioning System
GS	glide slope
HAT	height above touchdown
HIRL	high intensity runway lights
HSI	horizontal situation indicator
IAF	instrument approach fix
IAP	instrument approach procedure
IAS	indicated airspeed
IFR	instrument flight rules
ILS	instrument landing system
IM	inner marker (ILS)
IMC	instrument meteorological conditions
ISA	International Standard Atmosphere
KCAS	knots calibrated airspeed
KIAS	knots indicated airspeed
LAHSO	land and hold short operations
LDA	Localizer-Type Directional Aid
LMM	locator middle marker (ILS)
LNAV	lateral navigation
LOC	localizer (ILS)
LOM	locator outer marker (ILS)
LPV	localizer performance with vertical guidance
MAWP	missed approach waypoint
MCA	minimum crossing altitude
MDA	minimum decision altitude
MEA	minimum enroute altitude
METAR	aviation routine weather report
MHA	minimum holding altitude
MM	middle marker (ILS)
MOA	Military Operations Area
MOCA	minimum obstacle clearance altitude
MSA	minimum sector altitude
MSL	mean sea level
NAVAID	navigational aid
NDB	non-directional beacon
NM	nautical mile
NOTAM	Notice to Air Missions
NTSB	National Transportation Safety Board
OAT	outside air temperature
OBS	omni bearing selector

OCS	obstacle clearance surface
ODP	obstacle departure procedure
OM	outer marker (ILS)
PAPI	precision approach path indicator
PAR	precision approach radar
PFD	primary flight display
PIC	pilot-in-command
PIREP	pilot report
PRM	precision runway monitoring
PT	procedure turn
RAIM	receiver autonomous integrity monitoring
REIL	runway end identifier lights
RNAV	area navigation
RVR	runway visual range
SDF	Simplified Directional Facility
SIAP	standard instrument approach procedure
SIGMET	significant meteorological information
SM	statute mile
STAR	standard terminal arrival route
TAA	technically advanced aircraft
TACAN	tactical air navigation system
TAF	terminal aerodrome forecast
TAS	true airspeed
TCH	threshold crossing height
TDZE	touchdown zone elevation
TPP	Terminal Procedures Publication
UHF	ultra high frequency
UTC	Coordinated Universal Time
VASI	visual approach slope indicator
VDA	vertical descent angle
VDP	visual descent point
VFR	visual flight rules
VMC	visual meteorological conditions
VNAV	vertical navigation
VOR	VHF Omnidirectional Range
VORTAC	VOR-TACAN navigation system
VOT	VOR Test Facility
VSI	vertical speed indicator
WAAS	Wide Area Augmentation System
WW	severe weather watch bulletin

ASA Test Prep Layout

Sample FAA questions have been sorted into chapters according to subject matter. Within each chapter, similar questions are grouped together following introductory chapter text. Figures referenced in the chapter text are numbered with the appropriate chapter number, e.g., "Figure 1-1" is Chapter 1's first chapter text figure.

Some sample FAA questions refer to Figures or Legends immediately following the question number, e.g., "4201. (Refer to Figure 14.)." These are FAA Figures and Legends from the Airman Knowledge Testing Supplement (FAA-CT-8080-3F) that can be found at the back of this book. This supplement will be provided to you as a separate booklet when you take your FAA test.

Following each sample FAA test question is ASA's explanation in italics. The last line of the explanation contains a Learning Statement Code (LSC), for those tests referencing an FAA Practical Test Standard (PTS), or Airman Certification Standards (ACS) code, for those tests with an ACS, as well as a reference for further study. Some questions include an explanation for the incorrect answers for added clarity. When you encounter a difficult question, find the LSC or ACS code in Cross-Reference B, and then look for material relating to the subject description within the given reference(s). Refer to Cross-Reference B for more information on how to use LSCs or ACS codes for effective studying.

Answers to each question are found at the bottom of each page.

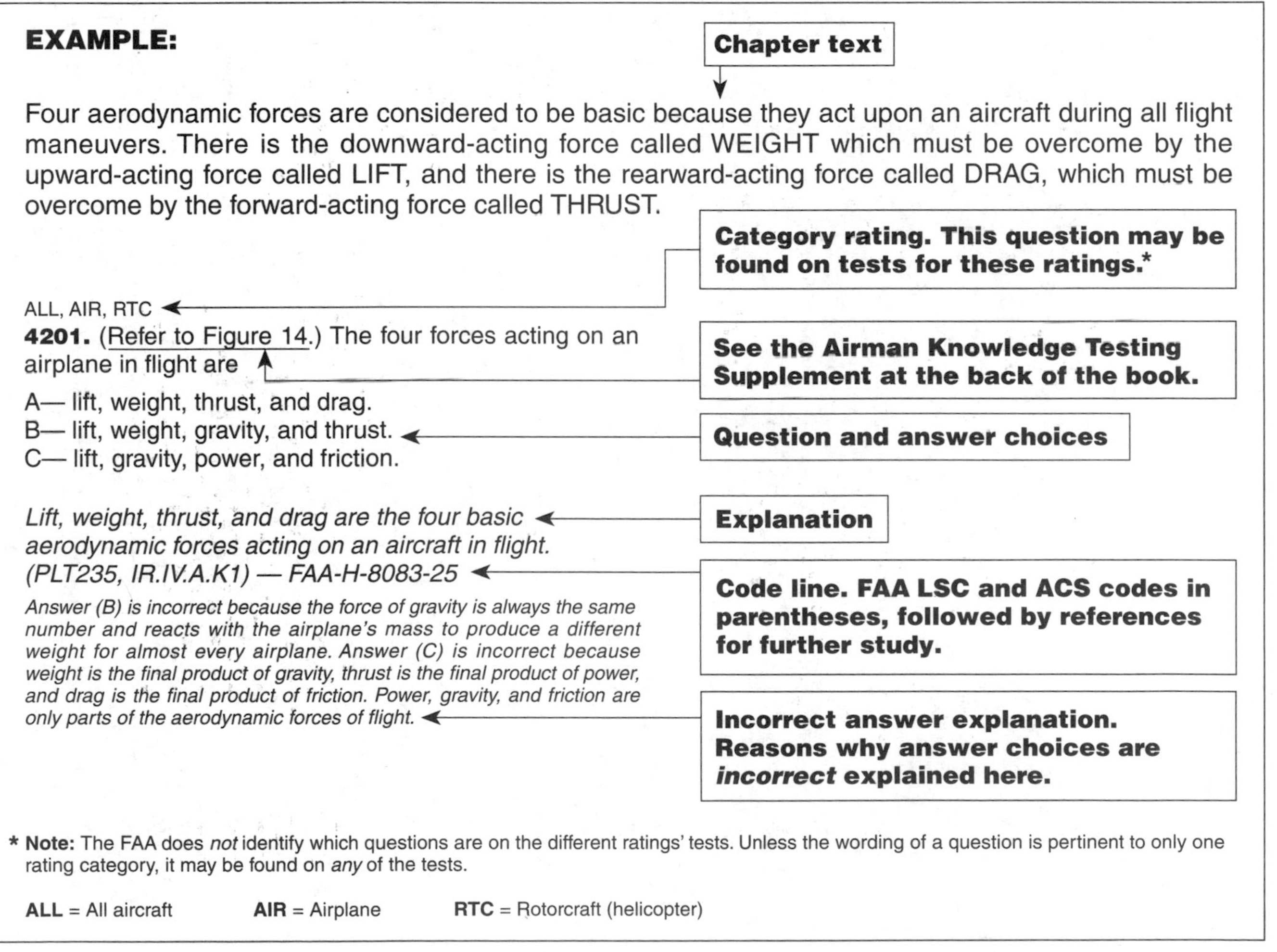

Chapter 1
Weather

The Earth's Atmosphere

We classify the atmosphere into layers, or spheres, by characteristics exhibited in these layers. The troposphere is the layer from the surface to an average altitude of about 7 miles (37,000 feet). It is characterized by an overall decrease of temperature with increasing altitude. The height of the troposphere varies with latitude and season. It slopes from about 20,000 feet over the poles to about 65,000 feet over the Equator; and it is higher in summer than in winter.

At the top of the troposphere is the tropopause, a very thin layer marking the boundary between the troposphere and the layer above. It is characterized by an abrupt change in temperature lapse rate.

Above the tropopause is the stratosphere. This layer is typified by relatively small changes in temperature with height except for a warming trend near the top. See Figure 1-1.

ALL
4097. A characteristic of the stratosphere is

A—an overall decrease of temperature with an increase in altitude.
B—a relatively even base altitude of approximately 35,000 feet.
C—relatively small changes in temperature with an increase in altitude.

Above the tropopause is the stratosphere. This layer is typified by relatively small changes in temperature with height except for a warming trend near the top. (PLT203, IR.I.B.K3a) — AC 00-6

Answer (A) is incorrect because temperature increases (not decreases) with an increase in altitude. Answer (B) is incorrect because the stratosphere fluctuates in altitude, as the base is higher at the equator compared to the poles.

ALL
4154. The average height of the troposphere in the middle latitudes is

A—20,000 feet.
B—25,000 feet.
C—37,000 feet.

The height of the troposphere varies with latitude and seasons. It slopes from about 20,000 feet over the poles, to an average of 37,000 feet over the mid-latitudes, to about 65,000 feet over the equator, and it is higher in summer than in winter. (PLT203, IR.I.B.K3a) — AC 00-6

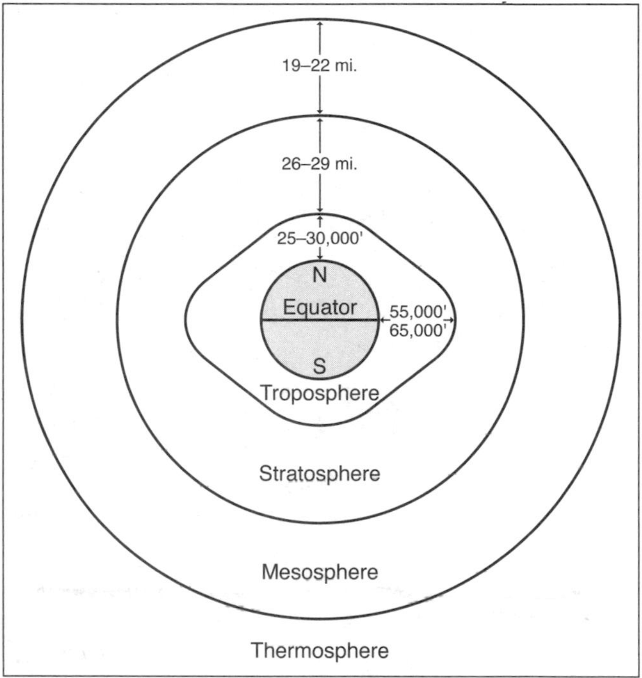

Figure 1-1. Layers of the atmosphere

ALL
4227. Which feature is associated with the tropopause?

A—Absence of wind and turbulent conditions.
B—Absolute upper limit of cloud formation.
C—Abrupt change in temperature lapse rate.

Temperature over the tropical tropopause increases with height, but temperatures over the polar tropopause remain almost constant. An abrupt change in temperature lapse rate characterizes the tropopause. (PLT203, IR.I.B.K3a) — AC 00-6

Answer (A) is incorrect because the winds are usually very strong in the tropopause. Answer (B) is incorrect because clouds can form above the tropopause.

Answers

4097 [C] 4154 [C] 4227 [C]

High Altitude Weather

The jet stream is a river of high speed winds (50 knots or more) associated with the tropopause. The location of the jet stream changes seasonally. In the winter, the jet stream moves south and increases in velocity. During the summer, the jet stream moves north and slows.

ALL
4155. A jet stream is defined as wind of

A—30 knots or greater.
B—40 knots or greater.
C—50 knots or greater.

A jetstream occurs in an area of intensified temperature gradients characteristic of the break in the tropopause. The concentrated winds, by arbitrary definition, must be 50 knots or greater to classify as a jetstream. (PLT302, IR.I.B.K3b) — AC 00-6

ALL
4168. The strength and location of the jet stream is normally

A—stronger and farther north in the winter.
B—weaker and farther north in the summer.
C—stronger and farther north in the summer.

In mid-latitudes, wind speed in the jetstream averages considerably stronger in winter than in summer. Also the jet shifts farther south in winter than in summer. (PLT302, IR.I.B.K3b) — AC 00-6

Temperature

The major source of all weather is the sun. Changes or variations of weather patterns are caused by the unequal heating of the Earth's surface. In aviation, surface and aloft temperature is measured in degrees Celsius (°C).

Standard temperature is 15°C at sea level. To calculate International Standard Atmosphere (ISA), use the average lapse rate of 2°C per 1,000 feet.

ALL
4096. The primary cause of all changes in the Earth's weather is

A—variation of solar energy received by the Earth's regions.
B—changes in air pressure over the Earth's surface.
C—movement of the air masses.

Every physical process of weather is accompanied by or is the result of a heat exchange. Differences in solar energy create temperature variations. These temperature variations create forces that drive the atmosphere in its endless motion. (PLT510, IR.I.B.K3a) — AC 00-6

Answer (B) is incorrect because changes in air pressure are due to temperature variations. Answer (C) is incorrect because movement of air masses is a result of varying temperatures and pressures.

ALL
4095. How much colder than standard temperature is the forecast temperature at 9,000 feet, as indicated in the following excerpt from the winds and temperature aloft forecast?

FT	6000	9000
	0737-04	1043-10

A—3°C.
B—10°C.
C—7°C.

According to the winds and temperatures aloft forecast, the temperature is -10°C at 9,000 feet. Using the average lapse rate of 2°C per 1,000 feet, the temperature change from sea level to 9,000 feet is 18°C. Standard sea level temperature is 15°C. Subtract 18°C from 15°C to get -3°C. Compared to the winds and temperatures aloft forecast for 9,000 feet, the difference is 7°C (10–3). (PLT492, IR.I.B.K3a) — AC 00-45

Answer (A) is incorrect because 3°C is the standard temperature at 9,000 feet, which is not what the question is asking for. Answer (B) is incorrect because 10°C is the given temperature at 9,000 feet, which is not what the question is asking for.

Answers

4155 [C] 4168 [B] 4096 [A] 4095 [C]

ALL

4113. If the air temperature is +8°C at an elevation of 1,350 feet and a standard (average) temperature lapse rate exists, what will be the approximate freezing level?

A—3,350 feet MSL.
B—5,350 feet MSL.
C—9,350 feet MSL.

Temperature normally decreases with increasing altitude throughout the troposphere. This decrease of temperature with altitude is defined as lapse rate. The average decrease of temperature (average lapse rate) in the troposphere is 2°C per 1,000 feet. An 8°C loss is necessary to reach 0°C, or freezing, in this situation. At 2°/1,000 feet the amount of altitude gain necessary would be:

1. 8°C ÷ 2 = 4 or 4,000 ft

2. 1,350 ft MSL (altitude at +8°C)
+ 4,000 ft (altitude gain necessary to reach 0°C)
5,350 ft MSL (approximate freezing level)

(PLT492, IR.I.B.K3a) — AC 00-6

ALL

4094. A common type of ground or surface based temperature inversion is that which is produced by

A—warm air being lifted rapidly aloft in the vicinity of mountainous terrain.
B—the movement of colder air over warm air, or the movement of warm air under cold air.
C—ground radiation on clear, cool nights when the wind is light.

An increase in temperature with altitude is defined as an inversion. An inversion often develops near the ground on clear, cool nights when wind is light. The ground radiates and cools much faster than the overlying air. Air in contact with the ground becomes cold while the temperature a few hundred feet above changes very little. Thus, temperature increases with height. (PLT301, IR.I.B.K3c) — AC 00-6

Answer (A) is incorrect because when warm air is lifted, an unstable situation occurs, and a temperature inversion requires stable conditions. Answer (B) is incorrect because warm air over cold air constitutes an inversion (not cold air over warm air).

ALL

4112. The most frequent type of ground- or surface-based temperature inversion is that produced by

A—radiation on a clear, relatively still night.
B—warm air being lifted rapidly aloft in the vicinity of mountainous terrain.
C—the movement of colder air under warm air, or the movement of warm air over cold air.

An inversion often develops near the ground on clear, cool nights when wind is light. The ground radiates and cools much faster than the overlying air. Air in contact with the ground becomes cold while the temperature a few hundred feet above changes very little. Thus, temperature increases with height. (PLT301, IR.I.B.K3c) — AC 00-6

Answer (B) is incorrect because it describes orographic lifting. Answer (C) is incorrect because it describes fronts.

ALL

4114. What feature is associated with a temperature inversion?

A—A stable layer of air.
B—An unstable layer of air.
C—Air mass thunderstorms.

A temperature inversion occurs when the temperature increases with altitude. A stable layer of air is characterized by warmer air lying above colder air. With an inversion, the layer is stable and convection is suppressed. (PLT301, IR.I.B.K3c) — AC 00-6

Answer (B) is incorrect because unstable air is characterized by a decrease in temperature with an increase in altitude. Answer (C) is incorrect because air mass thunderstorms are characteristic of unstable conditions.

ALL

4125. A temperature inversion will normally form only

A—in stable air.
B—in unstable air.
C—when a stratiform layer merges with a cumuliform mass.

If the temperature increases with altitude through a layer (an inversion), the layer is stable and convection is suppressed. Air may be unstable beneath the inversion. (PLT301, IR.I.B.K3c) — AC 00-6

Answer (B) is incorrect because unstable air has warmer air below colder air. Answer (C) is incorrect because when a stratiform layer merges with a cumuliform mass it is associated with a cold front occlusion.

Answers

4113 [B] 4094 [C] 4112 [A] 4114 [A] 4125 [A]

ALL

4200. Which weather conditions should be expected beneath a low-level temperature inversion layer when the relative humidity is high?

A—Smooth air and poor visibility due to fog, haze, or low clouds.

B—Light wind shear and poor visibility due to haze and light rain.

C—Turbulent air and poor visibility due to fog, low stratus-type clouds, and showery precipitation.

A ground-based inversion favors poor visibility by trapping fog, smoke, and other restrictions into low levels of the atmosphere. Wind just above the inversion may be relatively strong. A wind shear zone develops between the calm and the stronger winds above. Eddies in the shear zone cause airspeed fluctuations as an aircraft climbs or descends through the inversion. (PLT301, IR.I.B.K3c) — AC 00-6

Answer (B) is incorrect because wind shear may be expected within (not beneath) a low-level temperature inversion. Answer (C) is incorrect because inversions cause steady precipitation and create a stable layer of air, thus making it smooth (not turbulent).

Wind

The rules in the Northern Hemisphere are:

1. Air circulates in a clockwise direction around a high pressure system.
2. Air circulates in a counterclockwise direction around a low pressure system.
3. The closer the isobars are together, the stronger the wind speed.
4. Due to surface friction (up to about 2,000 feet AGL), surface winds do not exactly parallel the isobars, but move outward from the center of the high toward lower pressure.
5. Coriolis force is at a right angle to wind direction and directly proportional to wind speed. The force deflects air to the right in the Northern Hemisphere.

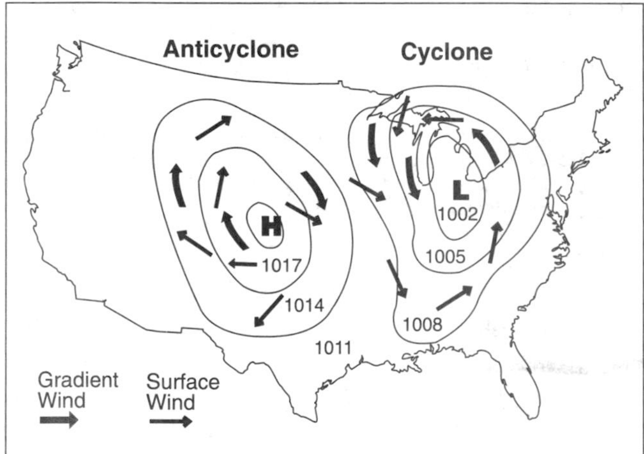

Figure 1-2. Gradient and surface wind

ALL

4105. What causes surface winds to flow across the isobars at an angle rather than parallel to the isobars?

A—Coriolis force.

B—Surface friction.

C—The greater density of the air at the surface.

Friction between the wind and the surface slows the wind. As frictional force slows the wind speed, Coriolis force decreases. However, friction does not affect pressure gradient force. Pressure gradient and Coriolis forces are no longer in balance. The stronger pressure gradient force turns the wind at an angle across the isobars toward lower pressure until the three forces balance. The angle of surface wind to isobars is about 10° over water, increasing with roughness of terrain. (PLT516, IR.I.B.K3b) — AC 00-6

Answer (A) is incorrect because as wind decreases, so does the Coriolis force. Answer (C) is incorrect because the density of the air has little effect on the relation to the winds and the isobars.

Answers

4200 [A]   4105 [B]

ALL
4106. Winds at 5,000 feet AGL on a particular flight are southwesterly while most of the surface winds are southerly. This difference in direction is primarily due to

A—a stronger pressure gradient at higher altitudes.
B—friction between the wind and the surface.
C—stronger Coriolis force at the surface.

Surface winds and winds at altitude can differ due to friction. Friction between the wind and the surface slows the wind. (PLT516, IR.I.B.K3b) — AC 00-6

Answer (A) is incorrect because the pressure gradient is relatively uniform at altitudes. Answer (C) is incorrect because the winds are weaker at the surface, therefore the Coriolis force is weaker.

ALL
4107. What relationship exists between the winds at 2,000 feet above the surface and the surface winds?

A—The winds at 2,000 feet and the surface winds flow in the same direction, but the surface winds are weaker due to friction.
B—The winds at 2,000 feet tend to parallel the isobars while the surface winds cross the isobars at an angle toward lower pressure and are weaker.
C—The surface winds tend to veer to the right of the winds at 2,000 feet and are usually weaker.

Close to the earth, wind direction is modified by the contours over which it passes and wind speed is reduced by friction with the surface. Also, the winds at the surface are at an angle across the isobars due to the stronger pressure gradient. At levels 2,000 feet above the surface, the speed is greater and the direction is usually parallel to the isobars. (PLT516, IR.I.B.K3b) — AC 00-6

Answer (A) is incorrect because the winds at 2,000 feet and those at the surface flow in different directions due to the Coriolis force being weaker at the surface. Answer (C) is incorrect because surface winds do not veer to the right of the winds at 2,000 feet, the winds at 2,000 feet veer to the right of the surface winds.

ALL
4108. Which force, in the Northern Hemisphere, acts at a right angle to the wind and deflects it to the right until parallel to the isobars?

A—Centrifugal.
B—Pressure gradient.
C—Coriolis.

Coriolis force is at a right angle to wind direction and directly proportional to wind speed. In the Northern Hemisphere, the air is deflected to the right. (PLT510, IR.I.B.K3b) — AC 00-6

Answer (A) is incorrect because centrifugal force acts outwardly to any moving objective in a curved path. Answer (B) is incorrect because pressure gradient causes the wind to move perpendicular to the isobars, but it is then deflected by Coriolis force.

Moisture and Precipitation

Air contains moisture (water vapor). The water vapor content of air can be expressed in two different ways: relative humidity and dew point.

Relative humidity relates the actual water vapor present in the air to that which could be present. Temperature largely determines the maximum amount of water vapor the air can hold. Warm air can hold more water vapor than cold air can. Air with 100 percent relative humidity is said to be saturated, and air with less than 100 percent is unsaturated.

Dew point is the temperature to which air must be cooled to become saturated by the water already present in the air.

When water vapor condenses on large objects, such as leaves, windshields, or airplanes, it will form dew. When it condenses on microscopic particles, such as salt, dust, or combustion by-products (condensation nuclei), it will form clouds or fog.

If the temperature and dew point spread is small and decreasing, condensation is about to occur. If the temperature is above freezing, fog or low clouds will be most likely to develop.

The growth rate of precipitation is enhanced by upward currents. Cloud particles collide and merge into a larger drop in the more rapid growth process. This process produces larger precipitation particles and does so more rapidly than the simple condensation growth process. Upward currents also support larger drops.

Answers

4106 [B] 4107 [B] 4108 [C]

If wet snow is encountered at your flight altitude, then the temperature is above freezing at your altitude. Since melting snow has been encountered, the freezing level must be at a higher altitude.

The presence of ice pellets at the surface is evidence that there is freezing rain at a higher altitude. Rain falling through colder air may become supercooled, freezing on impact as freezing rain; or it may freeze during its descent, falling as ice pellets.

ALL
4104. Clouds, fog, or dew will always form when

A—water vapor condenses.
B—water vapor is present.
C—the temperature and dew point are equal.

When temperature reaches the dew point, water vapor can no longer remain invisible but is forced to condense, becoming visible on the ground as dew, appearing in the air as fog or clouds, or falling to the earth as rain. (PLT512, IR.I.B.K3f) — AC 00-6

Answer (B) is incorrect because there is almost always water vapor present. Answer (C) is incorrect because even when the temperature and dew point are equal (100% humidity), sufficient condensation nuclei must be present for water vapor to condense.

ALL
4101. To which meteorological condition does the term "dew point" refer?

A—The temperature to which air must be cooled to become saturated.
B—The temperature at which condensation and evaporation are equal.
C—The temperature at which dew will always form.

Dew point is the temperature to which air must be cooled to become saturated by the water vapor already present in the air. Aviation weather reports normally include the air temperature and dew point temperature. Dew point, when related to air temperature, reveals qualitatively how close the air is to saturation. (PLT512, IR.I.B.K3c) — AC 00-6

Answer (B) is incorrect because it takes higher temperatures for water to evaporate, and lower temperatures for water vapor to condense. Answer (C) is incorrect because the formation of dew depends upon the temperatures of the surface and the relative humidity.

ALL
4103. The amount of water vapor which air can hold largely depends on

A—relative humidity.
B—air temperature.
C—stability of air.

Temperature largely determines the maximum amount of water vapor air can hold. Warm air can hold more water vapor than cool air. (PLT512, IR.I.B.K3c) — AC 00-6

Answer (A) is incorrect because relative humidity does not determine the amount of water vapor air can hold, but rather measures the existing amount of water vapor compared to the amount that could be held. Answer (C) is incorrect because stability of air pertains to the temperature lapse rate, not moisture.

ALL
4159. What enhances the growth rate of precipitation?

A—Advective action.
B—Upward currents.
C—Cyclonic movement.

Cloud particles collide and merge into a larger drop in the more rapid growth process. This process produces larger precipitation particles and does so more rapidly than the simple condensation growth process. Upward currents enhance the growth rate and also support larger drops. (PLT344, IR.I.B.K3d) — AC 00-6

ALL
4102. What temperature condition is indicated if wet snow is encountered at your flight altitude?

A—The temperature is above freezing at your altitude.
B—The temperature is below freezing at your altitude.
C—You are flying from a warm air mass into a cold air mass.

Wet snow at your altitude means that the temperature is above freezing since the snow has begun to melt. For snow to form, water vapor must go from the vapor state to the solid state (known as sublimation) with the temperature below freezing. Since melting snow has been encountered, the freezing level must be at a higher altitude. (PLT512, IR.I.B.K3c) — AC 00-6

Answer (B) is incorrect because wet snow requires a temperature above freezing (not below). Answer (C) is incorrect because the temperature is colder above you, but not necessarily in front of you.

Answers

4104 [A] 4101 [A] 4103 [B] 4159 [B] 4102 [A]

ALL
4099. The presence of ice pellets at the surface is evidence that

A—there are thunderstorms in the area.
B—a cold front has passed.
C—there is freezing rain at a higher altitude.

Rain falling through colder air may become supercooled, freezing on impact as freezing rain; or it may freeze during its descent, falling as ice pellets. Ice pellets always indicate freezing rain at higher altitude. (PLT344, IR.I.B.K3i) — AC 00-6

Answers (A) and (B) are incorrect because thunderstorms and cold fronts do not necessarily cause ice pellets.

ALL
4161. Which precipitation type normally indicates freezing rain at higher altitudes?

A—Snow.
B—Hail.
C—Ice pellets.

Ice pellets always indicate freezing rain at higher altitudes. (PLT344, IR.I.B.K3i) — AC 00-6

Answer (A) is incorrect because snow indicates that the air above is already below freezing. Answer (B) is incorrect because hail indicates instability where supercooled water droplets have begun to freeze.

Air Masses, Fronts, and Stability

Atmospheric stability is defined as the resistance of the atmosphere to vertical motion. A stable atmosphere resists any upward or downward movement. An unstable atmosphere allows an upward or downward disturbance to grow into a vertical (convective) current.

Characteristics of unstable air are: cumuliform clouds, showery precipitation, rough air (turbulence), and good visibility, except in blowing obstructions. Characteristics of stable air are: stratiform clouds and fog, continuous precipitation, smooth air, and fair to poor visibility in haze and smoke.

Determining the stability of the atmosphere requires measuring the difference between the actual existing (ambient) temperature lapse rate of a given parcel of air and the dry adiabatic (3°C per 1,000 feet) lapse rate.

When a body of air (or air mass) comes to rest, or moves slowly over a large geographical area that has fairly uniform properties of temperature and moisture, the air mass acquires the temperature/moisture properties of that area it covers.

As air masses move out of their source regions, they come in contact with other air masses of different properties. The zone between two different air masses is a frontal zone or front. Across this zone, temperature, humidity and wind often change rapidly over short distances. The three principal types of fronts are the cold front, the warm front, and the stationary front. Frontal waves and cyclones (areas of low pressure) usually form on slow-moving cold fronts or stationary fronts.

Unstable Air	Stable Air
Cumuliform clouds	Stratiform clouds and fog
Showery precipitation	Continuous precipitation
Rough air (turbulence)	Smooth air
Good visibility, except in blowing obstructions	Fair to poor visibility in haze and smoke

Figure 1-3. Properties of unstable and stable air

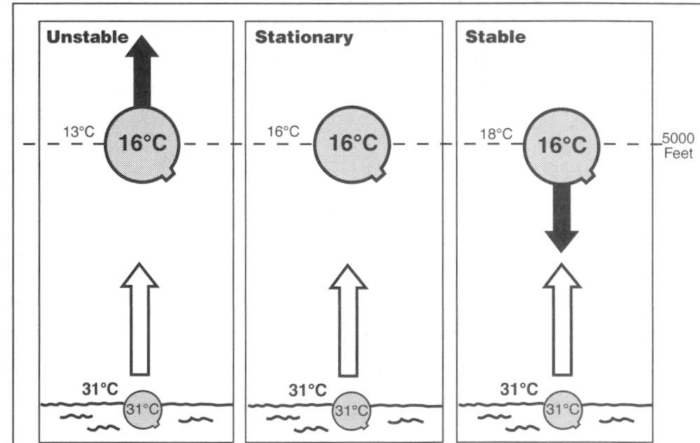

Figure 1-4. Temperature effects on ambient lapse rate

Answers
4099 [C]
4161 [C]

ALL

4121. Stability can be determined from which measurement of the atmosphere?

A—Low-level winds.
B—Ambient lapse rate.
C—Atmospheric pressure.

A change in ambient temperature lapse rate of an air mass can tip the balance between stable or unstable air. The ambient lapse rate is the rate of decrease in temperature with altitude. (PLT173, IR.I.B.K3a) — AC 00-6

Answer (A) is incorrect because stability cannot be determined from low-level winds. Answer (C) is incorrect because the atmospheric pressure does not affect the stability of the air.

ALL

4122. What determines the structure or type of clouds which form as a result of air being forced to ascend?

A—The method by which the air is lifted.
B—The stability of the air before lifting occurs.
C—The amount of condensation nuclei present after lifting occurs.

Cloud type or structure is determined by whether the air is stable or unstable within the layer forced upward. When stable air is forced upward, the air tends to retain horizontal flow and any cloudiness is flat and stratified. When unstable air is forced upward, the disturbance grows, and resulting cloudiness shows "heaped" or cumulus development. (PLT511, IR.I.B.K3f) — AC 00-6

Answers (A) and (C) are incorrect because the method in which air is lifted and the nuclei present do not determine cloud structure or type.

ALL

4124. Unsaturated air flowing up slope will cool at the rate of approximately (dry adiabatic lapse rate)

A—3°C per 1,000 feet.
B—2°C per 1,000 feet.
C—2.5°C per 1,000 feet.

Unsaturated air moving upward and downward cools and warms at about 3°C (5.4°F) per 1,000 feet. (PLT173, IR.I.B.K3a) — AC 00-6

Answer (B) is incorrect because 2°C per 1,000 feet is the lapse rate for stable air. Answer (C) is incorrect because 2.5°C per 1,000 feet is the rate of converging temperature and dew point in a convective current of unsaturated air.

ALL

4115. What type of clouds will be formed if very stable moist air is forced up slope?

A—First stratified clouds and then vertical clouds.
B—Vertical clouds with increasing height.
C—Stratified clouds with little vertical development.

When stable air is forced upward, the air tends to retain horizontal flow and any cloudiness is flat and stratified. When unstable air is forced upward, the disturbance grows and any resulting cloudiness shows extensive vertical development. (PLT511, IR.I.B.K3f) — AC 00-6

Answers (A) and (B) are incorrect because vertical clouds are not characteristic of stable air.

ALL

4118. What type clouds can be expected when an unstable air mass is forced to ascend a mountain slope?

A—Layered clouds with little vertical development.
B—Stratified clouds with considerable associated turbulence.
C—Clouds with extensive vertical development.

When stable air is forced upward, the air tends to retain horizontal flow and any cloudiness is flat and stratified. When unstable air is forced upward, the disturbance grows and any resulting cloudiness shows extensive vertical development. (PLT511, IR.I.B.K3f) — AC 00-6

Answers (A) and (B) are incorrect because layered and stratified clouds are characteristic of stable air.

ALL

4123. Which of the following combinations of weather producing variables would likely result in cumuliform-type clouds, good visibility, rain showers, and possible clear-type icing in clouds?

A—Unstable, moist air, and no lifting mechanism.
B—Stable, dry air, and orographic lifting.
C—Unstable, moist air, and orographic lifting.

Unstable air favors convection. A cumulus cloud forms in a convective updraft and builds upward. The initial lifting that triggers a cumuliform cloud can be either orographic (topographical, i.e., mountains) or by surface heating. For convective cumuliform clouds to develop, the air must be unstable after saturation. (PLT511, IR.I.B.K3f) — AC 00-6

Answer (A) is incorrect because without a lifting mechanism, clouds will not have vertical development, resulting in showery rain and icing in clouds. Answer (B) is incorrect because stable conditions result in stratiform clouds, and dry air does not result in showery rain or icing when lifted.

Answers

4121 [B]	4122 [B]	4124 [A]	4115 [C]	4118 [C]	4123 [C]

ALL

4158. An air mass is a body of air that

A—has similar cloud formations associated with it.
B—creates a wind shift as it moves across the Earth's surface.
C—covers an extensive area and has fairly uniform properties of temperature and moisture.

If a body of air (or air mass) comes to rest, or moves slowly over a large geographical area that has fairly uniform temperatures and moisture content, the body of air (or air mass) acquires the temperature/moisture properties of the geographical area it covers. Therefore, it becomes fairly uniform in these properties over an extensive area. (PLT511, IR.I.B.K3e) — AC 00-6

ALL

4116. The general characteristics of unstable air are

A—good visibility, showery precipitation, and cumuliform-type clouds.
B—good visibility, steady precipitation, and stratiform-type clouds.
C—poor visibility, intermittent precipitation, and cumuliform-type clouds.

The stability of an air mass determines its typical weather characteristics. When one type of air mass overlies another, conditions change with height. Characteristics typical of an unstable and a stable air mass are shown in the figure below. (PLT511, IR.I.B.K3a) — AC 00-6

Answers (B) and (C) are incorrect because steady precipitation, stratiform clouds, and poor visibility are characteristic of stable air.

ALL

4120. Some of the characteristics you would expect to see with an unstable air mass are

A—nimbostratus clouds and good surface visibility.
B—turbulence and poor surface visibility.
C—turbulence and good surface visibility.

The stability of an air mass determines its typical weather characteristics. When one type of air mass overlies another, conditions change with height. Characteristics typical of an unstable and a stable air mass are shown in the figure to the left. (PLT173, IR.I.B.K3e) — AC 00-6

Answers (A) and (B) are incorrect because nimbostratus clouds and poor surface visibility are characteristic of stable air.

ALL

4128. Which are characteristics of an unstable cold air mass moving over a warm surface?

A—Cumuliform clouds, turbulence, and poor visibility.
B—Cumuliform clouds, turbulence, and good visibility.
C—Stratiform clouds, smooth air, and poor visibility.

Cool air moving over a warm surface is heated from below, generating instability and increasing the possibility of showers. Stability of an air mass determines its typical weather characteristics. When one type of air mass overlies another, conditions change with height. Characteristics typical of an unstable air mass are cumuliform clouds, turbulence, and good visibility. See the figure to the left. (PLT511, IR.I.B.K3e) — AC 00-6

Answer (A) is incorrect because poor visibility is a characteristic of stable air. Answer (C) is incorrect because stratiform clouds, smooth air, and poor visibility are characteristics of stable air.

ALL

4117. Which is a characteristic of stable air?

A—Fair weather cumulus clouds.
B—Stratiform clouds.
C—Unlimited visibility.

The stability of an air mass determines its typical weather characteristics. When one type of air mass overlies another, conditions change with height. Characteristics typical of an unstable and a stable air mass are shown in the figure to the left. (PLT173, IR.I.B.K3a) — AC 00-6

Answers (A) and (C) are incorrect because fair weather cumulus clouds and unlimited visibility are characteristic of unstable air.

ALL

4119. What are the characteristics of stable air?

A—Good visibility, steady precipitation, and stratus-type clouds.
B—Poor visibility, intermittent precipitation, and cumulus-type clouds.
C—Poor visibility, steady precipitation, and stratus-type clouds.

The stability of an air mass determines its typical weather characteristics. When one type of air mass overlies another, conditions change with height. Characteristics typical of an unstable and a stable air mass are shown in the figure to the left. (PLT173, IR.I.B.K3a) — AC 00-6

Answers (A) and (B) are incorrect because good visibility, intermittent precipitation, and cumulus type clouds are all characteristics of unstable air.

Answers

4158 [C]	4116 [A]	4120 [C]	4128 [B]	4117 [B]	4119 [C]

ALL
4098. Steady precipitation, in contrast to showers, preceding a front is an indication of

A—stratiform clouds with moderate turbulence.
B—cumuliform clouds with little or no turbulence.
C—stratiform clouds with little or no turbulence.

Steady precipitation is a characteristic of stable air, which has little or no turbulence. Stratiform clouds are associated with stable air. (PLT511, IR.I.B.K3e) — AC 00-6

Answer (A) is incorrect because stratiform clouds are a characteristic of stable air, which has little or no turbulence. Answer (B) is incorrect because precipitation from cumuliform clouds is of a shower type and the clouds are turbulent.

ALL
4127. Frontal waves normally form on

A—slow moving cold fronts or stationary fronts.
B—slow moving warm fronts and strong occluded fronts.
C—rapidly moving cold fronts or warm fronts.

Frontal waves and cyclones (areas of low pressure) usually form on slow-moving cold fronts or stationary fronts. (PLT511, IR.I.B.K3e) — AC 00-6

ALL
4136. Which weather phenomenon is always associated with the passage of a frontal system?

A—A wind change.
B—An abrupt decrease in pressure.
C—Clouds, either ahead or behind the front.

Wind always changes across a front. Wind discontinuity may be in direction, in speed, or in both. Temperature and humidity also may change. (PLT511, IR.I.B.K3e) — AC 00-6

Answer (B) is incorrect because pressure will increase abruptly when flying into colder air and will decrease gradually when flying into warmer air. Answer (C) is incorrect because there may be insufficient moisture to produce clouds.

Clouds

Cloud types are divided into four families: high clouds, middle clouds, low clouds, and clouds with extensive vertical development. The first three families are further classified according to the way they are formed. The high cloud family is cirriform and includes cirrus, cirrocumulus, and cirrostratus. They are composed almost entirely of ice crystals. Clouds formed by vertical currents in unstable air are cumulus, meaning "accumulation or heap." They are characterized by their lumpy, billowy appearance. Clouds formed by the cooling of a stable layer are stratus, meaning "stratified or layered." They are characterized by their uniform, sheet-like appearance.

In addition to the above, the prefix nimbo or the suffix nimbus means "raincloud." A heavy, swelling cumulus type cloud which produces precipitation is a cumulonimbus. The high cloud family is cirriform and composed almost entirely of ice crystals.

Lenticular clouds are associated with a mountain wave. Crests of standing waves may be marked by stationary, lens-shaped clouds known as standing lenticular clouds. Mountain waves and lenticular clouds indicate strong turbulence.

Answers
4098 [C] 4127 [A] 4136 [A]

ALL
4131. The suffix "nimbus," used in naming clouds, means a

A—cloud with extensive vertical development.
B—rain cloud.
C—dark massive, towering cloud.

The prefix "nimbo-" or the suffix "-nimbus" means rain-cloud. Thus, stratified clouds from which rain is falling are called nimbostratus. A heavy, swelling cumulus-type cloud which produces precipitation is a cumulonimbus. (PLT192, IR.I.B.K3f) — AC 00-6

Answer (A) is incorrect because "cumulo" means a cloud with extensive vertical development. Answer (C) is incorrect because cumulonimbus is a dark massive, towering cloud.

ALL
4134. What are the four families of clouds?

A—Stratus, cumulus, nimbus, and cirrus.
B—Clouds formed by updrafts, fronts, cooling layers of air, and precipitation into warm air.
C—High, middle, low, and those with extensive vertical development.

For identification purposes, cloud types are divided into four families. The families are high clouds, middle clouds, low clouds, and clouds with extensive vertical development. (PLT192, IR.I.B.K3f) — AC 00-6

ALL
4157. A high cloud is composed mostly of

A—ozone.
B—condensation nuclei.
C—ice crystals.

The high cloud family is cirriform and includes cirrus, cirrocumulus, and cirrostratus. They are composed almost entirely of ice crystals. (PLT192, IR.I.B.K3f) — AC 00-6

ALL
4133. Which family of clouds is least likely to contribute to structural icing on an aircraft?

A—Low clouds.
B—High clouds.
C—Clouds with extensive vertical development.

Two conditions are necessary for structural icing in flight:

1. *The aircraft must be flying through visible water such as rain or cloud droplets, and*
2. *The temperature, at the point where the moisture strikes the aircraft must be 0°C or colder.*

The high cloud family is composed almost entirely of ice crystals. Because ice crystals are already frozen, they most likely won't stick to an aircraft. (PLT192, IR.I.B.K3f) — AC 00-6

ALL
4129. Which clouds have the greatest turbulence?

A—Towering cumulus.
B—Cumulonimbus.
C—Altocumulus castellanus.

Cumulonimbus clouds are the ultimate manifestation of instability. They are vertically developed clouds of large dimensions with dense boiling tops, often crowned with thick veils of dense cirrus (the anvil). Nearly the entire spectrum of flying hazards are contained in these clouds, including violent turbulence. They should be avoided at all times. (PLT192, IR.I.B.K3f) — AC 00-6

Answer (A) is incorrect because a towering cumulus has primarily updrafts. Answer (C) is incorrect because altocumulus castellanus are turbulent, but not nearly as turbulent as cumulonimbus clouds.

ALL
4130. Standing lenticular clouds, in mountainous areas, indicate

A—an inversion.
B—unstable air.
C—turbulence.

Standing lenticular altocumulus clouds are formed on the crests of waves created by barriers to the wind flow. The clouds show little movement, hence the name "standing." However, wind can be quite strong blowing through such clouds. The presence of these clouds is a good indication of very strong turbulence and should be avoided. (PLT263, IR.I.B.K3f) — AC 00-6

Answers

4131 [B] 4134 [C] 4157 [C] 4133 [B] 4129 [B] 4130 [C]

ALL
4132. The presence of standing lenticular altocumulus clouds is a good indication of

A—a jet stream.
B—very strong turbulence.
C—heavy icing conditions.

Standing lenticular altocumulus clouds are formed on the crests of waves created by barriers to the wind flow. The clouds show little movement, hence the name "standing." However, wind can be quite strong blowing through such clouds. The presence of these clouds is a good indication of very strong turbulence and they should be avoided. (PLT263, IR.I.B.K3f) — AC 00-6

ALL
4149. Fair weather cumulus clouds often indicate

A—turbulence at and below the cloud level.
B—poor visibility.
C—smooth flying conditions.

Fair weather cumulus clouds often indicate bumpy turbulence beneath and in the clouds but good visibility. The cloud tops indicate the approximate upper limit of convection; flight above is usually smooth. (PLT192, IR.I.B.K3f) — AC 00-6

Answer (B) is incorrect because fair weather cumulus clouds produce good visibility. Answer (C) is incorrect because fair weather cumulus clouds produce turbulence.

Fog

Fog is a surface-based cloud composed of either water droplets or ice crystals. Fog is the most frequent cause of surface visibility below 3 miles, and is one of the most common and persistent weather hazards encountered in aviation. Fog may form by cooling the air to its dew point or by adding moisture to the air near the ground. A small temperature/dew point spread is essential to the formation of fog. An abundance of condensation nuclei from combustion products makes fog prevalent in industrial areas. Fog is classified by the way it is formed:

1. Radiation fog (ground fog) is formed when terrestrial radiation cools the ground, which in turn cools the air in contact with it. When the air is cooled to its dew point (or within a few degrees), fog will form. This fog will form most readily in warm, moist air over low, flatland areas on clear, calm nights.
2. Advection fog (sea fog) is formed when warm, moist air moves (wind is required) over colder ground or water. An example is an air mass moving inland from the coast in winter.
3. Upslope fog is formed when moist, stable air is cooled to its dew point as it moves (wind is required) up sloping terrain. Cooling will be at the dry adiabatic lapse rate of approximately 3°C per 1,000 feet.

ALL
4163. Fog is usually prevalent in industrial areas because of

A—atmospheric stabilization around cities.
B—an abundance of condensation nuclei from combustion products.
C—increased temperatures due to industrial heating.

Abundant condensation nuclei enhance the formation of fog. Thus, fog is prevalent in industrial areas where byproducts of combustion provide a high concentration of these nuclei. (PLT226, IR.I.B.K3j) — AC 00-6

ALL
4156. Under which condition does advection fog usually form?

A—Moist air moving over colder ground or water.
B—Warm, moist air settling over a cool surface under no-wind conditions.
C—A land breeze blowing a cold air mass over a warm water current.

Advection fog forms when moist air moves over colder ground or water. (PLT226, IR.I.B.K3j) — AC 00-6

Answer (B) is incorrect because it describes radiation fog. Answer (C) is incorrect because it describes steam fog.

Answers

4132 [B]	4149 [A]	4163 [B]	4156 [A]

ALL

4164. In which situation is advection fog most likely to form?

A—An air mass moving inland from the coast in winter.
B—A light breeze blowing colder air out to sea.
C—Warm, moist air settling over a warmer surface under no-wind conditions.

Advection fog forms when moist air moves over colder ground or water. During the winter, advection fog over the central and eastern United States results when moist air from the Gulf of Mexico spreads northward over cold ground. The fog may extend as far north as the Great Lakes. (PLT226, IR.I.B.K3j) — AC 00-6

ALL

4165. In what localities is advection fog most likely to occur?

A—Coastal areas.
B—Mountain slopes.
C—Level inland areas.

Advection fog forms when moist air moves over colder ground or water. It is most common along coastal areas but often develops deep into continental areas. (PLT226, IR.I.B.K3j) — AC 00-6

ALL

4166. What types of fog depend upon a wind in order to exist?

A—Steam fog and down slope fog.
B—Precipitation-induced fog and ground fog.
C—Advection fog and up slope fog.

Advection fog forms when moist air moves over colder ground or water. Upslope fog forms as a result of moist, stable air being cooled adiabatically as it moves up sloping terrain. (PLT226, IR.I.B.K3j) — AC 00-6

ALL

4167. What situation is most conducive to the formation of radiation fog?

A—Warm, moist air over low, flatland areas on clear, calm nights.
B—Moist, tropical air moving over cold, offshore water.
C—The movement of cold air over much warmer water.

Conditions favorable for radiation fog are clear skies, little or no wind, and small temperature/dew point spread (high relative humidity). The fog forms almost exclusively at night or near daybreak. (PLT226, IR.I.B.K3j) — AC 00-6A

Answer (B) is incorrect because it describes advection fog. Answer (C) is incorrect because it describes steam fog.

ALL

4169. Which conditions are favorable for the formation of radiation fog?

A—Moist air moving over colder ground or water.
B—Cloudy sky and a light wind moving saturated warm air over a cool surface.
C—Clear sky, little or no wind, small temperature/dew point spread, and over a land surface.

Conditions favorable for radiation fog are clear skies, little or no wind, and small temperature/dew point spread (high relative humidity). The fog forms almost exclusively at night or near daybreak. (PLT226, IR.I.B.K3j) — AC 00-6

Answers (A) and (B) are incorrect because they both describe advection fog.

ALL

4162. Which weather condition can be expected when moist air flows from a relatively warm surface to a colder surface?

A—Increased visibility.
B—Convective turbulence due to surface heating.
C—Fog.

Advection fog forms when moist air moves over colder ground or water. (PLT226, IR.I.B.K3j) — AC 00-6

Answers

4164 [A]	4165 [A]	4166 [C]	4167 [A]	4169 [C]	4162 [C]

Turbulence

If severe turbulence is encountered either inside or outside of clouds, the airplane's airspeed should be reduced to maneuvering speed and the pilot should attempt to maintain a level flight attitude because the amount of excess load that can be imposed on the wing will be decreased. An attempt to maintain a constant altitude will greatly increase the stresses that are applied to the aircraft. See Figure 1-5.

Turbulence Reporting Criteria

Intensity	Aircraft reaction	Reaction inside aircraft	Reporting term definition
Light	Turbulence that momentarily causes slight, erratic changes in altitude and/or attitude (pitch, roll, yaw). Report as *Light Turbulence;** *or* Turbulence that causes slight, rapid and somewhat rhythmic bumpiness without appreciable changes in altitude or attitude. Report as *Light Chop.*	Occupants may feel a slight strain against belts or shoulder straps. Unsecured objects may be displaced slightly. Food service may be conducted and little or no difficulty is encountered in walking.	Occasional – less than 1/3 of the time. Intermittent – 1/3 to 2/3 of the time. Continuous – more than 2/3 of the time.
Moderate	Turbulence that is similar to Light Turbulence but of greater intensity. Changes in altitude and/or attitude occur but the aircraft remains in positive control at all times. It usually causes variations in indicated airspeed. Report as *Moderate Turbulence.** *or* Turbulence that is similar to Light Chop but of greater intensity. It causes rapid bumps or jolts without appreciable changes in aircraft altitude or attitude. Report as *Moderate Chop.*	Occupants feel definite strains against seat belts or shoulder straps. Unsecured objects are dislodged. Food service and walking are difficult.	NOTE 1. Pilots should report location(s), time (UTC), intensity, whether in or near clouds, altitude, type of aircraft and, when applicable, duration of turbulence. 2. Duration may be based on time between two locations or over a single location. All locations should be readily identifiable.
Severe	Turbulence that causes large, abrupt changes in altitude and/or attitude. It usually causes large variations in indicated airspeed. Aircraft may be momentarily out of control. Report as *Severe Turbulence.**	Occupants are forced violently against seat belts or shoulder straps. Unsecured objects are tossed about. Food service and walking are impossible.	
Extreme	Turbulence in which the aircraft is violently tossed about and is practically impossible to control. It may cause structural damage. Report as *Extreme Turbulence.**		

* High level turbulence (normally above 15,000 feet AGL) that is not associated with cumuliform cloudiness, including thunderstorms, should be reported as CAT (clear air turbulence) preceded by the appropriate intensity, or light or moderate chop.

Figure 1-5. Turbulence Reporting Criteria

ALL

4160. If you fly into severe turbulence, which flight condition should you attempt to maintain?

A—Constant airspeed (V_A).
B—Level flight attitude.
C—Constant altitude and constant airspeed.

When flying in severe turbulence, maintaining positive aircraft control may be nearly impossible to do. In attempting to maintain a constant altitude, the stresses applied to the aircraft are greatly increased. Stresses will be lessened if the aircraft is held in a constant attitude and allowed to "ride the waves." Wide fluctuations in airspeed will probably have to be tolerated in order to reduce aircraft stresses. (PLT263, IR.I.B.K3g) — AC 00-6

Answer (A) is incorrect because airspeed should be maintained at or below V_A. Answer (C) is incorrect because a constant attitude (not airspeed or altitude) should be maintained.

Answers
4160 [B]

ALL

4916. If severe turbulence is encountered during your IFR flight, the airplane should be slowed to the design maneuvering speed because the

A—maneuverability of the airplane will be increased.
B—amount of excess load that can be imposed on the wing will be decreased.
C—airplane will stall at a lower angle of attack, giving an increased margin of safety.

If during flight, rough air or severe turbulence is encountered, the airspeed should be reduced to maneuvering speed or less, to minimize the stress on the airplane structure. (PLT263, IR.I.B.K3g) — FAA-H-8083-25

Answer (A) is incorrect because the maneuverability will not be increased by slowing down the aircraft. Answer (C) is incorrect because the airplane will always stall at the same critical angle of attack.

ALL

4210. A pilot reporting turbulence that momentarily causes slight, erratic changes in altitude and/or attitude should report it as

A—light turbulence.
B—moderate turbulence.
C—light chop.

Light turbulence is defined as turbulence that momentarily causes slight, erratic changes in attitude and/or altitude. (PLT501, IR.I.B.K3g) — AC 00-45

Answer (B) is incorrect because moderate turbulence will cause greater changes in attitude and altitude. Answer (C) is incorrect because light chop is slight or moderate rhythmic bumps with negligible changes in attitude or altitude.

Thunderstorms

A thunderstorm is a local storm produced by a cumulonimbus cloud. It is always accompanied by lightning and thunder, usually with strong gusts of wind, heavy rain, and sometimes, with hail. Three conditions necessary for the formation of a thunderstorm are: sufficient water vapor, an unstable lapse rate, and an initial upward boost (lifting). The initial upward boost can be caused by heating from below, frontal lifting, or by mechanical lifting (wind blowing air upslope on a mountain).

There are three stages of a thunderstorm:

1. The **cumulus stage** is characterized by continuous updrafts, and these updrafts create low-pressure areas.
2. The **mature stage** is characterized by updrafts and downdrafts inside the cloud. Precipitation inside the cloud aids in the development of these downdrafts, and the start of rain from the base of the cloud signals the beginning of the mature stage. Thunderstorms reach their greatest intensity during the mature stage.
3. The **dissipating stage** is characterized predominantly by downdrafts.

Thunderstorms that generally produce the most intense hazard to aircraft are called squall-line thunderstorms. These nonfrontal, narrow bands of thunderstorms often develop ahead of a cold front.

Embedded thunderstorms are those that are obscured by massive cloud layers and cannot be seen.

ALL

4148. What are the requirements for the formation of a thunderstorm?

A—A cumulus cloud with sufficient moisture.
B—A cold front pushing into an area of moist, stable air.
C—Sufficient moisture, an unstable lapse rate, and a lifting action.

For a thunderstorm to form, the air must have:

1. *Sufficient water vapor,*
2. *An unstable lapse rate, and*
3. *An initial upward boost (lifting) to start the storm process in motion.*

(PLT495, IR.I.B.K3h) — AC 00-6

Answers

4916 [B] 4210 [A] 4148 [C]

ALL

4126. Which weather phenomenon signals the beginning of the mature stage of a thunderstorm?

A—The start of rain at the surface.
B—Growth rate of cloud is maximum.
C—Strong turbulence in the cloud.

Precipitation beginning to fall from the cloud base signals that a downdraft has developed and a cell has entered the mature stage. (PLT495, IR.I.B.K3h) — AC 00-6

Answer (B) is incorrect because maximum growth rate occurs during the cumulus stage. Answer (C) is incorrect because strong turbulence may occur during any stage of a thunderstorm.

ALL

4143. During the life cycle of a thunderstorm, which stage is characterized predominately by downdrafts?

A—Cumulus.
B—Dissipating.
C—Mature.

A thunderstorm cell during its life cycle progress through three stages: the cumulus, the mature, and the dissipating. Downdrafts characterize the dissipating stage. (PLT495, IR.I.B.K3h) — AC 00-6

Answer (A) is incorrect because the cumulus stage is characterized by updrafts. Answer (C) is incorrect because the mature stage is characterized by precipitation beginning to fall.

ALL

4147. What is an indication that downdrafts have developed and the thunderstorm cell has entered the mature stage?

A—The anvil top has completed its development.
B—Precipitation begins to fall from the cloud base.
C—A gust front forms.

Precipitation beginning to fall from the cloud base signals that a downdraft has developed and a cell has entered the mature stage. (PLT495, IR.I.B.K3h) — AC 00-6

Answer (A) is incorrect because the anvil top will normally complete development near the end of the mature stage. Answer (C) is incorrect because a gust front may be formed by any number of cells in a thunderstorm.

ALL

4137. Where do squall lines most often develop?

A—In an occluded front.
B—In a cold air mass.
C—Ahead of a cold front.

A squall line (instability line) is a nonfrontal, narrow band of active thunderstorms. Often it develops ahead of a cold front in moist, unstable air, but it may develop in unstable air far removed from any front. (PLT495, IR.I.B.K3h) — AC 00-6

ALL

4142. If squalls are reported at your destination, what wind conditions should you anticipate?

A—Sudden increases in wind speed of at least 16 knots, rising to 22 knots or more, lasting for at least 1 minute.
B—Peak gusts of at least 35 knots for a sustained period of 1 minute or longer.
C—Rapid variation in wind direction of at least 20° and changes in speed of at least 10 knots between peaks and lulls.

A squall is a sudden increase in speed of at least 16 knots to a sustained speed of 22 knots or more, lasting for at least one minute. (PLT475, IR.I.B.K3h) — AC 00-45

Answer (B) is incorrect because peak gusts of at least 35 knots refers to peak wind. Answer (C) is incorrect because squalls refer to wind speed (not direction) changes.

ALL

4145. Which thunderstorms generally produce the most severe conditions, such as heavy hail and destructive winds?

A—Warm front.
B—Squall line.
C—Air mass.

A squall line often contains severe steady-state thunderstorms and presents the single most intense weather hazard to aircraft. It usually forms rapidly, generally reaching maximum intensity during the late afternoon and the first few hours of darkness. Hail competes with turbulence as the greatest thunderstorm hazard to aircraft. (PLT495, IR.I.B.K3h) — AC 00-6

Answers

4126 [A]	4143 [B]	4147 [B]	4137 [C]	4142 [A]	4145 [B]

ALL

4141. What is indicated by the term "embedded thunderstorms"?

A—Severe thunderstorms are embedded within a squall line.
B—Thunderstorms are predicted to develop in a stable air mass.
C—Thunderstorms are obscured by massive cloud layers and cannot be seen.

Usually, thunderstorms are quite visible to the pilot. However, when a thunderstorm is present but not visible to the pilot due to cloud cover, such as a thick stratus layer, the thunderstorm is said to be embedded. (PLT495, IR.I.B.K3h) — AC 00-6

Answer (A) is incorrect because a squall line is a line of thunderstorms that can usually be seen. Answer (B) is incorrect because thunderstorms are virtually nonexistent in stable air masses.

ALL

4144. Which weather phenomenon is always associated with a thunderstorm?

A—Lightning.
B—Heavy rain showers.
C—Supercooled raindrops.

A thunderstorm is a local storm produced by a cumulonimbus cloud. It is always accompanied by lightning and thunder, usually with strong gusts of wind, heavy rain, and sometimes, with hail. (PLT495, IR.I.B.K3h) — AC 00-6

Answer (B) is incorrect because it may hail instead of rain in a thunderstorm. Answer (C) is incorrect because the occurrence of supercooled raindrops depends on the temperature.

ALL

4146. Which procedure is recommended if a pilot should unintentionally penetrate embedded thunderstorm activity?

A—Reverse aircraft heading or proceed toward an area of known VFR conditions.
B—Reduce airspeed to maneuvering speed and maintain a constant altitude.
C—Set power for recommended turbulence penetration airspeed and attempt to maintain a level flight attitude.

Following are some do's and don'ts during thunderstorm penetration:

1. *Do keep your eyes on your instruments. Looking outside the cockpit can increase the danger of temporary blindness from lightning.*
2. *Don't change power settings; maintain settings for reduced airspeed.*
3. *Do maintain a constant attitude; let the aircraft "ride the waves." Maneuvers that try to maintain constant altitude increase stresses on the aircraft.*
4. *Don't turn back once you are in the thunderstorm. A straight course through the storm most likely is the quickest way out of the hazards. In addition, turning maneuvers increase stresses on the aircraft.*

(PLT120, IR.I.B.K3h) — AC 00-6

Answer (A) is incorrect because turning maneuvers increase the load on the aircraft, and a straight path will be the most direct route out of the thunderstorm. Answer (B) is incorrect because the pilot should attempt to maintain a constant attitude (not airspeed or altitude).

ALL

4146-1. When approaching a cumulonimbus cell that is on your route of flight, a pilot should

A—circumnavigate the cell by at least 20 NM.
B—descend to an altitude that will allow the aircraft to fly under the cell.
C—attempt to fly under the anvil, as this will protect the aircraft from the most violent parts of the cell.

A pilot should avoid by at least 20 miles any thunderstorm identified as severe or giving an intense radar echo. This is especially true under the anvil of a large cumulonimbus where hail can be discharged. (PLT495, IR.I.B.K3h) — AIM ¶7-1-27

Answers

4141 [C]	4144 [A]	4146 [C]	4146-1 [A]

Microbursts

Microbursts are small-scale intense downdrafts which, as they get near the ground, spread outward from the center in all directions. Maximum downdrafts at the center of a microburst may be as strong as 6,000 feet per minute. As your aircraft approaches, encounters, and exits a microburst it will experience a sudden increase in performance due to a headwind followed by a strong downdraft at the microburst center and then a severe loss of performance as the downdraft becomes a sudden tailwind. Since the initial headwind may be 45 knots and the tailwind also 45 knots, the total wind shear passing across the microburst would be 90 knots.

An individual microburst will seldom last longer than 15 minutes from the time it strikes the ground until dissipation. The horizontal winds continue to increase during the first 5 minutes with the maximum intensity winds lasting approximately 2–4 minutes.

ALL

4251. What is the expected duration of an individual microburst?

A—Two minutes with maximum winds lasting approximately 1 minute.
B—One microburst may continue for as long as 2 to 4 hours.
C—Seldom longer than 15 minutes from the time the burst strikes the ground until dissipation.

An individual microburst will seldom last longer than 15 minutes from the time it strikes the ground until dissipation. However, there may be multiple microbursts in the area. (PLT317, IR.I.B.K3h) — AIM ¶7-1-25

ALL

4252. Maximum downdrafts in a microburst encounter may be as strong as

A—8,000 feet per minute.
B—7,000 feet per minute.
C—6,000 feet per minute.

The downdrafts can be as strong as 6,000 fpm in a microburst encounter. (PLT317, IR.I.B.K3h) — AIM ¶7-1-25

ALL

4253. An aircraft that encounters a headwind of 45 knots, within a microburst, may expect a total shear across the microburst of

A—40 knots.
B—80 knots.
C—90 knots.

Horizontal winds near the surface can be as strong as 45 knots resulting in a 90-knot shear (headwind to tailwind) across the microburst. These strong horizontal winds occur within a few hundred feet of the ground. (PLT317, IR.I.B.K3h) — AIM ¶7-1-25

ALL

4254. (Refer to Figure 13.) If involved in a microburst encounter, in which aircraft positions will the most severe downdraft occur?

A—4 and 5.
B—2 and 3.
C—3 and 4.

The strongest downdraft occurs at point 3. Although there is also downdraft at points 2 and 4, the correct answer is C (3 and 4) because the combination of downdraft and tailwind at 4 has a more negative effect on performance than the combination of downdraft and headwind at 2. (PLT317, IR.I.B.K3h) — AIM ¶7-1-25

ALL

4255. (Refer to Figure 13.) When penetrating a microburst, which aircraft will experience an increase in performance without a change in pitch or power?

A—3.
B—2.
C—1.

At position 1, the aircraft is in the outflow, initially experiencing a headwind with little or no downdraft resulting in a temporary performance increase. (PLT317, IR.I.B.K3h) — AIM ¶7-1-25

Answers

4251 [C]	4252 [C]	4253 [C]	4254 [C]	4255 [C]

ALL
4256. (Refer to Figure 13.) The aircraft in position 3 will experience which effect in a microburst encounter?

A—Decreasing headwind.
B—Increasing tailwind.
C—Strong downdraft.

Answer C is the best answer. Although all three answer choices are occurring, the strong downdraft is the most severe effect at point 3. (PLT317, IR.I.B.K3h) — AIM ¶7-1-25

ALL
4257. (Refer to Figure 13.) What effect will a microburst encounter have upon the aircraft in position 4?

A—Strong tailwind.
B—Strong updraft.
C—Significant performance increase.

In position 4, performance decreases from the strong tailwind and the strong downdraft. (PLT317, IR.I.B.K3h) — AIM ¶7-1-25

ALL
4258. (Refer to Figure 13.) How will the aircraft in position 4 be affected by a microburst encounter?

A—Performance increasing with a tailwind and updraft.
B—Performance decreasing with a tailwind and downdraft.
C—Performance decreasing with a headwind and downdraft.

At position 4, the aircraft experiences a severe performance decrease. The wind contours indicate a strong downdraft and increasing tailwind which may cause an aircraft to sink toward ground impact. (PLT317, IR.I.B.K3h) — AIM ¶7-1-25

Icing

One of the hazards to flight is aircraft icing. Pilots should be aware of the conditions conducive to icing, the types of icing, the effects of icing on aircraft control and performance, and the use and limitations of aircraft deice and anti-ice equipment. For ice to form, there must be moisture present in the air and the air must be cooled to a temperature of 0°C (32°F) or less. Aerodynamic cooling can lower the temperature of an airfoil to 0°C even though the ambient temperature is a few degrees warmer.

Ice is identified as clear, rime, or mixed. **Rime ice** forms if the droplets are small and freeze immediately when contacting the aircraft surface. This type of ice usually forms on areas such as the leading edges of wings or struts. It has a somewhat rough looking appearance and is a milky white color. **Clear ice** is usually formed from larger water droplets or freezing rain that can spread over a surface. This is the most dangerous type of ice since it is clear, hard to see, and can change the shape of the airfoil. **Mixed ice** is a mixture of clear ice and rime ice. It has the bad characteristics of both types and can form rapidly.

Structural and Induction Icing

There are two kinds of icing that are significant to aviation: structural icing and induction icing. **Structural icing** refers to the accumulation of ice on the exterior of the aircraft. **Induction icing** affects the powerplant operation. Structural icing occurs on an aircraft whenever supercooled droplets of water make contact with any part of the aircraft that is also at a temperature below freezing.

One inflight condition necessary for structural icing is visible moisture (clouds or raindrops). As the rain falls through air that is below freezing, its temperature begins to fall below freezing yet it does not freeze solid—i.e., freezing rain. The process requires the temperature of the rain to be above freezing before it becomes supercooled. Aircraft structural ice will most likely have the highest accumulation in freezing rain; therefore, an operational consideration if you fly into rain that freezes on impact is that temperatures are above freezing at some higher altitude.

Answers
4256 [C] 4257 [A] 4258 [B]

Hazards of Structural Icing

The most hazardous aspect of structural icing is its aerodynamic effects. Ice can alter the shape of an airfoil. This can cause control problems, change the angle of attack at which the aircraft stalls, and cause the aircraft to stall at a significantly higher airspeed. Ice can reduce the amount of lift that an airfoil will produce and increase amount of drag by several times. It can partially block or limit control surfaces, which will limit or make control movements ineffective. If the extra weight caused by ice accumulation is too great, the aircraft might not be able to become airborne, and if in flight, might not be able to maintain altitude.

For this reason, regulations prohibit takeoff when snow, ice, or frost is adhering to wings, propellers, or control surfaces of an aircraft. Yet another hazard of structural icing is the possible uncommanded and uncontrolled roll phenomenon referred to as roll upset, which is associated with severe inflight icing. Therefore, pilots flying airplanes certificated for flight in known icing conditions should be aware that *severe* icing is a condition that is outside of the airplane's certificated icing envelope.

Structural icing can also cause tailplane (empennage) stall. The tail can collect ice faster than the wing and because it is not visible to the pilot inflight, the situation could go undetected. A tailplane stall occurs when, same as with the wing, the critical angle of attack is exceeded. Since the horizontal stabilizer counters the natural nose-down tendency caused by the center of lift of the main wing, the airplane will react by pitching down, sometimes uncontrollably, when the tailplane is stalled. Application of flaps can aggravate or initiate the stall.

Because of this, the pilot should use caution when applying flaps during an approach if there is the possibility of icing on the tailplane. Ice buildup will cause the airplane to require more power to maintain cruise airspeed. Ice on the tailplane can cause diminished nose-up pitch control and heavy elevator forces, and the aircraft may buffet if flaps are applied. Ice on the rudder or ailerons can cause control oscillations or vibrations.

For an airplane to be approved for flight into icing conditions, the airplane must be equipped with systems that will adequately protect various components. Not all airplanes with these components are approved for flight into known icing; check your POH to know if your airplane has been certificated to operate in known icing conditions.

Frost and Snow

Frost is described as ice deposits formed on a surface when the temperature of the collecting surface is at or below the dew point of the adjacent air, and the dew point is below freezing. Frost causes early airflow separation on an airfoil resulting in a loss of lift. Therefore, all frost should be removed from the lifting surfaces of an airplane before flight or it could prevent the airplane from becoming airborne.

Test data indicate that ice, snow, or frost formations having a thickness and surface roughness similar to medium or course sandpaper on the leading edge and upper surface of a wing can reduce wing lift by as much as 30 percent, and increase drag by 40 percent.

Deice and Anti-Ice

Deicing is a procedure in which frost, ice, or snow is removed from the aircraft in order to provide clean surfaces. This is often accomplished with pneumatic boots. Anti-icing is a process that provides some protection against the formation of frost or ice for a limited period of time.

ALL

4100. Which conditions result in the formation of frost?

A—The temperature of the collecting surface is at or below freezing and small droplets of moisture are falling.

B—When dew forms and the temperature is below freezing.

C—Temperature of the collecting surface is below the dew point of surrounding air and the dew point is colder than freezing.

In order for frost to form, the surface temperature must be below the dew point and the dew point of the surrounding air must be colder than freezing. Water vapor will then sublimate directly as ice crystals or frost. (PLT493, IR.I.B.K3k) — AC 00-6

Answer (A) is incorrect because droplets of moisture are not necessary, and the dew point must also be colder than freezing. Answer (B) is incorrect because dew does not have to form, and the temperature must be below the dew point and the dew point below freezing.

ALL

4152. In which meteorological environment is aircraft structural icing most likely to have the highest rate of accumulation?

A—Cumulonimbus clouds.

B—High humidity and freezing temperature.

C—Freezing rain.

The condition most favorable for very hazardous icing is the presence of many large, supercooled water droplets, also called freezing rain. (PLT274, IR.I.B.K3i) — AC 00-6

Answer (A) is incorrect because due to temperature variations within them, cumulonimbus clouds (thunderstorms) do not necessarily cause structural icing to accumulate. Answer (B) is incorrect because high humidity alone can not produce structural icing; visible moisture must be present.

ALL

4153. What is an operational consideration if you fly into rain which freezes on impact?

A—You have flown into an area of thunderstorms.

B—Temperatures are above freezing at some higher altitude.

C—You have flown through a cold front.

As the rain falls through air that is below freezing, its temperature begins to fall below freezing yet without freezing solid. This is freezing rain. The process requires that the temperature of the rain must be above freezing before it becomes supercooled. Therefore, when freezing rain is encountered, it indicates that warmer temperatures are above. (PLT344, IR.I.B.K3i) — AC 00-6

ALL

4171. Test data indicate that ice, snow, or frost having a thickness and roughness similar to medium or coarse sandpaper on the leading edge and upper surface of an airfoil

A—reduce lift by as much as 50 percent and increase drag by as much as 50 percent.

B—increase drag and reduce lift by as much as 25 percent.

C—reduce lift by as much as 30 percent and increase drag by 40 percent.

Test data indicate that ice, snow, or frost formations having a thickness and surface roughness similar to medium or coarse sandpaper on the leading edge and upper surface of a wing can reduce wing lift by as much as 30 percent and increase drag by 40 percent. (PLT128, IR.I.B.K3i) — AC 91-74

ALL

4950. During an IFR cross-country flight you picked up rime icing which you estimate is 1/2" thick on the leading edge of the wings. You are now below the clouds at 2,000 feet AGL and are approaching your destination airport under VFR. Visibility under the clouds is more than 10 miles, winds at the destination airport are 8 knots right down the runway, and the surface temperature is 3°C. You decide to:

A—use a faster than normal approach and landing speed.

B—approach and land at your normal speed since the ice is not thick enough to have any noticeable effect.

C—fly your approach slower than normal to lessen the "wind chill" effect and break up the ice.

Ice will accumulate unevenly on the airplane. It will add weight and drag, and decrease thrust and lift. With ice accumulations, landing approaches should be made with a minimum wing flap setting and with an added margin of airspeed. Sudden and large configuration and airspeed changes should be avoided. (PLT493, IR.I.B.K3i) — FAA-H-8083-3

Answer (B) is incorrect because ice having a thickness similar to sandpaper on the leading edge and upper surface of a wing can reduce wing lift by as much as 30 percent and increase drag by 40 percent. Answer (C) is incorrect because ice will increase drag, requiring additional lift (airspeed); wind chill effect cannot be relied upon to melt/remove the ice that has already accumulated; flying slower than normal increases the possibility of a stall due to the decreased lift.

Answers

4100 [C] 4152 [C] 4153 [B] 4171 [C] 4950 [A]

ALL

4151. Why is frost considered hazardous to flight operation?

A—Frost changes the basic aerodynamic shape of the airfoil.
B—Frost decreases control effectiveness.
C—Frost causes early airflow separation resulting in a loss of lift.

Frost does not change the basic aerodynamic shape of the wing, but the roughness of its surface spoils the smooth flow of air, thus causing a slowing of the airflow. This slowing of the air causes early air flow separation over the affected airfoil, resulting in a loss of lift. (PLT493, IR.I.B.K3i) — AC 00-6

ALL

4151-1. The formation of frost on an airplane wing will cause

A—a change in the basic aerodynamic shape of the wing.
B—a disruption of the smooth airflow over the wing.
C—the airplane to become airborne at a slower speed.

Frost does not change the basic aerodynamic shape of the wing, but the roughness of its surface spoils the smooth flow of air, thus causing a slowing of the airflow. This slowing of the air causes early air flow separation over the affected airfoil, resulting in a loss of lift. (PLT344, IR.I.B.K3i) — AC 00-6

ALL

4958. When icing is detected, particularly while operating an aircraft without deicing equipment, the pilot should

A—fly to an area with liquid precipitation.
B—fly to a lower altitude.
C—leave the area of precipitation or go to an altitude where the temperature is above freezing.

When icing is detected, a pilot should do one of two things, particularly if the aircraft is not equipped with deicing equipment: leave the area of precipitation or go to an altitude where the temperature is above freezing. This warmer altitude may not always be a lower altitude. Proper preflight action includes obtaining information on the freezing level and the above-freezing levels in precipitation areas. (PLT493, IR.I.B.K3i) — FAA-H-8083-15

Answer (A) is incorrect because pilots should leave the area of any precipitation; even liquid precip can result in an icing scenario. Answer (B) is incorrect because a warmer altitude may not always be a lower altitude.

ALL

4959. Tailplane icing can be detected by

A—a slow and steady decrease in altitude.
B—flaps failing to operate.
C—a sudden change in elevator force or uncommanded nose-down pitch.

Since the tailplane is ordinarily thinner than the wing, it is a more efficient collector of ice. It is important the pilot be alert to the possibility of a tailplane stall, particularly on approach and landing. Any of the following symptoms, occurring singly or in combination, may be a warning of tailplane icing: elevator control pulsing, oscillations or vibrations; abnormal nose-down trim change; reduction or loss of elevator effectiveness; sudden change in elevator force; sudden uncommanded nose-down pitch. (PLT493, IR.I.B.K3i) — FAA-H-8083-15

Answer (A) is incorrect because tailplane ice or a taiplane stall typically results in a rapid change in pitch. Answer (B) is incorrect because flaps may operate even with tailplane icing, further aggravating or initiating a stall.

ALL

4960. If tailplane icing or a tailplane stall is detected, the pilot should

A—lower the flaps to decrease airspeed.
B—decrease power to V_{FE}.
C—retract flaps and increase power.

If a tailplane stall is suspected, the pilot should immediately retract flaps to the previous setting and apply appropriate nose-up elevator pressure; increase airspeed appropriately for the reduced flap extension setting; apply sufficient power for aircraft configuration and conditions; make nose-down pitch changes slowly; and if a pneumatic deicing system is used, operate the system several times in an attempt to clear the tailplane of ice. (PLT493, IR.I.B.K3i) — FAA-H-8083-15

Answer (A) is incorrect because flaps should not be used if tailplane ice is suspected. Answer (B) is incorrect because power should be increased if tailplane ice is suspected.

Answers

4151 [C]	4151-1 [B]	4958 [C]	4959 [C]	4960 [C]

ALL
4971. Which is true with regards to icing?

A—Heavy icing on the leading edge is not as bad as light icing on the upper surface.
B—Smooth ice on the upper surface will cause minimal if any problems.
C—Light icing is worse than heavy icing.

Ice on the leading edge can be removed using deicing systems. Ice on the upper surface is more dangerous because it is more difficult to remove. (PLT493, IR.I.B.K3i) — AC 91-74

Answer (B) is incorrect because smooth ice on the upper surface will disrupt laminar flow and is difficult to remove. Answer (C) is incorrect because heavy icing causes more aerodynamic problems than light icing.

AIR
4972. What is the most likely reason for buffeting or vibrations after extending the flaps during or exiting icing conditions?

A—Incipient tailplane stall.
B—Aerodynamic stall due to increased angle of attack.
C—Aerodynamic instability due to ice accumulation forward of the ailerons.

Any of the following symptoms, occurring singly or in combination, may be a warning of tailplane icing: elevator control pulsing, oscillations or vibrations; abnormal nose-down trim change; reduction or loss of elevator effectiveness; sudden change in elevator force; sudden uncommanded nose-down pitch. If any of the above symptoms occur, the pilot should immediately retract the flaps to the previous setting and apply appropriate nose-up elevator pressure. (PLT493, IR.I.B.K3i) — FAA-H-8083-15

ALL
4973. The best technique for using deicing boots is to

A—allow ice to build first to reduce likelihood of "ice bridging."
B—use them immediately upon visual detection of any ice.
C—cycle several times after exiting to obtain a clean wing.

The FAA recommends deicing systems be activated at the first indication of icing. (PLT493, IR.I.B.K3i) — FAA-H-8083-15

ALL
4974. How should deicing boots be used after exiting flight in icing conditions?

A—Boots do not need to be operated after leaving icing conditions.
B—Continue to cycle the boots several times to remove residual ice left behind after normal boot operation.
C—Only continue to cycle the boots if you are concerned ice may continue to accumulate.

Some residual ice continues to adhere between pneumatic boot system cycles. This residual ice increases as airspeed and/or temperature decreases. It may take many boot cycles to effectively shed the ice. (PLT493, IR.I.B.K3i) — AC 91-74

ALL
4969. The most hazardous aspect of structural icing is that

A—it can cause breakage of antennas.
B—it can cause blockage of the pitot tube and/or static ports affecting aircraft instruments.
C—it can result in aerodynamic degradation including loss of lift.

The most hazardous aspect of structural icing is its aerodynamic effects. Ice alters the shape of an airfoil, reducing the maximum coefficient of lift and angle of attack at which the aircraft stalls. (PLT493, IR.I.B.K3i) — FAA-H-8083-15

ALL
4970. Preventing ice from causing a hazard for aircraft certificated for flight into known icing conditions is accomplished by

1. Spraying alcohol or glycol solution on the aircraft before takeoff.
2. A deicing system on the aircraft.
3. An anti-icing system on the aircraft.

Which statement is true?

A—All three statements are true.
B—Only statements 2 and 3 are true.
C—Only statement 1 is true.

Pilots need an operational understanding of how to use the deicing and anti-icing systems before flying appropriately certified aircraft into known icing conditions. All of these statements are true regarding the reduction of the hazards associated with ice. (PLT493, IR.I.B.K3i) — FAA-H-8083-15

Answers

4971 [A]	4972 [A]	4973 [B]	4974 [B]	4969 [C]	4970 [A]

ALL

4971-1. What is the purpose of a weeping wing?

A—The weeping wing can be used in place of spoilers to slow the aircraft.
B—The weeping wing provides leading edge protection against icing.
C—The weeping wing provides additional camber for aerodynamic lifting.

An alternate type of leading edge protection that is not as common as thermal anti-ice and deicing boots is known as a "weeping wing." The weeping-wing design uses small holes located in the leading edge of the wing to prevent the formation and build-up of ice; it is both an anti-ice and a deicing system. An antifreeze solution is pumped to the leading edge and weeps out through the holes. Additionally, the weeping wing is capable of deicing an aircraft. When ice has accumulated on the leading edges, application of the antifreeze solution chemically breaks down the bond between the ice and airframe, allowing aerodynamic forces to remove the ice. (PLT493, IR.I.B.K3i) — FAA-H-8083-25

ALL

4960-1. What should pilots do if icing is detected while also experiencing a rolling condition?

A—Lower the flaps to decrease airspeed.
B—Set power and angle of attack for a controlled descent.
C—Retract flaps and increase power.

One hazard of structural icing is the possible uncommanded and uncontrolled roll phenomenon called roll upset, associated with severe in-flight icing. Roll upset may occur as a consequence of, or prior to, a wing stall due to anomalous forces that cause the ailerons to deflect or because the ailerons have lost effectiveness. Deflection of ailerons or loss of aileron effectiveness may be caused by ice accumulating in a sensitive area of the wing aft of areas protected by wing ice prevention systems. If roll upset occurs, pilots should reduce the angle of attack by increasing airspeed or extending wing flaps to first setting, set power for a controlled descent, not retract the flaps (if already extended), and verify operation of any wing ice protection or prevention systems. (PLT493, IR.I.B.K3i) — AC 91-74

Answer (A) is incorrect because airspeed should be increased, not decreased. Answer (C) is incorrect because flaps should not be retracted if they are already extended.

ALL

4960-2. What autopilot function should you turn off if icing is suspected?

A—HDG (heading) mode.
B—AUTO Approach (APP) mode.
C—Turn autopilot off.

If inflight icing is encountered, the pilot should disengage the autopilot and hand-fly the airplane. Using the autopilot during icing conditions may mask important cues relating to control or systems. Additionally, autopilots might self-disconnect and present unusual attitudes or control conditions in some icing encounters. (PLT493, IR.I.B.K3i) — AC 91-74

ALL

4960-3. A generally recommended practice for autopilot usage during cruise flight in icing conditions is

A—keeping the autopilot engaged while monitoring the system.
B—periodically disengaging the autopilot and hand flying the aircraft.
C—periodically disengaging and immediately reengaging the altitude hold function.

If inflight icing is encountered, the pilot should disengage the autopilot and hand-fly the aircraft. Using the autopilot during icing conditions may mask important cues relating to control or systems. (PLT128, IR.II.A.K1) — AC 91-74

ALL

4960-4. On initial climb-out after takeoff and with the autopilot engaged, you encounter icing conditions. In this situation you can expect

A—ice to accumulate on the underside of the wings due to the higher AOA.
B—the autopilot to hold the vertical speed, if the anti-icing boots are working.
C—the increased airflow under the wings to prevent the accumulation of ice.

Airplanes are vulnerable to ice accumulation during the initial climb-out in icing conditions because lower speeds often translate into a higher AOA. This exposes the underside of the airplane and its wings to the icing conditions and allows ice to accumulate further aft than it would in cruise flight. Consequently, any ice that forms may be out of the pilot's view and go undetected. Extreme vigilance should be exercised while climbing with the autopilot engaged. Climbing in Vertical Speed (VS) mode in icing conditions is highly discouraged. (PLT128, IR.I.B.K3i) — AC 91-74

Answers

4971-1 [B]	4960-1 [B]	4960-2 [C]	4960-3 [B]	4960-4 [A]

ALL

4961. If icing is suspected on an airplane equipped with deicing equipment, the pilot should

A—first confirm ice with the ice light prior to deploying the pneumatic boots.
B—operate the pneumatic deicing system several times to clear the ice.
C—operate the pneumatic deicing system once to allow time for the ice removal.

Pneumatic boots are one method capable of removing ice from an aircraft surface. This system is commonly used on smaller aircraft and usually provides ice removal for the wing and tail section by inflating a rubber boot. (PLT493, IR.II.A.K1) — FAA-H-8083-15

Answer (A) is incorrect because the deicing system should be used as soon as icing is suspected. Answer (C) is incorrect because the pneumatic boots should be inflated/deflated several times to try to remove the ice.

ALL

4984. When using inflight deicing systems in icing conditions, you should be aware that

A—there will be residual or some stage of intercycle ice on the wings.
B—residual or intercycle ice accumulation is unlikely if the deicing system is engaged prior to entering icing conditions.
C—ice accumulated during cruise flight can be expected to have little effect during approach or landing operations.

Because ice is permitted to accrete between cycles (called intercycle or residual ice) the wing or the tailplane is never entirely clean. Residual or intercycle ice is inherent in the use of any available deicing system, including pneumatic boots. Proper operation of the boots is necessary to minimize the effect of these types of ice. (PLT128, IR.II.A.K1) — AC 91-74

ALL

4962. The first place ice is likely to form on an aircraft is the

A—wings.
B—tailplane.
C—windshield.

Small and/or narrow objects are the best collectors of droplets and ice up most rapidly. This is why a small protuberance within sight of the pilot can be used as an "ice evidence probe." It is generally one of the first parts of the airplane on which an appreciable amount of ice forms. An aircraft's tailplane is a better collector than its wings, because the tailplane presents a thinner surface to the airstream. (PLT493, IR.I.B.K3i) — FAA-H-8083-15

Answer (A) is incorrect because the wings are thicker than the tailplane so not as likely to first build up with ice. Answer (C) is incorrect because the windshield does not protrude into the airstream as much as the control surfaces, so it is less likely than the tailplane to develop ice.

ALL

4964. If a pilot encounters freezing drizzle, he can assume that

A—there is warmer air above.
B—the freezing drizzle will accumulate as rime ice.
C—since freezing drizzle is supercooled it is not a concern for structural icing.

Freezing rain and freezing drizzle occur when the temperature of the surface is below freezing; the rain freezes on contact with the cooler surface. Ice associated with freezing rain or freezing drizzle can accumulate on and beyond the limits of an ice protection system. This kind of ice may not produce the familiar performance degradation; however, it may be hazardous. (PLT493, IR.I.B.K3i) — FAA-H-8083-15

Answer (B) is incorrect freezing drizzle is likely to accumulate as clear ice. Answer (C) is incorrect because freezing drizzle is a major concern for structural icing.

ALL

4965. When flying through supercooled water droplets, the first sign of structural ice accumulation would be

A—the leading edge of the wings.
B—on probes and antennas.
C—the windshield.

Small and/or narrow objects are the best collectors of droplets and ice up most rapidly. This is why a small protuberance within sight of the pilot can be used as an "ice evidence probe." It is generally one of the first parts of the airplane on which an appreciable amount of ice forms. (PLT493, IR.I.B.K3i) — FAA-H-8083-15

Answer (A) is incorrect because the wings are thicker so not as likely to build up with ice. Answer (C) is incorrect because the windshield does not protrude into the airstream, so it is less likely to develop ice first.

Answers

4961 [B]	4984 [A]	4962 [B]	4964 [A]	4965 [B]

ALL

4966. What actions should the pilot take in the event of suspected tailplane icing during an approach?

A—Leave the autopilot on to assist flying the approach.
B—Use partial or no flaps and no autopilot.
C—Hand fly the approach until the IAF and then use the autopilot.

When the autopilot is used in icing conditions, it can mask changes in performance due to the aerodynamic effects of icing that would otherwise be detected by the pilot if the airplane were being hand flown. Pilots should disengage the autopilot and hand fly the aircraft when operating in icing conditions. If tailplane icing is suspected, the pilot should immediately retract flaps to the previous setting and apply appropriate nose-up elevator pressure. (PLT493, IR.II.A.K1) — AC 91-74

Answers (A) and (C) are incorrect because you should not use the autopilot anytime during the approach when operating in icing conditions.

ALL

4967. Expect clear ice to form on the leading edge of airfoils when

A—liquid water and snow combine with ice.
B—temperatures are close to freezing, there is a large volume of liquid water precipitation, and the aircraft is at high airspeeds.
C—the precipitation is small droplets and the aircraft is at low airspeeds.

A glossy, transparent ice formed by the relatively slow freezing of supercooled water is referred to as clear ice. This type of ice is denser, harder, and sometimes more transparent than rime ice. Temperatures close to the freezing point, large amounts of liquid water, high aircraft velocities, and large droplets are conducive to the formation of clear ice. (PLT493, IR.I.B.K3i) — FAA-H-8083-15

Answer (A) is incorrect because this describes conditions conducive to mixed ice. Answer (C) is incorrect because this describes conditions conducive to rime ice.

ALL

4968. When flying through stratiform clouds, the best way to alleviate icing is by

A—changing altitude to one with above-freezing temperatures or where temperatures are colder than -10°C.
B—slowly climbing out of the icing layer.
C—always descending to find warm air below.

When icing is detected, a pilot should do one of two things: leave the area of precipitation or go to an altitude where the temperature is above freezing or colder than -10°C. This "warmer" altitude may not always be lower and "colder" altitude not always higher. Proper preflight action includes obtaining information on the freezing level and the above-freezing levels in precipitation areas. (PLT493, IR.I.B.K3i) — FAA-H-8083-15

Wind Shear

Wind shear is defined as a change in wind direction and/or speed in a very short distance in the atmosphere. This can occur at any level of the atmosphere and can be detected by the pilot as a sudden change in airspeed.

Low-level (low altitude) wind shear can be expected during strong temperature inversions, on all sides of a thunderstorm and directly below the cell. Low-level wind shear can also be found near frontal activity because winds can be significantly different in the two air masses which meet to form the front.

In warm front conditions, the most critical period is before the front passes. Warm front shear may exist below 5,000 feet for about 6 hours before surface passage of the front. The wind shear associated with a warm front is usually more extreme than that found in cold fronts.

The shear associated with cold fronts is usually found behind the front. If the front is moving at 30 knots or more, the shear zone will be 5,000 feet above the surface 3 hours after frontal passage.

Answers

4966 [B]   4967 [B]   4968 [A]

There are two potentially hazardous shear situations:

1. *Loss of tailwind*—A tailwind may shear to either a calm or headwind component. In this instance, initially the airspeed increases, the aircraft pitches up, and altitude increases. Lower than normal power would be required initially, followed by a further decrease as the shear is encountered, and then an increase as glide slope is regained.
2. *Loss of headwind*—A headwind may shear to a calm or tailwind component. Initially, the airspeed decreases, the aircraft pitches down, and altitude decreases.

ALL
4138. Where does wind shear occur?

A—Exclusively in thunderstorms.
B—Wherever there is an abrupt decrease in pressure and/or temperature.
C—With either a wind shift or a wind speed gradient at any level in the atmosphere.

Wind shear may be associated with either a wind shift or a wind speed gradient at any level in the atmosphere. (PLT518, IR.I.B.K3b) — AC 00-6

ALL
4139. What is an important characteristic of wind shear?

A—It is primarily associated with the lateral vortices generated by thunderstorms.
B—It usually exists only in the vicinity of thunderstorms, but may be found near a strong temperature inversion.
C—It may be associated with either a wind shift or a wind speed gradient at any level in the atmosphere.

Wind shear may be associated with either a wind shift or a wind speed gradient at any level in the atmosphere. Low-level wind shear may result from a frontal passage, thunderstorm activity, or low-level temperature inversion. Wind shear may also be found at higher altitudes in association with a frontal passage due to wind shift through the frontal zone. (PLT518, IR.I.B.K3b) — AC 00-6

ALL
4150. What is an important characteristic of wind shear?

A—It is an atmospheric condition that is associated exclusively with zones of convergence.
B—The Coriolis phenomenon in both high- and low-level air masses is the principal generating force.
C—It is an atmospheric condition that may be associated with a low-level temperature inversion, a jet stream, or a frontal zone.

Wind shear may be associated with either a wind shift or a wind speed gradient at any level in the atmosphere. Low-level wind shear may result from a frontal passage, thunderstorm activity, or low-level temperature inversion. Wind shear may also be found at higher altitudes in association with a frontal passage due to wind shift through the frontal zone. (PLT518, IR.I.B.K3b) — AC 00-6

ALL
4140. Which is a characteristic of low-level wind shear as it relates to frontal activity?

A—With a warm front, the most critical period is before the front passes the airport.
B—With a cold front, the most critical period is just before the front passes the airport.
C—Turbulence will always exist in wind-shear conditions.

Wind shear occurs with a cold front just after the front passes the airport and for a short period thereafter. If the front is moving 30 knots or more, the frontal surface will usually be 5,000 feet above the airport about three hours after the frontal passage. With a warm front, the most critical period is before the front passes the airport. Warm front wind shear may exist below 5,000 feet for approximately six hours. The problem ceases to exist after the front passes the airport. Data compiled on wind shear indicates that the amount of shear in warm fronts is much greater than that found in cold fronts. (PLT518, IR.I.B.K3b) — AC 00-6

Answer (B) is incorrect because cold front wind shear occurs as the front passes or just after (not before). Answer (C) is incorrect because turbulence may or may not exist in wind shear conditions.

Answers

4138 [C] 4139 [C] 4150 [C] 4140 [A]

ALL

4238. Hazardous wind shear is commonly encountered near the ground

A—during periods when the wind velocity is stronger than 35 knots.
B—during periods when the wind velocity is stronger than 35 knots and near mountain valleys.
C—during periods of strong temperature inversion and near thunderstorms.

You can be relatively certain of a shear zone in a low-level temperature inversion, if you know that the wind at 2,000 to 4,000 feet is 25 knots or more. Wind shear turbulence is also found near the ground outside thunderstorm clouds. See the following figure. (PLT518, IR.I.B.K3b) — AC 00-6

Answer (A) is incorrect because winds stronger than 35 knots are hazardous but not specifically due to wind shear. Answer (B) is incorrect because hazardous wind shear is normally located on the leeward side of mountains (not just mountain valleys).

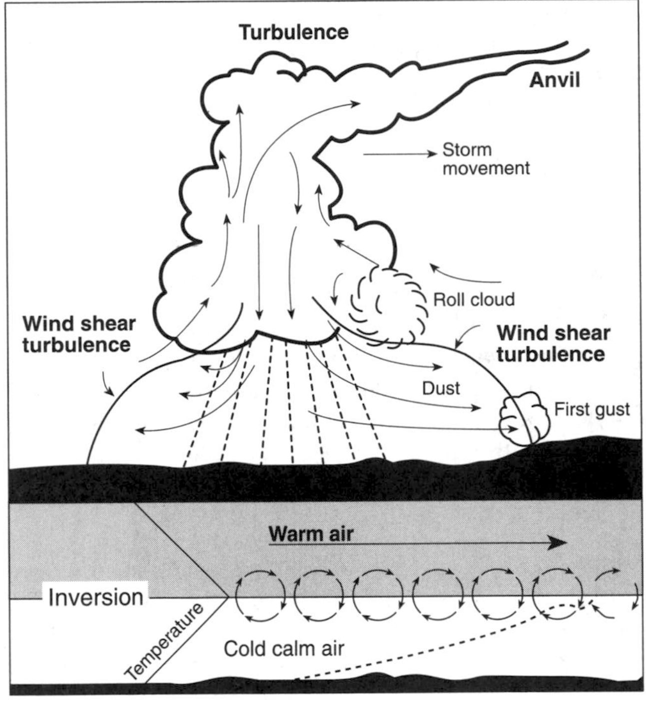

Question 4238

ALL

4135. Where can wind shear associated with a thunderstorm be found? Choose the most complete answer.

A—In front of the thunderstorm cell (anvil side) and on the right side of the cell.
B—In front of the thunderstorm cell and directly under the cell.
C—On all sides of the thunderstorm cell and directly under the cell.

The winds around a thunderstorm are complex. Wind shear can be found on all sides of a thunderstorm cell and in the downdraft directly under the cell. The wind shift line, or gust front, associated with thunderstorms can precede the actual storm by 15 nautical miles or more. (PLT518, IR.I.B.K3b) — AC 00-6

ALL

4720. When passing through an abrupt wind shear which involves a shift from a tailwind to a headwind, what power management would normally be required to maintain a constant indicated airspeed and ILS glide slope?

A—Higher than normal power initially, followed by a further increase as the wind shear is encountered, then a decrease.
B—Lower than normal power initially, followed by a further decrease as the wind shear is encountered, then an increase.
C—Higher than normal power initially, followed by a decrease as the shear is encountered, then an increase.

When on an approach in a tailwind condition that shears into a calm wind or headwind, initially the IAS and pitch will increase and the aircraft will balloon above the glide slope. Power should first be reduced to correct this condition. Power should be further reduced as the aircraft proceeds through the wind shear, then increased. (PLT518, IR.I.B.K3b) — AC 00-54

ALL

4727. While flying a 3° glide slope, a constant tailwind shears to a calm wind. Which conditions should the pilot expect?

A—Airspeed and pitch attitude decrease and there is a tendency to go below glide slope.
B—Airspeed and pitch attitude increase and there is a tendency to go below glide slope.
C—Airspeed and pitch attitude increase and there is a tendency to go above glide slope.

Answers

4238 [C]	4135 [C]	4720 [B]	4727 [C]

When an aircraft that is flying with a tailwind suddenly encounters calm air, it is the same as encountering a headwind. Initially, the IAS and pitch will increase and the aircraft will balloon above the glide slope. (PLT518, IR.I.B.K3b) — AC 00-54

Answer (A) is incorrect because the airspeed and pitch increase and there is a tendency to go above the glide slope. Answer (B) is incorrect because there is a tendency to go above the glide slope.

ALL

4739. Thrust is managed to maintain IAS, and glide slope is being flown. What characteristics should be observed when a headwind shears to be a constant tailwind?

A—PITCH ATTITUDE: Increases; REQUIRED THRUST: Increased, then reduced; VERTICAL SPEED: Increases; IAS: Increases, then decreases to approach speed.
B—PITCH ATTITUDE: Decreases; REQUIRED THRUST: Increased, then reduced; VERTICAL SPEED: Increases; IAS: Decreases, then increases to approach speed.
C—PITCH ATTITUDE: Increases; REQUIRED THRUST: Reduced, then increased; VERTICAL SPEED: Decreases; IAS: Decreases, then increases to approach speed.

When a headwind shears to a constant tailwind: the nose pitches down, thrust must be increased initially to resume normal approach speed and then reduced as the airspeed stabilizes, vertical speed increases, and indicated airspeed decreases and then increases to approach speed. See the following figure. (PLT518, IR.I.B.K3b) — AC 00-54

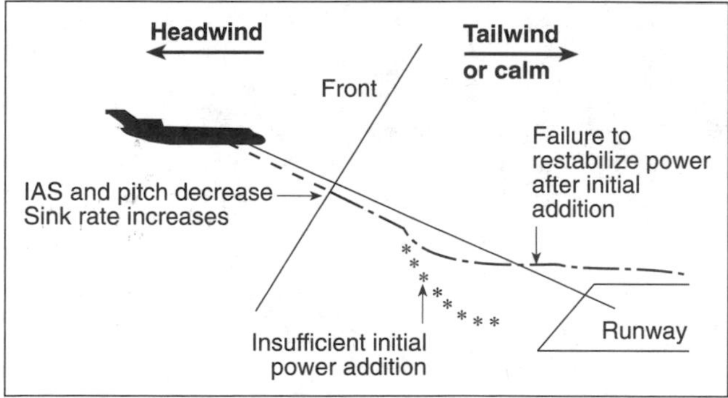

Question 4739

ALL

4755. While flying a 3° glide slope, a headwind shears to a tailwind. Which conditions should the pilot expect on the glide slope?

A—Airspeed and pitch attitude decrease and there is a tendency to go below glide slope.
B—Airspeed and pitch attitude increase and there is a tendency to go above glide slope.
C—Airspeed and pitch attitude decrease and there is a tendency to remain on the glide slope.

When a headwind shears to a tailwind the airspeed decreases, the nose pitches down, and the aircraft will begin to drop below the glide slope. See the following figure. (PLT518, IR.I.B.K3b) — AC 00-54

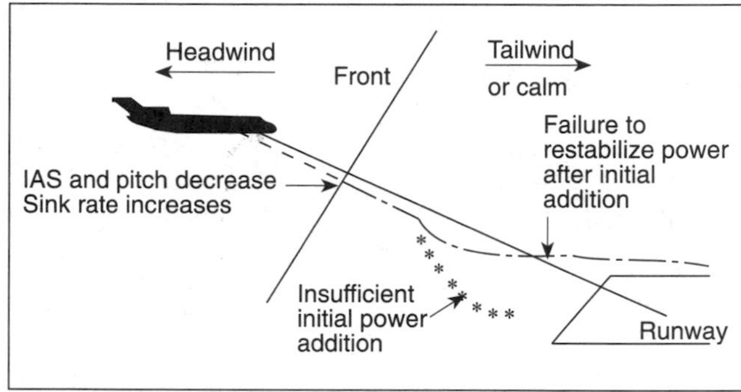

Question 4755

ALL

4917. When climbing or descending through a temperature inversion or an area of possible wind shear, the pilot should be aware of

A—a fast rate of climb and a slow rate of descent.
B—a rapid change of airspeed.
C—airframe icing.

There are two potentially hazardous shear situations:

1. *A tailwind may shear to either a calm or headwind component. In this instance, initially the airspeed increases, the aircraft pitches up and the altitude increases.*
2. *A headwind may shear to a calm or tailwind component. In this situation, initially the airspeed decreases, the aircraft pitches down, and the altitude decreases.*

(PLT518, IR.I.B.K3b) — AC 00-54

Answer (A) is incorrect because a fast rate of climb and a slow rate of descent is safer than the reverse situation. Answer (C) is incorrect because airframe icing does not vary with wind shear.

Answers

4739 [B] 4755 [A] 4917 [B]

Chapter 2
Weather Services

Aviation Routine Weather Report (METAR)

An international weather reporting code is used for weather reports (METAR) and forecasts (TAFs) worldwide. The reports follow the format shown in Figure 2-1.

For aviation purposes, the ceiling is the lowest broken or overcast layer, or vertical visibility into an obscuration.

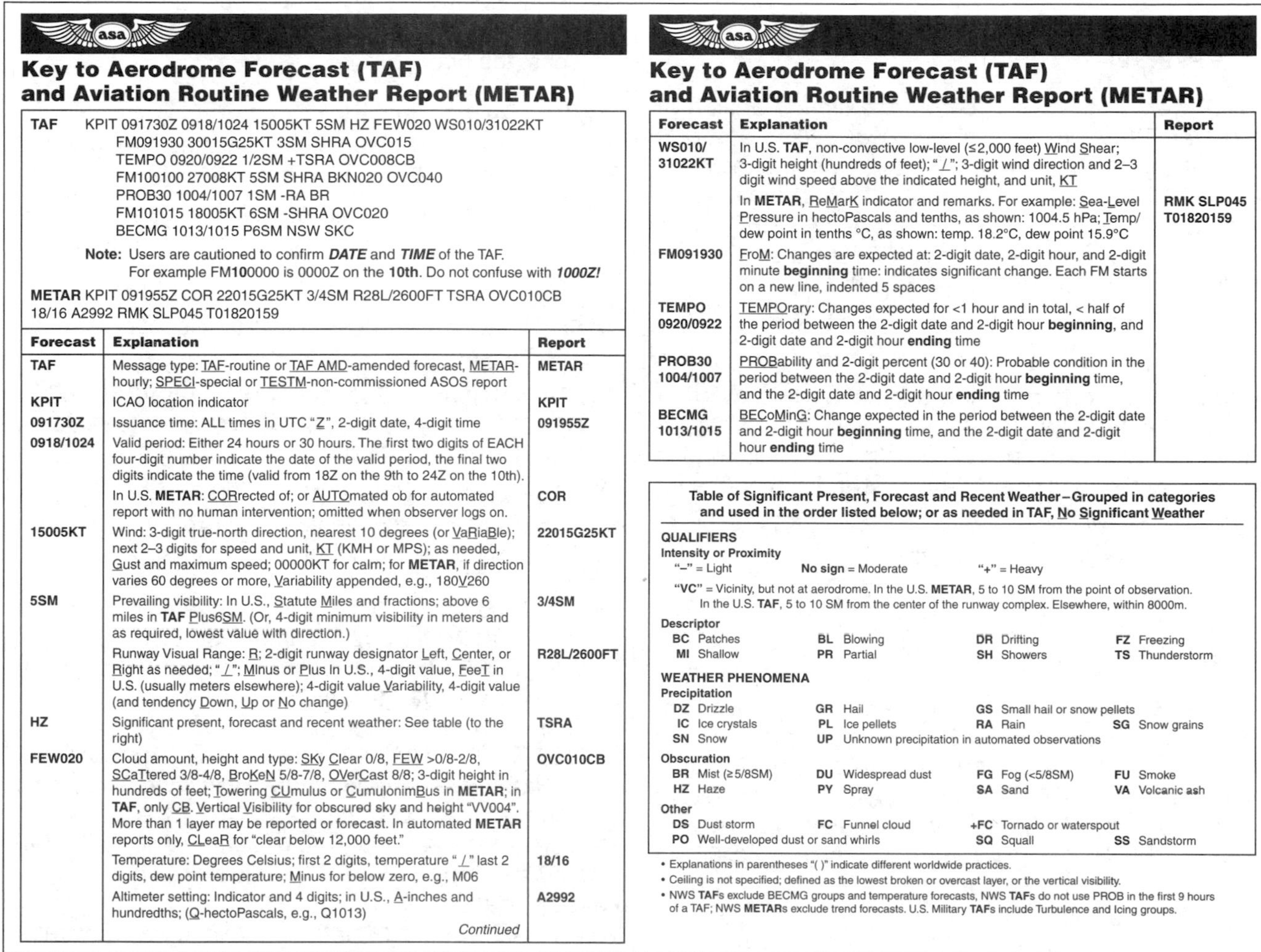

Key to Aerodrome Forecast (TAF) and Aviation Routine Weather Report (METAR)

TAF KPIT 091730Z 0918/1024 15005KT 5SM HZ FEW020 WS010/31022KT
FM091930 30015G25KT 3SM SHRA OVC015
TEMPO 0920/0922 1/2SM +TSRA OVC008CB
FM100100 27008KT 5SM SHRA BKN020 OVC040
PROB30 1004/1007 1SM -RA BR
FM101015 18005KT 6SM -SHRA OVC020
BECMG 1013/1015 P6SM NSW SKC

Note: Users are cautioned to confirm ***DATE*** and ***TIME*** of the TAF. For example FM**10**0000 is 0000Z on the **10th**. Do not confuse with ***1000Z!***

METAR KPIT 091955Z COR 22015G25KT 3/4SM R28L/2600FT TSRA OVC010CB 18/16 A2992 RMK SLP045 T01820159

Forecast	Explanation	Report
TAF	Message type: TAF-routine or TAF AMD-amended forecast, METAR-hourly; SPECI-special or TESTM-non-commissioned ASOS report	**METAR**
KPIT	ICAO location indicator	**KPIT**
091730Z	Issuance time: ALL times in UTC "Z", 2-digit date, 4-digit time	**091955Z**
0918/1024	Valid period: Either 24 hours or 30 hours. The first two digits of EACH four-digit number indicate the date of the valid period, the final two digits indicate the time (valid from 18Z on the 9th to 24Z on the 10th).	
	In U.S. **METAR**: CORrected of; or AUTOmated ob for automated report with no human intervention; omitted when observer logs on.	**COR**
15005KT	Wind: 3-digit true-north direction, nearest 10 degrees (or VaRiaBle); next 2–3 digits for speed and unit, KT (KMH or MPS); as needed, Gust and maximum speed; 00000KT for calm; for **METAR**, if direction varies 60 degrees or more, Variability appended, e.g., 180V260	**22015G25KT**
5SM	Prevailing visibility: In U.S., Statute Miles and fractions; above 6 miles in **TAF** Plus6SM. (Or, 4-digit minimum visibility in meters and as required, lowest value with direction.)	**3/4SM**
	Runway Visual Range: R; 2-digit runway designator Left, Center, or Right as needed; "/"; Minus or Plus in U.S., 4-digit value, FeeT in U.S. (usually meters elsewhere); 4-digit value Variability, 4-digit value (and tendency Down, Up or No change)	**R28L/2600FT**
HZ	Significant present, forecast and recent weather: See table (to the right)	**TSRA**
FEW020	Cloud amount, height and type: SKy Clear 0/8, FEW >0/8-2/8, SCaTtered 3/8-4/8, BroKeN 5/8-7/8, OVerCast 8/8; 3-digit height in hundreds of feet; Towering CUmulus or CumulonimBus in **METAR**; in **TAF**, only CB. Vertical Visibility for obscured sky and height "VV004". More than 1 layer may be reported or forecast. In automated **METAR** reports only, CLeaR for "clear below 12,000 feet."	**OVC010CB**
	Temperature: Degrees Celsius; first 2 digits, temperature "/" last 2 digits, dew point temperature; Minus for below zero, e.g., M06	**18/16**
	Altimeter setting: Indicator and 4 digits; in U.S., A-inches and hundredths; (Q-hectoPascals, e.g., Q1013)	**A2992**

Continued

Key to Aerodrome Forecast (TAF) and Aviation Routine Weather Report (METAR)

Forecast	Explanation	Report
WS010/31022KT	In U.S. **TAF**, non-convective low-level (≤2,000 feet) Wind Shear; 3-digit height (hundreds of feet); "/"; 3-digit wind direction and 2–3 digit wind speed above the indicated height, and unit, KT	
	In **METAR**, ReMarK indicator and remarks. For example: Sea-Level Pressure in hectoPascals and tenths, as shown: 1004.5 hPa; Temp/dew point in tenths °C, as shown: temp. 18.2°C, dew point 15.9°C	**RMK SLP045 T01820159**
FM091930	FroM: Changes are expected at: 2-digit date, 2-digit hour, and 2-digit minute **beginning** time: indicates significant change. Each FM starts on a new line, indented 5 spaces	
TEMPO 0920/0922	TEMPOrary: Changes expected for <1 hour and in total, < half of the period between the 2-digit date and 2-digit hour **beginning**, and 2-digit date and 2-digit hour **ending** time	
PROB30 1004/1007	PROBability and 2-digit percent (30 or 40): Probable condition in the period between the 2-digit date and 2-digit hour **beginning** time, and the 2-digit date and 2-digit hour **ending** time	
BECMG 1013/1015	BECoMinG: Change expected in the period between the 2-digit date and 2-digit hour **beginning** time, and the 2-digit date and 2-digit hour **ending** time	

Table of Significant Present, Forecast and Recent Weather–Grouped in categories and used in the order listed below; or as needed in TAF, No Significant Weather

QUALIFIERS

Intensity or Proximity

"–" = Light **No sign** = Moderate "+" = Heavy

"VC" = Vicinity, but not at aerodrome. In the U.S. **METAR**, 5 to 10 SM from the point of observation. In the U.S. **TAF**, 5 to 10 SM from the center of the runway complex. Elsewhere, within 8000m.

Descriptor

BC Patches	**BL** Blowing	**DR** Drifting	**FZ** Freezing
MI Shallow	**PR** Partial	**SH** Showers	**TS** Thunderstorm

WEATHER PHENOMENA

Precipitation

DZ Drizzle	**GR** Hail	**GS** Small hail or snow pellets	
IC Ice crystals	**PL** Ice pellets	**RA** Rain	**SG** Snow grains
SN Snow	**UP** Unknown precipitation in automated observations		

Obscuration

BR Mist (≥5/8SM)	**DU** Widespread dust	**FG** Fog (<5/8SM)	**FU** Smoke
HZ Haze	**PY** Spray	**SA** Sand	**VA** Volcanic ash

Other

DS Dust storm	**FC** Funnel cloud	**+FC** Tornado or waterspout	
PO Well-developed dust or sand whirls		**SQ** Squall	**SS** Sandstorm

- Explanations in parentheses "( )" indicate different worldwide practices.
- Ceiling is not specified; defined as the lowest broken or overcast layer, or the vertical visibility.
- NWS **TAFs** exclude BECMG groups and temperature forecasts, NWS **TAFs** do not use PROB in the first 9 hours of a TAF; NWS **METARs** exclude trend forecasts. U.S. Military **TAFs** include Turbulence and Icing groups.

Figure 2-1. TAF/METAR weather card

ALL

4202. A ceiling is defined as the height of the

A—highest layer of clouds aloft that covers over 6/10 of the sky.

B—lowest layer of clouds that contributed to the overall overcast.

C—lowest layer of clouds or obscuring phenomena aloft that is reported as broken or overcast.

Ceiling is defined as height of the lowest layer of clouds or obscuring phenomena aloft that is reported as broken or overcast and not classified as thin; or, as vertical visibility into surface-based obscuring phenomena that hides all the sky. (PLT026, IR.I.B.K3f) — AC 00-45

Answer (A) is incorrect because a ceiling is defined as the lowest layer of clouds. Answer (B) is incorrect because a ceiling is specifically the lowest layer of clouds which is broken or overcast.

Answers

4202 [C]

ALL

4196. The station originating the following weather report has a field elevation of 1,300 feet MSL. From the bottom of the overcast cloud layer, what is its thickness? (Tops of OVC are reported at 3,800 feet.)

SPECI KOKC 2228Z 28024G36KT 3/4SM BKN008 OVC020 28/23 A3000

A—500 feet.
B—1,700 feet.
C—2,500 feet.

Will Rogers Airport (KOKC) reports clouds broken at 800 feet (BKN008) and an overcast ceiling at 2,000 feet (OVC020). This means the bottom of the overcast layer is 3,300 feet (1,300 feet MSL + 2,000 feet AGL). The tops of the overcast are reported at 3,800 feet. Therefore, the overcast layer is 500 feet thick (3,800 – 3,300). (PLT059, IR.I.B.K2) — AC 00-45

ALL

4203. The reporting station originating this Aviation Routine Weather Report has a field elevation of 620 feet. If the reported sky cover is one continuous layer, what is its thickness? (Tops of OVC are reported at 6,500 feet.)

METAR KMDW 121856Z AUTO 32005KT 1 1/2SM +RABR OVC007 17/16 A2980

A—5,180 feet.
B—5,800 feet.
C—5,880 feet.

Chicago Midway Airport (KMDW) reports an overcast ceiling at 700 feet (OVC007). This means the bottom of the overcast layer is 1,320 feet (620 MSL + 700 feet AGL). The tops of the overcast layer are reported at 6,500 feet. Therefore, the overcast layer is 5,180 feet thick (6,500 – 1,320). (PLT059, IR.I.B.K2) — AC 00-45

ALL

4205. What is meant by the entry in the remarks section of METAR surface report for KBNA?

METAR KBNA 211250Z 33018KT 290V260 1/2SM R31/2700FT +SN

BLSNFG VV008 00/M03 A2991 RMK RAE42SNB42

A—The wind is variable from 290° to 360.
B—Heavy blowing snow and fog on runway 31.
C—Rain ended 42 past the hour, snow began 42 past the hour.

RMK — remarks follow
RAE42SNB42 — rain ended 42 past the hour (RAE42), snow began 42 past the hour (SNB42)

(PLT059, IR.I.B.K2) — AC 00-45

ALL

4182. What significant sky condition is reported in this METAR observation?

METAR KBNA 1250Z 33018KT 290V360 1/2SM R31/2700FT +SN BLSNFG VV008 00/M03 A2991 RMK RERAE42SNB42

A—Runway 31 ceiling is 2700 feet.
B—Sky is obscured with vertical visibility of 800 feet.
C—Measured ceiling is 300 feet overcast.

METAR KBNA 1250Z — routine weather report for Nashville Metro airport, time 1250 UTC
33018KT 290V360 — wind from 330° at 18 knots, variable between 290° and 360°
1/2SM — visibility 1/2 statute mile
R31/2700FT — RVR for runway 31 is 2,700 feet
+SN BLSNFG — heavy snow, visibility obstructed by blowing snow and fog
VV008 — sky obscured with vertical visibility of 800 feet
00/M03 — temperature 0°C, dew point -3°C
A2991 — altimeter setting 29.91"
RMK RAE42SNB42 — remarks follow, recent weather events, rain ended 42 past the hour, snow began 42 past the hour

(PLT059, IR.I.B.K2) — AC 00-45

Answers

4196 [A]   4203 [A]   4205 [C]   4182 [B]

Terminal Aerodrome Forecast (TAF)

A TAF is a concise statement of the expected meteorological conditions at an airport during a specified period (usually 24 hours). TAFs use the same code used in the METAR weather reports (See Figure 2-1, page 2-3).

TAFs are issued in the following format:

TYPE / LOCATION / ISSUANCE TIME / VALID TIME / FORECAST

Note: the "/" above are for separation purposes and do not appear in the actual TAFs.

ALL

4170. The body of a terminal aerodrome forecast (TAF) covers a geographical proximity within a

A—5 nautical mile radius of the center of an airport.
B—5 statute mile radius from the center of an airport runway complex.
C—5 to 10 statute mile radius from the center of an airport runway complex.

A TAF is a concise statement of the expected meteorological conditions within a 5 SM radius from the center of an airport's runway complex during a 24-hour time period. (PLT288, IR.I.B.K2) — AC 00-45

ALL

4170-1. Which weather product is a concise statement of the expected weather for an airport's runway complex?

A—Area forecast.
B—Weather depiction charts.
C—Terminal aerodrome forecast.

A TAF is a concise statement of the expected meteorological conditions within a 5 SM radius from the center of an airport's runway complex during a 24-hour time period. (PLT288, IR.I.B.K2) — AC 00-45

ALL

4177. A "VRB" wind entry in a TAF will be indicated when the wind is

A—3 knots or less.
B—6 knots or less.
C—9 knots or less.

A variable wind is encoded as "VRB" when wind direction fluctuates due to convective activity or low wind speeds (6 knots or less). (PLT288, IR.I.B.K2) — AC 00-45

ALL

4178. When the visibility is greater than 6 SM on a TAF it is expressed as

A—6PSM.
B—P6SM.
C—6SMP.

Expected visibilities greater than 6 miles are forecast as a Plus 6SM (P6SM). (PLT288, IR.I.B.K2) — AC 00-45

ALL

4180. What is the forecast wind at 1800Z in the following TAF?

KMEM 091740Z 1818 00000KT 1/2SM RAFG OVC005=

A—Calm.
B—Unknown.
C—Not recorded.

A calm wind is forecast as "00000KT." (PLT288, IR.I.B.K2) — AC 00-45

ALL

4228. From which primary source should you obtain information regarding the weather expected to exist at your destination at your estimated time of arrival?

A—Weather depiction chart.
B—Surface analysis charts.
C—Terminal aerodrome forecast.

A TAF is a prediction of weather conditions to be expected for a specific airport rather than a larger area. (PLT288, IR.I.B.K2) — AC 00-45

Answers (A) and (B) are incorrect because they are not forecasts, but rather reports of current or past conditions.

Answers

4170 [B] 4170-1 [C] 4177 [B] 4178 [B] 4180 [A] 4228 [C]

ALL

4204. What is the wind shear forecast in the following TAF?

TAF
KCVG 231051Z 231212 12012KT 4SM -RA BR OVC008
WS005/27050KT TEMPO 1719 1/2SM -RA FG
FM1930 09012KT 1SM -DZ BR VV003 BECMG 2021
5SM HZ=

A—5 feet AGL from 270° at 50 KT.
B—50 feet AGL from 270° at 50 KT.
C—500 feet AGL from 270° at 50 KT.

WS005/27050KT — low level wind shear at 500 feet, wind 270° at 50 knots.

(PLT288, IR.I.B.K2) — AC 00-45

Graphical Forecasts for Aviation (GFA)

The GFA is an online interactive map of observed and forecast weather information over the continental United States (CONUS), and can be accessed at **aviationweather.gov/gfa**. It is intended to give users a complete picture of weather critical to aviation safety. The GFA display shows user-selected weather categories each containing multiple fields of interest at altitudes from the surface up to FL480. Depending on the field of interest chosen, weather information is available from -6 hours in the past (observed) to +15 hours in the future (forecast).

The GFA is an aggregate of several existing weather products. The information and data from the various weather products are overlaid on a high-resolution basemap of the United States. The user selects flight levels and current time period for either observed or forecast weather information. Mouse-clicking or hovering over the map provides additional information in textual format, such as current METAR or TAF for a selected airport. The GFA replaces the textual area forecast (FA) for the CONUS and Hawaii with a more modern digital solution for obtaining weather information. The Aviation Surface Forecast and Aviation Cloud Forecast graphics are snapshot images derived from a subset of the aviation weather forecasts.

The Aviation Surface Forecast displays surface visibility with overlays of wind and gusts, predominant precipitation type (i.e., rain, snow, mix, ice, or thunderstorm) coincident with any cloud and predominant weather type (i.e., haze, fog, smoke, blowing dust/sand). The graphical AIRMETs for IFR and strong surface wind are overlaid. See FAA Figure 260. Forecast surface visibility is contoured for Low IFR (0–1 statute miles), IFR (1–3 statute miles), and Marginal VFR (MVFR; 3–5 statute miles) conditions. Visibilities in excess of 5 statute miles are not shown. Winds are depicted with a standard wind barb, in red when indicating gusts. See Figure 2-2.

The Aviation Cloud Forecast displays a cloud coverage fraction (few/scattered, broken, overcast) for clouds with bases below FL180 (18,000 feet MSL). Text overlays indicate cloud coverage and height in feet above MSL at that particular location. See FAA Figure 263. The fill fraction of the circle at each forecasted point depicts sky cloud coverage. Clear skies are annotated as SKC. Clouds above FL180 are indicated as cirrus or CI. The bases below FL180 of FEW/SCT, BKN, and OVC clouds are labeled. The tops of the highest BKN or OVC layer with bases below FL180 are labeled. When multiple layers of BKN or OVC clouds exist, the top of the highest layer will be given preceded by LYRD. Cirrus clouds above clouds with bases below FL180 are labeled as CI ABV. The graphical AIRMETs for icing and mountain obscuration are also overlaid.

Answers
4204 [C]

Dust or sand		
	FU VA	Smoke or volcanic ash
	HZ	Haze
	DU SA	Dust or sand
	BLDU BLSA	Blowing dust or Blowing sand
	PO	Well-developed Dust/Sand whirls
	VCSS	Sandstorm in the vicinity
Fog or special weather		
	BR	Mist
	MIFG	Shallow fog
	VCTS	Thunderstorm in the vicinity
	VIRGA	Virga
	VCSH	Showers in the vicinity
	TS	Thunderstorm
	SQ	Squalls
	FC	Funnel cloud or tornado
Blowing weather		
	SS	Sand or dust storm
	+SS	Strong sand or dust storm
	BLSN	Blowing snow
	DRSN	Drifting snow
Fog		
	VCFG	Fog in the vicinity
	BCFG	Patchy fog
	PRFG	Partial fog
	FG	Fog
	FZFG	Freezing fog
Drizzle		
	-DZ	Light drizzle
	DZ	Moderate drizzle
	+DZ	Heavy drizzle
	-FZDZ	Light freezing drizzle
	FZDZ +FZDZ	Moderate to heavy freezing drizzle
	-DZRA	Light drizzle and rain
	DZRA	Moderate to heavy drizzle and rain

Rain		
	-RA	Light rain
	RA	Moderate rain
	+RA	Heavy rain
	-FZRA	Light freezing rain
	FZRA +FZRA	Moderate to heavy freezing rain
	-RASN	Light rain and snow
	RASN +RASN	Moderate to heavy rain and snow
Snow and misc. frozen precipitation		
	-SN	Light snow
	SN	Moderate snow
	+SN	Heavy snow
	SG	Snow grains
	IC	Ice crystals
	PL	Ice pellets
Showery precipitation		
	-SHRA	Light rain showers
	SHRA +SHRA	Moderate to heavy rain showers
	-SHRASN	Light rain and snow showers
	SHRASN +SHRASN	Moderate to heavy rain and snow showers
	-SHSN	Light snow showers
	SHSN +SHSN	Moderate to heavy snow showers
	-SHGR	Light showers with hail
	SHGR	Moderate to heavy showers with hail
Thunderstorms		
	TSRA	Thunderstorm, rain
	TSGR	Thunderstorm, hail
	+TSRA	Thunderstorm, Heavy rain
	+TSGR	Heavy thunderstorm with hail

Figure 2-2. Weather symbols

ALL

4179. To best determine general forecast weather conditions covering a flight information region, the pilot should refer to

A—Graphical Forecast for Aviation (GFA).
B—Weather Depiction Charts.
C—Satellite Maps.

The GFA is intended to provide the necessary aviation weather information to give users a complete picture of the weather that may impact flight in the continental U.S. (CONUS). (PLT290, IR.I.B.K2) — AC 00-45

ALL

4259. (Refer to Figure 260.) What is the valid period for the aviation surface forecast CONUS?

A—1355 UTC.
B—1655 UTC.
C—1600 UTC.

The valid period for the static display is shown in the top right corner, VALID AT 1600 UTC WED 15 MAR 2017. (PLT290, IR.I.B.K2) — AC 00-45

ALL

4260. (Refer to Figure 261.) The precipitation type forecast to occur over southern ND (area C) is

A—Freezing rain.
B—Freezing drizzle.
C—Moderate snow.

The red symbol depicted over southern North Dakota (ND) identifies the type of precipitation, in this case freezing rain. (PLT290, IR.I.B.K2) — AC 00-45

ALL

4268. (Refer to Figure 260.) The surface visibility over the western part of Washington State (area A) forecast at +3 hr is predominantly

A—0–1 SM.
B—3–5 SM.
C—1–3 SM.

The shaded area along the western part of Washington State indicates marginal VFR conditions or 3–5 SM visibility. Note the scale in the bottom left portion of the GFA static image. (PLT290, IR.I.B.K2) — AC 00-45

ALL

4271. (Refer to Figure 262.) The weather conditions causing limited visibility along the coastal waters of Southern California (area B) are forecast to be

A—Moderate to heavy rain showers.
B—Partial fog.
C—Fog.

The three horizontal yellow lines is the weather symbol for fog. The limited visibility is due to foggy conditions along the coast and coastal waters. (PLT290, IR.I.B.K2) — AC 00-45

ALL

4273. (Refer to Figure 262.) The surface winds over eastern Washington State (area A) are forecasted to be

A—10 knots gusting to 30 knots.
B—20 knots gusting to 30 knots.
C—30 knots.

Winds are depicted with a standard wind barb, in red where showing gusts. The single black barb indicates a sustained wind of 10 knots with an additional 20 knots of gusting conditions or sustained winds of 10 gusting to 30 knots. (PLT290, IR.I.B.K2) — AC 00-45

ALL

4281. (Refer to Figure 263.) The ceilings over southern Texas (area C) are forecast to be

A—SCT.
B—BKN.
C—OVC.

Note the cloud coverage chart in the bottom left of the Aviation Cloud Forecast. The dark purple identifies an area of overcast conditions. (PLT290, IR.I.B.K2) — AC 00-45

ALL

4285. (Refer to Figure 266.) Precipitation throughout Washington and Oregon is predominantly

A—Light rain and rain showers.
B—Heavy rain showers.
C—Freezing rain.

The weather symbols over both Washington and Oregon are predominantly two filled-in circles indicating light rain and an upside down triangle with single filled-in circle above indicating rain showers. (PLT290, IR.I.B.K2) — AC 00-45

Answers

4179 [A]	4259 [C]	4260 [A]	4268 [B]	4271 [C]	4273 [A]
4281 [C]	4285 [A]				

ALL
4290. (Refer to Figure 268.) What forecast weather conditions should you expect along the coast of California (area C)?

A—Fog and visibility 0–1 SM.
B—Fog and visibility 3–5 SM.
C—Low overcast layer and IFR conditions.

The three horizontal yellow lines are the weather symbol for fog. The general area is shaded a blue color depicting marginal VFR and visibility 3–5 SM. Note the scale in the bottom left corner of the GFA static image. (PLT290, IR.I.B.K2) — AC 00-45

ALL
4299. (Refer to Figure 269.) The cloud coverage around area B on the Aviation Cloud Forecast is forecast to be

A—Bases at 6,000' tops at 7,000.
B—BRKN tops at 7,000'.
C—OVC at 7,000'.

The dark shaded purple indicates an area of predominantly overcast conditions. Note the scale in the bottom left corner of the GFA static image. The bases and tops are both given as OVC 060 / TOP 070. (PLT290, IR.I.B.K2) — AC 00-45

Pilot Reports (UA)

Aircraft in flight are the only means of directly observing cloud tops, icing, and turbulence; therefore, no observation is more timely than one made from the cockpit. While the FAA encourages pilots to report inflight weather, a report of any unforecast weather is required by regulation. A PIREP (UA) is usually transmitted in a prescribed format. See Figure 2-3 on the next page.

Pilots seeking weather avoidance assistance should keep in mind that ATC radar limitations and frequency congestion may limit the controller's capability to provide this service.

ALL
4092. Which is true regarding the use of airborne weather avoidance radar for the recognition of certain weather conditions?

A—The radarscope provides no assurance of avoiding instrument weather conditions.
B—The avoidance of hail is assured when flying between and just clear of the most intense echoes.
C—The clear area between intense echoes indicates that visual sighting of storms can be maintained when flying between the echoes.

Radar only detects precipitation. Not all clouds contain enough moisture to be detected by weather radar, which makes it possible to fly into instrument weather conditions despite using radar. (PLT105, IR.I.B.K2) — AC 00-45

Answer (B) is incorrect because hail can be thrown miles away from thunderstorms, and radar can only detect the actual storm. Answer (C) is incorrect because clouds and fog are not shown on radar, so clear areas on the radar do not guarantee VFR conditions.

ALL
4468. Pilots on IFR flights seeking ATC in-flight weather avoidance assistance should keep in mind that

A—ATC radar limitations and, frequency congestion may limit the controllers capability to provide this service.
B—circumnavigating severe weather can only be accommodated in the en route areas away from terminals because of congestion.
C—ATC Narrow Band Radar does not provide the controller with weather intensity capability.

The controller's primary function is to provide safe separation between aircraft. Any additional service, such as weather avoidance assistance, can only be provided to the extent that it does not degrade the primary function. The separation workload is generally greater than normal when weather disrupts the usual flow of traffic. ATC radar limitations and frequency congestion may also be a factor in limiting the controller's capability to provide additional service. (PLT172, IR.I.B.K2) — AIM ¶7-1-13

Answer (B) is incorrect because controllers can provide inflight weather avoidance in terminal areas when workload conditions permit. Answer (C) is incorrect because ATC Narrow Band Radar does provide weather intensity capability.

Answers

4290 [B]	4299 [A]	4092 [A]	4468 [A]

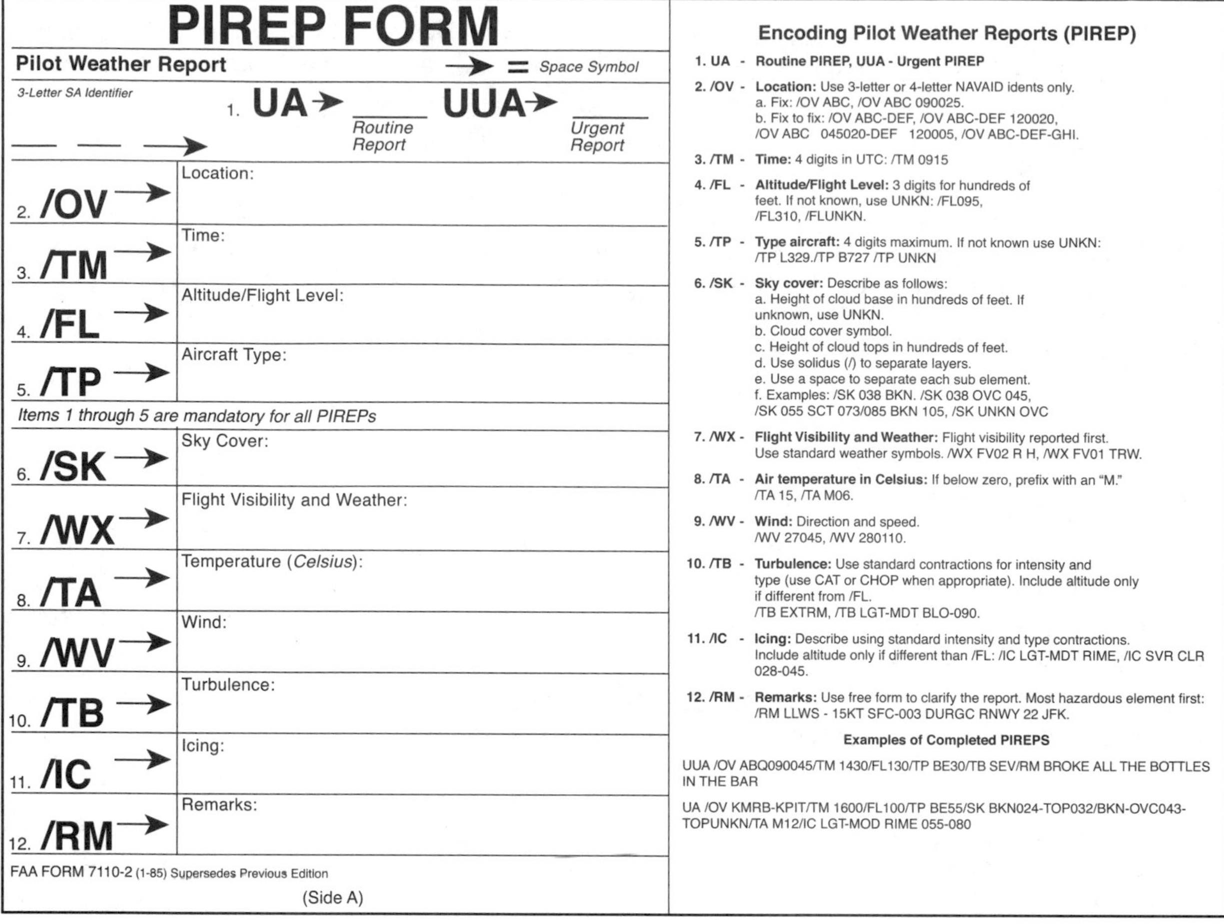

PIREP FORM

Pilot Weather Report → = *Space Symbol*

3-Letter SA Identifier

1. **UA**→ ____ **UUA**→ ____
Routine Report *Urgent Report*

— — →

2. **/OV** →	Location:
3. **/TM** →	Time:
4. **/FL** →	Altitude/Flight Level:
5. **/TP** →	Aircraft Type:
Items 1 through 5 are mandatory for all PIREPs	
6. **/SK** →	Sky Cover:
7. **/WX** →	Flight Visibility and Weather:
8. **/TA** →	Temperature (*Celsius*):
9. **/WV** →	Wind:
10. **/TB** →	Turbulence:
11. **/IC** →	Icing:
12. **/RM** →	Remarks:

FAA FORM 7110-2 (1-85) Supersedes Previous Edition

(Side A)

Encoding Pilot Weather Reports (PIREP)

1. UA - **Routine PIREP, UUA - Urgent PIREP**
2. /OV - **Location:** Use 3-letter or 4-letter NAVAID idents only.
   a. Fix: /OV ABC, /OV ABC 090025.
   b. Fix to fix: /OV ABC-DEF, /OV ABC-DEF 120020, /OV ABC 045020-DEF 120005, /OV ABC-DEF-GHI.
3. /TM - **Time:** 4 digits in UTC: /TM 0915
4. /FL - **Altitude/Flight Level:** 3 digits for hundreds of feet. If not known, use UNKN: /FL095, /FL310, /FLUNKN.
5. /TP - **Type aircraft:** 4 digits maximum. If not known use UNKN: /TP L329./TP B727 /TP UNKN
6. /SK - **Sky cover:** Describe as follows:
   a. Height of cloud base in hundreds of feet. If unknown, use UNKN.
   b. Cloud cover symbol.
   c. Height of cloud tops in hundreds of feet.
   d. Use solidus (/) to separate layers.
   e. Use a space to separate each sub element.
   f. Examples: /SK 038 BKN. /SK 038 OVC 045, /SK 055 SCT 073/085 BKN 105, /SK UNKN OVC
7. /WX - **Flight Visibility and Weather:** Flight visibility reported first. Use standard weather symbols. /WX FV02 R H, /WX FV01 TRW.
8. /TA - **Air temperature in Celsius:** If below zero, prefix with an "M." /TA 15, /TA M06.
9. /WV - **Wind:** Direction and speed. /WV 27045, /WV 280110.
10. /TB - **Turbulence:** Use standard contractions for intensity and type (use CAT or CHOP when appropriate). Include altitude only if different from /FL. /TB EXTRM, /TB LGT-MDT BLO-090.
11. /IC - **Icing:** Describe using standard intensity and type contractions. Include altitude only if different than /FL: /IC LGT-MDT RIME, /IC SVR CLR 028-045.
12. /RM - **Remarks:** Use free form to clarify the report. Most hazardous element first: /RM LLWS - 15KT SFC-003 DURGC RNWY 22 JFK.

Examples of Completed PIREPS

UUA /OV ABQ090045/TM 1430/FL130/TP BE30/TB SEV/RM BROKE ALL THE BOTTLES IN THE BAR

UA /OV KMRB-KPIT/TM 1600/FL100/TP BE55/SK BKN024-TOP032/BKN-OVC043-TOPUNKN/TA M12/IC LGT-MOD RIME 055-080

Figure 2-3

ALL

4468-1. If you encounter in-flight icing and ATC asks you to report your conditions, what are the official reportable icing values that you are expected to use?

A—Light, moderate, severe, extreme.
B—Trace, light, moderate, severe.
C—Few, light, moderate, severe.

The following classifies icing intensity according to its operational effects on aircraft: trace, light, moderate, severe. (PLT294, IR.I.B.K3i) — AC 00-45

ALL

4220. Interpret this PIREP.

MRB UA/OV MRB/TM1430/FL060/TPC182/SK BKN BL/WX RA/TB MDT

A—Ceiling 6,000 feet intermittently below moderate thundershowers; turbulence increasing westward.
B—FL 60,000, intermittently below clouds; moderate rain, turbulence increasing with the wind.
C—At 6,000 feet; between layers; moderate turbulence; moderate rain.

A pilot reported over (OV) MRB at 1430 Zulu time (TM 1430), at 6,000 feet (FL060) in a Cessna 182 (TPC182), the sky cover is broken between layers (SK BKN BL), the weather included rain (WX RA) and moderate turbulence (TB MDT). (PLT061, IR.I.B.K2) — AC 00-45

Answers

4468-1 [B] 4220 [C]

ALL
4198. Which response most closely interprets the following PIREP?

UA/OV OKC 063064/TM 1522/FL080/TP C172/TA M04/WV 245040/TB LGT/RM IN CLR

A—64 nautical miles on the 63° radial from Oklahoma City VOR at 1522 UTC, flight level 8,000 ft. Type of aircraft is a Cessna 172.
B—Reported by a Cessna 172, turbulence and light rime icing in climb to 8,000 ft.
C—63 nautical miles on the 64° radial from Oklahoma City, thunderstorm and light rain at 1522 UTC.

UA/OV OKC 063064 — pilot report, aircraft located 64 NM on the 63° radial from Oklahoma City VOR
TM 1522 — time is 1522 UTC
FL080 — reporting aircraft is at flight level 8,000 feet MSL
TP C172 — reporting aircraft type is Cessna 172
TA M04 — temperature -4°C
WV 245040 — wind is from 245° at 40 knots
TB LGT — light turbulence
RM IN CLR — remarks, in the clear

(PLT061, IR.I.B.K2) — AC 00-45

Winds and Temperatures Aloft Forecast (FB)

The winds and temperatures aloft forecast is displayed in a 6-digit format (DDffTT). It shows wind direction (DD), wind velocity (ff), and temperature (TT) that is forecast to exist at specified levels. For example, "234502" decodes as: winds from 230° true north, at 45 knots, temperature 2°C.

When the wind speed (ff) is between 100 and 199 knots, the wind direction (DD) portion of the code will be greater than 50. In cases such as this, you will need to subtract 50 from the coded wind direction, and add 100 to the coded wind speed in order to decipher the code. For example, "734502" decodes as: winds from 230° true north, at 145 knots, temperature 2°C. When the wind speed is 200 knots or greater, the speed will be indicated by 99. In this case, you will again need to subtract 50 from the coded wind direction and translate the 99 to "greater than 200 knots." For example, "739902" decodes as winds 230°, greater than 200 knots, temperature 2°C.

Temperatures with a negative symbol in front of them (DDff-37) are negative. For altitudes above 24,000 feet MSL, temperatures are always negative and will not have a negative symbol. Light and variable winds or wind speeds below 5 knots are indicated by 9900, followed by the forecast temperature. For example, the coded winds aloft forecast for FL270 is "990017" and decodes as: winds are light and variable, temperature -17°C.

ALL
4191. Which values are used for winds aloft forecasts?

A—Magnetic direction and knots.
B—Magnetic direction and mph.
C—True direction and knots.

The wind direction for all reports and forecasts is always given in relation to true north. The wind speed is always reported and forecast in knots. (PLT284, IR.I.B.K2) — AC 00-45

ALL
4172. What wind direction and speed is represented by the entry 9900+00 for 9,000 feet, on an Winds and Temperatures Aloft Forecast (FB)?

A—Light and variable; less than 5 knots.
B—Vortex winds exceeding 200 knots.
C—Light and variable; less than 10 knots.

When the forecast speed is less than 5 knots, the coded group is "9900" and reads "LIGHT AND VARIABLE." The "+00" is the outside air temperature for that altitude in degrees Celsius. (PLT284, IR.I.B.K2) — AC 00-45

Answers
4198 [A]   4191 [C]   4172 [A]

ALL

4188. When is the temperature at one of the forecast altitudes omitted at a specific location or station in the Winds and Temperatures Aloft Forecast (FB)?

A—When the temperature is standard for that altitude.
B—For the 3,000-foot altitude (level) or when the level is within 2,500 feet of station elevation.
C—Only when the winds are omitted for that altitude (level).

No temperatures are forecast for the 3,000-foot level or for a level within 2,500 feet of station elevation. (PLT284, IR.I.B.K2) — AC 00-45

ALL

4189. When is the wind-group at one of the forecast altitudes omitted at a specific location or station in the Winds and Temperatures Aloft Forecast (FB)? When the wind

A—is less than 5 knots.
B—is less than 10 knots.
C—at the altitude is within 1,500 feet of the station elevation.

No winds are forecast within 1,500 feet of station elevation. (PLT284, IR.I.B.K2) — AC 00-45

ALL

4190. Decode the excerpt from the Winds and Temperature Aloft Forecast (FB) for OKC at 39,000 feet.

FT	3000	6000	39000
OKC			830558

A—Wind 130° at 50 knots, temperature -58°C.
B—Wind 330° at 105 knots, temperature -58°C.
C—Wind 330° at 205 knots, temperature -58°C.

Encoded wind speeds 100 to 199 knots have 50 added to the direction code and 100 subtracted from the speed, so 830558 would be: wind direction 83 – 50 = 330°; wind speed 05 + 100 = 105 knots; temperatures are negative above 24,000 feet, so 58 becomes -58°C. (PLT284, IR.I.B.K2) — AC 00-45

ALL

4192. (Refer to Figure 2.) What approximate wind direction, speed, and temperature (relative to ISA) should a pilot expect when planning for a flight over PSB at FL 270?

A—260° magnetic at 93 knots; ISA +7°C.
B—280° true at 113 knots; ISA +3°C.
C—255° true at 93 knots; ISA +6°C.

To find the conditions at PSB at FL270, you must interpolate between 24,000 and 30,000:

Altitude	*Code*	*Wind direction*	*Wind speed*	*Temperature*
24,000	*2368-26*	*230°*	*68*	*-26°C*
30,000	*781939*	*280°*	*119*	*-39°C*
27,000		*255°*	*93*	*-33°C*

To find the temperature relative to ISA, multiply the standard temperature lapse rate (-2°C per 1,000 feet) times the altitude in thousands of feet (in this case 27), then add +15°C for standard day conditions:

1. -2°C x 27 = -54°C

2. -54°C + 15 = -39°C (ISA)

Therefore, -33°C (today) is 6°C warmer than -39°C, so the temperature is ISA + 6°C. (PLT284, IR.I.B.K2) — AC 00-45

ALL

4193. (Refer to Figure 2.) What approximate wind direction, speed, and temperature (relative to ISA) should a pilot expect when planning for a flight over ALB at FL 270?

A—270° magnetic at 97 knots; ISA -4°C.
B—260° true at 110 knots; ISA +5°C.
C—275° true at 97 knots; ISA +4°C.

To find the conditions at ALB at FL270, you must interpolate between 24,000 and 30,000:

Altitude	*Code*	*Wind direction*	*Wind speed*	*Temperature*
24,000	*2777-28*	*270°*	*77*	*-28°C*
30,000	*781842*	*280°*	*118*	*-42°C*
27,000		*275°*	*97*	*-35°C*

To find the temperature relative to ISA, multiply the standard temperature lapse rate (-2°C per 1,000 feet) times the altitude in thousands of feet (in this case 27), then add +15°C for standard day conditions:

1. -2°C x 27 = 54°C

2. -54°C + 15 = -39°C (ISA)

Therefore, -35°C (today) is 4°C warmer than -39°C, so the temperature is ISA + 4°C. (PLT284, IR.I.B.K2) — AC 00-45

Answers

4188 [B] 4189 [C] 4190 [B] 4192 [C] 4193 [C]

ALL
4194. (Refer to Figure 2.) What approximate wind direction, speed, and temperature (relative to ISA) should a pilot expect when planning for a flight over EMI at FL 270?

A—265° true; 100 knots; ISA +3°C.
B—270° true; 110 knots; ISA +5°C.
C—260° magnetic; 100 knots; ISA -5°C.

To find the conditions at EMI at FL270, you must interpolate between 24,000 and 30,000:

Altitude	*Code*	*Wind direction*	*Wind speed*	*Temperature*
24,000	*2891-30*	*280°*	*91*	*-30°C*
30,000	*751041*	*250°*	*110*	*-41°C*
27,000		*265°*	*100*	*-36°C*

To find the temperature relative to ISA, multiply the standard temperature lapse rate (-2°C per 1,000 feet) times the altitude in thousands of feet (in this case 27), then add +15°C for standard day conditions:

1. -2°C x 27 = 54°C

2. -54°C + 15 = -39°C (ISA)

Therefore, -36°C (today) is 3°C warmer than -39°C, so the temperature is ISA + 3°C. (PLT284, IR.I.B.K2) — AC 00-45

ALL
4199. A station is forecasting wind and temperature aloft at FL 390 to be 300° at 200 knots; temperature -54°C. How would this data be encoded in the FB?

A—300054.
B—809954.
C—309954.

Wind speed above 100 knots have 50 added to the direction code (first 2 digits). Wind speeds at 200 knots or greater are coded 99 (middle 2 digits). Temperatures above 24,000 feet are negative so the minus sign is omitted (last 2 digits). The 300° at 200 knots and 54° is a encoded as 809954. (PLT284, IR.I.B.K2) — AC 00-45

Answer (A) is incorrect because 300054 would be 300° at 0 knots and -54°C. Answer (C) is incorrect because 309954 would be 300° at 99 knots and -54°C.

Inflight Weather Advisories (WA, WS, WST)

Previously called Severe Weather Watch Bulletins (WW), the National Weather Service releases the Aviation Notification Watch Message (SAW) as needed. The SAW provides an area threat alert for the aviation meteorology community to forecast organized severe thunderstorms that may produce tornadoes, large hail, and/or convective damaging winds.

Inflight Weather Advisories advise pilots en route of the possibility of encountering hazardous flying conditions that may not have been forecast at the time of the preflight weather briefing.

AIRMETs (WA) contain information on weather that may be hazardous to single engine, other light aircraft, and VFR pilots. The items covered are moderate icing or turbulence, sustained winds of 30 knots or more at the surface, widespread areas of IFR conditions, and extensive mountain obscurement.

SIGMETs (WS) advise of weather potentially hazardous to all aircraft. A SIGMET may be issued when any of the following conditions occur or is expected to occur in an area affecting at least 3,000 square miles or an area deemed to have a significant effect on the safety of aircraft operations: thunderstorms (except for the contiguous U.S. where Convective SIGMETs are used instead), severe or greater turbulence, severe icing, widespread duststorm, widespread sandstorm, volcanic ash, or tropical cyclone.

SIGMETs and AIRMETs are broadcast upon receipt and at 30-minute intervals (H + 15 and H + 45) during the first hour. If the advisory is still in effect after the first hour, an alert notice will be broadcast. Pilots may contact the nearest FSS to ascertain whether the advisory is pertinent to their flights.

Answers
4194 [A] 4199 [B]

Convective SIGMETs (WST) cover weather developments such as tornadoes, lines of thunderstorms, and embedded thunderstorms, and they also imply severe or greater turbulence, severe icing, and low-level wind shear. Convective SIGMET Bulletins are issued hourly at H+55. Unscheduled Convective SIGMETs are broadcast upon receipt and at 15-minute intervals for the first hour (H + 15, H + 30, H + 45).

ALL

4186. When does the National Weather Service release an Aviation Notification Watch Message (SAW)?

A—At 0000 (UTC).
B—At 0000 and 1200 (UTC).
C—Unscheduled and issued as required.

A SAW provides threat alerts to forecast organized severe thunderstorms that may produce tornadoes, large hail, and/or convective damaging winds on an unscheduled and as-needed basis. (PLT316, IR.I.B.K1) — AC 00-45

ALL

4181. SIGMETs are issued as a warning of weather conditions potentially hazardous

A—particularly to light aircraft.
B—to all aircraft.
C—only to light aircraft operations.

A SIGMET advises of weather potentially hazardous to all aircraft other than convective activity. In the continental U.S., items covered are: severe icing, severe or extreme turbulence, duststorms, sandstorms, or volcanic ash lowering visibilities to less than 3 miles. (PLT290, IR.I.B.K2) — AC 00-45

Answer (A) is incorrect because SIGMETs apply to all aircraft. Answer (C) is incorrect because AIRMETs (not SIGMETs) apply only to light aircraft operations.

ALL

4183. Which meteorological condition is issued in the form of a SIGMET (WS)?

A—Widespread sand or dust storms affecting at least 3,000 square miles or an area deemed to have a significant effect on the safety of aircraft operations.
B—Moderate icing.
C—Sustained winds of 30 knots or greater at the surface.

A SIGMET advises of weather potentially hazardous to all aircraft. A SIGMET may be issued when any of the following conditions occur or is expected to occur in an area affecting at least 3,000 square miles or an area deemed to have a significant effect on the safety of aircraft operations: thunderstorms (except for the contiguous U.S.), severe or greater turbulence, severe icing, widespread duststorm, widespread sandstorm, volcanic ash, or tropical cyclone. (PLT290, IR.I.B.K2) — AC 00-45

Answer (B) is incorrect because SIGMETs advise of severe (not moderate) icing. Answer (C) is incorrect because AIRMETs (not SIGMETs) advise of sustained winds of 30 knots or greater at the surface.

ALL

4184. A pilot planning to depart at 1100Z on an IFR flight is particularly concerned about the hazard of icing. What sources reflect the most accurate information on icing conditions (current and forecast) at the time of departure?

A—Low-Level Significant Weather Prognostic Chart, and the Area Forecast.
B—The Area Forecast, and the Freezing Level Chart.
C—Pilot weather reports (PIREPs), AIRMETs, and SIGMETs.

Almost all of the listed reports and forecasts will contain information about icing hazards. SIGMETs and AIRMETs are issued when there is an icing hazard. PIREPs (pilot reports) contain information from pilots actually flying in the area forecast to have icing conditions. (PLT290, IR.I.B.K2) — AC 00-45

Answers (A) and (B) are incorrect because Low-Level Significant Weather Prognostic Charts are not issued for icing hazards. Area Forecasts only show basic icing forecasts, and Freezing Level Charts show the freezing level (not icing).

Answers

4186 [C]	4181 [B]	4183 [A]	4184 [C]

ALL

4187. What is the maximum forecast period for AIRMETs?

A—Two hours.
B—Four hours.
C—Six hours.

AIRMETs are issued with a maximum forecast period of 6 hours. If conditions persist beyond the 6-hour forecast period, the AIRMET must be updated and reissued. (PLT290, IR.I.B.K2) — AC 00-45

ALL

4467. AIRMETs are issued on a scheduled basis every

A—15 minutes after the hour only.
B—15 minutes until the AIRMET is canceled.
C—six hours.

AIRMETs are issued on a scheduled basis every six hours, with unscheduled amendments issued as required. (PLT290, IR.I.B.K2) — AIM ¶7-1-5

ALL

4980. Consider this AIRMET that includes your route of flight:

DFWS WA 211445 AIRMET IFR...OK TX FROM END TO TXK TO HOU TO LBB TO END CIG BELOW 010. CONDS ENDG 15-18Z.

This indicates

A—there will be icing in clouds below 1,000 feet MSL.
B—visibility will be less than 3 SM until 15Z.
C—the area will have low ceilings before 15Z.

This AIRMET IFR indicates ceilings below 10,000 feet with conditions ending between 1500–1800 Zulu (CIG BELOW 010 CONDS ENDG 15-18Z). (PLT290, IR.I.B.K2) — AC 00-45

ALL

4990. The use of airborne weather avoidance radar

A—provides no assurance of avoiding instrument weather conditions.
B—assures the avoidance of hail.
C—allows you to fly safely between echoes.

The ability of airborne weather radar to detect weather phenomena is limited in both direction and range. Additionally, weather radar detects only precipitation drops; it does not detect turbulence. Therefore, the radar display provides no assurance of avoiding turbulence. The radar display also does not provide assurance of avoiding instrument weather conditions from clouds and fog. (PLT105, IR.I.B.K4) — AC 00-6

ALL

4991. When does the National Weather Service release an Aviation Notification Watch Message (SAW)?

A—At 0000 (UTC).
B—0000 and 1200 (UTC).
C—Unscheduled and issued as required.

Watch Hazard Probabilities are non-scheduled, event driven products and can be issued at anytime to draw attention to a specific weather hazard. (PLT316, IR.I.B.K1) — AC 00-45

Answers

4187 [C]	4467 [C]	4980 [C]	4990 [A]	4991 [C]

Convective Outlook (AC)

A Convective Outlook (AC) describes the prospects for general thunderstorm activity during the following 24 hours. Areas in which there is a high, moderate, or slight risk of severe thunderstorms are included as well as areas where thunderstorms may approach severe limits. Convective Outlooks are produced at the Storm Prediction Center (SPC) in Norman, Oklahoma. Pilots should use an AC primarily for planning flights later in the day.

ALL

4215. What information is provided by a Convective Outlook (AC)?

A—It describes areas of probable severe icing and severe or extreme turbulence during the next 24 hours.
B—It provides prospects of both general and severe thunderstorm activity during the following 24 hours.
C—It indicates areas of probable convective turbulence and the extent of instability in the upper atmosphere (above 500 MB).

An AC describes prospects for general thunderstorm activity during the following 24 hours. Use the outlook primarily for planning flights later in the day. The charts show conditions as they are forecast to be at the valid time of the chart. (PLT051, IR.I.B.K2) — AC 00-45

Answer (A) is incorrect because SIGMETs (not Convective Outlooks) describe both severe turbulence and icing. Answer (C) is incorrect because a Constant Pressure Analysis Chart (not Convective Outlooks) indicates areas of turbulence and instability.

ALL

4226. Which weather forecast describes prospects for an area coverage of both severe and general thunderstorms during the following 24 hours?

A—Terminal Aerodrome Forecast.
B—Convective Outlook.
C—Radar Summary Chart.

An AC describes the prospects for general thunderstorm activity during the following 24 hours. (PLT051, IR.I.B.K2) — AC 00-45

Answer (A) is incorrect because TAFs are given for a specific airport. Answer (C) is incorrect because Radar Summary Charts are issued hourly and are valid until 35 minutes past the hour.

ALL

4175. What does a Convective Outlook (AC) describe for a following 24 hour period?

A—Areas of slight, moderate, or high risk of severe thunderstorms.
B—A severe weather watch bulletin.
C—When forecast conditions are expected to continue beyond the valid period.

The AC defines areas of slight risk (SLGT), moderate risk (MDT), or high risk (HIGH) of severe thunderstorms for a 24-hour period beginning at 1200 UTC. The Day 1 and Day 2 Convective Outlooks also depict areas of general thunderstorms (GEN TSTMS). (PLT051, IR.I.B.K2) — AC 00-45

Answers

4215 [B] 4226 [B] 4175 [A]

Surface Analysis Chart

The Surface Analysis Chart depicts frontal positions, pressure patterns, temperature, dew point, wind, weather, and obstructions to vision as of the valid time of the chart.

ALL

4209. The Surface Analysis Chart depicts

A—actual pressure systems, frontal locations, cloud tops, and precipitation at the time shown on the chart.
B—frontal locations and expected movement, pressure centers, cloud coverage, and obstructions to vision at the time of chart transmission.
C—actual frontal positions, pressure patterns, temperature, dew point, wind, weather, and obstructions to vision at the valid time of the chart.

The Surface Analysis Chart provides a ready means of locating pressure systems and fronts and also gives an overview of winds, temperatures and dew points as of the time of the plotted observations. The chart also shows weather and obstruction to vision symbols. It does not show cloud heights or tops or the expected movement of any item depicted. Expected movement would be contained in a forecast. (PLT071, IR.I.B.K2) — AC 00-45

Answer (A) is incorrect because cloud tops are not depicted by the Surface Analysis Chart. Answer (B) is incorrect because current conditions are depicted, not expected movement.

Constant Pressure Chart

A Constant Pressure Analysis Chart is an upper air weather map where all the information depicted is at the specified pressure of the chart. Each of the Constant Pressure Analysis Charts (850 MB, 700 MB, 500 MB, 300 MB, 250 MB, and 200 MB) can provide observed temperature, temperature/dew point spread, wind, height of the pressure surface, and the height changes over the previous 12-hour period.

ALL

4195. What flight planning information can a pilot derive from constant pressure charts?

A—Clear air turbulence and icing conditions.
B—Levels of widespread cloud coverage.
C—Winds and temperatures aloft.

Plotted at each reporting station (at the level of the specified pressure) on constant pressure charts are the observed temperature, temperature/dew point spread, wind, height of the pressure surface, as well as height changes over the previous 12-hour period. (PLT283, IR.I.B.K2) — AC 00-45

Answer (A) is incorrect because Low-Level Prognostic Charts indicate clear air turbulence. Answer (B) is incorrect because Weather Depiction and Surface Analysis Charts indicate areas and levels of widespread cloud coverage.

ALL

4173. What conclusion(s) can be drawn from a 500-millibar Constant Pressure Chart for a planned flight at FL 180?

A—Winds aloft at FL180 generally flow across the height contours.
B—Observed temperature, wind, and temperature/dew point spread along the proposed route can be approximated.
C—Upper highs, lows, troughs, and ridges will be depicted by the use of lines of equal pressure.

Plotted at each reporting station (at the level of the specified pressure) are the observed temperature, temperature/dew point spread, wind, and height of the pressure surface, as well as the height changes over the previous 12-hour period. (PLT283, IR.I.B.K2) — AC 00-45

Answer (A) is incorrect because winds generally flow parallel to the height contours. Answer (C) is incorrect because heights are identified by solid lines (contours) which depict high height centers and low height centers.

Answers

4209 [C] 4195 [C] 4173 [B]

Significant Weather (SIGWX) Forecast Charts

The Low-Level Significant Weather Prognostic Chart (FL240 and below) portrays forecast weather hazards that may influence flight planning, including those areas or activities of most significant turbulence and icing. It is a two-panel display representing a 12-hour forecast interval (left) and 24-hour forecast interval (right). Turbulence intensities are identified by standard symbols as shown in Figure 2-4. The vertical extent of turbulence layers is depicted by top and base heights separated by a slant and shown in hundreds of feet MSL (180/100 = 18,000 feet MSL to 10,000 feet MSL). Freezing levels above the surface will correspond with a given altitude in hundreds of feet MSL (080 = 8,000 feet MSL). Low-level SIGWX charts are issued four times daily, and valid time, date, and chart type are depicted in the lower left corner of each panel.

The High-Level Significant Weather Prognostic Chart (FL250 to FL630) outlines areas of forecast turbulence and cumulonimbus clouds, shows the expected height of the tropopause, and predicts jet stream location and velocity. The chart depicts clouds and turbulence as shown in Figure 2-5.

Symbol	Meaning	Symbol	Meaning
	Moderate Turbulence		Rain Shower
	Severe Turbulence		Snow Shower
	Moderate Icing		Thunderstorm
	Severe Icing		Freezing Rain
	Rain		Tropical Storm
	Snow		Hurricane (typhoon)
	Drizzle		

Note: Character of stable precipitation is the manner in which it occurs. It may be intermittent or continuous.

Examples:

	Intermittent	**Continuous**
Rain		
Drizzle		
Snow		

Depiction	Meaning
	Showery precipitation (Thunderstorms/rain showers) covering half or more of the area.
	Continuous precipitation (rain) covering half or more of the area.
	Showery precipitation (snow showers) covering less than half of the area.
	Intermittent precipitation (drizzle) covering less than half of the area.
	Showery precipitation (rain showers) embedded in an area of continuous rain covering more than half of the area.

Figure 2-4

Cumulonimbus cloud (CB) areas are enclosed by a red scalloped line. The height of the tropopause is shown in hundreds of feet MSL and enclosed in a rectangular box; centers of high (H) and low (L) heights are enclosed in polygons. Areas of turbulence are enclosed in yellow dashed lines and labeled with the appropriate severity symbol and top and base altitudes. A jet stream axis containing a wind speed of 80 knots or greater is identified by a bold green line and directional arrowhead. A standard wind symbol is placed on the jet stream to identify velocity and an associated flight level is placed adjacent to it. An omission of a base altitude (XXX) identifies that the weather phenomena exceeds the lower limit of the high-level SIGWX chart (FL250). See also FAA Figures 5, 7, and 18.

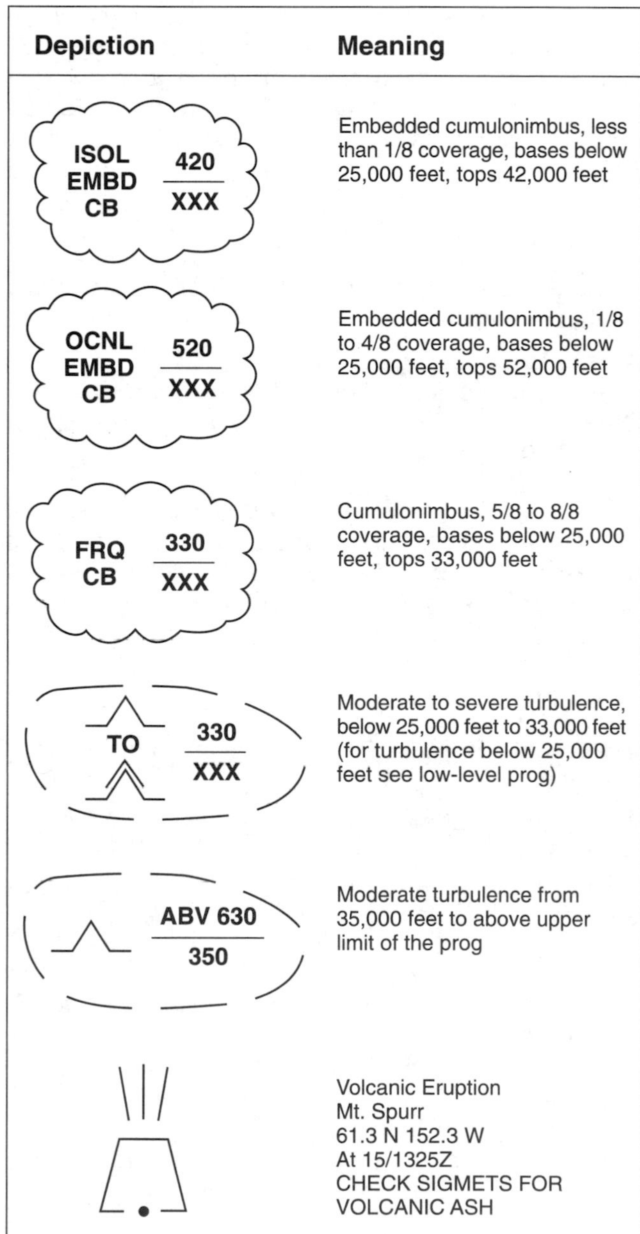

Depiction	Meaning
ISOL EMBD CB 420/XXX	Embedded cumulonimbus, less than 1/8 coverage, bases below 25,000 feet, tops 42,000 feet
OCNL EMBD CB 520/XXX	Embedded cumulonimbus, 1/8 to 4/8 coverage, bases below 25,000 feet, tops 52,000 feet
FRQ CB 330/XXX	Cumulonimbus, 5/8 to 8/8 coverage, bases below 25,000 feet, tops 33,000 feet
TO 330/XXX	Moderate to severe turbulence, below 25,000 feet to 33,000 feet (for turbulence below 25,000 feet see low-level prog)
ABV 630/350	Moderate turbulence from 35,000 feet to above upper limit of the prog
	Volcanic Eruption Mt. Spurr 61.3 N 152.3 W At 15/1325Z CHECK SIGMETS FOR VOLCANIC ASH

Figure 2-5

ALL

4211. The Low-Level Significant Weather Prognostic Chart depicts weather conditions

A—that are forecast to exist at a valid time shown on the chart.
B—as they existed at the time the chart was prepared.
C—that existed at the time shown on the chart which is about 3 hours before the chart is received.

The Low-Level Significant Weather Prognostic Chart is a four-panel chart. The two lower panels are 12- and 24-hour surface forecasts. The two upper panels are 12- and 24-hour forecasts of significant weather from the surface to 400 millibars (24,000 feet). The charts show conditions as they are forecast to be at the valid time of the chart. (PLT068, IR.I.B.K2) — AC 00-45

Answer (B) is incorrect because the Low-Level Prognostic charts contain 12 and 24-hour forecasts. Answer (C) is incorrect because the Low-Level Prognostic charts contain forecasts (not previous conditions).

ALL

4214. A prognostic chart depicts the conditions

A—existing at the surface during the past 6 hours.
B—which presently exist from the 1,000-millibar through the 700-millibar level.
C—forecast to exist at a specific time in the future.

The Low-Level Significant Weather Prognostic Chart depicts conditions as they are forecast to be at the valid time of the chart (12- and 24-hour forecasts). (PLT286, IR.I.B.K2) — AC 00-45

Answers (A) and (B) are incorrect because Low-Level Prognostic Charts indicate 12 and 24-hour forecasts (not current or past conditions).

Answers

4211 [A] 4214 [C]

ALL

4992. What is the time frame for the validity of Low-Level Significant Weather Prognostic Charts?

A—12 to 24 hours in the future.
B—From 3 hours before to 3 hours after the time on the chart.
C—Up to 48 hours in the future.

Low-Level Significant Weather Charts are issued four times daily and are valid at fixed times: 0000, 0600, 1200, and 1800 UTC. Each chart is divided into 12 (left) and 24 hour (right) forecast intervals. (PLT068, IR.I.B.K2) — AC 00-45

ALL

4212. Which meteorological conditions are depicted by a prognostic chart?

A—Conditions existing at the time of the observation.
B—Interpretation of weather conditions for geographical areas between reporting stations.
C—Conditions forecast to exist at a specific time shown on the chart.

The Low-Level Significant Weather Prognostic Chart depicts conditions as they are forecast to be at the valid time of the chart (12- and 24-hour forecasts). (PLT286, IR.I.B.K2) — AC 00-45

Answers (A) and (B) are incorrect because Low-Level Significant Weather Prognostic charts contain 12- and 24-hour forecasts (not existing conditions).

ALL

4221. (Refer to Figure 7.) What weather conditions are depicted around area 7?

A—Occasional cumulonimbus, 4/8 to 6/8 sky coverage, bases below 25,000 feet MSL, tops 53,000 feet MSL.
B—Moderate or severe turbulence up to FL530.
C—Occasional cumulonimbus, 5/8 to 8/8 sky coverage, tropopause height 53,000 feet MSL.

Scalloped lines enclose areas of expected cumulonimbus development. "OCNL CB" indicates 4/8 to 6/8 coverage of cumulonimbus. "530/XXX" indicates tops at 53,000 and bases below 25,000 feet MSL (below the prognostic chart forecast layer). (PLT068, IR.I.B.K2) — AC 00-45

ALL

4222. (Refer to Figure 7.) What type of weather can be expected in the red scalloped area near area 9?

A—2/8 to 6/8 coverage, occasional embedded thunderstorms, tops at FL330.
B—1/8 to 4/8 coverage, occasional embedded thunderstorms, maximum tops at 51,000 feet MSL.
C—Isolated embedded cumulonimbus with tops at FL330.

A significant weather prognostic chart provides a forecast of significant en route weather. "ISOL EMBD CB" indicates less than 1/8 coverage, embedded cumulonimbus clouds. "330/XXX" indicates tops at 33,000 feet MSL and bases below 25,000 feet MSL (below the chart's forecast layer). (PLT068, IR.I.B.K2) — AC 00-45

ALL

4223. (Refer to Figure 7.) What weather conditions are indicated within area 3?

A—Moderate CAT turbulence at FL370.
B—Severe turbulence from FL300 up to FL370.
C—Reported moderate turbulence from FL300 up to FL370.

Areas of moderate or greater turbulence are enclosed by bold dashed lines. The double hat symbol indicates severe turbulence. The "370/300" identifies a layer of turbulence from below FL300 to FL370. (PLT068, IR.I.B.K2) — AC 00-45

ALL

4224. (Refer to Figure 7.) What weather conditions are depicted within area 1?

A—Moderate turbulence from below FL250 up to FL360.
B—Moderate to severe turbulence at FL310.
C—Severe CAT up to FL360.

Areas of moderate or greater turbulence are enclosed by bold dashed lines. The hat symbol indicates moderate turbulence. The "360/XXX" identifies a layer of turbulence from below FL250 (lower limit of the High-Level Significant Weather Prognostic Chart) up to FL360. (PLT068, IR.I.B.K2) — AC 00-45

Answers

4992 [A]	4212 [C]	4221 [A]	4222 [C]	4223 [B]	4224 [A]

ALL

4243. (Refer to Figure 20.) What is the maximum wind velocity forecast in the jet stream shown on the High-Level Significant Weather Prognostic Chart over the southern United States?

A—50 knots
B—140 knots
C—90 knots

The maximum core speed along the jet stream is depicted by shafts, pennants, and feathers. The maximum wind velocity forecast in the jet stream can be found on the solid green line just NE of Texas. The one pennant (50 knots) and four lines (10 knots each) indicate a forecast maximum speed of 90 knots, at a height of 41,000 feet MSL (FL410). (PLT068, IR.I.B.K2) - AC 00-45

ALL

4244. (Refer to Figure 20.) What is the height of the tropopause over the northwest United States?

A—45,000 feet MSL.
B—45,000 meters.
C—450,000 feet MSL.

Tropopause heights are to be depicted in hundreds of feet MSL and are enclosed in small rectangular blocks. Altitudes are shown similar to flight levels, for example, FL450 = 45,000 feet MSL. Centers of high (H) and low (L) tropopause heights are enclosed by polygons. (PLT068, IR.I.B.K2) — AC 00-45

ALL

4242. (Refer to Figure 7.) The symbol on the U.S. High-Level Significant Weather Prognostic Chart indicated by number 5 represents the

A—Height of the tropopause.
B—Maximum height of CAT (FL530).
C—Height of the jet stream (53,000 feet MSL).

Tropopause heights are to be depicted in hundreds of feet MSL and are enclosed in small rectangular blocks. Centers of high (H) and low (L) tropopause heights are enclosed by polygons. (PLT068, IR.I.B.K2) — AC 00-45

ALL

4245. (Refer to Figure 7.) The area indicated by arrow 3 indicates

A—light turbulence below 34,000 feet.
B—isolated embedded cumulonimbus clouds with bases below FL180 and tops at FL340.
C—severe turbulence at and below 37,000 feet.

Areas of moderate or greater turbulence are enclosed by bold dashed lines. Turbulence intensities are identified by symbols. The vertical extent of turbulence layers is specified by top and base heights in hundreds of feet. Turbulence bases that extend below the layer of the chart are identified with "XXX." For example "370/XXX" identifies a layer of turbulence from below FL370 to FL300. (PLT068, IR.I.B.K2) — AC 00-45

ALL

4225. (Refer to Figure 7.) What information is indicated right of number 8?

A—The height of the tropopause in meters above sea level.
B—The maximum height of CAT.
C—The height of the tropopause in hundreds of feet above MSL.

Tropopause heights are to be depicted in hundreds of feet MSL and are enclosed in small rectangular blocks. Centers of high (H) and low (L) tropopause heights are enclosed by polygons. (PLT068, IR.I.B.K2) — AC 00-45

ALL

4229. (Refer to Figure 7.) What weather conditions are depicted within the area indicated by number 6?

A—Occasional embedded cumulonimbus clouds, bases below 25,000 feet MSL, tops 45,000 feet MSL.
B—Embedded cumulonimbus clouds, less than 1/8 coverage.
C—Embedded thunderstorm activity from the surface up to FL450.

Scalloped lines enclose areas of expected cumulonimbus development. "OCNL EMBD CB" indicates 1/8 to 4/8 coverage of embedded cumulonimbus. "450/XXX" indicates tops at 45,000 and bases below 25,000 feet MSL (below the prog's forecast layer). (PLT068, IR.I.B.K2) — AC 00-45

Answers

4243 [C]	4244 [A]	4242 [A]	4245 [C]	4225 [C]	4229 [A]

ALL

4201. (Refer to Figure 5.) On a Low-Level Significant Weather Prognostic Chart this symbol represents

A—Freezing rain.
B—Mixed precipitation.
C—Snow showers.

The left portion of this symbol represents light rain, two solid dots. The right portion has a solid dot above an unfilled upside-down triangle, which represents rain showers. This symbol is best described as mixed precipitation: light rain and rain showers in the general vicinity. (PLT068, IR.I.B.K2) — AC 00-45

ALL

4207. (Refer to Figure 18.) The right panel of the Significant Weather Prognostic Chart provides a forecast of selected aviation weather hazards up to FL240 until what time?

A—March 18th at 0600.
B—March 17th at 1800.
C—March 18th at 1800.

The right panel of Figure 18 is the 24-hour SIGWX prognostic chart. The bottom left corner lists the valid time for the chart as 1800Z (VT 18Z), March 17th. Therefore the chart would expire at 1800Z March 18th, or 24 hours from valid time. (PLT068, IR.I.B.K2) — AC 00-45

Answer (A) is incorrect because 0600 is only 12 hours from the start of the valid period. Answer (B) is incorrect because 1800 on March 17th is the beginning of the valid period for the chart.

ALL

4208. (Refer to Figure 19.) The next issuance of the 12-hour Significant Weather Prognostic Chart will become valid at

A—0000Z.
B—1200Z.
C—1800Z.

The 12-hour Low-Level Significant Weather Prognostic Charts are issued four times daily with valid times of 00Z, 06Z, 12Z, and 18Z. The bottom left corner of the 12-hour forecast in Figure 19 lists the VT as 18Z; therefore, the next chart issued will have a VT of 00Z. (PLT068, IR.I.B.K2) — AC 00-45

Answers

4201 [B] 4207 [C] 4208 [A]

Chapter 3
Flight Instruments

Airspeeds

Indicated airspeed (IAS)—the airspeed that is shown on the airspeed indicator. See Figure 3-1.

Calibrated airspeed (CAS)—the indicated airspeed corrected for position or installation error.

Equivalent airspeed (EAS)—calibrated airspeed corrected for compressibility. EAS will always be lower than CAS.

True airspeed (TAS)—the equivalent airspeed corrected for temperature and pressure altitude. At speeds below 200 knots, TAS can be found by correcting CAS for temperature and pressure altitude. A rule of thumb is that TAS is 2 percent more than CAS per 1,000 feet of altitude above sea level.

Mach number—the ratio of aircraft true airspeed to the speed of sound.

Figure 3-1. Airspeed indicator

ALL

4267. What CAS must be used to maintain the filed TAS of 155 knots at 8,000 feet MSL if the outside air temperature is -5°C?

A—134 KCAS.
B—139 KCAS.
C—142 KCAS.

To find CAS when TAS is known, the correct OAT and the pressure altitude are required. Since neither are available for the problem, substitute the uncorrected OAT and the planned flight altitude. Using a flight computer determine the CAS from the given information (Airspeed on FLT menu using a CX-3):

Altitude .... 8,000 feet
Temperature .... -5°C
TAS .... 155 knots

Therefore, CAS is 139 KCAS.

(PLT012, IR.I.C.K3a) — FAA-H-8083-25

ALL

4278. What CAS must be used to maintain the filed TAS of 180 knots at the flight planned altitude of 8,000 feet MSL if the outside air temperature is +8°C?

A—154 KCAS.
B—157 KCAS.
C—163 KCAS.

To find CAS when TAS is known, the correct OAT and the pressure altitude are required. Since neither are available for the problem, substitute the uncorrected OAT and the planned flight altitude. Using a flight computer determine the CAS from the given information (Airspeed on FLT menu using a CX-3):

Altitude .... 8,000 feet
Temperature .... +8°C
TAS .... 180 knots

Therefore, CAS is 157.4 KCAS.

(PLT012, IR.I.C.K3a) — FAA-H-8083-25

Answers

4267 [B] 4278 [B]

ALL

4289. What CAS must be used to maintain the filed TAS of 156 knots at 11,000 feet MSL if the outside air temperature is +05°C?

A—129 KCAS.
B—133 KCAS.
C—139 KCAS.

To find CAS when TAS is known, the correct OAT and the pressure altitude are required. Since neither are available for the problem, substitute the uncorrected OAT and the planned flight altitude. Using a flight computer determine the CAS from the given information (Airspeed on FLT menu using a CX-3):

Altitude .... 11,000 feet
Temperature .... +5°C
TAS .... 156 knots

Therefore, CAS is 129.4 KCAS.

(PLT012, IR.I.C.K3a) — FAA-H-8083-25

ALL

4301. What CAS must be used to maintain a filed TAS of 180 knots at 12,000 feet MSL if the outside air temperature is +5°C?

A—147 KCAS.
B—150 KCAS.
C—154 KCAS.

To find CAS when TAS is known, the correct OAT and the pressure altitude are required. Since neither are available for the problem, substitute the uncorrected OAT and the planned flight altitude. Using a flight computer determine the CAS from the given information (Airspeed on FLT menu using a CX-3):

Altitude .... 12,000 feet
Temperature .... +5°C
TAS .... 180 knots

Therefore, CAS is 146.6 KCAS.

(PLT012, IR.I.C.K3a) — FAA-H-8083-25

ALL

4313. What CAS must be used to maintain a filed TAS of 158 knots at 8,000 feet MSL if the outside air temperature is 0°C?

A—136 KCAS.
B—140 KCAS.
C—147 KCAS.

To find CAS when TAS is known, the correct OAT and the pressure altitude are required. Since neither are available for the problem, substitute the uncorrected OAT and the planned flight altitude. Using a flight computer determine the CAS from the given information (Airspeed on FLT menu using a CX-3):

Altitude .... 8,000 feet
Temperature .... 0°C
TAS .... 158 knots

Therefore, CAS is 140.1 KCAS.

(PLT012, IR.I.C.K3a) — FAA-H-8083-25

ALL

4345. What CAS must be used to maintain a filed TAS of 128 knots at 5,000 feet MSL if the outside air temperature is +5°C?

A—119 KCAS.
B—124 KCAS.
C—126 KCAS.

To find CAS when TAS is known, the correct OAT and the pressure altitude are required. Since neither are available for the problem, substitute the uncorrected OAT and the planned flight altitude. Using a flight computer determine the CAS from the given information (Airspeed on FLT menu using a CX-3):

Altitude .... 5,000 feet
Temperature .... +5°C
TAS .... 128 knots

Therefore, CAS is 118.9 KCAS.

(PLT012, IR.I.C.K3a) — FAA-H-8083-25

Answers

4289 [A] 4301 [A] 4313 [B] 4345 [A]

ALL
4359. What CAS must be used to maintain a filed TAS of 160 knots at 11,000 feet MSL if the outside air temperature is +5°C?

A—129 KCAS.
B—133 KCAS.
C—139 KCAS.

To find CAS when TAS is known, the correct OAT and the pressure altitude are required. Since neither are available for the problem, substitute the uncorrected OAT and the planned flight altitude. Using a flight computer determine the CAS from the given information (Airspeed on FLT menu using a CX-3):

Altitude .... 11,000 feet
Temperature .... +5°C
TAS .... 160 knots

Therefore, CAS is 132.8 KCAS.

(PLT012, IR.I.C.K3a) — FAA-H-8083-25

RTC
4323. What CAS must be used to maintain a filed TAS of 110 knots at 7,000 feet MSL if the outside air temperature is +5°C?

A—98 KCAS.
B—101 KCAS.
C—103 KCAS.

To find CAS when TAS is known, the correct OAT and the pressure altitude are required. Since neither are available for the problem, substitute the uncorrected OAT and the planned flight altitude. Using a flight computer determine the CAS from the given information (Airspeed on FLT menu using a CX-3):

Altitude .... 7,000 feet
Temperature .... +5°C
TAS .... 110 knots

Therefore, CAS is 98.4 KCAS.

(PLT002) — FAA-H-8083-25

Altitudes

Indicated altitude—the altitude above mean sea level indicated on an altimeter that is set to the current local altimeter setting. Better vertical separation of aircraft in a particular area results when all pilots use the local altimeter setting.

Pressure altitude—the altitude indicated on an altimeter when it is set to the standard sea level pressure of 29.92 inches of mercury ("Hg). Above 18,000 feet MSL, flight levels, which are pressure altitudes, are flown.

Density altitude—the result of a given pressure altitude that is corrected for a nonstandard temperature.

True altitude—the exact height above sea level. The altimeter setting yields true altitude at field elevation.

Pressure decreases with altitude most rapidly in cold air and least rapidly in warm air. However, the standard pressure lapse rate is a decrease of 1 "Hg for each 1,000 feet of increase in altitude. See Figures 3-2 and 3-3.

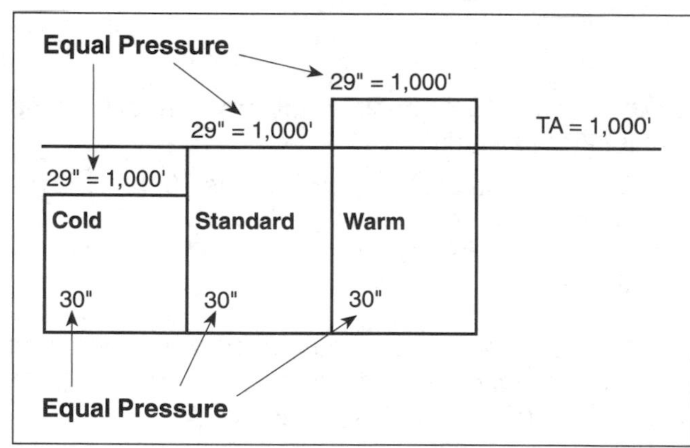

Figure 3-2

Answers
4359 [B] 4323 [A]

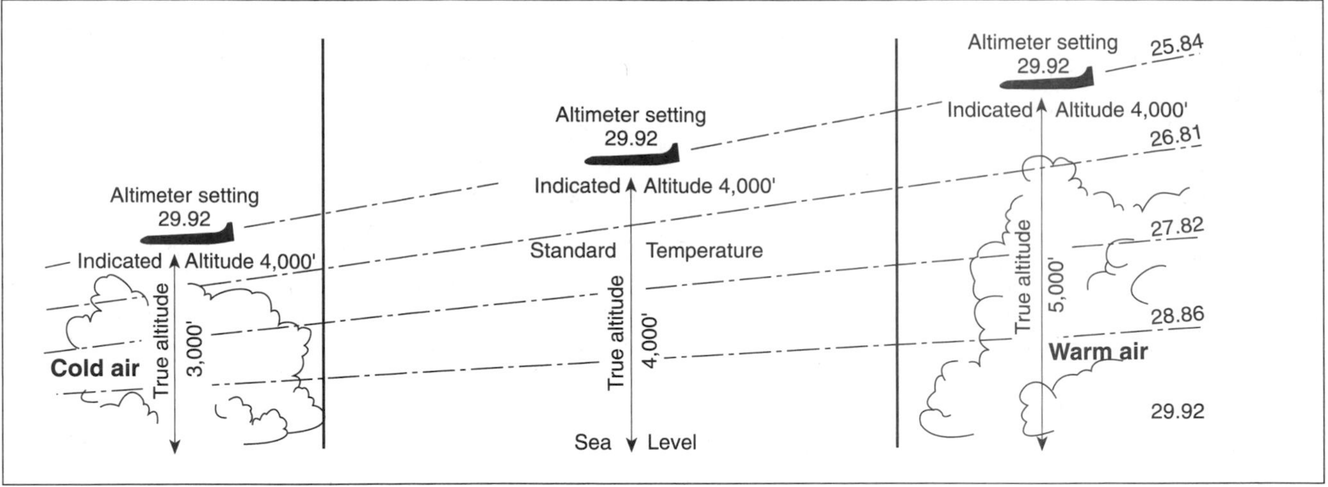

Figure 3-3

ALL

4089. Under what condition is pressure altitude and density altitude the same value?

A—At standard temperature.
B—When the altimeter setting is 29.92 "Hg.
C—When indicated, and pressure altitudes are the same value on the altimeter.

Density altitude is pressure altitude corrected for nonstandard temperature. Under standard atmospheric conditions, each level of air in the atmosphere has a specific density, and under standard conditions, pressure altitude and density altitude identify the same level. (PLT041, IR.I.C.K2) — AC 00-6

Answer (B) is incorrect because pressure altitude must be corrected for nonstandard temperature. Answer (C) is incorrect because pressure and indicated altitudes are not corrected for nonstandard temperature, and density altitude is.

ALL

4090. Under which condition will pressure altitude be equal to true altitude?

A—When the atmospheric pressure is 29.92 "Hg.
B—When standard atmospheric conditions exist.
C—When indicated altitude is equal to the pressure altitude.

Pressure altitude will be equal to true altitude when standard atmospheric conditions exist for the same altitude. (PLT023, IR.I.C.K2) — AC 00-6

Answer (A) is incorrect because it does not consider the possibility of nonstandard temperature. Answer (C) is incorrect because indicated altitude only considers air pressure, not both air pressure and temperature.

ALL

4091. Which condition would cause the altimeter to indicate a lower altitude than actually flown (true altitude)?

A—Air temperature lower than standard.
B—Atmospheric pressure lower than standard.
C—Air temperature warmer than standard.

Effects of nonstandard conditions can result in a difference of as much as 2,000 feet between true and indicated altitude. On a warm day, the pressure levels are raised, and the altimeter will indicate a lower altitude than the one actually flown (true altitude). (PLT165, IR.I.C.K2) — AC 00-6

Answer (A) is incorrect because air temperature colder than standard has lower pressure levels, and will cause the altimeter to indicate higher than true altitude. Answer (B) is incorrect because the altimeter will adjust for nonstandard pressure settings.

ALL

4109. Under what condition will true altitude be lower than indicated altitude with an altimeter setting of 29.92 "Hg?

A—In warmer than standard air temperature.
B—In colder than standard air temperature.
C—When density altitude is higher than indicated altitude.

Effects of nonstandard conditions can result in a difference of as much as 2,000 feet between true and indicated altitude. On a cold day, the pressure levels are lowered, and the altimeter will indicate a higher altitude than the one actually flown (true altitude). (PLT023, IR.I.C.K2) — AC 00-6

Answer (A) is incorrect because in warmer than standard air, the true altitude will be higher than the indicated altitude. Answer (C)

Answers

4089 [A]	4090 [B]	4091 [C]	4109 [B]

is incorrect because a high density altitude indicates warmer than standard air, which would mean that the true altitude will be higher than the indicated altitude.

ALL

4111. Altimeter setting is the value to which the scale of the pressure altimeter is set so the altimeter indicates

A—true altitude at field elevation.
B—pressure altitude at field elevation.
C—pressure altitude at sea level.

Since the altitude scale is adjustable, you can set the altimeter to read true altitude at some specified height. Takeoff and landing are the most critical phases of flight; therefore, airport elevation is the most desirable altitude for a true reading of the altimeter. Altimeter setting is the value to which the scale of the pressure altimeter is set so the altimeter indicates true altitude at the field elevation. (PLT041, IR.I.C.K2) — FAA-H-8083-15

Answers (B) and (C) are incorrect because altimeter setting is the value to which the scale of the pressure altimeter is set so the altimeter indicates true altitude (not pressure altitude) at field elevation.

ALL

4477. Below 18,000 feet, pressure altitude may be obtained by

A—setting the altimeter to 29.92 "Hg.
B—setting the altimeter to the local altimeter setting.
C—requesting the current pressure altitude for the area.

Pressure altitude can always be determined from the altimeter whether in flight or on the ground. Set the altimeter at the standard altimeter setting of 29.92 inches, and the altimeter will indicate pressure altitude. (PLT041, IR.I.C.K2) — FAA-H-8083-15

ALL

4478. How can you determine the pressure altitude on an airport without a tower or FSS?

A—Set the altimeter to 29.92 "Hg and read the altitude indicated.
B—Set the altimeter to the current altimeter setting of a station within 100 miles and correct this indicated altitude with local temperature.
C—Use your computer and correct the field elevation for temperature.

Pressure altitude can always be determined from the altimeter whether in flight or on the ground. Set the altimeter at the standard altimeter setting of 29.92 inches, and the altimeter will indicate pressure altitude. (PLT041, IR.I.C.K2) — FAA-H-8083-15

ALL

4479. Which altitude is indicated when the altimeter is set to 29.92 "Hg?

A—Density.
B—Pressure.
C—Standard.

With the altimeter set at the standard altimeter setting of 29.92 inches, the altimeter will indicate pressure altitude. (PLT041, IR.I.C.K2) — FAA-H-8083-15

ALL

4911. At an altitude of 6,500 feet MSL, the current altimeter setting is 30.42 "Hg. The pressure altitude would be approximately

A—7,500 feet.
B—6,000 feet.
C—6,500 feet.

Pressure altitude is the altitude indicated when the altimeter setting window is adjusted to 29.92 "Hg. (the theoretical standard datum plane). To find pressure altitude, follow these steps:

1. *Find the difference between the given pressure and standard pressure:*

   30.42 – 29.92 = 0.50 "Hg.

2. *Find the change in indicated altitude. The standard pressure lapse rate is about 1 inch per 1,000 feet:*

   0.50 × 1000 = 500 feet difference

3. *Find pressure altitude. The standard datum plane pressure is lower than the current station setting and therefore, pressure altitude will also be lower:*

   6,500 feet MSL – 500 feet =
   6,000 feet pressure altitude

(PLT166, IR.II.B.K1a) — FAA-H-8083-15

ALL

4912. The pressure altitude at a given location is indicated on the altimeter after the altimeter is set to

A—the field elevation.
B—29.92 "Hg.
C—the current altimeter setting.

Pressure altitude is the altitude read on the altimeter when the instrument is adjusted to indicate height above the standard datum plane. The standard datum plane is a theoretical level where the weight of the atmosphere is 29.92 "Hg. (PLT166, IR.II.B.K1a) — FAA-H-8083-15

Answer (A) is incorrect because the altimeter is set to standard pressure, not field elevation. Answer (C) is incorrect because the current altimeter setting would give indicated, not pressure, altitude.

Answers

4111 [A] 4477 [A] 4478 [A] 4479 [B] 4911 [B] 4912 [B]

ALL

4913. If the outside air temperature increases during a flight at constant power and at a constant indicated altitude, the true airspeed will

A—decrease and true altitude will increase.
B—increase and true altitude will decrease.
C—increase and true altitude will increase.

As temperature increases, pressure levels increase. An increase in pressure causes true airspeed and true altitude to increase. (PLT012, IR.I.C.K3a) — FAA-H-8083-15

Answer (A) is incorrect because true airspeed will increase (not decrease). Answer (B) is incorrect because true altitude will increase (not decrease).

ALL

4922. Altimeter setting is the value to which the scale of the pressure altimeter is set so the altimeter indicates

A—pressure altitude at sea level.
B—true altitude at field elevation.
C—pressure altitude at field elevation.

The altimeter setting broadcast by each FSS is a computed correction for nonstandard surface pressure only, for a specific location and elevation. Consequently, altimeter indications based upon a local altimeter setting indicate true altitude at field elevation. (PLT041, IR.I.C.K2) — FAA-H-8083-15

Answers (A) and (C) are incorrect because the altimeter setting causes the altimeter to indicate true (not pressure) altitude at field (not sea) level.

ALL

4923. Pressure altitude is the altitude read on your altimeter when the instrument is adjusted to indicate height above

A—sea level.
B—the standard datum plane.
C—ground level.

Pressure altitude is the altitude read on your altimeter when the instrument is adjusted to indicate height above the standard datum plane. The standard datum plane is a theoretical level where the weight of the atmosphere is 29.92 "Hg as measured by a barometer. As atmospheric pressure changes, the standard datum plane may be below, at, or above sea level. Pressure altitude is important as a basis for determining aircraft performance as well as for assigning flight levels to aircraft operating at high altitude. (PLT166, IR.II.B.K1a) — FAA-H-8083-15

Altimeter Settings

Before departure, the pilot should obtain the altimeter setting given for the local airport. En route, the pilot should set the altimeter to the closest station within 100 NM. The pilot will be periodically advised by ATC of the proper altimeter setting.

At or above 18,000 feet, all aircraft use 29.92 "Hg. The change to or from 29.92 "Hg should be made when passing through 18,000 feet. If this change is not made, the altimeter will read erroneously.

Aside from incorrectly setting an altimeter, one of the most common errors is to misread it. The small hand indicates thousand of feet. The long, thin hand indicates hundreds of feet. The very thin hand with the triangular tip indicates tens of thousand of feet. See Figure 3-4.

To preflight the altimeter, the current reported altimeter setting should be set in the Kollsman window. Note any variation between the known field elevation and the altimeter indication. If the variation exceeds ±75 feet, the accuracy of the altimeter is questionable and the problem should be referred to an appropriately rated repair station for evaluation and possible correction.

Answers

4913 [C] 4922 [B] 4923 [B]

Figure 3-4. Altimeter

ALL

4093. When an altimeter is changed from 30.11 "Hg to 29.96 "Hg, in which direction will the indicated altitude change and by what value?

A—Altimeter will indicate 15 feet lower.
B—Altimeter will indicate 150 feet lower.
C—Altimeter will indicate 150 feet higher.

The altimeter indication changes 1,000 feet for every one inch change in pressure. When the pressure setting is changed to a lower number, the altitude indicated on the altimeter will decrease. The altimeter setting in this question has changed 0.15 (30.11 – 29.96 = 0.15), which will cause a 150-foot change in the altimeter reading (0.15 × 1,000). (PLT041, IR.II.B.K1a) — AC 00-6

Answers (A) and (C) are incorrect because a 0.15" pressure change would cause the altimeter to indicate 150 (not 15) feet lower (not higher).

ALL

4445. En route at FL290, the altimeter is set correctly, but not reset to the local altimeter setting of 30.57 "Hg during descent. If the field elevation is 650 feet and the altimeter is functioning properly, what is the approximate indication upon landing?

A—715 feet.
B—1,300 feet.
C—Sea level.

En route at FL290, the pilot would have the altimeter set to 29.92 "Hg, since the altitude is at or above FL180. If the pilot failed to reset it to the local altimeter setting of 30.57 during descent, the altimeter will not indicate field elevation upon landing.

Since: 30.57
– 29.92
0.65

and since 1 inch per 1,000 feet equals 0.1 inch per 100 feet and 0.01 inch per 10 feet, the altimeter will, in this case, indicate an error of 650 feet. Because the flight went from a low-pressure area (29.92) to a higher-pressure area (30.57), the altimeter error is subtracted from the field elevation of 650 feet.

650 – 650 = 0 feet, or the altimeter will indicate sea level

(PLT166, IR.II.B.K1a) — FAA-H-8083-15

ALL

4481. En route at FL290, your altimeter is set correctly, but you fail to reset it to the local altimeter setting of 30.26 "Hg during descent. If the field elevation is 134 feet and your altimeter is functioning properly, what will it indicate after landing?

A—100 feet MSL.
B—474 feet MSL.
C—206 feet below MSL.

En route at FL290, the pilot would have the altimeter set to 29.92 inches, since the altitude is above FL180. Since the pilot failed to reset it to the local altimeter setting of 30.26 during descent, the altimeter will not indicate field elevation upon landing. Since:

30.26
– 29.92
0.34

and one inch per 1,000 feet equals 0.1 inch per 100 feet and 0.01 inch per 10 feet, the altimeter will, in this case, indicate an error of 340 feet.

Because the flight went from a low-pressure area (29.92) to a higher-pressure area (30.26), the altimeter error is subtracted from the field elevation of 134 feet.

134 airport elevation
– 340 error
-206 feet below sea level

(PLT166, IR.II.B.K1a) — FAA-H-8083-15

Answers

4093 [B] 4445 [C] 4481 [C]

ALL

4110. Which of the following defines the type of altitude used when maintaining FL210?

A—Indicated.
B—Pressure.
C—Calibrated.

At or above 18,000 feet MSL, the altimeter is set to 29.92 "Hg. You can always determine pressure altitude from your altimeter whether in flight or on the ground. Simply set the altimeter to 29.92 inches, and the altimeter indicates pressure altitude. (PLT023, IR.II.B.K1a) — AC 00-6

Answer (A) is incorrect because indicated altitude is what is read from the altimeter at any setting. Answer (C) is incorrect because all altimeters are calibrated.

ALL

4444. What is the procedure for setting the altimeter when assigned an IFR altitude of 18,000 feet or higher on a direct flight off airways?

A—Set the altimeter to 29.92 "Hg before takeoff.
B—Set the altimeter to the current altimeter setting until reaching the assigned altitude, then set to 29.92 "Hg.
C—Set the altimeter to the current reported setting for climb-out and 29.92 "Hg upon reaching 18,000 feet.

The cruising altitude or flight level of aircraft shall be maintained by reference to an altimeter which shall be set, when operating at or above 18,000 feet MSL, to 29.92 "Hg (standard setting). (PLT166, IR.II.B.K1a) — AIM ¶7-2-2

Answer (A) is incorrect because the local altimeter settings or indicated altitude should be used up to FL180. Answer (B) is incorrect because the altimeter should be set to 29.92 upon reaching FL180 (not the assigned altitude).

ALL

4446. While you are flying at FL250, you hear ATC give an altimeter setting of 28.92 "Hg in your area. At what pressure altitude are you flying?

A—24,000 feet.
B—25,000 feet.
C—26,000 feet.

Pressure altitude is the altitude indicated when the altimeter setting window is adjusted to 29.92. Because the pilot is flying at FL250 the altimeter will be set at 29.92 "Hg (since the pilot is above FL180). Consequently the pressure altitude will be 25,000 feet. (PLT041, IR.II.B.K1a) — FAA-H-8083-15

Answers (A) and (C) are incorrect because FL250 implies a pressure altitude of 25,000 feet, by definition.

ALL

4480. If you are departing from an airport where you cannot obtain an altimeter setting, you should set your altimeter

A—to 29.92 "Hg.
B—on the current airport barometric pressure, if known.
C—to the airport elevation.

In the case of an aircraft not equipped with a radio, set the altimeter to the elevation of the departure airport or use an appropriate altimeter setting available prior to departure. (PLT166, IR.II.B.K1a) — 14 CFR §91.121

ALL

4482. How does a pilot normally obtain the current altimeter setting during an IFR flight in Class E airspace below 18,000 feet?

A—The pilot should contact ARTCC at least every 100 NM and request the altimeter setting.
B—FSS's along the route broadcast the weather information at 15 minutes past the hour.
C—ATC periodically advises the pilot of the proper altimeter setting.

For flight below 18,000 feet MSL, the altimeter should be set to the current reported altimeter setting of a station along the route, and within 100 NM of the aircraft, or if there is no station within this area, the current reported altimeter setting of an appropriate available station. When an aircraft is en route on an instrument flight plan, ATC will furnish this information to the pilot at least once while the aircraft is in its area of jurisdiction. (PLT166, IR.II.B.K1a) — AIM ¶7-2-2

Answer (A) is incorrect because ATC provides the altimeter setting without being asked. Answer (B) is incorrect because the FSS is not responsible for broadcasting altimeter settings.

Answers

4110 [B]	4444 [C]	4446 [B]	4480 [C]	4482 [C]

ALL

4910. The local altimeter setting should be used by all pilots in a particular area, primarily to provide for

A—the cancellation of altimeter error due to nonstandard temperatures aloft.
B—better vertical separation of aircraft.
C—more accurate terrain clearance in mountainous areas.

The altimeter setting system provides the means that must be used to correct the altimeter for pressure variations. The system is necessary to ensure safe terrain clearance for instrument approaches and landings, and to maintain vertical separation between aircraft during instrument weather conditions. (PLT166, IR.II.B.K1a) — FAA-H-8083-25

Answer (A) is incorrect because a local altimeter setting does not cancel error due to nonstandard temperatures aloft. Answer (C) is incorrect because a local altimeter setting will not provide more accurate terrain clearance since it does not cancel error due to nonstandard temperatures aloft.

ALL

4402. How should you preflight check the altimeter prior to an IFR flight?

A—Set the altimeter to 29.92 "Hg. With current temperature and the altimeter indication, determine the true altitude to compare with the field elevation.
B—Set the altimeter first to 29.92 "Hg and then the current altimeter setting. The change in altitude should correspond to the change in setting.
C—Set the altimeter to the current altimeter setting. The indication should be within 75 feet of the actual elevation for acceptable accuracy.

With the altimeter set to the current reported altimeter setting, note any variation between the known field elevation and the altimeter indication. If the variation exceeds ±75 feet, the accuracy of the altimeter is questionable and the problem should be referred to an appropriately-rated repair station for evaluation and possible correction. (PLT337, IR.IV.A.K1a) — FAA-H-8083-15

Answer (A) is incorrect because setting the altimeter to 29.92 and adjusting for temperature give only the density (not true) altitude. Answer (B) is incorrect because only the indicated altitude (not change in altitude) is checked.

ALL

4880. How should you preflight check the altimeter prior to an IFR flight?

A—Set the altimeter to the current temperature. With current temperature and the altimeter indication, determine the calibrated altitude to compare with the field elevation.
B—Set the altimeter first to 29.92 "Hg and then the current altimeter setting. The change in altitude should correspond to the change in setting.
C—Set the altimeter to the current altimeter setting. The indication should be within 75 feet of the actual elevation for acceptable accuracy.

With the altimeter set to the current reported altimeter setting, note any variation between the known field elevation and the altimeter indication. If the variation exceeds ±75 feet, the accuracy of the altimeter is questionable and the problem should be referred to an appropriately-rated repair station for evaluation and possible correction. (PLT337, IR.IV.A.K3) — FAA-H-8083-15

Answer (A) is incorrect because setting the altimeter to 29.92 and adjusting for temperature would indicate density (not true) altitude. Answer (B) is incorrect because only the indicated altitude (not change in altitude) is checked.

Answers

4910 [B]   4402 [C]   4880 [C]

Vertical Speed Indicator

The vertical speed indicator (VSI) is designed to indicate the rate of climb or descent. Although not required by regulation to be on board, it is commonly found on instrument airplanes. A VSI pre-takeoff check is made to check for a "zero" reading. If it is indicating a climb or descent, note the error and apply it to readings in flight. See Figure 3-5.

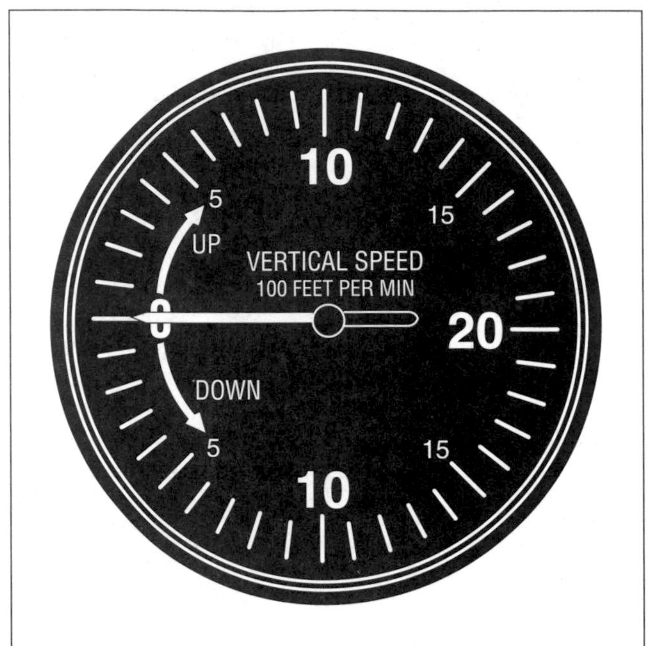

Figure 3-5. Vertical speed indicator (VSI)

ALL

4056. During taxi, the VSI indicates a 100 fpm descent. How does this indication affect your flight?

A—You may not operate under IFR until the VSI is repaired.

B—You may continue under IFR using the 100 fpm descent as the "zero" indication.

C—You may operate under IFR, but only if the weather is VMC.

The needle of the vertical velocity indicator should indicate zero when the aircraft is on the ground or maintaining a constant pressure level in flight. If this adjustment cannot be made, you must allow for the error when interpreting the indications in flight. Since the VSI is not a required instrument, there are no regulation requirements concerning calibration. (PLT445, IR.IV.A.K1) — FAA-H-8083-15

Answers (A) and (C) are incorrect because the VSI may be used by noting any discrepancies and accommodating for them in flight. A VSI is not required for instrument flight. Even if the VSI was completely inaccurate, the flight could still proceed under IFR in IMC under the regulations.

Attitude Indicator

Gyroscopes (gyros) exhibit two important principles: rigidity in space and precession. There are three instruments controlled by gyroscopes: attitude indicator, turn coordinator, and the heading indicator.

The attitude indicator provides an immediate, direct, and corresponding indication of any change of aircraft pitch and bank attitude in relation to the natural horizon. It is the pilot's primary instrument during transitions of pitch or bank attitudes. See Figure 3-6.

The attitude indicator exhibits several inherent errors:

- Following a 180° turn, it indicates a slight climb and bank in the opposite direction (turn error). Following a 360° turn, this error cancels itself out and is not apparent.
- During acceleration, the horizon bar moves down, indicating a climb (acceleration error).
- During deceleration, the horizon bar moves up, indicating a descent (deceleration error).

An attitude indicator pre-takeoff check verifies that the horizon bar stabilizes within five minutes, and does not dip more than 5° during taxiing turns.

Answers

4056 [B]

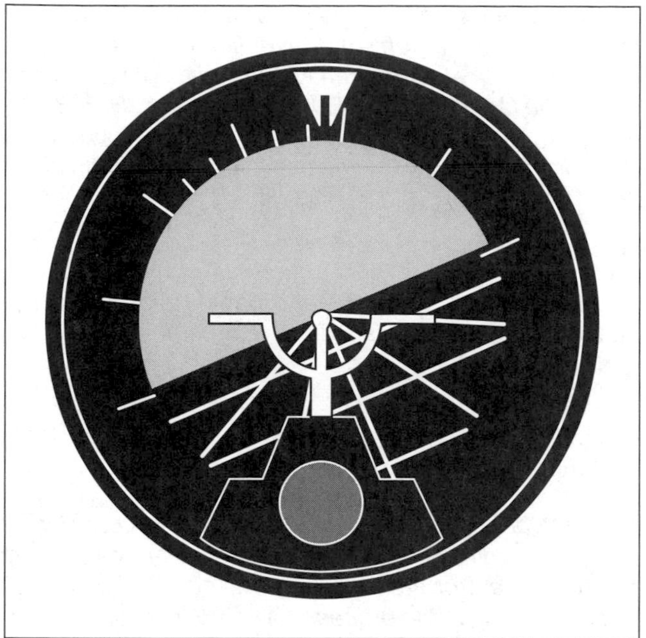

Figure 3-6. Attitude indicator

ALL

4902. One characteristic that a properly functioning gyro depends upon for operation is the

A—ability to resist precession 90° to any applied force.
B—resistance to deflection of the spinning wheel or disc.
C—deflecting force developed from the angular velocity of the spinning wheel.

Any rotating body exhibits gyroscopic properties according to Newton's laws of motion. The first law states: a body at rest will remain at rest; or if in motion in a straight line, it will continue in motion in a straight line unless acted upon by an outside force. The second law states: the deflection of a moving body is proportional to the deflective force applied and is inversely proportional to its weight and speed. A gyro is a wheel or disc designed to utilize these principles. (PLT118, IR.II.B.K1b) — FAA-H-8083-15

Answer (A) is incorrect because a gyro uses (not resists) precession. Answer (C) is incorrect because deflecting forces are applied (not developed) to gyros.

ALL

4901. If a 180° steep turn is made to the right and the aircraft is rolled out to straight-and-level flight by visual references, the attitude indicator

A—should immediately show straight-and-level flight.
B—will show a slight skid and climb to the right.
C—may show a slight climb and turn.

Attitude indicators are free from most errors, but there is a possibility of a small bank angle and pitch error after a 180° turn. (PLT278, IR.II.B.K1b) — FAA-H-8083-15

ALL

4820. As a rule of thumb, altitude corrections of less than 100 feet should be corrected by using a

A—full bar width on the attitude indicator.
B—half bar width on the attitude indicator.
C—two bar width on the attitude indicator.

As a rule-of-thumb, for errors less than 100 feet, use a half-bar-width correction. (PLT278, IR.II.B.K1b) — FAA-H-8083-15

ALL

4835. Which condition during taxi is an indication that an attitude indicator is unreliable?

A—The horizon bar tilts more than 5° while making taxi turns.
B—The horizon bar vibrates during warmup.
C—The horizon bar does not align itself with the miniature airplane after warmup.

If the attitude indicator's horizon bar erects to the horizontal position and remains at the correct position for the attitude of the airplane, or if it begins to vibrate after this attitude is reached and then slowly stops vibrating altogether, the instrument is operating properly. If the horizon bar fails to remain in the horizontal position during straight taxiing, or tips in excess of 5° during taxi turns, the instrument is unreliable. (PLT118, IR.II.B.K1b) — FAA-H-8083-15

Answer (B) is incorrect because during warm-up the horizon bar will normally vibrate as the gyros gather speed. Answer (C) is incorrect because the horizon bar will align itself with the center of the dial thus indicating level flight. At this point, the miniature airplane can be adjusted to align with the horizon bar from the pilot's viewpoint.

Answers

4902 [B] 4901 [C] 4820 [B] 4835 [A]

ALL

4842. What pretakeoff check should be made of the attitude indicator in preparation for an IFR flight?

A—The horizon bar does not vibrate during warmup.
B—The miniature airplane should erect and become stable within 5 minutes.
C—The horizon bar should erect and become stable within 5 minutes.

If the horizon bar erects to the horizontal position and remains at the correct position for the attitude of the airplane, or if it begins to vibrate after this attitude is reached and then slowly stops vibrating altogether, the instrument is operating properly. If the horizon bar fails to remain in the horizontal position during straight taxiing, or tips in excess of 5° during taxi turns, the instrument is unreliable. (PLT445, IR.II.B.K1b) — FAA-H-8083-15

Answer (A) is incorrect because during warm-up, the horizon will normally vibrate as the gyros begin to gather speed. Answer (B) is incorrect because the miniature airplane can be set manually.

ALL

4857. During normal operation of a vacuum-driven attitude indicator, what attitude indication should you see when rolling out from a 180° skidding turn to straight-and-level coordinated flight?

A—A straight-and-level coordinated flight indication.
B—A nose-high indication relative to level flight.
C—The miniature aircraft shows a turn in the direction opposite the skid.

After returning the aircraft to straight-and-level coordinated flight, the miniature aircraft shows a turn in the direction opposite the skid. (PLT118, IR.II.B.K1b) — FAA-H-8083-15

Answer (A) is incorrect because the attitude indicator shows a small turn in the opposite direction and does not reflect coordinated flight. Answer (B) is incorrect because a nose-high indication would be found when rolling out of a coordinated turn.

ALL

4860. During normal coordinated turns, what error due to precession should you observe when rolling out to straight-and-level flight from a 180° steep turn to the right?

A—A straight-and-level coordinated flight indication.
B—The miniature aircraft would show a slight turn indication to the left.
C—The miniature aircraft would show a slight descent and wings-level attitude.

If a 180° steep turn is made to the right and the aircraft is rolled-out to straight-and-level flight by visual references, the miniature aircraft will show a slight climb and turn to the left. (PLT278), IR.II.B.K1b — FAA-H-8083-15

Answer (A) is incorrect because the attitude indicator will show a slight climb to the left and does not reflect coordinated flight. Answer (C) is incorrect because it will show a slight climb and a turning error.

ALL

4900. Errors in both pitch and bank indication on an attitude indicator are usually at a maximum as the aircraft rolls out of a

A—180° turn.
B—270° turn.
C—360° turn.

Errors in both pitch and bank indications occur during normal coordinated turns. These errors are caused by the movement of the pendulous vanes by centrifugal force, resulting in the precession of the gyro towards the inside of the turn. The error is greatest in a 180° steep turn. (PLT278, IR.II.B.K1b) — FAA-H-8083-15

ALL

4918. When the aircraft accelerates, the attitude indicator may precess and incorrectly indicate a

A—climb.
B—descent.
C—right turn.

Acceleration and deceleration induce precession errors, depending upon the amount and extent of the force applied. During acceleration, the horizon bar moves down, indicating a climb. (PLT132, IR.II.B.K1b) — FAA-H-8083-15

ALL

4919. When an aircraft is decelerated, some attitude indicators will precess and incorrectly indicate a

A—left turn.
B—climb.
C—descent.

Acceleration and deceleration induce precession errors, depending upon the amount and extent of the force applied. During deceleration, the horizon bar moves up, indicating a descent. (PLT118, IR.II.B.K1b) — FAA-H-8083-15

Answers

4842 [C]	4857 [C]	4860 [B]	4900 [A]	4918 [A]	4919 [C]

ALL

4928. While cruising at 160 knots, you wish to establish a climb at 130 knots. When entering the climb (full panel), it is proper to make the initial pitch change by increasing back elevator pressure until the

A—attitude indicator, airspeed, and vertical speed indicate a climb.
B—vertical speed indication reaches the predetermined rate of climb.
C—attitude indicator shows the approximate pitch attitude appropriate for the 130-knot climb.

To enter a constant airspeed climb from cruising airspeed, raise the miniature aircraft on the attitude indicator to the approximate nose-high indication appropriate to the predetermined climb speed. The attitude will vary according to the type of airplane you are flying. (PLT185, IR.II.B.K1b) — FAA-H-8083-15

Answers (A) and (B) are incorrect because initial pitch changes should be made using the attitude indicator.

ALL

4929. While cruising at 190 knots, you wish to establish a climb at 160 knots. When entering the climb (full panel), it would be proper to make the initial pitch change by increasing back elevator pressure until the

A—attitude indicator shows the approximate pitch attitude appropriate for the 160-knot climb.
B—attitude indicator, airspeed, and vertical speed indicate a climb.
C—airspeed indication reaches 160 knots.

To enter a constant airspeed climb from cruising airspeed, raise the miniature aircraft on the attitude indicator to the approximate nose-high indication appropriate to the predetermined climb speed. The attitude will vary according to the type of airplane you are flying. (PLT185, IR.II.B.K1b) — FAA-H-8083-15

Answers (B) and (C) are incorrect because initial pitch changes should be made using the attitude indicator.

RTC

4841. Which initial pitch attitude change on the attitude indicator should be made to correct altitude while at normal cruise in a helicopter?

A—Two bar width.
B—One and one-half bar width.
C—One bar width.

When making initial pitch attitude corrections to maintain altitude, the changes of attitude should be small and smoothly applied. The initial movement of the horizon bar should not exceed one bar high or low. If further change is required, an additional correction of one-half bar will normally correct any deviation from the desired altitude. This correction (one and one-half bars) is normally the maximum. (PLT185) — FAA-H-8083-15

RTC

4846. During the initial acceleration on an instrument takeoff in a helicopter, what flight attitude should be established on the attitude indicator?

A—Level flight attitude.
B—Two bar widths low.
C—One bar width high.

During the initial acceleration, the pitch attitude of the helicopter, as read on the attitude indicator, should be one to two bar widths low. (PLT278) — FAA-H-8083-15

RTC

4852. During a stabilized autorotation, approximately what flight attitude should be established on the attitude indicator?

A—Two bar widths below the artificial horizon.
B—A pitch attitude that will give an established rate of descent of not more than 500 feet per minute.
C—Level flight attitude.

The pitch attitude of the helicopter should be approximately level as shown by the attitude indicator. (PLT175) — FAA-H-8083-15

RTC

4861. The primary reason the pitch attitude must be increased, to maintain a constant altitude during a coordinated turn, is because the

A—use of pedals has increased the drag.
B—vertical component of lift has decreased as the result of the bank.
C—thrust is acting in a different direction, causing a reduction in airspeed and loss of lift.

The primary reason the pitch attitude must be increased, to maintain a constant altitude during a coordinated turn, is because the vertical component of lift has decreased (and horizontal component of lift increased) as a result of the bank. (PLT235) — FAA-H-8083-15

Answers

4928 [C]	4929 [A]	4841 [C]	4846 [B]	4852 [C]	4861 [B]

Turn Coordinator

The turn coordinator is a gyroscopically operated instrument that is designed to show roll rate, rate of turn, and quality of turn. It acts as a backup system in case of a failure of the vacuum powered attitude indicator. See Figure 3-7.

Before starting the engine, the turn needle should be centered and the race full of fluid. During a taxiing turn, the needle will indicate a turn in the proper direction and the ball will show a skid.

An airplane turns because of the horizontal component of lift in a banked attitude. The greater the horizontal lift at any airspeed, the greater the rate of turn. The angle of attack must be increased to maintain altitude during a turn because the vertical component of lift decreases as a result of the bank. When airspeed is decreased in a turn, either a decrease in the bank angle or an increase in the angle of attack is required to maintain level flight. During a constant bank level turn, an increase in airspeed would result in a decrease in rate of turn and an increase in turn radius.

In a coordinated turn, horizontal lift and centrifugal force are equal. In a skid, the rate of turn is too great for the angle of bank, and excessive centrifugal force causes the ball to move to the outside of the turn. To correct to coordinated flight, the pilot should increase the bank or decrease the rate of turn, or a combination of both. In a slip, the rate of turn is too slow for the angle of bank, and the lack of centrifugal force causes the ball to move to the inside of the turn. To return to coordinated flight, the pilot needs to decrease the bank or increase the rate of turn, or a combination of both.

A standard rate turn (3° per second) takes 2 minutes to complete a 360° turn. A half-standard rate turn (1.5° per second) takes 4 minutes to complete a 360° turn.

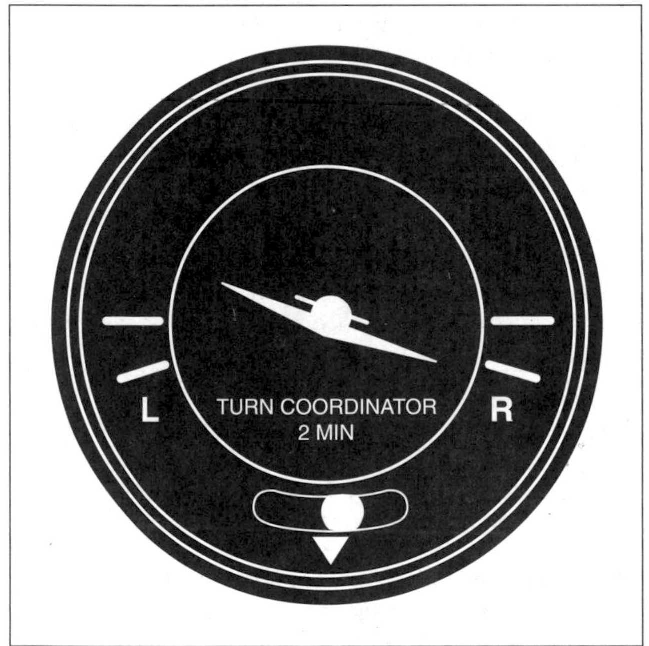

Figure 3-7. Turn coordinator

ALL

4882. Prior to starting an engine, you should check the turn-and-slip indicator to determine if the

A—needle indication properly corresponds to the angle of the wings or rotors with the horizon.
B—needle is approximately centered and the tube is full of fluid.
C—ball will move freely from one end of the tube to the other when the aircraft is rocked.

The following are items that should be checked before starting the engine(s):

1. *Check turn-and-slip indicator and magnetic compass for fluid level (should be full).*
2. *If instruments are electrical, turn on and listen for any unusual or irregular mechanical noise.*
3. *Check instruments for poor condition, mounting, marking, broken, or loose knobs. Also check the power-off indications of the instrument pointers and warning flags.*

(PLT187, IR.II.B.K1b) — FAA-H-8083-15

Answer (A) is incorrect because the needle is related to rate and direction of turn (not wings or rotors). Answer (C) is incorrect because the ball is checked during taxi and it is not necessary to rock the aircraft.

Answers

4882 [B]

ALL

4831. What indication should be observed on a turn coordinator during a left turn while taxiing?

A—The miniature aircraft will show a turn to the left and the ball remains centered.
B—The miniature aircraft will show a turn to the left and the ball moves to the right.
C—Both the miniature aircraft and the ball will remain centered.

When an aircraft makes a taxiing left turn, the turn coordinator will show the same indications as a level, no-bank left turn in flight. Those indications are: The miniature airplane will show a left turn (the direction of turn and rate) while the ball will show an uncoordinated turn (a skid), by moving to the right. (PLT118, IR.II.B.K1b) — FAA-H-8083-15

Answer (A) is incorrect because the ball would move to the outside of the turn due to centrifugal force. Answer (C) is incorrect because the miniature aircraft will show a turn to the left and the ball will move to the right.

ALL

4883. What indications should you observe on the turn-and-slip indicator during taxi?

A—The ball moves freely opposite the turn, and the needle deflects in the direction of the turn.
B—The needle deflects in the direction of the turn, but the ball remains centered.
C—The ball deflects opposite the turn, but the needle remains centered.

You should observe the following on the turn-and-slip indicator during taxi:

1. *Check and ensure the turn needle indicates proper direction of turn.*
2. *Check the ball for freedom of movement in the glass tube. Centrifugal force causes the ball to move to the outside of the turn.*

(PLT187, IR.II.B.K1b) — FAA-H-8083-15

Answer (B) is incorrect because the ball will move opposite to the direction of the turn. Answer (C) is incorrect because the needle moves in the direction of the turn.

ALL

4604. What indication should be observed on a turn coordinator during a right turn while taxiing?

A—The miniature aircraft will show a turn to the left and the ball remains centered.
B—The miniature aircraft will show a turn to the right and the ball moves to the left.
C—Both the miniature aircraft and the ball will remain centered.

When an aircraft makes a taxiing right turn, the turn coordinator will show the same indications as a level, no-bank right turn in flight. Those indications are: The miniature airplane will show a right turn (the direction of turn and rate) while the ball will show an uncoordinated turn (a skid), by moving to the left. (PLT118, IR.II.B.K1b) — FAA-H-8083-15

Answer (A) is incorrect because the ball would move to the outside of the turn due to centrifugal force. Answer (C) is incorrect because the miniature aircraft will show a turn to the right and the ball will move to the left.

ALL

4839. What does the miniature aircraft of the turn coordinator directly display?

A—Rate of roll and rate of turn.
B—Angle of bank and rate of turn.
C—Angle of bank.

The miniature aircraft of the turn coordinator displays rate of roll and rate of turn. (PLT187, IR.II.B.K1b) — FAA-H-8083-15

Answers (B) and (C) are incorrect because the miniature aircraft of the turn coordinator does not directly display the bank angle of the aircraft.

ALL

4847. What indications are displayed by the miniature aircraft of a turn coordinator?

A—Rate of roll and rate of turn.
B—Direct indication of bank angle and pitch attitude.
C—Indirect indication of bank angle and pitch attitude.

The miniature aircraft of the turn coordinator displays only rate-of-roll and rate-of-turn. It does not directly display the bank angle of the aircraft. (PLT187, IR.II.B.K1b) — FAA-H-8083-15

Answer (B) is incorrect because the turn coordinator is an indirect indication of bank angle and is not related to pitch attitude. Answer (C) is incorrect because the turn coordinator does not reflect pitch attitude.

Answers

4831 [B] 4883 [A] 4604 [B] 4839 [A] 4847 [A]

ALL

4856. What indication is presented by the miniature aircraft of the turn coordinator?

A—Indirect indication of the bank attitude.
B—Direct indication of the bank attitude and the quality of the turn.
C—Quality of the turn.

The miniature aircraft of the turn coordinator displays only rate-of-roll and rate-of-turn. It only indirectly displays the bank angle of the aircraft. (PLT187, IR.II.B.K1b) — FAA-H-8083-15

Answer (B) is incorrect because the turn coordinator does not provide a direct indication of bank. Answer (C) is incorrect because the ball in the turn coordinator displays the quality of the turn.

ALL

4884. Which instrument indicates the quality of a turn?

A—Attitude indicator.
B—Heading indicator or magnetic compass.
C—Ball of the turn coordinator.

The ball of the turn coordinator is a balance indicator, and is used as a visual aid to determine coordinated use of the aileron and rudder control. During a turn it indicates the relationship between the angle of bank and rate-of-turn. It indicates the quality of the turn, or whether the aircraft has the correct angle of bank for the rate-of-turn. When the ball is centered, the turn is coordinated, and neither slipping nor skidding. (PLT185, IR.II.B.K1b) — FAA-H-8083-15

Answer (A) is incorrect because the attitude indicator provides both pitch and bank information. Answer (B) is incorrect because the heading indicator and/or magnetic compass indicates the current or change in direction.

ALL

4870-1. What force causes an airplane to turn?

A—Rudder pressure or force around the vertical axis.
B—Vertical lift component.
C—Horizontal lift component.

An aircraft requires a sideward force to make it turn. In a normal turn, this force is supplied by banking the aircraft so that lift is exerted inward as well as upward. The horizontal lift component is the sideward force that causes the aircraft to turn. (PLT248, IR.IV.A.K1) — FAA-H-8083-15

Answer (A) is incorrect because rudder pressure is used to coordinate the airplane when it is banked. Answer (B) is incorrect because the vertical component of lift will act against weight, which affects altitude.

ALL

4843. The rate of turn at any airspeed is dependent upon

A—the horizontal lift component.
B—the vertical lift component.
C—centrifugal force.

The rate-of-turn at any given airspeed depends on the amount of sideward force causing the turn; that is, the horizontal lift component, which varies directly in proportion to bank in a correctly executed turn. (PLT237, IR.IV.A.K1) — FAA-H-8083-15; FAA-H-8083-21

Answer (B) is incorrect because the vertical lift component determines altitude and change in altitude. Answer (C) is incorrect because centrifugal force will act against the horizontal lift component.

ALL

4833-1. When airspeed is decreased in a turn, what must be done to maintain level flight?

A—Decrease the angle of bank and/or increase the angle of attack.
B—Increase the angle of bank and/or decrease the angle of attack.
C—Increase the angle of attack.

When airspeed is reduced, the vertical component of lift is reduced. To keep level flight you must either increase the angle of attack or reduce the angle of bank. (PLT185, IR.IV.A.K1) — FAA-H-8083-15

Answer (B) is incorrect because the increased vertical lift required must come from a decrease in angle of bank and/or increase in angle of attack. Answer (C) is incorrect because it is possible to decrease the angle of bank as well as increase the angle of attack.

ALL

4844. During a skidding turn to the right, what is the relationship between the component of lift, centrifugal force, and load factor?

A—Centrifugal force is less than horizontal lift and the load factor is increased.
B—Centrifugal force is greater than horizontal lift and the load factor is increased.
C—Centrifugal force and horizontal lift are equal and the load factor is decreased.

A skidding turn results from excess centrifugal force over the horizontal lift component, pulling the aircraft toward the outside of the turn. As centrifugal force increases, the load factor also increases. See the following figure. (PLT248, IR.IV.A.K1) — FAA-H-8083-15

Answer (A) is incorrect because a slipping turn will occur if centrifugal force is less than horizontal lift. Answer (C) is incorrect because centrifugal force and horizontal lift are equal in a coordinated turn and load factor will increase.

Answers

4856 [A] 4884 [C] 4870-1 [C] 4843 [A] 4833-1 [A] 4844 [B]

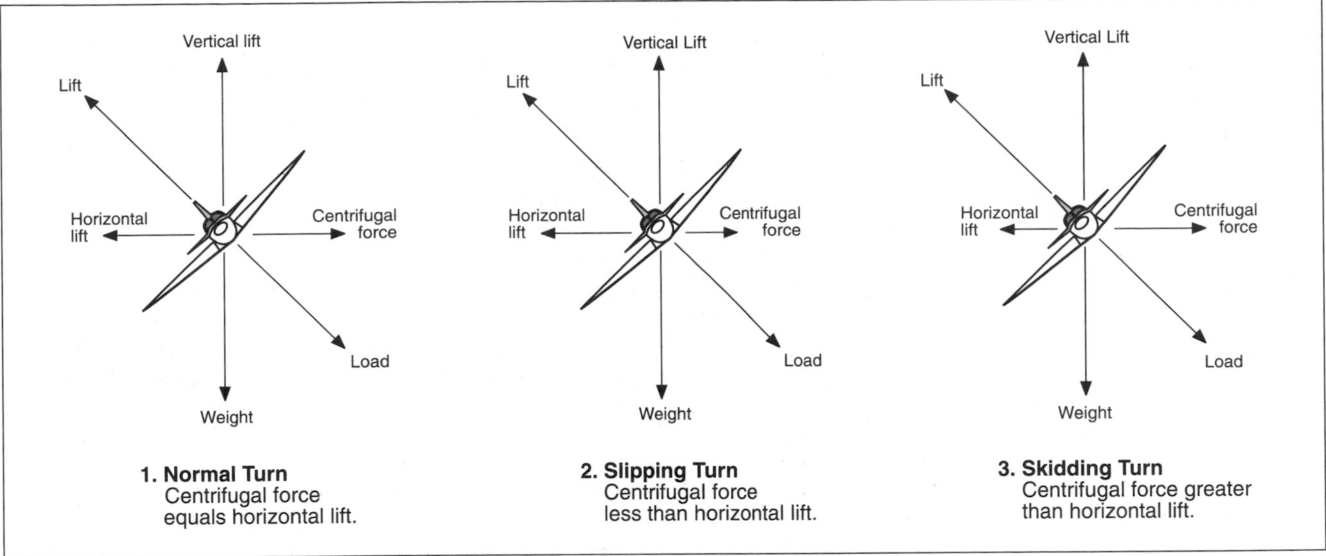

Question 4844

ALL

4868. What is the relationship between centrifugal force and the horizontal lift component in a coordinated turn?

A—Horizontal lift exceeds centrifugal force.
B—Horizontal lift and centrifugal force are equal.
C—Centrifugal force exceeds horizontal lift.

In a coordinated turn, horizontal lift equals centrifugal force. This is indicated by the ball on the turn-and-slip indicator being centered. See the following figure. (PLT242, IR.IV.A.K1) — FAA-H-8083-15; FAA-H-8083-21

Answer (A) is incorrect because if horizontal lift exceeds centrifugal force, a slipping turn will occur. Answer (C) is incorrect because if centrifugal force exceeds horizontal lift, a skidding turn will occur.

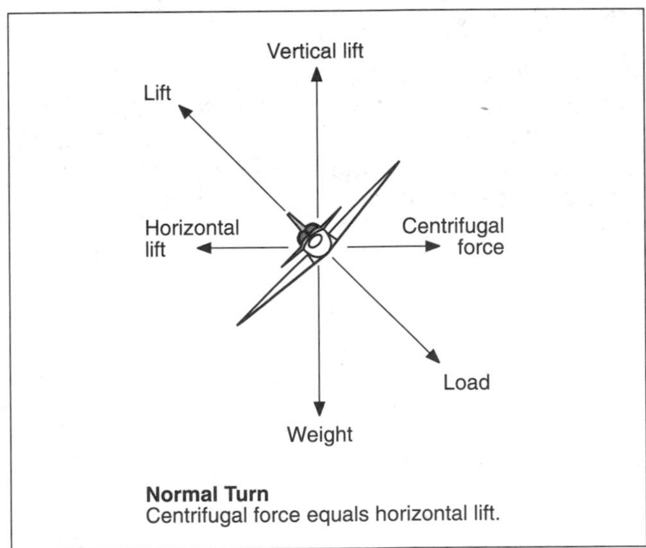

Question 4868

ALL

4878-1. When airspeed is increased in a turn, what must be done to maintain a constant altitude?

A—Decrease the angle of bank.
B—Increase the angle of bank and/or decrease the angle of attack.
C—Decrease the angle of attack.

As airspeed increases, the lift generated by the wings increases. Therefore to keep level, vertical lift must be decreased by either decreasing the total lift by decreasing the angle of attack, or by changing the vertical component when you tighten the turn. (PLT185, IR.IV.A.K1) — FAA-H-8083-15

Answer (A) is incorrect because the angle of bank must be increased. Answer (C) is incorrect because the angle of bank could also be increased.

ALL

4895. If a half-standard rate turn is maintained, how long will it take to turn 360°?

A—1 minute.
B—2 minutes.
C—4 minutes.

A standard rate turn (3° per second) takes 2 minutes to complete a 360° turn. A half-standard rate turn (1.5° per second) takes 4 minutes complete a 360° turn. (PLT185, IR.IV.A.K1) — FAA-H-8083-15

Answers

4868 [B] 4878-1 [B] 4895 [C]

ALL
4896. If a standard rate turn is maintained, how long would it take to turn 180°?

A—1 minute.
B—2 minutes.
C—3 minutes.

A standard rate turn is one during which the heading changes 3° per second. Therefore, at a rate of 3° of turn each second, 180° of turn would require 180/3 or 60 seconds (1 minute). (PLT185, IR.IV.A.K1) — FAA-H-8083-15

ALL
4897. If a half-standard rate turn is maintained, how much time would be required to turn clockwise from a heading of 090° to a heading of 180°?

A—30 seconds.
B—1 minute.
C—1 minute 30 seconds.

A half-standard rate turn is one in which the heading changes 1.5° per second. A heading change of 090° to 180° is a total turn of 90°. At a rate-of-turn of 1.5° each second would require 90/1.5 or 60 seconds (1 minute). (PLT185, IR.IV.A.K1) — FAA-H-8083-15

ALL
4898. During a constant-bank level turn, what effect would an increase in airspeed have on the rate and radius of turn?

A—Rate of turn would increase, and radius of turn would increase.
B—Rate of turn would decrease, and radius of turn would decrease.
C—Rate of turn would decrease, and radius of turn would increase.

Both the rate of turn and the radius of turn vary with changes in airspeed. If airspeed is increased, then the rate of turn is decreased, and the radius of the turn is increased. (PLT311, IR.IV.A.K1) — FAA-H-8083-15

Answer (A) is incorrect because rate of turn decreases. Answer (B) is incorrect because the radius of turn increases.

ALL
4903. If a standard rate turn is maintained, how much time would be required to turn to the right from a heading of 090° to a heading of 270°?

A—1 minute.
B—2 minutes.
C—3 minutes.

A standard rate turn is one during which the heading changes 3° per second. A heading change from 090° to 270° is a total turn of 180°. At a rate-of-turn of 3° each second, this turn would require 180/3 or 60 seconds (1 minute). (PLT185, IR.IV.A.K1) — FAA-H-8083-15

ALL
4904. If a standard rate turn is maintained, how much time would be required to turn to the left from a heading of 090° to a heading of 300°?

A—30 seconds.
B—40 seconds.
C—50 seconds.

A standard rate turn is one during which the heading changes 3° per second. A turn to the left from 090° to 300° is a total turn of 150°. At a turn rate of 3° each second, this turn would require 150/3 or 50 seconds. (PLT185, IR.IV.A.K1) — FAA-H-8083-15

ALL
4905. If a half-standard rate turn is maintained, how long would it take to turn 135°?

A—1 minute.
B—1 minute 20 seconds.
C—1 minute 30 seconds.

A standard rate turn is one during which the heading changes 3° per second. In this case, the aircraft is turning one-half that rate, or 1.5° per second. Therefore, a turn of 135° would require 135/1.5 or 90 seconds (1 minute 30 seconds). (PLT185, IR.IV.A.K1) — FAA-H-8083-15

Answers

4896 [A]	4897 [B]	4898 [C]	4903 [A]	4904 [C]	4905 [C]

ALL

4914. Rate of turn can be increased and radius of turn decreased by

A—decreasing airspeed and shallowing the bank.
B—decreasing airspeed and increasing the bank.
C—increasing airspeed and increasing the bank.

The horizontal component of lift varies directly in proportion to bank in a correctly executed turn. Thus, the rate of turn increases (and radius of turn decreases) as the angle of bank increases, and the airspeed decreases. (PLT311, IR.IV.A.K1) — FAA-H-8083-15

Answer (A) is incorrect because shallowing the bank would cause a decrease in the rate of turn. Answer (C) is incorrect because increasing the airspeed would cause a decreasing rate of turn.

ALL

4915. The primary reason the angle of attack must be increased, to maintain a constant altitude during a coordinated turn, is because the

A—thrust is acting in a different direction, causing a reduction in airspeed and loss of lift.
B—vertical component of lift has decreased as the result of the bank.
C—use of ailerons has increased the drag.

The division of lift into horizontal and vertical components during a turn reduces the amount of lift supporting the weight of the aircraft. Consequently, the reduced vertical component results in the loss of altitude unless the total lift is increased by:

1. *Increasing the angle of attack of the wing;*
2. *Increasing the airspeed; or*
3. *Increasing the angle of attack and airspeed in combination.*

(PLT168, IR.IV.A.K1) — FAA-H-8083-15

Answer (A) is incorrect because thrust does not act in a different direction during a turn. Answer (C) is incorrect because ailerons will only increase drag when entering or recovering from a turn.

ALL

4921. The displacement of a turn coordinator during a coordinated turn will

A—indicate the angle of bank.
B—remain constant for a given bank regardless of airspeed.
C—increase as angle of bank increases.

The miniature aircraft of the turn coordinator displays only rate-of-roll and rate-of-turn. It does not directly display the bank angle of the aircraft. The displacement of a turn coordinator increases as angle of bank increases. (PLT187, IR.IV.A.K1) — FAA-H-8083-15

Answer (A) is incorrect because the angle of bank is indirectly shown. Answer (B) is incorrect because the rate-of-turn varies with airspeed for any given bank angle, therefore the displacement of the turn coordinator will change with a change in airspeed.

ALL

4931. (Refer to Figure 144.) What changes in control displacement should be made so that "2" would result in a coordinated standard rate turn?

A—Increase left rudder and increase rate of turn.
B—Increase left rudder and decrease rate of turn.
C—Decrease left rudder and decrease angle of bank.

Illustration 2 shows a slipping, half-standard rate turn. To perform a coordinated standard rate turn, we must increase our rate-of-turn and correct the slip by applying additional left rudder. (PLT086, IR.IV.A.K1) — FAA-H-8083-15; FAA-H-8083-21

Answer (B) is incorrect because the rate of turn needs to be increased to obtain a standard rate turn. Answer (C) is incorrect because left rudder must be increased to correct for the current slipping condition.

ALL

4932. (Refer to Figure 144.) Which illustration indicates a coordinated turn?

A—3.
B—1.
C—2.

Illustration 3 indicates a coordinated turn, since the ball is centered. (PLT086, IR.IV.A.K1) — FAA-H-8083-15; FAA-H-8083-21

Answer (B) is incorrect because illustration 1 shows a skidding turn. Answer (C) is incorrect because illustration 2 shows a slipping turn.

Answers

4914 [B]	4915 [B]	4921 [C]	4931 [A]	4932 [A]

ALL

4933. (Refer to Figure 144.) Which illustration indicates a skidding turn?

A—2.
B—1.
C—3.

Illustration 1 indicates a skidding turn, since the ball is to the outside of the direction of the turn. In a skid, the rate of turn is too great for the angle of bank, and excessive centrifugal force causes the ball to move to the outside of the turn. (PLT086, IR.IV.A.K1) — FAA-H-8083-15; FAA-H-8083-21

Answer (A) is incorrect because illustration 2 shows a slipping turn. Answer (C) is incorrect because illustration 3 shows a coordinated turn.

ALL

4934. (Refer to Figure 144.) What changes in control displacement should be made so that "1" would result in a coordinated standard rate turn?

A—Increase right rudder and decrease rate of turn.
B—Increase right rudder and increase rate of turn.
C—Decrease right rudder and increase angle of bank.

Illustration 1 shows a skidding, half-standard rate turn. To perform a coordinated standard rate turn, we must increase our rate of turn and correct the skid by applying additional right rudder. (PLT086, IR.IV.A.K1) — FAA-H-8083-15

Answer (A) is incorrect because the rate of turn must be increased for a standard rate turn. Answer (C) is incorrect because the right rudder must be increased to correct the current skidding condition.

ALL

4935. (Refer to Figure 144.) Which illustration indicates a slipping turn?

A—1.
B—3.
C—2.

Illustration 2 indicates a slipping turn, since the ball is to the inside of the direction of the turn. In a slip, the rate of turn is too slow for the angle of bank, and the lack of centrifugal force causes the ball to move to the inside of the turn. (PLT086, IR.IV.A.K1) — FAA-H-8083-15; FAA-H-8083-21

Answer (A) is incorrect because illustration 1 shows a skidding turn. Answer (B) is incorrect because illustration 3 shows a coordinated turn.

ALL

4878-3. When airspeed is increased in a turn, what must be done to maintain a constant altitude?

A—Decrease the angle of attack.
B—Increase the angle of bank and/or decrease the pitch attitude.
C—Decrease the angle of bank.

During an increase in airspeed, you must increase the angle of bank and decrease the pitch attitude to maintain altitude and a standard-rate turn. (PLT185, IR.IV.A.K1) — FAA-H-8083-15

RTC

4833-2. When airspeed is decreased in a turn, what must be done to maintain level flight?

A—Increase the pitch attitude and/or increase the angle of bank.
B—Increase the angle of bank and/or decrease the pitch attitude.
C—Decrease the angle of bank and/or increase the pitch attitude.

During a reduction of airspeed, you must decrease the angle of bank and increase the pitch attitude to maintain altitude and a standard-rate turn. (PLT185) — FAA-H-8083-15

RTC

4870-2. What force causes a helicopter to turn in cruise flight?

A—Rudder pressure or force around the vertical axis.
B—Vertical lift component.
C—Horizontal lift component.

When the helicopter is banked, the rotor disc is tilted sideward resulting in lift being separated into two components. Lift acting vertically, in opposition to weight, is the vertical component of lift. Lift acting horizontally, in opposition to inertia (centrifugal force), is the horizontal component of lift (centripetal force). (PLT248) — FAA-H-8083-21

Answers

4933 [B]	4934 [B]	4935 [C]	4878-3 [B]	4833-2 [C]	4870-2 [C]

Heading Indicator

The heading indicator is a gyroscopically operated instrument. Its purpose is to indicate the aircraft's heading without the errors that are inherent in the magnetic compass. See Figure 3-8. Due to precessional error, however, the heading indicator should be regularly compared to the magnetic compass in flight.

The heading indicator pre-takeoff check is made by setting it and checking for proper alignment after making taxiing turns.

Figure 3-8. Heading indicator

ALL

4885. What pretakeoff check should be made of a vacuum-driven heading indicator in preparation for an IFR flight?

A—After 5 minutes, set the indicator to the magnetic heading of the aircraft and check for proper alignment after taxi turns.

B—After 5 minutes, check that the heading indicator card aligns itself with the magnetic heading of the aircraft.

C—Determine that the heading indicator does not precess more than 2° in 5 minutes of ground operation.

Allow 5 minutes after starting engines for the gyro rotor of the vacuum-operated heading indicator to attain normal operating speed. Before taxiing, or while taxiing straight, set the heading indicator to correspond with the magnetic compass heading. Be sure the instrument is fully uncaged if it has a caging feature. Before takeoff, recheck the heading indicator. If your magnetic compass and deviation card are accurate, the heading indicator should show the known taxiway or runway direction when the airplane is aligned with them (within 5°). (PLT445, IR.IV.A.K1) — FAA-H-8083-15

Answer (B) is incorrect because a non-slaved heading indicator must be set manually to the correct magnetic heading. Answer (C) is incorrect because a precession error of no greater than 3° (not 2°) in 15 minutes is acceptable.

Magnetic Compass

The magnetic compass is the only self-contained directional instrument in the aircraft. It is influenced by magnetic dip which causes northerly turning error and acceleration/deceleration error.

When northerly turning error occurs, the compass will lag behind the actual aircraft heading while turning through headings in the northern half of the compass rose, and lead the aircraft's actual heading in the southern half. The error is most pronounced when turning through north or south, and is approximately equal in degrees to the latitude. See Figure 3-9.

The acceleration/deceleration error is most pronounced on headings of east and west. When accelerating, the compass indicates a turn toward the north, and when decelerating it indicates a turn toward the south. The acronym ANDS is a good memory aid:

Answers

4885 [A]

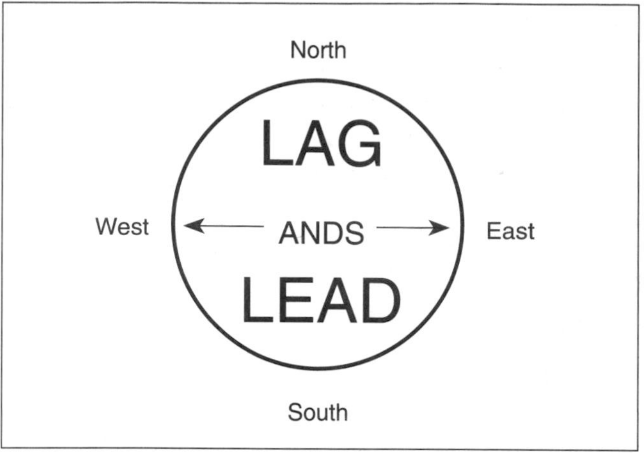

Figure 3-9

Accelerate
North
Decelerate
South

A magnetic compass pre-takeoff check verifies that:

1. The liquid chamber is full of fluid.
2. The compass is free turning.
3. No bubbles appear in the fluid.
4. The compass agrees with a known heading with radios and electrical systems on.

ALL
4834. On the taxi check, the magnetic compass should

A—swing opposite to the direction of turn when turning from north.
B—exhibit the same number of degrees of dip as the latitude.
C—swing freely and indicate known headings.

Check the magnetic compass card for freedom of movement and be sure that the bowl is full of fluid. Determine compass accuracy by comparing the indicated heading against a known heading, while the airplane is stopped or taxiing straight. (PLT215, IR.II.B.K1d) — FAA-H-8083-15

Answer (A) is incorrect because turning errors are only associated with an airplane that is airborne and in a bank. Answer (B) is incorrect because compass turning errors are the result of magnetic dip in flight.

ALL
4877. What should be the indication on the magnetic compass as you roll into a standard rate turn to the left from an east heading in the Northern Hemisphere?

A—The compass will initially indicate a turn to the right.
B—The compass will remain on east for a short time, then gradually catch up to the magnetic heading of the aircraft.
C—The compass will indicate the approximate correct magnetic heading if the roll into the turn is smooth.

When you are on an east or west heading, the compass indicates correctly as you start a turn in either direction. (PLT215, IR.II.B.K1d) — FAA-H-8083-15

Answer (A) is incorrect because the compass will initially indicate a turn in the opposite direction only when on a northerly heading. Answer (B) is incorrect because there will not be a lag time when turning from an east heading.

ALL
4886. What should be the indication on the magnetic compass as you roll into a standard rate turn to the right from an easterly heading in the Northern Hemisphere?

A—The compass will initially indicate a turn to the left.
B—The compass will remain on east for a short time, then gradually catch up to the magnetic heading of the aircraft.
C—The compass will indicate the approximate correct magnetic heading if the roll into the turn is smooth.

When on an east or west heading, no error is apparent while entering a turn to north or south. (PLT215, IR.II.B.K1d) — FAA-H-8083-25

Answer (A) is incorrect because the compass will initially indicate a turn in the opposite direction of a bank while on a northerly heading. Answer (B) is incorrect because there is no lag when turning from an east heading.

Answers

4834 [C] 4877 [C] 4886 [C]

ALL

4887. What should be the indication on the magnetic compass as you roll into a standard rate turn to the right from a south heading in the Northern Hemisphere?

A—The compass will indicate a turn to the right, but at a faster rate than is actually occurring.
B—The compass will initially indicate a turn to the left.
C—The compass will remain on south for a short time, then gradually catch up to the magnetic heading of the aircraft.

If on a southerly heading and a turn is made toward the east or west, the initial indication of the compass needle will indicate a greater amount of turn than is actually made. This lead diminishes as the turn progresses toward east or west where there is no turn error. (PLT215, IR.II.B.K1d) — FAA-H-8083-25

Answer (B) is incorrect because the compass will initially indicate a turn to the opposite direction if the turn is made from a north (not south) heading. Answer (C) is incorrect because the turn leads from a southerly heading (not lags).

ALL

4888. On what headings will the magnetic compass read most accurately during a level 360° turn, with a bank of approximately 15°?

A—135° through 225°.
B—90° and 270°.
C—180° and 0°.

A 15° bank is an approximate standard rate turn for most general aviation aircraft. Either lag or lead diminishes as the turn progresses toward east or west, where there is no turn error. (PLT215, IR.II.B.K1d) — FAA-H-8083-25; FAA-H-8083-21

Answer (A) is incorrect because the compass leads the heading through a southerly heading. Answer (C) is incorrect because the compass has the greatest turning errors at south and north headings.

ALL

4889. What causes the northerly turning error in a magnetic compass?

A—Coriolis force at the mid-latitudes.
B—Centrifugal force acting on the compass card.
C—The magnetic dip characteristic.

Northerly turning error is the most pronounced of the dip errors. Due to the mounting of the magnetic compass, its center of gravity is below the pivot point on the pedestal and the card is well balanced in the fluid. When the aircraft is banked, the card is also banked as a result of centrifugal force. While the card is in the banked attitude, the vertical component of the Earth's magnetic field causes the north-seeking ends of the compass to dip to the low side of the turn, giving an erroneous turn indication. (PLT215, IR.II.B.K1d) — FAA-H-8083-15

Answer (A) is incorrect because Coriolis force affects winds, not compass indications. Answer (B) is incorrect because centrifugal force does not cause turning errors in magnetic compasses.

ALL

4890. What should be the indication on the magnetic compass when you roll into a standard rate turn to the left from a south heading in the Northern Hemisphere?

A—The compass will indicate a turn to the left, but at a faster rate than is actually occurring.
B—The compass will initially indicate a turn to the right.
C—The compass will remain on south for a short time, then gradually catch up to the magnetic heading of the aircraft.

If on a southerly heading and a turn is made toward the east or west, the initial indication of the compass needle will indicate a greater amount of turn than is actually made. This lead diminishes as the turn progresses toward east or west where there is no turn error. (PLT215, IR.II.B.K1d) — FAA-H-8083-25

Answers (B) and (C) are incorrect because the magnetic compass will lead the heading during turns from the south or through southerly headings.

ALL

4891. What should be the indication on the magnetic compass as you roll into a standard rate turn to the right from a westerly heading in the Northern Hemisphere?

A—The compass will initially show a turn in the opposite direction, then turn to a northerly indication but lagging behind the actual heading of the aircraft.
B—The compass will remain on a westerly heading for a short time, then gradually catch up to the actual heading of the aircraft.
C—The compass will indicate the approximate correct magnetic heading if the roll into the turn is smooth.

When on an east or west heading, no error is apparent while entering a turn to north or south. (PLT215, IR.II.B.K1d) — FAA-H-8083-25

Answer (A) is incorrect because the magnetic compass will only indicate a turn in the opposite direction when turning from a north heading. Answer (B) is incorrect because the magnetic compass will only lag when turning from a north heading.

Answers

4887 [A]	4888 [B]	4889 [C]	4890 [A]	4891 [C]

ALL

4892. What should be the indication on the magnetic compass as you roll into a standard rate turn to the right from a northerly heading in the Northern Hemisphere?

A—The compass will indicate a turn to the right, but at a faster rate than is actually occurring.
B—The compass will initially indicate a turn to the left.
C—The compass will remain on north for a short time, then gradually catch up to the magnetic heading of the aircraft.

If on a northerly heading and a turn is made toward east or west, the initial indication of the compass lags or indicates a turn in the opposite direction. This lag diminishes as the turn progresses toward east or west where there is no turn error. (PLT215, IR.II.B.K1d) — FAA-H-8083-25

Answer (A) is incorrect because the compass will lead the turn only if turning from a southerly heading. Answer (C) is incorrect because the compass will only indicate the approximate correct heading if turning from the east or west.

ALL

4893. What should be the indication on the magnetic compass as you roll into a standard rate turn to the left from a west heading in the Northern Hemisphere?

A—The compass will initially indicate a turn to the right.
B—The compass will remain on west for a short time, then gradually catch up to the magnetic heading of the aircraft.
C—The compass will indicate the approximate correct magnetic heading if the roll into the turn is smooth.

When on an east or west heading, no error is apparent while entering a turn to north or south. (PLT215, IR.II.B.K1d) — FAA-H-8083-25

Answer (A) is incorrect because the compass will only indicate a turn in the opposite direction from a northerly heading. Answer (B) is incorrect because the compass will only lag the turn from a southerly heading.

ALL

4894. What should be the indication on the magnetic compass as you roll into a standard rate turn to the left from a north heading in the Northern Hemisphere?

A—The compass will indicate a turn to the left, but at a faster rate than is actually occurring.
B—The compass will initially indicate a turn to the right.
C—The compass will remain on north for a short time, then gradually catch up to the magnetic heading of the aircraft.

If on a northerly heading and a turn is made toward east or west, the initial indication of the compass lags or indicates a turn in the opposite direction. This lag diminishes as the turn progresses toward east or west where there is no turn error. (PLT215, IR.II.B.K1d) — FAA-H-8083-25

Answer (A) is incorrect because the compass will lead the turn only if turning from a southerly heading. Answer (C) is incorrect because the compass will initially indicate a turn in the opposite direction if turning from a northerly heading.

Answers

4892 [B] 4893 [C] 4894 [B]

Electronic Flight Instruments

Electronic flight instrument systems integrate many individual instruments into a single presentation called a primary flight display (PFD). Flight instrument presentations on a PFD differ from conventional instrumentation not only in format, but sometimes in location as well. For example, the attitude indicator on the PFD is often larger than conventional round-dial presentations of an artificial horizon. Airspeed and altitude indications are presented on vertical tape displays that appear on the left and right sides of the primary flight display. The vertical speed indicator is depicted using conventional analog presentation. Turn coordination is shown using a segmented triangle near the top of the attitude indicator. The rate-of-turn indicator appears as a curved line display at the top of the heading/navigation instrument in the lower half of the PFD.

Automatic Dependent Surveillance – Broadcast Out (ADS-B Out) is a function of an aircraft's onboard electronic equipment (avionics) that periodically broadcasts the aircraft's three-dimensional position and velocity along with additional identifying information prescribed by 14 CFR §91.227. If the aircraft is equipped with ADS-B Out, it must be in transmit mode at all times.

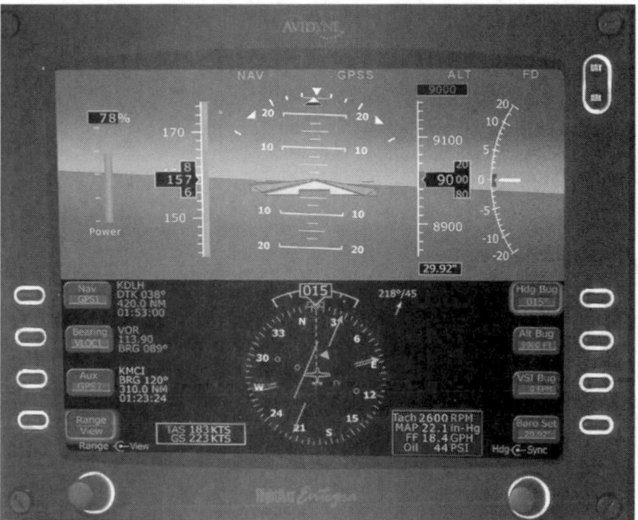

Figure 3-10. A typical primary flight display (PFD)

ALL

4979. The primary flight display (PFD) receives attitude and heading data from the

A—AHRS.
B—vacuum system.
C—pitot-static system.

The attitude and heading reference system (AHRS) is the engine that drives the attitude display. The AHRS unit is capable of precisely tracking minute changes in the pitch, bank, and yaw axes, thereby making the PFD very accurate and reliable. (PLT278, IR.II.B.K1c) — FAA-H-8083-15

ALL

4988. Each person operating an aircraft equipped with ADS-B Out must operate this equipment

A—in transmit mode at all times.
B—when on an IFR flight plan.
C—when on a VFR flight plan.

If an aircraft is equipped with ADS-B Out, it must be operated in transmit mode at all times regardless of the airspace or altitude. (PLT405, IR.II.B.K1c) — 14 CFR §91.225

Answers

4979 [A] 4988 [A]

Instrument Errors

The pitot-static system provides the source of air pressure for the operation of the altimeter, airspeed indicator, and vertical speed indicator. See Figure 3-11. Pitot-static system failures will present indications as shown in Figure 3-12.

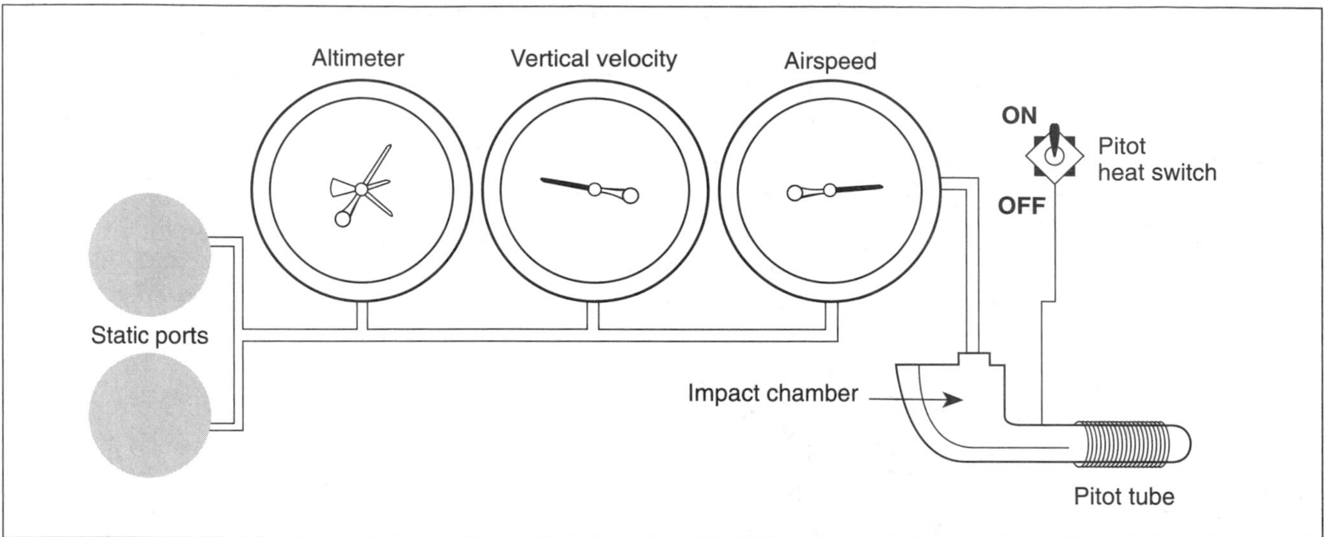

Figure 3-11. Pitot-static system

Situation	Airspeed	Altimeter	VSI
1. Blocked pitot.	zero	works	works
2. Blocked pitot and drain hole. Open static.	**high** in climb **low** in descent	works	works
3. Blocked static — open pitot.	**low** in climb **high** in descent	frozen	frozen
4. Using alternate cockpit static air.	reads high	reads high	momentarily shows a climb
5. Broken VSI glass.	reads high	reads high	reverses

Figure 3-12. Pitot-static system failures

ALL
4821. If both the ram air input and drain hole of the pitot system are blocked, what airspeed indication can be expected?

A—Increase of indicated airspeed during a climb.
B—Decrease of indicated airspeed during a climb.
C—Constant indicated airspeed during any change in altitude.

If both the ram air input and drainhole are completely blocked by ice, the pressure is trapped in the system and the airspeed indicator may react as an altimeter:

1. *During level flight, airspeed indication will not change even when actual airspeed is varied by large power changes.*
2. *During climb, airspeed indication will increase.*
3. *During descent, airspeed indication will decrease.*

(PLT088, IR.IV.A.K3) — FAA-H-8083-25

ALL
4830. If both the ram air input and the drain hole of the pitot system are blocked, what reaction should you observe on the airspeed indicator when power is applied and a climb is initiated out of severe icing conditions?

A—The indicated airspeed would show a continuous deceleration while climbing.
B—The airspeed would drop to, and remain at, zero.
C—No change until an actual climb rate is established, then indicated airspeed will increase.

If both the ram air input and the drain hole are blocked, the pressure is trapped in the system and the airspeed indicator may react as an altimeter:

Answers
4821 [A]
4830 [C]

1. *During level flight, the airspeed indication will not change even when actual airspeed is varied by large power changes;*
2. *During climb, the airspeed indication will increase; and*
3. *During descent, airspeed indication will decrease.*

(PLT337, IR.IV.A.K3) — FAA-H-8083-25

Answer (A) is incorrect because the airspeed indicator will show an increase in airspeed with an increase in altitude. Answer (B) is incorrect because this would only occur if the ram air input was blocked, not the drain hole.

ALL

4854. What indication should a pilot observe if an airspeed indicator ram air input and drain hole are blocked?

A—The airspeed indicator will react as an altimeter.
B—The airspeed indicator will show a decrease with an increase in altitude.
C—No airspeed indicator change will occur during climbs or descents.

If both the ram air input and the drain hole are blocked, the pressure is trapped in the system and the airspeed indicator may react as an altimeter:

1. *During level flight, the airspeed indication will not change even when actual airspeed is varied by large power changes;*
2. *During climb, the airspeed indication will increase; and*
3. *During descent, airspeed indication will decrease.*

(PLT337, IR.IV.A.K3) — FAA-H-8083-25

Answer (B) is incorrect because indicated airspeed will increase given an increase in altitude. Answer (C) is incorrect because the differential pressure between the pitot tube and static air source changes; therefore, so does the indicated airspeed.

ALL

4854-1. If the pitot tube ram air pressure hole and drain hole become obstructed, the airspeed indicator will operate

A—like an altimeter as the aircraft climbs and descends.
B—like a very sluggish airspeed indicator, lagging all changes by minutes.
C—normally due to the static port pressure changes.

If the pitot tube ram air pressure hole and drain hole become obstructed, the airspeed indicator will operate like an altimeter as the aircraft climbs and descends. (PLT041, IR.IV.B.K1) — FAA-H-8083-15

ALL

4879. What would be the indication on the VSI during entry into a 500 fpm actual descent from level flight if the static ports were iced over?

A—The indication would be in reverse of the actual rate of descent (500 fpm climb).
B—The initial indication would be a climb, then descent at a rate in excess of 500 fpm.
C—The VSI pointer would remain at zero regardless of the actual rate of descent.

The VSI operates by indicating a change in pressure between the instantaneous static pressure in the diaphragm and the trapped static pressure inside the case. If the static ports are iced over prior to entering a climb or descent, the VSI pointer will remain at zero because the diaphragm static pressure and the trapped static pressure inside the case remain equal to each other. (PLT088, IR.IV.A.K2) — FAA-H-8083-15

Answers (A) and (B) are incorrect because without a change in pressure, the VSI would remain at zero, indicating level flight.

ALL

4908. If, while in level flight, it becomes necessary to use an alternate source of static pressure vented inside the airplane, which of the following should the pilot expect?

A—The altimeter and airspeed indicator to become inoperative.
B—The gyroscopic instruments to become inoperative.
C—The vertical speed to momentarily show a climb.

If the alternate static source is vented inside the airplane, where static pressure is usually lower than outside static pressure, selection of the alternate source may result in the following instrument indications:

1. *The altimeter reads higher than normal;*
2. *Indicated airspeed greater than normal; and*
3. *The vertical-velocity indicator momentarily shows a climb.*

(PLT337, IR.IV.A.K3) — FAA-H-8083-15; FAA-H-8083-21

Answers

4854 [A]	4854-1 [A]	4879 [C]	4908 [C]

ALL

4909. During flight, if the pitot tube becomes clogged with ice, which of the following instruments would be affected?

A—The airspeed indicator only.
B—The airspeed indicator and the altimeter.
C—The airspeed indicator, altimeter, and VSI.

Clogging of the pitot opening by ice or dirt (or failure to remove the pitot cover) affects the airspeed indicator only. (PLT337, IR.IV.A.K3) — FAA-H-8083-15

Answers (B) and (C) are incorrect because the pitot tube is only connected to the airspeed indicator.

ALL

4930. If you need to use an alternate static source during level flight, you can expect to see

A—a higher indication on the altimeter.
B—a momentary descent on the VSI.
C—a lower indicated airspeed.

If the alternate static source is vented inside the airplane, where static pressure is usually lower than outside static pressure, selection of the alternate source may result in the following instrument indications:

1. *The altimeter reads higher than normal;*
2. *Indicated airspeed greater than normal; and*
3. *The vertical-velocity indicator momentarily shows a climb.*

(PLT337, IR.IV.A.K3) — FAA-H-8083-25; FAA-H-8083-21

ALL

4937. (Refer to Figure 146.) Identify the system that has failed and determine a corrective action to return the airplane to straight-and-level flight.

A—Static/pitot system is blocked; lower the nose and level the wings to level-flight attitude by use of attitude indicator.
B—Vacuum system has failed; reduce power, roll left to level wings, and pitchup to reduce airspeed.
C—Electrical system has failed; reduce power, roll left to level wings, and raise the nose to reduce airspeed.

In this situation, the vacuum instruments both show a climbing right turn. They are supported by the turn coordinator which shows a right turn, and the altimeter and VSI which indicate a climb. These are contradicted by the airspeed indicator which is rising (airspeed would not be increasing in this situation). The airspeed indicator then, is the one instrument which conflicts with the remaining unrelated systems and indicates that the pitot tube and drain holes are blocked, and the airspeed indicator is acting as an altimeter. The correct recovery procedure for a nose-high attitude is to lower the nose and level the wings to level flight attitude by use of the attitude indicator. (PLT297, IR.IV.B.K1) — FAA-H-8083-15

ALL

4941. (Refer to Figure 150.) What is the flight attitude? One instrument has malfunctioned.

A—Climbing turn to the right.
B—Climbing turn to the left.
C—Descending turn to the right.

The question states that one instrument (not system) has malfunctioned. The attitude indicator disagrees with both the turn coordinator and the heading indicator in its bank indication. It also disagrees with the altimeter, VSI, and airspeed indicator in its pitch indication. Elimination of the attitude indicator shows the aircraft to be in a climbing turn to the right. (PLT297, IR.IV.B.K1) — FAA-H-8083-15

ALL

4939. (Refer to Figure 148.) What is the flight attitude? One system which transmits information to the instruments has malfunctioned.

A—Climbing turn to left.
B—Climbing turn to right.
C—Level turn to left.

The attitude indicator and heading indicator show a right turn. The airspeed indicator, altimeter, and VSI show a climb. The turn coordinator (showing a lack of turn) is not in agreement with the other instruments. (PLT297, IR.IV.B.K1) — FAA-H-8083-15

Answers

4909 [A]	4930 [A]	4937 [A]	4941 [A]	4939 [B]

ALL
4940. (Refer to Figure 149.) What is the flight attitude? One system which transmits information to the instruments has malfunctioned.

A—Level turn to the right.
B—Level turn to the left.
C—Straight-and-level flight.

The attitude indicator and the heading indicator (both vacuum driven) are presenting conflicting indications. The attitude indicator shows a bank to the right, while the heading indicator shows a left turn; therefore, there must be a vacuum system malfunction. All other instruments are in agreement with straight-and-level flight. (PLT297, IR.IV.B.K1) — FAA-H-8083-15

RTC
4942. (Refer to Figure 151.) What is the flight attitude? One instrument has malfunctioned.

A—Climbing turn to the right.
B—Level turn to the right.
C—Level turn to the left.

The question states that one instrument (not system) has malfunctioned. Although the airspeed indicator shows a decrease, the other pitch instruments (attitude indicator, altimeter, and VSI) all agree and show the aircraft in level flight. The airspeed indicator has malfunctioned. The three bank instruments are in agreement, showing a level turn to the right. (PLT297) — FAA-H-8083-15

Fundamental Skills

During attitude instrument training, the pilot must develop three fundamental skills involved in all instrument flight maneuvers:

1. Instrument cross-check.
2. Instrument interpretation.
3. Aircraft control.

When executing an ILS approach, the pilot must keep the aircraft on an electronic glide slope. This requires the ability to establish the proper rate of descent for the ground speed. As ground speed increases, the rate of descent required to maintain the glide slope must be increased; as ground speed decreases, the rate of descent required to maintain the glide slope also decreases. By first cross-checking the instruments and then interpreting them, the pilot is able to precisely control the aircraft to a successful landing.

ALL
4840. What is the correct sequence in which to use the three skills used in instrument flying?

A—Attitude control, cross-check, and instrument interpretation.
B—Pitch controls, power control, and trim control.
C—Cross-check, instrument interpretation, and aircraft control.

During attitude instrument training, a pilot must develop three fundamental skills involved in all instrument flight maneuvers:

1. Instrument cross-check.

2. Instrument interpretation.

3. Aircraft control.

(PLT185, IR.IV.A.K2) — FAA-H-8083-15

Answer (A) is incorrect because aircraft control is the third skill used in instrument flying. Answer (B) is incorrect because instrument interpretation is the second skill and cross-check is the first skill used in instrument flying.

Answers

4940 [C]	4942 [B]	4840 [C]

ALL

4855. What are the three fundamental skills involved in attitude instrument flying?

A—Instrument interpretation, trim application, and aircraft control.
B—Cross-check, instrument interpretation, and aircraft control.
C—Cross-check, emphasis, and aircraft control.

The three fundamental skills involved in all instrument flight maneuvers are:

1. *Instrument cross-check.*
2. *Instrument interpretation.*
3. *Aircraft control.*

(PLT186, IR.IV.A.K2) — FAA-H-8083-15

Answer (A) is incorrect because application of trim is just one aspect of aircraft control. Answer (C) is incorrect because emphasis is a common error in instrument cross-checking.

ALL

4862. What is the first fundamental skill in attitude instrument flying?

A—Aircraft control.
B—Instrument cross-check.
C—Instrument interpretation.

The three fundamental skills involved in all instrument flight maneuvers are:

1. *Instrument cross-check.*
2. *Instrument interpretation.*
3. *Aircraft control.*

(PLT185, IR.IV.A.K2) — FAA-H-8083-15

Answer (A) is incorrect because aircraft control is the third fundamental skill in instrument flight. Answer (C) is incorrect because instrument interpretation is the second fundamental skill in instrument flight.

ALL

4721. What effect will a change in wind direction have upon maintaining a 3° glide slope at a constant true airspeed?

A—When ground speed decreases, rate of descent must increase.
B—When ground speed increases, rate of descent must increase.
C—Rate of descent must be constant to remain on the glide slope.

The VSI shows rate of change of altitude. The faster an aircraft descends, the greater the rate of descent shown on the VSI. The slower an aircraft descends, the slower the rate of descent shown on the VSI. The vertical speed required is dependent on the ground speed when flying on a fixed glide slope. Therefore, when ground speed increases, the rate of descent must increase. (PLT518, IR.I.B.K3b) — FAA-H-8083-15

ALL

4745. The rate of descent required to stay on the ILS glide slope

A—must be increased if the ground speed is decreased.
B—will remain constant if the indicated airspeed remains constant.
C—must be decreased if the ground speed is decreased.

The vertical speed required is dependent on the ground speed when flying on a fixed glide slope. In order to stay on the glide slope, the vertical speed must be decreased if the ground speed is decreased. (PLT277, IR.II.B.K2a) — FAA-H-8083-15

Answers (A) and (B) are incorrect because the rate of descent must be decreased with decreasing ground speed or increased with increasing ground speed.

ALL

4748. To remain on the ILS glidepath, the rate of descent must be

A—decreased if the airspeed is increased.
B—decreased if the ground speed is increased.
C—increased if the ground speed is increased.

The vertical speed required is dependent on the ground speed when flying on a fixed glide slope. In order to stay on the glide slope, the vertical speed must be increased if the ground speed is increased. (PLT277, IR.II.B.K2a) — FAA-H-8083-15

Answer (A) is incorrect because the rate of descent is dependent on ground speed (not airspeed). Answer (B) is incorrect because if the rate of descent is decreased when the ground speed increases, the aircraft will rise above the glidepath.

Answers

4855 [B] 4862 [B] 4721 [B] 4745 [C] 4748 [C]

ALL

4752. The rate of descent on the glide slope is dependent upon

A—true airspeed.
B—indicated airspeed.
C—ground speed.

The vertical speed required is dependent on the ground speed when flying on a fixed glide slope. For example, in order to stay on the glide slope, the vertical speed must be increased if the ground speed is increased. (PLT008, IR.IV.A.K2) — FAA-H-8083-15

Answers (A) and (B) are incorrect because the vertical speed is dependent on ground speed (not true or indicated airspeed).

ALL

4756. The glide slope and localizer are centered, but the airspeed is too fast. Which should be adjusted initially?

A—Pitch and power.
B—Power only.
C—Pitch only.

The heaviest demand on pilot technique occurs during descent from the outer marker to the middle marker, when you maintain the localizer course, adjust pitch attitude to maintain the proper rate of descent, and adjust power to maintain proper airspeed. (PLT415, IR.IV.A.K2) — FAA-H-8083-15

Answer (A) is incorrect because the pitch and power adjustments are closely coordinated, but the power should be adjusted first. Answer (C) is incorrect because a pitch adjustment only will cause you to fly above the glide path.

ALL

4772. During a precision radar or ILS approach, the rate of descent required to remain on the glide slope will

A—remain the same regardless of ground speed.
B—increase as the ground speed increases.
C—decrease as the ground speed increases.

The vertical speed required is dependent on the ground speed when flying on a fixed glide slope. For example, in order to stay on the glide slope, the vertical speed must be increased if the ground speed is increased. (PLT277, IR.II.B.K2a) — FAA-H-8083-15

Answer (A) is incorrect because vertical speed is dependent on ground speed. Answer (C) is incorrect because the vertical speed will increase (not decrease) if the ground speed increases.

ALL

4859. What is the third fundamental skill in attitude instrument flying?

A—Instrument cross-check.
B—Power control.
C—Aircraft control.

The three fundamental skills involved in all instrument flight maneuvers are:

1. *Instrument cross-check.*
2. *Instrument interpretation.*
3. *Aircraft control.*

(PLT185, IR.IV.A.K2) — FAA-H-8083-15

Answer (A) is incorrect because instrument cross-check is the first skill in instrument flying. Answer (B) is incorrect because the use of power control is only one aspect of aircraft control.

Answers

4752 [C]　4756 [B]　4772 [B]　4859 [C]

Attitude Instrument Flying

The attitude of an aircraft is controlled by movement around its lateral (pitch), longitudinal (roll), and vertical (yaw) axes. In instrument flying, attitude requirements are determined by correctly interpreting the flight instruments. Instruments are grouped as to how they relate to control, function, and aircraft performance. Attitude control is discussed in terms of pitch, bank, and power control. The three pitot-static instruments, the three gyroscopic instruments, and the tachometer or manifold pressure gauge are grouped into the following categories:

Pitch Instruments:

- Attitude indicator
- Altimeter
- Airspeed indicator
- Vertical speed indicator

Bank Instruments:

- Attitude indicator
- Heading indicator
- Turn coordinator

Power Instruments:

- Manifold pressure gauge
- Tachometer
- Airspeed indicator

When climbing and descending, it is necessary to begin level-off in enough time to avoid overshooting the desired altitude. The amount of lead to level-off from a climb varies with the rate of climb and pilot technique. If the aircraft is climbing at 1,000 feet per minute, it will continue to climb at a descending rate throughout the transition to level flight. An effective practice is to lead the altitude by 10 percent of the vertical speed (500 fpm would have a 50 foot lead; 1,000 fpm would have a 100 foot lead).

The amount of lead to level-off from a descent also depends upon the rate of descent and control technique. To level-off from a descent at descent airspeed, lead the desired altitude by approximately 10 percent. For level-off at an airspeed higher than descending airspeed, lead the level-off by approximately 25 percent.

When making initial pitch attitude corrections to maintain altitude during straight-and-level flight, the changes of attitude should be small and smoothly applied. As a rule-of-thumb for airplanes, use a half-bar-width correction for errors of less than 100 feet and a full-bar-width correction for errors in excess of 100 feet.

ALL

4869. In addition to the attitude indicator, the pitch control instruments are the

A—altimeter and airspeed indicator.
B—altimeter, turn coordinator, and VSI.
C—altimeter, airspeed indicator, and VSI.

In addition to the attitude indicator, the altimeter, airspeed indicator, and VSI provide pitch information. (PLT186, IR.IV.A.K2) — FAA-H-8083-15

Answer (A) is incorrect because the VSI and airspeed indicator also provide pitch information. Answer (B) is incorrect because the airspeed indicator also provides pitch information.

ALL

4876. Which instruments should be used to make a pitch correction when you have deviated from your assigned altitude?

A—Altimeter and VSI.
B—Manifold pressure gauge and VSI.
C—Attitude indicator, altimeter, and VSI.

The pitch instruments are the attitude indicator, the altimeter, the VSI, and the airspeed indicator. When a pitch error is detected, corrective action should be taken promptly, but with light control pressures. (PLT186, IR.IV.A.K2) — FAA-H-8083-15

Answer (A) is incorrect because an attitude indicator would also be used to make a pitch correction. Answer (B) is incorrect because the manifold pressure gauge is used as a power instrument (not pitch).

Answers

4869 [C] 4876 [C]

ALL

4899. Conditions that determine the pitch attitude required to maintain level flight are

A—airspeed, air density, wing design, and angle of attack.
B—flightpath, wind velocity, and angle of attack.
C—relative wind, pressure altitude, and vertical lift component.

Factors that affect the attitude in maintaining level flight include airspeed, air density, wing design, and angle of attack. (PLT186, IR.IV.A.K2) — FAA-H-8083-15

Answer (B) is incorrect because flight path and wind velocity do not determine pitch attitude. Answer (C) is incorrect because relative wind, pressure altitude, and vertical lift component do not determine the pitch attitude.

ALL

4906. Approximately what percent of the indicated vertical speed should be used to determine the number of feet to lead the level-off from a climb to a specific altitude?

A—10 percent.
B—20 percent.
C—25 percent.

The amount of lead varies with rate of climb and pilot technique. An effective practice is to lead the altitude by 10 percent of the vertical speed shown (500 fpm/50-foot lead—1,000 fpm/100-foot lead). (PLT185, IR.IV.A.K2) — FAA-H-8083-15

ALL

4907. To level off from a descent to a specific altitude, the pilot should lead the level-off by approximately

A—10 percent of the vertical speed.
B—30 percent of the vertical speed.
C—50 percent of the vertical speed.

The level-off from a descent at descent airspeed must be started before you reach the desired altitude. The amount of lead depends upon the rate of descent and control technique. With too little lead, you will tend to overshoot the selected altitude, unless your technique is rapid. An effective practice is to lead the altitude by 10 percent of the vertical speed shown. Assuming a 500-fpm rate of descent, lead the desired altitude by approximately 50 feet. (PLT185, IR.IV.A.K2) — FAA-H-8083-15

ALL

4920. For maintaining level flight at constant thrust, which instrument would be the least appropriate for determining the need for a pitch change?

A—Altimeter.
B—VSI.
C—Attitude indicator.

The attitude indicator would be the least appropriate instrument for determining the need for a pitch change in level flight at constant thrust. Until level flight, as indicated by the attitude indicator, is identified and established by reference to the altimeter and VSI, there is no way of knowing if it is truly level flight. With constant thrust, any change in the altimeter or VSI indications shows a need for a pitch change. (PLT278, IR.IV.A.K2) — FAA-H-8083-15

ALL

4924. To enter a constant-airspeed descent from level cruising flight and maintain cruising airspeed, the pilot should

A—first adjust the pitch attitude to a descent using the attitude indicator as a reference, then adjust the power to maintain the cruising airspeed.
B—first reduce power, then adjust the pitch using the attitude indicator as a reference to establish a specific rate on the VSI.
C—simultaneously reduce power and adjust the pitch using the attitude indicator as a reference to maintain the cruising airspeed.

The following method for entering descents is effective either with or without an attitude indicator:

1. *Reduce airspeed to your selected descent airspeed while maintaining straight-and-level flight, then make a further reduction in power (to a predetermined setting); and*
2. *As the power is adjusted, simultaneously lower the nose to maintain constant airspeed, and trim off control pressures.*

(PLT125, IR.IV.A.K2) — FAA-H-8083-15

Answer (A) is incorrect because adjusting the pitch attitude first will result in an increased airspeed. Answer (B) is incorrect because adjusting the power first will result in a decreased airspeed, and the airspeed indicator (not VSI) is used to maintain a constant airspeed.

Answers

4899 [A]	4906 [A]	4907 [A]	4920 [C]	4924 [C]

ALL

4925. To level off at an airspeed higher than the descent speed, the addition of power should be made, assuming a 500 fpm rate of descent, at approximately

A—50 to 100 feet above the desired altitude.
B—100 to 150 feet above the desired altitude.
C—150 to 200 feet above the desired altitude.

The level-off from a descent must be started before you reach the desired altitude. The amount of lead depends upon the rate of descent and control technique. Assuming a 500-fpm rate of descent, lead the altitude by 100–150 feet for level-off at an airspeed higher than descending speed. At the lead point, add power to the appropriate level flight cruise setting. (PLT125, IR.IV.A.K2) — FAA-H-8083-15

ALL

4926. To level off from a descent maintaining the descending airspeed, the pilot should lead the desired altitude by approximately

A—20 feet.
B—50 feet.
C—60 feet.

To level-off from a descent at descent airspeed, lead the desired altitude by approximately 50 feet, simultaneously adjusting the pitch attitude to level flight and adding power to a setting that will hold the airspeed constant. (PLT185, IR.IV.A.K2) — FAA-H-8083-15

Unusual Attitude Recoveries

When recovering from an unusual attitude without the aid of the attitude indicator, approximate level pitch attitude is reached when the airspeed indicator and altimeter stop moving and the vertical speed indicator reverses its trend.

The following procedures are accomplished to recover from a nose-low attitude:

1. Reduce power.
2. Level the wings.
3. Raise the nose to the horizon.

The following procedures are accomplished to recover from a nose-high attitude:

1. Add power.
2. Apply forward elevator pressure.
3. Level the wings.

ALL

4867. While recovering from an unusual flight attitude without the aid of the attitude indicator, approximate level pitch attitude is reached when the

A—airspeed and altimeter stop their movement and the VSI reverses its trend.
B—airspeed arrives at cruising speed, the altimeter reverses its trend, and the vertical speed stops its movement.
C—altimeter and vertical speed reverse their trend and the airspeed stops its movement.

When the rate of movement of altimeter and airspeed indicator needles decreases, and the VSI reverses its trend, the aircraft is approaching level pitch attitude. (PLT297, IR.IV.B.K1) — FAA-H-8083-15

Answer (B) is incorrect because the VSI will lag and only show a decrease in vertical movement when it has stopped. Answer (C) is incorrect because the altimeter must stop (not just reverse its trend) in order to indicate a level pitch attitude.

Answers

4925 [B]   4926 [B]   4867 [A]

ALL

4927. During recoveries from unusual attitudes, level flight is attained the instant

A—the horizon bar on the attitude indicator is exactly overlapped with the miniature airplane.
B—a zero rate of climb is indicated on the VSI.
C—the altimeter and airspeed needles stop prior to reversing their direction of movement.

A level-pitch attitude is indicated by the reversal and stabilization of the airspeed indicator and altimeter needles. (PLT297, IR.IV.B.K1) — FAA-H-8083-15

Answer (A) is incorrect because the precessing tendency of the attitude indicator makes it unreliable after recovery from an unusual attitude. Answer (B) is incorrect because the vertical speed indicator has a short lag time which does not allow it to show level flight at the instant it is achieved.

ALL

4936. (Refer to Figure 145.) What is the correct sequence for recovery from the unusual attitude indicated?

A—Reduce power, increase back elevator pressure, and level the wings.
B—Reduce power, level the wings, bring pitch attitude to level flight.
C—Level the wings, raise the nose of the aircraft to level flight attitude, and obtain desired airspeed.

The conditions associated with this unusual attitude are: airspeed is high, nose is below horizon, vertical speed shows excessive rate of descent, compass indicates right turn, and turn coordinator shows uncoordinated greater-than-standard rate turn to the right. To correct for this nose-low condition the correct sequence is: reduce power to prevent excessive airspeed and loss of altitude, correct the bank attitude with coordinated aileron and rudder pressure to straight flight by referring to the turn coordinator, and raise the nose to level flight attitude by smooth back elevator pressure. (PLT297, IR.IV.B.K1) — FAA-H-8083-15

Answer (A) is incorrect because the wings must be leveled before increasing the back elevator pressure to decrease the load factor. Answer (C) is incorrect because the power must be reduced before leveling the wings to prevent additional airspeed.

ALL

4938. (Refer to Figure 147.) Which is the correct sequence for recovery from the unusual attitude indicated?

A—Level wings, add power, lower nose, descend to original attitude and heading.
B—Add power, lower nose, level wings, return to original attitude and heading.
C—Stop turn by raising right wing and add power at the same time, lower the nose, and return to original attitude and heading.

The conditions associated with this unusual attitude are: airspeed is decreasing, altitude is increasing, nose is above the horizon, VSI shows an excessive rate of climb, compass indicates a right turn, and turn coordinator shows uncoordinated greater-than-standard rate turn to the right. To correct for this nose-high condition the correct sequence is: increase power, apply forward elevator pressure to lower the nose and prevent a stall, and correct the bank by applying coordinated aileron and rudder pressure to level the miniature aircraft and center the ball of the turn coordinator. (PLT297, IR.IV.B.K1) — FAA-H-8083-15

Answers (A) and (C) are incorrect because power should be increased and the nose lowered before leveling the wings.

AIR

4873-1. You enter an unusual attitude after failure of your attitude indicator. To recover, which Instruments do you consult for the best pitch information?

A—Turn indicator and VSI.
B—Airspeed, VSI, and altimeter.
C—VSI and airspeed to detect approaching V_{MO}.

As soon as the unusual attitude is detected, the recovery should be initiated primarily by reference to the airspeed indicator (for pitch attitude), altimeter (for pitch attitude), VSI, and turn coordinator. (PLT297, IR.IV.B.K1) — FAA-H-8083-15

Answer (A) is incorrect because the turn coordinator does not provide information about pitch attitude. Answer (C) is incorrect because the VSI is not as reliable as the altimeter in determining a climb or descent.

Answers

4927 [C] 4936 [B] 4938 [B] 4873-1 [B]

AIR

4875-1. Which is the correct sequence for recovery from a spiraling, nose-low, increasing airspeed, unusual flight attitude?

A—Increase pitch attitude, reduce power, and level wings.
B—Reduce power, correct the bank attitude, and raise the nose to a level attitude.
C—Reduce power, raise the nose to level attitude, and correct the bank attitude.

Reduce power to prevent excessive airspeed and loss of altitude, correct the bank attitude with coordinated aileron and rudder pressure to straight flight by referring to the turn coordinator. Raise the nose to level-flight attitude by smooth back-elevator pressure. (PLT297, IR.IV.B.K1) — FAA-H-8083-15

Answer (A) is incorrect because power should be decreased first and then wings leveled. Answer (C) is incorrect because the wings should be level before the nose is pulled up, in order to minimize the effects of an excessive load factor.

RTC

4873-2. If a helicopter is in an unusual flight attitude and the attitude indicator has exceeded its limits, which instruments should be relied on to determine pitch attitude before starting recovery?

A—Turn indicator and VSI.
B—Airspeed, VSI and altimeter.
C—VSI and airspeed to detect approaching V_{S1} or V_{MO}.

To recover from an unusual attitude, correct bank-and-pitch attitude, and adjust power as necessary. Pitch attitude should be corrected by reference to the altimeter, airspeed indicator, VSI, and attitude indicator. (PLT297) — FAA-H-8083-15

RTC

4875-2. Which is the correct sequence for recovery from a spiraling, nose low, increasing airspeed, unusual flight attitude?

A—Increase pitch attitude, reduce power, and level wings.
B—Correct the bank attitude, raise the nose to a level attitude and reduce power.
C—Reduce power, raise the nose to level attitude, and correct the bank attitude.

To recover from an usual attitude, correct bank-and-pitch attitude, and adjust power as necessary. (PLT297) — FAA-H-8083-15

ALL

4976. When a pilot believes advanced avionics enable operations closer to personal or environmental limits,

A—greater utilization of the aircraft is achieved.
B—risk is increased.
C—risk is decreased.

Advanced avionics can sometimes have a negative effect on pilot risk-taking behavior, where more information results in pilots taking more risk than they might be willing to accept without the information. Advanced avionics should be used to increase safety, not risk. (PLT104, IR.II.B.R1) — FAA-H-8083-6

ALL

4977. Automation in aircraft has proven

A—to present new hazards in its limitations.
B—that automation is basically flawless.
C—effective in preventing accidents.

Advanced avionics were designed to increase safety as well as the utility of the aircraft. However, the systems are not infallible. While automation does help prevent many existing types of errors, it has also created new kinds of errors. (PLT104, IR.II.B.R1) — FAA-H-8083-6

ALL

4977-1. An aircraft which is equipped with an Electronic Flight Display (EFD) can

A—compensate for an airman's lack of skill or knowledge.
B—offer new capabilities and simplify the basic flying task.
C—improve flight awareness by allowing the pilot to simply watch for alerts.

While an EFD cannot compensate for an airman's lack of skill or knowledge, it does offer new capabilities to include onboard weather, terrain information, chart overlays, and airport data along with primary flight displays and navigation tools. (PLT104, IR.II.B.R1) — FAA-H-8083-15

Answers

4875-1 [B]	4873-2 [B]	4875-2 [B]	4976 [B]	4977 [A]	4977-1 [B]

ALL
4978. The lighter workloads associated with glass (digital) flight instrumentation

A—are instrumental in decreasing flightcrew fatigue.
B—have proven to increase safety in operations.
C—may lead to complacency by the flightcrew.

Risk management is the last of the three flight management skills needed for mastery of the advanced avionics aircraft. The enhanced situational awareness and automation capabilities offered by a glass flight deck vastly expand its safety and utility, especially for personal transportation use. At the same time, there is some risk that lighter workloads could lead to complacency. (PLT104, IR.II.B.R1) — FAA-H-8083-2

ALL
4978-1. The advancement of avionics in light general aviation airplanes has enhanced situational awareness for properly trained pilots. However, there is concern that this technology could lead to

A—complacency.
B—fatigue.
C—resignation.

The enhanced situational awareness and automation capabilities offered by a glass flight deck vastly expand its safety and utility, especially for personal transportation use. At the same time, there is some risk that lighter workloads could lead to complacency. (PLT104, IR.II.B.R1) — FAA-H-8083-2

Answers
4978 [C]   4978-1 [A]

NAVAID Classes

VOR and VORTAC facilities are classed according to their operational use. There are three classes:

1. T (Terminal).
2. L (Low altitude).
3. H (High altitude).

The class defines the service volume of the NAVAID (which is the reception limit to which an unrestricted NAVAID may be used for random or unpublished route navigation).

The service volume of VOR/VORTACs can be found in the *Chart Supplements U.S.* and in the *AIM*. The NAVAID class and any restrictions to use (unusable radials) will also be found in the *Chart Supplements U.S.* See Figure 4-1.

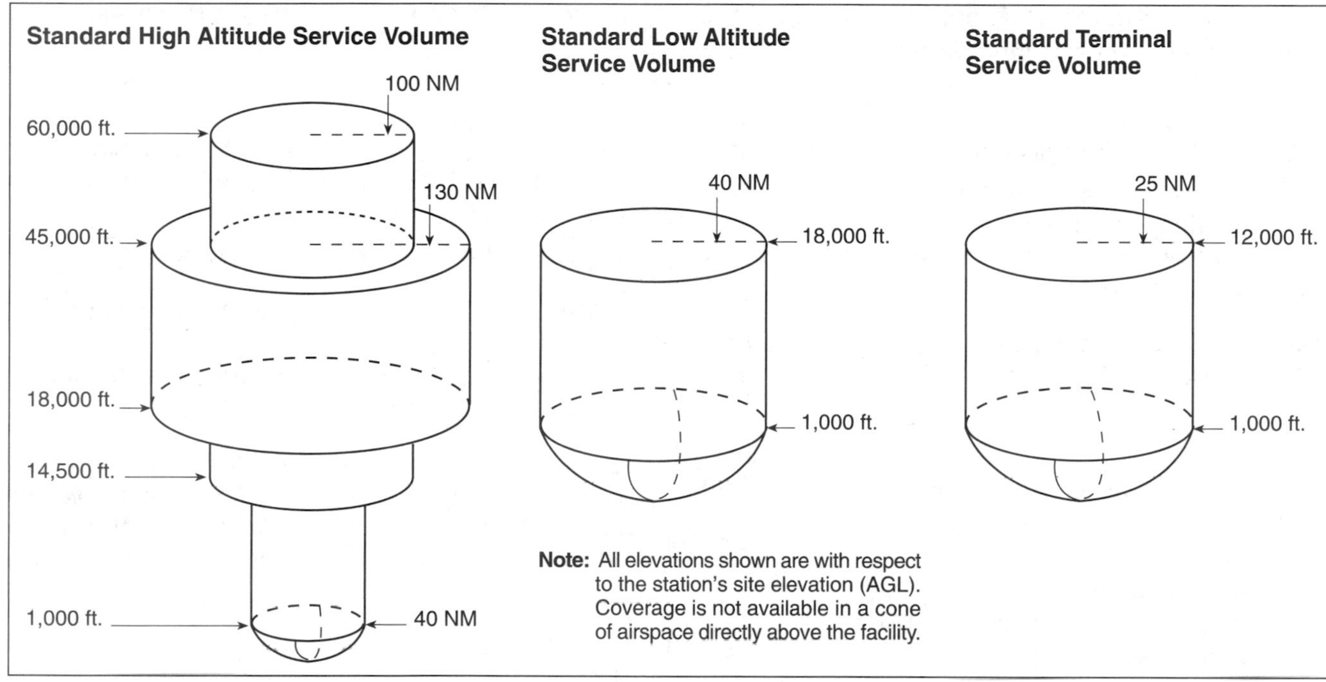

Figure 4-1

ALL

4400. For operations off established airways at 17,000 feet MSL in the contiguous U.S., (H) Class VORTAC facilities used to define a direct route of flight should be no farther apart than

A—75 NM.
B—100 NM.
C—200 NM.

Normal usable radius distance for high-altitude VOR/VORTAC NAVAIDS (H) within the contiguous United States between 14,500 feet and 17,999 feet is 100 NM. A direct-route flight should have a distance of no more than 200 NM between two H-class NAVAIDS. (PLT322, IR.II.B.K2a) — AIM ¶1-1-8

ALL

4400-1. You are planning an IFR flight off established airways below 18,000 feet MSL. If you use VOR navigation to define the route, the maximum distance between NAVAIDs should be

A—40 NM.
B—70 NM.
C—80 NM.

Pilots operating off established airways below 18,000 feet MSL should not use aids more than 80 NM apart. (PLT222, IR.II.B.K2a) — AIM ¶5-1-8

Answers

4400 [C] 4400-1 [C]

Distance Measuring Equipment (DME)

DME operates on the principle of a timed UHF signal that is transmitted from the aircraft to the ground station and back to the aircraft. This time is translated into a distance. The DME readout is presented in nautical miles (NM) and is slant range distance, not actual horizontal distance. When passing over a station, the range indicator will decrease until it indicates the height above the station. After crossing the station, it will start to increase. (If an aircraft passes over a station at 6,000 feet, the DME readout will be 1 NM.)

The greatest error in DME indications occur when an aircraft is very close to the station at a high altitude. The accuracy of the DME unit is valid only for 1 or more nautical miles from the ground facility for each 1,000 feet of altitude.

The identifier heard on the VORTAC or VOR-DME frequency is actually the identifiers of two separate radios on a time-shared basis. The DME portion identifies itself once every thirty seconds. The remaining identifiers are the VOR portion. Assuming both components are operating normally, there will be an uninterrupted series of identifiers.

ALL

4397. Which distance is displayed by the DME indicator?

A—Slant range distance in NM.
B—Slant range distance in SM.
C—Line-of-sight direct distance from aircraft to VORTAC in SM.

The DME indicator displays slant range distance in nautical miles. (PLT202, IR.II.B.K2a) — AIM ¶1-1-7

ALL

4399. Where does the DME indicator have the greatest error between ground distance to the VORTAC and displayed distance?

A—High altitudes far from the VORTAC.
B—High altitudes close to the VORTAC.
C—Low altitudes far from the VORTAC.

The greatest slant-range error occurs when flying directly over the DME facility (VORTAC, VOR/DME), when the displayed distance is the height above the facility in nautical miles. Slant-range error is negligible if the aircraft is 1 mile or more from the ground facility for each 1,000 feet of altitude above the elevation of the facility. (PLT202, IR.II.B.K2a) — AIM ¶1-1-7

ALL

4674. (Refer to Figure 240.) How should a pilot determine when the DME at Price/Carbon County Airport is inoperative?

A—The airborne DME will always indicate "0" mileage.
B—The airborne DME will "search," but will not "lock on."
C—The airborne DME may appear normal, but there will be no code tone.

A DME tone is heard once for each three or four VOR/LOC tones. A single code each 30 seconds indicates DME is operative. No ident indicates the NAVAID is unreliable even though signals are received. (PLT202, IR.II.B.K2a) — AIM ¶1-1-7

ALL

4674-1. (Refer to Figure 240.) How should a pilot determine when the DME at PUC airport is inoperative?

A—The airborne DME will always indicate "0" mileage.
B—The airborne DME will "search," but will not "lock on."
C—The airborne DME may appear normal, but there will be no code tone.

A DME tone is heard once for every three or four VOR/LOC tones. A single code every 30 seconds indicates DME is operative. No ident indicates the NAVAID is unreliable even though signals are received. (PLT202, IR.II.B.K2a) — AIM ¶1-1-7

Answers

4397 [A] 4399 [B] 4674 [C] 4674-1 [C]

ALL

4413. Which DME indication should you receive when you are directly over a VORTAC site at approximately 6,000 feet AGL?

A—0.
B—1.
C—1.3.

Distance information received from DME is slant range distance not actual horizontal distance. It is measured in nautical miles, and since 6,000 feet equals 1 NM, the DME will show 1.0 NM above the VORTAC. (PLT202, IR.II.B.K2a) — AIM ¶1-1-7

Answer (A) is incorrect because the DME would only indicate zero at ground level next to the VORTAC. Answer (C) is incorrect because 1.3 would indicate an altitude of approximately 8,000 feet AGL (6,000 × 1.3).

ALL

4472. As a rule of thumb, to minimize DME slant range error, how far from the facility should you be to consider the reading as accurate?

A—Two miles or more for each 1,000 feet of altitude above the facility.
B—One or more miles for each 1,000 feet of altitude above the facility.
C—No specific distance is specified since the reception is line-of-sight.

Slant-range error is negligible if the aircraft is 1 mile or more from the ground facility for each 1,000 feet of altitude above the elevation of the facility. (PLT202, IR.II.B.K2a) — FAA-H-8083-15

ALL

4663. When a VOR/DME is collocated under frequency pairings and the VOR portion is inoperative, the DME identifier will repeat at an interval of

A—20 second intervals at 1020 Hz.
B—30 second intervals at 1350 Hz.
C—60 second intervals at 1350 Hz.

VOR/DME, VORTAC, ILS/DME, and LOC/DME facilities are identified by synchronized identifications which are transmitted on a time share basis when either the VOR or the DME is inoperative. It is important to recognize which identifier is retained for the operative facility. A single coded identification with a repetition interval of approximately 30 seconds indicates that the DME is operative. DME is identified by a coded tone modulated at 1350 Hz. (PLT202, IR.II.B.K2a) — AIM ¶1-1-7

ALL

4412. What is the meaning of a single coded identification received only once approximately every 30 seconds from a VORTAC?

A—The VOR and DME components are operative.
B—VOR and DME components are both operative, but voice identification is out of service.
C—The DME component is operative and the VOR component is inoperative.

VOR/DME, VORTAC, ILS/DME, and LOC/DME facilities are identified by synchronized identifications which are transmitted on a timeshare basis. When either the VOR or the DME is inoperative, it is important to recognize which identifier is retained for the operative facility. A single-coded identification with a repetition interval of approximately 30 seconds indicates that the DME is operative. (PLT300, IR.II.B.K2a) — AIM ¶1-1-7

Answer (A) is incorrect because a constant series of identity codes indicates that the VOR and DME are both working properly. Answer (B) is incorrect because voice identification operates independently of the identity codes.

ALL

4320. (Refer to Figure 192.) As a guide in making range corrections, how many degrees of relative bearing change should be used for each one-half mile deviation from the desired arc?

A—2° to 3°.
B—5° maximum.
C—10° to 20°.

As a guide in making range corrections, change the relative bearing 10 to 20° for each 1/2-mile deviation from the desired arc. (PLT202, IR.II.B.K2a) — FAA-H-8083-15

ALL

4669. How does a pilot determine if DME is available on an ILS/LOC?

A—IAP indicate DME/TACAN channel in LOC frequency box.
B—LOC/DME are indicated on en route low altitude frequency box.
C—LOC/DME frequencies available in the Airman's Information Manual.

DME/TACAN channels are associated with LOC frequencies and are on the plan view of the approach chart. (PLT292, IR.III.B.K1) — AIM ¶1-1-9

Answers (B) and (C) are incorrect because the frequencies are on the instrument approach charts (not low altitude enroute charts or the AIM).

Answers

4413 [B]	4472 [B]	4663 [B]	4412 [C]	4320 [C]	4669 [A]

VHF Omnidirectional Range (VOR)

VOR accuracy may be checked by means of a VOR Test Facility (VOT), ground or airborne checkpoints, or by checking dual VORs against each other. A VOT location and frequency can be found in the *Chart Supplements U.S.* To use the VOT, tune to the appropriate frequency and center the course deviation indicator (CDI). The omni-bearing selector (OBS) should read 0° with a FROM indication, or 180° with a TO indication. The allowable error is ±4°. VOR receiver checkpoints are listed in the *Chart Supplements U.S.* With the appropriate frequency tuned and the OBS set to the published certified radial, the CDI should center with a FROM indication when the aircraft is over the designated check point. Allowable accuracy is ±4° for a ground check, and ±6° for an airborne check. If the aircraft is equipped with dual VORs, they may be checked against each other. The maximum permissible variation when tuned to the same VOR is 4°.

The pilot must log the results of the VOR accuracy test in the aircraft logbook or other record. The log must include the date, place, bearing error, if any, and a signature.

All VOR stations transmit an identifier. It is a three-letter Morse code signal interrupted only by a voice identifier on some stations, or to allow the controlling flight service station to speak on the frequency. Absence of a VOR identifier indicates maintenance is being performed on the station and the signal may not be reliable.

All VOR receivers have at least the essential components shown in Figure 4-2.

The pilot may select the desired course or radial by turning the OBS. The CDI centers when the aircraft is on the selected radial or its reciprocal. A full-scale deflection of the CDI from the center represents a deviation of approximately 10° to 12°. The TO/FROM Indicator (ambiguity indlcator) shows whether the selected course will take the aircraft TO or FROM the station. A TO indication shows that the OBS selection is on the other side of the VOR station. A FROM indication shows that the OBS selection and the aircraft are on the same side of the VOR station. When an aircraft flies over a VOR, the TO/FROM indicator will reverse, indicating station passage.

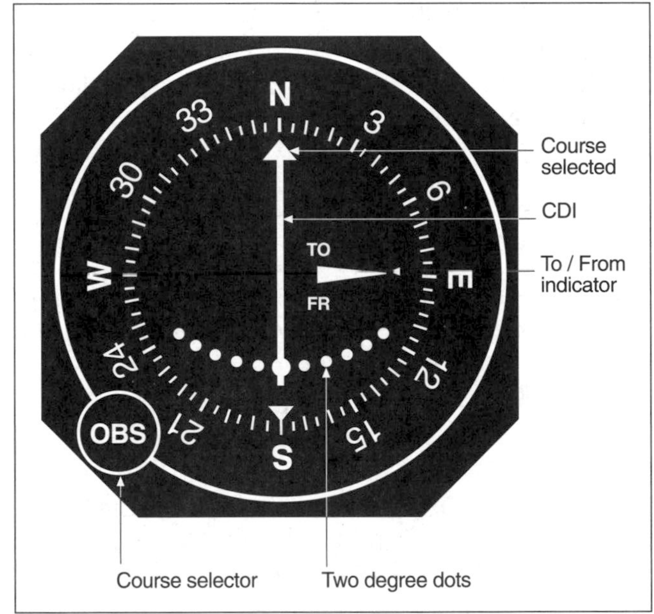

Figure 4-2. VOR indicators

The position of the aircraft can always be determined by rotating the OBS until the CDI centers with a FROM indication. The course displayed indicates the radial FROM the station. The VOR indicator displays information as though the aircraft were going in the direction of the course selected. However, actual heading does not influence the display. See Figure 4-3.

VOR radials, all of which originate at the VOR antenna, diverge as they radiate outward. For example, while the 011° radial and the 012° radial both start at the same point, 1 NM from the antenna, they are 100 feet apart. When they are 2 NM from the antenna, they are 200 feet apart. So at 60 NM, the radials would be 1 NM (6,000 feet) apart. See Figure 4-4.

The VOR indicator uses a series of dots to indicate any deviation from the selected course, with each dot equal to approximately 2° of deviation. Thus, a one-dot deviation at a distance of 30 NM from the station would indicate that the aircraft was 1 NM from the selected radial (200 feet × 30 = 6,000 feet).

To orient where the aircraft is in relation to the VOR, first determine which radial is selected (look at the OBS setting). Next, determine whether the aircraft is flying to or away from the station (look at the TO/FROM indicator), to find which hemisphere the aircraft is in. Last, determine how far off course the aircraft is from the selected course (look at the CDI needle deflection) to find which quadrant the aircraft is in. Remember that aircraft heading does not affect orientation to the VOR.

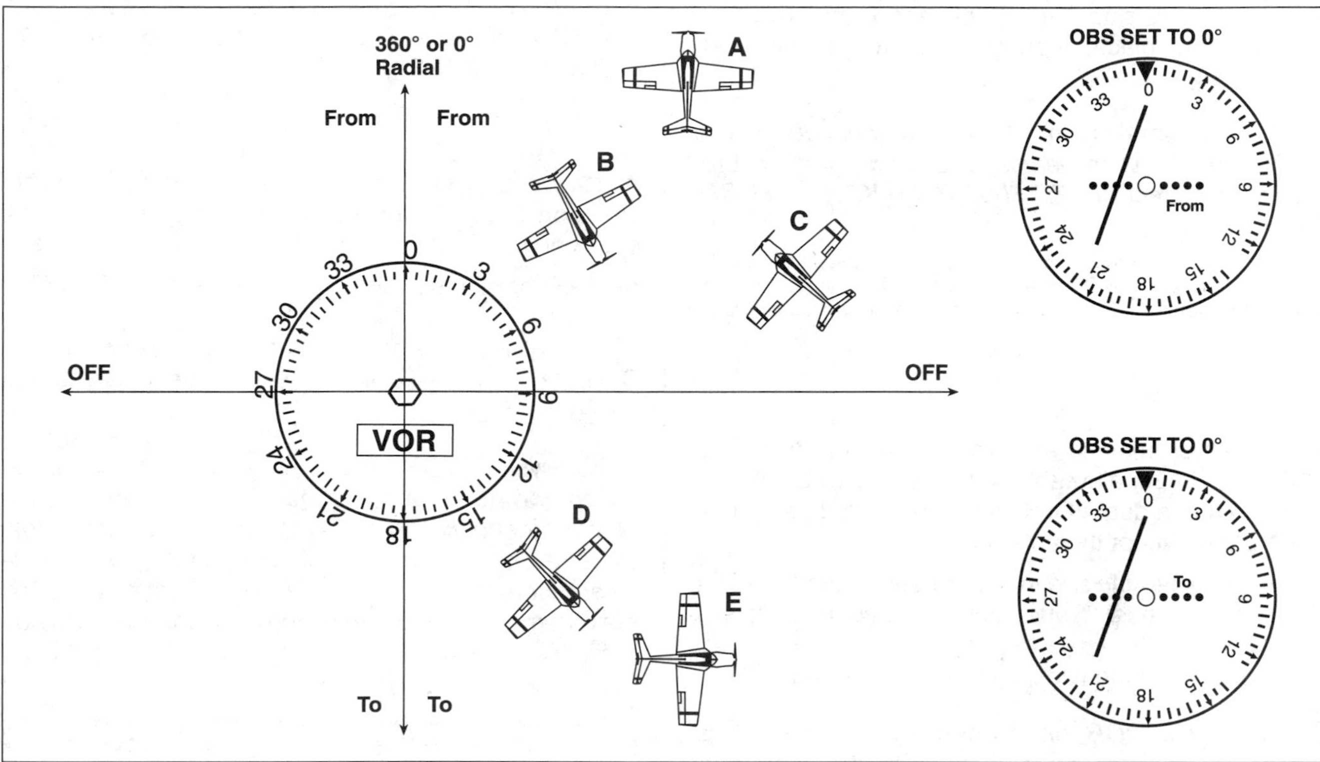

Figure 4-3. VOR display

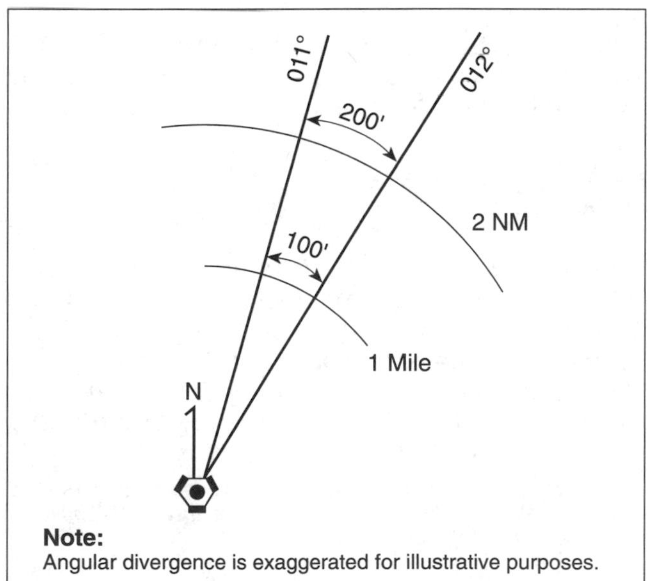

Figure 4-4. Radial divergence

ALL

4044. Which data must be recorded in the aircraft log or other appropriate log by a pilot making a VOR operational check for IFR operations?

A—VOR name or identification, date of check, amount of bearing error, and signature.
B—Place of operational check, amount of bearing error, date of check, and signature.
C—Date of check, VOR name or identification, place of operational check, and amount of bearing error.

Each person making the VOR operational check shall enter the date, place, bearing error, and sign the aircraft log or other record. (PLT508, IR.II.B.K2a) — 14 CFR §91.171

Answers (A) and (C) are incorrect because the VOR name or identification is not required.

Answers
4044 [B]

ALL

4046. What record shall be made in the aircraft log or other permanent record by the pilot making the VOR operational check?

A—The date, place, bearing error, and signature.
B—The date, frequency of VOR or VOT, number of flight hours since last check, and signature.
C—The date, place, bearing error, aircraft total time, and signature.

Each person making the VOR operational check shall enter the date, place, bearing error, and sign the aircraft log or other record. (PLT508, IR.II.B.K2a) — 14 CFR §91.171

Answer (B) is incorrect because it is not necessary to log the frequency of VOR or VOT, or the number of flight hours since last check. Answer (C) is incorrect because it is not necessary to log the aircraft total time.

ALL

4054. When making an airborne VOR check, what is the maximum allowable tolerance between the two indicators of a dual VOR system (units independent of each other except the antenna)?

A—4° between the two indicated bearings of a VOR.
B—Plus or minus 4° when set to identical radials of a VOR.
C—6° between the two indicated radials of a VOR.

If dual system VOR (units independent of each other except for the antenna) is installed in the aircraft, the pilot shall tune both systems to the same VOR ground facility and note the indicated bearings TO that station. The maximum permissible variation between the two indicated radials is 4° on the ground or in the air. (PLT300, IR.II.B.K2a) — 14 CFR §91.171

Answer (B) is incorrect because the VORs are not set to identical radials of a VOR, but rather the CDI is centered and the bearing noted. Answer (C) is incorrect because the maximum allowable tolerance between the two VORs is 4° (not 6°).

ALL

4362. (Refer to Figure 76.) Which indication would be an acceptable accuracy check of both VOR receivers when the aircraft is located on the VOR receiver checkpoint at the Helena Regional Airport?

A—A.
B—B.
C—C.

If a test signal is not available at the airport of intended departure, use a point on an airport surface designated as a VOR system checkpoint by the Administrator, the maximum permissible bearing error for a ground check is ±4°. The tail of the RMI will show which radial that the aircraft is on. The ground check point for Helena is located on the 237° radial from the HLN VOR, therefore, both RMI tails should be indicating 237° ±4°. (PLT507, IR.II.B.K2a) — AIM ¶1-1-4

ALL

4383. While airborne, what is the maximum permissible variation between the two indicated bearings when checking one VOR system against the other?

A—Plus or minus 4° when set to identical radials of a VOR.
B—4° between the two indicated bearings to a VOR.
C—Plus or minus 6° when set to identical radials of a VOR.

If dual system VOR (units independent of each other except for the antenna) is installed in the aircraft, the pilot may check one system against the other. Both systems shall be tuned to the same VOR ground facility and note the indicated bearings to that station. The maximum permissible variation between the two indicated bearings is 4° on the ground or in the air. (PLT507, IR.II.B.K2a) — AIM ¶1-1-4

Answer (A) is incorrect because the CDI needles must be centered (not set to identical radials). Answer (C) is incorrect because the maximum permissible variation is 4° (not 6°).

ALL

4382. (Refer to Figure 81.) When checking a dual VOR system by use of a VOT, which illustration indicates the VOR's are satisfactory?

A—1.
B—2.
C—4.

The maximum permissible indicated bearing error is ±4°, when using a VOT to check the equipment. A valid VOT signal should be indicated as the 360° radial FROM the station. Since RMI arrows point TO the station, an RMI should indicate 180° ±4° on any OBS setting when using a VOT facility, which is the case in RMI 1. (PLT363, IR.II.C.S1) — AIM ¶1-1-4

Answer (B) is incorrect because RMI 2 indicates 0° and 180° TO (not 360° FROM). Answer (C) is incorrect because RMI 4 indicates 001° and 0° TO (not 360° FROM).

Answers

4046 [A]	4054 [A]	4362 [C]	4383 [B]	4382 [A]

ALL

4377. How should the pilot make a VOR receiver check when the aircraft is located on the designated checkpoint on the airport surface?

A—Set the OBS on 180° plus or minus 4°; the CDI should center with a FROM indication.
B—Set the OBS on the designated radial. The CDI must center within plus or minus 4° of that radial with a FROM indication.
C—With the aircraft headed directly toward the VOR and the OBS set to 000°, the CDI should center within plus or minus 4° of that radial with a TO indication.

A VOR receiver ground checkpoint requires setting the OBS on a designated radial (found in the Chart Supplements U.S.) from a nearby VOR. It requires ±4° accuracy with a FROM indication. (PLT300, IR.II.B.K2a) — AIM ¶1-1-4

Answer (A) is incorrect because the designated radial (not 180°) is used. Answer (C) is incorrect because the aircraft heading does not affect the VOR indications.

ALL

4385. (Refer to Figure 82.) Which is an acceptable range of accuracy when performing an operational check of dual VOR's using one system against the other?

A—1.
B—2.
C—4.

Using an RMI to perform a dual VOR check, the bearing pointers must be within 4° of each other, which is the case in RMI 4. (PLT508, IR.II.B.K2a) — AIM ¶1-1-4

Answer (A) is incorrect because RMI 1 shows needles with 180° difference. Answer (B) is Incorrect because RMI 2 shows needles with 10° difference.

ALL

4386. Where can the VOT frequency for a particular airport be found?

A—On the IAP Chart and in the Chart Supplements U.S.
B—Only in the Chart Supplements U.S.
C—In the Chart Supplements U.S. and on the A/G Voice Communication Panel of the En Route Low Altitude Chart.

Locations of airborne checkpoints, ground checkpoints, and VOTs are published in the Chart Supplements U.S. (PLT363, IR.II.C.S1) — AIM ¶1-1-4

ALL

4387. Which indications are acceptable tolerances when checking both VOR receivers by use of the VOT?

A—360° TO and 003° TO, respectively.
B—001° FROM and 005° FROM, respectively.
C—176° TO and 003° FROM, respectively.

To test for VOR receiver accuracy center the CDI needle. The omnibearing selector should read 0° with the TO/FROM flag showing FROM and 180° with the flag showing TO. The allowable bearing error is ±4°. Therefore, a 176° TO indication for one of the VOR receivers and a 003° FROM for the other VOR is an acceptable combination. (PLT363, IR.II.C.S1) — AIM ¶1-1-4

ALL

4388. In which publication can the VOR receiver ground checkpoint(s) for a particular airport be found?

A—Aeronautical Information Manual.
B—En Route Low Altitude Chart.
C—Chart Supplements U.S.

A list of VOR receiver check points and VOTs can be found in the back of the Chart Supplements U.S. (PLT281, IR.III.B.K1) — AIM ¶1-1-4

ALL

4389. Which is the maximum tolerance for the VOR indication when the CDI is centered and the aircraft is directly over the airborne checkpoint?

A—Plus or minus 6° of the designated radial.
B—Plus 6° or minus 4° of the designated radial.
C—Plus or minus 4° of the designated radial.

The indicated VOR bearing when over the airborne (or over the ground point) checkpoint cannot be more than ±6° from the designated radial. The flag will have a FROM indication. (PLT300, IR.II.C.S1) — AIM ¶1-1-4

ALL

4372. What is the maximum tolerance allowed for an operational VOR equipment check when using a VOT?

A—Plus or minus 4°.
B—Plus or minus 6°.
C—Plus or minus 8°.

The maximum tolerance allowed for an operational VOR equipment check when using a VOT is ±4°. (PLT363, IR.II.C.S1) — 14 CFR §91.171

Answers

4377 [B]	4385 [C]	4386 [B]	4387 [C]	4388 [C]	4389 [A]
4372 [A]					

ALL

4384. How should the pilot make a VOR receiver check when the airplane is located on the designated checkpoint on the airport surface?

A—With the aircraft headed directly toward the VOR and the OBS set to 000°, the CDI should center within plus or minus 4° of that radial with a TO indication.

B—Set the OBS on the designated radial. The CDI must center within plus or minus 4° of that radial with a FROM indication.

C—Set the OBS on 180° plus or minus 4°; the CDI should center with a FROM indication.

If a test signal is not available at the airport of intended departure, use a point on the airport surface designated as a VOR system checkpoint. The maximum permissible bearing error is ±4° with a FROM indication. (PLT300, IR.II.C.S1) — AIM ¶1-1-4

Answer (A) is incorrect because the heading of the aircraft does not affect the VOR indications. Answer (C) is incorrect because the designated radial (not 180°) should be used.

ALL

4376. To correctly use a VOT for a VOR receiver check, the CDI should be centered with a TO indication and the OBS should indicate that the aircraft is on the

A—090 radial.

B—180 radial.

C—360 radial.

To use a VOT service, tune in the VOT frequency with the VOR receiver. With the CDI centered, the OBS should read 0° with a FROM flag, or 180° with a TO flag. The question asks for radial, so you are "0° or 360° FROM." (PLT363, IR.II.C.S1) — AIM ¶1-1-4

ALL

4378. When the CDI needle is centered during an airborne VOR check, the omni-bearing selector and the OBS indicator should read

A—within 4° of the selected radial.

B—within 6° of the selected radial.

C—0° TO, only if you are due south of the VOR.

If no check signal or point is available while in flight, select a VOR radial that lies along the centerline of an established VOR airway and maneuver the aircraft directly over a prominent ground point. Note the VOR bearing indicated by the receiver. The maximum permissible variation between the published radial and the indicated bearing is ±6°. (PLT507, IR.II.B.K2a) — AIM ¶1-1-4

ALL

4337. (Refer to Figure 64.) The course deviation indicator (CDI) are centered. Which indications on the No. 1 and No. 2 VOR receivers over the Lafayette Regional Airport would meet the requirements for the VOR receiver check?

	VOR No. 1	TO/FROM	VOR No. 2	TO/FROM
A—	162°	TO	346°	FROM
B—	160°	FROM	162°	FROM
C—	341°	FROM	330°	FROM

The top-half of the chart supplement excerpt for LFT contains the VOR receiver checkpoints. The Lafayette checkpoint is airborne at 1,000 feet over the rotating beacon and the azimuth from the VORTAC is on the R-343. Once established on R-343, the CDI needle should be centered with an OBS setting of 160° TO or 340° FROM, with an acceptable error being ±6°. (PLT090, IR.II.C.S1) — AIM ¶1-1-4

Answer (B) is incorrect because the radial from the station is 343° which would result in a TO indication with the OBS set to 163°. Answer (C) is incorrect because the No. 2 VOR OBS exceeds the acceptable error of ±6°.

ALL

4410. What indication should a pilot receive when a VOR station is undergoing maintenance and may be considered unreliable?

A—No coded identification, but possible navigation indications.

B—Coded identification, but no navigation indications.

C—A voice recording on the VOR frequency announcing that the VOR is out of service for maintenance.

The only positive method of identifying a VOR is by its Morse code identification or by the recorded automatic voice identification which is always indicated by use of "VOR" following the range's name. During periods of maintenance, the coded facility identification is removed. If a navigational signal is being received without the corresponding Morse code identification, the VOR is out for maintenance. (PLT507, IR.II.B.K2a) — AIM ¶1-1-3

Answer (B) is incorrect because the coded identification is unavailable when the station is undergoing maintenance. Answer (C) is incorrect because an out-of-service VOR is not identified by a voice recording.

Answers

4384 [B] 4376 [C] 4378 [B] 4337 [A] 4410 [A]

ALL
4411. A particular VOR station is undergoing routine maintenance. This is evidenced by

A—removal of the navigational feature.
B—broadcasting a maintenance alert signal on the voice channel.
C—removal of the identification feature.

The only positive method of identifying a VOR is by its Morse code identification or by the recorded automatic voice identification which is always indicated by use of "VOR" following the range's name. During periods of maintenance, the coded facility identification is removed. If a navigational signal is being received without the corresponding Morse code identification, the VOR is out for maintenance. (PLT507, IR.II.B.K2a) — AIM ¶1-1-3

Answer (A) is incorrect because the navigational signal may still be transmitted, although it will be inaccurate. Answer (B) is incorrect because an out-of-service VOR is not identified by a voice recording.

ALL
4548. What angular deviation from a VOR course centerline is represented by a full-scale deflection of the CDI?

A—4°.
B—5°.
C—10°.

Full-needle deflection from the center position to either side of the dial indicates the aircraft is 10° or more off course, assuming normal needle sensitivity. (PLT276, IR.II.C.S1) — FAA-H-8083-15

ALL
4549. When using VOR for navigation, which of the following should be considered as station passage?

A—The first movement of the CDI as the aircraft enters the zone of confusion.
B—The moment the TO-FROM indicator becomes blank.
C—The first positive, complete reversal of the TO-FROM indicator.

Approach to the station is indicated by flickering of the TO/FROM indicator and CDI as the aircraft flies into the "cone of confusion" (no-signal area). Station passage is shown by the first positive, complete reversal of the TO/FROM indicator. (PLT322, IR.II.B.K2a) — FAA-H-8083-15

Answer (A) is incorrect because the first movements of the CDI as the aircraft enters the zone of confusion indicates the aircraft is approaching the station. Answer (B) is incorrect because the moment the TO/FROM indicator becomes blank indicates the aircraft is in the cone of confusion over the VOR.

ALL
4550. Which of the following should be considered as station passage when using VOR?

A—The first flickering of the TO-FROM indicator and CDI as the station is approached.
B—The first full-scale deflection of the CDI.
C—The first complete reversal of the TO-FROM indicator.

Station passage is shown by the first positive, complete reversal of the TO/FROM indicator. (PLT322, IR.II.B.K2a) — FAA-H-8083-15

Answer (A) is incorrect because the first flickering of the TO/FROM indicator means the aircraft is approach the station. Answer (B) is incorrect because the first full-scale deflection of the CDI needle indicates the aircraft is in the cone of confusion.

ALL
4551. When checking the sensitivity of a VOR receiver, the number of degrees in course change as the OBS is rotated to move the CDI from center to the last dot on either side should be between

A—5° and 6°.
B—8° and 10°.
C—10° and 12°.

Course sensitivity may be checked by noting the number of degrees of change in the course selected as you rotate the OBS to move the CDI from center to the last dot on either side. This should be between 10° and 12°. (PLT507, IR.II.B.K2a) — FAA-H-8083-15

Answers

4411 [C]	4548 [C]	4549 [C]	4550 [C]	4551 [C]

ALL

4552. A VOR receiver with normal five-dot course sensitivity shows a three-dot deflection at 30 NM from the station. The aircraft would be displaced approximately how far from the course centerline?

A—2 NM.
B—3 NM.
C—5 NM.

Aircraft displacement from course is approximately 200 feet per dot per nautical mile. For example, at 30 NM from the station, one dot deflection indicates approximately 1 NM displacement of the aircraft from the course centerline. Therefore, a three-dot deflection would mean the aircraft is approximately 3 NM from the course centerline. (PLT091, IR.V.A.S2) — FAA-H-8083-3

Answers (A) and (C) are incorrect because 3 dots per 200 feet per 30 NM = 3 NM.

ALL

4553. An aircraft which is located 30 miles from a VOR station and shows a 1/2 scale deflection on the CDI would be how far from the selected course centerline?

A—1 1/2 miles.
B—2 1/2 miles.
C—3 1/2 miles.

Aircraft displacement from course is approximately 200 feet per dot per nautical mile. For example, at 30 NM from the station, a one-dot deflection indicates approximately 1 NM displacement from the course centerline. Assuming a receiver with normal course sensitivity and full-scale deflection being five dots, a half-scale deflection would be two-and-one-half dots. Therefore, at 30 NM, the aircraft would be approximately 2.5 NM from course centerline. (PLT507, IR.II.B.K2a) — FAA-H-8083-15

ALL

4554. What angular deviation from a VOR course centerline is represented by a 1/2 scale deflection of the CDI?

A—2°.
B—4°.
C—5°.

Full-needle deflection from the center position to either side of the dial indicates the aircraft is 10° or more off course, assuming normal needle sensitivity. Therefore, a half-scale deflection would indicate an angular deviation of one-half of 10°, or 5°. (PLT507, IR.II.B.K2a) — FAA-H-8083-15

ALL

4556. After passing a VORTAC, the CDI shows 1/2 scale deflection to the right. What is indicated if the deflection remains constant for a period of time?

A—The airplane is getting closer to the radial.
B—The OBS is erroneously set on the reciprocal heading.
C—The airplane is flying away from the radial.

Aircraft displacement from course is approximately 200 feet per dot per nautical mile. Therefore, in this instance, the aircraft is two and one-half dots, or 500 feet, from the radial per nautical mile from the station (at 10 miles, 5,000 feet; at 20 miles, 10,000 feet, and so on). The constant deflection indicates the airplane is flying away from the radial. (PLT507, IR.II.B.K2a) — FAA-H-8083-15

Answer (A) is incorrect because the deflection would have to decrease (not stay constant) to signify the airplane is getting closer to the radial. Answer (B) is incorrect because with the OBS set on the reciprocal heading, the CDI would give reverse indications (not stay constant).

ALL

4557. (Refer to Figure 95.) What is the lateral displacement of the aircraft in NM from the radial selected on the No. 1 NAV?

A—5.0 NM.
B—7.5 NM.
C—10.0 NM.

Aircraft displacement from course is approximately 200 feet per dot per nautical mile. For example, at 30 NM from the station, a one dot deflection indicates approximately a 1 NM displacement of the aircraft from the course centerline. In this case, the CDI is displaced two-and-one-half dots at 60 NM, which equals 2 NM times two-and-one-half dots, or approximately a 5 NM displacement from course centerline. (PLT049, IR.V.A.S2) — FAA-H-8083-3

Answer (B) is incorrect because 7.5 NM would be indicated by a 3/4 needle deflection. Answer (C) is incorrect because 10 NM would be indicated by full needle deflection.

ALL

4558. (Refer to Figure 95.) On which radial is the aircraft as indicated by the No. 1 NAV?

A—R-175.
B—R-165.
C—R-345.

The TO/FROM indictor is the triangular shaped pointer(s) (▲). When the indicator points to the head of the course arrow, it indicates that the course selected, if properly

Answers

4552 [B]	4553 [B]	4554 [C]	4556 [C]	4557 [A]	4558 [C]

intercepted and flown, will take the aircraft TO the selected facility, and vice versa. In this case, the indicator is pointing to the TAIL of the course arrow, so if flown, the course selected (350) would take the aircraft away FROM the selected facility. Each dot represents 2°. In this case, the aircraft is two-and-one-half dots (5°) to the LEFT of the selected course, therefore the aircraft is on R-345. (PLT049, IR.V.A.S2) — FAA-H-8083-15

ALL
4559. (Refer to Figure 95.) Which OBS selection on the No. 1 NAV would center the CDI and change the TO/FROM indication to a TO?

A—175°.
B—165°.
C—345°.

Currently, the course selector is set to 350 (the arrow head of the needle is pointing to 350), with a FROM indication (the triangular shaped pointers are pointing to the tail of the needle), and a left two-and-one-half dot needle deflection (5° left of course). This means the aircraft is on R-345 (350 – 5). To center the CDI and change the ambiguity indication to a TO, the OBS should be turned to the reciprocal of 345° (345 – 180), or 165°. (PLT091, IR.V.A.S2) — FAA-H-8083-15

ALL
4560. (Refer to Figure 95.) What is the lateral displacement in degrees from the desired radial on the No. 2 NAV?

A—1°.
B—2°.
C—4°.

Full-scale deflection is 10°, so each dot represents 2°. The CDI is displaced two dots, therefore the lateral displacement is 4°. (PLT091, IR.V.A.S2) — FAA-H-8083-15

ALL
4561. (Refer to Figure 95.) Which OBS selection on the No. 2 NAV would center the CDI?

A—174°.
B—166°.
C—335°.

Full-scale deflection is 10°, so each dot represents 2°. The CDI is displaced two dots (4°). The OBS is set at 170° with a FROM indication, and the aircraft is 4° to the RIGHT of course (or on the 174° radial). Simply rotating the OBS to 174° would center the CDI. (PLT091, IR.V.A.S2) — FAA-H-8083-15

ALL
4562. (Refer to Figure 95.) Which OBS selection on the No. 2 NAV would center the CDI and change the TO/FROM indication to a TO?

A—166°.
B—346°.
C—354°.

Rotating the OBS until the reciprocal of 170° (350°) is shown under the course arrow will cause the ambiguity indication to change to TO. The CDI now indicates that the aircraft is 4° to the right of course (or on the 354° course TO the selected facility). Simply rotating the OBS to 354° will center the CDI. (PLT091, IR.V.A.S2) — FAA-H-8083-15

ALL
4601. (Refer to Figure 106.) The course selector of each aircraft is set on 360°. Which aircraft would have a FROM indication on the TO/FROM indicator and the CDI pointing left of center?

A—1.
B—2.
C—3.

A FROM indication, with a 360° course selection, means the aircraft is in the northern hemisphere. A left CDI needle means the aircraft is in the right quadrant. Airplane 2 fits this description. Remember that the VOR works without regard to the aircraft heading. (PLT091, IR.V.A.S2) — FAA-H-8083-15

Answer (A) is incorrect because aircraft 1 would have the CDI pointing right (not left) of center. Answer (C) is incorrect because aircraft 3 would have a TO (not FROM) indication, and the CDI would be pointing right (not left) of center.

ALL
4666. Full scale deflection of a CDI occurs when the course deviation bar or needle

A—deflects from left side of the scale to right side of the scale.
B—deflects from the center of the scale to either far side of the scale.
C—deflects from half scale left to half scale right.

Full-scale deflection of the CDI represents 10° or more or a five-dot deflection to one side or the other from center. This will be indicated when the needle moves from the center of the scale to either far side of the scale. (PLT507, IR.III.A.S5) — FAA-H-8083-15

Answers

4559 [B]	4560 [C]	4561 [A]	4562 [C]	4601 [B]	4666 [B]

ALL

4338. (Refer to Figures 65 and 66.) What is your position relative to GRICE intersection?

A—Right of V552 and approaching GRICE intersection.
B—Right of V552 and past GRICE intersection.
C—Left of V552 and approaching GRICE intersection.

The #1 VOR (set to TIBBY VOR) shows you should fly left to get back on course (heading eastbound on V552). Consequently, you are right of course. The #2 NAV indicator is tuned to a localizer, which is why there is no TO/FROM indication. The CDI position indicates that if you were inbound on the localizer, the course centerline would be to your left. This corresponds to a position approaching GRICE intersection. (PLT090, IR.II.B.K2a) — Enroute Low Altitude Chart

Answer (B) is incorrect because the CDI on the #2 NAV indicator would be to the right if you had passed GRICE. Answer (C) is incorrect because the CDI on the #1 NAV indicator would be to the right if you were left of course.

ALL

4347. (Refer to Figures 71 and 71A.) What is your position relative to the Flosi intersection Northbound on V213?

A—West of V213 and approaching the Flosi intersection.
B—East of V213 and approaching the Flosi intersection.
C—West of V213 and past the Flosi intersection.

The #1 VOR is tuned to Kingston VORTAC (IGN). With the OBS set to 265, a FROM indication, and the CDI deflected to the right, the aircraft is south of the 265 radial and approaching the FLOSI intersection. The #2 VOR is tuned to Sparta VORTAC (SAX). With the OBS set to 029, a FROM indication, and the CDI deflected to the right, the aircraft is west of the 029 radial. (PLT079, IR.II.B.K2a) — Enroute Low Altitude Chart

Answer (B) is incorrect because the #2 VOR would have a left deflection of the CDI needle, if the aircraft was east of V213. Answer (C) is incorrect because the #1 VOR would have a left-deflected CDI needle, if the aircraft was past the FLOSI intersection.

ALL

4246. (Refer to Figures 86 and 87.) What two indications show you left of V20 and west of MOCKS intersection?

A—1 and 3.
B—1 and 4.
C—3 and 4.

The #1 VOR (set to BPT VOR) has a selected radial of 249° and FROM indication. You would turn right to get back on course (heading west on V20). The #4 VOR (set to DAS) has a selected radial of 153° and FROM indication. You would turn left to get back on course, putting you on the west side of MOCKS or past MOCKS intersection while westbound on V20. (PLT090, IR.II.B.K2a) — FAA-H-8083-15

ALL

4495. (Refer to Figures 87 and 88.) What is your relationship to the airway while heading west on V222?

A—South of V222 and approaching FALSE intersection.
B—North of V222 and approaching FALSE intersection.
C—South of V222 and past FALSE intersection.

The OBS #1 indicates you are to the left of V222 (264° radial FROM BPT) which coincides with OBS #2's indication that you are to the left of 139° radial FROM DAS or approaching FALSE. (PLT 100, IR.II.B.K2a) — Enroute Low Altitude Chart.

ALL

4507. (Refer to Figures 89 and 90.) What is your relationship to the airway while en route from BCE VORTAC to HVE VORTAC on V8?

A—Left of course on V8.
B—Left of course on V382.
C—Right of course on V8.

The OBS #1 indicates you are to the right of V382 (033° radial FROM BCE) which coincides with OBS #2's indication that you to the left of V8 (046° radial TO HVE). (PLT100, IR.II.B.K2a) — Enroute Low Altitude Chart

Answers

4338 [A]	4347 [A]	4246 [B]	4495 [A]	4507 [A]

ALL

4606. (Refer to Figure 109.) In which general direction from the VORTAC is the aircraft located?

A—Northeast.
B—Southeast.
C—Southwest.

The course selected is 180° and the TO/FROM indicator is pointing to the course, which means the aircraft is north of the course. The CDI needle is deflected to the right, which means the aircraft is left (or east) of course. Therefore, the aircraft is northeast of the VORTAC. See the figure below. (PLT091, IR.V.A.S2) — FAA-H-8083-15

Answer (B) is incorrect because if the aircraft was southeast there would be a FROM indication. Answer (C) is incorrect because if the aircraft was southwest there would be a FROM indication, and the CDI needle would be deflected to the left.

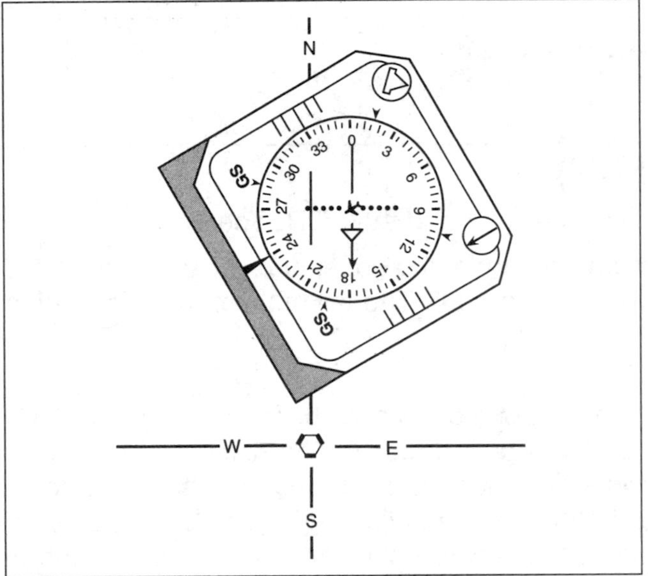

Question 4606

ALL

4607. (Refer to Figure 110.) In which general direction from the VORTAC is the aircraft located?

A—Southwest.
B—Northwest.
C—Northeast.

The course selected is 060° and the TO/FROM indicator is pointing away from the course, which means the aircraft is northeast of the course. The CDI needle is deflected right, which means the aircraft is left (or north) of course. Therefore, the aircraft is northeast of the VORTAC. See the figure below. (PLT091, IR.V.A.S2) — FAA-H-8083-15

Answer (A) is incorrect because if the aircraft was southwest there would be a TO indication. Answer (B) is incorrect because if the aircraft was northwest the CDI needle would be fully deflected to the right.

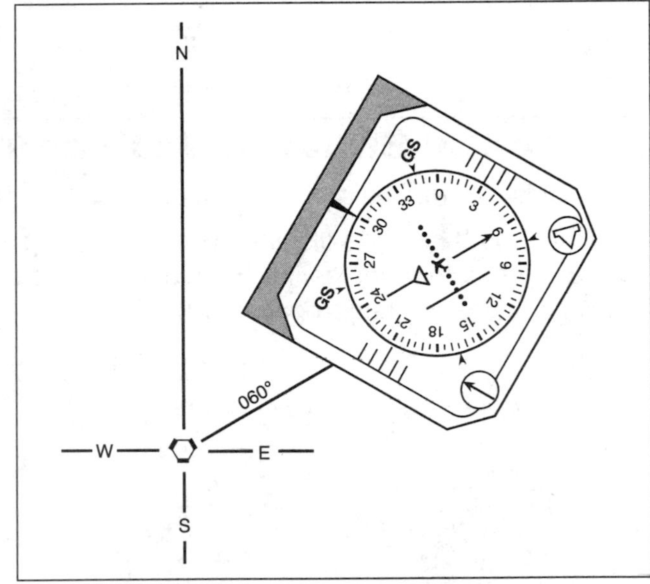

Question 4607

Answers

4606 [A]
4607 [C]

ALL

4608. (Refer to Figure 111.) In which general direction from the VORTAC is the aircraft located?

A—Northeast.
B—Southeast.
C—Northwest.

The course selected is 360° and the TO/FROM indicator is pointing away from the course, which means the aircraft is north of the course. The CDI needle is deflected to the right, which means the aircraft is left (or west) of course. Therefore, the aircraft is northwest of the VORTAC. See the figure below. (PLT091, IR.V.A.S2) — FAA-H-8083-15

Answer (A) is incorrect because if the aircraft was northeast the CDI needle would be deflected to the left. Answer (B) is incorrect because if the aircraft was southeast there would be a TO indication.

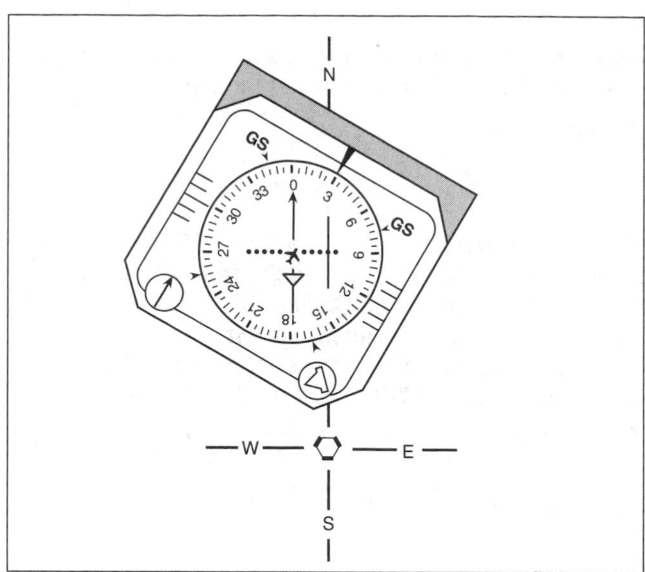

Question 4608

Horizontal Situation Indicator (HSI)

The HSI is a combination of two instruments: the heading indicator and the VOR. See Figure 4-5.

The aircraft heading displayed on the rotating azimuth card under the upper lubber line in Figure 4-5 is 330°. The course indicating arrowhead that is shown is set to 300°. The tail of the course indicating arrow indicates the reciprocal, or 120°.

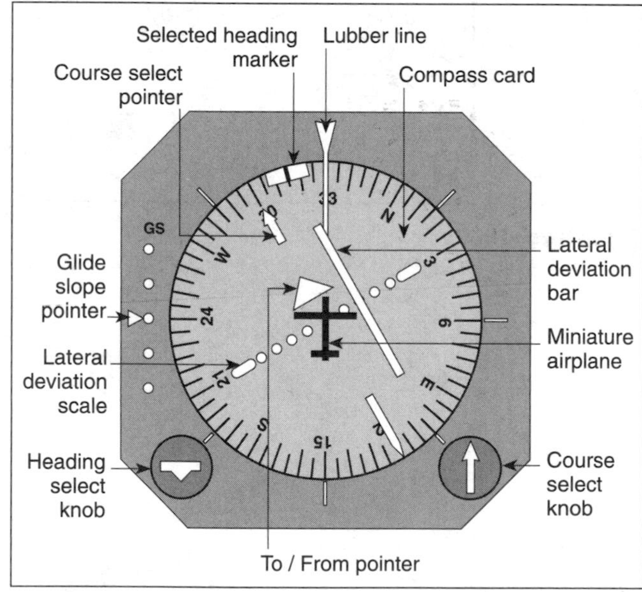

Figure 4-5. Horizontal situation indicator (HSI)

The course deviation bar operates with a VOR/LOC navigation receiver to indicate either left or right deviations from the course that is selected with the course indicating arrow. It moves left or right to indicate deviation from the centerline in the same manner that the angular movement of a conventional VOR/LOC needle indicates deviation from course.

The desired course is selected by rotating the course indicating arrow in relation to the azimuth card by means of the course set knob. This gives the pilot a pictorial presentation. The fixed aircraft symbol and the course deviation bar display the aircraft relative to the selected course as though the pilot was above the aircraft looking down.

The TO/FROM indicator is a triangular-shaped pointer. When this indicator points to the head of the course arrow, it indicates that the course selected, if properly intercepted and flown, will take the aircraft TO the selected facility, and vice versa.

Answers
4608 [C]

The glide slope deviation pointer indicates the relationship of the aircraft to the glide slope. When the pointer is below the center position, the aircraft is above the glide slope and an increased rate of descent is required.

To orient where the aircraft is in relation to the facility, first determine which radial is selected (look at the arrowhead). Next, determine whether the aircraft is flying to or away from the station (look at the TO/FROM indicator) to find which hemisphere the aircraft is in. Next, determine how far from the selected course the aircraft is (look at the deviation bar) to find which quadrant the aircraft is in. Last, consider the aircraft heading (under the lubber line) to determine the aircraft's position within the quadrant. Note that you will have reverse sensing if you're flying the back course. You will know if you're on the back course if the HSI is tuned to the reciprocal of where the localizer is positioned. For example, if the HSI is tuned to 090 but the localizer is on the 270 extension, then you are on the back course and will have reverse sensing.

ALL

4563. (Refer to Figures 96 and 97.) To which aircraft position(s) does HSI presentation "A" correspond?

A—9 and 6.
B—9 only.
C—6 only.

HSI Indicator "A" is set up with the head of the arrow pointing to 270°. The CDI is centered; therefore, the aircraft is on the extended centerline of RW #9 and #27. With a heading of 360°, Indicator "A" represents an airplane at position #6 or #9. See the figure below. (PLT056, IR.V.A.S2) — FAA-H-8083-15

Answers (B) and (C) are incorrect because HSI indicator A corresponds to both aircraft positions 6 and 9.

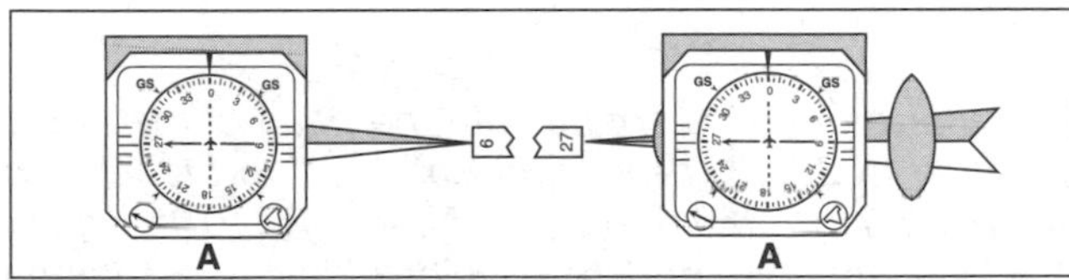

Question 4563

ALL

4564. (Refer to Figures 96 and 97.) To which aircraft position(s) does HSI presentation "B" correspond?

A—11.
B—5 and 13.
C—7 and 11.

HSI Indicator "B" is set up with the head of the arrow pointing to 090°. The CDI indication is reversed and the aircraft is actually to the south of the extended centerline. Indicator "B" then, with the aircraft flying on a heading of 090°, could be at position #13 and #5. Remember that the localizer receiver does not know where you are in relation to the antenna site. Note that you're flying the backcourse (the HSI is turned to 090 but the localizer is on the 270 extension as depicted in Figure 96) so you have reverse sensing. See the figure below. (PLT056, IR.V.A.S2) — FAA-H-8083-15

Answers (A) and (C) are incorrect because aircrafts 11 and 7 have a 270° heading (not 90°).

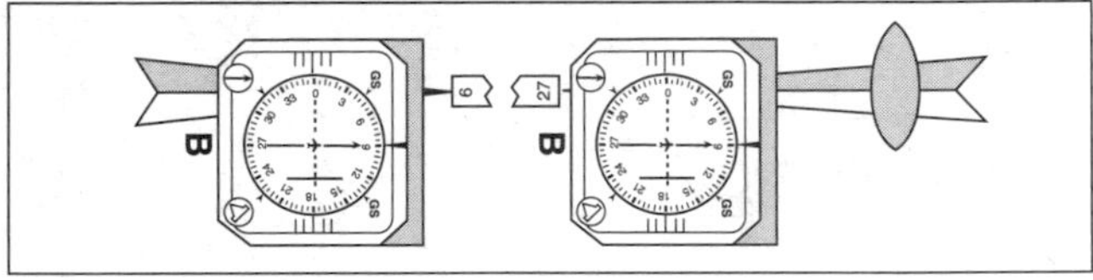

Question 4564

ALL

4565. (Refer to Figures 96 and 97.) To which aircraft position does HSI presentation "C" correspond?

A—9.
B—4.
C—12.

HSI Indicator "C" is set up with the head of the arrow pointing to 090°. With the CDI centered, the aircraft is obviously on the extended centerline. With a heading of 090°, position #12 is the only one which would have that indication. See the figure below. (PLT056, IR.V.A.S2) — FAA-H-8083-15

Answer (A) is incorrect because aircraft 9 has a 360° heading (not 090°). Answer (B) is incorrect because aircraft 4 has a 270° heading (not 090°).

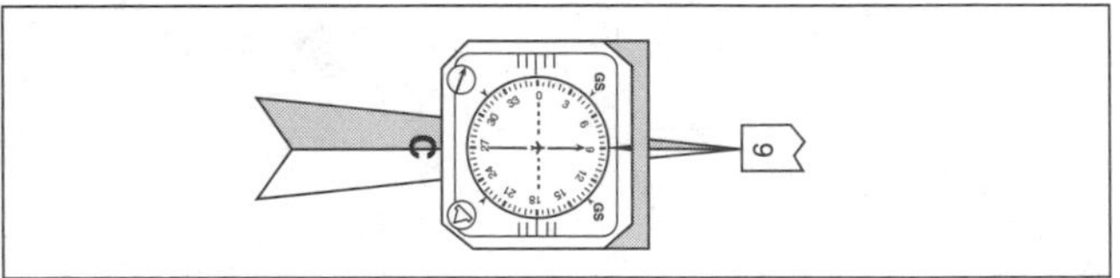

Question 4565

Answers

4563 [A] 4564 [B] 4565 [C]

ALL

4566. (Refer to Figures 96 and 97.) To which aircraft position does HSI presentation “D” correspond?

A—1.
B—10.
C—2.

HSI Indicator “D” is set up with the head of the arrow pointing to 090°. The CDI is using reverse sensing, placing the aircraft to the south of course on a heading of 315°, making position #2 the only possible choice. See the figure below. — (PLT056, IR.V.A.S2) — FAA-H-8083-15

Answer (A) is incorrect because aircraft 1 has a heading of 225° (not 315°). Answer (B) is incorrect because aircraft 10 has a heading of 135° (not 315°).

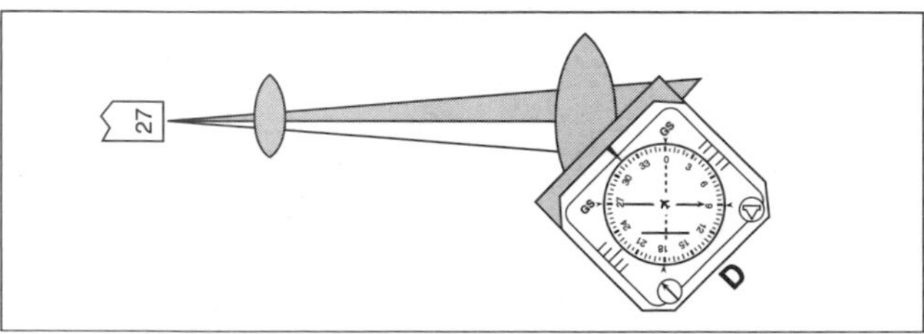

Question 4566

ALL

4567. (Refer to Figures 96 and 97.) To which aircraft position(s) does HSI presentation “E” correspond?

A—8 only.
B—3 only.
C—8 and 3.

HSI Indicator “E” is set up with the head of the arrow pointing to 090°. The aircraft is to the south of the extended centerline, with position #8 or #3 being the only possible answer for an aircraft on the heading of 045°. See the figure below. (PLT056, IR.V.A.S2) — FAA-H-8083-15

Answers (A) and (B) are incorrect because both aircraft 8 and 3 are positioned south of the course with a 045° heading.

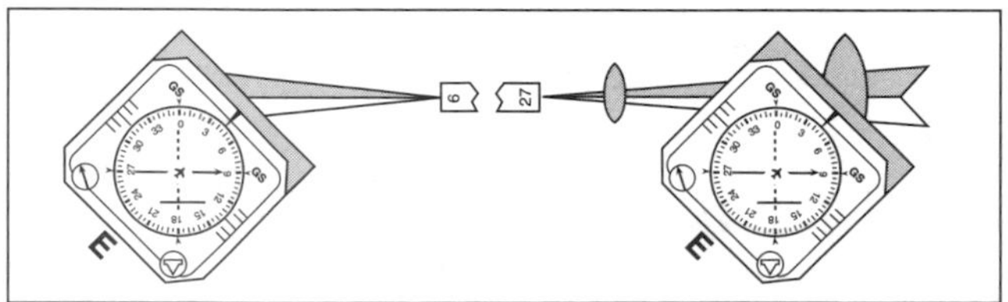

Question 4567

ALL

4568. (Refer to Figures 96 and 97.) To which aircraft position does HSI presentation “F” correspond?

A—4.
B—11.
C—5.

HSI Indicator “F” is set up with the head of the arrow pointing to 270°, and the CDI centered so the aircraft is on the extended centerline. Position #4 is the only one that would be correct for an aircraft on a heading of 270°. See the figure below. (PLT056, IR.V.A.S2) — FAA-H-8083-15

Answer (B) is incorrect because aircraft 11 has a left course deviation bar. Answer (C) is incorrect because aircraft 5 has a 090° heading (not 270°).

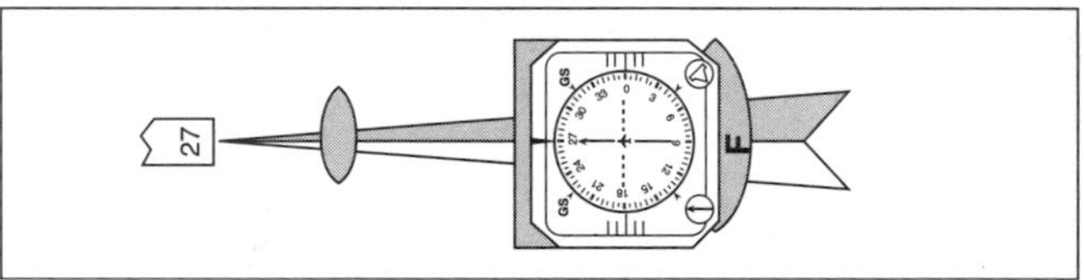

Question 4568

ALL

4569. (Refer to Figures 96 and 97.) To which aircraft position(s) does HSI presentation “G” correspond?

A—7 only.
B—7 and 11.
C—5 and 13.

HSI Indicator “G” is set up with the head of the arrow pointing to 270°. The CDI is deflected to the left, so the aircraft is to the north on a heading of 270°. Again, the indicator does not know which side of the antenna you are on, so position #7 or #11 would be appropriate selections. See the figure below. (PLT056, IR.V.A.S2) — FAA-H-8083-15

Answer (A) is incorrect because aircraft 11 would also have the indication of HSI “G”. Answer (C) is incorrect because aircraft 5 and 13 have a 090° heading (not 270°), and are south (not north) of the course.

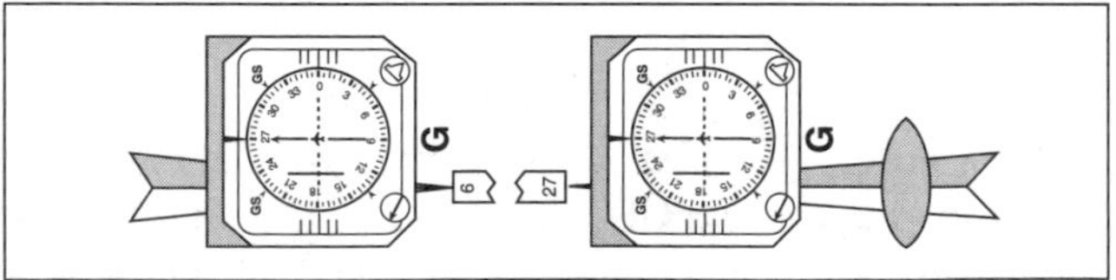

Question 4569

Answers

4566 [C] 4567 [C] 4568 [A] 4569 [B]

ALL

4570. (Refer to Figures 96 and 97.) To which aircraft position does HSI presentation "H" correspond?

A—8.
B—1.
C—2.

HSI Indicator "H" is set up with the head of the arrow pointing to 270°. The CDI is deflected to the left, so the aircraft is to the north on a heading of 215°. Position #1 is the only position corresponding to the CDI presentation. See the figure below. (PLT056, IR.V.A.S2) — FAA-H-8083-15

Answer (A) is incorrect because aircraft 8 has a 045° heading (not 215°). Answer (C) is incorrect because aircraft 2 has a 315° heading (not 215°).

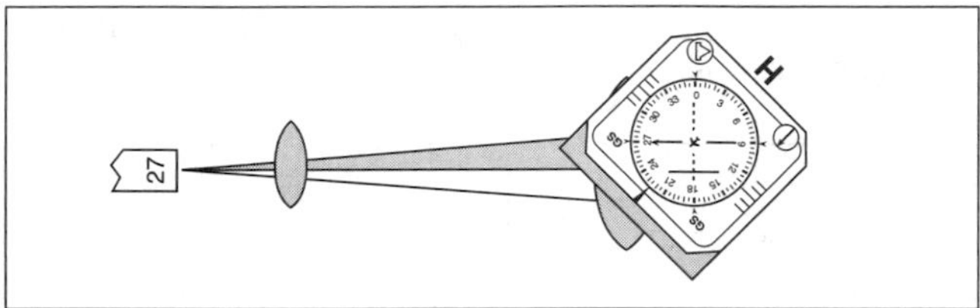

Question 4570

ALL

4571. (Refer to Figures 96 and 97.) To which aircraft position does HSI presentation "I" correspond?

A—4.
B—12.
C—11.

HSI Indicator "I" is set up with the head of the arrow pointing to 090°. The aircraft is to the north of the extended centerline on a heading of 270°. The CDI is using reverse sensing, so position #7 or #11 would be appropriate. See the figure below. (PLT056, IR.V.A.S2) — FAA-H-8083-15

Answer (A) is incorrect because aircraft 4 has a centered CDI, so it is on the extended centerline (not to the north). Answer (B) is incorrect because aircraft 12 heading a 090° heading (not 270°) and is on the extended centerline (not to the north).

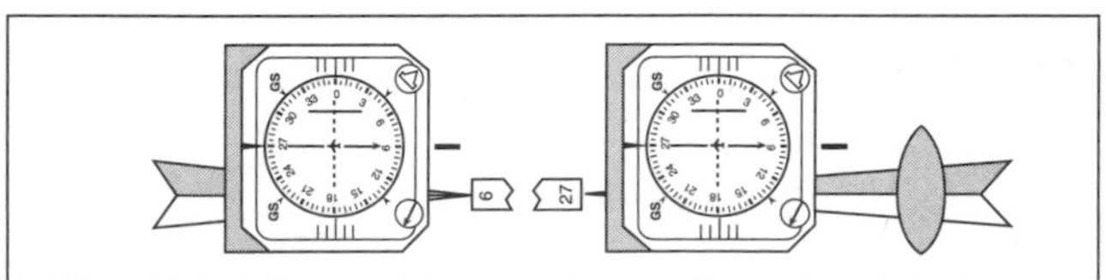

Question 4571

ALL

4572. (Refer to Figures 98 and 99.) To which aircraft position does HSI presentation "D" correspond?

A—4.
B—15.
C—17.

HSI Indicator "D" has a course selection of 180°, and the TO/FROM indicator is pointing to the tail of the course arrow. So the aircraft is flying away FROM the station, and is south of R-270 and R-090. The CDI bar is to the left, which means the aircraft is west of R-180. The aircraft heading is 180°, which describes aircraft 17. See the figure below. (PLT056, IR.V.A.S2) — FAA-H-8083-15

Answer (A) is incorrect because aircraft 4 would have a TO (not FROM) indication since it is north of R-270 and R-090. Answer (B) is incorrect because aircraft 15 is on a 360° heading (not 180°), and the CDI would be centered (not to the left).

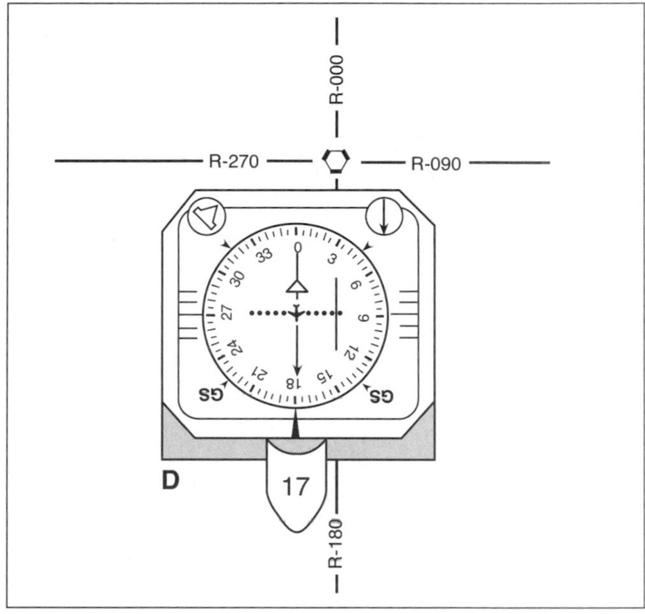

Question 4572

Answers

4570 [B] 4571 [C] 4572 [C]

ALL

4573. (Refer to Figures 98 and 99.) To which aircraft position does HSI presentation "E" correspond?

A—5.
B—6.
C—15.

HSI Indicator "E" has a course selection of 360°, and the TO/FROM indicator is pointing to the tail of the course arrow. So the aircraft is flying away FROM the station, and is north of R-270 and R-090. The CDI bar is to the left, which means the aircraft is east of R-000. The aircraft heading is 360°, which describes aircraft 6. See the figure below. (PLT056, IR.V.A.S2) — FAA-H-8083-15

Answer (A) is incorrect because aircraft 5 has a 180° heading (not 360°), and the CDI would be centered (not deflected to the left). Answer (C) is incorrect because aircraft 15 would have a TO indication (not FROM) and the CDI would be centered (not deflected to the left).

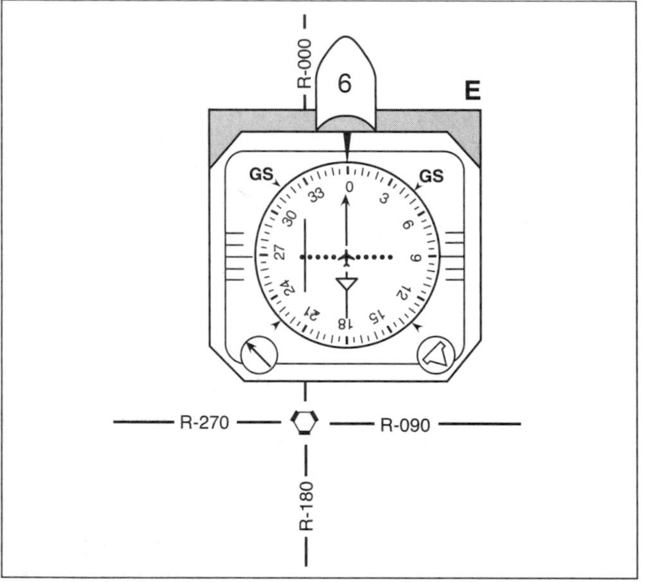

Question 4573

ALL

4573-1. (Refer to Figure 99.) The GPS waypoint information displayed on HSI "E" indicates that your position is

A—southwest, on the 350° bearing to the waypoint.
B—west, on the 010° bearing to the waypoint.
C—north, on the 190° bearing to the waypoint.

HSI indicator "E" has a course selection of 360°, and the TO/FROM indicator is pointing to the tail of the course arrow. So the aircraft is flying away FROM the station, and is north of R-270 and R090. The CDI bar is to the left, which means the aircraft is east of R-000. (PLT091, IR.V.A.S2) — FAA-H-8083-15

ALL

4574. (Refer to Figures 98 and 99.) To which aircraft position does HSI presentation "F" correspond?

A—10.
B—14.
C—16.

HSI Indicator "F" has a course selection of 180°, and the TO/FROM indicator is pointing to the tail of the course arrow. So the aircraft is flying away FROM the station, and is south of R-270 and R-090. The CDI bar is centered, which means the aircraft is on the extended centerline. The aircraft heading is 045°, which describes aircraft 16. See the following figure. (PLT056, IR.V.A.S2) — FAA-H-8083-15

Answer (A) is incorrect because aircraft 10 would have a CDI bar deflection to the left (not centered) and a TO (not FROM) indication. Answer (B) is incorrect because aircraft 14 would have a CDI bar deflection to the left (not centered).

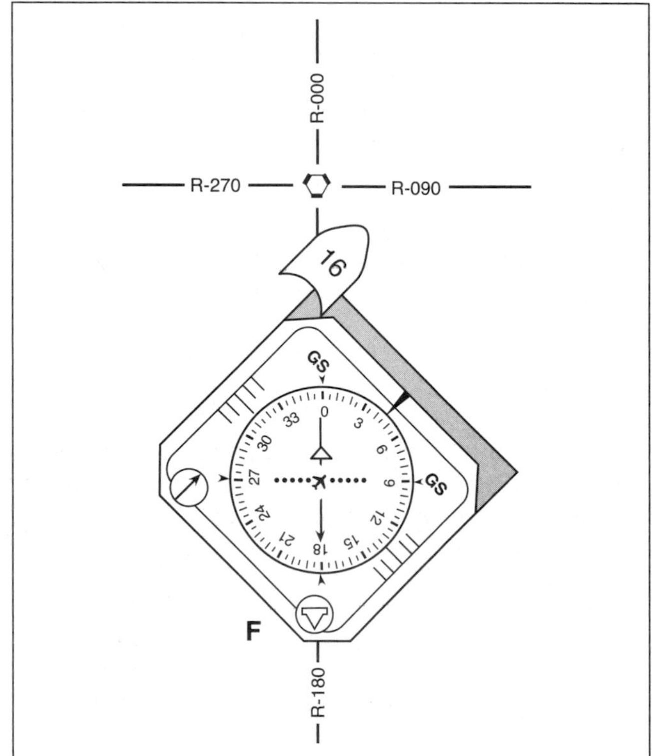

Question 4574

Answers

4573 [B] 4573-1 [C] 4574 [C]

ALL

4575. (Refer to Figures 98 and 99.) To which aircraft position does HSI presentation "A" correspond?

A—1.
B—8.
C—11.

HSI Indicator "A" has a course selection of 090°, and the TO/FROM indicator is pointing to the head of the course arrow. So the aircraft is flying TO the station, and is west R-000 and R-180. The CDI is deflected to the right, which means the aircraft is north of R-270. The aircraft heading is 205°, which describes aircraft 1. See the following figure. (PLT056, IR.V.A.S2) — FAA-H-8083-15

Answer (B) is incorrect because aircraft 8 would have a FROM (not TO) indication. Answer (C) is incorrect because aircraft 11 would have FROM (not TO) indication and the CDI bar would be deflected to the left (not right).

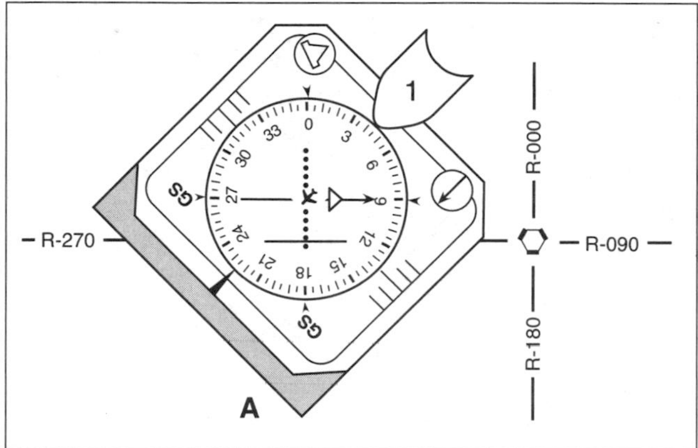

Question 4575

ALL

4576. (Refer to Figures 98 and 99.) To which aircraft position does HSI presentation "B" correspond?

A—9.
B—13.
C—19.

HSI Indicator "B" has a course selection of 270°, and the TO/FROM indicator is pointing to the tail of the course arrow. So the aircraft is flying FROM the station, and is west of R-000 and R-180. The CDI is deflected right, which means the aircraft is south of R-270. The aircraft heading is 135°, which describes aircraft 19. See the following figure. (PLT275, IR.V.A.S2) — FAA-H-8083-15

Answer (A) is incorrect because aircraft 9 would have a TO (not FROM) indication, and the CDI bar would be deflected to the left (not right). Answer (B) is incorrect because aircraft 13 would have a TO (not FROM) indication.

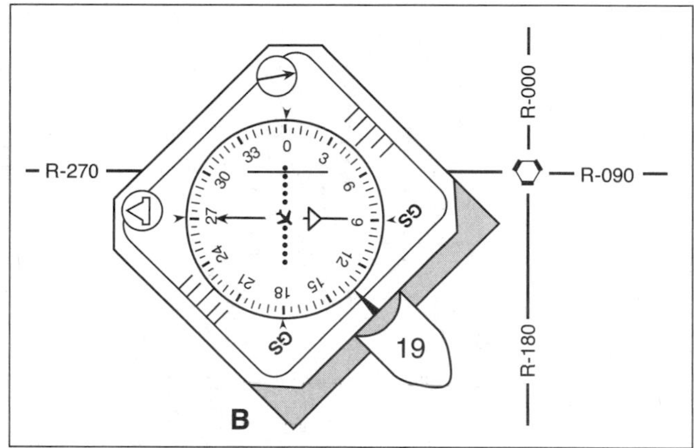

Question 4576

Answers

4575 [A]
4576 [C]

ALL

4577. (Refer to Figures 98 and 99.) To which aircraft position does HSI presentation "C" correspond?

A—6.
B—7.
C—12.

HSI Indicator "C" has a course selection of 360°, and the TO/FROM indicator is pointing to the head of the course arrow. So the aircraft is flying TO the station, and is south of R-270 and R-090. The CDI is deflected left, which means the aircraft is east of R-180. The aircraft heading is 310°, which describes aircraft 12. See the figure below. (PLT091, IR.V.A.S2) — FAA-H-8083-15

Answer (A) is incorrect because aircraft 6 would have a 360° (not 310°) heading, and a FROM (not TO) indication. Answer (B) is incorrect because aircraft 7 would have a FROM (not TO) indication.

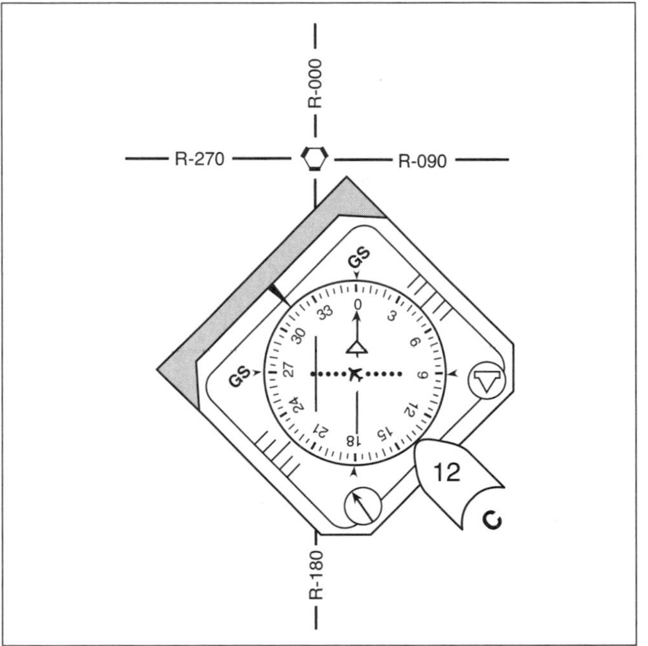

Question 4577

ALL

4240. (Refer to Figures 47 and 48.) What is your position relative to relative to Yakima VOR?

A—Northwest of V468 flying away from the VOR.
B—North of V448 flying to the VOR.
C—Approaching TAMPO intersection.

The HSI is tuned to the 206° radial of Yakima VOR which identifies V468. The TO/FROM indication is pointing to the tail of the course arrow. So the aircraft is flying away from the VOR. You location is still northwest of the selected radial and are flying on a 130° magnetic heading to intercept. (PLT091, IR.V.A.S2) — FAA-8083-15

Answer (B) is incorrect because the TO/FROM indication is pointing to the tail of the course arrow. Answer (C) is incorrect because you have a course deflection of 2 dots and you're only 9 miles from the station; therefore you are already south of TAMPO intersection flying away.

Area Navigation (RNAV)

RNAV is a system of navigation which allows a pilot to fly a selected course without the need to overfly ground- or space-based navigation aids. To fly either an RNAV route or to execute an RNAV approach under IFR, the aircraft must have an approved RNAV receiver.

A **waypoint** is a predetermined geographical position used for route definition and/or progress reporting purposes.

Answers

4577 [C] 4240 [A]

ALL

4069. What is a way point when used for an IFR flight?

A—A predetermined geographical position used for an RNAV route or an RNAV instrument approach.
B—A reporting point defined by the intersection of two VOR radials.
C—A location on a victor airway which can only be identified by VOR and DME signals.

Waypoint: A predetermined geographical position used for route/instrument approach definition, or progress reporting purposes, that is defined relative to a VORTAC station, or in terms of latitude/longitude coordinates. (PLT354, IR.VI.A.K1) — FAA-H-8083-15, Glossary

Answer (B) is incorrect because it describes an intersection, not a waypoint. Answer (C) is incorrect because it describes a DME fix, not a waypoint.

ALL

4684. (Refer to Figure 242.) What minimum airborne equipment is required to be operative for RNAV RWY 36 approach at Adams Field?

A—An approved RNAV receiver that provides both horizontal and vertical guidance.
B—A transponder and an approved RNAV receiver that provides both horizontal and vertical guidance.
C—Any approved RNAV receiver.

An approved RNAV receiver is required for RNAV approaches. (PLT083, IR.VI.A.K1) — Instrument Approach Procedures

Answer (A) is incorrect because RNAV approaches do not require RNAV equipment with vertical guidance capability. Answer (B) is incorrect because ATC may authorize continued flight with an inoperative transponder, and vertical guidance capability is not required.

ALL

4684-1. What are the primary benefits of satellite based area navigation (RNAV)?

A—Provides optimal routing and altitudes.
B—Radio tuning and controller communication is minimized.
C—Standard Terminal Arrival Routes and Departure Procedures are not required.

RNAV procedures are used to develop new routes that reduce flow complexity by permitting aircraft to fly optimum routes with minimal controller intervention. (PLT354, IR.VI.A.K1) — FAA-H-8083-16

RTC

4684-2. In what circumstances would a BARO-VNAV approach not be authorized?

A—When the ground-based NAVAIDs, such as the ILS, are out of service.
B—In areas of hazardous terrain or when a remote altimeter setting is required.
C—When the lower limit of the published temperature is -20°C and the outside temperature is -15°C.

Baro-VNAV must be flown using the local altimeter setting only. Where no local altimeter is available, the LNAV/VNAV line will still be published for use by WAAS receivers with a note that BARO-VNAV is not authorized. In addition, reliance on barometric pressure for vertical guidance is not authorized near hazardous terrain. (PLT354) — AIM ¶5-4-5

Answer (A) is incorrect because the RNAV approach does not use the ILS glideslope signal. Answer (C) is incorrect because the minimum and maximum temperature limitation is published on procedures which authorize BARO-VNAV operation; these temperatures will vary by procedure.

RTC

4684-3. How does BARO-VNAV provide vertical guidance during an RNAV approach?

A—GPS-equipped airplanes use the existing ILS glideslope signal for vertical guidance during BARO-VNAV approaches.
B—By defined vertical angles or altitudes as fixes using the local altimeter setting.
C—Using a series of step-down fixes.

Baro-VNAV must be flown using the local altimeter setting only. Where no local altimeter is available, the LNAV/VNAV line will still be published for use by WAAS receivers with a note that BARO-VNAV is not authorized. (PLT354) — AIM ¶5-4-5

Answer (A) is incorrect because the RNAV approach does not use the ILS glideslope signal. Answer (C) is incorrect because BARO-VNAV approaches use a constant descent angle, not step-down fixes.

Answers

4069 [A]	4684 [C]	4684-1 [A]	4684-2 [B]	4684-3 [B]

ALL

4684-5. Your avionics system offers advisory VNAV functions, but does not use WAAS or BARO-VNAV systems. Which statement is true?

A—You may use your avionics system to execute approaches to LNAV/VNAV minimums.
B—Your avionics system cannot be used to execute approaches to LNAV/VNAV minimums.
C—You may use your avionics system to execute approaches to LNAV/VNAV and LPV minimums.

Required navigational performance for vertical navigation is based upon barometric VNAV or WAAS. (PLT354, IR.VI.A.K1) — AIM ¶1-2-2

Instrument Landing System (ILS)

An ILS consists of a localizer, a glide slope, marker beacons, and approach lights. See Figure 4-6 and FAA CT-8080-3 Legend 38. The localizer provides azimuth information, furnishing the pilot with course guidance to the runway centerline. The approach course is called the front course and the localizer signal is transmitted from approximately 1,000 feet past the far end of the runway. At the runway threshold, the course width is adjusted to 700 feet. When tracking inbound on the localizer, drift corrections should be small and should be reduced as the course narrows. When the outer marker is reached, enough drift correction should be established so as to allow completion of the approach with heading corrections no greater than 2°. The localizer identification, which consists of a three-letter identifier preceded by the letter "I", is transmitted in Morse code on the localizer frequency.

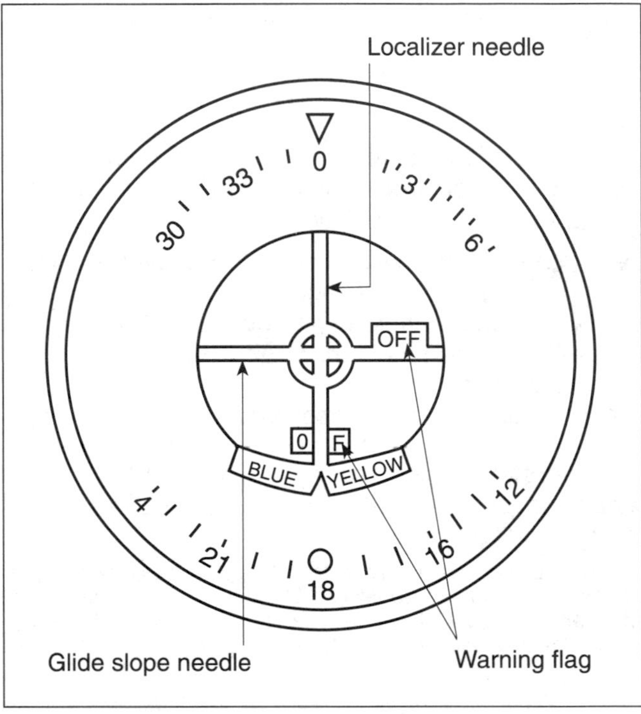

Figure 4-6. Localizer and glide slope needles

The glide slope transmitter is automatically tuned when the localizer frequency is selected. Offset from the runway approximately 1,000 feet from the approach end, it projects a beam 1.4° from full-scale. The glide slope angle is normally adjusted to 3° above horizontal so that it intersects the middle marker approximately 200 feet AGL, and is usable to a distance of about 10 NM. Figures 4-7 and 4-8 depict typical indications that a pilot would see during localizer and/or glide slope operations.

Low-powered transmitters called marker beacons are located along the ILS approach course. These beacons transmit their signals vertically upward in a very narrow beam across the localizer course. When an aircraft flies through the beam a receiver is activated which informs the pilot of the aircraft's position relative to the runway. The marker beacon farthest from the runway is the outer marker (OM). Passing over the OM the pilot will hear a series of dashes, and a blue (or purple) light will illuminate on the instrument panel. Located 4 to 7 miles from the runway, the OM indicates a position at which an aircraft at the appropriate altitude on the localizer course will intercept the glide slope. Approximately 3,500 feet from the landing threshold, an aircraft on the glide slope will cross the middle marker (MM) at an altitude of

Answers
4684-5 [B]

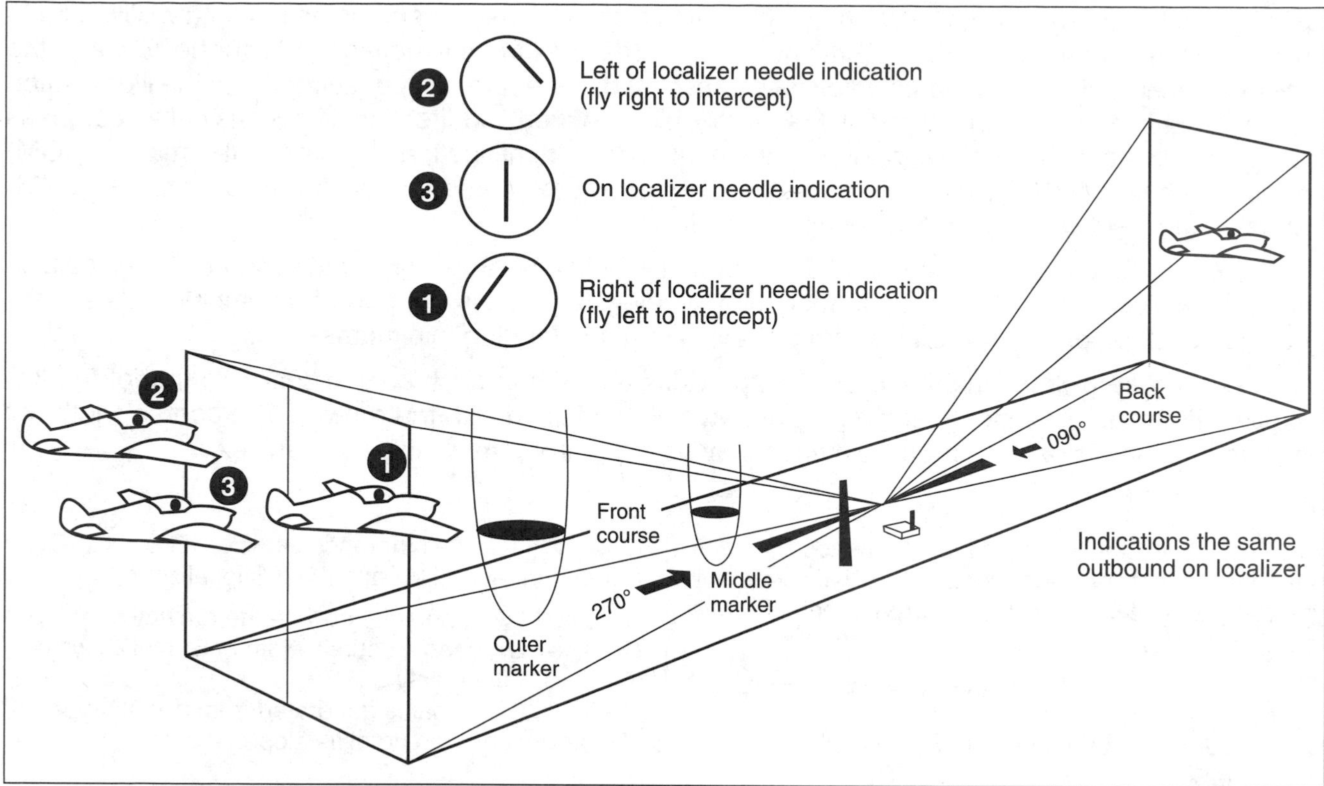

Figure 4-7. Localizer course indications

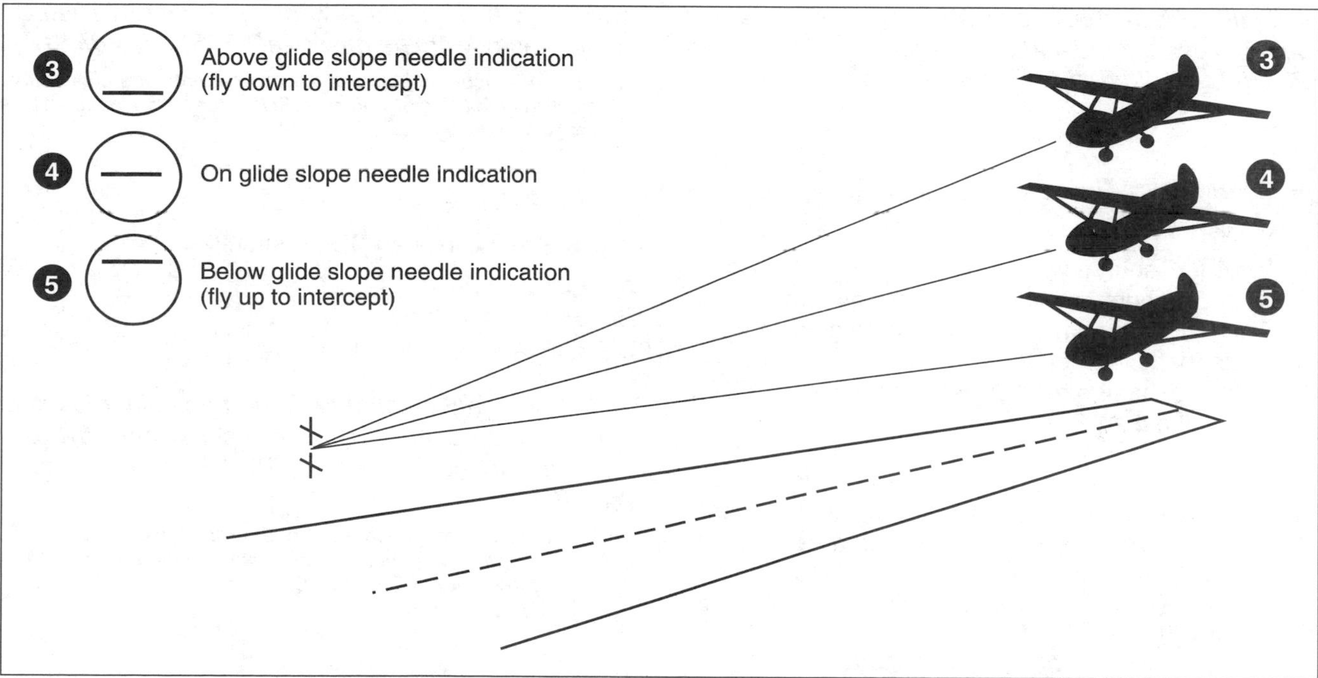

Figure 4-8. Glide slope indications

approximately 200 feet. The pilot will hear alternating dots and dashes, and an amber light will illuminate on the instrument panel. At some locations, an inner marker (IM) is installed between the MM and the runway threshold. The IM is identified by dots transmitted at the rate of 4 per second and the illumination of a white light on the instrument panel. Frequently, low-powered nondirectional beacons called compass locators are co-located with outer and middle markers. For identification, a locator outer marker (LOM) transmits the first two letters of the localizer identification group, and the locator middle marker (LMM) transmits the last two letters of the localizer identifier.

A Localizer-Type Directional Aid (LDA) approach is of comparable utility and accuracy to a localizer. Like the localizer, it has a course width of approximately 5°, but it is not part of a complete ILS system and it is not aligned with the runway. It may have straight-in landing minimums.

The Simplified Directional Facility (SDF) provides a final approach course similar to that of the ILS localizer. It has no glide slope, and it may or may not be aligned with the runway. The course width will be fixed at either 6° or 12°, and the antenna may be offset from the runway centerline.

RTC
4353. (Refer to Figure 210.) Which sequence of marker beacon indicator lights, and their respective codes, will you receive on the ILS RWY 6 approach procedure to the MAP?

A—Blue—alternate dots and dashes; amber—dashes.
B—Amber—alternate dots and dashes; blue—dashes.
C—White—rapid dots.

Figure 210 depicts an IM for this approach. The IM is identified with continuous dots keyed at the rate of four dots per second and a white marker beacon light. (PLT083) — AIM ¶1-1-9

RTC
4702. What is a difference between an SDF and an LDA facility?

A—The SDF course width is either 6° or 12° while the LDA course width is approximately 5°.
B—The SDF course has no glide slope guidance while the LDA does.
C—The SDF has no marker beacons while the LDA has at least an OM.

An LDA is of comparable utility and accuracy to a localizer but is not part of a complete ILS. The LDA usually provides a more precise approach course than the SDF, which may have a course width of 6° or 12°. The LDA course widths are from 3° to 6°. (PLT361) — AIM ¶1-1-9 and ¶1-1-10

Answer (B) is incorrect because neither the SDF or the LDA are equipped with glide slope guidance. Answer (C) is incorrect because both the SDF or LDA may be equipped with marker beacons.

RTC
4703. What is the difference between a Localizer-Type Directional Aid (LDA) and the ILS localizer?

A—The LDA is not aligned with the runway.
B—The LDA uses a course width of 6° or 12°, while an ILS uses only 5°.
C—The LDA signal is generated from a VOR-type facility and has no glide slope.

An LDA is of comparable utility and accuracy to a localizer but is not part of a complete ILS. The LDA usually provides a more precise approach course than the SDF, which may have a course width of 6° or 12°. The LDA is not aligned with the runway. (PLT357) — AIM ¶1-1-9

Answer (B) is incorrect because the course width of a LDA and an ILS are the same (3° to 6°). Answer (C) is incorrect because an LDA is a localizer-type signal (not a VOR-type).

ALL
4704. How wide is an SDF course?

A—Either 3° or 6°.
B—Either 6° or 12°.
C—Varies from 5° to 10°.

The SDF signal emitted from the transmitter is either 6° or 12° wide as needed to provide maximum flyability and optimum course quality. (PLT361, IR.II.B.K2a) — AIM ¶1-1-10

Answer (A) is incorrect because 3° or 6° is half the course width for the SDF. Answer (C) is incorrect because a course of 5° to 10° is not related to an SDF, LDA, or an ILS.

Answers

4353 [C]	4702 [A]	4703 [A]	4704 [B]

ALL

4705. What are the main differences between the SDF and the localizer of an ILS?

A—The useable off-course indications are limited to 35° for the localizer and up to 90° for the SDF.
B—The SDF course may not be aligned with the runway and the course may be wider.
C—The course width for the localizer will always be 5° while the SDF course will be between 6° and 12°.

The SDF course may not be aligned with the runway and the course may be wider than an ILS localizer course. The ILS localizer course width varies between 3° and 6° and is tailored to provide 700 feet at the threshold (full-scale limits). (PLT361, IR.II.B.K2a) — AIM ¶1-1-10

Answer (A) is incorrect because both approaches are limited to 35° for off-course indications. Answer (C) is incorrect because the course width for a localizer is usually between 3° and 6° while the SDF is either 6° or 12° (not between).

ALL

4747. If the ILS outer marker is inoperative, you may substitute

A—a compass locator or precision radar.
B—VOR radials that identify the location.
C—Distant measuring equipment (DME).

Precision radar, or compass locators located at the OM or MM, may be substituted for marker beacons. DME, only when specified in the procedure, may be substituted for the OM. (PLT321, IR.VI.B.K1) — AIM ¶1-1-9

ALL

4773. When tracking inbound on the localizer, which of the following is the proper procedure regarding drift corrections?

A—Drift corrections should be accurately established before reaching the outer marker and completion of the approach should be accomplished with heading corrections no greater than 2°.
B—Drift corrections should be made in 5° increments after passing the outer marker.
C—Drift corrections should be made in 10° increments after passing the outer marker.

Drift corrections should be small and reduced proportionately as the course narrows. By the time you reach the outer marker, your drift correction should be established accurately enough on a well-executed approach to permit completion of the approach with heading corrections no greater than 2°. (PLT170, IR.VI.C.K1) — FAA-H-8083-15

Answers (B) and (C) are incorrect because drift corrections should be no greater than 2° (not 5° or 10°).

ALL

4987. (Refer to Figure 61.) Determine your position relative to the glide slope and localizer course.

A—Below the glide slope and right of the localizer course.
B—Above the glide slope and left of the localizer course.
C—Above the glide slope and right of the localizer course.

The CDI is one dot to the left, indicating we are right of course. The glide slope is one dot down, indicating we are above the glideslope. (PLT049, IR.V.A.S2) — FAA-H-8083-15

ALL

4824. (Refer to Figures 139 and 140.) Which displacement from the localizer and glide slope at the 1.9 NM point is indicated?

A—710 feet to the left of the localizer centerline and 140 feet below the glide slope.
B—710 feet to the right of the localizer centerline and 140 feet above the glide slope.
C—430 feet to the right of the localizer centerline and 28 feet above the glide slope.

With the CDI two dots to the left, we are to the right of course, and according to FAA Figure 139, at the 1.9 NM location 710 feet to the right of course. With the glide slope indication two dots below, we are above the glide slope and at the 1.9 NM mark on FAA Figure 139, that would put you 140 feet above the glide slope. (PLT049, IR.V.A.S2) — FAA-H-8083-15

Answers

4705 [B] 4747 [A] 4773 [A] 4987 [C] 4824 [B]

ALL
4825. (Refer to Figures 139 and 141.) Which displacement from the localizer centerline and glide slope at the 1,300-foot point from the runway is indicated?

A—21 feet below the glide slope and approximately 320 feet to the right of the runway centerline.
B—28 feet above the glide slope and approximately 250 feet to the left of the runway centerline.
C—21 feet above the glide slope and approximately 320 feet to the left of the runway centerline.

With the CDI one-and-one-half dots to the right, we are to the left of course, and according to FAA Figure 139, at the 1,300-foot location (you must interpolate between 500 feet and 1,500 feet AGL), we are 322.5 feet to the left of course. The glide slope indication is a dot and a half above the glide slope and at the 1,300-foot location; that would put you 21 feet above the glide slope. (PLT049, IR.V.A.S2) — FAA-H-8083-15

ALL
4826. (Refer to Figures 139 and 142.) Which displacement from the localizer and glide slope at the outer marker is indicated?

A—1,550 feet to the left of the localizer centerline and 210 feet below the glide slope.
B—1,550 feet to the right of the localizer centerline and 210 feet above the glide slope.
C—775 feet to the left of the localizer centerline and 420 feet below the glide slope.

With the CDI two dots to the right, we are to the left of course, and according to FAA Figure 139, at the 5.6 NM location 1,550 feet to the left of course. The glide slope indication is one dot below the glide slope and at the 5.6 NM mark, that would put you 210 feet below the glide slope. (PLT049, IR.V.A.S2) — FAA-H-8083-15

RTC
4685. (Refer to Figure 244.) How does an LDA facility, such as the one at Roanoke Regional, differ from a standard ILS approach facility?

A—The LOC is wider.
B—The LOC is offset from the runway.
C—The GS is unusable beyond the MM.

The LDA is not aligned with the runway. Straight-in minimums may be published where alignment does not exceed 30° between the course and runway. Circling minimums only are published where this alignment exceeds 30°. (PLT083) — FAA-H-8083-15

ALL
4981. (Refer to Figure 227.) You are executing the Centennial Airport (APA) ILS RWY 35R approach. What is your crossing altitude at the outer marker?

A—2,092 feet MSL.
B—7,977 feet MSL.
C—8,000 feet MSL.

The locator outer marker is shown on the profile view of the approach chart as indicated by "LOM." The altitude is shown below as 7,977 feet MSL. (PLT083, IR.V.A.S2) — Instrument Approach Procedures

ALL
4982. You have been given the following approach clearance: "N696US you are cleared for the ILS Runway 7 left approach, side-step Runway 7 right." At what point are you expected to commence the side-step maneuver?

A—At the published minimum altitude for a circling approach.
B—As soon as possible after the runway or runway environment is in sight.
C—At the localizer MDA minimum and when the runway is in sight.

Side-step maneuvers should be executed as soon as possible after spotting the runway environment. Compliance with minimum altitudes associated with step-down fixes is expected even after the side-step maneuver is initiated. (PLT083, IR.VI.E.K1) — FAA-H-8083-16

Answers

4825 [C]	4826 [A]	4685 [B]	4981 [B]	4982 [B]

Global Positioning System (GPS)

GPS is a satellite-based radio navigational, positioning, and time transfer system. The GPS receiver verifies the integrity (usability) of the signals received from the GPS satellites through receiver autonomous integrity monitoring (RAIM) to determine if a satellite is providing corrupted information. Without RAIM capability, the pilot has no assurance of the accuracy of the GPS position. If RAIM is not available, another type of navigation and approach system must be used, another destination selected, or the trip delayed until RAIM is predicted to be available on arrival.

The database may not contain all of the transitions or departures from all runways and some GPS receivers do not contain DPs in the data base. It is necessary that helicopter procedures be flown at 70 knots or less since helicopter departure procedures and missed approaches use a 20:1 obstacle clearance surface (OCS), which is double the fixed-wing OCS, and turning areas are based on this speed as well. Any required alternate airport must have an approved instrument approach procedure other than GPS, which is anticipated to be operational and available at the estimated time of arrival and which the aircraft is equipped to fly.

ALL

4799. If receiver autonomous integrity monitoring (RAIM) is not available prior to beginning a GPS approach, the pilot should

A—use a navigation or approach system other than GPS for an approach.
B—continue to the MAP and hold until the satellites are recaptured.
C—continue the approach, expecting to recapture the satellites before reaching the FAF.

If RAIM is not available, another type of navigation and approach system must be used, another destination selected, or the trip delayed until RAIM is predicted to be available on arrival. (PLT354, IR.VI.A.K1) — AIM ¶1-1-19

ALL

4799-1. While on a GPS approach, you receive a RAIM annunciation about the status of RAIM reliability. You should

A—execute an immediate missed approach regardless of where you are on the approach path.
B—execute an immediate missed approach only if you are past the FAWP.
C—continue the approach since you have up to 5 minutes of GPS accuracy to complete the approach after you receive the annunciation.

If at any time RAIM is not available, another type of navigation and approach system must be used, another destination selected, or the trip delayed until RAIM is predicted to be available on arrival. (PLT354, IR.VI.A.K1) — AIM ¶1-1-19

ALL

4799-2. As part of your GPS preflight planning, RAIM prediction should be verified. This means that

A—RAIM availability is assured for your entire route of flight including the GPS approach at your destination.
B—RAIM is predicted to be available for your entire route of flight including the GPS approach at your destination.
C—if RAIM is predicted to be available, you must still have ILS capability to use a GPS approach.

During the preflight planning phase, RAIM prediction must be performed. GPS RAIM availability must be confirmed for the intended route of flight (route and time) using current GPS satellite information. In the event of a predicted, continuous loss of RAIM of more than five minutes for any part of the intended flight, the flight should be delayed, canceled, or re-routed to where RAIM requirements can be met. (PLT354, IR.VI.A.K1) — AIM ¶5-1-15

Answer (A) is incorrect because the RAIM availability may change during the flight. Answer (C) is incorrect because ILS capability is not required to execute a GPS approach.

Answers

4799 [A] 4799-1 [A] 4799-2 [B]

ALL

4801. When using GPS for navigation and instrument approaches, any required alternate airport must have

A—authorization to fly approaches under IFR using GPS avionics systems.
B—a GPS approach that is anticipated to be operational and available at the ETA.
C—an approved operational instrument approach procedure other than GPS.

Any required alternate airport must have an approved instrument approach procedure other than GPS, which is anticipated to be operational and available at the estimated time of arrival and which the aircraft is equipped to fly. (PLT354, IR.VI.A.K1) — AIM ¶1-1-19

ALL

4801-1. Your onboard GPS-based FMS/RNAV unit is IFR certified under TSO-C129 or TSO-C196. Your destination is below minimums for the GPS RNAV approach and you proceed to your filed alternate. You know that

A—GPS units certified under TSO-C129 are not authorized for alternate approach requirements; subsequently, you must use an approach procedure based on ground based NAVAIDS.
B—once diverted to the alternate airport, you may fly a GPS-based approach as long as there is an operational ground-based NAVAID and appropriate airborne receiver for use as a backup.
C—if your aircraft is equipped with a second TSO-C129 certified GPS as a backup in place of a ground-based NAVAID receiver, you may complete the approach even if the IAP is based on ground-based NAVAIDS.

Any required alternate airport must have an approved instrument approach procedure other than GPS, which is anticipated to be operational and available at the estimated time of arrival and which the aircraft is equipped to fly. (PLT354, IR.VI.A.K1) — AIM ¶1-1-18(g)

ALL

4947. Hand-held GPS systems, and GPS systems certified for VFR operation, may be used during IFR operations as

A—the principal reference to determine enroute waypoints.
B—an aid to situational awareness.
C—the primary source of navigation.

VFR and hand-held GPS systems are not authorized for IFR navigation, instrument approaches, or as a principal instrument flight reference. During IFR operations they may be considered only an aid to situational awareness. (PLT354, IR.VI.A.K1) — AIM ¶1-1-19

ALL

4947-1. A hand-held GPS is

A—authorized for IFR use under VMC.
B—authorized for IFR use under IMC until the runway is in sight.
C—not authorized for IFR use.

VFR and hand-held GPS are not authorized for IFR navigation, instrument approaches, or as a principle instrument flight reference. During IFR operations they may be considered only an aid to situational awareness. (PLT354, IR.VI.A.K1) — AIM ¶1-1-19

ALL

4947-2. A hand-held GPS system

A—may be used for IFR operations in VFR weather conditions.
B—is not authorized for IFR navigation.
C—may be used in IFR weather conditions only for en route navigation.

VFR and hand-held GPS systems are not authorized for IFR navigation, instrument approaches, or as a principle instrument flight reference. During IFR operations they may be considered as only an aid to situational awareness. (PLT354, IR.VI.A.K1) — AIM ¶1-1-19

Answers

4801 [C]	4801-1 [B]	4947 [B]	4947-1 [C]	4947-2 [B]

ALL

4948. During IFR en route and terminal operations using an approved GPS system for navigation, ground based navigational facilities

A—are only required during the approach portion of the flight.
B—must be operational along the entire route.
C—must be operational only if RAIM predicts an outage.

The avionics necessary to receive all of the ground-based facilities appropriate for the route to the destination airport and any required alternate airport must be installed and operational. Ground-based facilities necessary for these routes must also be operational. (PLT354, IR.VI.A.K1) — AIM ¶1-1-19

Answer (A) is incorrect because ground-based facilities must be operational for the whole route, not just the approach. Answer (C) is incorrect because ground-based facilities must be operational regardless of RAIM status (although active monitoring is only required if RAIM predicts an outage).

ALL

4949. During IFR en route operations using an approved TSO-C129 or TSO-C196 GPS system for navigation,

A—no other navigation system is required.
B—active monitoring of an alternate navigation system is always required.
C—the aircraft must have an approved and operational alternate navigation system appropriate for the route.

Procedures must be established for use in the event that GPS integrity outages are predicted to occur (RAIM annunciation). In these situations, the flight must rely on other approved equipment; this may require the aircraft to be equipped with operational NDB and/or DME receivers. Otherwise, the flight must be rerouted, delayed, canceled or conducted VFR. (PLT354, IR.VI.A.K1) — AIM ¶1-1-19

ALL

4949-1. On a GPS approach, the GPS/HSI shows an LNAV/VNAV flag. What should you do?

A—Descend to the LNAV MDA missed approach point.
B—Follow the glideslope to the LNAV/VNAV DA.
C—Execute the missed approach.

WAAS receivers do not "fail down" to lower levels of service once the approach has been activated. If only the vertical off flag appears, the pilot may elect to use the LNAV minima if the rules under which the flight is operating allow changing the type of approach being flown after commencing the procedure. If the lateral integrity limit is exceeded on an LPV, LNAV/VNAV, or LNAV approach, a missed approach will be necessary since there is no way to reset the lateral alarm limit while the approach is active. With the LNAV/VNAV flag indicating full failure pilots should execute the missed approach. (PLT354, IR.VI.A.K1) — AIM ¶1-1-20

ALL

4949-2. Changing the default sensitivity on your GPS approach will

A—deselect the altitude mode.
B—deselect the altitude and heading mode.
C—disable the GPS annunciator.

Overriding an automatically selected sensitivity during an approach will cancel the approach mode annunciation. The RAIM and CDI sensitivity will not ramp down, and the pilot should not descend to MDA, but fly to the MAWP and execute a missed approach. (PLT354, IR.VI.A.K1) — AIM ¶1-1-19

ALL

4949-3. In a Technically Advanced Aircraft (TAA), the typical warning message is a

A—flashing red indication with a repeating tone.
B—yellow indication with a single tone.
C—white or green indication with no tone.

In a G1000-equipped TAA, the typical warning message is a flashing red indication with a repeating tone. (PLT354, IR.VI.A.K1) — FAA-H-8083-15

Answer (B) is incorrect because while yellow is often used as an onscreen warning, it often does not include an accompanying tone. Answer (C) is incorrect because white or green is not used to indicate a warning.

Answers

4948 [B]	4949 [C]	4949-1 [C]	4949-2 [C]	4949-3 [A]

ALL

4949-4. On a WAAS-capable GPS approach, what is the significance of "LNAV+V" being displayed?

A—Advisory vertical guidance is provided to the pilot that must be used in lieu of published step-down fixes on the instrument approach.
B—Advisory vertical guidance is provided as an aid to the pilot during the descent to the runway.
C—Approved vertical guidance to descend to the decision height is provided to the pilot.

LNAV+V provides advisory vertical guidance that may be used in lieu of the published step-down fixes on the IAP. (PLT354, IR.VI.A.K1) — AIM ¶1-1-20

Answer (A) is incorrect because LNAV+V may, not must, be used. Answer (C) is incorrect because LNAV+V provides advisory, not approved, vertical guidance.

RTC

4800. For a helicopter GPS instrument approach to be practical in a metropolitan area, airspeed must be limited to

A—90 knots.
B—70 knots.
C—60 knots.

It is necessary that helicopter procedures be flown at 70 knots or less since helicopter departure procedures and missed approaches use a 20:1 obstacle clearance surface. (PLT354) — AIM ¶1-1-19

Answers

4949-4 [B] 4800 [B]

Chapter 5
Regulations and Procedures

Requirements for Instrument Rating

Although FAR is used as the acronym for Federal Aviation Regulations, and can be seen used throughout the regulations themselves and hundreds of other publications, the FAA is now actively discouraging its use. FAR also stands for Federal Acquisition Regulations. To eliminate any possible confusion, the FAA cites the Federal Aviation Regulations with reference to Title 14 of the Code of Federal Regulations. For example, "FAR Part 91.3" is referred to as "14 CFR Part 91 Section 3" or "14 CFR §91.3."

Federal Aviation Regulations Part 61 stipulates that no person may act as pilot-in-command (PIC) of a civil aircraft under IFR or in weather conditions less than the minimums prescribed for VFR unless the pilot holds an Instrument Rating. The rating must be for the category of aircraft to be flown; e.g., airplane or rotorcraft.

In addition, any flight in Class A airspace (from 18,000 feet MSL up to and including FL600) requires an Instrument Rating. VFR flight is not allowed in Class A airspace.

Commercial airplane pilots who carry passengers for hire at night, or on cross-country flights of more than 50 NM, are also required to hold an Instrument Rating.

Student, recreational, and private pilot operations other than glider and balloon pilots require a third-class medical certificate, or if operating without a medical certificate, compliance with Part 68, referred to as BasicMed. BasicMed privileges apply to persons exercising student, recreational, and private pilot privileges when acting as PIC. They also apply to persons exercising flight instructor privileges when acting as PIC. BasicMed cannot be used to fly as a safety pilot, except when the pilot is acting as PIC. When operating under BasicMed, pilots are limited to:

1. Fly with no more than five passengers.
2. Fly an aircraft with a maximum certificated takeoff weight of no more than 6,000 lbs.
3. Fly an aircraft that is authorized to carry no more than six occupants.
4. Flights within the United States at an indicated airspeed of 250 knots or less, and at an altitude at or below 18,000 feet MSL.
5. You may not fly for compensation or hire.

If operating beyond these limitations, pilots must obtain an FAA Medical Certificate.

ALL

4983. What conditions allow a pilot who is exercising the privileges of BasicMed to act as a PIC under instrument flight rules (IFR)?

A—Flight in IMC is not permitted under BasicMed.
B—When the PIC is instrument rated and current.
C—When there is a safety pilot who shares the PIC responsibilities.

BasicMed privileges apply to persons exercising student, recreational, and private pilot privileges when acting as PIC. (PLT538, IR.I.A.K3) — 14 CFR §61.113

ALL

4024. When are you required to have an Instrument Rating for flight in VMC?

A—Flight through an MOA.
B—Flight into an ADIZ.
C—Flight into Class A airspace.

Each person operating an aircraft in Class A airspace must conduct that operation under IFR. (PLT161, IR.I.C.K2) — 14 CFR §61.3, §91.135

Answer (A) is incorrect because an Instrument Rating is not required for VMC flight through an MOA. Answer (B) is incorrect because an Instrument Rating is not required for VMC flight into an ADIZ.

Answers

4983 [B]   4024 [C]

ALL

4025. The pilot-in-command of a civil aircraft must have an Instrument Rating only when operating

A—under IFR in positive control airspace.
B—under IFR, in weather conditions less than the minimum for VFR flight, and in a Class A airspace.
C—in weather conditions less than the minimum prescribed for VFR flight.

No person may act as PIC of a civil aircraft under IFR, or in weather conditions less than the minimums prescribed for VFR flight unless:

1. *In the case of an airplane, the pilot holds an Instrument Rating or an Airline Transport Pilot Certificate with an Airplane Category Rating on it; or*
2. *In the case of a helicopter, the pilot holds a Helicopter Instrument Rating or an Airline Transport Pilot Certificate with a Rotorcraft Category and Helicopter Class Rating not limited to VFR.*

Also, each person operating an aircraft in Class A airspace must conduct that operation under IFR. (PLT448, IR.I.A.K2) — 14 CFR §61.3, §91.135

Answer (A) is incorrect because it doesn't address the requirement for an Instrument Rating if flying in IFR conditions in uncontrolled airspace. Answer (C) is incorrect because it doesn't address the option of flying in VFR conditions with an IFR clearance.

ALL

4028. A certificated commercial pilot who carries passengers for hire at night or in excess of 50 NM is required to have at least

A—a type rating.
B—a First Class Medical Certificate.
C—an Instrument Rating in the same category and class of aircraft.

A commercial pilot applicant must hold an Instrument Rating, or the Commercial Pilot Certificate that is issued is endorsed with a limitation prohibiting the carriage of passengers for hire in aircraft on cross-country flights of more than 50 NM, or at night. (PLT443, IR.I.A.K2) — 14 CFR §61.133

Answer (A) is incorrect because regardless of whether the aircraft needs a type rating, an Instrument Rating is required to carry passengers for hire at night. Answer (B) is incorrect because a commercial pilot does not need a First Class Medical Certificate, but rather a Second Class Medical Certificate.

ALL

4031. Under which condition must the pilot-in-command of a civil aircraft have at least an Instrument Rating?

A—When operating in Class E airspace.
B—For a flight in VFR conditions while on an IFR flight plan.
C—For any flight above an altitude of 1,200 feet AGL, when the visibility is less than 3 miles.

No person may act as PIC of a civil aircraft under IFR, or in weather conditions less than the minimums prescribed for VFR flight unless:

1. *In the case of an airplane, the pilot holds an Instrument Rating or an Airline Transport Pilot Certificate with an Airplane Category Rating on it; or*
2. *In the case of a helicopter, the pilot holds a Helicopter Instrument Rating or an Airline Transport Pilot Certificate with a Rotorcraft Category and Helicopter Class Rating not limited to VFR.*

Also, each person operating an aircraft in Class A airspace must conduct that operation under IFR. (PLT448, IR.I.A.K2) — 14 CFR §61.3

Answer (A) is incorrect because an Instrument Rating is required for flight in Class A airspace, not in the Continental Control Area. Answer (C) is incorrect because VFR is allowed in uncontrolled airspace during the day with as little as 1 SM visibility when more than 1,200 feet AGL but less than 10,000 feet MSL.

AIR

4029. You intend to carry passengers for hire on a night VFR flight in a single-engine airplane within a 25-mile radius of the departure airport. You are required to possess at least which rating(s)?

A—A Commercial Pilot Certificate with a Single-Engine Land Rating.
B—A Commercial Pilot Certificate with a Single-Engine and Instrument (airplane) Rating.
C—A Private Pilot Certificate with a Single-Engine Land and Instrument Airplane Rating.

A Commercial Certificate, with Single-Engine Airplane Class, is required to carry passengers for hire in that class of aircraft. In addition, the applicant must hold an Instrument Rating (airplane), or the Commercial Pilot Certificate is endorsed with a limitation prohibiting the carriage of passengers for hire in airplanes on cross-country flights of more than 50 NM, or at night. (PLT451, IR.I.A.K2) — 14 CFR §61.133

Answer (A) is incorrect because in order to carry passengers for hire at night, an Instrument Rating is required in addition to a Commercial Pilot Certificate. Answer (C) is incorrect because a Commercial Certificate (not Private) is required to carry passengers for hire.

Answers

4025 [B]	4028 [C]	4031 [B]	4029 [B]

AIR
4002. What limitation is imposed on a newly certificated commercial airplane pilot if that person does not hold an instrument pilot rating?

A—The carrying of passengers or property for hire on cross-country flights at night is limited to a radius of 50 NM.
B—The carrying of passengers for hire on cross-country flights is limited to 50 NM for night flights, but not limited for day flights.
C—The carrying of passengers for hire on cross-country flights is limited to 50 NM and the carrying of passengers for hire at night is prohibited.

The commercial pilot applicant must hold an Instrument Rating (airplane), or the Commercial Pilot Certificate that is issued is endorsed with a limitation prohibiting the carriage of passengers for hire in airplanes on cross-country flights of more than 50 NM, or at night. (PLT448, IR.I.A.K2) — 14 CFR §61.133

Answer (A) is incorrect because the carriage of any property is not prohibited at night. Answer (B) is incorrect because passengers may not be carried during night and flight is limited to 50 NM for flights without an Instrument Rating.

AIR
4034. Which limitation is imposed on the holder of a Commercial Pilot Certificate if that person does not hold an Instrument Rating?

A—That person is limited to private pilot privileges at night.
B—The carrying of passengers or property for hire on cross-country flights at night is limited to a radius of 50 NM.
C—The carrying of passengers for hire on cross-country flights is limited to 50 NM and the carrying of passengers for hire at night is prohibited.

The commercial pilot applicant must hold an Instrument Rating (airplane), or the Commercial Pilot Certificate that is issued is endorsed with a limitation prohibiting the carriage of passengers for hire in airplanes on cross-country flights of more than 50 NM, or at night. (PLT451, IR.I.A.K2) — 14 CFR §61.133

Answer (A) is incorrect because the pilot may exercise commercial pilot privileges at night, but with limitations imposed. Answer (B) is incorrect because no passengers may be carried at night without an Instrument Rating.

AIR
4035. To carry passengers for hire in an airplane on cross-country flights of more than 50 NM from the departure airport, the pilot-in-command is required to hold at least

A—a Category II pilot authorization.
B—a First Class Medical certificate.
C—a Commercial Pilot Certificate with an Instrument Rating.

In order to fly for hire, the PIC must hold a Commercial Pilot Certificate. In addition commercial pilots must hold an Instrument Rating (airplane), or they will be prohibited to carry passengers for hire in airplanes on cross-country flights of more than 50 NM, or at night. (PLT451, IR.I.A.K2) — 14 CFR §61.133

Answer (A) is incorrect because Category II pilot authorization is in reference to an authorization for reduced ILS approach minimums. Answer (B) is incorrect because a First Class Medical Certificate is only required for airline transport pilots.

AIR
4030-2. Do regulations permit you to act as pilot-in-command of an airplane in IMC if you hold a Private Pilot Certificate with ASEL, Rotorcraft category, with helicopter class rating and instrument helicopter rating?

A—No, however, you may do so if you hold an Airline Transport Pilot-Airplane Certificate, limited to VFR.
B—No, you must hold either an unrestricted Airline Transport Pilot-Airplane Certificate or an Airplane Instrument Rating.
C—Yes, if you comply with the recent IFR experience requirements for a helicopter.

No person may act as PIC of an airplane unless the pilot has a valid pilot certificate with airplane category. In addition, to operate IFR, the PIC must have either an Airplane Instrument Rating or an Airline Transport Pilot Certificate with airplane category not limited to VFR. Along with the appropriate ratings, a pilot must have the required recent experience set forth in 14 CFR §61.57. (PLT448, IR.I.A.K2) — 14 CFR §61.3, §61.57

Answer (A) is incorrect because even with the ATP-Helicopter certificate, it must be unrestricted, to allow flight in IMC. Answer (C) is incorrect because the pilot must hold the appropriate certificate, in addition to meeting the currency requirements.

Answers

4002 [C] 4034 [C] 4035 [C] 4030-2 [B]

RTC
4018. Under which condition may you act as pilot-in-command of a helicopter under IFR?

Your certificates and ratings: Private Pilot Certificate with AMEL and Airplane Instrument, Rotorcraft Category Rating, and Helicopter Class Rating.

A—If a certificated helicopter instrument flight instructor is on board.
B—If you meet the recent helicopter IFR experience requirements.
C—If you acquire a Helicopter Instrument Rating and meet IFR currency requirements.

No person may act as PIC of a helicopter unless he/she has a valid pilot certificate with rotorcraft category and helicopter class ratings. In addition, to operate IFR, the PIC must have either a Helicopter Instrument Rating or an Airline Transport Pilot Certificate with Rotorcraft Category and Helicopter Class Rating not limited to VFR. In addition to having the appropriate ratings, a pilot must have the required recent experience set forth in 14 CFR §61.57. (PLT411) — 14 CFR §61.57

Answer (A) is incorrect because the pilot must have the appropriate category, class, and Instrument Ratings in order to operate as PIC of an instrument flight, regardless of who is accompanying the flight. Answer (B) is incorrect because the pilot must have the Helicopter Instrument Rating and meet the currency requirements in order to operate as PIC of an instrument flight.

RTC
4030-1. Do regulations permit you to act as pilot-in-command of a helicopter in IMC if you hold a Private Pilot Certificate with ASEL, Airplane Instrument Rating, Rotorcraft Category, and Helicopter Class Rating?

A—Yes, if you comply with the recent IFR experience requirements for a helicopter.
B—No, you must hold either an unrestricted Airline Transport Pilot-Helicopter Certificate or a helicopter instrument rating.
C—No, however, you may do so if you hold an Airline Transport Pilot-Helicopter Certificate, limited to VFR.

No person may act as PIC of a helicopter unless the pilot has a valid pilot certificate with rotorcraft category and helicopter class ratings. In addition, to operate IFR, the PIC must have either an Instrument Helicopter Rating or an Airline Transport Pilot Certificate with Rotorcraft Category, and Helicopter Class Rating not limited to VFR. Along with the appropriate ratings, a pilot must have the required recent experience set forth in 14 CFR §61.57. (PLT411) — 14 CFR §61.3, §61.57

Answer (A) is incorrect because the pilot must hold the appropriate certificate, in addition to meeting the currency requirements. Answer (C) is incorrect because even with the ATP-Helicopter Certificate, it must be unrestricted, to allow flight in IMC.

Instrument Currency Requirements

No person may act as PIC under IFR or in weather conditions less than the minimums prescribed for VFR, unless within the preceding 6 calendar months, that person has performed and logged under actual or simulated instrument conditions:

1. At least six instrument approaches made in an aircraft, flight simulator, or flight training device;
2. Holding procedures; and
3. Intercepting and tracking courses through the use of navigation systems.

Satisfactory accomplishment (within the last 6 calendar months) of an instrument proficiency check in the category of aircraft to be flown will also meet this recency requirements.

If the recent instrument experience for 6 calendar months is not met, the pilot may not act as PIC under IFR until an instrument proficiency check (IPC) in the category of aircraft involved has been passed. This check must be given by an approved FAA examiner, instrument instructor, or FAA inspector.

Answers
4018 [C]   4030-1 [B]

ALL

4012. To meet the minimum instrument experience requirements, within the last 6 calendar months you need

A—six instrument approaches, holding procedures, and intercepting and tracking courses in the appropriate category of aircraft.
B—six hours in the same category aircraft.
C—six hours in the same category aircraft, and at least 3 of the 6 hours in actual IFR conditions.

To act as PIC under IFR, a pilot must have logged, in the past 6 calendar months, at least six instrument approaches, holding procedures, and intercepting and tracking courses through the use of navigation systems, in the appropriate category of aircraft for the instrument privileges sought. (PLT442, IR.I.A.K1) — 14 CFR §61.57

Answers (B) and (C) are incorrect because pilots are not required to fly a specified amount of flight time under IFR conditions.

ALL

4013. After your recent IFR experience lapses, how much time do you have before you must pass an instrument proficiency check to act as pilot-in-command under IFR?

A—6 months.
B—90 days.
C—12 months.

A pilot who does not meet the recent instrument experience requirements during the prescribed time, has 6 months thereafter to meet the experience requirements or pass an instrument proficiency check in the category of aircraft involved. (PLT442, IR.I.A.K1) — 14 CFR §61.57

Answer (B) is incorrect because "90 days" refers to the takeoff and landing currency requirements to carry passengers. Answer (C) is incorrect because 12 months is the time from when you gain IFR currency to when you need another instrument proficiency check (assuming you have not maintained currency).

ALL

4014. An instrument rated pilot, who has not logged any instrument time in 1 year or more, cannot serve as pilot-in-command under IFR, unless the pilot

A—completes the required 6 hours and six approaches, followed by an instrument proficiency check given by an FAA-designated examiner.
B—passes an instrument proficiency check in the category of aircraft involved, given by an approved FAA examiner, instrument instructor, or FAA inspector.
C—passes an instrument proficiency check in the category of aircraft involved, followed by 6 hours and six instrument approaches, 3 of those hours in the category of aircraft involved.

A pilot who does not meet the recent instrument experience requirements during the prescribed time, has 6 months thereafter to pass an instrument proficiency check in the category of aircraft involved, given by an approved FAA Examiner, instrument instructor, or FAA inspector. (PLT442, IR.I.A.K1) — 14 CFR §61.57

Answers (A) and (C) are incorrect because an instrument proficiency check alone provides currency. Additional hours and approaches are not required.

ALL

4015. A pilot's recent IFR experience expires on July 1 of this year. What is the latest date the pilot can meet the IFR experience requirement without having to take an instrument proficiency check?

A—December 31, this year.
B—June 30, next year.
C—July 31, this year.

A pilot who does not meet the recent instrument experience requirements during the prescribed time, has 6 months thereafter to pass an instrument proficiency check in the category of aircraft involved. If a pilot's IFR currency expires on July 1 of this year, that pilot would have 6 months, or until December 31, this year, to gain the IFR experience before an instrument proficiency check would be required. (PLT442, IR.I.A.K1) — 14 CFR §61.57

Answer (B) is incorrect because this is a 12-month period, not the required 6 months. Answer (C) is incorrect because this is 1 month, not the required 6 months.

Answers

4012 [A] 4013 [A] 4014 [B] 4015 [A]

ALL

4015-1. An instrument rated pilot is planning a flight under IFR on July 10, this year. Before conducting the flight, the pilot must have

A—performed and logged the prescribed tasks and repetitions required for instrument currency no earlier than January 1, this year.
B—performed and logged the prescribed tasks and repetitions required for instrument currency no earlier than February 10, this year.
C—passed an instrument proficiency check between August 1 last year and July 1 this year.

To act as PIC under IFR, a pilot must have logged, in the past 6 calendar months, at least six instrument approaches, holding procedures, and intercepting and tracking courses through the use of navigation systems, in the appropriate category of aircraft for the instrument privileges sought. A pilot who does not meet the recent instrument experience requirements during the prescribed time, has 6 months thereafter to meet the experience requirements or pass an instrument proficiency check in the category of aircraft involved. (PLT442, IR.I.A.K1) — 14 CFR §61.57

Answer (B) is incorrect because the prescribed tasks and repetitions must have been logged in the past 6 calendar months from the planned flight date. Answer (C) is incorrect because the PIC would have between July and December to complete the prescribed tasks and repetitions before completing the IPC in January.

ALL

4017. What minimum conditions are necessary for the instrument approaches required for IFR currency?

A—The approaches may be made in an aircraft, flight simulator, or flight training device.
B—At least three approaches must be made in the same category of aircraft to be flown.
C—At least three approaches must be made in the same category and class of aircraft to be flown.

The minimum conditions necessary for the instrument approaches is to complete six within the past 6 months, to be completed in an aircraft, flight simulator, or flight training device. (PLT442, IR.I.A.K1) — 14 CFR §61.57

Answers (B) and (C) are incorrect because it is not necessary to complete three approaches in the same category and class of aircraft; they can be in an approved instrument ground trainer, as well.

ALL

4020. How may a pilot satisfy the recent flight experience requirement necessary to act as pilot-in-command in IMC in powered aircraft? Within the previous 6 calendar months, logged

A—six instrument approaches and 3 hours under actual or simulated IFR conditions within the last 6 months; three of the approaches must be in the category of aircraft involved.
B—six instrument approaches, holding procedures, and intercepting and tracking courses using navigational systems.
C—6 hours of instrument time under actual or simulated IFR conditions within the last 3 months, including at least six instrument approaches of any kind. Three of the 6 hours must be in flight in any category aircraft.

To act as pilot-in-command under IFR, a pilot must have logged, in the past 6 calendar months, at least six instrument approaches, holding procedures, and intercepting and tracking courses through the use of navigation systems, in the appropriate category of aircraft for the instrument privileges sought. (PLT442, IR.I.A.K1) — 14 CFR §61.57

ALL

4021. How long does a pilot meet the recency of experience requirements for IFR flight after successfully completing an instrument competency check if no further IFR flights are made?

A—90 days.
B—6 calendar months.
C—12 calendar months.

A pilot who does not meet the recent instrument experience requirements during the prescribed time, may not serve as PIC under IFR until that pilot passes an instrument competency check in the category of aircraft involved. If no other instrument flight is conducted, that instrument competency check will remain current for 6 months. (PLT442, IR.I.A.K1) — 14 CFR §61.57

Answer (A) is incorrect because 90 days refers to the takeoff and landing requirements for carrying passengers. Answer (C) is incorrect because 12 months is the time after which another instrument competency check will be required.

Answers

4015-1 [A]	4017 [A]	4020 [B]	4021 [B]

ALL

4027. To meet the minimum required instrument flight experience to act as pilot-in-command of an aircraft under IFR, you must have logged within the preceding 6 calendar months in the same category of aircraft: six instrument approaches,

A—holding procedures, intercepting and tracking courses through the use of navigation systems.
B—and 6 hours of instrument time in any aircraft.
C—three of which must be in the same category and class of aircraft to be flown, and 6 hours of instrument time in any aircraft.

To act as PIC under IFR, a pilot must have logged, in the past 6 calendar months, at least six instrument approaches, holding procedures, and intercepting and tracking courses through the use of navigation systems in the appropriate category of aircraft for the instrument privileges sought. (PLT442, IR.I.A.K1) — 14 CFR §61.57

ALL

4001. No pilot may act as pilot-in-command of an aircraft under IFR or in weather conditions less than the minimums prescribed for VFR unless that pilot has, within the preceding 6 calendar months, completed at least

A—three instrument approaches and logged 3 hours.
B—six instrument flights under actual IFR conditions.
C—six instrument approaches, holding procedures, intercepting and tracking courses using navigational systems, or passed an instrument proficiency check.

To act as PIC under IFR, a pilot must have logged, in the past 6 calendar months, at least six instrument approaches, holding procedures, and intercepting and tracking courses through the use of navigation systems, in the appropriate category of aircraft for the instrument privileges sought. (PLT442, IR.I.A.K1) — 14 CFR §61.57

ALL

4001-1. Enroute weather conditions are IMC. However, during the descent to your destination for an ILS approach, you encounter VMC weather conditions prior to reaching the initial approach fix. You know that to log the ILS approach toward instrument currency requirements,

A—the flight must remain on an IFR flight plan throughout the approach and landing.
B—the ILS approach can be credited only if you use a view-limiting device.
C—the ILS approach can be credited regardless of actual weather if you are issued an IFR clearance.

To meet instrument currency requirements, the required tasks and iterations must be completed in actual weather conditions, or under simulated conditions using a view-limiting device. (PLT442, IR.I.A.K1) — 14 CFR §61.57

AIR

4023. What recent instrument flight experience requirements must be met before you may act as pilot-in-command of an airplane under IFR?

A—A minimum of six instrument approaches in an airplane, or an approved simulator (airplane) or ground trainer, within the preceding 6 calendar months.
B—A minimum of six instrument approaches, at least three of which must be in an aircraft within the preceding 6 calendar months.
C—A minimum of six instrument approaches in an aircraft, at least three of which must be in the same category within the preceding 6 calendar months.

The minimum conditions necessary for the instrument approaches is to complete six within the past 6 months, to be completed in an aircraft, approved instrument ground trainer, or any combination of these. (PLT442, IR.I.A.K1) —14 CFR §61.57

Answers (B) and (C) are incorrect because all six approaches can be in an approved instrument ground trainer, and all must be in the same category of aircraft.

Answers

4027 [A] 4001 [C] 4001-1 [B] 4023 [A]

AIR

4026. What additional instrument experience is required for you to meet the recent flight experience requirements to act as pilot-in-command of an airplane under IFR?

Your present instrument experience within the preceding 6 calendar months is:

1. 3 hours with holding, intercepting and tracking courses in an approved airplane flight simulator.
2. two instrument approaches in an airplane.

A—Three hours of simulated or actual instrument flight time in a helicopter, and two instrument approaches in an airplane or helicopter.
B—Three instrument approaches in an airplane.
C—Four instrument approaches in an airplane, or an approved airplane flight simulator or training device.

To act as PIC under IFR, a pilot must have logged, in the past 6 calendar months, at least six instrument approaches, holding procedures, and intercepting and tracking courses through the use of navigation systems in the appropriate category of aircraft for the instrument privileges sought. (PLT451, IR.I.A.K1) — 14 CFR §61.57

RTC

4016. What additional instrument approaches, if any, must you perform to meet the recent flight experience requirements for IFR operation in a helicopter?

Within the preceding 6 calendar months, you have accomplished:

One approach in a helicopter.

Two approaches in an airplane.

Two approaches in an approved airplane simulator.

A—One approach in an airplane, helicopter, or approved simulator.
B—None.
C—Five approaches in a helicopter or an approved rotorcraft simulator.

To act as PIC under IFR, a pilot must have logged, in the past 6 calendar months, at least six instrument approaches, holding procedures, and intercepting and tracking courses through the use of navigation systems, in the appropriate category of aircraft for the instrument privileges sought. (PLT442) — 14 CFR §61.57

RTC

4019. What additional flight hours within the preceding 6 calendar months are required to maintain IFR currency in a helicopter, if you already have 3 hours in an instrument simulator?

A—None, but 6 instrument approaches, holding procedures and tracking courses must be accomplished.
B—None, but three instrument approaches must also be accomplished.
C—3 hours of actual or simulated instrument time in the same type helicopter.

To act as PIC under IFR, a pilot must have logged, in the past 6 calendar months, at least six instrument approaches, holding procedures, and intercepting and tracking courses through the use of navigation systems, in the appropriate category of aircraft for the instrument privileges sought. (PLT442) — 14 CFR §61.57

Answer (B) is incorrect because six approaches (not three) must be accomplished, along with holding procedures and tracking courses. Answer (C) is incorrect because pilots are not required to fly a specified amount of flight time under IFR conditions.

RTC

4022. Which additional instrument experience is required before you may act as pilot-in-command of a helicopter under IFR?

Your instrument experience within the preceding 6 calendar months is:

2 hours and one instrument approach in an approved helicopter simulator with holding, intercepting and tracking procedures, and one instrument approach in an airplane.

A—Three instrument approaches in an airplane or helicopter.
B—1 hour of simulated instrument flight time and two instrument approaches in a helicopter.
C—Five instrument approaches in a helicopter or an approved helicopter simulator.

To act as PIC under IFR, a pilot must have logged, in the past 6 calendar months, at least six instrument approaches, holding procedures, and intercepting and tracking courses through the use of navigation systems, in the appropriate category of aircraft for the instrument privileges sought. (PLT442) — 14 CFR §61.57

Answers (A) and (B) are incorrect because a total of six approaches must be accomplished all in the aircraft category for the instrument privileges sought, and pilots are not required to fly a specified amount of flight time under IFR conditions.

Answers

4026 [C] 4016 [C] 4019 [A] 4022 [C]

Equipment Requirements

For IFR flight, the following instruments and equipment are required:

1. All VFR day and night equipment.
2. Two-way radio and navigational equipment appropriate to the ground facilities to be used.
3. Gyroscopic rate-of-turn indicator.
4. Slip-skid indicator.
5. Gyroscopic attitude indicator.
6. Gyroscopic heading indicator.
7. Sensitive altimeter.
8. Clock with sweep-second hand or digital display.
9. Generator of adequate capacity.
10. Mode C transponder with encoding altimeter (above 10,000 feet MSL in controlled airspace).
11. DME when at or above FL240 using VORs for navigation. Should the DME fail at or above 24,000 feet MSL, the PIC shall report the failure to ATC immediately and may then continue at and above 24,000 feet MSL to the next airport of intended landing.

ALL

4037. In the 48 contiguous states, excluding the airspace at or below 2,500 feet AGL, an operable coded transponder equipped with Mode C capability is required in all controlled airspace at and above

A—12,500 feet MSL.
B—10,000 feet MSL.
C—Flight level (FL) 180.

A coded transponder with altitude reporting (Mode C) is required for all operations within the 48 contiguous states and the District of Columbia above an altitude of 10,000 feet MSL. Operations in airspace below 2,500 feet AGL are excluded from this rule. (PLT161, IR.I.C.K2) — 14 CFR §91.215

Answer (A) is incorrect because 12,500 feet MSL is not an altitude which defines airspace. Answer (C) is incorrect because FL180 is the floor of Class A airspace.

ALL

4038. A coded transponder equipped with altitude reporting capability is required in all controlled airspace

A—at and above 10,000 feet MSL, excluding at and below 2,500 feet AGL.
B—at and above 2,500 feet above the surface.
C—below 10,000 feet MSL, excluding at and below 2,500 feet AGL.

A coded transponder with altitude reporting (Mode C) is required for all operations within the 48 contiguous states and the District of Columbia above an altitude of 10,000 feet MSL. Operations in airspace below 2,500 feet AGL are excluded from this rule. (PLT161, IR.I.C.K2) — 14 CFR §91.215

ALL

4051. An aircraft operated under 14 CFR Part 91 IFR is required to have which of the following?

A—Radar altimeter.
B—Dual VOR system.
C—Gyroscopic direction indicator.

For IFR flight, the following instruments and equipment are required:

1. *Instruments and equipment specified for VFR flight (and those required for night flight, if applicable).*
2. *Two-way radio communications system and navigational equipment appropriate to the ground facilities to be used.*
3. *Gyroscopic rate-of-turn indicator (with certain exceptions).*
4. *Slip-skid indicator.*
5. *Sensitive altimeter adjustable for barometric pressure.*

(continued)

Answers

4037 [B] 4038 [A] 4051 [C]

6. *A clock displaying hours, minutes and seconds with a sweep-second pointer or digital presentation.*
7. *Generator or alternator of adequate capacity.*
8. *Gyroscopic pitch and bank indicator (artificial horizon).*
9. *Gyroscopic direction indicator (heading indicator or equivalent).*

(PLT405, IR.II.C.K2) — 14 CFR §91.205

Answer (A) is incorrect because a sensitive (not radar) altimeter is required for IFR flight. Answer (B) is incorrect because, if VOR navigation is being used, only a single VOR is required.

ALL

4055. What minimum navigation equipment is required for IFR flight?

A—VOR/LOC receiver, transponder, and DME.
B—VOR receiver and, if in ARTS III environment, a coded transponder equipped for altitude reporting.
C—Navigation equipment appropriate to the ground facilities to be used.

Two-way radio communications system and navigational equipment appropriate to the ground facilities to be used is required for IFR flight. (PLT322, IR.II.B.K2a) — 14 CFR §91.205

Answer (A) is incorrect because a VOR/LOC receiver and DME are only required if that is the primary means of navigation used for this flight (and a transponder is not a navigation system). Answer (B) is incorrect because a VOR is only required if that is the primary means of navigation (and a transponder is not a navigation system).

ALL

4050. Where is DME required under IFR?

A—At or above 24,000 feet MSL if VOR navigational equipment is required.
B—In positive control airspace.
C—Above 18,000 feet MSL.

DME is required if VOR is used for navigation on flights at or above 24,000 feet MSL. (PLT202, IR.II.B.K2a) — 14 CFR §91.205

Answers (B) and (C) are incorrect because Class A airspace begins at 18,000 feet MSL and DME is required for flights at or above 24,000 feet MSL, if using VOR for navigation.

ALL

4448. What action should you take if your DME fails at FL240?

A—Advise ATC of the failure and land at the nearest available airport where repairs can be made.
B—Notify ATC that it will be necessary for you to go to a lower altitude, since your DME has failed.
C—Notify ATC of the failure and continue to the next airport of intended landing where repairs can be made.

For flight at and above 24,000 feet MSL, if VOR navigational equipment is required, no person may operate a U.S. registered civil aircraft within the 50 states, and the District of Columbia, unless that aircraft is equipped with approved DME. When DME fails at and above FL240, the PIC of the aircraft shall notify ATC immediately, and may then continue operations at and above FL240 to the next airport of intended landing at which repairs or replacement of the equipment can be made. (PLT202, IR.II.B.K2a) — 14 CFR §91.205

Answer (A) is incorrect because it is not necessary to land at the nearest airport; the pilot may continue the flight to the destination. Answer (B) is incorrect because it is not necessary to descend; the pilot may continue the flight at or above FL240.

ALL

4459. What is the procedure when the DME malfunctions at or above 24,000 feet MSL?

A—Notify ATC immediately and request an altitude below 24,000 feet.
B—Continue to your destination in VFR conditions and report the malfunction.
C—After immediately notifying ATC, you may continue to the next airport of intended landing where repairs can be made.

For flight at and above 24,000 feet MSL, if VOR navigational equipment is required, no person may operate a U.S.-registered civil aircraft within the 50 states, and the District of Columbia, unless that aircraft is equipped with approved DME. When DME fails at and above FL240, the PIC of the aircraft shall notify ATC immediately, and may then continue operations at and above FL240 to the next airport of intended landing at which repairs or replacement of the equipment can be made. (PLT202, IR.II.B.K2a) — 14 CFR §91.205

Answer (A) is incorrect because it is not necessary to descent to a lower altitude; the pilot may continue the flight at or above 24,000 feet. Answer (B) is incorrect because it is not necessary to fly only in VFR conditions; the pilot may continue the flight as normal.

Answers

4055 [C] 4050 [A] 4448 [C] 4459 [C]

ALL
4007. If the aircraft's transponder fails during flight within Class B airspace,

A—the pilot should immediately request clearance to depart the Class B airspace.
B—ATC may authorize deviation from the transponder requirement to allow aircraft to continue to the airport of ultimate destination.
C—aircraft must immediately descend below 1,200 feet AGL and proceed to destination.

ATC may authorize deviations from transponder requirements to allow an aircraft with an inoperative transponder to continue to the airport of ultimate destination, including any intermediate stops, or to proceed to a place where suitable repairs can be made. (PLT405, IR.II.B.K1c) — 14 CFR §91.215

Answer (A) is incorrect because ATC can authorize a deviation from the transponder requirement and does not require the pilot to request clearance to depart Class B airspace. Answer (C) is incorrect because a pilot may only descend after a clearance from ATC is obtained.

ALL
4438. When an aircraft is not equipped with a transponder, what requirement must be met before ATC will authorize a flight within Class B airspace?

A—A request for the proposed flight must be made to ATC at least 1 hour before the flight.
B—The proposed flight must be conducted when operating under instrument flight rules.
C—The proposed flight must be conducted in visual meteorological conditions (VMC).

ATC may authorize deviations on a continuing or individual basis for operations of aircraft without a transponder, in which case the request for a deviation must be submitted to the ATC facility having jurisdiction over the airspace concerned at least 1 hour before the proposed operation. (PLT162, IR.II.B.K1c) — 14 CFR §91.215

ALL
4043. Aircraft being operated under IFR are required to have, in addition to the equipment required for VFR and night, at least

A—distance measuring equipment.
B—dual VOR receivers.
C—a slip-skid indicator.

For IFR flight, the following instruments and equipment are required:

1. *Instruments and equipment specified for VFR flight (and those required for night flight, if applicable).*
2. *Two-way radio communications system and navigational equipment appropriate to the ground facilities to be used.*
3. *Gyroscopic rate-of-turn indicator (with certain exceptions).*
4. *Slip-skid indicator.*
5. *Sensitive altimeter adjustable for barometric pressure.*
6. *A clock displaying hours, minutes and seconds with a sweep-second pointer or digital presentation.*
7. *Generator or alternator of adequate capacity.*
8. *Gyroscopic pitch and bank indicator (artificial horizon).*
9. *Gyroscopic direction indicator (heading indicator or equivalent).*

(PLT405, IR.II.C.K2) — 14 CFR §91.205

Answers (A) and (B) are incorrect because distance measuring equipment and dual VOR receivers are not mandatory for instrument flight, although they may be helpful.

Answers
4007 [B] 4438 [A] 4043 [C]

ALL

4057. To meet the requirements for flight under IFR, an aircraft must be equipped with certain operable instruments and equipment. One of those required is

A—a clock with sweep-second pointer or digital presentation.
B—a radar altimeter.
C—a transponder with altitude reporting capability.

For IFR flight, the following instruments and equipment are required:

1. *Instruments and equipment specified for VFR flight (and those required for night flight, if applicable)*
2. *Two-way radio communications system and navigational equipment appropriate to the ground facilities to be used.*
3. *Gyroscopic rate-of-turn indicator (with certain exceptions).*
4. *Slip-skid indicator.*
5. *Sensitive altimeter adjustable for barometric pressure.*
6. *A clock displaying hours, minutes and seconds with a sweep-second pointer or digital presentation.*
7. *Generator or alternator of adequate capacity.*
8. *Gyroscopic pitch and bank indicator (artificial horizon).*
9. *Gyroscopic direction indicator (heading indicator or equivalent).*

(PLT405, IR.II.C.K2) — 14 CFR §91.205

Answer (B) is incorrect because a sensitive altimeter (not radar) is required. Answer (C) is incorrect because a transponder is not required for instrument flight, but rather for flight at specified altitudes and airspaces.

ALL

4653. (Refer to Figure 230.) What minimum navigation equipment is required to complete the VOR/DME-A procedure?

A—One VOR receiver.
B—One VOR receiver and DME.
C—Two VOR receivers and DME.

VOR/DME procedure number means that both operative VOR and DME receivers and ground equipment in normal operation are required to use the procedure. In the VOR/DME procedure, when either the VOR or DME is inoperative, the procedure is not authorized. (PLT083, IR.II.B.K2a) — Instrument Approach Procedures

ALL

4375. Your transponder is inoperative. What are the requirements for flying in Class D airspace?

A—The entry into Class D is prohibited.
B—Continue the flight as planned.
C—Pilot must immediately request priority handling to proceed to destination.

ATC may authorize deviations from transponder requirements immediately to allow an aircraft with an inoperative transponder to continue to the airport of ultimate destination, including any intermediate stops, or to proceed to a place where suitable repairs can be made. Within Class D airspace there are no transponder requirements, therefore if the aircraft's transponder fails while in Class D airspace, no deviation will be necessary. (PLT161, IR.I.C.K2) — 14 CFR §91.215

Answers (A) and (C) are incorrect because there are no transponder requirements within Class D airspace, therefore no deviation or priority handling will be necessary.

ALL

4426. In addition to a VOR receiver and two-way communications capability, which additional equipment is required for IFR operation in Class B airspace?

A—DME and an operable coded transponder having Mode C capability.
B—Standby communications receiver, DME, and coded transponder.
C—An operable coded transponder having Mode C capability.

No person may operate an aircraft within Class B airspace unless that aircraft is equipped with:

1. *For IFR operations, an operable VOR or TACAN receiver; and*
2. *For all operations, an operable two-way radio capable of communications with ATC on appropriate frequencies for that Class B airspace area and a transponder having Mode C capability.*

(PLT161, IR.I.C.K2) — 14 CFR §91.131

Answer (A) is incorrect because DME is not required, and the transponder must have Mode C capability. Answer (B) is incorrect because a standby radio receiver and DME are not required, and the transponder must have Mode C capability.

Answers

4057 [A] 4653 [B] 4375 [B] 4426 [C]

ALL

4439. Prior to operating an aircraft not equipped with a transponder in Class B airspace, a request for a deviation must be submitted to the

A—FAA Administrator at least 24 hours before the proposed operation.
B—nearest FAA General Aviation District Office 24 hours before the proposed operation.
C—controlling ATC facility at least 1 hour before the proposed flight.

ATC may authorize deviations on a continuing or individual basis for operation of an aircraft that is not equipped with a transponder. The request must be made at least one hour before the proposed operation. (PLT161, IR.I.C.K2) — 14 CFR §91.215

Answers (A) and (B) are incorrect because the ATC facility having jurisdiction over Class B airspace (not the FAA Administrator or the nearest GADO) can authorize deviations from the transponder requirements, and the request must be made at least one hour before the proposed operation.

ALL

4440. Which of the following is required equipment for operating an aircraft within Class B airspace?

A—A 4096 code transponder with automatic pressure altitude reporting equipment.
B—A VOR receiver with DME.
C—A 4096 code transponder.

No person may operate an aircraft in Class B airspace unless the aircraft is equipped with:

1. *For IFR operations, an operable VOR or TACAN receiver; and*
2. *For all operations, an operable two-way radio capable of communications with ATC on appropriate frequencies for that Class B airspace area, and a transponder with Mode C capability.*

(PLT161, IR.I.C.K2) — 14 CFR §91.131

Answer (B) is incorrect because DME is not required and a VOR receiver is only required for IFR operations. Answer (C) is incorrect because the transponder must also have Mode C capability.

ALL

4004. The use of certain portable electronic devices is prohibited on aircraft that are being operated under

A—IFR.
B—VFR.
C—DVFR.

With certain exceptions, no person may operate, nor may any operator or pilot-in-command of an aircraft allow the operation of any portable electronic device on U.S. registered civil aircraft operated in IFR conditions. (PLT415, IR.II.A.K1) — 14 CFR §91.21

ALL

4284. How can a pilot determine if a Global Positioning System (GPS) installed in an aircraft is approved for IFR enroute and IFR approaches?

A—Flight manual supplement.
B—GPS operator's manual.
C—Aircraft owner's handbook.

An appropriate airplane or rotorcraft flight manual supplement (or, for aircraft without an FAA approved flight manual, a supplemental flight manual) containing the limitations and operating procedures applicable to the equipment installed, should be provided for each installation of GPS navigation equipment for IFR approval. A flight manual supplement may be necessary for installations limited to VFR use only, depending upon the complexity of the installation and the need to identify necessary limitations and operating procedures. (PLT354, IR.VI.A.K1) — AC 20-138, page 21

RTC

4329. (Refer to Figure 59.) Unless otherwise authorized by ATC, what is the minimum equipment for navigation of helicopters on an IFR cross-country flight when in the immediate vicinity of the HUMBLE VORTAC?

A—VOR receiver, transponder with Mode C capability and two-way communications.
B—Transponder with Mode C capability and two-way communications.
C—VOR (or TACAN) and two-way communications.

At HUMBLE VORTAC the helicopter would be in Class B airspace. Unless otherwise authorized by ATC, no person may operate an aircraft within a Class B airspace unless that aircraft is equipped with an operable two-way radio, and the applicable operating transponder and automatic altitude reporting equipment. Because the question states "on an IFR cross-country flight," VOR is also required. (PLT429) — 14 CFR §91.131 and §91.205

Answers

4439 [C] 4440 [A] 4004 [A] 4284 [A] 4329 [A]

Inspection Requirements

The altimeter, transponder, static system, and encoder must be checked every 24 calendar months.

The emergency locator transmitter (ELT) batteries must be replaced when 50% of their shelf life has expired, or after 1 hour of cumulative use. Check the date on the outside of the transmitter case.

The VOR receiver(s) must be checked within 30 days and found to be within limits.

ALL

4047. Your aircraft had the static pressure system and altimeter tested and inspected on January 5, of this year, and was found to comply with FAA standards. These systems must be reinspected and approved for use in controlled airspace under IFR by

A—January 5, next year.
B—January 5, 2 years hence.
C—January 31, 2 years hence.

No person may operate an airplane or helicopter in controlled airspace under IFR unless within the preceding 24 calendar months, each static pressure system, each altimeter instrument, and each automatic pressure altitude reporting system has been tested and inspected. (PLT454, IR.II.C.K2) — 14 CFR §91.411

Answer (A) is incorrect because it is 24 months (not 12). Answer (B) is incorrect because the test is valid until the end of the month.

ALL

4048. Which checks and inspections of flight instruments or instrument systems must be accomplished before an aircraft can be flown under IFR?

A—VOR within 30 days, altimeter systems within 24 calendar months, and transponder within 24 calendar months.
B—ELT test within 30 days, altimeter systems within 12 calendar months, and transponder within 24 calendar months.
C—VOR within 24 calendar months, transponder within 24 calendar months, and altimeter system within 12 calendar months.

No person may operate a civil aircraft under IFR using the VOR system of radio navigation unless the VOR equipment of that aircraft has been operationally checked within the preceding 30 days and was found to be within the limits of the permissible indicated bearing error.

No person may operate an airplane in controlled airspace under IFR unless within the preceding 24 calendar months, each static pressure system, each altimeter instrument, and each automatic pressure altitude reporting system has been tested and inspected. No person may use an ATC transponder unless, within the preceding 24 calendar months, that ATC transponder has been tested and inspected. (PLT508, IR.II.C.K2) — 14 CFR §91.171, §91.413 and §91.411

Answer (B) is incorrect because the altimeter must be checked every 24 (not 12) month, and ELTs are maintained in accordance with the manufacturer's requirements (only ELT batteries must be replaced on a specified time interval). Answer (C) is incorrect because VORs must be checked within 30 days (not 24 months), and altimeter systems within 24 months (not 12).

ALL

4049. An aircraft altimeter system test and inspection must be accomplished within

A—12 calendar months.
B—18 calendar months.
C—24 calendar months.

No person may operate an airplane or helicopter in controlled airspace under IFR unless the aircraft altimeter system test and inspection has been accomplished within the preceding 24 calendar months. (PLT454, IR.II.C.K2) — 14 CFR §91.411

Answers (A) and (B) are incorrect because the altimeter system must be checked every 24 calendar months (not 18 or 12).

ALL

4039. Who is responsible for determining that the altimeter system has been checked and found to meet 14 CFR Part 91 requirements for a particular instrument flight?

A—Owner.
B—Operator.
C—Pilot-in-command.

The PIC of an aircraft is directly responsible for, and is the final authority as to, the operation of that aircraft. (PLT454, IR.II.C.K2) — 14 CFR §91.3

Answers (A) and (B) are incorrect because the owner or operator is primarily responsible for maintaining the aircraft, but the PIC is responsible for determining that the aircraft is airworthy.

Answers

4047 [C] 4048 [A] 4049 [C] 4039 [C]

AIR
4036. When must an operational check on the aircraft VOR equipment be accomplished when used to operate under IFR?

A—Within the preceding 10 days or 10 hours of flight time.
B—Within the preceding 30 days or 30 hours of flight time.
C—Within the preceding 30 days.

No person may operate a civil aircraft under IFR using the VOR system of radio navigation unless the VOR equipment of that aircraft:

1. *Is maintained, checked, and inspected under an approved procedure; or*
2. *Has been operationally checked within the preceding 30 days and was found to be within the limits of the permissible indicated bearing error.*

(PLT508, IR.II.C.K2) — 14 CFR §91.171

Answer (A) is incorrect because the VOR must be checked every 30 (not 10) days. Answer (B) is incorrect because there is no requirement for regarding hours in operation.

Oxygen Requirements

Pilots are encouraged to use supplemental oxygen above 5,000 feet MSL at night. 14 CFR §91.211 stipulates that the required flight crew must use oxygen after 30 minutes at cabin pressure altitudes above 12,500 feet MSL, and at all times at cabin pressure altitudes above 14,000 feet MSL. Every occupant of the aircraft must be provided with supplemental oxygen at cabin pressure altitudes above 15,000 feet MSL.

Hypoxia is a state of oxygen deficiency, and impairs functions of the brain and other organs. Headache, drowsiness, dizziness, and euphoria are all symptoms of hypoxia. Hyperventilation, a deficiency of carbon dioxide within the body, can be the result of rapid or extra deep breathing due to emotional tension, anxiety, or fear. Symptoms will subside after the rate and depth of breathing are brought under control. Anxiety is an uneasiness over an impending or anticipated ill, or a fearful concern.

ALL
4042. If an unpressurized aircraft is operated above 12,500 feet MSL, but not more than 14,000 feet MSL, for a period of 2 hours 20 minutes, how long during that time is the minimum flightcrew required to use supplemental oxygen?

A—2 hours 20 minutes.
B—1 hour 20 minutes.
C—1 hour 50 minutes.

No person may operate a civil aircraft of U.S. registry at cabin pressure altitudes above 12,500 feet MSL up to and including 14,000 feet MSL unless the required minimum flight crew is provided with and uses supplemental oxygen for that part of the flight at those altitudes that is of more than 30 minutes duration.

Solution:

2 hours 20 minutes
– 30 minutes
1 hour 50 minutes

(PLT438, IR.II.C.K2) — 14 CFR §91.211

Answer (A) is incorrect because a pilot can fly for 30 minutes before using oxygen between these altitudes. Answer (B) is incorrect because a pilot can fly for 30 minutes (not 1 hour) before using oxygen between these altitudes.

ALL
4045. What is the maximum cabin pressure altitude at which a pilot can fly for longer than 30 minutes without using supplemental oxygen?

A—10,500 feet.
B—12,000 feet.
C—12,500 feet.

No person may operate a civil aircraft of U.S. registry at cabin pressure altitudes above 12,500 feet MSL up to and including 14,000 feet MSL unless the required minimum flight crew is provided with and uses supplemental oxygen for that part of the flight at those altitudes that is of more than 30 minutes duration. (PLT438, IR.II.C.K2) — 14 CFR §91.211

Answers (A) and (B) are incorrect because 12,500 is the highest altitude at which the pilot can fly for longer than 30 minutes without using supplemental oxygen.

Answers
4036 [C] 4042 [C] 4045 [C]

ALL

4052. What is the maximum IFR altitude you may fly in an unpressurized aircraft without providing passengers with supplemental oxygen?

A—12,500 feet.
B—14,000 feet.
C—15,000 feet.

No person may operate a civil aircraft of U.S. registry at cabin pressure altitudes above 15,000 feet MSL unless each occupant of the aircraft is provided with supplemental oxygen. (PLT438, IR.II.C.K2) — 14 CFR §91.211

Answer (A) is incorrect because between cabin pressure altitudes 12,500 feet and 14,000 feet MSL, only the flight crew must use supplemental oxygen, and only for that part of the flight more than 30 minutes duration. Answer (B) is incorrect because at cabin pressure altitudes 14,000 feet MSL and above, only the flight crew is required to use supplemental oxygen.

ALL

4053. What is the oxygen requirement for an unpressurized aircraft at 15,000 feet?

A—All occupants must use oxygen for the entire time at this altitude.
B—Crew must start using oxygen at 12,000 feet and passengers at 15,000 feet.
C—Crew must use oxygen for the entire time above 14,000 feet and passengers must be provided supplemental oxygen only above 15,000 feet.

No person may operate a civil aircraft of U.S. registry at cabin pressure altitudes above 15,000 feet MSL unless each occupant of the aircraft is provided with supplemental oxygen. (PLT438, IR.II.C.K2) — 14 CFR §91.211

Answer (A) is incorrect because all occupants must only be provided with oxygen, and crew must use oxygen above 14,000 feet MSL. Answer (B) is incorrect because the crew must begin using oxygen at cabin pressure altitudes above 14,000 feet MSL or at 12,500 feet MSL for those parts of the flight more than 30 minutes duration.

ALL

4503. (Refer to Figure 89.) What are the oxygen requirements for an IFR flight northeast-bound from Milford Municipal on V244 at the lowest appropriate altitude in an unpressurized aircraft?

A—The required minimum crew must be provided and use supplemental oxygen for that part of the flight of more than 30 minutes.
B—The required minimum crew must be provided and use supplemental oxygen for that part of the flight of more than 30 minutes, and the passengers must be provided supplemental oxygen.
C—The required minimum crew must be provided and use supplemental oxygen, and all occupants must be provided supplemental oxygen for the entire flight above 15,000 feet.

The lowest appropriate altitude northeast bound on V244 is 16,000 feet (MEA). At altitudes above 14,000 feet MSL, the minimum flight crew must be provided with and use supplemental oxygen during the entire flight time at those altitudes. At altitudes above 15,000 feet MSL, each occupant of the aircraft must be provided with supplemental oxygen. (PLT079, IR.II.C.K2) — 14 CFR §91.211

ALL

4513. (Refer to Figure 91.) What are the oxygen requirements for an IFR flight eastbound on V520 from DBS VORTAC in an unpressurized aircraft at the MEA?

A—The required minimum crew must be provided and use supplemental oxygen for that part of the flight of more than 30 minutes.
B—The required minimum crew must be provided and use supplemental oxygen for that part of the flight of more than 30 minutes, and the passengers must be provided supplemental oxygen.
C—Required crewmembers must use oxygen at all times and passengers must be provided with supplemental oxygen.

Eastbound V520 is in the bottom, center of FAA Figure 91. The MEA for V520 eastbound from DBS VORTAC is 15,300 feet; therefore the required crew must be provided with, and use, supplemental oxygen and all passengers must be provided supplemental oxygen. (PLT079, IR.II.C.K2) — 14 CFR §91.211

Answer (A) is incorrect because this implies the oxygen requirement for flights between 12,500 feet MSL and 14,000 feet MSL. Answer (B) is incorrect because the crew must use supplemental oxygen at all times above 14,000 feet MSL, and passengers must be provided with oxygen only above 15,000 feet MSL.

Answers

4052 [C] 4053 [C] 4503 [C] 4513 [C]

ALL

4809. Why is hypoxia particularly dangerous during flights with one pilot?

A—Night vision may be so impaired that the pilot cannot see other aircraft.
B—Symptoms of hypoxia may be difficult to recognize before the pilot's reactions are affected.
C—The pilot may not be able to control the aircraft even if using oxygen.

The effects of hypoxia are usually difficult to recognize, especially when they occur gradually. (PLT330, IR.II.C.K2) — AIM ¶8-1-2

Answer (A) is incorrect because hypoxia affects more than just night vision. Answer (C) is incorrect because hypoxia will not occur if oxygen is properly used.

ALL

4816. What action should be taken if hyperventilation is suspected?

A—Breathe at a slower rate by taking very deep breaths.
B—Consciously breathe at a slower rate than normal.
C—Consciously force yourself to take deep breaths and breathe at a faster rate than normal.

The symptoms of hyperventilation subside within a few minutes after the rate and depth of breathing are consciously brought back under control. The buildup of carbon dioxide in the body can be hastened by controlled breathing in and out with a paper bag held over the nose and mouth. (PLT332, IR.II.C.K2) — AIM ¶8-1-3

Answers (A) and (C) are incorrect because taking very deep breaths and breathing at a faster rate will further aggravate hyperventilation.

Logbook Requirements

Pilots are authorized to log both simulated and actual instrument time, but only for that period during which the pilot operates the aircraft solely by reference to instruments. An instrument instructor may log instrument time when instruction is given during actual instrument weather conditions. Each logbook entry must include the place and type of each instrument approach, and for each flight in simulated instrument conditions, the name of the safety pilot.

A safety pilot must occupy the other control seat when the PIC is operating the aircraft solely by reference to instruments. The safety pilot is required to be an appropriately rated pilot, but there is no requirement to have an Instrument Rating.

ALL

4008. To meet instrument experience requirements of 14 CFR §61.57(c), a pilot enters the condition of flight in the pilot logbook as simulated instrument conditions. What other qualifying information must be entered?

A—Location and type of each instrument approach completed and name of safety pilot.
B—Number and type of instrument approaches completed and route of flight.
C—Name and pilot certificate number of safety pilot and type of approaches completed.

Each instrument flight entry must include the place and type of each instrument approach completed, and the name of the safety pilot for each simulated instrument flight. (PLT442, IR.I.A.K1) — 14 CFR §61.51

Answer (B) is incorrect because the number of instrument approaches completed and the route of flight is not required in the logbook entry. Answer (C) is incorrect because the pilot certificate number of the safety pilot is not required in the logbook entry.

ALL

4010. Which flight time may be logged as instrument time when on an instrument flight plan?

A—All of the time the aircraft was not controlled by ground references.
B—Only the time you controlled the aircraft solely by reference to flight instruments.
C—Only the time you were flying in IFR weather conditions.

A pilot may log as instrument flight time only that time during which the pilot operates the aircraft solely by reference to instruments under actual or simulated instrument flight conditions. (PLT409, IR.I.A.K1) — 14 CFR §61.51

Answer (A) is incorrect because VFR-on-top can be conducted without reference to ground reference. The regulations specifically state flight must be conducted solely by reference to the instruments. Answer (C) is incorrect because flight conducted solely by reference to the instruments can be done in actual as well as simulated IFR weather conditions.

Answers

4809 [B] 4816 [B] 4008 [A] 4010 [B]

ALL

4011. What are the minimum qualifications for a person who occupies the other control seat as safety pilot during simulated instrument flight?

A—Private Pilot Certificate with appropriate category and class ratings for the aircraft.
B—Private pilot with Instrument Rating.
C—Private pilot with appropriate category, class, and instrument ratings.

No person may operate a civil aircraft in simulated instrument flight unless the other control seat is occupied by a safety pilot who possesses at least a Private Pilot Certificate with category and class ratings appropriate to the aircraft being flown. (PLT443, IR.I.A.K2) — 14 CFR §91.109

Answer (B) is incorrect because a private helicopter pilot may not act as safety pilot in an airplane. The safety pilot's certificate must have the appropriate category and class rating. Answers (B) and (C) are incorrect because a safety pilot is not required to be instrument rated.

ALL

4009. What portion of dual instruction time may a certificated instrument flight instructor log as instrument flight time?

A—All time during which the instructor acts as instrument instructor, regardless of weather conditions.
B—All time during which the instructor acts as instrument instructor in actual instrument weather conditions.
C—Only the time during which the instructor flies the aircraft by reference to instruments.

Instrument flight instructors may log as instrument flight time that time during which they act as instrument flight instructor in actual instrument weather conditions. (PLT442, IR.I.A.K2) — 14 CFR §61.51

Answers (A) and (C) are incorrect because the flight conditions must be IMC for the instructor to enter flight instruction as instrument time.

Preflight Requirements

Before beginning a flight, the PIC is required to become familiar with all available information concerning that flight. This must include:

1. Weather reports and forecasts.
2. Fuel requirements.
3. Alternatives available if the flight cannot be completed as planned.
4. Any known traffic delays.
5. Runway lengths.
6. Expected takeoff and landing distances.

ALL

4003. Before beginning any flight under IFR, the pilot-in-command must become familiar with all available information concerning that flight including:

A—all instrument approaches at the destination airport.
B—an alternate airport and adequate takeoff and landing performance at the destination airport.
C—the runway lengths at airports of intended use, and the aircraft's takeoff and landing data.

Each PIC shall, before beginning a flight, become familiar with all available information concerning that flight. This information must include:

1. *For a flight under IFR or a flight not in the vicinity of an airport, weather reports and forecasts, fuel requirements, alternatives available if the planned flight cannot be completed, and any known traffic delays of which the pilot has been advised by ATC.*
2. *For any flight, runway lengths at airports of intended use, and takeoff and landing distance information.*
3. *For civil aircraft for which an approved airplane or rotorcraft flight manual containing takeoff and landing distance data is required, the takeoff and landing distance data contained therein.*

(PLT445, IR.IV.A.K1) — 14 CFR §91.103

Answer (A) is incorrect because it is not a required preflight action to know what approaches are available (but it is a good idea to know what a pilot's options will be). Answer (B) is incorrect because listing an alternate airport is only required when the destination is forecast to have ceilings below 2,000 feet and visibility less than 3 SM.

Answers

4011 [A] 4009 [B] 4003 [C]

ALL

4033. Before beginning any flight under IFR, the pilot-in-command must become familiar with all available information concerning that flight. In addition, the pilot must

A—list an alternate airport on the flight plan and become familiar with the instrument approaches to that airport.

B—list an alternate airport on the flight plan and confirm adequate takeoff and landing performance at the destination airport.

C—be familiar with the runway lengths at airports of intended use, and the alternatives available if the flight cannot be completed.

Each PIC shall, before beginning a flight, become familiar with all available information concerning the flight. This information must include:

1. *For a flight under IFR or a flight not in the vicinity of an airport, weather reports and forecasts, fuel requirements, alternatives available if the planned flight cannot be completed, and any known traffic delays of which the pilot has been advised by ATC.*
2. *For any flight, runway lengths at airports of intended use.*
3. *For civil aircraft for which an approved airplane or rotorcraft flight manual containing takeoff and landing distance data is required, the takeoff and landing distance data contained therein.*

(PLT445, IR.IV.A.K1) — 14 CFR §91.103

Answers (A) and (B) are incorrect because listing an alternate airport is not required for all IFR flights, but only when the destination is forecast to have ceilings below 2,000 feet AGL and visibility less than 3 SM.

Airspace

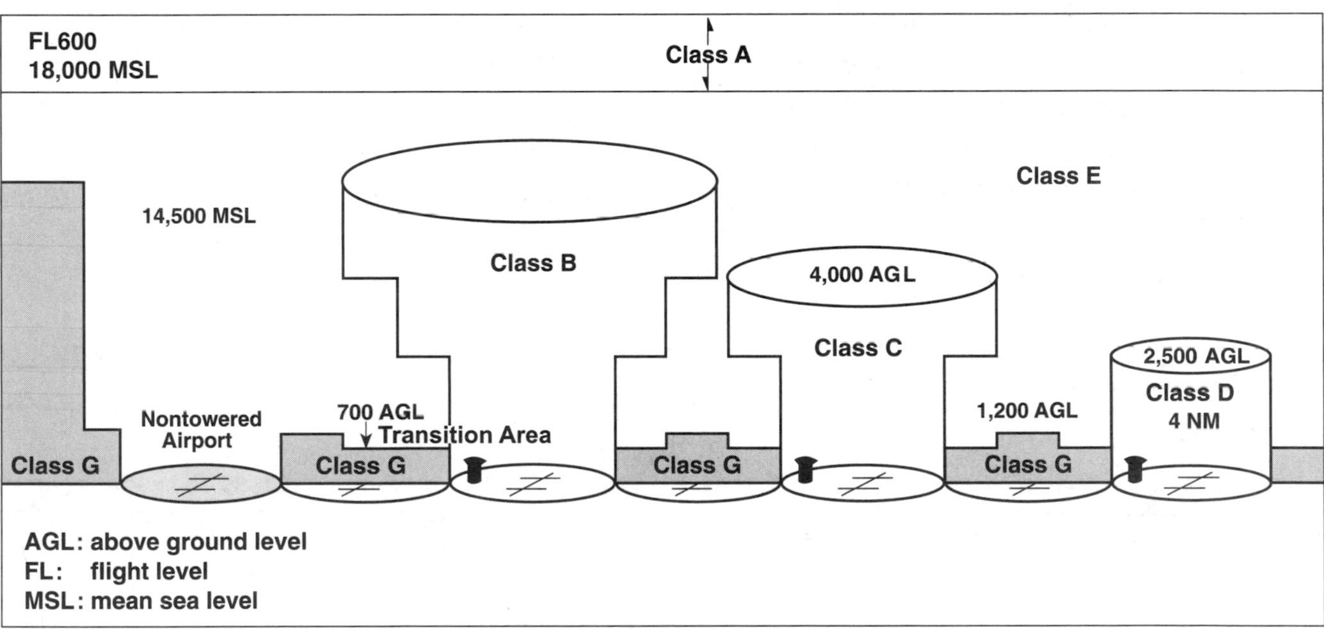

Figure 5-1

Class A—Class A airspace extends from 18,000 feet MSL to and including FL600. No VFR flight, including VFR-on-top, is authorized in Class A airspace. With altimeter set to 29.92, you fly at pressure altitude.

Class B—Class B airspace consists of controlled airspace within which all aircraft are subject to certain operating rules as well as pilot and equipment requirements. Each location will contain at least one primary airport. ATC clearance is required prior to operating within Class B airspace. In addition,

Answers

4033 [C]

each aircraft must be equipped with: two-way radio with appropriate ATC frequencies, a VOR or TACAN receiver unless flying VFR, and a Mode C transponder (there are some local exceptions when operating to non-primary airports). ATC may authorize deviations from the transponder requirements. Requests for deviation must be submitted to the controlling ATC facility at least 1 hour prior to the proposed operation. A pilot landing or taking off from an airport within Class B airspace must hold at least a Private Pilot Certificate, or meet stringent student pilot requirements. When operating to or from the primary airport, large turbine-powered airplanes must remain at or above the floor of Class B airspace.

Class C—Class C airspace is controlled airspace surrounding designated airports within which ATC provides radar vectoring and sequencing for all IFR and VFR aircraft. Two-way radio is required, and communication with ATC must be maintained while flying within Class C airspace. A Mode C transponder is required within, and up to 10,000 feet MSL over Class C airspace.

Class D—Class D airspace exists only when and where an airport traffic control tower is in operation. It usually extends for a 5 SM radius (4 NM) from the center of the airport and from the surface up to, but not including, 2,500 feet AGL. The actual dimensions may be different, as needed. ATC authorization is required for all operations within the airspace. When the control tower is not operating, the Class D airspace becomes Class E or Class G, as appropriate.

Class E—Class E airspace is controlled airspace that has not been designated Class A, B, C, or D.

Class G—Class G airspace is the portion of airspace that has not been designated Class A, B, C, D, or E airspace. It is uncontrolled; ATC has neither the authority nor the responsibility for exercising control over air traffic in these areas.

Transition Area—Class E airspace which begins at 700 feet AGL or at 1,200 feet AGL and is used as a transition to/from the terminal environment.

Alert Area—contains a high volume of pilot training or other unusual aerial activity.

Military Operations Area (MOA)—designated to separate or segregate certain military activities from IFR traffic and to let VFR traffic know where these activities are taking place.

Prohibited and Restricted Areas—denote the presence of unusual, often invisible, hazards to flight.

Warning Areas—contain the same sort of hazardous activities as those in Restricted Areas, but are located in international airspace.

ALL
4526. What is the floor of Class E airspace when designated in conjunction with an airway?

A—700 feet AGL.
B—1,200 feet AGL.
C—1,500 feet AGL.

The floor of Class E airspace when designated in conjunction with an airway is 1,200 feet AGL. (PLT161, IR.I.C.K2) — AIM ¶3-2-1

Answer (A) is incorrect because 700 feet AGL is the floor of Class E airspace when designated in conjunction with an airport which has an approved instrument approach procedure. Answer (C) is incorrect because 1,200 (not 1,500) feet AGL is the floor of Class E airspace when designated in conjunction with an airway.

ALL
4528. What is the floor of Class E airspace when designated in conjunction with an airport which has an approved IAP?

A—500 feet AGL.
B—700 feet AGL.
C—1,200 feet AGL.

Assuming Class E airspace has not been designated to the surface, the floor of Class E airspace is 700 feet AGL when designated in conjunction with an airport which has an approved instrument approach procedure. (PLT161, IR.I.C.K2) — AIM ¶3-2-6

Answer (A) is incorrect because the floor is 700 (not 500) feet. Answer (C) is incorrect because 1,200 feet AGL is the floor of Class E airspace when designated in conjunction with an airway.

Answers
4526 [B]   4528 [B]

ALL

4530. What is the maximum altitude that Class G airspace will exist? (Does not include airspace less than 1,500 feet AGL.)

A—18,000 feet MSL.
B—14,500 feet MSL.
C—14,000 feet MSL.

The maximum altitude Class G airspace exists is 14,500 feet MSL. (PLT161, IR.I.C.K2) — AIM ¶3-2-1

Answer (A) is incorrect because 18,000 feet MSL is where Class A airspace begins, not where Class G airspace ends. Answer (C) is incorrect because 14,000 feet MSL does not define an airspace.

ALL

4531. What is generally the maximum altitude for Class B airspace?

A—4,000 feet MSL.
B—10,000 feet MSL.
C—14,500 feet MSL.

The shape of Class B airspace is individually tailored to fit the specific requirements of the terrain and traffic flows. However, the vertical dimension is generally from the surface to 10,000 feet MSL. (PLT161, IR.I.C.K2) — AIM ¶3-2-3

ALL

4532. What are the normal lateral limits for Class D airspace?

A—8 NM.
B—5 NM.
C—4 NM.

The normal lateral limits for Class D airspace is 4 NM. (PLT161, IR.I.C.K2) — AIM ¶3-2-5

ALL

4533. What is the floor of Class A airspace?

A—10,000 feet MSL.
B—14,500 feet MSL.
C—18,000 feet MSL.

Class A airspace exists from 18,000 feet MSL up to and including FL600. (PLT161, IR.I.C.K2) — AIM ¶3-2-2

ALL

4434. MOAs are established to

A—prohibit all civil aircraft because of hazardous or secret activities.
B—separate certain military activities from IFR traffic.
C—restrict civil aircraft during periods of high-density training activities.

MOAs consist of airspace of defined vertical and lateral limits established for the purpose of separating certain military training activities from IFR traffic. (PLT161, IR.I.C.K2) — AIM ¶3-4-5

Answer (A) is incorrect because a Prohibited Area (not MOA) would prohibit all aircraft because of hazardous or secret activities. Answer (C) is incorrect because a Restricted Area (not MOA) would be used to restrict aircraft during period of high-density training activities.

ALL

4473. Which airspace is defined as a transition area when designated in conjunction with an airport which has a prescribed IAP?

A—The Class E airspace extending upward from 700 feet or more above the surface and terminating at the base of the overlying controlled airspace.
B—That Class D airspace extending from the surface and terminating at the base of the continental control area.
C—The Class C airspace extending from the surface to 700 or 1,200 feet AGL, where designated.

A Transition Area is Class E airspace starting from 700 feet or more above the surface when designated in conjunction with an airport for which an instrument approach procedure has been prescribed, and extends up to the overlying controlled airspace. (PLT162, IR.I.C.K2) — AIM ¶3-2-6

ALL

4529. Which altitude is the upper limit for Class A airspace?

A—14,500 feet MSL.
B—18,000 feet MSL.
C—60,000 feet MSL.

Class A airspace is that airspace from 18,000 feet MSL up to and including FL600, including that airspace overlying the waters within 12 NM of the coast of the 48 contiguous states and Alaska. (PLT161, IR.I.C.K2) — AIM ¶3-2-2

Answers

4530 [B] 4531 [B] 4532 [C] 4533 [C] 4434 [B] 4473 [A]
4529 [C]

ALL

4474. The vertical extent of the Class A airspace throughout the conterminous U.S. extends from

A—18,000 feet to and including FL450.
B—18,000 feet to and including FL600.
C—12,500 feet to and including FL600.

Class A airspace includes airspace within the continental U.S. from 18,000 feet MSL up to and including FL600. (PLT161, IR.I.C.K2) — AIM ¶3-2-2

ALL

4475. Class G airspace is that airspace where

A—ATC does not control air traffic.
B—ATC controls only IFR flights.
C—the minimum visibility for VFR flight is 3 miles.

Class G airspace is that portion of the airspace that has not been designated as Class A, B, C, D, or E airspace. If flight is conducted outside of these areas, ATC does not exercise control over that flight. (PLT161, IR.I.C.K2) — AIM ¶3-3-1

ALL

4476. What are the vertical limits of a transition area that is designated in conjunction with an airport having a prescribed IAP?

A—Surface to 700 feet AGL.
B—1,200 feet AGL to the base of the overlying controlled airspace.
C—700 feet AGL or more to the base of the overlying controlled airspace.

A Transition Area is Class E airspace starting from 700 feet or more above the surface when designated in conjunction with an airport for which an instrument approach procedure has been prescribed, and extends up to the overlying controlled airspace. (PLT161, IR.I.C.K2) — AIM ¶3-2-6

ALL

4485. Unless otherwise specified on the chart, the minimum en route altitude along a jet route is

A—18,000 feet MSL.
B—24,000 feet MSL.
C—10,000 feet MSL.

A jet route is a route designed to serve aircraft operations from 18,000 feet MSL up to, and including FL450. (PLT220, IR.I.C.K2) — AIM ¶5-3-4

ALL

4527. Which altitude is the normal upper limit for Class D airspace?

A—1,000 feet AGL.
B—2,500 feet AGL.
C—4,000 feet AGL.

Class D airspace is that airspace from the surface to 2,500 feet above the airport elevation (charted in MSL) surrounding those airports that have an operational control tower. (PLT161, IR.I.C.K2) — AIM ¶3-2-5

ALL

4539. What minimum aircraft equipment is required for operation within Class C airspace?

A—Two-way communications and Mode C transponder.
B—Two-way communications.
C—Transponder and DME.

A Mode C transponder and two-way communications are required in order to operate within Class C airspace. (PLT161, IR.I.C.K2) — AIM ¶3-2-4

Answer (B) is incorrect because a Mode C transponder is also required in Class C airspace. Answer (C) is incorrect because DME is not required, and two-way radio is required, to operate in Class C airspace.

Answers

4474 [B]	4475 [A]	4476 [C]	4485 [A]	4527 [B]	4539 [A]

Cloud Clearance and Visibility Requirements

When operating under VFR, or when operating with a VFR-on-top clearance, the pilot must maintain the required visibility and cloud clearance appropriate to the altitude flown. See Figures 5-2 and 5-3.

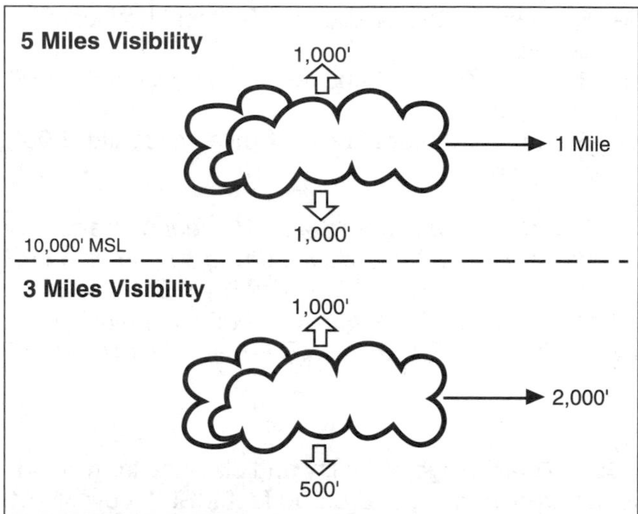

Figure 5-2. Visibility and cloud clearance

Airspace	Flight Visibility	Distance from Clouds
Class A	Not applicable	Not applicable
Class B	3 statute miles	Clear of clouds
Class C	3 statute miles	500 feet below 1,000 feet above 2,000 feet horizontal
Class D	3 statute miles	500 feet below 1,000 feet above 2,000 feet horizontal
Class E: Less than 10,000 feet MSL	3 statute miles	500 feet below 1,000 feet above 2,000 feet horizontal
At or above 10,000 feet MSL	5 statute miles	1,000 feet below 1,000 feet above 1 statute mile horizontal
Class G: **1,200 feet or less** above the surface (regardless of MSL altitude)		
Day except as provided in § 91.155(b)	1 statute mile	Clear of clouds
Night except as provided in § 91.155(b)	3 statute miles	500 feet below 1,000 feet above 2,000 feet horizontal
More than 1,200 feet above the surface **but less than 10,000**		
Day	1 statute mile	500 feet below 1,000 feet above 2,000 feet horizontal
Night	3 statute miles	500 feet below 1,000 feet above 2,000 feet horizontal
More than 1,200 feet above the surface and at or above 10,000 feet MSL	5 statute miles	1,000 feet below 1,000 feet above 1 statute mile horizontal

Figure 5-3. Basic VFR weather minimums

ALL

4518. What is the minimum flight visibility and distance from clouds for flight at 10,500 feet with a VFR-on-top clearance during daylight hours? (Class E airspace.)

A—3 SM, 1,000 feet above, 500 feet below, and 2,000 feet horizontal.
B—5 SM, 1,000 feet above, 1,000 feet below, and 1 mile horizontal.
C—5 SM, 1,000 feet above, 500 feet below, and 1 mile horizontal.

In Class E airspace, at or above 10,000 feet MSL, the VFR weather minimums are flight visibility 5 SM, and cloud clearance of 1,000 feet below, 1,000 feet above, and 1 SM horizontal. (PLT163, IR.I.B.K3) — 14 CFR §91.155

Answers
4518 [B]

ALL

4519. What is the required flight visibility and distance from clouds if you are operating in Class E airspace at 9,500 feet MSL with a VFR-on-top clearance during daylight hours?

A—3 SM, 1,000 feet above, 500 feet below, and 2,000 feet horizontal.
B—5 SM, 500 feet above, 1,000 feet below, and 2,000 feet horizontal.
C—3 SM, 500 feet above, 1,000 feet below, and 2,000 feet horizontal.

In Class E airspace, less than 10,000 feet MSL, the VFR weather minimums are flight visibility 3 SM, and cloud clearance of 500 feet below, 1,000 feet above, and 2,000 feet horizontal. (PLT163, IR.I.B.K3) — 14 CFR §91.155

ALL

4520. What is the minimum in-flight visibility and distance from clouds required for a VFR-On-Top flight at 9,500 feet MSL (above 1,200 feet AGL) during daylight hours in Class E airspace?

A—2,000 feet; 1,000 feet above; 2,000 feet horizontal; 500 feet below.
B—5 miles; 1,000 feet above; 2,000 feet horizontal; 500 feet below.
C—3 miles; 1,000 feet above; 2,000 feet horizontal; 500 feet below..

In Class E airspace, less than 10,000 feet MSL, the VFR weather minimums are flight visibility 3 SM, and cloud clearance of 500 feet below, 1,000 feet above, and 2,000 feet horizontal (regardless of whether it is day or night). (PLT163, IR.I.B.K3) — 14 CFR §91.155

ALL

4521. A flight is to be conducted in VFR-On-Top conditions at 12,500 feet MSL (above 1,200 feet AGL). What is the in-flight visibility and distance from clouds required for operation in Class E airspace during daylight hours?

A—5 miles; 1,000 feet above; 2,000 feet horizontal; 500 feet below.
B—5 miles; 1,000 feet above; 1 mile horizontal; 1,000 feet below.
C—3 miles; 1,000 feet above; 2,000 feet horizontal; 1,000 feet below.

In Class E airspace, at or above 10,000 feet MSL, the VFR weather minimums are flight visibility 5 SM, and cloud clearance of 1,000 feet below, 1,000 feet above, and 1 SM horizontal (regardless of whether it is day or night). (PLT163, IR.I.B.K3) — 14 CFR §91.155

ALL

4522. What is the minimum in-flight visibility and distance from clouds required in VFR conditions above clouds at 13,500 feet MSL (above 1,200 feet AGL) in Class G airspace during daylight hours?

A—5 miles; 1,000 feet above; 2,000 feet horizontal; 500 feet below.
B—3 miles; 1,000 feet above; 1 mile horizontal; 1,000 feet below.
C—5 miles; 1,000 feet above; 1 mile horizontal; 1,000 feet below.

In Class G airspace, more than 1,200 feet AGL and at or above 10,000 feet MSL, during daylight hours, the VFR weather minimums are flight visibility 5 SM, and cloud clearance of 1,000 feet above, 1,000 feet below, and 1 SM horizontal. (PLT163, IR.I.B.K3) — 14 CFR §91.155

ALL

4523. What in-flight visibility and distance from clouds is required for a flight at 8,500 feet MSL (above 1,200 feet AGL) in Class G airspace in VFR conditions during daylight hours?

A—1 mile; 1,000 feet above; 2,000 feet horizontal; 500 feet below.
B—3 miles; 1,000 feet above; 2,000 feet horizontal; 500 feet below.
C—5 miles; 1,000 feet above; 1 mile horizontal; 1,000 feet below.

In Class G airspace, more than 1,200 feet AGL but less than 10,000 feet MSL, during daylight hours, the VFR weather minimums are flight visibility 1 SM, and cloud clearance of 1,000 feet above, 500 feet below, and 2,000 feet horizontal. (PLT163, IR.I.B.K3) — 14 CFR §91.155

ALL

4524. What is the minimum in-flight visibility and distance from clouds required for an airplane operating less than 1,200 feet AGL in Class G airspace during daylight hours?

A—3 miles; 1,000 feet above; 2,000 feet horizontal; 500 feet below.
B—1 mile; clear of clouds.
C—1 mile; 500 feet above; 1,000 feet horizontal; 500 feet below.

In Class G airspace, less than 1,200 feet AGL, during daylight hours, the VFR weather minimums are flight visibility 1 SM, and the pilot must stay clear of clouds. (PLT163, IR.I.B.K3) — 14 CFR §91.155

Answers

4519 [A] 4520 [C] 4521 [B] 4522 [C] 4523 [A] 4524 [B]

ALL
4525. What is the minimum in-flight visibility and distance from clouds required for an airplane operating less than 1,200 feet AGL under Special VFR in Class E airspace during daylight hours?

A—1 mile; 2,000 feet above; 2,000 feet horizontal; 500 feet below.
B—3 miles; clear of clouds.
C—1 mile; clear of clouds.

Special VFR operations require the pilot to remain clear of clouds, and ground visibility must be at least 1 SM, or if ground visibility is not reported, flight visibility must be at least 1 SM. (PLT163, IR.I.B.K3) — 14 CFR §91.157

ALL
4985. If you enter VMC while on an IFR flight plan, you must

A—report VFR conditions to ATC.
B—request clearance for VFR-on-top.
C—see and avoid other traffic.

Pilots operating VFR-on-top/VFR conditions may receive traffic information from ATC on other pertinent IFR or VFR aircraft. However, when operating in VFR weather conditions, it is the pilot's responsibility to be vigilant to see and avoid other aircraft. (PLT444, IR.III.A.K1) — FAA-H-8083-15

Aircraft Accident/Incident Reporting and NOTAMs

Reports are required following an aircraft accident, if an aircraft is overdue and is believed to have been involved in an accident, or after any of a number of listed incidents. The reporting procedures are set forth in NTSB Part 830.

Notices to Air Missions (NOTAMs) provide the most current information available. They provide time-critical information on airports and changes that affect the NAS and are of concern to IFR operations. NOTAM information is classified into five categories: NOTAM (D) or distant, Flight Data Center (FDC) NOTAMs, pointer NOTAMs, Special Activity Airspace (SAA) NOTAMs, and military NOTAMs.

NOTAM (D)s are attached to hourly weather reports and are available at flight service stations (AFSS/FSS). FDC NOTAMs are issued by the National Flight Data Center and contain regulatory information, such as temporary flight restrictions or an amendment to instrument approach procedures.

Pointer NOTAMs highlight or point out another NOTAM, such as an FDC or NOTAM (D). This type of NOTAM will assist pilots in cross-referencing important information that may not be found under an airport or NAVAID identifier. Military NOTAMs pertain to U.S. Air Force, Army, Marine, and Navy NAVAIDs/airports that are part of the NAS.

SAA NOTAMs are issued when Special Activity Airspace will be active outside the published schedule times and when required by the published schedule. Pilots and other users are still responsible to check published schedule times for Special Activity Airspace as well as any NOTAMs for that airspace.

Prior to any flight, pilots should check for any NOTAMs that could affect their intended flight.

ALL
4088. Which publication covers the procedures required for aircraft accident and incident reporting responsibilities for pilots?

A—FAR Part 61.
B—FAR Part 91.
C—NTSB Part 830.

NTSB Part 830 contains regulations pertaining to notification and reporting of aircraft accidents or incidents and overdue aircraft, and preservation of aircraft wreckage, mail, cargo, and records. (PLT366, IR.I.C.K1) — NTSB Part 830

Answer (A) is incorrect because Part 61 contains regulations on certification of pilots. Answer (B) is incorrect because Part 91 contains regulations on general operating and flight rules.

Answers
4525 [C]   4985 [C]   4088 [C]

ALL

4079. Which sources of aeronautical information, when used collectively, provide the latest status of airport conditions (e.g., runway closures, runway lighting, snow conditions)?

A—Aeronautical Information Manual, aeronautical charts, and Distant (D) Notice to Air Missions (NOTAMs).
B—Chart Supplements U.S. and FDC NOTAMs
C—Chart Supplements U.S. and Distant (D) NOTAMs

The Chart Supplements U.S. provides current airport conditions known. NOTAM (D)s provide the latest status of airport conditions, for those items too recent or temporary to be published in the Chart Supplements U.S. (PLT445, IR.I.C.K1) — AIM ¶5-1-3

Answer (A) is incorrect because the AIM does not provide specific airport information, and aeronautical charts do not provide current runway conditions. Answer (B) is incorrect because FDC NOTAMs provide information on regulatory changes, not airport conditions.

ALL

4080. What is the purpose of FDC NOTAMs?

A—To provide the latest information on the status of navigation facilities to all FSS facilities for scheduled broadcasts.
B—To issue notices for all airports and navigation facilities in the shortest possible tlme.
C—To advise of changes in flight data which affect instrument approach procedure (IAP), aeronautical charts, and flight restrictions prior to normal publication.

FDC NOTAMs are regulatory in nature, and contain such things as amendments to published IAPs and other current aeronautical charts. They are also used to advertise temporary flight restrictions caused by such things as natural disasters or large-scale public events that may generate a congestion of air traffic over a site. (PLT323, IR.I.C.K1) — AIM ¶5-1-3

Answers (A) and (B) are incorrect because they describe the purpose of NOTAM (D)s.

ALL

4406. From what source can you obtain the latest FDC NOTAMs?

A—Notice to Air Missions Publications.
B—FAA AFSS/FSS.
C—Chart Supplements U.S.

FDC NOTAMs are published as needed by the National Flight Data Center and are kept on file at the FSS until published or canceled. (PLT323, IR.I.C.K1) — AIM ¶5-1-3

Answer (A) is incorrect because NTAP are only published every 28 days and the FSS may have more current data. Answer (C) is incorrect because the Chart Supplements U.S. only includes changes that are permanent and were known at the time of publication.

Answers

4079 [C]	4080 [C]	4406 [B]

Spatial Disorientation

Illusions caused by the motion-sensing system of the body are most commonly encountered during instrument flight. The system may be stimulated by motion of the aircraft or by head or body movement. It is not capable of distinguishing between centrifugal force and gravity, nor can it detect small changes in velocity. This system may also produce false sensations, such as interpreting deceleration as a turn in the opposite direction. These illusions and false sensations may lead to spatial disorientation.

The most common form of spatial disorientation is "the leans," resulting from a banked attitude not being perceived by the pilot. Abrupt correction of a banked attitude may stimulate the motion-sensing fluid of the inner ear, creating the sensation of banking in the opposite direction. The pilot may roll the aircraft back to its original attitude until he or she thinks the aircraft is straight and level, or if level flight is maintained, will still feel compelled to align his or her body with the perceived vertical.

The motion-sensing system may lead to a false perception of the true vertical. For example, in a well-coordinated turn without visual reference, the only sensation is that of the body being pressed into the seat, a sensation normally associated with a climb, and the pilot may falsely interpret it as such. On the other hand, recovering from turns reduces pressure on the seat and may lead the pilot to believe the aircraft is descending.

Spatial disorientation can happen to anyone since it is due to the normal function and limitations of the senses of balance. It only becomes dangerous when the pilot fails to suppress the false sensations and place complete reliance on the indications of the flight instruments. Eventually, as instrument flight experience is acquired, the onset of spatial disorientation lessens as trust in the flight instruments is built up.

An abrupt change from climb to straight-and-level flight can create the illusion of tumbling backwards. The disoriented pilot will push the aircraft abruptly into a nose-low attitude, possibly intensifying this illusion. This is called an inversion illusion. A rapid acceleration during takeoff can create the illusion of being in a nose-up attitude. The disoriented pilot will push the aircraft into a nose-low, or dive attitude. This is called a somatogravic illusion.

ALL

4810. The sensations which lead to spatial disorientation during instrument flight conditions

A—are frequently encountered by beginning instrument pilots, but never by pilots with moderate instrument experience.
B—occur, in most instances, during the initial period of transition from visual to instrument flight.
C—must be suppressed and complete reliance placed on the indications of the flight instruments.

The sensations which lead to illusions during instrument flight conditions are normal perceptions experienced by normal individuals. These undesirable sensations cannot be completely prevented, but they can and must be ignored or sufficiently suppressed by developing absolute reliance upon what the flight instruments are telling about the attitude of the aircraft. (PLT334, IR.IV.A.R2) — AIM ¶8-1-5

Answers (A) and (B) are incorrect because spatial disorientation can occur to anyone at all levels of experience.

ALL

4811. How can an instrument pilot best overcome spatial disorientation?

A—Rely on kinesthetic sense.
B—Use a very rapid cross-check.
C—Read and interpret the flight instruments, and act accordingly.

To overcome spatial orientation, pilots must become proficient in the use of flight instruments and rely upon them. Sight is the only reliable sense during instrument flight. (PLT334, IR.IV.A.R2) — AIM ¶8-1-5

Answer (A) is incorrect because kinesthetic senses cause spatial disorientation, and they must be ignored. Answer (B) is incorrect because it is not beneficial to use a very rapid cross-check.

Answers

4810 [C] 4811 [C]

ALL

4814. A pilot is more subject to spatial disorientation if

A—kinesthetic senses are ignored.
B—eyes are moved often in the process of cross-checking the flight instruments.
C—body signals are used to interpret flight attitude.

Illusions that lead to spatial disorientation are created by information received from our motion-sensing system located in each inner ear. In flight, the system may be stimulated by motion of the aircraft alone, or in combination with head and body movement. Sight is the only reliable sense when flying solely by reference to flight instruments. (PLT334, IR.IV.A.R2) — AIM ¶8-1-5

Answer (A) is incorrect because ignoring the kinesthetic senses is a method of overcoming spatial disorientation. Answer (B) is incorrect because proper cross-checking of the instruments is a method for overcoming spatial disorientation.

ALL

4815. Which procedure is recommended to prevent or overcome spatial disorientation?

A—Reduce head and eye movements to the extent possible.
B—Rely on the kinesthetic sense.
C—Rely on the indications of the flight instruments.

Spatial disorientation cannot be completely prevented, but it can and must be ignored or sufficiently suppressed by developing absolute reliance upon what the flight instruments are telling about the attitude of the aircraft. (PLT334, IR.IV.A.R2) — AIM ¶8-1-5

Answer (A) is incorrect because eye movement is necessary for proper instrument scan. Answer (B) is incorrect because kinesthetic senses cause spatial disorientation and must be ignored.

ALL

4813. How can an instrument pilot best overcome spatial disorientation?

A—Use a very rapid cross-check.
B—Properly interpret the flight instruments and act accordingly.
C—Avoid banking in excess of 30°.

To overcome spatial orientation, pilots must become proficient in the use of flight instruments and rely upon them. Sight is the only reliable sense during instrument flight. (PLT334, IR.IV.A.R2) — AIM ¶8-1-5

Answer (A) is incorrect because it is important to properly interpret the instruments. Answer (C) is incorrect because even in banks less than 30°, pilots can still experience spatial disorientation.

ALL

4802. Without visual aid, a pilot often interprets centrifugal force as a sensation of

A—rising or falling.
B—turning.
C—motion reversal.

A pilot often interprets centrifugal force as a sensation of rising or falling. (PLT280, IR.IV.A.R2) — FAA-H-8083-15

Answer (B) is incorrect because centrifugal force is caused by turning. Answer (C) is incorrect because is often interpreted as a vertical movement (not motion reversal).

ALL

4805. Abrupt head movement during a prolonged constant rate turn in IMC or simulated instrument conditions can cause

A—Coriolis illusion.
B—false horizon.
C—elevator illusion.

An abrupt head movement in a prolonged constant rate turn that has ceased stimulating the motion-sensing system can create the illusion of rotation or movement on an entirely different axis. The disoriented pilot will maneuver the aircraft into a dangerous attitude in an attempt to stop rotation. This most overwhelming of all illusions (called the Coriolis illusion) may be prevented by not making any sudden, extreme head movements, particularly during prolonged constant-rate turns under IFR conditions. (PLT334, IR.IV.A.R2) — AIM ¶8-1-5

Answer (B) is incorrect because a false horizon is created by sloping cloud formations, an obscured horizon, a dark scene spread with ground lights and stars, or certain geometric patterns of ground light. Answer (C) is incorrect because elevator illusion is caused by an abrupt vertical acceleration, usually an updraft.

ALL

4807. An abrupt change from climb to straight-and-level flight can create the illusion of

A—tumbling backwards.
B—a noseup attitude.
C—a descent with the wings level.

An abrupt change from climb to straight-and-level flight can create the illusion of tumbling backwards. The disoriented pilot will push the aircraft abruptly into a nose-low attitude, possibly intensifying this illusion. This is called an inversion illusion. (PLT280, IR.IV.A.R2) — AIM ¶8-1-5

Answers

4814 [C]	4815 [C]	4813 [B]	4802 [A]	4805 [A]	4807 [A]

ALL
4808. A rapid acceleration during takeoff can create the illusion of

A—spinning in the opposite direction.
B—being in a noseup attitude.
C—diving into the ground.

A rapid acceleration during takeoff can create the illusion of being in a nose-up attitude. The disoriented pilot will push the aircraft into a nose-low, or dive attitude. This is called a somatogravic illusion. (PLT280, IR.IV.A.R2) — AIM ¶8-1-5

ALL
4808-1. Tunnel vision and cyanosis are symptoms of

A—hypoxia.
B—hyperventilation.
C—carbon monoxide poisoning.

Hypoxia is a state of oxygen deficiency in the body sufficient to impair functions of the brain and other organs. The symptoms of hypoxia vary with the individual, but common symptoms include cyanosis (blue fingernails and lips), headache, decreased reaction time, impaired judgment, euphoria, visual impairment, drowsiness, lightheaded or dizzy sensation, tingling in fingers and toes, and numbness. As hypoxia worsens, the field of vision begins to narrow, and instrument interpretation can become difficult. (PLT330, IR.IV.A.R1) — FAA-H-8083-25

Optical Illusions

Various atmospheric and surface features encountered while landing may create the illusion of incorrect distance from, or height above, the landing runway. Some of the more common illusions are:

Runway width illusion—A runway that is narrower-than-usual can create the illusion that the aircraft is at a higher altitude that it actually is, causing the pilot to fly a lower than normal approach. A wider-than-usual runway can have the opposite effect.

Runway and terrain slopes illusion—An upsloping runway or upsloping terrain can create the illusion that the aircraft is at a higher altitude than it actually is, while a down-sloping runway will have the opposite effect.

Atmospheric illusion—Atmospheric haze can create the illusion of being at a greater distance from the runway. Rain on the windshield can create an illusion of greater height. The pilot who does not recognize these illusions will fly a lower approach.

False horizon illusion—Sloping cloud formations, an obscured horizon, a dark scene spread with ground lights and stars, or certain geometric patterns of ground light can create illusions of not being aligned correctly with the actual horizon. The disoriented pilot will place the aircraft in a dangerous position.

ALL
4806. A sloping cloud formation, an obscured horizon, and a dark scene spread with ground lights and stars can create an illusion known as

A—elevator illusions.
B—autokinesis.
C—false horizons.

Sloping cloud formations, an obscured horizon, a dark scene spread with ground lights and stars, or certain geometric patterns of ground light can create illusions of not being aligned correctly with the actual horizon. The disoriented pilot will place the aircraft in a dangerous position. This is called the false horizon illusion. (PLT280, IR.IV.A.R2) — AIM ¶8-1-5

Answer (A) is incorrect because elevator illusion is caused by an abrupt vertical acceleration, usually an updraft, giving the sensation of being in a climb. Answer (B) is incorrect because autokinesis is caused by staring at a static light for many seconds, which creates the illusion the light is moving.

Answers

4808 [B] 4808-1 [A] 4806 [C]

ALL
4803. Due to visual illusion, when landing on a narrower-than-usual runway, the aircraft will appear to be

A—higher than actual, leading to a lower-than-normal approach.
B—lower than actual, leading to a higher-than-normal approach.
C—higher than actual, leading to a higher-than-normal approach.

A narrower-than-usual runway can create the illusion that the aircraft is at a higher altitude than it actually is. The pilot who does not recognize this illusion will fly a lower approach, with the risk of striking objects along the approach path or landing short. (PLT280, IR.IV.A.R2) — AIM ¶8-1-5

Answer (B) is incorrect because wider (not narrower) runways give a lower-than-actual illusion. Answer (C) is incorrect because a narrower runway appears to be higher than actual, which leads to a lower (not higher) than normal approach.

ALL
4804. What visual illusion creates the same effect as a narrower-than-usual runway?

A—An upsloping runway.
B—A wider-than-usual runway.
C—A downsloping runway.

An upsloping runway, upsloping terrain, or both can create the illusion that the aircraft is at a higher altitude than it actually is. The pilot who does not recognize this illusion will fly a lower approach. This is the same effect as a narrower-than-usual runway. (PLT280, IR.IV.A.R2) — AIM ¶8-1-5

Answers (B) and (C) are incorrect because wider-than-usual runways and downsloping runways create an illusion that the aircraft is lower than it is. The narrower-than-usual runway creates an illusion that the aircraft is higher than it is.

ALL
4819. What effect does haze have on the ability to see traffic or terrain features during flight?

A—Haze causes the eyes to focus at infinity, making terrain features harder to see.
B—The eyes tend to overwork in haze and do not detect relative movement easily.
C—Haze creates the illusion of being a greater distance than actual from the runway, and causes pilots to fly a lower approach.

Atmospheric haze causes the illusion of being a greater distance from the runway. The pilot who does not recognize this illusion will fly a lower approach. (PLT280, IR.IV.A.R2) — AIM ¶8-1-5

Cockpit Lighting and Scanning

Dark adaptation, during which vision becomes more sensitive to light, can be achieved to a moderate degree within 20 minutes under dim red cockpit lighting. After that, any exposure to white light, even for a few seconds, will seriously impair night vision.

Only a very small portion of the eye has the ability to send clear messages to the brain. Because the eyes focus on only a narrow viewing area, effective scanning is accomplished with a series of short, regularly spaced eye movements that bring successive areas of the sky into the central viewing area of the retina. Each movement should not exceed 10°, and each area should be observed for at least 1 second to enable the eyes to detect a moving or contrasting object.

Pilots should execute gentle banks, at a frequency which permits continuous visual scanning of the airspace about them, during climbs and descents in flight conditions which permit visual detection of other traffic.

Answers

4803 [A] 4804 [A] 4819 [C]

ALL

4812. Which statement is correct regarding the use of cockpit lighting for night flight?

A—Reducing the lighting intensity to a minimum level will eliminate blind spots.
B—The use of regular white light, such as a flashlight, will impair night adaptation.
C—Coloration shown on maps is least affected by the use of direct red lighting.

In darkness, vision becomes more sensitive to light through a process called dark adaptation. Since any degree of dark adaptation is lost within a few seconds of viewing a bright light, the pilot should avoid it or close one eye when using white light. (PLT333, IR.IV.A.K1) — AIM ¶8-1-6

Answer (A) is incorrect because reducing the lighting intensity to a minimum level will be insufficient to read charts, instruments, etc. Answer (C) is incorrect because red lighting distorts colors on maps.

ALL

4817. Which use of cockpit lighting is correct for night flight?

A—Reducing the interior lighting intensity to a minimum level.
B—The use of regular white light, such as a flashlight, will not impair night adaptation.
C—Coloration shown on maps is least affected by the use of direct red lighting.

In darkness, vision becomes more sensitive to light through a process called dark adaptation. Since any degree of dark adaptation is lost within a few seconds of viewing a bright light, the pilot should avoid it or close one eye when using bright light. (PLT333, IR.IV.A.K1) — AIM ¶8-1-6

Answer (B) is incorrect because white light will impair night vision within a few seconds. Answer (C) is incorrect because red light significantly distorts color.

ALL

4818. Which technique should a pilot use to scan for traffic to the right and left during straight-and-level flight?

A—Systematically focus on different segments of the sky for short intervals.
B—Concentrate on relative movement detected in the peripheral vision area.
C—Continuous sweeping of the windshield from right to left.

While the eyes can observe an approximate 200° arc of the horizon at one glance, only a very small center area called the fovea, in the rear of the eye, has the ability to send clear, sharply focused messages to the brain. Because the eyes can focus only on this narrow viewing area, effective scanning is accomplished with a series of short, regularly spaced eye movements that bring successive areas of the sky into the central visual field. Each movement should not exceed 10°, and each area should be observed for at least one second to enable detection. (PLT194, IR.IV.A.K1) — AIM ¶8-1-6

ALL

4993. Having appropriate instrument lighting will

A—enable better recognition of outside references.
B—make a proper instrument scan difficult.
C—result in unnecessary eye strain.

Flight deck lighting should be kept as low as possible so that the light does not monopolize night vision. This includes readjustment of instrument lights and orientation to allow for better night adaptation to see outside references. (PLT333, IR.IV.A.R1) — FAA-H-8083-25

ALL

4634. What is expected of you as pilot on an IFR flight plan if you are descending or climbing in VFR conditions?

A—If on an airway, climb or descend to the right of the centerline.
B—Advise ATC you are in visual conditions and will remain a short distance to the right of the centerline while climbing.
C—Execute gentle banks, left and right, at a frequency which permits continuous visual scanning of the airspace about you.

During climbs and descents in flight conditions which permit visual detection of other traffic, pilots should execute gentle banks left and right at a frequency which permits continuous visual scanning of the airspace about them. (PLT194, IR.V.B.K1) — AIM ¶4-4-15

Answers (A) and (B) are incorrect because the pilot is required to remain on the centerline (not to the right) of the airway unless in VFR conditions and maneuvering to avoid other traffic, and the pilot is not required to advise ATC when in visual conditions.

Answers

4812 [B]	4817 [A]	4818 [A]	4993 [A]	4634 [C]

Altitude and Course Requirements

During IFR operations in mountainous terrain, pilots may not operate below 2,000 feet above the highest obstacle, within a horizontal distance of 4 NM from the course to be flown (except for takeoff or landing). During IFR operations in nonmountainous terrain, pilots may not operate below 1,000 feet above the highest obstacle.

VFR cruising altitudes are based on magnetic course.

ALL

4428. Unless otherwise prescribed, what is the rule regarding altitude and course to be maintained during an IFR off-airways flight over mountainous terrain?

A—1,000 feet above the highest obstacle within a horizontal distance of 4 NM of course.
B—2,000 feet above the highest obstacle within a horizontal distance of 5 NM of course.
C—2,000 feet above the highest obstacle within 4 NM of course.

In the case of operations over an area designated as mountainous terrain, no person may operate an aircraft under IFR (except when necessary for takeoff or landing) below an altitude of 2,000 feet above the highest obstacle, within a horizontal distance of 4 NM from the course to be flown. (PLT430, IR.I.C.K2) — 14 CFR §91.177

ALL

4425. Unless otherwise prescribed, what is the rule regarding altitude and course to be maintained during an off-airways IFR flight over nonmountainous terrain?

A—1,000 feet above the highest obstacle within 4 NM of course.
B—2,000 feet above the highest obstacle within 5 SM of course.
C—1,000 feet above the highest obstacle within 3 NM of course.

Except when necessary for takeoff or landing, or unless otherwise authorized by the Administrator, no person may operate an aircraft in nonmountainous terrain under IFR below an altitude 1,000 feet above the highest obstacle within a horizontal distance of 4 NM from the course to be flown (4.6 SM). (PLT430, IR.I.C.K2) — 14 CFR §91.177

ALL

4441. Which procedure is recommended while climbing to an assigned altitude on the airway?

A—Climb on the centerline of the airway except when maneuvering to avoid other air traffic in VFR conditions.
B—Climb slightly on the right side of the airway when in VFR conditions.
C—Climb far enough to the right side of the airway to avoid climbing or descending traffic coming from the opposite direction if in VFR conditions.

Unless otherwise authorized by ATC, no person may operate an aircraft within controlled airspace under IFR except as follows:

1. *On a federal airway, along the centerline of that airway.*
2. *On any other route, along the direct course between the navigational aids or fixes defining that route.*

However, this section does not prohibit maneuvering the aircraft to pass well clear of other air traffic or maneuvering the aircraft in VFR conditions to clear the intended flight path both before and during climb or descent. (PLT414, IR.V.B.K1) — 14 CFR §91.181

Answers (B) and (C) are incorrect because the pilot is required to maintain the centerline (not on the right side) while operating on a federal airway.

ALL

4541. In the case of operations over an area designated as a mountainous area where no other minimum altitude is prescribed, no person may operate an aircraft under IFR below an altitude of

A—500 feet above the highest obstacle.
B—1,000 feet above the highest obstacle.
C—2,000 feet above the highest obstacle.

Except when necessary for takeoff or landing, or unless otherwise authorized by the Administrator, no person may operate an aircraft in an area designated as a mountainous area under IFR below an altitude of 2,000 feet above the highest obstacle within a horizontal distance of 4 NM from the course to be flown. (PLT430, IR.I.C.K2) — 14 CFR §91.177

Answers

4428 [C]	4425 [A]	4441 [A]	4541 [C]

ALL

4543. If, while in Class E airspace, a clearance is received to "maintain VFR conditions on top," the pilot should maintain a VFR cruising altitude based on the direction of the

A—true course.
B—magnetic heading.
C—magnetic course.

Each person operating an aircraft under the ATC clearance "VFR conditions on-top" shall maintain an altitude or flight level appropriate to the magnetic course. (PLT430, IR.I.C.K2) — 14 CFR §91.159

ALL

4006. Except when necessary for takeoff or landing or unless otherwise authorized by the Administrator, the minimum altitude for IFR flight is

A—3,000 feet over all terrain.
B—3,000 feet over designated mountainous terrain; 2,000 feet over terrain elsewhere.
C—2,000 feet above the highest obstacle over designated mountainous terrain; 1,000 feet above the highest obstacle over terrain elsewhere.

Except when necessary for takeoff or landing, no person may operate an aircraft under IFR below an altitude of 2,000 feet above the highest obstacle within 4 NM for mountainous areas, and in any other case, 1,000 feet above. (PLT430, IR.I.C.K2) — 14 CFR §91.177

Answer (A) is incorrect because the minimum IFR altitude is not 3,000 feet over all terrain, but 2,000 feet while over mountainous terrain, and 1,000 feet over terrain elsewhere. Answer (B) is incorrect because the minimum IFR altitude while over mountainous terrain is 2,000 feet and 1,000 feet over terrain elsewhere.

ALL

4765. In the case of operations over an area designated as a mountainous area, no person may operate an aircraft under IFR below 2,000 feet above the highest obstacle within a horizontal distance of

A—3 SM from the course flown.
B—4 SM from the course flown.
C—4 NM from the course flown.

Except when necessary for takeoff or landing, or unless otherwise authorized by the Administrator, no person may operate an aircraft in a designated mountainous area under IFR below an altitude of 2,000 feet above the highest obstacle within a horizontal distance of 4 nautical miles from the course to be flown. (PLT430, IR.I.C.K2) — 14 CFR §91.177

Answers

4543 [C]	4006 [C]	4765 [C]

Communication Reports

The PIC of an aircraft operating under IFR in controlled airspace is required to report the following items as soon as possible:

1. Any unforecast weather.
2. The time and altitude passing each designated reporting point (including fixes used to define direct routes) except when in radar contact. (Resume normal position reporting when advised "radar contact lost" or "radar service terminated.")
3. Any other information relating to the safety of flight.

The pilot should also advise ATC immediately should any of the following malfunctions occur in flight:

1. Loss of VOR or ADF capability.
2. Complete or partial panel of ILS receiver capability.
3. Impairment of air/ground communications capability.

Some additional reports should be made without specific request from ATC. These include:

1. When an approach has been missed.
2. When leaving a previously assigned altitude for a newly assigned altitude.
3. When unable to climb or descend at a rate of at least 500 fpm.
4. Changing altitude when operating VFR-on-top.
5. Change in average true airspeed of ±5 percent or 10 knots (whichever is greater) from that filed in the flight plan.
6. Time and altitude when reaching a holding fix or clearance limit.
7. When leaving holding.

Additionally, when not in radar contact, a report should be made upon leaving the final approach fix inbound on final, and should a previously submitted estimate be made more than 3 minutes in error, a corrected estimate should be given to ATC.

ALL

4456. Which report should be made to ATC without a specific request when not in radar contact?

A—Entering instrument meteorological conditions.
B—When leaving final approach fix inbound on final approach.
C—Correcting an ETA, any time a previous ETA is in error in excess of 2 minutes.

The following reports should be made to ATC or FSS facilities without a specific ATC request when not in radar contact:

1. *When leaving final approach fix inbound on final approach.*
2. *A corrected estimate at anytime it becomes apparent that an estimate previously submitted is in error in excess of 3 minutes.*

(PLT171, IR.III.A.K1) — AIM ¶5-3-3

Answer (A) is incorrect because a report should be made to the ATC controller any time (not only in IMC) when leaving any assigned holding fix or point. Answer (C) is incorrect because a report should be made to the ATC controller any time a previous ETA is in error in excess of 3 minutes.

Answers

4456 [B]

ALL

4071. While on an IFR flight plan, you should notify ATC of a variation in speed when

A—ground speed changes more than 5 knots.
B—average TAS changes 10 knots or 5 percent.
C—ground speed changes by 10 mph or more.

The pilot of an IFR flight should report changes in the average true airspeed (at cruising altitude) of 5 percent or 10 knots (whichever is greater) from that filed in the flight plan. (PLT440, IR.V.B.K2) — AIM ¶5-3-3

Answers (A) and (C) are incorrect because the pilot should notify ATC if the true airspeed (not ground speed) changes more than 10 knots (not 5 knots or 10 mph).

ALL

4379. What does declaring "minimum fuel" to ATC imply?

A—Traffic priority is needed to the destination airport.
B—Emergency handling is required to the nearest useable airport.
C—Merely an advisory that indicates an emergency situation is possible should any undue delay occur.

"Minimum fuel" indicates that an aircraft's fuel supply has reached a state where, upon reaching the destination, it can accept little or no delay. This is not an emergency situation, but merely indicates an emergency situation is possible should any undue delay occur. (PLT318, IR.III.A.K1) — AIM ¶5-5-15

Answers (A) and (B) are incorrect because priority may be issued only when declaring an emergency, and minimum fuel is not an emergency.

ALL

4380. When ATC has not imposed any climb or descent restrictions and aircraft are within 1,000 feet of assigned altitude, pilots should attempt to both climb and descend at a rate of between

A—500 feet per minute and 1,000 feet per minute.
B—500 feet per minute and 1,500 feet per minute.
C—1,000 feet per minute and 2,000 feet per minute.

When ATC has not used the phrase "at pilot's discretion" nor imposed any climb or descent restrictions, pilots should initiate climb or descent promptly on acknowledgment of the clearance. Descend or climb at an optimum rate consistent with the operating characteristics of the aircraft to 1,000 feet above or below the assigned altitude, and then attempt to descend or climb at a rate of between 500 and 1,500 fpm until the assigned altitude is reached. (PLT133, IR.III.A.K1) — AIM ¶4-4-10

ALL

4078. For IFR planning purposes, what are the compulsory reporting points when using VOR/DME or VORTAC fixes to define a direct route not on established airways?

A—Fixes selected to define the route.
B—There are no compulsory reporting points unless advised by ATC.
C—At the changeover points.

When a pilot is on a direct flight, pilots shall report over each reporting point used in the flight plan to define the route of flight. (PLT322, IR.III.A.K1) — AIM ¶5-3-2

Answer (B) is incorrect because the compulsory points on a direct flight are those fixes used to define the route. Answer (C) is incorrect because some direct flights do not require changeover points; for example, flights using GPS.

ALL

4460. What action should you take if your No. 1 VOR receiver malfunctions while operating in controlled airspace under IFR? Your aircraft is equipped with two VOR receivers. The No. 1 receiver has VOR/Localizer/Glide Slope capability, and the No. 2 has only VOR/Localizer capability.

A—Report the malfunction immediately to ATC.
B—Continue the flight as cleared; no report is required.
C—Continue the approach and request a VOR or NDB approach.

The PIC of each aircraft operated in controlled airspace under IFR shall report as soon as practical to ATC any malfunctions of navigational, approach, or communication equipment occurring in flight. (PLT391, IR.V.A.S7) — 14 CFR §91.187

Answer (B) is incorrect because a report must be made to ATC regarding the situation. Answer (C) is incorrect because ATC will know a VOR or NDB approach will be necessary if you report the ILS receiver inoperative.

Answers

4071 [B]	4379 [C]	4380 [B]	4078 [A]	4460 [A]

ALL

4381. During an IFR flight in IMC, a distress condition is encountered (fire, mechanical, or structural failure). The pilot should

A—not hesitate to declare an emergency and obtain an amended clearance.
B—wait until the situation is immediately perilous before declaring an emergency.
C—contact ATC and advise that an urgency condition exists and request priority consideration.

Pilots should not hesitate to declare an emergency when faced with a distress condition, such as fire, mechanical failure, or structural damage. A distress condition is defined as being threatened by serious and/or imminent danger and requiring immediate assistance. (PLT208, IR.VII.A.K1) — AIM ¶6-1-2

Answer (B) is incorrect because a distress condition is perilous and an emergency condition should be declared. Answer (C) is incorrect because the pilot should contact ATC and advise that an emergency condition exists and obtain an amended clearance.

ALL

4605. During the en route phase of an IFR flight, the pilot is advised "Radar service terminated." What action is appropriate?

A—Set transponder to code 1200.
B—Resume normal position reporting.
C—Activate the IDENT feature of the transponder to re-establish radar contact.

Pilots should resume normal position reporting when ATC advises "radar contact lost," or "radar service terminated." (PLT044, IR.III.A.K3) — AIM ¶5-3-2

Answer (A) is incorrect because squawking 1200 is for VFR flights only. Answer (C) is incorrect because the IDENT feature of the transponder should only be used upon request by ATC.

ALL

4605-1. A pilot or crew may not perform any activities except those required to safely operate the aircraft during

A—the preflight walk-around of the aircraft.
B—fueling of the aircraft.
C—critical phases of flight.

Commonly known as the sterile cockpit rule, regulations require 121 and 135 flight crewmembers to refrain from nonessential activities during critical phases of flight. Critical phases of flight are all ground operations involving taxi, takeoff, and landing, and all other flight operations below 10,000 feet except cruise flight. Nonessential activities include eating, reading a newspaper, and chatting. While the regulation grew out of accidents in the airline industry, it holds true for the entire aviation community. Pilots can improve flight safety significantly by reducing distractions during critical phases of flight. (PLT440, IR.V.B.K2) — FAA-H-8083-16

ALL

4605-2. The "sterile cockpit" rule is good practice not just for airline pilots but for all pilots because

A—keeping the cockpit neat and clean keeps you better organized.
B—it greatly reduces distractions during critical phases of flight.
C—it keeps radio transmissions to a minimum.

Commonly known as the sterile cockpit rule, regulations require 121 and 135 flight crewmembers to refrain from nonessential activities during critical phases of flight. Critical phases of flight are all ground operations involving taxi, takeoff, and landing, and all other flight operations below 10,000 feet except cruise flight. Nonessential activities include eating, reading a newspaper, and chatting. While the regulation grew out of accidents in the airline industry, it holds true for the entire aviation community. Pilots can improve flight safety significantly by reducing distractions during critical phases of flight. (PLT440, IR.V.B.K2) — FAA-H-8083-16

Answers

4381 [A]   4605 [B]   4605-1 [C]   4605-2 [B]

Lost Communication Requirements

If unable to contact ATC on a newly assigned frequency, the pilot should go back to the previous frequency. If contact is lost on that frequency also, the pilot should attempt to establish contact with the nearest FSS. If it becomes apparent that two-way communication has been lost, the pilot should change the transponder to code 7600.

If communications are lost in VFR conditions, the pilot should remain in VFR and land as soon as practicable.

Should the communication failure occur in IFR conditions, the pilot should proceed to the destination by:

1. *Route:*
   a. The route assigned in the last ATC clearance;
   b. If being radar vectored, by the direct route to the fix, route, or airway specified in the vector clearance;
   c. If no route has been assigned, by the route the pilot was told to expect; or
   d. In the absence of any of the above, by the route filed in the flight plan.
2. *Altitude*—at the highest of the following altitudes for the route segment being flown:
   a. The altitude assigned in the last clearance received;
   b. The altitude ATC has advised may be expected in a further clearance; or
   c. The minimum enroute altitude (MEA).

If given holding instructions or a clearance limit, the pilot should leave that fix at the expect further clearance (EFC) time given. If holding is necessary in the terminal area, it should be depicted, or, if none is depicted, at the initial approach fix (IAF). If no holding was required en route, the pilot should proceed to the terminal area without delay and hold, maintaining the enroute altitude.

Descent for approach may begin upon arrival at the IAF, but not before the ETA shown on the flight plan, as amended with ATC. If an expect approach clearance (EAC) time has been received, begin descent for the approach at that time.

ALL

4462. During an IFR flight in IMC, you enter a holding pattern (at a fix that is not the same as the approach fix) with an EFC time of 1530. At 1520 you experience complete two-way communications failure. Which procedure should you follow to execute the approach to a landing?

A—Depart the holding fix to arrive at the approach fix as close as possible to the EFC time and complete the approach.

B—Depart the holding fix at the EFC time and complete the approach.

C—Depart the holding fix at the earliest of the flight planned ETA or the EFC time and complete the approach.

If the clearance limit is not a fix from which an approach begins, leave the clearance limit at the EFC time if one has been received. Then proceed to a fix from which an approach begins and commence descent, or descent and approach, as close as possible to the ETA as calculated from the filed, or amended (with ATC), estimated time en route. (PLT391, IR.VII.A.K1) — 14 CFR §91.185

Answer (A) is incorrect because the pilot is to leave for (not arrive at) the approach fix at the EFC time. Answer (C) is incorrect because the EFC time takes priority over the flight plan ETA.

Answers

4462 [B]

ALL

4463. Which procedure should you follow if you experience two-way communications failure while holding at a holding fix with an EFC time? (The holding fix is not the same as the approach fix.)

A—Depart the holding fix to arrive at the approach fix as close as possible to the EFC time.
B—Depart the holding fix at the EFC time.
C—Proceed immediately to the approach fix and hold until EFC.

If the clearance limit is not a fix from which an approach begins, leave the clearance limit at the EFC time if one has been received. Then proceed to a fix from which an approach begins and commence descent, or descent and approach, as close as possible to the ETA as calculated from the filed, or amended (with ATC), estimated time en route. (PLT391, IR.VII.A.K1) — 14 CFR §91.185

Answer (A) is incorrect because the pilot is to leave for (not arrive at) the approach fix at the EFC time. Answer (C) is incorrect because the pilot should not leave the holding fix for the approach fix until the EFC time.

ALL

4464. You are in IMC and have two-way radio communications failure. If you do not exercise emergency authority, what procedure are you expected to follow?

A—Set transponder to code 7600, continue flight on assigned route, and fly at the last assigned altitude or the MEA, whichever is higher.
B—Set transponder to code 7700 for 1 minute, then to 7600, and fly to an area with VFR weather conditions.
C—Set transponder to 7700 and fly to an area where you can let down in VFR conditions.

If an aircraft with a coded radar beacon transponder experiences a loss of two-way radio capability, the pilot should set transponder to code 7600. During a flight in IMC, the pilot should continue flight on the assigned route and fly at the last assigned altitude or the MEA, whichever is higher. (PLT391, IR.VII.A.K1) — AIM ¶6-4-2

Answers (B) and (C) are incorrect because code 7700 is not used in lost communication procedures, and if VFR conditions prevail, the flight should continue and land as soon as practicable.

ALL

4465. Which procedure should you follow if, during an IFR flight in VFR conditions, you have two-way radio communications failure?

A—Continue the flight under VFR and land as soon as practicable.
B—Continue the flight at assigned altitude and route, start approach at your ETA, or, if late, start approach upon arrival.
C—Land at the nearest airport that has VFR conditions.

If the failure occurs in VFR conditions, or if VFR conditions are encountered after the failure, the pilot shall continue the flight under VFR and land as soon as practicable. (PLT391, IR.VII.A.K1) — AIM ¶6-4-1

Answer (B) is incorrect because it only applies if in IMC. Answer (C) is incorrect because the pilot is may continue the flight and land as soon as practicable.

ALL

4466. What altitude and route should be used if you are flying in IMC and have two-way radio communications failure?

A—Continue on the route specified in your clearance, fly at an altitude that is the highest of last assigned altitude, altitude ATC has informed you to expect, or the MEA.
B—Fly direct to an area that has been forecast to have VFR conditions, fly at an altitude that is at least 1,000 feet above the highest obstacles along the route.
C—Descend to MEA and, if clear of clouds, proceed to the nearest appropriate airport. If not clear of clouds, maintain the highest of the MEA's along the clearance route.

If two-way radio communications are lost in IMC, the flight should be continued via the last assigned route by ATC, the route ATC advised or may be expected to advise, or by the flight plan. The altitude to be used is the highest of the altitude assigned in the last ATC clearance, the MEA, or the flight level ATC may be expected to assign. (PLT391, IR.VII.A.K1) — AIM ¶6-4-1

Answer (B) is incorrect because the pilot should maintain the assigned route. Answer (C) is incorrect because the highest altitude assigned, expected to be assigned, or the MEA should be used.

Answers

4463 [B] 4464 [A] 4465 [A] 4466 [A]

ALL

4505. In the event of two way radio communications failure while operating on an IFR clearance in VFR conditions the pilot should continue

A—by the route assigned in the last ATC clearance received.
B—the flight under VFR and land as soon as practical.
C—the flight by the most direct route to the fix specified in the last clearance.

If a two-way radio communication failure occurs in VFR conditions, or if VFR conditions are encountered after the failure, each pilot shall continue the flight under VFR and land as soon as practicable. (PLT391, IR.VII.A.K1) — 14 CFR §91.185

ALL

4500. (Refer to Figure 87.) While holding at the 10 DME fix east of LCH for an ILS approach to RWY 15 at Lake Charles Muni airport, ATC advises you to expect clearance for the approach at 1015. At 1000 you experience two-way radio communications failure. Which procedure should be followed?

A—Squawk 7600 and listen on the LOM frequency for instructions from ATC. If no instructions are received, start your approach at 1015.
B—Squawk 7700 for 1 minute, then 7600. After 1 minute, descend to the minimum final approach fix altitude. Start your approach at 1015.
C—Squawk 7600; plan to begin your approach at 1015.

If a pilot experiences a loss of two-way radio capability while on an IFR flight, the pilot should:

1. *Adjust the transponder to code 7600.*
2. *Leave the clearance limit to begin the approach as close as possible to the EFC time.*

(PLT391, IR.VII.A.K1) — AIM ¶6-4-1

Answer (A) is incorrect because there is no LOM for Lake Charles Muni Airport. Answer (B) is incorrect because 7700 should be squawked in an emergency situation, and altitude should be maintained until the EFC time (the time at which you begin the approach).

ALL

4374. While flying on an IFR flight plan, you experience two-way communications radio failure while in VFR conditions. In this situation, you should continue your flight under

A—VFR and land as soon as practicable.
B—VFR and proceed to your flight plan destination.
C—IFR and maintain the last assigned route and altitude to your flight plan destination.

If the failure occurs in VFR conditions, or if VFR conditions are encountered after the failure, each pilot shall continue the flight under VFR and land as soon as practicable. (PLT391, IR.VII.A.K1) — AIM ¶6-4-1

Answers

4505 [B] 4500 [C] 4374 [A]

Chapter 6
Departure

Flight Plan Requirements

Prior to operating an aircraft in controlled airspace under IFR, the PIC must have filed an IFR flight plan and received an appropriate ATC clearance. Become familiar with the FAA International Flight Plan form, used for both domestic and international operations under VFR or IFR (see Figure 6-1 on the next page). Review AIM paragraph 5-1-9 to understand how to complete the flight plan in preparation for future FAA Knowledge Exam testing on this subject. Note: For domestic IFR flights entirely in U.S. domestic airspace you may still file using FAA Form 7233-1, however filers utilizing this form may not be eligible for assignment of RNAV, SID and STAR procedures.

The most current en route and destination flight information for planning an instrument flight should be obtained from an FSS.

IFR flight plans should be filed with the FSS at least 30 minutes prior to the estimated time of departure in order to preclude any delay in receiving a clearance from ATC when ready to depart. If a pilot wishes to file an IFR flight plan while airborne, the pilot should contact the nearest FSS, submit the request, and remain VFR until a clearance is received.

Once a pilot elects to proceed to a selected alternate airport, that airport becomes the destination. The landing minimums for the new destination are the minimums that are published for the procedure to be flown.

ALL

4062. When is an IFR flight plan required?

A—When less than VFR conditions exist in either Class E or Class G airspace and in Class A airspace.

B—In all Class E airspace when conditions are below VFR, in Class A airspace, and in defense zone airspace.

C—In Class E airspace when IMC exists or in Class A airspace.

No person may operate an aircraft in controlled airspace under IFR unless the person has:

1. *Filed an IFR flight plan; and*
2. *Received an appropriate ATC clearance.*

No person may operate an aircraft within Class A airspace unless that aircraft is:

1. *Operated under IFR at a specific flight level assigned by ATC;*
2. *Equipped with instruments and equipment required for IFR operations; and*
3. *Flown by a pilot rated for instrument flight.*

(PLT455, IR.I.C.K4) — 14 CFR §91.173, §91.135

Answer (A) is incorrect because an IFR flight plan is not required in Class G airspace. Answer (B) is incorrect because defense zone airspace does not require an IFR flight plan in VFR conditions.

ALL

4063. Prior to which operation must an IFR flight plan be filed and an appropriate ATC clearance received?

A—Flying by reference to instruments in controlled airspace.

B—Entering controlled airspace when IMC exists.

C—Takeoff when IFR weather conditions exist.

No person may operate an aircraft in controlled airspace under IFR unless that person has:

1. *Filed an IFR flight plan; and*
2. *Received an appropriate ATC clearance.*

(PLT455, IR.I.C.K4) — 14 CFR §91.173

Answer (A) is incorrect because a pilot may fly with reference to instruments in controlled airspace in VFR conditions with a safety pilot without an IFR flight plan or clearance. Answer (C) is incorrect because an IFR flight plan is only required in controlled airspace.

Answers

4062 [C] 4063 [B]

Approved OMB No. 2120-0026
Exp. 7/31/2020

U S Department of Transportation
Federal Aviation Administration

International Flight Plan

PRIORITY
<=FF

ADDRESSEE(S)

<=

FILING TIME

ORIGINATOR

<=

SPECIFIC IDENTIFICATION OF ADDRESSEE(S) AND / OR ORIGINATOR

3 MESSAGE TYPE
<=(FPL

7 AIRCRAFT IDENTIFICATION
—

8 FLIGHT RULES
—

TYPE OF FLIGHT
—

<=

9 NUMBER
—

TYPE OF AIRCRAFT

WAKE TURBULENCE CAT.
/

10 EQUIPMENT
— /

<=

13 DEPARTURE AERODROME
—

TIME

<=

15 CRUISING SPEED
—

LEVEL

ROUTE

<=

16 DESTINATION AERODROME

TOTAL EET
HR MIN

ALTN AERODROME

2ND ALTN AERODROME

<=

18 OTHER INFORMATION
—

<=

SUPPLEMENTARY INFORMATION (NOT TO BE TRANSMITTED IN FPL MESSAGES)

19 ENDURANCE
HR MIN
—**E/**

PERSONS ON BOARD
P/

EMERGENCY RADIO
UHF VHF ELT
R/ U V E

SURVIVAL EQUIPMENT
POLAR DESERT MARITIME JUNGLE
/ P D M J

JACKETS
LIGHT FLUORES UHF VHF
/ L F U V

DINGHIES
NUMBER CAPACITY COVER
D / C

COLOR

<=

AIRCRAFT COLOR AND MARKINGS
A/

REMARKS
N /

<=

PILOT-IN-COMMAND
C/

)<=

FILED BY

ACCEPTED BY

ADDITIONAL INFORMATION

FAA Form 7233-4 (7/15)

Figure 6-1. FAA International Flight Plan Form 7233-4

ALL

4064. To operate under IFR below 18,000 feet, a pilot must file an IFR flight plan and receive an appropriate ATC clearance prior to

A—entering controlled airspace.
B—entering weather conditions below VFR minimums.
C—takeoff.

No person may operate an aircraft in controlled airspace under IFR unless that person has:

1. *Filed an IFR flight plan; and*
2. *Received an appropriate ATC clearance.*

(PLT455, IR.I.C.K4) — 14 CFR §91.173

Answers (B) and (C) are incorrect because an IFR flight plan and clearance is only required in controlled airspace.

ALL

4065. To operate an aircraft under IFR, a flight plan must have been filed and an ATC clearance received prior to

A—controlling the aircraft solely by use of instruments.
B—entering weather conditions in any airspace.
C—entering controlled airspace.

No person may operate an aircraft in controlled airspace under IFR unless that person has:

1. *Filed an IFR flight plan; and*
2. *Received an appropriate ATC clearance.*

(PLT455, IR.I.C.K4) — 14 CFR §91.173

Answer (A) is incorrect because a pilot may fly with reference to instruments in controlled airspace in VFR conditions with a safety pilot without an IFR flight plan or clearance. Answer (B) is incorrect because an IFR flight plan and clearance is only required in controlled airspace.

ALL

4066. When is an IFR clearance required during VFR weather conditions?

A—When operating in the Class E airspace.
B—When operating in a Class A airspace.
C—When operating in airspace above 14,500 feet.

No person may operate an aircraft within Class A airspace (regardless of the weather conditions) unless that aircraft is:

1. *Operated under IFR at a specific flight level assigned by ATC;*
2. *Equipped with instruments and equipment required for IFR operations; and*
3. *Flown by a pilot rated for instrument flight.*

(PLT370, IR.VI.B.K1) — 14 CFR §91.135

Answers (A) and (C) are incorrect because an IFR clearance is only required in Class E airspace when conditions are below VMC (Class E airspace includes that airspace from 14,000 feet up to but not including 18,000 feet MSL).

ALL

4067. Operation in which airspace requires filing an IFR flight plan?

A—Any airspace when the visibility is less than 1 mile.
B—Class E airspace with IMC and Class A airspace.
C—Positive control area, Continental Control Area, and all other airspace, if the visibility is less than 1 mile.

No person may operate in controlled airspace under IFR unless that person has:

1. *Filed an IFR flight plan; and*
2. *Received an appropriate ATC clearance.*

Each person operating an aircraft within Class A airspace must conduct that operation under IFR with an ATC clearance received prior to entering the airspace. (PLT455, IR.I.C.K4) — 14 CFR §91.173, §91.135

Answers (A) and (C) are incorrect because an IFR flight plan is only required in controlled airspace.

ALL

4068. When departing from an airport located outside controlled airspace during IMC, you must file an IFR flight plan and receive a clearance before

A—takeoff.
B—entering IFR conditions.
C—entering Class E airspace.

No person may operate an aircraft in controlled airspace under IFR unless that person has:

1. *Filed an IFR flight plan; and*
2. *Received an appropriate ATC clearance.*

(PLT161, IR.I.C.K2) — 14 CFR §91.173

Answers (A) and (B) are incorrect because an IFR flight plan and clearance is only required in controlled airspace.

Answers

4064 [A] 4065 [C] 4066 [B] 4067 [B] 4068 [C]

ALL

4427. No person may operate an aircraft in controlled airspace under IFR unless he/she files a flight plan

A—and receives a clearance by telephone prior to takeoff.
B—prior to takeoff and requests the clearance upon arrival on an airway.
C—and receives a clearance prior to entering controlled airspace.

No person may operate an aircraft in controlled airspace under IFR unless that person has:

1. *Filed an IFR flight plan; and*
2. *Received an appropriate ATC clearance.*

(PLT161, IR.I.C.K2) — 14 CFR §91.173

Answer (A) is incorrect because it does not matter how the clearance is obtained. Answer (B) is incorrect because an IFR flight plan must have been filed before the pilot can operate in controlled airspace.

ALL

4427-1. When may VFR waypoints be used on an IFR flight plan?

A—Never.
B—Always.
C—When filing a composite flight plan.

VFR waypoints shall not be used to plan flights under IFR. VFR waypoints will not be recognized by the IFR system and will be rejected for IFR routing purposes. (PLT161, IR.I.C.K2) — AIM ¶1-1-19

AIR

4005-1. During your preflight planning for an IFR flight, you determine that the first airport of intended landing has no instrument approach prescribed in 14 CFR Part 97. The weather forecast for one hour before through one hour after your estimated time of arrival is 3000' scattered with 5 miles visibility. To meet the fuel requirements for this flight, you must be able to fly to the first airport of intended landing,

A—then to the alternate airport, and then for 30 minutes at normal cruising speed.
B—then to the alternate airport, and then for 45 minutes at normal cruising speed.
C—and then fly for 45 minutes at normal cruising speed.

No person may operate in IFR conditions unless the aircraft carries enough fuel (considering weather reports, forecasts, and conditions) to complete the flight to the first airport of intended landing, fly from that airport to the alternate airport and fly after that for 45 minutes at normal cruising speed. (PLT413, IR.I.C.K4) — 14 CFR §91.167

RTC

4005-2. During your preflight planning for an IFR flight in a helicopter, you determine that the first airport of intended landing has no instrument approach prescribed in 14 CFR Part 97. The weather forecast for one hour before through one hour after your estimated time of arrival is 3,000 feet scattered with 6 miles visibility. To meet the fuel requirements for this flight, you must be able to fly to the first airport of intended landing,

A—then to the alternate airport, and then for 30 minutes at normal cruising speed.
B—then to the alternate airport, and then for 45 minutes at normal cruising speed.
C—and then fly for 45 minutes at normal cruising speed.

No person may operate a helicopter in IFR conditions unless the aircraft carries enough fuel (considering weather reports, forecasts, and conditions) to complete the flight to the first airport of intended landing, fly from that airport to the alternate airport, and fly after that for 30 minutes at normal cruising speed. (PLT413) — 14 CFR §91.167

AIR

4032. What are the minimum fuel requirements in IFR conditions, if the first airport of intended landing is forecast to have a 1,500-foot ceiling and 3 miles visibility at flight-planned ETA? Fuel to fly to the first airport of intended landing,

A—and fly thereafter for 45 minutes at normal cruising speed.
B—fly to the alternate, and fly thereafter for 45 minutes at normal cruising speed.
C—fly to the alternate, and fly thereafter for 30 minutes at normal cruising speed.

No person may operate a civil aircraft in IFR conditions unless it carries enough fuel (considering weather reports and forecasts, and weather conditions) to:

1. *Complete the flight to the first airport of intended landing;*
2. *Fly from that airport to the alternate airport; and*

Answers

4427 [C]	4427-1 [A]	4005-1 [B]	4005-2 [A]	4032 [B]

3. *Fly after that for 45 minutes at normal cruising speed.*

The above does not apply if:

1. *There is a standard instrument approach procedure for the first airport of intended landing; and*
2. *For at least 1 hour before and 1 hour after the ETA at the airport, the weather reports or forecasts or any combination of them, indicate:*
   a. *The ceiling will be at least 2,000 feet above the airport elevation; and*
   b. *Visibility will be at least 3 SM.*

An alternate, and fuel for flight to the alternate, plus 45 minutes reserve is required for this question because the forecast weather (1,500-foot ceiling) does not meet the 2,000-foot ceiling exemption. (PLT413, IR.I.C.K4) — 14 CFR §91.167, §91.169

Answer (A) is incorrect because an alternate is required since the destination has a forecast ceiling of less than 2,000 feet AGL. Answer (C) is incorrect because the fuel reserve required after the alternate is 45 minutes (not 30 minutes).

RTC
4032-1. What are the minimum fuel requirements in IFR conditions, if the first airport of intended landing is forecast to have a 1,500-foot ceiling and 3 miles visibility at flight-planned ETA? Fuel to fly to the first airport of intended landing,

A—and fly thereafter for 45 minutes at normal cruising speed.
B—fly to the alternate, and fly thereafter for 45 minutes at normal cruising speed.
C—fly to the alternate, and fly thereafter for 30 mlnutes at normal cruising speed.

No person may operate a civil helicopter ln IFR conditions unless it carries enough fuel (considering weather reports and forecasts, and weather conditions) to:

1. *Complete the flight to the first airport of intended landing;*
2. *Fly from that airport to the alternate airport; and*
3. *Fly after that for 30 minutes at normal cruising speed.*

(PLT413) — 14 CFR §91.167, §91.169

ALL
4061. What is the recommended procedure for transitioning from VFR to IFR on a composite flight plan?

A—Prior to transitioning to IFR, contact the nearest FSS, close the VFR portion, and request ATC clearance.
B—Upon reaching the proposed point for change to IFR, contact the nearest FSS and cancel your VFR flight plan, then contact ARTCC and request an IFR clearance.
C—Prior to reaching the proposed point for change to IFR, contact ARTCC, request your IFR clearance, and instruct them to cancel the VFR flight plan.

When VFR flight is conducted for the first part of a composite flight, close the VFR portion and request ATC clearance from the FSS nearest the point at which the change from VFR to IFR is proposed. (PLT224, IR.I.C.K5) — AIM ¶5-1-7

Answer (B) is incorrect because the pilot must obtain an IFR clearance before the point where IFR operations begin. Answer (C) is incorrect because the VFR flight plan should be canceled with FSS, not ARTCC.

ALL
4081. What minimum weather conditions must be forecast for your ETA at an alternate airport, that has only a VOR approach with standard alternate minimums, for the airport to be listed as an alternate on the IFR flight plan?

A—800-foot ceiling and 1 statute mile visibility.
B—800-foot ceiling and 2 statute miles visibility.
C—1,000-foot ceiling and visibility to allow descent from minimum enroute altitude (MEA), approach, and landing under basic VFR.

No person may include an airport as an alternate in an IFR flight plan unless current weather forecasts indicate that, at the estimated time of arrival at the alternate airport, the ceiling and visibility at that airport will be at or above the following alternate airport weather minimums:

1. *Precision approach procedure (ILS): ceiling 600 feet and visibility 2 SM.*
2. *Nonprecision approach procedure (VOR, NDB, LOC): ceiling 800 feet and visibility 2 SM.*

If an instrument approach procedure has been published for that airport, use the alternate airport minimums specified in that procedure. (PLT379, IR.I.C.K1) — 14 CFR §91.169

Answer (A) is incorrect because the visibility requirements is 2 (not 1) SM. Answer (C) is incorrect because the ceiling and visibility minimums are those allowing descent from the MEA, approach, and landing under basic VFR (not a 1,000-foot ceiling).

Answers

4032-1 [C] 4061 [A] 4081 [B]

ALL

4081-1. An airport may not be qualified for alternate use if

A—the airport has only AWOS-3 weather reporting.
B—the airport is next to a restricted or prohibited area.
C—the only standard approach procedure is GPS.

Not all airports can be used as an alternate. An airport may not be qualified for alternate use if the airport NAVAID is unmonitored, is GPS-based, or if it does not have weather reporting capability. (PLT455, IR.I.C.K1) — FAA-H-8083-16

Answer (A) is incorrect because an airport can qualify for alternate use if it has any weather reporting capability. Answer (B) is incorrect because an airport can qualify for alternate use even if it is located in a restricted or prohibited area.

ALL

4081-2. When your aircraft is equipped with a TSO-C129 or TSO-C196 GPS, an airport may not be qualified for alternate use if

A—the only standard approach procedure is GPS at the destination and alternate.
B—the airport has only AWOS-3 weather reporting and no LAAS equipment operational.
C—the airport is next to a restricted or prohibited area.

The requirement for an alternate depends on the aircraft category, equipment installed, approach NAVAID and forecast weather. For example, airports with only a GPS approach procedure cannot be used as an alternate by TSO-C129/129A users. (PLT455, IR.I.C.K4) — FAA-H-8083-16

AIR

4760-1. What are the alternate minimums for an airport with a precision approach procedure?

A—400-foot ceiling and 2 miles visibility.
B—600-foot ceiling and 2 miles visibility.
C—800-foot ceiling and 2 miles visibility.

Unless otherwise authorized by the Administrator, no person may include an alternate airport in an IFR flight plan that has a precision (ILS) approach unless current weather forecasts indicate that, at the estimated time of arrival at the alternate airport, the ceiling will be at least 600 feet and visibility 2 SM. (PLT379, IR.I.C.K1) — 14 CFR §91.169

Answer (A) is incorrect because 400 feet is not an alternative airport minimum. Answer (C) is incorrect because an 800-foot ceiling is the minimum for airports with nonprecision approaches.

AIR

4760-2. When an alternate airport is required, what are the weather minimums that must be forecast at the ETA for an alternate airport that has a precision approach procedure?

A—Ceiling 200 feet above the approach minimums and at least 1 statute mile visibility, but not less than the minimum visibility for the approach.
B—600 foot ceiling and 2 statute miles visibility.
C—Ceiling 200 feet above field elevation and visibility 1 statute mile, but not less than the minimum visibility for the approach.

Unless otherwise authorized by the Administrator, no person may include an alternate airport in an IFR flight plan that has a precision (ILS) approach unless current weather forecasts indicate that, at the estimated time of arrival at the alternate airport, the ceiling will be at least 600 feet and visibility 2 SM. (PLT382, IR.I.C.K4) — 14 CFR §91.169

RTC

4760-3. When an alternate airport is required, for helicopters, what are the weather minimums that must be forecast at the ETA for an alternate airport that has a precision approach procedure?

A—Ceiling 200 feet above the approach minimums and at least 1 statute mile visibility, but not less than the minimum visibility for the approach.
B—Ceiling 200 feet above field elevation and visibility 1 statute mile, but not less than the minimum visibility for the approach.
C—600 foot ceiling and 2 statute miles visibility.

Unless otherwise authorized by the Administrator, no person may include an alternate airport in an IFR flight plan in a helicopter that has a precision (ILS) approach unless current weather forecasts indicate that, at the estimated time of arrival at the alternate airport, the ceiling will be at least 200 feet above the minimum approach to be flown, and visibility at least 1 SM but never less than the minimum visibility for the approach to be flown. (PLT382) — 14 CFR §91.169

Answers

4081-1 [C] 4081-2 [A] 4760-1 [B] 4760-2 [B] 4760-3 [A]

ALL
4086. What are the minimum weather conditions that must be forecast to list an airport as an alternate when the airport has no approved IAP?

A—The ceiling and visibility at ETA, 2,000 feet and 3 miles, respectively.
B—The ceiling and visibility from 2 hours before until 2 hours after ETA, 2,000 feet and 3 miles, respectively.
C—The ceiling and visibility at ETA must allow descent from MEA, approach, and landing, under basic VFR.

If no instrument approach procedure has been published for that airport, the ceiling and visibility minimums are those allowing descent from the MEA, approach, and landing, under basic VFR. (PLT379, IR.I.C.K1) — 14 CFR §91.169

Answers (A) and (B) are incorrect because they describe the minimums when an alternate airport is required (inaccurately, because the alternate airport weather conditions apply 1 hour before and 1 hour after ETA).

ALL
4719. When a pilot elects to proceed to the selected alternate airport, which minimums apply for landing at the alternate?

A—600-1 if the airport has an ILS.
B—Ceiling 200 feet above the published minimum; visibility 2 miles.
C—The landing minimums for the approach to be used.

If the pilot elects to proceed to the selected alternate airport, the alternate ceiling and visibility minimums are disregarded, and the published landing minimum is applicable for the new destination, utilizing facilities as appropriate to the procedure. In other words, the alternate airport becomes a new destination, and the pilot uses the landing minimum appropriate to the type of procedure selected. (PLT379, IR.I.C.K1) — 14 CFR §91.169

ALL
4630. If a pilot elects to proceed to the selected alternate, the landing minimums used at that airport should be the

A—minimums specified for the approach procedure selected.
B—alternate minimums shown on the approach chart.
C—minimums shown for that airport in a separate listing of "IFR Alternate Minimums."

If the pilot elects to proceed to the selected alternate airport, the alternate ceiling and visibility minimums are disregarded, and the published landing minimums are applicable for the new destination, utilizing facilities as appropriate to the procedure. In other words, the alternate airport becomes a new destination, and the pilot uses the landing minimums appropriate to the type of procedure selected. (PLT379, IR.I.C.K1) — 14 CFR §91.169

Answers (B) and (C) are incorrect because alternate minimums shown on the approach chart refer to the weather conditions required to list that airport as an alternate on your IFR flight plan (not to land there).

ALL
4637. When making an instrument approach at the selected alternate airport, what landing minimums apply?

A—Standard alternate minimums (600-2 or 800-2).
B—The IFR alternate minimums listed for that airport.
C—The landing minimums published for the type of procedure selected.

If the pilot elects to proceed to the selected alternate airport, the alternate ceiling and visibility minimums are disregarded, and the published landing minimums are applicable for the new destination, utilizing facilities as appropriate to the procedure. In other words, the alternate airport becomes a new destination, and the pilot uses the landing minimums appropriate to the type of procedure selected. (PLT379, IR.I.C.K1) — 14 CFR §91.169

Answers (A) and (B) are incorrect because alternate minimums shown on the approach chart refer to the weather conditions required to list that airport as an alternate on your IFR flight plan (not to land there).

Answers
4086 [C] 4719 [C] 4630 [A] 4637 [C]

ALL

4769. An airport without an authorized IAP may be included on an IFR flight plan as an alternate, if the current weather forecast indicates that the ceiling and visibility at the ETA will

A—allow for descent from the IAF to landing under basic VFR conditions.
B—be at least 1,000 feet and 1 mile.
C—allow for a descent from the MEA, approach, and a landing under basic VFR conditions.

If no instrument approach procedure has been published for that airport, the ceiling and visibility minimums are those allowing descent from the MEA, approach, and landing, under basic VFR conditions. (PLT379, IR.I.C.K1) — 14 CFR §91.169

ALL

4070. Preferred IFR routes beginning with a fix indicate that departing aircraft will normally be routed to the fix by

A—the established airway(s) between the departure airport and the fix.
B—an instrument departure procedure (DP) or radar vectors.
C—direct route only.

Preferred IFR routes beginning/ending with a fix indicate that aircraft may be routed to/from these fixes via a DP route, radar vectors (RV), or a Standard Terminal Arrival Route (STAR). (PLT224, IR.I.C.K5) — Chart Supplements U.S.

Answer (A) is incorrect because established airway(s) may not even exist between the airport and the fix, or other routes may be more efficient. Answer (C) is incorrect because obstructions or traffic may prevent direct routing.

ALL

4275. (Refer to Figure 190.) What are the hours of operation (local standard time) of the control tower at Santa Barbara Muni (SBA)?

A—5:30am – 10:00pm
B—0600 – 2300
C—1400 – 0700

The hours of operation for the control tower at Santa Barbara Muni are listed on the Chart Supplement page for SBA and shown in UTC in parentheses after the tower frequency, "TOWER: 119.7 (1400-0700Z)." The first line of the page for SBA lists the number of hours to subtract from UTC to obtain local standard time ("UTC-8 (-7DT)") for both standard and daylight saving time.

1400Z – 0800 = 0600 or 6 a.m. local standard time

0700Z – 0800 = 2300 or 11 p.m. local standard time

Therefore the tower is open 0600–2300 local standard time based on the 24-hour clock, or 6 a.m.–11 p.m. (PLT281, IR.I.C.K4) — Chart Supplement U.S.

Answer (A) is incorrect because this is the local standard time the airport is attended, which differs from the operating hours of the control tower. Answer (C) is incorrect because this is the Zulu time for when the airport is attended.

ALL

4305. (Refer to Figure 184.) What are the hours of operation (local time) of the Class D service for the Yakima Air Terminal when daylight savings time is in effect?

A—0500 to 2100 local.
B—0700 to 2300 local.
C—0600 to 2200 local.

The hours of operation for Class D service at Yakima Air Terminal are listed on the Chart Supplements U.S. page for YKM and shown in UTC in the airspace section, "CLASS D svc 1400-0600Z‡." The first line of the page for YKM lists the number of hours to subtract from UTC to obtain local time ("UTC-8 (-7DT)") for both standard and daylight saving time. The ‡ symbol after the Z indicates that during daylight saving time the hours will be 1 hour earlier then shown. Therefore class D service is actually from 1300 – 0500 UTC.

1300Z – 0700 = 0600

0500Z – 0700 = 2200

(PLT281, IR.I.C.K4) — Chart Supplement U.S.

ALL

4405. The most current en route and destination flight information for planning an instrument flight should be obtained from the

A—ATIS broadcast.
B—AFSS.
C—Notice to Air Missions publications.

Every pilot is urged to receive a preflight briefing and to file a flight plan. This briefing should consist of the latest or most current weather, airport, and enroute NAVAID information. Briefing service may be obtained from an FSS either by telephone or interphone, by radio when airborne, or by a personal visit to the station. (PLT455, IR.I.C.K4) — AIM ¶5-1-1

Answer (A) is incorrect because the ATIS broadcasts only information referring to landing and departing operations at one airport. Answer (C) is incorrect because Class II NOTAMs is a biweekly publication containing current NOTAMs and is only one part of a complete flight briefing.

Answers

4769 [C]	4070 [B]	4275 [B]	4305 [C]	4405 [B]

ALL

4761. What point at the destination should be used to compute estimated time en route on an IFR flight plan?

A—The final approach fix on the expected instrument approach.

B—The initial approach fix on the expected instrument approach.

C—The point of first intended landing.

Unless otherwise authorized by ATC, each person filing an IFR or VFR flight plan shall include in it the point of first intended landing and the estimated elapsed time until over that point. (PLT455, IR.I.C.K4) — 14 CFR §91.169

Answers (A) and (B) are incorrect because it is not possible to accurately tell which approach will be used.

AIR

4085-1. For aircraft other than helicopters, what forecast weather minimums are required to list an airport as an alternate on an IFR flight plan if the airport has VOR approach only?

A—Ceiling and visibility at ETA, 800 feet and 2 miles, respectively.

B—Ceiling and visibility from 2 hours before until 2 hours after ETA, 800 feet and 2 miles, respectively.

C—Ceiling and visibility at ETA, 600 feet and 2 miles, respectively.

An alternate airport with a VOR approach only (a nonprecision approach) can be used only if the current weather conditions indicate that at the ETA the alternate airport ceiling is at least 800 feet and the visibility is at least 2 SM. (PLT379, IR.I.C.K1) — 14 CFR §91.169

Answer (B) is incorrect because the alternate airport must have the specified minimums at the ETA (not 2 hours before until 2 hours after). Answer (C) is incorrect because 600 feet and 2 miles applies to alternate airports with precision approach procedures (ILS).

AIR

4087-1. For aircraft other than helicopters, what minimum weather conditions must be forecast for your ETA at an alternate airport that has a precision approach procedure, with standard alternate minimums, in order to list it as an alternate for the IFR flight?

A—600-foot ceiling and 2 SM visibility at your ETA.

B—600-foot ceiling and 2 SM visibility from 2 hours before to 2 hours after your ETA.

C—800-foot ceiling and 2 SM visibility at your ETA.

An alternate airport with a precision approach can be used only if the current weather conditions indicate that at the ETA the alternate airport ceiling is at least 600 feet and the visibility is at least 2 SM. (PLT379, IR.I.C.K1) — 14 CFR §91.169

Answer (B) is incorrect because the current weather conditions must specify the minimum requirements at the ETA (not 2 hours before to 2 hours after ETA). Answer (C) is incorrect because 800-foot ceilings and 2 SM visibility is the minimum for nonprecision approaches.

AIR

4082-2. For aircraft other than helicopters, is an alternate airport required for an IFR flight to ATL (Atlanta Hartsfield) if the proposed ETA is 1930Z?

TAF KATL 121720Z 121818 20012KT 5SM HZ BKN030
FM2000 3SM TSRA OVC025CB
FM2200 33015G20KT P6SM BKN015 OVC040 BECMG
0608 02008KT BKN040 BECMG 1012
00000KT P6SM CLR=

A—No, because the ceiling and visibility are forecast to be at or above 2,000 feet and 3 miles within 1 hour before to 1 hour after the ETA.

B—No, because the ceiling and visibility are forecast to remain at or above 1,000 feet and 3 miles, respectively.

C—Yes, because the ceiling could fall below 2,000 feet within 2 hours before to 2 hours after the ETA.

An alternate airport is required on an IFR flight plan unless, from 1 hour before to 1 hour after the ETA at the destination airport, weather reports and forecasts indicate that at the destination:

1. *The ceiling will be at least 2,000 feet above the airport elevation; and*
2. *The visibility will be at least 3 SM.*

In the forecast for Atlanta, the chance of reduced conditions occurs before and after the 1 hour before to 1 hour after ETA. (PLT379, IR.I.C.K1) — 14 CFR §91.169

Answers (B) and (C) are incorrect because the time frame for alternates is 1 hour before and after ETA.

Answers

4761 [C]	4085-1 [A]	4087-1 [A]	4082-2 [A]

AIR

4083-1. For aircraft other than helicopters, what minimum conditions must exist at the destination airport to avoid listing an alternate airport on an IFR flight plan when a standard IAP is available?

A—From 2 hours before to 2 hours after ETA, forecast ceiling 2,000, and visibility 2 and 1/2 miles.

B—From 2 hours before to 2 hours after ETA, forecast ceiling 3,000, and visibility 3 miles.

C—From 1 hour before to 1 hour after ETA, forecast ceiling 2,000, and visibility 3 miles.

An alternate airport is required on an IFR flight plan unless, from 1 hour before to 1 hour after the ETA at the destination airport, weather reports and forecasts indicate that at the destination:

1. *The ceiling will be at least 2,000 feet above the airport elevation; and*
2. *The visibility will be at least 3 SM.*

(PLT379, IR.I.C.K1) — 14 CFR §91.169

AIR

4083-3. For aircraft other than helicopters, under what conditions are you not required to list an alternate airport on an IFR flight plan if 14 CFR Part 97 prescribes a standard IAP for the destination airport?

A—When the ceiling is forecast to be at least 1,000 feet above the lowest of the MEA, MOCA, or initial approach altitude and the visibility is 2 miles more than the minimum landing visibility within 2 hours of your ETA at the destination airport.

B—When the weather reports or forecasts indicate the ceiling and visibility will be at least 2,000 feet and 3 miles for 1 hour before to 1 hour after your ETA at the destination airport.

C—When the ceiling is forecast to be at least 1,000 feet above the lowest of the MEA, MOCA, or initial approach altitude within 2 hours of your ETA at the destination airport.

An alternate airport is required on an IFR flight plan unless, from 1 hour before to 1 hour after the ETA at the destination airport, weather reports and forecasts indicate that at the destination:

1. *The ceiling will be at least 2,000 feet above the airport elevation; and*
2. *The visibility will be at least 3 SM.*

(PLT379, IR.I.C.K1) — 14 CFR §91.169

RTC

4085-2. For helicopters, what forecast weather minimums are required to list an airport as an alternate on an IFR flight plan if the airport has VOR approach only?

A—Ceiling 200 feet above the approach minimums and visibility 1 statute mile, but not less than the minimum visibility for the approach, at the alternate airport ETA.

B—Ceiling and visibility at ETA, 800 feet and 2 miles, respectively.

C—Ceiling 1,000 feet above airport elevation and 2 statute miles visibility for 1 hour after the alternate airport ETA.

An alternate airport can be used only if the current weather conditions indicate that at the ETA the alternate airport ceiling is 200 feet above the minimum for the approach to be flown and visibility at least 1 SM, but never less than the minimum visibility for the approach to be flown. (PLT379) — 14 CFR §91.169

RTC

4087-2. For helicopters, what minimum weather conditions must be forecast for your ETA at an alternate airport that has a precision approach procedure, with standard alternate minimums, in order to list it as an alternate for the IFR flight?

A—600 foot ceiling and 2 SM visibility at your ETA.

B—200 foot ceiling above the airport elevation and 1 SM visibility from 1 hour before to 1 hour after your ETA.

C—200 foot ceiling above the approach minimums and 1 SM visibility, but not less than the visibility minimums for the approach, at your ETA.

An alternate airport can be used only if the current weather conditions indicate that at the ETA the alternate airport ceiling is 200 feet above the minimum for the approach to be flown and visibility at least 1 SM, but never less than the minimum visibility for the approach to be flown. (PLT379) — 14 CFR §91.169

Answers

4083-1 [C] 4083-3 [B] 4085-2 [A] 4087-2 [C]

RTC
4082-1. For helicopters, is an alternate airport required for an IFR flight to ATL (Atlanta Hartsfield) if the proposed ETA is 1930Z?

TAF KATL 121720Z 121818 20012KT 5SM HZ
BKN030
FM2000 3SM TSRA OVC025CB
FM2200 33015G20KT P6SM BKN015 OVC040
BECMG 0608
02008KT BKN040 BECMG 1012 00000KT
P6SM CLR=

A—Yes, because the ceiling could fall below 2,000 feet within 2 hours before to 2 hours after the ETA.
B—No, because the ceiling and visibility are forecast to remain at or above 1,000 feet and 3 miles, respectively.
C—No, because the ceiling and visibility are forecast to be at or above 1,000 feet above the airport elevation (and 400 feet above the approach minima) with 3 miles visibility at the ETA to 1 hour thereafter.

An alternate airport is required on a helicopter IFR flight plan unless, at the estimated time of arrival and for 1 hour thereafter weather reports and forecasts indicate that at the destination:

1. *The ceiling will be at least 1,000 feet above the airport elevation; or at least 400 feet above the approach minima.*
2. *The visibility will be at least 2 SM.*

In the forecast for Atlanta, the chance of reduced conditions occurs before and after the time frame. (PLT379) — 14 CFR §91.169

RTC
4083-2. For helicopters, what minimum conditions must exist at the destination airport to avoid listing an alternate airport on an IFR flight plan when a standard IAP is available?

A—From 1 hour before to 1 hour after ETA, forecast ceiling 2,000, and visibility 3 miles.
B—From 1 hour before to 1 hour after ETA, reports and forecasts indicate a ceiling of 1,000 feet above the airport elevation and visibility 2 miles.
C—From the ETA to 1 hour after the ETA, reports and forecasts indicate a ceiling 1,000 feet above the airport elevation, or at least 400 feet above the lowest applicable approach minima, whichever is higher, and visibility 2 statute miles.

An alternate airport is required on helicopter IFR flight plans unless at the estimated time of arrival and for 1 hour after the ETA, weather reports and forecasts indicate that at the destination:

1. *The ceiling will be at least 1,000 feet above the airport elevation, or at least 400 feet above the approach minima;*
2. *The visibility will be at least 2 SM.*

(PLT379) — 14 CFR §91.169

RTC
4040. What are the fuel requirements for a night IFR flight in a helicopter when an alternate airport is not required?

A—Enough fuel to complete the flight to the first airport of intended landing and fly after that for 30 minutes.
B—Enough fuel to complete the flight to the first airport of intended landing, and fly thereafter for 45 minutes at cruising speed.
C—Enough fuel to complete the flight to the first airport of intended landing, make an approach, and fly thereafter for 45 minutes at cruising speed.

No person may operate a civil helicopter in IFR conditions unless it carries enough fuel (considering weather reports and forecasts, and weather conditions) to:

1. *Complete the flight to the first airport of intended landing;*
2. *Fly from that airport to the alternate airport; and*
3. *Fly after that for 30 minutes at normal cruising speed.*

(PLT413) — 14 CFR §91.167

Answer (B) is incorrect because a helicopter must be able to fly 30 minutes after the alternate (45 minutes is the requirement for airplanes). Answer (C) is incorrect because a helicopter must be able to fly to the destination, alternate, and fly after that for 30 minutes.

Answers
4082-1 [C]   4083-2 [C]   4040 [A]

RTC

4041. When an alternate airport is required for helicopters on the flight plan, you must have sufficient fuel to complete the flight to the first airport of intended landing, fly to the alternate, and thereafter fly for at least

A—30 minutes at normal cruising speed.
B—45 minutes at holding speed.
C—45 minutes at normal cruising speed.

No person may operate a civil helicopter in IFR conditions unless it carries enough fuel (considering weather reports and forecasts, and weather conditions) to:

1. *Complete the flight to the first airport of intended landing;*
2. *Fly from that airport to the alternate airport; and*
3. *Fly after that for 30 minutes at normal cruising speed.*

(PLT413) — 14 CFR §91.167

Answers (B) and (C) are incorrect because the helicopter must be able to fly to the destination, alternate, and fly after that for 30 minutes at normal cruise.

RTC

4084-1. For helicopters, what minimum weather conditions must be forecast for your ETA at an alternate airport that has only a VOR approach with standard alternate minimums, for the airport to be listed as an alternate on the IFR flight plan?

A—Ceiling 200 feet above the minimums for the approach to be flown and 1 SM visibility, but not less than the minimum visibility for the approach to be flown.
B—800 foot ceiling and 2 SM visibility.
C—800 foot ceiling and 1 SM visibility.

No person may include an airport as an alternate in a helicopter IFR flight plan unless current weather forecasts indicate that, at the ETA at the alternate airport, the ceiling and visibility at that airport will be at or above the following alternate airport weather minimums: ceiling 200 feet above the minimum for the approach to be flown and visibility at least 1 SM, but never less than the minimum visibility for the approach to be flown. (PLT379) — 14 CFR §91.169

RTC

4084-2. When 14 CFR Part 97 prescribes a standard IAP for the destination airport, under what conditions are you not required to list an alternate airport on an IFR flight plan for an IFR flight in a helicopter?

A—When the weather reports or forecasts indicate the ceiling and visibility will be at least 2,000 feet and 3 miles for 1 hour before to 1 hour after your ETA at the destination airport.
B—When the ceiling is forecast to be at least 1,000 feet above the lowest of the MEA, MOCA, or initial approach altitude within 2 hours of your ETA at the destination airport.
C—At your ETA and for 1 hour after your ETA, the ceiling is forecast to be at least 1,000 feet above the field elevation, or at least 400 feet above the lowest applicable approach minima, whichever is higher, and visibility of at least 2 statute miles.

An alternate airport is required on a helicopter IFR flight plan unless at the estimated time of arrival and for 1 hour after the ETA, weather reports and forecasts indicate that at the destination:

1. *The ceiling will be at least 1,000 feet above the airport elevation or at least 400 feet above the approach minima; and*
2. *The visibility will be at least 2 SM.*

(PLT379) — 14 CFR §91.169

ALL

4248. (Refer to Figure 165.) What are the hours of operation (local standard time) of the Cascade Approach/Departure Control when flying into Medford Airport?

A—1400 – 0730.
B—0600 – 2330.
C—0730 – 1400.

The hours of operation of the Cascade App/Dep Control are listed on the Chart Supplement U.S. excerpt, Figure 165. Hours of operation are expressed in UTC and are shown as "Z" time or Zulu. The top line of this Medford page gives the number of hours to be subtracted from UTC to obtain local standard time (UTC -8 (-7DT)):

Published time of operation	*1400 Z*	*to*	*0730 Z*
Time zone correction	*–800*		*–800*
Local standard time hours of operation	*0600*	*to*	*2330*

(PLT281, IR.I.B.S4) — Chart Supplement U.S.

Answers

4041 [A] 4084-1 [A] 4084-2 [C] 4248 [B]

Clearance Requirements

If a PIC deviates from any ATC clearance or instruction, that pilot must notify ATC of the deviation as soon as possible.

If operating VFR, and compliance with an ATC clearance would cause a violation of a regulation, pilots should advise ATC and obtain a revised clearance.

ALL

4407. When may ATC request a detailed report of an emergency even though a rule has not been violated?

A—When priority has been given.
B—Any time an emergency occurs.
C—When the emergency occurs in controlled airspace.

Each PIC who, though not deviating from a rule, is given priority by ATC in an emergency, shall submit a detailed report of that emergency within 48 hours to the manager of that ATC facility, if requested by ATC. (PLT171, IR.III.A.K1) — 14 CFR §91.123

Answer (B) is incorrect because a written report may be requested when priority has been granted, not any time an emergency occurs. Answer (C) is incorrect because a written report may be requested when priority has been granted in an emergency, regardless of where the emergency occurs.

ALL

4461. While on an IFR flight, a pilot has an emergency which causes a deviation from an ATC clearance. What action must be taken?

A—Notify ATC of the deviation as soon as possible.
B—Squawk 7700 for the duration of the emergency.
C—Submit a detailed report to the chief of the ATC facility within 48 hours.

Each PIC who, in an emergency, deviates from an ATC clearance or instruction shall notify ATC of that deviation as soon as possible. (PLT403, IR.III.A.K1) — 14 CFR §91.123

Answer (B) is incorrect because the pilot must also notify ATC (not just squawk 7700) in an emergency causing deviation from a clearance. Answer (C) is incorrect because the requirement to submit a report within 48 hours only applies if given priority and/or ATC requests it.

ALL

4758. If you are performing a VFR practice instrument approach and radar approach control assigns an altitude or heading that will cause you to enter the clouds, what action should you take?

A—Continue as directed.
B—Advise "unable" and remain clear of clouds.
C—Deviate as needed; then rejoin the approach.

If operating VFR and compliance with any radar vector or altitude would cause a violation of any regulation, pilots should advise ATC and obtain a revised clearance or instruction. (PLT141, IR.III.A.K1) — AIM ¶5-5-6

ALL

4758-1. You have been issued a clearance void time for an IFR departure at a non-towered airport but are not yet airborne within the prescribed time. You must notify ATC of your failure to depart

A—as soon as possible.
B—within 30 minutes.
C—within 60 minutes.

A pilot who does not depart prior to the clearance void time must advise ATC as soon as possible of their intentions. ATC will normally advise the pilot of the time allotted to contact ATC of a failure to depart and this time may not exceed 30 minutes. (PLT141, IR.III.A.K1) — AIM ¶5-2-7

Answer choice (B) is incorrect, ATC may not issue a time exceeding 30 minutes, while the pilot must notify ATC as soon as possible. Answer choice (c) is incorrect, anything exceeding 30 minutes will result in the aircraft being overdue and a search and rescue mission initiated.

Answers

4407 [A]	4461 [A]	4758 [B]	4758-1 [A]

ATC Clearance/Separations

All IFR clearances follow this same basic format:

1. Clearance limit.
2. Departure procedure (as appropriate).
3. Route of flight.
4. Initial altitude to be flown.
5. Additional instructions as necessary.

If the route of flight filed in the flight plan can be approved with little or no revision, ATC will issue an abbreviated clearance. The abbreviated clearance will always contain the instrument departure procedure (DP) name, number, and transition (if appropriate) after the phrase "cleared to (destination) airport" and then the words "as filed."

There is no requirement for a pilot to read back an ATC clearance unless requested to do so. However, pilots of airborne aircraft should read back without request those parts of clearances containing altitude assignments or vectors.

The ATC IFR clearance may be received in many different ways, depending upon the point of departure. At locations not served by a control tower, the clearance may contain a void time. If the flight does not depart prior to the void time, ATC must be notified of the pilot's intentions as soon as possible, but no later than 30 minutes.

ATC may use the term "cruise" to authorize flight at any altitude from the minimum IFR altitude up to and including the altitude specified. However, once the pilot starts descent, and verbally reports leaving an altitude in the block, they may not return to that altitude without additional ATC clearance. Climb, descent, and level-off within the block is at the pilot's discretion.

ALL

4395. What response is expected when ATC issues an IFR clearance to pilots of airborne aircraft?

A—Read back the entire clearance as required by regulation.

B—Read back those parts containing altitude assignments or vectors and any part requiring verification.

C—Read-back should be unsolicited and spontaneous to confirm that the pilot understands all instructions.

Pilots of airborne aircraft should read back those parts of ATC clearances and instructions containing altitude assignments or vectors as a means of mutual verification. The readback of the "numbers" serves as a double check between pilots and controllers and reduces the kinds of communications errors that occur when a number is either misheard or is incorrect. (PLT171, IR.III.A.S1) — AIM ¶4-4-7

Answers (A) and (C) are incorrect because the readback is an expected, not required, procedure and only those parts containing assigned altitudes or vectors should be read back (not the entire clearance).

ALL

4396. Which clearance items are always given in an abbreviated IFR departure clearance? (Assume radar environment.)

A—Altitude, destination airport, and one or more fixes which identify the initial route of flight.

B—Destination airport, altitude, and DP name, number, and/or transition, if appropriate.

C—Clearance limit, and DP name, number, and/or transition, if appropriate.

The clearance as issued will include the destination airport filed in the flight plan. An enroute altitude will be stated in the clearance or the pilot will be advised to expect an assigned or filed altitude within a given time frame or at a certain point after departure. ATC procedures now require the controller to state the DP name, the current number, and the DP transition name. (PLT370, IR.V.B.K1) — AIM ¶5-2-5

Answer (A) is incorrect because the fixes are included in the flight plan and will not be repeated in an abbreviated clearance. Answer (C) is incorrect because an enroute altitude is also given in an abbreviated clearance.

Answers

4395 [B] 4396 [B]

ALL
4398. On the runup pad, you receive the following clearance from ground control:

CLEARED TO THE DALLAS LOVE AIRPORT AS FILED—MAINTAIN SIX THOUSAND—SQUAWK ZERO SEVEN ZERO FOUR JUST BEFORE DEPARTURE—DEPARTURE CONTROL WILL BE ONE TWO FOUR POINT NINER.

An abbreviated clearance, such as this, will always contain the

A—departure control frequency.
B—destination airport and route.
C—requested enroute altitude.

The clearance as issued will include the destination airport filed in the flight plan. (PLT044, IR.III.A.S1) — AIM ¶5-2-5

ALL
4414. Which information is always given in an abbreviated departure clearance?

A—DP or transition name and altitude to maintain.
B—Name of destination airport or specific fix and altitude.
C—Altitude to maintain and code to squawk.

An abbreviated clearance always includes the name of the destination airport or clearance limit, altitude, and if a DP is to be flown, the DP name, current DP number, and the DP transition name. (PLT370, IR.VI.B.K1) — AIM ¶5-2-5

Answer (A) is incorrect because the DP or transition name and altitude is only included when a DP is to be flown, and the name of destination or specific fix and altitude must be included. Answer (C) is incorrect because the abbreviated clearance must also include the name of destination airport or specific fix, and it does not have to include a code to squawk.

ALL
4486. An abbreviated departure clearance "...CLEARED AS FILED..." will always contain the name

A—and number of the STAR to be flown when filed in the flight plan.
B—of the destination airport filed in the flight plan.
C—of the first compulsory reporting point if not in a radar environment.

The abbreviated clearance will include the destination airport filed in the flight plan. (PLT370, IR.VI.B.K1) — AIM ¶5-2-5

Answer (A) is incorrect because STARs are considered a part of the filed route of flight and will not normally be stated in an initial departure clearance. Answer (C) is incorrect because compulsory reporting points are not given in an abbreviated clearance.

ALL
4394. When departing from an airport not served by a control tower, the issuance of a clearance containing a void time indicates that

A—ATC will assume the pilot has not departed if no transmission is received before the void time.
B—the pilot must advise ATC as soon as possible, but no later than 30 minutes, of their intentions if not off by the void time.
C—ATC will protect the airspace only to the void time.

If operating from an airport not served by a control tower, the pilot may receive a clearance containing a provision that if the flight has not departed by a specific time, the clearance is void. In this situation, the pilot who does not depart prior to the void time must advise ATC as soon as possible, but no later than 30 minutes, of their intentions. (PLT370, IR.VI.B.K1) — AIM ¶5-2-6

Answer (A) is incorrect because ATC will assume the pilot has departed unless they hear from the pilot. Answer (C) is incorrect because the airspace is protected until ATC hears from the pilot.

ALL
4392. What is the significance of an ATC clearance which reads "... CRUISE SIX THOUSAND ..."?

A—The pilot must maintain 6,000 feet until reaching the IAF serving the destination airport, then execute the published approach procedure.
B—Climbs may be made to, or descents made from, 6,000 feet at the pilot's discretion.
C—The pilot may utilize any altitude from the MEA/MOCA to 6,000 feet, but each change in altitude must be reported to ATC.

A cruise clearance is used in an ATC clearance to authorize a pilot to conduct flight at any altitude from the minimum IFR altitude up to, and including, the altitude specified in the clearance. The pilot may level-off at any intermediate altitude within this block of airspace. Climb/descent within the block is to be made at the discretion of the pilot. However, once the pilot starts descent, and verbally reports leaving an altitude in the block, they may not return to that altitude without additional ATC clearance. (PLT044, IR.III.A.S1) — AIM ¶4-4-3

Answer (A) is incorrect because the pilot does not have to maintain 6,000 feet. Answer (C) is incorrect because all airspace between the minimum IFR altitude and 6,000 feet is protected, and the pilot need not report altitude changes to ATC.

Answers

4398 [B]	4414 [B]	4486 [B]	4394 [B]	4392 [B]

ALL

4458. A "CRUISE FOUR THOUSAND FEET" clearance would mean that the pilot is authorized to

A—vacate 4,000 feet without notifying ATC.
B—climb to, but not descend from 4,000 feet, without further ATC clearance.
C—use any altitude from minimum IFR to 4,000 feet, but must report leaving each altitude.

A cruise clearance is used in an ATC clearance to authorize a pilot to conduct flight at any altitude from the minimum IFR altitude up to and including the altitude specified in the clearance. The pilot may level-off at any intermediate altitude within this block of airspace. Climb/descent within the block is to be made at the discretion of the pilot. However, once the pilot starts descent and verbally reports leaving an altitude in the block, they may not return to that altitude without additional ATC clearance. (PLT044, IR.III.A.S1) — AIM ¶4-4-3

Answer (B) is incorrect because any airspace between the minimum IFR altitude and 4,000 feet MSL may be utilized without further ATC clearance. Answer (C) is incorrect because cruise clearances do not necessitate reporting a change in altitude to ATC.

ALL

4393. What is the recommended climb procedure when a nonradar departure control instructs a pilot to climb to the assigned altitude?

A—Maintain a continuous optimum climb until reaching assigned altitude and report passing each 1,000 foot level.
B—Climb at a maximum angle of climb to within 1,000 feet of the assigned altitude, then 500 feet per minute the last 1,000 feet.
C—Maintain an optimum climb on the centerline of the airway without intermediate level-offs until 1,000 feet below assigned altitude, then 500 to 1500 feet per minute.

When ATC has not used the phrase "at pilot's discretion" nor imposed any climb or descent restrictions, pilots should initiate climb or descent promptly and acknowledgment of the clearance. Descend or climb at an optimum rate consistent with the operating characteristics of the aircraft to 1,000 feet above or below the assigned altitude, and then attempt to descend or climb at a rate of between 500 and 1,500 fpm until the assigned altitude is reached. (PLT044, IR.III.A.S1) — AIM ¶4-4-10

Answer (A) is incorrect because the pilot is not required to report passing each 1,000 feet of altitude. Answer (B) is incorrect because cruise climb (not maximum angle of climb) should be used.

ALL

4555. To comply with ATC instructions for altitude changes of more than 1,000 feet, what rate of climb or descent should be used?

A—As rapidly as practicable to 500 feet above/below the assigned altitude, and then at 500 feet per minute until the assigned altitude is reached.
B—1,000 feet per minute during climb and 500 feet per minute during descents until reaching the assigned altitude.
C—As rapidly as practicable to 1,000 feet above/below the assigned altitude, and then between 500 and 1,500 feet per minute until reaching the assigned altitude.

When ATC has not used the term "at pilot's discretion," nor imposed any climb or descent restrictions, pilots should initiate climb or descent promptly on acknowledgment of the clearance. Descend or climb at an optimum rate consistent with the operating characteristics of the aircraft to 1,000 feet above or below the assigned altitude, and then attempt to descend or climb at a rate of 500 to 1,500 fpm until the assigned altitude is reached. (PLT004, IR.III.A.S1) — AIM ¶4-4-10

ALL

4442. Which clearance procedures may be issued by ATC without prior pilot request?

A—DPs, STARs, and contact approaches.
B—Contact and visual approaches.
C—DPs, STARs, and visual approaches.

Contact approaches will only be authorized when requested by the pilot and the reported ground visibility at the destination airport is at least 1 SM. ATC may initiate a visual approach when it will be operationally beneficial and certain conditions can be met. DPs and STARs are assigned as determined necessary by ATC. (PLT044), IR.III.A.S1 — AIM ¶5-2-5, ¶5-4-1, ¶5-4-24

Answers (A) and (B) are incorrect because contact approaches may not be issued unless the pilot requests one.

Answers

4458 [A]	4393 [C]	4555 [C]	4442 [C]

ALL

4443. What is the significance of an ATC clearance which reads "...CRUISE SIX THOUSAND..."?

A—The pilot must maintain 6,000 until reaching the IAF serving the destination airport, then execute the published approach procedure.
B—It authorizes a pilot to conduct flight at any altitude from minimum IFR altitude up to and including 6,000.
C—The pilot is authorized to conduct flight at any altitude from minimum IFR altitude up to and including 6,000, but each change in altitude must be reported to ATC.

A cruise clearance is used in an ATC clearance to authorize a pilot to conduct flight at any altitude from the minimum IFR altitude up to and including the altitude specified in the clearance. The pilot may level-off at any intermediate altitude within this block of airspace. Climb/descent within the block is to be made at the discretion of the pilot. However, once the pilot starts descent and verbally reports leaving an altitude in the block, they may not return to that altitude without additional ATC clearance. (PLT044, IR.III.A.S1) — AIM ¶4-4-3

Answer (A) is incorrect because the pilot is not required to maintain 6,000 feet. Answer (C) is incorrect because the pilot may change altitude without reporting to ATC.

RTC

4644. Does the ATC term "cleared to cruise" apply to helicopter IFR operations?

A—No, this term applies to airplane IFR operations only.
B—Yes, but the pilot must report leaving an altitude.
C—Yes, in part, it authorizes the pilot to commence the approach at the destination airport at pilot's discretion.

The term "cruise" may be used instead of "maintain" to assign a block of airspace, to a pilot, from the minimum IFR altitude up to and including the altitude specified in the cruise clearance. The pilot may level off at any intermediate altitude within this block of airspace. Climb/descent within the block is to be made at the discretion of the pilot. However, once the pilot starts descent and verbally reports leaving an altitude in the block, they may not return to that altitude without additional ATC clearance. (PLT044) — AIM ¶4-4-3

Departure Procedures (DPs)

To simplify ATC clearance delivery, DPs have been established at certain airports. Pilots may be issued a DP whenever ATC deems it appropriate. If the PIC does not wish to use a DP, the pilot is expected to so advise ATC. If the pilot does elect to use a DP, they must possess at least the textual description. Figure 6-2 on the next page shows a DP for Detroit, Michigan.

On some DPs a climb gradient may be specified. The pilot can convert climb gradient per nautical mile to rate of climb in feet per minute by using the rate of climb table in FAA Legend 16.

When ready for departure, the pilot will receive takeoff clearance from the tower. The pilot should remain on the tower frequency until directed to contact departure control.

Answers

4443 [B] 4644 [C]

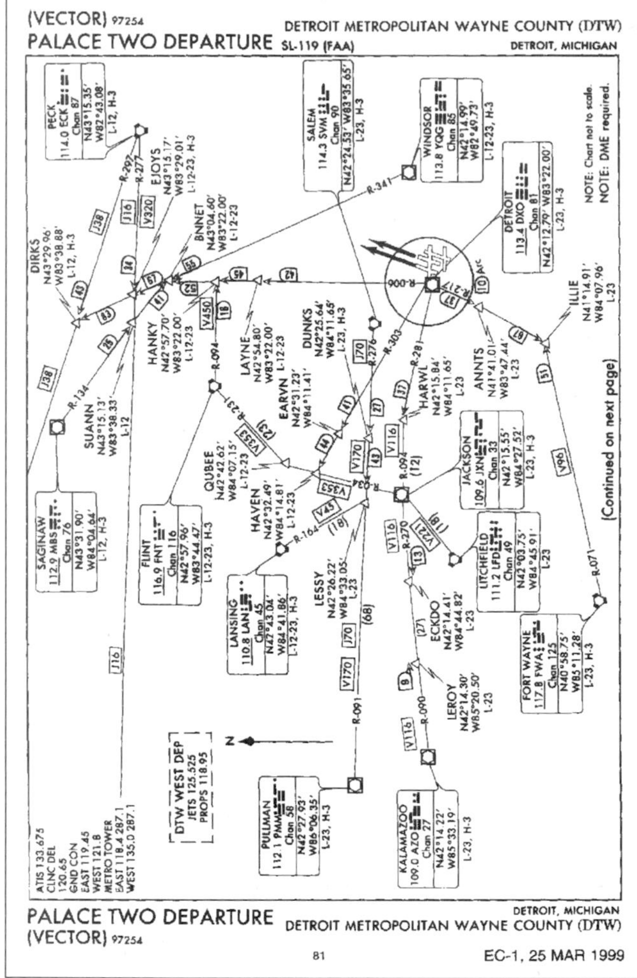

Figure 6-2. Departure Procedure, Detroit, Michigan

ALL

4270-1. Unless otherwise stated, instrument procedures use the standard IFR climb gradient of

A—500 feet per minute.
B—400 feet per nautical mile.
C—200 feet per nautical mile.

Pilots must pre-plan to determine if the aircraft can meet the climb gradient (expressed in feet per nautical mile) required by the departure procedure, and be aware that flying at a higher than anticipated ground speed increases the climb rate requirement in feet per minute. Higher than standard climb gradients are specified by a note on the departure procedure chart for graphic DPs or in the Take-Off Minimums and (Obstacle) Departure Procedures section of the U.S. Terminal Procedures booklet for textual ODPs. The required (or higher) climb gradient must be maintained to the specified altitude or fix, then the standard climb gradient of 200 feet per NM can be resumed. A table for the conversion of climb gradient (feet per nautical mile) to climb rate (feet per minute), at a given ground speed, is included in the U.S. Terminal Procedures booklets. (PLT133, IR.V.B.K1) — AIM ¶5-2-8

ALL

4270. (Refer to Figures 163 and 164.) Using an average ground speed of 120 knots, what minimum rate of climb must be maintained to meet the required climb rate (feet per NM) to 6,800 feet as specified on the instrument departure procedure for RWY 32?

A—800 feet per minute.
B—400 feet per minute.
C—600 feet per minute.

Note the takeoff minimums on Figure 163 in the bottom left corner of the departure chart. Runway 32 requires a minimum 400 feet per NM up to 6,800. Using this standard formula you can determine the required rate of climb needed. Additionally, you can interpolate the answer using Legend 27.

1. *Ground speed × climb rate required ÷ 60 = rate of climb needed*
2. *120 × 400 feet/NM ÷ 60 = 800 fpm*

(PLT004, IR.V.B.K1) — FAA-H-8083-15

ALL

4303. (Refer to Legend 27 and Figure 182.) Using an average ground speed of 140 knots, what minimum indicated rate of climb must be maintained to meet the required climb rate (feet per NM) to 6,300 feet for RWY 22 as specified on the instrument departure procedure?

A—916 feet per minute.
B—886 feet per minute.
C—380 feet per minute.

The note on the plan view of the DP states the takeoff minimums for Runway 22: a climb of 380 feet per NM is required to 6,300 feet. Using this standard formula you can determine the required rate of climb needed. Additionally, you can interpolate the answer using Legend 27.

1. *Ground speed × climb rate required ÷ 60 = rate of climb needed*
2. *140 × 380 feet/NM ÷ 60 = 886 fpm*

(PLT004, IR.V.B.K1) — U.S. Terminal Procedures, IAP Chart

Answers

4270-1 [C] 4270 [A] 4303 [B]

ALL

4316. (Refer to Figure 189.) Using an average ground speed of 100 knots, what minimum rate of climb would meet the required minimum climb rate per NM as specified by the instrument departure procedure?

A—425 feet per minute.
B—580 feet per minute.
C—641 feet per minute.

The note on the plan view of the HABUT FOUR DEPARTURE indicates this departure requires a minimum climb rate of 385 feet per NM to 6,000. Using this standard formula you can determine the required rate of climb needed. Additionally, you can interpolate the answer using Legend 27.

1. *Ground speed × climb rate required ÷ 60 = rate of climb needed*
2. *100 × 385 feet/NM ÷ 60 = 641 fpm*

(PLT052, IR.V.B.K1) — U.S. Terminal Procedures, IAP Chart

ALL

4316-1. (Refer to Figure 216.) Departing Runway 34L or 34R with weather minimums for takeoff and a climb ground speed of 150 knots, what minimum rate of climb would be required to 8,700 feet?

A—1,200 feet per minute.
B—1,125 feet per minute.
C—1,225 feet per minute.

The note on the plan view of the RENO NINE DEPARTURE indicates this departure requires a minimum climb rate of 480 feet per NM to 8,700. The Rate-of-Climb Table (FAA Legend 27) is used to convert this to a rate of climb (fpm).

1. *Find 450 feet per NM in the left-hand column. Move right to intercept the 150-knot ground speed column and read 1,125 fpm rate of climb.*
2. *Find 500 feet per NM in the left-hand column. Move right to intercept the 150-knot ground speed column and read 1,250 fpm rate of climb.*
3. *Interpolate the difference between 450 and 500, then find the rate of climb for 480: 1,200 fpm.*

(PLT052, IR.V.B.K1) — U.S. Terminal Procedures, IAP Chart

ALL

4361. (Refer to Figure 211.) At which point does the basic instrument departure procedure terminate?

A—When Helena Departure Control establishes radar contact.
B—At STAKK intersection.
C—Over the BOZEMAN VOR.

The heavy black lines with arrows portray the Departure Route, which, in this case, terminates at STAKK INT. Note also in the textual description all the transitions are indicated with the following statement, "...localizer course to STAKK. INT at or above 8,400 feet. Thence..." (PLT052, IR.V.B.K1) — U.S. Terminal Procedures, DP Chart Legend

Answer (A) is incorrect because Helena Departure Control will establish contact shortly after leaving the runway. Answer (C) is incorrect because the BOZEMAN VOR is the end of the BOZEMAN transition.

ALL

4363. (Refer to Figure 211.) At which minimum altitude should you cross the STAKK intersection?

A—11,800 feet MSL.
B—10,800 feet MSL.
C—10,200 feet MSL.

The departure route descriptions for the STAKK THREE DEPARTURE state "... cross STAKK at or above 10,200" for either runway. (PLT052, IR.V.B.K1) — U.S. Terminal Procedures, DP Chart Legend

ALL

4364. (Refer to Figure 211.) Using an average ground speed of 140 knots, what minimum rate of climb would meet the required minimum climb rate per NM as specified on the instrument departure procedure for RWY 9?

A—933 feet per minute.
B—1,050 feet per minute.
C—968 feet per minute.

The note on the plan view of the STAKK Three Departure indicates a departure from Rwy 9 requires a minimum climb rate of 415 feet per NM to 10,200. Using this standard formula you can determine the required rate of climb needed. Additionally, you can interpolate the answer using Legend 27.

1. *Ground speed × climb rate required ÷ 60 = rate of climb needed*
2. *140 × 415 feet/NM ÷ 60 = 968 fpm*

(PLT052, IR.V.B.K1) — U.S. Terminal Procedures

Answers

4316 [C]	4316-1 [A]	4361 [B]	4363 [C]	4364 [C]

ALL

4364-1. (Refer to Figures 163 and 164.) Departing runway 32 for takeoff with an average ground speed of 120 knots, what minimum rate of climb must be maintained to meet the required climb rate to 6,800 feet as specified on the instrument departure procedure?

A—700 feet per minute.
B—800 feet per minute.
C—900 feet per minute.

The note on the GNATS SIX DEPARTURE indicates this departure requires a minimum climb rate of 400 feet per NM to 6,800 feet for runway 32. Use the Rate-of-Climb Table (FAA Legend 16) to convert this to a rate of climb (fpm). Find 400 feet per NM in the left-hand column. Move right in that row to intercept the 120-knot ground speed column and read 800 feet per minute rate of climb. (PLT052, IR.V.B.K1) — U.S. Terminal Procedures, IAP Chart

ALL

4417. What action is recommended if a pilot does not wish to use an instrument departure procedure?

A—Advise clearance delivery or ground control before departure.
B—Advise departure control upon initial contact.
C—Enter "No DP" in the REMARKS section of the IFR flight plan.

If, for any reason, the pilot does not wish to use a DP, he/she is expected to advise ATC. Notification may be accomplished by writing "NO DP" in the remarks section of the flight plan, or by the less desirable method of verbally advising ATC. (PLT201, IR.V.B.K1) — AIM ¶5-2-8

Answers (A) and (B) are incorrect because entering "No DP" in the flight plan is preferred over a verbal request.

ALL

4418. A particular instrument departure procedure requires a minimum climb rate of 210 feet per NM to 8,000 feet. If you climb with a ground speed of 140 knots, what is the rate of climb required in feet per minute?

A—210.
B—450.
C—490.

The question can be solved using the Rate-of-Climb Table (FAA Legend 16). At a ground speed of 140 knots, a climb rate of 210 feet per NM must be interpolated between 200 and 250: 583 – 467 = 116 × 20% = 23.2, added to 467 fpm equals 490.2 fpm. (PLT004, IR.V.B.K1) — AIM ¶5-2-8

ALL

4419. Which procedure applies to instrument departure procedures?

A—Instrument departure clearances will not be issued unless requested by the pilot.
B—The pilot-in-command must accept an instrument departure procedure when issued by ATC.
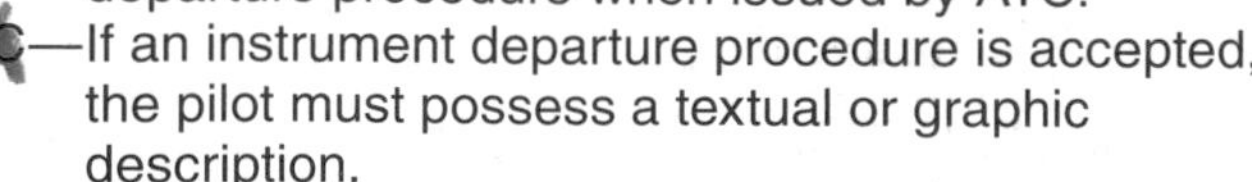
C—If an instrument departure procedure is accepted, the pilot must possess a textual or graphic description.

The use of a DP requires pilot possession of a textual description or graphic depiction of the approved effective DP. (PLT201, IR.V.B.K1) — AIM ¶5-2-8

Answer (A) is incorrect because ATC will issue DP clearances when DP procedures exist. Answer (B) is incorrect because a DP clearance must be rejected if the pilot does not have the textual description of the DP or if it is otherwise unacceptable.

ALL

4488. (Refer to Figure 155.) Which restriction to use the BRICK transition would be applicable to the Grand Junction Six Departure (JNC6.BRICK)?

A—Minimum climb of 300' per NM to 9300.
B—Dual VOR receivers.
C—DME.

On the plan view of the instrument departure procedure under the Note at right, it states: "BRICK and DIRDY TRANSITIONS: DME required." (PLT052, IR.V.B.K1) — U.S. Terminal Procedures

Answer (A) is incorrect because the minimum climb is a takeoff minimum for Runway 11, it does not apply to the actual transitions unless you are specifically departing from that runway. Answer (B) is incorrect because the DP does not state dual VORs are required.

ALL

4489. (Refer to Figures 216 and 216A.) What route should you take if cleared for the RENO Nine Departure with filed routing to V6, takeoff from Runway 25?

A—Climb on heading 254° to 5,000 feet MSL, then climbing right turn heading 340° and expect radar vectors to V6.
B—Climb on runway heading to 5,000 feet MSL, then climbing right turn heading 340° to 9,700 feet MSL, then direct V6.
C—Climb on heading 254° to 5,000 feet MSL, then climbing left turn to intercept V6.

Answers

4364-1 [B]	4417 [C]	4418 [C]	4419 [C]	4488 [C]	4489 [A]

Note the takeoff route description on Figure 216A for Runway 25, "Climb heading 254° to 5000 then climbing right turn heading 340°. Thence..." Below that the note states "...Expect RADAR vectors to assigned route/fix." (PLT052, IR.V.B.K1) — AIM ¶5-2-5

Answer (B) is incorrect because the departure procedure and description specifically states 254°, not runway heading. 9,700 feet MSL are the takeoff minimums for runway 25, and routing is stated to expect radar vectors not direct. Answer (C) is incorrect because the departure procedure calls for a right turn heading 340° upon reaching 5,000 feet MSL, not a left turn.

ALL

4490. (Refer to Figures 216 and 216A.) What procedure should be followed if communication is not established with departure control 1 minute after takeoff from Runway 34L?

A—Turn right direct FMG VORTAC, then via assigned route.
B—Maintain 330° heading up to 10,000 feet MSL, then right turn direct FMG VORTAC, then via assigned route.
C—Turn right direct FMG VORTAC and hold until reaching 8,700 feet MSL, then via assigned route.

Figure 216A states, "If not in contact with departure control within 1 minute after takeoff, maintain assigned heading until passing 10000..." If departing from Runway 34L, you should then "Turn right direct FMG VORTAC, then via assigned route." (PLT052, IR.V.B.K1) — AIM ¶5-2-6

Answers (A) and (C) are incorrect because you are not permitted to turn until passing through 10,000 feet MSL on the assigned heading of 330° when departing Runway 34L.

ALL

4491. (Refer to Figures 216 and 216A.) What is the minimum rate of climb per NM to 9,700 feet departing Runway 25?

A—500 feet.
B—450 feet.
C—400 feet.

The DP in Figure 216 lists takeoff minimums for each runway. For Runway 25 it states, "Standard with a minimum climb of 500 feet per NM to 9700." (PLT052, IR.V.B.K1) — AIM ¶5-2-8

ALL

4492. (Refer to Figures 216 and 216A.) Of the following, which is the minimum acceptable rate of climb (feet per minute) to meet the takeoff minimums for Runway 25 with a departure ground speed of 140 knots?

A—970 feet per minute.
B—1,225 feet per minute.
C—1,167 feet per minute.

The RENO Nine Departure lists the takeoff minimums for each runway. For Runway 25, 500 feet per NM to 9,700 is required. The question lists a GS of 140 knots, which is required to answer the question. Using this standard formula, you can determine the required rate of climb needed. Additionally, you can interpolate the answer using Legend 27.

1. *Ground speed × climb rate required ÷ 60 = rate of climb needed*
2. *140 x 500 feet/NM ÷ 60 = 1,167 fpm*

(PLT052, IR.V.B.K1) — AIM ¶5-2-8

ALL

4683. (Refer to Figures 182 and 183.) All transitions on the GROMO Three Departure require

A—a minimum climb to 8100.
B—DME.
C—a climb-in-hold to 8100 before proceeding on course.

The first note in Figure 182 states that DME is required for this departure procedure. (PLT052, IR.V.B.K1) — U.S. Terminal Procedures Chart

Answers (A) and (C) are incorrect because these two requirements are only noted for the TAMPO transition.

ALL

4638. Which is true regarding the use of an instrument-departure procedure chart?

A—The use of instrument departure procedures is mandatory.
B—To use an instrument departure procedure, the pilot must possess at least the textual description of the approved standard departure.
C—To use an instrument departure procedure, the pilot must possess both the textual and graphic form of the approved procedure.

The use of a DP requires pilot possession of at least the textual description of the approved effective DP. (PLT293, IR.V.B.K1) — AIM ¶5-2-8

Answer (A) is incorrect because DP usage is not mandatory for IFR departures. Answer (C) is incorrect because the pilot must possess only a textual description of the approved effective DP.

Answers

4490 [B]	4491 [A]	4492 [C]	4683 [B]	4638 [B]

Services Available to Pilots

At some locations within airspace defined as Terminal Radar Service Areas, ATC provides separation between all IFR aircraft and all participating VFR aircraft. Pilot participation is urged, but is not mandatory.

Controllers will issue traffic information with reference to a 12-hour clock. The traffic advisories are based on the radar position, and does not take into consideration any heading correction to account for a wind.

"Resume own navigation" means the pilot is to resume his/her own navigational responsibility. It is issued after a radar vector or when radar contact is lost.

"Radar contact" means ATC has identified the aircraft on the radar display and radar flight following will be provided until radar identification is terminated.

ALL
4409. What service is provided by departure control to an IFR flight when operating within the outer area of Class C airspace?

A—Separation from all aircraft.
B—Position and altitude of all traffic within 2 miles of the IFR pilot's line of flight and altitude.
C—Separation from all IFR aircraft and participating VFR aircraft.

Class C Service provides approved separation between IFR and VFR aircraft, and sequencing of VFR arrivals to the primary airport. (PLT161, IR.I.C.K2) — AIM ¶4-1-18

Answer (A) is incorrect because separation from nonparticipating VFR aircraft cannot be provided. Answer (B) is incorrect because ATC will provide traffic advisories (to the extent possible in relation to higher priorities) in relation to your airplane's track, and may include altitude if known.

ALL
4390. When should your transponder be on Mode C while on an IFR flight?

A—Only when ATC requests Mode C.
B—At all times if the equipment has been calibrated, unless requested otherwise by ATC.
C—When passing 12,500 feet MSL.

Adjust transponder to reply on the Mode A/3 code specified by ATC and, if equipped, to reply on Mode C with altitude reporting capability activated; that is, unless deactivation is directed by ATC, or unless the installed aircraft equipment has not been tested and calibrated as required by 14 CFR §91.413. (PLT497, IR.II.B.K1c) — AIM ¶4-1-20

ALL
4421. During a flight, the controller advises "traffic two o'clock 5 miles southbound." The pilot is holding 20° correction for a crosswind from the right. Where should the pilot look for the traffic?

A—40° to the right of the aircraft's nose.
B—20° to the right of the aircraft's nose.
C—Straight ahead.

Radar traffic information is given by the controller based on azimuth from the aircraft's ground track (not the heading) in terms of a 12-hour clock. Each clock position is 30°. Two o'clock is about 60° from the aircraft's course, but since the pilot is already holding a 20° right crosswind, the pilot will only have to look 40° to the right of the aircraft's nose. (PLT370, IR.VI.B.K1) — AIM ¶4-1-15

Answer (B) is incorrect because 20° to the right of the aircraft nose would be between one and two o'clock. Answer (C) is incorrect because straight ahead would be between twelve and one o'clock.

ALL
4422. What is meant when departure control instructs you to "resume own navigation" after you have been vectored to a victor airway?

A—You should maintain the airway by use of your navigation equipment.
B—Radar service is terminated.
C—You are still in radar contact, but must make position reports.

"Resume own navigation" is used by ATC to advise a pilot to resume his/her own navigational responsibility. It is issued after completion of a radar vector or when radar contact is lost while the aircraft is being radar vectored. (PLT370, IR.VI.B.K1) — Pilot/Controller Glossary

Answer (B) is incorrect because "resume own navigation" means the radar controller will stop issuing vectors, but will not stop observing. Answer (C) is incorrect because position reports are not necessary when in radar contact.

Answers

4409 [C] 4390 [B] 4421 [A] 4422 [A]

ALL

4423. What does the ATC term "radar contact" signify?

A—Your aircraft has been identified and you will receive separation from all aircraft while in contact with this radar facility.
B—Your aircraft has been identified on the radar display and radar flight-following will be provided until radar identification is terminated.
C—You will be given traffic advisories until advised the service has been terminated or that radar contact has been lost.

Radar contact is used by ATC to inform an aircraft that it is identified on the radar display and radar flight following will be provided until radar identification is terminated. Radar service may also be provided within the limits of necessity and capability. When a pilot is informed of "radar contact," they discontinue reporting over compulsory reporting points. (PLT044, IR.III.A.K3) — Pilot/ Controller Glossary

Answer (A) is incorrect because separation from all aircraft only occurs in Class A, B, and C airspaces. Answer (C) is incorrect because traffic advisory service is only provided to the extent possible.

ALL

4424. Upon intercepting the assigned radial, the controller advises you that you are on the airway and to "RESUME OWN NAVIGATION." This phrase means that

A—you are still in radar contact, but must make position reports.
B—radar services are terminated and you will be responsible for position reports.
C—you are to assume responsibility for your own navigation.

"Resume own navigation" is used by ATC to advise a pilot to resume their own navigational responsibility. It is issued after completion of a radar vector or when radar contact is lost while the aircraft is being radar vectored. (PLT370, IR.VI.B.K1) — Pilot/Controller Glossary

Answer (A) is incorrect because position reports are not necessary when in radar contact. Answer (B) is incorrect because "resume own navigation" means the radar controller will stop issuing vectors but will not stop observing.

ALL

4736. When is radar service terminated during a visual approach?

A—Automatically when ATC instructs the pilot to contact the tower.
B—Immediately upon acceptance of the approach by the pilot.
C—When ATC advises, "Radar service terminated; resume own navigation."

On a visual approach, radar service is automatically terminated without advising the pilot, when the aircraft is instructed to contact the tower. (PLT170, IR.VI.C.K1) — AIM ¶5-5-11

Answer (B) is incorrect because approach clearance is given long before radar service is terminated. Answer (C) is incorrect because "resume own navigation" is normally an enroute instruction.

ALL

4420. During a takeoff into IFR conditions with low ceilings, when should the pilot contact departure control?

A—Before penetrating the clouds.
B—When advised by the tower.
C—Upon completing the first turn after takeoff.

The pilot should contact departure control on the assigned frequency upon release from the control tower. (PLT222, IR.III.A.K1) — AIM ¶5-2-7

Answers (A) and (C) are incorrect because tower control will advise the pilot when to contact departure control, which may or may not be before penetrating the clouds, upon completion of the first turn after takeoff, or upon establishing cruise climb on a straight-out departure.

Answers

4423 [B] 4424 [C] 4736 [A] 4420 [B]

Pilot/Controller Roles and Responsibilities

The PIC is responsible to see and avoid other traffic whenever meteorological conditions permit, regardless of the type of flight plan to be flown.

The PIC is responsible for complying with speed adjustments within ±10 knots or .02 Mach number of the specified speed.

ATC cannot issue a VFR clearance to a pilot on an IFR flight plan, unless that pilot requests it or to comply with noise abatement routes or altitudes.

ALL

4471. What responsibility does the pilot-in-command of an IFR flight assume upon entering VFR conditions?

A—Report VFR conditions to ARTCC so that an amended clearance may be issued.
B—Use VFR operating procedures.
C—To see and avoid other traffic.

When meteorological conditions permit, regardless of type of flight plan or whether or not under control of a radar facility, the pilot is responsible to see and avoid other traffic, terrain, or obstacles. (PLT444, IR.III.A.K1) — AIM ¶5-5-8

Answer (A) is incorrect because it is not required to report VFR conditions unless requested to do so by ATC. Answer (B) is incorrect because the pilot must follow IFR procedures when on an IFR flight.

ALL

4373. When is a pilot on an IFR flight plan responsible for avoiding other aircraft?

A—At all times when not in radar contact with ATC.
B—When weather conditions permit, regardless of whether operating under IFR or VFR.
C—Only when advised by ATC.

When weather conditions permit, regardless of whether an operation is conducted under IFR or VFR, vigilance shall be maintained by each person operating an aircraft so as to see and avoid other aircraft in compliance with this section. (PLT444, IR.III.A.K1) — 14 CFR §91.113

Answers (A) and (C) are incorrect because if weather conditions permit, each pilot is responsible for seeing and avoiding other aircraft.

ALL

4538. When should pilots state their position on the airport when calling the tower for takeoff?

A—When visibility is less than 1 mile.
B—When parallel runways are in use.
C—When departing from a runway intersection.

Pilots should state their position on the airport when calling the tower for takeoff from a runway intersection. (PLT222, IR.III.A.K1) — AIM ¶4-3-10

ALL

4633. Under which of the following circumstances will ATC issue a VFR restriction to an IFR flight?

A—Whenever the pilot reports the loss of any navigational aid.
B—When it is necessary to provide separation between IFR and special VFR traffic.
C—When the pilot requests it.

ATC may not authorize VFR-on-top/VFR conditions operations unless the pilot requests the VFR operation, or a clearance to operate in VFR conditions will result in noise abatement benefits where part of the IFR departure route does not conform to an FAA-approved noise abatement route or altitude. (PLT044, IR.III.A.K3) — AIM ¶4-4-8

Answer (A) is incorrect because a pilot would only report a malfunction of navigation equipment to ATC. Answer (B) is incorrect because Special VFR traffic would be found in Class D airspace that is currently experiencing IMC, so ATC would not issue a VFR restriction to an IFR flight.

Answers

4471	[C]	4373	[B]	4538	[C]	4633	[C]

ALL

4633-1. During a takeoff into IMC with low ceilings, you should contact departure

A—before entering the clouds.
B—when the tower instructs the change.
C—upon reaching traffic pattern altitude.

Following takeoff, contact departure control on the assigned frequency when advised to do so by the control tower. (PLT222, IR.III.A.K1) — FAA-H-8083-15

ALL

4725. What is the pilot-in-command's responsibility when flying a propeller aircraft within 20 miles of the airport of intended landing and ATC requests the pilot to reduce speed to 160? (Pilot complies with speed adjustment.)

A—Reduce TAS to 160 knots and maintain until advised by ATC.
B—Reduce IAS to 160 MPH and maintain until advised by ATC.
C—Reduce IAS to 160 knots and maintain that speed within 10 knots.

When complying with speed adjustments assignment, maintain an indicated airspeed within ±10 knots or .02 Mach number of the specified speed. (PLT170, IR.VI.C.K1) — AIM ¶5-5-9

Answer (A) is incorrect because the speed restrictions issued by ATC are based on indicated (not true) airspeed. Answer (B) is incorrect because MPH are not used in ATC instructions.

Airport Lighting, Signs, and Marking Aids

The visual approach slope indicator (VASI) is a system of lights arranged to provide visual descent guidance information during the approach to a runway. These lights are visible from 3 to 5 miles during the day and up to 20 miles or more at night. The visual glide path of the VASI provides safe obstruction clearance within ±10° of the extended runway centerline and to 4 NM from the runway threshold. Descent using the VASI should not be initiated until the aircraft is visually aligned with the runway. Lateral course guidance is provided by the runway or runway lights. See Figure 6-3.

The precision approach path indicator (PAPI) uses light units similar to the VASI, but they are installed in a single row of either two- or four-light units. These systems have an effective visual range of about 5 miles during the day and up to 20 miles at night. The row of light units is usually installed on the left side of the runway, and the glide path indications are as depicted. See Figure 6-4.

Runway lighting is described in FAA Legends 30 and 31.

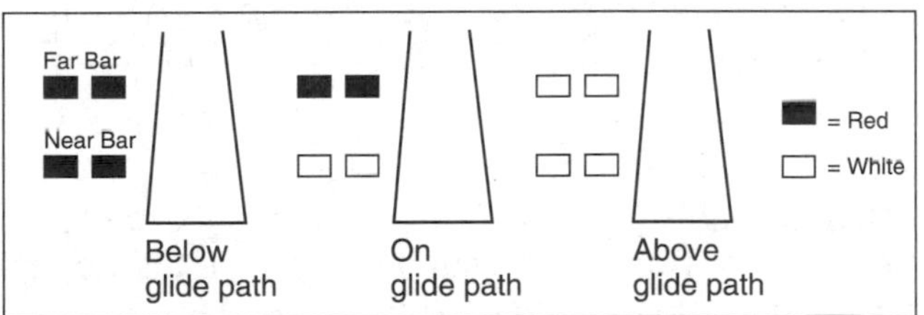

Figure 6-3

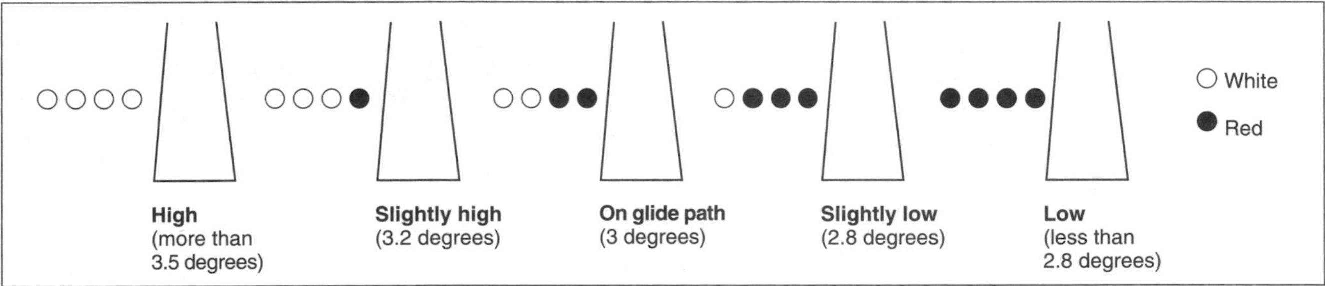

Figure 6-4

Answers

4633-1 [B]
4725 [C]

ALL

4534. (Refer to Figure 94.) Mandatory airport instruction signs are designated by having

A—yellow lettering with a black background.
B—white lettering with a red background.
C—black lettering with a yellow background.

Mandatory instruction signs have a red background with a white inscription and are used to denote:

1. *An entrance to a runway or critical area; and*
2. *Areas where an aircraft is prohibited from entering.*

(PLT141, IR.VI.E.K2) — AIM ¶2-3-8

ALL

4535. (Refer to Figure 94.) What sign is designated by illustration 7?

A—Location sign.
B—Mandatory instruction sign.
C—Direction sign.

The holding position sign is a mandatory instruction sign, used to hold an aircraft on a taxiway located in the approach or departure area for a runway so the aircraft does not interfere with operations on that runway. (PLT141, IR.VI.E.K2) — AIM ¶2-3-8

ALL

4536. (Refer to Figure 94.) What colors are runway holding position signs?

A—White with a red background.
B—Red with a white background.
C—Yellow with a black background.

Holding position signs are mandatory instruction signs and have a red background with a white inscription. (PLT141, IR.VI.E.K2) — AIM ¶2-3-8

ALL

4537. (Refer to Figure 94.) Hold line markings at the intersection of taxiways and runways consist of four lines that extend across the width of the taxiway. These lines are

A—white and the dashed lines are nearest the runway.
B—yellow and the dashed lines are nearest the runway.
C—yellow and the solid lines are nearest the runway.

Holding position markings indicate where an aircraft is supposed to stop. They consist of four yellow lines: two solid and two dashed, spaced six inches apart and extending across the width of the taxiway or runway. The solid lines are always on the side where the aircraft is to hold. (PLT141, IR.VI.E.K2) — AIM ¶2-3-5

ALL

4537-1. Which lines should you cross when exiting the runway?

A—Solid lines.
B—Striped lines.
C—Both solid and striped lines.

Holding position markings indicate where an aircraft is supposed to stop. Referred typically to as "hold short lines," they consist of four yellow lines: two solid and two dashed, spaced six inches apart and extending across the width of the taxiway or runway. The solid lines are always on the side where the aircraft is to hold. An aircraft exiting a runway is not clear of the runway until all parts of the aircraft have crossed the applicable holding position marking. (PLT141, IR.I.C.K2) — AIM ¶2-3-5

ALL

4774. (Refer to Figure 134.) Unless a higher angle is necessary for obstacle clearance, what is the normal glidepath angle for a 2-bar VASI?

A—2.75°.
B—3.00°.
C—3.25°.

Two-bar VASI installations provide one visual glidepath which is normally set at 3°. (PLT147, IR.VI.E.K2) — AIM ¶2-1-2

Answers

4534 [B]	4535 [B]	4536 [A]	4537 [B]	4537-1 [C]	4774 [B]

ALL

4775. Which of the following indications would a pilot see while approaching to land on a runway served by a 2-bar VASI?

A—If on the glidepath, the near bars will appear red, and the far bars will appear white.
B—If departing to the high side of the glidepath, the far bars will change from red to white.
C—If on the glidepath, both near bars and far bars will appear white.

When on the glidepath with a two-bar VASI (four light units shown), the pilot will see red-over-white. As the airplane levels off and deviates above the visual glidepath, it flies through the transition zone for the far bars. The far bars will turn from red to white, and the airplane will be above the glidepath. See the figure below. (PLT147, IR.VI.E.K2) — AIM ¶2-1-2

Answer (A) is incorrect because this type of indication is not possible. Answer (C) is incorrect because both bars must be white to indicate the aircraft above (not on) the glidepath.

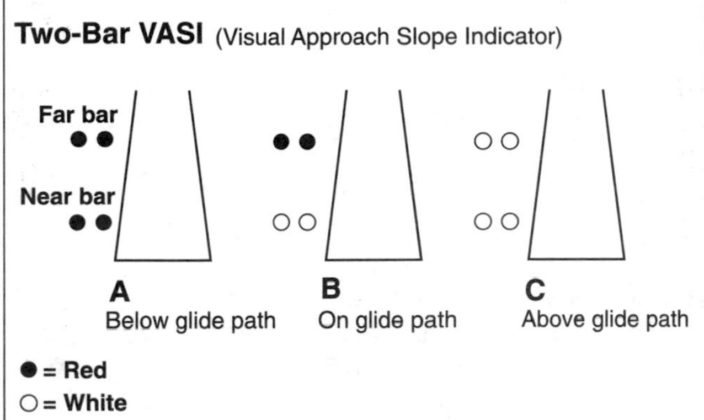

Questions 4775 and 4778

ALL

4776. The middle and far bars of a 3-bar VASI will

A—both appear white to the pilot when on the upper glidepath.
B—constitute a 2-bar VASI for using the lower glidepath.
C—constitute a 2-bar VASI for using the upper glidepath.

Three-bar VASI installations provide two visual glidepaths. The lower path is provided by the near and middle bars and is normally set at 3° higher, while the upper path, provided by the middle and far bars, is normally 1/4 degree higher. (PLT147, IR.VI.E.K2) — AIM ¶2-1-2

Answer (A) is incorrect because if a pilot was on the upper glidepath, the middle bar would be white and the far bar would be red. Answer (B) is incorrect because the middle and far bars are for the upper glidepath.

ALL

4778. When on the proper glidepath of a 2-bar VASI, the pilot will see the near bar as

A—white and the far bar as red.
B—red and the far bar as white.
C—white and the far bar as white.

When on the glidepath with a two-bar VASI, the pilot will see red-over-white. See the figure on the previous page. (PLT147, IR.VI.E.K2) — AIM ¶2-1-2

ALL

4779. If an approach is being made to a runway that has an operating 3-bar VASI and all the VASI lights appear red as the airplane reaches the MDA, the pilot should

A—start a climb to reach the proper glidepath.
B—continue at the same rate of descent if the runway is in sight.
C—level off momentarily to intercept the proper approach path.

See the figure below. An airplane approaching to land on a runway served by a visual approach slope indicator, shall maintain an altitude at or above the glide slope until a lower altitude is necessary for a safe landing. If the VASI is indicating all red lights, the aircraft is below the glidepaths, and the pilot should level-off momentarily to intercept the proper approach path. (PLT147, IR.VI.E.K2) — AIM ¶2-1-2

Answer (A) is incorrect because climbing is not necessary to acquire the proper glldepath. Answer (B) is incorrect because if you continue your present rate of descent, you will remain below the glidepath.

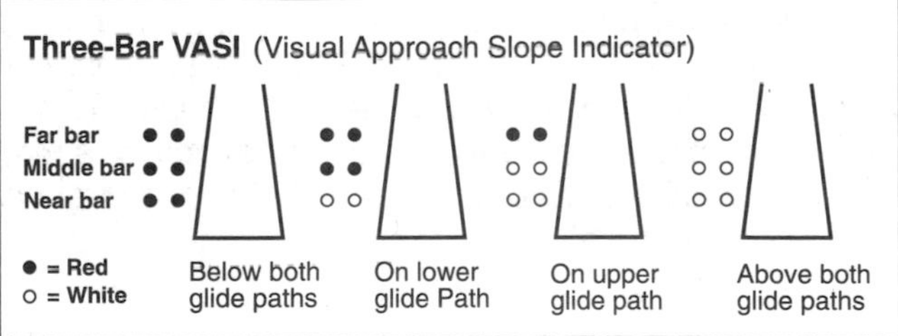

Question 4779

Answers

4775 [B]	4776 [C]	4778 [A]	4779 [C]

ALL
4781. Which approach and landing objective is assured when the pilot remains on the proper glidepath of the VASI?

A—Continuation of course guidance after transition to VFR.
B—Safe obstruction clearance in the approach area.
C—Course guidance from the visual descent point to touchdown.

The VASI is a system of lights arranged to provide visual descent guidance information during the approach to a runway. These lights are visible from 3 to 5 miles during the day, and up to 20 miles or more at night. The visual glidepath of the VASI provides safe obstruction clearance within ±10° of the extended runway centerline and to 4 NM from the runway threshold. (PLT147, IR.VI.E.K2) — AIM ¶2-1-2

Answers (A) and (C) are incorrect because a VASI does not provide course guidance.

ALL
4782. (Refer to Figure 135.) Unless a higher angle is required for obstacle clearance, what is the normal glidepath for a 3-bar VASI?

A—2.3°.
B—2.75°.
C—3.0°.

Three-bar VASI installations provide two visual glidepaths. The lower glidepath is provided by the near and middle bars and is normally set at 3° while the upper glidepath, provided by the middle and far bars, is normally 1/4-degree higher. This higher glidepath is intended for use only by high cockpit aircraft to provide a sufficient threshold-crossing height. Although normal glidepath angles are 3°, angles at some locations may be as high as 4.5° to give proper obstacle clearance. (PLT147, IR.VI.E.K2) — AIM ¶2-1-2

ALL
4783. (Refer to Figure 135.) Which illustration would a pilot observe when on the lower glidepath?

A—4.
B—5.
C—6.

On a lower glidepath of a three-bar VASI, the near lights will be white and the middle and far bars will be red, which is illustration 5. See the figure below. (PLT147, IR.VI.E.K2) — AIM ¶2-1-2

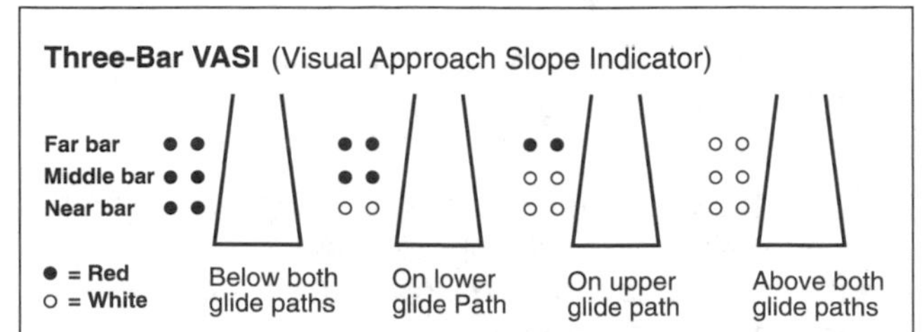

Questions 4783, 4784 and 4785

ALL
4784. (Refer to Figure 135.) Which illustration would a pilot observe if the aircraft is above both glidepaths?

A—5.
B—6.
C—7.

Above a glidepath of a three-bar VASI, all of the lights will be white, which is illustration 7. See the figure above. (PLT147, IR.VI.E.K2) — AIM ¶2-1-2

ALL
4785. (Refer to Figure 135.) Which illustration would a pilot observe if the aircraft is below both glidepaths?

A—4.
B—5.
C—6.

Below a glidepath of a three-bar VASI, all of the lights will be red, which is illustration 4. See the figure above. (PLT147, IR.VI.E.K2) — AIM ¶2-1-2

ALL
4786. (Refer to Figure 136.) Which illustration depicts an "on glidepath" indication?

A—8.
B—10.
C—11.

The PAPI uses light units similar to the VASI, but are installed in a single row of either two- or four-light units. The on-glidepath indication will have two red lights and two white lights, which is illustration 10. (PLT147, IR.VI.E.K2) — AIM ¶2-1-2

Answers

4781 [B] 4782 [C] 4783 [B] 4784 [C] 4785 [A] 4786 [B]

ALL

4787. (Refer to Figure 136.) Which illustration depicts a "slightly low" (2.8°) indication?

A—9.
B—10.
C—11.

The PAPI uses light units similar to the VASI, but are installed in a single row of either two- or four-light units. The slightly low position will be indicated with three red lights and one white light, which is illustration 11. (PLT147, IR.VI.E.K2) — AIM ¶2-1-2

ALL

4790. (Refer to Figure 136.) Which illustration would a pilot observe if the aircraft is less than 2.5°?

A—10.
B—11.
C—12.

The PAPI uses light units similar to the VASI, but are installed in a single row of either two- or four-light units. The low-glidepath indication will have all red lights, which is illustration 12. (PLT147, IR.VI.E.K2) — AIM ¶2-1-2

ALL

4994. (Refer to Figure 136.) As you emerge from the clouds during an instrument approach and make visual contact with the runway environment, you see PAPI lights corresponding to those depicted in illustration 12. You are

A—on the glidepath.
B—above the glidepath.
C—below the glidepath.

PAPI uses light units similar to the VASI, but are installed in a single row of either two- or four-light units. The low-glidepath indication will have all red lights, which is depicted in illustration 12. (PLT147, IR.VI.E.K2) — AIM ¶2-1-2

ALL

4795. Which type of runway lighting consists of a pair of synchronized flashing lights, one on each side of the runway threshold?

A—MALSR.
B—HIRL.
C—REIL.

REIL are installed for rapid and positive identification of the approach end of a runway. The system consists of a pair of synchronized flashing lights, located laterally one on each side of the runway threshold facing the approach area. See the figure below. (PLT145, IR.VI.E.K2) — AIM ¶2-1-3

Answer (A) is incorrect because MALSR are medium-intensity approach lights. Answer (B) is incorrect because HIRL are high-intensity runway lights, which is a runway edge lighting system.

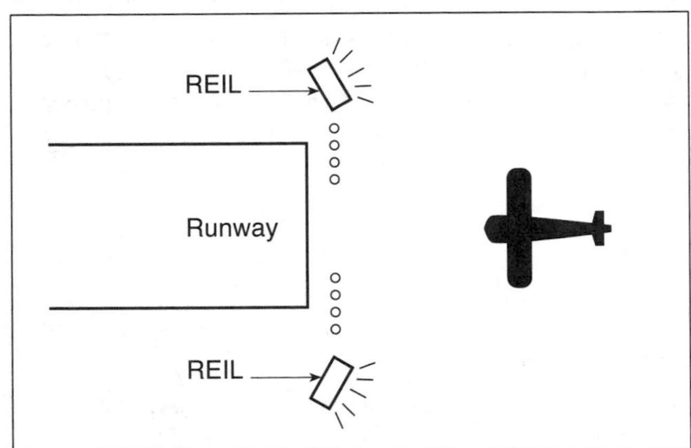

Question 4795

ALL

4796. The primary purpose of runway end identifier lights, installed at many airfields, is to provide

A—rapid identification of the approach end of the runway during reduced visibility.
B—a warning of the final 3,000 feet of runway remaining as viewed from the takeoff or approach position.
C—rapid identification of the primary runway during reduced visibility.

REIL are installed for rapid and positive identification of the approach end of a runway. The system consists of a pair of synchronized flashing lights, located laterally one on each side of the runway threshold facing the approach area. (PLT145, IR.VI.E.K2) — AIM ¶2-1-3

Answers

4787 [C]	4790 [C]	4994 [C]	4795 [C]	4796 [A]

ALL

4791. (Refer to Figure 137.) What is the distance (A) from the beginning of the runway to the fixed distance marker?

A—500 feet.
B—1,000 feet.
C—1,500 feet.

The aiming point marking (or fixed distance marker) serves as a visual aiming point for a landing aircraft. These two rectangular markings consist of a broad white stripe located on each side of the runway centerline and approximately 1,000 feet from the landing threshold. (PLT141, IR.VI.E.K2) — AIM ¶2-3-3

ALL

4302. (Refer to Figure 162.) You have accepted a visual approach to RWY 16L at EUG at night. As you approach the runway, you notice runway centerline lights. This indicates

A—you are on the centerline for your assigned runway.
B—you are too low on the approach.
C—you have lined up with the wrong runway.

According to the Chart Supplement for EUG, Runway 16L does not have runway centerline lights, only Runway 16R/34L does. You are therefore lined up on the wrong runway. Runway centerline lights are shown on the airport visual depiction with white ticks down the center of the runway and noted as CL under the runway information in the textual section. (PLT281, IR.VI.E.K2) — Chart Supplement U.S. Legend

ALL

4792. (Refer to Figure 137.) What is the distance (B) from the beginning of the runway to the touchdown zone marker?

A—250 feet.
B—500 feet.
C—750 feet.

The touchdown zone markings identify the touchdown zone for landing operations and are coded to provide distance information in 500-foot increments. These markings consist of groups of one, two, and three rectangular bars symmetrically arranged in pairs about the runway centerline. (PLT141, IR.VI.E.K2) — AIM ¶2-3-3

ALL

4793. (Refer to Figure 137.) What is the distance (C) from the beginning of the touchdown zone marker to the beginning of the fixed distance marker?

A—1,000 feet.
B—500 feet.
C—250 feet.

The touchdown zone marker is 500 feet from the runway threshold, and the fixed distance marker is 1,000 feet from the runway threshold. Therefore, the distance from the beginning of the touchdown zone marker to the beginning of the fixed distance marker is 500 feet (1,000 – 500). (PLT141, IR.VI.E.K2) — AIM ¶2-3-3

ALL

4794. Which runway marking indicates a displaced threshold on an instrument runway?

A—Arrows leading to the threshold mark.
B—Centerline dashes starting at the threshold.
C—Red chevron marks in the nonlanding portion of the runway.

A displaced threshold is a threshold that is not at the beginning of the full strength runway pavement. The paved area behind the displaced runway threshold is available for taxiing, the landing rollout, and the takeoff of aircraft. White arrows are located along the centerline in the area between the beginning of the runway and the displaced threshold. (PLT141, IR.VI.E.K2) — AIM ¶2-3-3

ALL

4797. (Refer to Figure 138.) What night operations, if any, are authorized between the approach end of the runway and the threshold lights?

A—No aircraft operations are permitted short of the threshold lights.
B—Only taxi operations are permitted in the area short of the threshold lights.
C—Taxi and takeoff operations are permitted, providing the takeoff operations are toward the visible green threshold lights.

On displaced thresholds, runway edge lights emit red light toward the runway to indicate the end of the runway to a departing aircraft, and green light outward from the runway end to indicate the threshold to landing aircraft. The area behind the displaced threshold is available for taxiing, landing rollout, and takeoff. (PLT141, IR.VI.E.K2) — AIM ¶2-1-4

Answers

4791 [B]	4302 [C]	4792 [B]	4793 [B]	4794 [A]	4797 [C]

ALL
4943. The "runway hold position" sign denotes

A—intersecting runways.
B—an entrance to runway from a taxiway.
C—an area protected for an aircraft approaching a runway.

The runway holding position sign is a mandatory instruction sign which is used to denote an entrance to a runway or critical area. (PLT141, IR.VI.E.K2) — AIM ¶2-3-8

ALL
4944. "Runway hold position" markings on the taxiway

A—identifies where aircraft hold short of the runway.
B—identifies area where aircraft are prohibited.
C—allows an aircraft permission onto the runway.

For runways, runway holding position markings indicate where an aircraft is supposed to stop. (PLT141, IR.VI.E.K2) — AIM ¶2-3-5

ALL
4945. The "No Entry" sign identifies

A—the exit boundary for the runway protected area.
B—an area that does not continue beyond intersection.
C—paved area where aircraft entry is prohibited.

The no entry sign prohibits an aircraft from entering an area. Typically, this sign would be located on a taxiway intended to be used in only one direction or at an intersection of vehicle roadways with runways, taxiways or aprons where the roadway may be mistaken as a taxiway or other aircraft movement surface. (PLT141, IR.VI.E.K2) — AIM ¶2-3-8

ALL
4946. When turning onto a taxiway from another taxiway, the "taxiway directional sign" indicates

A—direction to the takeoff runway.
B—designation and direction of taxiway leading out of an intersection.
C—designation and direction of exit taxiway from runway.

Direction signs have a yellow background with a black inscription. The inscription identifies the designation(s) of the intersecting taxiway(s) leading out of the intersection that a pilot would normally be expected to turn onto or hold short of. (PLT141, IR.VI.E.K2) — AIM ¶2-3-10

ALL
4954. When exiting the runway, what is the purpose of the runway exit sign?

A—Indicates designation and direction of exit taxiway from runway.
B—Indicates designation and direction of taxiway leading out of an intersection.
C—Indicates direction to take-off runway.

Runway exit signs provide the direction to turn to exit the runway onto the named taxiway. (PLT141, IR.VI.E.K2) — FAA-H-8083-25

Answer (B) is incorrect because this is the purpose of the taxiway directional sign. Answer (C) is incorrect because this is the purpose of the direction sign.

ALL
4954-1. A runway exit sign

A—points toward a named taxiway that leads off the runway.
B—designated an intersection of two or more runways.
C—indicates the direction to exit from a named taxiway onto a runway.

Runway exit signs provide direction to turn to exit runway onto named taxiway. (PLT141, IR.VI.E.K2) — FAA-H-8083-25

ALL
4250. (Refer to Figure 185.) What is identified by HS 1 and HS 2 on the PDX airport diagram?

A—Hot Spot.
B—Increased Helicopter Activity.
C—Restricted Area.

A hot spot is defined as a location on an airport movement area with a history of potential risk of collision or runway incursion, and where heightened attention by pilots and drivers is necessary. These hot spots are identified by HS and sequentially numbered. (PLT141, IR.VI.E.K2) — FAA-H-8083-25

Answers

4943 [B]	4944 [A]	4945 [C]	4946 [B]	4954 [A]	4954-1 [A]
4250 [A]					

ALL

4304. (Refer to Figure 254.) Which of the signs in the figure is a mandatory instruction sign?

A—Top red.
B—Middle yellow.
C—Bottom yellow.

Mandatory instruction signs are red with white lettering. (PLT141, IR.VI.E.K2) — AIM ¶2-3-8

ALL

4951. (Refer to Figure 256.) You have requested taxi instructions for takeoff using Runway 16. The controller issues the following taxi instructions: "N123, Taxi to Runway 16." Where are you required to stop in order to be in compliance with the controller's instructions?

A—5 (Five).
B—6 (Six).
C—9 (Nine).

When ATC clears an aircraft to "taxi to" an assigned takeoff runway, the absence of holding instructions does not authorize the aircraft to "cross" all runways which the taxi route intersects except the assigned takeoff runway. A clearance must be obtained prior to crossing any runway. It does not include authorization to "taxi onto" or "cross" the assigned takeoff runway at any point. You should taxi and hold short of Runway 16, which is position 5. (PLT141, IR.VI.E.K2) — AIM ¶4-3-18

Answer (B) is incorrect because "taxi to" does not authorize the aircraft to "taxi onto" the assigned takeoff runway. Answer (C) is incorrect because the airplane should taxi the most direct route to the assigned runway unless instructed otherwise; position 9 would not be encountered for the airplane at the west ramp to taxi to Runway 16.

ALL

4952. In the movement area of an airport, what does a "Destination" sign indicate?

A—Direction to the takeoff runway.
B—Direction from taxiway to runway.
C—Direction from ramp to taxiway.

Destination signs have a yellow background with a black inscription indicating a destination at the airport. These signs always have an arrow showing the direction of the taxiing route to that destination and provide information on locating things, such as runways, terminals, cargo areas, and civil aviation areas. Outbound destination signs define directions to takeoff runways. Inbound destination signs define directions for arriving aircraft. (PLT141, IR.VI.E.K2) — AIM ¶2-3-11

ALL

4963. The ILS critical area markings denote

A—where you are clear of the runway.
B—where you must be to start your ILS procedure.
C—where you are clear of the ILS critical area.

The ILS critical area sign is located adjacent to the ILS holding position marking on the pavement and can be seen by pilots leaving the critical area. The sign is intended to provide pilots with another visual cue which they can use as a guide in deciding when they are clear of the ILS critical area. (PLT141, IR.VI.E.K2) — AIM ¶2-3-9

ALL

4963-1. (Refer to Figure 259.) While clearing an active runway, you are clear of the ILS critical area when you pass which sign?

A—D.
B—G.
C—H.

Sign H depicts the ILS critical area. ILS critical areas are markings depicted with two yellow solid lines spaced two feet apart connected by two solid lines spaced ten feet apart, and extending across the width of the taxiway. The ILS critical area is not clear until all parts of the aircraft have crossed the applicable holding position marking. (PLT141, IR.VI.E.K2) — AIM ¶2-3-5

Answers

4304 [A]	4951 [A]	4952 [A]	4963 [C]	4963-1 [C]

VFR-On-Top

A pilot operating in VMC while on an IFR flight plan may wish to select a different altitude. The pilot may request VFR-on-top, and if the request is approved, select an appropriate VFR altitude based on the magnetic course being flown at or above the minimum IFR altitude (0° through 179°, odd thousands plus 500 feet; 180° through 359°, even thousands plus 500 feet).

ATC may provide traffic information on other IFR or VFR aircraft to pilots operating VFR-on-top, but when in VMC, it is the pilot's responsibility to see and avoid other aircraft.

Pilots should advise ATC prior to any altitude change to ensure the exchange of accurate traffic information.

VFR-on-top will not be authorized at or above 18,000 feet MSL.

ALL

4430. What altitude may a pilot on an IFR flight plan select upon receiving a VFR-on-top clearance?

A—Any altitude at least 1,000 feet above the meteorological condition.
B—Any appropriate VFR altitude at or above the MEA in VFR weather conditions.
C—Any VFR altitude appropriate for the direction of flight at least 500 feet above the meteorological condition.

The VFR-on-top clearance is the ATC authorization for an IFR aircraft to operate in VFR conditions at any appropriate VFR altitude (as specified in 14 CFR and as restricted by ATC). A pilot receiving this authorization must comply with VFR visibility, distance from cloud criteria, and the minimum IFR altitudes. (PLT298, IR.I.C.K2) — 14 CFR §91.159

Answers (A) and (C) are incorrect because with a VFR-on-top clearance, the pilot is not restricted to 500 feet above the meteorological condition.

ALL

4431. When must a pilot fly at a cardinal altitude plus 500 feet on an IFR flight plan?

A—When flying above 18,000 feet in VFR conditions.
B—When flying in VFR conditions above clouds.
C—When assigned a VFR-On-Top clearance.

A pilot operating on an IFR flight plan in VFR conditions with an ATC authorization to "maintain VFR-on-top, maintain VFR conditions," must fly at appropriate VFR altitudes which are VFR cardinal altitudes plus 500 feet. (PLT044, IR.I.C.K2) — 14 CFR §91.179

Answer (A) is incorrect because VFR-on-top is not permitted in Class A airspace, which is from 18,000 feet MSL up to and including FL600. Answer (B) is incorrect because a pilot on a IFR flight plan can only utilize VFR altitudes when assigned a VFR-on-top clearance.

ALL

4433. You have filed an IFR flight plan with a VFR-On-Top clearance in lieu of an assigned altitude. If you receive this clearance and fly a course of 180°, at what altitude should you fly? (Assume VFR conditions.)

A—Any IFR altitude which will enable you to remain in VFR conditions.
B—An odd thousand-foot MSL altitude plus 500 feet.
C—An even thousand-foot MSL altitude plus 500 feet.

A pilot operating on an IFR flight plan in VFR conditions with a VFR-on-top clearance must fly at appropriate VFR altitudes, which are VFR cardinal altitudes plus 500 feet. On a magnetic course of 180° through 359°, any even thousand-foot MSL altitude plus 500 feet must be flown. (PLT298, IR.I.C.K2) — 14 CFR §91.179

Answer (A) is incorrect because when operating under a VFR-on-top clearance, the pilot must use VFR (not IFR) altitudes. Answer (B) is incorrect because odd thousand-foot altitudes plus 500 feet must be flown on a magnetic course of 0° through 179°.

ALL

4447. Where are VFR-on-top operations prohibited?

A—In Class A airspace.
B—During off-airways direct flights.
C—When flying through Class B airspace.

VFR-on-top is not permitted in Class A airspace. Consequently, IFR flights operating VFR-on-top are not allowed to operate above FL180. (PLT298, IR.I.C.K2) — AIM ¶4-4-7

Answers (B) and (C) are incorrect because VFR-on-top operations are allowed (not prohibited) while flying during off-airways direct flights or when flying through Class B airspace.

Answers

4430 [B] 4431 [C] 4433 [C] 4447 [A]

ALL

4449. Which rules apply to the pilot-in-command when operating on a VFR-On-Top clearance?

A—VFR only.
B—VFR and IFR.
C—VFR when "in the clear" and IFR when "in the clouds."

When operating in VFR conditions with an ATC authorization to "maintain VFR-on-top/maintain VFR conditions," pilots on IFR flight plans must:

1. *Fly at the appropriate VFR altitude as prescribed in 14 CFR §91.159.*
2. *Comply with the VFR visibility and distance from cloud criteria in 14 CFR §91.155 (basic VFR weather minimums).*
3. *Comply with instrument flight rules that are applicable to this flight (i.e., minimum IFR altitudes, position reporting, radio communications, course to be flown, adherence to ATC clearance, etc.).*

(PLT298, IR.I.C.K2) — AIM ¶4-4-8

Answer (A) is incorrect because a VFR-on-top clearance does not cancel the IFR flight plan. Answer (C) is incorrect because a VFR-on-top clearance does not permit a pilot to fly in IMC.

ALL

4450. When can a VFR-On-Top clearance be assigned by ATC?

A—Only upon request of the pilot when conditions are indicated to be suitable.
B—Any time suitable conditions exist and ATC wishes to expedite traffic flow.
C—When VFR conditions exist, but there is a layer of clouds below the MEA.

ATC may not authorize VFR-on-top operations unless the pilot requests the VFR operation while operating in VMC weather. (PLT298, IR.I.C.K2) — AIM ¶4-4-8

Answers (B) and (C) are incorrect because ATC can only issue a VFR-on-top clearance upon a pilot's request.

ALL

4451. Which ATC clearance should instrument-rated pilots request in order to climb through a cloud layer or an area of reduced visibility and then continue the flight VFR?

A—To VFR-On-Top.
B—Special VFR to VFR Over-the-Top.
C—VFR Over-the-Top.

Pilots desiring to climb through a cloud, haze, smoke, or other meteorological formation, and then either cancel their IFR flight plan or operate VFR-on-top, may request a climb to VFR-on-top. (PLT298, IR.I.C.K2) — AIM ¶4-4-8

Answer (B) is incorrect because a special VFR clearance is issued in Class D airspace, and the pilot must remain clear of clouds (not climb through them). Answer (C) is incorrect because the pilot must request a VFR-on-top (not VFR Over-the-Top) clearance.

ALL

4452. When on a VFR-On-Top clearance, the cruising altitude is based on

A—true course.
B—magnetic course.
C—magnetic heading.

When operating on a VFR-on-top clearance, the pilot must fly VFR cruising altitudes which are based on magnetic course. (PLT298, IR.I.C.K2) — AIM ¶4-4-8

ALL

4453. In which airspace is VFR-On-Top operation prohibited?

A— Class B airspace.
B— Class E airspace.
C— Class A airspace.

ATC will not authorize VFR or VFR-on-top operations in Class A airspace. (PLT298, IR.I.C.K2) — AIM ¶4-4-8

Answers (A) and (B) are incorrect because VFR-on-top is allowed (not prohibited) in Class B and E airspace.

Answers

4449 [B]	4450 [A]	4451 [A]	4452 [B]	4453 [C]

ALL

4454. What cruising altitude is appropriate for VFR on Top on a westbound flight below 18,000 feet?

A—Even thousand-foot levels.
B—Even thousand-foot levels plus 500 feet, but not below MEA.
C—Odd thousand-foot levels plus 500 feet, but not below MEA.

When operating on a VFR-on-top clearance, the pilot must fly appropriate VFR cruising altitudes. On a magnetic course of 180° through 359°, the pilot must fly any even thousand-foot MSL altitude plus 500 feet. (PLT298, IR.I.C.K2) — AIM ¶4-4-8

Answer (A) is incorrect because an even thousand-foot level is an IFR cruising altitude and VFR-on-top requires VFR altitudes. Answer (C) is incorrect because odd thousand-foot levels plus 500 feet are for eastbound flights.

ALL

4510. (Refer to Figure 91.) What are the two limiting cruising altitudes useable on V343 for a VFR-On-Top flight from DBS VORTAC to RANEY intersection?

A—14,500 and 16,500 feet.
B—15,000 and 17,000 feet.
C—15,500 and 17,500 feet.

The eastbound course on V343 from DBS VORTAC to RANEY intersection requires VFR-on-top odd altitudes plus 500 feet above the MEA (15,000 feet MSL) and below Class A (18,000 feet MSL). (PLT100, IR.I.C.K2) — Enroute Low Altitude Chart Legend

ALL

4455. What reports are required of a flight operating on an IFR clearance specifying VFR-on-top in a nonradar environment?

A—The same reports that are required for any IFR flight.
B—All normal IFR reports except vacating altitudes.
C—Only the reporting of any unforecast weather.

When operating in VFR conditions with an ATC authorization to "maintain VFR-on-top" pilots on IFR flight plans must comply with instrument flight rules that are applicable to this flight (i.e., minimum IFR altitudes, position reporting, radio communications, course to be flown, adherence to ATC clearance, etc.). (PLT298, IR.I.C.K2) — AIM ¶4-4-8

Answer (B) is incorrect because all normal IFR reports are required while flying on a VFR-on-top clearance, including any altitude change. Answer (C) is incorrect because all IFR reports, not only unforecast weather, must be made while flying on a VFR-on-top clearance.

ALL

4457. What minimums must be considered in selecting an altitude when operating with a VFR-On-Top clearance?

A—At least 500 feet above the lowest MEA, or appropriate MOCA, and at least 1,000 feet above the existing meteorological condition.
B—At least 1,000 feet above the lowest MEA, appropriate MOCA, or existing meteorological condition.
C—Minimum IFR altitude, minimum distance from clouds, and visibility appropriate to altitude selected.

VFR-on-top flight must be conducted at or above the minimum IFR altitude and in basic VFR weather conditions. (PLT298, IR.I.C.K2) — AIM ¶4-4-8

Answers (A) and (B) are incorrect because the pilot must fly at or above (not a specified distance from) the minimum IFR altitude and the pilot may fly above, below, or between layers of the existing weather conditions.

Answers

4454 [B]	4510 [C]	4455 [A]	4457 [C]

ALL

4643. When operating under IFR with a VFR-On-Top clearance, what altitude should be maintained?

A—The last IFR altitude assigned by ATC.
B—An IFR cruising altitude appropriate to the magnetic course being flown.
C—A VFR cruising altitude appropriate to the magnetic course being flown and as restricted by ATC.

If the ATC clearance assigns "VFR conditions on top" the pilot shall maintain an appropriate VFR altitude or flight level as prescribed by 14 CFR §91.159 (which describes the VFR hemispheric rule). (PLT298, IR.I.C.K2) — AIM ¶4-4-8

ALL

4643-1. ATC has approved your request for VFR-on-top while on an IFR clearance. Therefore, you

A—should set your transponder to code 1200.
B—must fly appropriate IFR altitudes.
C—must fly appropriate VFR altitudes.

When operating in VFR conditions with an ATC authorization to "maintain VFR-on-top/maintain VFR conditions," pilots on IFR flight plans must:

1. *Fly at the appropriate VFR altitude as prescribed in 14 CFR §91.159.*
2. *Comply with the VFR visibility and distance from cloud criteria in 14 CFR §91.155 (basic VFR weather minimums).*
3. *Comply with instrument flight rules that are applicable to this flight (i.e., minimum IFR altitudes, position reporting, radio communications, course to be flown, adherence to ATC clearance, etc.).*

(PLT161, IR.I.C.K2) — AIM ¶4-4-8

Answers

4643 [C] 4643-1 [C]

Chapter 7
En Route

Instrument Altitudes

Minimum enroute altitude (MEA) is the lowest published altitude between radio fixes which ensures acceptable navigational signal coverage and meets obstacle clearance requirements between those fixes.

Minimum reception altitude (MRA) is the lowest altitude at which an intersection can be determined.

Minimum crossing altitude (MCA) is the lowest altitude at certain fixes at which an aircraft must cross when proceeding in the direction of a higher minimum enroute IFR altitude.

Minimum obstruction clearance altitude (MOCA) is the lowest published altitude in effect between radio fixes on VOR airways, off-airway routes, or route segments which meets obstacle clearance requirements for the entire route segment, and which ensures acceptable navigational signal coverage within 25 SM (22 NM) of a VOR.

Minimum sector altitude (MSA) is the lowest altitude which may be used under emergency conditions which will provide a minimum clearance of 1,000 feet above all obstacles located in an area contained within a 25 NM sector centered on a radio aid to navigation.

ALL

4429. What is the definition of MEA?

A—The lowest published altitude which meets obstacle clearance requirements and assures acceptable navigational signal coverage.
B—The lowest published altitude which meets obstacle requirements, assures acceptable navigational signal coverage, two-way radio communications, and provides adequate radar coverage.
C—An altitude which meets obstacle clearance requirements, assures acceptable navigation signal coverage, two-way radio communications, adequate radar coverage, and accurate DME mileage.

The MEA is the lowest published altitude between radio fixes which assures acceptable navigational signal coverage and meets obstacle clearance requirements between those fixes. The MEA prescribed for a federal airway or segment thereof, area navigation low or high route or other direct route applies to the entire width of the airway, segment, or route between the radio fixes defining the airway, segment or route. (PLT033, IR.I.C.K2) — Pilot/Controller Glossary

Answers (B) and (C) are incorrect because the MEA does not guarantee that two-way radio communications are adequate radar coverage.

ALL

4432. The altitude that provides acceptable navigational signal coverage for the route, and meets obstacle clearance requirements, is the minimum

A—enroute altitude.
B—reception altitude.
C—obstacle clearance altitude.

The MEA is the lowest published altitude between radio fixes that ensures acceptable navigational signal coverage and meets obstacle clearance requirements between those fixes. (PLT033, IR.I.C.K2) — Pilot/Controller Glossary

ALL

4435. Reception of signals from an off-airway radio facility may be inadequate to identify the fix at the designated MEA. In this case, which altitude is designated for the fix?

A—MRA.
B—MCA.
C—MOCA.

The MRA is the lowest altitude required to receive adequate signals to determine specific fixes. Reception of signals from a radio facility located off the airway being flown may be inadequate at the designated MEA, in which case, a MRA is designated for the fix. (PLT033, IR.I.C.K2) — Pilot/Controller Glossary

Answer (B) is incorrect because MCA is the lowest altitude at a fix at which an aircraft must cross when flying in the direction of a higher MEA. Answer (C) is incorrect because the MOCA is the lowest published altitude which meets the obstacle clearance requirements of the entire route segment and also ensures acceptable navigation signal coverage only within 22 NM of a VOR.

Answers

4429 [A] 4432 [A] 4435 [A]

ALL

4436. Which condition is guaranteed for all of the following altitude limits: MAA, MCA, MRA, MOCA, and MEA? (Non-mountainous area.)

A—Adequate navigation signals.
B—Adequate communications.
C—1,000-foot obstacle clearance.

Obstruction clearance is normally at least 1,000 feet in nonmountainous areas above the highest terrain or obstruction 4 NM either side of centerline of the airway or route. (PLT430, IR.I.C.K2) — 14 CFR §91.177

Answer (A) is incorrect because the MOCA is the only altitude which assures acceptable navigational signals within 22 NM of a VOR. Answer (B) is incorrect because minimum IFR altitudes do not assure adequate communications coverage.

ALL

4437. If no MCA is specified, what is the lowest altitude for crossing a radio fix, beyond which a higher minimum applies?

A—The MEA at which the fix is approached.
B—The MRA at which the fix is approached.
C—The MOCA for the route segment beyond the fix.

If a normal climb, commenced immediately after passing a fix beyond which a higher MEA applies, would not assure adequate obstruction clearance, then a MCA is specified. Otherwise, cross the radio fix at the MEA at which it is approached, and then climb to the next higher MEA. (PLT033, IR.I.C.K2) — Pilot/Controller Glossary

ALL

4542. MEA is an altitude which assures

A—obstacle clearance, accurate navigational signals from more than one VORTAC, and accurate DME mileage.
B—a 1,000-foot obstacle clearance within 2 miles of an airway and assures accurate DME mileage.
C—acceptable navigational signal coverage and meets obstruction clearance requirements.

The MEA is the lowest published altitude which assures acceptable navigational signal coverage and meets obstacle clearance requirements between those fixes. (PLT033, IR.I.C.K2) — Pilot/Controller Glossary

ALL

4544. Reception of signals from a radio facility, located off the airway being flown, may be inadequate at the designated MEA to identify the fix. In this case, which altitude is designated for the fix?

A—MOCA.
B—MRA.
C—MCA.

The MRA is the lowest altitude required to receive adequate signals to determine specific fixes. Reception of signals from a radio facility located off the airway being flown may be inadequate at the designated MEA, in which case, an MRA is designated for the fix. (PLT033, IR.I.C.K2) — Pilot/Controller Glossary

Answer (A) is incorrect because MOCA is the lowest altitude which meets obstacle clearance requirements for the entire route segment and which assures acceptable navigation coverage only within 22 NM of a VOR. Answer (C) is incorrect because MCA is the lowest altitude at a fix which an aircraft must cross when proceeding in the direction of a higher MEA.

ALL

4545. ATC may assign the MOCA when certain special conditions exist, and when within

A—22 NM of a VOR.
B—25 NM of a VOR.
C—30 NM of a VOR.

The MOCA is the lowest published altitude in effect between radio fixes on VOR airways, off-airway routes, or route segments which meets obstacle clearance requirements for the entire route segment and which assures acceptable navigational signal coverage only within 25 SM (22 NM) of a VOR. (PLT033, IR.I.C.K2) — Pilot/Controller Glossary

Answers (B) and (C) are incorrect because ATC may assign the MOCA as an altitude only with 22 NM of a VOR.

Answers

4436 [C] 4437 [A] 4542 [C] 4544 [B] 4545 [A]

ALL

4953. The lowest published altitude which meets obstacle clearance requirements and assures acceptable navigational signal coverage is the

A—MEA.
B—MRA.
C—MOCA.

The MEA is the lowest published altitude which ensures acceptable navigational signal coverage and meets obstacle clearance requirements between those fixes. (PLT033, IR.I.C.K2) — Pilot/Controller Glossary

Answer (B) is incorrect because MRA is the lowest altitude required to receive adequate signals to determine specific fixes. Answer (C) is incorrect because MOCA is the lowest altitude which meets obstacle clearance requirements for the entire route segment and which ensures acceptable navigation coverage only within 22 NM of a VOR.

ALL

4547. Acceptable navigational signal coverage at the MOCA is assured for a distance from the VOR of only

A—12 NM.
B—22 NM.
C—25 NM.

The MOCA is the lowest published altitude in effect between radio fixes on VOR airways, off-airway routes, or route segments which meets obstacle clearance requirements for the entire route segment and which assures acceptable navigational signal coverage only within 25 SM (22 NM) of a VOR. (PLT033, IR.I.C.K2) — Pilot/Controller Glossary

Answers (A) and (C) are incorrect because the MOCA is only acceptable when within 25 SM (22 NM) of a VOR.

ALL

4540. What obstacle clearance and navigation signal coverage is a pilot assured with the minimum sector altitudes depicted on the IAP charts?

A—1,000 feet and acceptable navigation signal coverage within a 25 NM radius of the navigation facility.
B—1,000 feet within a 25 NM radius of the navigation facility but not acceptable navigation signal coverage.
C—500 feet and acceptable navigation signal coverage within a 10 NM radius of the navigation facility.

MSAs provide at least 1,000 feet of clearance above the highest obstacle in the defined sector to a distance of 25 NM from the facility. Navigational course guidance is not assured at the MSA. (PLT292, IR.III.B.K1) — AIM ¶5-4-5

Answer (A) is incorrect because MSAs do not provide acceptable navigation signal coverage. Answer (C) is incorrect because MSAs provide at least 1,000 feet (not 500) of obstacle clearance, up to a distance of 25 NM (not 10) from the facility, and they do not provide acceptable navigation signal coverage.

Enroute Low Altitude Chart

The Enroute Low Altitude Charts are valid for use up to, but not including, 18,000 feet MSL. You should become familiar with FAA Legends 33, 34, and 35, which depict the legends for the charts. These will be available to you when you take the FAA Knowledge Test.

ALL

4546. Which aeronautical chart depicts Military Training Routes (MTR) above 1,500 feet?

A—IFR Planning Chart.
B—IFR Low Altitude En Route Chart.
C—IFR High Altitude En Route Chart.

MTRs are charted on IFR Low Altitude Enroute charts, VFR Sectional charts, and Area Planning charts. (PLT100, IR.I.C.K1) — AIM ¶3-5-2

Answer (A) is incorrect because MTRs are charted on Area (not IFR) Planning charts. Answer (C) is incorrect because MTRs are charted on IFR Low (not High) Altitude Enroute charts.

Answers

4953 [A] 4547 [B] 4540 [B] 4546 [B]

ALL

4365. (Refer to Figure 214.) Which enroute low altitude navigation chart would cover proposed IFR routing departing from Billing Logan Intl. (BIL)?

A—H-1E
B—L-13D
C—Billings Sectional Chart

In the top right corner of the Billings-Logan entry in the Chart Supplement, the letter-number combinations indicate the charts where the airport and surrounding area are found. FAA Figure 214 lists "L-13D" as the chart to cover the Billings area. (PLT100, IR.I.C.K1) — U.S. Terminal Procedures, DP Chart Legend

Answer (A) is incorrect because H-1E is the high altitude enroute chart. Answer (C) is incorrect because the Billings Sectional covers VFR navigation, not IFR routing.

ALL

4339. (Refer to Figures 65 and 67.) What is the significance of the symbol at GRICE intersection?

A—It signifies a localizer-only approach is available at Harry P. Williams Memorial.
B—The localizer has an additional navigation function.
C—GRICE intersection also serves as the FAF for the ILS approach procedure to Harry P. Williams Memorial.

The localizer symbol at GRICE INT indicates that the localizer has a navigation function in addition to course guidance. See FAA Legend 33. (PLT100, IR.V.B.K1) — Enroute Low Altitude Chart Legend

ALL

4506. (Refer to Figure 89.) What is the ARTCC discrete frequency at the COP on V208 southwest bound from HVE to PGA VOR/DME?

A—122.1.
B—122.4.
C—127.55.

Discrete frequencies are normally designated for each control sector in enroute terminal facilities. Since the COP for southwest-bound traffic between Hanksville and Page on V208 is still in Salt Lake City ARTCC's boundary, the frequency should be the one contained in the Hanksville Remote Site scalloped box by the Hanksville VORTAC: 127.55. (PLT100, IR.V.B.K1) — Enroute Low Altitude Chart Legend

ALL

4645. (Refer to Figure 47.) En route on V112 from BTG VORTAC to LTJ VORTAC, the minimum altitude crossing Gymme intersection is

A—6,400 feet.
B—6,500 feet.
C—7,000 feet.

In the absence of a minimum crossing altitude, you would cross at the MEA. Looking at GYMME intersection, the minimum enroute altitude eastbound is 7,000 feet and westbound is 6,500 feet. Since the question asks the altitude while traveling west to east, 7,000 is the minimum altitude to be flown crossing GYMME. (PLT089, IR.V.B.K1) — Enroute Low Altitude Chart Legend

Answer (A) is incorrect because 6,400 is the MOCA along V112. Answer (B) is incorrect because 6,500 is the MEA for a westbound (not eastbound) flight on V112.

ALL

4646. (Refer to Figure 47.) When en route on V448 from YKM VORTAC to BTG VORTAC, what minimum navigation equipment is required to identify ANGOO intersection?

A—One VOR receiver.
B—One VOR receiver and DME.
C—Two VOR receivers.

Magnetic bearings are read directly from the VOR indicator. You can easily identify ANGOO intersection while on the radial of YKM with one VOR. Identify the intersecting radial of DLS simply by alternately tuning the single VOR to each station. (PLT100, IR.V.B.K1) — Enroute Low Altitude Chart Legend

ALL

4647. (Refer to Figure 47.) En route on V468 from BTG VORTAC to YKM VORTAC, the minimum altitude at TROTS intersection is

A—7,100 feet.
B—10,000 feet.
C—11,500 feet.

TROTS intersection has a flag with an "x" in it, which means that there is an MCA. Under the intersection name the MCA is shown as 11,500 on V468 when proceeding to the northeast. (PLT089, IR.V.B.K1) — Enroute Low Altitude Chart Legend

Answer (A) is incorrect because 7,100 feet is the MOCA along V468. Answer (B) is incorrect because 10,000 feet is the MEA west of TROTS intersection.

Answers

4365 [B] 4339 [B] 4506 [C] 4645 [C] 4646 [A] 4647 [C]

ALL

4077. Which types of airspace are depicted on the En Route Low Altitude Chart?

A—Limits of controlled airspace, military training routes and special use airspace.
B—Class A, special use airspace, Class D and Class E.
C—Special use airspace, Class E, Class D, Class A, Class B and Class C.

Limits of controlled airspace, MTRs, and special use airspace, all up to 18,000 feet MSL, are shown on low altitude enroute charts. (PLT100, IR.V.B.K1) — AIM ¶9-1-4

Answers (B) and (C) are incorrect because Class A airspace is not shown on low altitude enroute charts.

ALL

4287. (Refer to Figure 34.) For planning purposes, what is the highest useable altitude for an IFR flight on V573 from the HOT VORTAC to the TXK VORTAC?

A—16,000 feet MSL.
B—14,500 feet MSL.
C—13,999 feet MSL.

The Enroute Low Altitude U.S. IFR Chart is for use up to, but not including, 18,000 feet. In controlled airspace, each person operating an aircraft under IFR in level cruising flight shall maintain the altitude assigned by ATC or the regulatory IFR altitudes. Flying on V573 from HOT VORTAC to the TXK VORTAC is a westerly course which requires an even-thousands altitude. (PLT079, IR.V.B.K1) — Enroute Low Altitude Chart

Answer (B) is incorrect because 14,500 feet MSL is a VFR cruising altitude. Answer (C) is incorrect because IFR flight requires rounded-off odd or even thousands of feet (13,999 is neither).

ALL

4501. (Refer to Figure 89.) When flying from Milford Municipal to Bryce Canyon via V235 and V293, what minimum altitude should you be at when crossing Cedar City VOR?

A—11,400 feet.
B—12,000 feet.
C—13,000 feet.

The MCA is the lowest altitude at which an aircraft must cross when proceeding in the direction of a higher MEA. The MCA southbound on V235 is 11,400 feet and 12,000 feet eastbound on V293. The 12,000 feet eastbound must be reached by the Cedar City VOR. (PLT100, IR.V.B.K1) — Enroute Low Altitude Chart Legend

ALL

4291. (Refer to Figure 40.) For planning purposes, what is the highest useable altitude for an IFR flight on V16 from BGS VORTAC to ABI VORTAC?

A—17,000 feet MSL.
B—18,000 feet MSL.
C—6,500 feet MSL.

The Enroute Low Altitude U.S. IFR Chart is for use up to, but not including, 18,000 feet. (PLT100, IR.V.B.K1) — Enroute Low Altitude Chart

Answer (B) is incorrect because the airways go up to 17,999 feet, not including 18,000 feet. Answer (C) is incorrect because the 6,500 feet is the MRA at LORAN intersection.

ALL

4317. (Refer to Figure 53.) Where is the VOR COP on V27 between the GVO and MQO VORTACs?

A—20 DME from GVO VORTAC.
B—20 DME from MQO VORTAC.
C—30 DME from SBA VORTAC.

The COP is located 20 NM from GVO or 34 NM from MQO. (PLT079, IR.V.B.K1) — Enroute Low Altitude Chart Legend

ALL

4263. (Refer to Figure 24.) At what point should a VOR changeover be made from JNC VOR to MANCA intersection southbound on V187?

A—36 NM south of JNC.
B—52 NM south of JNC.
C—74 NM south of JNC.

The changeover should be made at the changeover symbol if depicted, where there is a change in the direction of the airway, or in the absence of these, at the halfway point between the VORs. In this case, the COP is indicated with a symbol, and should be made 52 miles from JNC and 90 miles from the next VOR. (PLT090, IR.V.B.K1) — Enroute Low Altitude Chart Legend

Answer (A) is incorrect because 36 NM south of JNC is just south of HERRM intersection. Answer (C) is incorrect because 74 NM south of JNC is a little over halfway between the VORs, which is incorrect since there is a specifically designated COP.

Answers

4077 [A]	4287 [A]	4501 [B]	4291 [A]	4317 [A]	4263 [B]

ALL

4336. (Refer to Figure 65.) Which point would be the appropriate VOR COP on V552 from the LFT to the TBD VORTACs?

A—CLYNT intersection.
B—HATCH intersection.
C—34 DME from the LFT VORTAC.

The total distance between LFT and TBD is 68 NM (shown in the box between NAVAIDs). The COP is half of 68, or 34 NM from LFT. VOR COPs are where the pilot should change navigation receiver frequency from the station behind the aircraft to the station ahead and are:

1. *Halfway between the VORs, if no other designation is given;*
2. *At a course change; or*
3. *At the COP symbol.*

(PLT079, IR.V.B.K1) — Enroute Low Altitude Chart Legend

Answers (A) and (B) are incorrect because they are not the halfway points, and there is no symbol designating these locations as the COP.

ALL

4516. (Refer to Figure 91.) Where should you change VOR frequencies when en route from DBS VORTAC to JAC VOR/DME on V520?

A—35 NM from DBS VORTAC.
B—60 NM from DBS VORTAC.
C—60 NM from JAC VOR/DME.

The COP symbol indicates the point where the pilot should change navigation receiver frequency from the station behind the aircraft to the station ahead. The distance from each VORTAC can be read above and below the symbol, pointing to the VORTAC which it is referring to. The COP from DBS to JAC on V520 is 60 NM from DBS VORTAC. (PLT100, IR.V.B.K1) — Enroute Low Altitude Chart Legend

ALL

4366. (Refer to Figure 78.) What is the maximum altitude that you may flight plan an IFR flight on V-86 EASTBOUND between BOZEMAN and BILLINGS VORTACs?

A—14,500 feet MSL.
B—17,000 feet MSL.
C—18,000 feet MSL.

The Enroute Low Altitude U.S. IFR Chart is for use up to, but not including, 18,000 feet. (PLT100, IR.V.B.K1) — Enroute Low Altitude Chart Legend

Answer (A) is incorrect because 14,500 feet is a VFR (not IFR) cruising altitude. Answer (C) is incorrect because victor airways extend up to, but not including FL180.

ALL

4370-1. (Refer to Figure 78.) What is the minimum crossing altitude over the BOZEMAN VORTAC for a flight southeast bound on V86?

A—10,900 feet MSL.
B—10,200 feet MSL.
C—10,500 feet MSL.

Bozeman (BZN) has a flag with an X in it, which indicates it has an MCA. Below the Bozeman communications box is the list of MCAs. For a flight southeast bound on V86, the MCA is 10,200 feet MSL. (PLT058, IR.V.B.K1) — Enroute Low Altitude Chart Legend

Answer (A) is incorrect because 10,900 feet MSL is the MEA on V86 at ZUBLI INT. Answer (C) is incorrect because 10,500 feet MSL is the MCA South on V343.

ALL

4370-2. (Refer to Figure 78.) When eastbound on V86 between Whitehall and Livingston, the minimum altitude that you should cross BZN is

A—10,200 feet MSL.
B—8,500 feet MSL.
C—9,100 feet MSL.

Bozeman (BZN) has a flag with an X in it, indicating an MCA. Below the BZN communications box is the list of MCAs. For a flight eastbound on V86, the MCA is 10,200 feet MSL. (PLT058, IR.V.B.K1) — Enroute Low Altitude Chart Legend

Answer (B) is incorrect because 8,500 feet MSL is the MEA from Whitehall to Bozeman VORTACs. Answer (C) is incorrect because 9,100 feet MSL is the MCA over HIA VORTAC on V86 Westbound.

Answers

4336 [C] 4516 [B] 4366 [B] 4370-1 [B] 4370-2 [A]

ALL

4280. (Refer to Figure 34.) At which altitude and location on V573 would you expect the navigational signal of the HOT VOR/DME to be unreliable?

A—3,000 feet at APINE intersection.
B—2,700 feet at MARKI intersection.
C—4,000 feet at ELMMO intersection.

The navigational signal at APINE intersection would be unreliable below 3,500 feet because the MEA and MOCA are 3,500 and 2,500 feet, respectively. Since APINE is further than 22 NM from the HOT VOR, navigational signal is only assured with the MEA. (PLT090, IR.V.B.K1) — Enroute Low Altitude Chart Legend

Answer (B) is incorrect because MARKI should have a reliable VOR signal down to the MOCA (which is 2,700 feet), since it is within 22 NM from HOT VOR. Answer (C) is incorrect because the signal at ELMMO would be reliable at the MEA, which is 3,500 feet.

ALL

4493. (Refer to Figure 87.) Where is the VOR COP when flying east on V306 from Daisetta to Lake Charles?

A—50 NM east of DAS.
B—40 NM east of DAS.
C—30 NM east of DAS.

VOR COPs are the points at which the pilot should change navigation receiver frequency from the station behind the aircraft to the station ahead and are:

1. *halfway between stations, if no other designation is given;*
2. *at a course change in the route;*
3. *at the COP symbol.*

In this case, the COP symbol indicates the change should be made 30 NM from Daisetta (DAS). (PLT079, IR.V.B.K1) — AIM ¶5-3-6

ALL

4496. (Refer to Figure 87.) What is indicated by the localizer course symbol at Jack Brooks Rgnl Airport?

A—A published LDA localizer course with voice capability.
B—A published SDF localizer course with back course capability.
C—A published ILS localizer course, which has an additional navigation function.

The localizer course symbol at Jack Brooks Rgnl indicates an ILC Localizer Course with ATC function is available. (PLT058, IR.VII.A.K1) — Enroute Low Altitude Chart Legend

Answer (A) is incorrect because although it could be used for an LDA approach, this symbol is not representative of a strictly LDA approach. Answer (B) is incorrect because SDF sites do not have back courses, and this symbol is accompanied by the words "back course."

RTC

4498. (Refer to Figure 87.) Why is the localizer back course at Jefferson Jack Brooks Rgnl depicted?

A—The back course is not aligned with a runway.
B—The back course has a glide slope.
C—The back course has an additional navigation function.

An ILS Localizer Course at Jack Brooks Rgnl with an additional navigation function is available. The feathered side indicates Blue Sector. The "back course" indicates that it is a back course ILS localizer course with additional navigation function. (PLT100) — Enroute Low Altitude Chart Legend

Answers

4280 [A]	4493 [C]	4496 [C]	4498 [C]

ALL

4499. (Refer to Figure 87.) Where is the VOR changeover point on V70 between Sabine Pass and Lake Charles?

A—Halfway point.
B—POPEY intersection.
C—Back course localizer.

The COP is located midway between the navigation facilities for straight route segments. In the case of dogleg route segments, the COP is located at the intersection of radials or courses forming the dogleg. When the COP is not located at the midway point, the location will be identified with a COP symbol, giving the mileage to the radio aids. There is no COP symbol on this route segment; therefore, the COP is at the halfway point or 28 miles from Sabine Pass. (PLT079, IR.V.B.K1) — Enroute Low Altitude Chart Legend

Answers (B) and (C) are incorrect because they are not halfway between Sabine Pass and Lake Charles.

ALL

4261. (Refer to Figure 24.) While passing near the CORTEZ VOR, southbound on V187, contact is lost with Denver Center. You should attempt to reestablish contact with Denver Center on

A—118.575 MHz.
B—108.4 MHz.
C—122.3 MHz.

ARTCC names and frequencies are shown on low altitude charts enclosed in a box with postage-stamp style lines. Just left of the Cortez VOR symbol is the box showing Denver Center available at Cortez, using frequency 118.575. (PLT058, IR.V.B.K1) — Enroute Low Altitude Chart Legend

ALL

4517. (Refer to Figure 91.) What is the minimum crossing altitude at SABAT intersection when eastbound from DBS VORTAC on V298?

A—8,300 feet.
B—11,100 feet.
C—13,000 feet.

SABAT Intersection has a flag with an "X" in it, indicating an MCA. The MCA at SABAT when eastbound from DBS VORTAC on V298 is 11,100 feet. (PLT100, IR.V.B.K1) — Enroute Low Altitude Chart Legend

ALL

4509. (Refer to Figure 91.) What is the minimum crossing altitude at DBS VORTAC for a northbound IFR flight on V257?

A—7,500 feet.
B—8,600 feet.
C—11,100 feet.

DBS VORTAC can be found in the bottom left-hand quadrant of the FAA figure. The MCA is identified in the middle of the DBS VORTAC compass rose, beneath the flag with the "X" inside. The minimum crossing altitude at DBS VORTAC for an IFR flight northbound on V257 is 8,600 feet. (PLT058, IR.VII.A.K1) — Enroute Low Altitude Chart Legend

Answer (A) is incorrect because 7,500 feet is the MEA on V257. Answer (C) is incorrect because 11,100 feet is the MOCA on V210257.

ALL

4512. (Refer to Figure 91.) What lighting is indicated on the chart for Jackson Hole Airport?

A—Lights on prior request.
B—No lighting available.
C—Pilot controlled lighting.

The Jackson Hole Airport is located in the bottom right quadrant of FAA Figure 91. The "L" in the circle indicates pilot controlled lighting. (PLT100, IR.V.B.K1) — Enroute Low Altitude Chart Legend

ALL

4515. (Refer to Figure 91.) What is the function of the Great Falls RCO (Yellowstone vicinity)?

A—Long range communications outlet for Great Falls Center.
B—Remote communications outlet for Great Falls FSS.
C—Satellite remote controlled by Salt Lake Center with limited service.

An RCO is an un-manned communications facilities remotely controlled by air traffic personnel. RCOs serve FSS's. An RCO may be UHF or VHF and will extend the communications range of the air traffic facility. (PLT100, IR.V.B.K1) — Enroute Low Altitude Chart Legend

Answers

4499 [A]	4261 [A]	4517 [B]	4509 [B]	4512 [C]	4515 [B]

ALL
4262. (Refer to Figure 24.) For planning purposes, what would be the highest MEA on V187 between Grand Junction Regional (GJT) and Durango Animas Air Park (00C)?

A—12,400 feet.
B—12,100 feet.
C—15,000 feet.

The highest published MEA shown on V187 is 15,000 feet MSL, between Grand Junction VOR and MANCA intersections. (PLT100, IR.V.B.K1) — Enroute Low Altitude Chart Legend

Answers (A) and (B) are both incorrect because they are listed as MOCAs along V187.

ALL
4264. (Refer to Figure 24.) What is the MOCA between JNC and HERRM intersection on V187?

A—15,000 feet.
B—12,400 feet.
C—12,100 feet.

If an altitude is written under the MEA with an asterisk (*), this altitude represents the MOCA. In this case, 12,100 feet MSL is the MOCA on that portion of V187. (PLT100, IR.V.B.K1) — Enroute Low Altitude Chart Legend

ALL
4239. (Refer to Figure 31.) Identifying DRAIN INT along V448 will require you to be at a minimum altitude of

A—3,900.
B—5,000.
C—6,000.

When a flag with an R is shown above an intersection it is the symbol for MRA. This is the altitude required to identify that particular intersection and in this case, DRAIN requires 6,000 feet MSL. (PLT100, IR.V.B.K1) — Enroute Low Altitude Chart Legend

Answer (A) is incorrect because 3,900 is the MOCA from EUG to DRAIN along V448. Answer (B) is incorrect because 5,000 is the MEA along V448 from EUG to RBG VORTACs.

ALL
4639. For IFR operations off of established airways below 18,000 feet, VOR navigational aids used to describe the "route of flight" should be no more than

A—40 NM apart.
B—70 NM apart.
C—80 NM apart.

For operation off established airways below 18,000 feet MSL, pilots should use aids not more than 80 NM apart. These aids are depicted on Enroute Low Altitude Charts. (PLT322, IR.II.B.K2a) — AIM ¶5-1-8

Holding

Holding may be necessary when ATC is unable to clear a flight to its destination. VORs, NDBs, airway intersections, and DME fixes may all be used as holding points. Flying a holding pattern involves two turns and two straight-and-level legs as shown in Figure 7-1.

At and below 14,000 feet MSL (no wind), the aircraft flies the specified course inbound to the fix, turns to the right 180°, flies a parallel course outbound for 1 minute, again turns 180° to the right, and flies 1 minute inbound to the fix. Above 14,000 feet MSL, the inbound leg length is 1-1/2 minutes. If a nonstandard pattern is to be flown, ATC will specify left turns.

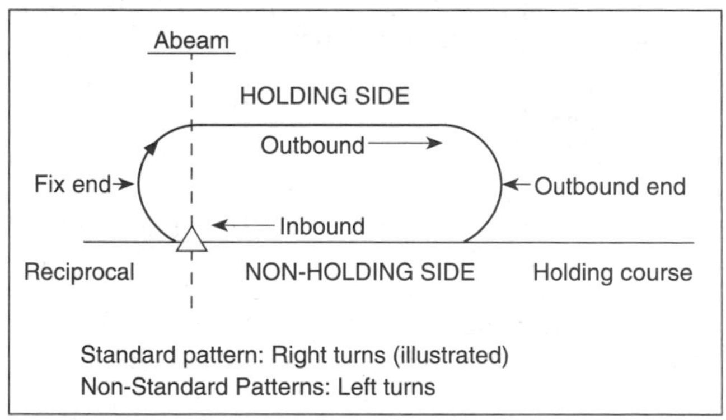

Figure 7-1

When 3 minutes or less from the holding fix, the pilot is expected to start a speed reduction so as to cross the fix at or below the maximum holding airspeed. For all aircraft between minimum holding altitude (MHA) and 6,000 feet MSL, holding speed is 200 KIAS. For all aircraft between 6,001 and 14,000 feet MSL, holding speed is 230 KIAS. For all aircraft 14,001 feet MSL and above, holding speed is 265 KIAS. Exceptions to these speeds will be indicated by an icon.

Answers

4262 [C] 4264 [C] 4239 [C] 4639 [C]

The aircraft is holding as of the initial time of arrival over the fix, and that time should be reported to ATC. The initial outbound leg is flown for 1 minute at or below 14,000 feet MSL. Subsequently, timing of the outbound leg should be adjusted as necessary to arrive at the proper inbound leg length. Timing of the outbound leg begins over or abeam the fix, whichever occurs later. If the abeam position cannot be determined, start timing when the turn to outbound is completed. The same entry and holding procedures apply to DME holding, except distances in nautical miles are used to establish leg length.

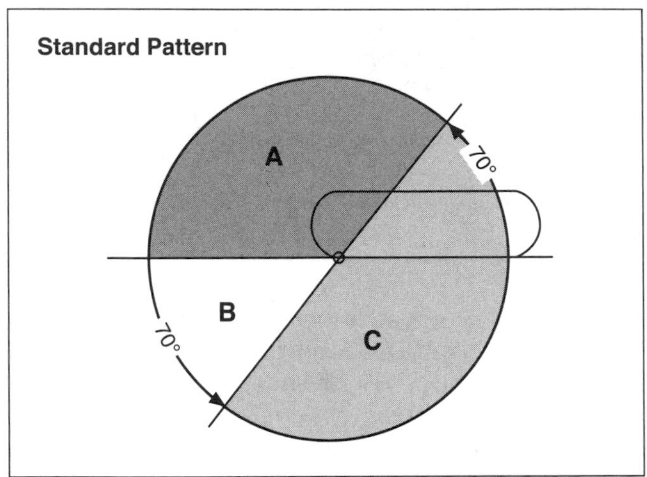

Figure 7-2

The FAA has three recommended methods for entering a holding pattern, as shown in Figure 7-2. An aircraft approaching from within sector (A) would fly a parallel entry by turning left to parallel the outbound course, making another left turn to remain in protected airspace, and returning to the holding fix. Aircraft approaching from sector (B) would fly a teardrop entry, by flying outbound on a track of 30° or less to the holding course, and then making a right turn to intercept the holding course inbound to the fix. Those approaching from within sector (C) would fly a direct entry by turning right to fly the pattern.

If the holding pattern is charted, the controller may omit all holding instructions, except the holding direction and the statement "as published." Pilots are expected to hold in the pattern depicted even if it means crossing the clearance limit. If the holding pattern to be used is not depicted on charts, ATC will issue general holding instructions. The holding clearance will include the following information: direction of holding from the fix in terms of the eight cardinal compass points; holding fix; radial, course, bearing, airway, or route on which the aircraft is to hold; leg length in miles if DME or RNAV is to be used; direction of turn if left turns are to be made; time to expect further clearance and any pertinent additional delay information.

ALL

4494. (Refer to Figure 87.) At STRUT intersection headed eastbound, ATC instructs you to hold west on the 10 DME fix west of LCH on V306, standard turns, what entry procedure is recommended?

A—Direct.
B—Teardrop.
C—Parallel.

Determine the holding pattern by placing your pencil on the holding fix and dragging it on the holding radial given by ATC, then returning back to the fix. Then draw the pattern from the fix with turns in the direction specified. In this question, ATC has specified standard turns (right turns).

The entry procedure is based on the aircraft's heading. To determine which entry procedure to use, draw a line at a 70° angle from the holding fix, and cutting the outbound leg at about one-third its length. With the aircraft at STRUT intersection heading eastbound, we are in the largest piece of the pie, so a direct entry would be used. See the figure. (PLT100, IR.III.B.K1) — AIM ¶5-3-7

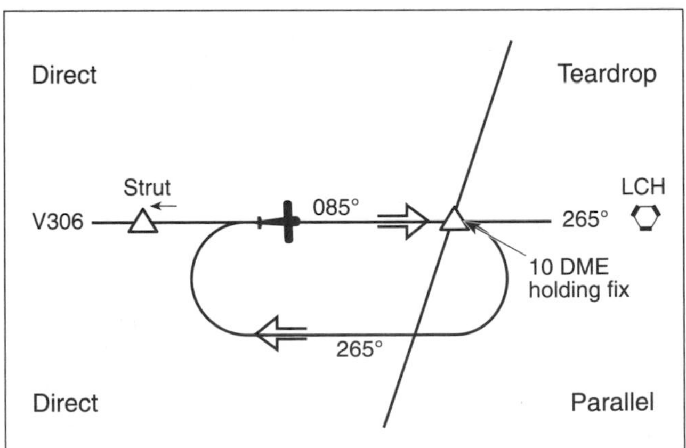

Question 4494

Answers
4494 [A]

ALL

4609. (Refer to Figure 112.) You arrive at the 15 DME fix on a heading of 350°. Which holding pattern correctly complies with the ATC clearance below, and what is the recommended entry procedure?

"...HOLD WEST OF THE ONE FIVE DME FIX ON THE ZERO EIGHT SIX RADIAL OF THE ABC VORTAC, FIVE MILE LEGS, LEFT TURNS..."

A—1; teardrop entry.
B—1; direct entry.
C—2; direct entry.

Determine the holding pattern by placing your pencil on the holding fix and dragging it on the holding radial given by ATC, then returning back to the fix. Then draw the pattern from the fix with turns in the direction specified. In this question, ATC has specified left-hand turns, which corresponds to holding pattern 1.

The entry procedure is based on the aircraft's heading. To determine which entry procedure to use, draw a line at a 70° angle from the holding fix, and cutting the outbound leg at about one-third its length. With a heading of 350°, we are in the largest piece of the pie, so a direct entry would be used. See the figure below. (PLT146, IR.III.B.K1) — AIM ¶5-3-7

Answer (A) is incorrect because a heading of 350° requires a direct entry. Answer (C) is incorrect because the second holding pattern does not have the holding fix at the end of the inbound leg.

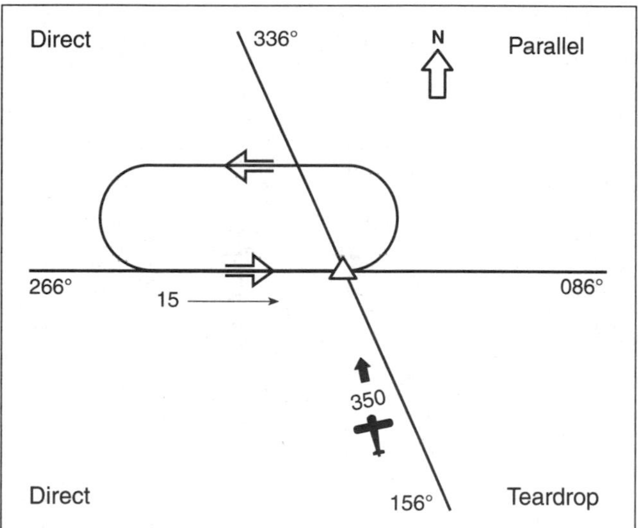

Question 4609

ALL

4610. (Refer to Figure 113.) You receive this ATC clearance:

"...HOLD EAST OF THE ABC VORTAC ON THE ZERO NINER ZERO RADIAL, LEFT TURNS..."

What is the recommended procedure to enter the holding pattern?

A—Parallel only.
B—Direct only.
C—Teardrop only.

Determine the holding pattern by placing your pencil on the holding fix and dragging it on the holding radial given by ATC, then returning back to the fix. Then draw the pattern from the fix with turns in the direction specified. Holding east on the 090° radial with left turns means you will be south of R-090.

The entry procedure is based on the aircraft's heading. To determine which entry procedure to use, draw a line at a 70° angle from the holding fix, and cutting the outbound leg at about one-third its length. With a heading of 055°, we are in the second-largest piece of the pie, so a parallel entry would be used. See the figure below. (PLT146, IR.III.B.K1) — AIM ¶5-3-7

Answer (B) is incorrect because a direct entry would only be appropriate between the 340° and 160° radials. Answer (C) is incorrect because a teardrop entry would only be appropriate between the 270° and 340° radials.

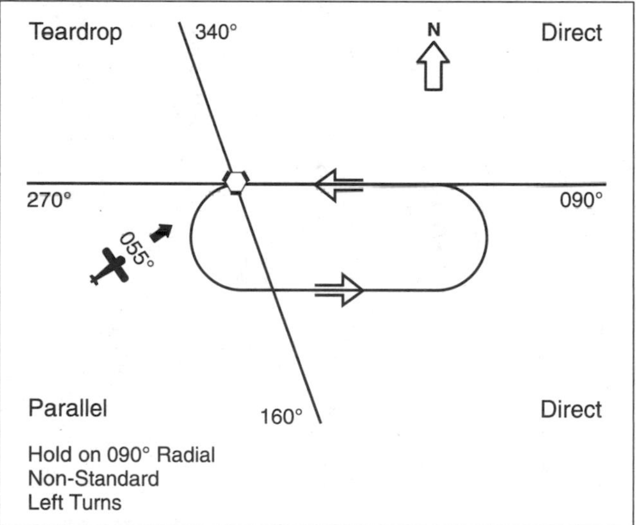

Question 4610

Answers

4609 [B] 4610 [A]

ALL

4611. (Refer to Figure 113.) You receive this ATC clearance:

"...CLEARED TO THE ABC VORTAC. HOLD SOUTH ON THE ONE EIGHT ZERO RADIAL..."

What is the recommended procedure to enter the holding pattern?

A—Teardrop only.
B—Direct only.
C—Parallel only.

Determine the holding pattern by placing your pencil on the holding fix and dragging it on the holding radial given by ATC, then returning back to the fix. Then draw the pattern from the fix with turns in the direction specified. Holding south on the 180° radial with right turns means you will be east of R-180.

The entry procedure is based on the aircraft's heading. To determine which entry procedure to use, draw a line at a 70° angle from the holding fix, and cutting the outbound leg at about one-third its length. With a heading of 055°, we are in the largest piece of the pie, so a direct entry would be used. See the figure below. (PLT146, IR.III.B.K1) — AIM ¶5-3-7

Answer (A) is incorrect because a teardrop entry would only be appropriate between the 290° and 360° radials. Answer (C) is incorrect because a parallel entry would only be appropriate between the 360° and 110° radials.

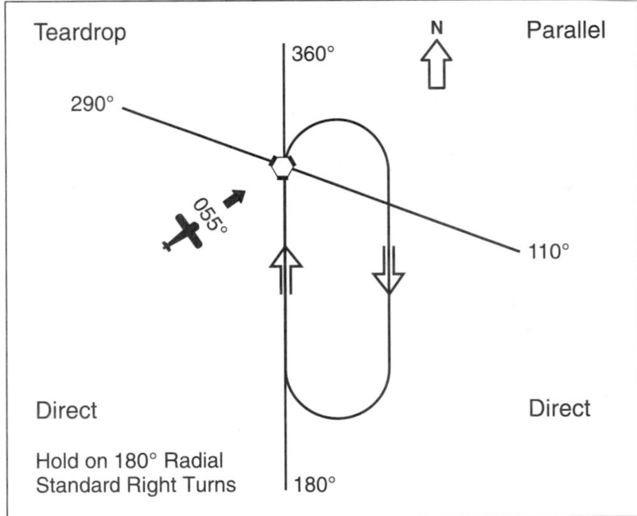

Question 4611

ALL

4612. (Refer to Figure 113.) You receive this ATC clearance:

"...CLEARED TO THE XYZ VORTAC. HOLD NORTH ON THE THREE SIX ZERO RADIAL, LEFT TURNS..."

What is the recommended procedure to enter the holding pattern.

A—Parallel only.
B—Direct only.
C—Teardrop only.

Determine the holding pattern by placing your pencil on the holding fix and dragging it on the holding radial given by ATC, then returning back to the fix. Then draw the pattern from the fix with turns in the direction specified. Holding north on the 360° radial with left turns means you will be east of R-360.

The entry procedure is based on the aircraft's heading. To determine which entry procedure to use, draw a line at a 70° angle from the holding fix, and cutting the outbound leg at about one-third its length. With a heading of 055°, we are in the smallest piece of the pie, so a teardrop entry would be used. See the figure below. (PLT146, IR.III.B.K1) — AIM ¶5-3-7

Answer (A) is incorrect because a parallel entry would only be appropriate between the 070° and 180° radials. Answer (B) is incorrect because a direct entry would only be appropriate between the 070° and 250° radials.

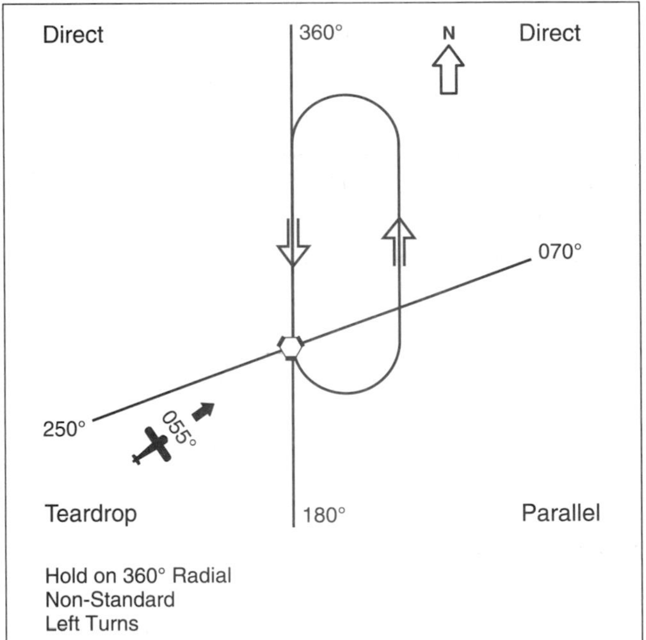

Question 4612

Answers

4611 [B]

4612 [C]

ALL

4613. (Refer to Figure 113.) You receive this ATC clearance:

"...CLEARED TO THE ABC VORTAC. HOLD WEST ON THE TWO SEVEN ZERO RADIAL..."

What is the recommended procedure to enter the holding pattern?

A—Parallel only.
B—Direct only.
C—Teardrop only.

Determine the holding pattern by placing your pencil on the holding fix and dragging it on the holding radial given by ATC, then returning back to the fix. Then draw the pattern from the fix with turns in the direction specified. Holding west on the 270° radial with right turns means you will be south of R-270.

The entry procedure is based on the aircraft's heading. To determine which entry procedure to use, draw a line at a 70° angle from the holding fix, and cutting the outbound leg at about one-third its length. With a heading of 055°, we are in the largest piece of the pie, so a direct entry would be used. See the figure below. (PLT146, IR.III.B.K1) — AIM ¶5-3-7

Answer (A) is incorrect because a parallel entry would only be appropriate between the 090° and 200° radials. Answer (C) is incorrect because a teardrop entry would only be appropriate between the 020° and 090° radials.

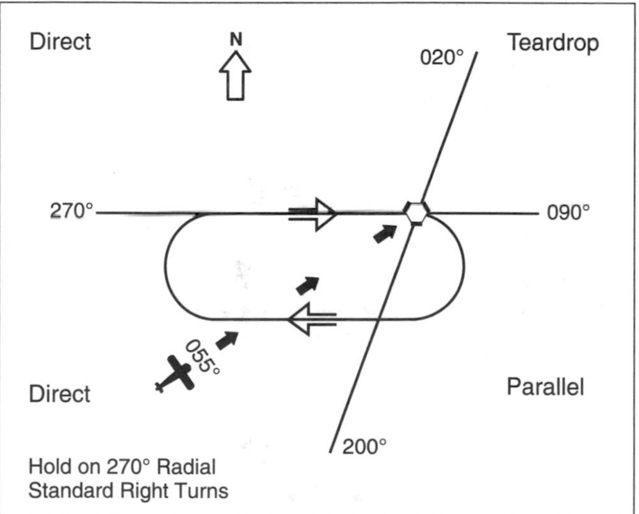

Question 4613

ALL

4614. (Refer to Figure 114.) A pilot receives this ATC clearance:

"...CLEARED TO THE ABC VORTAC. HOLD WEST ON THE TWO SEVEN ZERO RADIAL..."

What is the recommended procedure to enter the holding pattern?

A—Parallel or teardrop.
B—Parallel only.
C—Direct only.

Determine the holding pattern by placing your pencil on the holding fix and dragging it on the holding radial given by ATC, then returning back to the fix. Then draw the pattern from the fix with turns in the direction specified. Holding west on the 270° radial with right turns means you will be south of R-270.

The entry procedure is based on the aircraft's heading. To determine which entry procedure to use, draw a line at a 70° angle from the holding fix, and cutting the outbound leg at about one-third its length. With a heading of 155°, we are in the largest piece of the pie, so a direct entry would be used. See the figure below. (PLT146, IR.III.B.K1) — AIM ¶5-3-7

Answer (A) is incorrect because either the parallel or teardrop entry is only appropriate when on the 090° radial. Answer (B) is incorrect because a parallel entry would only be appropriate between the 090° and 200° radials.

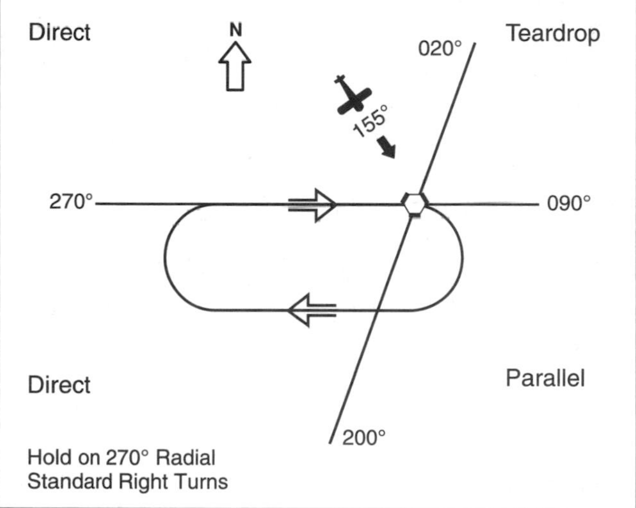

Question 4614

Answers

4613 [B]
4614 [C]

ALL

4616. (Refer to Figure 114.) A pilot receives this ATC clearance:

"...CLEARED TO THE ABC VORTAC. HOLD SOUTH ON THE ONE EIGHT ZERO RADIAL..."

What is the recommended procedure to enter the holding pattern?

A—Teardrop only.
B—Parallel only.
C—Direct only.

Determine the holding pattern by placing your pencil on the holding fix and dragging it on the holding radial given by ATC, then returning back to the fix. Then draw the pattern from the fix with turns in the direction specified. Holding south on the 180° radial with right turn means you will be east of R-180.

The entry procedure is based on the aircraft's heading. To determine which entry procedure to use, draw a line at a 70° angle from the holding fix, and cutting the outbound leg at about one-third its length. With a heading of 155°, we are in the smallest piece of the pie, so a teardrop entry would be used. See the figure below. (PLT146, IR.III.B.K1) — AIM ¶5-3-7

Answer (B) is incorrect because a parallel entry would only be appropriate between the 360° and 110° radials. Answer (C) is incorrect because a direct entry would only be appropriate between the 110° and 290° radials.

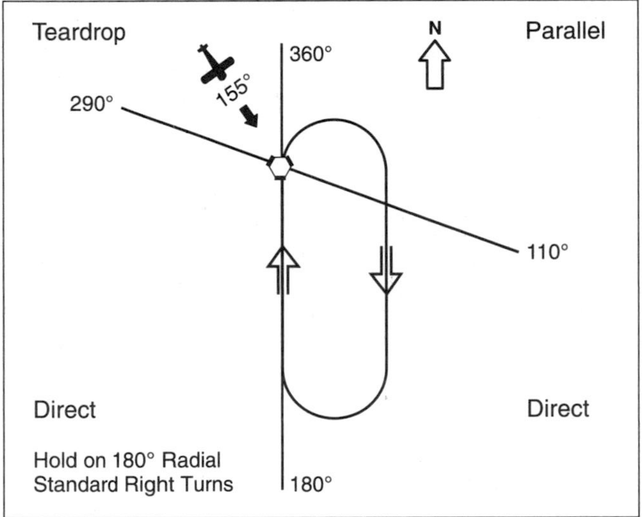

Question 4616

ALL

4618. (Refer to Figure 115.) You receive this ATC clearance:

"...HOLD WEST OF THE ONE FIVE DME FIX ON THE ZERO NINE ZERO RADIAL OF ABC VORTAC, FIVE MILE LEGS, LEFT TURNS..."

You arrive at the 15 DME fix on a heading of 350°. Which holding pattern correctly complies with these instructions, and what is the recommended entry procedure?

A—1; teardrop.
B—2; direct.
C—1; direct.

Determine the holding pattern by placing your pencil on the holding fix and dragging it on the holding radial given by ATC, then returning back to the fix. Then draw the pattern from the fix with turns in the direction specified. In this question, ATC has specified left-hand turns, which corresponds to holding pattern 1.

The entry procedure is based on the aircraft's heading. To determine which entry procedure to use, draw a line at a 70° angle from the holding fix, and cutting the outbound leg at about one-third its length. With a heading of 350°, we are in the largest piece of the pie, so a direct entry would be used. See the figure below. (PLT146, IR.III.B.K1) — AIM ¶5-3-7

Answer (A) is incorrect because a heading of 350° requires a direct entry. Answer (B) is incorrect because the second holding pattern does not have the holding fix at the end of the inbound leg.

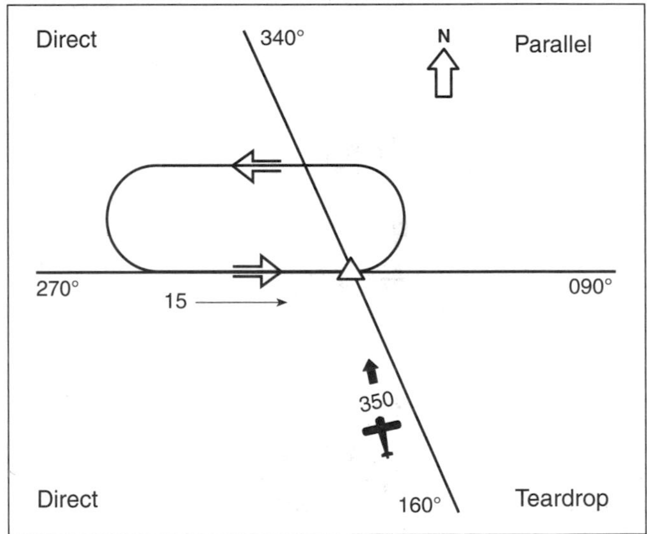

Question 4618

Answers

4616 [A] 4618 [C]

ALL

4619. (Refer to Figure 116.) You arrive over the 15 DME fix on a heading of 350°. Which holding pattern correctly complies with the ATC clearance below, and what is the recommended entry procedure?

"...HOLD WEST OF THE ONE FIVE DME FIX ON THE TWO SIX EIGHT RADIAL OF THE ABC VORTAC, FIVE MILE LEGS, LEFT TURNS..."

A—1; teardrop entry.
B—2; direct entry.
C—1; direct entry.

Determine the holding pattern by placing your pencil on the holding fix and dragging it on the holding radial given by ATC, then returning back to the fix. Then draw the pattern from the fix with turns in the direction specified. In this question, ATC has specified left-hand turns, which corresponds to holding pattern 2.

The entry procedure is based on the aircraft's heading. To determine which entry procedure to use, draw a line at a 70° angle from the holding fix, and cutting the outbound leg at about one-third its length. With a heading of 350°, we are in the largest piece of the pie, so a direct entry would be used. See the figure below. (PLT146, IR.III.B.K1) — AIM ¶5-3-7

Answer (A) is incorrect because a heading of 350° requires a direct entry, and the first holding pattern does not have the holding fix at the end of the inbound leg. Answer (C) is incorrect because the first holding pattern does not have the holding fix at the end of the inbound leg.

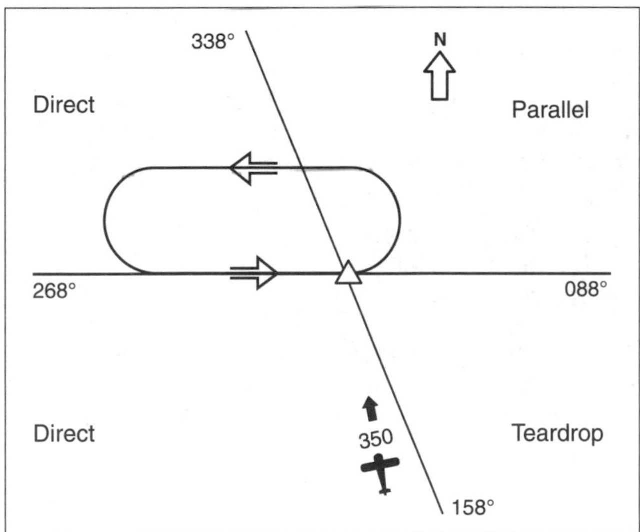

Question 4619

ALL

4624. What timing procedure should be used when performing a holding pattern at a VOR?

A—Timing for the outbound leg begins over or abeam the VOR, whichever occurs later.
B—Timing for the inbound leg begins when initiating the turn inbound.
C—Adjustments in timing of each pattern should be made on the inbound leg.

Outbound leg timing begins over/abeam the fix, whichever occurs later. (PLT146, IR.III.B.K1) — AIM ¶5-3-7

Answers (B) and (C) are incorrect because timing procedures coordinate with the outbound (not inbound) leg.

ALL

4620. At what point should the timing begin for the first leg outbound in a nonstandard holding pattern?

A—Abeam the holding fix, or wings level, whichever occurs last.
B—When the wings are level at the completion of the 180° turn outbound.
C—When over or abeam the holding fix, whichever occurs later.

Outbound leg timing begins over/abeam the fix, whichever occurs later. If the abeam position cannot be determined, start timing when the turn to the outbound is completed. (PLT146, IR.III.B.K1) — AIM ¶5-3-7

Answer (A) is incorrect because timing begins on the outbound leg when the wings are level only if the abeam point cannot be determined. Answer (B) is incorrect because you may roll wings level before abeam the fix.

ALL

4617. To ensure proper airspace protection while in a holding pattern, what is the maximum airspeed above 14,000 feet for civil turbojet aircraft?

A—230 knots.
B—265 knots.
C—200 knots.

The maximum airspeed above 14,000 feet is 265 KIAS. (PLT146, IR.III.B.K1) — AIM ¶5-3-7

Answers

4619 [B]	4624 [A]	4620 [C]	4617 [B]

ALL

4626. To ensure proper airspace protection while holding at 5,000 feet in a civil aircraft, what is the maximum indicated airspeed a pilot should use?

A—230 knots.
B—200 knots.
C—210 knots.

The maximum holding airspeed between MHA and 6,000 feet MSL is 200 KIAS. (PLT296, IR.III.B.K1) — AIM ¶5-3-7

ALL

4766. To ensure proper airspace protection while in a holding pattern, what is the maximum indicated airspeed above 14,000 feet?

A—220 knots.
B—265 knots.
C—200 knots.

While in a holding pattern, the maximum indicated airspeed above 14,000 feet is 265 KIAS. (PLT296, IR.III.B.K1) — AIM ¶5-3-7

ALL

4668. When more than one circuit of the holding pattern is needed to lose altitude or become better established on course, the additional circuits can be made

A—at pilot's discretion.
B—only in an emergency.
C—only if pilot advises ATC and ATC approves.

If timed approaches are in use, aircraft are expected to proceed inbound on final approach when clearance is received. Pilots are responsible for advising ATC if they elect to make additional circuits to lose altitude or become established on course. There is no AIM language regarding ATC approval, but it is implied. (PLT296, IR.III.B.K1) — AIM ¶5-4-9

Answer (A) is incorrect because although additional circuits may be made at your discretion, you must advise ATC. Answer (B) is incorrect because it is not necessary to declare an emergency.

ALL

4681. (Refer to Figure 242.) What type of entry is recommended to the missed approach holding pattern if your magnetic heading is 050°?

A—Direct.
B—Parallel.
C—Teardrop.

The missed approach procedure is to fly direct to HIGHS. The holding pattern depicted is left-hand turns, so the pilot should execute a teardrop turn to enter the holding pattern. (PLT083, IR.III.B.K1) — AIM ¶5-3-7

Answer (A) is incorrect because a direct entry would be used if the pilot were coming from the north. Answer (B) is incorrect because a parallel entry would be used if the pilot were coming from the southeast.

ALL

4698. (Refer to Figure 247.) What type of entry is recommended for the missed approach holding pattern at Riverside Municipal?

A—Teardrop or Direct.
B—Direct or Teardrop.
C—Parallel or Teardrop.

The pilot can use either a parallel or teardrop entry for the holding pattern at Riverside Municipal. The missed approach procedures route the pilot directly to R-076 where they can join the depicted holding pattern. (PLT296, IR.III.B.K1) — AIM ¶5-4-9

ALL

4675. (Refer to Figure 240.) What type entry is recommended for the missed approach holding pattern depicted on the VOR/DME RWY 36 approach chart for Price/Carbon County Airport?

A—Parallel or teardrop.
B—Direct or parallel.
C—Teardrop or direct.

The missed approach takes you outbound on the PUC R-164° which sets you up for either a parallel or teardrop entry into the holding pattern. (PLT083, IR.III.B.K1) — AIM ¶5-3-7

Answers

4626 [B]	4766 [B]	4668 [C]	4681 [C]	4698 [C]	4675 [A]

ALL

4675-1. (Refer to Figure 245.) You are executing the missed approach at CQX from the RNAV (GPS)-B approach. How will you enter the holding pattern?

A—Direct.
B—Teardrop.
C—Parallel.

You'll use a direct entry into the holding pattern to comply with the missed approach notes, which state execute a climbing left turn to 3000 direct CEPUL and hold. (PLT083, IR.III.Bk1) — AIM ¶5-3-7

AIR

4615. (Refer to Figure 114.) A pilot receives this ATC clearance:

"...CLEARED TO THE XYZ VORTAC. HOLD NORTH ON THE THREE SIX ZERO RADIAL, LEFT TURNS..."

What is the recommended procedure to enter the holding pattern?

A—Teardrop only.
B—Parallel only.
C—Direct only.

Determine the holding pattern by placing your pencil on the holding fix and dragging it on the holding radial given by ATC, then returning back to the fix. Then draw the pattern from the fix with turns in the direction specified. Holding north on the 360° radial with left turn means you will be east of R-360.

The entry procedure is based on the aircraft's heading. To determine which entry procedure to use, draw a line at a 70° angle from the holding fix, and cutting the outbound leg at about one-third its length. With a heading of 055°, we are in the largest piece of the pie, so a direct entry would be used. See the figure below. (PLT146, IR.III.B.K1) — AIM ¶5-3-7

Answer (A) is incorrect because a teardrop entry would only be appropriate between the 180° and 250° radials. Answer (B) is incorrect because a parallel entry would only be appropriate between the 360° and 250° radials.

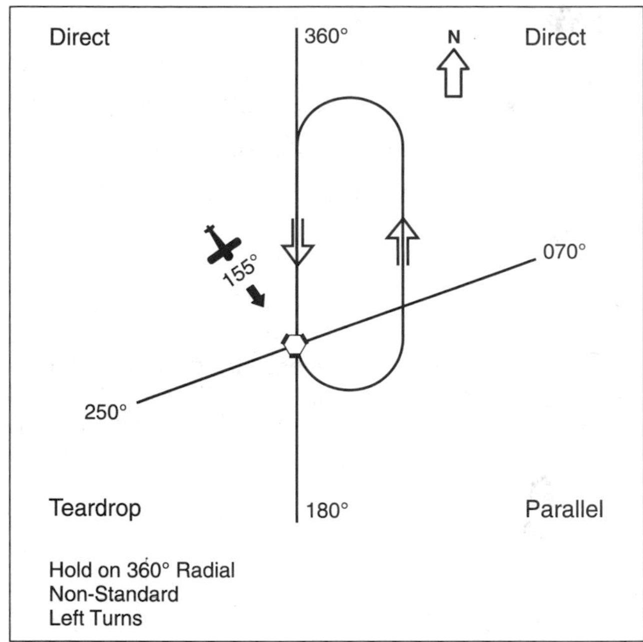

Question 4615

ALL

4986. (Refer to Figure 234.) The control tower at LNK has instructed you: "in the event of a missed approach, hold as published." What holding entry procedure will you use?

A—Teardrop.
B—Direct.
C—Parallel.

Figure 234 states the missed approach instructions as climb to 1700 then climbing right turn to 3000 direct LNK VORTAC and hold. Follow the depicted holding pattern using a parallel entry. (PLT234, IR.III.B.K1) — AIM ¶5-3-7

Answers

4675-1 [A] 4615 [C] 4986 [C]

Fuel Consumption

In order to calculate fuel consumption, you must complete the flight log provided with each question. Each question will go through the following steps:

1. Calculate the ground speed.
2. Find the time en route for the flight.
3. Calculate the total fuel burn.

ALL

4265. (Refer to Figure 24.) Your original route of flight was CEZ V391 JNC. However, due to thunderstorms en route, ATC revises your route to CEZ V391 DVC V68 MTJ V26 JNC. Calculate how much additional fuel you will consume given the following:

Winds = 230 @40 kts
TAS = 130 kts
GPH = 17

A—13.2 gallons.
B—5.5 gallons.
C—9.1 gallons.

For both routes of flight, determine the magnetic headings and distances for each leg as published on the Low Altitude Chart segment. Then using a flight computer, determine ground speed, time, and fuel burn for each leg.

Totals Route 1
Distance: 106 NM
Time En Route: 46:38
Fuel Burn: 13.2 GPH

Totals Route 2
Distance: 152 NM
Time En Route: 01:09:29
Fuel Burn: 19.7 GPH

A difference of 6.5 GPH, the closest available answer choice for this question is 5.5 GPH. (PLT012, IR.I.C.K3c) — FAA-H-8083-25, Low Altitude En Route Legend

ALL

4265-1. (Refer to Figure 47.) Due to thunderstorms along your planned route, you decide to file Battle Ground (BTG) VORTAC, V520 to OGYAJ intersection, KLICKITAT (LTJ) VORTAC, V25 to YAKIMA (YKM) VORTAC. Calculate the time and fuel burn for the route with the following conditions:

TAS = 140 kts
Reported winds = 270 at 30 kts
Fuel burn rate = 17 GPH

A—49 minutes, 13.7 gallons.
B—53 minutes, 15.1 gallons.
C—60 minutes, 17 gallons.

Determine your magnetic heading and distance as published on the Low Altitude Chart segment. Then using a flight computer, determine ground speed, leg time, and fuel burn.

Distance: 124 NM
Time En Route: 0:48:36
Fuel Burn: 13.77 GPH

(PLT012, IR.I.C.K3c) — FAA-H-8083-25, Low Altitude Enroute Chart

Answers

4265 [B] 4265-1 [A]

Chapter 8
Arrival and Approach

Standard Terminal Arrivals (STARs)

STARs are used in much the same way as DPs—to relieve frequency congestion and to expedite the arrival of aircraft into the terminal area. Like DPs, STARs may be issued by ATC whenever it is deemed appropriate. As with DPs, the PIC may either accept or decline a STAR, but if the STAR is accepted, the pilot must possess at least the textual description of the procedure. Should the pilot not wish to use a STAR, a notation to that effect in the remarks section of the flight plan will make ATC aware of the PIC's decision.

The STAR is depicted by a procedural track with a corresponding textual arrival descirption for each transition route as shown in Figure 8-1, GLEN ROSE Nine Arrival. Familiarize yourself with FAA Legends 22 through 24, as they have information on STARs which will be available for you during the FAA Knowledge Exam.

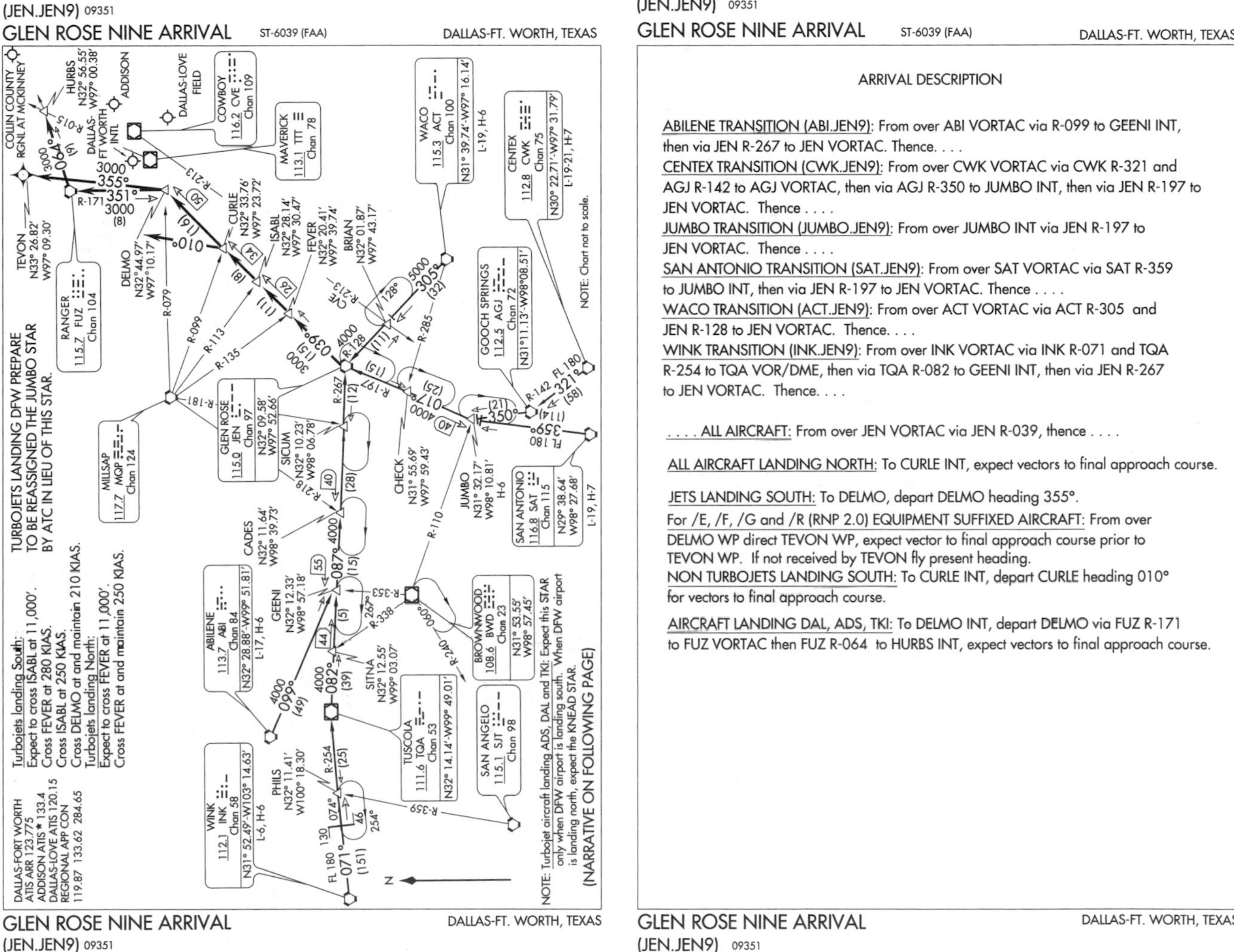

(JEN.JEN9) 09351
GLEN ROSE NINE ARRIVAL ST-6039 (FAA) DALLAS-FT. WORTH, TEXAS

ARRIVAL DESCRIPTION

ABILENE TRANSITION (ABI.JEN9): From over ABI VORTAC via R-099 to GEENI INT, then via JEN R-267 to JEN VORTAC. Thence. . . .
CENTEX TRANSITION (CWK.JEN9): From over CWK VORTAC via CWK R-321 and AGJ R-142 to AGJ VORTAC, then via AGJ R-350 to JUMBO INT, then via JEN R-197 to JEN VORTAC. Thence . . . .
JUMBO TRANSITION (JUMBO.JEN9): From over JUMBO INT via JEN R-197 to JEN VORTAC. Thence . . . .
SAN ANTONIO TRANSITION (SAT.JEN9): From over SAT VORTAC via SAT R-359 to JUMBO INT, then via JEN R-197 to JEN VORTAC. Thence . . . .
WACO TRANSITION (ACT.JEN9): From over ACT VORTAC via ACT R-305 and JEN R-128 to JEN VORTAC. Thence. . . .
WINK TRANSITION (INK.JEN9): From over INK VORTAC via INK R-071 and TQA R-254 to TQA VOR/DME, then via TQA R-082 to GEENI INT, then via JEN R-267 to JEN VORTAC. Thence. . . .

. . . . ALL AIRCRAFT: From over JEN VORTAC via JEN R-039, thence . . . .

ALL AIRCRAFT LANDING NORTH: To CURLE INT, expect vectors to final approach course.

JETS LANDING SOUTH: To DELMO, depart DELMO heading 355°.
For /E, /F, /G and /R (RNP 2.0) EQUIPMENT SUFFIXED AIRCRAFT: From over DELMO WP direct TEVON WP, expect vector to final approach course prior to TEVON WP. If not received by TEVON fly present heading.
NON TURBOJETS LANDING SOUTH: To CURLE INT, depart CURLE heading 010° for vectors to final approach course.

AIRCRAFT LANDING DAL, ADS, TKI: To DELMO INT, depart DELMO via FUZ R-171 to FUZ VORTAC then FUZ R-064 to HURBS INT, expect vectors to final approach course.

GLEN ROSE NINE ARRIVAL DALLAS-FT. WORTH, TEXAS
(JEN.JEN9) 09351

Figure 8-1. Standard terminal arrival (STAR)

ALL
4640. Which is true regarding STARs?

A—STARs are used to separate IFR and VFR traffic.
B—STARs are established to simplify clearance delivery procedures.
C—STARs are used at certain airports to decrease traffic congestion.

STARs have been established to simplify clearance delivery procedures for arriving aircraft at certain areas having high density traffic. (PLT080, IR.V.B.K1) — AIM ¶5-4-1

ALL
4286. (Refer to Figures 167 and 168.) At which point does the BYP.BYP6 arrival begin?

A—At the LIT VORTAC.
B—At GLOVE intersection.
C—At the BYP VORTAC.

The heavy black lines with arrows portray the Arrival Route, which, in this case, begins at the Bonham VOR (BYP). Note also, in the textual description, all the transitions end with the following statement, "To BYP VORTAC. Thence..." (PLT102, IR.V.B.K1) — STAR Chart

ALL
4292. (Refer to Figures 174 and 175.) At which point does the JEN.JEN9 arrival begin?

A—TEVON Waypoint.
B—INK VORTAC.
C—JEN VORTAC.

Heavy lines ending in arrows are arrival routes, thin lines are transition routes. Also, arrival descriptions in FAA Figure 175 state that transitions end and arrivals begin ("Thence...") at JEN VORTAC. (PLT080, IR.V.B.K1) — U.S. Terminal Procedures, STAR Legend

Answer (A) is incorrect because TEVON is simply a GPS waypoint on the arrival route. Answer (B) is incorrect because INK VORTAC is the beginning of the WINK Transition (INK.JEN9) which transitions you to the beginning of the arrival route at JEN VORTAC.

ALL
4294. (Refer to Figures 174 and 175.) On which heading should you plan to depart CURLE INT if landing Addison Airport (ADS)?

A—039°
B—010°
C—355°

Figure 175 states "AIRCRAFT LANDING DAL, ADS, TKI: To DELMO INT..." Therefore you would depart CURLE INT heading 039° to DELMO INT as shown from JEN VORTAC. (PLT102, IR.V.B.K1) — U.S. Terminal Procedures, STAR Legend

Answer (B) is incorrect because 010° is the heading from CURLE INT for Non Turbo Jet aircraft landing south at DFW. Answer (C) is incorrect because 355° is a heading shown from DELMO INT.

ALL
4349. (Refer to Figures 208 and 209.) At which location or condition does the AUDIL.STELA1 transition begin?

A—CANAN Intersection.
B—RKA VORTAC.
C—AUDILE Intersection.

Figure 208 shows both arrival and transition routes. The heavy black lines with arrows portray the arrival route, in this case beginning at CANAN intersection. Transition routes are depicted as thin black lines with arrows. The AUDILE transition (AUDILE.STELA1) begins at AUDILE intersection. Also note the textual description in Figure 209, which states that the transition begins "over AUDIL INT" ending at CANAN INT where the arrival route begins. (PLT080, IR.V.B.K1) — U.S. Terminal Procedures, STAR Chart Legend

ALL
4751. Under which condition does ATC issue a STAR?

A—To all pilots wherever STAR's are available.
B—Only if the pilot requests a STAR in the "Remarks" section of the flight plan.
C—When ATC deems it appropriate, unless the pilot requests "No STAR."

Pilots of IFR civil aircraft destined to locations for which STARs have been published may be issued a clearance containing a STAR whenever ATC deems it appropriate. Use of STARs requires pilot possession of at least the approved textual description. As with any ATC clearance or portion thereof, it is the responsibility of each pilot to accept or refuse an issued STAR. A pilot should notify ATC if they do not wish to use a STAR by placing "NO STAR" in the remarks section of the flight plan, or by the less desirable method of verbally stating the same to ATC. (PLT172, IR.V.B.K1) — AIM ¶5-4-1

Answer (A) is incorrect because STARs are not mandatory to pilots or ATC. Answer (B) is incorrect because a request is only necessary when the pilot does not wish to use a STAR.

Answers

4640 [B]	4286 [C]	4292 [C]	4294 [A]	4349 [C]	4751 [C]

Communications During Arrival

Should the pilot elect to cancel the IFR flight plan and proceed VFR to the destination, the pilot is expected to monitor the ATIS (if available) for non-control information regarding runway in use, weather, etc. The ATIS broadcast will be updated upon receipt of any official weather. Should the visibility exceed 5 statute miles, or the ceiling be above 5,000 feet AGL, those items may be omitted. If inbound to an airport with an operating air traffic control tower, a pilot who has canceled their IFR flight plan must contact the tower at least 5 miles from the airport to comply with Class D airspace requirements. If Class B or Class C airspace exists at the destination, remaining VFR requirements for those must also be met.

As the IFR flight enters the terminal area, it is common to receive radar vectors to the final approach course, or be constantly reassigned altitudes. Climbs and descents should be made at an optimum rate of between 500 and 1,500 feet per minute. If at any time, the aircraft is unable to climb or descend at 500 feet, ATC must be advised. During a radar vector to the final approach course, it is good operating practice to read back the portions of clearances which contain heading and altitude assignments.

In order to avoid excessive vectoring in the terminal environment, ATC may request pilots to adjust their speed. ATC will express all speeds in terms of knots indicated airspeed (KIAS) and use only 10-knot increments. Pilots complying with such a request are expected to maintain that indicated speed within ±10 knots. If unable to comply with the request, the pilot is expected to advise ATC immediately of the speed that will be used.

If radar vectored and about to pass through the final approach course, the pilot may not turn inbound unless an approach clearance has been received. Instead, the pilot should maintain the course and query ATC. ATC occasionally needs to vector an aircraft through the approach course, and in such cases the controllers should state their intentions to do so. Controllers are required to advise you if they will be vectoring you across the localizer.

If ATC uses the phrase "cleared for approach," the pilot may use any authorized instrument approach for the airport as long as the entire procedure is followed. If cleared for a specific procedure, such as "cleared for the ILS Runway 31R approach," the pilot must execute only that ILS approach.

If the pilot is being radar vectored or operating on an unpublished route when approach clearance is received, the pilot must maintain the last assigned altitude until established on a segment of a published route or instrument approach procedure.

LAHSO stands for land and hold short operations. These operations include landing and holding short of an intersecting runway, an intersecting taxiway, or some other designated point on a runway other than an intersecting runway or taxiway. At controlled airports, ATC may clear a pilot to land and hold short. The PIC has the final authority to accept or decline any land and hold short clearance. The safety and operation of the aircraft remain the responsibility of the pilot. To conduct LAHSO, pilots should become familiar with all available information concerning LAHSO at their destination airport. Pilots should have, readily available, the published available landing distance (ALD) and runway slope information for all LAHSO runway combinations at each airport of intended landing. Additionally, knowledge about landing performance data permits the pilot to readily determine that the ALD for the assigned runway is sufficient for safe LAHSO. If, for any reason, such as difficulty in discerning the location of a LAHSO intersection, wind conditions, aircraft condition, etc., the pilot elects to request to land on the full length of the runway, to land on another runway, or to decline LAHSO, a pilot is expected to promptly inform ATC, ideally even before the clearance is issued. Once accepted, a LAHSO clearance must be adhered to just as any other ATC clearance, unless an amended clearance is obtained or an emergency occurs. However, a LAHSO clearance does not preclude a rejected landing. The airport markings, signage, and lighting associated with LAHSO consist of a three-part system of yellow hold-short markings, red and white signage, and, in certain cases, in-pavement lighting.

ALL

4403. When are ATIS broadcasts updated?

A—Every 30 minutes if weather conditions are below basic VFR; otherwise, hourly.
B—Upon receipt of any official weather, regardless of content change or reported values.
C—Only when the ceiling and/or visibility changes by a reportable value.

ATIS broadcasts shall be updated upon the receipt of any official weather, regardless of content change and reported values. A new recording will also be made when there is a change in other pertinent data such as runway change, instrument approach in use, etc. (PLT196, IR.V.B.K2) — AIM ¶4-1-13

Answer (A) is incorrect because the ATIS updates are not different under VFR or IFR conditions. Answer (C) is incorrect because the recording will be updated when official weather is received, even if there is no change.

ALL

4403-1. What is the rule for a pilot receiving a Land and Hold Short Operation (LAHSO) clearance?

A—The pilot is required to accept the controller's clearance in visual meteorological conditions.
B—The pilot must accept the clearance if the pavement is dry and the stopping distance is adequate.
C—The pilot has the option to accept or reject all LAHSO clearances regardless of the meteorological conditions.

LAHSO operations are permitted only on dry runways under acceptable weather conditions and limited to airports where a clearance depends on what is happening on the other runway, or where approved rejected landing procedures are in place. A dependent procedure example is when a landing airplane is a minimum distance from the threshold and an airplane is departing an intersecting runway, the LAHSO clearance can be issued because even in the event of a rejected landing, separation is assured. It is always the pilot's option to reject a LAHSO clearance. (PLT140, IR.V.B.K2) — FAA-H-8083-16

Answers (A) and (B) are incorrect because pilots always have the option to decline a LAHSO clearance.

ALL

4404. Absence of the sky condition and visibility on an ATIS broadcast specifically implies that

A—the ceiling is more than 5,000 feet and visibility is 5 miles or more.
B—the sky condition is clear and visibility is unrestricted.
C—the ceiling is at least 3,000 feet and visibility is 5 miles or more.

If the weather is above a ceiling/sky condition of 5,000 feet and the visibility is 5 miles or more, inclusion of the ceiling/sky condition, visibility, and obstructions to vision in the ATIS message is optional. (PLT196, IR.V.B.K2) — AIM ¶4-1-13

Answers (B) and (C) are incorrect because the absence of the sky conditions and visibility on an ATIS broadcast means the ceilings are more than 5,000 feet and visibility 5 SM or better.

ALL

4293. (Refer to Figures 174 and 175.) When DFW is landing to the north, at CURLE expect

A—to be instructed to maintain 200 knots.
B—to fly a course of 010°.
C—radar vectors.

Figure 175 includes the note "ALL AIRCRAFT LANDING NORTH: To CURLE INT, expect vectors to final approach course." (PLT102, IR.V.B.K2) — U.S. Terminal Procedures, STAR Legend

ALL

4295. (Refer to Figures 174, 176, and 176A.) Approaching DFW from Abilene, which frequencies should you expect to use for Regional Approach Control, Control Tower, and Ground Control respectively?

A—119.87; 126.55; 121.65.
B—119.87; 124.15; 121.85.
C—125.025; 126.55; 121.65.

On FAA Figure 174 you can see that ABI VORTAC is west of DFW airport, therefore aircraft approaching DFW from ABI would be approaching from the west. Figure 176A lists the common frequencies for aircraft approaching from either the west (W) or east (E) right underneath the airport remarks section. Those frequencies likely to be given to aircraft approaching from the west are followed by (W). (PLT102, IR.V.B.K2) — U.S. Terminal Procedures

Answers (A) and (C) are incorrect because the tower and ground frequencies shown are likely to be assigned to those aircraft approaching and landing from the East.

Answers

4403 [B] 4403-1 [C] 4404 [A] 4293 [C] 4295 [B]

ALL

4469. When are you required to establish communications with the tower, (Class D airspace) if you cancel your IFR flight plan 10 miles from the destination?

A—Immediately after canceling the flight plan.
B—When advised by ARTCC.
C—Before entering Class D airspace.

When flying in Class D airspace, communications must be established with the tower. Class D airspace has a radius of at least 4.4 NM, which equals 5 SM. (PLT162, IR.V.B.K2) — 14 CFR §91.129

Answer (A) is incorrect because it not necessary to contact tower 10 miles out. Answer (B) is incorrect because the pilot is only required to contact tower prior to entering the Class D airspace.

ALL

4726. You have not yet been cleared for the approach, but you are being vectored to the ILS approach course. It is clear that you will pass through the localizer course unless you take action. You should

A—turn outbound and complete the procedure turn.
B—continue as assigned and query ATC.
C—turn inbound and join the final approach course.

Radar vectors and altitude/flight levels will be issued as required for spacing and separating aircraft; therefore, you must not deviate from the headings as issued by approach control. You will normally be informed when it becomes necessary to vector you across the final approach course for spacing or other reasons. If you determine that approach course crossing is imminent and you have not been informed that you will be vectored across it, you should question the controller. You should not turn inbound on the final approach course unless you have received an approach clearance. (PLT370, IR.VI.B.K1) — AIM ¶5-4-3

ALL

4734. When being radar vectored for an ILS approach, at what point may you start a descent from your last assigned altitude to a lower minimum altitude if cleared for the approach?

A—When established on a segment of a published route or IAP.
B—You may descend immediately to published glide slope interception altitude.
C—Only after you are established on the final approach unless informed otherwise by ATC.

When operating on an unpublished route or while being radar vectored, the pilot, when an approach clearance is received, shall maintain the last altitude assigned to that pilot until the aircraft is established on a segment of a published route or instrument approach procedure, unless a different altitude is assigned by ATC. (PLT420, IR.V.B.K1) — AIM ¶5-4-3

Answer (B) is incorrect because the pilot must be on part of the published approach in order to descend. Answer (C) is incorrect because the pilot should follow the prescribed altitude whenever on a segment of a published route or IAP.

ALL

4757. While being vectored, if crossing the ILS final approach course becomes imminent and an approach clearance has not been issued, what action should be taken by the pilot?

A—Turn outbound on the final approach course, execute a procedure turn, and inform ATC.
B—Turn inbound and execute the missed approach procedure at the outer marker if approach clearance has not been received.
C—Maintain the last assigned heading and query ATC.

Radar vectors and altitude/flight levels will be issued as required for spacing and separating aircraft; therefore, pilots must not deviate from the headings as issued by approach control. Aircraft will normally be informed when it becomes necessary to vector across the final approach course for spacing or other reasons. If approach course crossing is imminent and the pilot has not been informed that the aircraft will be vectored across the final approach course, the pilot should query the controller. (PLT277, IR.V.B.K2) — AIM ¶5-4-3

Answers (A) and (B) are incorrect because the pilot should not deviate from headings or altitudes issued by approach control until an amended clearance has been received.

Answers

4469 [C] 4726 [B] 4734 [A] 4757 [C]

ALL

4641. While being radar vectored, an approach clearance is received. The last assigned altitude should be maintained until

A—reaching the FAF.
B—advised to begin descent.
C—established on a segment of a published route or IAP.

Upon receipt of an approach clearance while on an unpublished route or being radar vectored, the pilots must maintain the last assigned altitude until established on a segment of a published route or IAP, at which time published altitudes apply. (PLT170, IR.V.B.K2) — AIM ¶5-5-4

Answer (A) is incorrect because published altitudes may be used as soon as the aircraft is on a published route, which should be before the FAF. Answer (B) is incorrect because once ATC issues an approach clearance, descent to published altitudes is left to the discretion of the pilot.

ALL

4249. (Refer to Figure 178.) On what frequency should you expect to contact Regional Approach Control while flying the ILS or LOC Y RWY 13L approach to DAL?

A—124.3.
B—125.2.
C—123.7.

The top of the IAP lists several of the common frequencies associated with the approach at DAL. Since you are approaching DAL from the North, landing to the South you would contact Regional Approach Control on 124.3. (PLT102, IR.VI.C.K1) — U.S. Terminal Procedures

Instrument Approach Terms and Abbreviations

The **decision height (DH)** is the altitude at which, on a precision approach, a decision must be made to either continue the approach or execute a missed approach.

The **minimum descent altitude (MDA)** is the lowest altitude, expressed in feet above MSL, to which descent is authorized on final approach or during circle-to-land maneuvering in execution of a standard instrument approach procedure where no electronic glide slope is provided.

The **final approach fix (FAF)** identifies the beginning of the final approach segment of an instrument approach procedure. The FAF for nonprecision approaches is designated by a Maltese cross. On precision approaches, a lightning bolt symbol indicates the FAF. If ATC directs a glide slope intercept altitude which is lower than that published, the actual point of glide slope intercept becomes the FAF.

The **final approach point (FAP)** applies only to nonprecision approaches with no designated FAF, such as an on-airport VOR or NDB. It is the point at which an aircraft has completed the procedure turn, is established inbound on the final approach course, and may start the final descent. The FAP serves as the FAF and identifies the beginning of the final approach segment.

The **glide slope (GS)** or glide path provides vertical guidance for aircraft during approach and landing. Applying the glide slope angle and the ground speed to the rate of descent table gives a recommended vertical speed.

An **instrument approach procedure (IAP)** is a series of predetermined maneuvers for the orderly transfer of an aircraft under instrument flight conditions, from the beginning of the initial approach to a landing or to a point from which a landing may be made visually.

A **nonprecision approach** is a standard instrument approach procedure in which no electronic glide slope is provided; for example, NDB, VOR, TACAN, ASR, LDA, or SDF approaches.

A **precision approach** is a standard instrument approach procedure in which an electronic glide slope/glide path is provided; for example, ILS, MLS, or PAR approaches.

Answers

4641 [C] 4249 [A]

A **procedure turn (PT)** is the maneuver prescribed when it is necessary to reverse direction in order to establish an aircraft on the intermediate approach segment or on the final approach course. A procedure turn (and the initial approach segment) begins by overheading a facility or fix. The maximum speed for a PT is 200 KIAS.

In the case of a radar vector to a final approach fix, or position or a timed approach from a holding fix, or where the procedure is specified "NoPT," no pilot may make a procedure turn unless, upon receiving the final approach clearance, the pilot so advises ATC and a clearance is received.

A barb indicates the direction or side of the outbound course on which the procedure turn is made. If no barb is depicted then a procedure turn is not authorized. Headings are provided for course reversal using the 45°-type procedure turn. However, the point at which the turn may be commenced and the type and rate of turn is left to the discretion of the pilot. When a teardrop procedure turn is depicted and a course reversal is required, this type of turn must be executed. When a one-minute holding pattern replaces the procedure turn, the standard entry and the holding pattern must be followed, except when radar vectoring is provided or when "NoPT" is shown on the approach course. The holding maneuver must be executed within the 1-minute time limitation or within the published leg length.

A **straight-in approach** is one in which the final approach segment is begun without first having executed a procedure turn (such as a holding pattern, teardrop, or 45°-type). Radar vectors to final are straight-in approaches. The straight-in approach may be followed by either a straight-in landing or a circle-to-land maneuver.

Straight-in landing minimums are published when the runway alignment and the IAP final approach course are within 30° of each other, and will be identified by the letter "S" followed by designation of the runway to which they apply; for example, "S-ILS 34."

The same IAP may furnish circling minimums for use if it is necessary to land on a runway other than the one aligned with the final approach course. These will be identified by the word "circling" and no runway will be designated.

In some cases, the IAP final approach course may not be within 30 of alignment with a runway. Then, only circling minimums will be published.

The **initial approach fix (IAF)** is the point at which the procedure turn begins, or any fix labeled "IAF" that identifies the beginning of the initial approach segment of an instrument approach procedure. Follow the published feeder route unless instructed otherwise.

The **initial approach segment** is the segment of an IAP between IAF and the intermediate fix, or the point where the aircraft is established on the intermediate or final approach course. The intermediate approach segment is the segment between the intermediate fix or point and the final approach fix. The final approach segment is the segment between the final approach fix or point and the runway or missed approach point. The missed approach segment is the segment between the missed approach point or the point of arrival at decision height and the missed approach fix at the prescribed altitude.

The **visual descent point (VDP)** is a point on a final approach course of a nonprecision approach from which a normal descent from the MDA to the runway can be commenced, provided the pilot has the runway, lights, etc., identified.

The **side-step maneuver** is one that ATC may authorize to a runway that is within 1,200 feet of an adjacent parallel runway. Pilots are expected to commence the side-step maneuvers as soon as possible after the runway, or runway environment is in sight.

ALL

4740. When cleared to execute a published side-step maneuver for a specific approach and landing on the parallel runway, at what point is the pilot expected to commence this maneuver?

A—At the published minimum altitude for a circling approach.
B—As soon as possible after the runway or runway environment is in sight.
C—At the localizer MDA minimum and when the runway is in sight.

Aircraft that execute a side-step maneuver will be cleared for a specified approach and landing on the adjacent parallel runway. Example, "Cleared for ILS runway 07 left approach, side-step to runway 07 right." Pilots are expected to commence the side-step maneuver as soon as possible after the runway or runway environment is in sight. (PLT221, IR.VI.E.K1) — AIM ¶5-4-19

ALL

4715. How can an IAF be identified on a Standard Instrument Approach Procedure (SIAP) Chart?

A—All fixes that are labeled IAF.
B—Any fix illustrated within the 10 mile ring other than the FAF or stepdown fix.
C—The procedure turn and the fixes on the feeder facility ring.

The instrument approach commences at the IAP. Initial approach fixes are specifically identified with "IAF." (PLT083, IR.I.C.K1) — Instrument Approach Procedure Legend

ALL

4746. Which fixes on the IAP Charts are initial approach fixes?

A—Any fix on the en route facilities ring, the feeder facilities ring, and those at the start of arc approaches.
B—Only the fixes at the start of arc approaches and those on either the feeder facilities ring or en route facilities ring that have a transition course shown to the approach procedure.
C—Any fix that is identified by the letters IAF.

Initial approach fixes are the fixes depicted on the Instrument Approach Procedure Charts that identify the beginning of the initial approach segment(s). The letters IAF identify initial approach fixes on instrument approach charts. (PLT083, IR.I.C.K1) — Pilot/Controller Glossary

Answers (A) and (B) are incorrect because the instrument approach fixes are specifically identified with "IAF" with the exception of the procedure turn approach pattern.

ALL

4632. When the approach procedure involves a procedure turn, the maximum speed should not be greater than

A—180 knots IAS.
B—200 knots IAS.
C—250 knots IAS.

When the approach procedure involves a procedure turn, a maximum speed no more than 200 KIAS should be observed, and the turn should be executed within the distance specified in the profile view. (PLT170, IR.VI.C.K1) — AIM ¶5-4-9

ALL

4636. What does the absence of the procedure turn barb on the plan view on an approach chart indicate?

A—A procedure turn is not authorized.
B—Teardrop-type procedure turn is authorized.
C—Racetrack-type procedure turn is authorized.

The absence of the procedure turn barb in the plan view indicates that a procedure turn is not authorized for that procedure. (PLT292, IR.III.B.K1) — Instrument Approach Procedures

ALL

4767. Where a holding pattern is specified in lieu of a procedure turn, the holding maneuver must be executed within

A—the 1 minute time limitation or DME distance as specified in the profile view.
B—a radius of 5 miles from the holding fix.
C—10 knots of the specified holding speed.

Where a holding pattern is specified in lieu of a procedure turn, the holding maneuver must be executed within the 1 minute time limitation or DME distance as specified in the profile view. The maneuver is completed when the aircraft is established on the inbound course after executing the appropriate holding pattern entry. (PLT170, IR.VI.C.K1) — AIM ¶5-4-9

Answers

4740 [B]	4715 [A]	4746 [C]	4632 [B]	4636 [A]	4767 [A]

ALL

4771. Assume this clearance is received:
"CLEARED FOR ILS RUNWAY 07 LEFT APPROACH, SIDE-STEP TO RUNWAY 07 RIGHT."

When would the pilot be expected to commence the side-step maneuver?

A—As soon as possible after the runway environment is in sight.
B—Any time after becoming aligned with the final approach course of Runway 07 left, and after passing the final approach fix.
C—After reaching the circling minimums for Runway 07 right.

Aircraft that execute a side-step maneuver will be cleared for a specified approach and landing on the adjacent parallel runway. Pilots are expected to commence the side-step maneuver as soon as possible after the runway or runway environment is in sight. (PLT044, IR.VI.E.K1) — AIM ¶5-4-19

Answer (B) is incorrect because the pilot has only been cleared for runway 07 left, and should commence as soon as the runway environment is in sight. Answer (C) is incorrect because the side-step should commence as soon as the runway environment is in sight.

ALL

4670. When simultaneous approaches are in progress, how does each pilot receive radar advisories on final?

A—On tower frequency.
B—On approach control frequency.
C—One pilot on tower frequency and the other on approach control frequency.

Pilots will monitor tower frequency for advisories and instructions when simultaneous approaches are in progress. (PLT420, IR.V.B.K2) — AIM ¶5-4-15

ALL

4670-1. Precision Runway Monitoring (PRM) is

A—an airborne radar system for monitoring approaches to two runways.
B—a radar system for monitoring approaches to closely spaced parallel runways.
C—a high update rate radar system for monitoring multiple aircraft to a single runway.

PRM is a high update-rate radar surveillance system, certified to provide simultaneous independent approaches to closely spaced parallel runways. (PLT292, IR.III.B.K1) — FAA-H-8083-16

Answer (A) is incorrect because PRM is not an airborne radar system; it is ground based. Answer (C) is incorrect because PRM monitors simultaneous approaches to two closely spaced parallel runways.

ALL

4670-2. A Precision Runway Monitoring (PRM) approach may require

A—monitoring of two communication frequencies simultaneously.
B—special training and monitoring of two ILS receivers simultaneously.
C—tracking performance parameters within the "decision region" of: 1/3 dot localizer and 1/2 dot glideslope displacement.

Approval for ILS PRM approaches requires the airport to have a precision runway monitoring system and a final monitor controller who can only communicate with aircraft on the final approach course. Additionally, two tower frequencies are required to be used and the controller broadcasts over both frequencies to reduce the chance of instructions being missed. Pilot training is also required for pilots using the PRM system. (PLT292, IR.III.B.K1) — FAA-H-8083-16

Answers

4771 [A]	4670 [A]	4670-1 [B]	4670-2 [A]

Instrument Approach Procedures (IAP) Chart

A pilot adhering to the altitudes, flight paths, and weather minimums depicted on the IAP chart, or vectors and altitudes issued by the radar controller, is assured of terrain and obstruction clearance and runway or airport alignment during approach for landing.

The IAP chart may be divided into four distinct areas: the plan view, showing the route to the airport; the profile view, showing altitude and descent information; the minimums section, showing approach categories, minimum altitudes, and visibility requirements; and the airport diagram, showing runway alignments, runway lights, and approach lighting systems.

1. The **plan view** is that portion of the IAP chart depicted at "A" in Figure 8-2. Above the IAP chart is the procedure identifications which will depict the A/C equipment necessary to execute the approach, the runway alignment, the name of the airport, the city and state of airport location. See Figure 8-2, #1. An ILS approach, for example, requires the aircraft to have an operable localizer, glide slope, and marker beacon receiver. A LOC/DME approach would require the aircraft to be equipped with both a localizer receiver and DME. If the approach is aligned within 30° of the centerline, the runway number listed at the top of the approach chart means straight-in landing minimums are published for that runway. If the approach course is not within 30° of the runway centerline, an alphabetic code will be assigned to tie IAP identification (for example, NDB-A, VOR-C), indicating that only circle-to-land minimums are published. This would not preclude a pilot from landing straight-in, however, if the pilot has the runway in sight in sufficient time to make a normal approach for landing, and has been cleared to land.

   The IAP plan view will list in either upper corner, the approach control, tower, and other communications frequencies a pilot will need. Some listings may include a direction (for example, North 120.2, South 120.8).

   The IAP plan view may contain an MSA diagram. The diagram shows the altitude that would provide obstacle clearance of at least 1,000 feet in the defined sector while within 25 NM of the primary omnidirectional NAVAID; usually a VOR or NDB. See Figure 8-2, #2.

   An IAP may include a procedural track around a DME arc to intercept a radial. An arc-to-radial altitude restriction applies while established on that segment of the IAP.

2. The **profile view** is that portion of the IAP chart depicted at "B" in Figure 8-2. The profile view shows a side view of the procedures. This view includes the minimum altitude and maximum distance for the procedure turn, altitudes over prescribed fixes, distances between fixes, and the missed approach procedure.
3. The **minimums section** is that portion of the IAP chart depicted at "C" in Figure 8-2. The categories listed on instrument approach charts are based on aircraft speed. The speed is 1.3 times V_{SO} at maximum certificated gross landing weight.
4. The **aerodrome data** is that portion of the IAP chart which includes an airport diagram, and depicts runway alignments, runway lights, approach lights, and other important information, such as the touchdown zone elevation (TDZE) and airport elevation. See area "D" in Figure 8-2.

See FAA Legends 20, 21, 24, 25, 26, and 29 for IAP legends, which will be available for you to use during the FAA Knowledge tests.

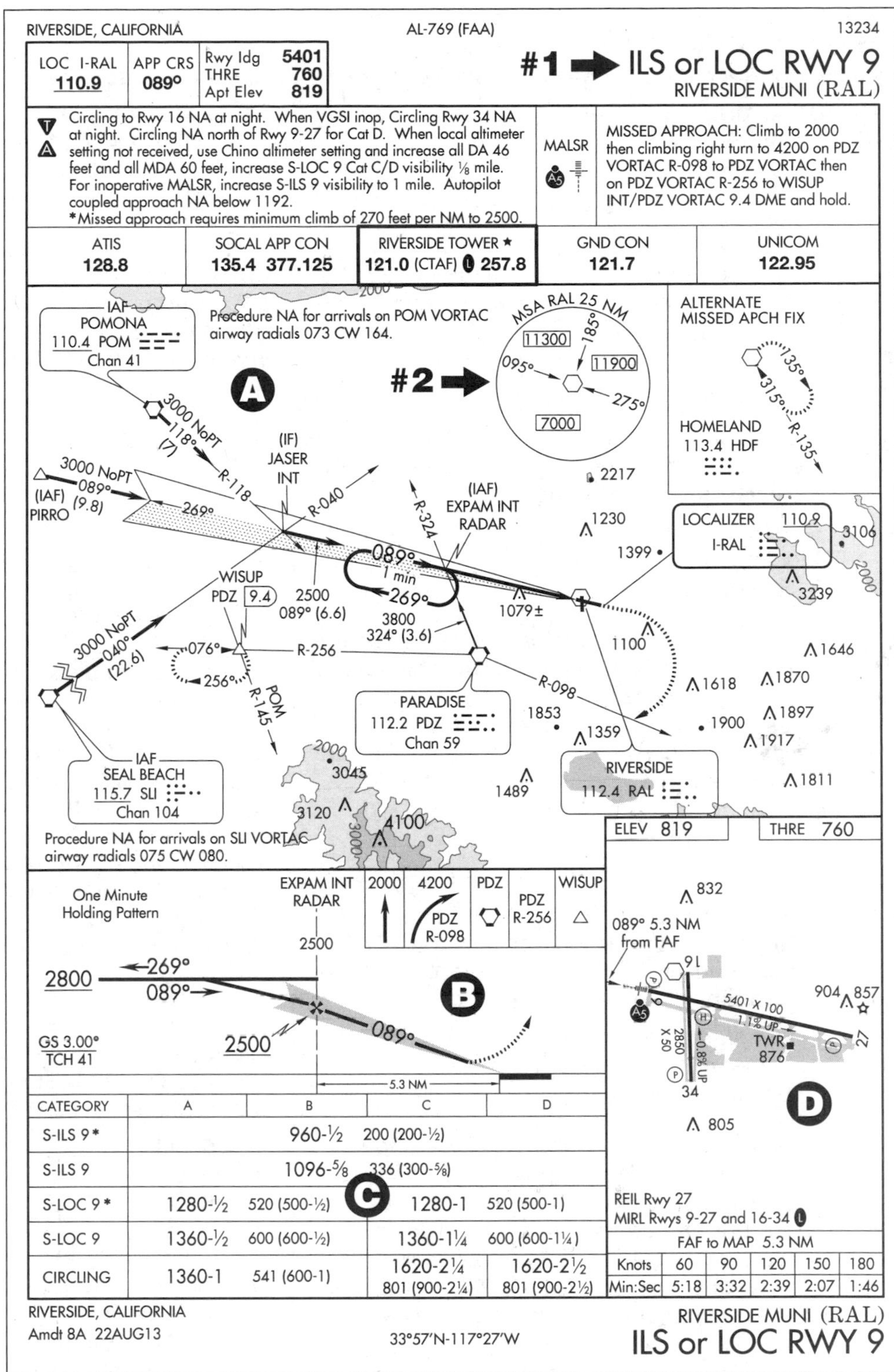

Figure 8-2. Instrument Approach Procedures (IAP) Chart

ALL

4274. (Refer to Figures 161 and 162.) What is the TDZ elevation for RWY 16R at Eugene/Mahlon Sweet Field?

A—363 feet MSL.
B—365 feet MSL.
C—396 feet MSL.

The TDZE of 363 feet for Runway 16R is shown on the airport sketch of FAA Figure 161 in the bottom right corner of the approach plate: TDZE 363. (PLT083, IR.VI.B.K1) — Instrument Approach Procedures

ALL

4276. (Refer to Figure 161 and Legend 27.) Using a ground speed of 90 knots on the ILS final approach course, what rate of descent should be used as a reference to maintain the ILS glide slope?

A—415 feet per minute.
B—478 feet per minute.
C—555 feet per minute.

On FAA Figure 161, find the glide slope angle of descent on the profile view, in this case, 3°. Enter the rate of descent table (FAA Legend 27) at the 3° point in the angle of descent column. Move directly to the right until intercepting the 90-knot ground speed column and read the rate of descent, 478 fpm. (PLT008, IR.VI.B.K1) — Instrument Approach Procedures

ALL

4276-1. (Refer to Figures 160, 162, and Legend 27.) Using a ground speed of 90 knots on the ILS RWY 16L final approach course, what rate of descent should be used as a reference to maintain the ILS glide slope?

A—415 feet per minute.
B—478 feet per minute.
C—555 feet per minute.

On FAA Figure 160, find the glide slope angle-of-descent on the profile view, in this case, 3°. Enter the rate of descent table (FAA Legend 27) at the 3° point in the angle-of-descent column. Move directly to the right until intercepting the 90-knot ground speed column and read the rate of descent, in this case, 478 fpm. (PLT008, IR.VI.B.K1) — Instrument Approach Procedures

ALL

4283. (Refer to Figure 171.) What are the MDA and visibility criteria, respectively, for landing on runway 33?

A—596 feet MSL; 1 NM.
B—1240 feet MSL; 1 SM.
C—600 feet MSL; 1 SM.

FAA Figure 171 indicates the LNAV MDA and visibility criteria for Runway 33 approach to be 1,240 feet and 1 SM with the Addison altimeter. Visibility requirements are always given in statue miles. The first altitude listed is given in MSL (1,240) and the second altitude is given in AGL (596). (PLT202, IR.VI.B.K1) — FAA-H-8083-15

ALL

4296. (Refer to Figure 177.) Which navigational information and services would be available to the pilot when using the localizer frequency?

A—Localizer and glide slope, DME, TACAN with no voice capability.
B—Localizer information only, ATIS and DME are available.
C—Localizer and glide slope, DME, and no voice capability.

"Converging ILS RWY 36L" provides localizer and glide slope (since an ILS approach requires these components). DME is available, as indicated by the channel numbers. "No voice capability" is indicated by the underline on the I-BXN 111.9 frequency. (PLT083, IR.VI.B.K1) — U.S. Terminal Procedures, IAP Chart

Answer (A) is incorrect because TACAN is not available. Answer (B) is incorrect because glide slope information is also available.

ALL

4297. (Refer to Figure 177.) What is the difference in elevation (in feet MSL) between the airport elevation and the threshold elevation?

A—25 feet.
B—30 feet.
C—35 feet.

The airport elevation and threshold elevation are shown on the airport diagram and displayed as "ELEV 607" and "THRE 582." The same information is also shown on the top of the approach chart just left of the approach name. 607 – 582 = 25 feet. (PLT083, IR.VI.B.K1) — U.S. Terminal Procedures, IAP Chart

Answers

4274 [A]	4276 [B]	4276-1 [B]	4283 [B]	4296 [C]	4297 [A]

ALL

4298. (Refer to Legend 27 and Figure 170.) What rate of descent should you plan to use initially to establish the glide path for the ILS or LOC RWY 33 approach at a ground speed of 120 knots?

A—425 feet per minute.
B—530 feet per minute.
C—637 feet per minute.

The bottom-right corner of the profile view indicates a 3° glide slope, "GS 3.00°." Enter the Rate-of-Descent Table (FAA Legend 27) in the left-hand column at the given glide slope angle of descent (3.0°). Move horizontally to the right to the 120-knot ground speed column and read the recommended rate of descent, 637 fpm. (PLT083, IR.VI.B.K1) — U.S. Terminal Procedures, IAP Chart

ALL

4307. (Refer to Figure 188.) What are the MDA and visibility criteria for a straight-in LOC/DME RWY 21 approach at Portland International, assuming an approach ground speed of 100 knots?

A—1,120 feet MSL; visibility 1 SM.
B—700 feet MSL; visibility 1 SM.
C—700 feet MSL; visibility 1 NM.

Look at FAA Figure 188 to find the straight-in minimums for Runway 21 (S-21). An approach speed of 100 knots would classify you as Category B (91 to 120 knots). Category B is 700 feet MSL and 1 SM visibility. (PLT083, IR.VI.B.K1) — Instrument Approach Procedures

ALL

4975. (Refer to Figure 188.) When conducting a missed approach from the LOC/DME RWY 21 approach at PDX, what is the Minimum Safe Altitude (MSA) while maneuvering between the runway and BTG VORTAC?

A—4,000 feet MSL.
B—3,500 feet MSL.
C—6,200 feet MSL.

The MSA is depicted in the top left corner of the plan view in the circle. When maneuvering between the runway and BTG VORTAC, the MSA is 3,500 feet MSL. (PLT083, IR.VI.B.K1) — Instrument Approach Procedures

ALL

4309. (Refer to Figure 188.) You have been cleared to the CREAK intersection via the BTG 054° radial at 7,000 feet. Approaching CREAK, you are cleared for the LOC/DME RWY 21 approach to PDX. Descent to procedure turn altitude should not begin prior to

A—completion of the procedure turn, and established on the localizer.
B—CREAK outbound.
C—intercepting the glide slope.

If you are above the altitude designated for the course reversal, you may begin descent as soon as you cross the IAF, which is CREAK intersection. (PLT083, IR.VI.B.K1) — Instrument Approach Procedures

ALL

4310. (Refer to Figure 188.) With a ground speed of 120 knots, approximately what minimum rate of descent will be required between I-GPO 11.3 DME fix (COVDU) and the I-GPO 14.3 DME fix (YIPYU)?

A—1,200 fpm.
B—600 fpm.
C—900 fpm.

Use the profile view of Figure 188 to calculate the rate of descent:

1. *Use a flight computer to calculate the leg time given a distance of 3 NM and ground speed of 120 knots (00:01:30 or 1 minute, 30 seconds).*
2. *Compute the altitude to be lost (4,400 – 3,500 = 900 feet).*
3. *Compute the rate of descent: 900 feet in 00:01:30 (900/1.5 = 600 fpm).*

(PLT083, IR.VI.B.K1) — Instrument Approach Procedures

ALL

4311. (Refer to Figure 188.) What is the usable runway length for landing on Runway 21 at PDX?

A—6,000 feet.
B—7,000 feet.
C—7,900 feet.

Figure 188 indicates the usable runway length for landing on Runway 21 is 6,000 feet. (PLT083, IR.VI.B.K1) — Instrument Approach Procedures

Answers

4298 [C] 4307 [B] 4975 [B] 4309 [B] 4310 [B] 4311 [A]

ALL

4319. (Refer to Figure 192.) Using an average ground speed of 90 knots, what constant rate of descent from 3,100 feet MSL at the 6 DME fix would enable the aircraft to arrive at 2,400 feet MSL at the FAF?

A—350 feet per minute.
B—700 feet per minute.
C—233 feet per minute.

The distance between the 6 DME and the FAF is 3 NM as shown in the profile view. The aircraft will cover that distance in 2 minutes, at 90 knots. Therefore, the aircraft must lose 700 feet (3,100 – 2,400) in 2 minutes, or 350 feet per minute. Computation:

1. *Apply the following formula:*

   Distance × 60 ÷ ground speed = time

   or:

   3 × 60 ÷ 90 = 2 minutes

2. *Compute the altitude to be lost:*

   3,100 feet – 2,400 feet = 700 feet (altitude to be lost)

3. *Compute the time:*

   700 feet in 2 minutes = 350 feet per minute.

(PLT083, IR.VI.B.K1) — FAA-H-8083-25

ALL

4332. (Refer to Figure 196.) What is the elevation of the TDZE for RWY 4?

A—46
B—44
C—70

TDZE is the highest elevation in the first 3,000 feet of the landing surface. TDZE is indicated on the IAP chart when straight-in landing minimums are authorized. The TDZE is 44 feet MSL, and can be found in the top portion of the airport overview. (PLT080, IR.VI.B.K1) — Instrument Approach Procedures

Answer (A) is incorrect because 46 feet is the airport elevation. Answer (C) is incorrect because it is the height of an obstruction on the approach end of the runway.

ALL

4995. (Refer to Figure 235.) What is the LPV decision altitude for the LNK RNAV (GPS) RWY 32?

A—1,563 feet MSL.
B—1,429 feet MSL.
C—1,760 feet MSL.

Figure 235 shows an LPV DA of 1,429 feet MSL for Runway 32. (PLT083, IR.VI.B.K1) — Instrument Approach Procedures

ALL

4350. (Refer to Figure 195.) How many precision approach procedures are published for William P Hobby (HOU)?

A—3
B—4
C—5

The bottom of the Chart Supplement excerpt lists the available approaches:

ILS/DME Rwy 04
ILS/DME Rwy 12R
LOC/DME Rwy 22
ILS/DME Rwy 30L

Three of these are precision approaches (ILS/DME). The LOC/DME is a nonprecision approach. (PLT080, IR.VI.B.K1) — Chart Supplement U.S.

ALL

4351. (Refer to Figure 210.) What is the minimum altitude at which you should intercept the glide slope on the ILS RWY 6 approach procedure?

A—3,000 feet MSL.
B—1,800 feet MSL.
C—1,080 feet MSL.

The glide slope intercept and final approach fix for a precision approach is identified with a lightning bolt (on the NOS chart) on the profile view of the approach. The minimum altitude to intercept the glide slope on the ILS RWY 6 approach is 1,800 feet MSL. (PLT083, IR.VI.B.K1) — U.S. Terminal Procedures, IAP Legend; FAA-H-8083-15

Answer (A) is incorrect because 3,000 feet MSL is the minimum altitude in the holding pattern at PENNA intersection. Answer (C) is incorrect because 1,080 feet MSL is the minimum altitude at JETIX when conducting the LOC RWY 6 approach.

Answers

4319 [A] 4332 [B] 4995 [B] 4350 [A] 4351 [B]

ALL

4354. (Refer to Figure 210.) Using an average ground speed of 90 knots on the final approach segment, what rate of descent should be used initially to establish the glidepath for the ILS RWY 6 approach procedure?

A—395 feet per minute.
B—480 feet per minute.
C—555 feet per minute.

Enter the Rate-of-Descent Table (FAA Legend 27) in the left-hand column at the given glide slope angle of descent (3.0°, found on the profile view of the approach). Move horizontally to the right to the 90-knot ground speed column and read the recommended rate of descent 478 fpm (approximately 480). (PLT083, IR.VI.B.K1) — U.S. Terminal Procedures, IAP Chart

Answer (A) is incorrect because 395 fpm is the required descent rate for 75 (not 90) knots ground speed. Answer (C) is incorrect because 555 fpm is the required descent rate for 105 (not 90) knots.

ALL

4355. (Refer to Figure 210.) What is the touchdown zone elevation for RWY 6?

A—173 feet MSL.
B—200 feet AGL.
C—270 feet MSL.

The upper right box of the airport sketch shows the TDZE for RWY 6 as 173 feet MSL. TDZE is the highest elevation in the first 3,000 feet of the approach end of the runway starting at the threshold. It also happens to be the same altitude as the airport elevation (ELEV). (PLT083, IR.VI.B.K1) — U.S. Terminal Procedures, IAP Chart Legend

Answer (B) is incorrect because 200 feet AGL is the height above touchdown (HAT). Answer (C) is incorrect because 270 feet MSL is the height of an obstruction near the approach end of RWY 6.

ALL

4357. (Refer to Figure 210.) Which runway and landing environment lighting is available for approach and landing on RWY 6 at Bradley International?

A—HIRL, REIL, and VASI.
B—HIRL and VASI.
C—ALSF2 and HIRL.

Looking at the airport sketch in the IAP, there is an "A" in a circle, with a dot above it, near the approach end of Runway 6. FAA Legend 30 indicates this means ALSF-2 approach lighting. Also, at the bottom of the airport sketch, it indicates Runway 6 has HIRL. (PLT083, IR.VI.B.K1) — U.S. Terminal Procedures, IAP Legend

ALL

4197. (Refer to Figure 213.) What is the THRE for landing on RWY 28R?

A—3,652 feet MSL.
B—3,661 feet MSL.
C—3,488 feet MSL.

The instrument approach plate shows the threshold elevation (THRE) in the airport diagram (bottom, right-hand quadrant): THRE 3488. (PLT083, IR.VI.B.K1) — U.S. Terminal Procedures

Answer (A) is incorrect because 3,652 is the airport elevation which often differs from the THRE elevation. Answer (B) is incorrect because 3,661 feet MSL is the elevation of the control tower on the airfield.

ALL

4369. (Refer to Figure 213.) Which aircraft approach category should be used for a circling approach for a landing on RWY 28R, with an aircraft V_{S0} of 72 knots?

A—C.
B—A.
C—B.

The approach category is based on 1.3 times V_{S0}. For this problem, $1.3 \times 72 = 93.6$ knots, so the aircraft would be Category B (91–120 knots). (PLT083, IR.VI.B.K1) — U.S. Terminal Procedures, IAP Legend

ALL

4470. What does the symbol T within a black triangle in the minimums section of the IAP for a particular airport indicate?

A—Takeoff minimums are 1 mile for aircraft having two engines or less and 1/2 mile for those with more than two engines.
B—Instrument takeoffs are not authorized.
C—Takeoff minimums are not standard and/or departure procedures are published.

A "T" within a black triangle in the minimums section of the instrument approach plate indicates that takeoff minimums are not standard and/or departure procedures are published. (PLT102, IR.VI.B.K1) — FAA-H-8083-15

Answers

4354 [B]	4355 [A]	4357 [C]	4197 [C]	4369 [C]	4470 [C]

ALL

4635. (Refer to Figure 217.) During the approach to DSM before you can begin the ILS RWY 13 procedure, the glide slope fails and you are cleared for the LOC RWY 13 at DSM, what altitude minimum applies?

A—1,420 feet.
B—1,380 feet.
C—1,121 feet.

When the glide slope becomes inoperative on a precision approach, the approach, if continued, becomes a localizer approach. Looking at the minimums section of the chart for S-LOC, 13 indicates an MDA of 1,380 would be applicable for all categories assuming a straight-in landing. (PLT292, IR.VI.B.K1) — Instrument Approach Procedures

Answer (A) is incorrect because 1,420 feet is the circling MDA for categories B and C. Answer (C) is incorrect because 1,121 feet is the DH for the ILS, which is not applicable with the glide slope inoperative.

ALL

4642. (Refer to Figure 221.) The final approach fix for the precision approach is located at

A—DENAY intersection.
B—Glide slope intercept (lightning bolt).
C—ROMEN intersection/locator outer marker.

The FAF is the fix from which the final approach (IFR) to an airport is executed and which identifies the beginning of the final approach segment. On government charts it is designated by the Maltese cross for nonprecision approaches and by the lightning bolt symbol or glide slope intercept for precision approaches. The profile view of FAA Figure 221 depicts the lightning bolt symbol pointing from the glide slope intercept altitude of 2200 to its position on the glidepath. This is close to the ROMEN LOF (nonprecision FAF) but is not coincident with it. (PLT083, IR.VI.B.K1) — Pilot/Controller Glossary

Answer (A) is incorrect because Denay intersection is an initial approach fix (not the final approach fix). Answer (C) is incorrect because ROMEN intersection/locator outer marker is the final approach fix for the nonprecision (not precision) approach.

ALL

4648. (Refer to Figure 227.) Refer to the DEN ILS RWY 35R procedure. The FAF intercept altitude is

A—7,080.
B—8,000.
C—9,000.

The FAF identifies the beginning of the final approach segment. On precision approaches, a lightning bolt symbol indicates the FAF. For APA ILS RWY 35R, the FAF intercept altitude is 8,000 feet. (PLT083, IR.VI.B.K1) — U.S. Terminal Procedures, IAP Legend

Answer (A) is incorrect because 7,080 feet is the LOC altitude at LECET. Answer (C) is incorrect because 9,000 feet is the altitude at FIRPI.

ALL

4648-1. (Refer to Figure 227.) Refer to the DEN ILS RWY 35R procedure. The FAF intercept altitude is

A—7,080 feet MSL.
B—7,977 feet MSL.
C—8,000 feet MSL.

The FAF identifies the beginning of the final approach segment. On precision approaches, a lightning bolt symbol indicates the FAF. For DEN ILS RWY 35R, the FAF intercept altitude is 8,000 feet. (PLT083, IR.VI.B.K1) — IAP Legend

ALL

4649. (Refer to Figure 227.) The ILS RWY 35R procedure at APA depicts a symbol on the plan view that represents a minimum safe altitude sector within 25 NM of

A—the FIRPI intersection.
B—CASSE NDB/LOM.
C—the I-APA Localizer.

The MSA is defined as altitudes depicted on approach charts that provide at least 1,000 feet of obstacle clearance within a 25-mile radius, upon which the procedure is predicated. In this case, it is the LOM CASSE. MSA DEN 25 NM. (PLT083, IR.VI.B.K1) — U.S. Terminal Procedures, IAP Legend

Answers

4635 [B]	4642 [B]	4648 [B]	4648-1 [C]	4649 [B]

ALL

4650. (Refer to Figure 223.) During the ILS RWY 30R procedure at DSM, the minimum altitude for glide slope interception is

A—2,365 feet MSL.
B—2,400 feet MSL.
C—3,000 feet MSL.

Glide slope intercept altitude is defined as the minimum altitude to intercept the glide slope/path on a precision approach. The intersection of the published intercept altitude with the glide slope/path is designated on government charts by the lightning bolt symbol which is 2,400 feet MSL for the ILS RWY 30R procedure at DSM. (PLT083, IR.VI.B.K1) — U.S. Terminal Procedures, IAP Legend

Answer (A) is incorrect because 2,365 feet is the glide slope altitude over FOREM LOM. Answer (C) is incorrect because 3,000 feet is the MSA south of the LOM.

ALL

4654. (Refer to Figure 230.) The symbol on the plan view of the VOR/DME or GPS-A procedure at Baldwin (7D3) represents a minimum safe sector altitude within 25 NM of

A—DEANI intersection.
B—White Cloud VOR/DME.
C—Baldwin Municipal Airport.

The MSA is identified in the bottom right quadrant of the VOR/DME or GPS-A procedure at 7D3. The symbol in the middle of the MSA circle indicates the type of navigation aid the altitude is based. The statement above the circle, "MSA HIC 25 NM," indicates White Cloud VOR/DME (HIC) as the facility identifier for the MSA. (PLT083, IR.VI.B.K1) — Pilot/Controller Glossary

ALL

4655. (Refer to Figure 234.) What options are available concerning the teardrop course reversal for LOC RWY 18 approach to Lincoln?

A—If a course reversal is required, only the teardrop can be executed.
B—The point where the turn is begun and the type and rate of turn are optional.
C—A normal procedure turn may be made if the 10 DME limit is not exceeded.

When a teardrop procedure turn is depicted and a course reversal is required, this type turn must be executed. (PLT083, IR.VI.B.K1) — Instrument Approach Procedures

ALL

4996. (Refer to Figure 243.) What is the minimum altitude to cross CLAMM intersection while conducting the RNAV (GPS) RWY 6 approach at ROA?

A—4,300 MSL.
B—5,200 MSL.
C—2,700 MSL.

CLAMM is the FAF and needs to be crossed at or above 4,300 feet MSL as shown on the profile view of the approach chart. (PLT083, IR.VI.A.K1) — U.S. Terminal Procedures

ALL

4657. (Refer to Figure 234.) If your aircraft was cleared for the ILS RWY 18 at Lincoln Municipal and crossed the Lincoln VOR at 5,000 feet MSL, at what point in the teardrop could a descent to 3,200 feet commence?

A—As soon as intercepting LOC inbound.
B—Immediately.
C—Only at the point authorized by ATC.

Once the pilot is cleared for the approach and established on part of the published route or procedure, the pilot may descend to the published altitude. LNK is the IAF, and upon crossing LNK the pilot may commence the approach. (PLT083, IR.VI.B.K1) — AIM ¶5-4-7

Answer (A) is incorrect because a descent to 3,200 feet may begin once the pilot is LNK VORTAC outbound (not inbound). Answer (C) is incorrect because published altitudes apply when the pilot is on a published route or procedure and has been cleared for the approach.

ALL

4658. (Refer to Figure 234.) If cleared for an S-LOC 18 approach at Lincoln Municipal from over HUSKR, it means the flight should

A—land straight in on Runway 18.
B—comply with straight in landing minimums.
C—begin final approach without making procedure turn.

When cleared for an approach, the pilot has authorization to execute the specific approach cleared for. When cleared for the S-LOC 18 approach from over HUSKR Intersection, the approach specifies an interception of the localizer with no procedure turn allowed (NoPT). (PLT083, IR.VI.B.K1) — AIM ¶5-4-7

Answer (A) is incorrect because the pilot could request to land on a different runway. Answer (B) is incorrect because circling minimums may apply if the pilot requests (or is assigned) a different runway.

Answers

4650 [B]	4654 [B]	4655 [A]	4996 [A]	4657 [B]	4658 [C]

ALL

4659. (Refer to Figure 236.) What landing minimums apply for a 14 CFR Part 91 operator at Dothan, AL using a category C aircraft during a circling LOC 32 approach at 120 knots? (Dual VOR receivers available.)

A—MDA 860 feet MSL and visibility 2 SM.
B—MDA 860 feet MSL and visibility 1 and 1/2 SM.
C—MDA 720 feet MSL and visibility 3/4 SM.

Under the DME minimums for a circling approach for RWY 31, Category C aircraft are required to use the MDA of 860 feet MSL and 1-1/2 statute mile visibility. (PLT083, IR.VI.B.K1) — Instrument Approach Procedures

Answer (A) is incorrect because 2 SM is the visibility requirement for Category D aircraft. Answer (C) is incorrect because 720 feet and 3/4 SM are the requirements for Category D aircraft and straight-in localizer approach.

ALL

4660. (Refer to Figure 236.) If cleared for a straight-in LOC approach from over OALDY, it means the flight should

A—land straight-in on runway 32.
B—comply with straight-in landing minimums.
C—begin final approach without making a procedure turn.

A straight-in approach is one begun without first having executed a procedure turn, not necessarily completed with a straight-in landing or made to straight-in landing minimums. (PLT083, IR.VI.B.K1) — Pilot/Controller Glossary

Answer (A) is incorrect because the pilot may request a different runway. Answer (B) is incorrect because the circling minimums may be used.

ALL

4672. During an instrument precision approach, terrain and obstacle clearance depends on adherence to

A—minimum altitude shown on the IAP.
B—terrain contour information.
C—natural and man-made reference point information.

A pilot adhering to the altitudes, flight paths, and weather minimums depicted on the IAP chart is assured terrain and obstruction clearance and runway or airport alignment during approach for landing. (PLT170, IR.VI.C.K1) — AIM ¶5-4-5

Answer (B) is incorrect because the IAP takes terrain contour information into account. Answer (C) is incorrect because instrument (not visual) information is used as reference points.

ALL

4677. (Refer to Figure 240.) At which point may you initiate a descent to the next lower minimum altitude when cleared for the VOR/DME RWY 36 approach, from the PUC R-009 IAF (DME operative)?

A—Start descent from 8900 when established on the PUC R-009 at 12 DME.
B—Start descent from 8900 when established on the PUC R-009 at 8.3 DME.
C—Descent to 6,240 can be made once reaching the PUC 12.0 DME.

At the VOR/DME RWY 36 IAF you should be at 8,900 feet MSL and begin a descent to the next lower minimum altitude reaching the 8.3 DME no lower than 8,000 feet MSL. (PLT083, IR.VI.A.K1) — Instrument Approach Procedures

Answer (B) is incorrect because a descent can be made to 8,000 feet prior to reaching the 8.3 DME. Answer (C) is incorrect because you cannot make an immediate descent to the MDA of 6,240 until reaching the 5.1 DME.

ALL

4678. (Refer to Figure 240.) What is the purpose of the 10,600 MSA on the Price/Carbon County Airport Approach Chart?

A—It provides safe clearance above the highest obstacle in the defined sector out to 25 NM.
B—It provides and altitude above which navigational course guidance is assured.
C—It is the minimum vectoring altitude for aircraft in that defined sector.

MSAs are published for emergency use on approach procedure charts, utilizing NDB or VOR type facilities. The altitude shown provides at least 1,000 feet of clearance above the highest obstacle in the defined sector to a distance of 25 NM from the facility upon which the procedure is predicated. As many as four sectors may be depicted with different altitudes for each sector displayed in rectangular boxes in the plan view of the chart. (PLT083, IR.VI.A.K1) — Pilot/Controller Glossary

Answer (B) is incorrect because navigational course guidance is not assured at the MSA within these sectors. Answer (C) is incorrect because the MSA provides safe clearance (not vector) altitudes.

Answers

4659 [B]	4660 [C]	4672 [A]	4677 [A]	4678 [A]

ALL

4680. (Refer to Figure 242.) What indication should you get when it is time to turn inbound while in the procedure turn at FEHXE?

A—4 DME miles from FEHXE.
B—10 DME miles from the MAP.
C—12 DME miles from LIT VORTAC.

DME holding patterns and procedure turn entries follow the usual rules except that distances (nautical miles) are used in lieu of time values. The DME will indicate 4 NM (see the holding pattern in the plan view) from FEHXE when it is time to turn inbound. (PLT083, IR.VI.A.K1) — AIM ¶5-3-7

ALL

4682-1. (Refer to Figure 242 and Legend 27.) You have been cleared for the RNAV RWY 36 approach to LIT. At a ground speed of 90 knots, what are the vertical descent angle and rate of descent on final approach?

A—2.8 degrees and 280 feet per nautical mile.
B—3.0 degrees and 478 feet per minute.
C—3.2 degrees and 510 feet per minute.

The VDA found on nonprecision approach charts provides the pilot with information required to establish a stabilized approach descent from the FAF or stepdown fix to the TCH. Pilots can use the published angle and estimated or actual ground speed to find a target rate of descent using the rate of descent table in the back of the TPP. On the profile view of the IAP find the VDA of 3.00° just below KAGBE fix. Using FAA Legend 27 enter the right side of the chart at 3.0, move right to intersect the 90 knot GS column, and read a descent rate of 478 feet per minute. (PLT083, IR.VI.A.K1) — Instrument Approach Procedures

ALL

4682-2. (Refer to Figure 242 and Legend 27.) You have been cleared for the RNAV (GPS) RWY 36 approach to LIT. At a ground speed of 105 knots, what are the vertical descent angle and rate of descent on final approach?

A—2.82 degrees and 524 feet per minute.
B—3.00 degrees and 557 feet per minute.
C—4.00 degrees and 550 feet per nautical mile.

The VDA found on nonprecision approach charts provides the pilot with information required to establish a stabilized approach descent from the FAF, or stepdown fix, to the TCH. Pilots can use the published angle and estimated or actual ground speed to find a target rate of descent using the rate-of-descent table in the back of the U.S. Terminal Procedures Publication. (PLT083, IR.VI.A.K1) — Instrument Approach Procedures

RTC

4686. (Refer to Figure 244.) What are the procedure turn restrictions on the LDA RWY 6 approach at Roanoke Regional?

A—Restrict holding pattern to one minute legs.
B—Remain within 10 NM of EXUNE INT.
C—Remain within 25 NM of the airport.

The upper left corner of the profile view denotes a one-minute holding pattern. (PLT083) — Instrument Approach Procedures

RTC

4687. (Refer to Figure 244.) What are the restrictions regarding circle to land procedures for LDA RWY/GS 6 approach at Roanoke Regional?

A—Circling to runway 24 not authorized.
B—Circling not authorized NW of RWY 6-24.
C—Visibility increased 1/2 mile for circling approach.

See the note under in the remarks section of the instrument approach. Circling not authorized northwest of runway 6/24. (PLT083) — Instrument Approach Procedures

RTC

4688. (Refer to Figure 244.) At what minimum altitude should you cross RAMKE intersection during the S-LDA 6 approach at Roanoke Regional?

A—5300.
B—4300.
C—2720.

The minimum altitude at the FAF fix RAMKE INT 9.7 DME is 4,300 feet MSL. (PLT083) — Instrument Approach Procedures

Answer (A) is incorrect because 5,300 is the minimum altitude at EXUNE INT. Answer (C) is incorrect because 2,720 is the MDA for S-LDA 6.

Answers

4680 [A]	4682-1 [B]	4682-2 [B]	4686 [A]	4687 [B]	4688 [B]

ALL

4690. (Refer to Figure 179.) What is the landing distance available for the ILS or LOC RWY 31 at RBD?

A—7,251.
B—7,000.
C—6,451.

The top right box of the IAP lists the runway landing distance available: 6,451. (PLT083, IR.V.B.K2) — Instrument Approach Procedures

ALL

4692. Which of the following statements is true regarding Parallel ILS approaches?

A—Parallel ILS approach runway centerlines are separated by at least 4,300 feet and standard IFR separation is provided on the adjacent runway.
B—Parallel ILS approaches provide aircraft a minimum of 1-1/2 miles radar separation between successive aircraft on the adjacent localizer course.
C—Landing minimums to the adjacent runway will be higher than the minimums to the primary runway, but will normally be lower than the published circling minimums.

Parallel ILS approaches provide aircraft a minimum of 1-1/2 miles separation between successive aircraft on the adjacent localizer course. (PLT277, IR.V.B.K2) — AIM ¶5-4-14

ALL

4671. During an instrument approach, under what conditions, if any, is the holding pattern course reversal not required?

A—When radar vectors are provided.
B—When cleared for the approach.
C—None, since it is always mandatory.

Holding pattern course reversal is not required with radar vectoring or when "NoPT" is shown on the approach course. (PLT296, IR.V.B.K2) — AIM ¶5-4-9

Answer (B) is incorrect because a course reversal may be required when cleared for the approach. Answer (C) is incorrect because a course reversal is not required when being radar vectored or if NoPT is shown on the approach chart.

ALL

4696. (Refer to Figure 247.) How should a pilot reverse course to get established on the inbound course of the ILS RWY 9, if radar vectoring or the IAFs are not utilized?

A—Execute a standard 45° procedure turn toward Seal Beach VORTAC or Pomona VORTAC.
B—Make an appropriate entry to the depicted pattern at EXPAM INT.
C—Use any type of procedure turn, but remain within 10 NM of Riverside VOR.

A procedure turn need not be established when an approach can be made from a properly aligned holding pattern. In such cases, the holding pattern is established over an IAF or a FAF. The holding pattern maneuver is completed when the aircraft is established on the inbound course after executing the appropriate entry. (PLT170, IR.VI.C.K1) — AIM ¶5-4-9

Answer (A) is incorrect because it is not an appropriate procedure. Answer (C) is incorrect because the pilot must follow the depicted holding pattern.

ALL

4700. (Refer to Figure 131.) If the required visual references are in sight, at what point on the approach may you begin a descent below the MDA?

A—Upon reaching the BOS VOR/DME.
B—When the required visibility has been met and the runway is in sight.
C—Upon reaching the BOS 1.2 DME.

The solid V at the BOS 1.2 DME indicates a VDP. The VDP is a defined point on a straight-in, nonprecision approach from which you can descend below the MDA, as long as you have the required visual reference. Do not descend below MDA before reaching the VDP. (PLT083, IR.V.B.K2) — Instrument Approach Procedures

ALL

4701. (Refer to Figure 247.) What is the minimum altitude descent procedure if cleared for the S-ILS 9 approach from Seal Beach VORTAC?

A—Descend and maintain 3,000 to JASER INT, descend to and maintain 2,500 until crossing EXPAM, descend to MDA of 1,280.
B—Descend and maintain 3,000 to JASER INT, descend to 2,800 when established on the LOC course, intercept and maintain the GS to 960 (DH).
C—Descend and maintain 3,000 to JASER INT, descend to 2,500 while established on the LOC course inbound and intercept the glide slope at 2,500 feet crossing EXPAM.

Answers

4690 [C]	4692 [B]	4671 [A]	4696 [B]	4700 [C]	4701 [C]

Maintain the last altitude assigned until the aircraft is established on a segment of a published route or instrument approach procedure, unless a different altitude is assigned by ATC. Once cleared from Seal Beach VORTAC, descend and maintain 3,000 feet to JASER INT, then descend to 2,500 feet once established on the localizer course inbound, then intercept and maintain the glide slope to the decision height (960 feet). (PLT083, IR.V.B.K2) — Instrument Approach Procedures

ALL

4997. (Refer to Figure 245.) While flying at an assigned altitude of 5,000 feet MSL, you are cleared to CEPUL for the RNAV (GPS)-B at CQX. At what point may you leave 5,000 feet MSL?

A—Upon crossing UMANE inbound for the approach.
B—Upon crossing UMANE for the procedure turn.
C—Upon crossing CEPUL.

Once you have crossed CEPUL and established the approach, you can begin a descent to 2,000 feet MSL. (PLT102, IR.V.B.K2) — AIM ¶5-4-9

Answer (A) is incorrect because you can begin a descent to 2,000 feet MSL prior to reaching UMANE, but you may not descend below 2,000 feet MSL until reaching the FAF. Answer (B) is incorrect because the approach chart notes NoPT (no procedure turn) from the CEPUL.

ALL

4714. Which procedure should be followed by a pilot who is circling to land in a Category B airplane, but is maintaining a speed 5 knots faster than the maximum specified for that category?

A—Use the approach minimums appropriate for Category C.
B—Use Category B minimums.
C—Use Category D minimums since they apply to all circling approaches.

If it is necessary to maneuver at speeds in excess of the upper limit of the speed range for each category, the minimum for the next higher approach category should be used. (PLT420, IR.V.B.K2) — AIM ¶5-4-7

Answer (B) is incorrect because the pilot should use the minimums in the category appropriate to the approach speed being flown. Answer (C) is incorrect because not all circling approaches have a Category D.

ALL

4717. Aircraft approach categories are based on

A—certificated approach speed at maximum gross weight.
B—1.3 times the stall speed in landing configuration at maximum gross landing weight.
C—1.3 times the stall speed at maximum gross weight.

Aircraft approach category means a grouping of aircraft based on a speed of 1.3 VSO and the maximum certificated landing weight are those values as established for the aircraft by the certificating authority of the country of registry. (PLT170, IR.VI.C.K1) — AIM ¶5-4-7

ALL

4717-1. The instrument approach criteria for a Category A aircraft is based on a maximum airspeed of

A—100 knots.
B—90 knots.
C—80 knots.

Aircraft approach category means a grouping of aircraft based on a speed of V_{REF}, if specified, or if V_{REF} is not specified, 1.3 V_{S0} at the maximum certificated weight. The category speeds are defined as follows:

Category A: speed less than 91 knots.

Category B: speed 91 knots or more but less than 121 knots.

Category C: speed 121 knots or more but less than 141 knots.

Category D: speed 141 knots or more but less than 166 knots.

Category E: speed 166 knots or more.

(PLT382, IR.VI.A.K1) — AIM ¶5-4-7

Answers

4997 [C] 4714 [A] 4717 [B] 4717-1 [B]

ALL

4749. When may a pilot make a straight-in landing, if using an IAP having only circling minimums?

A—A straight-in landing may not be made, but the pilot may continue to the runway at MDA and then circle to land on the runway.
B—The pilot may land straight-in if the runway is the active runway and he has been cleared to land.
C—A straight-in landing may be made if the pilot has the runway in sight in sufficient time to make a normal approach for landing, and has been cleared to land.

When either the normal rate of descent or the runway alignment factor of 30° is exceeded, a straight-in minimum is not published and a circling minimum applies. The fact that a straight-in minimum is not published does not preclude the pilot from landing straight-in, if the active runway is in sight and there is sufficient time to make a normal approach for landing. (PLT296, IR.VI.C.K1) — AIM ¶5-4-20

Answer (A) is incorrect because a straight-in landing can be made if there is sufficient time and the runway is in sight. Answer (B) is incorrect because in addition to having the runway in sight, there must also be sufficient time to make a normal approach for landing.

ALL

4763. If during an ILS approach in IFR conditions, the approach lights are not visible upon arrival at the DH, the pilot is

A—required to immediately execute the missed approach procedure.
B—permitted to continue the approach and descend to the localizer MDA.
C—permitted to continue the approach to the approach threshold of the ILS runway.

No pilot may operate an aircraft at any airport below the authorized MDA, or continue an approach below the authorized DH unless at least one of the following visual references for the intended runway is distinctly visible and identifiable to the pilot. If the approach lights are not visible upon arrival at the DH, then the pilot must execute the missed approach procedure. (PLT170, IR.VI.C.K1) — 14 CFR §91.175

Answer (B) is incorrect because the DH is lower than the localizer MDA, and is used as the missed approach point on an ILS approach. Answer (C) is incorrect because the pilot may only continue the approach below the DH if the required visual references are distinctly visible and identifiable.

ALL

4763-1. How can the pilot determine, for an ILS runway equipped with MALSR, that there may be penetration of the obstacle identification surfaces (OIS), and care should be taken in the visual segment to avoid any obstacles?

A—The runway has a visual approach slope indicator (VASI).
B—The published visibility for the ILS is no lower than 3/4 SM.
C—The approach chart has a visual descent point (VDP) published.

The visibility published on an approach chart is dependent on many variables, including the height above touchdown for straight-in approaches, or height above airport elevation for circling approaches. Other factors include the approach light system coverage, and type of approach procedure, such as precision, nonprecision, circling or straight-in. Another factor determining the minimum visibility is the penetration of the 34:1 and 20:1 surfaces. These surfaces are inclined planes that begin 200 feet out from the runway and extend outward to 10,000 feet. If there is a penetration of the 34:1 surface, the published visibility can be no lower than 3/4 SM. If there is penetration of the 20:1 surface, the published visibility can be no lower than 1 SM with a note prohibiting approaches to the affected runway at night (both straight-in and circling). Pilots should be aware of these penetrating obstacles when entering the visual and/or circling segments of an approach and take adequate precautions to avoid them. (PLT321, IR.VI.B.K1) — FAA-H-8083-16

Answers (A) and (C) are incorrect because a VASI or VDP are not indicators to a possible penetration of the OIS.

ALL

4764. Immediately after passing the final approach fix inbound during an ILS approach in IFR conditions, the glide slope warning flag appears. The pilot is

A—permitted to continue the approach and descend to the DH.
B—permitted to continue the approach and descend to the localizer MDA.
C—required to immediately begin the prescribed missed approach procedure.

When the glide slope fails, the ILS reverts to a nonprecision localizer approach. With a glide slope failure, the pilot is permitted to switch to a localizer approach and descend to the localizer MDA. (PLT083, IR.VI.B.K1) — 14 CFR §91.175

Answer (A) is incorrect because without a glide slope, the localizer

Answers

4749 [C] 4763 [A] 4763-1 [B] 4764 [B]

becomes a nonprecision approach which has a MDA (not a DH). Answer (C) is incorrect because the missed approach procedure should only be executed upon reaching the missed approach point.

RTC

4764-1. (Refer to Figure 249.) Why is there a note stating a temperature limitation for executing this approach with BARO-VNAV equipment?

A—The descent gradient exceeds the maximum standard of 400-foot per nautical mile at low temperatures.
B—The decision altitude and final approach segment height above obstacles or terrain is unsafe when temperatures are lower than charted.
C—The missed approach climb gradient exceeds the airplane maximum standard of 40 to 1 at low temperatures.

The note is in the upper left corner of the approach plate. Baro-VNAV is a navigational system that presents computed vertical guidance to the pilot referenced to a specified VPA. If a flight crew is authorized to conduct VNAV approaches using an RNAV system that falls into this category, the Baro-VNAV temperature limitations listed in the notes section of the approach procedure apply. Considering the pronounced effect of cold temperatures on Baro-VNAV operations, a minimum temperature limitation is published for each procedure for which Baro-VNAV minimums are published. This temperature represents the airport temperature below which the use of Baro-VNAV is not authorized to the LNAV/VNAV DA. The note "Baro-VNAV systems, LNAV/VNAV NA below -23°C (-9°F)" implies that the approach may not be flown using Baro-VNAV when the temperature is below -23°C. However, Baro-VNAV may be used for approach guidance down to the published LNAV MDA. (PLT354) — FAA-H-8083-16

ALL

4955. (Refer to Figure 249). At what point is the pilot authorized to descend to 4,700 feet when cleared to the AJCIZ waypoint from the west?

A—30 NM from AJCIZ.
B—15 NM from AJCIZ.
C—15 NM from LBF.

The plan view of the approach plate shows that the pilot can descend below 5,300 feet to 4,700 when at a point 15 NM to AJCIZ. (PLT083, IR.V.B.K1) — Instrument Approach Procedures

ALL

4956. (Refer to Figure 249.) What waypoints are designated as fly-over waypoints?

A—AJCIZ, BEMXI, and WIVGO.
B—RW30.
C—AGHAN.

The RW30 missed approach is depicted with the four-pointed star enclosed in a circle, which indicates these are fly-over waypoints. This type of waypoint is used to denote a missed approach point, a missed approach holding point, or other specific points in space that must be flown over. (PLT083, IR.V.B.K1) — Instrument Approach Procedures

ALL

4956-1. (Refer to Figure 249.) How do you enter the approach if the aircraft is 27 DME from the AJCIZ intersection heading 300°?

A—Begin final approach with a procedure turn.
B—Begin final approach without a procedure turn.
C—Continue to LNAV minimums after completing the procedure turn.

When cleared for the RNAV (GPS) RWY 30 approach from over AJCIZ Intersection, the approach specifies no procedure turn is required when intercepting the localizer within that sector (NoPT). (PLT083, IR.V.B.K1) — Instrument Approach Procedures

ALL

4956-2. Why would the required visibility minimums for LNAV/VNAV be higher than that for LNAV alone?

A—The location of obstacles along the descent path.
B—An LNAV/VNAV procedure always has higher visibility minimums.
C—The location of the MAP in relation to the MDA for LNAV procedure requires lower visibility minimums.

The LNAV/VNAV procedure usually has lower visibility minima than LNAV alone. The reverse is true when obstacle clearance cannot be assured to the missed approach point. In this case, the lower LNAV visibility indicates there are obstacles below the MDA. (PLT354, IR.V.B.K1) — AIM ¶5-4-5

Answer (B) is incorrect because an LNAV/VNAV procedure usually has lower visibility minimum due to the benefit of the stabilized approach descent provided by the vertical navigation. Answer (C) is incorrect the location of the missed approach point does not affect the required visibility minima for the LNAV procedure.

Answers

4764-1 [B]	4955 [B]	4956 [B]	4956-1 [B]	4956-2 [A]

ALL

4956-3. (Refer to Figure 250.) For a stabilized approach, the aircraft must be in an approved configuration for landing

A—with the engines spooled up, before descending below 1,768 feet MSL.
B—with the correct speed and on glide path before descending below 1,268 feet MSL.
C—with a descent rate of less than 1,000 fpm below 1,080 feet MSL and bank angles of less than 15° below 500 feet AGL.

A stabilized approach is required 1,000 feet above TDZE which is listed as 268. Therefore, at 1,268 MSL you need to be established in a stabilized approach.

Answer (A) is incorrect because engines don't need to be spooled up until 1,000 feet above TDZE minimum. Answer (C) is incorrect because it is listing the MDA for this approach.

(PLT170, IR.VI.C.K1) — FAA-H-8083-16

ALL

4956-4. (Refer to Figure 250.) For a stabilized approach, the aircraft would be in a configuration for approach or landing and descending at about

A—480 feet per minute to MDA.
B—480 feet per nautical mile below 1,580 feet MSL.
C—a descent rate of less than 1,000 fpm below 1,080 feet MSL and bank angles of less than 15° below 500 feet AGL.

For turbojets, the airplane must be in an approved configuration for landing or circling, if appropriate, with the engines spooled up, and on the correct speed and flight path with a descent rate of less than 1,000 fpm before descending below the following minimum stabilized approach heights:

- *For all straight-in instrument approaches (this includes contact approaches) in IFR weather conditions, the approach must be stabilized before descending below 1,000 feet above the airport or TDZE.*
- *For visual approaches and straight-in instrument approaches in VFR weather conditions, the approach must be stabilized before descending below 500 feet above the airport elevation.*
- *For the final segment of a circling approach maneuver, the approach must be stabilized 500 feet above the airport elevation or at the MDA, whichever is lower.*

(PLT170, IR.VI.C.K1) — FAA-H-8083-16

RTC

4342. (Refer to Figure 199.) What is the visual glide slope indicator angle for RWY 12 at Houma-Terrebonne?

A—3.0.
B—2.8.
C—2.0.

The VGSI angle is shown on the top portion of the profile view of the approach procedure. "VGSI Angle 3.00/TCH 44": visual glide slope indicator angle 3.00°/ threshold crossing height 44 feet. (PLT147) — Chart Supplement U.S.

RTC

4343. (Refer to Figure 199.) What would be the approach minimums if using New Orleans Intl. altimeter?

A—431 – ¾.
B—440 – ¾.
C—520 – ¾.

In the remarks section of the IAP, it states that when the local altimeter is not available, use the New Orleans International altimeter setting and increase MDA 80 feet: 440 + 80 = 520' MDA, and the visibility remains the same 3/4 SM. (PLT102) — Instrument Approach Procedures

RTC

4673. (Refer to Figure 240.) What is the helicopter landing minimum for the VOR RWY 36 approach at Price/ Carbon County Airport?

A—500-foot ceiling and 1/2 mile visibility.
B—1-mile visibility.
C—one-half mile visibility.

Choppers use Category A MDA or DH with half the published visibility (but equal to or not less than 1,200 RVR or 1/4 mile). The visibility minimums for the VOR RWY 36 approach, Category A are one mile, so the helicopter minimum is one-half mile visibility. (PLT083) — 14 CFR §97.3

Answers

4956-3 [B] 4956-4 [C] 4342 [A] 4343 [C] 4673 [C]

RTC
4676. (Refer to Figure 240.) What is the helicopter MDA for a straight-in VOR RWY 36 approach at Price/Carbon County Airport (VOR only)?

A—6,660 feet MSL.
B—405 feet MSL.
C—6,240 feet MSL.

Choppers use category A MDA or DH with half the published visibility (but equal to or not less than 1,200 RVR or 1/4 mile). The MDA for a straight-in VOR/DME RWY 36 approach, category A, is 6,240 feet MSL. (PLT382) — 14 CFR §97.3

RTC
4679. (Refer to Figure 242.) As you approach FEHXE during a straight-in RNAV RWY 36 approach in a helicopter, Little Rock Approach Control advises that the ceiling is 400 feet and the visibility is 1/4 mile. Do regulations permit you to continue the approach and land?

A—No, you may not reduce the visibility prescribed for Category A airplanes by more than 50 percent.
B—Yes, only a 1/4 mile visibility or an RVR of 1,200 feet is required for any approach, including RNAV.
C—No, neither the ceiling nor the visibility meet regulatory requirements.

Helicopters use Category A MDA or DH with half the published visibility (but equal to or not less than 1,200 RVR or 1/4 mile). The visibility minimum for RNAV RWY 36, Category A, is 1 mile. So for helicopters, the minimum is one-half mile. The visibility is below this, so the helicopter is not permitted to continue to approach and land. (PLT382) — 14 CFR §91.175(d)(2)

RTC
4679-1. Which of the following are required for a helicopter ILS approach with a decision height lower than 200 feet HAT?

A—Special aircrew training and aircraft certification.
B—Both a marker beacon and a radio altimeter.
C—ATP helicopter certificate and CAT II certification.

While there are helicopter ILS precision approaches to CAT I facilities with DAs no lower than a 200-foot HAT, there are helicopter approaches to CAT II facilities with a 100-foot HAT and 1/4 SM visibility. These approaches with a HAT below 200 feet require special aircrew and aircraft certification. The procedure to apply for this certification is available from your local FSDO. (PLT420) — FAA-H-8083-16, Appendix C

RTC
4697. (Refer to Figure 247.) If the Chino altimeter setting is used, what is the MDA and visibility for a helicopter if cleared for the S-LOC 9 approach at Riverside Municipal?

A—1,340 – ¼ mile.
B—1,420 – ½ mile.
C—1,280 – ½ mile.

Helicopters may use airplane approach procedures in the Category A MDA or DH. The required visibility minimum may be reduced to one-half the published visibility minimum for Category A aircraft, but it must not in any case be reduced to less than one-quarter mile or 1,200 feet RVR. The S-LOC 9 MDA is 1,280. The note section requires a 60-foot increase in MDA if the Chino altimeter is used. 1,280 + 60 = 1,340 MDA. The visibility can be reduced from one-half mile to one-quarter mile for helicopters. (PLT083) — U.S. Terminal Procedures, IAP Legend*

RTC
4713. During a precision instrument approach (using Category A minimums) a helicopter may not be operated below DH unless

A—the ceiling is forecast to be at or above landing minimums prescribed for that procedure.
B—positioned such that a normal approach to the runway of intended landing can be made.
C—the visibility is forecast to be at or above the landing minimums prescribed for that procedure.

Where a DH or MDA is applicable, no pilot may operate an aircraft at any airport below the authorized MDA or continue an approach below the authorized DH unless the aircraft is continuously in a position from which a descent to a landing on the intended runway can be made at a normal rate of descent using normal maneuvers. (PLT420) — 14 CFR §91.175

RTC
4722. Upon what maximum airspeed is the instrument approach criteria for a helicopter based?

A—100 knots.
B—90 knots.
C—80 knots.

Helicopters use Category A procedures, which requires a speed less than 91 knots. (PLT382) — 14 CFR §97.3

Answers

4676 [C]	4679 [A]	4679-1 [A]	4697 [A]	4713 [B]	4722 [B]

RTC
4723. All helicopters are considered to be in which approach category for a helicopter IAP?

A—A.
B—A or B, depending upon weight.
C—B.

When helicopters use instrument flight procedures designed for fixed-wing aircraft, approach Category A approach minima shall apply, regardless of helicopter weight. (PLT420) — 14 CFR §97.3

RTC
4724. What reduction, if any, to visibility requirements is authorized when using a fixed-wing IAP for a helicopter instrument approach?

A—All visibility requirements may be reduced by one-half.
B—All visibility requirements may be reduced by one-fourth.
C—The visibility requirements may be reduced by one-half, but in no case lower than 1,200 RVR or 1/4 mile.

The required visibility minimum may be reduced to one-half the published visibility minimum for Category A aircraft, but must not in any case be reduced to less than one-quarter mile or 1,200 feet RVR. (PLT170) — 14 CFR §97.3

Radar Approaches

Precision approach radar (PAR) provides elevation (glide path) guidance in addition to azimuth and range information.

On occasion, a no-gyro radar approach may be provided. The controller will direct the pilot when to start and stop turns. All turns should be executed at standard rate, except on final approach. On final approach, all turns will be half-standard rate.

Radar service is automatically terminated upon completion of the radar approach. Pilots are authorized to use any radar IAP for which civil minimums are published.

ALL
4728. How is ATC radar used for instrument approaches when the facility is approved for approach control service?

A—Precision approaches, weather surveillance, and as a substitute for any inoperative component of a navigation aid used for approaches.
B—ASR approaches, weather surveillance, and course guidance by approach control.
C—Course guidance to the final approach course, ASR and PAR approaches, and the monitoring of nonradar approaches.

Where radar is approved for approach control service, it is used not only for radar approaches (ASR and PAR), but is also used to provide vectors in conjunction with published instrument approach procedures predicated on radio NAVAIDs such as ILS, VOR, and NDB. (PLT172, IR.VI.B.K1) — AIM ¶5-4-3

Answers (A) and (B) are incorrect because approach control radar is not designed for weather surveillance.

ALL
4822. During a "no-gyro" approach and prior to being handed off to the final approach controller, the pilot should make all turns

A—one-half standard rate unless otherwise advised.
B—any rate not exceeding a 30° bank.
C—standard rate unless otherwise advised.

During a no-gyro approach and prior to being handed off to the final approach controller, the pilot should make all turns at standard rate and should execute the turn immediately upon receipt of instructions. (PLT170, IR.VI.C.K1) — AIM ¶5-4-11

Answers

4723 [A] 4724 [C] 4728 [C] 4822 [C]

ALL

4823. After being handed off to the final approach controller during a "no-gyro" surveillance or precision approach, the pilot should make all turns

A—one half standard-rate.
B—based upon the ground speed of the aircraft.
C—standard-rate.

After being handed off to the final approach controller during a no-gyro approach, the pilot should make all turns at one-half standard rate and should execute the turn immediately upon receipt of instructions. (PLT170, IR.VI.C.K1) — AIM ¶5-4-11

Visual and Contact Approaches

Under certain conditions, a pilot on an IFR flight plan may be authorized to deviate from the published IAP and proceed to the destination airport visually, while remaining on an IFR flight plan and in the IFR system.

A **visual approach** may be assigned by ATC or requested by the pilot if:

1. Surface visibility is at least 3 miles and the ceiling is at least 500 feet above the minimum vectoring altitude;
2. The pilot has reported the airport or the preceding aircraft in sight; and
3. The aircraft will remain in VFR conditions.

A **contact approach** must be requested by the pilot, provided:

1. The aircraft remains clear of clouds;
2. The pilot has at least 1 mile flight visibility; and
3. The pilot can reasonably expect to continue to the airport in the specified conditions.

Controllers may honor the pilot's request for a contact approach if reported ground visibility is at least 1 mile, the airport has an IAP, and separation from other aircraft can be maintained.

ALL

4718. What are the main differences between a visual approach and a contact approach?

A—The pilot must request a contact approach; the pilot may be assigned a visual approach and higher weather minimums must exist.
B—The pilot must request a visual approach and report having the field in sight; ATC may assign a contact approach if VFR conditions exist.
C—Any time the pilot reports the field in sight, ATC may clear the pilot for a contact approach; for a visual approach, the pilot must advise that the approach can be made under VFR conditions.

Visual approaches are initiated by ATC to reduce pilot/controller workload and expedite traffic by shortening flight paths to the airport. Contact approaches are initiated by the pilot and are provided if the pilot will remain clear of clouds and have at least 1 mile flight visibility. (PLT292, IR.III.A.K1) — AIM ¶5-4-22, ¶5-4-24

Answer (B) is incorrect because a visual approach may be assigned and a contact approach must be requested. Answer (C) is incorrect because a contact approach must be requested.

ALL

4735. What are the requirements for a contact approach to an airport that has an approved IAP, if the pilot is on an instrument flight plan and clear of clouds?

A—The controller must determine that the pilot can see the airport at the altitude flown and can remain clear of clouds.
B—The pilot must agree to the approach when given by ATC and the controller must have determined that the visibility was at least 1 mile and be reasonably sure the pilot can remain clear of clouds.
C—The pilot must request the approach, have at least 1-mile visibility, and be reasonably sure of remaining clear of clouds.

Pilots operating in accordance with an IFR flight plan, provided they are clear of clouds and have at least 1 mile flight visibility and can reasonably expect to continue to the destination airport in those conditions, may request ATC authorization for a contact approach. Controllers may authorize a contact approach if it is specifically

Answers

4823 [A] 4718 [A] 4735 [C]

requested by the pilot. ATC cannot initiate this approach. (PLT292, IR.III.B.K1) — AIM ¶5-4-24

Answer (A) is incorrect because the pilot (not the controller) must determine whether the flight can continue to the airport. Answer (B) is incorrect because only the pilot can request a contact approach.

ALL

4737. When may you obtain a contact approach?

A—ATC may assign a contact approach if VFR conditions exist or you report the runway in sight and are clear of clouds.
B—ATC may assign a contact approach if you are below the clouds and the visibility is at least 1 mile.
C—ATC will assign a contact approach only upon request if the reported visibility is at least 1 mile.

Pilots operating in accordance with an IFR flight plan, provided they are clear of clouds and have at least 1 mile flight visibility and can reasonably expect to continue to the destination airport in those conditions, may request ATC authorization for a contact approach. (PLT420, IR.III.A.K1) — AIM ¶5-4-24

ALL

4750. A contact approach is an approach procedure that may be used

A—in lieu of conducting a SIAP.
B—if assigned by ATC and will facilitate the approach.
C—in lieu of a visual approach.

A contact approach is an approach wherein an aircraft on an IFR flight plan, having an air traffic control authorization, operating clear of clouds with at least 1 mile flight visibility and a reasonable expectation of continuing to the destination airport on those conditions, may deviate from the SIAP and proceed to the destination airport by visual reference to the surface. This approach will only be authorized when requested by the pilot and the reported ground visibility at the destination airport is at least 1 SM. (PLT292, IR.III.B.K1) — AIM ¶5-4-24

Answer (B) is incorrect because a contact approach can only be authorized when requested by the pilot. Answer (C) is incorrect because a contact approach would not be necessary if a visual approach is already in progress.

ALL

4743. What conditions are necessary before ATC can authorize a visual approach?

A—You must have the preceding aircraft in sight, and be able to remain in VFR weather conditions.
B—You must have the airport in sight or the preceding aircraft in sight, and be able to proceed to, and land in IFR conditions.
C—You must have the airport in sight or a preceding aircraft to be followed, and be able to proceed to the airport in VFR conditions.

When it will be operationally beneficial, ATC may authorize an aircraft to conduct a visual approach to an airport or to follow another aircraft when flight to, and landing at, the airport can be accomplished in VFR weather. The pilot must have the airport or the identified aircraft in sight before the clearance is issued. (PLT172, IR.III.A.K1) — AIM ¶5-4-22

Answer (A) is incorrect because the pilot could have either the preceding aircraft in sight or the airport. Answer (B) is incorrect because the landing must be made in VFR conditions.

ALL

4712. You arrive at your destination airport on an IFR flight plan. Which is a prerequisite condition for the performance of a contact approach?

A—Clear of clouds and at least 1 SM flight visibility.
B—A ground visibility of at least 2 SM.
C—A flight visibility of at least 1/2 NM.

Pilots operating in accordance with an IFR flight plan, provided they are clear of clouds and have at least 1 mile flight visibility and can reasonably expect to continue to the destination airport in those conditions, may request ATC authorization for a contact approach. Controllers may authorize a contact approach provided the contact approach is specifically requested by the pilot. ATC cannot initiate this approach. (PLT434, IR.III.A.K1) — AIM ¶5-4-24

Answer (B) is incorrect because flight visibility is the requirement for a contact approach. Answer (C) is incorrect because a flight visibility of 1 SM is needed.

Answers

4737 [C] 4750 [A] 4743 [C] 4712 [A]

Missed Approach

When executing an early missed approach, fly the IAP as specified to the MAP, at or above the MDA or DH, before executing a turning maneuver.

If visual contact is lost during a circling maneuver, make an initial climbing turn toward the approach runway and continue the turn until established on the missed approach course.

ALL

4667. If an early missed approach is initiated before reaching the MAP, the following procedure should be used unless otherwise cleared by ATC.

A—Proceed to the missed approach point at or above the MDA or DH before executing a turning maneuver.
B—Begin a climbing turn immediately and follow missed approach procedures.
C—Maintain altitude and continue past MAP for 1 minute or 1 mile whichever occurs first.

When an early missed approach is executed, pilots should fly the IAP as specified on the approach plate to the missed approach point at or above the MDA or DH before executing a turning maneuver to ensure terrain/obstacle clearance. (PLT170, IR.VI.C.K1) — AIM ¶5-4-21

Answer (B) is incorrect because the pilot should not execute any turns prior to the missed approach point. Answer (C) is incorrect because the pilot need only proceed to (not past) the MAP.

ALL

4631. If the pilot loses visual reference while circling to land from an instrument approach and ATC radar service is not available, the missed approach action should be to

A—execute a climbing turn to parallel the published final approach course and climb to the initial approach altitude.
B—climb to the published circling minimums then proceed direct to the final approach fix.
C—make a climbing turn toward the landing runway and continue the turn until established on the missed approach course.

If visual reference is lost while circling to land from an instrument approach, the missed approach specified for that particular procedure must be followed (unless an alternate missed approach procedure is specified by ATC). To become established on the prescribed missed approach course, the pilot should make an initial climbing turn toward the landing runway and continue the turn until he/she is established on the missed approach course. (PLT296, IR.VI.C.K1) — AIM ¶5-4-21

Answers (A) and (B) are incorrect because the climbing turn should be toward the landing runway and then execute the published missed approach procedure.

ALL

4998. (Refer to Figure 247 and Legend 27.) ATC assigns the RAL Runway 9 ILS. In the event that a missed approach is necessary, you determine you will climb with 120 knots groundspeed. What would the missed approach rate of climb be?

A—540 feet per minute minimum.
B—200 feet per nautical mile.
C—540 feet per nautical mile.

The notes box on Figure 247 states a minimum rate of climb of 270 feet per NM is required up to 2,500 feet MSL. Using Legend 27, determine the rate of climb to be 540 fpm based on a 270 feet per NM rate of climb and GS of 120 knots. (PLT083, IR.VI.C.K1) — U.S. Terminal Procedures

ALL

4999. (Refer to Figure 253.) While executing the RNAV (GPS) RWY 18 LNAV approach at OSH, how would the missed approach point be identified?

A—RW18 waypoint.
B—1.1 NM from RW18 waypoint.
C—1,040 feet MSL indicated.

On an LNAV, the missed approach point is the last waypoint depicted in the profile view (RW18). (PLT083, IR.VI.C.K1) — U.S. Terminal Procedures

ALL

4282. (Refer to Figure 171.) You are briefing the RNAV (GPS) RWY33 approach at ADS. Where would you plan to execute the missed approach?

A—4.1 DME from PORTR.
B—RW33 waypoint.
C—1,240 feet indicated on altimeter.

The missed approach point is identified by the RW33 waypoint as shown on the profile view followed by the dashed line and arrow. (PLT083, IR.V.B.K1) — U.S. Terminal Procedures

Answers

4667 [A]	4631 [C]	4998 [A]	4999 [A]	4282 [B]

RTC

4684-4. The missed approach for the BARO-VNAV and LNAV is initiated at the

A—decision height.
B—missed approach point.
C—final approach fix.

BARO-VNAV and LNAV approaches are terminated at the missed approach point, which is where the missed approach segment begins. (PLT354) — AIM ¶5-4-5

ALL

4306. (Refer to Figure 188.) What determines the MAP on the LOC/DME RWY 21 approach at Portland International Airport?

A—I-GPO 1.2 DME.
B—5.8 NM from ROBOT FAF.
C—160° radial of BTG VORTAC.

The missed approach point is determined by I-GPO 1.2 DME. (PLT083, IR.VI.B.K1) — Instrument Approach Procedures

ALL

4321. (Refer to Figure 192.) Under which condition should a missed approach procedure be initiated if the runway environment (Paso Robles Municipal Airport) is not in sight?

A—After descending to 1,440 feet MSL.
B—After descent to 1,440 feet or reaching the 1 NM DME, whichever occurs first.
C—When you reach the established missed approach point and determine the visibility is less than 1 mile.

The established missed approach point is the PRB VOR. If, upon reaching it, the runway environment is not in sight and the visibility is less than 1 mile, the missed approach procedure should be commenced. (PLT083, IR.VI.B.K1) — Instrument Approach Procedures

Answers (A) and (B) are incorrect because neither describe the published missed approach point.

ALL

4352. (Refer to Figure 210.) At which indication or occurrence should you initiate the published missed approach procedure for the ILS RWY 6 approach provided the runway environment is not in sight?

A—When reaching 373 feet MSL indicated altitude.
B—When 3 minutes (at 90 knots ground speed) have expired or reaching 373 feet MSL, whichever occurs first.
C—Upon reaching 373 feet AGL.

With respect to the operation of aircraft, decision height (DH) means the height at which a decision must be made during an ILS or PAR instrument approach to either continue the approach or to execute a missed approach. The DH for the ILS RWY 6 approach is 373 feet MSL. (PLT083, IR.VI.B.K1) — U.S. Terminal Procedures, IAP Chart Legend

Answer (B) is incorrect because timing is used for localizer approaches, or as a backup to ILS approaches. Answer (C) is incorrect because the DH is 373 feet MSL (not AGL).

ALL

4682. (Refer to Figure 242.) How should the missed approach point be identified when executing the RNAV RWY 36 approach at Adams Field?

A—When the TO-FROM indicator changes.
B—Upon arrival at 760 feet on the glidepath.
C—When time has expired for 5 NM past the FAF.

The MAP is a waypoint and the TO/FROM indicator will show passage of the "phantom station." (PLT083, IR.VI.A.K1) — Instrument Approach Procedures

Answer (B) is incorrect because the pilot will be at 760 feet on the RWY 36 approach prior to reaching the MAP. Answer (C) is incorrect because on the RNAV, the MAP is designated, so it is to be used (not the time).

RTC

4689. (Refer to Figure 244.) How should the pilot identify the missed approach point for the S-LDA GS 6 approach to Roanoke Regional?

A—Arrival at 2,720 feet MSL.
B—Arrival at JOKNI INT 1.4 DME.
C—Arrival at 1,605 feet MSL.

LDA RWY GS 6 is an approach with vertical guidance (APV); therefore, the missed approach point is the DH which is 1,605 feet. (PLT083) — Instrument Approach Procedures

Answers

4684-4 [B]	4306 [A]	4321 [C]	4352 [A]	4682 [A]	4689 [C]

ALL

4694. (Refer to Figure 131.) During a missed approach from the VOR/DME RWY 33L approach at BOS, what course should be flown to the missed approach holding waypoint?

A—Climbing right turn to heading 030°.
B—030° Radial from BOS.
C—Direct WAXEN INT.

The missed approach procedures are in the upper right corner of the approach plate. The missed approach procedure for VOR/DME RWY 33L states: climb to 3000 via BOS R-030 to WAXEN INT/BOS 14 DME and hold. (PLT083, IR.V.B.K2) — Instrument Approach Procedures

Answer (A) is incorrect because the missed approach does not state fly a magnetic heading of 030°. Answer (C) is incorrect because the missed approach requires you to fly to WAXEN INT via the 030 Radial from BOS.

ALL

4744. If you do not see the required visual references on an ILS approach, you must execute the missed approach procedure no later than

A—decision altitude.
B—middle marker.
C—minimum descent altitude.

An ILS approach is a precision approach procedure, because it has an electronic glide slope. The MAP on a precision approach is always the DH. (PLT277, IR.VI.C.K1) — AIM ¶5-5-5

Answer (B) is incorrect because the MM is not the MAP. Answer (C) is incorrect because the time listed on the approach chart for the missed approach is used for a localizer approach when the glide slope has failed.

Runway Visual Range (RVR)

RVR is an instrumentally derived value that represents the maximum horizontal distance down a specific runway at which a pilot can see and identify standard high intensity runway lights. It is reported in hundreds of feet.

If minimum visibility for an IAP is stated as an RVR value, and RVR is not available, use the comparable values table shown in FAA Legend 11 to get the corresponding value in statute miles.

ALL

4401. What does the RVR value, depicted on certain straight-in IAP Charts, represent?

A—The slant range distance the pilot can see down the runway while crossing the threshold on glide slope.
B—The horizontal distance a pilot should see when looking down the runway from a moving aircraft.
C—The slant visual range a pilot should see down the final approach and during landing.

RVR is the maximum horizontal distance down a specified instrument runway at which a pilot can see and identify standard high-intensity runway lights. It is always determined using a transmissiometer and is reported in hundreds of feet. (PLT292, IR.III.B.K1) — AIM ¶7-1-14

Answers (A) and (C) are incorrect because RVR is the horizontal (not slant range) distance the pilot will be able to see down the runway.

ALL

4716. RVR minimums for landing are prescribed in an IAP, but RVR is inoperative and cannot be reported for the intended runway at the time. Which of the following would be an operational consideration?

A—RVR minimums which are specified in the procedures should be converted and applied as ground visibility.
B—RVR minimums may be disregarded, providing the runway has an operative HIRL system.
C—RVR minimums may be disregarded, providing all other components of the ILS system are operative.

If RVR minimums for takeoff or landing are prescribed in an instrument approach procedure, but RVR is not reported for the runway of intended operation, the RVR minimum shall be converted to ground visibility and shall be the visibility minimum for takeoff or landing on that runway. (PLT382, IR.III.A.K1) — 14 CFR §91.175

Answers (B) and (C) are incorrect because the RVR minimums should not be disregarded, instead they should be converted to ground visibility.

Answers

4694 [B]	4744 [A]	4401 [B]	4716 [A]

ALL

4754. If the RVR is not reported, what meteorological value should you substitute for 2,400 RVR?

A—A ground visibility of 1/2 NM.
B—A slant range visibility of 2,400 feet for the final approach segment of the published approach procedure.
C—A ground visibility of 1/2 SM.

Use the RVR/Meteorological Visibility Comparable Values in FAA Legend 11 to convert RVR (feet) to visibility (statute miles). 2,400 RVR can be substituted for a ground visibility of 1/2 SM. (PLT382, IR.III.A.K1) — 14 CFR §91.175

Answer (A) is incorrect because the RVR value is converted into statute (not nautical) miles. Answer (B) is incorrect because when RVR is not reported, the ground visibility is substituted.

ALL

4759. The RVR minimums for takeoff or landing are published in an IAP, but RVR is inoperative and cannot be reported for the runway at the time. Which of the following would apply?

A—RVR minimums which are specified in the procedure should be converted and applied as ground visibility.
B—RVR minimums may be disregarded, providing the runway has an operative HIRL system.
C—RVR minimums may be disregarded, providing all other components of the ILS system are operative.

If RVR minimums for takeoff or landing are prescribed in an instrument approach procedure, but RVR is not reported for the runway of intended operation, the RVR minimum shall be converted to ground visibility and shall be the visibility minimum for takeoff or landing on that runway. See FAA Legend 11 for the RVR/Meteorological Visibility Comparable Values. (PLT382, IR.III.A.K1) — 14 CFR §91.175

Answers (B) and (C) are incorrect because the RVR minimums must be converted to ground visibility (not disregarded).

ALL

4762. If the RVR equipment is inoperative for an IAP that requires a visibility of 2,400 RVR, how should the pilot expect the visibility requirement to be reported in lieu of the published RVR?

A—As a slant range visibility of 2,400 feet.
B—As an RVR of 2,400 feet.
C—As a ground visibility of 1/2 SM.

If RVR minimums for takeoff or landing are prescribed in an instrument approach procedure, but RVR is not reported for the runway of intended operation, the RVR minimum shall be converted to ground visibility and shall be the visibility minimum for takeoff or landing on that runway. See FAA Legend 11 for the RVR/Meteorological Visibility Comparable Values. (PLT382, IR.III.A.K1) — 14 CFR §91.175

Answers (A) and (B) are incorrect because if the RVR equipment is inoperative, the pilot can expect to receive the visibility requirement reported as ground visibility.

ALL

4999-1. (Refer to Figure 178 and Legend 21.) You have been cleared for the straight-in localizer approach for Runway 13L at DAL. Prior to reaching the final approach fix, ATC advises you the RVR is not available and that the visibility is 1/2 SM. You may

A—convert the RVR to statute miles and continue the approach.
B—convert the RVR to statute miles and use the next higher minimums.
C—request the ILS approach and disregard the RVR value.

If RVR minimums for takeoff or landing are prescribed in an instrument approach procedure but RVR is not reported for the runway of intended operation, the RVR minimum shall be converted to ground visibility and shall be the visibility minimum for takeoff or landing on that runway. (PLT382, IR.VI.E.K1) — 14 CFR §91.175

RTC

4328. (Refer to Figure 161.) To which value may the visibility criteria be reduced, if any, for the S-ILS 16R approach? (Assuming an aircraft type Bell 206 Helicopter.)

A—RVR 20.
B—RVR 16.
C—RVR 12.

Helicopters may also use the Category A MDA or DH. The required visibility minimum may be reduced to one-half the published visibility minimum for Category A aircraft, but in no case may it be reduced to less than one-quarter mile or 1,200 feet RVR. Looking at FAA Figure 161, the RVR is given as 18, so the acceptable visibility may be reduced to RVR 12. (PLT083, IR.III.A.K1) – Instrument Approach Procedures

Answers

4754 [C] 4759 [A] 4762 [C] 4999-1 [A] 4328 [C]

Inoperative Components

When the localizer fails, an ILS approach is not authorized. When the glide slope fails, the ILS reverts to a nonprecision localizer approach. See the inoperative component table in the Terminal Procedures Publication (TPP), for adjustments to minimums due to inoperative airborne or ground system equipment.

RTC
4699. (Refer to Figure 247.) What action should the pilot take if the aircraft is not capable of a minimum climb rate of 270 feet per NM up to 2,500?

A—The pilot is not permitted to fly the approach.
B—The pilot must increase MDA or DA by 10%.
C—The pilot will be required to fly the higher prescribed ILS or LOC minimums.

The asterisk next to the S-ILS 9 and S-LOC* denotes a minimum climb of 270 feet per NM up to 2,500. If the aircraft is not able to meet the minimum climb gradient, the pilot must use the higher set of the two minimums displayed, in this case 1,096 for the ILS and 1,360 for the LOC. (PLT083) — 14 CFR §91.175*

ALL
4731. Which pilot action is appropriate if more than one component of an ILS is unusable?

A—Use the highest minimum required by any single component that is unusable.
B—Request another approach appropriate to the equipment that is useable.
C—Raise the minimums a total of that required by each component that is unusable.

If more than one component is inoperative, each minimum is raised to the highest minimum required by any single component that is inoperative. (PLT382, IR.II.C.K3) — Instrument Approach Procedures

Answer (B) is incorrect because although an approach may have inoperative components, it may still be usable. Answer (C) is incorrect because only the highest minimum is required as a result of any component being inoperative.

ALL
4770. Which substitution is appropriate during an ILS approach?

A—A VOR radial crossing the outer marker site may be substituted for the outer marker.
B—LOC minimums should be substituted for ILS minimums whenever the glide slope becomes inoperative.
C—DME, when located at the localizer antenna site, should be substituted for either the outer or middle marker.

Inoperative ILS components:
Localizer—when the localizer fails, an ILS approach is not authorized.
Glide slope—when the glide slope fails, the ILS reverts to a nonprecision localizer approach, and localizer minimums apply.
(PLT357, IR.II.C.K3) — AIM ¶1-1-9

Answer (A) is incorrect because unless the VOR radial is authorized in the standard approach procedure, the VOR radial may not be used. Answer (C) is incorrect because DME can not be substituted for the middle marker.

ALL
4706. A pilot is making an ILS approach and is past the OM to a runway which has a VASI. What action should the pilot take if an electronic glide slope malfunction occurs and the pilot has the VASI in sight?

A—The pilot should inform ATC of the malfunction and then descend immediately to the localizer DH and make a localizer approach.
B—The pilot may continue the approach and use the VASI glide slope in place of the electronic glide slope.
C—The pilot must request an LOC approach, and may descend below the VASI at the pilot's discretion.

As long as the flight visibility in not less than the visibility prescribed for the approach, the pilot should continue the approach and use the VASI. (PLT406, IR.II.C.K3) — 14 CFR §91.175

Answer (A) is incorrect because once the necessary visual references are in sight, the approach may continue visually. Answer (C) is incorrect because once the necessary visual references are in sight, the approach may continue visually, and the pilot may descend below the VASI glidepath only when it is necessary for a safe landing.

Answers

4699 [C] 4731 [A] 4770 [B] 4706 [B]

RTC
4330. (Refer to Figure 196.) What is the DA and visibility criteria for a helicopter for the ILS RWY 4 approach if the MM is inoperative?

A—244/18.
B—244/12.
C—480/24.

Since helicopters can decrease RVR by 50% but not less than 1,200, and no adjustment is necessary to the DA (no adjustment is necessary for the MM out), the correct choice is 244/12. (PLT083) — Instrument Approach Procedures

Hazards On Approach

Hydroplaning will radically reduce braking effectiveness. It is most likely to occur in conditions of standing water, slush, high speed and smooth runway texture. The best technique to use when landing under such conditions is to apply moderate braking after the wheels have had time to "spin up." Anti-skid should be on.

Wake turbulence is caused by high-pressure air circulating outward, upward, and around a wing tip. These wing-tip vortices are at their greatest strength when the generating aircraft is heavy, clean and slow.

When the vortices of a large aircraft are close to ground level, they tend to move laterally. Thus, if a large aircraft is landing or taking off, a light crosswind or a light quartering tailwind would tend to hold the upwind vortex over the runway. If landing behind a large aircraft, plan to land past its touchdown point. If departing behind a large aircraft, lift off prior to its rotation point. Climb above and upwind of its flight path.

ALL
4408. The operation of an airport rotating beacon during daylight hours may indicate that

A—the In-flight visibility is less than 3 miles and the ceiling is less than 1,500 feet within Class E airspace.
B—the ground visibility is less than 3 miles and/or the ceiling is less than 1,000 feet in Class B, C, or D airspace.
C—an IFR clearance is required to operate within the airport traffic area.

In Class B, C, D, or E airspace, operation of the airport beacon during the hours of daylight often indicates that the ground visibility is less than 3 miles and/or the ceiling is less than 1,000 feet. Pilots should not rely solely on the operation of the airport beacon to indicate if weather conditions are IFR or VFR. (PLT141, IR.VI.E.K2) — AIM ¶2-1-9

ALL
4707. What wind condition prolongs the hazards of wake turbulence on a landing runway for the longest period of time?

A—Direct headwind.
B—Direct tailwind.
C—Light quartering tailwind.

A tailwind condition can move the vortices of the preceding aircraft forward into the touchdown zone. The light quartering tailwind requires maximum caution. Pilots should be alert to large aircraft upwind from their approach and takeoff flight paths. (PLT509, IR.VI.E.K1) — AIM ¶7-4-4

Answer (A) is incorrect because a direct headwind will move the vortices to the sides of the runway. Answer (B) is incorrect because a direct tailwind will move the vortices to the sides of the runway.

ALL
4708. Wake turbulence is near maximum behind a jet transport just after takeoff because

A—the engines are at maximum thrust output at slow airspeed.
B—the gear and flap configuration increases the turbulence to maximum.
C—of the high angle of attack and high gross weight.

The strength of the vortex is governed by the weight, speed, and shape of the wing of the generating aircraft. The greatest vortex strength occurs when the generating aircraft is heavy, clean, and slow. (PLT509, IR.VI.E.K1) — AIM ¶7-4-3

Answer (A) is incorrect because vortices are related to airflow around the wing tips (not engines). Answer (B) is incorrect because when the gear and flap configuration changes, the characteristics of the vortex change, and the basic factor increasing vortex strength is weight.

Answers

4330 [B]	4408 [B]	4707 [C]	4708 [C]

ALL

4709. What effect would a light crosswind of approximately 7 knots have on vortex behavior?

A—The light crosswind would rapidly dissipate vortex strength.
B—The upwind vortex would tend to remain over the runway.
C—The downwind vortex would tend to remain over the runway.

A crosswind will decrease the lateral movement of the upwind vortex and increase the movement of the downwind vortex. Thus, a light wind of 3 to 7 knots could result in the upwind vortex remaining in the touchdown zone for a period of time and hasten the drift of the downwind vortex toward another runway. (PLT509, IR.VI.E.K1) — AIM ¶7-4-4

Answer (A) is incorrect because a strong wind would help dissipate vortex strength quicker than a light wind. Answer (C) is incorrect because the upwind vortex would remain over the runway in a light crosswind.

ALL

4709-1. (Refer to Figure 158.) With winds reported as from 330° at 4 knots, you are given instructions to taxi to runway 4 for departure and to expect takeoff after an airliner departs from Runway 29. What effect would you expect from that airliner's vortices?

A—The winds will push the vortices southeast of your takeoff path.
B—The upwind vortex would tend to remain over the runway.
C—The downwind vortex will rapidly dissipate.

When the vortices of a large aircraft are close to ground level, they tend to move laterally. Thus, if a large aircraft is taking off, a light crosswind would tend to hold the upwind vortex over the runway. If departing behind a large aircraft, lift off prior to its rotation point and climb above and upwind of its flight path. (PLT509, IR.IV.B.R1) — AIM ¶7-4-3

ALL

4710. When landing behind a large jet aircraft, at which point on the runway should you plan to land?

A—If any crosswind, land on the windward side of the runway and prior to the jet's touchdown point.
B—At least 1,000 feet beyond the jet's touchdown point.
C—Beyond the jet's touchdown point.

When landing behind a large aircraft on the same runway, stay at or above the large aircraft's final approach flight path. Note the touchdown point and land beyond it. (PLT509, IR.VI.E.K1) — AIM ¶7-4-6

Answer (A) is incorrect because the pilot should land beyond the jet's touchdown point (not prior). Answer (B) is incorrect because there is no specific minimum distance behind a jet's touchdown point that the pilot should land.

ALL

4738. Under which conditions is hydroplaning most likely to occur?

A—When rudder is used for directional control instead of allowing the nosewheel to contact the surface early in the landing roll on a wet runway.
B—During conditions of standing water, slush, high speed, and smooth runway texture.
C—During a landing on any wet runway when brake application is delayed until a wedge of water begins to build ahead of the tires.

Hydroplaning may occur as a result of aircraft speed and water on the runway. As the speed of the aircraft and the depth of the water increase, the water layer builds up an increasing resistance to displacement, resulting in the formation of a wedge of water beneath the tire. Dynamic hydroplaning occurs when there is standing water on the runway surface. Water about one-tenth of an inch deep acts to lift the tire off the runway. (PLT144, IR.VI.E.K1) — AC 91-6A, page 5

Answer (A) is incorrect because the nosewheel cannot hydroplane if it is not on the ground. Answer (C) is incorrect because brake timing does not affect hydroplaning.

Answers

4709 [B] 4709-1 [B] 4710 [C] 4738 [B]

Closing the Flight Plan

If landing at an airport with an operating control tower, the tower will automatically close the IFR flight plan. When landing at any other airport, it is the pilot's responsibility to close the flight plan with the last controller or the nearest FSS. Flight service stations will provide airport advisories at non-tower airports.

ALL

4076. You may cancel an IFR flight plan

A—at any time as long as you advise ATC.
B—only in an emergency.
C—if in VMC outside Class A airspace.

An IFR flight plan may be canceled at any time the flight is operating in VFR conditions outside Class A airspace by stating "cancel my IFR flight plan" to the controller or air/ground station. (PLT224, IR.I.C.K5) — AIM ¶5-1-14

Answer (A) is incorrect because the pilot must be in VFR conditions and outside Class A airspace before canceling an IFR flight plan. Answer (B) is incorrect because ATC will provide assistance in an emergency while under an IFR flight plan.

Answers

4076 [C]

Cross-Reference A
Question Number and Page Number

This cross-reference lists all of the questions in this book in sequential order. Use this list in co… with Cross-Reference B to find specific questions to aid your studies. For more information about th… questions included in ASA Test Preps, please see pages vi–vii and xvii.

Question Number	Page Number
[illegible]53	1–23
4154	1–3
4155	1–4
4156	1–14
4157	1–13
4158	1–11
4159	1–8
4160	1–16
4161	1–9
4162	1–15
4163	1–14
4164	1–15
4165	1–15
4166	1–15
4167	1–15
4168	1–4
4169	1–15
4170	2–5
4170-1	2–5
4171	1–23
4172	2–11
4173	2–17
4175	2–16
4177	2–5
4178	2–5
4179	2–8
4180	2–5
4181	2–14
4182	2–4
4183	2–14
4184	2–14
4186	2–14
4187	2–15
4188	2–12
4189	2–12
4190	2–12
4191	2–11
4192	2–12
4193	2–12
4194	2–13
4195	2–17
4196	2–4
4198	2–11
4199	2–13
4200	1–6
4201	2–22
4202	2–3
4203	2–4
4204	2–6
4205	2–4
4207	2–22
4208	2–22
4209	2–17
4210	1–17
4211	2–19
4212	2–20
4214	2–19
4215	2–16
4220	2–10
4221	2–20
4222	2–20
4223	2–20
4224	2–20
4225	2–21
4226	2–16
4227	1–3
4228	2–5
4229	2–21
4238	1–30
4240	4–22
4242	2–21
4243	2–21
4244	2–21
4245	2–21
4250	6–33
4251	1–20
4252	1–20
4253	1–20
4254	1–20
4255	1–20
4256	1–21
4257	1–21
4258	1–21
4259	2–8
4260	2–8
4261	7–10
4262	7–11
4263	7–7
4264	7–11
4265	7–20
4265-1	7–20
4267	3–3
4268	2–8
4270	6–20
4270-1	6–20
4271	2–8
4273	2–8
4274	8–14
4275	6–10
4276	8–14
4276-1	8–14
4278	3–3
4280	7–9
4281	2–8
4282	8–31
4283	8–14
4284	5–15
4285	2–8
4286	8–4
4287	7–7
4289	3–4
4290	2–9
4291	7–7
4292	8–4
4293	8–6
4294	8–4
4295	8–6
4296	8–14
4297	8–14
4298	8–15
4299	2–9
4301	3–4
4303	6–20
4304	6–34
4305	6–10
4306	8–32
4307	8–15
4309	8–15
4310	8–15
4311	8–15
4313	3–4
4316	6–21
4316-1	6–21
4317	7–7
4319	8–16
4320	4–5
4321	8–32
4323	3–5
4328	8–34
4329	5–15
4330	8–36
4332	8–16
4336	7–8
4337	4–10
4338	4–14
4339	7–6
4342	8–26
4343	8–26
4345	3–4
4347	4–14
4349	8–4
4350	8–16
4351	8–16
4352	8–32
4353	4–26
4354	8–17
4355	8–17
4357	8–17
4359	3–5
4361	6–21
4362	4–8
4363	6–21
4364	6–21
4364-1	6–22
4365	7–6
4366	7–8
4369	8–17
4370-1	7–8
4370-2	7–8
4372	4–9
4373	6–26
4374	5–41
4375	5–14
4376	4–10
4377	4–9
4378	4–10
4379	5–37
4380	5–37
4381	5–38
4382	4–8
4383	4–8
4384	4–10
4385	4–9
4386	4–9
4387	4–9
4388	4–9
4389	4–9
4390	6–24
4392	6–17
4393	6–18
4394	6–17
4395	6–16
4396	6–16
4397	4–4
4398	6–17
4399	4–4

Question Number	Page Number
4631	8–31
4632	8–10
4633	6–26
4633-1	6–27
4634	5–33
4635	8–18
4636	8–10
4637	6–9
4638	6–23
4639	7–11
4640	8–4
4641	8–8
4642	8–18
4643	6–38
4643-1	6–38
4644	6–19
4645	7–6
4646	7–6
4647	7–6
4648	8–18
4648-1	8–18
4649	8–18
4650	8–19
4653	5–14
4654	8–19
4655	8–19
4657	8–19
4658	8–19
4659	8–20
4660	8–20
4663	4–5
4666	4–13
4667	8–31
4668	7–18
4669	4–5
4670	8–11
4670-1	8–11
4670-2	8–11
4671	8–22
4672	8–20
4673	8–26
4674	4–4
4674-1	4–4
4675	7–18
4675-1	7–19
4676	8–27
4677	8–20
4678	8–20
4679	8–27
4679-1	8–27
4680	8–21
4681	7–18
4682	8–32
4682-1	8–21
4682-2	8–21
4684	4–23
4684-1	4–23
4684-2	4–23
4684-3	4–23
4684-4	8–32
4684-5	4–24
4685	4–28
4686	8–21
4687	8–21
4688	8–21
4689	8–32
4690	8–22
4692	8–22
4694	8–33
4696	8–22
4697	8–27
4698	7–18
4699	8–35
4700	8–22
4701	8–22
4702	4–26
4703	4–26
4704	4–26
4705	4–27
4706	8–35
4707	8–36
4708	8–36
4709	8–37
4709-1	8–37
4710	8–37
4712	8–30
4713	8–27
4714	8–23
4715	8–10
4716	8–33
4717	8–23
4717-1	8–23
4718	8–29
4719	6–9
4720	1–30
4721	3–32
4722	8–27
4723	8–28
4724	8–28
4725	6–27
4726	8–7
4727	1–30
4728	8–28
4731	8–35
4734	8–7
4735	8–29
4736	6–25
4737	8–30
4738	8–37
4739	1–31
4740	8–10
4743	8–30
4744	8–33
4745	3–32
4746	8–10
4747	4–27
4748	3–32
4749	8–24
4750	8–30
4751	8–4
4752	3–33
4754	8–34
4755	1–31
4756	3–33
4757	8–7
4758	6–15
4758-1	6–15
4759	8–34
4760-1	6–8
4760-2	6–8
4760-3	6–8
4761	6–11
4762	8–34
4763	8–24
4763-1	8–24
4764	8–24
4764-1	8–25
4765	5–35
4766	7–18
4767	8–10
4769	6–10
4770	8–35
4771	8–11
4772	3–33
4773	4–27
4774	6–28
4775	6–29
4776	6–29
4778	6–29
4779	6–29
4781	6–30
4782	6–30
4783	6–30
4784	6–30
4785	6–30
4786	6–30
4787	6–31
4790	6–31
4791	6–32
4792	6–32
4793	6–32
4794	6–32
4795	6–31
4796	6–31
4797	6–32
4799	4–29
4799-1	4–29
4799-2	4–29
4800	4–32
4801	4–30
4801-1	4–30
4802	5–30
4803	5–32
4804	5–32
4805	5–30
4806	5–31
4807	5–30
4808	5–31
4808-1	5–31
4809	5–19
4810	5–29
4811	5–29
4812	5–33
4813	5–30
4814	5–30
4815	5–30
4816	5–19
4817	5–33
4818	5–33
4819	5–32
4820	3–13
4821	3–28
4822	8–28
4823	8–29
4824	4–27
4825	4–28

Cross-Reference B

Airman Knowledge Test Report Codes and Question Numbers

When you take the applicable FAA Knowledge Exam required for an airman certificate or rating, you will receive an Airman Knowledge Test Report (AKTR). This test report will list the Learning Statement Codes (LSC) or Airman Certification Codes (ACS) for questions you have answered incorrectly. Match the codes given on your AKTR to the ones listed in this cross-reference. Use Cross-Reference A in this book to find the page number for the question numbers listed below.

Your AKTR will list the codes accordingly:

- If an ACS exists for the certificate or rating you're seeking, the report will list an ACS code. Reference the ACS specific to the certificate or rating to determine the subject you missed on the test: **faa.gov/training_testing/testing/acs/**
- If an ACS does not yet exist for the certificate or rating you're seeking, the report will list an LSC. Reference the Learning Statement Reference Guide to determine the subject you missed on the test: **faa.gov/training_testing/testing/media/LearningStatementReferenceGuide.pdf**

Your instructor is required to provide instruction on each of the areas of deficiency listed on your AKTR and give you an endorsement for this instruction. The AKTR must be presented to the examiner conducting your practical test. During the oral portion of the practical test, the examiner is required to evaluate the noted areas of deficiency.

If you received a code on your AKTR that is not listed in this cross-reference, email ASA at **cfi@asa2fly.com**. We will provide the definition so you can review that subject area.

Learning Statement Codes and Question Numbers

LSC Code	*FAA Reference*	***Subject Description** (or **Topic** 〉 **Content** 〉 **Specific** classification)* ***Question Numbers***
PLT002	FAA-H-8083-25	Instrument Procedures 〉 Enroute 〉 CAS Calculations *4323*
PLT004	AIM FAA-H-8083-25 U.S. Terminal Procedures	Instrument Procedures 〉 Flight Planning 〉 Departure Climb *4270, 4303, 4418, 4555*
PLT008	FAA-H-8083-25	Aircraft Performance 〉 Computations 〉 Landing Distance *4276, 4276-1, 4752*
PLT012	FAA-H-8083-15 FAA-H-8083-25	Aircraft Systems 〉 Pitot/Static 〉 Temperature Instrument Procedures 〉 Enroute 〉 CAS Calculations Instrument Procedures 〉 Flight Planning 〉 Enroute *4265, 4265-1, 4267, 4278, 4289, 4301, 4313, 4345, 4359, 4913*
PLT023	AC 00-6	Weather 〉 Meteorology 〉 Pressure *4090, 4109, 4110*
PLT026	AC 00-45	Weather 〉 Aeronautical Weather Reports 〉 METAR *4202*

LSC Code	*FAA Reference*	*Subject Description (or Topic 〉 Content 〉 Specific classification)* *Question Numbers*
PLT033	AIM FAA-H-8083-15	Instrument Procedures 〉 Enroute 〉 Altitudes *4429, 4432, 4435, 4437, 4542, 4544, 4545, 4547, 4953*
PLT041	AC 00-6 AIM FAA-H-8083-15 FAA-H-8083-25	Aircraft Systems 〉 Flight Instruments 〉 Altimeter Aircraft Systems 〉 Pitot/Static 〉 Altimeter Instrument Procedures 〉 Basic Flight Instruments 〉 Altimeter Instrument Procedures 〉 Enroute 〉 Altimeter Settings *4089, 4093, 4111, 4446, 4477, 4478, 4479, 4854-1, 4922*
PLT044	AIM	Airport Operations 〉 Marking/Signs 〉 Runway Instrument Procedures 〉 Air Traffic Control 〉 ATC Clearance Instrument Procedures 〉 Communications 〉Terminology *4392, 4393, 4398, 4423, 4431, 4442, 4443, 4458, 4605, 4633, 4644, 4771*
PLT049	FAA-H-8083-15	Navigation 〉 Radio 〉 ILS *4557, 4558, 4824, 4825, 4826, 4987*
PLT051	AC 00-45	Weather 〉 Charts/Maps 〉 Convective Outlook Charts *4175, 4215, 4226*
PLT052	U.S. Terminal Procedures	Flight Operations 〉 Emergency Procedures 〉 Lost Communications Instrument Procedures 〉 Departure 〉 Departure Procedures Charts Instrument Procedures 〉 Flight Planning 〉 Departure Climb *4316, 4316-1, 4361, 4363, 4364, 4364-1, 4488, 4489, 4490, 4491, 4492, 4683*
PLT056	FAA-H-8083-15	Interpret information on a Horizontal Situation Indicator (HSI) *4563, 4564, 4565, 4566, 4567, 4568, 4569, 4570, 4571, 4572, 4573, 4574, 4575*
PLT058	Enroute Low Altitude Chart	Instrument Procedures 〉 Enroute 〉 VFR on Top Navigation 〉 Radio 〉 VOR Publications 〉 Aeronautical Charts 〉 IFR En Route *4261, 4370-1, 4370-2, 4496, 4509*
PLT059	AC 00-45	Weather 〉 Aeronautical Weather Reports 〉 METAR *4182, 4196, 4203, 4205*
PLT061	AC 00-45	Weather 〉 Aeronautical Weather Reports 〉 PIREP *4198, 4220*
PLT068	AC 00-45	Weather 〉 Charts/Maps 〉 High-Level Significant Weather Program Weather 〉 Charts/Maps 〉 Low-Level Significant Weather Program *4201, 4207, 4208, 4211, 4221, 4222, 4223, 4224, 4225, 4229, 4242, 4243, 4244, 4245, 4992*
PLT071	AC 00-45	Weather 〉 Charts/Maps 〉 Surface Analysis Charts *4209*
PLT079	Enroute Low Altitude Chart	Instrument Procedures 〉 Enroute 〉 Altitudes *4287, 4317, 4336, 4347, 4370-1, 4370-2, 4493, 4499, 4503, 4513*
PLT080	Chart Suppl. U.S.	Publications 〉 Aeronautical Charts 〉 Terminal Procedures Publications 〉 Chart Supplements U.S. 〉 Radio Aids to Navigation *4292, 4349, 4350, 4640*

LSC Code	*FAA Reference*	*Subject Description (or Topic 〉 Content 〉 Specific classification)* *Question Numbers*
PLT083	AIM IAP Charts FAA-H-8083-15 FAA-H-8083-16	Flight Operations 〉 Approach 〉 Descent Rate Instrument Procedures 〉 Approach Procedures 〉 Course Reversal; Descent; GPS; Holding; Minimums; Timed Approach Navigation 〉 Radio 〉 GPS Publications 〉 Aeronautical Charts 〉 Terminal Procedures Publications 〉 AIM 〉 Navigation Aids *4197, 4274, 4296, 4297, 4298, 4306, 4307, 4309, 4310, 4311, 4319, 4321, 4328, 4330, 4332, 4351, 4352, 4353, 4354, 4355, 4357, 4369, 4642, 4648, 4648-1, 4649, 4650, 4653, 4654, 4655, 4657, 4658, 4659, 4660, 4673, 4675, 4675-1, 4677, 4678, 4680, 4681, 4682, 4682-1, 4682-2, 4684, 4685, 4686, 4687, 4688, 4689, 4690, 4694, 4697, 4698, 4699, 4700, 4701, 4715, 4746, 4764, 4955, 4956, 4956-2, 4975, 4981, 4982, 4995, 4996, 4998, 4999, 4282*
PLT086	FAA-H-8083-15	Instrument Procedures 〉 Attitude Instrument Flying 〉 Fundamental Skills Instrument Procedures 〉 Basic Flight Instruments 〉 Turn-and-Slip Indicator *4931, 4932, 4933, 4934, 4935*
PLT088	FAA-H-8083-15	Aircraft Systems 〉 Pitot/Static 〉 Blockage *4821, 4879*
PLT089	Enroute Low Altitude Chart	Interpret Takeoff Speeds Chart *4645, 4647*
PLT090	AIM Enroute Low Altitude Chart FAA-H-8083-15	Navigation 〉 Radio 〉 VOR *4246, 4263, 4280, 4337, 4338, 4495*
PLT091	FAA-H-8083-15	Navigation 〉 Radio 〉 ADF/NDB; ILS; VOR *4552, 4559, 4560, 4561, 4562, 4573-1, 4577, 4601, 4606, 4607, 4608*
PLT100	AIM	Flight Operations 〉 Emergency Procedures 〉 Lost Communications Publications 〉 Aeronautical Charts 〉 IFR En Route Publications 〉 AIM 〉 Navigation Aids *4077, 4239, 4262, 4264, 4291, 4339, 4365, 4366, 4494, 4495, 4498, 4501, 4506, 4507, 4510, 4512, 4515, 4516, 4517, 4546, 4646*
PLT102	AIM Chart Suppl. U.S.	Instrument Procedures 〉 Terminal Area Operations 〉 STAR Publications 〉 Aeronautical Charts 〉 Terminal Procedures *4249, 4286, 4293, 4294, 4295, 4343, 4470, 4997*
PLT104	FAA-H-8083-2	Human Factors 〉 ADM 〉 Judgement *4976, 4977, 4977-1, 4978, 4978-1*
PLT105	AC 00-6	Aircraft Systems 〉 Avionics 〉 Radar *4092, 4990*
PLT118	FAA-H-8083-15	Aircraft Systems 〉 Flight Instruments 〉 Attitude Indicator; Heading Indicator; Terminal Procedures; Turn Indicator Instrument Procedures 〉 Basic Flight Instruments 〉 Attitude Indicator *4604, 4831, 4835, 4857, 4902, 4919*
PLT120	AC 00-6	Weather 〉 Meteorology 〉 Turbulence *4146*
PLT125	AIM FAA-H-8083-15 FAA-H-8083-16	Instrument Procedures 〉 Air Traffic Control 〉 Collision Avoidance Instrument Procedures 〉 Approach Procedures 〉 GPS Instrument Procedures 〉 Attitude Instrument Flying 〉 Descent *4924, 4925*

LSC Code	*FAA Reference*	*Subject Description (or Topic 〉 Content 〉 Specific classification)* *Question Numbers*
PLT128	AC 91-51	Aerodynamics 〉 Flight Characteristics 〉 Icing Flight Operations 〉 Approach 〉 Icing Conditions Flight Operations 〉 Climb 〉 Autopilot Operation Weather 〉 Hazardous 〉 Icing *4171, 4960-3, 4690-4, 4984*
PLT132	FAA-H-8083-15	Recall aircraft performance—instrument markings/airspeed/definitions/indications *4918*
PLT133	AIM	Instrument Procedures 〉 Enroute 〉 Climb *4270-1, 4380*
PLT140	FAA-H-8083-16	Recall airport operations—LAHSO *4403-1*
PLT141	AIM	Airport Operations 〉 Lighting 〉 Rotating Beacon Airport Operations 〉 Marking/Signs 〉 Displaced Threshold; Runway; Taxiway *4250, 4304, 4408, 4534, 4535, 4536, 4537, 4537-1, 4758, 4758-1, 4791, 4792, 4793, 4794, 4797, 4943, 4944, 4945, 4946, 4951, 4952, 4954, 4954-1, 4963, 4963-1*
PLT144	FAA-H-8083-3	Airport Operations 〉 Runway Conditions 〉 Hydroplaning *4738*
PLT145	AIM	Airport Operations 〉 Lighting 〉 REIL *4795, 4796*
PLT146	AIM	Recall airport operations—traffic pattern procedures *4609, 4610, 4611, 4612, 4613, 4614, 4615, 4616, 4617, 4618, 4619, 4620, 4624*
PLT147	AIM	Airport Operations 〉 Lighting 〉 VASI *4342, 4774, 4775, 4776, 4778, 4779, 4781, 4782, 4783, 4784, 4785, 4786, 4787, 4790, 4994*
PLT161	14 CFR 91 AIM	Airspace 〉 Controlled 〉 Class A; Class B; Class C; Class D; Class E Airspace 〉 Special Use 〉 MOA Airspace 〉 Uncontrolled 〉 Class G Instrument Procedures 〉 Enroute 〉 VFR on Top Regulations 〉 14 CFR Part 91 〉 Clearance/Flight Plan; Instrument Rating; Transponder *4024, 4037, 4038, 4068, 4375, 4409, 4426, 4427, 4427-1, 4434, 4439, 4440, 4474, 4475, 4476, 4526, 4527, 4528, 4529, 4530, 4531, 4532, 4533, 4539, 4643-1*
PLT162	AIM	Airspace 〉 Controlled 〉 Class E *4438, 4469, 4473*
PLT163	14 CFR 91	Airspace 〉 Controlled 〉 Class E Airspace 〉 Uncontrolled 〉 Class G Instrument Procedures 〉 Enroute 〉 VFR on Top *4518, 4519, 4520, 4521, 4522, 4523, 4524, 4525*
PLT165	AC 00-6	Weather 〉 Meteorology 〉 Temperature *4091*
PLT166	AIM FAA-H-8083-15 FAA-H-8083-25	Aircraft Systems 〉 Flight Instruments 〉 Altimeter Instrument Procedures 〉 Attitude Instrument Flying 〉 Airspeed Changes Instrument Procedures 〉 Enroute 〉 Altimeter Settings *4444, 4445, 4480, 4481, 4482, 4910, 4911, 4912, 4923*

LSC Code	*FAA Reference*	*Subject Description (or Topic 〉 Content 〉 Specific classification)* *Question Numbers*
PLT168	FAA-H-8083-3	Aerodynamics 〉 Principles of Flight 〉 Vertical Component of Lift *4915*
PLT170	14 CFR 91 AIM FAA-H-8083-15 FAA-H-8083-16	Flight Operations 〉 Approach 〉 Descent Rate; Drift Correction Instrument Procedures 〉 Approach Procedures 〉 Approach Category; Course Reversal; Descent; ILS; ILS/DME; Minimums; Missed Approach; Radar Approach *4632, 4641, 4667, 4672, 4696, 4717, 4724, 4725, 4736, 4763, 4767, 4773, 4822, 4823, 4956-3, 4956-4*
PLT171	AIM	Instrument Procedures 〉 Air Traffic Control 〉 Reporting *4395, 4407, 4456*
PLT172	AIM	Instrument Procedures 〉 Air Traffic Control 〉 Weather Avoidance Assistance Instrument Procedures 〉 Approach Procedures 〉 Radar Approach; Timed Approach; Visual/Contact Instrument Procedures 〉 Enroute 〉 Climb *4468, 4728, 4743, 4751*
PLT173	AC 00-6	Weather 〉 Meteorology 〉 Air Masses Weather 〉 Meteorology 〉 Stability *4117, 4119, 4120, 4121, 4124*
PLT175	FAA-H-8083-15	Instrument Procedures 〉 Attitude Instrument Flying 〉 Pitch *4852*
PLT185	FAA-H-8083-15	Instrument Procedures 〉 Attitude Instrument Flying 〉 Airspeed Changes; Bank; Fundamental Skills; Power *4833-1, 4833-2, 4840, 4841, 4859, 4862, 4878-1, 4878-3, 4884, 4895, 4896, 4897, 4903, 4904, 4905, 4906, 4907, 4926, 4928, 4929*
PLT186	FAA-H-8083-15	Aerodynamics 〉 Principles of Flight 〉 Pitch Attitude Instrument Procedures 〉 Attitude Instrument Flying 〉 Bank; Pitch *4855, 4869, 4876, 4899*
PLT187	FAA-H-8083-15	Instrument Procedures 〉 Attitude Instrument Flying 〉 Bank Instrument Procedures 〉 Basic Flight Instruments 〉 Turn Coordinator; Turn-and-Slip Indicator *4839, 4847, 4856, 4882, 4883, 4921*
PLT192	AC 00-6	Weather 〉 Meteorology 〉 Clouds; Icing *4129, 4131, 4133, 4134, 4149, 4157*
PLT194	AIM	Human Factors 〉 Aero-medical 〉 Visual Scanning *4634, 4818*
PLT196	AIM	Weather 〉 Aeronautical Weather Reports 〉 ATIS *4403, 4404*
PLT201	AIM	Recall departure procedures—ODP/SID *4417, 4419*
PLT202	AIM FAA-H-8083-15	Navigation 〉 Radio 〉 DME; DME ARC *4050, 4283, 4320, 4397, 4399, 4413, 4448, 4459, 4472, 4663, 4674, 4674-1*
PLT203	AC 00-6	Weather 〉 Meteorology 〉 Upper Air Data *4097, 4154, 4227*

LSC Code	*FAA Reference*	***Subject Description*** *(or **Topic** 〉 **Content** 〉 **Specific** classification)* ***Question Numbers***
PLT208	AIM	Flight Operations 〉 Emergency Procedures 〉 Declare an Emergency; Lost Communications *4381*
PLT215	FAA-H-8083-15 FAA-H-8083-25	Aircraft Systems 〉 Flight Instruments 〉 Compass Instrument Procedures 〉 Basic Flight Instruments 〉 Magnetic Compass *4834, 4877, 4886, 4887, 4888, 4889, 4890, 4891, 4892, 4893, 4894*
PLT220	AIM	Instrument Procedures 〉 Enroute 〉 Altitudes *4485*
PLT221	AIM	Recall flight operations—takeoff/landing maneuvers *4740*
PLT222	AIM	Recall flight operations—takeoff procedures *4400-1, 4420, 4538, 4633-1*
PLT224	AIM Chart Suppl. U.S.	Instrument Procedures 〉 Air Traffic Control 〉 ATC Clearance Instrument Procedures 〉 Departure 〉 Departure Procedures Charts Instrument Procedures 〉 Flight Planning 〉 Flight Plan *4061, 4070, 4076*
PLT226	AC 00-6	Weather 〉 Meteorology 〉 Fog *4156, 4162, 4163, 4164, 4165, 4166, 4167, 4169*
PLT235	FAA-H-8083-15	Recall forces acting on aircraft—aerodynamics *4861*
PLT237	FAA-H-8083-3	Aerodynamics 〉 Principles of Flight 〉 Horizontal Lift *4843*
PLT242	FAA-H-8083-21	Recall forces acting on aircraft—lift/drag/thrust/weight/stall/limitations *4868*
PLT248	FAA-H-8083-3	Aerodynamics 〉 Principles of Flight 〉 Horizontal Lift *4844, 4870-1, 4870-2*
PLT263	AC 00-6 FAA-H-8083-25	Weather 〉 Meteorology 〉 Turbulence *4130, 4132, 4160, 4916*
PLT274	AC 00-6 AC 91-51	Aerodynamics 〉 Flight Characteristics 〉 Icing Weather 〉 Hazardous 〉 Icing *4152*
PLT275	FAA-H-8083-15	Navigation 〉 Radio 〉 ILS; VOR *4576*
PLT276	FAA-H-8083-15	Navigation 〉 Radio 〉 VOR *4548*
PLT277	AIM	Flight Operations 〉 Approach 〉 Descent Rate Instrument Procedures 〉 Approach Procedures 〉 ILS Navigation 〉 Radio 〉 ILS *4692, 4744, 4745, 4747, 4748, 4757, 4772*
PLT278	FAA-H-8083-15	Instrument Procedures 〉 Attitude Instrument Flying 〉 Airspeed Changes; Bank; Climb; Pitch *4820, 4846, 4860, 4900, 4901, 4920, 4979*

LSC Code	***FAA Reference***	***Subject Description*** *(or* ***Topic*** 〉 ***Content*** 〉 ***Specific*** *classification)* ***Question Numbers***
PLT280	FAA-H-8083-15	Human Factors 〉 Aero-medical 〉 Illusions in Flight *4802, 4803, 4804, 4806, 4807, 4808, 4819*
PLT281	Chart Suppl. U.S.	Publications 〉 Chart Supplements U.S. 〉 Weather Data Sources *4248, 4275, 4302, 4305, 4388*
PLT283	AC 00-45	Weather 〉 Charts/Maps 〉 Constant Pressure Analysis Charts *4173, 4195*
PLT284	AC 00-45	Weather 〉 Aeronautical Weather Forecasts 〉 Winds/Temperatures Aloft Forecast (FD) *4172, 4188, 4189, 4190, 4191, 4192, 4193, 4194, 4199*
PLT286	AC 00-45	Recall information on a Significant Weather Prognostic Chart *4212, 4214*
PLT288	AC 00-45	Weather 〉 Aeronautical Weather Forecasts 〉 TAF *4170, 4170-1, 4177, 4178, 4180, 4204, 4228*
PLT290	AC 00-45 AIM	Weather 〉 Aeronautical Weather Reports 〉 AIRMETs; Icing; SIGMETs *4179, 4181, 4183, 4184, 4187, 4259, 4260, 4268, 4271, 4273, 4281, 4285, 4290, 4299, 4467, 4980*
PLT292	AIM	Instrument Procedures 〉 Approach Procedures 〉 Timed Approach; Visual/Contact Publications 〉 Aeronautical Charts 〉 Terminal Procedures *4401, 4540, 4635, 4636, 4669, 4670-1, 4670-2, 4718, 4735, 4750, 4986*
PLT293	AIM	Instrument Procedures 〉 Departure 〉 Departure Procedure Charts *4638*
PLT294	AC 00-45	Recall information on Inflight Aviation Weather Advisories *4468-1*
PLT296	AIM IAP Charts	Flight Operations 〉 Landing 〉 Circling Instrument Procedures 〉 Approach Procedures 〉 Holding; Minimums; Missed Approach Instrument Procedures 〉 Enroute 〉 Holding *4626, 4631, 4668, 4671, 4749, 4766*
PLT297	FAA-H-8083-15	Instrument Procedures 〉 Attitude Instrument Flying 〉 Instrument Malfunction; Unusual Attitude Recovery *4867, 4873-1, 4873-2, 4875-1, 4875-2, 4927, 4936, 4937, 4938, 4939, 4940, 4941, 4942*
PLT298	AIM	Airspace 〉 Controlled 〉 Class A Instrument Procedures 〉 Air Traffic Control 〉 Reporting Instrument Procedures 〉 Enroute 〉 VFR on Top *4430, 4433, 4447, 4449, 4450, 4451, 4452, 4453, 4454, 4455, 4457, 4643*
PLT300	14 CFR 91 AIM FAA-H-8083-15	Navigation 〉 Radio 〉 DME; VOR; VOR Check Regulations 〉 14 CFR Part 91 〉 VOR Check *4054, 4377, 4384, 4389, 4412*
PLT301	AC 00-6	Weather 〉 Meteorology 〉 Temperature *4094, 4112, 4114, 4125, 4200*
PLT302	AC 00-6	Weather 〉 Meteorology 〉 Jet Stream *4155, 4168*

LSC Code	*FAA Reference*	*Subject Description (or Topic 〉 Content 〉 Specific classification)* *Question Numbers*
PLT311	FAA-H-8083-15	Recall load factor—effect of airspeed *4898, 4914*
PLT316	AC 00-45	Weather 〉 Aeronautical Weather Forecasts 〉 Severe Weather Watch Bulletin (WW) *4186, 4991*
PLT317	AIM	Weather 〉 Hazardous 〉 Microburst; Windshear *4251, 4252, 4253, 4254, 4255, 4256, 4257, 4258*
PLT318	AIM	Instrument Procedures 〉 Air Traffic Control 〉 Reporting *4379*
PLT321	AIM	Instrument Procedures 〉 Approach Procedures 〉 ILS; Parallel Approaches *4763-1*
PLT322	AIM FAA-H-8083-15	Navigation 〉 Radio 〉 VOR *4055, 4078, 4400, 4549, 4550, 4639*
PLT323	AIM	Air Traffic Control Procedures 〉 Arrival 〉 NOTAMs Instrument Procedures 〉 Flight Planning 〉 NOTAMs *4080, 4406*
PLT330	AIM	Human Factors 〉 Aero-medical 〉 Physiological *4808-1, 4809*
PLT332	AIM	Human Factors 〉 Aero-medical 〉 Physiological *4816*
PLT333	FAA-H-8083-3	Human Factors 〉 Aero-medical 〉 Night Vision *4812, 4817, 4993*
PLT334	FAA-H-8083-15	Human Factors 〉 Aero-medical 〉 Spatial Disorientation *4805, 4810, 4811, 4813, 4814, 4815*
PLT337	FAA-H-8083-25	Aircraft Systems 〉 Pitot/Static 〉 Alternate Static Source *4402, 4830, 4854, 4880, 4908, 4909, 4930*
PLT344	AC 00-6	Weather 〉 Meteorology 〉 Precipitation *4099, 4151-1, 4153, 4159, 4161*
PLT354	AIM FAA-H-8083-15 FAA-H-8083-16	Instrument Procedures 〉 Approach Procedures 〉 GPS Navigation 〉 Radio 〉 GPS Publications 〉 AIM 〉 Navigation Aids *4069, 4284, 4684-1, 4684-2, 4684-3, 4684-4, 4684-5, 4764-1, 4799, 4799-1, 4799-2, 4800, 4801, 4801-1, 4947, 4947-1, 4947-2, 4948, 4949, 4949-1, 4949-2, 4949-3, 4949-4*
PLT357	AIM	Navigation 〉 Radio 〉 SDF/LDA *4703, 4770*
PLT361	AIM	Publications 〉 AIM 〉 Navigation Aids *4702, 4704, 4705*
PLT363	AIM	Navigation 〉 Radio 〉 VOR Check *4372, 4376, 4382, 4386, 4387*
PLT366	49 CFR 830	Regulations 〉 49 CFR Part 830 〉 Accident/Incident Reporting *4088*

LSC Code	***FAA Reference***	***Subject Description** (or **Topic** 〉 **Content** 〉 **Specific** classification)* ***Question Numbers***
PLT370	14 CFR 91 AIM	Instrument Procedures 〉 Air Traffic Conrol 〉 ATC Clearance; Collision Avoidance Regulations 〉 14 CFR Part 91 〉 Clearance/Flight Plan *4066, 4394, 4396, 4414, 4421, 4422, 4424, 4486, 4726*
PLT379	14 CFR 91	Regulations 〉 14 CFR Part 91 〉 Alternate Airport *4081, 4082-1, 4082-2, 4083-1, 4083-2, 4083-3, 4084-1, 4084-2, 4085-1, 4085-2, 4086, 4087-1, 4087-2, 4630, 4637, 4719, 4760-1, 4769*
PLT382	14 CFR 91	Instrument Procedures 〉 Approach Procedures 〉 Minimums *4676, 4679, 4716, 4722, 4731, 4754, 4759, 4760-2, 4760-3, 4762, 4717-1*
PLT391	AIM	Flight Operations 〉 Emergency Procedures 〉 Lost Communications Instrument Procedures 〉 Communications 〉 Reports *4374, 4460, 4462, 4463, 4464, 4465, 4466, 4500, 4505*
PLT403	AIM	Flight Operations 〉 Emergency Procedures 〉 Clearance Deviation *4461*
PLT405	14 CFR 91	Regulations 〉 14 CFR Part 91 〉 Instrument/Equipment Requirements *4007, 4043, 4051, 4057, 4988*
PLT406	14 CFR 91	Instrument Procedures 〉 Approach Procedures 〉 VASI Regulations 〉 14 CFR Part 91 〉 Instrument/Equipment Requirements *4706*
PLT409	14 CFR 61	Regulations 〉 14 CFR Part 61 〉 Logging Instrument Flight Time *4010*
PLT411	14 CFR 61	Regulations 〉 14 CFR Part 61 〉 Currency; Limitations *4018, 4030-1*
PLT413	14 CFR 91	Regulations 〉 14 CFR 91 〉 Fuel Requirements *4005, 4005-2, 4032, 4032-1, 4040, 4041*
PLT414	14 CFR 91	Recall regulations—general right-of-way rules *4441*
PLT415	14 CFR 91 FAA-H-8083-15	Instrument Procedures 〉 Attitude Instrument Flying 〉 Power Regulations 〉 14 CFR Part 91 〉 Portable Electronic Devices *4004, 4756*
PLT420	AIM	Instrument Procedures 〉 Approach Procedures 〉 Parallel Approaches *4670, 4679-1, 4713, 4714, 4723, 4734, 4737*
PLT429	14 CFR 91	Regulations 〉 14 CFR Part 91 〉 Instrument/Equipment Requirements *4329*
PLT430	14 CFR 91	Regulations 〉 14 CFR Part 91 〉 IFR Minimum Altitudes *4006, 4425, 4428, 4436, 4541, 4543, 4765*
PLT434	AIM	Air Traffic Control Procedures 〉 Communications 〉 Airport Advisory Service *4712*
PLT438	14 CFR 91	Regulations 〉 14 CFR Part 91 〉 Supplemental Oxygen *4042, 4045, 4052, 4053*
PLT440	FAA-H-8083-16	Recall regulations—pilot crew duties and responsibilities *4071, 4605-1, 4605-2*

LSC Code	*FAA Reference*	*Subject Description (or Topic ⟩ Content ⟩ Specific classification)* *Question Numbers*
PLT442	14 CFR 61	Regulations ⟩ 14 CFR Part 61 ⟩ Currency; Logging Instrument Flight Time *4001, 4001-1, 4008, 4009, 4012, 4013, 4014, 4015, 4015-1, 4016, 4017, 4019, 4020, 4021, 4022, 4023, 4027*
PLT443	14 CFR 61	Regulations ⟩ 14 CFR Part 61 ⟩ Limitations *4011, 4028*
PLT444	14 CFR 91 AIM	Instrument Procedures ⟩ Air Traffic Control ⟩ ATC Clearance; Collision Avoidance Regulations ⟩ 14 CFR Part 91 ⟩ Pre-flight Action *4373, 4471, 4985*
PLT445	14 CFR 91 AIM FAA-H-8083-15	Instrument Procedures ⟩ Basic Flight Instruments ⟩ Heading Indicator Publications ⟩ AIM ⟩ Aeronautical Information Regulations ⟩ 14 CFR 91 ⟩ Pre-flight Action *4003, 4033, 4056, 4079, 4842, 4885*
PLT448	14 CFR 61 14 CFR 91	Recall regulations—privileges/limitations of pilot certificates *4002, 4025, 4030-2, 4031*
PLT451	14 CFR 61	Regulations ⟩ 14 CFR Part 61 ⟩ Limitations *4026, 4029, 4034, 4035*
PLT454	14 CFR 91	Regulations ⟩ 14 CFR Part 91 ⟩ Altimeter System Test; VOR Check *4039, 4047, 4049*
PLT455	14 CFR 91 AIM	Publications ⟩ AIM ⟩ FSS Regulations ⟩ 14 CFR Part 91 ⟩ Clearance/Flight Plan *4062, 4063, 4064, 4065, 4067, 4081-1, 4081-2, 4405, 4761*
PLT475	AC 00-45	Weather ⟩ Meteorology ⟩ Squalls *4142*
PLT492	AC 00-6	Weather ⟩ Meteorology ⟩ Temperature *4095, 4113*
PLT493	AC 00-6 FAA-H-8083-25	Aerodynamics ⟩ Flight Characteristics ⟩ Icing Weather ⟩ Meteorology ⟩ Icing *4100, 4151, 4950, 4958, 4959, 4960, 4960-1, 4960-2, 4961, 4962, 4964, 4965, 4966, 4967, 4968, 4969, 4970, 4971, 4971-1, 4972, 4973, 4974*
PLT495	AC 00-6	Weather ⟩ Meteorology ⟩ Thunderstorms *4126, 4137, 4141, 4143, 4144, 4145, 4146-1, 4147, 4148*
PLT497	AIM	Recall transponder—codes/operations/usage *4390*
PLT501	AIM	Weather ⟩ Aeronautical Weather Reports ⟩ PIREP *4210*
PLT507	AIM FAA-H-8083-15	Navigation ⟩ Radio ⟩ VOR; VOR Check *4362, 4378, 4383, 4410, 4411, 4551, 4553, 4554, 4556, 4666*
PLT508	14 CFR 91 AIM	Navigation ⟩ Radio ⟩ VOR Check Regulations ⟩ 14 CFR Part 91 ⟩ Altimeter System Test; VOR Check *4036, 4044, 4046, 4048, 4385*
PLT509	AIM	Flight Operations ⟩ Wake Turbulence ⟩ Drift; Landing; Takeoff *4707, 4708, 4709, 4709-1, 4710*

LSC Code	*FAA Reference*	*Subject Description (or Topic 〉 Content 〉 Specific classification)* *Question Numbers*
PLT510	AC 00-6	Weather 〉 Meteorology 〉 Solar Energy *4096, 4108*
PLT511	AC 00-6	Weather 〉 Meteorology 〉 Air Masses; Fronts *4098, 4115, 4116, 4118, 4122, 4123, 4127, 4128, 4136, 4158*
PLT512	AC 00-6	Weather 〉 Meteorology 〉 Moisture *4101, 4102, 4103, 4104*
PLT516	AC 00-6	Weather 〉 Meteorology 〉 Wind *4105, 4106, 4107*
PLT518	AC 00-6 AIM	Weather 〉 Hazardous 〉 Wind Shear Weather 〉 Meteorology 〉 Thunderstorms; Wind Shear *4135, 4138, 4139, 4140, 4150, 4238, 4720, 4721, 4727, 4739, 4755, 4917*
PLT538	14 CFR 61	Regulations 〉 14 CFR Part 61 〉 Medical Certificates *4983*

Airman Certification Codes and Question Numbers

ACS Code	*Question Numbers*
IR.I.A.K1	*4001, 4001-1, 4008, 4010, 4012, 4013, 4014, 4015, 4015-1, 4017, 4020, 4021, 4023, 4026, 4027*
IR.I.A.K2	*4002, 4009, 4011, 4025, 4028, 4029, 4030-2, 4031, 4034, 4035*
IR.I.A.K3	*4983*
IR.I.B.K1	*4186, 4991*
IR.I.B.K2	*4092, 4170, 4170-1, 4172 , 4173, 4175, 4177, 4178, 4179, 4180, 4181, 4182, 4183, 4184, 4187, 4188, 4189, 4190, 4191, 4192, 4193, 4194, 4195, 4196, 4198, 4199, 4201, 4203, 4204, 4205, 4207, 4208, 4209, 4211, 4212, 4214, 4215, 4220, 4221, 4222, 4223, 4224, 4225, 4226, 4228, 4229, 4242, 4243, 4244, 4245, 4259, 4260, 4268, 4271, 4273, 4281, 4285, 4290, 4299, 4467, 4468, 4980, 4992*
IR.I.B.K3	*4518, 4519, 4520, 4521, 4522, 4523, 4524, 4525*
IR.I.B.K3a	*4095, 4096, 4097, 4113, 4116, 4117, 4119, 4121, 4124, 4154, 4227*
IR.I.B.K3b	*4105, 4106, 4107, 4108, 4135, 4138, 4139, 4140, 4150, 4155, 4168, 4238, 4720, 4721, 4727, 4739, 4755, 4917*
IR.I.B.K3c	*4094, 4101, 4102, 4103, 4112, 4114, 4125, 4200*
IR.I.B.K3d	*4159*
IR.I.B.K3e	*4098, 4120, 4127, 4128, 4136, 4158*
IR.I.B.K3f	*4104, 4115, 4118, 4122, 4123, 4129, 4130, 4131, 4132, 4133, 4134, 4149, 4157, 4202*
IR.I.B.K3g	*4160, 4210, 4916*
IR.I.B.K3h	*4126, 4137, 4141, 4142, 4143, 4144, 4145, 4146, 4146-1, 4147, 4148, 4251, 4252, 4253, 4254, 4255, 4256, 4257, 4258*
IR.I.B.K3i	*4099, 4151, 4151-1, 4152, 4153, 4161, 4171, 4468-1, 4950, 4958, 4959, 4960, 4960-1, 4960-2, 4960-4, 4962, 4964, 4965, 4967, 4968, 4969, 4970, 4971, 4971-1, 4972, 4973, 4974*
IR.I.B.K3j	*4156, 4162, 4163, 4164, 4165, 4166, 4167, 4169*

ACS Code	Question Numbers
IR.I.B.K3k	*4100*
IR.I.B.K4	*4990*
IR.I.B.S4	*4248*
IR.I.C.K1	*4079, 4080, 4081, 4081-1, 4082-2, 4083-1, 4083-3, 4085-1, 4086, 4087-1, 4088, 4365, 4406, 4546, 4630, 4637, 4715, 4719, 4746, 4760-1, 4769*
IR.I.C.K2	*4006, 4024, 4037, 4038, 4042, 4045, 4052, 4053, 4068, 4089, 4090, 4091, 4109, 4111, 4375, 4409, 4425, 4426, 4427, 4427-1, 4428, 4429, 4430, 4431, 4432, 4433, 4434, 4435, 4436, 4437, 4439, 4440, 4447, 4449, 4450, 4451, 4452, 4453, 4454, 4455, 4457, 4473, 4474, 4475, 4476, 4477, 4478, 4479, 4485, 4503, 4510, 4513, 4526, 4527, 4528, 4529, 4530, 4531, 4532, 4533, 4537-1, 4539, 4541, 4542, 4543, 4544, 4545, 4547, 4643, 4643-1, 4765, 4809, 4816, 4922, 4953*
IR.I.C.K3a	*4267, 4278, 4289, 4301, 4313, 4345, 4359, 4913*
IR.I.C.K3c	*4265, 4265-1*
IR.I.C.K4	*4005-1, 4032, 4062, 4063, 4064, 4065, 4067, 4081-2, 4275, 4305, 4405, 4760-2, 4761*
IR.I.C.K5	*4061, 4070*
IR.II.A.K1	*4004, 4960-3, 4961, 4966, 4984*
IR.II.B.K1a	*4093, 4110, 4402, 4444, 4445, 4446, 4480, 4481, 4482, 4910, 4911, 4912, 4923*
IR.II.B.K1b	*4604, 4820, 4831, 4835, 4839, 4842, 4847, 4856, 4857, 4860, 4882, 4883, 4884, 4900, 4901, 4902, 4918, 4919, 4928, 4929*
IR.II.B.K1c	*4007, 4390, 4438, 4979, 4988*
IR.II.B.K1d	*4834, 4877, 4886, 4887, 4888, 4889, 4890, 4891, 4892, 4893, 4894*
IR.II.B.K2a	*4044, 4046, 4050, 4054, 4055, 4246, 4320, 4338, 4347, 4362, 4377, 4378, 4383, 4385, 4397, 4399, 4400, 4400-1, 4410, 4411, 4412, 4413, 4448, 4459, 4472, 4495, 4507, 4549, 4550, 4551, 4553, 4554, 4556, 4639, 4653, 4663, 4674, 4674-1, 4704, 4705, 4745, 4748, 4772*
IR.II.B.R1	*4976, 4977, 4977-1, 4978, 4978-1*
IR.II.C.K2	*4036, 4039, 4043, 4047, 4048, 4049, 4051, 4057*
IR.II.C.K3	*4706, 4731, 4770*
IR.II.C.S1	*4337, 4372, 4376, 4382, 4384, 4386, 4387, 4389, 4548*
IR.III.A.K1	*4078, 4328, 4373, 4379, 4380, 4407, 4420, 4456, 4461, 4471, 4538, 4633-1, 4712, 4716, 4718, 4737, 4743, 4754, 4758, 4758-1, 4759, 4762, 4985*
IR.III.A.K3	*4423, 4605, 4633*
IR.III.A.S1	*4392, 4393, 4395, 4398, 4442, 4443, 4458, 4555*
IR.III.A.S5	*4666*
IR.III.B.K1	*4388, 4401, 4494, 4540, 4609, 4610, 4611, 4612, 4613, 4614, 4615, 4616, 4617, 4618, 4619, 4620, 4624, 4626, 4636, 4668, 4669, 4670-1, 4670-2, 4675, 4675-1, 4681, 4698, 4735, 4750, 4766, 4986*
IR.IV.A.K1	*4003, 4033, 4056, 4812, 4817, 4818, 4833-1, 4843, 4844, 4868, 4870-1, 4878-1, 4878-3, 4885, 4895, 4896, 4897, 4898, 4903, 4904, 4905, 4914, 4915, 4921, 4931, 4932, 4933, 4934, 4935*
IR.IV.A.K2	*4752, 4756, 4840, 4855, 4859, 4862, 4869, 4876, 4879, 4899, 4906, 4907, 4920, 4924, 4925, 4926*
IR.IV.A.K3	*4821, 4830, 4854, 4880, 4908, 4909, 4930*
IR.IV.A.R1	*4808-1, 4993*
IR.IV.A.R2	*4802, 4803, 4804, 4805, 4806, 4807, 4808, 4810, 4811, 4813, 4814, 4815, 4819*

ACS Code	Question Numbers
IR.IV.B.K1	4854-1, 4867, 4873-1, 4875-1, 4927, 4936, 4937, 4938, 4939, 4940, 4941
IR.IV.B.R1	4709-1
IR.V.A.S2	4240, 4552, 4557, 4558, 4559, 4560, 4561, 4562, 4563, 4564, 4565, 4566, 4567, 4568, 4569, 4570, 4571, 4572, 4573, 4573-1, 4574, 4575, 4576, 4577, 4601, 4606, 4607, 4608, 4824, 4825, 4826, 4981, 4987
IR.V.A.S7	4460
IR.V.B.K1	4077, 4239, 4261, 4262, 4263, 4264, 4270, 4270-1, 4280, 4282, 4286, 4287, 4291, 4292, 4294, 4303, 4316, 4316-1, 4317, 4336, 4339, 4349, 4361, 4363, 4364, 4364-1, 4366, 4370-1, 4370-2, 4396, 4417, 4418, 4419, 4441, 4488, 4489, 4490, 4491, 4492, 4493, 4499, 4501, 4506, 4512, 4515, 4516, 4517, 4634, 4638, 4640, 4645, 4646, 4647, 4683, 4734, 4751, 4955, 4956, 4956-1, 4956-2
IR.V.B.K2	4071, 4293, 4295, 4403, 4403-1, 4404, 4469, 4605-1, 4605-2, 4641, 4670, 4671, 4690, 4692, 4694, 4700, 4701, 4714, 4757, 4997
IR.VI.A.K1	4069, 4284, 4677, 4678, 4680, 4682, 4682-1, 4682-2, 4684, 4684-1, 4684-5, 4717-1, 4799, 4799-1, 4799-2, 4801, 4801-1, 4947, 4947-1, 4947-2, 4948, 4949, 4949-1, 4949-2, 4949-3, 4949-4, 4996
IR.VI.B.K1	4066, 4197, 4274, 4276, 4276-1, 4283, 4296, 4297, 4298, 4306, 4307, 4309, 4310, 4311, 4319, 4321, 4332, 4350, 4351, 4352, 4354, 4355, 4357, 4369, 4394, 4414, 4421, 4422, 4424, 4470, 4486, 4635, 4642, 4648, 4648-1, 4649, 4650, 4654, 4655, 4657, 4658, 4659, 4660, 4726, 4728, 4747, 4763-1, 4764, 4975, 4995
IR.VI.C.K1	4249, 4631, 4632, 4667, 4672, 4696, 4717, 4725, 4736, 4744, 4749, 4763, 4767, 4773, 4822, 4823, 4956-3, 4956-4, 4998, 4999
IR.VI.E.K1	4707, 4708, 4709, 4710, 4738, 4740, 4771, 4982
IR.VI.E.K2	4250, 4302, 4304, 4408, 4534, 4535, 4536, 4537, 4774, 4775, 4776, 4778, 4779, 4781, 4782, 4783, 4784, 4785, 4786, 4787, 4790, 4791, 4792, 4793, 4794, 4795, 4796, 4797, 4943, 4944, 4945, 4946, 4951, 4952, 4954, 4954-1, 4963, 4963-1, 4994
IR.VII.A.K1	4374, 4381, 4462, 4463, 4464, 4465, 4466, 4496, 4500, 4505, 4509

FAA-CT-8080-3F

Airman Knowledge Testing Supplement for Instrument Rating

2017

U.S. Department of Transportation
FEDERAL AVIATION ADMINISTRATION
Flight Standards Service

Preface

This Airman Knowledge Testing Supplement is designed by the Federal Aviation Administration (FAA) Flight Standards Service. It is intended for use by Airman Knowledge Testing (AKT) Organization Designation Authorization (ODA) Holders and other entities approved and/or authorized to administer airman knowledge tests on behalf of the FAA in the following knowledge areas:

Instrument Rating—Airplane (IRA)
Instrument Rating—Rotorcraft/Helicopter (IRH)
Instrument Rating—Powered Lift (IPL)
Instrument Flight Instructor—Powered Lift (IPI)
Instrument Rating—Foreign Pilot (IFP)
Instrument Flight Instructor—Airplane (FII)
Instrument Flight Instructor—Rotorcraft/Helicopter - (FIH)
Instrument Flight Instructor—Airplane (added rating) (AIF)
Instrument Flight Instructor—Rotorcraft/Helicopter (added rating) (HIF)
Ground Instructor—Instrument (IGI)

FAA-CT-8080-3F supercedes FAA-CT-8080-3E, Computer Testing Supplement for Instrument Rating, dated 2005.

Comments regarding this supplement, or any AFS-630 publication, should be sent in email form to the following address:

AFS630comments@faa.gov

Contents

Appendix 2 ... 49

APPENDIX 1

4

GENERAL INFORMATION

ABBREVIATIONS

The following abbreviations/acronyms are those commonly used within this Directory. Other abbreviations/acronyms may be found in the Legend and are not duplicated below. The abbreviations presented are intended to represent grammatical variations of the basic form. (Example–"req" may mean "request", "requesting", "requested", or "requests").

Abbreviation	Description
A/G	air/ground
AAF	Army Air Field
AAS	Airport Advisory Service
AB	Airbase
abm	abeam
ABn	Aerodrome Beacon
abv	above
ACC	Air Combat Command Area Control Center
acft	aircraft
ACLS	Automatic Carrier Landing System
act	activity
ACWS	Aircraft Control and Warning Squadron
ADA	Advisory Area
ADCC	Air Defense Control Center
ADCUS	Advise Customs
addn	addition
ADF	Automatic Direction Finder
adj	adjacent
admin	administration
ADR	Advisory Route
advs	advise
advsy	advisory
AEIS	Aeronautical Enroute Information Service
AER	approach end rwy
AFA	Army Flight Activity
AFB	Air Force Base
afct	affect
AFFF	Aqueous Film Forming Foam
AFHP	Air Force Heliport
AFIS	Aerodrome Flight Information Service
afld	airfield
AFOD	Army Flight Operations Detachment
AFR	Air Force Regulation
AFRC	Armed Forces Reserve Center/Air Force Reserve Command
AFRS	American Forces Radio Stations
AFS	Air Force Station
AFSS	Automated Flight Service Station
AFTN	Aeronautical Fixed Telecommunication Network
AG	Agriculture
A–G, A–GEAR	Arresting Gear
agcy	Agency
AGL	above ground level
AHP	Army heliport
AID	Airport Information Desk
AIS	Aeronautical Information Services
AL	Approach and Landing Chart
ALF	Auxiliary Landing Field
ALS	Approach Light System
ALSF–1	High Intensity ALS Category I configuration with sequenced Flashers (code)
ALSF–2	High Intensity ALS Category II configuration with sequenced Flashers (code)
alt	altitude
altn	alternate

Abbreviation	Description
AM	Amplitude Modulation, midnight til noon
AMC	Air Mobility Command
amdt	amendment
AMSL	Above Mean Sea Level
ANGS	Air National Guard Station
ant	antenna
AOE	Airport/Aerodrome of Entry
AP	Area Planning
APAPI	Abbreviated Precision Approach Path Indicator
apch	approach
apn	apron
APP	Approach Control
Apr	April
aprx	approximate
APU	Auxiliary Power Unit
apv, apvl	approve, approval
ARB	Air Reserve Base
ARCAL (CANADA)	Aircraft Radio Control of Aerodrome Lighting
ARFF	Aircraft Rescue and Fire Fighting
ARINC	Aeronautical Radio Inc
arng	arrange
arpt	airport
arr	arrive
ARS	Air Reserve Station
ARSA	Airport Radar Service Area
ARSR	Air Route Surveillance Radar
ARTCC	Air Route Traffic Control Center
AS	Air Station
ASAP	as soon as possible
ASDA	Accelerate–Stop Distance Available
ASDE	Airport Surface Detection
ASDE–X	Airport Surface Detection Equipment–Model X
asgn	assign
ASL	Above Sea Level
ASOS	Automated Surface Observing System
ASR	Airport Surveillance Radar
ASSC	Airport Surface Surveillance Capability
ASU	Aircraft Starting Unit
ATA	Actual Time of Arrival
ATC	Air Traffic Control
ATCC	Air Traffic Control Center
ATCT	Airport Traffic Control Tower
ATD	Actual Time of Departure Along Track Distance
ATIS	Automatic Terminal Information Service
ATS	Air Traffic Service
attn	attention
Aug	August
auth	authority
auto	automatic
AUW	All Up Weight (gross weight)
aux	auxiliary
AVASI	abbreviated VASI
avbl	available
AvGas	Aviation gasoline
avn	aviation
AvOil	aviation oil

LEGEND 1.—Abbreviations.

GENERAL INFORMATION 5

Abbreviation	Description
AWOS	Automatic Weather Observing System
AWSS	Automated Weather Sensor System
awt	await
awy	airway
az	azimuth
BA	braking action
BASH	Bird Aircraft Strike Hazard
BC	back course
bcn	beacon
bcst	broadcast
bdry	boundary
bldg	building
blkd	blocked
blo, blw	below
BOQ	Bachelor Officers Quarters
brg	bearing
btn	between
bus	business
byd	beyond
C	Commercial Circuit (Telephone)
CAC	Centralized Approach Control
cap	capacity
cat	category
CAT	Clear Air Turbulence
CCW or cntclkws	counterclockwise
ceil	ceiling
CERAP	Center Radar Approach Control
CG	Coast Guard
CGAF	Coast Guard Air Facility
CGAS	Coast Guard Air Station
CH, chan	channel
CHAPI	Chase Helicopter Approach Path Indicator
chg	change
cht	chart
cir	circle, circling
CIV, civ	Civil, civil, civilian
ck	check
CL	Centerline Lighting System
cl	class
clnc	clearance
clsd	closed
CNATRA	Chief of Naval Air Training
cnl	cancel
cntr	center
cntrln	centerline
Co	Company, County
CO	Commanding Officer
com	communication
comd	command
Comdr	Commander
coml	commercial
compul	compulsory
comsn	commission
conc	concrete
cond	condition
const	construction
cont	continue
CONUS	Continental United States
convl	conventional
coord	coordinate
copter	helicopter
corr	correct
CPDLC	Controller Pilot Data Link Communication

Abbreviation	Description
crdr	corridor
cros	cross
CRP	Compulsory Reporting Point
crs	course
CS	call sign
CSTMS	Customs
CTA	Control Area
CTAF	Common Traffic Advisory Frequency
ctc	contact
ctl	control
CTLZ	Control Zone
CVFR	Controlled Visual Flight Rules Areas
CW	Clockwise, Continuous Wave, Carrier Wave
dalgt	daylight
D–ATIS	Digital Automatic Terminal Information Service
daylt	daylight
db	decibel
DCL	Departure Clearance
Dec	December
decom	decommission
deg	degree
del	delivery
dep	depart
DEP	Departure Control
destn	destination
det	detachment
DF	Direction Finder
DH	Decision Height
DIAP	DoD Instrument Approach Procedure
direc	directional
disem	disseminate
displ	displace
dist	district, distance
div	division
DL	Direct Line to FSS
dlt	delete
dly	daily
DME	Distance Measuring Equipment (UHF standard, TACAN compatible)
DNVT	Digital Non–Secure Voice Telephone
DoD	Department of Defense
drct	direct
DSN	Defense Switching Network (Telephone)
DSN	Defense Switching Network
dsplcd	displaced
DT	Daylight Savings Time
dur	during
durn	duration
DV	Distinguished Visitor
E	East
ea	each
EAT	Expected Approach Time
ECN	Enroute Change Notice
EFAS	Enroute Flight Advisory Service
eff	effective, effect
E–HA	Enroute High Altitude
E–LA	Enroute Low Altitude
elev	elevation
ELT	Emergency Locator Transmitter
EMAS	Engineered Material Arresting System
emerg	emergency
eng	engine

LEGEND 1A.—Abbreviations.

6 GENERAL INFORMATION

Abbreviation	Description
EOR	End of Runway
eqpt	equipment
ERDA	Energy Research and Development Administration
E–S	Enroute Supplement
est	estimate
estab	establish
ETA	Estimated Time of Arrival
ETD	Estimated Time of Departure
ETE	Estimated Time Enroute
ETS	European Telephone System
EUR	European (ICAO Region)
ev	every
evac	evacuate
exc	except
excld	exclude
exer	exercise
exm	exempt
exp	expect
extd	extend
extn	extension
extv	extensive
F/W	Fixed Wing
FAA	Federal Aviation Administration
fac	facility
FAWS	Flight Advisory Weather Service
fax	facsimile
FBO	Fixed Base Operator
FCC	Flight Control Center
FCG	Foreign Clearance Guide
FCLP	field carrier landing practice
fcst	forecast
Feb	February
FIC	Flight Information Center
FIH	Flight Information Handbook
FIR	Flight Information Region
FIS	Flight Information Service
FL	flight level
fld	field
flg	flashing
FLIP	Flight Information Publication
flt	flight
flw	follow
FM	Fan Marker, Frequency Modulation
FOC	Flight Operations Center
FOD	Foreign Object Damage
fone	telephone
FPL	Flight Plan
fpm	feet per minute
fr	from
freq	frequency, frequent
Fri	Friday
frng	firing
FSC	Flight Service Center
FSS	Flight Service Station
ft	foot
ftr	fighter
GA	Glide Angle
gal	gallon
GAT	General Air Traffic (Europe–Asia)
GCA	Ground Control Approach
GCO	Ground Communication Outlet
gldr	glider
GND	Ground Control
gnd	ground

Abbreviation	Description
govt	government
GP	Glide Path
Gp	Group
GPI	Ground Point of Intercept
grad	gradient
grd	guard
GS	glide slope
GWT	gross weight
H	Enroute High Altitude Chart (followed by identification)
H+	Hours or hours plus...minutes past the hour
H24	continuous operation
HAA	Height Above Airport/Aerodrome
HAL	Height Above Landing Area
HAR	Height Above Runway
HAT	Height Above Touchdown
haz	hazard
hdg	heading
HDTA	High Density Traffic Airport/Aerodrome
HF	High Frequency (3000 to 30,000 KHz)
hgr	hangar
hgt	height
hi	high
HIRL	High Intensity Runway Lights
HIWAS	Hazardous Inflight Weather Advisory Service
HO	Service available to meet operational requirements
hol	holiday
HOLF	Helicopter Outlying Field
hosp	hospital
HQ	Headquarters
hr	hour
HS	Service available during hours of scheduled operations
hsg	housing
hvy	heavy
HW	Heavy Weight
hwy	highway
HX	station having no specific working hours
Hz	Hertz (cycles per second)
I	Island
IAP	Instrument Approach Procedure
IAS	Indicated Air Speed
IAW	in accordance with
ICAO	International Civil Aviation Organization
ident	identification
IFF	Identification, Friend or Foe
IFR	Instrument Flight Rules
IFR–S	FLIP IFR Supplement
IFSS	International Flight Service Station
ILS	Instrument Landing System
IM	Inner Marker
IMC	Instrument Meteorological Conditions
IMG	Immigration
immed	immediate
inbd	inbound
Inc	Incorporated
incl	include
incr	increase
indef	indefinite
info	information
inop	inoperative
inst	instrument

LEGEND 1B.—Abbreviations.

GENERAL INFORMATION

Abbreviation	Description
instl	install
instr	instruction
int	intersection
intcntl	intercontinental
intcp	intercept
intl	international
intmt	intermittent
ints	intense, intensity
invof	in the vicinity of
irreg	Irregularly
Jan	January
JASU	Jet Aircraft Starting Unit
JATO	Jet Assisted Take–Off
JOAP	Joint Oil Analysis Program
JOSAC	Joint Operational Support Airlift Center
JRB	Joint Reserve Base
Jul	July
Jun	June
K or Kt	Knots
kHz	kilohertz
KIAS	Knots Indicated Airspeed
KLIZ	Korea Limited Identification Zone
km	Kilometer
kw	kilowatt
L	Compass locator (Component of ILS system) under 25 Watts, 15 NM, Enroute Low Altitude Chart (followed by identification)
L	Local Time
LAA	Local Airport Advisory
LAHSO	Land and Hold–Short Operations
L–AOE	Limited Airport of Entry
LAWRS	Limited Aviation Weather Reporting Station
lb, lbs	pound (weight)
LC	local call
lcl	local
LCP	French Peripheral Classification Line
lctd	located
lctn	location
lctr	locator
LCVASI	Low Cost Visual Approach Slope Indicator
lczr	localizer
LD	long distance
LDA	Landing Distance Available
ldg	landing
LDIN	Lead–in Lights
LDOCF	Long Distance Operations Control Facility
len	length
lgt, lgtd, lgts	light, lighted, lights
LIRL	Low Intensity Runway Lights
LLWAS	Low–Level Wind Shear Alert System
LLZ	Localizer (Instrument Approach Procedures Identification only)
LMM	Compass locator at Middle Marker ILS
lo	low
LoALT or LA	Low Altitude
LOC	Localizer
LOM	Compass locator at Outer Marker ILS
LR	Long Range, Lead Radial
LRA	Landing Rights Airport
LRRS	Long Range RADAR Station

Abbreviation	Description
LSB	lower side band
ltd	limited
M	meters, magnetic (after a bearing), Military Circuit (Telephone)
MACC	Military Area Control Center
mag	magnetic
maint	maintain, maintenance
maj	major
MALS	Medium Intensity Approach Lighting System
MALSF	MALS with Sequenced Flashers
MALSR	MALS with Runway Alignment Indicator Lights
Mar	March
MARA	Military Activity Restricted Area
MATO	Military Air Traffic Operations
MATZ	Military Aerodrome Traffic Zone
max	maximum
mb	millibars
MCAC	Military Common Area Control
MCAF	Marine Corps Air Facility
MCALF	Marine Corps Auxiliary Landing Field
MCAS	Marine Corps Air Station
MCB	Marine Corps Base
MCC	Military Climb Corridor
MCOLF	Marine Corps Outlying Field
MDA	Minimum Descent Altitude
MEA	Minimum Enroute Altitude
med	medium
MEHT	Minimum Eye Height over Threshold
mem	memorial
MET	Meteorological, Meteorology
METAR	Aviation Routine Weather Report (in international MET figure code)
METRO	Pilot–to–Metro voice cell
MF	Medium Frequency (300 to 3000 KHz), Mandatory Frequency (Canada)
MFA	Minimum Flight Altitude
mgmt	Management
mgr	manager
MHz	Megahertz
mi	mile
MID/ASIA	Middle East/Asia (ICAO Region)
MIJI	Meaconing, Intrusion, Jamming, and Interference
Mil, mil	military
min	minimum, minute
MIRL	Medium Intensity Runway Lights
misl	missile
mkr	marker (beacon)
MM	Middle Marker of ILS
mnt	monitor
MOA	Military Operations Area
MOCA	Minimum Obstruction Clearance Altitude
mod	modify
MOG	Maximum (aircraft) on the Ground
Mon	Monday
MP	Maintenance Period
MR	Medium Range
MRA	Minimum Reception Altitude
mrk	mark, marker
MSAW	minimum safe altitude warning
msg	message
MSL	Mean Sea Level
msn	Mission

LEGEND 1C.—Abbreviations.

8 **GENERAL INFORMATION**

Abbreviation	Description
mt	mount, mountain
MTAF	Mandatory Traffic Advisory Frequency
MTCA	Military Terminal Control Area
mthly	monthly
MUAC	Military Upper Area Control
muni	municipal
MWARA	Major World Air Route Area
N	North
N/A	not applicable
NA	not authorized (For Instrument Approach Procedure take–off and alternate MINIMA only)
NAAS	Naval Auxiliary Air Station
NADC	Naval Air Development Center
NADEP	Naval Air Depot
NAEC	Naval Air Engineering Center
NAES	Naval Air Engineering Station
NAF	Naval Air Facility
NALCO	Naval Air Logistics Control Office
NALF	Naval Auxiliary Landing Field
NALO	Navy Air Logistics Office
NAS	Naval Air Station
NAT	North Atlantic (ICAO Region)
natl	national
nav	navigation
navaid	navigation aid
NAVMTO	Navy Material Transportation Office
NAWC	Naval Air Warfare Center
NAWS	Naval Air Weapons Station
NCRP	Non–Compulsory Reporting Point
NDB	Non–Directional Radio Beacon
NE	Northeast
nec	necessary
NEW	Net Explosives Weight
ngt	night
NM	nautical miles
nml	normal
NMR	nautical mile radius
No or Nr	number
NOLF	Naval Outlying Field
NORDO	Lost communications or no radio installed/available in aircraft
NOTAM	Notice to Airmen
Nov	November
npi	non precision instrument
Nr or No	number
NS	Naval Station
NS ABTMT	Noise Abatement
NSA	Naval Support Activity
NSF	Naval Support Facility
NSTD, nstd	nonstandard
ntc	notice
NVD	Night Vision Devices
NVG	Night Vision Goggles
NW	Northwest
NWC	Naval Weapons Center
O/A	On or about
O/S	out of service
O/R	On Request
OAT	Operational Air Traffic
obsn	observation
obst	obstruction
OCA	Oceanic Control Area
ocnl	occasional
Oct	October

Abbreviation	Description
ODALS	Omnidirectional Approach Lighting System
ODO	Operations Duty Officer
offl	official
OIC	Officer In Charge
OLF	Outlying Field
OLS	Optical Landing System
OM	Outer Marker, ILS
opr	operate, operator, operational
OPS, ops	operations
orig	original
OROCA	Off Route Obstruction Clearance Altitude
ORTCA	Off Route Terrain Clearance Altitude
OT	other times
OTS	out of service
outbd	outbound
ovft	overflight
ovrn	overrun
OX	oxygen
P/L	plain language
PAC	Pacific (ICAO Region)
PAEW	personnel and equipment working
PALS	Precision Approach and Landing System (NAVY)
PAPI	Precision Approach Path Indicator
PAR	Precision Approach Radar
para	paragraph
parl	parallel
pat	pattern
PAX	Passenger
PCL	pilot controlled lighting
pent	penetrate
perm	permanent
perms	permission
pers	personnel
PFC	Porous Friction Courses
PJE	Parachuting Activities/Exercises
p–line	power line
PM	Post meridian, noon til midnight
PMRF	Pacific Missile Range Facility
PMSV	Pilot–to–Metro Service
PN	prior notice
POB	persons on board
POL	Petrol, Oils and Lubricants
posn	position
PPR	prior permission required
prcht	parachute
pref	prefer
prev	previous
prim	primary
prk	park
PRM	Precision Runway Monitor
pro	procedure
proh	prohibited
pt	point
PTD	Pilot to Dispatcher
pub	publication
publ	publish
PVASI	Pulsating Visual Approach Slope Indicator
pvt	private
pwr	power
QFE	Altimeter Setting above station

Legend 1D.—Abbreviations.

GENERAL INFORMATION

Abbreviation	Description
QNE	Altimeter Setting of 29.92 inches which provides height above standard datum plane
QNH	Altimeter Setting which provides height above mean sea level
qtrs	quarters
quad	quadrant
R/T	Radiotelephony
R/W	Rotary/Wing
RACON	Radar Beacon
rad	radius, radial
RAIL	Runway Alignment Indicator Lights
RAMCC	Regional Air Movement Control Center
R–AOE	Regular Airport of Entry
RAPCON	Radar Approach Control (USAF)
RATCF	Radar Air Traffic Control Facility (Navy)
RCAG	Remote Center Air to Ground Facility
RCAGL	Remote Center Air to Ground Facility Long Range
RCL	runway centerline
RCLS	Runway Centerline Light System
RCO	Remote Communications Outlet
rcpt	reception
RCR	Runway Condition Reading
rcv	receive
rcvr	receiver
rdo	radio
reconst	reconstruct
reful	refueling
reg	regulation, regular
REIL	Runway End Identifier Lights
rel	reliable
relctd	relocated
REP	Reporting Point
req	request
RETIL	Rapid Exit Taxiway Indicator Light
Rgn	Region
Rgnl	Regional
rgt	right
rgt tfc	right traffic
rlgd	realigned
RLLS	Runway Lead-in Light System
rmk	remark
rng	range, radio range
RNP	Required Navigation Performance
RON	Remain Overnight
Rot Lt or Bcn	Rotating Light or Beacon
RPI	Runway Point of Intercept
rpt	report
rqr	require
RR	Railroad
RRP	Runway Reference Point
RSC	Runway Surface Condition
RSDU	Radar Storm Detection Unit
RSE	Runway Starter Extension/Starter Strip
RSRS	Reduced Same Runway Separation
rstd	restricted
rte	route
ruf	rough
RVR	Runway Visual Range
RVSM	Reduced Vertical Separation Minima
rwy	runway
S	South
S/D	Seadrome
SALS	Short Approach Lighting System

Abbreviation	Description
SAR	Search and Rescue
Sat	Saturday
SAVASI	Simplified Abbreviated Visual Approach Slope Indicator
SAWRS	Supplement Aviation Weather Reporting Station
sby	standby
Sched	scheduled services
sctr	sector
SDF	Simplified Directional Facility
SE	Southeast
sec	second, section
secd	secondary
SELCAL	Selective Calling System
SELF	Strategic Expeditionary Landing Field
SEng	Single Engine
Sep	September
SFA	Single Frequency Approach
sfc	surface
SFL	Sequence Flashing Lights
SFRA	Special Flight Rules Area
SID	Standard Instrument Departure
SIDA	Secure Identification Display Area
SIF	Selective Identification Feature
sked	schedule
SM	statute miles
SOAP	Spectrometric Oil Analysis Program
SOF	Supervisor of Flying
SPB	Seaplane Base
SR	sunrise
SRE	Surveillance Radar Element of GCA (Instrument Approach Procedures Identification only)
SS	sunset
SSALS/R	Simplified Short Approach Lighting System/with RAIL
SSB	Single Sideband
SSR	Secondary Surveillance Radar
STA	Straight-in Approach
std	standard
stn	station
stor	storage
str–in	Straight–in
stu	student
subj	subject
sum	summer
Sun	Sunday
sur	surround
survl	survival, surveillance
suspd	suspended
svc	service
svcg	servicing
SW	Southwest
sys	system
TA	Transition Altitude
TAC	Tactical Air Command
TAF	Aerodrome (terminal or alternate) forecast in abbreviated form
TALCE	Tanker Aircraft Control Element
TCA	Terminal Control Area
TCH	Threshold Crossing Height
TCTA	Transcontinental Control Area
TD	Touchdown
TDWR	Terminal Doppler Weather Radar
TDZ	Touchdown Zone
TDZL	Touchdown Zone Lights

LEGEND 1E.—Abbreviations.

10 **GENERAL INFORMATION**

Abbreviation	Description
tfc	traffic
thld	threshold
thou	thousand
thru	through
Thu	Thursday
til	until
tkf, tkof	take–off
TLv	Transition Level
tmpry	temporary
TODA	Take–Off Distance Available
TORA	Take–Off Run Available
TP	Tire Pressure
TPA	Traffic Pattern Altitude
TRACON	Terminal Radar Approach Control (FAA)
tran	transient
trans	transmit
trml	terminal
trng	training
trns	transition
TRSA	Terminal Radar Service Area
Tue	Tuesday
TV	Television
TWEB	Transcribed Weather Broadcast
twr	tower
twy	taxiway
UACC	Upper Area Control Center (used outside US)
UAS	Unmanned Aerial Systems
UC	Under Construction
UCN	Urgent Change Notice
UDA	Upper Advisory Area
UDF	Ultra High Frequency Direction Finder
UFN	until further notice
UHF	Ultra High Frequency (300 to 3000 MHz)
UIR	Upper Flight Information Region
unauthd	unauthorized
unavbl	unavailable
unctl	uncontrolled
unk	unknown
unlgtd	unlighted
unltd	unlimited
unmrk	unmarked
unmto	unmonitored
unrel	unreliable
unrstd	unrestricted
unsatfy	unsatisfactory
unsked	unscheduled
unsvc	unserviceable
unuse, unusbl	unusable
USA	United States Army
USAF	United States Air Force
USB	Upper Side Band
USCG	United States Coast Guard
USMC	United States Marine Corps
USN	United States Navy
UTA	Upper Control Area
UTC	Coordinated Universal Time
V	Defense Switching Network (telephone, formerly AUTOVON)
V/STOL	Vertical and Short Take–off and Landing aircraft
VAL	Visiting Aircraft Line
var	variation (magnetic variation)
VASI	Visual Approach Slope Indicator

Abbreviation	Description
vcnty	vicinity
VDF	Very High Frequency Direction Finder
veh	vehicle
vert	vertical
VFR	Visual Flight Rules
VFR–S	FLIP VFR Supplement
VHF	Very High Frequency (30 to 300 MHz)
VIP	Very Important Person
vis	visibility
VMC	Visual Meteorological Conditions
VOIP	Voice Over Internet Protocol
VOLMET	Meteorological Information for Aircraft in Flight
VOT	VOR Receiver Testing Facility
W	Warning Area (followed by identification), Watts, West, White
WCH	Wheel Crossing Height
Wed	Wednesday
Wg	Wing
WIE	with immediate effect
win	winter
WIP	work in progress
WSO	Weather Service Office
WSFO	Weather Service Forecast Office
wk	week
wkd	weekday
wkly	weekly
wng	warning
wo	without
WSP	Weather System Processor
wt	weight
wx	weather
yd	yard
yr	year
Z	Greenwich Mean Time (time groups only)

LEGEND 1F.—Abbreviations.

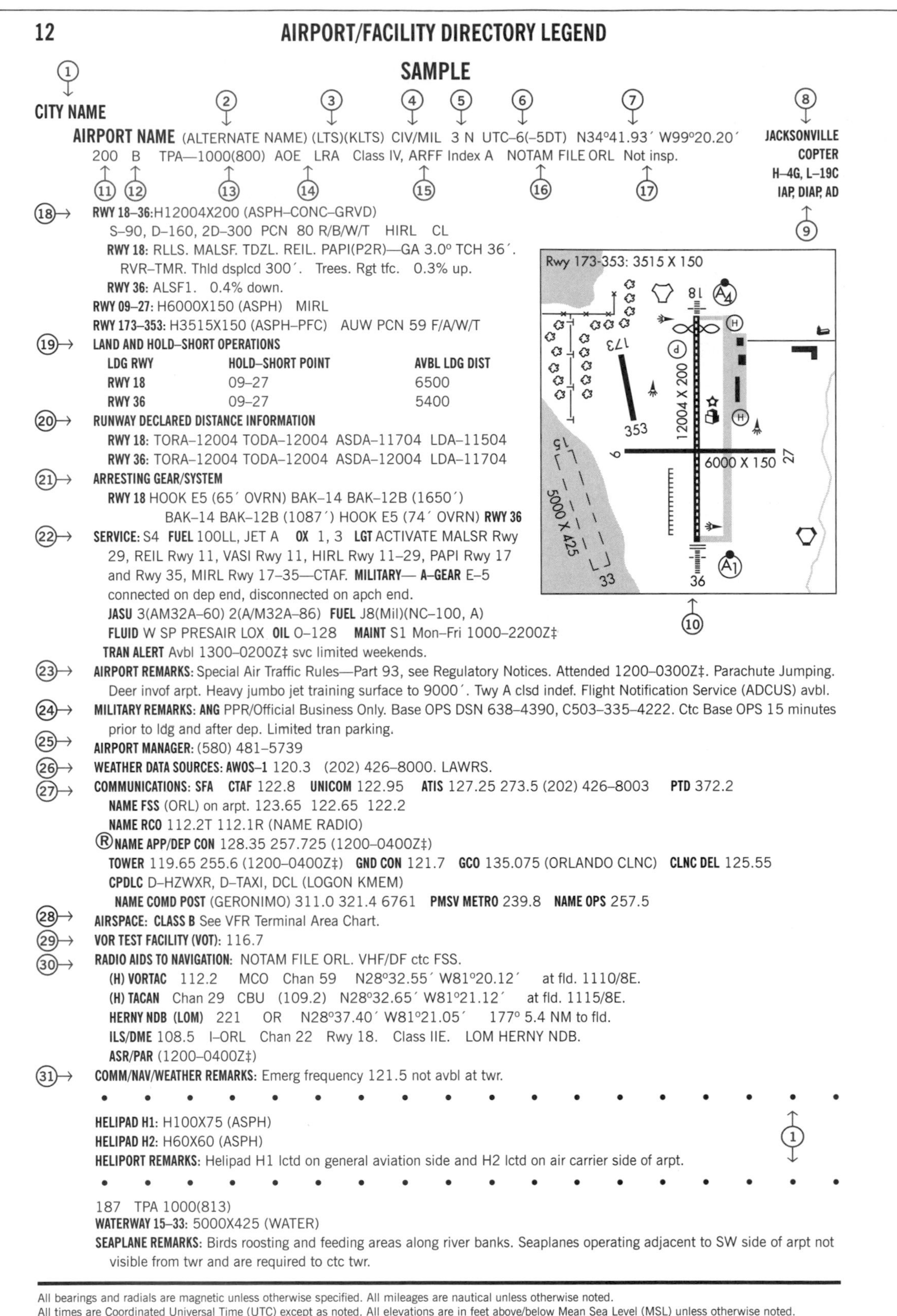

12 **AIRPORT/FACILITY DIRECTORY LEGEND**

SAMPLE

(1) **CITY NAME**

(2) (3) (4) (5) (6) (7) (8)

AIRPORT NAME (ALTERNATE NAME) (LTS)(KLTS) CIV/MIL 3 N UTC–6(–5DT) N34°41.93′ W99°20.20′ **JACKSONVILLE COPTER H–4G, L–19C IAP, DIAP, AD**

200 B TPA—1000(800) AOE LRA Class IV, ARFF Index A NOTAM FILE ORL Not insp.

(11) (12) (13) (14) (15) (16) (17) (9)

(18)→ **RWY 18–36:** H12004X200 (ASPH–CONC–GRVD)
S–90, D–160, 2D–300 PCN 80 R/B/W/T HIRL CL
RWY 18: RLLS. MALSF. TDZL. REIL. PAPI(P2R)—GA 3.0° TCH 36′.
RVR–TMR. Thld dsplcd 300′. Trees. Rgt tfc. 0.3% up.
RWY 36: ALSF1. 0.4% down.
RWY 09–27: H6000X150 (ASPH) MIRL
RWY 173–353: H3515X150 (ASPH–PFC) AUW PCN 59 F/A/W/T

(19)→ **LAND AND HOLD–SHORT OPERATIONS**

LDG RWY	HOLD–SHORT POINT	AVBL LDG DIST
RWY 18	09–27	6500
RWY 36	09–27	5400

(20)→ **RUNWAY DECLARED DISTANCE INFORMATION**
RWY 18: TORA–12004 TODA–12004 ASDA–11704 LDA–11504
RWY 36: TORA–12004 TODA–12004 ASDA–12004 LDA–11704

(21)→ **ARRESTING GEAR/SYSTEM**
RWY 18 HOOK E5 (65′ OVRN) BAK–14 BAK–12B (1650′)
BAK–14 BAK–12B (1087′) HOOK E5 (74′ OVRN) **RWY 36**

(22)→ **SERVICE:** S4 **FUEL** 100LL, JET A **OX** 1, 3 **LGT** ACTIVATE MALSR Rwy 29, REIL Rwy 11, VASI Rwy 11, HIRL Rwy 11–29, PAPI Rwy 17 and Rwy 35, MIRL Rwy 17–35—CTAF. **MILITARY— A–GEAR** E–5 connected on dep end, disconnected on apch end.
JASU 3(AM32A–60) 2(A/M32A–86) **FUEL** J8(Mil)(NC–100, A)
FLUID W SP PRESAIR LOX **OIL** O–128 **MAINT** S1 Mon–Fri 1000–2200Z‡
TRAN ALERT Avbl 1300–0200Z‡ svc limited weekends.

(23)→ **AIRPORT REMARKS:** Special Air Traffic Rules—Part 93, see Regulatory Notices. Attended 1200–0300Z‡. Parachute Jumping. Deer invof arpt. Heavy jumbo jet training surface to 9000′. Twy A clsd indef. Flight Notification Service (ADCUS) avbl.

(24)→ **MILITARY REMARKS: ANG** PPR/Official Business Only. Base OPS DSN 638–4390, C503–335–4222. Ctc Base OPS 15 minutes prior to ldg and after dep. Limited tran parking.

(25)→ **AIRPORT MANAGER:** (580) 481–5739

(26)→ **WEATHER DATA SOURCES: AWOS–1** 120.3 (202) 426–8000. LAWRS.

(27)→ **COMMUNICATIONS: SFA CTAF** 122.8 **UNICOM** 122.95 **ATIS** 127.25 273.5 (202) 426–8003 **PTD** 372.2
NAME FSS (ORL) on arpt. 123.65 122.65 122.2
NAME RCO 112.2T 112.1R (NAME RADIO)
®**NAME APP/DEP CON** 128.35 257.725 (1200–0400Z‡)
TOWER 119.65 255.6 (1200–0400Z‡) **GND CON** 121.7 **GCO** 135.075 (ORLANDO CLNC) **CLNC DEL** 125.55
CPDLC D–HZWXR, D–TAXI, DCL (LOGON KMEM)
NAME COMD POST (GERONIMO) 311.0 321.4 6761 **PMSV METRO** 239.8 **NAME OPS** 257.5

(28)→ **AIRSPACE: CLASS B** See VFR Terminal Area Chart.

(29)→ **VOR TEST FACILITY (VOT):** 116.7

(30)→ **RADIO AIDS TO NAVIGATION:** NOTAM FILE ORL. VHF/DF ctc FSS.
(H) VORTAC 112.2 MCO Chan 59 N28°32.55′ W81°20.12′ at fld. 1110/8E.
(H) TACAN Chan 29 CBU (109.2) N28°32.65′ W81°21.12′ at fld. 1115/8E.
HERNY NDB (LOM) 221 OR N28°37.40′ W81°21.05′ 177° 5.4 NM to fld.
ILS/DME 108.5 I–ORL Chan 22 Rwy 18. Class IIE. LOM HERNY NDB.
ASR/PAR (1200–0400Z‡)

(31)→ **COMM/NAV/WEATHER REMARKS:** Emerg frequency 121.5 not avbl at twr.

• •

HELIPAD H1: H100X75 (ASPH)
HELIPAD H2: H60X60 (ASPH) (1)
HELIPORT REMARKS: Helipad H1 lctd on general aviation side and H2 lctd on air carrier side of arpt.

• •

187 TPA 1000(813)
WATERWAY 15–33: 5000X425 (WATER)
SEAPLANE REMARKS: Birds roosting and feeding areas along river banks. Seaplanes operating adjacent to SW side of arpt not visible from twr and are required to ctc twr.

All bearings and radials are magnetic unless otherwise specified. All mileages are nautical unless otherwise noted.
All times are Coordinated Universal Time (UTC) except as noted. All elevations are in feet above/below Mean Sea Level (MSL) unless otherwise noted.
The horizontal reference datum of this publication is North American Datum of 1983 (NAD83), which for charting purposes is considered equivalent to World Geodetic System 1984 (WGS 84).

Legend 2.—Airport/Facility Directory.

(10)

SKETCH LEGEND

RUNWAYS/LANDING AREAS

Hard Surfaced . . . .

Metal Surface . . . .

Sod, Gravel, etc. . . . .

Light Plane, ...
Ski Landing Area or Water

Under Construction . . . . .

Closed . . . .

Helicopter Landings Area . . . . (H)

Displaced Threshold . . . .

Taxiway, Apron and Stopways . .

RADIO AIDS TO NAVIGATION

VORTAC . . .

VOR . . . .

VOR/DME . .

NDB . . . .

TACAN . . . .

NDB/DME . . . .

DME . . . .

MISCELLANEOUS AERONAUTICAL FEATURES

Airport Beacon . . . .

Wind Cone . . . .

Landing Tee . . . .

Tetrahedron . . . .

Control Tower . . . . or TWR

When control tower and rotating beacon are co-located beacon symbol will be used and further identified as TWR.

MISCELLANEOUS BASE AND CULTURAL FEATURES

Buildings . . . .

Power Lines . . . . –T——T–

Fence . . . .

Towers . . . .

Wind Turbine. . . . .

Tanks . . . .

Oil Well . . . .

Smoke Stack . . . .

Obstruction 5812

Controlling Obstruction . . . . +5812

Trees . . . .

Populated Places . . . .

Cuts and Fills . . . . . . Cut Fill

Cliffs and Depressions . .

Ditch . . . .

Hill . . . .

APPROACH LIGHTING SYSTEMS

A dot "•" portrayed with approach lighting letter identifier indicates sequenced flashing lights (F) installed with the approach lighting system e.g. (A1) Negative symbology, e.g., (A1) (V) indicates Pilot Controlled Lighting (PCL).

Runway Centerline Lighting . . . . .

(A) Approach Lighting System ALSF-2 . .

(A1) Approach Lighting System ALSF-1 . .

(A2) Short Approach Lighting System SALS/SALSF . . . .

(A3) Simplified Short Approach Lighting System (SSALR) with RAIL . . . . .

(A4) Medium Intensity Approach Lighting System (MALS and MALSF)/(SSALS and SSALF) . . . .

(A5) Medium Intensity Approach Lighting System (MALSR) and RAIL . . . . . .

Omnidirectional Approach Lighting System (ODALS) . . . .

(D) Navy Parallel Row and Cross Bar . . .

Air Force Overrun . . . .

(V) Visual Approach Slope Indicator with Standard Threshold Clearance provided

(V2) Pulsating Visual Approach Slope Indicator (PVASI)

(V3) Visual Approach Slope Indicator with a threshold crossing height to accomodate long bodied or jumbo aircraft

(V4) Tri-color Visual Approach Slope Indicator (TRCV)

(V5) Approach Path Alignment Panel (APAP)

(P) Precision Approach Path Indicator (PAPI)

LEGEND 3.—Airport/Facility Directory.

AIRPORT/FACILITY DIRECTORY LEGEND

LEGEND

This directory is a listing of data on record with the FAA on public–use airports, military airports and selected private–use airports specifically requested by the Department of Defense (DoD) for which a DoD Instrument Approach Procedure has been published in the U.S. Terminal Procedures Publication. Additionally this listing contains data for associated terminal control facilities, air route traffic control centers, and radio aids to navigation within the conterminous United States, Puerto Rico and the Virgin Islands. Civil airports and joint Civil/Military airports which are open to the public are listed alphabetically by state, associated city and airport name and cross–referenced by airport name. Military airports and private–use (limited civil access) joint Military/Civil airports are listed alphabetically by state and official airport name and cross–referenced by associated city name. Navaids, flight service stations and remote communication outlets that are associated with an airport, but with a different name, are listed alphabetically under their own name, as well as under the airport with which they are associated.

The listing of an airport as open to the public in this directory merely indicates the airport operator's willingness to accommodate transient aircraft, and does not represent that the airport conforms with any Federal or local standards, or that it has been approved for use on the part of the general public. Military airports, private–use airports, and private–use (limited civil access) joint Military/Civil airports are open to civil pilots only in an emergency or with prior permission. See Special Notice Section, Civil Use of Military Fields.

The information on obstructions is taken from reports submitted to the FAA. Obstruction data has not been verified in all cases. Pilots are cautioned that objects not indicated in this tabulation (or on the airports sketches and/or charts) may exist which can create a hazard to flight operation. Detailed specifics concerning services and facilities tabulated within this directory are contained in the Aeronautical Information Manual, Basic Flight Information and ATC Procedures.

The legend items that follow explain in detail the contents of this Directory and are keyed to the circled numbers on the sample on the preceding pages.

① CITY/AIRPORT NAME

Civil and joint Civil/Military airports which are open to the public are listed alphabetically by state and associated city. Where the city name is different from the airport name the city name will appear on the line above the airport name. Airports with the same associated city name will be listed alphabetically by airport name and will be separated by a dashed rule line. A solid rule line will separate all others. FAA approved helipads and seaplane landing areas associated with a land airport will be separated by a dotted line. Military airports and private–use (limited civil access) joint Military/Civil airports are listed alphabetically by state and official airport name.

② ALTERNATE NAME

Alternate names, if any, will be shown in parentheses.

③ LOCATION IDENTIFIER

The location identifier is a three or four character FAA code followed by a four–character ICAO code, when assigned, to airports. If two different military codes are assigned, both codes will be shown with the primary operating agency's code listed first. These identifiers are used by ATC in lieu of the airport name in flight plans, flight strips and other written records and computer operations. Zeros will appear with a slash to differentiate them from the letter "O".

④ OPERATING AGENCY

Airports within this directory are classified into two categories, Military/Federal Government and Civil airports open to the general public, plus selected private–use airports. The operating agency is shown for military, private–use and joint use airports. The operating agency is shown by an abbreviation as listed below. When an organization is a tenant, the abbreviation is enclosed in parenthesis. No classification indicates the airport is open to the general public with no military tenant.

A	US Army	MC	Marine Corps
AFRC	Air Force Reserve Command	MIL/CIV	Joint Use Military/Civil Limited Civil Access
AF	US Air Force	N	Navy
ANG	Air National Guard	NAF	Naval Air Facility
AR	US Army Reserve	NAS	Naval Air Station
ARNG	US Army National Guard	NASA	National Air and Space Administration
CG	US Coast Guard	P	US Civil Airport Wherein Permit Covers Use by Transient Military Aircraft
CIV/MIL	Joint Use Civil/Military Open to the Public		
DND	Department of National Defense Canada	PVT	Private Use Only (Closed to the Public)

⑤ AIRPORT LOCATION

Airport location is expressed as distance and direction from the center of the associated city in nautical miles and cardinal points, e.g., 4 NE.

⑥ TIME CONVERSION

Hours of operation of all facilities are expressed in Coordinated Universal Time (UTC) and shown as "Z" time. The directory indicates the number of hours to be subtracted from UTC to obtain local standard time and local daylight saving time UTC–5(–4DT). The symbol ‡ indicates that during periods of Daylight Saving Time (DST) effective hours will be one hour earlier than shown. In those areas where daylight saving time is not observed the (–4DT) and ‡ will not be shown. Daylight saving time is in effect from 0200 local time the second Sunday in March to 0200 local time the first Sunday in November. Canada and all U.S. Conterminous States observe daylight saving time except Arizona and Puerto Rico, and the Virgin Islands. If the state observes daylight saving time and the operating times are other than daylight saving times, the operating hours will include the dates, times and no ‡ symbol will be shown, i.e., April 15–Aug 31 0630–1700Z, Sep 1–Apr 14 0600–1700Z.

LEGEND 4.—Airport/Facility Directory.

AIRPORT/FACILITY DIRECTORY LEGEND 15

⑦ GEOGRAPHIC POSITION OF AIRPORT—AIRPORT REFERENCE POINT (ARP)

Positions are shown as hemisphere, degrees, minutes and hundredths of a minute and represent the approximate geometric center of all usable runway surfaces.

⑧ CHARTS

Charts refer to the Sectional Chart and Low and High Altitude Enroute Chart and panel on which the airport or facility is located. Helicopter Chart locations will be indicated as COPTER. IFR Gulf of Mexico West and IFR Gulf of Mexico Central will be depicted as GOMW and GOMC.

⑨ INSTRUMENT APPROACH PROCEDURES, AIRPORT DIAGRAMS

IAP indicates an airport for which a prescribed (Public Use) FAA Instrument Approach Procedure has been published. DIAP indicates an airport for which a prescribed DoD Instrument Approach Procedure has been published in the U.S. Terminal Procedures. See the Special Notice Section of this directory, Civil Use of Military Fields and the Aeronautical Information Manual 5–4–5 Instrument Approach Procedure Charts for additional information. AD indicates an airport for which an airport diagram has been published. Airport diagrams are located in the back of each Chart Supplement volume alphabetically by associated city and airport name.

⑩ AIRPORT SKETCH

The airport sketch, when provided, depicts the airport and related topographical information as seen from the air and should be used in conjunction with the text. It is intended as a guide for pilots in VFR conditions. Symbology that is not self–explanatory will be reflected in the sketch legend. The airport sketch will be oriented with True North at the top. Airport sketches will be added incrementally.

⑪ ELEVATION

The highest point of an airport's usable runways measured in feet from mean sea level. When elevation is sea level it will be indicated as "00". When elevation is below sea level a minus "–" sign will precede the figure.

⑫ ROTATING LIGHT BEACON

B indicates rotating beacon is available. Rotating beacons operate sunset to sunrise unless otherwise indicated in the AIRPORT REMARKS or MILITARY REMARKS segment of the airport entry.

⑬ TRAFFIC PATTERN ALTITUDE

Traffic Pattern Altitude (TPA)—The first figure shown is TPA above mean sea level. The second figure in parentheses is TPA above airport elevation. Multiple TPA shall be shown as "TPA—See Remarks" and detailed information shall be shown in the Airport or Military Remarks Section. Traffic pattern data for USAF bases, USN facilities, and U.S. Army airports (including those on which ACC or U.S. Army is a tenant) that deviate from standard pattern altitudes shall be shown in Military Remarks.

⑭ AIRPORT OF ENTRY, LANDING RIGHTS, AND CUSTOMS USER FEE AIRPORTS

U.S. CUSTOMS USER FEE AIRPORT—Private Aircraft operators are frequently required to pay the costs associated with customs processing.

AOE—Airport of Entry. A customs Airport of Entry where permission from U.S. Customs is not required to land. However, at least one hour advance notice of arrival is required.

LRA—Landing Rights Airport. Application for permission to land must be submitted in advance to U.S. Customs. At least one hour advance notice of arrival is required.

NOTE: Advance notice of arrival at both an AOE and LRA airport may be included in the flight plan when filed in Canada or Mexico. Where Flight Notification Service (ADCUS) is available the airport remark will indicate this service. This notice will also be treated as an application for permission to land in the case of an LRA. Although advance notice of arrival may be relayed to Customs through Mexico, Canada, and U.S. Communications facilities by flight plan, the aircraft operator is solely responsible for ensuring that Customs receives the notification. (See Customs, Immigration and Naturalization, Public Health and Agriculture Department requirements in the International Flight Information Manual for further details.)

U.S. CUSTOMS AIR AND SEA PORTS, INSPECTORS AND AGENTS

Northeast Sector (New England and Atlantic States—ME to MD)	407–975–1740
Southeast Sector (Atlantic States—DC, WV, VA to FL)	407–975–1780
Central Sector (Interior of the US, including Gulf states—MS, AL, LA)	407–975–1760
Southwest East Sector (OK and eastern TX)	407–975–1840
Southwest West Sector (Western TX, NM and AZ)	407–975–1820
Pacific Sector (WA, OR, CA, HI and AK)	407–975–1800

⑮ CERTIFICATED AIRPORT (14 CFR PART 139)

Airports serving Department of Transportation certified carriers and certified under 14 CFR part 139 are indicated by the Class and the ARFF Index; e.g. Class I, ARFF Index A, which relates to the availability of crash, fire, rescue equipment. Class I airports can have an ARFF Index A through E, depending on the aircraft length and scheduled departures. Class II, III, and IV will always carry an Index A.

AIRPORT CLASSIFICATIONS

Type of Air Carrier Operation	Class I	Class II	Class III	Class IV
Scheduled Air Carrier Aircraft with 31 or more passenger seats	X			
Unscheduled Air Carrier Aircraft with 31 or more passengers seats	X	X		X
Scheduled Air Carrier Aircraft with 10 to 30 passenger seats	X	X	X	

LEGEND 5.—Airport/Facility Directory.

16

AIRPORT/FACILITY DIRECTORY LEGEND

INDICES AND AIRCRAFT RESCUE AND FIRE FIGHTING EQUIPMENT REQUIREMENTS

Airport Index	Required No. Vehicles	Aircraft Length	Scheduled Departures	Agent + Water for Foam
A	1	<90′	≥1	500#DC or HALON 1211 or 450#DC + 100 gal H_2O
B	1 or 2	≥90′, <126′ ≥126′, <159′	≥5 <5	Index A + 1500 gal H_2O
C	2 or 3	≥126′, <159′ ≥159′, <200′	≥5 <5	Index A + 3000 gal H_2O
D	3	≥159′, <200′ >200′	 <5	Index A + 4000 gal H_2O
E	3	≥200′	≥5	Index A + 6000 gal H_2O

> Greater Than; < Less Than; ≥ Equal or Greater Than; ≤ Equal or Less Than; H_2O–Water; DC–Dry Chemical.

NOTE: The listing of ARFF index does not necessarily assure coverage for non–air carrier operations or at other than prescribed times for air carrier. ARFF Index Ltd.—indicates ARFF coverage may or may not be available, for information contact airport manager prior to flight.

⑯ NOTAM SERVICE

All public use landing areas are provided NOTAM service. A NOTAM FILE identifier is shown for individual landing areas, e.g., "NOTAM FILE BNA". See the AIM, Basic Flight Information and ATC Procedures for a detailed description of NOTAMs. Current NOTAMs are available from flight service stations at 1–800–WX–BRIEF (992–7433) or online through the FAA PilotWeb at https://pilotweb.nas.faa.gov. Military NOTAMs are available using the Defense Internet NOTAM Service (DINS) at https://www.notams.faa.gov. Pilots flying to or from airports not available through the FAA PilotWeb or DINS can obtain assistance from Flight Service.

⑰ FAA INSPECTION

All airports not inspected by FAA will be identified by the note: Not insp. This indicates that the airport information has been provided by the owner or operator of the field.

⑱ RUNWAY DATA

Runway information is shown on two lines. That information common to the entire runway is shown on the first line while information concerning the runway ends is shown on the second or following line. Runway direction, surface, length, width, weight bearing capacity, lighting, and slope, when available are shown for each runway. Multiple runways are shown with the longest runway first. Direction, length, width, and lighting are shown for sea–lanes. The full dimensions of helipads are shown, e.g., 50X150. Runway data that requires clarification will be placed in the remarks section.

RUNWAY DESIGNATION

Runways are normally numbered in relation to their magnetic orientation rounded off to the nearest 10 degrees. Parallel runways can be designated L (left)/R (right)/C (center). Runways may be designated as Ultralight or assault strips. Assault strips are shown by magnetic bearing.

RUNWAY DIMENSIONS

Runway length and width are shown in feet. Length shown is runway end to end including displaced thresholds, but excluding those areas designed as overruns.

RUNWAY SURFACE AND SURFACE TREATMENT

Runway lengths prefixed by the letter "H" indicate that the runways are hard surfaced (concrete, asphalt, or part asphalt–concrete). If the runway length is not prefixed, the surface is sod, clay, etc. The runway surface composition is indicated in parentheses after runway length as follows:

(AFSC)—Aggregate friction seal coat
(AM2)—Temporary metal planks coated with nonskid material
(ASPH)—Asphalt
(CONC)—Concrete
(DIRT)—Dirt
(GRVD)—Grooved
(GRVL)—Gravel, or cinders
(MATS)—Pierced steel planking, landing mats, membranes
(PEM)—Part concrete, part asphalt
(PFC)—Porous friction courses
(PSP)—Pierced steel plank
(RFSC)—Rubberized friction seal coat
(SAND)—Sand
(TURF)—Turf
(TRTD)—Treated
(WC)—Wire combed

LEGEND 6.—Airport/Facility Directory.

AIRPORT/FACILITY DIRECTORY LEGEND 17

RUNWAY WEIGHT BEARING CAPACITY

Runway strength data shown in this publication is derived from available information and is a realistic estimate of capability at an average level of activity. It is not intended as a maximum allowable weight or as an operating limitation. Many airport pavements are capable of supporting limited operations with gross weights in excess of the published figures. Permissible operating weights, insofar as runway strengths are concerned, are a matter of agreement between the owner and user. When desiring to operate into any airport at weights in excess of those published in the publication, users should contact the airport management for permission. Runway strength figures are shown in thousand of pounds, with the last three figures being omitted. Add 000 to figure following S, D, 2S, 2T, AUW, SWL, etc., for gross weight capacity. A blank space following the letter designator is used to indicate the runway can sustain aircraft with this type landing gear, although definite runway weight bearing capacity figures are not available, e.g., S, D. Applicable codes for typical gear configurations with S=Single, D=Dual, T=Triple and Q=Quadruple:

CURRENT	NEW	NEW DESCRIPTION
S	S	Single wheel type landing gear (DC3), (C47), (F15), etc.
D	D	Dual wheel type landing gear (BE1900), (B737), (A319), etc.
T	D	Dual wheel type landing gear (P3, C9).
ST	2S	Two single wheels in tandem type landing gear (C130).
TRT	2T	Two triple wheels in tandem type landing gear (C17), etc.
DT	2D	Two dual wheels in tandem type landing gear (B707), etc.
TT	2D	Two dual wheels in tandem type landing gear (B757, KC135).
SBTT	2D/D1	Two dual wheels in tandem/dual wheel body gear type landing gear (KC10).
None	2D/2D1	Two dual wheels in tandem/two dual wheels in tandem body gear type landing gear (A340–600).
DDT	2D/2D2	Two dual wheels in tandem/two dual wheels in double tandem body gear type landing gear (B747, E4).
TTT	3D	Three dual wheels in tandem type landing gear (B777), etc.
TT	D2	Dual wheel gear two struts per side main gear type landing gear (B52).
TDT	C5	Complex dual wheel and quadruple wheel combination landing gear (C5).

AUW—All up weight. Maximum weight bearing capacity for any aircraft irrespective of landing gear configuration.

SWL—Single Wheel Loading. (This includes information submitted in terms of Equivalent Single Wheel Loading (ESWL) and Single Isolated Wheel Loading).

PSI—Pounds per square inch. PSI is the actual figure expressing maximum pounds per square inch runway will support, e.g., (SWL 000/PSI 535).

Omission of weight bearing capacity indicates information unknown.

The ACN/PCN System is the ICAO standard method of reporting pavement strength for pavements with bearing strengths greater than 12,500 pounds. The Pavement Classification Number (PCN) is established by an engineering assessment of the runway. The PCN is for use in conjunction with an Aircraft Classification Number (ACN). Consult the Aircraft Flight Manual, Flight Information Handbook, or other appropriate source for ACN tables or charts. Currently, ACN data may not be available for all aircraft. If an ACN table or chart is available, the ACN can be calculated by taking into account the aircraft weight, the pavement type, and the subgrade category. For runways that have been evaluated under the ACN/PCN system, the PCN will be shown as a five–part code (e.g. PCN 80 R/B/W/T). Details of the coded format are as follows:

NOTE: Prior permission from the airport controlling authority is required when the ACN of the aircraft exceeds the published PCN or aircraft tire pressure exceeds the published limits.

(1) The PCN NUMBER—The reported PCN indicates that an aircraft with an ACN equal or less than the reported PCN can operate on the pavement subject to any limitation on the tire pressure.

(2) The type of pavement:
- R — Rigid
- F — Flexible

(3) The pavement subgrade category:
- A — High
- B — Medium
- C — Low
- D — Ultra–low

(4) The maximum tire pressure authorized for the pavement:
- W — Unlimited, no pressure limit
- X — High, limited to 254 psi (1.75 MPa)
- Y — Medium, limited to 181 psi (1.25MPa)
- Z — Low, limited to 73 psi (0.50 MPa)

(5) Pavement evaluation method:
- T — Technical evaluation
- U — By experience of aircraft using the pavement

RUNWAY LIGHTING

Lights are in operation sunset to sunrise. Lighting available by prior arrangement only or operating part of the night and/or pilot controlled lighting with specific operating hours are indicated under airport or military remarks. At USN/USMC facilities lights are available only during airport hours of operation. Since obstructions are usually lighted, obstruction lighting is not included in this code. Unlighted obstructions on or surrounding an airport will be noted in airport or military remarks. Runway lights nonstandard (NSTD) are systems for which the light fixtures are not FAA approved L–800 series: color, intensity, or spacing does not meet FAA standards. Nonstandard runway lights, VASI, or any other system not listed below will be shown in airport remarks or military

LEGEND 7.—Airport/Facility Directory.

service. Temporary, emergency or limited runway edge lighting such as flares, smudge pots, lanterns or portable runway lights will also be shown in airport remarks or military service. Types of lighting are shown with the runway or runway end they serve.

NSTD—Light system fails to meet FAA standards.
LIRL—Low Intensity Runway Lights.
MIRL—Medium Intensity Runway Lights.
HIRL—High Intensity Runway Lights.
RAIL—Runway Alignment Indicator Lights.
REIL—Runway End Identifier Lights.
CL—Centerline Lights.
TDZL—Touchdown Zone Lights.
ODALS—Omni Directional Approach Lighting System.
AF OVRN—Air Force Overrun 1000′ Standard Approach Lighting System.
MALS—Medium Intensity Approach Lighting System.
MALSF—Medium Intensity Approach Lighting System with Sequenced Flashing Lights.
MALSR—Medium Intensity Approach Lighting System with Runway Alignment Indicator Lights.
RLLS—Runway Lead–in Light System
SALS—Short Approach Lighting System.
SALSF—Short Approach Lighting System with Sequenced Flashing Lights.
SSALS—Simplified Short Approach Lighting System.
SSALF—Simplified Short Approach Lighting System with Sequenced Flashing Lights.
SSALR—Simplified Short Approach Lighting System with Runway Alignment Indicator Lights.
ALSAF—High Intensity Approach Lighting System with Sequenced Flashing Lights.
ALSF1—High Intensity Approach Lighting System with Sequenced Flashing Lights, Category I, Configuration.
ALSF2—High Intensity Approach Lighting System with Sequenced Flashing Lights, Category II, Configuration.
SF—Sequenced Flashing Lights.
OLS—Optical Landing System.
WAVE–OFF.

NOTE: Civil ALSF2 may be operated as SSALR during favorable weather conditions. When runway edge lights are positioned more than 10 feet from the edge of the usable runway surface a remark will be added in the "Remarks" portion of the airport entry. This is applicable to Air Force, Air National Guard and Air Force Reserve Bases, and those joint use airfields on which they are tenants.

VISUAL GLIDESLOPE INDICATORS

APAP—A system of panels, which may or may not be lighted, used for alignment of approach path.

PNIL	APAP on left side of runway	PNIR	APAP on right side of runway

PAPI—Precision Approach Path Indicator

P2L	2–identical light units placed on left side of runway	P4L	4–identical light units placed on left side of runway
P2R	2–identical light units placed on right side of runway	P4R	4–identical light units placed on right side of runway

PVASI—Pulsating/steady burning visual approach slope Indlcator, normally a single light unit projecting two colors.

PSIL	PVASI on left side of runway	PSIR	PVASI on right side of runway

SAVASI—Simplified Abbreviated Visual Approach Slope Indicator

S2L	2–box SAVASI on left side of runway	S2R	2–box SAVASI on right side of runway

TRCV—Tri–color visual approach slope indicator, normally a single light unit projecting three colors.

TRIL	TRCV on left side of runway	TRIR	TRCV on right side of runway

VASI—Visual Approach Slope Indicator

V2L	2–box VASI on left side of runway	V6L	6–box VASI on left side of runway
V2R	2–box VASI on right side of runway	V6R	6–box VASI on right side of runway
V4L	4–box VASI on left side of runway	V12	12–box VASI on both sides of runway
V4R	4–box VASI on right side of runway	V16	16–box VASI on both sides of runway

NOTE: Approach slope angle and threshold crossing height will be shown when available; i.e., –GA 3.5° TCH 37′.

PILOT CONTROL OF AIRPORT LIGHTING

Key Mike	Function
7 times within 5 seconds	Highest intensity available
5 times within 5 seconds	Medium or lower intensity (Lower REIL or REIL–Off)
3 times within 5 seconds	Lowest intensity available (Lower REIL or REIL–Off)

Available systems will be indicated in the Service section, e.g., **LGT** ACTIVATE HIRL Rwy 07–25, MALSR Rwy 07, and VASI Rwy 07—122.8.

Where the airport is not served by an instrument approach procedure and/or has an independent type system of different specification installed by the airport sponsor, descriptions of the type lights, method of control, and operating frequency will be explained in clear text. See AIM, "Basic Flight Information and ATC Procedures," for detailed description of pilot control of airport lighting.

RUNWAY SLOPE

When available, runway slope data will be provided. Runway slope will be shown only when it is 0.3 percent or greater. On runways less than 8000 feet, the direction of the slope up will be indicated, e.g., 0.3% up NW. On runways 8000 feet or greater, the slope will be shown (up or down) on the runway end line, e.g., RWY 13: 0.3% up., RWY 31: Pole. Rgt tfc. 0.4% down.

Legend 8.—Airport/Facility Directory.

AIRPORT/FACILITY DIRECTORY LEGEND 19

RUNWAY END DATA

Information pertaining to the runway approach end such as approach lights, touchdown zone lights, runway end identification lights, visual glideslope indicators, displaced thresholds, controlling obstruction, and right hand traffic pattern, will be shown on the specific runway end. "Rgt tfc"—Right traffic indicates right turns should be made on landing and takeoff for specified runway end. Runway Visual Range shall be shown as "RVR" appended with "T" for touchdown, "M" for midpoint, and "R" for rollout; e.g., RVR-TMR.

⑲ LAND AND HOLD–SHORT OPERATIONS (LAHSO)

LAHSO is an acronym for "Land and Hold–Short Operations" These operations include landing and holding short of an intersection runway, an intersecting taxiway, or other predetermined points on the runway other than a runway or taxiway. Measured distance represents the available landing distance on the landing runway, in feet.

Specific questions regarding these distances should be referred to the air traffic manager of the facility concerned. The Aeronautical Information Manual contains specific details on hold–short operations and markings.

⑳ RUNWAY DECLARED DISTANCE INFORMATION

TORA—Take–off Run Available. The length of runway declared available and suitable for the ground run of an aeroplane take–off.

TODA—Take–off Distance Available. The length of the take–off run available plus the length of the clearway, if provided.

ASDA—Accelerate–Stop Distance Available. The length of the take–off run available plus the length of the stopway, if provided.

LDA—Landing Distance Available. The length of runway which is declared available and suitable for the ground run of an aeroplane landing.

㉑ ARRESTING GEAR/SYSTEMS

Arresting gear is shown as it is located on the runway. The a–gear distance from the end of the appropriate runway (or into the overrun) is indicated in parentheses. A–Gear which has a bi–direction capability and can be utilized for emergency approach end engagement is indicated by a (B). Up to 15 minutes advance notice may be required for rigging A–Gear for approach and engagement. Airport listing may show availability of other than US Systems. This information is provided for emergency requirements only. Refer to current aircraft operating manuals for specific engagement weight and speed criteria based on aircraft structural restrictions and arresting system limitations.

Following is a list of current systems referenced in this publication identified by both Air Force and Navy terminology:

BI–DIRECTIONAL CABLE (B)

TYPE	DESCRIPTION
BAK–9	Rotary friction brake.
BAK–12A	Standard BAK–12 with 950 foot run out, 1–inch cable and 40,000 pound weight setting. Rotary friction brake.
BAK–12B	Extended BAK–12 with 1200 foot run, 1¼ inch Cable and 50,000 pounds weight setting. Rotary friction brake.
E28	Rotary Hydraulic (Water Brake).
M21	Rotary Hydraulic (Water Brake) Mobile.

The following device is used in conjunction with some aircraft arresting systems:

BAK–14	A device that raises a hook cable out of a slot in the runway surface and is remotely positioned for engagement by the tower on request. (In addition to personnel reaction time, the system requires up to five seconds to fully raise the cable.)
H	A device that raises a hook cable out of a slot in the runway surface and is remotely positioned for engagement by the tower on request. (In addition to personnel reaction time, the system requires up to one and one–half seconds to fully raise the cable.)

UNI–DIRECTIONAL CABLE

TYPE	DESCRIPTION
MB60	Textile brake—an emergency one–time use, modular braking system employing the tearing of specially woven textile straps to absorb the kinetic energy.
E5/E5–1/E5–3	Chain Type. At USN/USMC stations E–5 A–GEAR systems are rated, e.g., E–5 RATING–13R–1100 HW (DRY), 31L/R–1200 STD (WET). This rating is a function of the A–GEAR chain weight and length and is used to determine the maximum aircraft engaging speed. A dry rating applies to a stabilized surface (dry or wet) while a wet rating takes into account the amount (if any) of wet overrun that is not capable of withstanding the aircraft weight. These ratings are published under Service/Military/A-Gear in the entry.

FOREIGN CABLE

TYPE	DESCRIPTION	US EQUIVALENT
44B–3H	Rotary Hydraulic (Water Brake)	
CHAG	Chain	E–5

UNI–DIRECTIONAL BARRIER

TYPE	DESCRIPTION
MA–1A	Web barrier between stanchions attached to a chain energy absorber.
BAK–15	Web barrier between stanchions attached to an energy absorber (water squeezer, rotary friction, chain). Designed for wing engagement.

NOTE: Landing short of the runway threshold on a runway with a BAK–15 in the underrun is a significant hazard. The barrier in the down position still protrudes several inches above the underrun. Aircraft contact with the barrier short of the runway threshold can cause damage to the barrier and substantial damage to the aircraft.

OTHER

TYPE	DESCRIPTION
EMAS	Engineered Material Arresting System, located beyond the departure end of the runway, consisting of high energy absorbing materials which will crush under the weight of an aircraft.

Legend 9.—Airport/Facility Directory.

AIRPORT/FACILITY DIRECTORY LEGEND

㉒ SERVICE

SERVICING—CIVIL

S1: Minor airframe repairs.
S2: Minor airframe and minor powerplant repairs.
S3: Major airframe and minor powerplant repairs.
S4: Major airframe and major powerplant repairs.
S5: Major airframe repairs.
S6: Minor airframe and major powerplant repairs.
S7: Major powerplant repairs.
S8: Minor powerplant repairs.

FUEL—CIVIL

CODE	FUEL
80	Grade 80 gasoline (Red)
100	Grade 100 gasoline (Green)
100LL	100LL gasoline (low lead) (Blue)
115	Grade 115 gasoline (115/145 military specification) (Purple)
A	Jet A, Kerosene, without FS–II*, FP** minus 40° C.
A+	Jet A, Kerosene, with FS–II*, FP** minus 40°C.
A++	Jet A, Kerosene, with FS–II*, CI/LI#, SDA##, FP** minus 40°C.
A++100	Jet A, Kerosene, with FS–II*, CI/LI#, SDA##, FP** minus 40°C, with +100 fuel additive that improves thermal stability characteristics of kerosene jet fuels.
A1	Jet A–1, Kerosene, without FS–II*, FP** minus 47°C.
A1+	Jet A–1, Kerosene with FS–II*, FP** minus 47° C.
B	Jet B, Wide–cut, turbine fuel without FS–II*, FP** minus 50° C.
B+	Jet B, Wide–cut, turbine fuel with FS–II*, FP** minus 50° C
J4 (JP4)	(JP–4 military specification) FP** minus 58° C.
J5 (JP5)	(JP–5 military specification) Kerosene with FS–II, FP** minus 46°C.
J8 (JP8)	(JP–8 military specification) Jet A–1, Kerosene with FS–II*, CI/LI#, SDA##, FP** minus 47°C.
J8+100	(JP–8 military specification) Jet A–1, Kerosene with FS–II*, CI/LI#, SDA##,FP** minus 47°C, with +100 fuel additive that improves thermal stability characteristics of kerosene jet fuels.
J	(Jet Fuel Type Unknown)
MOGAS	Automobile gasoline which is to be used as aircraft fuel.

*(Fuel System Icing Inhibitor) **(Freeze Point) # (Corrosion Inhibitors/Lubricity Improvers) ## (Static Dissipator Additive)

NOTE: Certain automobile gasoline may be used in specific aircraft engines if a FAA supplemental type certificate has been obtained. Automobile gasoline, which is to be used in aircraft engines, will be identified as "MOGAS", however, the grade/type and other octane rating will not be published.

Data shown on fuel availability represents the most recent information the publisher has been able to acquire. Because of a variety of factors, the fuel listed may not always be obtainable by transient civil pilots. Confirmation of availability of fuel should be made directly with fuel suppliers at locations where refueling is planned.

OXYGEN—CIVIL

OX 1 High Pressure
OX 2 Low Pressure
OX 3 High Pressure—Replacement Bottles
OX 4 Low Pressure—Replacement Bottles

SERVICE—MILITARY

Specific military services available at the airport are listed under this general heading. Remarks applicable to any military service are shown in the individual service listing.

JET AIRCRAFT STARTING UNITS (JASU)—MILITARY

The numeral preceding the type of unit indicates the number of units available. The absence of the numeral indicates ten or more units available. If the number of units is unknown, the number one will be shown. Absence of JASU designation indicates non–availability.

The following is a list of current JASU systems referenced in this publication:

USAF JASU (For variations in technical data, refer to T.O. 35–1–7.)

ELECTRICAL STARTING UNITS:

A/M32A–86	AC: 115/200v, 3 phase, 90 kva, 0.8 pf, 4 wire DC: 28v, 1500 amp, 72 kw (with TR pack)
MC–1A	AC: 115/208v, 400 cycle, 3 phase, 37.5 kva, 0.8 pf, 108 amp, 4 wire DC: 28v, 500 amp, 14 kw
MD–3	AC: 115/208v, 400 cycle, 3 phase, 60 kva, 0.75 pf, 4 wire DC: 28v, 1500 amp, 45 kw, split bus
MD–3A	AC: 115/208v, 400 cycle, 3 phase, 60 kva, 0.75 pf, 4 wire DC: 28v, 1500 amp, 45 kw, split bus
MD–3M	AC: 115/208v, 400 cycle, 3 phase, 60 kva, 0.75 pf, 4 wire DC: 28v, 500 amp, 15 kw
MD–4	AC: 120/208v, 400 cycle, 3 phase, 62.5 kva, 0.8 pf, 175 amp, "WYE" neutral ground, 4 wire, 120v, 400 cycle, 3 phase, 62.5 kva, 0.8 pf, 303 amp, "DELTA" 3 wire, 120v, 400 cycle, 1 phase, 62.5 kva, 0.8 pf, 520 amp, 2 wire

LEGEND 10.—Airport/Facility Directory.

AIRPORT/FACILITY DIRECTORY LEGEND 21

AIR STARTING UNITS

AM32–95	150 +/– 5 lb/min (2055 +/– 68 cfm) at 51 +/– 2 psia
AM32A–95	150 +/– 5 lb/min @ 49 +/– 2 psia (35 +/– 2 psig)
LASS	150 +/– 5 lb/min @ 49 +/– 2 psia
MA–1A	82 lb/min (1123 cfm) at 130° air inlet temp, 45 psia (min) air outlet press
MC–1	15 cfm, 3500 psia
MC–1A	15 cfm, 3500 psia
MC–2A	15 cfm, 200 psia
MC–11	8,000 cu in cap, 4000 psig, 15 cfm

COMBINED AIR AND ELECTRICAL STARTING UNITS:

AGPU	AC: 115/200v, 400 cycle, 3 phase, 30 kw gen
	DC: 28v, 700 amp
	AIR: 60 lb/min @ 40 psig @ sea level
AM32A–60*	AIR: 120 +/– 4 lb/min (1644 +/– 55 cfm) at 49 +/– 2 psia
	AC: 120/208v, 400 cycle, 3 phase, 75 kva, 0.75 pf, 4 wire, 120v, 1 phase, 25 kva
	DC: 28v, 500 amp, 15 kw
AM32A–60A	AIR: 150 +/– 5 lb/min (2055 +/– 68 cfm at 51 +/– psia
	AC: 120/208v, 400 cycle, 3 phase, 75 kva, 0.75 pf, 4 wire
	DC: 28v, 200 amp, 5.6 kw
AM32A–60B*	AIR: 130 lb/min, 50 psia
	AC: 120/208v, 400 cycle, 3 phase, 75 kva, 0.75 pf, 4 wire
	DC: 28v, 200 amp, 5.6 kw

*NOTE: During combined air and electrical loads, the pneumatic circuitry takes preference and will limit the amount of electrical power available.

USN JASU

ELECTRICAL STARTING UNITS:

NC–8A/A1	DC: 500 amp constant, 750 amp intermittent, 28v;
	AC: 60 kva @ .8 pf, 115/200v, 3 phase, 400 Hz.
NC–10A/A1/B/C	DC: 750 amp constant, 1000 amp intermittent, 28v;
	AC: 90 kva, 115/200v, 3 phase, 400 Hz.

AIR STARTING UNITS:

GTC–85/GTE–85	120 lbs/min @ 45 psi.
MSU–200NAV/A/U47A–5	204 lbs/min @ 56 psia.
WELLS AIR START SYSTEM	180 lbs/min @ 75 psi or 120 lbs/min @ 45 psi. Simultaneous multiple start capability.

COMBINED AIR AND ELECTRICAL STARTING UNITS:

NCPP–105/RCPT	180 lbs/min @ 75 psi or 120 lbs/min @ 45 psi. 700 amp, 28v DC. 120/208v, 400 Hz AC, 30 kva.

ARMY JASU

59B2–1B	28v, 7.5 kw, 280 amp.

OTHER JASU

ELECTRICAL STARTING UNITS (DND):

CE12	AC 115/200v, 140 kva, 400 Hz, 3 phase
CE13	AC 115/200v, 60 kva, 400 Hz, 3 phase
CE14	AC/DC 115/200v, 140 kva, 400 Hz, 3 phase, 28vDC, 1500 amp
CE15	DC 22–35v, 500 amp continuous 1100 amp intermittent
CE16	DC 22–35v, 500 amp continuous 1100 amp intermittent soft start

AIR STARTING UNITS (DND):

CA2	ASA 45.5 psig, 116.4 lb/min

COMBINED AIR AND ELECTRICAL STARTING UNITS (DND)

CEA1	AC 120/208v, 60 kva, 400 Hz, 3 phase DC 28v, 75 amp
	AIR 112.5 lb/min, 47 psig

ELECTRICAL STARTING UNITS (OTHER)

C–26	28v 45kw 115–200v 15kw 380–800 Hz 1 phase 2 wire
C–26–B, C–26–C	28v 45kw: Split Bus: 115–200v 15kw 380–800 Hz 1 phase 2 wire
E3	DC 28v/10kw

AIR STARTING UNITS (OTHER):

A4	40 psi/2 lb/sec (LPAS Mk12, Mk12L, Mk12A, Mk1, Mk2B)
MA–1	150 Air HP, 115 lb/min 50 psia
MA–2	250 Air HP, 150 lb/min 75 psia

CARTRIDGE:

MXU–4A	USAF

LEGEND 11.—Airport/Facility Directory.

22 **AIRPORT/FACILITY DIRECTORY LEGEND**

FUEL—MILITARY

Fuel available through US Military Base supply, DESC Into–Plane Contracts and/or reciprocal agreement is listed first and is followed by (Mil). At commercial airports where Into–Plane contracts are in place, the name of the refueling agent is shown. Military fuel should be used first if it is available. When military fuel cannot be obtained but Into–Plane contract fuel is available, Government aircraft must refuel with the contract fuel and applicable refueling agent to avoid any breach in contract terms and conditions. Fuel not available through the above is shown preceded by NC (no contract). When fuel is obtained from NC sources, local purchase procedures must be followed. The US Military Aircraft Identaplates DD Form 1896 (Jet Fuel), DD Form 1897 (Avgas) and AF Form 1245 (Avgas) are used at military installations only. The US Government Aviation Into–Plane Reimbursement (AIR) Card (currently issued by AVCARD) is the instrument to be used to obtain fuel under a DESC Into–Plane Contract and for NC purchases if the refueling agent at the commercial airport accepts the AVCARD. A current list of contract fuel locations is available online at https://cis.energy.dla.mil/ip_cis/. See legend item 14 for fuel code and description.

SUPPORTING FLUIDS AND SYSTEMS—MILITARY

CODE	
ADI	Anti–Detonation Injection Fluid—Reciprocating Engine Aircraft.
W	Water Thrust Augmentation—Jet Aircraft.
WAI	Water–Alcohol Injection Type, Thrust Augmentation—Jet Aircraft.
SP	Single Point Refueling.
PRESAIR	Air Compressors rated 3,000 PSI or more.
De–Ice	Anti–icing/De–icing/Defrosting Fluid (MIL–A–8243).

OXYGEN:

LPOX	Low pressure oxygen servicing.
HPOX	High pressure oxygen servicing.
LHOX	Low and high pressure oxygen servicing.
LOX	Liquid oxygen servicing.
OXRB	Oxygen replacement bottles. (Maintained primarily at Naval stations for use in acft where oxygen can be replenished only by replacement of cylinders.)
OX	Indicates oxygen servicing when type of servicing is unknown.

NOTE: Combinations of above items is used to indicate complete oxygen servicing available;

LHOXRB	Low and high pressure oxygen servicing and replacement bottles;
LPOXRB	Low pressure oxygen replacement bottles only, etc.

NOTE: Aircraft will be serviced with oxygen procured under military specifications only. Aircraft will not be serviced with medical oxygen.

NITROGEN:

LPNIT — Low pressure nitrogen servicing.

HPNIT — High pressure nitrogen servicing.

LHNIT — Low and high pressure nitrogen servicing.

OIL—MILITARY

US AVIATION OILS (MIL SPECS):

CODE	GRADE, TYPE
O–113	1065, Reciprocating Engine Oil (MIL–L–6082)
O–117	1100, Reciprocating Engine Oil (MIL–L–6082)
O–117+	1100, O–117 plus cyclohexanone (MIL–L–6082)
O–123	1065, (Dispersant), Reciprocating Engine Oil (MIL–L–22851 Type III)
O–128	1100, (Dispersant), Reciprocating Engine Oil (MIL–L–22851 Type II)
O–132	1005, Jet Engine Oil (MIL–L–6081)
O–133	1010, Jet Engine Oil (MIL–L–6081)
O–147	None, MIL–L–6085A Lubricating Oil, Instrument, Synthetic
O–148	None, MIL–L–7808 (Synthetic Base) Turbine Engine Oil
O–149	None, Aircraft Turbine Engine Synthetic, 7.5c St
O–155	None, MIL–L–6086C, Aircraft, Medium Grade
O–156	None, MIL–L–23699 (Synthetic Base), Turboprop and Turboshaft Engines
JOAP/SOAP	Joint Oil Analysis Program. JOAP support is furnished during normal duty hours, other times on request. (JOAP and SOAP programs provide essentially the same service, JOAP is now the standard joint service supported program.)

TRANSIENT ALERT (TRAN ALERT)—MILITARY

Tran Alert service is considered to include all services required for normal aircraft turn–around, e.g., servicing (fuel, oil, oxygen, etc.), debriefing to determine requirements for maintenance, minor maintenance, inspection and parking assistance of transient aircraft. Drag chute repack, specialized maintenance, or extensive repairs will be provided within the capabilities and priorities of the base. Delays can be anticipated after normal duty hours/holidays/weekends regardless of the hours of transient maintenance operation. Pilots should not expect aircraft to be serviced for TURN–AROUNDS during time periods when servicing or maintenance manpower is not available. In the case of airports not operated exclusively by US military, the servicing indicated by the remarks will not always be available for US military aircraft. When transient alert services are not shown, facilities are unknown. NO PRIORITY BASIS—means that transient alert services will be provided only after all the requirements for mission/tactical assigned aircraft have been accomplished.

Legend 12.—Airport/Facility Directory.

AIRPORT/FACILITY DIRECTORY LEGEND 23

㉓ AIRPORT REMARKS

The Attendance Schedule is the months, days and hours the airport is actually attended. Airport attendance does not mean watchman duties or telephone accessibility, but rather an attendant or operator on duty to provide at least minimum services (e.g., repairs, fuel, transportation).

Airport Remarks have been grouped in order of applicability. Airport remarks are limited to those items of information that are determined essential for operational use, i.e., conditions of a permanent or indefinite nature and conditions that will remain in effect for more than 30 days concerning aeronautical facilities, services, maintenance available, procedures or hazards, knowledge of which is essential for safe and efficient operation of aircraft. Information concerning permanent closing of a runway or taxiway will not be shown. A note "See Special Notices" shall be applied within this remarks section when a special notice applicable to the entry is contained in the Special Notices section of this publication.

Parachute Jumping indicates parachute jumping areas associated with the airport. See Parachute Jumping Area section of this publication for additional Information.

Landing Fee indicates landing charges for private or non–revenue producing aircraft. In addition, fees may be charged for planes that remain over a couple of hours and buy no services, or at major airline terminals for all aircraft.

Note: Unless otherwise stated, remarks including runway ends refer to the runway's approach end.

㉔ MILITARY REMARKS

Joint Civil/Military airports contain both Airport Remarks and Military Remarks. Military Remarks published for these airports are applicable only to the military. Military and joint Military/Civil airports contain only Military Remarks. Remarks contained in this section may not be applicable to civil users. When both sets of remarks exist, the first set is applicable to the primary operator of the airport. Remarks applicable to a tenant on the airport are shown preceded by the tenant organization, i.e., (A) (AF) (N) (ANG), etc. Military airports operate 24 hours unless otherwise specified. Airport operating hours are listed first (airport operating hours will only be listed if they are different than the airport attended hours or if the attended hours are unavailable) followed by pertinent remarks in order of applicability. Remarks will include information on restrictions, hazards, traffic pattern, noise abatement, customs/agriculture/immigration, and miscellaneous information applicable to the Military.

Type of restrictions:

CLOSED: When designated closed, the airport is restricted from use by all aircraft unless stated otherwise. Any closure applying to specific type of aircraft or operation will be so stated. USN/USMC/USAF airports are considered closed during non–operating hours. Closed airports may be utilized during an emergency provided there is a safe landing area.

OFFICIAL BUSINESS ONLY: The airfield is closed to all transient military aircraft for obtaining routine services such as fueling, passenger drop off or pickup, practice approaches, parking, etc. The airfield may be used by aircrews and aircraft if official government business (including civilian) must be conducted on or near the airfield and prior permission is received from the airfield manager.

AF OFFICIAL BUSINESS ONLY OR NAVY OFFICIAL BUSINESS ONLY: Indicates that the restriction applies only to service indicated.

PRIOR PERMISSION REQUIRED (PPR): Airport is closed to transient aircraft unless approval for operation is obtained from the appropriate commander through Chief, Airfield Management or Airfield Operations Officer. Official Business or PPR does not preclude the use of US Military airports as an alternate for IFR flights. If a non–US military airport is used as a weather alternate and requires a PPR, the PPR must be requested and confirmed before the flight departs. The purpose of PPR is to control volume and flow of traffic rather than to prohibit it. Prior permission is required for all aircraft requiring transient alert service outside the published transient alert duty hours. All aircraft carrying hazardous materials must obtain prior permission as outlined in AFJI 11–204, AR 95–27, OPNAVINST 3710.7.

Note: OFFICIAL BUSINESS ONLY AND PPR restrictions are not applicable to Special Air Mission (SAM) or Special Air Resource (SPAR) aircraft providing person or persons on aboard are designated Code 6 or higher as explained in AFJMAN 11–213, AR 95–11, OPNAVINST 3722–8J. Official Business Only or PPR do not preclude the use of the airport as an alternate for IFR flights.

㉕ AIRPORT MANAGER

The phone number of the airport manager.

㉖ WEATHER DATA SOURCES

Weather data sources will be listed alphabetically followed by their assigned frequencies and/or telephone number and hours of operation.

ASOS—Automated Surface Observing System. Reports the same as an AWOS–3 plus precipitation identification and intensity, and freezing rain occurrence;

AWOS—Automated Weather Observing System

AWOS–A—reports altimeter setting (all other information is advisory only).

AWOS–AV—reports altimeter and visibility.

AWOS–1—reports altimeter setting, wind data and usually temperature, dew point and density altitude.

AWOS–2—reports the same as AWOS–1 plus visibility.

AWOS–3—reports the same as AWOS–1 plus visibility and cloud/ceiling data.

AWOS–3P reports the same as the AWOS–3 system, plus a precipitation identification sensor.

AWOS–3PT reports the same as the AWOS–3 system, plus precipitation identification sensor and a thunderstorm/lightning reporting capability.

LEGEND 13.—Airport/Facility Directory.

AIRPORT/FACILITY DIRECTORY LEGEND

AWOS–3T reports the same as AWOS–3 system and includes a thunderstorm/lightning reporting capability.

See AIM, Basic Flight Information and ATC Procedures for detailed description of Weather Data Sources.

AWOS–4—reports same as AWOS–3 system, plus precipitation occurrence, type and accumulation, freezing rain, thunderstorm and runway surface sensors.

HIWAS—See RADIO AIDS TO NAVIGATION

LAWRS—Limited Aviation Weather Reporting Station where observers report cloud height, weather, obstructions to vision, temperature and dewpoint (in most cases), surface wind, altimeter and pertinent remarks.

LLWAS—indicates a Low Level Wind Shear Alert System consisting of a center field and several field perimeter anemometers.

SAWRS—identifies airports that have a Supplemental Aviation Weather Reporting Station available to pilots for current weather information.

SWSL—Supplemental Weather Service Location providing current local weather information via radio and telephone.

TDWR—indicates airports that have Terminal Doppler Weather Radar.

WSP—indicates airports that have Weather System Processor.

When the automated weather source is broadcast over an associated airport NAVAID frequency (see NAVAID line), it shall be indicated by a bold ASOS, AWOS, or HIWAS followed by the frequency, identifier and phone number, if available.

㉗ COMMUNICATIONS

Airport terminal control facilities and radio communications associated with the airport shall be shown. When the call sign is not the same as the airport name the call sign will be shown. Frequencies shall normally be shown in descending order with the primary frequency listed first. Frequencies will be listed, together with sectorization indicated by outbound radials, and hours of operation. Communications will be listed in sequence as follows:

Single Frequency Approach (SFA), Common Traffic Advisory Frequency (CTAF), Aeronautical Advisory Stations (UNICOM) or (AUNICOM), and Automatic Terminal Information Service (ATIS) along with their frequency is shown, where available, on the line following the heading "COMMUNICATIONS." When the CTAF and UNICOM frequencies are the same, the frequency will be shown as CTAF/UNICOM 122.8.

The FSS telephone nationwide is toll free 1–800–WX–BRIEF (1–800–992–7433). When the FSS is located on the field it will be indicated as "on arpt". Frequencies available at the FSS will follow in descending order. Remote Communications Outlet (RCO) providing service to the airport followed by the frequency and FSS RADIO name will be shown when available. FSS's provide information on airport conditions, radio aids and other facilities, and process flight plans. Airport Advisory Service (AAS) is provided on the CTAF by FSS's for select non–tower airports or airports where the tower is not in operation.

(See AIM, Para 4–1–9 Traffic Advisory Practices at Airports Without Operating Control Towers or AC 90–42C.)

Aviation weather briefing service is provided by FSS specialists. Flight and weather briefing services are also available by calling the telephone numbers listed.

Remote Communications Outlet (RCO)—An unmanned air/ground communications facility that is remotely controlled and provides UHF or VHF communications capability to extend the service range of an FSS.

Civil Communications Frequencies–Civil communications frequencies used in the FSS air/ground system are operated on 122.0, 122.2, 123.6; emergency 121.5; plus receive–only on 122.1.

a. 122.0 is assigned as the Enroute Flight Advisory Service frequency at selected FSS RADIO outlets.
b. 122.2 is assigned as a common enroute frequency.
c. 123.6 is assigned as the airport advisory frequency at select non–tower locations. At airports with a tower, FSS may provide airport advisories on the tower frequency when tower is closed.
d. 122.1 is the primary receive–only frequency at VOR's.
e. Some FSS's are assigned 50 kHz frequencies in the 122–126 MHz band (eg. 122.45). Pilots using the FSS A/G system should refer to this directory or appropriate charts to determine frequencies available at the FSS or remoted facility through which they wish to communicate.

Emergency frequency 121.5 and 243.0 are available at all Flight Service Stations, most Towers, Approach Control and RADAR facilities.

Frequencies published followed by the letter "T" or "R", indicate that the facility will only transmit or receive respectively on that frequency. All radio aids to navigation (NAVAID) frequencies are transmit only.

TERMINAL SERVICES

SFA—Single Frequency Approach.

CTAF—A program designed to get all vehicles and aircraft at airports without an operating control tower on a common frequency.

ATIS—A continuous broadcast of recorded non–control information in selected terminal areas.

D–ATIS—Digital ATIS provides ATIS information in text form outside the standard reception range of conventional ATIS via landline & data link communications and voice message within range of existing transmitters.

AUNICOM—Automated UNICOM is a computerized, command response system that provides automated weather, radio check capability and airport advisory information selected from an automated menu by microphone clicks.

UNICOM—A non–government air/ground radio communications facility which may provide airport information.

PTD—Pilot to Dispatcher.

APP CON—Approach Control. The symbol Ⓡ indicates radar approach control.

TOWER—Control tower.

GCA—Ground Control Approach System.

GND CON—Ground Control.

Legend 14.—Airport/Facility Directory.

AIRPORT/FACILITY DIRECTORY LEGEND 25

GCO—Ground Communication Outlet—An unstaffed, remotely controlled, ground/ground communications facility. Pilots at uncontrolled airports may contact ATC and FSS via VHF to a telephone connection to obtain an instrument clearance or close a VFR or IFR flight plan. They may also get an updated weather briefing prior to takeoff. Pilots will use four "key clicks" on the VHF radio to contact the appropriate ATC facility or six "key clicks" to contact the FSS. The GCO system is intended to be used only on the ground.

DEP CON—Departure Control. The symbol Ⓡ indicates radar departure control.

CLNC DEL—Clearance Delivery.

CPDLC—Controller Pilot Data Link Communication. FANS ATC data communication capability from the aircraft to the ATC Data Link system.

PRE TAXI CLNC—Pre taxi clearance.

VFR ADVSY SVC—VFR Advisory Service. Service provided by Non-Radar Approach Control.
Advisory Service for VFR aircraft (upon a workload basis) ctc APP CON.

COMD POST—Command Post followed by the operator call sign in parenthesis.

PMSV—Pilot-to-Metro Service call sign, frequency and hours of operation, when full service is other than continuous. PMSV installations at which weather observation service is available shall be indicated, following the frequency and/or hours of operation as "Wx obsn svc 1900–0000Z‡" or "other times" may be used when no specific time is given. PMSV facilities manned by forecasters are considered "Full Service". PMSV facilities manned by weather observers are listed as "Limited Service".

OPS—Operations followed by the operator call sign in parenthesis.

CON

RANGE

FLT FLW—Flight Following

MEDIVAC

NOTE: Communication frequencies followed by the letter "X" indicate frequency available on request.

㉘ AIRSPACE

Information concerning Class B, C, and part-time D and E surface area airspace shall be published with effective times, if available.

CLASS B—Radar Sequencing and Separation Service for all aircraft in CLASS B airspace.

CLASS C—Separation between IFR and VFR aircraft and sequencing of VFR arrivals to the primary airport.

TRSA—Radar Sequencing and Separation Service for participating VFR Aircraft within a Terminal Radar Service Area.

Class C, D, and E airspace described in this publication is that airspace usually consisting of a 5 NM radius core surface area that begins at the surface and extends upward to an altitude above the airport elevation (charted in MSL for Class C and Class D). Class E surface airspace normally extends from the surface up to but not including the overlying controlled airspace.

When part-time Class C or Class D airspace defaults to Class E, the core surface area becomes Class E. This will be formatted as:
AIRSPACE: CLASS C svc "times" ctc **APP CON** other times CLASS E:
or
AIRSPACE: CLASS D svc "times" other times CLASS E.

When a part-time Class C, Class D or Class E surface area defaults to Class G, the core surface area becomes Class G up to, but not including, the overlying controlled airspace. Normally, the overlying controlled airspace is Class E airspace beginning at either 700′ or 1200′ AGL and may be determined by consulting the relevant VFR Sectional or Terminal Area Charts. This will be formatted as:
AIRSPACE: CLASS C svc "times" ctc **APP CON** other times CLASS G, with CLASS E 700′ (or 1200′) AGL & abv:
or
AIRSPACE: CLASS D svc "times" other times CLASS G with CLASS E 700′ (or 1200′) AGL & abv:
or
AIRSPACE: CLASS E svc "times" other times CLASS G with CLASS E 700′ (or 1200′) AGL & abv.

NOTE: AIRSPACE SVC "TIMES" INCLUDE ALL ASSOCIATED ARRIVAL EXTENSIONS. Surface area arrival extensions for instrument approach procedures become part of the primary core surface area. These extensions may be either Class D or Class E airspace and are effective concurrent with the times of the primary core surface area. For example, when a part-time Class C, Class D or Class E surface area defaults to Class G, the associated arrival extensions will default to Class G at the same time. When a part-time Class C or Class D surface area defaults to Class E, the arrival extensions will remain in effect as Class E airspace.

NOTE: CLASS E AIRSPACE EXTENDING UPWARD FROM 700 FEET OR MORE ABOVE THE SURFACE, DESIGNATED IN CONJUNCTION WITH AN AIRPORT WITH AN APPROVED INSTRUMENT PROCEDURE.
Class E 700′ AGL (shown as magenta vignette on sectional charts) and 1200′ AGL (blue vignette) areas are designated when necessary to provide controlled airspace for transitioning to/from the terminal and enroute environments. Unless otherwise specified, these 700′/1200′ AGL Class E airspace areas remain in effect continuously, regardless of airport operating hours or surface area status. These transition areas should not be confused with surface areas or arrival extensions.

(See Chapter 3, AIRSPACE, in the Aeronautical Information Manual for further details)

LEGEND 15.—Airport/Facility Directory.

AIRPORT/FACILITY DIRECTORY LEGEND

㉙ VOR TEST FACILITY (VOT)

The VOT transmits a signal which provided users a convenient means to determine the operational status and accuracy of an aircraft VOR receiver while on the ground. Ground based VOTs and the associated frequency shall be shown when available. VOTs are also shown with identifier, frequency and referenced remarks in the VOR Receiver Check section in the back of this publication.

㉚ RADIO AIDS TO NAVIGATION

The Airport/Facility Directory section of the Chart Supplement lists, by facility name, all Radio Aids to Navigation that appear on FAA, Aeronautical Information Services Visual or IFR Aeronautical Charts and those upon which the FAA has approved an Instrument Approach Procedure, with exception of selected TACANs. All VOR, VORTAC, TACAN and ILS equipment in the National Airspace System has an automatic monitoring and shutdown feature in the event of malfunction. Unmonitored, as used in this publication, for any navigational aid, means that monitoring personnel cannot observe the malfunction or shutdown signal. The NAVAID NOTAM file identifier will be shown as "NOTAM FILE IAD" and will be listed on the Radio Aids to Navigation line. When two or more NAVAIDS are listed and the NOTAM file identifier is different from that shown on the Radio Aids to Navigation line, it will be shown with the NAVAID listing. NOTAM file identifiers for ILSs and its components (e.g., NDB (LOM) are the same as the associated airports and are not repeated. Automated Surface Observing System (ASOS), Automated Weather Observing System (AWOS), and Hazardous Inflight Weather Advisory Service (HIWAS) will be shown when this service is broadcast over selected NAVAIDs.

NAVAID information is tabulated as indicated in the following sample:

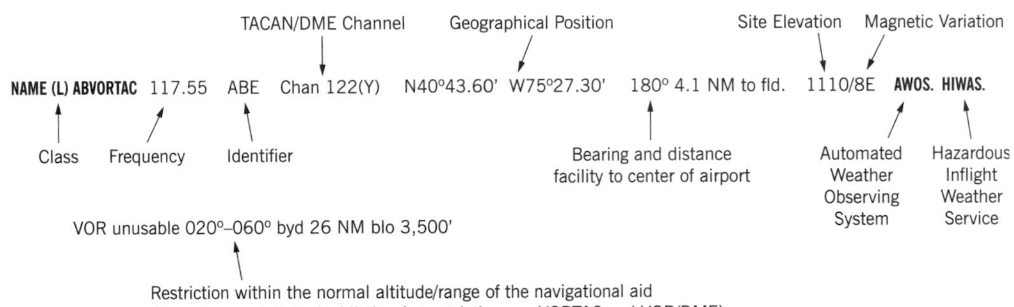

Note: Those DME channel numbers with a (Y) suffix require TACAN to be placed in the "Y" mode to receive distance information.

HIWAS—Hazardous Inflight Weather Advisory Service is a continuous broadcast of inflight weather advisories including summarized SIGMETs, convective SIGMETs, AIRMETs and urgent PIREPs. HIWAS is presently broadcast over selected VOR's throughout the U.S.

ASR/PAR—Indicates that Surveillance (ASR) or Precision (PAR) radar instrument approach minimums are published in the U.S. Terminal Procedures. Only part-time hours of operation will be shown.

LEGEND 16.—Airport/Facility Directory.

AIRPORT/FACILITY DIRECTORY LEGEND 27

RADIO CLASS DESIGNATIONS

VOR/DME/TACAN Standard Service Volume (SSV) Classifications

SSV Class	Altitudes	Distance (NM)
(T) Terminal	1000′ to 12,000′	25
(L) Low Altitude	1000′ to 18,000′	40
(H) High Altitude	1000′ to 14,500′	40
	14,500′ to 18,000′	100
	18,000′ to 45,000′	130
	45,000′ to 60,000′	100

NOTE: Additionally, (H) facilities provide (L) and (T) service volume and (L) facilities provide (T) service. Altitudes are with respect to the station's site elevation. Coverage is not available in a cone of airspace directly above the facility.

The term VOR is, operationally, a general term covering the VHF omnidirectional bearing type of facility without regard to the fact that the power, the frequency protected service volume, the equipment configuration, and operational requirements may vary between facilities at different locations.

AB	Automatic Weather Broadcast.
DF	Direction Finding Service.
DME	UHF standard (TACAN compatible) distance measuring equipment.
DME(Y)	UHF standard (TACAN compatible) distance measuring equipment that require TACAN to be placed in the "Y" mode to receive DME.
GS	Glide slope.
H	Non–directional radio beacon (homing), power 50 watts to less than 2,000 watts (50 NM at all altitudes).
HH	Non–directional radio beacon (homing), power 2,000 watts or more (75 NM at all altitudes).
H–SAB	Non–directional radio beacons providing automatic transcribed weather service.
ILS	Instrument Landing System (voice, where available, on localizer channel).
IM	Inner marker.
LDA	Localizer Directional Aid.
LMM	Compass locator station when installed at middle marker site (15 NM at all altitudes).
LOM	Compass locator station when installed at outer marker site (15 NM at all altitudes).
MH	Non–directional radio beacon (homing) power less than 50 watts (25 NM at all altitudes).
MM	Middle marker.
OM	Outer marker.
S	Simultaneous range homing signal and/or voice.
SABH	Non–directional radio beacon not authorized for IFR or ATC. Provides automatic weather broadcasts.
SDF	Simplified Direction Facility.
TACAN	UHF navigational facility–omnidirectional course and distance information.
VOR	VHF navigational facility–omnidirectional course only.
VOR/DME	Collocated VOR navigational facility and UHF standard distance measuring equipment.
VORTAC	Collocated VOR and TACAN navigational facilities.
W	Without voice on radio facility frequency.
Z	VHF station location marker at a LF radio facility.

LEGEND 17.—Airport/Facility Directory.

28

AIRPORT/FACILITY DIRECTORY LEGEND

ILS FACILITY PEFORMANCE CLASSIFICATION CODES

Codes define the ability of an ILS to support autoland operations. The two portions of the code represent Official Category and farthest point along a Category I, II, or III approach that the Localizer meets Category III structure tolerances.

Official Category: I, II, or III; the lowest minima on published or unpublished procedures supported by the ILS.

Farthest point of satisfactory Category III Localizer performance for Category I, II, or III approaches: A – 4 NM prior to runway threshold, B – 3500 ft prior to runway threshold, C – glide angle dependent but generally 750–1000 ft prior to threshold, T – runway threshold, D – 3000 ft after runway threshold, and E – 2000 ft prior to stop end of runway.

ILS information is tabulated as indicated in the following sample:

ILS/DME 108.5 I-ORL Chan 22 Rwy 18. Class IIE. LOM HERNY NDB.

ILS Facility Performance Classification Code

FREQUENCY PAIRING TABLE

VHF FREQUENCY	TACAN CHANNEL	VHF FREQUENCY	TACAN CHANNEL	VHF FREQUENCY	TACAN CHANNEL	VHF FREQUENCY	TACAN CHANNEL
108.10	18X	108.55	22Y	111.05	47Y	114.85	95Y
108.30	20X	108.65	23Y	111.15	48Y	114.95	96Y
108.50	22X	108.75	24Y	111.25	49Y	115.05	97Y
108.70	24X	108.85	25Y	111.35	50Y	115.15	98Y
108.90	26X	108.95	26Y	111.45	51Y	115.25	99Y
109.10	28X	109.05	27Y	111.55	52Y	115.35	100Y
109.30	30X	109.15	28Y	111.65	53Y	115.45	101Y
109.50	32X	109.25	29Y	111.75	54Y	115.55	102Y
109.70	34X	109.35	30Y	111.85	55Y	115.65	103Y
109.90	36X	109.45	31Y	111.95	56Y	115.75	104Y
110.10	38X	109.55	32Y	113.35	80Y	115.85	105Y
110.30	40X	109.65	33Y	113.45	81Y	115.95	106Y
110.50	42X	109.75	34Y	113.55	82Y	116.05	107Y
110.70	44X	109.85	35Y	113.65	83Y	116.15	108Y
110.90	46X	109.95	36Y	113.75	84Y	116.25	109Y
111.10	48X	110.05	37Y	113.85	85Y	116.35	110Y
111.30	50X	110.15	38Y	113.95	86Y	116.45	111Y
111.50	52X	110.25	39Y	114.05	87Y	116.55	112Y
111.70	54X	110.35	40Y	114.15	88Y	116.65	113Y
111.90	56X	110.45	41Y	114.25	89Y	116.75	114Y
108.05	17Y	110.55	42Y	114.35	90Y	116.85	115Y
108.15	18Y	110.65	43Y	114.45	91Y	116.95	116Y
108.25	19Y	110.75	44Y	114.55	92Y	117.05	117Y
108.35	20Y	110.85	45Y	114.65	93Y	117.15	118Y
108.45	21Y	110.95	46Y	114.75	94Y	117.25	119Y

FREQUENCY PAIRING TABLE

The following is a list of paired VOR/ILS VHF frequencies with TACAN channels.

TACAN CHANNEL	VHF FREQUENCY	TACAN CHANNEL	VHF FREQUENCY	TACAN CHANNEL	VHF FREQUENCY	TACAN CHANNEL	VHF FREQUENCY
2X	134.5	25X	108.80	36X	109.90	47X	111.00
2Y	134.55	25Y	108.85	36Y	109.95	47Y	111.05
11X	135.4	26X	108.90	37X	110.00	48X	111.10
11Y	135.45	26Y	108.95	37Y	110.05	48Y	111.15
12X	135.5	27X	109.00	38X	110.10	49X	111.20
12Y	135.55	27Y	109.05	38Y	110.15	49Y	111.25
17X	108.00	28X	109.10	39X	110.20	50X	111.30
17Y	108.05	28Y	109.15	39Y	110.25	50Y	111.35
18X	108.10	29X	109.20	40X	110.30	51X	111.40
18Y	108.15	29Y	109.25	40Y	110.35	51Y	111.45
19X	108.20	30X	109.30	41X	110.40	52X	111.50
19Y	108.25	30Y	109.35	41Y	110.45	52Y	111.55
20X	108.30	31X	109.40	42X	110.50	53X	111.60
20Y	108.35	31Y	109.45	42Y	110.55	53Y	111.65
21X	108.40	32X	109.50	43X	110.60	54X	111.70
21Y	108.45	32Y	109.55	43Y	110.65	54Y	111.75
22X	108.50	33X	109.60	44X	110.70	55X	111.80
22Y	108.55	33Y	109.65	44Y	110.75	55Y	111.85
23X	108.60	34X	109.70	45X	110.80	56X	111.90
23Y	108.65	34Y	109.75	45Y	110.85	56Y	111.95
24X	108.70	35X	109.80	46X	110.90	57X	112.00
24Y	108.75	35Y	109.85	46Y	110.95	57Y	112.05

LEGEND 18.—Airport/Facility Directory.

AIRPORT/FACILITY DIRECTORY LEGEND

TACAN CHANNEL	VHF FREQUENCY	TACAN CHANNEL	VHF FREQUENCY	TACAN CHANNEL	VHF FREQUENCY	TACAN CHANNEL	VHF FREQUENCY
58X	112.10	77X	113.00	96X	114.90	115X	116.80
58Y	112.15	77Y	113.05	96Y	114.95	115Y	116.85
59X	112.20	78X	113.10	97X	115.00	116X	116.90
59Y	112.25	78Y	113.15	97Y	115.05	116Y	116.95
60X	133.30	79X	113.20	98X	115.10	117X	117.00
60Y	133.35	79Y	113.25	98Y	115.15	117Y	117.05
61X	133.40	80X	113.30	99X	115.20	118X	117.10
61Y	133.45	80Y	113.35	99Y	115.25	118Y	117.15
62X	133.50	81X	113.40	100X	115.30	119X	117.20
62Y	133.55	81Y	113.45	100Y	115.35	119Y	117.25
63X	133.60	82X	113.50	101X	115.40	120X	117.30
63Y	133.65	82Y	113.55	101Y	115.45	120Y	117.35
64X	133.70	83X	113.60	102X	115.50	121X	117.40
64Y	133.75	83Y	113.65	102Y	115.55	121Y	117.45
65X	133.80	84X	113.70	103X	115.60	122X	117.50
65Y	133.85	84Y	113.75	103Y	115.65	122Y	117.55
66X	133.90	85X	113.80	104X	115.70	123X	117.60
66Y	133.95	85Y	113.85	104Y	115.75	123Y	117.65
67X	134.00	86X	113.90	105X	115.80	124X	117.70
67Y	134.05	86Y	113.95	105Y	115.85	124Y	117.75
68X	134.10	87X	114.00	106X	115.90	125X	117.80
68Y	134.15	87Y	114.05	106Y	115.95	125Y	117.85
69X	134.20	88X	114.10	107X	116.00	126X	117.90
69Y	134.25	88Y	114.15	107Y	116.05	126Y	117.95
70X	112.30	89X	114.20	108X	116.10		
70Y	112.35	89Y	114.25	108Y	116.15		
71X	112.40	90X	114.30	109X	116.20		
71Y	112.45	90Y	114.35	109Y	116.25		
72X	112.50	91X	114.40	110X	116.30		
72Y	112.55	91Y	114.45	110Y	116.35		
73X	112.60	92X	114.50	111X	116.40		
73Y	112.65	92Y	114.55	111Y	116.45		
74X	112.70	93X	114.60	112X	116.50		
74Y	112.75	93Y	114.65	112Y	116.55		
75X	112.80	94X	114.70	113X	116.60		
75Y	112.85	94Y	114.75	113Y	116.65		
76X	112.90	95X	114.80	114X	116.70		
76Y	112.95	95Y	114.85	114Y	116.75		

(31) **COMM/NAV/WEATHER REMARKS:** These remarks consist of pertinent information affecting the current status of communications, NAVAIDs and weather.

LEGEND 19.—Airport/Facility Directory.

12320

TERMS/LANDING MINIMA DATA

IFR LANDING MINIMA

The United States Standard for Terminal Instrument Procedures (TERPS) is the approved criteria for formulating instrument approach procedures. Landing minima are established for six aircraft approach categories (ABCDE and COPTER). In the absence of COPTER MINIMA, helicopters may use the CAT A minimums of other procedures.

LANDING MINIMA FORMAT

In this example airport elevation is 1179, and runway touchdown zone elevation is 1152.

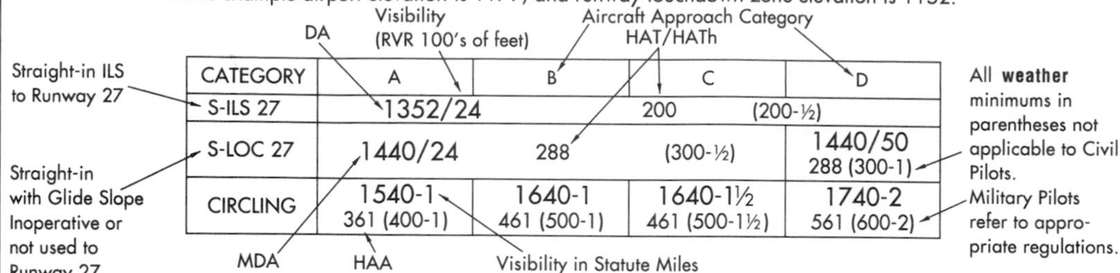

CATEGORY	A	B	C	D
S-ILS 27	1352/24		200	(200-½)
S-LOC 27	1440/24	288	(300-½)	1440/50 288 (300-1)
CIRCLING	1540-1 361 (400-1)	1640-1 461 (500-1)	1640-1½ 461 (500-1½)	1740-2 561 (600-2)

COPTER MINIMA ONLY

CATEGORY	COPTER
H-176°	680-½ 363 (400-½)

Copter Approach Direction

Height of MDA/DA Above Landing Area (HAL)

No circling minimums are provided

RNAV (GPS) MINIMA EXAMPLE

CATEGORY	A	B	C	D
LPV DA	1540/24 258 (300-½)			
LNAV/VNAV DA	1600/24 318 (400-½)			1600/40 318 (400-¾)
LNAV MDA	1840/24 558 (600-½)		1840/50 558 (600-1)	1840/60 558 (600-1 ¼)
CIRCLING	1840-1 545 (600-1)		1840-1½ 545 (600-1½)	1860-2 565 (600-2)

NOTE: The W symbol indicates outages of the WAAS vertical guidance may occur daily at this location due to initial system limitations. WAAS NOTAMS for vertical outages are not provided for this approach. Use LNAV minima for flight planning at these locations, whether as a destination or alternate. For flight operations at these locations, when the WAAS avionics indicate that LNAV/VNAV or LPV service is available, then vertical guidance may be used to complete the approach using the displayed level of service. Should an outage occur during the procedure, reversion to LNAV minima may be required. As the WAAS coverage is expanded, the W will be removed.

RNAV minimums are dependent on navigation equipment capability, as stated in the applicable AFM, AFMS, or other FAA approved document. See AIM paragraph 5-4-5, AC 90-105 and AC 90-107 for detailed requirements for each line of minima.

AIRCRAFT APPROACH CATEGORIES

Aircraft approach category indicates a grouping of aircraft based on a speed of VREF, if specified, or if VREF not specified, 1.3 VSO at the maximum certificated landing weight. VREF, VSO, and the maximum certificated landing weight are those values as established for the aircraft by the certification authority of the country of registry. Helicopters are Category A aircraft. An aircraft shall fit in only one category. However, if it is necessary to operate at a speed in excess of the upper limit of the speed range for an aircraft's category, the minimums for the category for that speed shall be used. For example, an airplane which fits into Category B, but is circling to land at a speed of 145 knots, shall use the approach Category D minimums. As an additional example, a Category A airplane (or helicopter) which is operating at 130 knots on a straight-in approach shall use the approach Category C minimums. See following category limits:

MANEUVERING TABLE

Approach Category	A	B	C	D	E
Speed (Knots)	0-90	91-120	121-140	141-165	Abv 165

TERMS/LANDING MINIMA DATA

LEGEND 20.—Instrument Approach Procedures Explanation of Terms.

13122

TERMS/LANDING MINIMA DATA

CIRCLING APPROACH OBSTACLE PROTECTED AIRSPACE

The circling MDA provides vertical clearance from obstacles when conducting a circle-to-land maneuver within the obstacle protected area. Circling approach obstacle protected areas extend laterally and longitudinally from the centerlines and ends of all runways at an airport by the distances shown in the following tables. The areas are technically defined by the tangential connection of arcs drawn at the radius distance shown from each runway end.

STANDARD CIRCLING APPROACH MANEUVERING RADIUS

Circling approach protected areas developed prior to late 2012 used the radius distances shown in the following table, expressed in nautical miles (NM), dependent on aircraft approach category. The approaches using standard circling approach areas can be identified by the absence of the C symbol on the circling line of minima.

Circling MDA in feet MSL	Approach Category and Circling Radius (NM)				
	CAT A	CAT B	CAT C	CAT D	CAT E
All Altitudes	1.3	1.5	1.7	2.3	4.5

C EXPANDED CIRCLING APPROACH MANEUVERING AIRSPACE RADIUS

Circling approach protected areas developed after late 2012 use the radius distance shown in the following table, expressed in nautical miles (NM), dependent on aircraft approach category, and the altitude of the circling MDA, which accounts for true airspeed increase with altitude. The approaches using expanded circling approach areas can be identified by the presence of the C symbol on the circling line of minima.

Circling MDA in feet MSL	Approach Category and Circling Radius (NM)				
	CAT A	CAT B	CAT C	CAT D	CAT E
1000 or less	1.3	1.7	2.7	3.6	4.5
1001-3000	1.3	1.8	2.8	3.7	4.6
3001-5000	1.3	1.8	2.9	3.8	4.8
5001-7000	1.3	1.9	3.0	4.0	5.0
7001-9000	1.4	2.0	3.2	4.2	5.3
9001 and above	1.4	2.1	3.3	4.4	5.5

Comparable Values of RVR and Visibility

The following table shall be used for converting RVR to ground or flight visibility. For converting RVR values that fall between listed values, use the next higher RVR value; do not interpolate. For example, when converting 1800 RVR, use 2400 RVR with the resultant visibility of ½ mile.

RVR (feet)	Visibility (statute miles)	RVR (feet)	Visibility (statute miles)
1600	¼	4500	⅞
2400	½	5000	1
3200	⅝	6000	1¼
4000	¾		

RADAR MINIMA

	RWY	GS/TCH/RPI	CAT	DA/ MDA-VIS	HAT/ HATh/ HAA	CEIL-VIS	CAT	DA/ MDA-VIS	HAT/ HATh/ HAA	CEIL-VIS
PAR	10	2.5°/42/1000	ABCDE	**195**/16	100	(100-¼)				
	28	2.5°/48/1068	ABCDE	**187**/16	100	(100-¼)				
ASR	10		ABC	**560**/40	463	(500-¾)	DE	**560**/50	463	(500-1)
	28		AB	**600**/50	513	(600-1)	CDE	**600**/60	513	(600-1¼)
CIR	10		AB	**560**-1¼	463	(500-1¼)	CDE	**560**-1½	463	(500-1½)
	28		AB	**600**-1¼	503	(600-1¼)	CDE	**600**-1½	503	(600-1½)

Visibility (RVR 100's of feet)

Visibility in Statute Miles

All minimums in parentheses not applicable to Civil Pilots. Military Pilots refer to appropriate regulations.

Radar Minima:

1. Minima shown are the lowest permitted by established criteria. Pilots should consult applicable directives for their category of aircraft.
2. The circling MDA and weather minima to be used are those for the runway to which the final approach is flown- not the landing runway. In the above RADAR MINIMA example, a category C aircraft flying a radar approach to runway 10, circling to land on runway 28, must use an MDA of 560 feet with weather minima of 500-1½.

NOTE: Military RADAR MINIMA may be shown with communications symbology that indicates emergency frequency monitoring capability by the radar facility as follows:

(E) VHF and UHF emergency frequencies monitored
(V) VHF emergency frequency (121.5) monitored
(U) UHF emergency frequency (243.0) monitored

Additionally, unmonitored frequencies which are available on request from the controlling agency may be annotated with an "x".

A Alternate Minimums not standard. Civil users refer to tabulation. USA/USN/USAF pilots refer to appropriate regulations.

A NA Alternate minimums are Not Authorized due to unmonitored facility or absence of weather reporting service.

T Takeoff Minimums not standard and/or Departure Procedures are published. Refer to tabulation.

TERMS/LANDING MINIMA DATA

LEGEND 21.—Instrument Approach Procedures Explanation of Terms.

13290
GENERAL INFO

GENERAL INFORMATION

This publication is issued every 56 days and includes Standard Instrument Approach Procedures (SIAPS), Standard Instrument Departures (SIDs), Standard Terminal Arrivals (STARs), IFR Takeoff Minimums and (Obstacle) Departure Procedures (ODPs), IFR Alternate Minimums, and Radar Instrument Approach Minimums for use by civil and military aviation. The organization responsible for SIAPs, Radar Minimums, SIDs, STARs and graphic ODPs is identified in parentheses in the top margin of the procedure; e.g., (FAA), (FAA-O), (USA), (USAF), (USN). SIAPS with the (FAA) and (FAA-O) designation are regulated under 14 CFR, Part 97. SIAPs with the (FAA-O) designation have been developed under Other Transaction Agreement (OTA) by private providers and have been certified by the FAA. See 14 CFR, Part 91.175 (a) and the AIM for further details. 14 CFR, Part 91.175 (g) and the Special Notices section of the Airport/Facility Directory contains information on civil operations at military airports.

STANDARD TERMINAL ARRIVALS AND DEPARTURE PROCEDURES

The use of the associated codified STAR/DP and transition identifiers are requested of users when filing flight plans via teletype and are required for users filing flight plans via computer interface. It must be noted that when filing a STAR/DP with a transition, the first three coded characters of the STAR and the last three coded characters of the DP are replaced by the transition code. Examples: ACTON SIX ARRIVAL, file (AQN.AQN6); ACTON SIX ARRIVAL, EDNAS TRANSITION, file (EDNAS.AQN6). FREEHOLD THREE DEPARTURE, file (FREH3.RBV), FREEHOLD THREE DEPARTURE, ELWOOD CITY TRANSITION, file (FREH3.EWC).

RNAV DP and STAR. Effective March 15,2007, these procedures, formerly identified as Type-A and Type-B, will be designated as RNAV 1 in accordance with amended Advisory Circular (AC) and ICAO terminology.

Refer to AC 90-100A U.S. TERMINAL AND EN ROUTE AREA NAVIGATION (RNAV) OPERATIONS and the Aeronautical Information Manual for additional guidance regarding these procedures.

Standard RNAV 1 Procedure Chart Notes

NOTE: RNAV 1
NOTE: DME/DME/IRU or GPS required

Some procedures may require use of GPS and will be identified by a "GPS required" note.

RNAV 1 Procedure Characteristics and Operations

1. Require use of an RNAV system with DME/DME/IRU, and/or GPS inputs.
2. Require use of a CDI, flight director, and/or autopilot, in lateral navigation mode, for flight guidance while operating on RNAV paths (track, course, or direct leg). Other methods providing an equivalent level of performance may be acceptable.
3. RNAV paths may start as low as 500 feet above airport elevation.

GENERAL INFO
13290

LEGEND 22.—General Information.

14149

GENERAL INFO

ABBREVIATIONS

AAUP....Attention All Users Page
ADF....Automatic Direction Finder
AFIS....Automatic Flight Information Service
ALS....Approach Light System
ALSF....Approach Light System with Sequenced Flashing Lights
AP....Autopilot System
APCH....Approach
APP CON....Approach Control
ARR....Arrival
ASOS....Automated Surface Observing System
ASR/PAR....Published Radar Minimums at this Airport
ATIS....Automatic Terminal Information Service
AUNICOM....Automated UNICOM
AWOS....Automated Weather Observing System
AZ....Azimuth
BC....Back Course
BND....Bound
C....Circling
CAT....Category
CCW....Counter Clockwise
CDI....Course Deviation Indicator
Chan....Channel
CIR....Circling
CLNC DEL....Clearance Delivery
CNF....Computer Navigation Fix
CTAF....Common Traffic Advisory Frequency
CW....Clockwise
DA....Decision Altitude
DER....Departure End of Runway
DH....Decision Height
DME....Distance Measuring Equipment
DTHR....Displaced Threshold
ELEV....Elevation
EMAS....Engineered Material Arresting System
FAF....Final Approach Fix
FD....Flight Director System
FM....Fan Marker
FMS....Flight Management System
GCO....Ground Communications Outlet
GLS....Ground Based Augmentation System Landing System
GPI....Ground Point of Interception
GPS....Global Positioning System
GS....Glide Slope
HAA....Height above Airport
HAL....Height above Landing
HAT....Height above Touchdown
HATh....Height Above Threshold
HGS....Head-up Guidance System
HIRL....High Intensity Runway Lights
HUD....Head-up Display
IAF....Initial Approach Fix
ICAO....International Civil Aviation Organization
IF....Intermediate Fix
IM....Inner Marker
INT....Intersection
LAAS....Local Area Augmentation System
LDA....Localizer Type Directional Aid
Ldg....Landing
LIRL....Low Intensity Runway Lights
LNAV....Lateral Navigation
LOC....Localizer
LP....Localizer Performance
LPV....Localizer Performance with Vertical Guidance
LR....Lead Radial. Provides at least 2 NM (Copter 1 NM) of lead to assist in turning onto the intermediate/final course.
MAA....Maximum Authorized Altitude
MALS....Medium Intensity Approach Light System
MALSR....Medium Intensity Approach Light System with RAIL
MAP....Missed Approach Point
MDA....Minimum Descent Altitude
MIRL....Medium Intensity Runway Lights
MLS....Microwave Landing System
MM....Middle Marker
MRA....Minimum Reception Altitude
N/A....Not Applicable
NA....Not Authorized
NDB....Non-directional Radio Beacon
NFD....National Flight Database
NM....Nautical Mile
NoPT....No Procedure Turn Required (Procedure Turn shall not be executed without ATC clearance)
ODALS....Omnidirectional Approach Light System
ODP....Obstacle Departure Procedure
OM....Outer Marker
PRM....Precision Runway Monitor

GENERAL INFO
14149

LEGEND 23.—Abbreviations.

14149

GENERAL INFO

ABBREVIATIONS

R.. Radial
RA.. Radio Altimeter setting height
RAIL.. Runway Alignment Indicator Lights
RCLS.. Runway Centerline Light System
REIL.. Runway End Identifier Lights
RF.. Radius-to-Fix
RLLS.. Runway Lead-in Light System
RNAV.. Area Navigation
RNP.. Required Navigation Performance
RPI.. Runway Point of Intercept(ion)
RRL.. Runway Remaining Lights
Rwy.. Runway
RVR.. Runway Visual Range
S.. Straight-in
SALS.. Short Approach Light System
SSALR.. Simplified Short Approach Light System with RAIL
SDF.. Simplified Directional Facility
SM.. Statute Mile
SOIA.. Simultaneous Offset Instrument Approach
TAA.. Terminal Arrival Area
TAC.. TACAN
TCH.. Threshold Crossing Height (height in feet Above Ground level)
TDZ.. Touchdown Zone
TDZE.. Touchdown Zone Elevation
TDZ/CL.. Touchdown Zone and Runway Centerline Lighting
TDZL.. Touchdown Zone Lights
THR.. Threshold
THRE.. Threshold Elevation
TODA.. Takeoff Distance Available
TORA.. Takeoff Run Available
TR.. Track
VASI.. Visual Approach Slope Indicator
VCOA.. Visual Climb Over Airport
VDP.. Visual Descent Point
VGSI.. Visual Glide Slope Indicator
VNAV.. Vertical Navigation
WAAS.. Wide Area Augmentation System
WP/WPT.. Waypoint (RNAV)

GENERAL INFO
14149

LEGEND 23A.—Abbreviations.

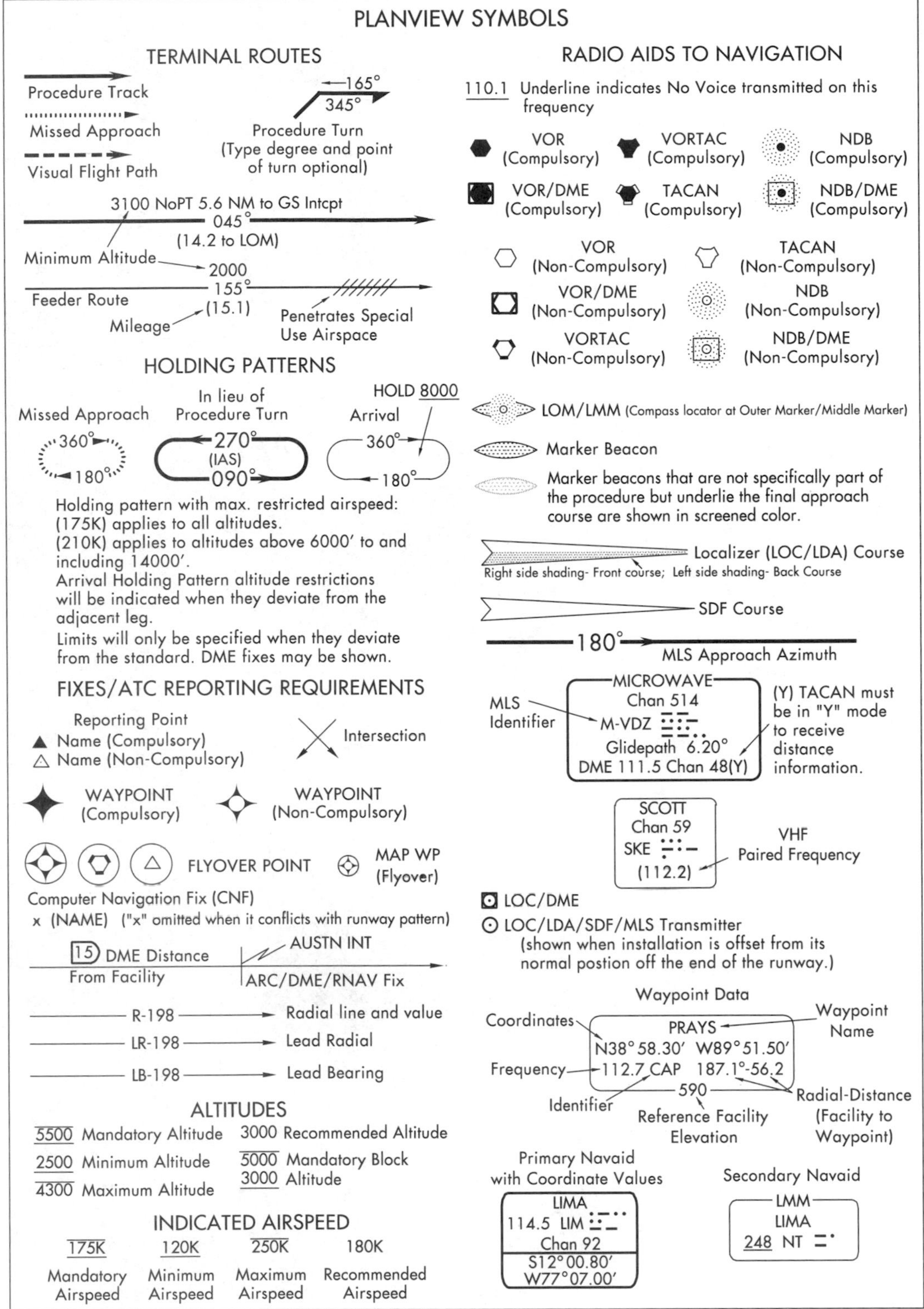

LEGEND 24.—Instrument Approach Procedures (Symbols).

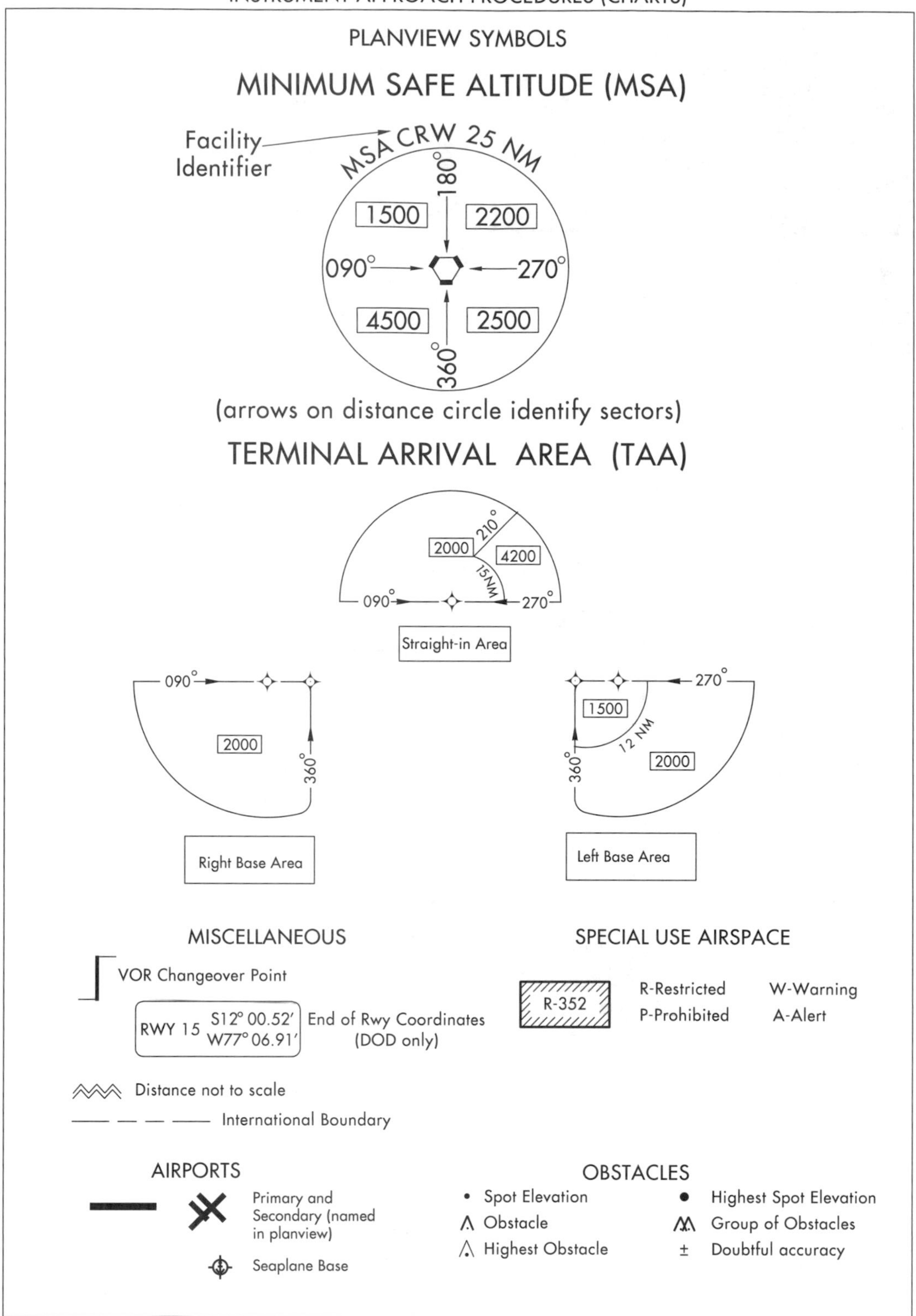

LEGEND 25.—Instrument Approach Procedures (Symbols).

13346
LEGEND

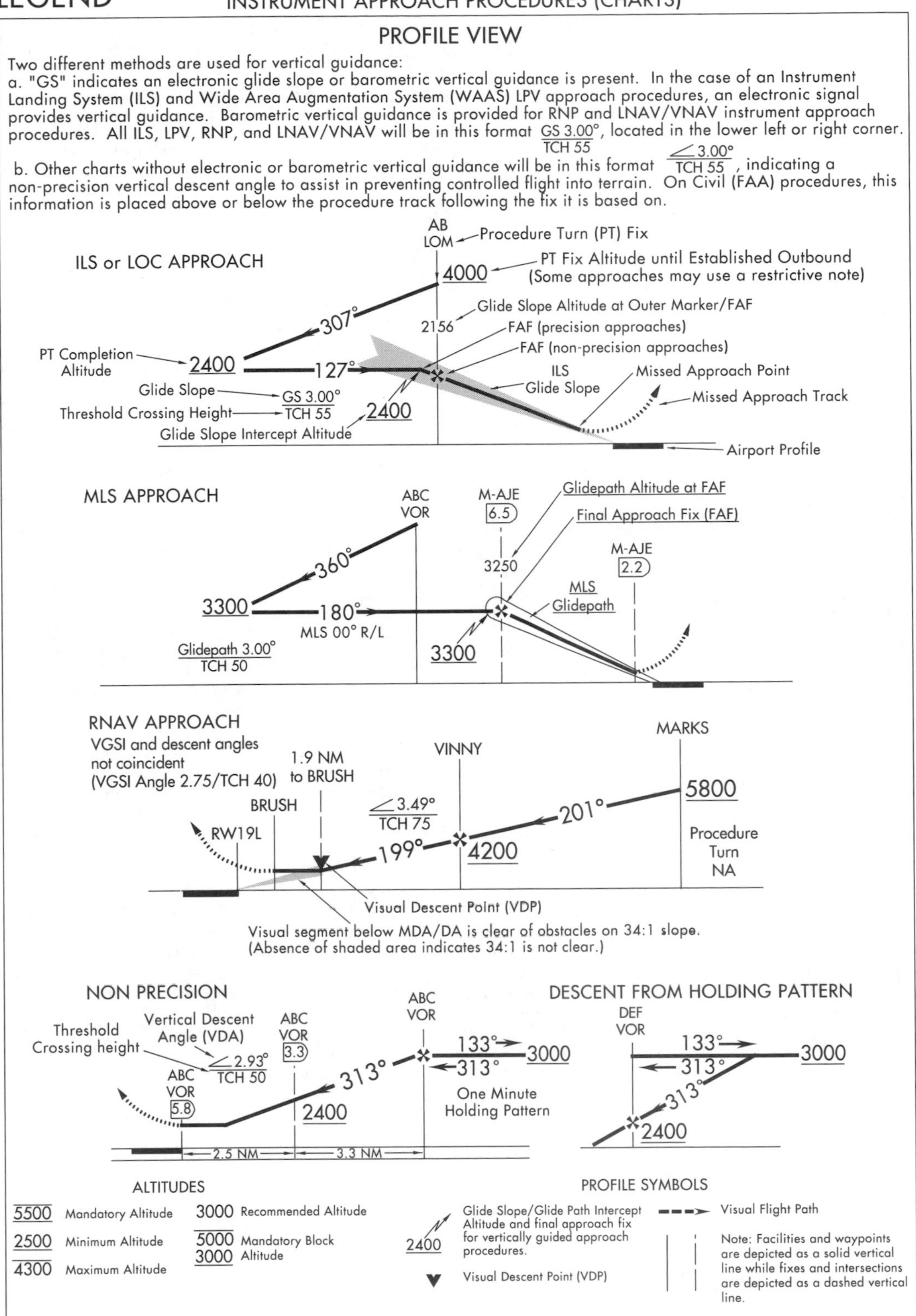

LEGEND
13346

LEGEND 26.—Instrument Approach Procedures (Profile).

CLIMB/DESCENT TABLE 10042

INSTRUMENT TAKEOFF OR APPROACH PROCEDURE CHARTS
RATE OF CLIMB/DESCENT TABLE

(ft. per min)

A rate of climb/descent table is provided for use in planning and executing climbs or descents under known or approximate ground speed conditions. It will be especially useful for approaches when the localizer only is used for course guidance. A best speed, power, altitude combination can be programmed which will result in a stable glide rate and altitude favorable for executing a landing if minimums exist upon breakout. Care should always be exercised so that minimum descent altitude and missed approach point are not exceeded.

CLIMB/ DESCENT ANGLE (degrees and tenths)	ft/NM	GROUND SPEED (knots)										
		60	90	120	150	180	210	240	270	300	330	360
2.0	210	210	320	425	530	635	743	850	955	1060	1165	1275
2.5	265	265	400	530	665	795	930	1060	1195	1325	1460	1590
VERTICAL PATH ANGLE 2.7	287	287	430	574	717	860	1003	1147	1290	1433	1576	1720
2.8	297	297	446	595	743	892	1041	1189	1338	1486	1635	1783
2.9	308	308	462	616	770	924	1078	1232	1386	1539	1693	1847
3.0	318	318	478	637	797	956	1115	1274	1433	1593	1752	1911
3.1	329	329	494	659	823	988	1152	1317	1481	1646	1810	1975
3.2	340	340	510	680	850	1020	1189	1359	1529	1699	1869	2039
3.3	350	350	526	701	876	1052	1227	1402	1577	1752	1927	2103
3.4	361	361	542	722	903	1083	1264	1444	1625	1805	1986	2166
3.5	370	370	555	745	930	1115	1300	1485	1670	1860	2045	2230
4.0	425	425	640	850	1065	1275	1490	1700	1915	2125	2340	2550
4.5	480	480	715	955	1195	1435	1675	1915	2150	2390	2630	2870
5.0	530	530	795	1065	1330	1595	1860	2125	2390	2660	2925	3190
5.5	585	585	880	1170	1465	1755	2050	2340	2635	2925	3220	3510
6.0	640	640	960	1275	1595	1915	2235	2555	2875	3195	3510	3830
6.5	690	690	1040	1385	1730	2075	2425	2770	3115	3460	3805	4155
7.0	745	745	1120	1490	1865	2240	2610	2985	3355	3730	4105	4475
7.5	800	800	1200	1600	2000	2400	2800	3200	3600	4000	4400	4800
8.0	855	855	1280	1710	2135	2560	2990	3415	3845	4270	4695	5125
8.5	910	910	1360	1815	2270	2725	3180	3630	4085	4540	4995	5450
9.0	960	960	1445	1925	2405	2885	3370	3850	4330	4810	5295	5775
9.5	1015	1015	1525	2035	2540	3050	3560	4065	4575	5085	5590	6100
10.0	1070	1070	1605	2145	2680	3215	3750	4285	4820	5355	5890	6430

CLIMB/DESCENT TABLE 10042

LEGEND 27.—Instrument Takeoff or Approach Procedure Charts, Rate-of-Climb/Descent Table.

12320
LEGEND

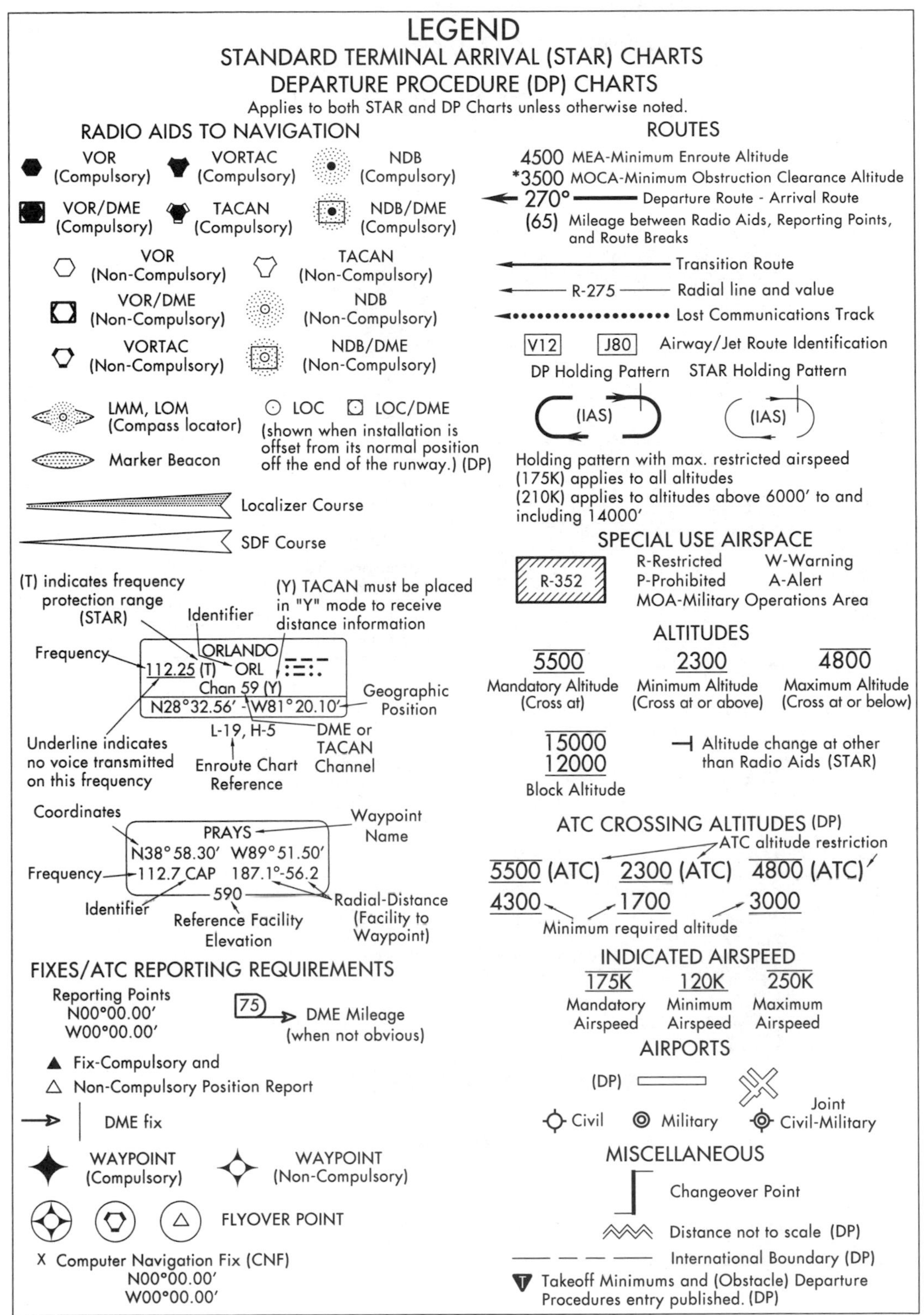

LEGEND

LEGEND 28.—Standard Arrival/Departure Charts.

13010

LEGEND

INSTRUMENT APPROACH PROCEDURES (CHARTS)

AIRPORT DIAGRAM/AIRPORT SKETCH

Runways

Hard Surface | Other Than Hard Surface | Stopways, Taxiways, Parking Areas, Water Runways | Displaced Threshold

Closed Runway | Closed Taxiway | Under Construction | Metal Surface

ARRESTING GEAR: Specific arresting gear systems; e.g., BAK12, MA-1A etc., shown on airport diagrams, not applicable to Civil Pilots. Military Pilots refer to appropriate DOD publications.

uni-directional | bi-directional | Jet Barrier

ARRESTING SYSTEM

REFERENCE FEATURES

Buildings..

24-Hour Self-Serve Fuel ##..............................

Tanks...

Obstructions..

Airport Beacon #...

Runway Radar Reflectors.................................

Hot Spot ....

Control Tower #...TWR

When Control Tower and Rotating Beacon are co-located, Beacon symbol will be used and further identified as TWR.

A fuel symbol is shown to indicate 24-hour self-serve fuel available, see appropriate A/FD, Alaska or Pacific Supplement for information.

Runway length depicted is the physical length of the runway (end-to-end, including displaced thresholds if any) but excluding areas designated as stopways.

A D symbol is shown to indicate runway declared distance information available, see appropriate A/FD, Alaska or Pacific Supplement for distance information.

Helicopter Alighting Areas

Negative Symbols used to identify Copter Procedures landing point....................

Runway Threshold elevation...........THRE 123

Runway TDZ elevation...................TDZE 123

0.3% DOWN

Runway Slope...............................0.8% UP

(shown when runway slope is greater than or equal to 0.3%)

NOTE:

Runway Slope measured to midpoint on runways 8000 feet or longer.

U.S. Navy Optical Landing System (OLS) "OLS" location is shown because of its height of approximately 7 feet and proximity to edge of runway may create an obstruction for some types of aircraft.

Approach light symbols are shown in the Flight Information Handbook.

Airport diagram scales are variable.

True/magnetic North orientation may vary from diagram to diagram

Coordinate values are shown in 1 or ½ minute increments. They are further broken down into 6 second ticks, within each 1 minute increments.

Positional accuracy within ±600 feet unless otherwise noted on the chart.

NOTE:

All new and revised airport diagrams are shown referenced to the World Geodetic System (WGS) (noted on appropriate diagram), and may not be compatible with local coordinates published in FLIP. (Foreign Only)

Runway Weight Bearing Capacity/or PCN Pavement Classification Number is shown as a codified expression.
Refer to the appropriate Supplement/Directory for applicable codes e.g.,
RWY 14-32 PCN 80 F/D/X/U S-75, D-185, 2S-175, 2D-325

Runway Slope
FIELD ELEV 174
Displaced Threshold
HS 1
BAK-12
0.7% UP
Runway Identification
EMAS
20
2
ELEV 164
9000 X 200
023.2°
1000 X 200
Runway End Elevation
Runway Dimensions (in feet)
Runway Heading (Magnetic)
Movement Area Dimensions (in feet)

SCOPE

Airport diagrams are specifically designed to assist in the movement of ground traffic at locations with complex runway/taxiway configurations. Airport diagrams are not intended to be used for approach and landing or departure operations. For revisions to Airport Diagrams: Consult FAA Order 7910.4.

LEGEND

LEGEND 29.—Airport Diagram.

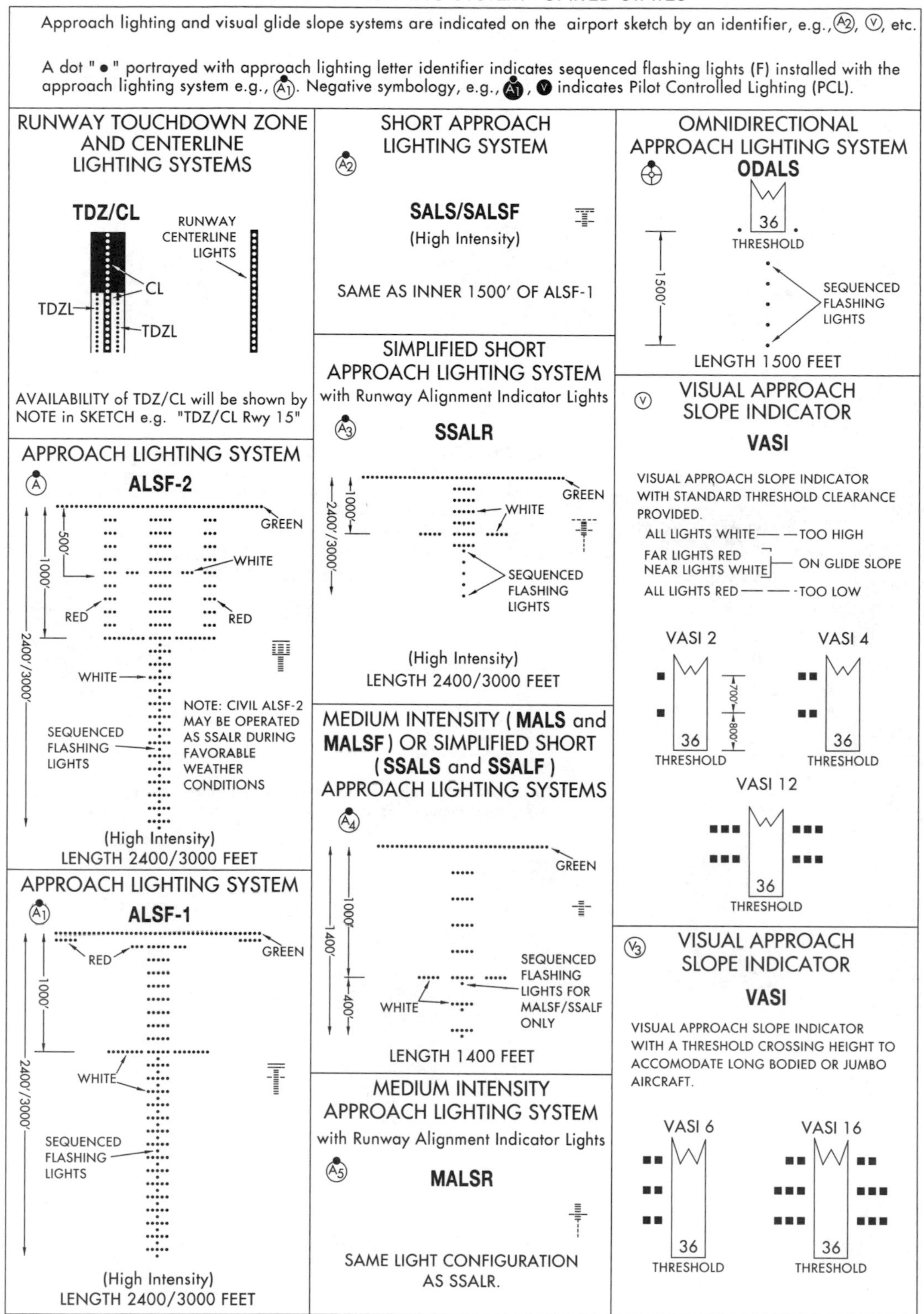

LEGEND 30.—Approach Lighting Systems.

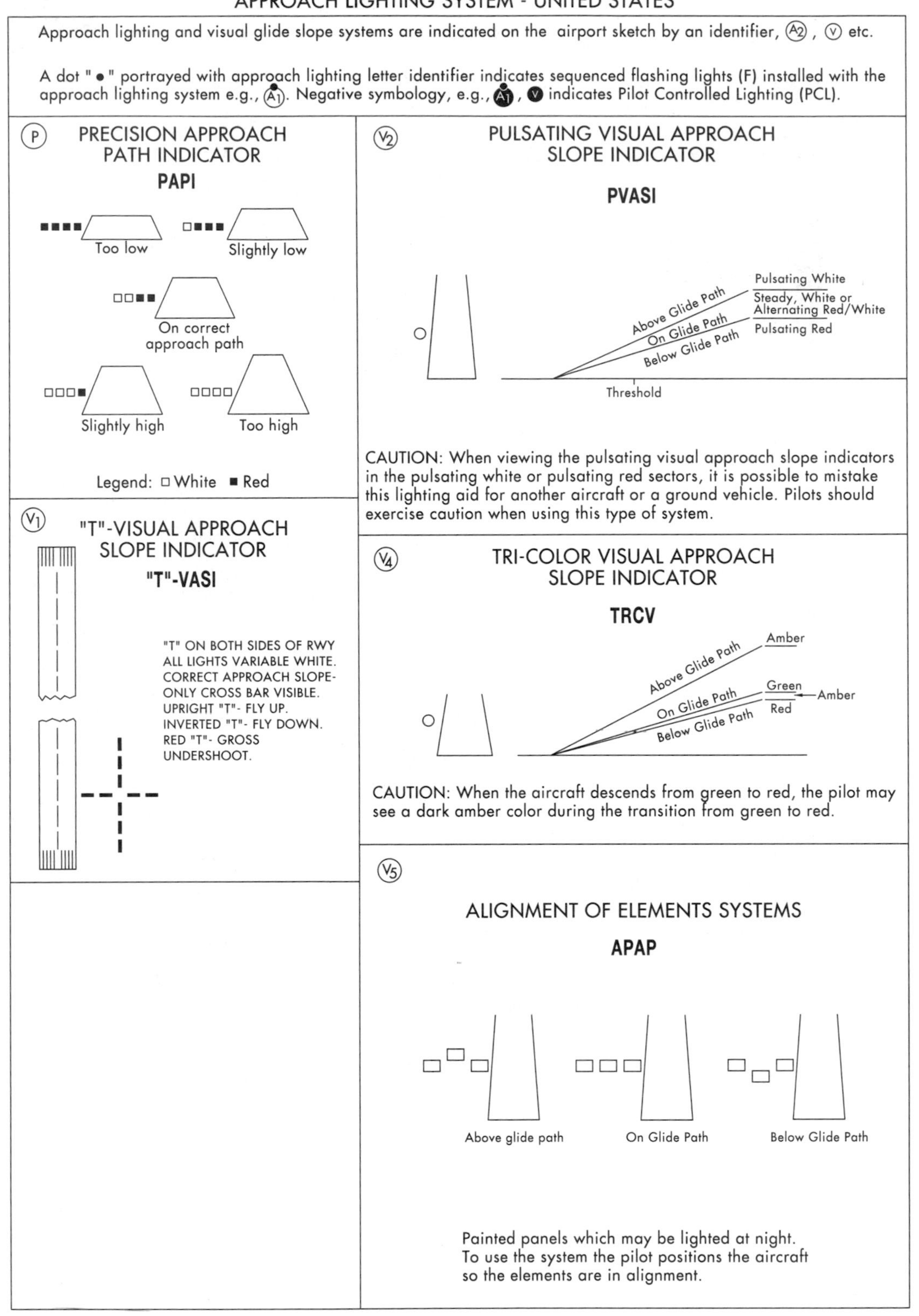

LEGEND 31.—Approach Lighting System.

13122

INOP COMPONENTS

INOPERATIVE COMPONENTS OR VISUAL AIDS TABLE

Landing minimums published on instrument approach procedure charts are based upon full operation of all components and visual aids associated with the particular instrument approach chart being used. Higher minimums are required with inoperative components or visual aids as indicated below. If more than one component is inoperative, each minimum is raised to the highest minimum required by any single component that is inoperative. ILS glide slope inoperative minimums are published on the instrument approach charts as localizer minimums. This table may be amended by notes on the approach chart. Such notes apply only to the particular approach category(ies) as stated. See legend page for description of components indicated below.

(1) ILS, MLS, PAR and RNAV (LPV line of minima)

Inoperative Component or Aid	Approach Category	Increase Visibility
ALSF 1 & 2, MALSR, & SSALR	ABCD	¼ mile

(2) ILS with visibility minimum of 1,800 RVR

ALSF 1 & 2, MALSR, & SSALR	ABCD	To 4000 RVR
TDZL RCLS	ABCD	To 2400 RVR*
RVR	ABCD	To ½ mile

*1800 RVR authorized with the use of FD or AP or HUD to DA.

(3) VOR, VOR/DME, TACAN, LOC, LOC/DME, LDA, LDA/DME, SDF, SDF/DME, GPS, ASR and RNAV (LNAV/VNAV, LP, LNAV lines of minima)

Inoperative Visual Aid	Approach Category	Increase Visibility
ALSF 1 & 2, MALSR, & SSALR	ABCD	½ mile
SSALS,MALS, & ODALS	ABC	¼ mile

(4) NDB

ALSF 1 & 2, MALSR, & SSALR	C	½ mile
	ABD	¼ mile
MALS, SSALS, ODALS	ABC	¼ mile

INOP COMPONENTS

LEGEND 32.—Inoperative Components or Visual Aids Table.

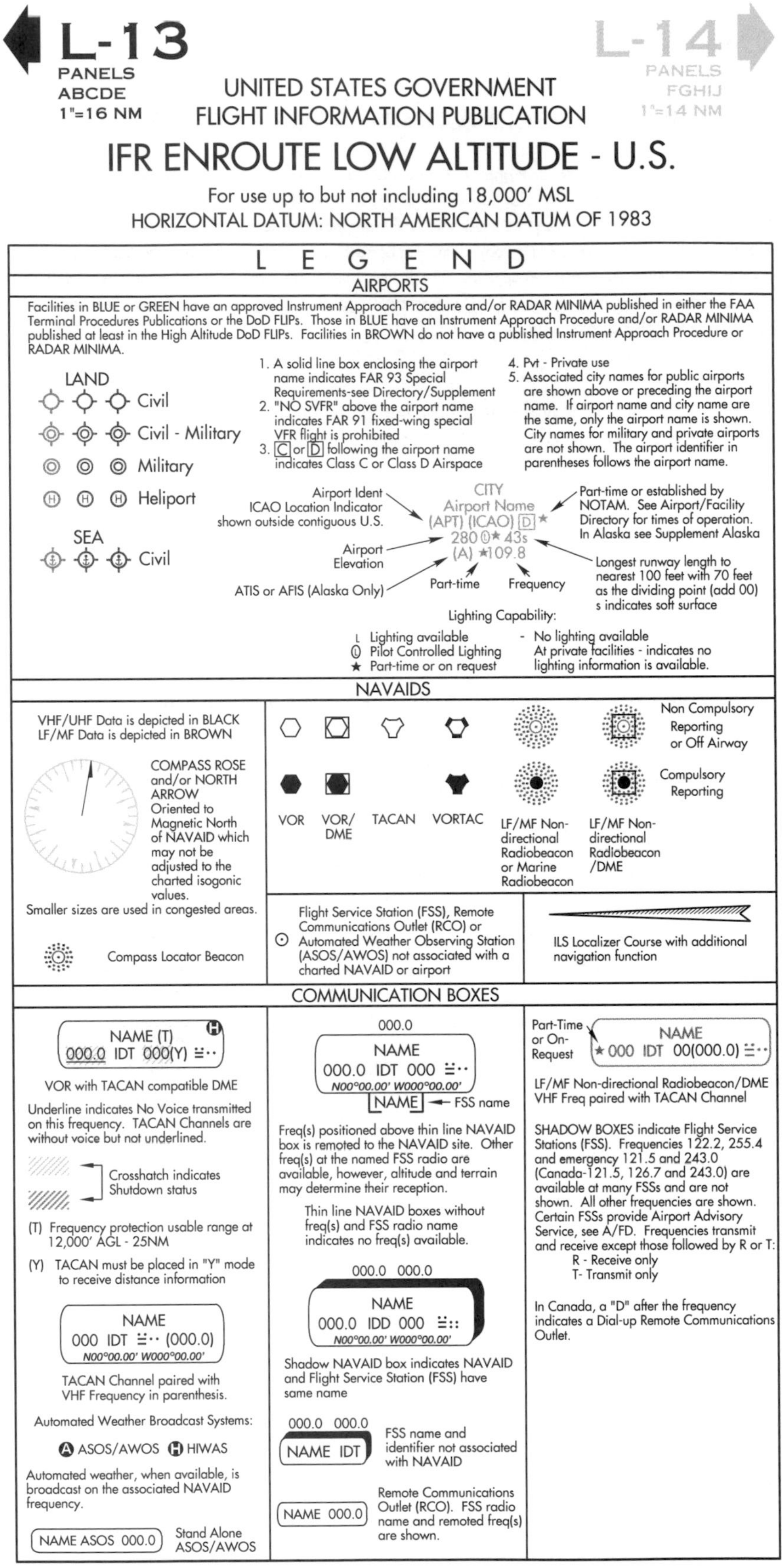

UNITED STATES GOVERNMENT
FLIGHT INFORMATION PUBLICATION

IFR ENROUTE LOW ALTITUDE - U.S.

For use up to but not including 18,000' MSL
HORIZONTAL DATUM: NORTH AMERICAN DATUM OF 1983

L E G E N D

AIRPORTS

Facilities in BLUE or GREEN have an approved Instrument Approach Procedure and/or RADAR MINIMA published in either the FAA Terminal Procedures Publications or the DoD FLIPs. Those in BLUE have an Instrument Approach Procedure and/or RADAR MINIMA published at least in the High Altitude DoD FLIPs. Facilities in BROWN do not have a published Instrument Approach Procedure or RADAR MINIMA.

LAND
Civil
Civil - Military
Military
Heliport

SEA
Civil

1. A solid line box enclosing the airport name indicates FAR 93 Special Requirements-see Directory/Supplement
2. "NO SVFR" above the airport name indicates FAR 91 fixed-wing special VFR flight is prohibited
3. C or D following the airport name indicates Class C or Class D Airspace
4. Pvt - Private use
5. Associated city names for public airports are shown above or preceding the airport name. If airport name and city name are the same, only the airport name is shown. City names for military and private airports are not shown. The airport identifier in parentheses follows the airport name.

CITY
Airport Name
(APT) (ICAO) D ★
280 Ⓛ★ 43s
(A) ★109.8

Airport Ident
ICAO Location Indicator shown outside contiguous U.S.
Airport Elevation
ATIS or AFIS (Alaska Only)
Part-time
Frequency
Part-time or established by NOTAM. See Airport/Facility Directory for times of operation. In Alaska see Supplement Alaska
Longest runway length to nearest 100 feet with 70 feet as the dividing point (add 00) s indicates soft surface

Lighting Capability:
L Lighting available
Ⓛ Pilot Controlled Lighting
★ Part-time or on request
\- No lighting available
At private facilities - indicates no lighting information is available.

NAVAIDS

VHF/UHF Data is depicted in BLACK
LF/MF Data is depicted in BROWN

COMPASS ROSE and/or NORTH ARROW Oriented to Magnetic North of NAVAID which may not be adjusted to the charted isogonic values.

Smaller sizes are used in congested areas.

Compass Locator Beacon

VOR
VOR/DME
TACAN
VORTAC
LF/MF Non-directional Radiobeacon or Marine Radiobeacon
LF/MF Non-directional Radiobeacon /DME

Non Compulsory Reporting or Off Airway
Compulsory Reporting

⊙ Flight Service Station (FSS), Remote Communications Outlet (RCO) or Automated Weather Observing Station (ASOS/AWOS) not associated with a charted NAVAID or airport

ILS Localizer Course with additional navigation function

COMMUNICATION BOXES

NAME (T) Ⓗ
000.0 IDT 000(Y)

VOR with TACAN compatible DME

Underline indicates No Voice transmitted on this frequency. TACAN Channels are without voice but not underlined.

Crosshatch indicates Shutdown status

(T) Frequency protection usable range at 12,000' AGL - 25NM

(Y) TACAN must be placed in "Y" mode to receive distance information

NAME
000 IDT (000.0)
N00°00.00' W000°00.00'

TACAN Channel paired with VHF Frequency in parenthesis.

Automated Weather Broadcast Systems:

Ⓐ ASOS/AWOS Ⓗ HIWAS

Automated weather, when available, is broadcast on the associated NAVAID frequency.

NAME ASOS 000.0 — Stand Alone ASOS/AWOS

000.0
NAME
000.0 IDT 000
N00°00.00' W000°00.00'
NAME ← FSS name

Freq(s) positioned above thin line NAVAID box is remoted to the NAVAID site. Other freq(s) at the named FSS radio are available, however, altitude and terrain may determine their reception.

Thin line NAVAID boxes without freq(s) and FSS radio name indicates no freq(s) available.

000.0 000.0
NAME
000.0 IDD 000
N00°00.00' W000°00.00'

Shadow NAVAID box indicates NAVAID and Flight Service Station (FSS) have same name

000.0 000.0
NAME IDT — FSS name and identifier not associated with NAVAID

NAME 000.0 — Remote Communications Outlet (RCO). FSS radio name and remoted freq(s) are shown.

Part-Time or On-Request
NAME
★000 IDT 00(000.0)

LF/MF Non-directional Radiobeacon/DME
VHF Freq paired with TACAN Channel

SHADOW BOXES indicate Flight Service Stations (FSS). Frequencies 122.2, 255.4 and emergency 121.5 and 243.0 (Canada-121.5, 126.7 and 243.0) are available at many FSSs and are not shown. All other frequencies are shown. Certain FSSs provide Airport Advisory Service, see A/FD. Frequencies transmit and receive except those followed by R or T:
R - Receive only
T- Transmit only

In Canada, a "D" after the frequency indicates a Dial-up Remote Communications Outlet.

LEGEND 33.—IFR En Route Low Altitude (U.S.)

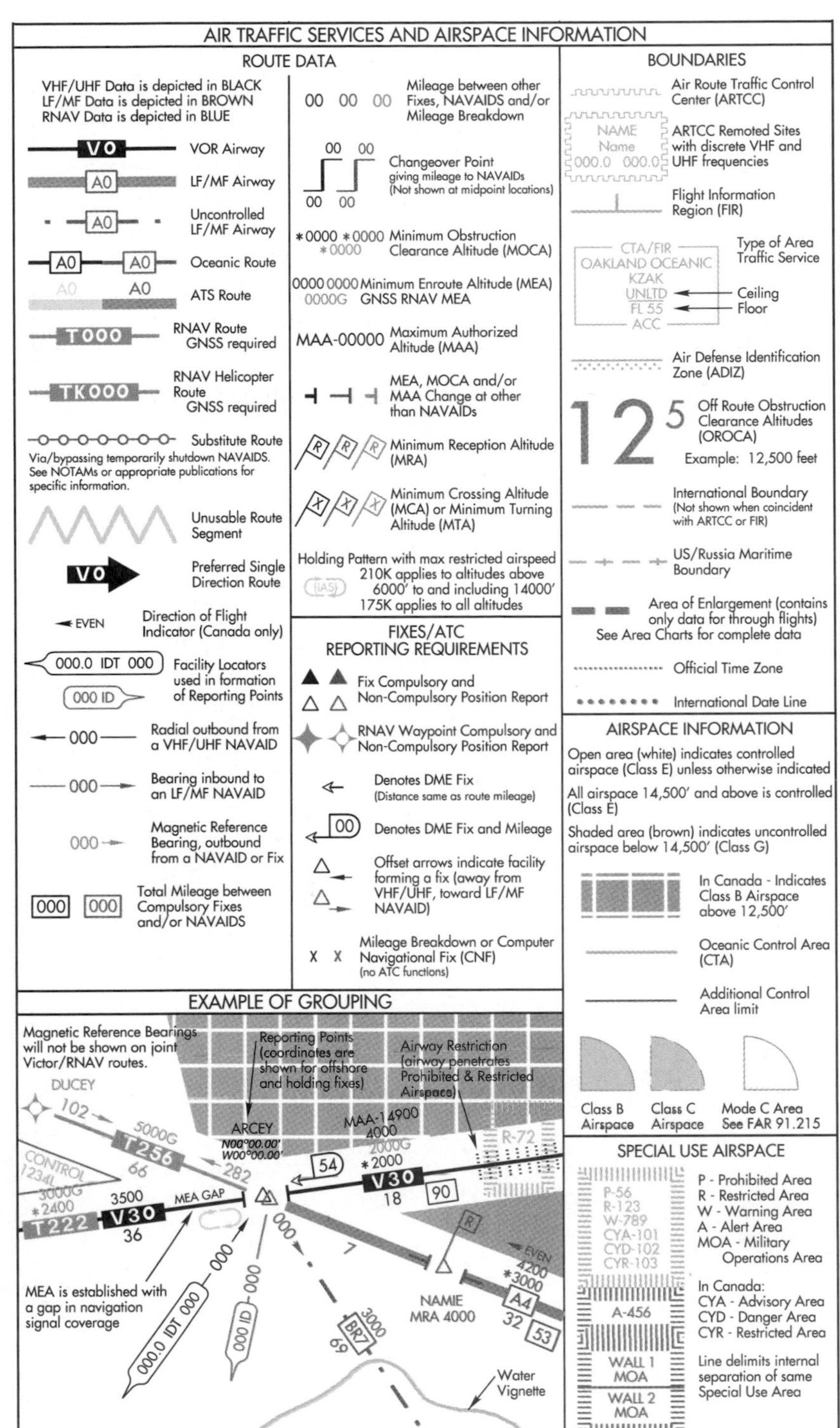

LEGEND 34.—IFR En Route Low Altitude (U.S.)

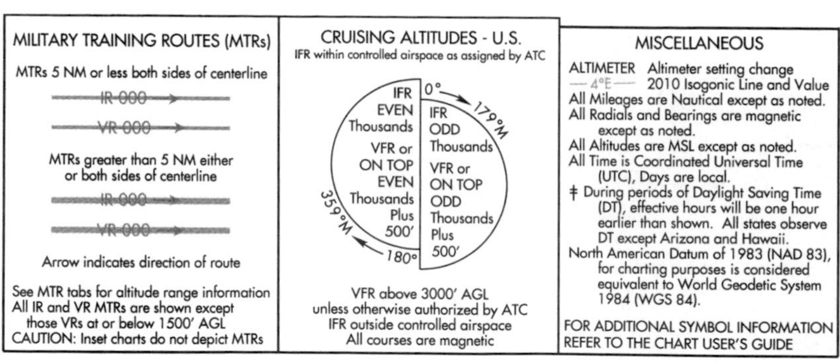

LEGEND 35.—IFR En Route Low Altitude (U.S.)

AIRCRAFT EQUIPMENT SUFFIXES	
SUFFIX	Aircraft Equipment Suffixes
	NO DME
/X	No transponder
/T	Transponder with no Mode C
/U	Transponder with Mode C
	DME
/D	No transponder
/B	Transponder with no Mode C
/A	Transponder with Mode C
	TACAN ONLY
/M	No transponder
/N	Transponder with no Mode C
/P	Transponder with Mode C
	AREA NAVIGATION (RNAV)
/Y	LORAN, VOR/DME, or INS with no transponder
/C	LORAN, VOR/DME, or INS, transponder with no Mode C
/I	LORAN, VOR/DME, or INS, transponder with Mode C
	ADVANCED RNAV WITH TRANSPONDER AND MODE C (if an aircraft is unable to operate with a transponder and/or Mode C, it will revert to the appropriate code listed above under Area Navigation.)
/E	Flight Management System (FMS) with en route, terminal, and approach capability. Equipment requirements are: (a) Dual FMS which meets the specifications of AC 25-15, Approval of Flight Management Systems in Transport Category Airplanes; AC 20-129, Airworthiness Approval of Vertical Navigation (VNAV) Systems for use in the U.S. NAS and Alaska; AC 20-130, Airworthiness Approval of Navigation or Flight Management Systems Integrating Multiple Navigation Sensors; or equivalent criteria as approved by Flight Standards. (b) A flight director and autopilot control system capable of following the lateral and vertical FMS flight path. (c) At least dual inertial reference units (IRU's). (d) A database containing the waypoints and speed/altitude constraints for the route and/or procedure to be flown that is automatically loaded into the FMS flight plan. (e) An electronic map. (U.S. and U.S. territories only unless otherwise authorized.)
/F	A single FMS with en route, terminal, and approach capability that meets the equipment requirements of /E, (a) through (d), above. (U.S. and U.S. territories only unless otherwise authorized.)
/G	Global Positioning System (GPS)/Global Navigation Satellite System (GNSS) equipped aircraft with en route and terminal capability.
/R	Required Navigational Performance (Denotes capability to operate in RNP designated airspace and routes)
/W	Reduced Vertical Separation Minima (RVSM)

LEGEND 36.—Aircraft Equipment Suffixes.

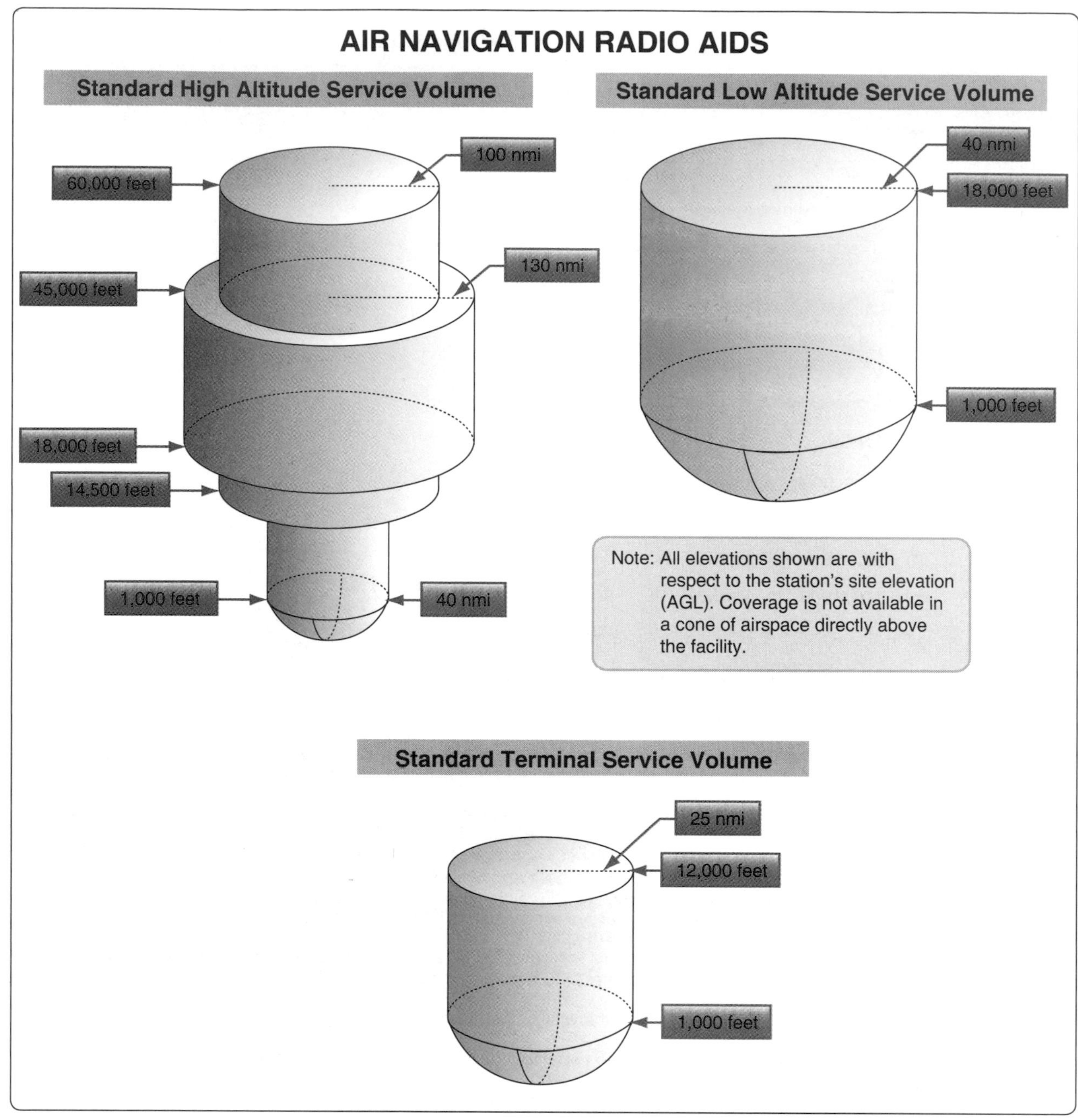

LEGEND 37.—Air Navigation Radio Aids.

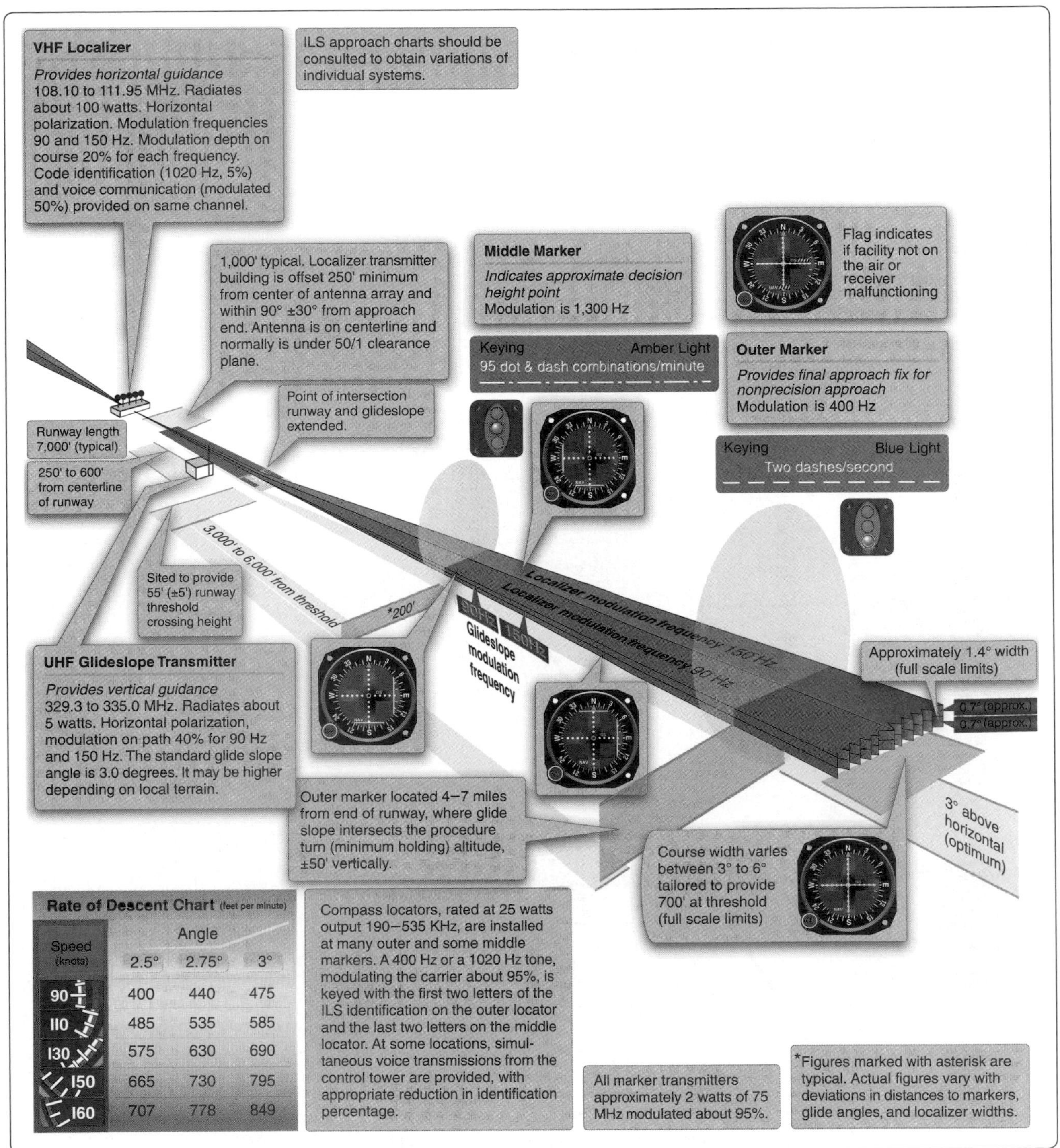

Speed (knots)	Angle 2.5°	2.75°	3°
90	400	440	475
110	485	535	585
130	575	630	690
150	665	730	795
160	707	778	849

Legend 38.—ILS Standard Characteristics and Terminology.

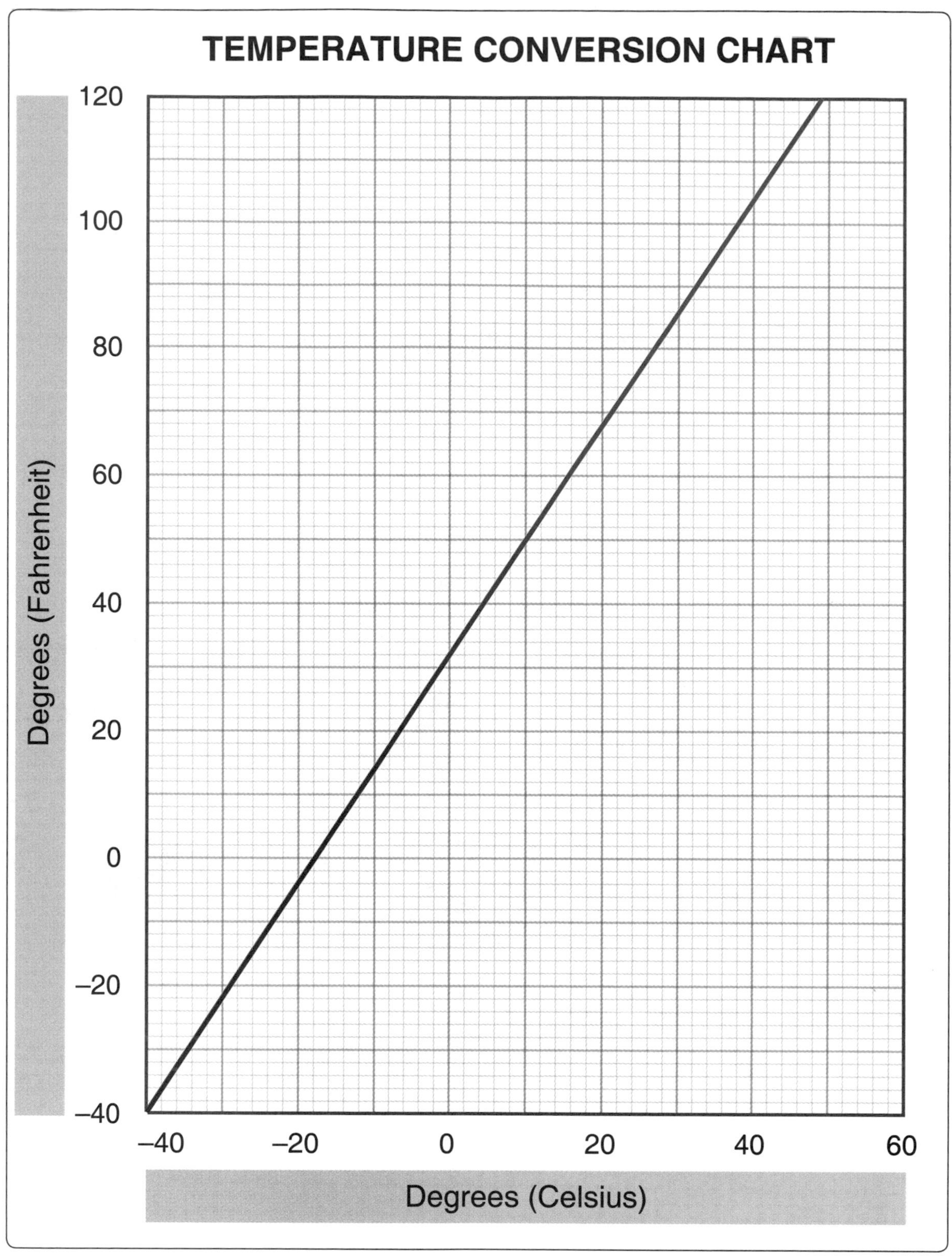

LEGEND 39.—Temperature Conversion Chart.

APPENDIX 2

VALID 1600Z FOR USE 0900-1500Z. TEMPS NEG ABV 24000									
FT	3000	6000	9000	12000	18000	24000	30000	34000	39000
EMI	2807	2715-07	2728-10	2842-13	2867-21	2891-30	751041	771150	780855
ALB	0210	9900-07	2714-09	2728-12	2656-19	2777-28	781842	760150	269658
PSB		1509+04	2119+01	2233-04	2262-14	2368-26	781939	760850	780456
STL	2308	2613+02	2422-03	2431-08	2446-19	2461-30	760142	782650	760559

FIGURE 2.—Wind and Temperatures Aloft Forecast.

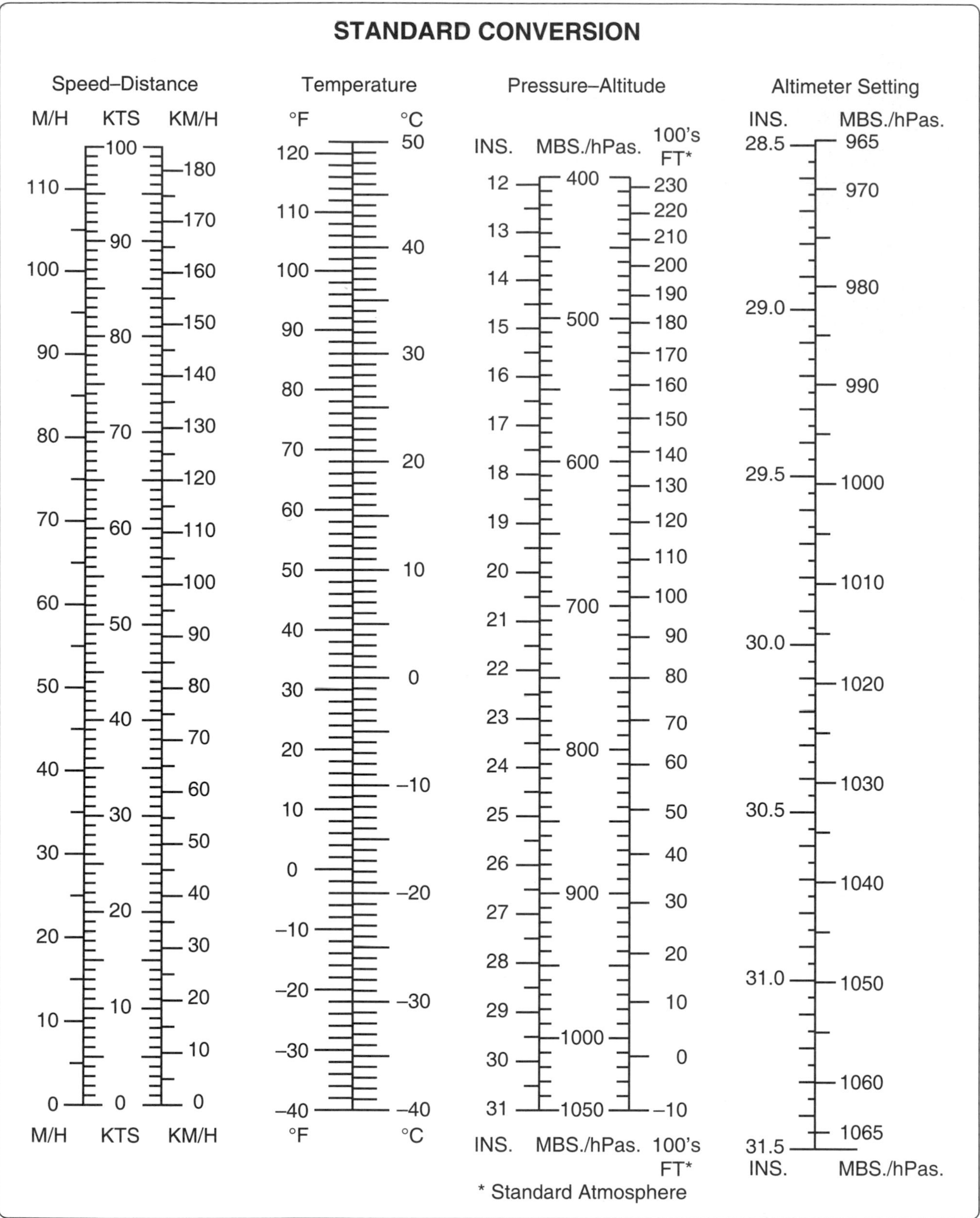

FIGURE 3.—Standard Conversion Chart.

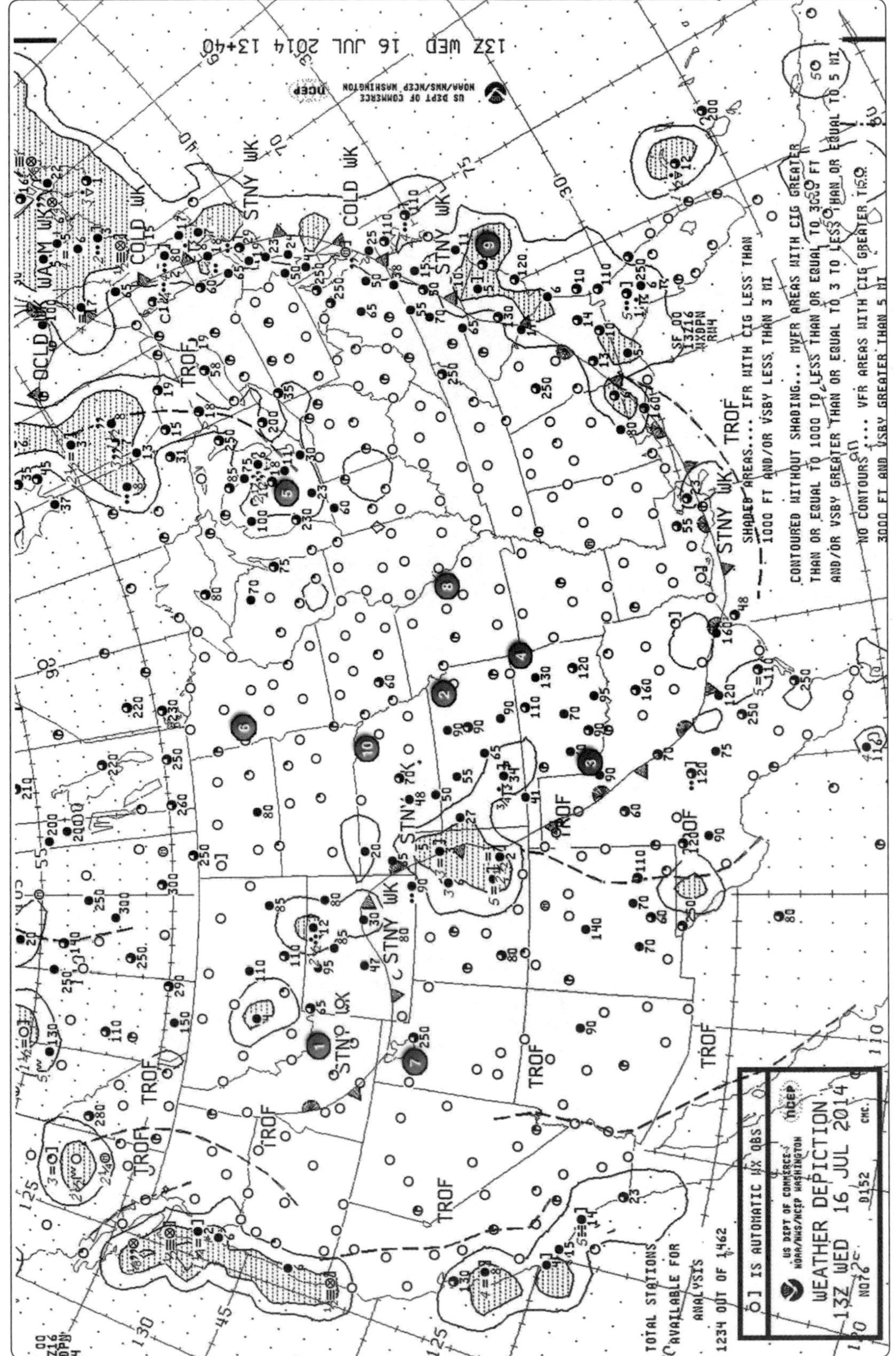

FIGURE 4.—Weather Depiction Chart.

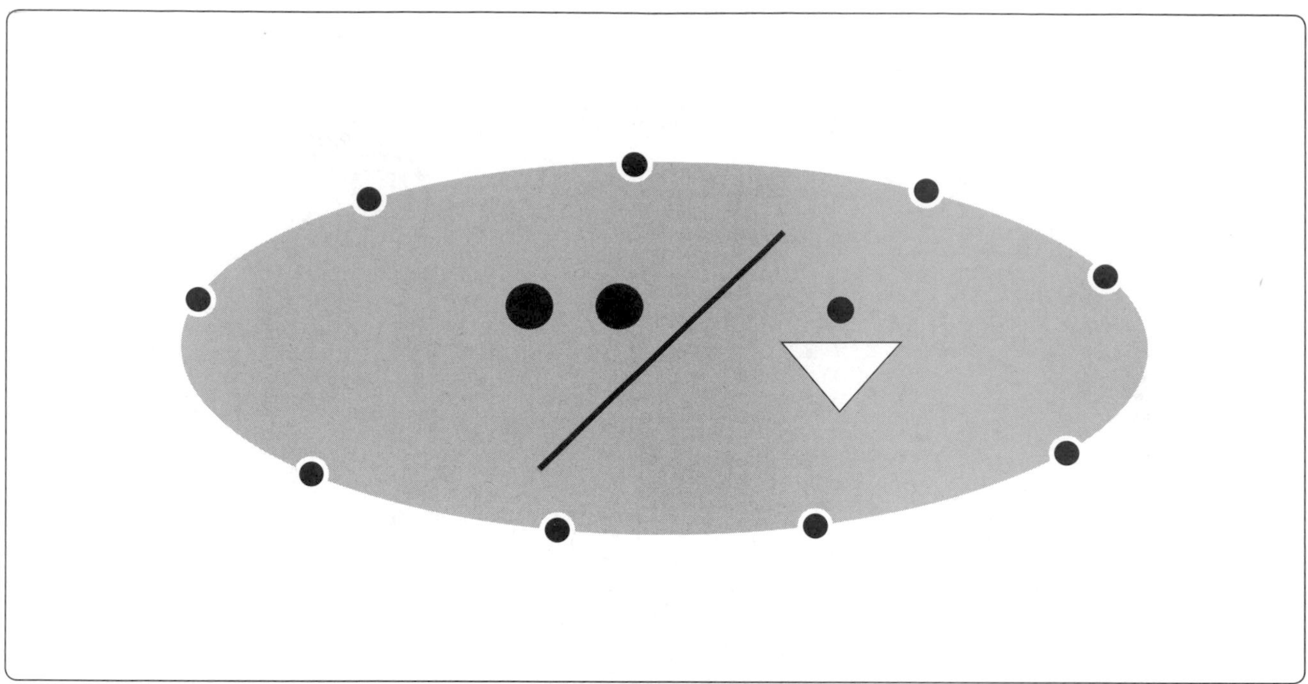

FIGURE 5.—Symbol Used on Low-Level Significant Weather Prognostic Chart.

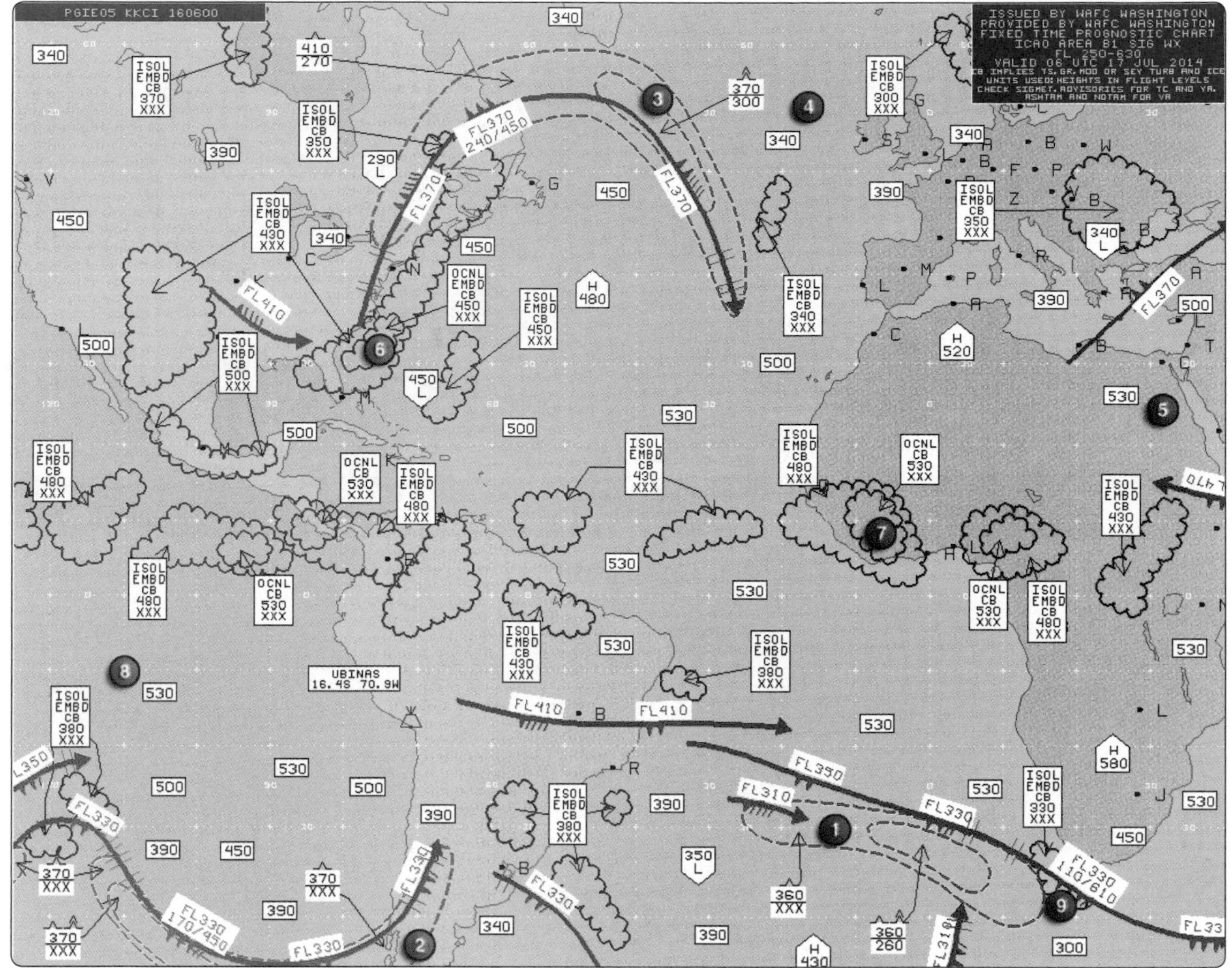

FIGURE 7.—High-Level Significant Weather Prognostic Chart.

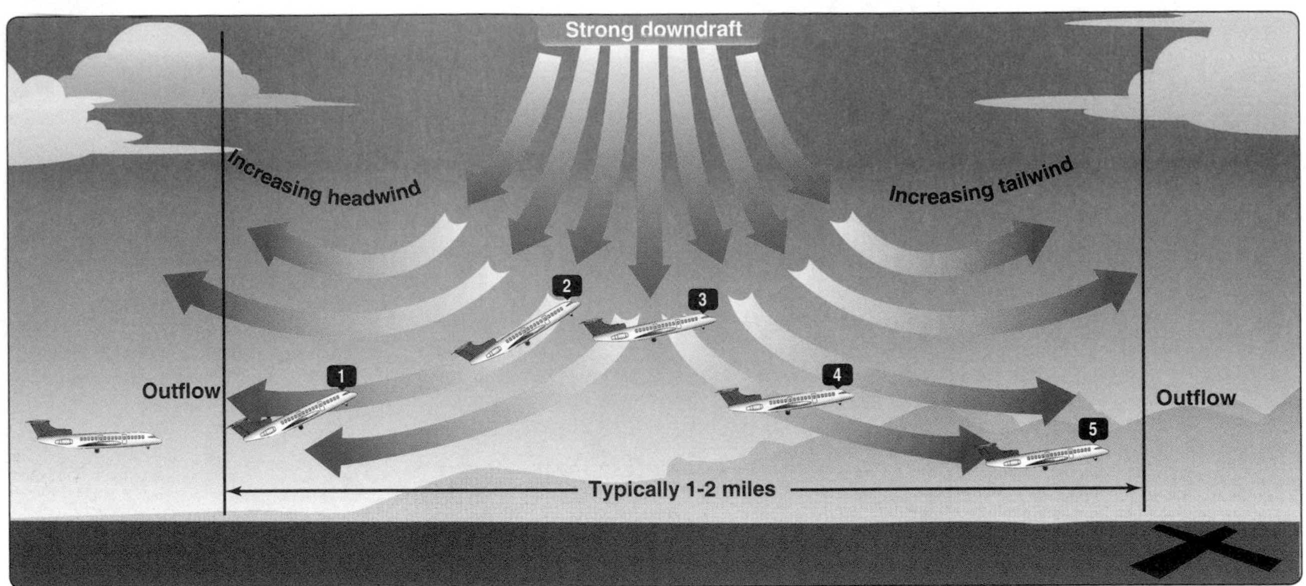

FIGURE 13.—Microburst Section Chart.

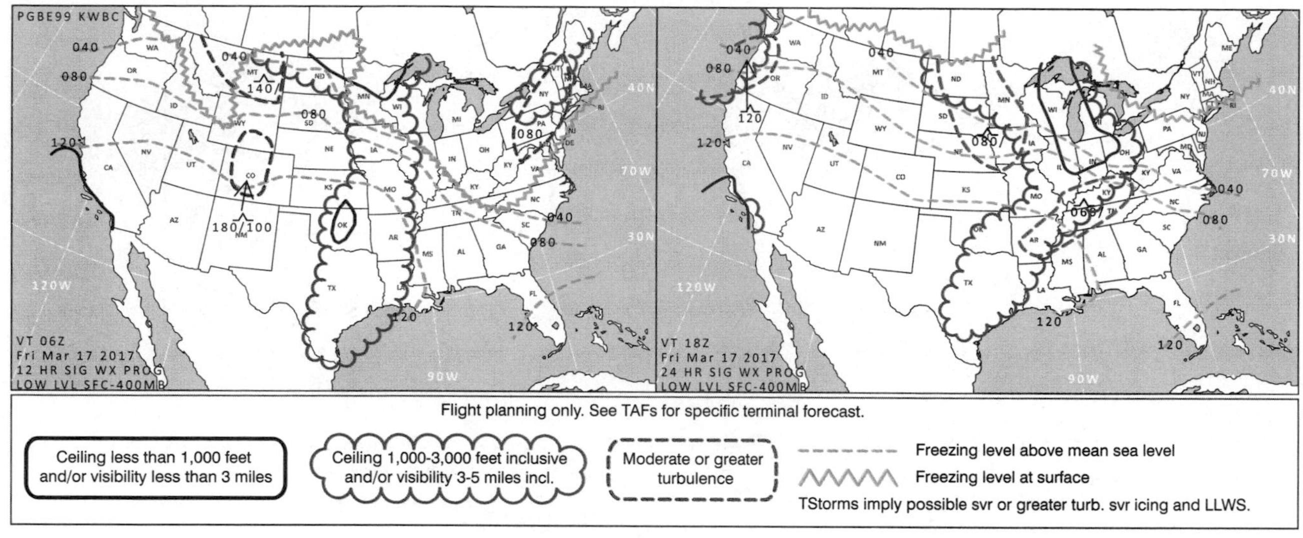

FIGURE 18.—U.S. Low-Level Significant Weather Prognostic Charts.

Appendix 2

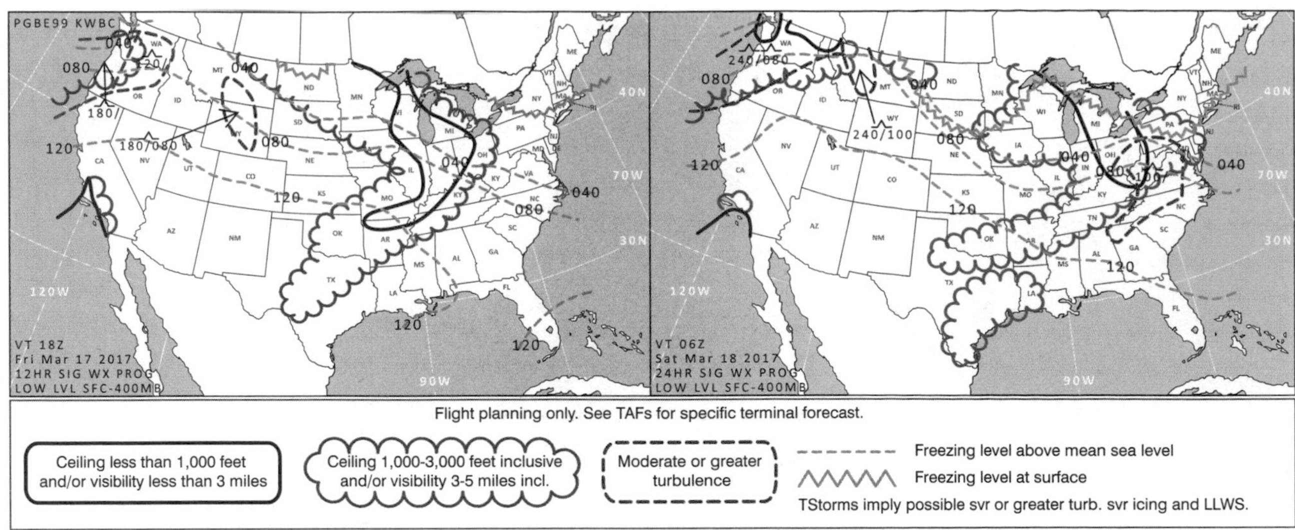

FIGURE 19.—U.S. Low-Level Significant Weather Prognostic Charts.

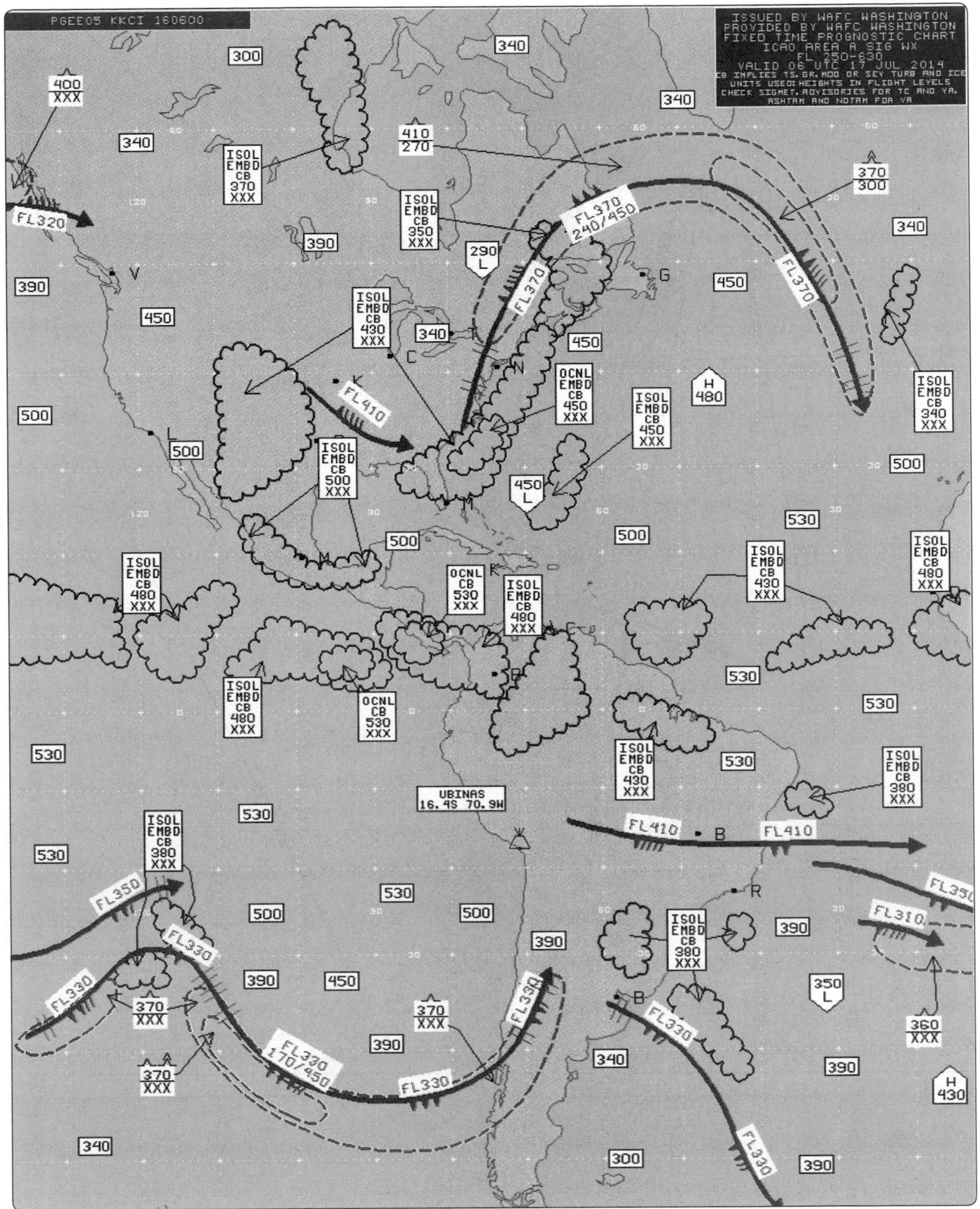

FIGURE 20.—High-Level Significant Weather Prognostic Chart.

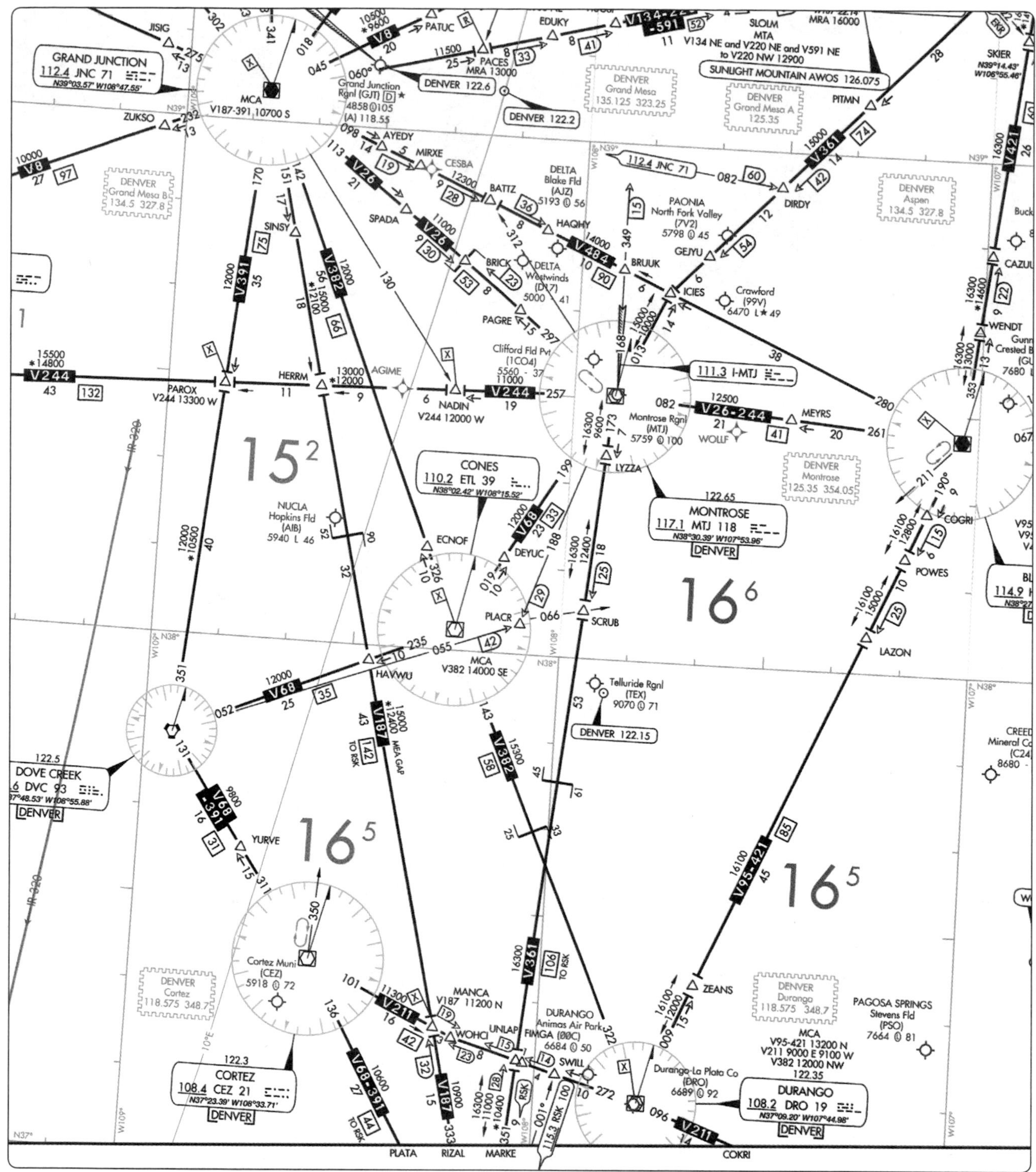

FIGURE 24.—En Route Low-Altitude Chart Segment.
NOTE: Chart is not to scale and should not be used for navigation. Chart is for testing purposes only.

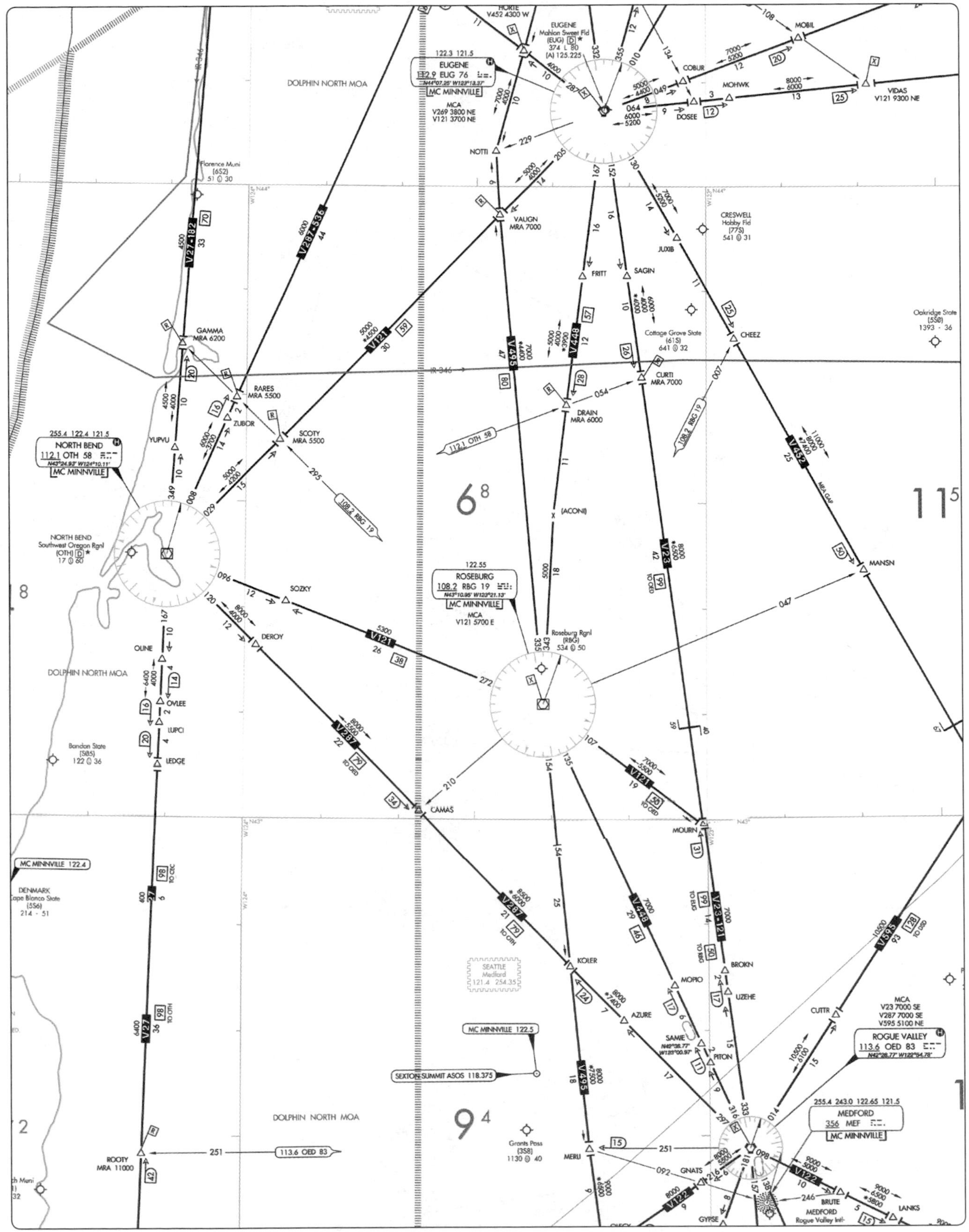

FIGURE 31.—En Route Low-Altitude Chart Segment.
NOTE: Chart is not to scale and should not be used for navigation. Chart is for testing purposes only.

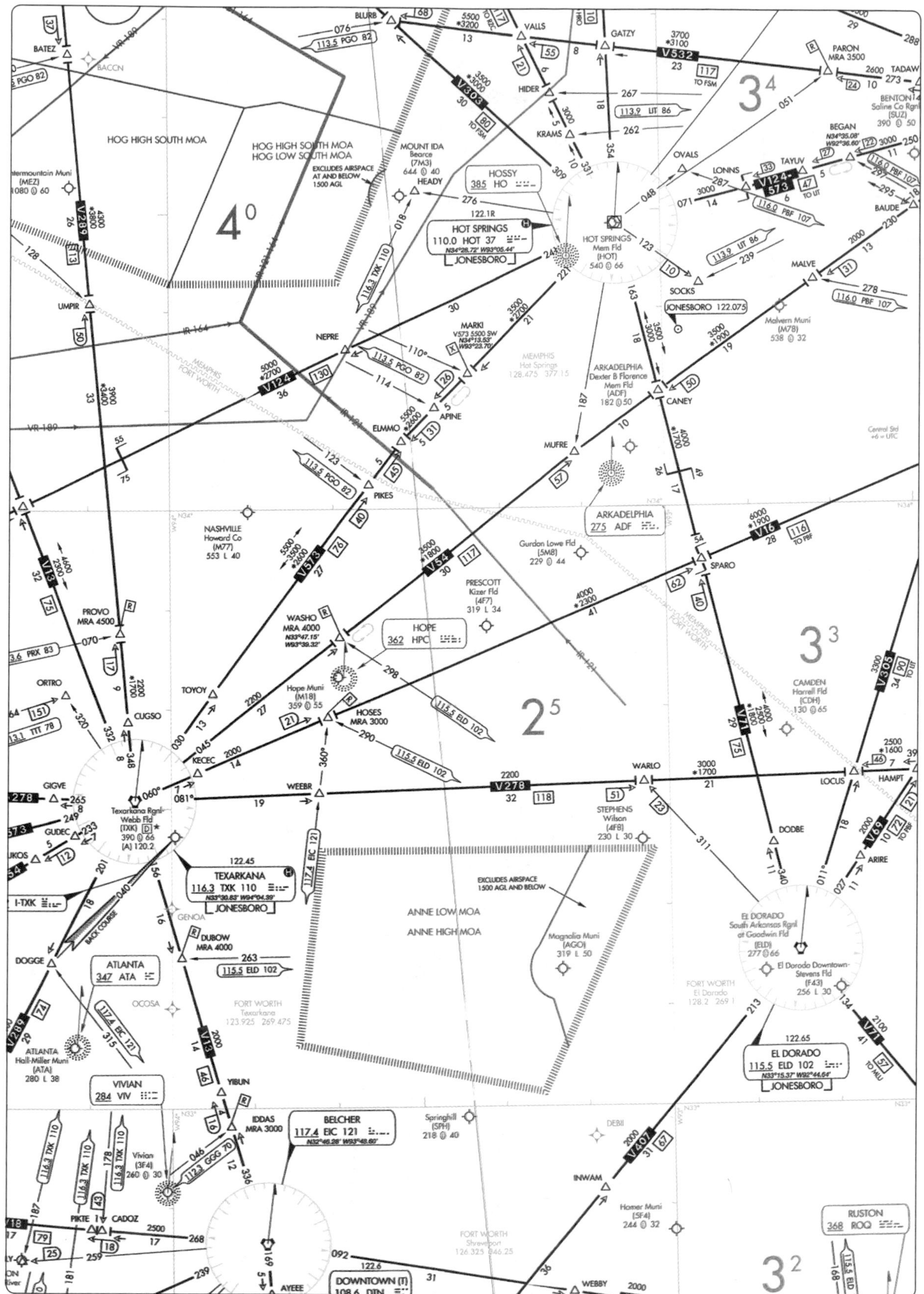

FIGURE 34.—En Route Low-Altitude Chart Segment.

NOTE: Chart is not to scale and should not be used for navigation. Chart is for testing purposes only.

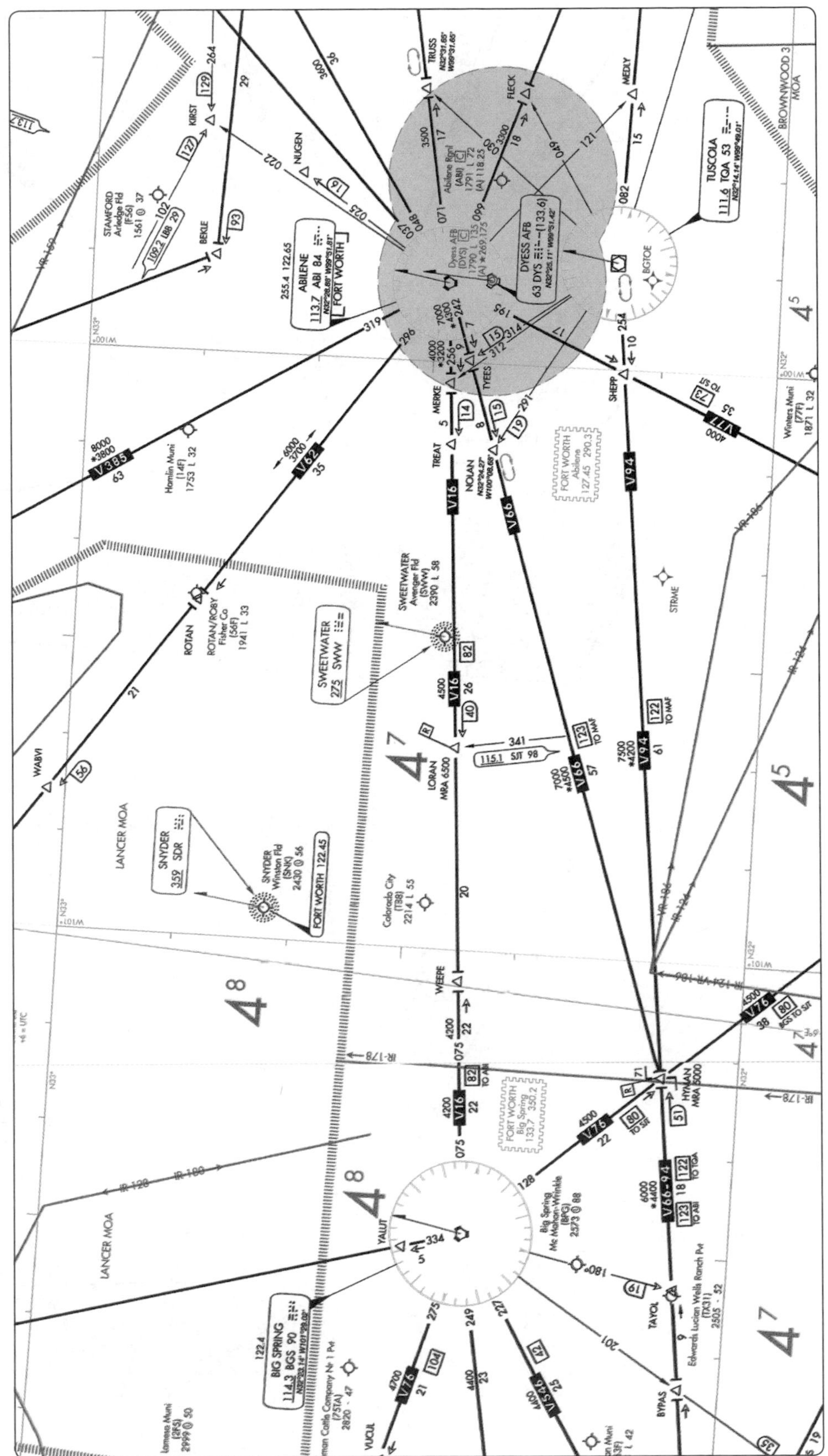

FIGURE 40.—En Route Low-Altitude Chart Segment.
NOTE: Chart is not to scale and should not be used for navigation. Chart is for testing purposes only.

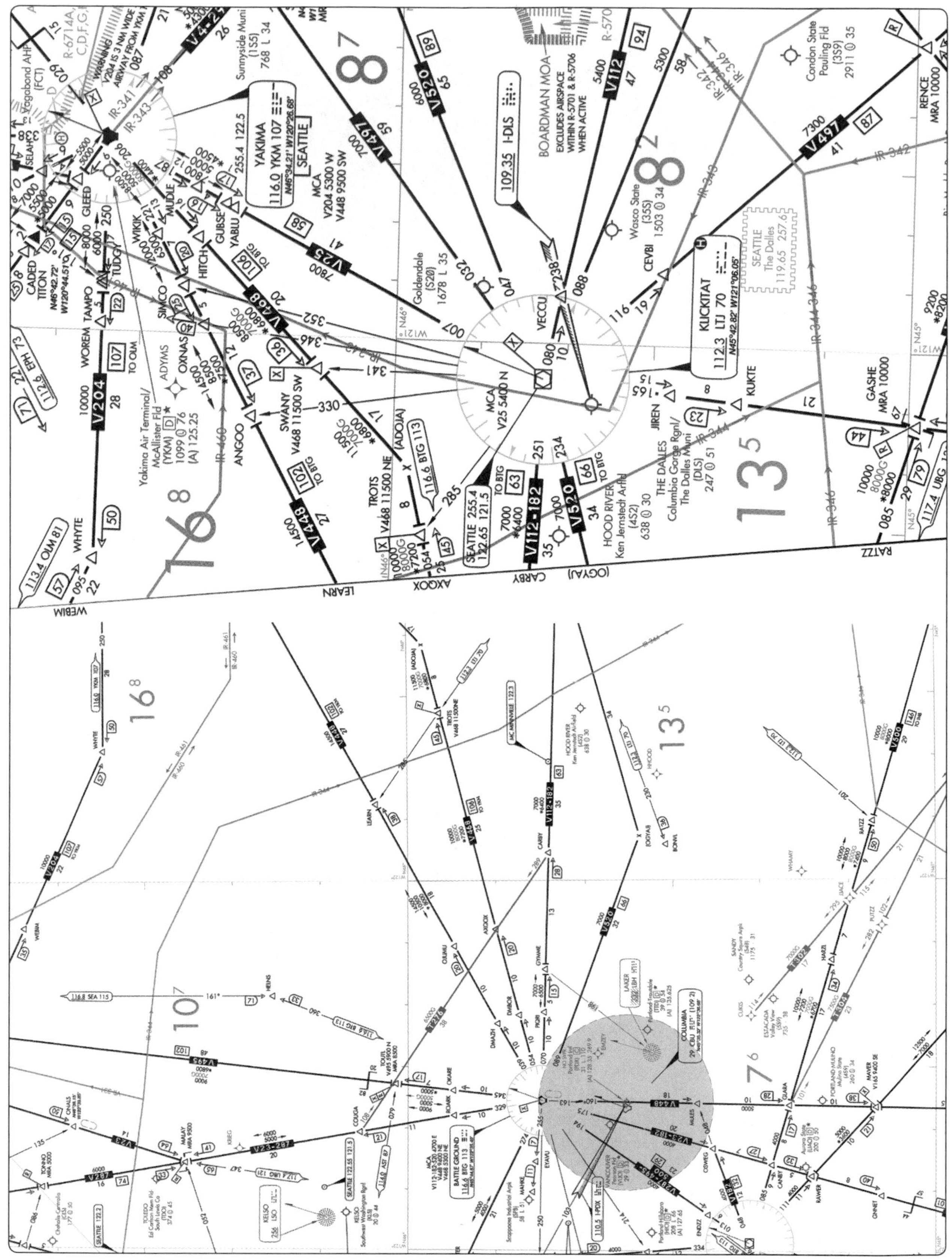

FIGURE 47.—En Route Low-Altitude Chart Segment.
NOTE: Chart is not to scale and should not be used for navigation. Chart is for testing purposes only.

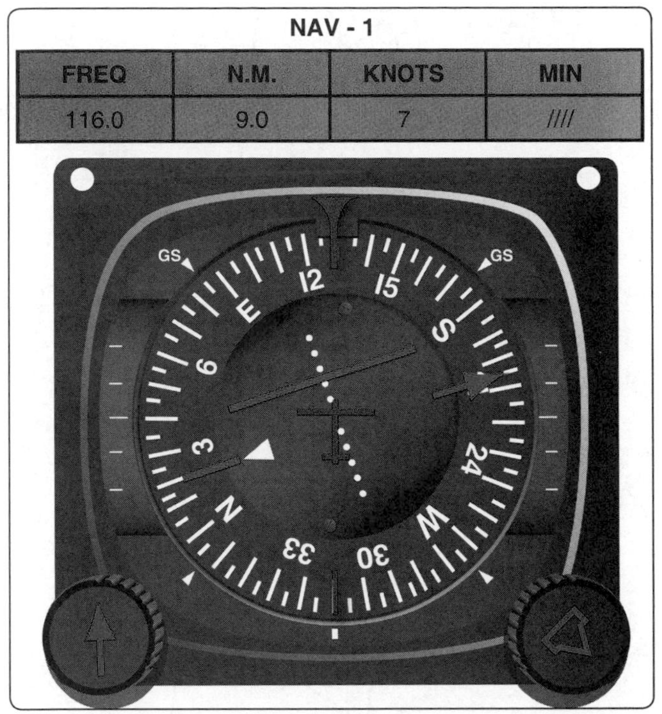

FIGURE 48.—CDI—NAV 1.

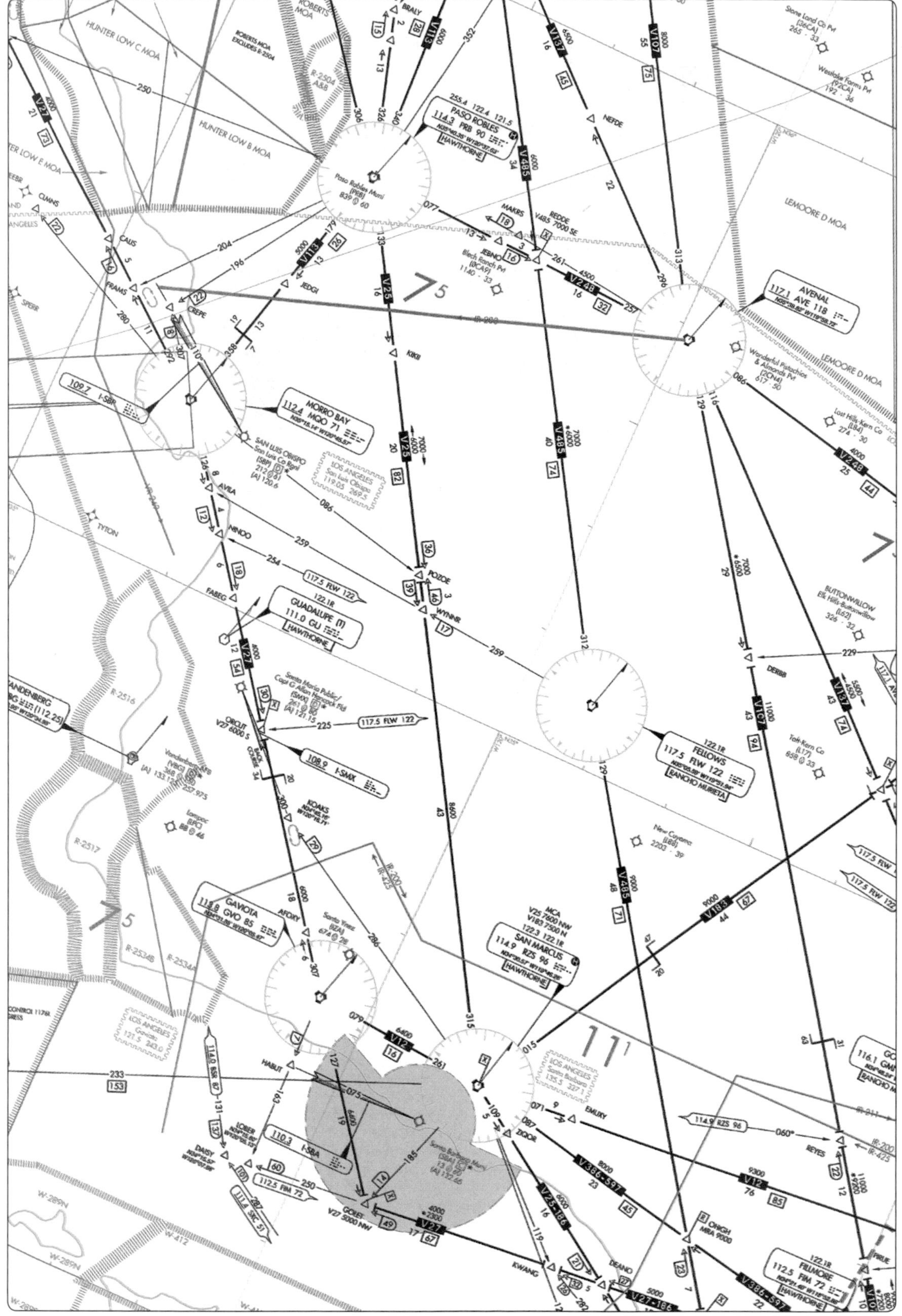

FIGURE 53.—En Route Low-Altitude Chart Segment.
NOTE: Chart is not to scale and should not be used for navigation. Chart is for testing purposes only.

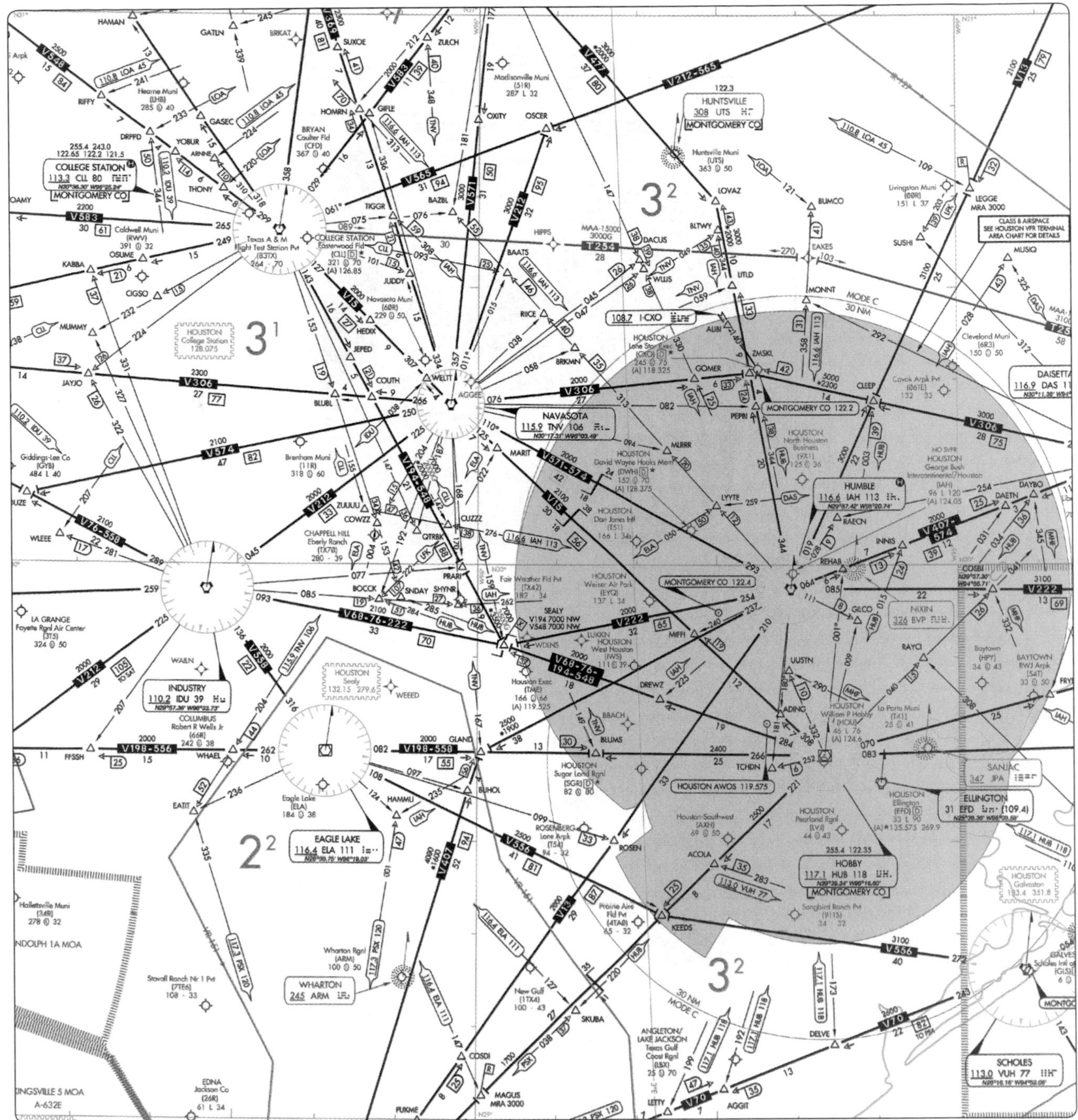

FIGURE 59.—En Route Low-Altitude Chart Segment.
NOTE: Chart is not to scale and should not be used for navigation. Chart is for testing purposes only.

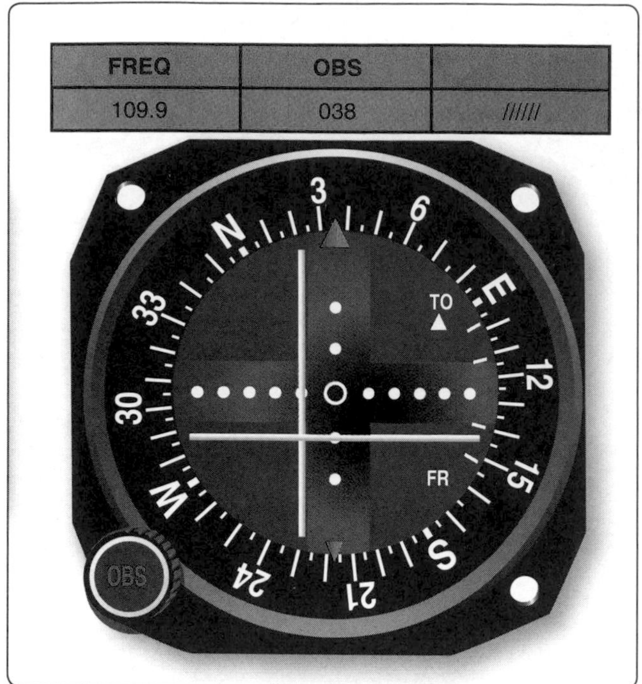

FIGURE 61.—CDI Indicator.

LOUISIANA
VOR RECEIVER CHECKPOINTS

Facility Name (Arpt Name)	Freq/Ident	Type Check Pt. Gnd. AB/ALT	Azimuth from Fac. Mag	Dist. from Fac. N.M.	Checkpoint Description
Alexandria (Alexandria Intl)	116.1/AEX	G	328	4.3	On runup Rwy 32.
Baton Rouge (Baton Rouge Metro, Ryan).	116.5/BTR	A/1500	063	7.2	Over water tank W side of arpt.
Lafayette (Lafayette Rgnl/Paul Fournet Fld)	109.8/LFT	A/1000	343	22.1	Over rotating beacon at St. Landry Parish–Ahart Fld. arpt.
	109.8/LFT	G	355	0.5	On Twy F run up area Rwy 04L.
	109.8/LFT	G	341	0.9	On Twy B run up area Rwy 11.
	109.8/LFT	G	025	1.4	On Twy J run up area Rwy 22L.
	109.8/LFT	G	039	0.8	On Twy B run up area Rwy 29.
Lake Charles (Lake Charles Rgnl)	113.4/LCH	A/1000	253	6.2	Over rotg bcn on twr.
Monroe (Monroe Rgnl)...........................	117.2/MLU	G	212	0.7	On Twy G South of twr.
Natchez (Concordia Parish)....................	110.0/HEZ	A/1000	247	10.5	Over hangar NW end of fld.
Reserve (St John The Baptist Parish).......	110.8 RQR	A/1500	270	16.8	Over center of bridge.
Tibby (Houma–Terrebonne)	112.0/TBD	A/1000	121	10.7	Over intersection of Rwys 18–36 and 12–30.
Tibby (Thibodaux Muni).........................	112.0/TBD	A/1000	356	5.0	Over microwave twr near arpt.

84 **LOUISIANA**

LAFAYETTE RGNL (LFT) 2 SE UTC–6(–5DT) N30°12.30´ W91°59.27´ **HOUSTON**
42 B S4 **FUEL** 100LL, JET A OX 1, 4 Class I, ARFF Index B NOTAM FILE LFT **H–7D, L–21B, 22E, GOMC**
RWY 04R–22L: H8001X150 (ASPH–GRVD) S–140, D–170, 2S–175, 2D–290 HIRL **IAP, AD**
RWY 04R: REIL. PAPI(P4L)—GA 3.0° TCH 53´. Pole. Rgt tfc.
RWY 22L: MALSR. PAPI(P4L)—GA 3.0° TCH 52´. Thld dsplcd 342´. Trees.
RWY 11–29: H5401X148 (ASPH–GRVD) S–85, D–110, 2S–140, 2D–175 MIRL
RWY 11: REIL. PAPI(P4L)—GA 3.0° TCH 35´. Trees. Rgt tfc.
RWY 29: REIL. PAPI(P4L)—GA 3.0° TCH 35´. Tree.
RWY 04L–22R: H4099X75 (ASPH) S–25, D–32 MIRL
RWY 04L: REIL. PAPI(P2L)—GA 3.0° TCH 26´. Tree.
RWY 22R: REIL. PAPI(P2L)—GA 3.0° TCH 27´. Tree. Rgt tfc.

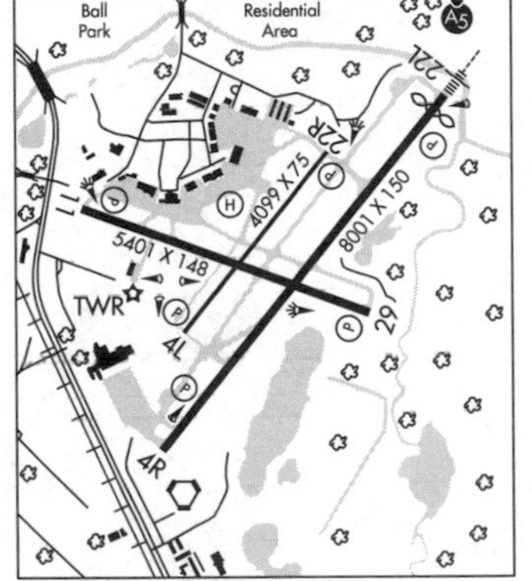

RUNWAY DECLARED DISTANCE INFORMATION

RWY 04L: TORA–4099	TODA–4099	ASDA–4099	LDA–4099
RWY 04R: TORA–8001	TODA–8001	ASDA–8001	LDA–8001
RWY 11: TORA–5401	TODA–5401	ASDA–5401	LDA–5401
RWY 22L: TORA–8001	TODA–8001	ASDA–8001	LDA–7659
RWY 22R: TORA–4099	TODA–4099	ASDA–4099	LDA–4099
RWY 29: TORA–5401	TODA–5401	ASDA–5401	LDA–5401

ARRESTING GEAR/SYSTEM
RWY 04R: EMAS
RWY 22L: EMAS

AIRPORT REMARKS: Attended continuously. Numerous birds on and invof arpt. PPR for unscheduled air carrier ops with more than 30 passenger seats call arpt manager 337–266–4400. Rwy 04L–22R not avbl for air carrier ops with more than 30 passenger seats. Ctc ground control prior to push back from terminal. 155´ oil rig 1 NM southeast of arpt. Rwy 22L runway visual range touchdown avbl. Twy B between Twy C and Twy D clsd to acft with wingspan over 80´. Twy F south of Twy B clsd to single wheel acft over 25,000 lbs and dual wheel acft over 32,000 lbs. Twy F south of Twy B reduces to 40´ wide. When twr clsd ACTIVATE MALSR Rwy 22L—CTAF, MIRL Rwy 04L–22R not avbl.

WEATHER DATA SOURCES: ASOS (337) 237–8153 **HIWAS** 109.8 LFT.

COMMUNICATIONS: CTAF 118.5 **ATIS** 134.05 **UNICOM** 122.95
RCO 122.35 (DE RIDDER RADIO)
Ⓡ **APP/DEP CON** 121.1 (020°–210°) 128.7 (211°–019°) (1130–0430Z‡)
Ⓡ **HOUSTON CENTER APP/DEP CON** 126.35 (0430–1130Z‡)
TOWER 118.5 (1130–0430Z‡) **GND CON** 121.8 **CLNC DEL** 125.55

AIRSPACE: CLASS C svc ctc **APP CON** svc 1130–0430Z‡ other times CLASS E.

RADIO AIDS TO NAVIGATION: NOTAM FILE LFT.
(L) VORTACW 109.8 LFT Chan 35 N30°11.63´ W91°59.55´ at fld. 36/3E. **HIWAS.**
LAFFS NDB (LOM) 375 LF N30°17.36´ W91°54.48´ 216° 6.5 NM to fld. Unmonitored when ATCT clsd.
ILS/DME 110.9 I–TYN Chan 46 Rwy 04R. Class IE.
ILS/DME 109.5 I–LFT Chan 32 Rwy 22L. Class IE. LOM LAFFS NDB. ILS and LOM unmonitored when ATCT clsd.
ASR (1130–0430Z‡)

FIGURE 64.—Excerpt from Chart Supplement (LFT).

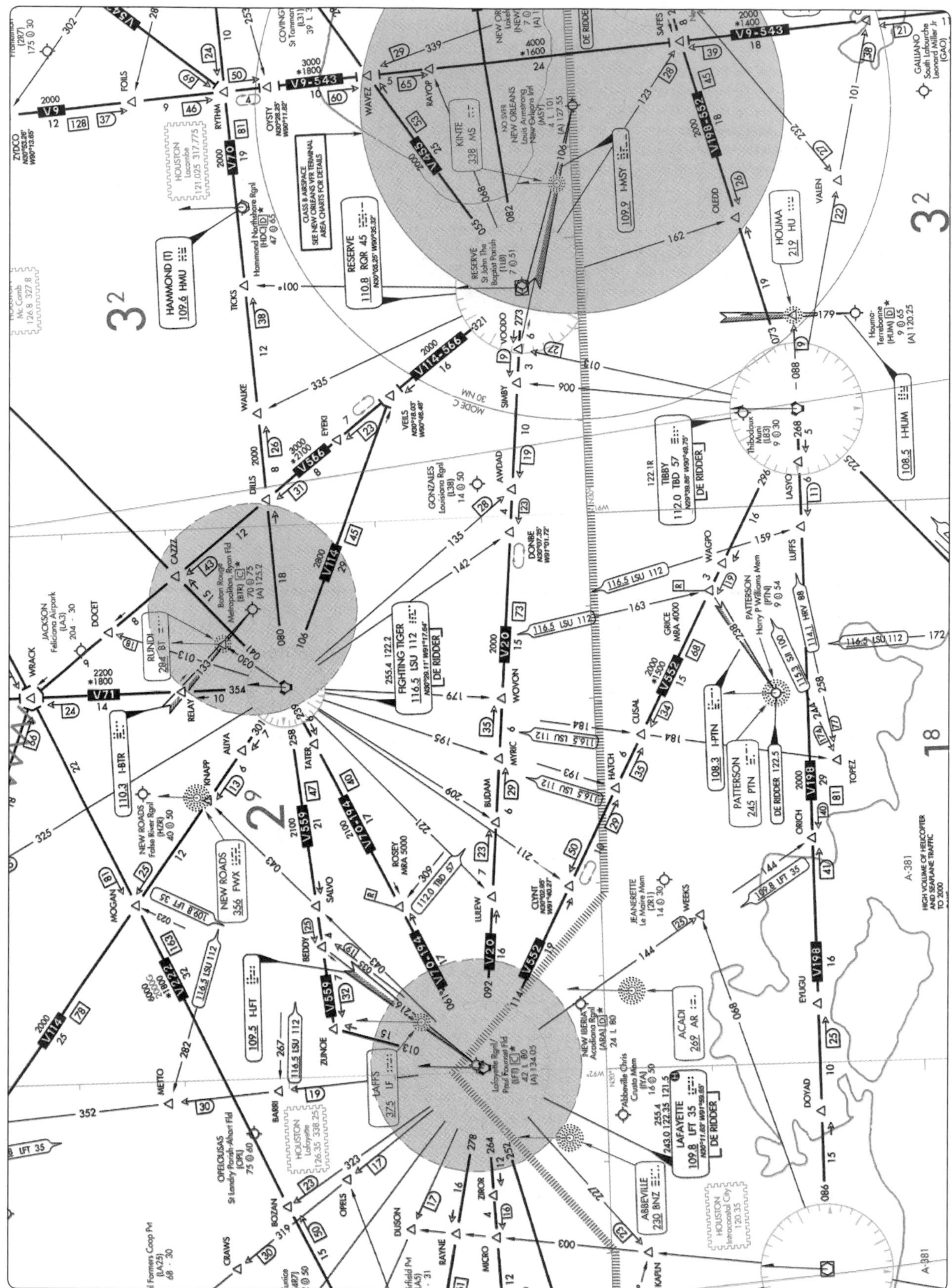

FIGURE 65.—En Route Low-Altitude Chart Segment.
NOTE: Chart is not to scale and should not be used for navigation. Chart is for testing purposes only.

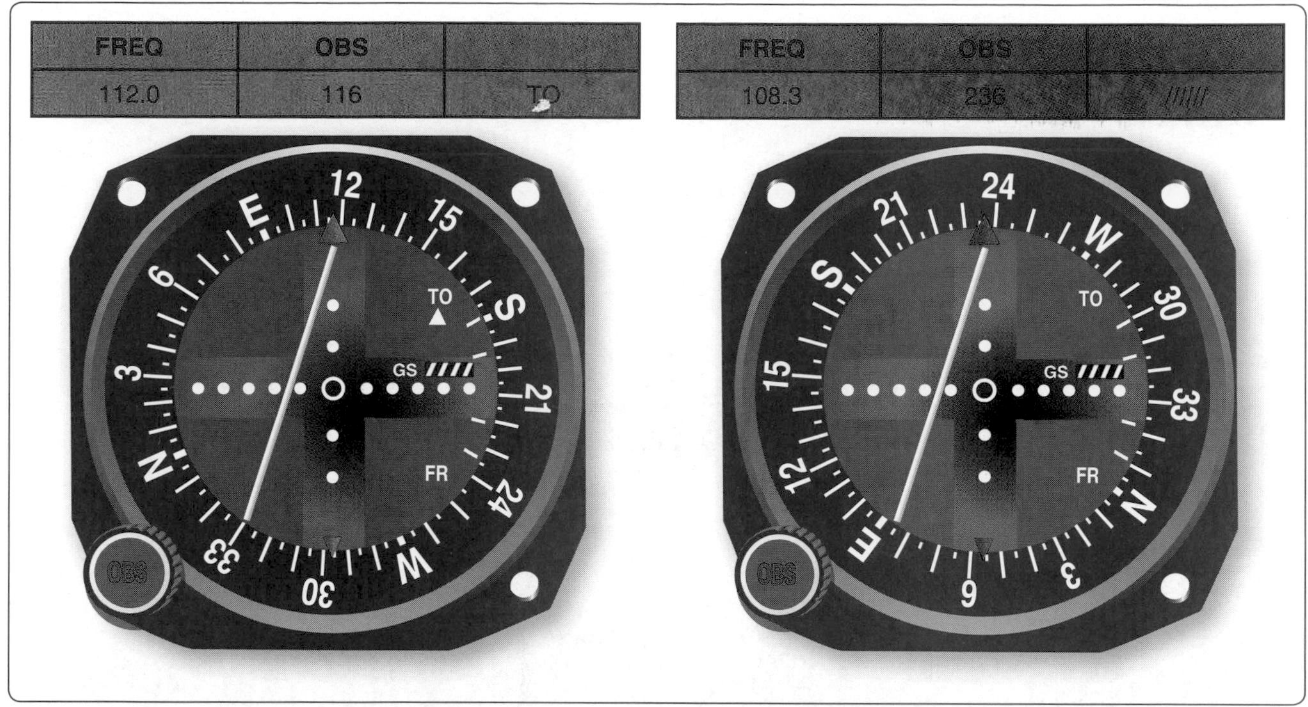

FIGURE 66.—CDI and OBS Indicators.

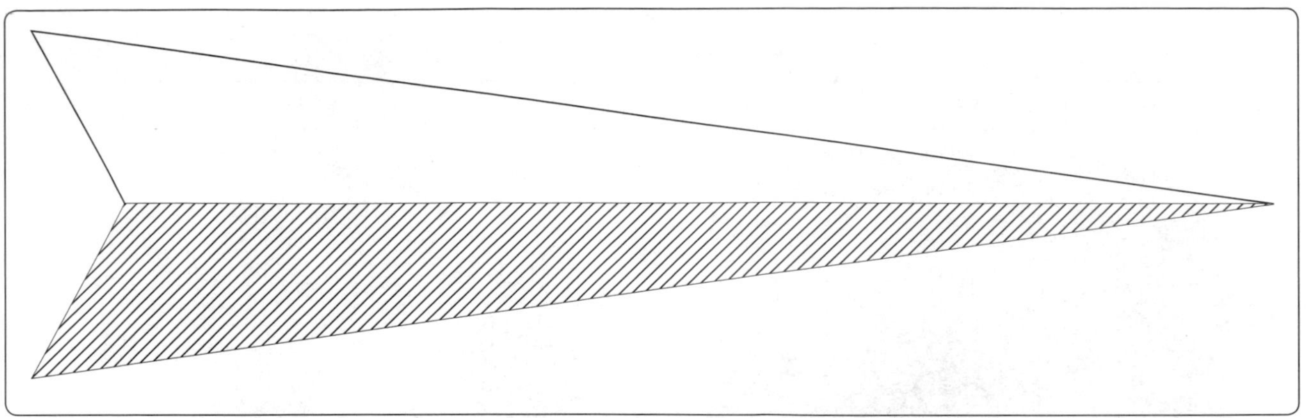

FIGURE 67.—Localizer Symbol.

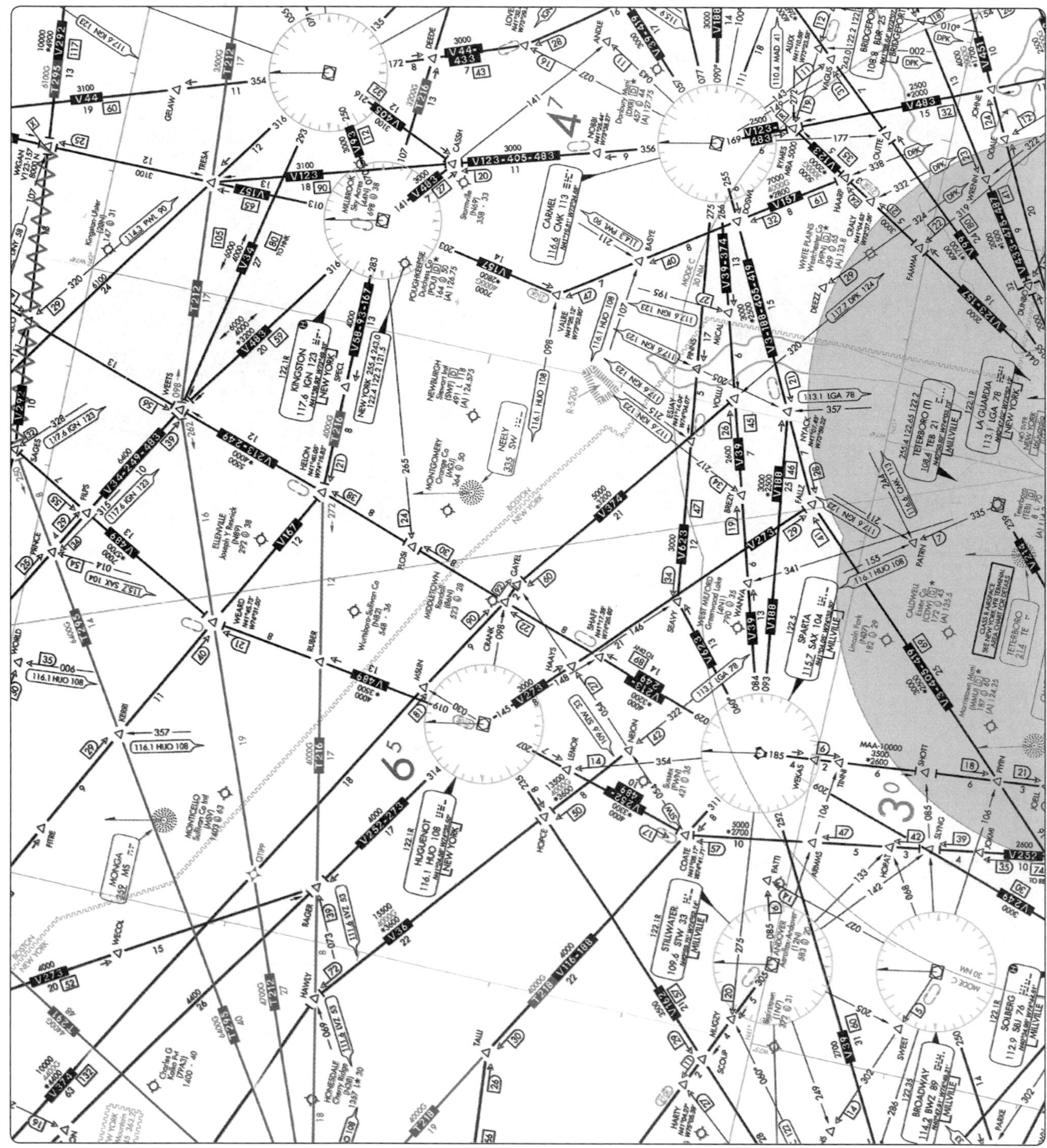

FIGURE 71.—En Route Low-Altitude Chart Segment.
NOTE: Chart is not to scale and should not be used for navigation. Chart is for testing purposes only.

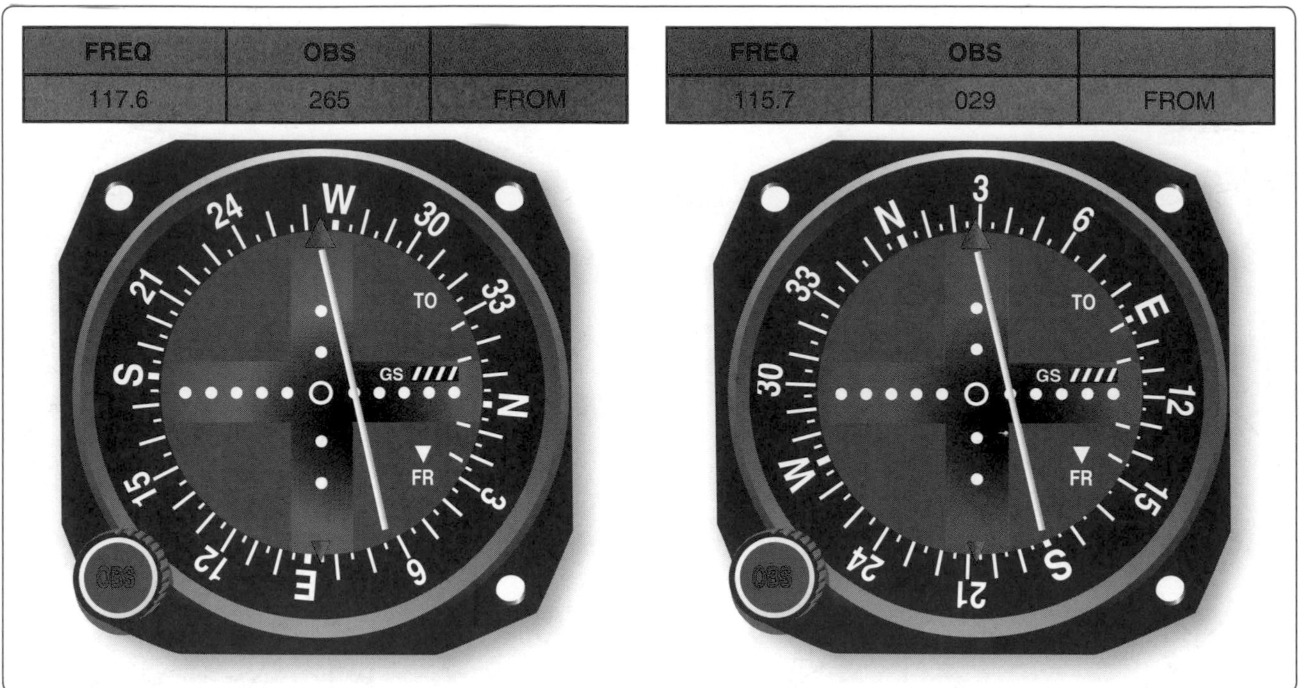

FIGURE 71A.—CDI and OBS Indicators.

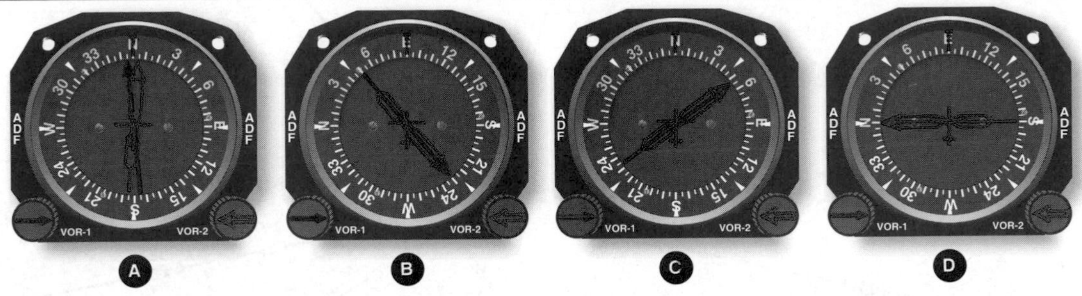

HELENA RGNL (HLN)(KHLN) P (ARNG) 2 NE UTC–7(–6DT) N46°36.41′ W111°58.97′ **GREAT FALLS**
3877 B S4 **FUEL** 80, 100, 100LL, JET A OX 1, 3 LRA Class I, ARFF Index B NOTAM FILE HLN **H–1D, L–13C**
IAP, DIAP, AD

RWY 09–27: H9000X150 (ASPH–PFC) S–100, D–160, 2S–175, 2D–250 HIRL
RWY 09: REIL. VASI(V4L)—GA 3.0° TCH 45′. Ground. 0.3% down.
RWY 27: MALSR. VASI(V4L)—GA 3.0° TCH 47′. Rgt tfc.
RWY 05–23: H4644X75 (ASPH–PFC) S–21, D–30 MIRL 1.2% up SW
RWY 05: Road.
RWY 23: PAPI(P2L)—GA 3.0° TCH 49′. Fence. Rgt tfc.
RWY 16–34: H2989X75 (ASPH–PFC) S–21, D–30 MIRL 1.7% up SE
RWY 34: Ground. Rgt tfc.

Rwy 16-34: 2989 X 75

MILITARY SERVICE: FUEL A+, J8 (C406–442–2190. Opr 1200–0600Z‡, OT $150 fee, 90 min PPR.) (NC–80, 100, 100LL)

AIRPORT REMARKS: Attended 1200–0800Z‡. ARFF coverage provided for scheduled Part 121 air carriers only exc with prior approval—call 406–442–2821. Landing rights customs available call 406–449–5506. Rwy 16–34 and Rwy 05–23 (except between Twy F and Rwy 09–27) not available for air carrier use by acft with greater than 30 passenger seats. Twys A, B, and C between Twy A and Rwy 34 not available for air carrier use by acft with greater than 30 passenger seats. When tower closed ACTIVATE HIRL Rwy 09–27, MIRL Rwy 05–23 and Rwy 16–34, REIL Rwy 09. MALSR Rwy 27—CTAF. Ldg fee for all commercial acft and all acft over 10,000 pounds. Flight Notification Service (ADCUS) avbl. NOTE: See SPECIAL NOTICE.

MILITARY REMARKS: ARNG Opr Mon–Fri 1400–0030Z‡, except holidays. Exercise caution while taxiing, AASF ramp not stressed for large acft. Ctc flight ops for ramp advisory 126.2, DSN 324–3055/56, C406–324–3055/56. No trans svc Sat, Sun, holidays or after 2300Z‡ Mon–Fri.

WEATHER DATA SOURCES: ASOS (406) 443–4317

COMMUNICATIONS: CTAF 118.3 **ATIS** 120.4 **UNICOM** 122.95
RCO 122.55 255.4 (GREAT FALLS RADIO)
APP/DEP CON 119.5 229.4 (1300–0500Z‡)
SALT LAKE CENTER APP/DEP CON 133.4 285.4 (0500–1300Z‡)
TOWER 118.3 257.8 (1300–0500Z‡) **GND CON** 121.9
ARNG OPS 40.65 126.2 321.45

AIRSPACE: CLASS D svc 1300–0500Z‡ other times CLASS E.

RADIO AIDS TO NAVIGATION: NOTAM FILE HLN.
(H) VORTACW 117.7 HLN Chan 124 N46°36.41′ W111°57.21′ 254° 1.2 NM to fld. 3823/16E.

VOR portion unusable:
035°–050° byd 35 NM blo 12,000′
105°–165° byd 25 NM blo 17,000′
165°–185° byd 25 NM blo 13,500′
185°–230° byd 25 NM blo 17,500′
203°–213° byd 22 NM blo 13,000′
230°–270° byd 25 NM blo 12,500′

TACAN AZIMUTH and DME unusable:
035°–070° byd 35 NM blo 13,000′
165°–185° byd 25 NM blo 13,500′
250°–300° byd 25 NM blo 14,000′
320°–035° byd 25 NM blo 13,000′

TACAN DME unusable:
035°–070° byd 35 NM blo 13,000′
105°–150° byd 25 NM
105°–210° byd 15 NM blo 11,100′
105°–210° byd 20 NM blo 12,000′
150°–165° byd 25 NM blo 17,000′
165°–185° byd 25 NM blo 13,500′
185°–210° byd 25 NM
203°–213° byd 22 NM blo 13,000′
210°–250° byd 15 NM blo 12,000′
210°–250° byd 25 NM blo 17,500′
250°–300° byd 25 NM blo 14,000′
320°–035° byd 25 NM blo 13,000′

TACAN AZIMUTH unusable:
105°–150° byd 15 NM
150°–165° byd 15 NM blo 17,000′
185°–210° byd 15 NM
210°–250° byd 15 NM blo 17,500′

CAPITOL NDB (HW) 335 CVP N46°36.40′ W111°56.23′ 258° 1.9 NM to fld. NDB unmonitored when ATCT clsd.
HAUSER NDB (MHW) 386 HAU N46°34.13′ W111°45.48′ 268° 9.6 NM to fld. NDB unmonitored when HLN ATCT clsd.
ILS 110.1 I–HLN Rwy 27. Unmonitored when ATCT closed. Localizer backcourse unusable byd 22° rgt of course, unusable within 2.7 DME.

VOR RECEIVER CHECKPOINTS

Facility Name (Arpt Name)	Freq/Ident	Type Check Pt. Gnd. AB/ALT	Azimuth from Fac. Mag	Dist. from Fac. N.M.	Checkpoint Description
Helena (Helena Rgnl)	117.7/HLN	G	238	0.7	On Twy E on South side of Rwy 27.
Kalispell (Glacier Park Intl)	113.2/FCA	A/4000	316	6.4	Over apch end Rwy 30.
Lewistown (Lewistown Muni)	112.0/LWT	A/5200	075	5.6	Over apch end Rwy 07.
Livingston	116.1/LVM	A/6500	237	5.5	Over northern most radio twr NE of city.
Miles City (Frank Wiley Field)	112.1/MLS	G	036	4.2	On twy leading to Rwy 30.
Missoula (Missoula Intl)	112.8/MSO	G	344	0.6	Terminal ramp east of Twy D.

FIGURE 76.—VOR Indications and Excerpts from Chart Supplement (HLN).

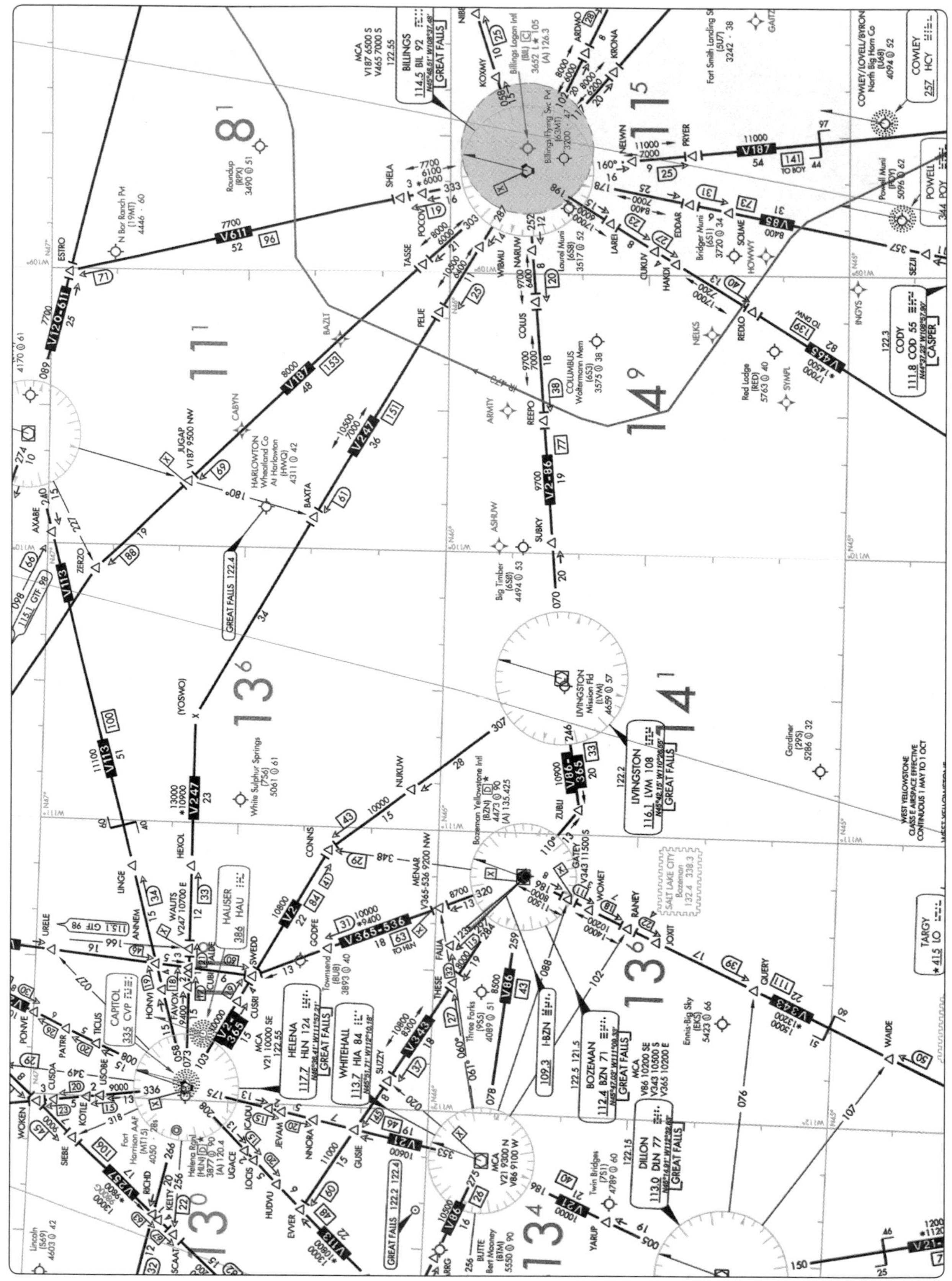

FIGURE 78.—En Route Low-Altitude Chart Segment.

NOTE: Chart is not to scale and should not be used for navigation. Chart is for testing purposes only.

FIGURE 81.—Dual VOR System, VOT Check.

FIGURE 82.—Dual VOR System, Accuracy Check.

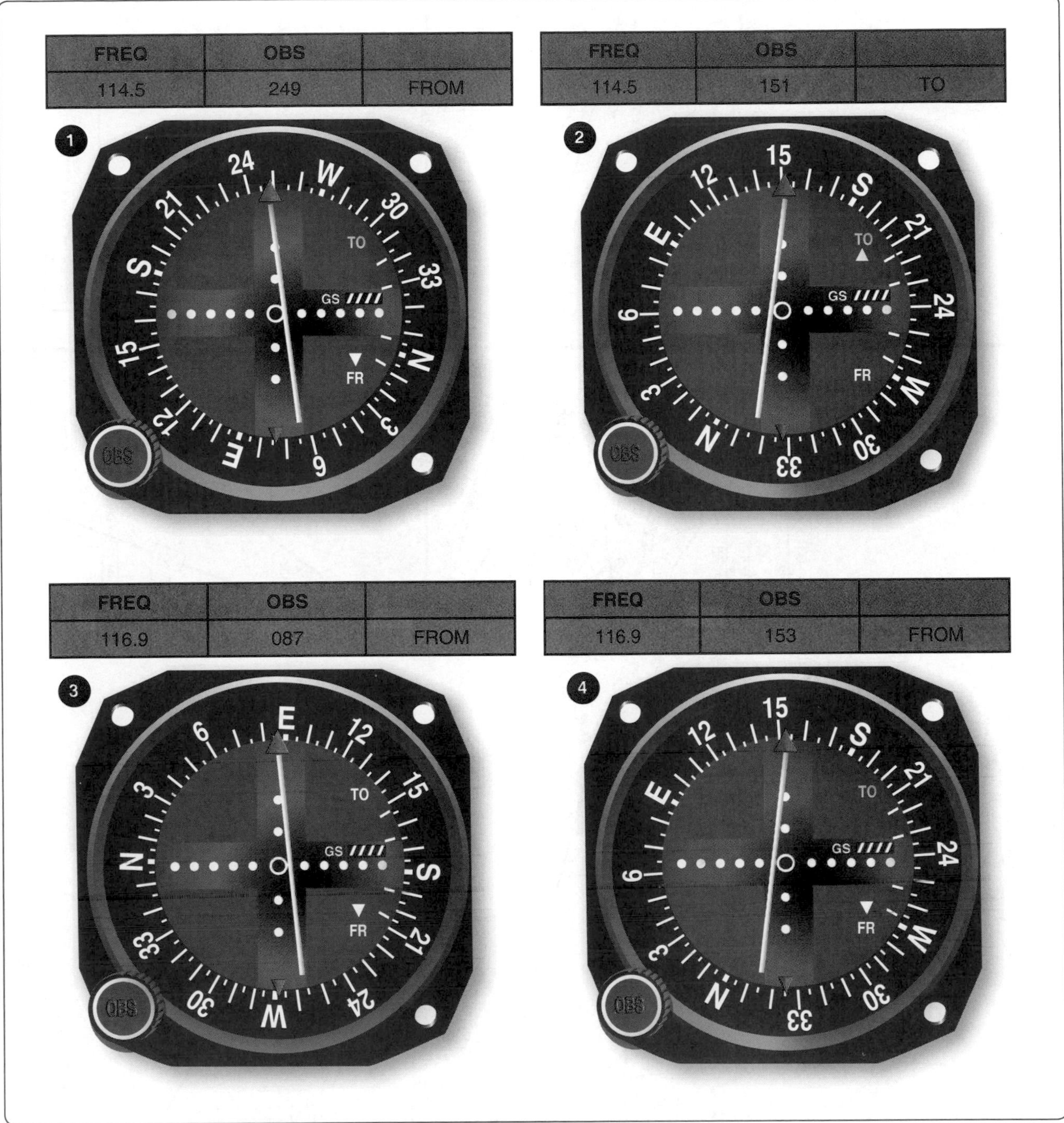

FIGURE 86.—CDI and OBS Indicators.

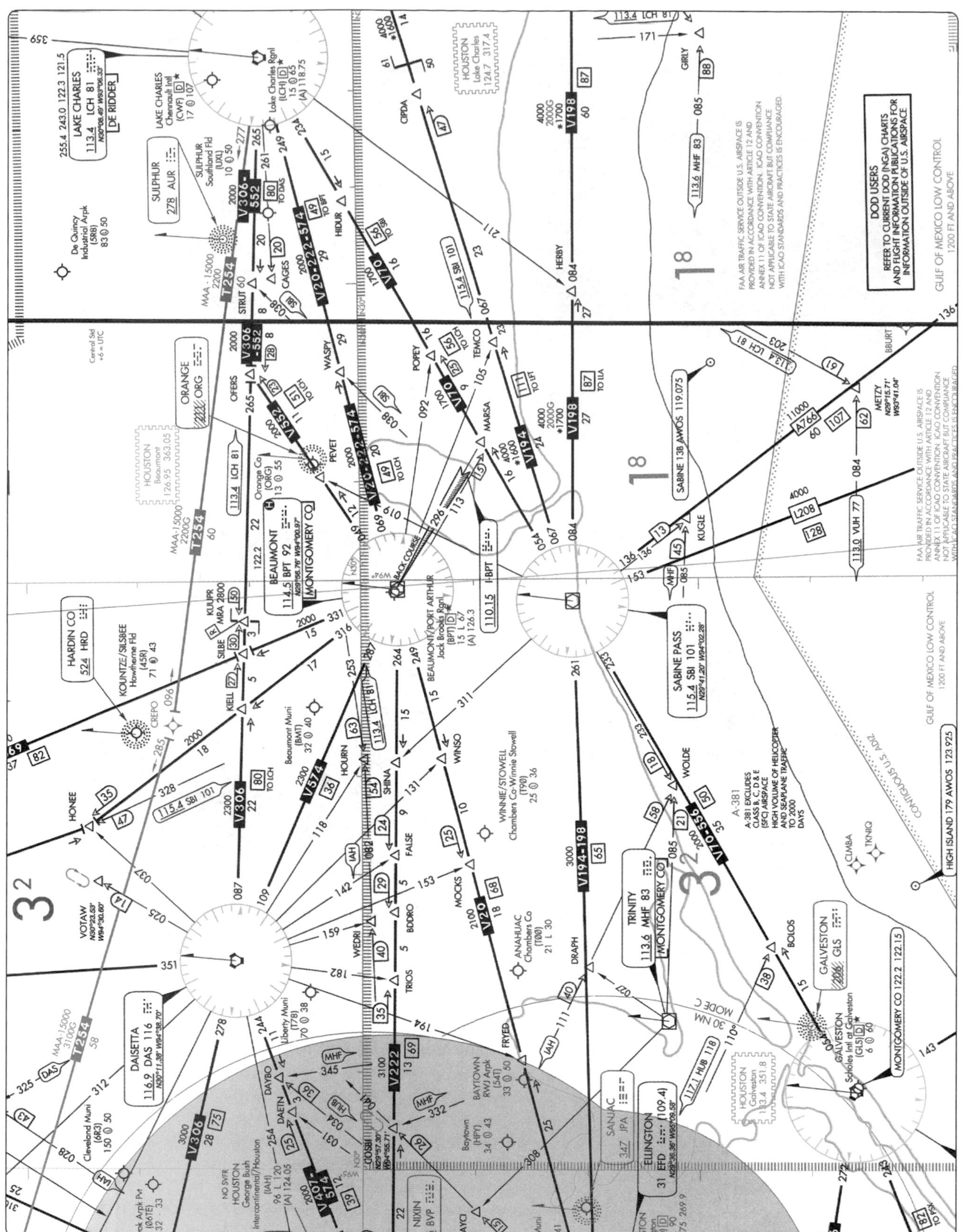

FIGURE 87.—En Route Low-Altitude Chart Segment.
NOTE: Chart is not to scale and should not be used for navigation. Chart is for testing purposes only.

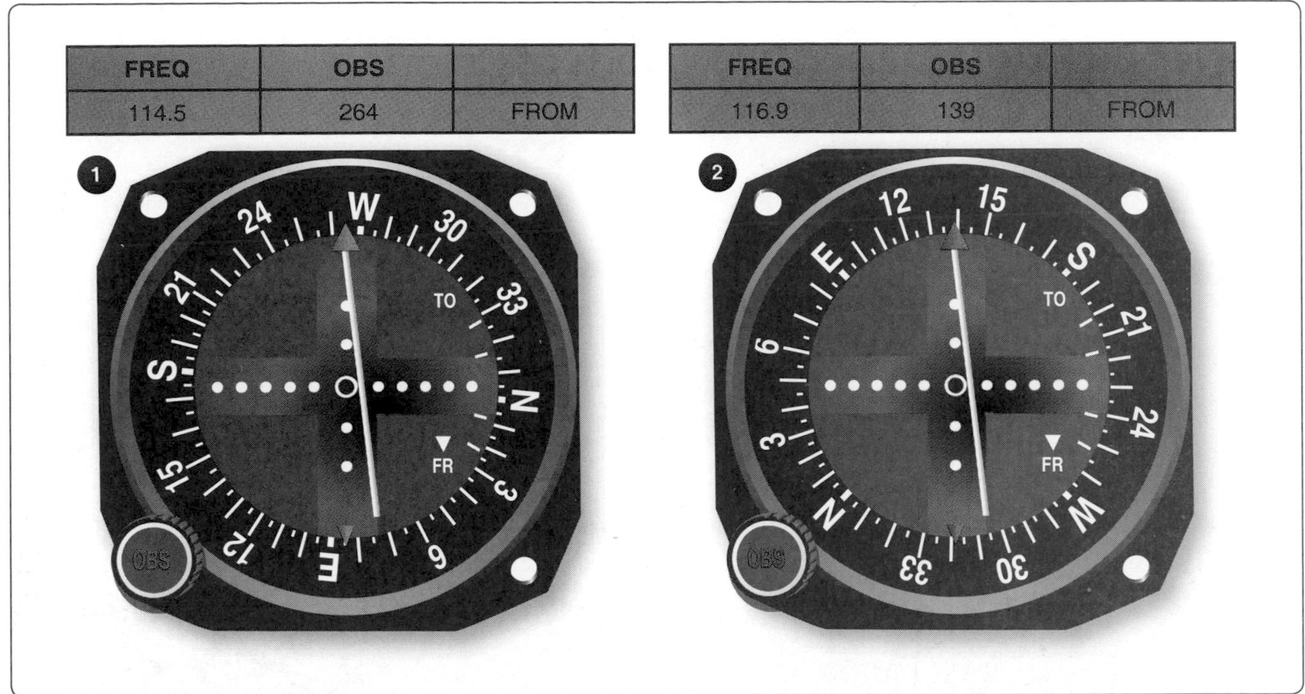

FIGURE 88.—CDI and OBS Indicators.

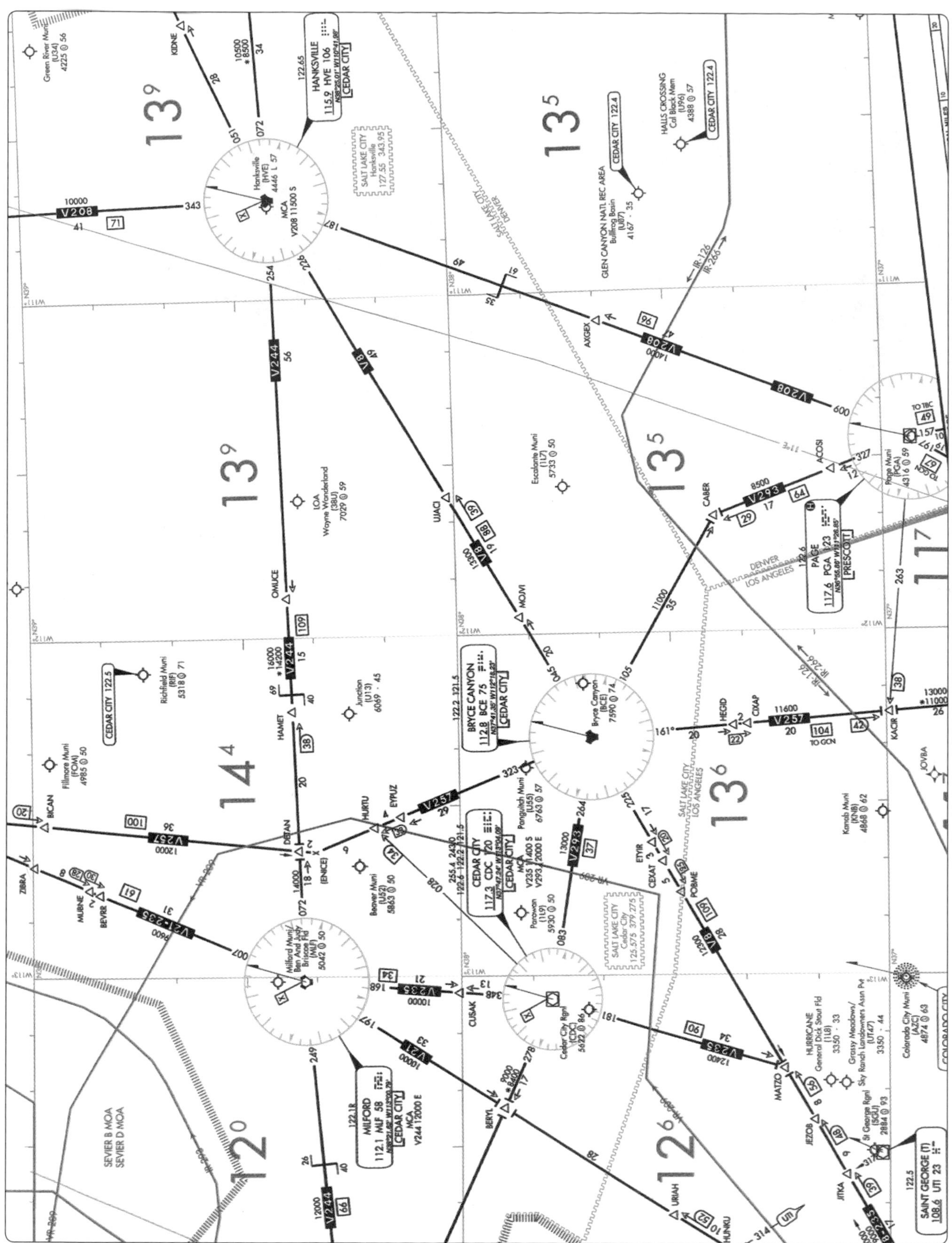

FIGURE 89.—En Route Low-Altitude Chart Segment.
NOTE: Chart is not to scale and should not be used for navigation. Chart is for testing purposes only.

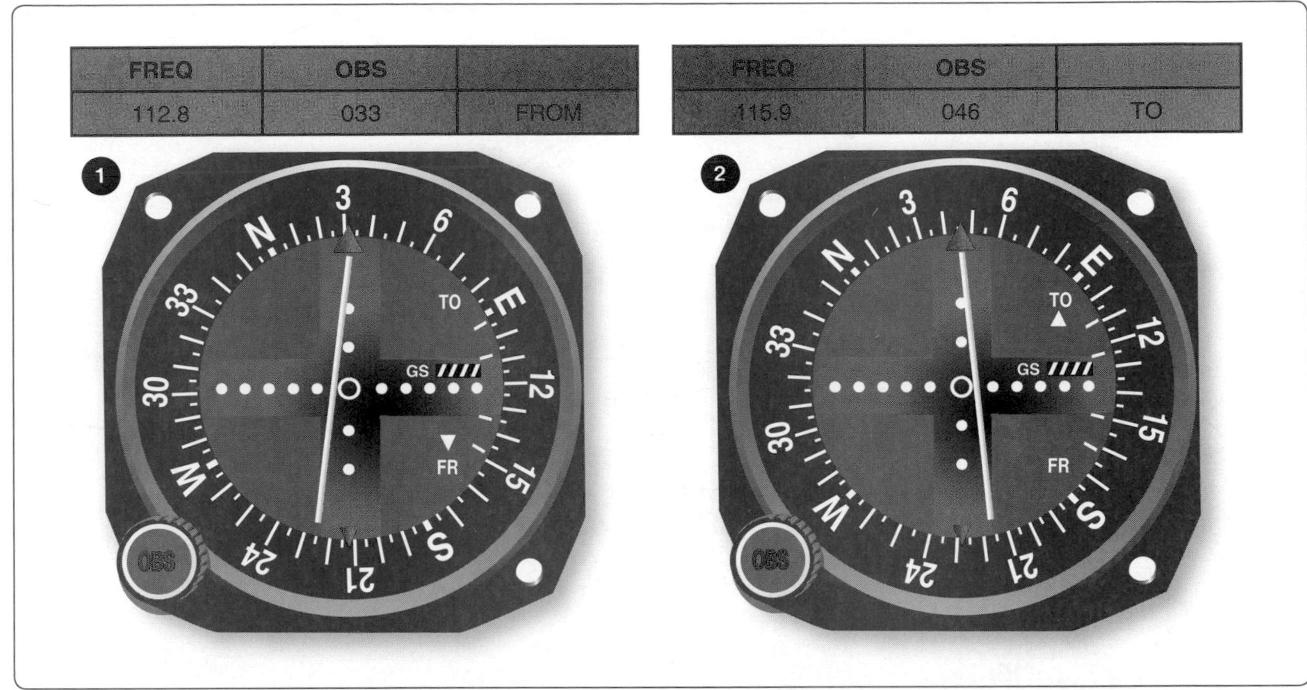

Figure 90.—CDI/OBS Indicators.

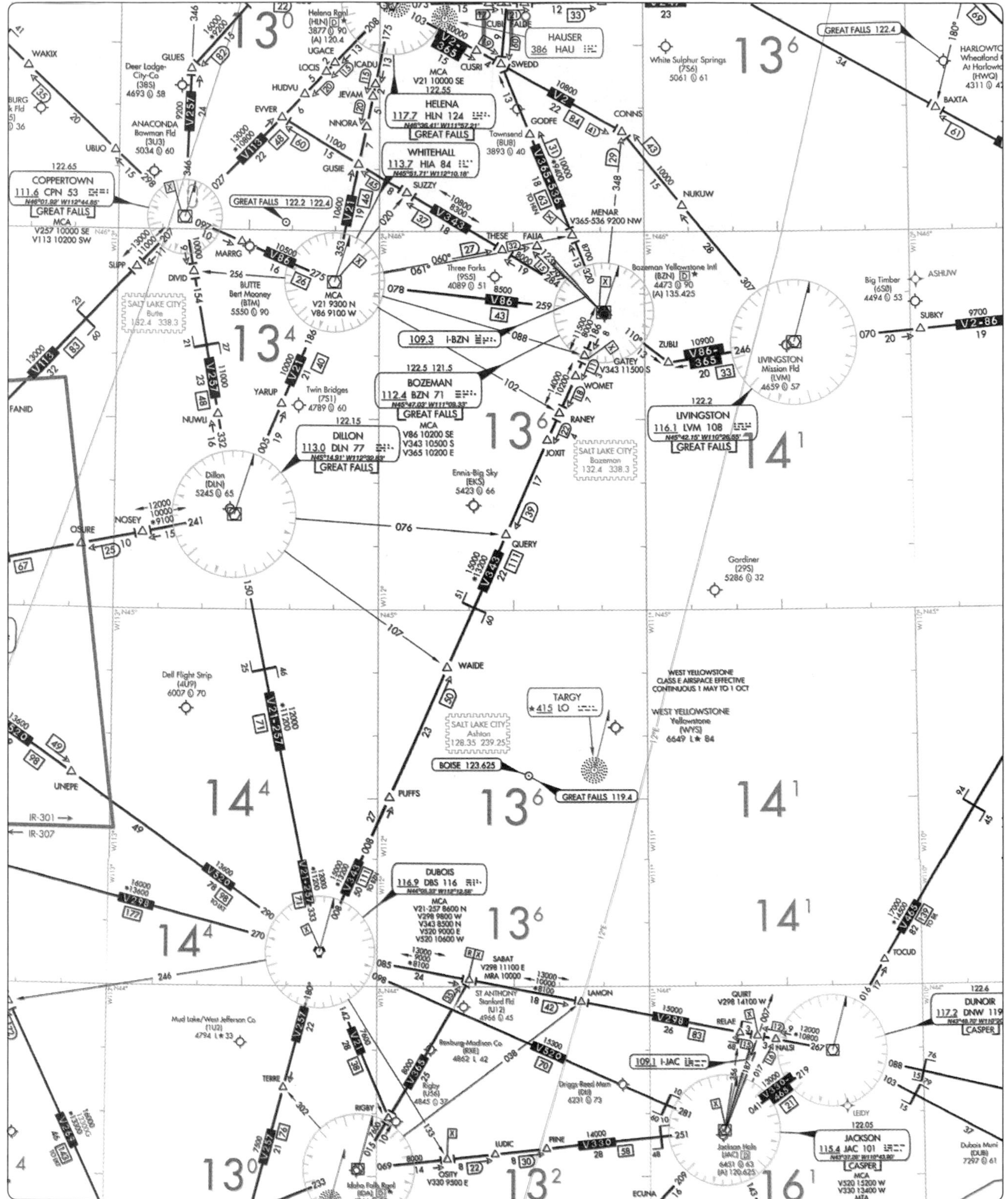

FIGURE 91.—En Route Low-Altitude Chart Segment.

NOTE: Chart is not to scale and should not be used for navigation. Chart is for testing purposes only.

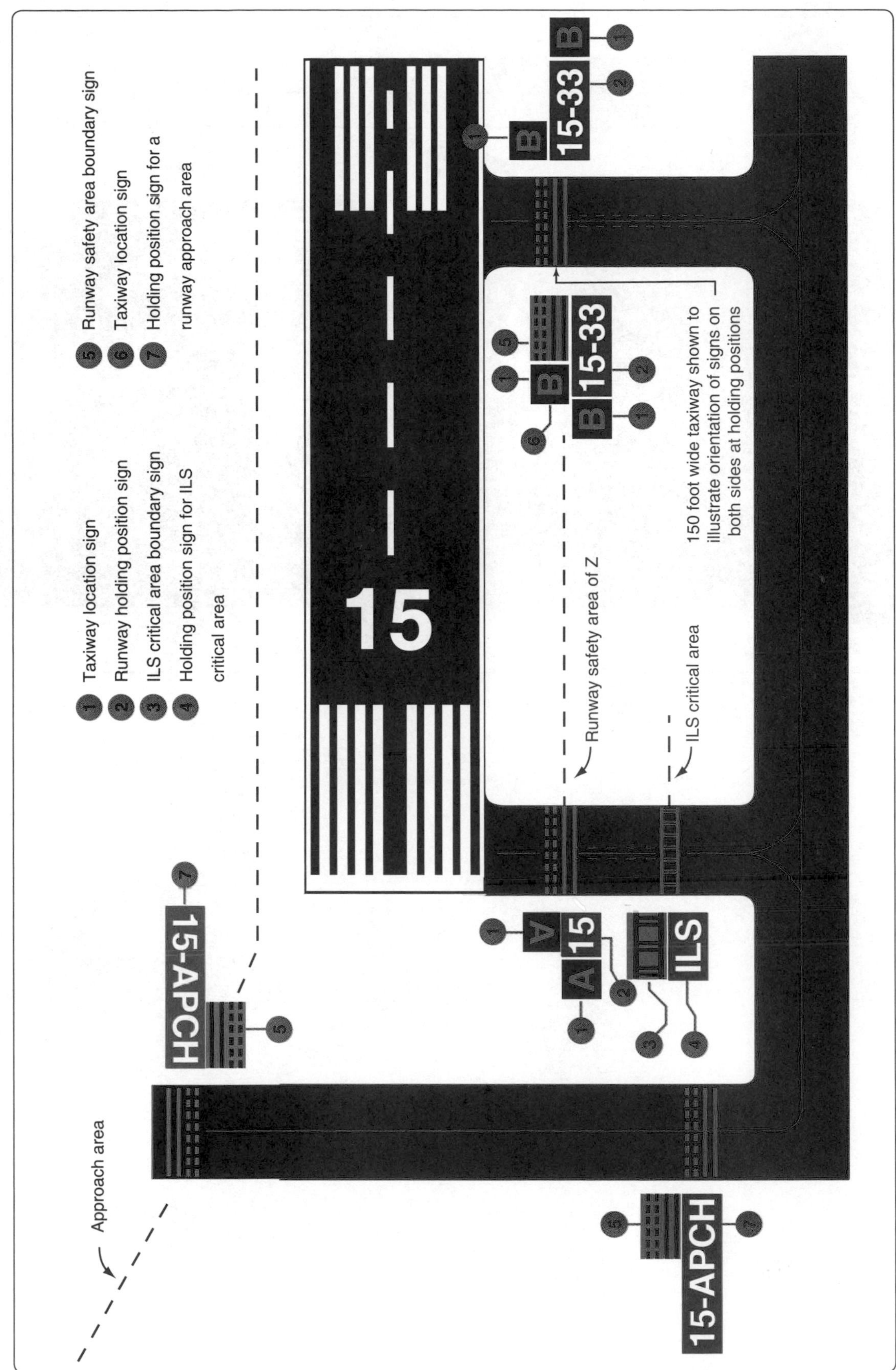

FIGURE 94.—Application Examples for Holding Positions.

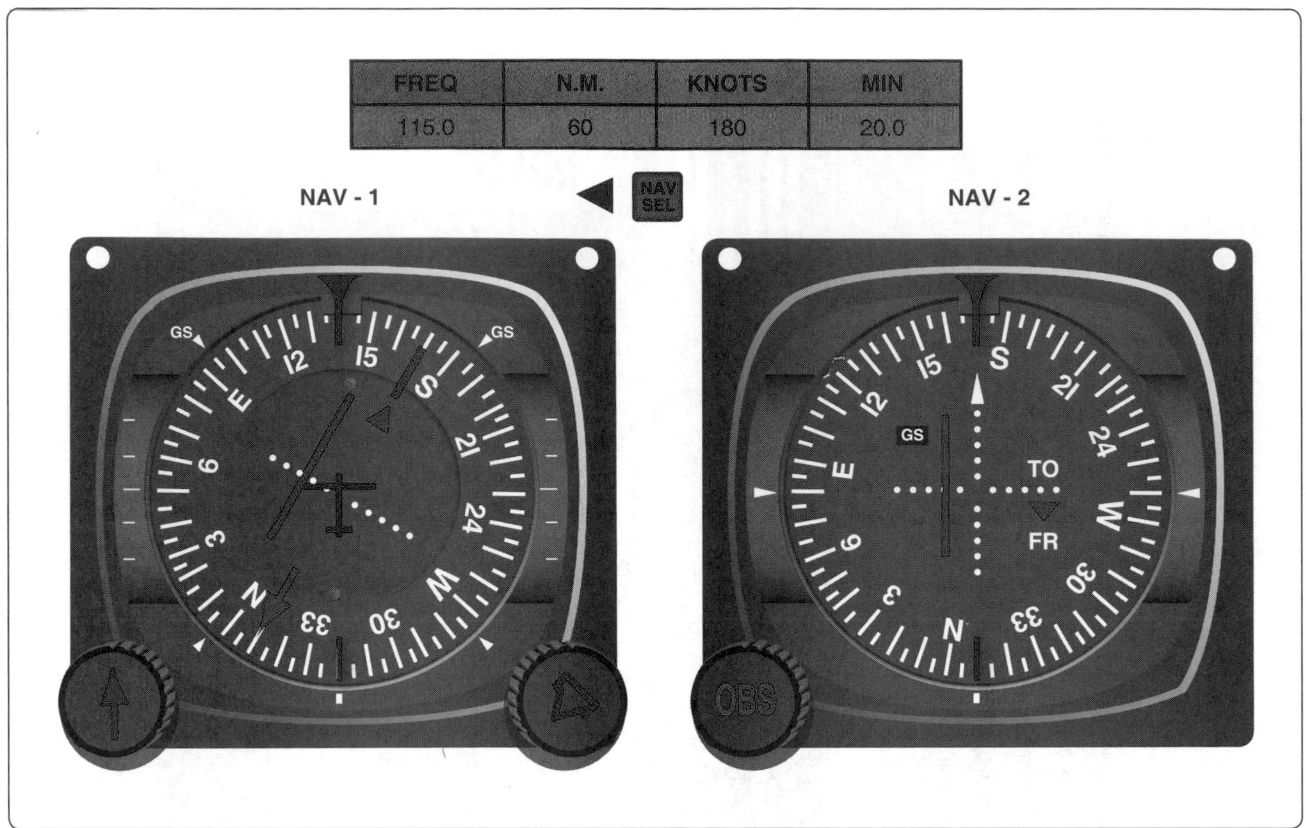

FIGURE 95.—No. 1 and No. 2 NAV Presentation.

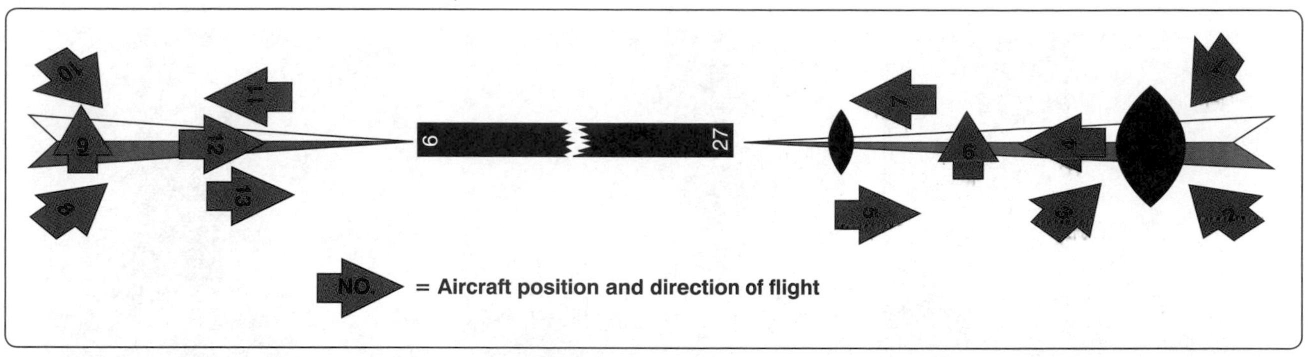

FIGURE 96.—Aircraft Position and Direction of Flight.

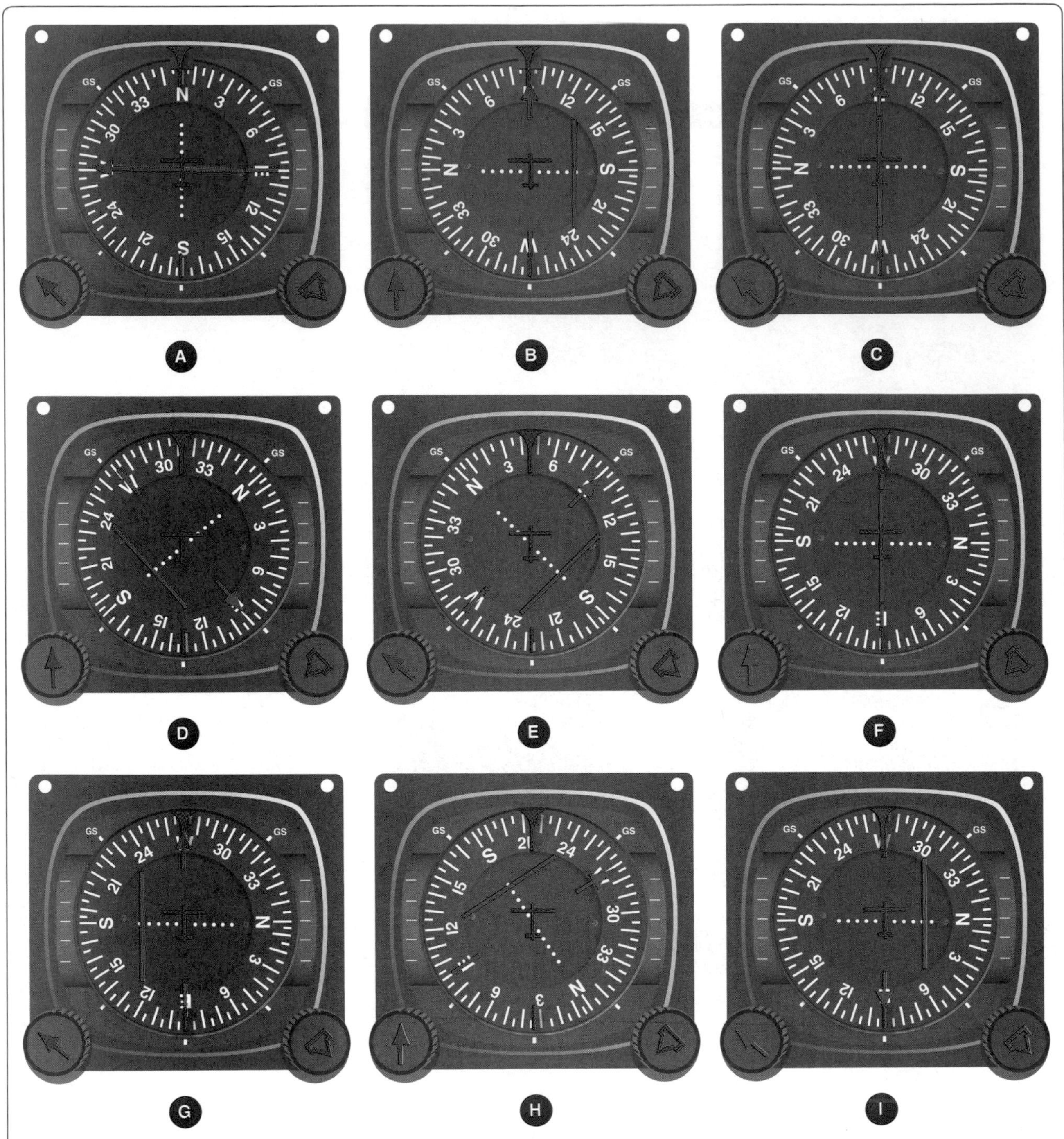

FIGURE 97.—HSI Presentation.

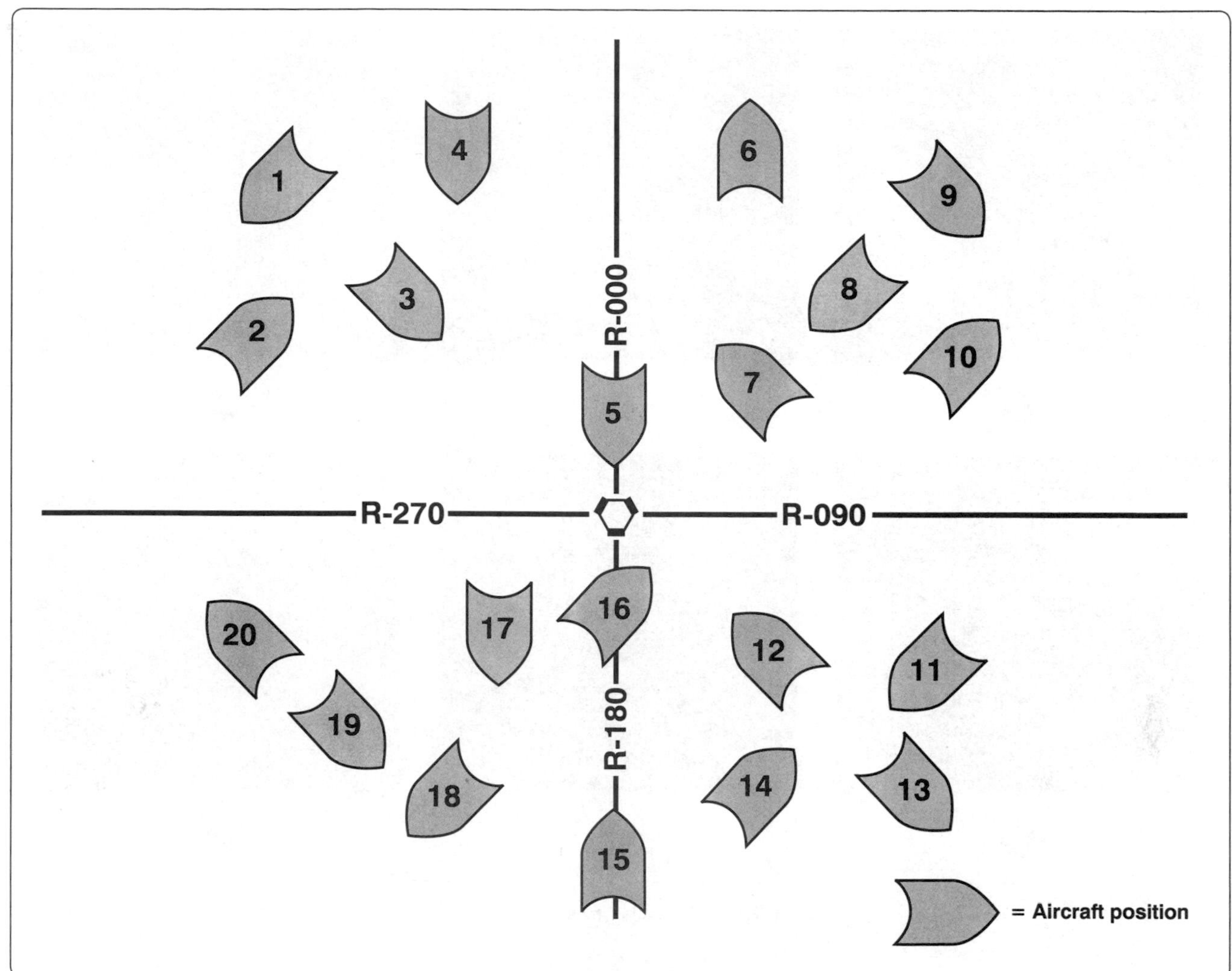

FIGURE 98.—Aircraft Position.

FIGURE 99.—HSI Presentation.

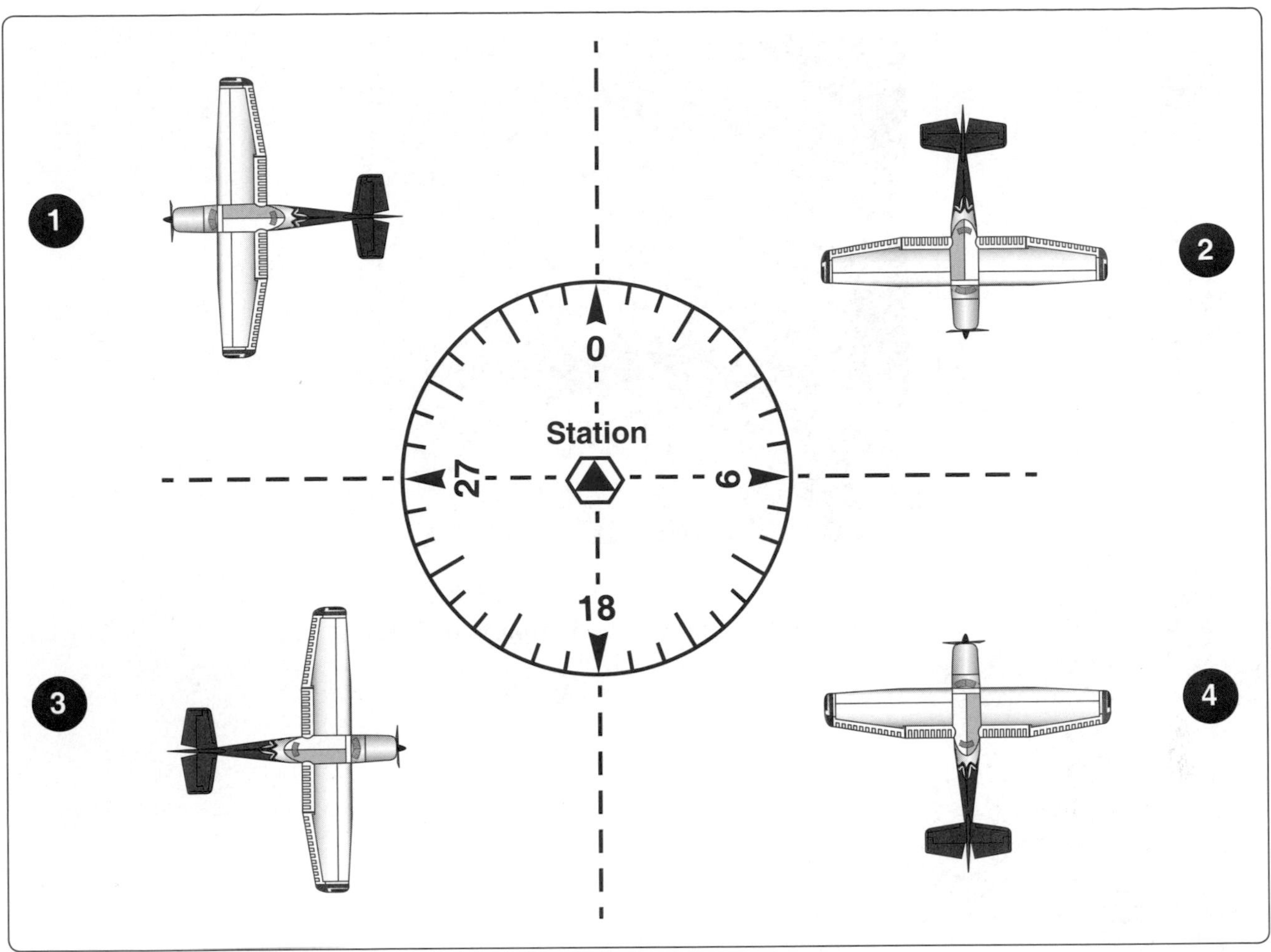

FIGURE 106.—Aircraft Location Relative to VOR.

FIGURE 109.—CDI Direction from VORTAC.

FIGURE 110.—CDI Direction from VORTAC.

FIGURE 111.—CDI Direction from VORTAC.

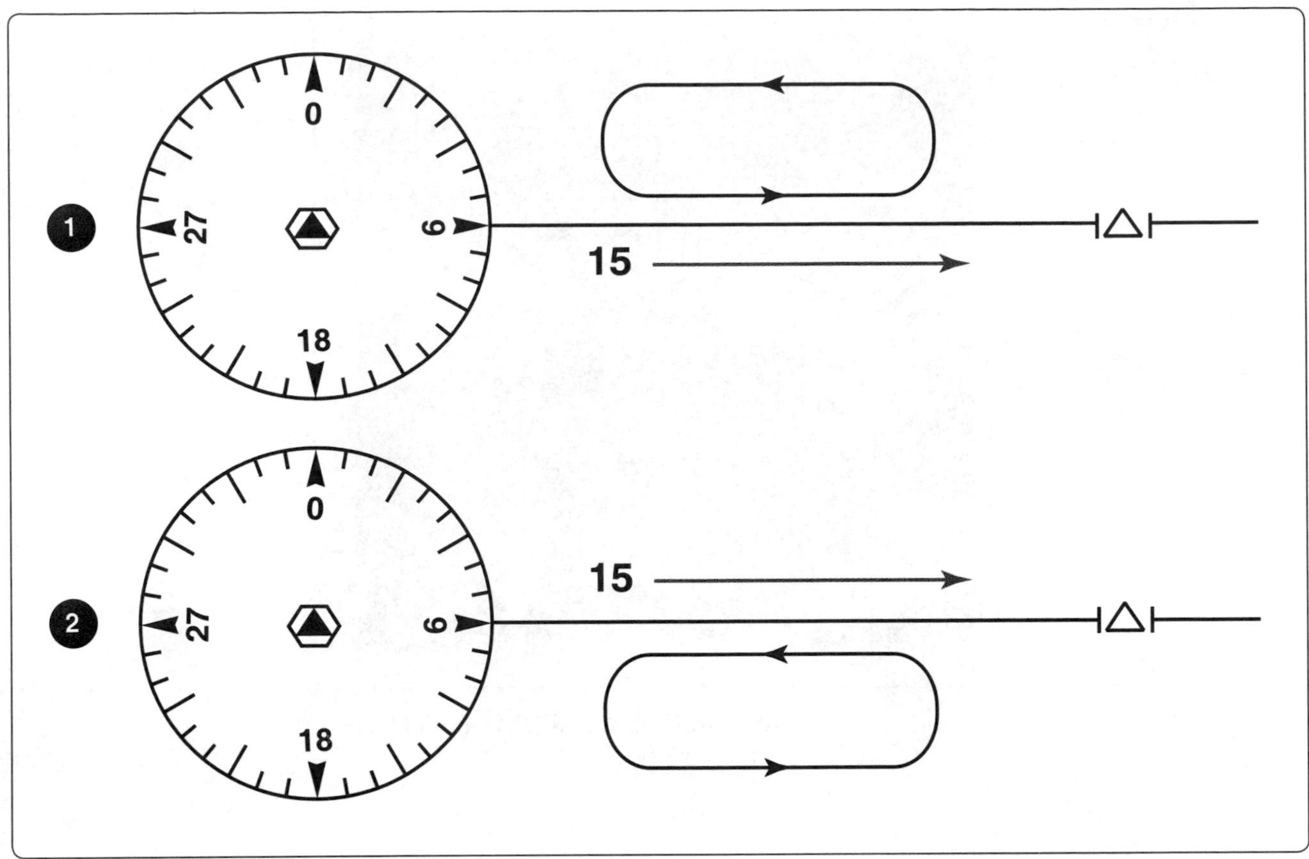

FIGURE 112.—Holding Entry Procedure.

FIGURE 113.—Aircraft Course and DME Indicator.

FIGURE 114.—Aircraft Course and DME Indicator.

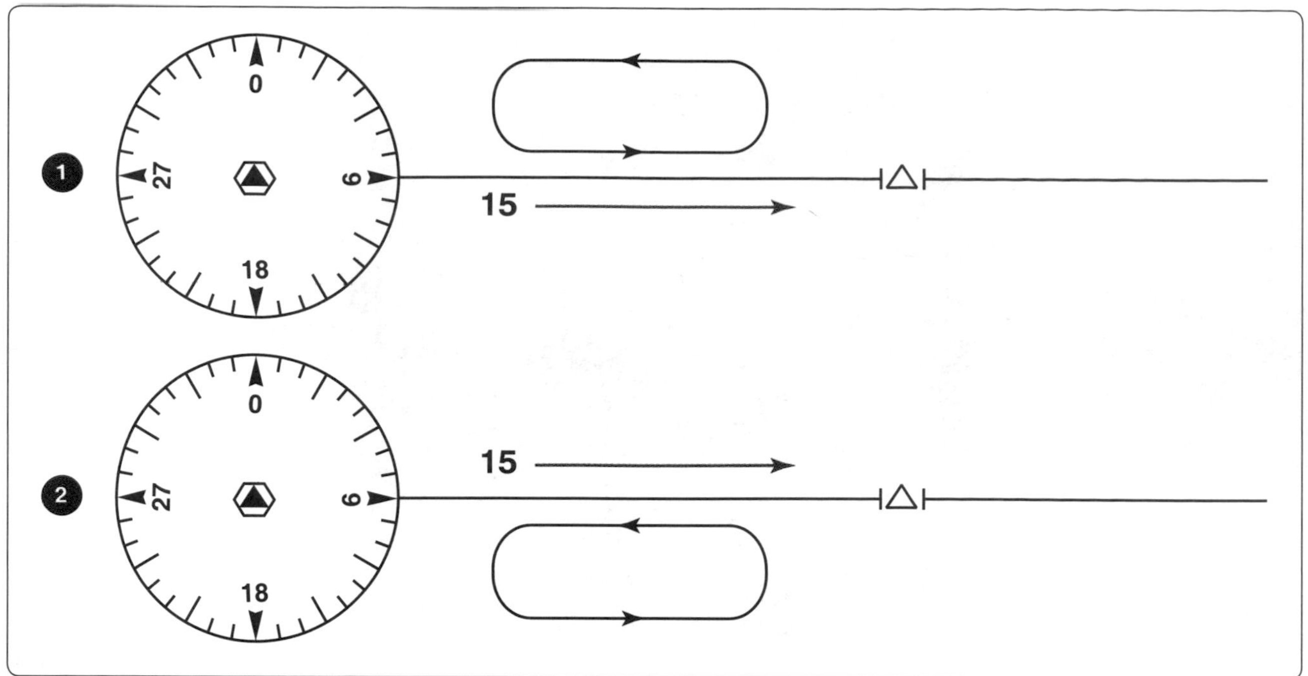

FIGURE 115.—DME Fix with Holding Pattern.

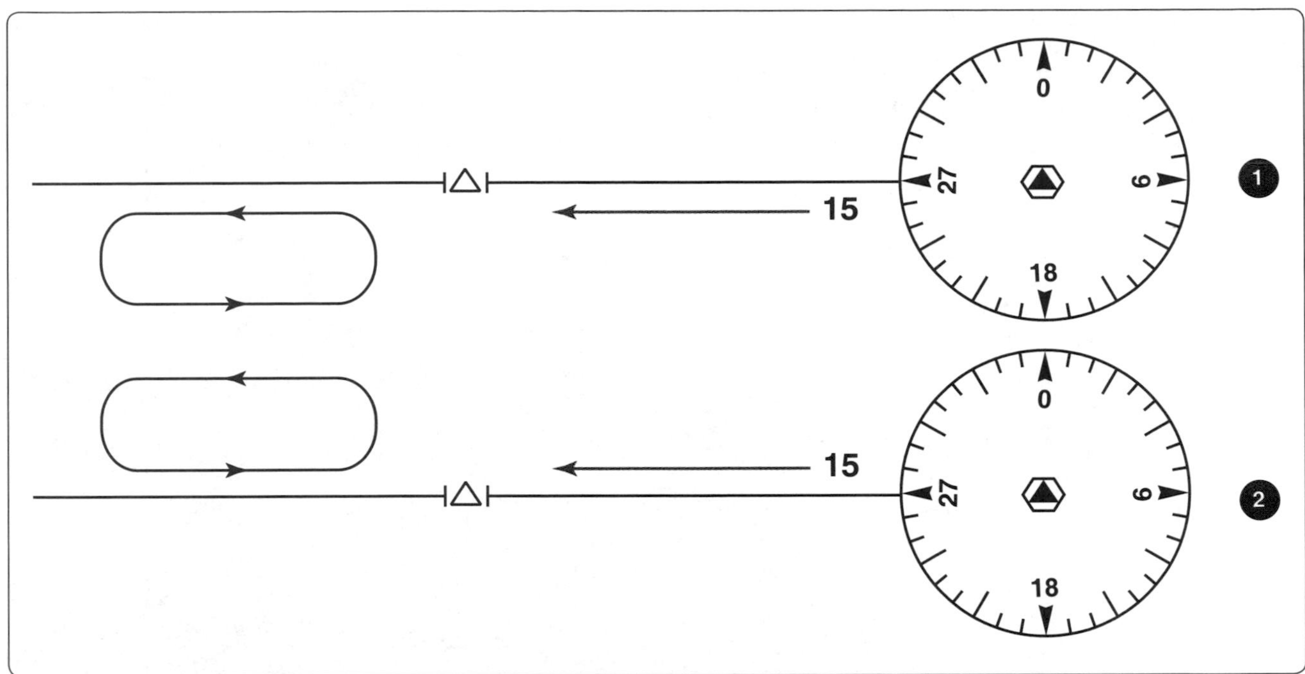

FIGURE 116.—Holding Entry Procedure.

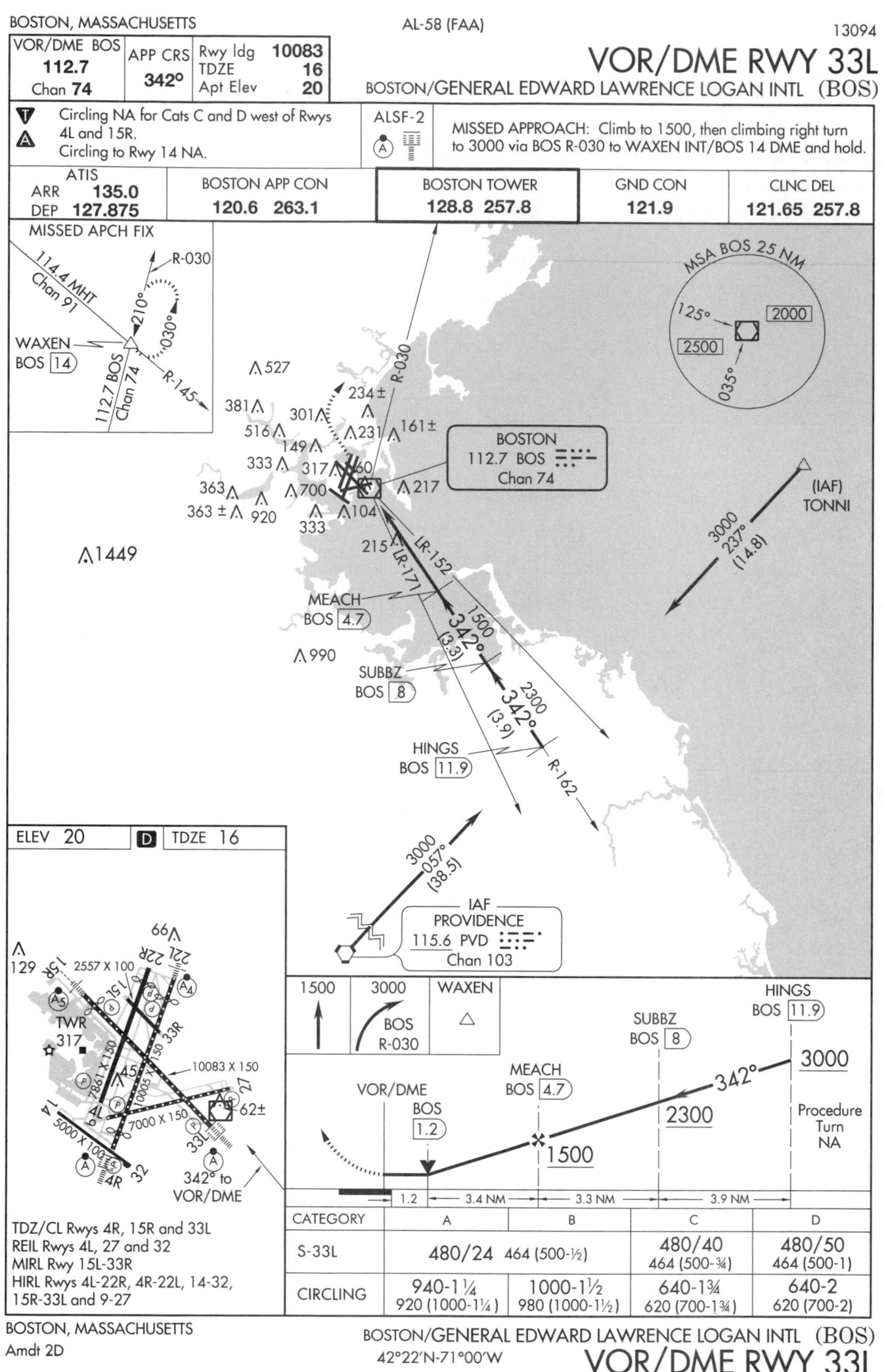

CATEGORY	A	B	C	D
S-33L	480/24 464 (500-½)		480/40 464 (500-¾)	480/50 464 (500-1)
CIRCLING	940-1¼ 920 (1000-1¼)	1000-1½ 980 (1000-1½)	640-1¾ 620 (700-1¾)	640-2 620 (700-2)

Figure 131.—VOR/DME RWY 33L.

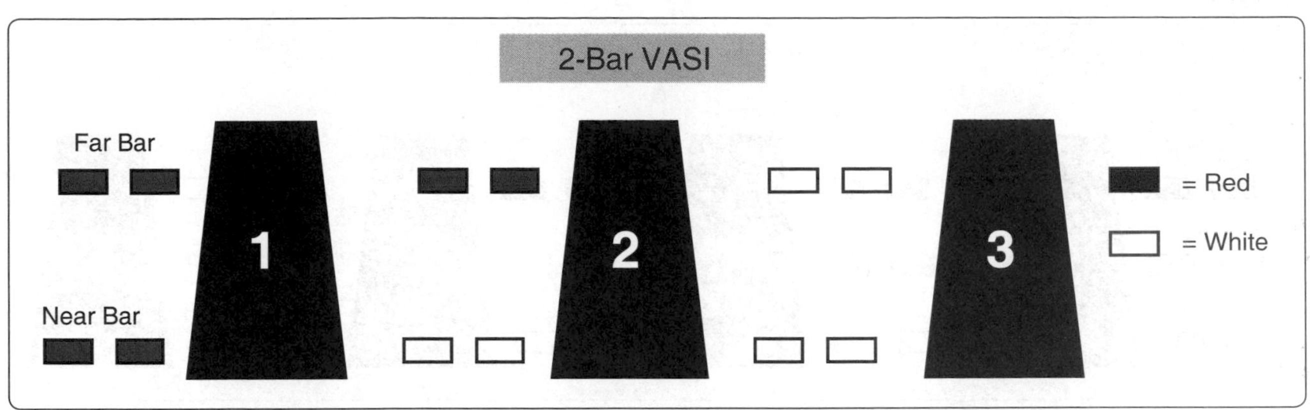

FIGURE 134.—2-BAR VASI.

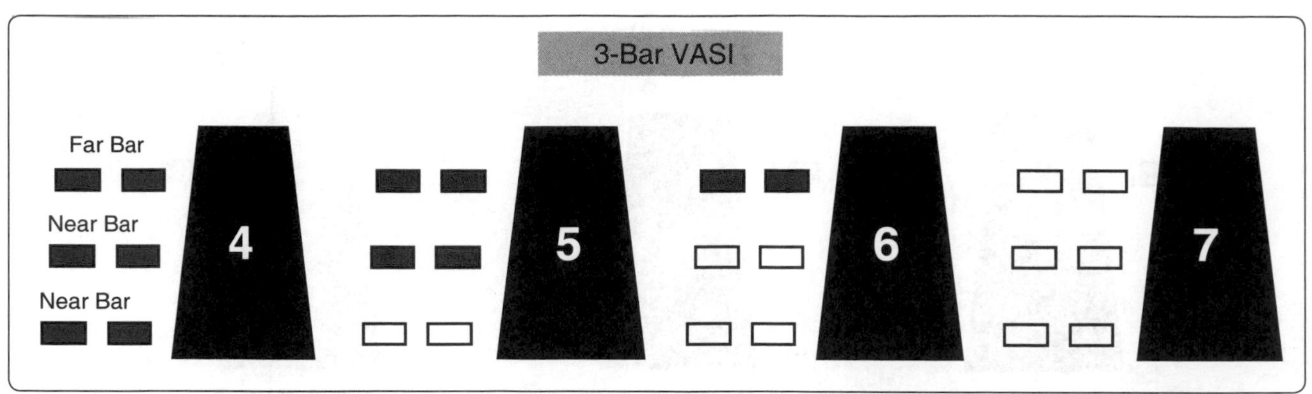

FIGURE 135.—3-BAR VASI.

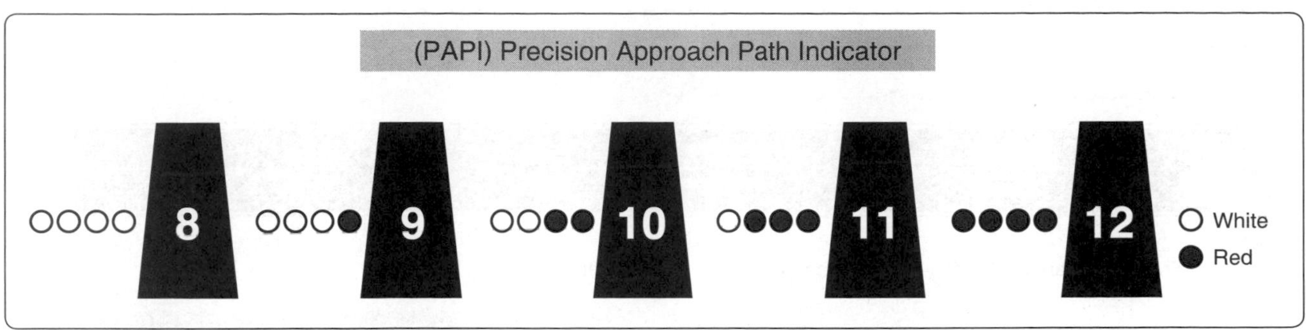

FIGURE 136.—Precision Approach Path Indicator (PAPI).

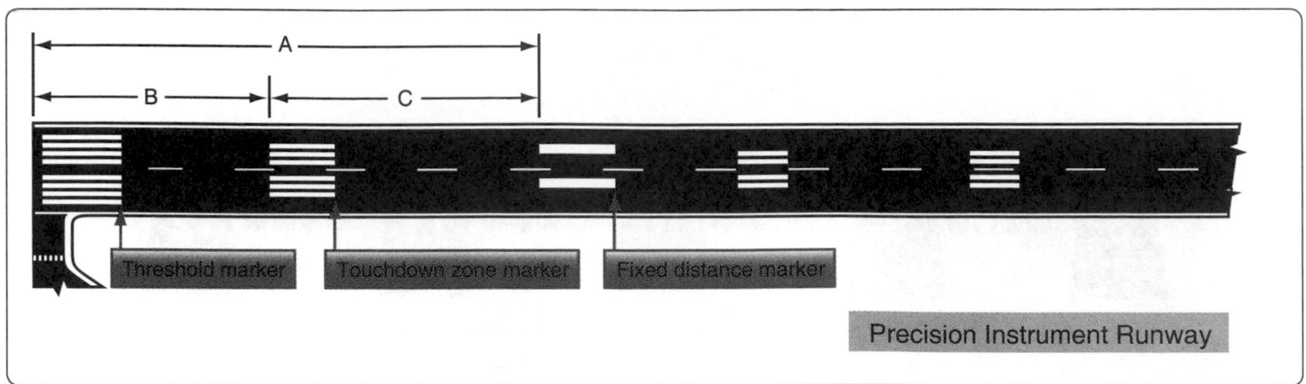

FIGURE 137.—Precision Instrument Runway.

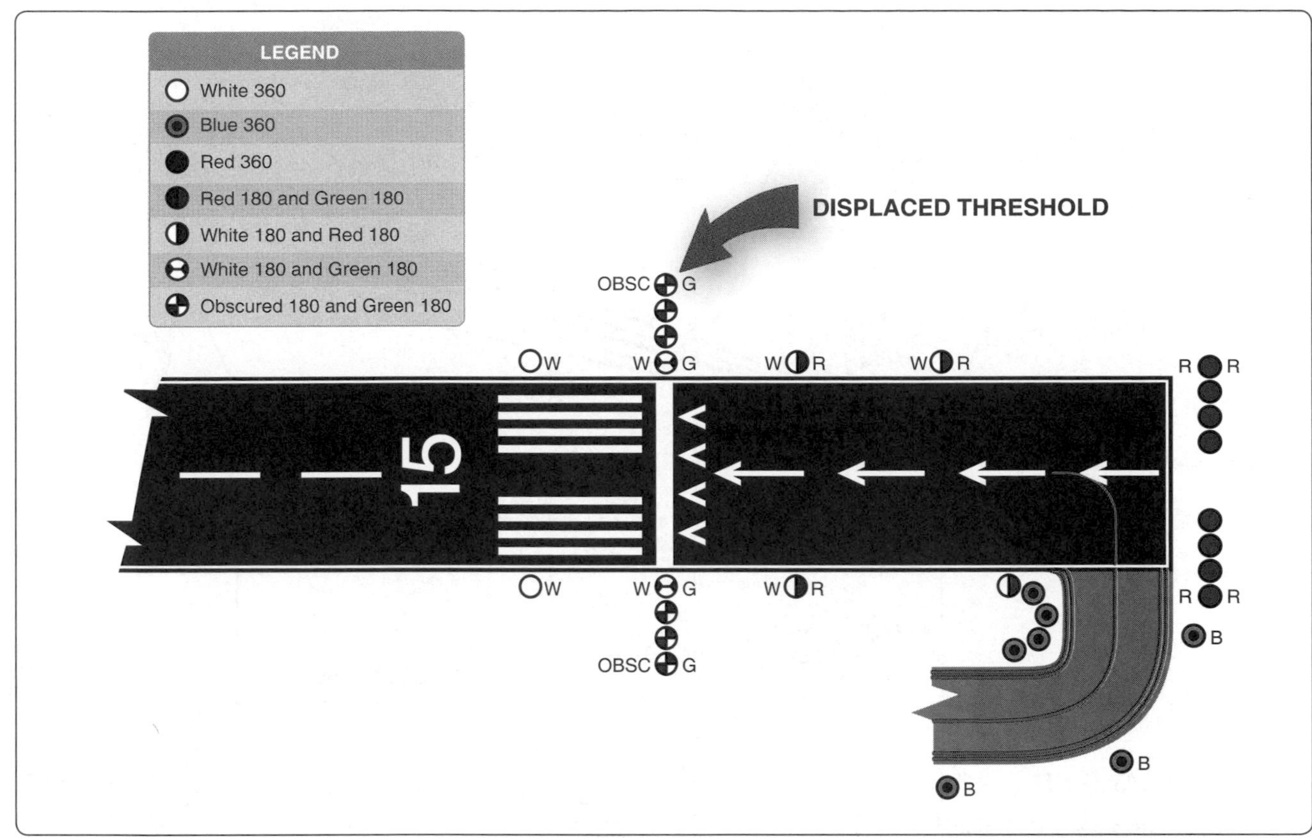

FIGURE 138.—Runway Legend.

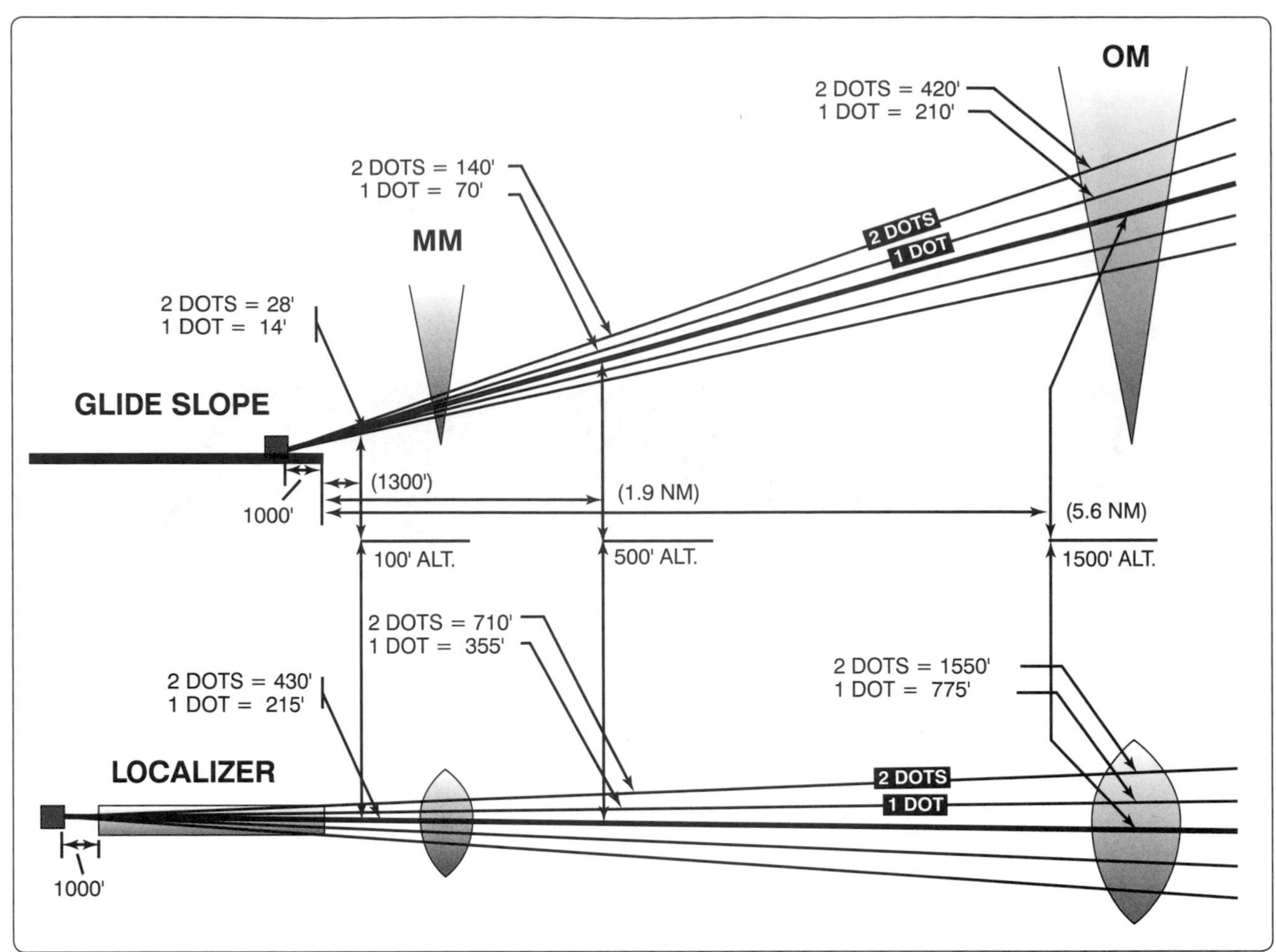

FIGURE 139.—Glide Slope and Localizer Illustration.

FIGURE 140.—OBS, ILS, and GS Displacement.

FIGURE 141.—OBS, ILS, and GS Displacement.

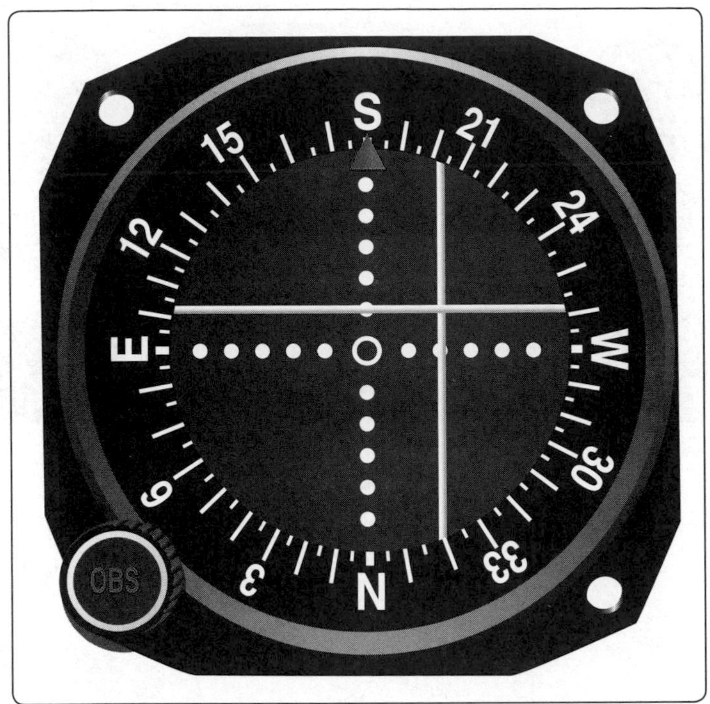

FIGURE 142.—OBS, ILS, and GS Displacement.

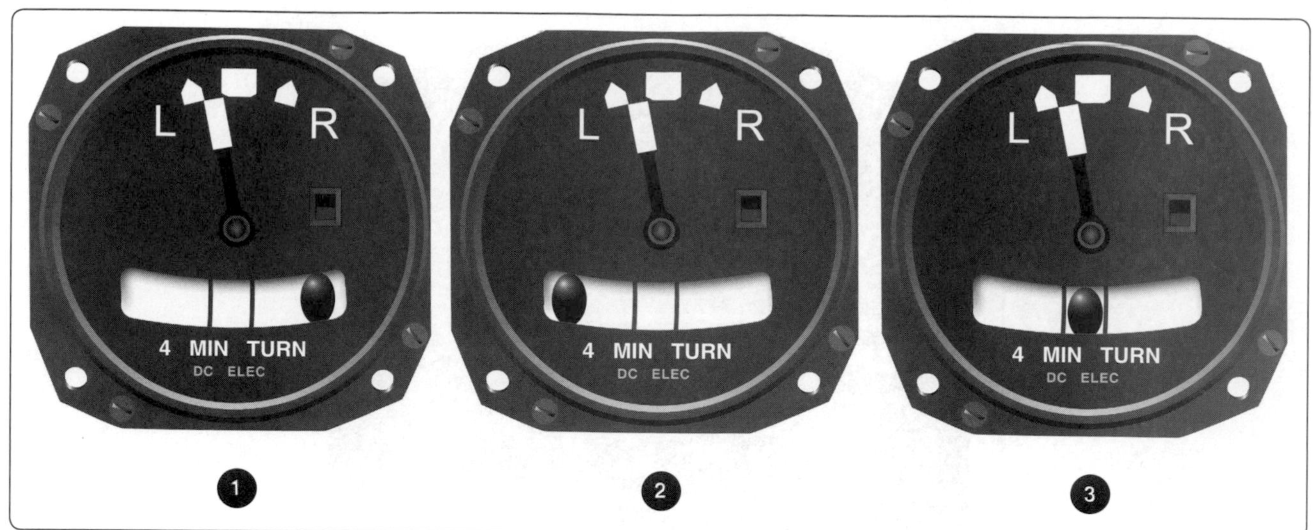

FIGURE 144.—Turn-and-Slip indicator.

FIGURE 145.—Instrument Sequence (Unusual Attitude).

FIGURE 146.—Instrument Sequence (System Failed).

FIGURE 147.—Instrument Sequence (Unusual Attitude).

FIGURE 148.—Instrument Interpretation (System Malfunction).

FIGURE 149.—Instrument Interpretation (System Malfunction).

FIGURE 150.—Instrument Interpretation (Instrument Malfunction).

FIGURE 151.—Instrument Interpretation (Instrument Malfunction).

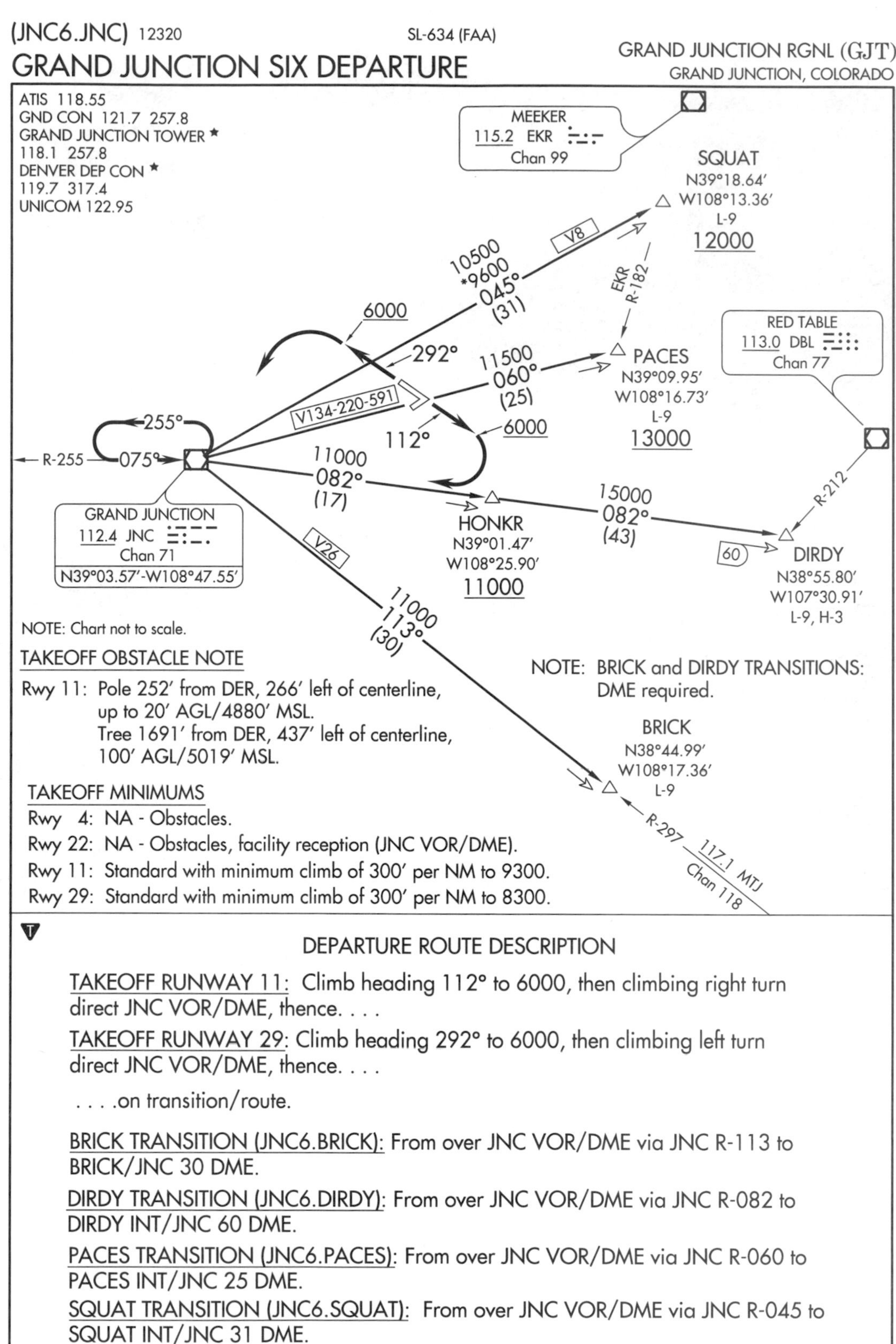

Figure 155.—Grand Junction Six Departure (JNC6.JNC).

HOT SPOTS

An "airport surface hot spot" is a location on an aerodrome movement area with a history or potential risk of collision or runway incursion, and where heightened attention by pilots/drivers is necessary.

A "hot spot" is a runway safety related problem area on an airport that presents increased risk during surface operations. Typically it is a complex or confusing taxiway/taxiway or taxiway/runway intersection. The area of increased risk has either a history of or potential for runway incursions or surface incidents, due to a variety of causes, such as but not limited to: airport layout, traffic flow, airport marking, signage and lighting, situational awareness, and training. Hot spots are depicted on airport diagrams as open circles or polygons designated as "HS 1", "HS 2", etc. and tabulated in the list below with a brief description of each hot spot. Hot spots will remain charted on airport diagrams until such time the increased risk has been reduced or eliminated.

CITY/AIRPORT	HOT SPOT	DESCRIPTION*
ALAMOGORDO, NM		
HOLLOMAN AFB (HMN)	HS1	Twy R, Twy G, and Twy L have multiple hold lines for Rwy 07-25 and Rwy 04-22. Contact tower if confused or lost.
	HS2	Hold line on Twy /EOR A and Twy/EOR H have multiple POV access roads, possibility of high vehicle traffic.
	HS3	Hold line on Twy /EOR B and Twy C for Rwy 07-25 have multiple POV access roads, possibility of high vehicle traffic.
	HS4	Multiple hold lines at intersecting rwys. Landing/departing aircraft disregard hold lines, taxiing aircraft contact tower prior to crossing hold lines.
	HS5	Multiple hold lines where rwys intersect. Hold line also at Twy D. Contact tower if confused or lost.
	HS6	POV crossing controlled by tower. Hold line located on each side of Rwy 07-25. Possibility of high vehicular traffic.
ALBUQUERQUE, NM		
ALBUQUERQUE INTL SUNPORT (ABQ)	HS 1	Hold Position Marking on Twy E1 for Rwy 08 and Rwy 12.
	HS 2	Twy G1 from Cutter Aviation ramp and Rwy 12-30.
	HS 3	Complex int at Twy F, Twy C, Twy G. Twy G and Rwy 03-21
ASPEN, CO		
ASPEN-PITKIN COUNTY / SARDY FIELD (ASE)	HS 1	Twy A2. Short taxi distance from ramp to rwy.
	HS 2	Twy A3. Short taxi distance from ramp to rwy.
	HS 3	Twy A4. Short taxi distance from ramp to rwy.
COLORADO SPRINGS, CO		
CITY OF COLORADO SPRINGS (COS)	HS 1	The apch ends of Rwy 13 and Rwy 17R; and Twy A1.
	HS 2	Twy A4 and Twy G at Rwy 17R-35L.
	HS 3	Int of Twy E4, Twy G, Twy H and Twy E.
	HS 4	Apch ends of Rwy 35R and Rwy 35L.
DENVER, CO		
CENTENNIAL (APA)	HS 1	Rwy 17L at Twy A1.
	HS 2	Twy A, Twy A8, Twy A9 and Twy C1 congested INT.
	HS 3	Twy C1 and Twy D1 close proximity to Rwy 10.
DENVER, CO		
DENVER INTL (DEN)	HS 1	Rwy 35L hold signs may not be visible from Twy SC or Twy A until entering Twy M, pilots sometimes enter Rwy 35L without authorization.
	HS 2	Rwy 17R Apch Hold Position.
DENVER, CO		
ROCKY MOUNTAIN METROPOLITAN (BJC)	HS 1	Frequent helicopter operations.
	HS 2	Multiple hold lines in close proximity. Hold line on Twy B south of Rwy 11R-29L is prior to Twy D.
EAGLE, CO		
EAGLE COUNTY RGNL (EGE)	HS 1	High density parking area.
GRAND JUNCTION, CO		
GRAND JUNCTION RGNL (GJT)	HS 1	Rwy 22 and Rwy 29 close proximity, wrong rwy departure risk.

FIGURE 156.—Grand Junction Hot Spots.

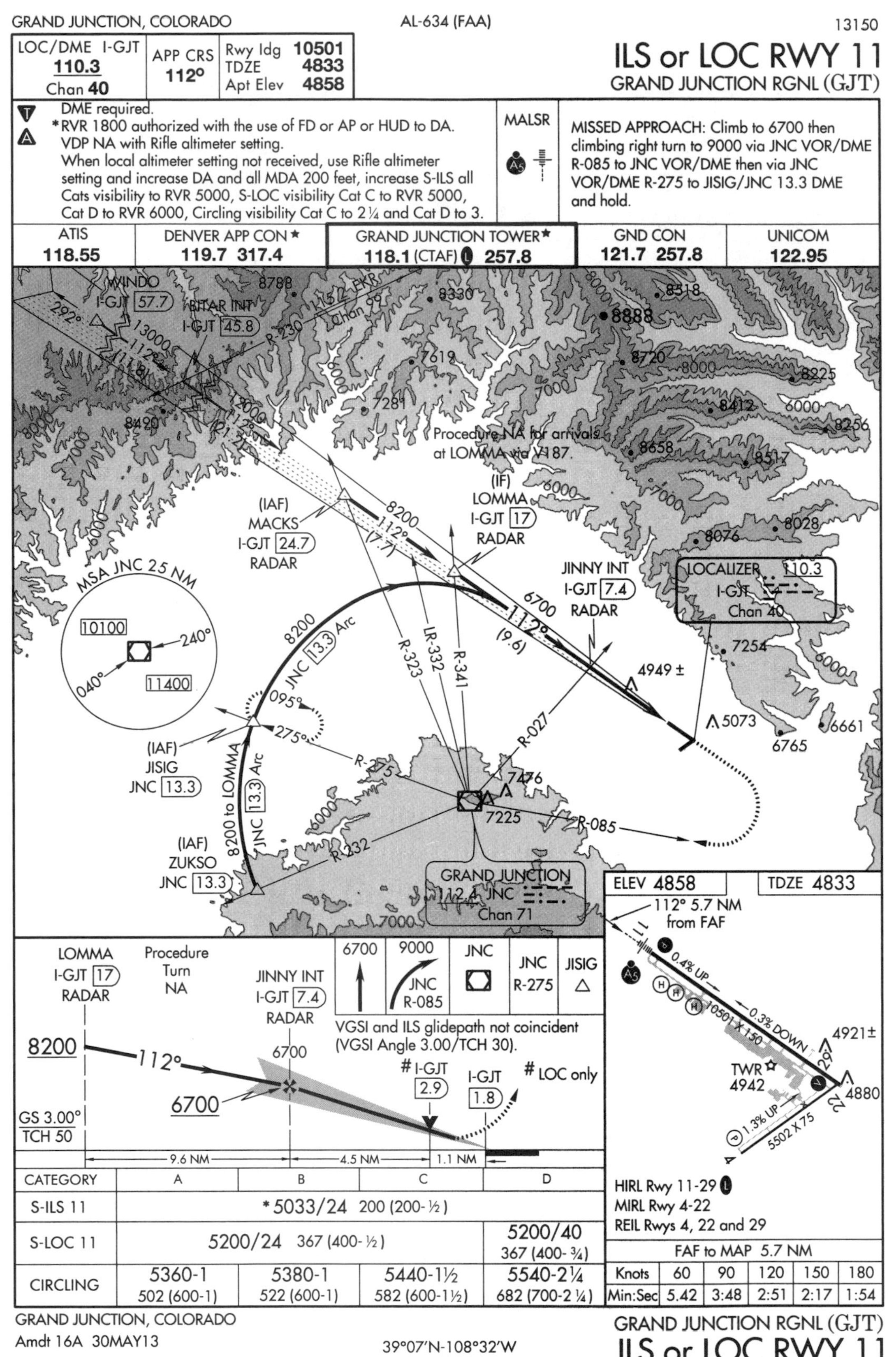

FIGURE 157.—ILS RWY 11 (GJT).

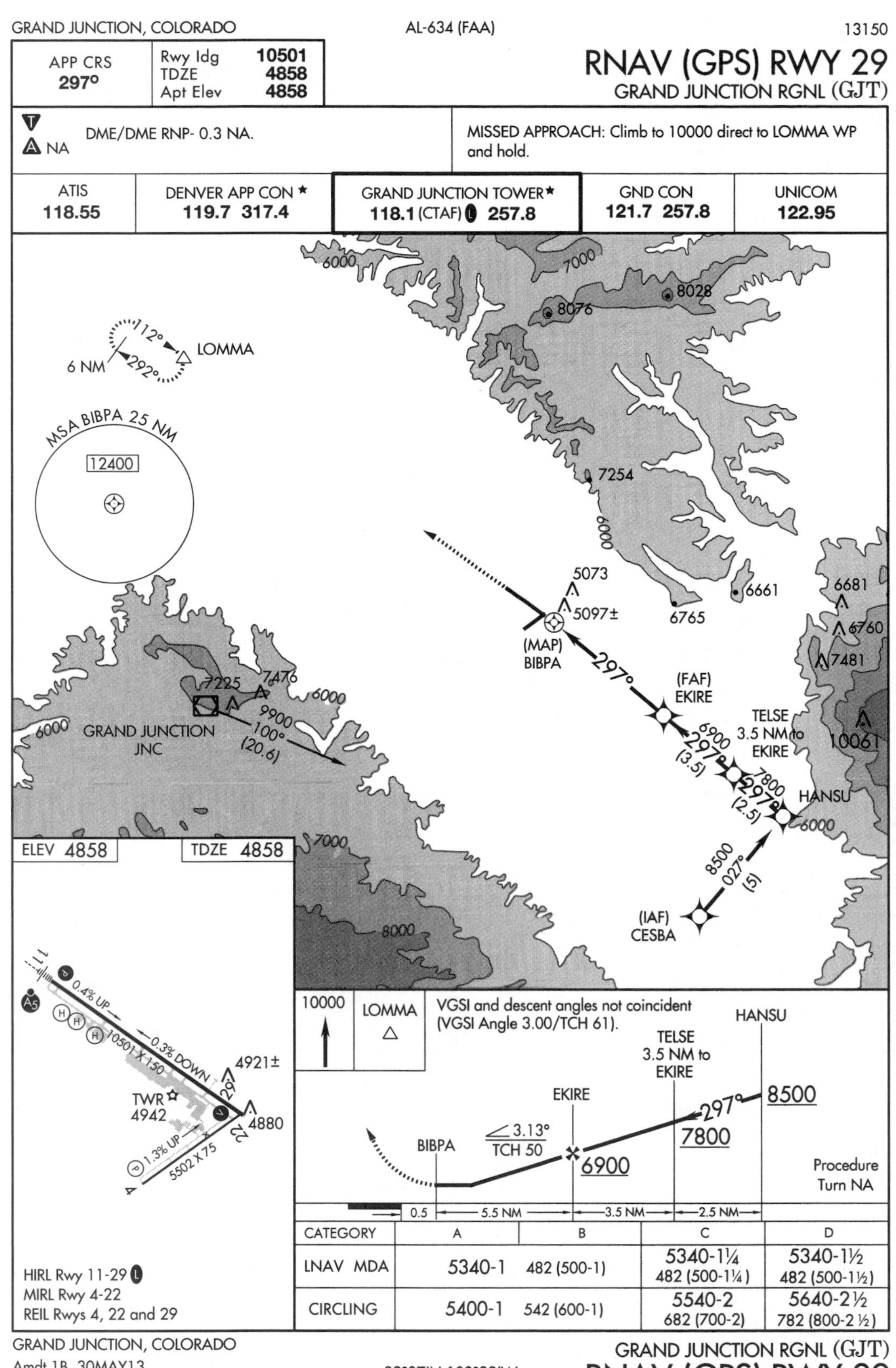

CATEGORY	A	B	C	D
LNAV MDA	5340-1	482 (500-1)	5340-1¼ 482 (500-1¼)	5340-1½ 482 (500-1½)
CIRCLING	5400-1	542 (600-1)	5540-2 682 (700-2)	5640-2½ 782 (800-2½)

FIGURE 158.—ILS RWY 11 (GJT).

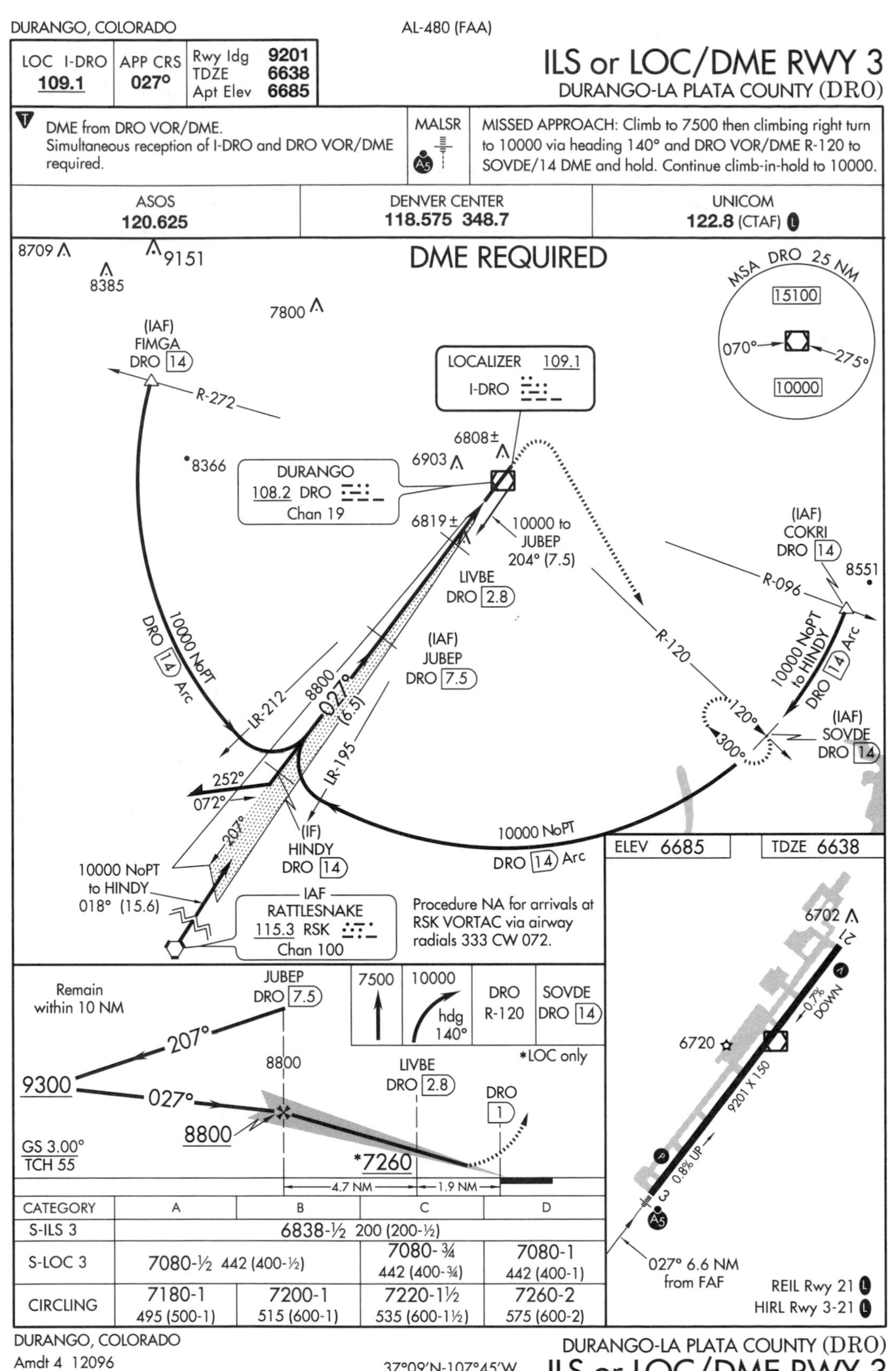

CATEGORY	A	B	C	D
S-ILS 3	6838-½ 200 (200-½)			
S-LOC 3	7080-½ 442 (400-½)		7080-¾ 442 (400-¾)	7080-1 442 (400-1)
CIRCLING	7180-1 495 (500-1)	7200-1 515 (600-1)	7220-1½ 535 (600-1½)	7260-2 575 (600-2)

FIGURE 159.—ILS/DME RWY 3 (DRO).

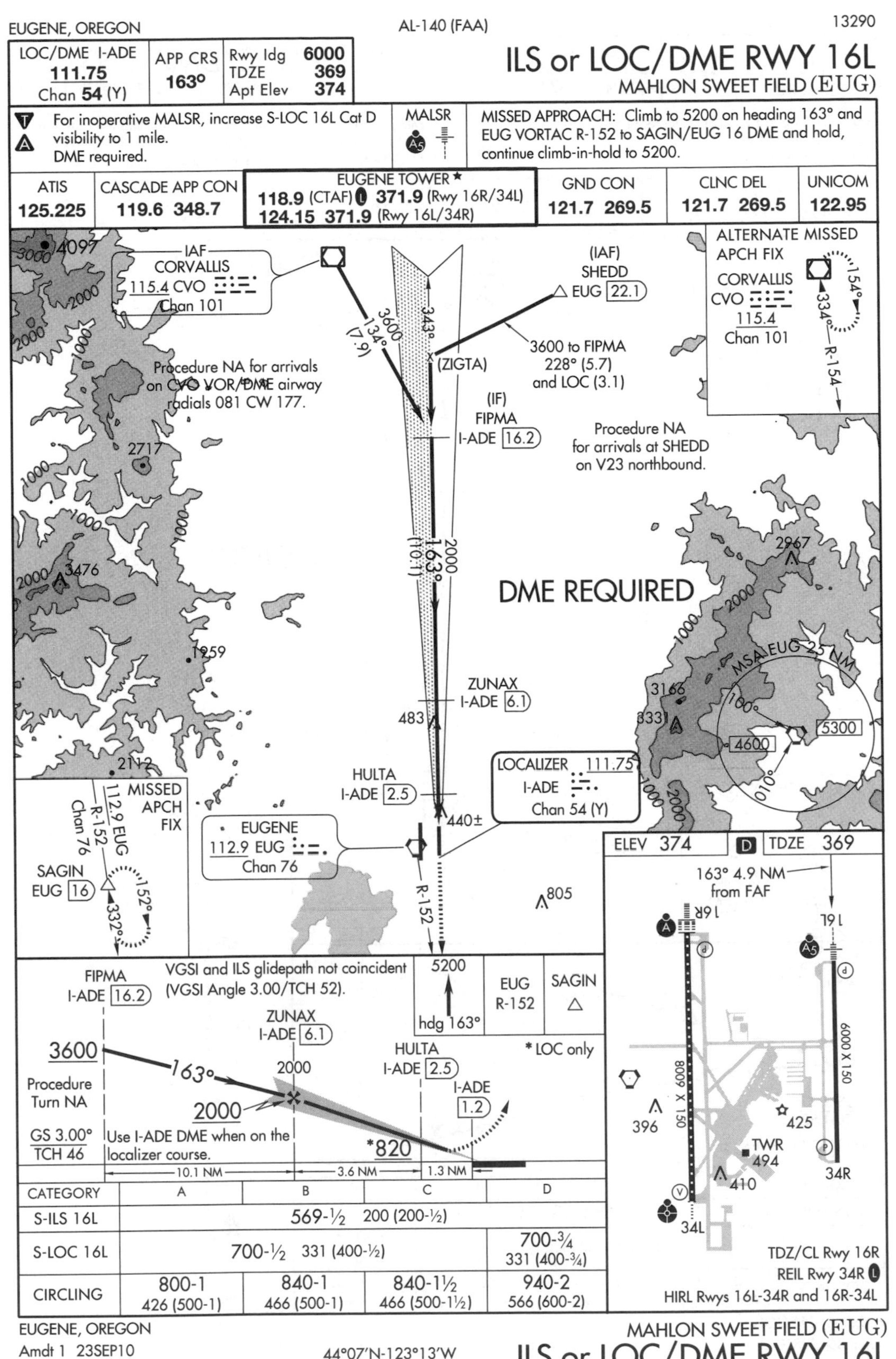

CATEGORY	A	B	C	D
S-ILS 16L	569-½ 200 (200-½)			
S-LOC 16L	700-½ 331 (400-½)			700-¾ 331 (400-¾)
CIRCLING	800-1 426 (500-1)	840-1 466 (500-1)	840-1½ 466 (500-1½)	940-2 566 (600-2)

FIGURE 160.—ILS or LOC/DME RWY 16L (EUG).

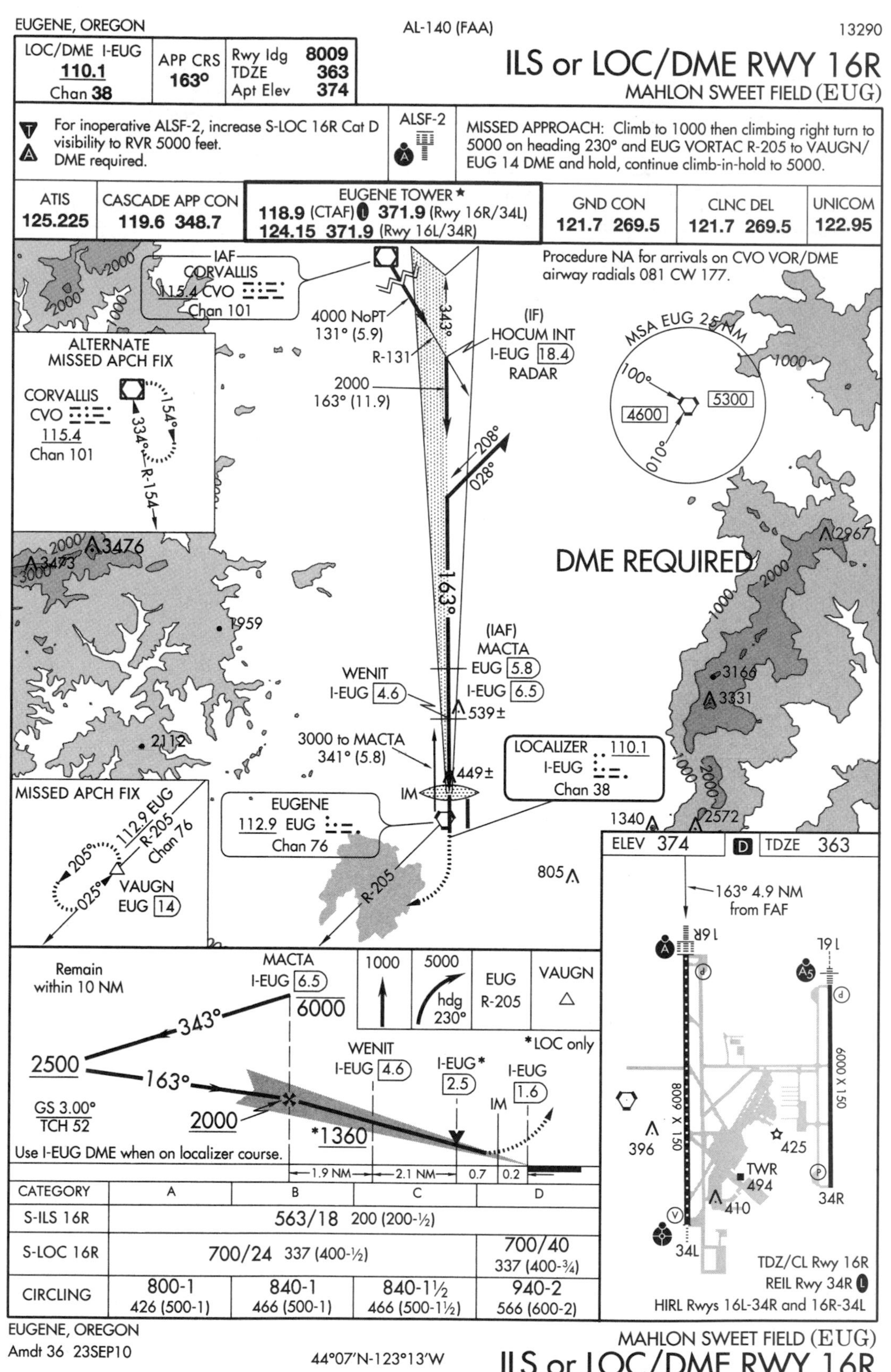

CATEGORY	A	B	C	D
S-ILS 16R	563/18 200 (200-½)			
S-LOC 16R	700/24 337 (400-½)			700/40 337 (400-¾)
CIRCLING	800-1 426 (500-1)	840-1 466 (500-1)	840-1½ 466 (500-1½)	940-2 566 (600-2)

FIGURE 161.—ILS or LOC/DME RWY 16R (EUG).

EUGENE

MAHLON SWEET FLD (EUG) 7 NW UTC–8(–7DT) N44°07.48′ W123°12.72′ **KLAMATH FALLS**

374 B S4 **FUEL** 100LL, JET A OX 1, 2, 3, 4 TPA—1174(800) Class I, ARFF Index B **H–1B, L–1B**

NOTAM FILE EUG **IAP, AD**

RWY 16R–34L: H8009X150 (ASPH–GRVD) S–75, D–200, 2D–400 HIRL CL

RWY 16R: ALSF2. TDZL. PAPI(P4L)—GA 3.0° TCH 50′.

RWY 34L: ODALS. VASI(V4L)—GA 3.0° TCH 53′.

RWY 16L–34R: H6000X150 (ASPH–GRVD) S–105, D–175, 2D–240 HIRL

RWY 16L: MALSR. PAPI(P4L)—GA 3.0° TCH 52′.

RWY 34R: REIL. PAPI(P4L)—GA 3.0° TCH 50′.

RUNWAY DECLARED DISTANCE INFORMATION

RWY 16L:TORA–6000 TODA–6000 ASDA–6000 LDA–6000

RWY 16R:TORA–8009 TODA–8009 ASDA–8009 LDA–8009

RWY 34L:TORA–8009 TODA–8009 ASDA–8009 LDA–8009

RWY 34R:TORA–6000 TODA–6000 ASDA–6000 LDA–6000

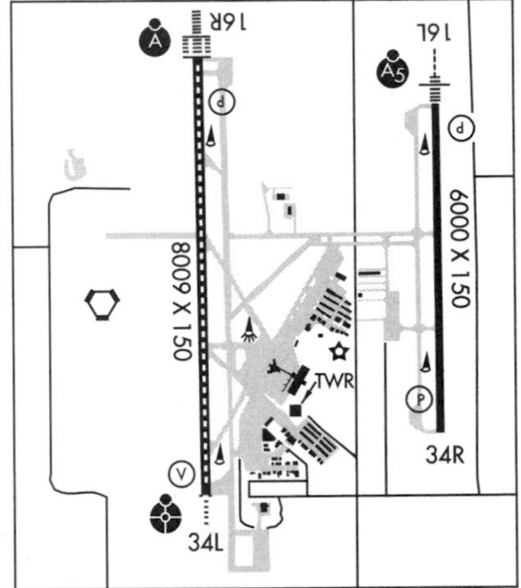

AIRPORT REMARKS: Attended continuously. Migratory waterfowl and other birds on and invof arpt. PPR for unscheduled air carrier ops with more than 30 passenger seats call 541–682–5430. ARFF svcs unavailable 0000–0500 local except PPR 541–682–5430. No access to Rwy 34L byd Twy A9. Helicopters ldg and departing avoid overflying the airline passenger terminal and ramp located E of Rwy 16R–34L. Helipad west of Rwy 16R restricted, PPR phone 541–682–5430. Twys H and K unavailable to acft 21,000 pounds single weight and 40,000 pounds dual gross weight. Terminal apron closed to acft except scheduled air carriers and flights with prior permission. PAPI Rwy 16R and Rwy 16L and 34R and VASI Rwy 34L opr 24 hrs. When twr clsd HIRL Rwy 16L–34R and Rwy 16R–34L preset medium ints. When twr clsd ACTIVATE ALSF2 Rwy 16R, ODALS Rwy 34L MALSR Rwy 16L and REIL Rwy 34R—CTAF.

WEATHER DATA SOURCES: ASOS (541) 461–3114 **HIWAS** 112.9 EUG.

COMMUNICATIONS: CTAF 118.9 **ATIS** 125.225 541–607–4699 **UNICOM** 122.95

EUGENE RCO 122.3 (MC MINNVILLE RADIO)

Ⓡ **CASCADE APP/DEP CON** 119.6 (340°–159°) 120.25 (160°–339°) (1400–0730Z‡)

Ⓡ **SEATTLE CENTER APP/DEP CON** 125.8 (0730–1400Z‡)

EUGENE TOWER 118.9 (Rwy 16R– 34L) 124.15 (Rwy 16L– 34R) (1400–0730Z‡) **GND CON** 121.7 **CLNC DEL** 121.7

AIRSPACE: CLASS D svc 1400–0730Z‡ other times CLASS E.

RADIO AIDS TO NAVIGATION: NOTAM FILE EUG.

EUGENE (H) VORTACW 112.9 EUG Chan 76 N44°07.25′ W123°13.37′ at fld. 364/20E. **HIWAS.**

ILS/DME 111.75 I–ADE Chan 54(Y) Rwy 16L. Class IE.

ILS/DME 110.1 I–EUG Chan 38 Rwy 16R. Class IIIE. Unmonitored when ATCT clsd.

FLORENCE

FLORENCE MUNI (6S2) 1 N UTC–8(–7DT) N43°58.97′ W124°06.68′ **KLAMATH FALLS**

51 B **FUEL** 100LL, JET A TPA—1051(1000) NOTAM FILE MMV **L–1A**

RWY 15–33: H3000X60 (ASPH) S–12.5 MIRL 0.4% up NW

RWY 15: Hill. Rgt tfc.

RWY 33: PAPI(P2L)—GA 3.0° TCH 40′. Trees.

AIRPORT REMARKS: Attended 1630–0030Z‡. Birds, deer and wildlife on and invof arpt. ACTIVATE MIRL Rwy 15–33—CTAF. PAPI Rwy 33 opr 24 hrs.

WEATHER DATA SOURCES: AWOS–3 118.225 (541) 997–8664.

COMMUNICATIONS: CTAF/UNICOM 122.8

RADIO AIDS TO NAVIGATION: NOTAM FILE OTH.

NORTH BEND (L) VORTACW 112.1 OTH Chan 58 N43°24.93′ W124°10.11′ 346° 34.1 NM to fld. 707/18E. **HIWAS.**

VORTAC unusable:

012°–087° byd 30 NM blo 5,000′

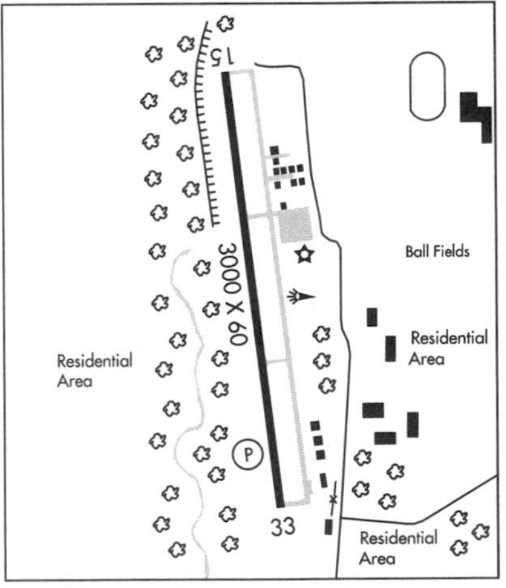

Figure 162.—Excerpt from Chart Supplement.

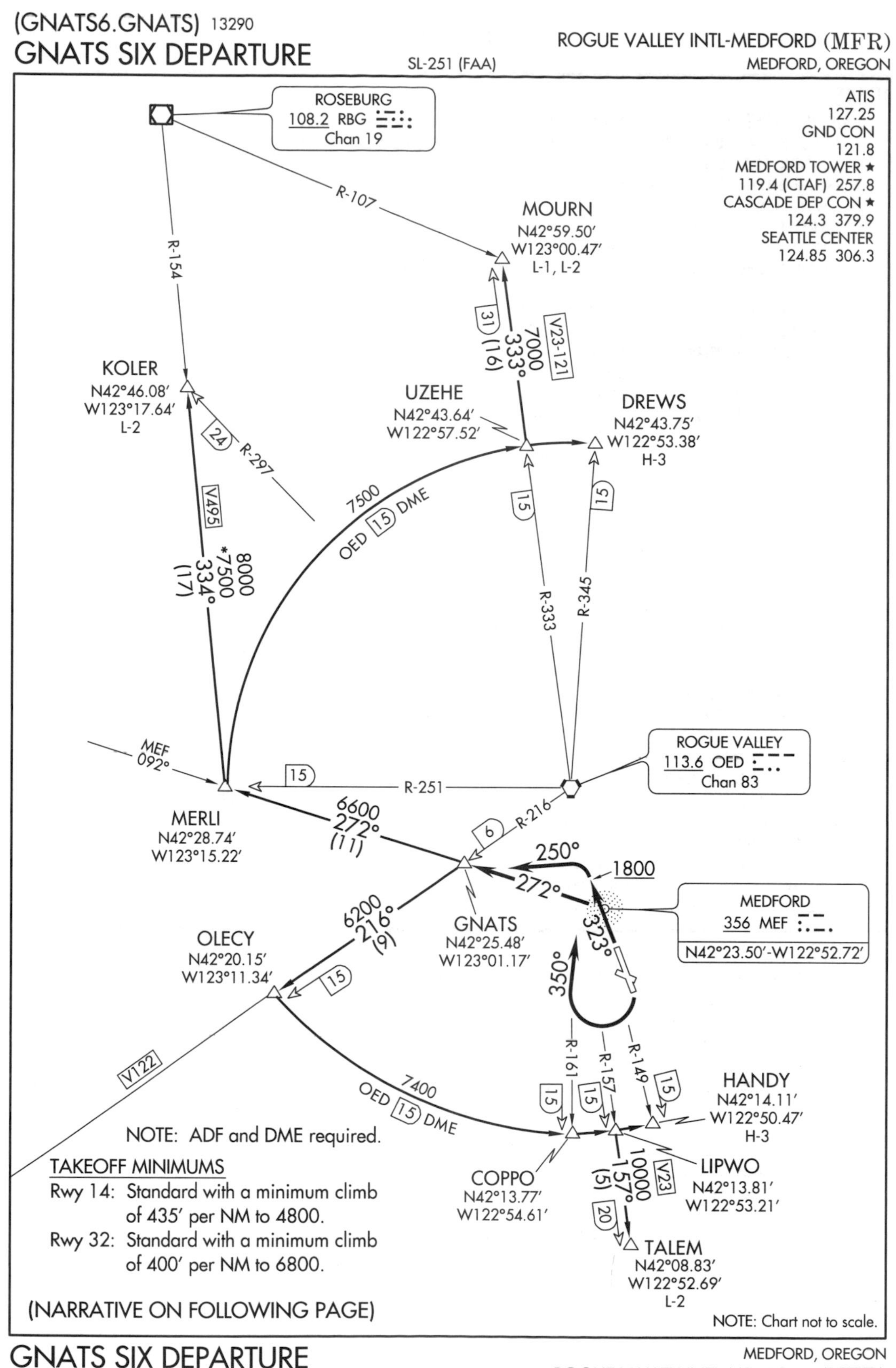

FIGURE 163.—GNATS Six Departure (GNATS6.GNATS).

(GNATS6.GNATS) 13290

GNATS SIX DEPARTURE

SL-251 (FAA)

ROGUE VALLEY INTL-MEDFORD (MFR)
MEDFORD, OREGON

DEPARTURE ROUTE DESCRIPTION

TAKEOFF RUNWAY 14: Climbing right turn on heading 350° to intercept bearing 272° from MEF NDB to GNATS INT. Thence . . . .

TAKEOFF RUNWAY 32: Climb on heading 323° to 1800 then climbing left turn on heading 250° to intercept bearing 272° from MEF NDB to GNATS INT. Thence . . . .

. . . . via (transition) or (assigned route). Maintain 11000 or assigned lower altitude.

COPPO TRANSITION (GNATS6.COPPO): From over GNATS INT via OED VORTAC R-216 to OLECY DME, then via the OED VORTAC 15 DME Arc CCW to COPPO DME.

DREWS TRANSITION (GNATS6.DREWS): From over GNATS INT via MEF NDB 272° to MERLI INT, then via the OED VORTAC 15 DME Arc CW to DREWS DME.

HANDY TRANSITION (GNATS6.HANDY): From over GNATS INT via the OED VORTAC R-216 to OLECY DME, then via the OED VORTAC 15 DME Arc CCW to HANDY DME.

KOLER TRANSITION (GNATS6.KOLER): From over GNATS INT via MEF NDB 272° to MERLI INT, then via RBG VOR/DME R-154 to KOLER INT.

MOURN TRANSITION (GNATS6.MOURN): From over GNATS INT via MEF NDB 272° to MERLI INT, then via the OED VORTAC 15 DME Arc CW to UZEHE DME, then via OED VORTAC R-333 to MOURN INT.

TALEM TRANSITION (GNATS6.TALEM): From over GNATS INT via OED VORTAC R-216 to OLECY DME, then via the OED VORTAC 15 DME Arc CCW to LIPWO DME, then via OED VORTAC R-157 to TALEM DME.

GNATS SIX DEPARTURE
(GNATS6.GNATS) 13290

MEDFORD, OREGON
ROGUE VALLEY INTL-MEDFORD (MFR)

FIGURE 164.—GNATS Six Departure (GNATS6.GNATS).

MEDFORD

ROGUE VALLEY INTL – MEDFORD (MFR) 3 N UTC–8(–7DT) N42°22.45′ W122°52.41′ **KLAMATH FALLS**
1335 B S4 **FUEL** 100LL, JET A OX 1, 3 TPA—See Remarks Class I, ARFF Index B **H–3B, L–2I**
NOTAM FILE MFR **IAP, AD**

RWY 14–32: H8800X150 (ASPH-GRVD) S–200, D–200, 2S–175, 2D–400 HIRL CL
RWY 14: MALSR. TDZL. PAPI(P4L)—GA 3.0° TCH 73′. 0.4% up.
RWY 32: REIL. PAPI(P4R)—GA 3.0° TCH 50′. 0.5% down.

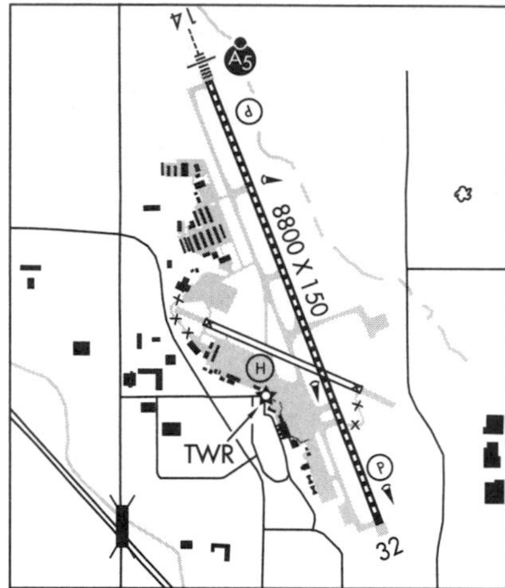

RUNWAY DECLARED DISTANCE INFORMATION
RWY 14: TORA-8800 TODA-8800 ASDA-8800 LDA-8800
RWY 32: TORA-8800 TODA-8800 ASDA-8800 LDA-8800

AIRPORT REMARKS: Attended 1300–0800Z‡. For fuel after hrs call 541–779–5451, or 541–842–2254. Bird haz large flocks of migratory waterfowl in vicinity Nov–May. Terminal apron clsd to acft exc scheduled air carrier and flts with prior permission. PPR for unscheduled ops with more than 30 passenger seats, call arpt ops 541–776–7228. Tran tie-downs avbl thru FBOs only. Rwy 32 preferred for tkfs and ldgs when twr clsd. TPA—2304(969) for propeller acft, 2804(1469) for turbo acft. PAPI Rwy 14 and VASI Rwy 32 on continuously. ACTIVATE HIRL Rwy 14–32, MALSR Rwy 14, REIL Rwy 32, TDZL Rwy 14, centerline lgts Rwy 14 and Rwy 32, and twy lgts—CTAF. Ldg fee applies to all corporate acft and all other acft with weight exceeding 12,500 lbs.

WEATHER DATA SOURCES: **ASOS** (541) 776–1238 SAWRS.

COMMUNICATIONS: CTAF 119.4 **ATIS** 127.25 **UNICOM** 122.95
MEDFORD RCO 122.65 (MC MINNVILLE RADIO)
Ⓡ **CASCADE APP/DEP CON** 124.3 (1400–0730Z‡)
SEATTLE CENTER APP/DEP CON 124.85 (0730–1400Z‡)
TOWER 119.4 (1400–0500Z‡) **GND CON** 121.8

AIRSPACE: **CLASS D** svc 1400–0500Z‡ other times CLASS E.

VOR TEST FACILITY (VOT) 117.2

RADIO AIDS TO NAVIGATION: NOTAM FILE MFR.
(H) VORTACW 113.6 OED Chan 83 N42°28.77′ W122°54.78′ 145° 6.6 NM to fld. 2083/19E. **HIWAS.**
VOR portion unusable:
260°–270° byd 35 NM blo 9,000′
290°–300° byd 35 NM blo 8,500′
MEDFORD NDB (MHW) 356 MEF N42°23.50′ W122°52.73′ 151° 1.1 NM to fld.
NDB unusable:
220°–240° byd 15 NM
PUMIE NDB (LOM) 373 MF N42°27.06′ W122°54.80′ 143° 4.9 NM to fld. LOM unusable 260°–270° beyond 10 NM. Unmonitored when ATCT closed.
ILS/DME 110.3 I–MFR Chan 40 Rwy 14. Class IA. LOM PUMIE NDB. LOM unusable 260°–270° beyond 10 NM. Unmonitored when ATCT closed. Localizer backcourse unusable byd 11 NM blo 7,000′, byd 13 NM blo 8,300′, byd 17 NM blo 8,700′. Localizer backcourse unusable byd 20° left of course.

MEMALOOSE (See IMNAHA on page 122)

MILLER MEM AIRPARK (See VALE on page 145)

MONUMENT MUNI (12S) 1 NW UTC–8(–7DT) N44°49.89′ W119°25.78′ **SEATTLE**
2323 TPA—3323(1000) NOTAM FILE MMV
RWY 14–32: H2104X29 (ASPH)
RWY 14: Hill.
AIRPORT REMARKS: Unattended. Intermittently clsd winters due to snow. Wildlife on and invof arpt. Rwy ends marked at each corner by a single white tire.
COMMUNICATIONS: CTAF 122.9

MULINO STATE (See PORTLAND–MULINO on page 137)

FIGURE 165.—Excerpt from Chart Supplement.

HOSSY N34°25.35′ W93°11.38′ NOTAM FILE HOT. **MEMPHIS**
NDB (HW/LOM) 385 HO 050° 5.7 NM to Mem Fld. **L–17E**

HOT SPRINGS

MEMORIAL FLD (HOT) 3 SW UTC–6(–5DT) N34°28.68′ W93°05.77′ **MEMPHIS**
540 B S4 **FUEL** 100LL, JET A Class II, ARFF Index A NOTAM FILE HOT **H–6I, L–17E**
IAP

RWY 05–23: H6595X150 (ASPH–GRVD) S–75, D–125, 2S–158, 2D–210, 2D/2D2–400 HIRL 0.6% up NE
RWY 05: MALSR. Rgt tfc.
RWY 23: PAPI(P4L)—GA 3.0° TCH 40′. Pole.
RWY 13–31: H4098X100 (ASPH) S–28, D–36, 2D–63 MIRL 0.4% up NW
RWY 13: REIL. Trees. Rgt tfc.
RWY 31: Pole.

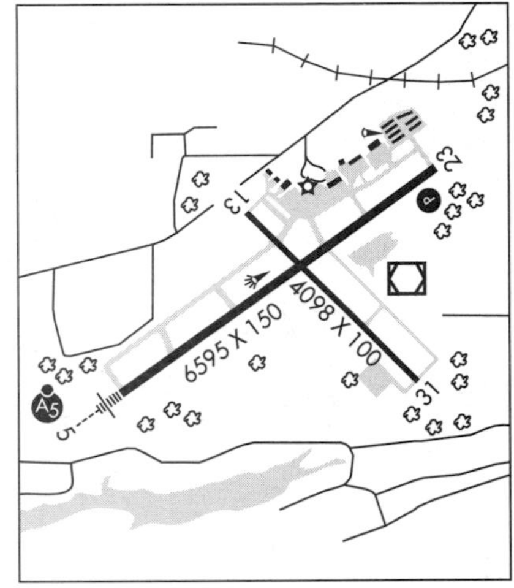

RUNWAY DECLARED DISTANCE INFORMATION
RWY 05: TORA–6595 TODA–6595 ASDA–6595 LDA–6595
RWY 13: TORA–4100 TODA–4100 ASDA–4100 LDA–4100
RWY 23: TORA–6595 TODA–6595 ASDA–6595 LDA–6595
RWY 31: TORA–4100 TODA–4100 ASDA–4100 LDA–4100

AIRPORT REMARKS: Attended 1100–0400Z‡. For fuel after hrs call 501–617–0324 or 501–617–4908. Rwy 23 PAPI OTS indef. ACTIVATE HIRL Rwy 05–23, MIRL Rwy 13–31, MALSR Rwy 05, PAPI Rwy 23 and REIL Rwy 13—CTAF.

WEATHER DATA SOURCES: ASOS 119.925 (501) 624–7633. **HIWAS** 110.0 HOT.

COMMUNICATIONS: CTAF/UNICOM 123.0
RCO 122.1R 110.0T (JONESBORO RADIO)
®**MEMPHIS CENTER APP/DEP CON** 128.475

AIRSPACE: CLASS E svc 1200–0400Z‡ other times CLASS G.

RADIO AIDS TO NAVIGATION: NOTAM FILE HOT.
HOT SPRINGS (L) VOR/DME 110.0 HOT Chan 37 N34°28.72′ W93°05.44′ at fld. 529/4E. **HIWAS.**
VOR unusable:
056°–140° byd 20 NM blo 6,500′
141°–227° byd 20 NM blo 3,500′
141°–227° byd 26 NM blo 5,500′
228°–311° byd 20 NM blo 3,500′
312°–345° byd 15 NM blo 5,500′
312°–345° byd 32 NM blo 9,500′
346°–055° byd 20 NM blo 3,500′
DME unusable:
310°–035° byd 10 NM blo 11,000′
310°–035° byd 25 NM blo 12,000′
310°–035° byd 30 NM blo 17,000′
HOSSY NDB (LOM) 385 HO N34°25.36′ W93°11.38′ 050° 5.7 NM to fld. Unmonitored.
ILS/DME 111.5 I–HOT Chan 52 Rwy 05. Class IT. LOM HOSSY NDB. ILS and LOM unmonitored.

HOWARD CO (See NASHVILLE on page 55)

FIGURE 166.—Chart Supplement (HOT).

(BYP.BYP6) 13178 ST-6039 (FAA)

DALLAS-FORT WORTH INTL (DFW)

BONHAM SIX ARRIVAL Transition Routes

DALLAS-FORT WORTH, TEXAS

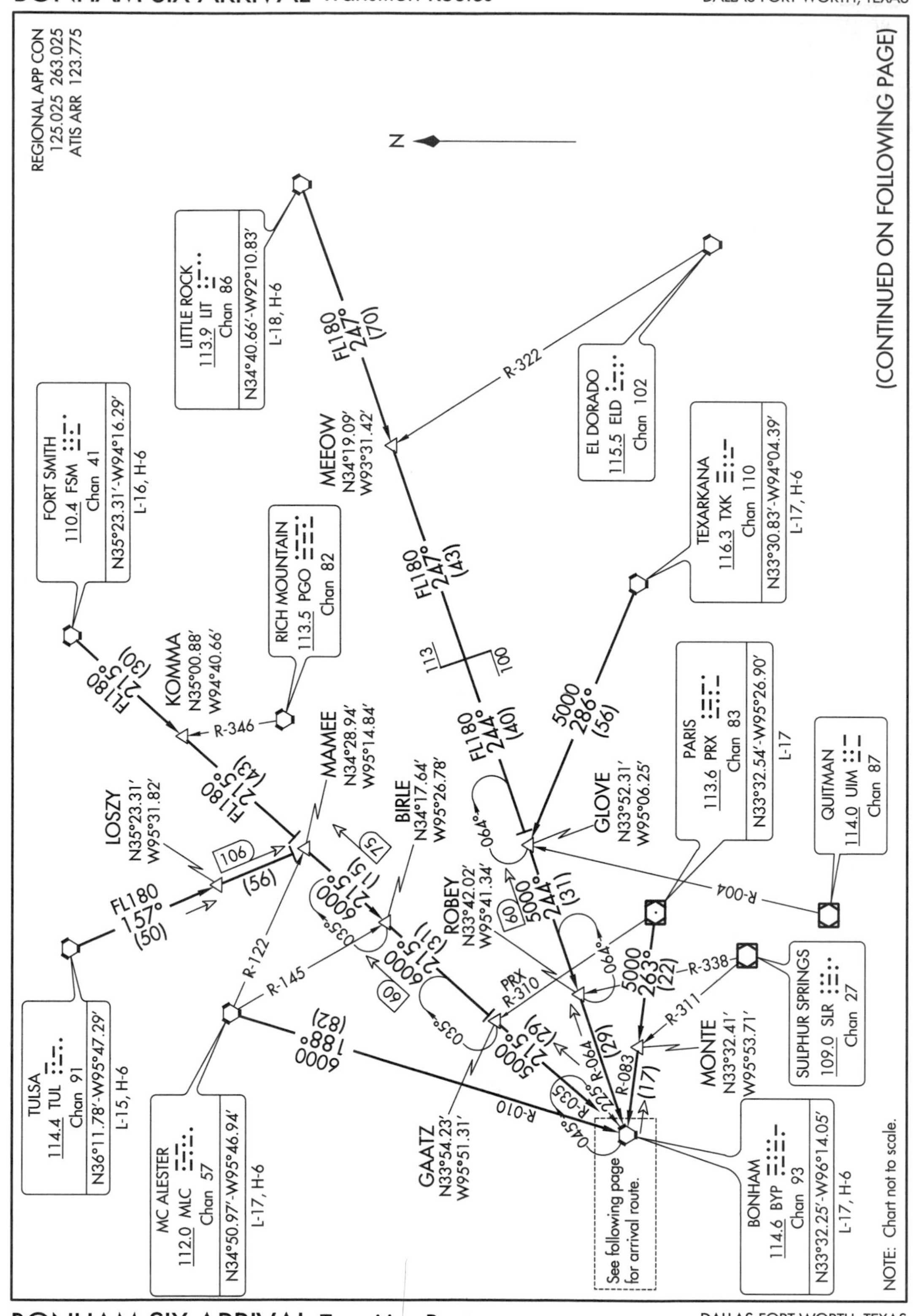

BONHAM SIX ARRIVAL Transition Routes

(BYP.BYP6) 13178

DALLAS-FORT WORTH, TEXAS

DALLAS-FORT WORTH INTL (DFW)

FIGURE 167.—BONHAM Six Arrival Transition Routes (BYP.BYP6) (DFW).

(BYP.BYP6) 13178 ST-6039 (FAA)

BONHAM SIX ARRIVAL Arrival Routes

DALLAS-FORT WORTH INTL (DFW)
DALLAS-FORT WORTH, TEXAS

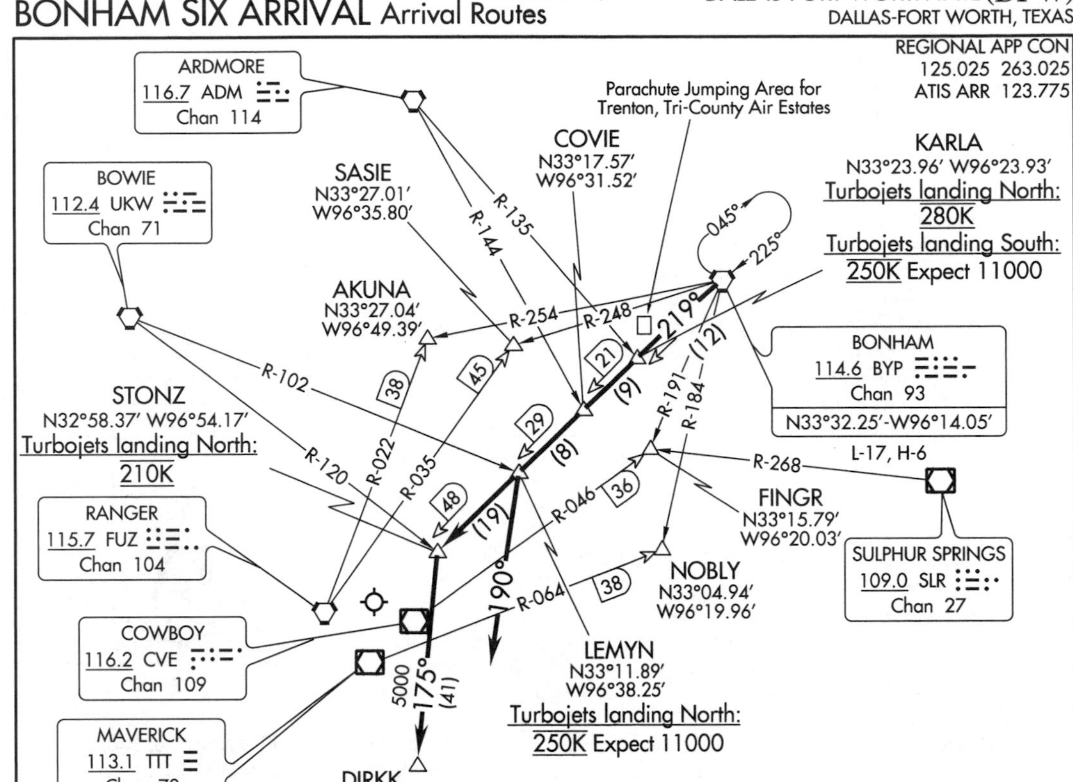

ARRIVAL DESCRIPTION

FORT SMITH TRANSITION (FSM.BYP6): From over FSM VORTAC on FSM R-215 to MAMEE INT, then on BYP R-035 to BYP VORTAC. Thence. . . .
LITTLE ROCK TRANSITION (LIT.BYP6): From over LIT VORTAC on LIT R-247 to MEEOW INT then on LIT R-247 and BYP R-064 to GLOVE INT, then on BYP R-064 to BYP VORTAC. Thence. . .
MC ALESTER TRANSITION (MLC.BYP6): From over MLC VORTAC on MLC R-188 and BYP R-010 to BYP VORTAC. Thence. . . .
PARIS TRANSITION (PRX.BYP6): From over PRX VOR/DME on PRX R-263 to MONTE INT then on BYP R-083 to BYP VORTAC. Thence. . . .
TEXARKANA TRANSITION (TXK.BYP6): From over TXK VORTAC on TXK R-286 to GLOVE INT then on BYP R-064 to BYP VORTAC. Thence. . . .
TULSA TRANSITION (TUL.BYP6): From over TUL VORTAC on TUL R-157 to MAMEE INT, then on BYP R-035 to BYP VORTAC. Thence. . . .

. . . . ALL AIRCRAFT: From over BYP VORTAC on BYP R-219, thence. . . .

ALL AIRCRAFT LANDING SOUTH: To LEMYN INT, expect vectors to final approach course.
JETS LANDING NORTH: FOR /E, /F, /G, and /R (RNP-2.0) EQUIPPED AIRCRAFT: From over STONZ INT direct DIRKK, expect vector to final approach course prior to DIRKK, if not received by DIRKK fly present heading.
ALL OTHERS: To STONZ depart STONZ heading 175° for vector to final approach course.
PROPS LANDING NORTH: Depart LEMYN INT heading 190°, expect vectors to final approach course.

BONHAM SIX ARRIVAL Arrival Routes

(BYP.BYP6) 13178

DALLAS-FORT WORTH, TEXAS
DALLAS-FORT WORTH INTL (DFW)

FIGURE 168.—BONHAM Six Arrival Routes (BYP.BYP6) (DFW).

DALLAS

ADDISON (ADS) 9 N UTC–6(–5DT) N32°58.11′ W96°50.19′ **DALLAS–FT WORTH**
645 B S4 **FUEL** 100LL, JET A OX 2, 3 TPA—See Remarks LRA NOTAM FILE ADS **COPTER**
RWY 15–33: H7203X100 (ASPH–GRVD) S–60, D–120 HIRL **H–6H, L–17C, A**
RWY 15: MALSR. PAPI(P4R)—GA 3.0° TCH 60′. Thld dsplcd 979′. Pole. **IAP, AD**
RWY 33: REIL. PAPI(P4L)—GA 3.0° TCH 60′. Thld dsplcd 772′. Bldg. 
RUNWAY DECLARED DISTANCE INFORMATION
RWY 15: TORA–7202 TODA–7202 ASDA–6592 LDA–5613
RWY 33: TORA–7202 TODA–7202 ASDA–7202 LDA–6431
AIRPORT REMARKS: Attended continuously. Birds on and invof arpt. No touch and go landings without arpt managers approval. Numerous 200′ buildings within 1 mile East, and South of arpt, transmission towers and water tanks West of arpt. Noise sensitive areas surround arpt. Pilots requested to use NBAA std noise procedures. TPA—1600 (956) for light acft, 2000 (1356) for large acft. Be alert: Rwy holding position markings located at the west edge of Twy A. ACTIVATE HIRL Rwy 15–33 and MALSR Rwy 15—CTAF. Flight Notification Service (ADCUS) available.
WEATHER DATA SOURCES: AWOS–3 (972) 386–4855 LAWRS.
COMMUNICATIONS: CTAF 126.0 **ATIS** 133.4 972–628–2439
UNICOM 122.95
®**REGIONAL APP/DEP CON** 124.3
TOWER 126.0 (1200–0400Z‡) **GND CON** 121.6 **CLNC DEL** 119.55
AIRSPACE: CLASS D svc 1200–0400Z‡, other times CLASS G.
RADIO AIDS TO NAVIGATION: NOTAM FILE FTW.
MAVERICK (H) VORW/DME 113.1 TTT Chan 78 N32°52.15′ W97°02.43′ 054° 11.9 NM to fld. 540/6E.
All acft arriving DFW are requested to turn DME off until departure due to traffic overload of Maverick DME
ILS/DME 110.1 I–ADS Chan 38 Rwy 15. Class IT. Unmonitored when ATCT closed. DME also serves Rwy 33.
ILS/DME 110.1 I–TBQ Chan 38 Rwy 33. Class IB. Localizer unmonitored when ATCT closed. DME also serves Rwy 15.

TWR
15
33
7203 X 100

AIR PARK–DALLAS (F69) 16 NE UTC–6(–5DT) N33°01.41′ W96°50.22′ **DALLAS–FT WORTH**
695 S4 **FUEL** 100LL TPA—1890(1195) NOTAM FILE FTW **COPTER**
RWY 16–34: H3080X30 (ASPH) LIRL(NSTD) **L–17C, A**
RWY 16: Thld dsplcd 300′. Pole.
RWY 34: Tree. Rgt tfc.
AIRPORT REMARKS: Uattended. For fuel call 972–248–4265 prior to arrival. Rwy 16–34 extensive cracking, loose asph and stones rwy. Rwy 16–34 NSTD LIRL, south 2780′ of rwy lgtd. Rwy 16 and Rwy 34 NSTD centerline marking incorrect size and spacing, dsplcd thld yellow. Rwy numbers 25′ tall. ACTIVATE LIRL Rwy 16–34—CTAF.
COMMUNICATIONS: CTAF 122.9
RADIO AIDS TO NAVIGATION: NOTAM FILE FTW.
MAVERICK (H) VORW/DME 113.1 TTT Chan 78 N32°52.15′ W97°02.43′ 042° 13.8 NM to fld. 540/6E.
All acft arrlving DFW are requested to turn DME off until departure due to traffic overload of Maverick DME

AIRPARK EAST (1F7) 23 E UTC–6(–5DT) N32°48.78′ W96°21.12′ **DALLAS–FT WORTH**
510 B S4 NOTAM FILE FTW **COPTER**
RWY 13–31: H2630X30 (ASPH) LIRL
RWY 13: Tree. Rgt tfc.
RWY 31: Tree.
AIRPORT REMARKS: Unattended. ACTIVATE LIRL Rwy 13–31—122.9.
COMMUNICATIONS: CTAF/UNICOM 122.7

FIGURE 169.—Excerpt from Chart Supplement (ADS).

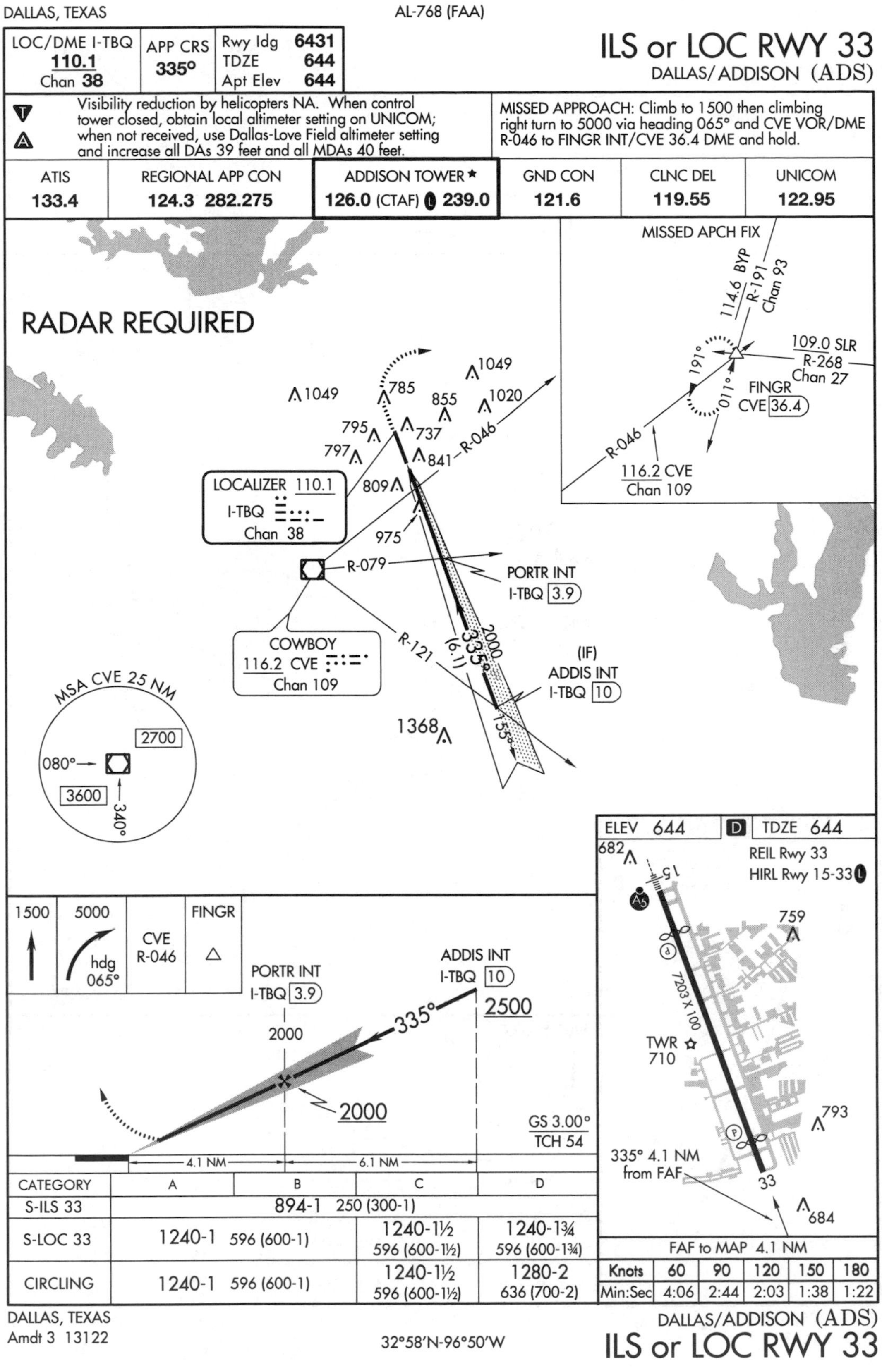

DALLAS, TEXAS AL-768 (FAA)

LOC/DME I-TBQ 110.1 Chan 38	APP CRS 335°	Rwy ldg 6431 TDZE 644 Apt Elev 644

ILS or LOC RWY 33

DALLAS/ADDISON (ADS)

Visibility reduction by helicopters NA. When control tower closed, obtain local altimeter setting on UNICOM; when not received, use Dallas-Love Field altimeter setting and increase all DAs 39 feet and all MDAs 40 feet.

MISSED APPROACH: Climb to 1500 then climbing right turn to 5000 via heading 065° and CVE VOR/DME R-046 to FINGR INT/CVE 36.4 DME and hold.

ATIS	REGIONAL APP CON	ADDISON TOWER ★	GND CON	CLNC DEL	UNICOM
133.4	124.3 282.275	126.0 (CTAF) 239.0	121.6	119.55	122.95

CATEGORY	A	B	C	D
S-ILS 33	894-1 250 (300-1)			
S-LOC 33	1240-1 596 (600-1)		1240-1½ 596 (600-1½)	1240-1¾ 596 (600-1¾)
CIRCLING	1240-1 596 (600-1)		1240-1½ 596 (600-1½)	1280-2 636 (700-2)

FAF to MAP 4.1 NM

Knots	60	90	120	150	180
Min:Sec	4:06	2:44	2:03	1:38	1:22

DALLAS, TEXAS
Amdt 3 13122

32°58′N-96°50′W

DALLAS/ADDISON (ADS)
ILS or LOC RWY 33

FIGURE 170.—ILS or LOC RWY 33 (ADS).

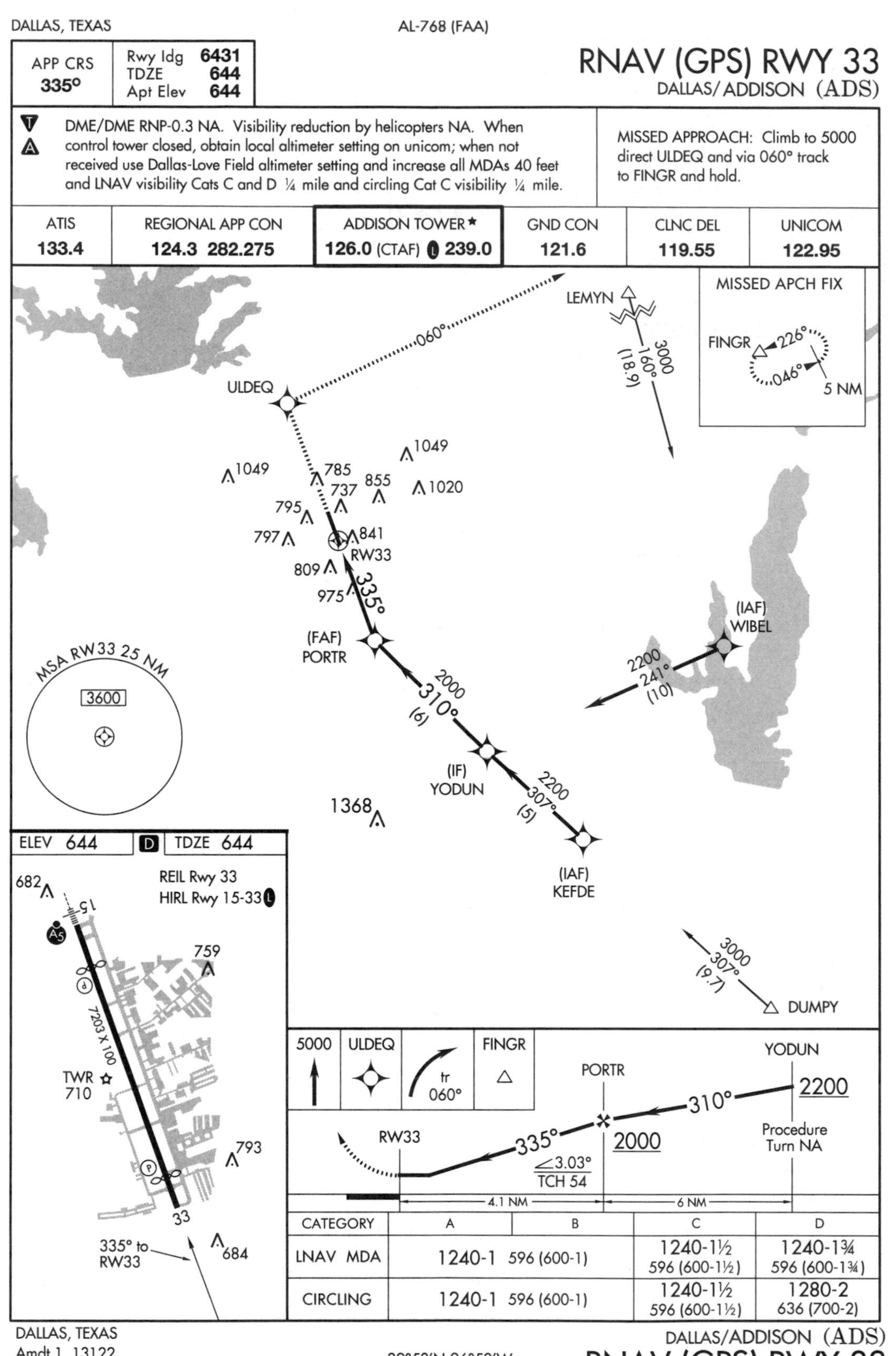

CATEGORY	A	B	C	D
LNAV MDA	1240-1 596 (600-1)		1240-1½ 596 (600-1½)	1240-1¾ 596 (600-1¾)
CIRCLING	1240-1 596 (600-1)		1240-1½ 596 (600-1½)	1280-2 636 (700-2)

FIGURE 171.—RNAV (GPS) RWY 33 (ADS).

84 **MONTANA**

HELENA RGNL (HLN)(KHLN) P (ARNG) 2 NE UTC–7(–6DT) N46°36.41′ W111°58.97′ **GREAT FALLS**
3877 B S4 **FUEL** 80, 100, 100LL, JET A OX 1, 3 LRA Class I, ARFF Index B NOTAM FILE HLN **H–1D, L–13C**
RWY 09–27: H9000X150 (ASPH–PFC) S–100, D–160, 2S–175, 2D–250 HIRL **IAP, DIAP, AD**
RWY 09: REIL. VASI(V4L)—GA 3.0° TCH 45′. Ground. 0.3% down.
RWY 27: MALSR. VASI(V4L)—GA 3.0° TCH 47′. Rgt tfc.
RWY 05–23: H4644X75 (ASPH–PFC) S–21, D–30 MIRL 1.2% up SW
RWY 05: Road.
RWY 23: PAPI(P2L)—GA 3.0° TCH 49′. Fence. Rgt tfc.
RWY 17–35: H2989X75 (ASPH–PFC) S–21, D–30 MIRL 1.7% up SE
RWY 35: Ground. Rgt tfc.
MILITARY SERVICE: LGT When twr clsd, ACTIVATE–HIRL Rwy 09–27, MIRL Rwy 05–23 and 16–34, REIL Rwy 09, MALSR Rwy 27 – CTAF. **FUEL** A+, J8 (C406–442–2190. Opr 1200–0600Z‡, OT $150 fee, 90 min PPR.) (NC–80, 100, 100LL)
AIRPORT REMARKS: Attended 1200–0800Z‡. ARFF coverage provided for scheduled Part 121 air carriers only exc with prior approval, call 406–442–2821. Ldg rights customs avbl call 406–449–5506. Rwy 17–35 and Rwy 05–23 (exc between Twy F and Rwy 09–27) not avbl for air carrier use by acft with greater than 30 passenger seats. Twy A, Twy B, and Twy C between Twy A and Rwy 35 not avbl for air carrier use by acft with greater than 30 passenger seats. When twr clsd ACTIVATE HIRL Rwy 09–27, MIRL Rwy 05–23 and Rwy 17–35, REIL Rwy 09, MALSR Rwy 27—CTAF. Ldg fee for all commercial acft and all acft over 10,000 lbs. Flight Notification Service (ADCUS) avbl. NOTE: See SPECIAL NOTICE.
MILITARY REMARKS: ARNG Opr Mon–Fri 1400–0030Z‡, exc holidays. Exercise caution while taxiing, AASF ramp not stressed for large acft. Ctc flt ops for ramp advisory 126.2, DSN 324–3055/56, C406–324–3055/56. No tran svc Sat, Sun, holidays or after 2300Z‡ Mon–Fri.
WEATHER DATA SOURCES: ASOS (406) 443–4317
COMMUNICATIONS: CTAF 118.3 **ATIS** 120.4 **UNICOM** 122.95
RCO 122.55 255.4 (GREAT FALLS RADIO)
APP/DEP CON 119.5 229.4 (1300–0500Z‡)
SALT LAKE CENTER APP/DEP CON 133.4 285.4 (0500–1300Z‡)
TOWER 118.3 257.8 (1300–0500Z‡) **GND CON** 121.9
ARNG OPS 40.65 126.2 321.45
AIRSPACE: CLASS D svc 1300–0500Z‡ other times CLASS E.
RADIO AIDS TO NAVIGATION: NOTAM FILE HLN.
(H) VORTACW 117.7 HLN Chan 124 N46°36.41′ W111°57.21′ 254° 1.2 NM to fld. 3823/16E.
VOR portion unusable:
035°–050° byd 35 NM blo 12,000′
105°–165° byd 25 NM blo 17,000′
165°–185° byd 25 NM blo 13,500′
185°–230° byd 25 NM blo 17,500′
203°–213° byd 22 NM blo 13,000′
230°–270° byd 25 NM blo 12,500′
TACAN AZIMUTH and DME unusable:
035°–070° byd 35 NM blo 13,000′
165°–185° byd 25 NM blo 13,500′
250°–300° byd 25 NM blo 14,000′
320°–035° byd 25 NM blo 13,000′
TACAN DME unusable:
035°–070° byd 35 NM blo 13,000′
105°–150° byd 25 NM
105°–210° byd 15 NM blo 11,100′
105°–210° byd 20 NM blo 12,000′
150°–165° byd 25 NM blo 17,000′
165°–185° byd 25 NM blo 13,500′
185°–210° byd 25 NM
203°–213° byd 22 NM blo 13,000′
210°–250° byd 15 NM blo 12,000′
210°–250° byd 25 NM blo 17,500′
250°–300° byd 25 NM blo 14,000′
320°–035° byd 25 NM blo 13,000′
TACAN AZIMUTH unusable:
105°–150° byd 15 NM
150°–165° byd 15 NM blo 17,000′
185°–210° byd 15 NM
210°–250° byd 15 NM blo 17,500′

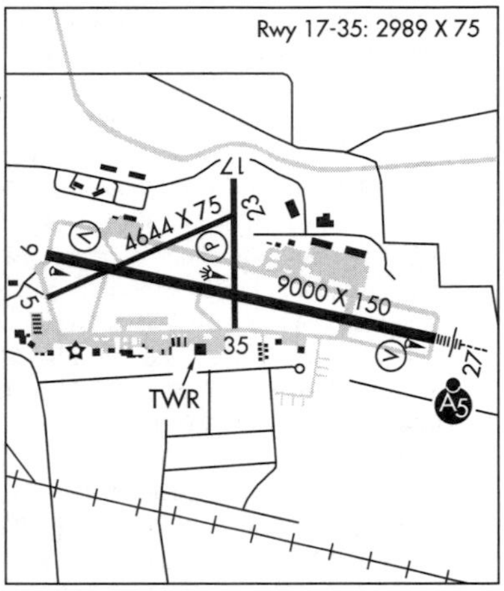

CONTINUED ON NEXT PAGE

FIGURE 172.—Excerpt from Chart Supplement.

BIG SPRING MC MAHON–WRINKLE (BPG) 2 SW UTC–6(–5DT) N32°12.76′ W101°31.30′ **DALLAS–FT WORTH**
2573 B S4 **FUEL** 100LL, JET A NOTAM FILE BPG **H–6G, L–6H**
RWY 17–35: H8802X100 (CONC) S–60, D–150, 2D–200 MIRL **IAP**
RWY 17: SSALS. PAPI(P4L)—GA 3.0° TCH 45′. Rgt tfc.
RWY 35: PAPI(P4L)—GA 3.0° TCH 36′.
RWY 06–24: H4601X75 (ASPH) MIRL 0.6% up NE
RWY 06: PVASI(PSIL)—GA 2.97° TCH 47′. Rgt tfc.
RWY 24: PVASI(PSIL)—GA 3.55° TCH 35′.
AIRPORT REMARKS: Attended Mon–Sat 1400–2300Z‡. For fuel after hours call 432–267–8952 or 432–935–3395. Prairie dogs on rwys and twys. Extensive agricultural ops invof arpt. Sandhill Cranes crossing in the spring and fall. MIRL Rwy 06–24 and Rwy 17–35 preset low ints, to increase ints and ACTIVATE SSALS Rwy 17 and PVASI Rwy 06, Rwy 24, and PAPI Rwy 17 and Rwy 35—CTAF.
WEATHER DATA SOURCES: AWOS–3 118.025 (432) 263–3842.
COMMUNICATIONS: CTAF/UNICOM 122.8
RCO 122.4 (SAN ANGELO RADIO)
FORT WORTH CENTER APP/DEP CON 133.7
RADIO AIDS TO NAVIGATION: NOTAM FILE BPG.
(L) VORTACW 114.3 BGS Chan 90 N32°23.14′ W101°29.02′ 180° 10.5 NM to fld. 2670/11E.

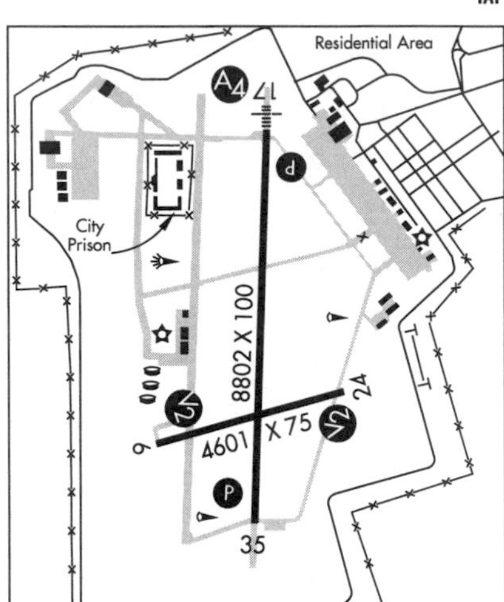

BIGGS AAF (FORT BLISS) (BIF)(KBIF) A 5 NE UTC–7(–6DT) N31°50.97′ W106°22.80′ **EL PASO**
3948 B TPA—See Remarks NOTAM FILE ABQ Not insp. **H–4L, L–6F**
RWY 03–21: H13554X150 (PEM) PCN 120 R/C/W/T HIRL **DIAP, AD**
RWY 03: PAPI(P4L)—GA 3.0° TCH 71′.
RWY 21: ALSF1. PAPI(P4L)—GA 3.0° TCH 71′. Rgt tfc. 0.3% down.
MILITARY SERVICE: LGT When unattended ACTIVATE 3–step HIRL Rwy 03–21, High Intensity ALS Category I configuration with sequenced Flashers (code) Rwy 21 and PAPI Rwy 21–127.9. **JASU** 4(A/M32A–86) 2(A/M32–95) **FUEL** A+ (Atlantic Avn, 1200–0400Z‡ Mon–Sun, C915–779–2831, 1 hr prior notice, after hr C915–861–2390, after hr call out fee $100.)
FLUID SP **TRAN ALERT** 1300–0500Z‡ Mon–Sun, exc holidays.
MILITARY REMARKS: Attended Mon–Sun 1300–0500Z‡, except holidays. See FLIP AP/1 Supplementary Arpt Remark. **RSTD** PPR all acft. 24 hr prior notice, ctc Airfield Ops DSN 621–8811/8330, C915–744–8811/8330. Twr and svcs avbl for all acft with PPR. PPR time valid +/— 1 hr. All acft ctc Afld Ops via PTD 30 min prior to arr. Twr and svcs unavbl before 1 hr prior to PPR sked arr. **CAUTION** El Paso Intl Rwy 22 2 NM SE can be mistaken for Rwy 21. Coyote hazard. **TFC PAT** Fixed Wing 5002(1054), Fixed Wing Category BCDE turbo prop 5502(1554), Rotary Wing 4502(554), Jet 6002(2054).
NS ABTMT VFR west arr/dep via mountain pass 15 NM NW of Biggs AAF. Avoid VFR over flight of city. Fly 1500′ AGL, 1500′ horizontal distance from mountain dwellings. **MISC** Approval required for access to ramp. Temporary storage of classified material avbl at Afld Ops. Intl garbage cap ltd. Expect delays unless placed in garbage bags prior to arrival. Hangar space extremely limited for transient acft. KBIF manual obsn and wx forecaster avbl Mon–Fri 1300–0500Z‡, clsd holidays. DSN 621–1215/1214, C915–744–1215/1214, OT 25th OWS, Davis Monthan AFB, DSN 228–6598/6599.
COMMUNICATIONS: ATIS 120.0 254.3 (C915–772–9412) **PTD** 122.7
® **EL PASO APP CON** 119.15 353.5 (South of V16) 124.25 298.85 (North of V16)
TOWER 127.9 342.25 (Mon–Sun 1300–0500Z‡, except holidays). Advisory svc twr freq other times.
® **EL PASO DEP CON** 121.3 263.0
EL PASO CLNC DEL 125.0 379.1
AIRSPACE: CLASS D svc 1300–0500Z‡ Mon–Sat except holidays other times CLASS E.
RADIO AIDS TO NAVIGATION: NOTAM FILE ABQ.
NEWMAN (L) VORTACW 112.4 EWM Chan 71 N31°57.10′ W106°16.34′ 210° 8.2 NM to fld. 4040/12E.
DME portion unusable:
220°–255° byd 25 NM blo 12,000′
COMM/NAV/WEATHER REMARKS: Radar—See Terminal FLIP for Radar Minima.

BIRD DOG AIRFIELD (See KRUM on page 297)

BISHOP (See DECATUR on page 245)

FIGURE 172A.—Excerpt from Chart Supplement.

CONTINUED FROM PRECEDING PAGE

CAPITOL NDB (HW) 335 CVP N46°36.40′ W111°56.23′ 258° 1.9 NM to fld. NDB unmonitored when ATCT clsd.
HAUSER NDB (MHW) 386 HAU N46°34.13′ W111°45.48′ 268° 9.6 NM to fld. NDB unmonitored when HLN ATCT clsd.
ILS 110.1 I–HLN Rwy 27. Unmonitored when ATCT closed. Localizer backcourse unusable byd 22° rgt of course, unusable within 2.7 DME.

HINSDALE (6U5) 0 SE UTC–7(–6DT) N48°23.28′ W107°05.00′ **BILLINGS**
2220 NOTAM FILE GTF
RWY 07–25: 2200X75 (TURF) LIRL(NSTD) 0.7% up W
RWY 07: Road.
RWY 10–28: 2160X200 (TURF) 0.3% up W
RWY 10: Road.
RWY 16–34: 1960X75 (TURF) 1.5% up S
RWY 16: P–line.
RWY 34: Fence.
AIRPORT REMARKS: Unattended. Rwys soft when wet. Hay bales and farm equipment adjacent to rwy. Rwys not clearly defined. Rwy 16–34, Rwy 07–25 and Rwy 10–28 marked with white cones full length of rwy. Rwy 16 p–lines marked with globes. Rwy 07–25 NSTD LIRL 335′ spacing between lgts, one thld lgt each end. For rwy lgts phone 406–364–2272/2387.
COMMUNICATIONS: CTAF 122.9

HOGELAND (6U6) 1 NW UTC–7(–6DT) N48°51.61′ W108°39.66′ **BILLINGS**
3139 B NOTAM FILE GTF
RWY 07–25: 3140X60 (TRTD) 0.6% up W
RWY 16–34: 1230X50 (TURF)
RWY 34: Bldg.
AIRPORT REMARKS: Unattended. Rwy 16–34 for emerg use only, road and drainage ditch parallel rwy on east side. Rwy 07–25 patches of loose aggregate and grvl.
COMMUNICATIONS: CTAF 122.9

HOT SPRINGS (SØ9) 2 E UTC–7(–6DT) N47°36.75′ W114°36.81′ **GREAT FALLS**
2763 B NOTAM FILE GTF
RWY 06–24: H3550X45 (ASPH–TRTD) MIRL
RWY 24: Thld dsplcd 411′. Road.
AIRPORT REMARKS: Unattended. Ultralights on and in vicinity of arpt. Occasional snow removal. Rwy 06–24 asph grvl composition full length. Rwy 24 has 411′ unlighted, 2169′ lgtd at ngt. Rwy 06–24 cones adjacent to MIRL full length and dsplcd thld marked with white cones. Rwy 06 and Rwy 24 numbers 4′x 8′ in measure, thld line and rwy lines NSTD.
COMMUNICATIONS: CTAF 122.9

HYSHAM (6U7) 2 E UTC–7(–6DT) N46°17.61′ W107°11.60′ **BILLINGS**
2624 B NOTAM FILE GTF
RWY 07–25: H3060X45 (ASPH–TRTD) LIRL
AIRPORT REMARKS: Unattended. 1030′ dirt extension east of Rwy 07 thld soft when wet. Rwy 07 basic markings NSTD numbers and stripes, markings are faded. Rwy 25 basic markings NSTD small numbers and stripes, markings are faded. Numerous rwy lgts inop. ACTIVATE LIRL Rwy 07–25—CTAF.
COMMUNICATIONS: CTAF 122.9

JORDAN (JDN) 2 NW UTC–7(–6DT) N47°19.73′ W106°57.16′ **BILLINGS**
2662 B NOTAM FILE JDN **L–13D**
RWY 10–28: H4300X75 (ASPH–PFC) S–12.5 MIRL
RWY 28: PAPI(P2L)—GA 3.0° TCH 29′.
AIRPORT REMARKS: Unattended. ACTIVATE MIRL Rwy 10–28 and PAPI Rwy 28—CTAF.
COMMUNICATIONS: CTAF 122.9
RADIO AIDS TO NAVIGATION: NOTAM FILE GGW.
GLASGOW (H) VORW/DME 113.9 GGW Chan 86 N48°12.92′ W106°37.53′ 180° 54.8 NM to fld. 2283/14E.
NDB (MHW) 263 JDN N47°20.00′ W106°56.29′ at fld. NOTAM FILE JDN. VFR only.

JUDITH MOUNTAIN N47°13.03′ W109°13.31′ **GREAT FALLS**
RCO 122.2 (GREAT FALLS RADIO) **L–13D**

FIGURE 173.—Excerpt from Chart Supplement.

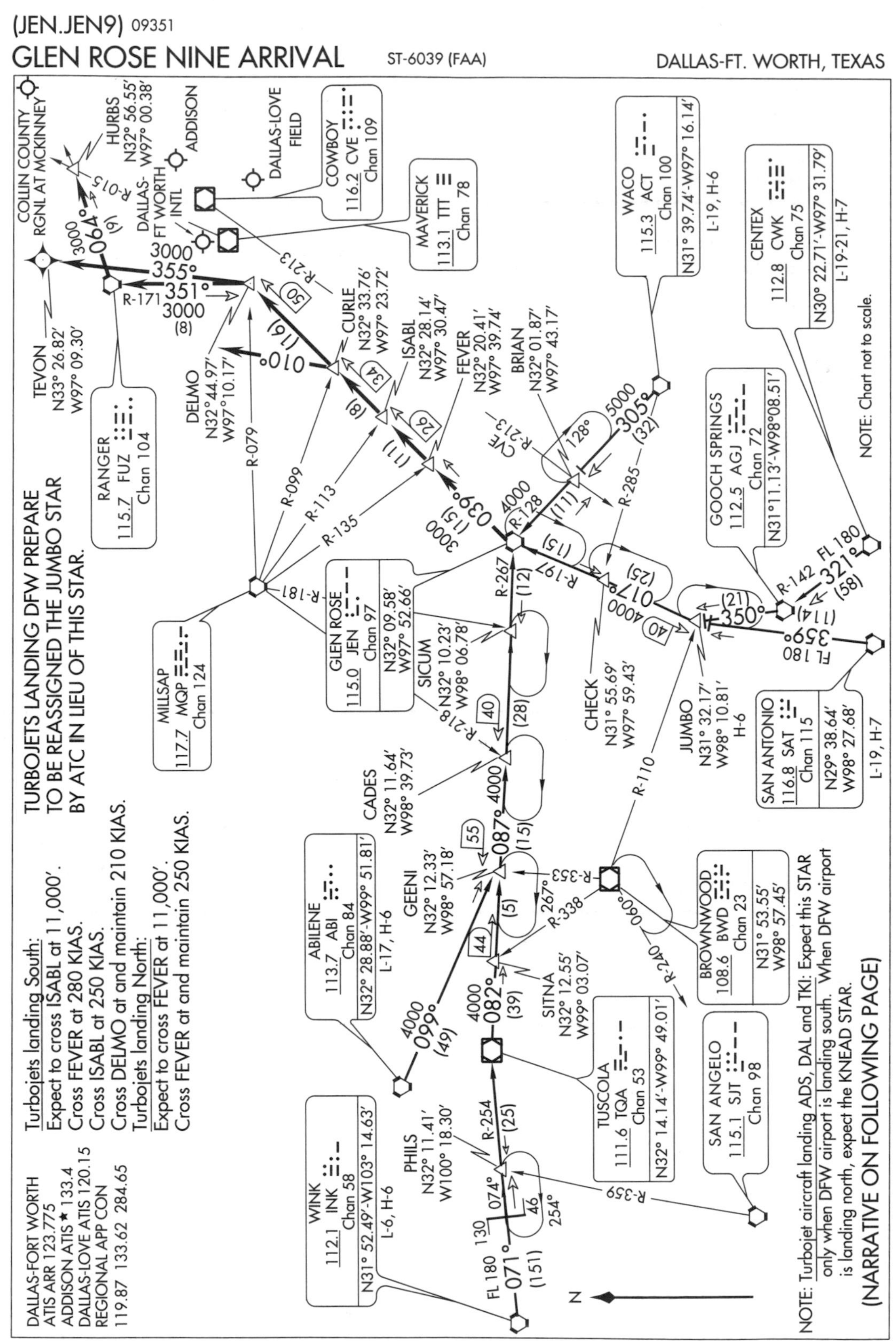

FIGURE 174.—GLEN ROSE Nine Arrival (JEN.JEN9).

(JEN.JEN9) 09351

GLEN ROSE NINE ARRIVAL ST-6039 (FAA) DALLAS-FT. WORTH, TEXAS

ARRIVAL DESCRIPTION

ABILENE TRANSITION (ABI.JEN9): From over ABI VORTAC via R-099 to GEENI INT, then via JEN R-267 to JEN VORTAC. Thence. . . .
CENTEX TRANSITION (CWK.JEN9): From over CWK VORTAC via CWK R-321 and AGJ R-142 to AGJ VORTAC, then via AGJ R-350 to JUMBO INT, then via JEN R-197 to JEN VORTAC. Thence . . . .
JUMBO TRANSITION (JUMBO.JEN9): From over JUMBO INT via JEN R-197 to JEN VORTAC. Thence . . . .
SAN ANTONIO TRANSITION (SAT.JEN9): From over SAT VORTAC via SAT R-359 to JUMBO INT, then via JEN R-197 to JEN VORTAC. Thence . . . .
WACO TRANSITION (ACT.JEN9): From over ACT VORTAC via ACT R-305 and JEN R-128 to JEN VORTAC. Thence. . . .
WINK TRANSITION (INK.JEN9): From over INK VORTAC via INK R-071 and TQA R-254 to TQA VOR/DME, then via TQA R-082 to GEENI INT, then via JEN R-267 to JEN VORTAC. Thence. . . .

. . . . ALL AIRCRAFT: From over JEN VORTAC via JEN R-039, thence . . . .

ALL AIRCRAFT LANDING NORTH: To CURLE INT, expect vectors to final approach course.

JETS LANDING SOUTH: To DELMO, depart DELMO heading 355°.
For /E, /F, /G and /R (RNP 2.0) EQUIPMENT SUFFIXED AIRCRAFT: From over DELMO WP direct TEVON WP, expect vector to final approach course prior to TEVON WP. If not received by TEVON fly present heading.
NON TURBOJETS LANDING SOUTH: To CURLE INT, depart CURLE heading 010° for vectors to final approach course.

AIRCRAFT LANDING DAL, ADS, TKI: To DELMO INT, depart DELMO via FUZ R-171 to FUZ VORTAC then FUZ R-064 to HURBS INT, expect vectors to final approach course.

GLEN ROSE NINE ARRIVAL DALLAS-FT. WORTH, TEXAS
(JEN.JEN9) 09351

Figure 175.—GLEN ROSE Nine Arrival (JEN.JEN9).

DALLAS–FORT WORTH

DALLAS/FORT WORTH INTL (DFW) 12 NW UTC–6(–5DT) N32°53.81´ W97°02.28´ **DALLAS–FT WORTH**
607 B **FUEL** 100LL, JET A OX 1, 3 AOE Class I, ARFF Index E NOTAM FILE DFW **COPTER**
RWY 17C–35C: H13401X150 (CONC–GRVD) S–120, D–200, 2S–175, 2D–600, 2D/2D2–850 HIRL CL **H–6H, L–17C, A**
IAP, AD
RWY 17C: ALSF2. TDZL. PAPI(P4L)—GA 3.0° TCH 74´.
RWY 35C: ALSF2. TDZL. PAPI(P4L)—GA 3.0° TCH 76´.
RWY 17R–35L: H13401X200 (CONC–GRVD) S–120, D–200, 2S–175, 2D–600, 2D/2D2–850 HIRL CL
RWY 17R: MALSR. TDZL. PAPI(P4L)—GA 3.0° TCH 68´.
RWY 35L: MALSR. TDZL. PAPI(P4L)—GA 3.0° TCH 63´.
RWY 18L–36R: H13400X200 (CONC–GRVD) S–120, D–200, 2S–175, 2D–600, 2D/2D2–850 HIRL CL
RWY 18L: MALSR. TDZL. PAPI(P4L)—GA 3.0° TCH 70´.
RWY 36R: MALSR. TDZL. PAPI(P4L)—GA 3.0° TCH 66´.
RWY 18R–36L: H13400X150 (CONC–GRVD) S–120, D–200, 2S–175, 2D–600, 2D/2D2–850 HIRL CL
RWY 18R: ALSF2. TDZL. PAPI(P4L)—GA 3.0° TCH 74´.
RWY 36L: MALSR. TDZL. PAPI(P4L)—GA 3.0° TCH 72´.
RWY 13R–31L: H9301X150 (CONC–GRVD) S–120, D–200, 2S–175, 2D–600, 2D/2D2–850 HIRL CL
RWY 13R: MALSR. TDZL. PAPI(P4L)—GA 3.0° TCH 71´.
RWY 31L: REIL. PAPI(P4L)—GA 3.13° TCH 72´.
RWY 13L–31R: H9000X200 (CONC–GRVD) S–120, D–200, 2S–175, 2D–600, 2D/2D2–850 HIRL CL
RWY 13L: REIL. PAPI(P4L)—GA 3.0° TCH 82´. Thld dsplcd 625´. 0.5% down.
RWY 31R: MALSR. TDZL. PAPI(P4L)—GA 3.0° TCH 69´. 0.5% up.
RWY 17L–35R: H8500X150 (CONC–GRVD) S–120, D–200, 2S–175, 2D–600, 2D/2D2–850 HIRL CL
RWY 17L: ALSF2. TDZL. PAPI(P4L)—GA 3.0° TCH 77´. Antenna. 0.6% up.
RWY 35R: ALSF2. TDZL. PAPI(P4R)—GA 3.0° TCH 73´. 0.6% down.

LAND AND HOLD–SHORT OPERATIONS

LDG RWY	HOLD–SHORT POINT	AVBL LDG DIST
RWY 17C	TWY B	10460
RWY 18R	TWY B	10100
RWY 35C	TWY EJ	9050
RWY 36L	TWY Z	10650

RUNWAY DECLARED DISTANCE INFORMATION

RWY 13L:	TORA–9000	TODA–9000	ASDA–9000	LDA–8375
RWY 13R:	TORA–9301	TODA–9301	ASDA–9301	LDA–9301
RWY 17C:	TORA–13401	TODA–13401	ASDA–13401	LDA–13401
RWY 17L:	TORA–8500	TODA–8500	ASDA–8500	LDA–8500
RWY 17R:	TORA–13401	TODA–13401	ASDA–13401	LDA–13401
RWY 18L:	TORA–13400	TODA–13400	ASDA–13400	LDA–13400
RWY 18R:	TORA–13400	TODA–13400	ASDA–13400	LDA–13400
RWY 31L:	TORA–9301	TODA–9301	ASDA–9301	LDA–9301
RWY 31R:	TORA–8375	TODA–8375	ASDA–8375	LDA–8375
RWY 35C:	TORA–13401	TODA–13401	ASDA–13401	LDA–13401
RWY 35L:	TORA–13401	TODA–13401	ASDA–13401	LDA–13401
RWY 35R:	TORA–8500	TODA–8500	ASDA–8500	LDA–8500
RWY 36L:	TORA–13400	TODA–13400	ASDA–13400	LDA–13400
RWY 36R:	TORA–13400	TODA–13400	ASDA–13400	LDA–13400

CONTINUED ON NEXT PAGE

FIGURE 176.—ILS-1 RWY 36L, Dallas-Fort Worth Intl.

CONTINUED FROM PRECEDING PAGE

AIRPORT REMARKS: Attended continuously. Rwy 17L–35R CLOSED 0400–1200Z‡ except PPR. Rwy 13R–31L CLOSED 0400–1200Z‡ except PPR. Rwy 13L–31R CLOSED 0400–1200Z‡ except PPR. Rwy 31R last 625´ CLOSED indef. Visual screen 20´ AGL 1180´ south AER 35C. Visual screen 22´ AGL 1179´ south AER 35L. ASDE–X SURVEILLANCE system in use: Pilots should opr transponders with mode C on all twys and rwys. PPR for acft with wingspan 215´ or greater (GROUP VI), call arpt ops 972–973–3112 for follow me services while taxiing to and from ramp and rwys. Rwy 13L, Rwy 17L, Rwy 31R, and Rwy 35R rwy visual range touchdown, midpoint and rollout avbl. Rwy 31L and Rwy 31R runway visual range touchdown and rollout avbl. Arpt under construction, PAEW in movement areas. Birds on and in vicinity of arpt. Tkf distance for Rwy 17L from Twy Q2 is 8196´. Tkf distance for Rwy 35R from Twy Q9 is 8196´. Tkf distance for Rwy 17R from Twy EG is 13082´ and from Twy EH is 12816´. Tkf distance for Rwy 35L from Twy EQ is 13084´ and from Twy EP is 12811´. Tkf distance for Rwy 36R from Twy WP is 12815´, from Twy WQ is 13082´. Tkf distance for Rwy 18L from Twy WG is 13082´, from Twy WH is 12815´. Tkf distance for Rwy 17C from Twy EG is 13,082´. Tkf distance for Rwy 18R from Twy WG is 13,082´. Land and hold–short signs on Rwy 17C at Twy B 10,460´ south of Rwy 17C thld, Rwy 18R at Twy B 10,100´ south of Rwy 18R thld, Rwy 35C at Twy EJ 9050´ north of Rwy 35C thld, Rwy 36L at Twy Z 10,650´ north of Rwy 36L thld, lgtd and marked with in–pavement pulsating white lgts. Twy G11 east of Twy G clsd to acft with wingspan 125´ and greater. Acft using gates D6–D17 must obtain approval from DFW ramp twr 129.95 prior to entering ramp and prior to pushback 1130–0430Z‡. Use extreme care at other times. Apron Terminal E ramp work in progress, ctc DFW ramp on 131.0 1530–1200Z‡ for Terminal E procedure change. Apron entrance/exit Points 32, 33, 34, 35, 36, 37, 38 and 39 clsd to acft with wingspan greater than 135´. Acft pushing back or powering back on Terminal B Apron have right of way. Frequent ground support equip under escort crossing Twys A and B at Twy HA. Apron entrance/exit points 5, 7, 42 and 44 clsd to acft with wingspan 118´ and greater. Apron entrance/exit points 42 and 44 clsd to acft with wingspan greater than 118´. Terminal B apron taxilane btn apron entrance/exit point taxilanes 110 and 115 clsd to acft with wingspan 118´ and greater. Apron entrance/exit points 22, 24, 105, 107 and 122 clsd to acft with wingspan 125´ and greater. Apron entrance/exit point 124 clsd to acft with wingspan 200´ and greater. Twy A5 clsd to acft with wingspan 171´ and greater. Twys may require judgemental oversteering for large acft. Apron entrance/exit points 52 and 53 clsd to acft with wingspan 171´ and greater. Acft exiting via apron entrance/exit points 42, 43 and 44 ctc Gnd Con prior to taxiing. PPR general aviation ops 0400–1200Z‡, call arpt ops 972–973–3112. PPR from arpt ops for general aviation acft to proceed to airline terminal gate except to general aviation facility. PPR from the primary tenant airlines to operate within the central terminal area. Proper minimum object free area distances may not be maintained for ramp/apron taxi lanes. Twy edge reflectors along all twys. Landing fee. Flight Notification Service (ADCUS) available. NOTE: See Land and Hold Short Operations, Intersection Departures During Periods of Darkness, Noise Abatement Procedures and Continuous Power Facilities.

WEATHER DATA SOURCES: ASOS (972) 453–0992 LLWAS.

COMMUNICATIONS: D–ATIS ARR 123.775 (972) 615–2701 **D–ATIS DEP** 135.925 (972) 615–2701 **UNICOM** 122.95

® **RGNL APP CON** 125.025 133.525 (E) 119.875 133.625 (W)

DFW TOWER 126.55 127.5 (E) 124.15 134.9 (W) **GND CON** 121.65 121.8 (E) 121.85 (W)

CLNC DEL 128.25

® **RGNL DEP CON** 118.55 (E) 126.475 (W) 124.825 (N) 125.125 (S)

AIRSPACE: CLASS B See VFR Terminal Area Chart

RADIO AIDS TO NAVIGATION: NOTAM FILE FTW.

MAVERICK (H) VORW/DME 113.1 TTT Chan 78 N32°52.15´ W97°02.43´ 358° 1.7 NM to fld. 540/6E.

ILS/DME 109.5 I–LWN Chan 32 Rwy 13R. Class IE.

ILS/DME 110.3 I–FLQ Chan 40 Rwy 17C. Class IIIE. DME also serves Rwy 35C.

ILS/DME 111.75 I–PPZ Chan 54(Y) Rwy 17L. Class IIIE. DME also serves Rwy 35R.

ILS/DME 111.35 I–JHZ Chan 50(Y) Rwy 17R. Class IE. DME also serves Rwy 35L.

ILS/DME 110.55 I–CIX Chan 42(Y) Rwy 18L. Class IE. DME also serves Rwy 36R.

ILS/DME 111.9 I–VYN Chan 56 Rwy 18R. Class IIIE. DME also serves Rwy 36L.

ILS/DME 110.9 I–RRA Chan 46 Rwy 31R. Class IE.

ILS/DME 110.3 I–PKQ Chan 40 Rwy 35C. Class IIIE. DME also serves Rwy 17C. OM/comlo also serves Rwy 35L.

ILS/DME 111.35 I–UWX Chan 50(Y) Rwy 35L. Class IE. OM/comlo also serves Rwy 35R. LOC unusable byd 14 NM blo 3,400´. DME also serves Rwy 17R.

ILS/DME 111.75 I–AJQ Chan 54(Y) Rwy 35R. Class IIIE. DME also serves Rwy 17L. LOC unusable byd 16 NM 5° right of course.

ILS/DME 111.9 I–BXN Chan 56 Rwy 36L. Class ID. DME also serves Rwy 18R. OM also serves Rwy 36R. LOC unusable byd 15 NM 5° right of course.

ILS/DME 110.55 I–FJN Chan 42(Y) Rwy 36R. Class IE. OM also serves Rwy 36L. DME also serves Rwy 18L.

COMM/NAV/WEATHER REMARKS: All acft arriving DFW are requested to turn DME off until dep due to tfc overload of Maverick DME.

DALLAS/FORT WORTH INTL (See DALLAS–FORT WORTH on page 243)

DAN E RICHARDS MUNI (See PADUCAH on page 325)

DAN JONES INTL (See HOUSTON on page 279)

FIGURE 176A.—ILS-1 RWY 36L, Dallas-Fort Worth Intl.

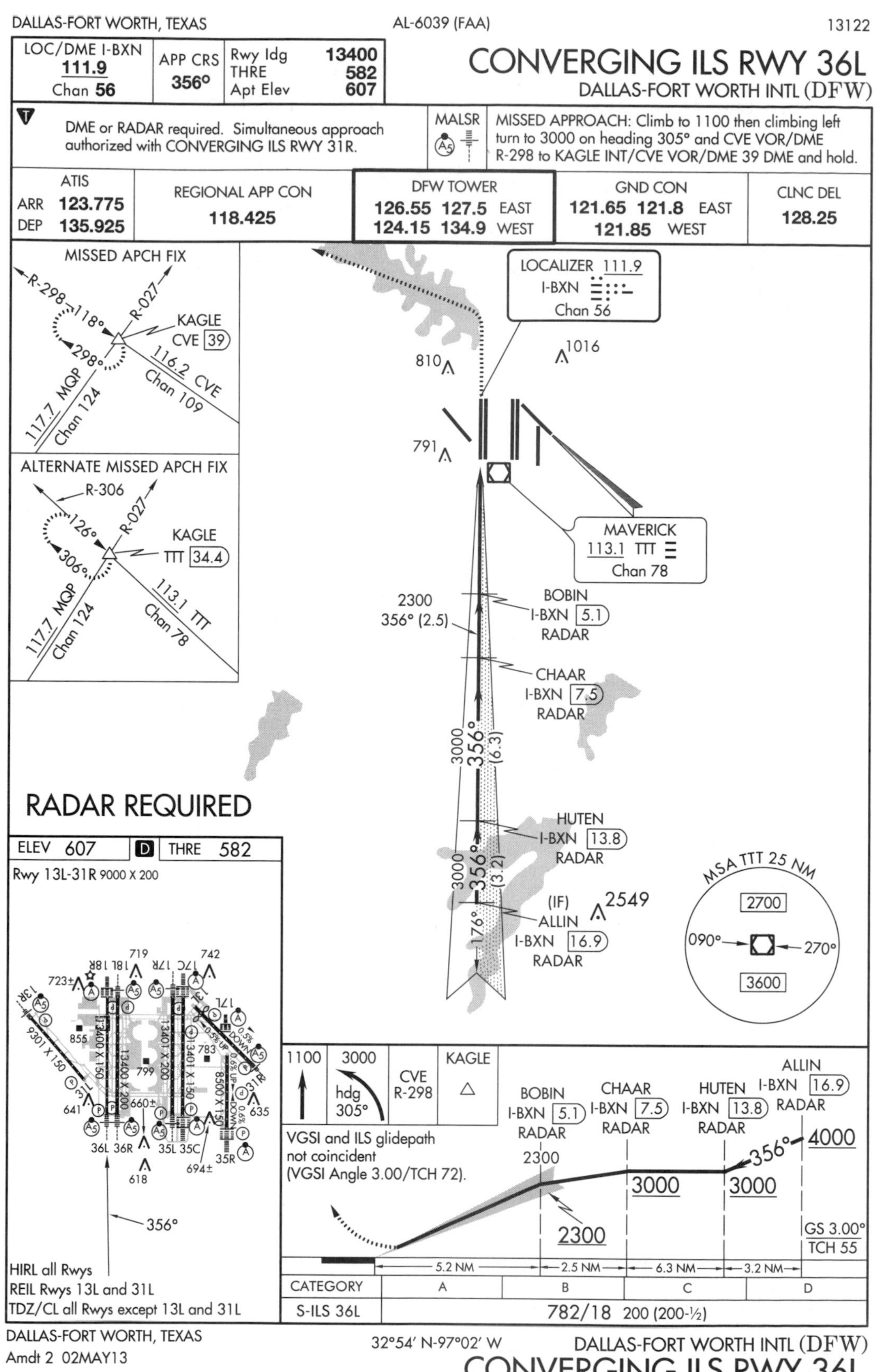

FIGURE 177.—Converging ILS RWY 36L (DFW).

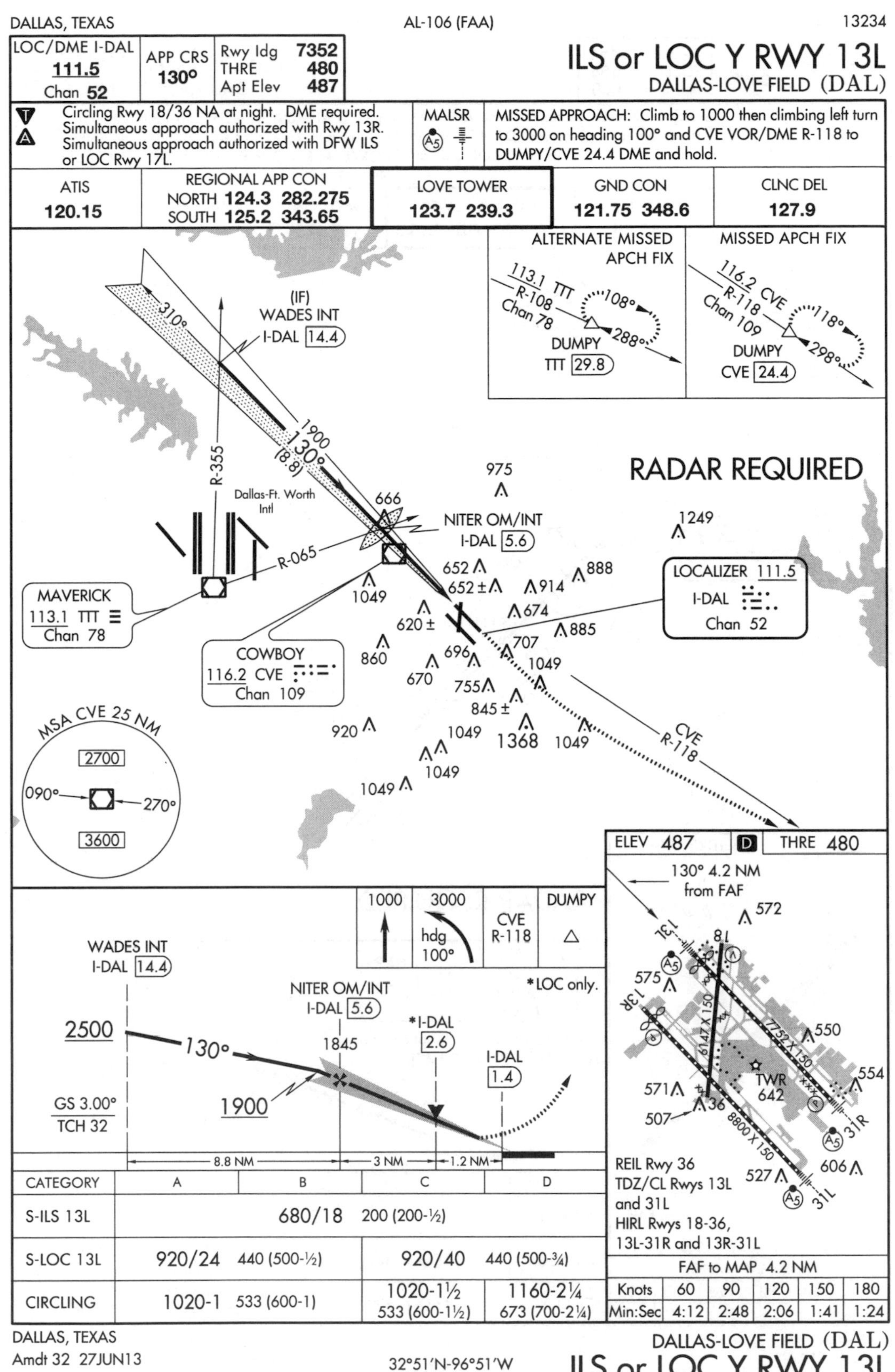

CATEGORY	A	B	C	D
S-ILS 13L	680/18 200 (200-½)			
S-LOC 13L	920/24 440 (500-½)		920/40 440 (500-¾)	
CIRCLING	1020-1 533 (600-1)		1020-1½ 533 (600-1½)	1160-2¼ 673 (700-2¼)

FAF to MAP 4.2 NM					
Knots	60	90	120	150	180
Min:Sec	4:12	2:48	2:06	1:41	1:24

FIGURE 178.—ILS or LOC Y RWY 13L (DAL).

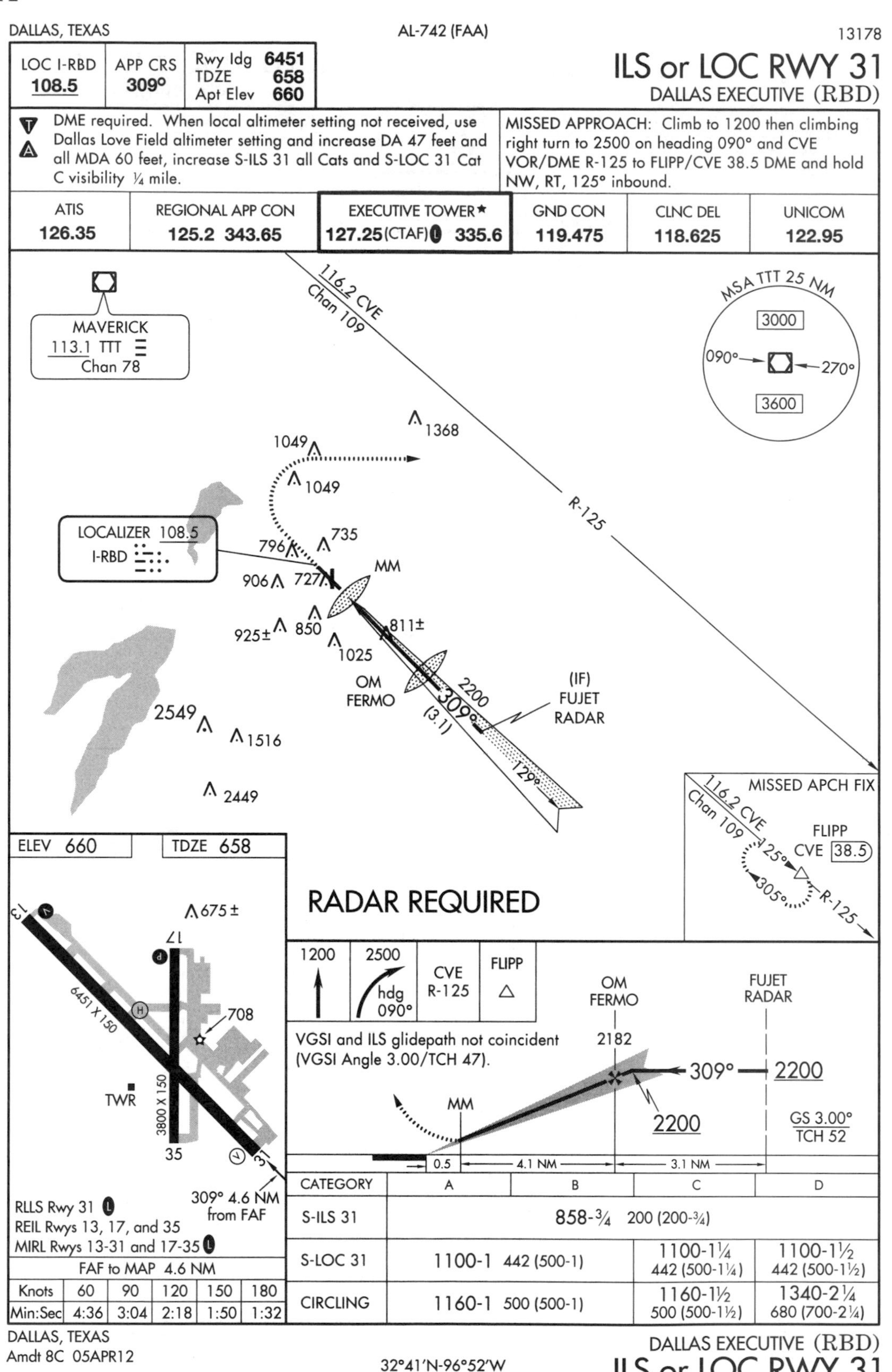

FAF to MAP 4.6 NM					
Knots	60	90	120	150	180
Min:Sec	4:36	3:04	2:18	1:50	1:32

CATEGORY	A	B	C	D
S-ILS 31	858-¾ 200 (200-¾)			
S-LOC 31	1100-1 442 (500-1)		1100-1¼ 442 (500-1¼)	1100-1½ 442 (500-1½)
CIRCLING	1160-1 500 (500-1)		1160-1½ 500 (500-1½)	1340-2¼ 680 (700-2¼)

FIGURE 179.—ILS or LOC RWY 31 (RBD).

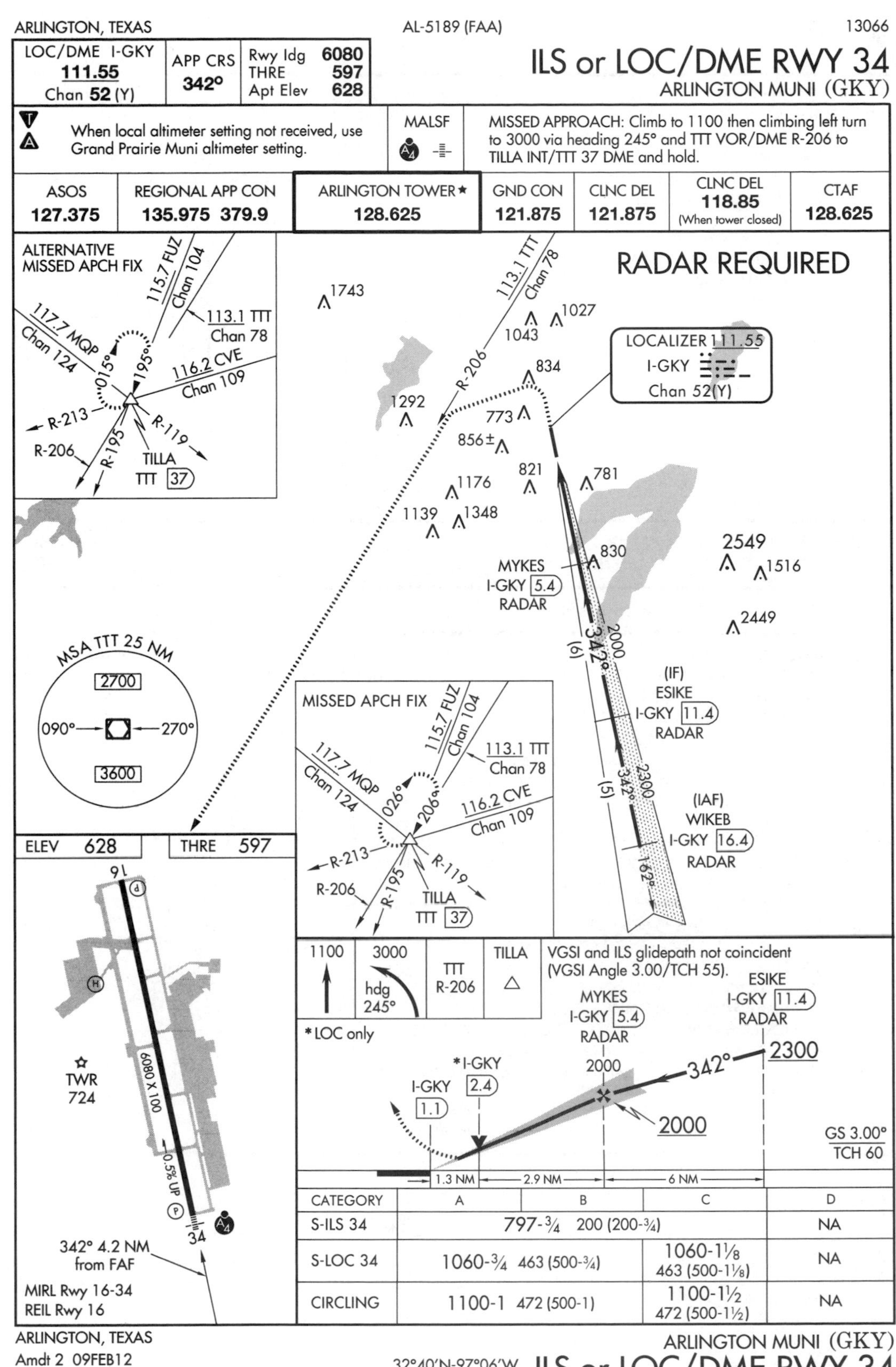

CATEGORY	A	B	C	D
S-ILS 34	797-¾ 200 (200-¾)			NA
S-LOC 34	1060-¾ 463 (500-¾)		1060-1⅛ 463 (500-1⅛)	NA
CIRCLING	1100-1 472 (500-1)		1100-1½ 472 (500-1½)	NA

FIGURE 180.—ILS or LOC/DME RWY 34 (GKY).

ARCHER CITY MUNI (T39) 1 SE UTC–6(–5DT) N33°34.94′ W98°37.12′ **DALLAS–FT WORTH**
1065 S2 NOTAM FILE FTW **L–17B**
RWY 17–35: H3200X60 (ASPH) S–12.5
RWY 17: Road.
AIRPORT REMARKS: Unattended. Wildlife on and invof arpt. 70′ AGL drilling rig 700′ northwest of Rwy 17–35. Rwy 17–35 loose grvl, tall grass and pot holes on rwy.
COMMUNICATIONS: CTAF 122.9
RADIO AIDS TO NAVIGATION: NOTAM FILE SPS.
WICHITA FALLS (H) VORTACW 112.7 SPS Chan 74 N33°59.24′ W98°35.61′ 173° 24.3 NM to fld. 1133/10E.

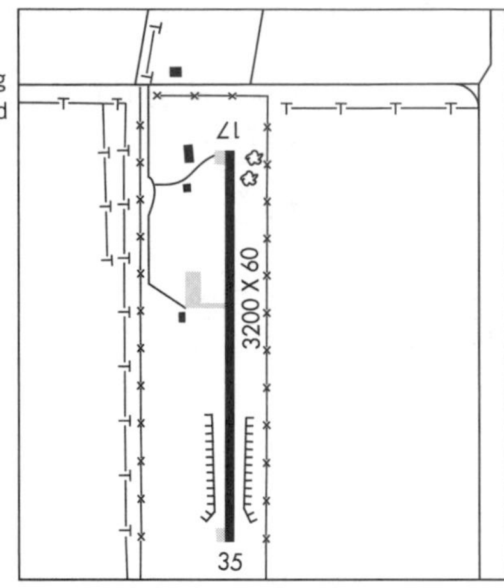

ARDYTH N27°38.54′ W99°27.48′ NOTAM FILE SJT. **BROWNSVILLE**
NDB (MHW) 405 AGH 174° 5.9 NM to Laredo Intl. **L–20G**

ARLEDGE FLD (See STAMFORD on page 351)

ARLINGTON MUNI (GKY) 4 S UTC–6(–5DT) N32°39.83′ W97°05.66′ **DALLAS–FT WORTH**
628 B S4 **FUEL** 100LL, JET A OX 4 TPA—1628(1000) NOTAM FILE GKY **COPTER**
RWY 16–34: H6080X100 (CONC) S–60 MIRL 0.5% up NW **H–6H, L–17C, A**
RWY 16: REIL. PAPI(P4L)—GA 3.0° TCH 42′. **IAP, AD**
RWY 34: MALSF. PAPI(P4L)—GA 3.0° TCH 55′.
AIRPORT REMARKS: Attended continuously. Self serve fuel with major credit card. Helicopter test facility at arpt mostly from private helipad adjoining ldg area. Extensive helicopter traffic west of rwy. Rwy 34 PAPI unusable byd 8° right of centerline. MIRL Rwy 16–34 preset medium ints, higher ints by twr request. When twr clsd ACTIVATE MALSF Rwy 34—CTAF. PAPI Rwy 16 and Rwy 34 opr continuously.
WEATHER DATA SOURCES: ASOS 127.375 (817) 557–0251.
COMMUNICATIONS: CTAF 128.625
Ⓡ **REGIONAL APP/DEP CON** 135.975
TOWER 128.625 (1300–0300Z‡) **GND CON/CLNC DEL** 121.875
CLNC DEL 118.85 (RGNL APP CON when twr clsd)
AIRSPACE: CLASS D svc 1300–0300Z‡ other times CLASS G.
RADIO AIDS TO NAVIGATION: NOTAM FILE FTW.
MAVERICK (H) VORW/DME 113.1 TTT Chan 78 N32°52.15′ W97°02.43′ 186° 12.6 NM to fld. 540/6E.
All acft arriving DFW are requested to turn DME off until departure due to traffic overload of Maverick DME
ILS/DME 111.55 I–GKY Chan 52(Y) Rwy 34. Class IE. LOC unusable byd 15° right of course. Unmonitored when ATCT clsd.

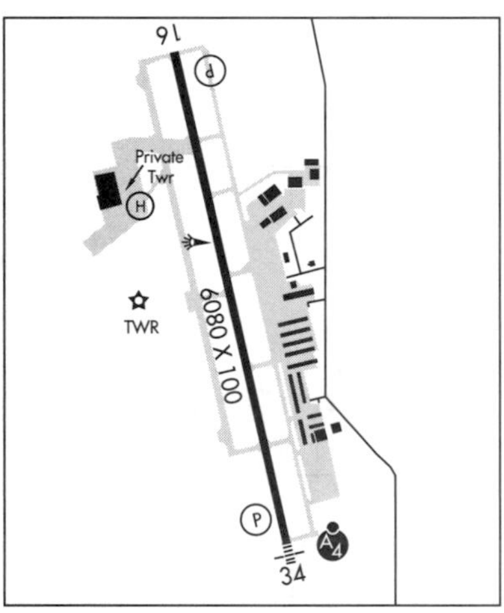

FIGURE 181.—Excerpt from Chart Supplement.

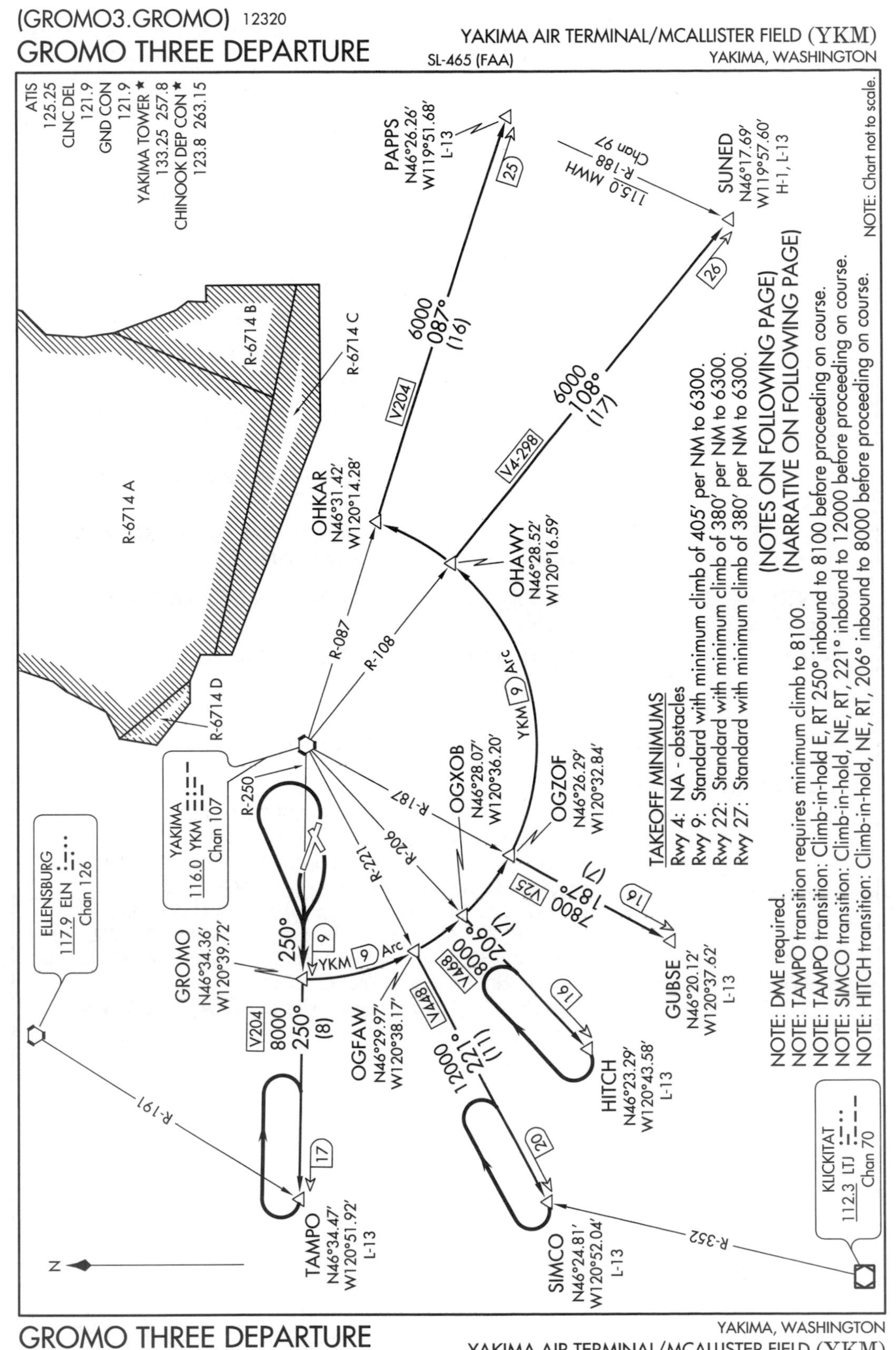

FIGURE 182.—GROMO Three Departure (GROMO3.GROMO).

(GROMO3.GROMO) 12208
GROMO THREE DEPARTURE

SL-465 (FAA)

YAKIMA AIR TERMINAL/MCALLISTER FIELD (YKM)
YAKIMA, WASHINGTON

DEPARTURE ROUTE DESCRIPTION

TAKEOFF RUNWAY 9,27: Climbing left turn thence. . . .
TAKEOFF RUNWAY 22: Climbing right turn thence. . . .

. . . . intercept and proceed via YKM R-250 to GROMO/YKM 9 DME, then on assigned transition.

GUBSE TRANSITION (GROMO3.GUBSE): From over GROMO DME Fix via YKM 9 DME Arc to OGZOF DME fix and YKM VORTAC R-187 to GUBSE DME fix.

HITCH TRANSITION (GROMO3.HITCH): From over GROMO DME Fix via YKM 9 DME Arc to OGXOB DME fix and YKM VORTAC R-206 to HITCH DME fix.

PAPPS TRANSITION (GROMO3.PAPPS): From over GROMO DME Fix via YKM 9 DME Arc to OKHAR DME fix and YKM VORTAC R-087 to PAPPS DME fix.

SIMCO TRANSITION (GROMO3.SIMCO): From over GROMO DME Fix via YKM 9 DME Arc to OGFAW DME fix and YKM VORTAC R-221 to SIMCO INT.

SUNED TRANSITION (GROMO3.SUNED): From over GROMO DME Fix via 9 DME Arc to OHAWY DME fix and KM R-108 to SUNED INT.

TAMPO TRANSITION (GROMO3.TAMPO): From over GROMO DME Fix via YKM VORTAC R-250 to TAMPO INT.

TAKEOFF OBSTACLE NOTES

Rwy 9: OL on building 27′ from DER, 507′ right of centerline, 34′ AGL/1074′ MSL.
Pole 388′ from DER, 561′ right of centerline, 34′ AGL/1073′ MSL.
Trees beginning 586′ from DER, 550′ right of centerline, up to 100′ AGL/1139′ MSL.

Rwy 22: Fence beginning 27′ from DER, 435′ right of centerline, up to 10′ AGL/1085′ MSL.
Trees beginning 570′ from DER, 228′ left of centerline, up to 100′ AGL/1199′ MSL.
Trees beginning 3195′ from DER, 202′ right of centerline, up to 100′ AGL/1199′ MSL.
Trees beginning 1 NM from DER, 732′ left of centerline, up to 100′ AGL/1239′ MSL.

Rwy 27: Ant on building 398′ from DER, 282′ left of centerline, 15′ AGL/1117′ MSL.
Trees beginning 3893′ from DER, 1341′ right of centerline, up to 100′ AGL/1239′ MSL.

GROMO THREE DEPARTURE
(GROMO3.GROMO) 12208

YAKIMA, WASHINGTON
YAKIMA AIR TERMINAL/MCALLISTER FIELD (YKM)

FIGURE 183.—GROMO Three Departure (GROMO3.GROMO).

YAKIMA AIR TERMINAL/MCALLISTER FLD (YKM) 3 S UTC–8(–7DT) N46°34.09′ W120°32.64′ **SEATTLE**
1099 B S4 **FUEL** 100LL, JET A OX 1, 3 Class I, ARFF Index A NOTAM FILE YKM **H–1C, L–13A**
RWY 09–27: H7604X150 (ASPH–GRVD) S–95, D–160, 2S–175, 2D–220, 2D/2D2–550 PCN 33 F/C/X/T **IAP, DIAP, AD**
HIRL 0.7% up W
RWY 09: REIL. VASI(V4L)—GA 3.0° TCH 50′.
RWY 27: MALSR. PAPI(P4L)—GA 3.0° TCH 57′.
RWY 04–22: H3835X150 (ASPH–PFC) S–70, D–80, 2S–102, 2D–120 PCN 28 F/C/X/T MIRL 0.5% up SW
RWY 04: REIL. PAPI(P4L)—GA 3.0° TCH 57′.
RWY 22: REIL. PAPI(P4L)—GA 3.0° TCH 45′.
RUNWAY DECLARED DISTANCE INFORMATION
RWY 04: TORA–3835 TODA–3835 ASDA–3835 LDA–3835
RWY 09: TORA–7604 TODA–7604 ASDA–7604 LDA–7604
RWY 22: TORA–3835 TODA–3835 ASDA–3535 LDA–3835
RWY 27: TORA–7604 TODA–7604 ASDA–7604 LDA–7604
AIRPORT REMARKS: Attended 1400–0400Z‡. Sfc conditions unmonitored 0800–1330Z‡. Be alert, birds invof Yakima River 5 NM east of apch to Rwy 27. Reflectors on Twy C only. Rwy 04–22 some spalling and raveling. PPR for unscheduled air carrier ops with more than 30 passenger seats, call arpt manger 509–575–6149/6150. Twy B from apch end of Rwy 22 to Twy A rstd to acft with wingspans 79′ or less. MIRL Rwy 04–22, REIL Rwy 04 and Rwy 22, PAPI Rwy 04 and Rwy 22 OTS when twr clsd. Twy B1 and Twy B2 twy lgts OTS when twr clsd. Twy B lgts south of Rwy 09–27 OTS when twr clsd. When twr clsd ACTIVATE HIRL Rwy 09–27 and MALSR Rwy 27—CTAF.
WEATHER DATA SOURCES: ASOS (509) 248–1502
COMMUNICATIONS: CTAF 133.25 **ATIS** 125.25 **UNICOM** 122.95
RCO 122.5 (SEATTLE RADIO)
Ⓡ **CHINOOK APP/DEP CON** 123.8 (1400–0600Z‡)
Ⓡ **SEATTLE CENTER APP/DEP CON** 132.6 (0600–1400Z‡)
TOWER 133.25 (1400–0600Z‡) **GND CON** 121.9 **CLNC DEL** 121.9
AIRSPACE: CLASS D svc 1400–0600Z‡ other times CLASS E.
RADIO AIDS TO NAVIGATION: NOTAM FILE YKM.
(H) VORTACW 116.0 YKM Chan 107 N46°34.21′ W120°26.68′ 247° 4.1 NM to fld. 984/21E.
DME unusable:
095°–115° byd 26 NM blo 8,000′
095°–115° byd 35 NM
115°–207° byd 20 NM blo 8,500′
115°–207° byd 36 NM blo 10,000′
207°–230° byd 20 NM blo 10,000′
290°–315° byd 20 NM blo 11,000′
315°–080° byd 12 NM blo 15,000′
VOR portion unusable:
025°–035° byd 5 NM blo 6,000′
080°–105° byd 35 NM blo 6,000′
105°–107° byd 25 NM blo 6,000′
109°–135° byd 25 NM blo 6,000′
135°–180° byd 30 NM blo 7,500′
195°–225° byd 30 NM blo 8,500′
305°–335° byd 30 NM blo 9,000′
350°–080° byd 25 NM blo 9,000′
DONNY NDB (LOM) 371 YK N46°31.54′ W120°22.33′ 274° 7.6 NM to fld. Unmonitored when ATCT closed.
ILS 110.1 I–YKM Rwy 27. LOM DONNY NDB. Unmonitored when ATCT closed.
COMM/NAV/WEATHER REMARKS: During hrs twr is clsd all ops in vicinity of arpt rstd to acft with VHF radio capability, unless an emerg exist necessitating UHF equipped acft to land.

FIGURE 184.—Excerpt from Chart Supplement.

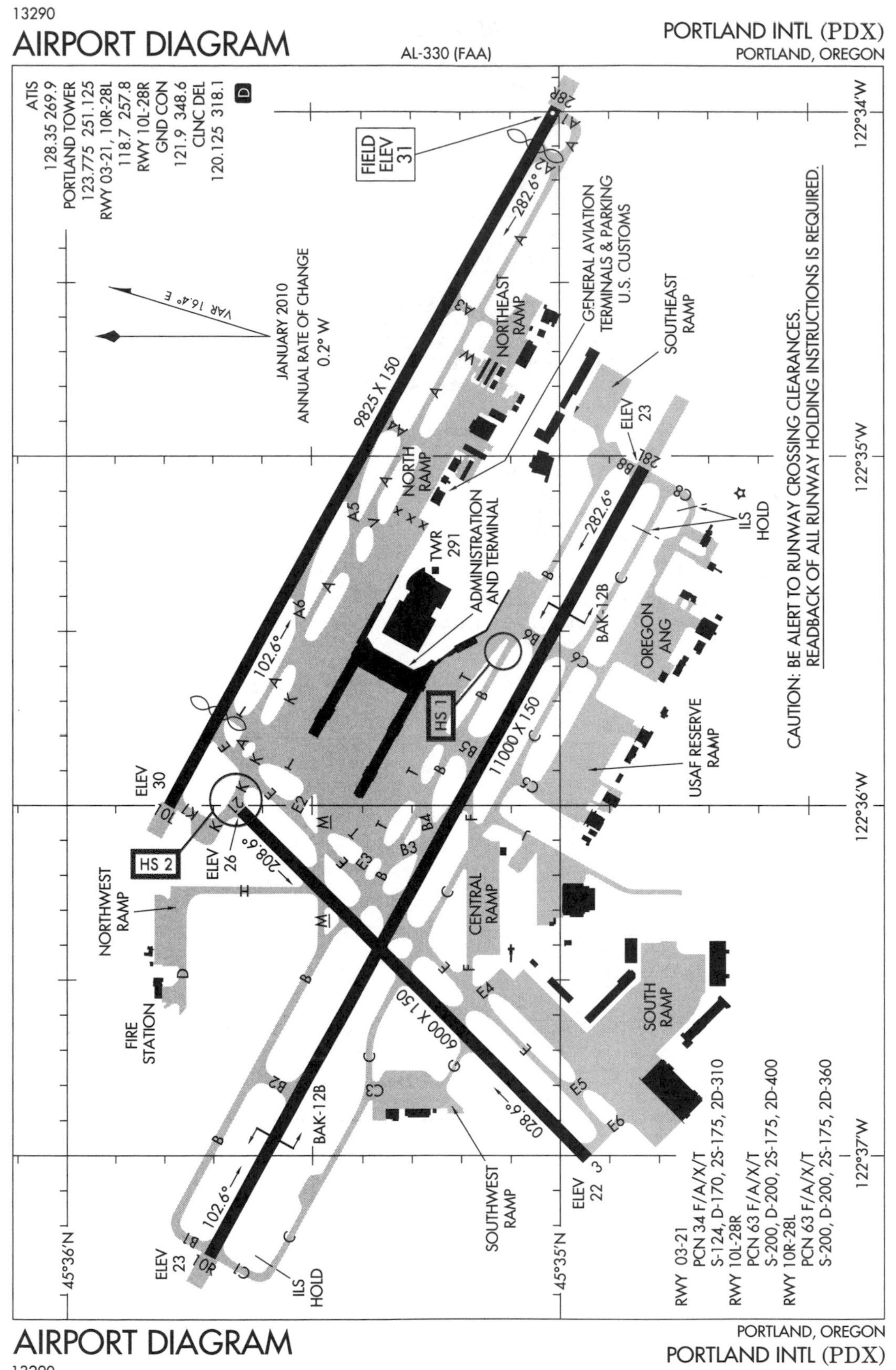

FIGURE 185.—Airport Diagram - Portland INTL (PDX).

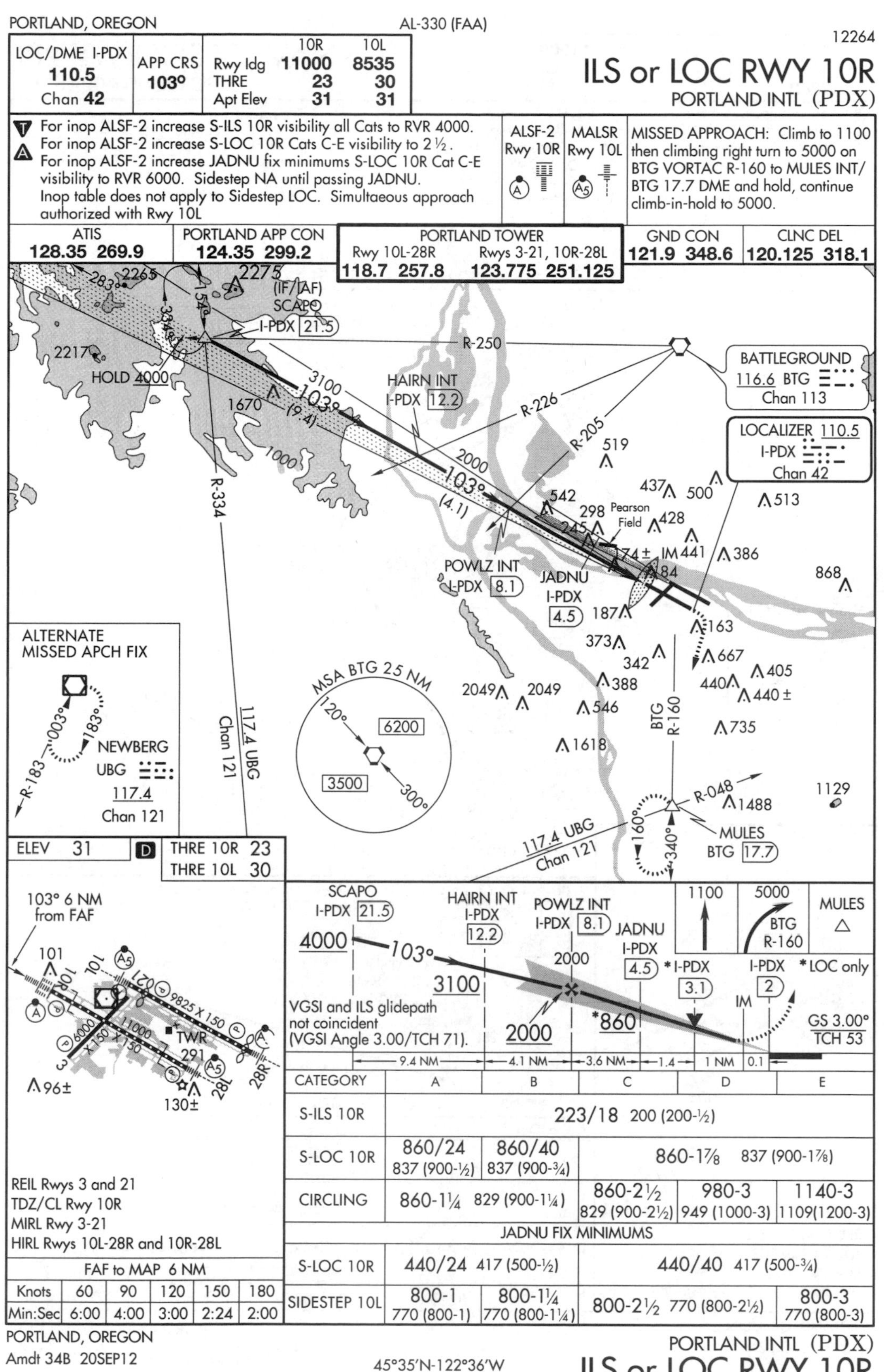

FAF to MAP 6 NM					
Knots	60	90	120	150	180
Min:Sec	6:00	4:00	3:00	2:24	2:00

CATEGORY	A	B	C	D	E
S-ILS 10R	223/18 200 (200-½)				
S-LOC 10R	860/24 837 (900-½)	860/40 837 (900-¾)	860-1⅞ 837 (900-1⅞)		
CIRCLING	860-1¼ 829 (900-1¼)		860-2½ 829 (900-2½)	980-3 949 (1000-3)	1140-3 1109(1200-3)
JADNU FIX MINIMUMS					
S-LOC 10R	440/24 417 (500-½)		440/40 417 (500-¾)		
SIDESTEP 10L	800-1 770 (800-1)	800-1¼ 770 (800-1¼)	800-2½ 770 (800-2½)		800-3 770 (800-3)

FIGURE 186.—ILS or LOC RWY 10R (PDX).

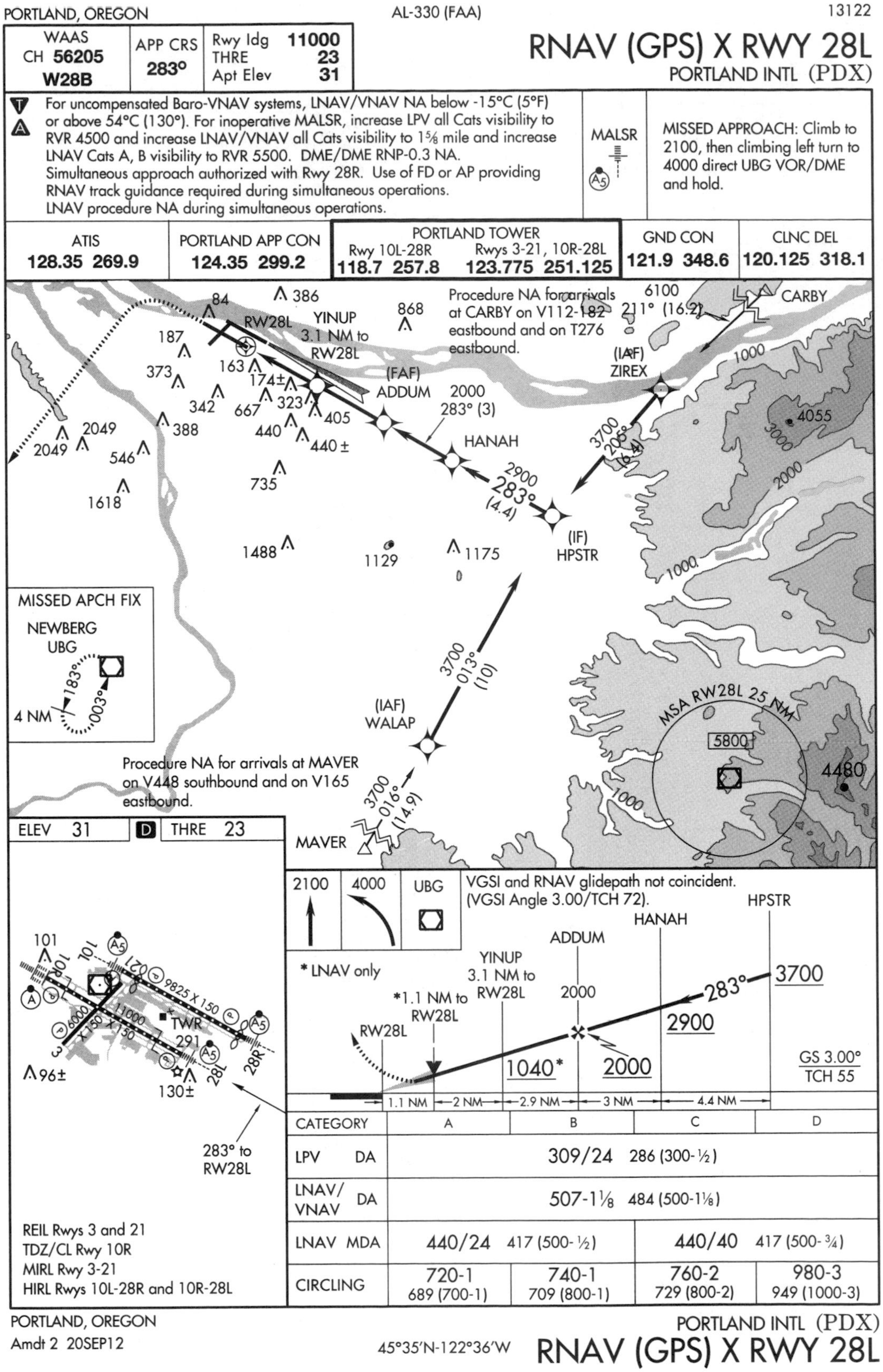

PORTLAND, OREGON
AL-330 (FAA)
13122
WAAS CH 56205 W28B
APP CRS 283°
Rwy ldg 11000
THRE 23
Apt Elev 31
RNAV (GPS) X RWY 28L
PORTLAND INTL (PDX)
For uncompensated Baro-VNAV systems, LNAV/VNAV NA below -15°C (5°F) or above 54°C (130°). For inoperative MALSR, increase LPV all Cats visibility to RVR 4500 and increase LNAV/VNAV all Cats visibility to 1⅝ mile and increase LNAV Cats A, B visibility to RVR 5500. DME/DME RNP-0.3 NA.
Simultaneous approach authorized with Rwy 28R. Use of FD or AP providing RNAV track guidance required during simultaneous operations.
LNAV procedure NA during simultaneous operations.
MALSR
MISSED APPROACH: Climb to 2100, then climbing left turn to 4000 direct UBG VOR/DME and hold.
ATIS 128.35 269.9
PORTLAND APP CON 124.35 299.2
PORTLAND TOWER Rwy 10L-28R 118.7 257.8 Rwys 3-21, 10R-28L 123.775 251.125
GND CON 121.9 348.6
CLNC DEL 120.125 318.1
Procedure NA for arrivals at CARBY on V112-182 eastbound and on T276 eastbound.
6100 211° (16.2)
CARBY
(IAF) ZIREX
3700 205° (6.4)
YINUP 3.1 NM to RW28L
RW28L
(FAF) ADDUM
2000 283° (3)
HANAH
2900 283° (4.4)
(IF) HPSTR
4055
MISSED APCH FIX
NEWBERG UBG
183°
003°
4 NM
3700 013° (10)
(IAF) WALAP
Procedure NA for arrivals at MAVER on V448 southbound and on V165 eastbound.
3700 016° (14.9)
MAVER
MSA RW28L 25 NM
5800
4480
ELEV 31
THRE 23
REIL Rwys 3 and 21
TDZ/CL Rwy 10R
MIRL Rwy 3-21
HIRL Rwys 10L-28R and 10R-28L
283° to RW28L
TWR
9825 X 150
11000 X 150
6000 X 150
2100
4000
UBG
VGSI and RNAV glidepath not coincident. (VGSI Angle 3.00/TCH 72).
* LNAV only
*1.1 NM to RW28L
YINUP 3.1 NM to RW28L
ADDUM 2000
HANAH
HPSTR
283° 3700
2900
1040*
2000
GS 3.00° TCH 55
1.1 NM 2 NM 2.9 NM 3 NM 4.4 NM
CATEGORY A B C D
LPV DA 309/24 286 (300-½)
LNAV/VNAV DA 507-1⅛ 484 (500-1⅛)
LNAV MDA A, B: 440/24 417 (500-½); C, D: 440/40 417 (500-¾)
CIRCLING A: 720-1 689 (700-1); B: 740-1 709 (800-1); C: 760-2 729 (800-2); D: 980-3 949 (1000-3)
PORTLAND, OREGON
Amdt 2 20SEP12
45°35′N-122°36′W
PORTLAND INTL (PDX)
RNAV (GPS) X RWY 28L

FIGURE 187.—RNAV (GPS) X RWY 28L (PDX).

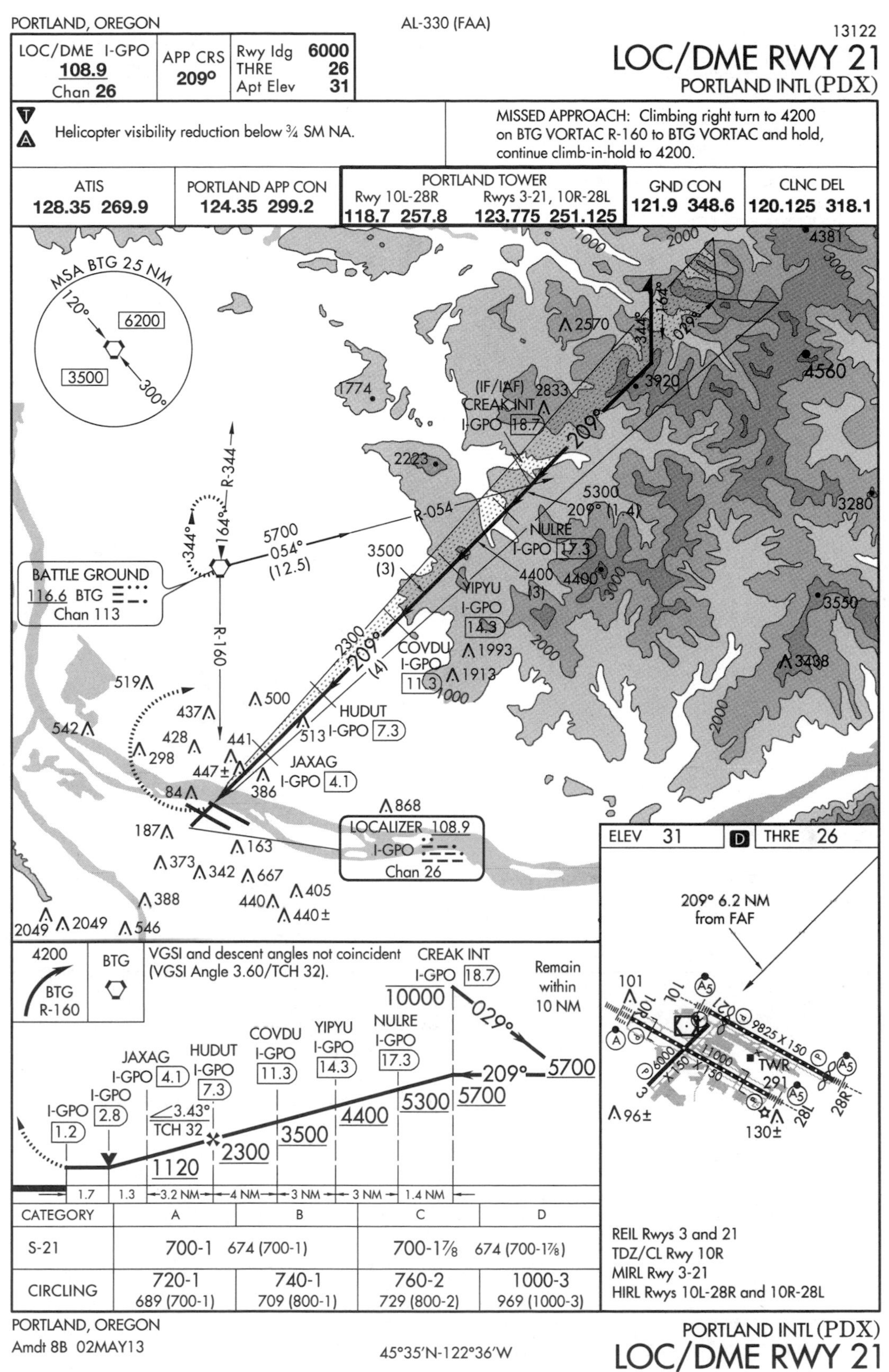

CATEGORY	A	B	C	D
S-21	700-1 674 (700-1)		700-1⅞ 674 (700-1⅞)	
CIRCLING	720-1 689 (700-1)	740-1 709 (800-1)	760-2 729 (800-2)	1000-3 969 (1000-3)

FIGURE 188.—LOC/DME RWY 21 (PDX).

(HABUT4.GVO) 13122

HABUT FOUR DEPARTURE

SL-378 (FAA)

SANTA BARBARA MUNI (SBA)
SANTA BARBARA, CALIFORNIA

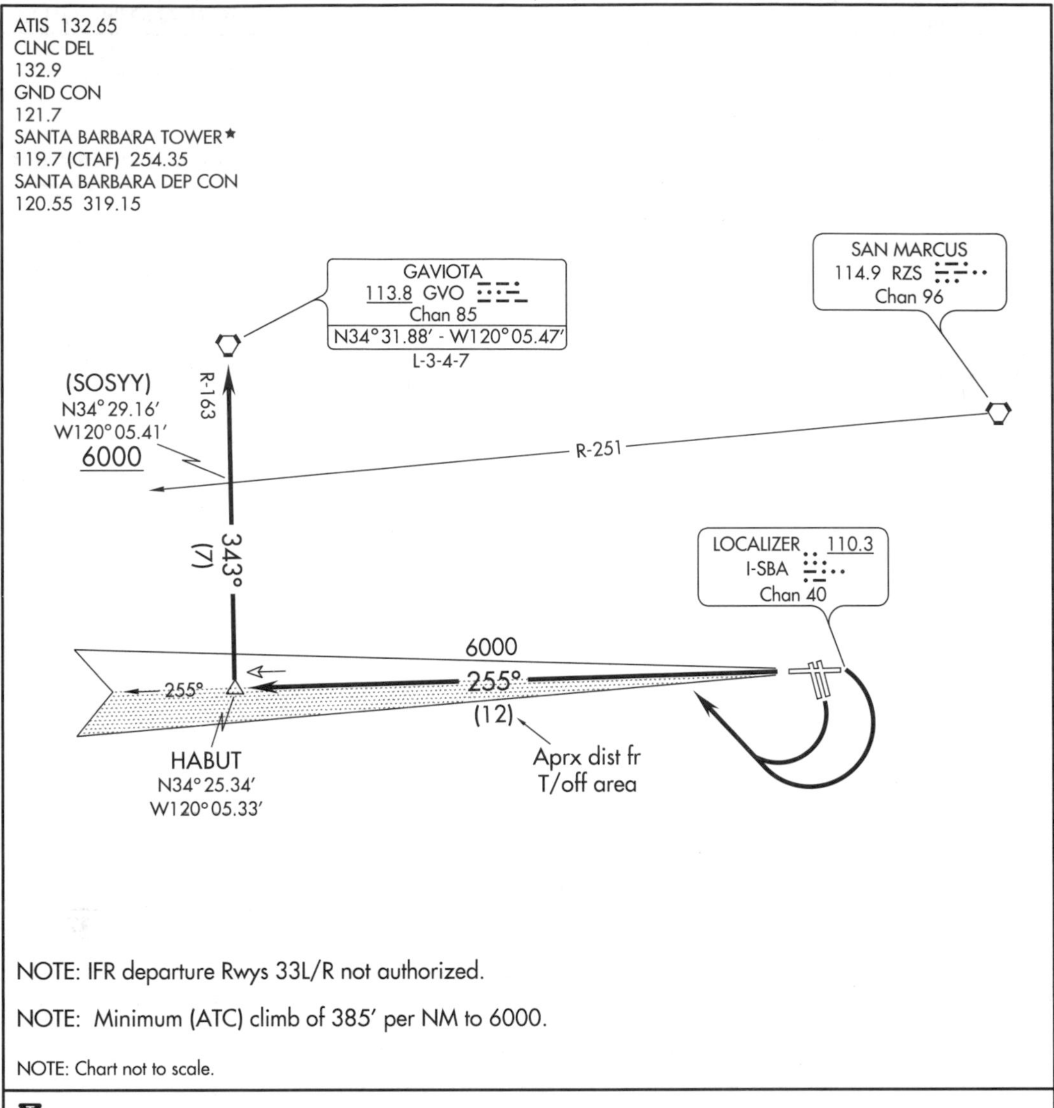

DEPARTURE ROUTE DESCRIPTION

TAKE-OFF RUNWAYS 7 and 15L/R: Turn right, intercept I-SBA west course to HABUT INT, thence via GVO R-163 to GVO VORTAC. Cross RZS R-251 at or above 6000′.

TAKE-OFF RUNWAY 25: Intercept I-SBA west course to HABUT INT, thence via GVO R-163 to GVO VORTAC. Cross RZS R-251 at or above 6000′.

HABUT FOUR DEPARTURE
(HABUT4.GVO) 13122

SANTA BARBARA, CALIFORNIA
SANTA BARBARA MUNI (SBA)

FIGURE 189.—HABUT Four Departure (HABUT4.GVO) (SBA).

SANTA BARBARA MUNI (SBA) 7 W UTC–8(–7DT) N34°25.57´ W119°50.49´ **LOS ANGELES**
13 B S4 **FUEL** 100LL, JET A OX 1, 2, 3, 4 TPA—See Remarks LRA Class I, ARFF Index C **H–4H, L–3D, 4F, 7A**
NOTAM FILE SBA **IAP, AD**

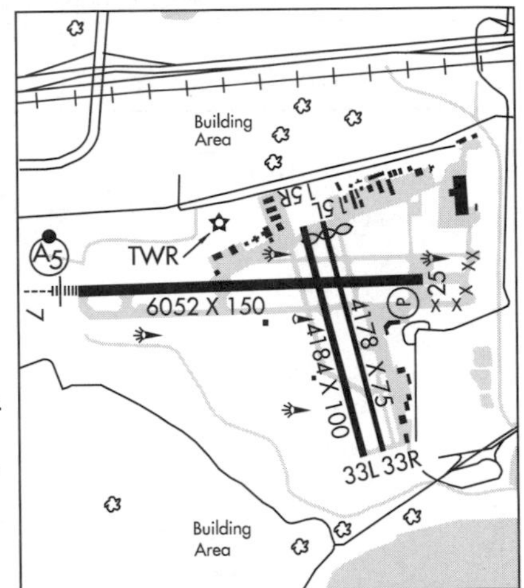

RWY 07–25: H6052X150 (ASPH–PFC) S–110, D–160, 2S–175, 2D–245 HIRL
RWY 07: MALSR. Tree. Rgt tfc.
RWY 25: REIL. PAPI(P4L)—GA 3.0° TCH 50´. Fence.
RWY 15R–33L: H4184X100 (ASPH) S–48, D–63, 2S–80, 2D–100 MIRL
RWY 15R: REIL. Tree.
RWY 33L: Tree. Rgt tfc.
RWY 15L–33R: H4178X75 (ASPH) S–35, D–41, 2S–80, 2D–63
RWY 15L: Thld dsplcd 217´. Bldg.
RWY 33R: Rgt tfc.
AIRPORT REMARKS: Attended 1330–0600Z‡. 100LL fuel 24 hr credit card svc avbl. Fee for Jet A fuel after hrs call 805–964–6733 or 967–5608. Numerous flocks of birds on and invof arpt. Deep creek located 300´ from rwy end Rwy 07, Rwy 33L and Rwy 33R. Rwy 15L–33R dalgt hrs only. Arpt has noise abatement procedures ctc arpt ops 805–692–6005. Due to ltd ramp space at the airline terminal non–scheduled transport category acft with more than 30 passenger seats are required to ctc arpt ops 805–692–6005 24 hour PPR to arrival. Commercial airline ramp clsd to all General Aviation acft. No customs personnel or facilities are avbl and international acft will not be allowed to land unless an emerg exists. TPA—1003(990) small acft, 1503(1490) large acft. Pure jet touch/go or low approaches prohibited. When twr clsd ACTIVATE MIRL Rwy 15R–33L, REIL Rwy 15R—CTAF. MALSR Rwy 07, PAPI Rwy 25 and REIL Rwy 25 opr continuously. CTAF. Ldg fee for all PART 135 opr and transient acft with maximum gross weight 10,000 lbs or more. Fees collected at FBO.
WEATHER DATA SOURCES: ASOS (805) 681–0583
COMMUNICATIONS: CTAF 119.7 **ATIS** 132.65 **UNICOM** 122.95
Ⓡ **APP/DEP CON** 120.55 (151°–329°) 125.4 (330°–150°) 124.15 127.725 (1400–0700Z‡)
Ⓡ **L.A. CENTER APP/DEP CON** 119.05 (0700–1400Z‡)
TOWER 119.7 (1400–0700Z‡) **GND CON** 121.7 **CLNC DEL** 132.9
AIRSPACE: CLASS C svc ctc **APP CON** svc 1400–0700Z‡ other times CLASS E.
RADIO AIDS TO NAVIGATION: NOTAM FILE HHR.
SAN MARCUS (H) VORTAC 114.9 RZS Chan 96 N34°30.57´ W119°46.26´ 201° 6.1 NM to fld. 3623/14E. **HIWAS.**
VOR unusable:
140°–178° byd 27 NM
GAVIOTA (L) VORTACW 113.8 GVO Chan 85 N34°31.88´ W120°05.47´ 101° 13.9 NM to fld. 2616/16E.
VORTAC unusable:
117°–137° byd 35 NM
310°–095° byd 10 NM blo 8,500´
360°–095° byd 20 NM blo 12,500´
ILS/DME 110.3 I–SBA Chan 40 Rwy 07. Class IA. Unmonitored when ATCT clsd.

SANTA CATALINA N33°22.50´ W118°25.19´ NOTAM FILE HHR. **LOS ANGELES**
(L) VORTACW 111.4 SXC Chan 51 352° 1.8 NM to Catalina. 2090/15E. **H–4I, L–3E, 4G**

FIGURE 190.—Excerpt from Chart Supplement.

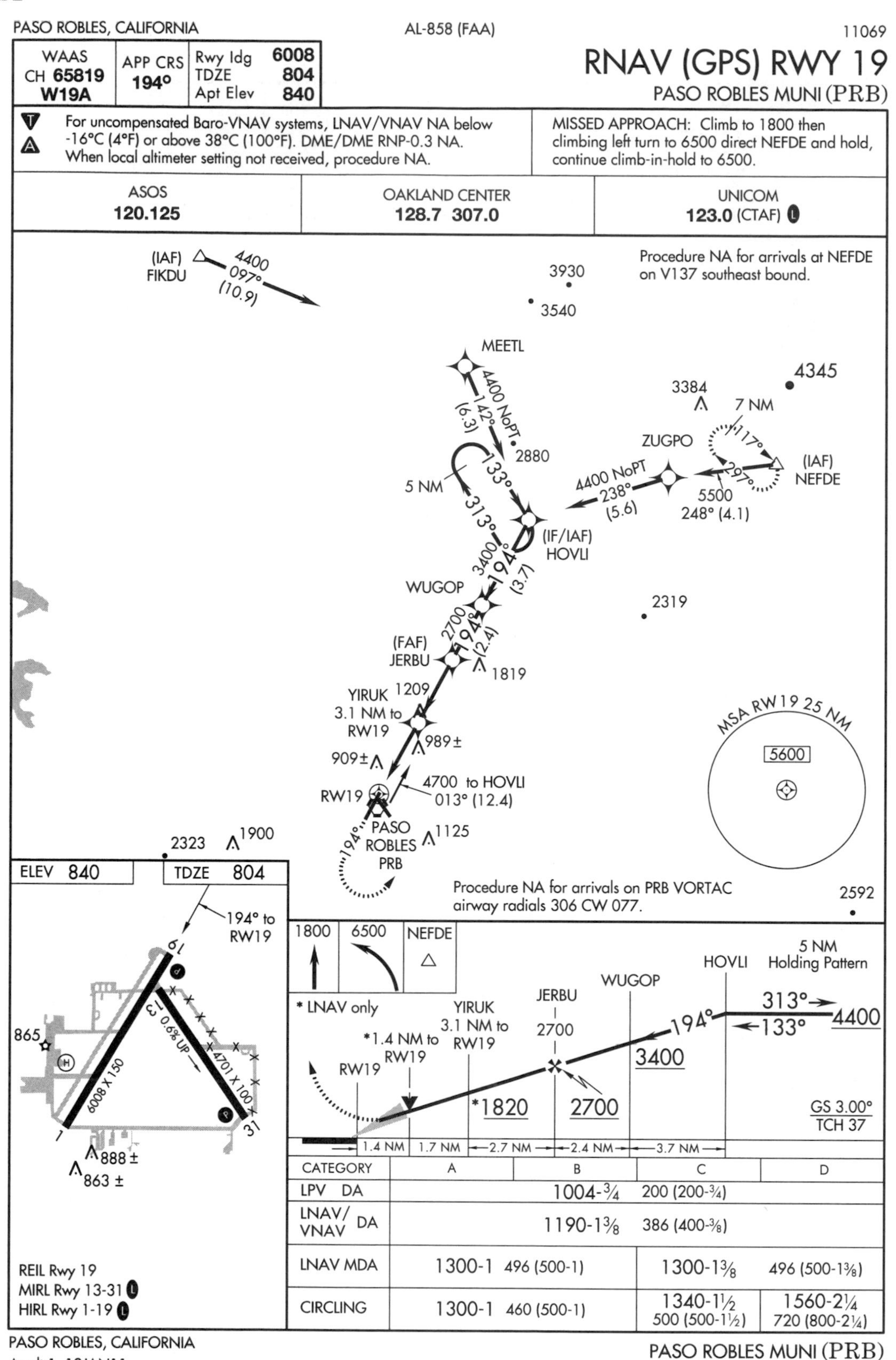

CATEGORY	A	B	C	D
LPV DA	1004-¾ 200 (200-¾)			
LNAV/VNAV DA	1190-1⅜ 386 (400-⅜)			
LNAV MDA	1300-1 496 (500-1)		1300-1⅜ 496 (500-1⅜)	
CIRCLING	1300-1 460 (500-1)		1340-1½ 500 (500-1½)	1560-2¼ 720 (800-2¼)

FIGURE 191.—RNAV (GPS) RWY 19 (PRB).

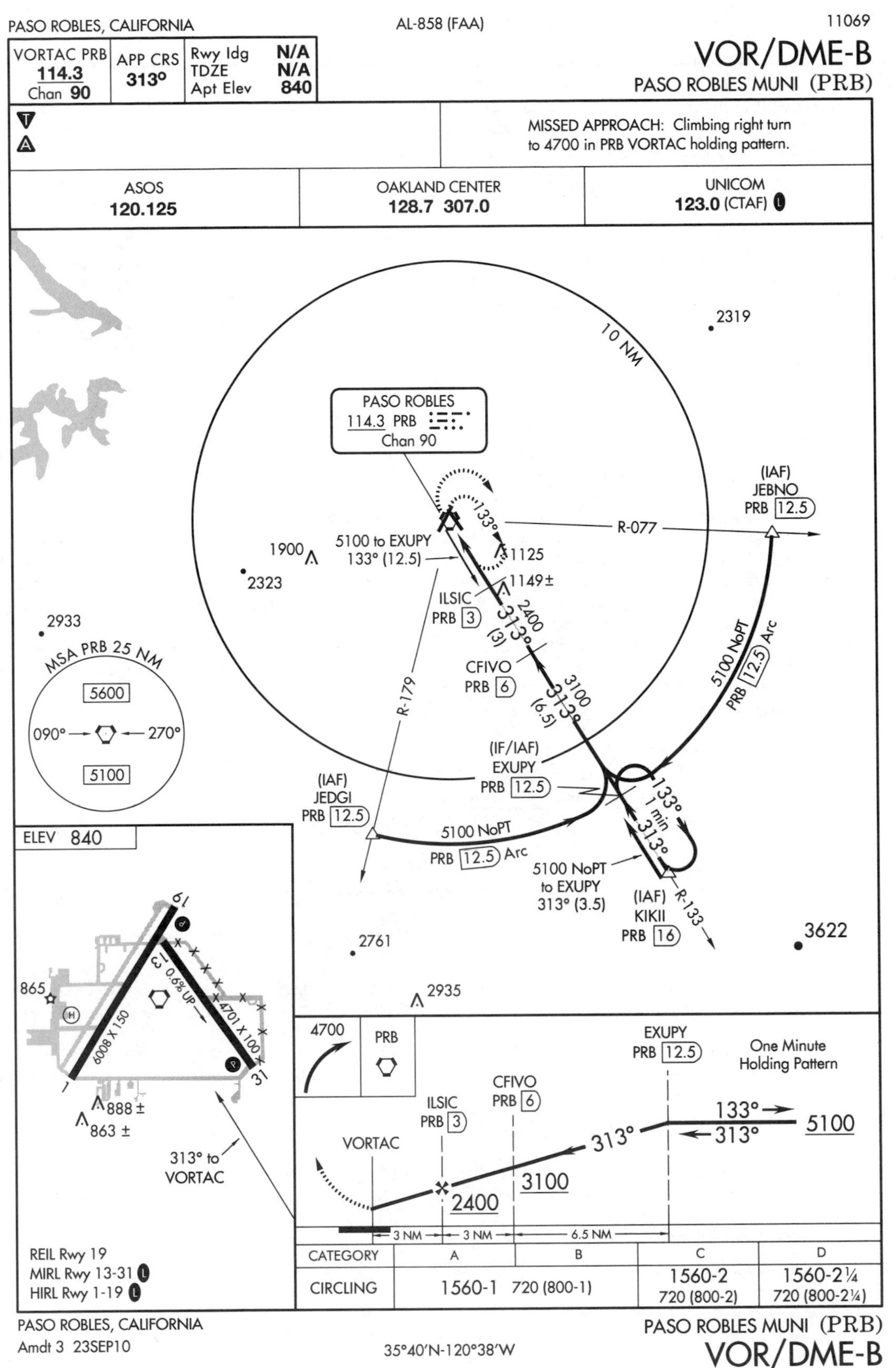

FIGURE 192.—VOR/DME-B (PRB).

COLLEGE STATION

EASTERWOOD FLD (CLL) 3 SW UTC–6(–5DT) N30°35.32′ W96°21.83′ **HOUSTON**
321 B S4 **FUEL** 100LL, JET A Class I, ARFF Index A NOTAM FILE CLL **H–7C, L–19D, 21A**
RWY 16–34: H7000X146 (ASPH–CONC–GRVD) S–70, D–90, 2S–114, 2D–150 HIRL **IAP, AD**
RWY 16: VASI(V4R)—GA 3.0° TCH 51′. Tree.
RWY 34: MALSR.
RWY 10–28: H5158X150 (ASPH–GRVD) S–27, D–50, 2D–87 MIRL
RWY 10: VASI(V4L)—GA 3.0° TCH 50′. Tree.
RWY 28: REIL. VASI(V4L)—GA 3.0° TCH 54′. Tree.
RWY 04–22: H5150X150 (CONC) S–27, D–50, 2D–87
RWY 04: Tree.
RWY 22: Tree. 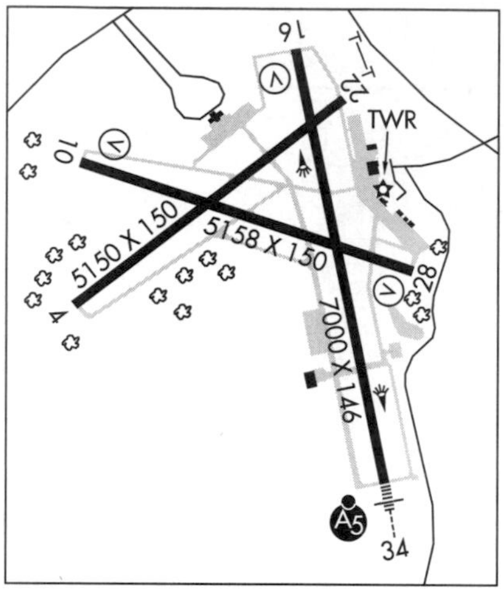
RUNWAY DECLARED DISTANCE INFORMATION
RWY 04: TORA–5149 TODA–5149 ASDA–5149 LDA–5149
RWY 10: TORA–5159 TODA–5159 ASDA–5159 LDA–5159
RWY 16: TORA–7000 TODA–7000 ASDA–7000 LDA–7000
RWY 22: TORA–5149 TODA–5149 ASDA–5149 LDA–5149
RWY 28: TORA–5159 TODA–5159 ASDA–5159 LDA–5159
RWY 34: TORA–7000 TODA–7000 ASDA–7000 LDA–7000
AIRPORT REMARKS: Attended 1200–0400Z‡. For fuel after hours PPR call 979–845–4811 or ctc Texas A and M University police 979–845–2345; late ngt fee. CLOSED to unscheduled air carrier ops with more than 30 passenger seats except 24 hours PPR call arpt manager 979–845–4811. Rwy 04–22 day VFR ops only. Rwy 10–28 mandatory hold short sign on Rwy 16–34 unlgtd. Itinerant acft park in front of twr, overnight parking fee. Ldg fee scheduled FAR 135 and all FAR 121 ops. Rwy 04–22 and Twy E S of Rwy 10–28 not avbl for air carrier acft with over 30 passenger seats. Rwy 16–34 first 1850′ Rwy 34 conc. PAEW adjacent all twys 1200–2200Z‡. When twr clsd ACTIVATE HIRL Rwy 16–34 and MALSR Rwy 34—CTAF. MIRL Rwy 10–28 and REIL Rwy 28 preset low ints only.
WEATHER DATA SOURCES: **ASOS** (979) 846–1708 **HIWAS** 113.3 CLL.
COMMUNICATIONS: **CTAF** 118.5 **ATIS** 126.85 **UNICOM** 122.95
COLLEGE STATION RCO 122.65 122.2 (MONTGOMERY COUNTY RADIO).
Ⓡ **HOUSTON APP/DEP CON** 134.3
TOWER 118.5 (1400–0300Z‡) **GND CON/CLNC DEL** 128.7 **CLNC DEL** 120.4 (when twr clsd)
AIRSPACE: **CLASS D** svc 1400–0300Z‡ other times CLASS E.

16
22
TWR
10
5150 X 150
5158 X 150
28
4
7000 X 146
A5
34

VOR RECEIVER CHECK

TEXAS

VOR RECEIVER CHECKPOINTS

Facility Name (Arpt Name)	Freq/Ident	Type Check Pt. Gnd. AB/ALT	Azimuth from Fac. Mag	Dist. from Fac. N.M.	Checkpoint Description
Abilene (Abilene Rgnl)	113.7/ABI	A/2800	047	10.1	Over silos in center of Ft Phantom Lake.
Alice (Alice International)	114.5/ALI	G	272	0.5	On twy near FBO.
Borger (Hutchinson Co)	108.6/BGD	G	173	6.7	On twy intersection at N end of ramp.
Brownsville (Brownsville/South Padre Island Intl)	116.3/BRO	G	247	3.2	3.2 NM on hold line Rwy 13R.
Brownwood (Brownwood Rgnl)	108.6/BWD	A/2600	169	6.2	Over rotating bcn.
Childress Muni	117.6/CDS	G	353	3.7	At the apron and the twy from Rwy 04–22.
College Station (Easterwood Fld)	113.3/CLL	G	97	3.2	On west edge of parking ramp.
Corpus Christi (Alfred C 'Bubba' Thomas)	115.5/CRP	A/1000	318	9.3	Over Rwy 32 thld.
Corpus Christi (Corpus Christi Intl)	115.5/CRP	A/1100	187	7.5	Over grain elevator.
Daisetta (Liberty Muni)	116.9/DAS	A/1200	195	7.5	Over hangar S of arpt.
Dalhart (Dalhart Muni)	112.0/DHT	A/5000	176	4.1	Over water tower on arpt.
Eagle Lake (Eagle Lake)	116.4/ELA	A/1200	180	4.1	Over water tank 0.4 NM SW of arpt.

FIGURE 193.—Excerpts from Chart Supplement.

CONTINUED FROM PRECEDING PAGE

RADIO AIDS TO NAVIGATION: NOTAM FILE CLL.
COLLEGE STATION (L) VORTACW 113.3 CLL Chan 80 N30°36.30′ W96°25.24′ 100° 3.1 NM to fld. 264/8E.
HIWAS.
DME unusable:
101°–130° byd 25 NM blo 2,500′
131°–148° byd 30 NM blo 2,500′
149°–160° byd 30 NM blo 2,000′
325°–349° byd 30 NM blo 2,500′
350°–100° byd 25 NM blo 3,500′
VOR portion unusable:
131°–189° blo 7,000′
ROWDY NDB (LOM) 260 CL N30°29.62′ W96°20.26′ 341° 5.8 NM to fld. Unmonitored when ATCT clsd.
ILS/DME 111.7 I–CLL Chan 54 Rwy 34. Class IB. LOM ROWDY NDB. Unmonitored when ATCT clsd. DME unmonitored. Glideslope unusable for coupled apchs blo 1,050′ MSL.

COLLIN CO RGNL AT MC KINNEY (See DALLAS on page 241)

COLLINSVILLE

SUDDEN STOP (T32) 1 NE UTC–6(–5DT) N33°34.29′ W96°54.43′ **DALLAS–FT WORTH**
720 NOTAM FILE FTW
RWY 17–35: 1550X60 (TURF)
RWY 17: Trees.
RWY 35: Road.
AIRPORT REMARKS: Attended continuously. Student training prohibited.
COMMUNICATIONS: CTAF 122.9

COLORADO CITY (T88) 6 NW UTC–6(–5DT) N32°28.11′ W100°55.27′ **DALLAS–FT WORTH H–6G, L–17A**
2214 B NOTAM FILE FTW
RWY 17–35: H5479X60 (ASPH) S–50 LIRL
RWY 35: Tree.
AIRPORT REMARKS: Attended irregularly. Rwy 17–35 pavement from Rwy 35 thld lgts southward used as a twy and not maintained.
COMMUNICATIONS: CTAF 122.9
RADIO AIDS TO NAVIGATION: NOTAM FILE BPG.
BIG SPRING (L) VORTACW 114.3 BGS Chan 90 N32°23.14′ W101°29.02′ 069° 29.0 NM to fld. 2670/11E.

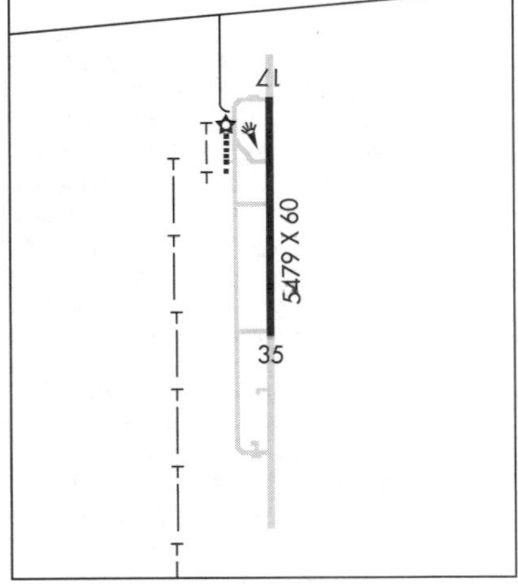

COLUMBUS

ROBERT R WELLS JR (66R) 3 S UTC–6(–5DT) N29°38.49′ W96°30.96′ **HOUSTON L–19D, 21A**
242 B **FUEL** 100LL, JET A NOTAM FILE CXO
RWY 15–33: H3800X60 (ASPH) S–12.5 MIRL
RWY 15: REIL. PAPI(P2L). Thld dsplcd 305′. Fence.
RWY 33: REIL. PAPI(P2L). Thld dsplcd 177′. Brush.
AIRPORT REMARKS: Unattended. Self svc fuel with major credit card. Ultra–light activity on and invof arpt. Rwy 33 REIL OTS indef. ACTIVATE MIRL Rwy 15–33—CTAF.
COMMUNICATIONS: CTAF 122.9
RADIO AIDS TO NAVIGATION: NOTAM FILE CXO.
INDUSTRY (L) VORTACW 110.2 IDU Chan 39 N29°57.36′ W96°33.73′ 165° 19.0 NM to fld. 419/8E.

FIGURE 194.—Excerpts from Chart Supplement.

WESTHEIMER AIR PARK (OØ7) 20 W UTC–6(–5DT) N29°41.68′ W95°47.68′ **HOUSTON**
117 B S2 **FUEL** 100LL NOTAM FILE CXO
RWY 11–29: H2500X28 (CONC) LIRL
RWY 11: Trees.
RWY 29: Tree.
AIRPORT REMARKS: Attended 1400–0000Z‡. 90′ P–line 1500′ from Rwy 11 thld. Grass in cracks on rwy sfc. ACTIVATE rotating bcn—CTAF. ACTIVATE LIRL Rwy 11–29—CTAF.
COMMUNICATIONS: CTAF/UNICOM 122.7

WILLIAM P HOBBY (HOU) 8 SE UTC–6(–5DT) N29°38.73′ W95°16.73′ **HOUSTON**
46 B S2 **FUEL** 100LL, JET A, A1 OX 1, 2, 3, 4 LRA Class I, ARFF Index C **COPTER**
NOTAM FILE HOU **H–7C, L–19E, 21A, GOMW**
RWY 04–22: H7602X150 (CONC–GRVD) S–75, D–200, 2S–168, 2T–461, 2D–400, 2D/D1–444, C5–717 HIRL CL **IAP, AD**
RWY 04: ALSF2. TDZL. PAPI(P4R)—GA 3.0° TCH 57′.
RWY 22: MALS. VASI(V4L)—GA 3.0° TCH 52′. Pole.
RWY 12R–30L: H7602X150 (ASPH–GRVD) S–75, D–195, 2S–168, 2T–461, 2D–220, 2D/D1–444, C5–717 HIRL CL
RWY 12R: MALSR. TDZL. PAPI(P4R)—GA 3.0° TCH 52′. Thld dsplcd 1034′. Pole.
RWY 30L: TDZL. REIL. PAPI(P4L)—GA 3.0° TCH 71′. Road.
RWY 17–35: H6000X150 (ASPH–CONC–GRVD) S–75, D–121, 2S–153, 2D–195 MIRL
RWY 17: VASI(V4L)—GA 3.0° TCH 38′. Antenna.
RWY 35: REIL. VASI(V4R)—GA 3.0° TCH 41′. Bldg.
RWY 12L–30R: H5148X100 (CONC–GRVD) S–30, D–45, 2D–80 MIRL
RWY 12L: PAPI(P4L)—GA 3.0° TCH 60′.

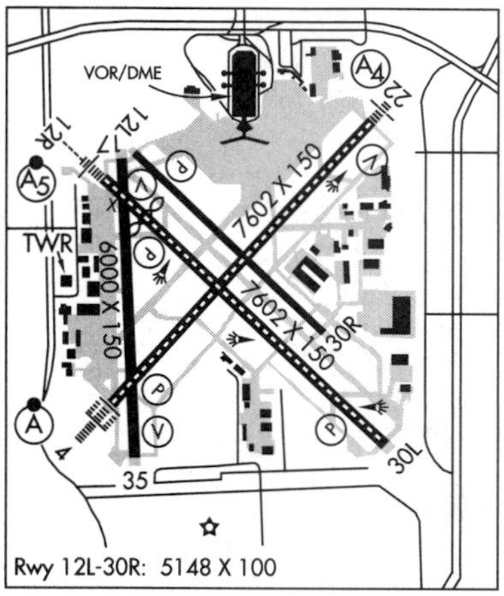

RUNWAY DECLARED DISTANCE INFORMATION

RWY 04:	TORA–7602	TODA–7602	ASDA–7602	LDA–7602
RWY 12L:	TORA–5148	TODA–5148	ASDA–5148	LDA–5148
RWY 12R:	TORA–7602	TODA–7602	ASDA–7602	LDA–6568
RWY 17:	TORA–6000	TODA–6000	ASDA–6000	LDA–6000
RWY 22:	TORA–7602	TODA–7602	ASDA–7602	LDA–7602
RWY 30L:	TORA–7602	TODA–7602	ASDA–7602	LDA–7602
RWY 30R:	TORA–5148	TODA–5148	ASDA–5148	LDA–5148
RWY 35:	TORA–6000	TODA–6000	ASDA–6000	LDA–6000

AIRPORT REMARKS: Attended continuously. Arpt CLOSED to acft with wingspan over 125′ except 24 hours PPR, call arpt manager 713–640–3000. Numerous birds on and invof arpt. ASDE–X Surveillance System in use: pilots should operate transponders with Mode C on all twys and rwys. Customs ramp has multiple obstructions, recommend large acft use customs overflow ramp. Acft in tkf position on Rwy 22 be alert for possible radio interference or null on frequency 118.7. Use upper antenna if so equipped. Rwy 04 runway visual range touchdown, midfield, rollout avbl. Rwy 22 runway visual range touchdown, midfield, rollout avbl. Rwy 12R runway visual range touchdown avbl. Rwy 30L runway visual range touchdown avbl. Twy G centerline to parked acft on W side only 68′. Twy G centerline to edge of adjacent svc vehicle road on W side only 48′. Due to complex rwy configuration, when taxiing to thlds 12L and 12R and 17 check compass heading before departing. Acft southbound on Twy C to Rwy 30L thld use extreme care, Twy C makes a 45° dogleg to the left crossing Twy K. PAPI Rwy 30L unusable byd 8° left and right of course. Flight Notification Service (ADCUS) available. NOTE: See Special Notices—U.S. Special Customs Requirement.
WEATHER DATA SOURCES: ASOS (713) 847–1462 TDWR.
COMMUNICATIONS: D–ATIS 124.6 (713) 847–1491 **UNICOM** 122.95
HOBBY RCO 122.35 (MONTGOMERY COUNTY RADIO)
Ⓡ **HOUSTON APP CON** 134.45 (South) 124.35 (West) 120.05 (East)
HOBBY TOWER 118.7
HOUSTON GND CON 121.9 **CLNC DEL** 125.45 **PRE–TAXI CLNC** 125.45
Ⓡ **HOUSTON DEP CON** 134.45 (South) 123.8 (West) 119.7 (North)
AIRSPACE: CLASS B See VFR Terminal Area Chart
VOR TEST FACILITY (VOT) 108.4
RADIO AIDS TO NAVIGATION: NOTAM FILE HOU.
HOBBY (H) VORW/DME 117.1 HUB Chan 118 N29°39.34′ W95°16.60′ at fld. 47/5E.
ILS/DME 109.9 I–HUB Chan 36 Rwy 04. Class IIIE. DME also serves Rwy 22.
ILS/DME 111.3 I–PRQ Chan 50 Rwy 12R. Class IE. DME also serves Rwy 30L.
LOC/DME 109.9 I–OIB Chan 36 Rwy 22. DME also serves Rwy 04. DME unusable byd 17° right of course.
ILS/DME 111.3 I–UPU Chan 50 Rwy 30L. Class IE. DME also serves Rwy 12R.

HOUSTON MCJ N29°42.83′ W95°23.80′ **HOUSTON**
AWOS–3 119.575 **H–7C, L–19E, 21A, GOMW**

Figure 195.—Excerpt from Chart Supplement.

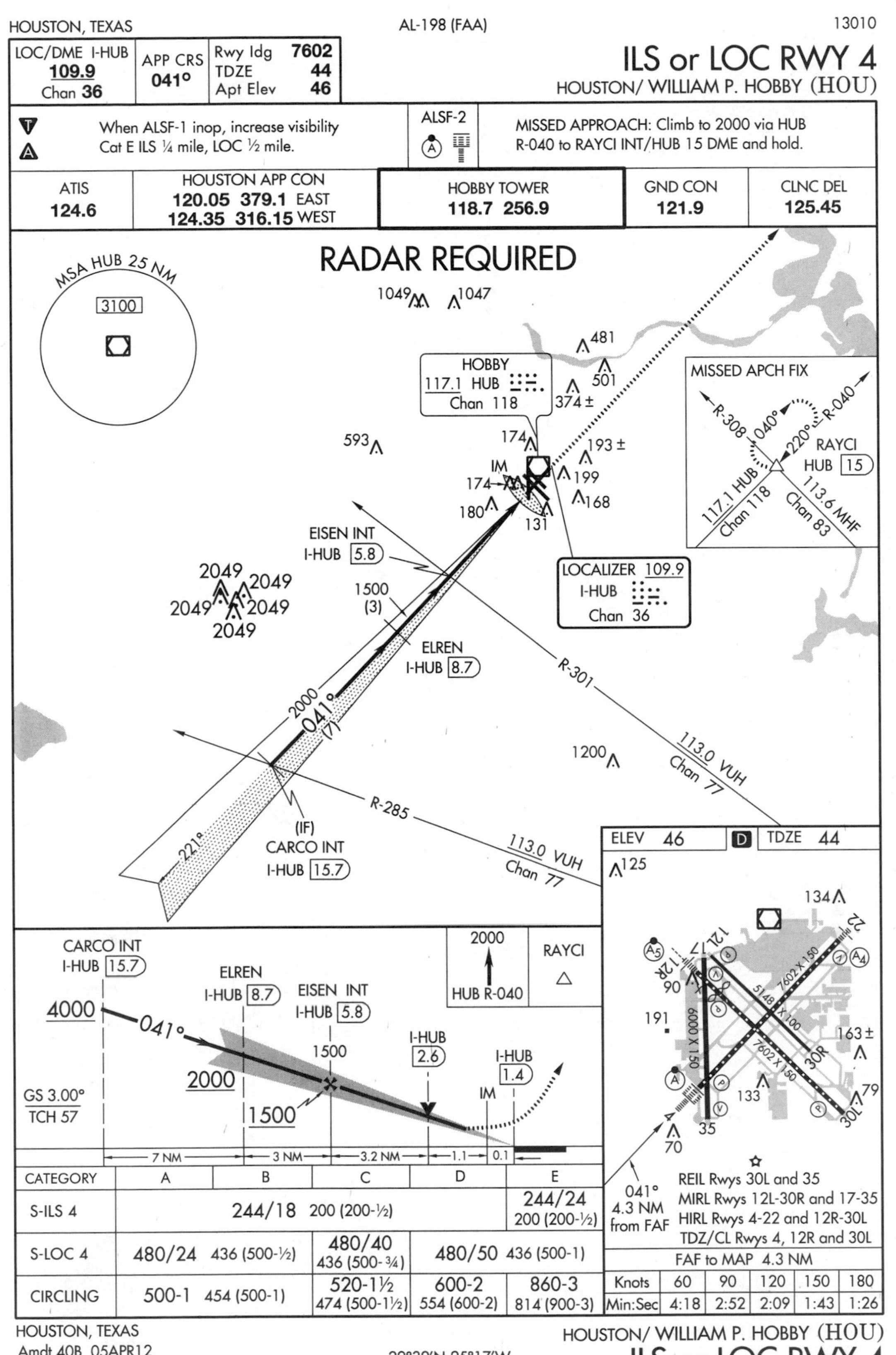

FIGURE 196.—ILS or LOC RWY 4 (HOU).

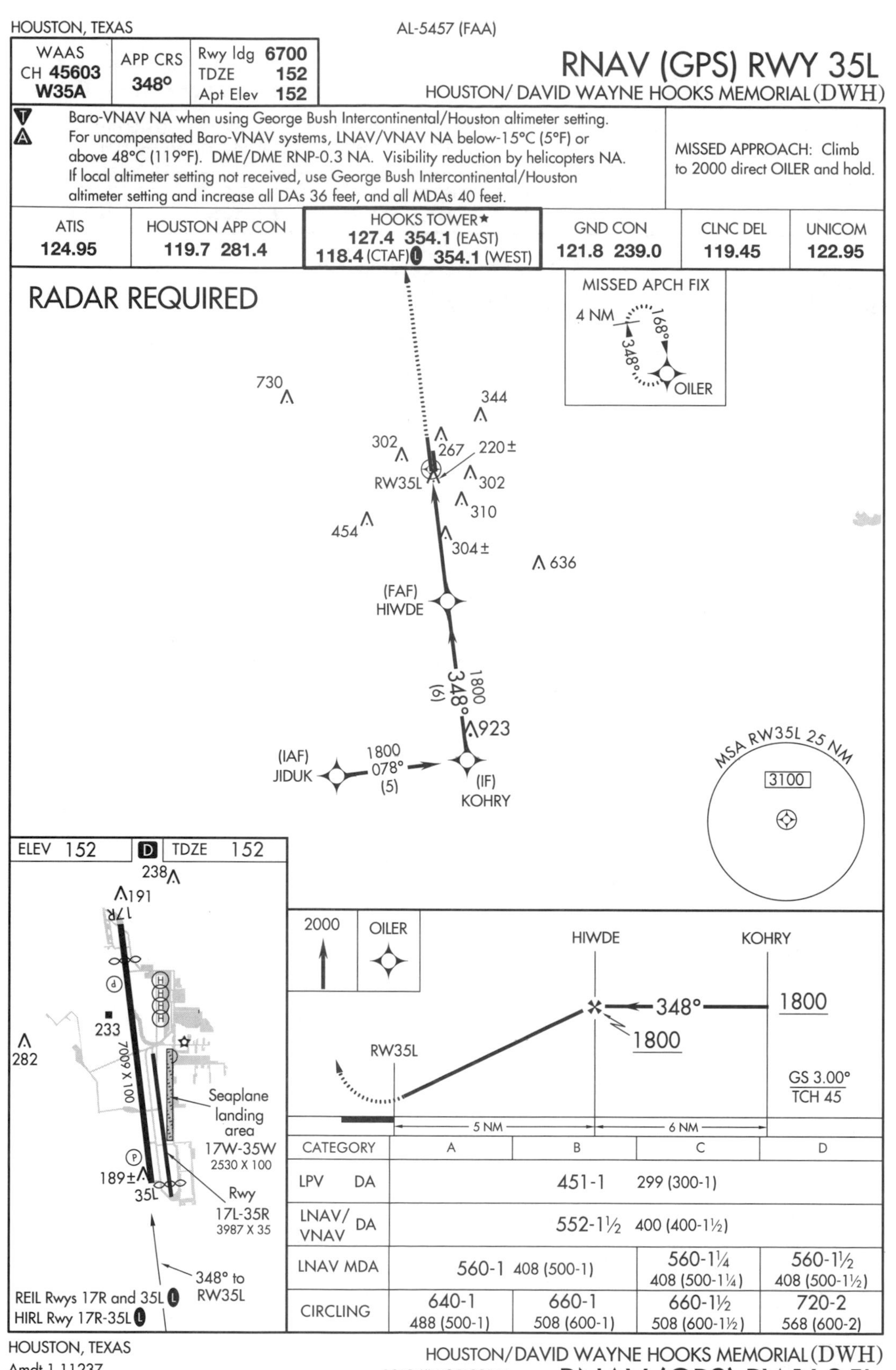

CATEGORY	A	B	C	D
LPV DA	451-1 299 (300-1)			
LNAV/VNAV DA	552-1½ 400 (400-1½)			
LNAV MDA	560-1 408 (500-1)		560-1¼ 408 (500-1¼)	560-1½ 408 (500-1½)
CIRCLING	640-1 488 (500-1)	660-1 508 (600-1)	660-1½ 508 (600-1½)	720-2 568 (600-2)

FIGURE 197.—RNAV (GPS) RWY 35L(DWH).

LAFAYETTE RGNL (LFT) 2 SE UTC–6(–5DT) N30°12.30′ W91°59.27′ **HOUSTON**
42 B S4 **FUEL** 100LL, JET A OX 1, 4 Class I, ARFF Index B NOTAM FILE LFT **H–7D, L–21B, 22E, GOMC**
IAP, AD

RWY 04R–22L: H8001X150 (ASPH–GRVD) S–140, D–170, 2S–175, 2D–290 HIRL
RWY 04R: REIL. PAPI(P4L)—GA 3.0° TCH 53′. Pole. Rgt tfc.
RWY 22L: MALSR. PAPI(P4L)—GA 3.0° TCH 52′. Thld dsplcd 342′. Trees.
RWY 11–29: H5401X148 (ASPH–GRVD) S–85, D–110, 2S–140, 2D–175 MIRL
RWY 11: REIL. PAPI(P4L)—GA 3.0° TCH 35′. Trees. Rgt tfc.
RWY 29: REIL. PAPI(P4L)—GA 3.0° TCH 35′. Tree.
RWY 04L–22R: H4099X75 (ASPH) S–25, D–32 MIRL
RWY 04L: REIL. PAPI(P2L)—GA 3.0° TCH 26′. Tree.
RWY 22R: REIL. PAPI(P2L)—GA 3.0° TCH 27′. Tree. Rgt tfc.

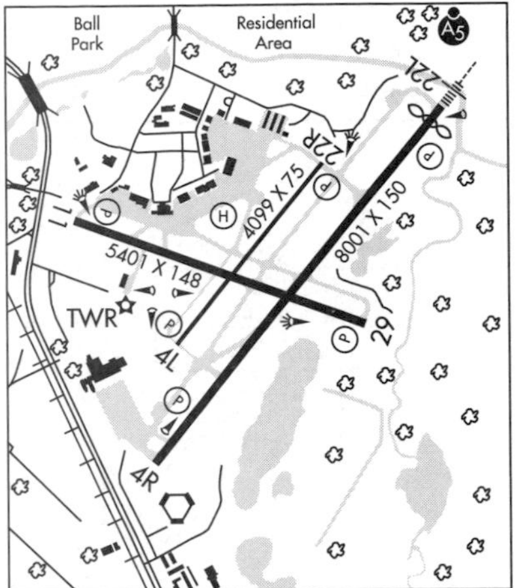

RUNWAY DECLARED DISTANCE INFORMATION

RWY 04L:	TORA–4099	TODA–4099	ASDA–4099	LDA–4099
RWY 04R:	TORA–8001	TODA–8001	ASDA–8001	LDA–8001
RWY 11:	TORA–5401	TODA–5401	ASDA–5401	LDA–5401
RWY 22L:	TORA–8001	TODA–8001	ASDA–8001	LDA–7659
RWY 22R:	TORA–4099	TODA–4099	ASDA–4099	LDA–4099
RWY 29:	TORA–5401	TODA–5401	ASDA–5401	LDA–5401

ARRESTING GEAR/SYSTEM
RWY 04R: EMAS
RWY 22L: EMAS

AIRPORT REMARKS: Attended continuously. Numerous birds on and invof arpt. PPR for unscheduled air carrier ops with more than 30 passenger seats call arpt manager 337–266–4400. Rwy 04L–22R not avbl for air carrier ops with more than 30 passenger seats. Ctc ground control prior to push back from terminal. 155′ oil rig 1 NM southeast of arpt. Rwy 22L runway visual range touchdown avbl. Twy B between Twy C and Twy D clsd to acft with wingspan over 80′. Twy F south of Twy B clsd to single wheel acft over 25,000 lbs and dual wheel acft over 32,000 lbs. Twy F south of Twy B reduces to 40′ wide. When twr clsd ACTIVATE MALSR Rwy 22L—CTAF, MIRL Rwy 04L–22R not avbl.

WEATHER DATA SOURCES: ASOS (337) 237–8153 **HIWAS** 109.8 LFT.

COMMUNICATIONS: CTAF 118.5 **ATIS** 134.05 **UNICOM** 122.95
RCO 122.35 (DE RIDDER RADIO)
Ⓡ **APP/DEP CON** 121.1 (020°–210°) 128.7 (211°–019°) (1130–0430Z‡)
Ⓡ **HOUSTON CENTER APP/DEP CON** 126.35 (0430–1130Z‡)
TOWER 118.5 (1130–0430Z‡) **GND CON** 121.8 **CLNC DEL** 125.55

AIRSPACE: CLASS C svc ctc **APP CON** svc 1130–0430Z‡ other times CLASS E.

RADIO AIDS TO NAVIGATION: NOTAM FILE LFT.
(L) VORTACW 109.8 LFT Chan 35 N30°11.63′ W91°59.55′ at fld. 36/3E. **HIWAS.**
LAFFS NDB (LOM) 375 LF N30°17.36′ W91°54.48′ 216° 6.5 NM to fld. Unmonitored when ATCT clsd.
ILS/DME 110.9 I–TYN Chan 46 Rwy 04R. Class IE.
ILS/DME 109.5 I–LFT Chan 32 Rwy 22L. Class IE. LOM LAFFS NDB. ILS and LOM unmonitored when ATCT clsd.
ASR (1130–0430Z‡)

• •

HELIPAD H1: H50X50 (ASPH)
HELIPAD H1: RLLS.
HELIPORT REMARKS: Rwy H1 circular pad. Helipad H1 perimeter lgts. Heliport ops to/from helipad between Twys B and F and the terminal ramp, avoid overflight of the terminal and other buildings in the 270°–020° quadrant from the helipad. Lead–in lgts two ingress paths. Helicopter parking pads avbl.

LAFFS N30°17.36′ W91°54.48′ NOTAM FILE LFT. **HOUSTON**
NDB (LOM) 375 LF 216° 6.5 NM to Lafayette Rgnl. Unmonitored when ATCT clsd. **L–21B, 22E**

FIGURE 198.—Excerpt from Chart Supplement.

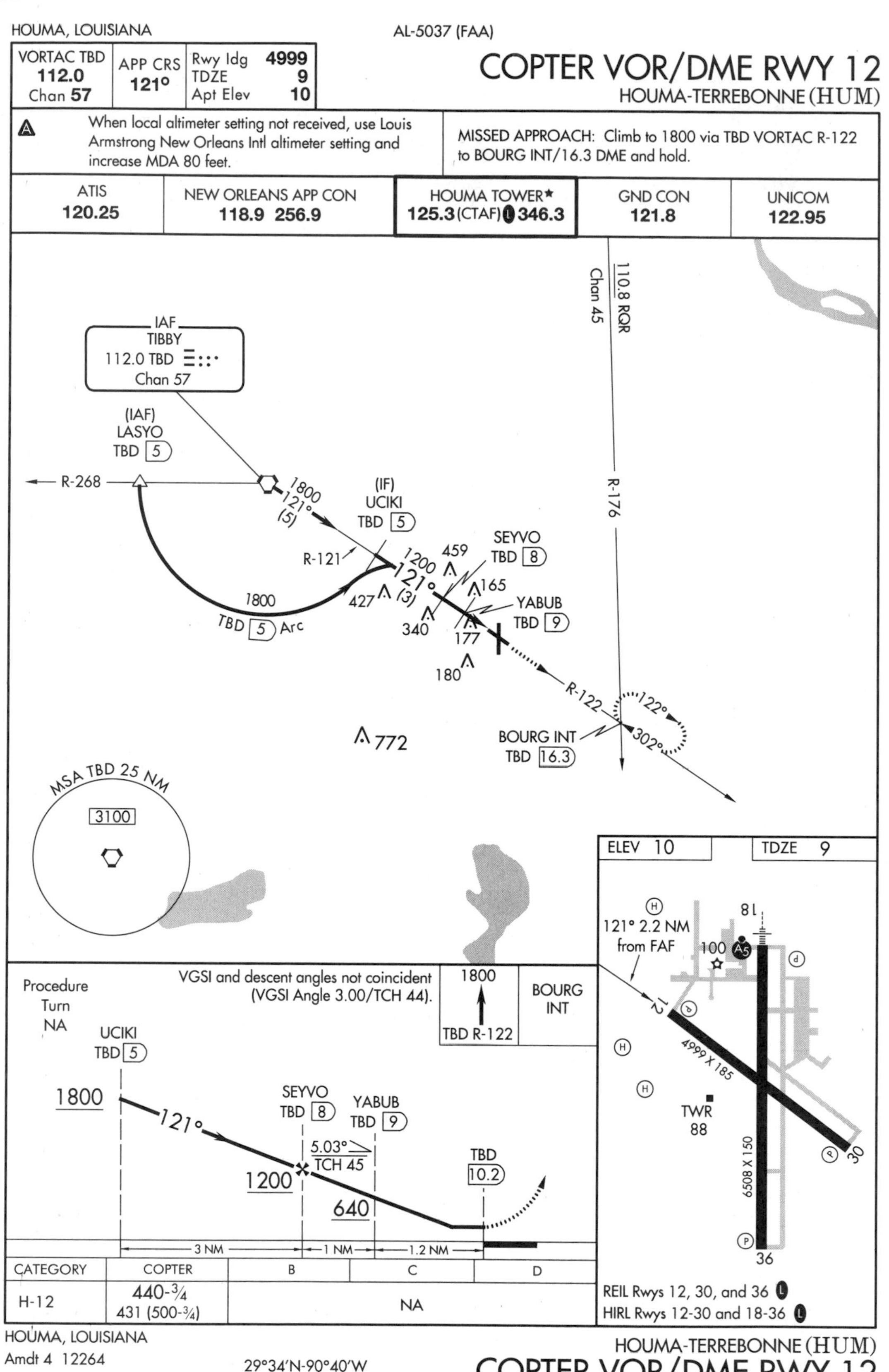

FIGURE 199.—COPTER VOR/DME RWY 12 (HUM).

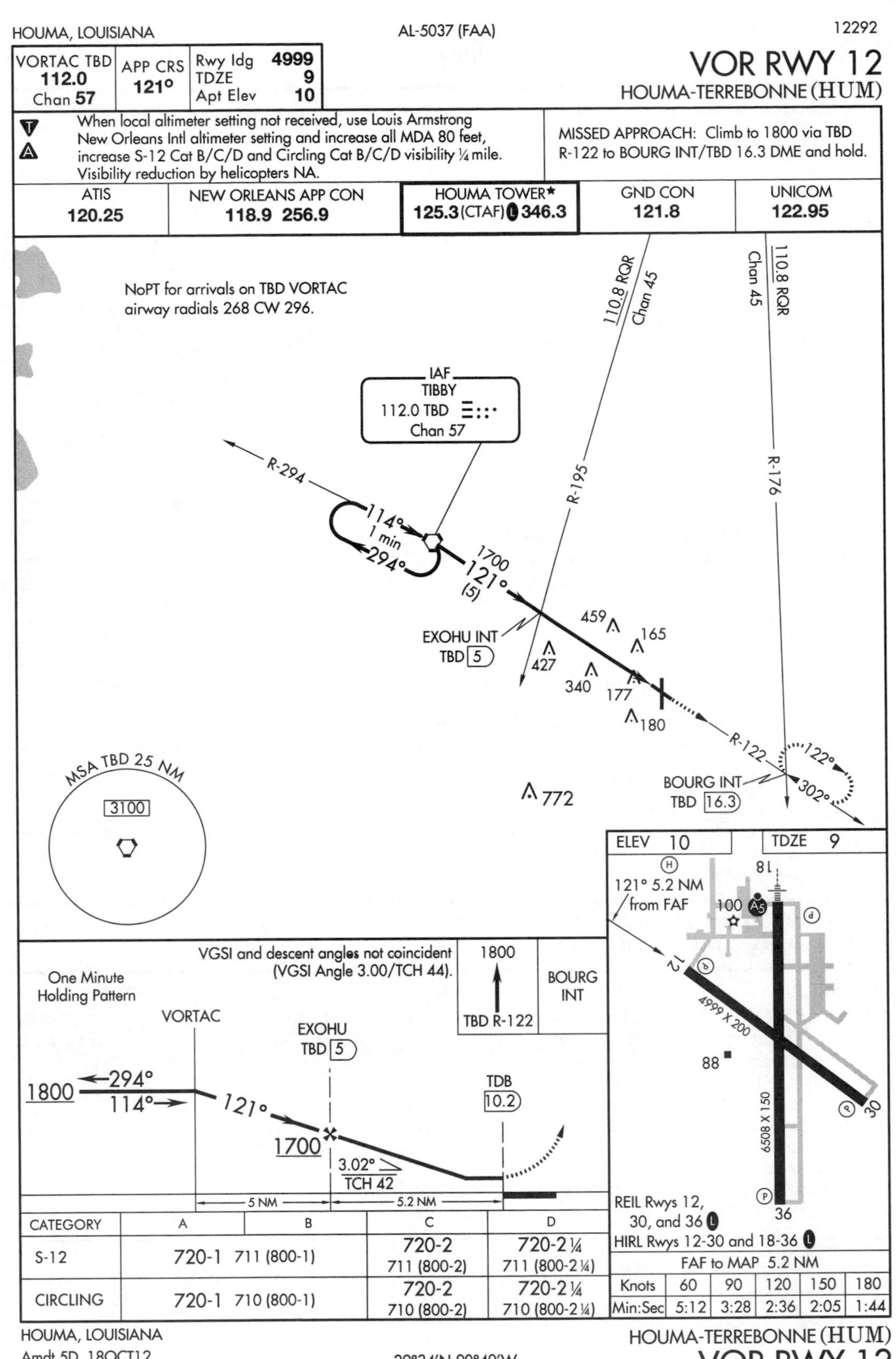

FIGURE 200.—VOR RWY 12 (HUM).

HOUMA–TERREBONNE (HUM) 3 SE UTC–6(–5DT) N29°33.99´ W90°39.63´ **NEW ORLEANS**
9 B S4 **FUEL** 100LL, JET A OX 1, 2, 3, 4 TPA—1009(1000) NOTAM FILE HUM **H–7D, L–21B, 22F**
RWY 18–36: H6508X150 (CONC–GRVD) S–50, D–70, 2S–89, 2D–137 HIRL **IAP, AD**
RWY 18: MALSR. PAPI(P2L)—GA 3.0° TCH 52´. Trees.
RWY 36: REIL. PAPI(P2L)—GA 3.0° TCH 50´. Trees.
RWY 12–30: H4999X185 (CONC) S–50, D–70, 2S–89, 2D–137 HIRL
RWY 12: REIL. PAPI(P2L)—GA 3.0° TCH 44´. Trees.
RWY 30: REIL. PAPI(P2L)—GA 3.0° TCH 39´.
AIRPORT REMARKS: Attended 1200–0100Z‡. Fuel avbl 24 hrs with credit card. Birds on and invof arpt. Numerous birds 500´AGL and blo 2.8 NM south southwest AER 36, avoidance advised. Extensive helicopter ops south thru west of arpt. Rwy 12–30 surface skid resistance fair when wet. ACTIVATE HIRL Rwy 12–30 and Rwy 18–36 and MALSR Rwy 18 and REIL Rwy 12, Rwy 30 and Rwy 36—CTAF.
WEATHER DATA SOURCES: AWOS–3PT 120.25 (985) 876–4055. LAWRS.
COMMUNICATIONS: CTAF 125.3 **ATIS** 120.25 **UNICOM** 122.95
RCO 122.45 (DE RIDDER RADIO)
®**NEW ORLEANS APP/DEP CON** 118.9
TOWER 125.3 (1200–0100Z‡) **GND CON** 121.8
AIRSPACE: CLASS D svc 1200–0100Z‡ other times CLASS G.
RADIO AIDS TO NAVIGATION: NOTAM FILE DRI.
TIBBY (L) VORTAC 112.0 TBD Chan 57 N29°39.86´ W90°49.75´ 122° 10.6 NM to fld. 10/2E.
VORTAC unusable:
byd 30 NM blo 2,000´
TACAN DME unusable:
byd 30 NM blo 2,000´
HOUMA NDB (LOM) 219 HU N29°39.80´ W90°39.58´ 179° 5.8 NM to fld. LOM unmonitored. Unmonitored when ATCT clsd.
ILS 108.5 I–HUM Rwy 18. LOM HOUMA NDB. LOM unmonitored. Unmonitored when ATCT clsd.

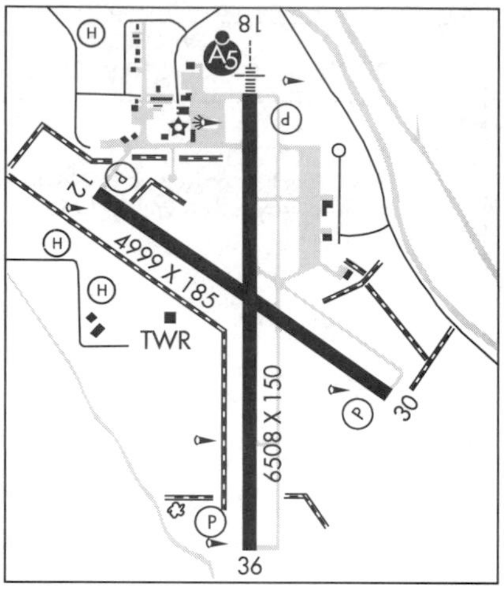

IDA'S HELIPORT (L87) 0 N UTC–6(–5DT) N33°00.26´ W93°53.59´ **MEMPHIS**
286 NOTAM FILE DRI
HELIPAD H1: H40X40 (CONC)
HELIPORT REMARKS: Attended continuously. Helipad H1 perimeter lgts. Helipad H1 100´ water twr 300´ E and 149´ radio twr 500´ S of pad. For perimeter lgts call 318–284–3231. Helipad H1 apch 180°–departure 000°.
COMMUNICATIONS: CTAF 122.9

INDEPENDENCE IPN N28°05.10´ W87°59.15´
AWOS–3 118.125 Winds unreliable.

JEANERETTE

LE MAIRE MEM (2R1) 1 S UTC–6(–5DT) N29°53.94´ W91°39.96´ **HOUSTON**
14 B **FUEL** 100LL NOTAM FILE DRI **L–21B, 22F**
RWY 04–22: H3000X75 (ASPH) S–6 MIRL
RWY 04: REIL. PAPI(P2L)—GA 3.0° TCH 50´. Trees.
RWY 22: REIL. PAPI(P2L)—GA 3.0° TCH 50´. Thld dsplcd 603´. Tree.
AIRPORT REMARKS: Unattended. For arpt attended call 337–365–7202. Fuel avbl 24 hrs self svc with credit card. MIRL Rwy 04–22 and REIL Rwys 04 and 22 preset low ints dusk to dawn, to incr ints ACTIVATE–CTAF.
COMMUNICATIONS: CTAF 122.9
RADIO AIDS TO NAVIGATION: NOTAM FILE LFT.
LAFAYETTE (L) VORTACW 109.8 LFT Chan 35 N30°11.63´ W91°59.55´ 133° 24.5 NM to fld. 36/3E. **HIWAS.**

FIGURE 201.—Excerpt from Chart Supplement.

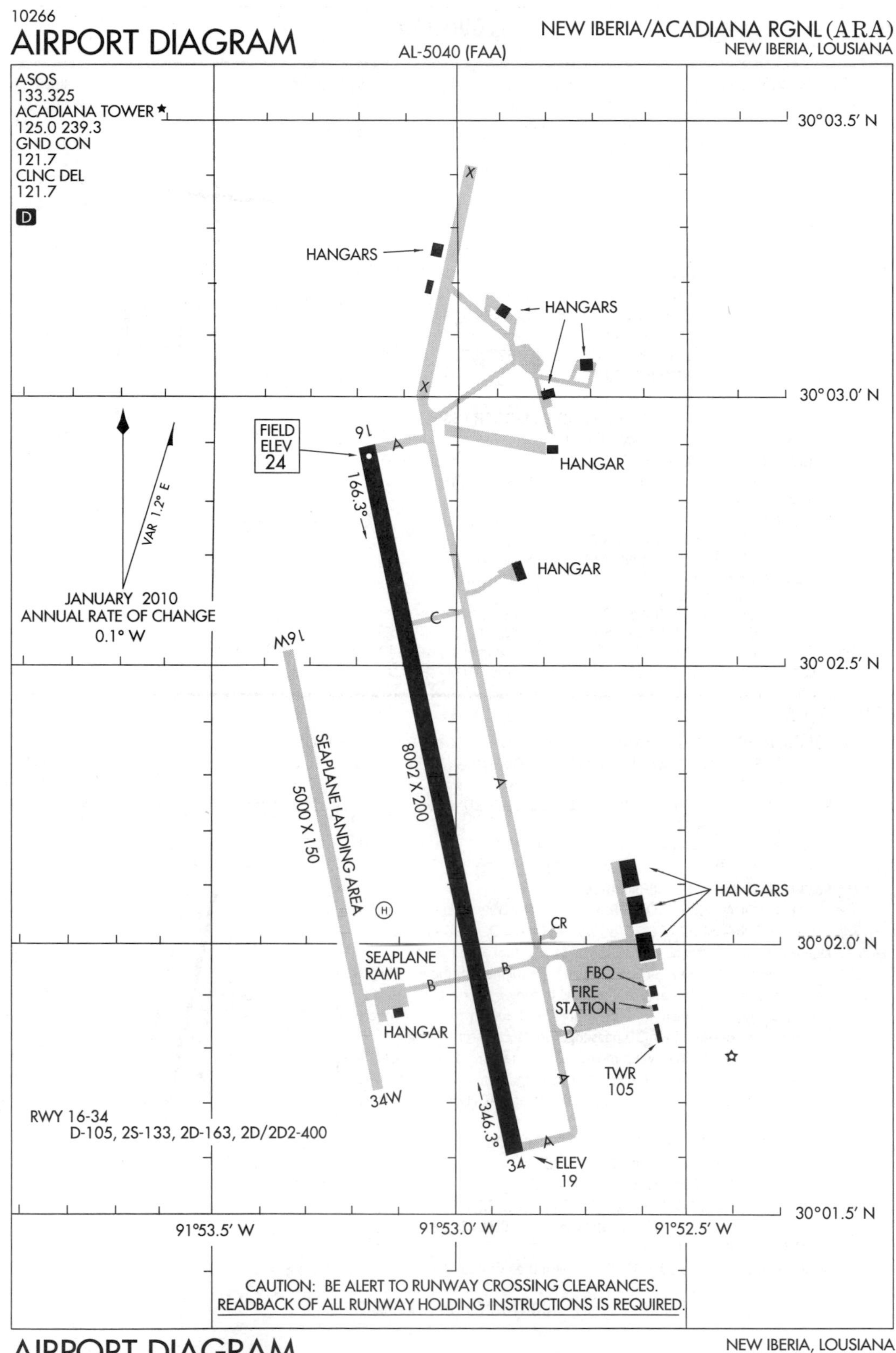

FIGURE 202.—Airport Diagram: New Iberia/Acadiana RGNL (ARA).

NATCHITOCHES RGNL (IER) 2 S UTC–6(–5DT) N31°44.14´ W93°05.95´ **HOUSTON**
121 B S4 **FUEL** 100LL, JET A1+ NOTAM FILE IER **H–6I, L–22E**
IAP
RWY 17–35: H5003X150 (ASPH) S–30 MIRL
RWY 17: REIL. PAPI(P4L)—GA 3.0° TCH 45´. Tree.
RWY 35: ODALS. PAPI(P4L)—GA 3.0° TCH 43´. Trees.
RWY 07–25: H4000X100 (ASPH) S–21 MIRL
RWY 07: Trees.
RWY 25: P–line.
AIRPORT REMARKS: Attended dawn–dusk. For arpt attendant after hrs call 318–471–2106. Fuel avbl 24 hr with credit card. MIRL Rwy 17–35 and REIL Rwy 17 preset low ints dusk to dawn, to increase ints and ACTIVATE MIRL Rwy 07–25—CTAF. Rwy 35 ODALS operate low ints continuously, to increase ints ACTIVATE—CTAF.
WEATHER DATA SOURCES: AWOS–3 119.025 (318) 352–1575.
COMMUNICATIONS: CTAF/UNICOM 122.8
Ⓡ **POLK APP/DEP CON** 125.4
GCO 135.075 (FORT POLK APCH AND DE RIDDER FSS)
RADIO AIDS TO NAVIGATION: NOTAM FILE AEX.
ALEXANDRIA (H) VORTACW 116.1 AEX Chan 108 N31°15.40´ W92°30.06´ 310° 42.0 NM to fld. 80/3E. **HIWAS.**
VOR unusable:
035°–065° blo 2,000´
066°–094° byd 35 NM blo 3,000´
185°–200° byd 35 NM blo 3,000´
201°–214° byd 35 NM blo 2,000´
215°–260° blo 2,000´
261°–285° byd 35 NM blo 2,000´
357°–034° byd 35 NM blo 3,000´
NDB (MHW) 407 OOC N31°39.45´ W93°04.66´ 343° 4.8 NM to fld. NOTAM FILE IER.
LOC 110.5 I–IER Rwy 35. LOC unmonitored 0000–1200Z‡.

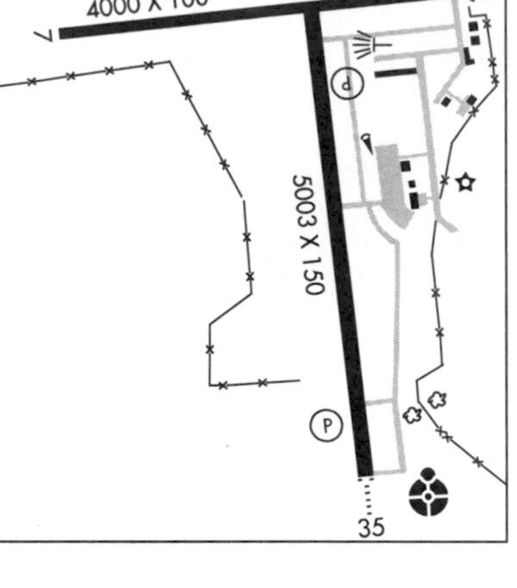

NEW IBERIA

ACADIANA RGNL (ARA) 4 NW UTC–6(–5DT) N30°02.27´ W91°53.03´ **HOUSTON**
24 B S2 **FUEL** 100LL, JET A OX 4 TPA—1024(1000) Class IV, ARFF Index A **H–7D, L–21B, 22E, GOMC**
NOTAM FILE ARA **IAP, AD**
RWY 16–34: H8002X200 (CONC) D–105, 2S–133, 2D–163, 2D/2D2–400 HIRL
RWY 16: ODALS. PAPI(P4L)—GA 3.0° TCH 51´.
RWY 34: MALSR. PAPI(P4L)—GA 3.0° TCH 52´. Rgt tfc.
RUNWAY DECLARED DISTANCE INFORMATION
RWY 16: TORA–8002 TODA–8002 ASDA–8002 LDA–8002
RWY 34: TORA–8002 TODA–8002 ASDA–8002 LDA–8002
AIRPORT REMARKS: Attended 1300–0300Z‡. For fuel after hrs call 337–367–1401, FAX 337–367–1404. Seaplane landing area (water channel) West of and adjacent/parallel to runway. Rwy 16W–34W seaway edge lgts green; thld lgts amber. Bird activity on and invof arpt. ARFF PPR for more than 30 passenger seats call arpt manager 337–365–7202. Rotor wing movement and landing area between the rwy and seaway. Intensive helicopter training. When twr closed HIRL Rwy 16–34 preset low ints, to increase ints and ACTIVATE MALSR Rwy 34—CTAF.
WEATHER DATA SOURCES: ASOS 133.325 (337) 365–0128.
COMMUNICATIONS: CTAF 125.0 **UNICOM** 122.95
Ⓡ **LAFAYETTE APP/DEP CON** 121.1 (1130–0430Z‡)
HOUSTON CENTER APP/DEP CON 126.35 (0430–1130Z‡)
TOWER 125.0 (1200–0300Z‡) **GND CON** 121.7 **CLNC DEL** 121.7
LAFAYETTE CLNC DEL 118.05
AIRSPACE: CLASS D svc 1200–0300Z‡ other times CLASS G.

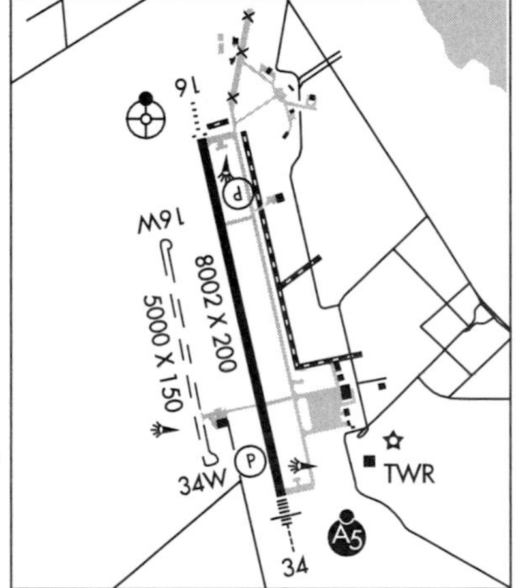

CONTINUED ON NEXT PAGE

FIGURE 203.—Excerpt from Chart Supplement.

LOUISIANA

CONTINUED FROM PRECEDING PAGE

RADIO AIDS TO NAVIGATION: NOTAM FILE LFT.
LAFAYETTE (L) VORTACW 109.8 LFT Chan 35 N30°11.63′ W91°59.55′ 146° 10.9 NM to fld. 36/3E. **HIWAS.**
ACADI NDB (MHW/LOM) 269 AR N29°57.38′ W91°51.80′ 345° 5.0 NM to fld. NOTAM FILE ARA.
ILS 108.9 I–ARA Rwy 34. Class IA. LOM ACADI NDB.

• • • • • • • • • • • • • • • • • •

WATERWAY 16W–34W: 5000X150 (WATER) MIRL
WATERWAY 16W: Rgt tfc.
RUNWAY DECLARED DISTANCE INFORMATION
RWY 16W:TORA–5000 TODA–5000 ASDA–5000 LDA–5000
RWY 34W:TORA–5000 TODA–5000 ASDA–5000 LDA–5000
SEAPLANE REMARKS: Waterway 16–34 seaway edge lgts green, thld lgts amber. ACTIVATE seaway edge lgts Waterway 16–34—122.7. 3 clicks on 7 clicks off.

NEW ORLEANS

LAKEFRONT (NEW) 4 NE UTC–6(–5DT) N30°02.55′ W90°01.70′ — **NEW ORLEANS**
7 B S4 **FUEL** 100LL, JET A OX 1, 3 LRA NOTAM FILE NEW — **H–7E, 8F, L–21B, 22F, GOMC**
RWY 18R–36L: H6879X150 (ASPH–GRVD) S–60, D–175, 2S–175, 2D–200, 2D/2D2–350 MIRL — **IAP, AD**

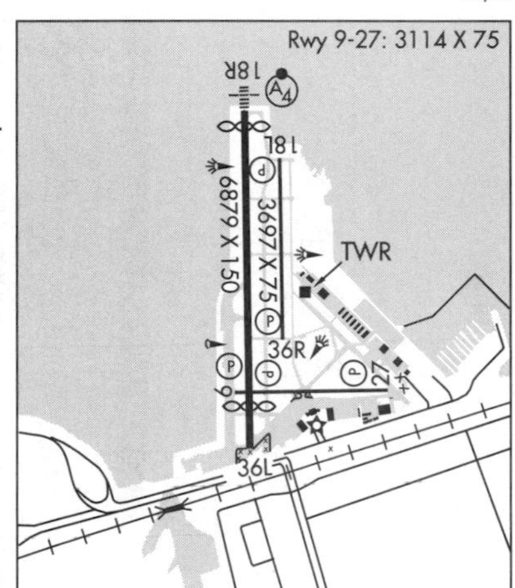

RWY 18R: MALSF. PAPI(P4L)—GA 3.0° TCH 51′. Thld dsplcd 239′. Pier. Rgt tfc.
RWY 36L: REIL. PAPI(P4L)—GA 3.0° TCH 50′. Thld dsplcd 820′. Wall.
RWY 18L–36R: H3697X75 (ASPH) S–35, D–55, 2D–80 MIRL
RWY 18L: REIL.
RWY 36R: REIL. PAPI(P4L)—GA 3.0° TCH 45′. Bldg. Rgt tfc.
RWY 09–27: H3114X75 (ASPH) S–50, D–80, 2S–102, 2D–100 MIRL
RWY 09: REIL. PAPI(P4L)—GA 3.0° TCH 40′. Berm.
RWY 27: PAPI(P4R)—GA 3.0° TCH 40′. Road. Rgt tfc.
RUNWAY DECLARED DISTANCE INFORMATION
RWY 09: TORA–3113 TODA–3113 ASDA–3113 LDA–3113
RWY 18L:TORA–3697 TODA–3697 ASDA–3697 LDA–3697
RWY 18R:TORA–6880 TODA–6880 ASDA–6035 LDA–5510
RWY 27: TORA–3113 TODA–3113 ASDA–3113 LDA–3113
RWY 36L:TORA–6880 TODA–6880 ASDA–5955 LDA–5135
RWY 36R:TORA–3697 TODA–3697 ASDA–3697 LDA–3697
AIRPORT REMARKS: Attended continuously. For field conditions after 2200Z‡ ctc arpt manager on 504–914–5721. Birds on and invof arpt. Boats as high as 80′ pass within 400′ of Rwy 09 thld. Rwy 18R–36L few low spots near intersection of Rwy 09–27 holding water. When twr clsd MIRL Rwy 18R–36L preset med ints and twy lgts for Twys A, B, D, E, F and H preset on medium. ARFF capability equivalent to Index B. Acft transporting any items listed in Part 175 title 49 PPR to land. Landing fee. Landing fee waived with minimum fuel purchase. Flight Notification Service (ADCUS) temporarily not available. NOTE: See Special Notices—U.S. Special Customs Requirement.
WEATHER DATA SOURCES: ASOS (504) 245–4366 LAWRS.
COMMUNICATIONS: CTAF 119.9 **ATIS** 124.9
NEW ORLEANS RCO 122.6 (DE RIDDER RADIO)
Ⓡ **NEW ORLEANS APP/DEP CON** 133.15 (North) 123.85 (South)
TOWER 119.9 (1400–0000Z‡) **GND CON** 121.7 **CLNC DEL** 127.4 (NEW ORLEANS APP/DEP CON when twr clsd)
AIRSPACE: CLASS D svc 1400–0000Z‡ other times CLASS E.
RADIO AIDS TO NAVIGATION: NOTAM FILE NEW.
HARVEY (H) VORTACW 114.1 HRV Chan 88 N29°51.01′ W90°00.18′ 351° 11.6 NM to fld. 2/2E.
VORTAC unusable:
004°–125° byd 30 NM blo 2,000′
126°–136° byd 25 NM blo 3,000′
137°–174° byd 30 NM blo 2,000′
175°–190° byd 30 NM blo 3,000′
191°–239° byd 30 NM blo 2,000′
240°–255° byd 25 NM blo 6,000′
256°–279° byd 30 NM blo 2,000′
280°–290° byd 30 NM
291°–352° byd 30 NM blo 2,000′
353°–003° byd 30 NM blo 3,000′
ILS/DME 111.3 I–NEW Chan 50 Rwy 18R.

FIGURE 203A.—Excerpt from Chart Supplement.

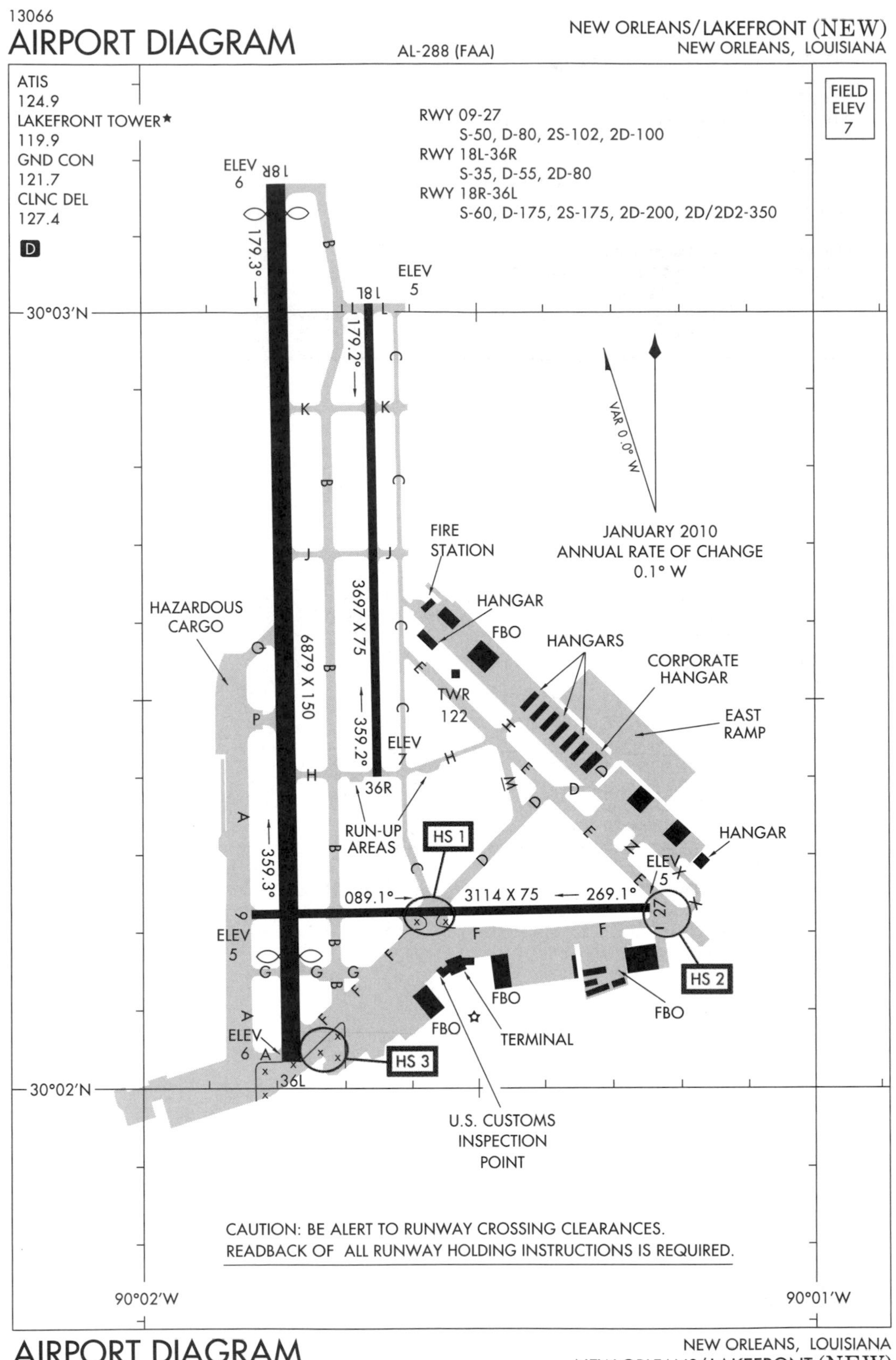

FIGURE 204.—Airport Diagram: New ORLEANS/LAKEFRONT (NEW).

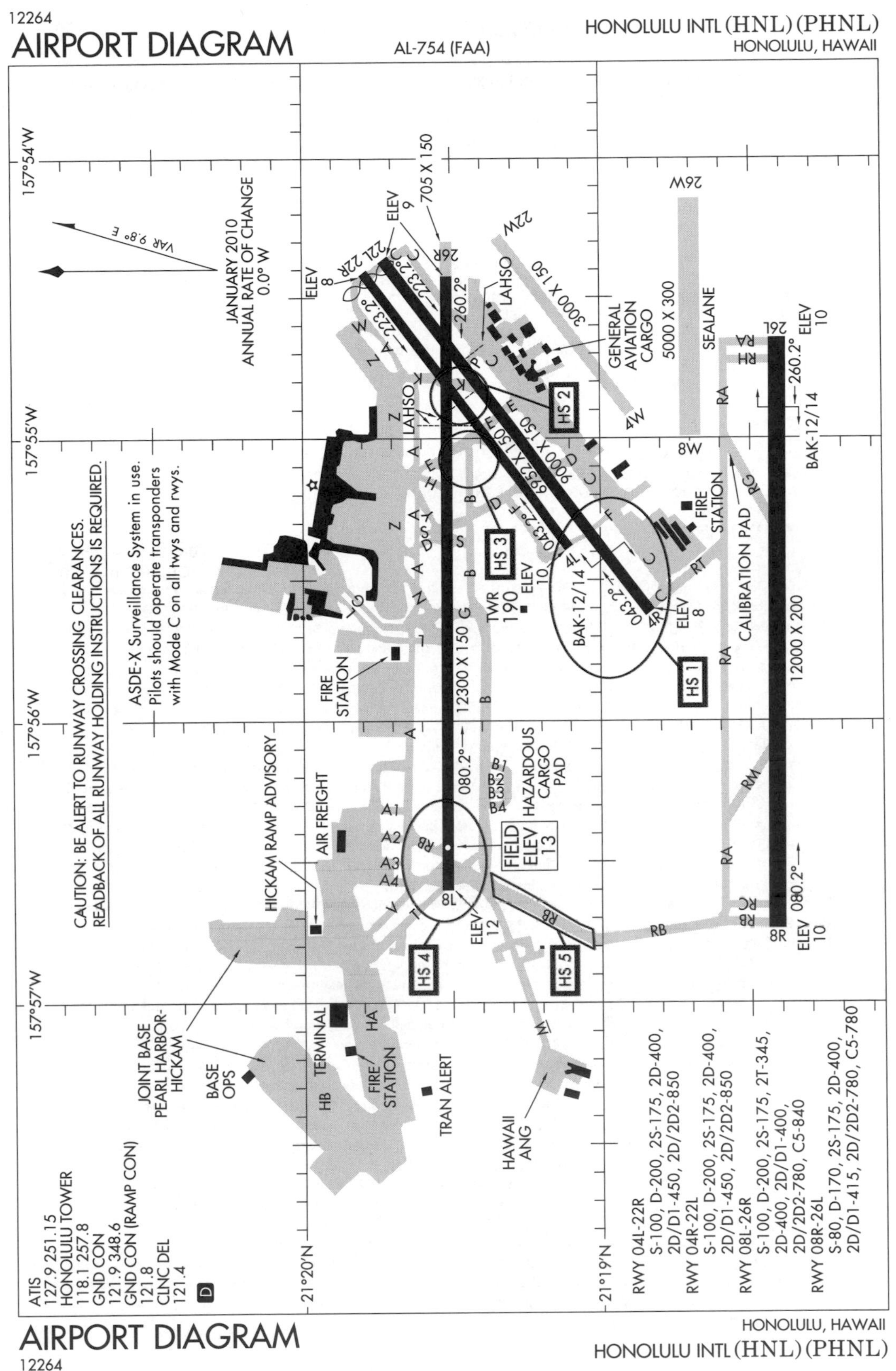

FIGURE 205.—Airport Diagram: Honolulu Intl (HNL) (PHNL).

HONOLULU INTL (JOINT BASE PEARL HARBOR–HICKAM) (HNL)(PHNL) 3 NW UTC–10 **HAWAIIAN–MARIANA**
N21°19.12′ W157°55.35′ **P–1C, 2G**
13 B S4 **FUEL** 80, 100, JET A, A1+, B OX 1, 2, 3, 4 TPA—See Remarks **IAP**
LRA Class I, ARFF Index E NOTAM FILE HNL
RWY 08L–26R: H12300X150 (ASPH-GRVD) S–100, D–200, 2S–175, 2T–345, 2D–400, 2D/D1–400, D2D/2D2–780 HIRL
RWY 08L: MALSR. PAPI(P4L)—GA 3.0° TCH 80′.
RWY 26R: REIL. PAPI(P4L)—GA 3.0 TCH 71′.
RWY 08R–26L: H12000X200 (ASPH-GRVD) S–80, D–170, 2S–175, 2D–400, D/2D2–780 HIRL
RWY 08R: REIL. PAPI(P4L)—GA 3.25° TCH 99′.
RWY 26L: MALSF. PAPI(P4L)—GA 3.0° TCH 75′. 3 cranes.
RWY 04R–22L: H9000X150 (ASPH–GRVD) S–100, D–200, 2S–175, 2D–400, D/2D2–850 HIRL
RWY 04R: MALSR. PAPI(P4L)—GA 3.0° TCH 71′. Tree.
RWY 22L: REIL. PAPI(P4L)—GA 3.44° TCH 80′. Stack.
RWY 04L–22R: H6952X150 (ASPH) S–100, D–200, 2S–175, 2D–400, D/2D2–850 MIRL
RWY 04L: REIL. PAPI(P4L)—GA 3.0° TCH 50′. **RWY 22R:** REIL. Antenna. Thld dsplcd 150′.

LAND AND HOLD-SHORT OPERATIONS

LDG RWY	HOLD-SHORT POINT	AVBL LDG DIST
RWY 04L	08L–26R	3700
RWY 04R	08L–26R	6250
RWY 08L	04L–22R	9300

RUNWAY DECLARED DISTANCE INFORMATION

RWY 04R: TORA–9000 TODA–9000 ASDA–8950 LDA–8950
RWY 22L: TORA–9000 TODA–9000 ASDA–8937 LDA–8937

ARRESTING GEAR/SYSTEMS

RWY 04R BAK–14 BAK–12B (1500′)

HOOK MB 60 (200′) → **RWY 26R**
BAK–14 BAK 12B(B) (1500) **RWY 26L**

AIRPORT REMARKS: Attended continuously. 80 and 100 octane fuel avbl thru FBO. Bird strike hazard all runways. Mil acft opr during Bird Watch Condition MODERATE (initial tkof or full stop ldg only, no multiple IFR/VFR approaches) and SEVERE (tkof and ldg prohibited w/o 15 OG/CC approval or 154 OG/CC approval for HIANG acft) ctc HIK ramp, PTD, 15 WG command post, 735 AMC command post, 154 WG command post for current conditions. See FLIP AP/3 Supplementary arpt information, route and area rstd, and Oakland FIR flt haz. Use caution for obstruction 76′ from Twy M centerline on Oceanside, approximately 200′ from parking apron. Crane 290′ AGL approximately 2,600′ north of Rwy 08L, 2500′ west of Inter Island Terminal 1630–0330Z daily. PAEW 600′–1300′E Rwy 22L and Rwy 22R thld, 1700–0130Z Mon–Fri. Rwys CLOSED 1730–0630 every month as follows: Rwy 04R–22L first Tue; Rwy 08R–26L second Tue; and Rwy 08L–26R third Tue. Rwy 08R–26L 200′ pavement width with lgts outside, pavement striped 150′ wide. Thld of Rwy 08L difficult to determine due to Twy T. All jet acft ctc ramp control prior to engine start at gate or hard stand. Foreign object debris hazard exits on all movement areas east of Twy S. Fighter acft exercise extreme caution when taxiing. To minimize foreign object damage potential, all acft should use minimum thrust, especially outboard engines, when taxiing past the F–22 alert facility on Twy T. Twys G and L between Twy A and Inter–Island ramp clsd to wide–bodied and 4–engine turbo–jet acft under power without PPR from arpt ops manager 808–836–6428 Mon–Fri 1745–0230Z. Twy K not a high speed exit twy. Wide body and 4 engine turbojets ldg on Rwy 04R roll to end of rwy, no left turn at Twy K without approval. Tfc pattern overhead altitude 2000(1987), restricted to HIANG acft. Rwy 04R–22L and Rwy 08R–26L sfc grvd within 10′ of A–G system. Potential for fighter acft tail hook skip exists. Due to sensitivities of citizens, fighter acft and water–augmented acft dep only authorized from Mon–Sat 1700–0700Z, and Sun and holidays 1800–0700Z. All request for waivers will be sent to the 15/OG/CC at least 5 working days in advance. Waivers will be granted on extreme necessary. If short notice mission essential waivers are necessary, ctc 15OG/CC by phone thru 15 WG Comd Post (15 WG/CP). 15 WG Comd Post will pass approval to Hickam flight svc and Hickam ramp advisory. Tfc pattern altitude for small acft entering from NW 800(787). Tfc pattern altitude for small acft entering from S 1000(987). Tfc pattern altitude for large acft entering from S 1500(1487). No F–16 transient support avbl in accordance with Area Control Center LSET flash safety 06–02. Transient F–16 units should provide their own maintenance support. PPR all acft units planning to stage ops from Hickam AFB must ctc 15 OSS/OSX DSN 315–449–1596/1597 at least 60 days prior to arrival. All military acft rqr Customs/Agriculture/Immigration inspection must ctc 15 WG command post or if Air Mobility Command ctc Hickam AMCC, no later than 3 hrs prior to arrival with departure location estimated block time, number of aircrew, Civilian/Military Passengers/Foreign Nationals/and Distinguished Visitor codes. JBPH–H is PPR to all non–AMC acft and AMC trng msn (QEN, KEN, PEN, AEN, and ANC C130′s). All tran acft not on an AMC/TWCF msn and home stn acft terminating at JBPH–H, will provide a 3 hr out call (COMM 808–448–6900) as well as a 20–30 min out call on 292.5 to the 15 WG/CP (KOA CONTROL). All transient acft, not on an Air Mobility Command mission, will provide a 2–3 hr out call, as well as 20–30 minute out call on 292.5 to the 15 WG/CP (KOA Control). 15 WG can provide eqpt but crews must provide own pers when needed. Upon arrival, crews will proceed directly to Command Post (Bldg 2050) and complete an outbound setup sheet to facilitate departure requirements. No COMSEC material avbl thru Hickam Airfield Ops. Transient aircrews should plan to arrive with appropriate amount of COSMEC to complete entire mission. Arfld

CONTINUED ON NEXT PAGE

FIGURE 206.—Excerpt from Chart Supplement.

This page is intentionally left blank

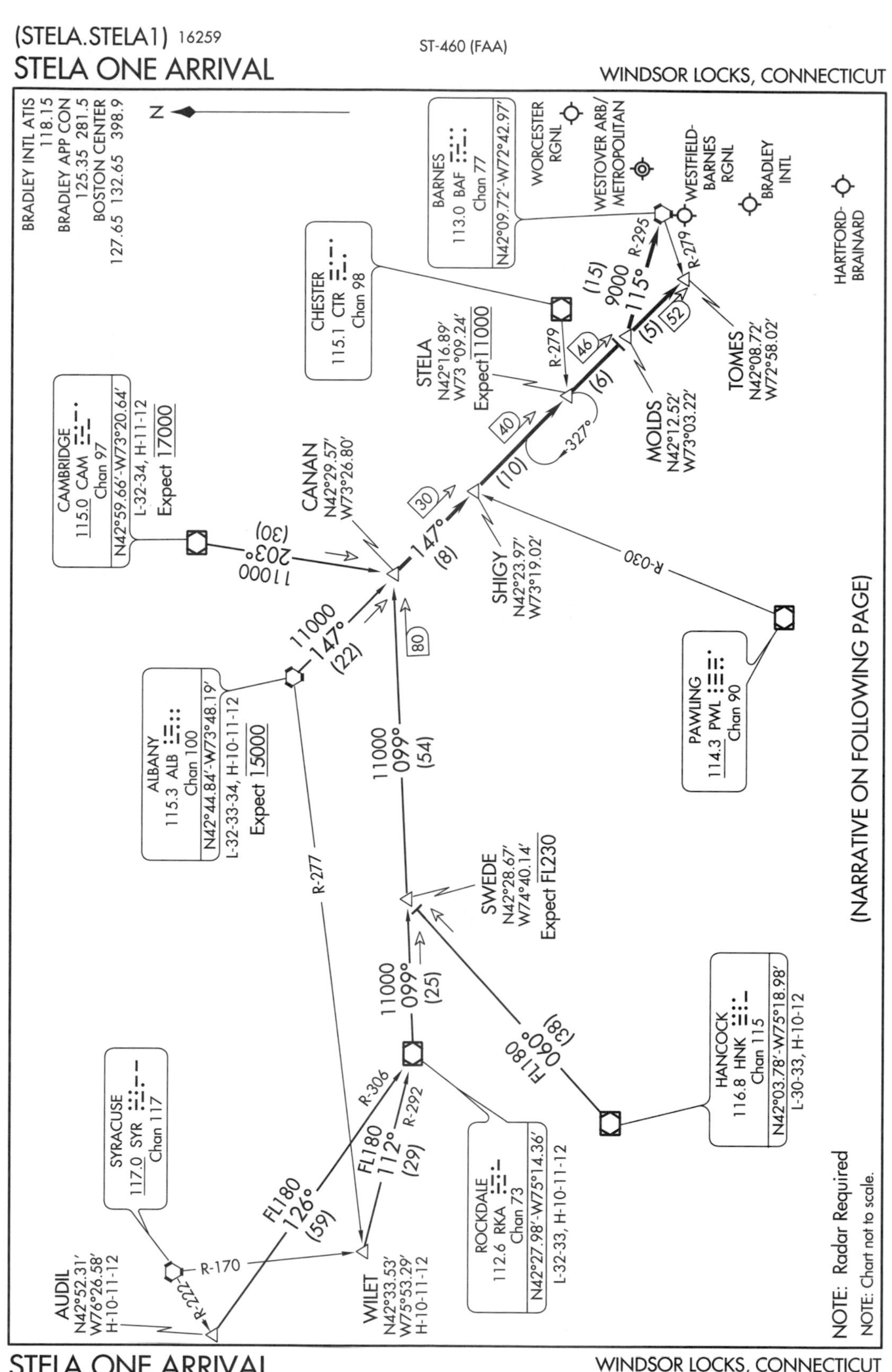

FIGURE 208.—STELA One Arrival (STELA.STELA1).

(STELA.STELA1) 16259 ST-460 (FAA)

STELA ONE ARRIVAL WINDSOR LOCKS, CONNECTICUT

ARRIVAL ROUTE DESCRIPTION

ALBANY TRANSITION (ALB.STELA1): From over ALB VORTAC via ALB R-147 to CANAN INT. Thence. . . .
AUDIL TRANSITION (AUDIL.STELA1): From over AUDIL INT via RKA R-306 to RKA VOR/DME, then via RKA R-099 to CANAN INT. Thence. . . .
CAMBRIDGE TRANSITION (CAM.STELA1): From over CAM VOR/DME via CAM R-203 to CANAN INT. Thence. . . .
HANCOCK TRANSITION (HNK.STELA1): From over HNK VOR/DME via HNK R-060 to SWEDE INT, then via RKA R-099 to CANAN INT. Thence. . . .
WILET TRANSITION (WILET.STELA1): From over WILET INT via RKA R-292 to RKA VOR/DME, then via RKA R-099 TO CANAN INT. Thence. . . .

KBDL and KHFD ARRIVALS: From over CANAN INT via ALB R-147 to TOMES INT. Expect radar vectors to final approach course prior to TOMES INT.

KBAF, KCEF and KORH ARRIVALS: From over CANAN INT via ALB R-147 to MOLDS INT. Then via BAF R-295 to BAF VORTAC. Expect radar vectors to final approach course prior to BAF VORTAC.

STELA ONE ARRIVAL WINDSOR LOCKS, CONNECTICUT
(STELA.STELA1) 31MAY12

FIGURE 209.—STELA One Arrival (STELA.STELA1).

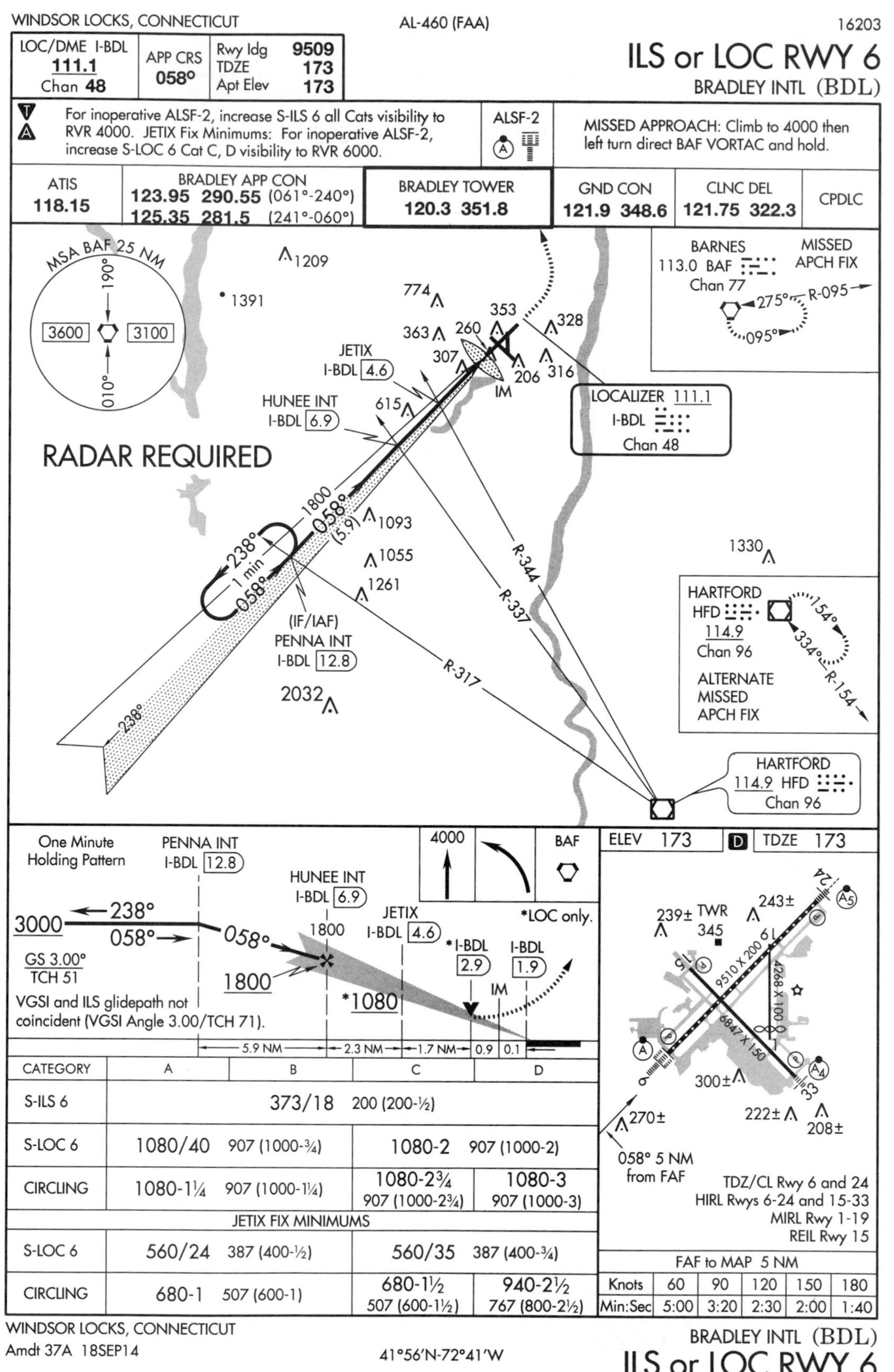

FIGURE 210.—ILS or LOC RWY 6 (CAT I) (BDL).

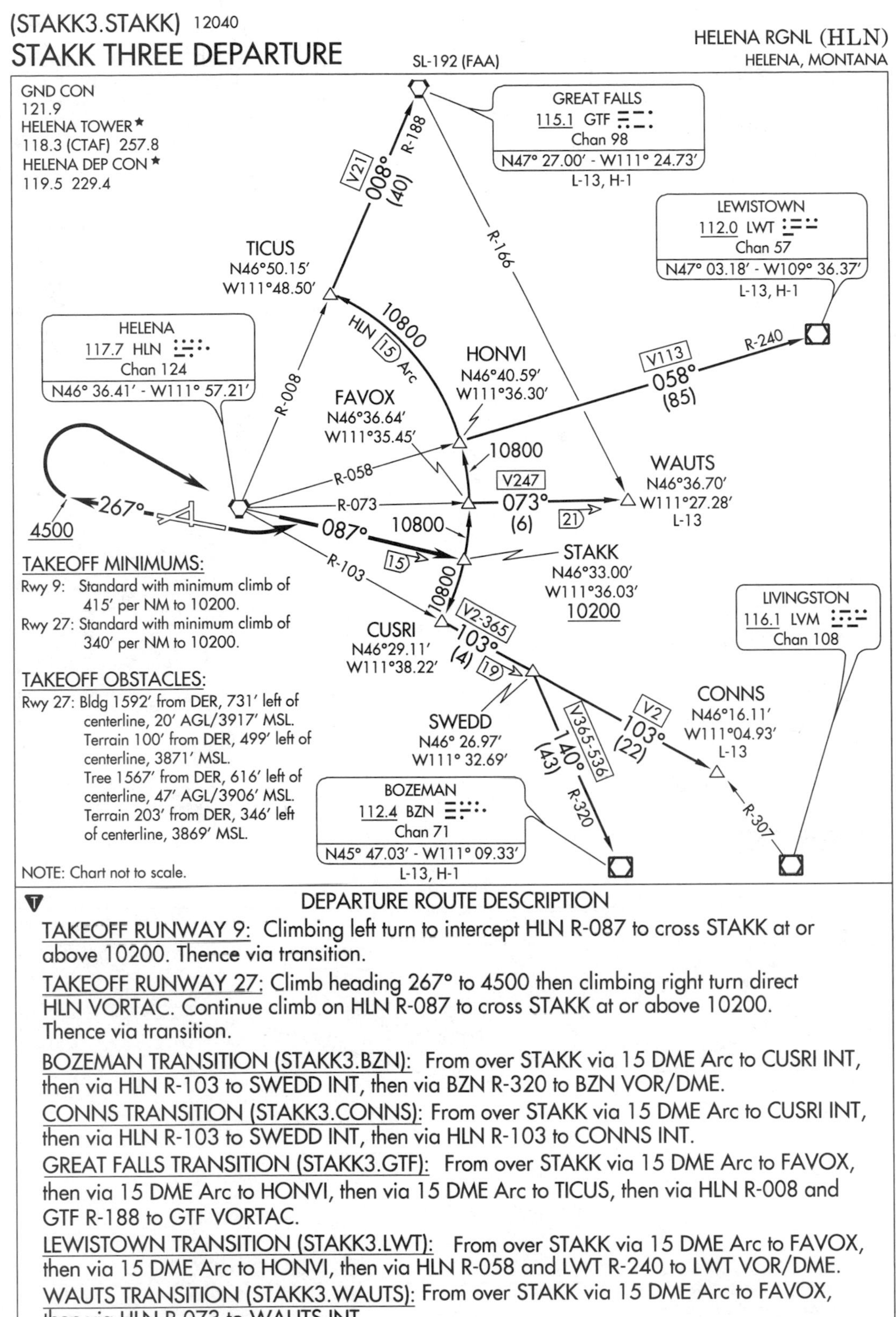

FIGURE 211.—STAKK Three Departure (STAKK3.STAKK) (HLN).

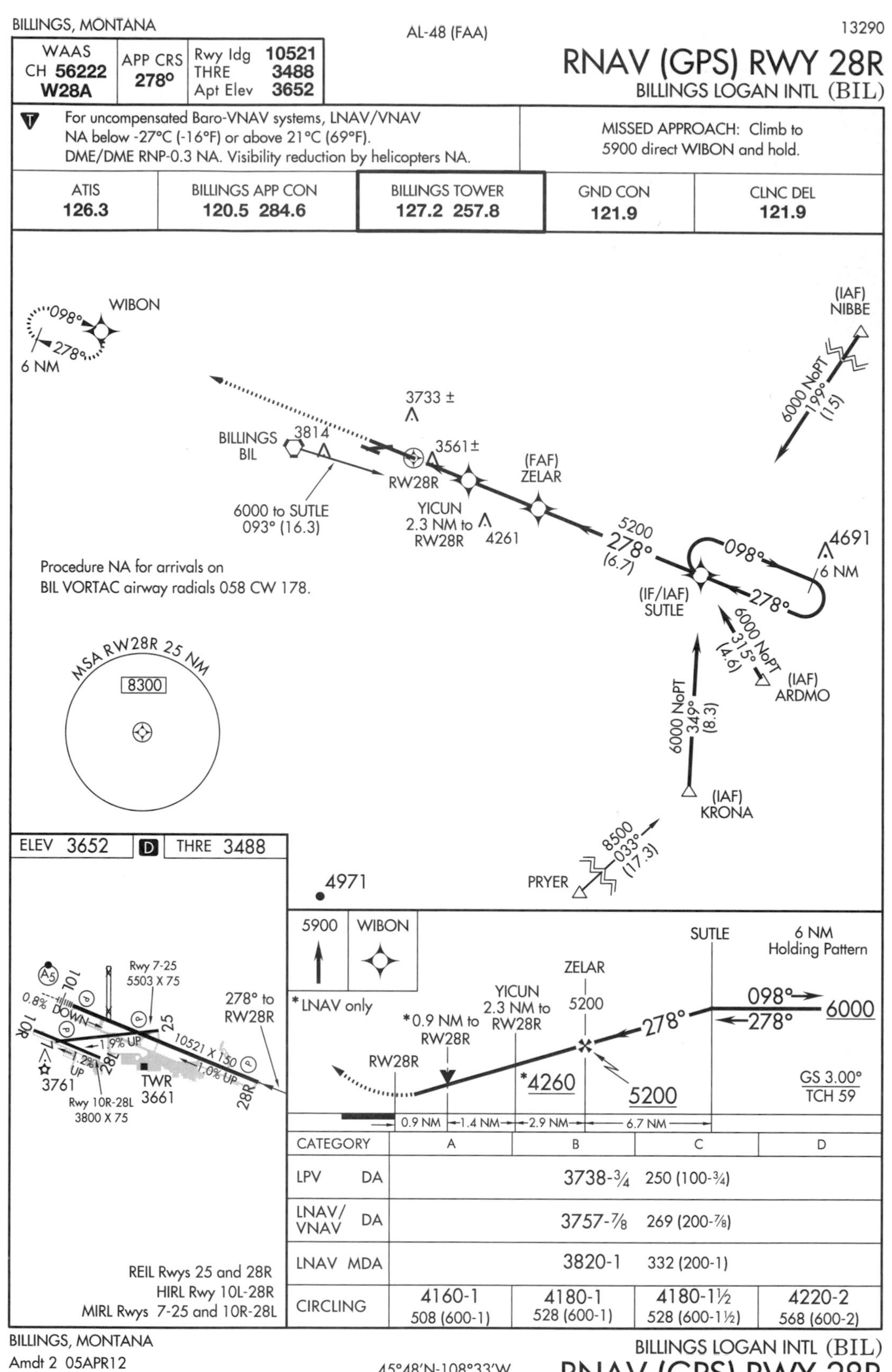

CATEGORY	A	B	C	D
LPV DA	3738-¾ 250 (100-¾)			
LNAV/VNAV DA	3757-⅞ 269 (200-⅞)			
LNAV MDA	3820-1 332 (200-1)			
CIRCLING	4160-1 508 (600-1)	4180-1 528 (600-1)	4180-1½ 528 (600-1½)	4220-2 568 (600-2)

BILLINGS, MONTANA
Amdt 2 05APR12
45°48′N-108°33′W
BILLINGS LOGAN INTL (BIL)
RNAV (GPS) RWY 28R

FIGURE 212.—RNAV (GPS) RWY 28R (BIL).

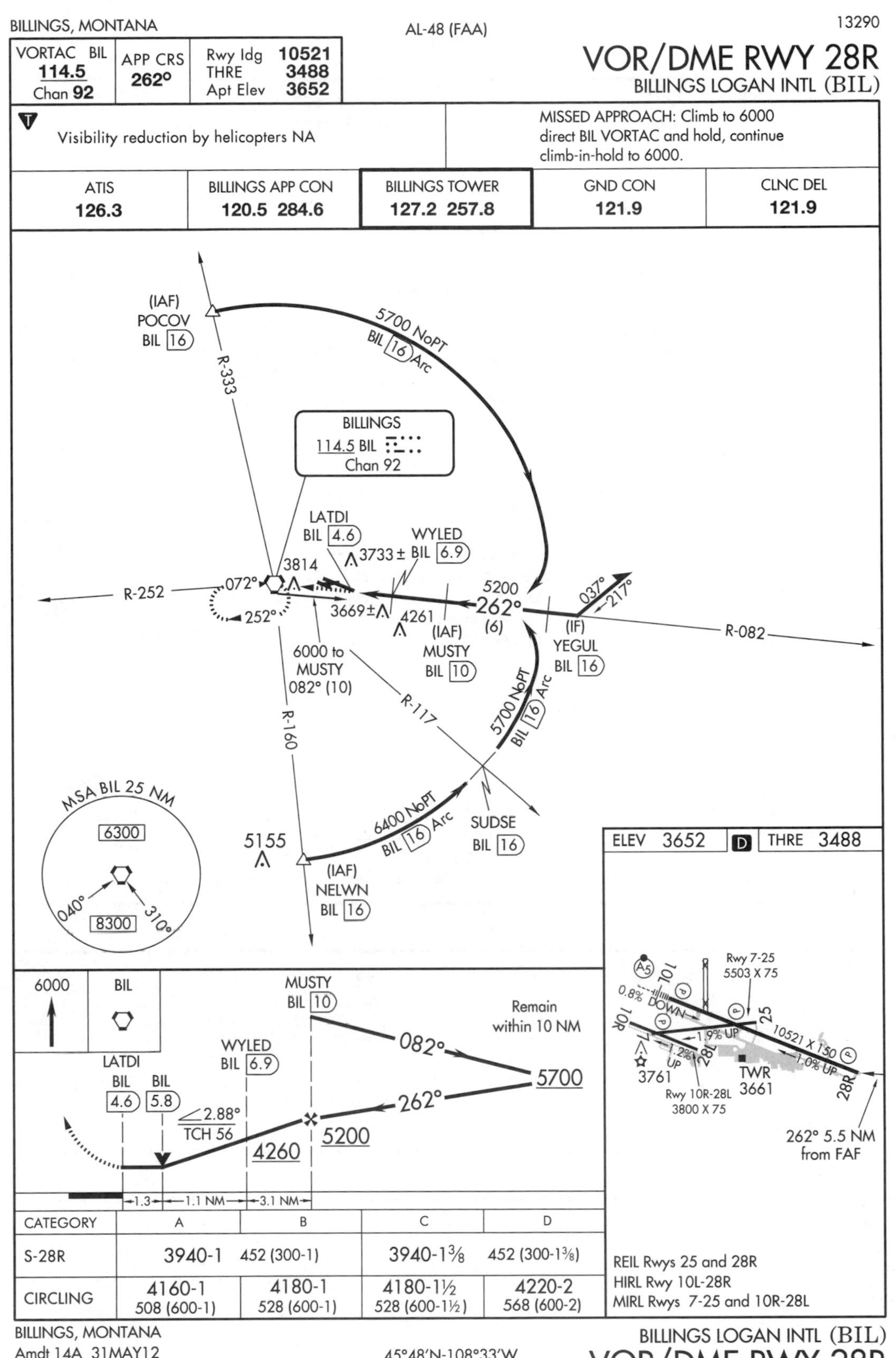

CATEGORY	A	B	C	D
S-28R	3940-1	452 (300-1)	3940-1⅜	452 (300-1⅜)
CIRCLING	4160-1 508 (600-1)	4180-1 528 (600-1)	4180-1½ 528 (600-1½)	4220-2 568 (600-2)

FIGURE 213.—VOR/DME RWY 28R (BIL).

BILLINGS LOGAN INTL (BIL) 2 NW UTC–7(–6DT) N45°48.46´ W108°32.57´ **BILLINGS**
3652 B S4 **FUEL** 100LL, JET A OX 1, 2, 3, 4 ARFF Index—See Remarks NOTAM FILE BIL **H–1E, L–13D**
RWY 10L–28R: H10521X150 (ASPH–GRVD) S–130, D–170, 2S–175, 2D–285 HIRL **IAP, AD** 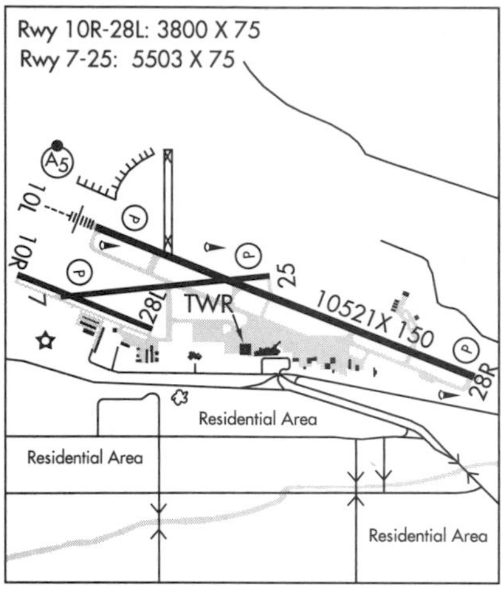
RWY 10L: MALSR. PAPI(P4L)—GA 3.0° TCH 51´. 0.8% down.
RWY 28R: REIL. PAPI(P4R)—GA 3.0° TCH 56´. Ground. 1.0% up.
RWY 07–25: H5503X75 (ASPH–GRVD) S–12.5 MIRL 1.9% up SW
RWY 07: PAPI(P4L)—GA 3.0° TCH 31´. Ground.
RWY 25: REIL. PAPI(P4R)—GA 3.0° TCH 36´.
RWY 10R–28L: H3800X75 (ASPH) S–12.5 MIRL 1.2% up NW
RWY 10R: Ground.

RUNWAY DECLARED DISTANCE INFORMATION
RWY 07: TORA–5503 TODA–5503 ASDA–5503 LDA–5503
RWY 10L: TORA–10521 TODA–10521 ASDA–10521 LDA–10521
RWY 10R: TORA–3800 TODA–3800 ASDA–3800 LDA–3800
RWY 25: TORA–5503 TODA–5503 ASDA–5503 LDA–5503
RWY 28L: TORA–3800 TODA–3800 ASDA–3800 LDA–3800
RWY 28R: TORA–10521 TODA–10521 ASDA–10521 LDA–10521

AIRPORT REMARKS: Attended continuously. Rwy 07–25 and Rwy 10R–28L CLOSED to acft over 12,500 lbs. No customs, remote acft parking, ltd ground handling svc. Migratory waterfowl invof arpt. Twy D 35´ wide clsd to acft over 12,500 lbs. Class I, ARFF Index C. PPR unscheduled air carrier ops with more than 30 passenger seats ctc arpt ops 406–657–8496. ARFF Index B from 0900–1300Z‡. 180° turns Rwy 10L–28R by acft over 25,000 lbs prohibited. For MIRL Rwy 10R–28L and Rwy 07–25, HIRL Rwy 10L–28R, MALSR Rwy 10L and REIL Rwy 25 and Rwy 28R ctc twr.
WEATHER DATA SOURCES: ASOS (406) 248–2773 LLWAS.
COMMUNICATIONS: ATIS 126.3 **UNICOM** 122.95
RCO 122.55 (GREAT FALLS RADIO)
Ⓡ **APP/DEP CON** 119.2 (EAST) 120.5 (WEST)
TOWER 127.2 **GND CON** 121.9 **CLNC DEL** 121.9
PRE TAXI CLNC 121.9
AIRSPACE: CLASS C svc ctc **APP CON**
RADIO AIDS TO NAVIGATION: NOTAM FILE BIL.
(H) VORTACW 114.5 BIL Chan 92 N45°48.51´ W108°37.48´ 077° 3.4 NM to fld. 3811/14E.
SAIGE NDB (LOM) 251 BI N45°51.13´ W108°41.67´ 099° 6.9 NM to fld.
ILS 110.3 I–BIL Rwy 10L. Class IB. LOM SAIGE NDB.
ILS/DME 111.5 I–BMO Chan 52 Rwy 28R. Class IA. Localizer unusable beyond 20° left and right of course.

BLACK BUTTE NORTH (See WINIFRED on page 106)

BOULDER (3U9) 2 S UTC–7(–6DT) N46°12.70´ W112°06.46´ **GREAT FALLS**
4968 NOTAM FILE GTF
RWY 11–29: 3675X72 (TURF) 1.6% up W
RWY 11: Hill.
RWY 29: Road.
AIRPORT REMARKS: Unattended. No snow removal. Rwy 11–29 thlds marked with faded red cones, edges marked with white cones. –2´ drainage ditch +1´ berm W side of rwy full length, 43´ from Rwy 11–29 centerline.
COMMUNICATIONS: CTAF 122.9

BOWMAN FLD (See ANACONDA on page 62)

FIGURE 214.—Excerpt from Chart Supplement.

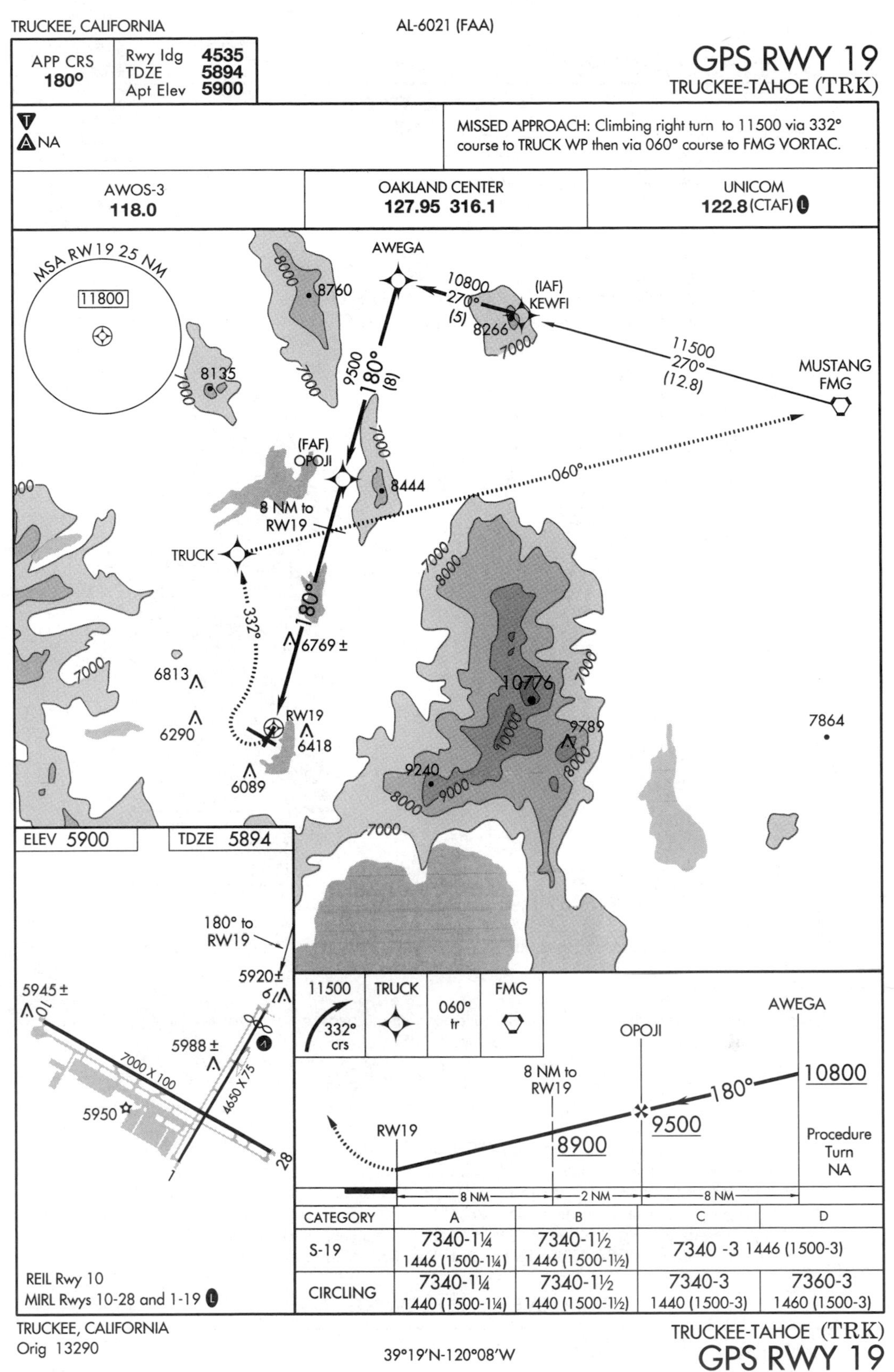

CATEGORY	A	B	C	D
S-19	7340-1¼ 1446 (1500-1¼)	7340-1½ 1446 (1500-1½)	7340 -3 1446 (1500-3)	
CIRCLING	7340-1¼ 1440 (1500-1¼)	7340-1½ 1440 (1500-1½)	7340-3 1440 (1500-3)	7360-3 1460 (1500-3)

FIGURE 215.—GPS RWY 19 (TRK).

(RENO9.FMG) 16035

RENO NINE DEPARTURE

SL-346 (FAA)

RENO/TAHOE INTL (RNO)
RENO, NEVADA

TOP ALTITUDE: FL190

ATIS 135.8 363.0
CLNC DEL 124.9 370.85
GND CON 121.9 348.6
RENO TOWER 118.7 257.8

TAKEOFF MINIMUMS

Rwy 7: NA- Obstacles.
Rwy 16L: Standard with minimum climb of 730′ per NM to 10900, or 600-1¼ with minimum climb of 352′ per NM to 10900.
Rwy 16R: Standard with minimum climb of 460′ per NM to 10900, or 300-1 with minimum climb of 395′ per NM to 10900.
Rwy 25: Standard with minimum climb of 500′ per NM to 9700.
Rwys 34L/R: Standard with mimimum climb of 480′ per NM to 8700, or 500-1½ with minimum climb of 430′ per NM to 8700.

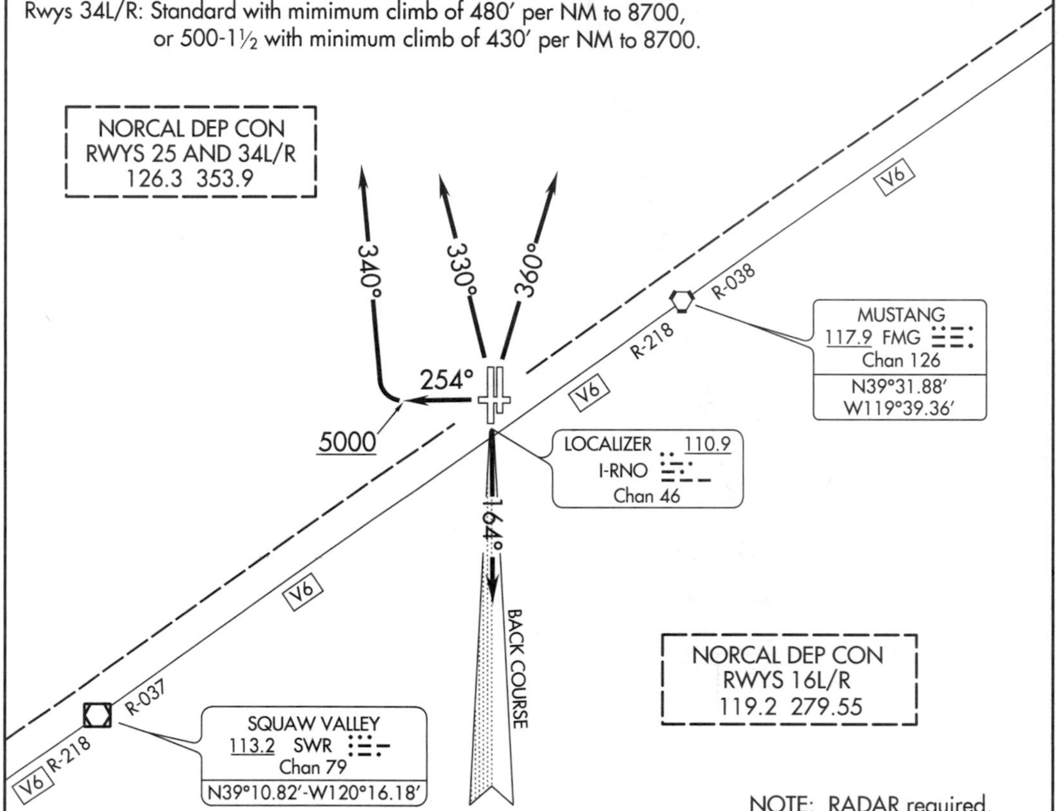

NOTE: RADAR required.

TAKEOFF OBSTACLE NOTES

Rwy 16L: Multiple poles, trees, bushes, terrain and buildings with antennas and cameras beginning 618′ from DER, 131′ left of centerline, up to 20′ AGL/4959′ MSL.
Rwy 16R: Multiple trees beginning 2784′ from DER, 171′ right of centerline, 20′ AGL/4510′ MSL.
Multiple trees and terrain beginning 746′ from DER, 380′ left of centerline, up to 20′ AGL/4723′ MSL.
Rwy 25: Multiple trees, poles, fence, and vent on building beginning 222′ from DER, 201′ right of centerline, up to 103′ AGL/4608′ MSL.
Multiple trees, poles and sign beginning 500′ from DER, 31′ left of centerline, up to 20′ AGL/4506′ MSL.
Rwy 34L: Multiple trees and pole beginning 1229′ from DER, 180′ right of centerline, up to 20′ AGL/4498′ MSL.
Multiple trees beginning 1193′ from DER, 331′ left of centerline, up to 20′ AGL/4489′ MSL.
Rwy 34R: Multiple trees and poles beginning 1067′ from DER, 172′ right of centerline, up to 20′ AGL/4497′ MSL.
Multiple trees beginning 1230′ from DER, 350′ left of centerline, up to 20′ AGL/4498′ MSL.
Building 1.2 NM from DER, 1730′ right of centerline, 363′ AGL/4780′ MSL.

(NARRATIVE ON FOLLOWING PAGE)

NOTE: Chart not to scale.

RENO NINE DEPARTURE
(RENO9.FMG) 04FEB16

RENO, NEVADA
RENO/TAHOE INTL (RNO)

FIGURE 216.—RENO Nine Departure (RENO9.FMG) (RNO).

(RENO9.FMG) 16035

RENO/TAHOE INTL (RNO)
RENO, NEVADA

RENO NINE DEPARTURE

SL-346 (FAA)

DEPARTURE ROUTE DESCRIPTION

TAKEOFF RUNWAYS 16L/R: Climb on heading 164° and I-RNO localizer south course. Thence. . . .

TAKEOFF RUNWAY 25: Climb heading 254° to 5000 then climbing right turn heading 340°. Thence. . . .

TAKEOFF RUNWAYS 34L/R: Climb heading 330° CW 360° as assigned by ATC. Thence. . . .

. . . .All aircraft maintain FL190 or assigned altitude. Expect clearance to requested altitude 5 minutes after departure. Expect RADAR vectors to assigned route/fix.

LOST COMMUNICATIONS: If not in contact with departure control within one minute after takeoff, maintain assigned heading until passing 10000, thence. . . .

. . . .RUNWAYS 16L/R DEPARTURES: Turn left direct FMG VORTAC, then via assigned route.

. . . .RUNWAYS 25 and 34L/R DEPARTURES: Turn right direct FMG VORTAC, then via assigned route.

RENO NINE DEPARTURE
(RENO9.FMG) 04FEB16

RENO, NEVADA
RENO/TAHOE INTL (RNO)

FIGURE 216A.—RENO Nine Departure (RENO9.FMG) (RNO).

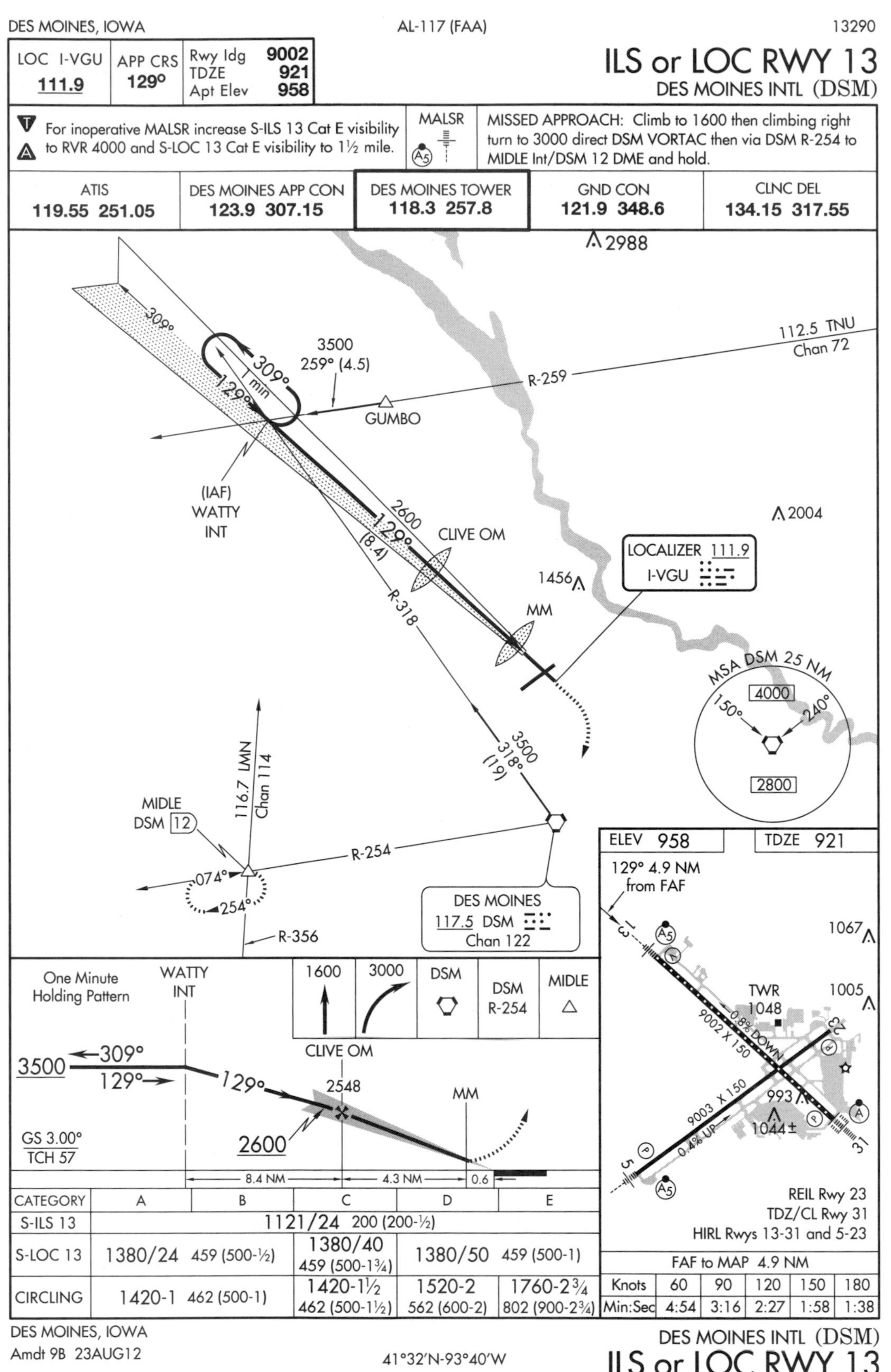

FIGURE 217.—ILS or LOC RWY 13 (DSM).

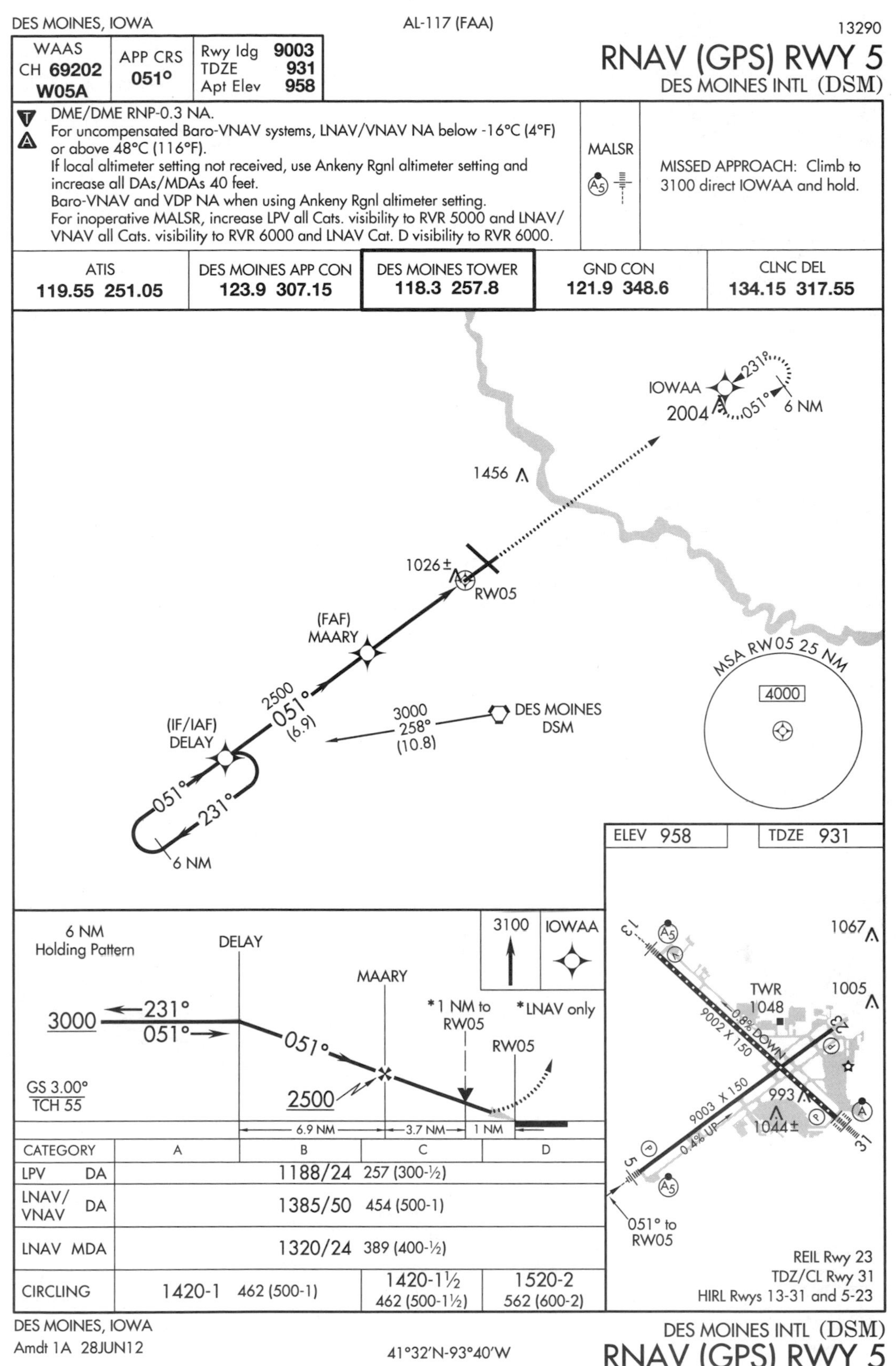

FIGURE 218.—RNAV (GPS) RWY 5 (DSM).

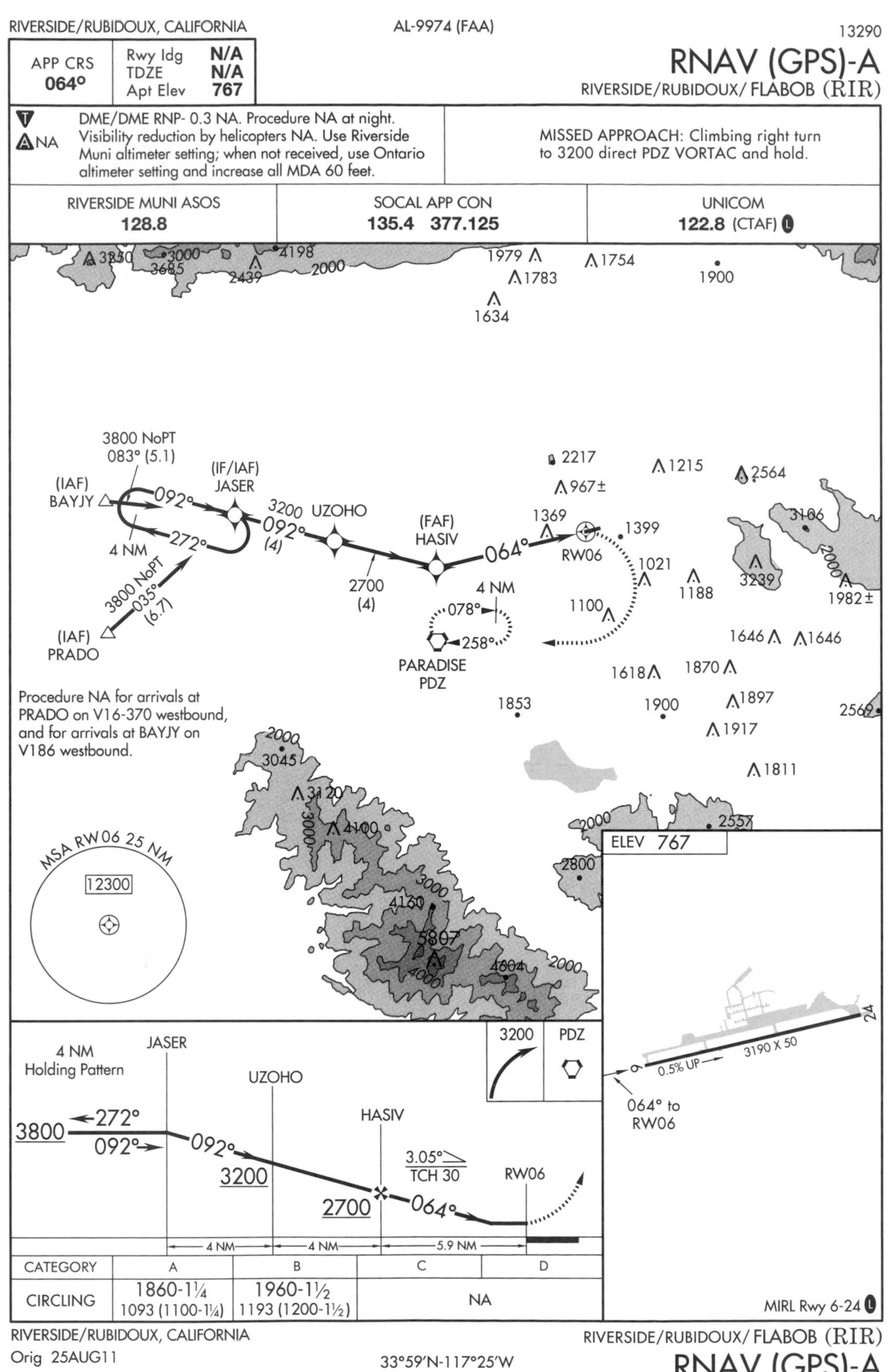

CATEGORY	A	B	C	D
CIRCLING	1860-1¼ 1093 (1100-1¼)	1960-1½ 1193 (1200-1½)	NA	

FIGURE 219.—RNAV (GPS)-A (RIR).

L11

TAKEOFF MINIMUMS AND (OBSTACLE) DEPARTURE PROCEDURES

13234

RIVERSIDE/RUBIDOUX, CA

FLABOB (RIR)

ORIG 11181 (FAA)

TAKEOFF MINIMUMS: **Rwy 6,** std. w/min. climb of 670' per NM to 4000 or 400-2 w/min. climb of 480' per NM to 4000 or 2100-3 for climb in visual conditions. **Rwy 24,** std. w/min. climb of 630' per NM to 3000 or 800-2¾ w/min. climb of 305' per NM to 4600 or 2100-3 for climb in visual conditions.

DEPARTURE PROCEDURE: **Rwy 6,** climb via heading 064° to 4000 then right turn direct PDZ VORTAC, or for climb in visual conditions cross Flabob Airport Southwest bound at or above 2700 then via PDZ R-039 to PDZ VORTAC. **Rwy 24,** climb via heading 244° and PDZ R-031 to PDZ VORTAC, or for climb in visual conditions cross Flabob airport Southwest bound at or above 2700 then via PDZ R-039 to PDZ VORTAC.

All aircraft climb in PDZ VORTAC holding pattern (hold East, right turns, 258° inbound) to cross PDZ VORTAC at or above MEA for direction of flight before proceeding on course.

NOTE: **Rwy 6,** trees beginning 3763' from DER, 1152' right of centerline, up to 40' AGL/1119' MSL. **Rwy 24,** antenna on tank 6193' from DER, 2057' right of centerline, 38' AGL/1237' MSL. Trees beginning 2494' from DER, 434' right of centerline, up to 40' AGL/1519' MSL. Pole 6261' from DER, 1950' right of centerline, 30' AGL/1230' MSL. Building 1.52 NM from DER, 1154' right of centerline, up to 29' AGL/1369' MSL. Antenna on tank 1.26 NM from DER, 2047' right of centerline, 54' AGL/1254' MSL. Tank 4043' from DER, 794' right of centerline, 66' AGL/961' MSL. Tree 1.79 NM from DER, 434' right of centerline, 58' AGL/1138' MSL.

SAN BERNARDINO, CA

SAN BERNARDINO INTL (SBD)

ORIG 93343 (FAA)

TAKEOFF MINIMUMS: **Rwy 6,** CAT A,B 2100-2 or std. with a min. climb of 340' per NM to 3700. CAT C,D 3100-2 or std. with a min. climb of 480' per NM to 4600.

DEPARTURE PROCEDURE: **Rwy 6,** climbing right turn. **Rwy 24,** climbing left turn. **All aircraft** climb direct PDZ VORTAC. Aircraft departing PDZ R-091 CW R-140 and R-231 CW R-280 climb on course. All others continue climb in PDZ holding pattern (Hold NE, right turns, 210° inbound) to cross PDZ VORTAC at or above: R-281 CW R-090, 7700; R-141 CW R-230, 4900.

SAN CLEMENTE ISLAND NALF (FREDERICK SHERMAN FLD)(KNUC)

SAN CLEMENTE ISLAND, CA 12208

Rwy 5: Diverse departures authorized 090° to 233° CCW.

Rwy 23: Diverse departures authorized 160° to 053° CW.

TAKE-OFF OBSTACLES: **Rwy 5,** Pylon 198' MSL, 44' from DER, 274' left of centerline. Terrain 192' MSL, 50' from DER, 500' right of centerline. Terrain 194' MSL, 264' from DER, 509' right of centerline. Terrain 209' MSL, 824' from DER, 721' right of centerline. Terrain 199' MSL, 957' from DER, 612' right of centerline.

SAN DIEGO, CA

BROWN FIELD MUNI (SDM)

AMDT 4 10154(FAA)

TAKEOFF MINIMUMS: **Rwy 8L,** std. w/ min. climb of 570' per NM to 3100. **Rwys 8R,26L,** NA - ATC.

DEPARTURE PROCEDURE: **Rwy 8L,** climbing left turn, thence...**Rwy 26R,** climbing right turn, thence...

...via heading 280° to intercept MZB R-160 to MZB VORTAC.

NOTE: **Rwy 26R,** tree 1284' from DER, 778' left of centerline, 52' AGL/561' MSL.

MONTGOMERY FIELD (MYF)

AMDT 3A 10210 (FAA)

TAKEOFF MINIMUMS: **Rwy 5,** 1500-2 or std. with a min. climb of 290' per NM to 1700.

DEPARTURE PROCEDURE: **Rwys 5, 10L/R,** climbing right turn. **Rwys 28L/R,** climbing left turn. **All aircraft** climb direct to MZB VORTAC. Aircraft departing MZB R-090 CW R-360 climb on course. All others climb in MZB holding pattern (W, right turns, 075° inbound) to cross MZB VORTAC at or above 1800.

NOTE: **Rwy 5,** trees and bushes beginning 244' from DER, 161' left of centerline, up to 99' AGL/524' MSL. Tree 1287' from DER, 103' right of centerline, up to 49' AGL/474' MSL. **Rwy 23,** tree, flag pole, and transmission towers beginning 1594' from DER, 82' right of centerline, up to 125' AGL/545' MSL. Transmission towers beginning 2627' from DER, 414' left of centerline up to 125' AGL/524' MSL. **Rwy 10L,** trees beginning 230' from DER, 494' left of centerline, up to 57' AGL/486' MSL. Trees beginning 1172' from DER, 591' right of centerline, up to 69' AGL/488' MSL. **Rwy 10R,** rod on electrical equipment 40' from DER, 66' left of centerline, 7' AGL/426' MSL. Trees beginning 2107' from DER, 199' right of centerline, up to 69' AGL/488' MSL. **Rwy 28L,** bushes and poles beginning 35' from DER, 160' right of centerline, up to 37' AGL/451' MSL. Trees beginning 1008' from DER, 7' left of centerline, up to 37' AGL/451' MSL.**Rwy 28R,** bushes, trees, and poles beginning 34' from DER, 162' left of centerline, up to 38' AGL/451' MSL. Trees, signs, and poles beginning 768' from DER, 98' right of centerline, up to 67' AGL/488' MSL.

13234

TAKEOFF MINIMUMS AND (OBSTACLE) DEPARTURE PROCEDURES

FIGURE 220.—Takeoff Minimums and (Obstacle) Departure Procedures.

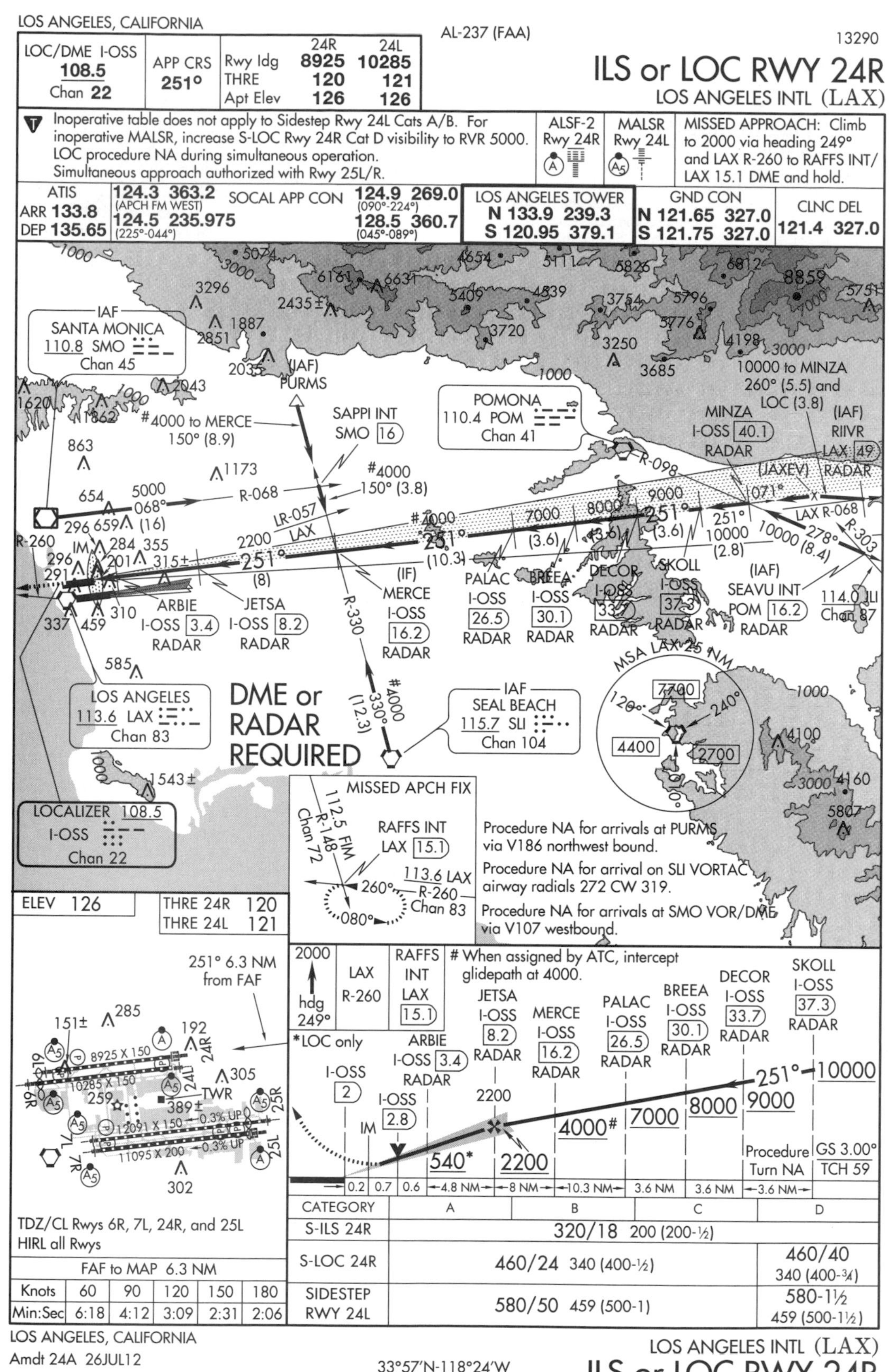

FAF to MAP 6.3 NM					
Knots	60	90	120	150	180
Min:Sec	6:18	4:12	3:09	2:31	2:06

CATEGORY	A	B	C	D
S-ILS 24R	320/18 200 (200-½)			
S-LOC 24R	460/24 340 (400-½)			460/40 340 (400-¾)
SIDESTEP RWY 24L	580/50 459 (500-1)			580-1½ 459 (500-1½)

FIGURE 221.—ILS or LOC RWY 24R (LAX).

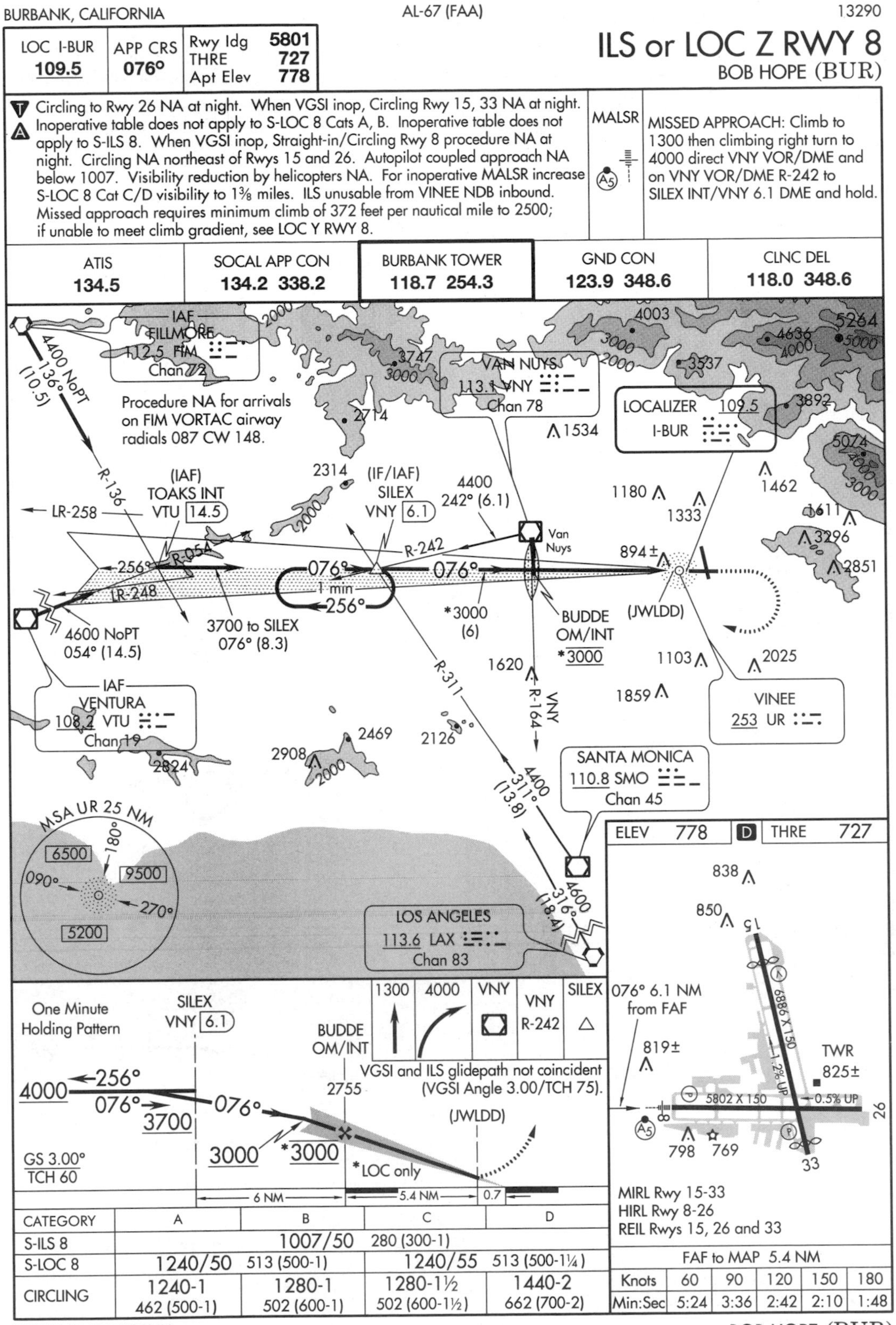
BURBANK, CALIFORNIA
AL-67 (FAA)
13290
LOC I-BUR 109.5
APP CRS 076°
Rwy ldg 5801
THRE 727
Apt Elev 778
ILS or LOC Z RWY 8
BOB HOPE (BUR)
Circling to Rwy 26 NA at night. When VGSI inop, Circling Rwy 15, 33 NA at night. Inoperative table does not apply to S-LOC 8 Cats A, B. Inoperative table does not apply to S-ILS 8. When VGSI inop, Straight-in/Circling Rwy 8 procedure NA at night. Circling NA northeast of Rwys 15 and 26. Autopilot coupled approach NA below 1007. Visibility reduction by helicopters NA. For inoperative MALSR increase S-LOC 8 Cat C/D visibility to 1⅜ miles. ILS unusable from VINEE NDB inbound. Missed approach requires minimum climb of 372 feet per nautical mile to 2500; if unable to meet climb gradient, see LOC Y RWY 8.
MALSR
MISSED APPROACH: Climb to 1300 then climbing right turn to 4000 direct VNY VOR/DME and on VNY VOR/DME R-242 to SILEX INT/VNY 6.1 DME and hold.
ATIS 134.5
SOCAL APP CON 134.2 338.2
BURBANK TOWER 118.7 254.3
GND CON 123.9 348.6
CLNC DEL 118.0 348.6
IAF FILLMORE 112.5 FIM Chan 72
Procedure NA for arrivals on FIM VORTAC airway radials 087 CW 148.
4400 NoPT 136° (10.5)
VAN NUYS 113.1 VNY Chan 78
LOCALIZER 109.5 I-BUR
(IAF) TOAKS INT VTU 14.5
(IF/IAF) SILEX VNY 6.1
4400 242° (6.1)
LR-258
R-136
R-242
R-054
R-248
076°
256°
1 min
3700 to SILEX 076° (8.3)
4600 NoPT 054° (14.5)
*3000 (6)
BUDDE OM/INT *3000
(JWLDD)
Van Nuys
R-311
R-164
IAF VENTURA 108.2 VTU Chan 19
VINEE 253 UR
SANTA MONICA 110.8 SMO Chan 45
4400 311° (13.8)
4600 316° (18.4)
LOS ANGELES 113.6 LAX Chan 83
MSA UR 25 NM
6500
9500
5200
180°
090°
270°
ELEV 778
THRE 727
838
850
076° 6.1 NM from FAF
819±
TWR 825±
5802 X 150
6886 X 150
1.2% UP
0.5% UP
798
769
15
33
26
MIRL Rwy 15-33
HIRL Rwy 8-26
REIL Rwys 15, 26 and 33
One Minute Holding Pattern
SILEX VNY 6.1
BUDDE OM/INT
1300
4000
VNY
VNY R-242
SILEX
VGSI and ILS glidepath not coincident (VGSI Angle 3.00/TCH 75).
4000
256°
076°
3700
2755
3000
*3000
*LOC only
(JWLDD)
GS 3.00° TCH 60
6 NM
5.4 NM
0.7

CATEGORY	A	B	C	D
S-ILS 8	1007/50 280 (300-1)			
S-LOC 8	1240/50 513 (500-1)		1240/55 513 (500-1¼)	
CIRCLING	1240-1 462 (500-1)	1280-1 502 (600-1)	1280-1½ 502 (600-1½)	1440-2 662 (700-2)

FAF to MAP 5.4 NM					
Knots	60	90	120	150	180
Min:Sec	5:24	3:36	2:42	2:10	1:48

BURBANK, CALIFORNIA
Amdt 37 05APR12
34°12′N-118°22′W
BOB HOPE (BUR)
ILS or LOC Z RWY 8

FIGURE 222.—ILS or LOC Z RWY 8 (BUR).

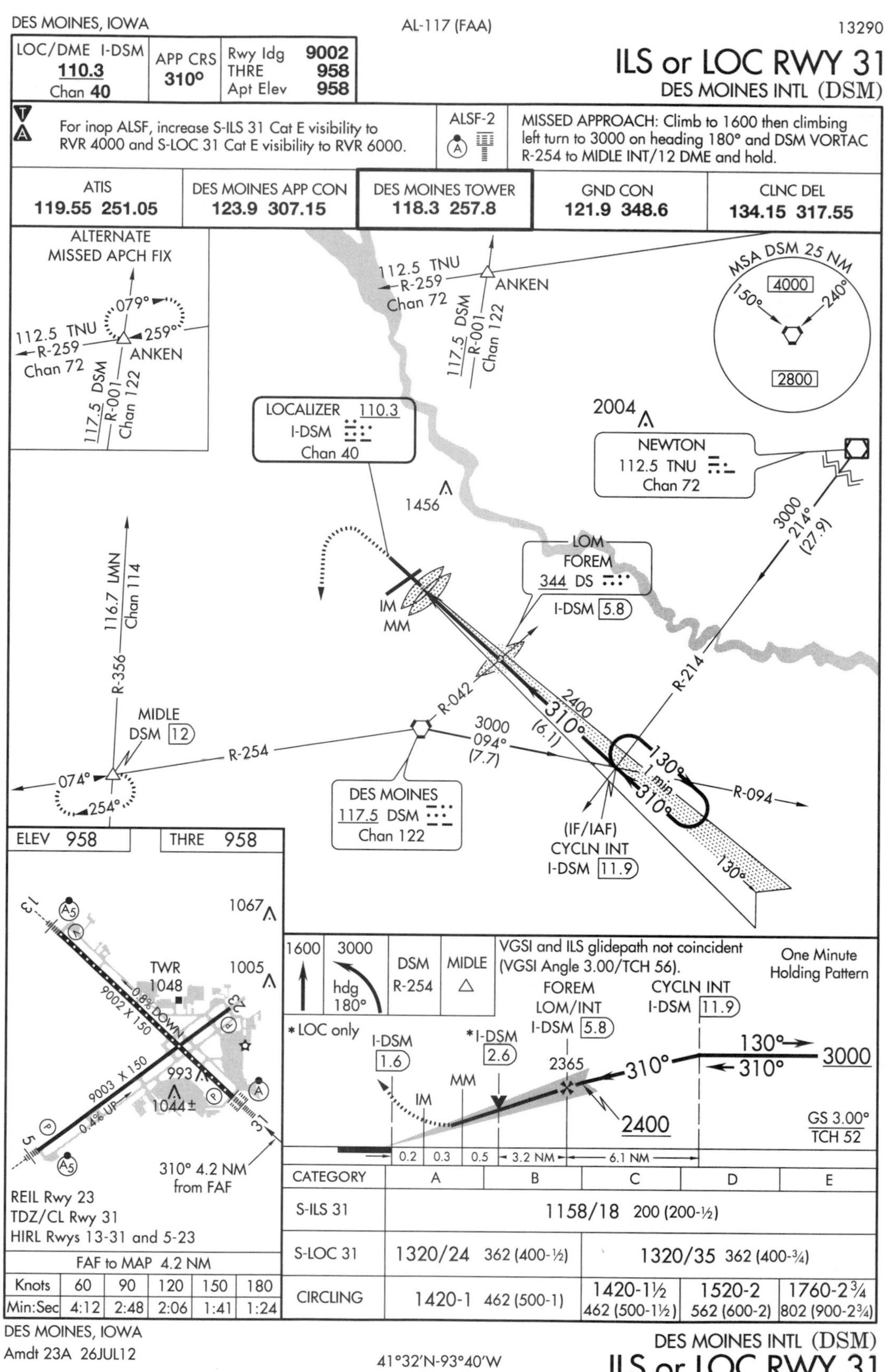

FIGURE 223.—ILS or LOC RWY 31 (DSM).

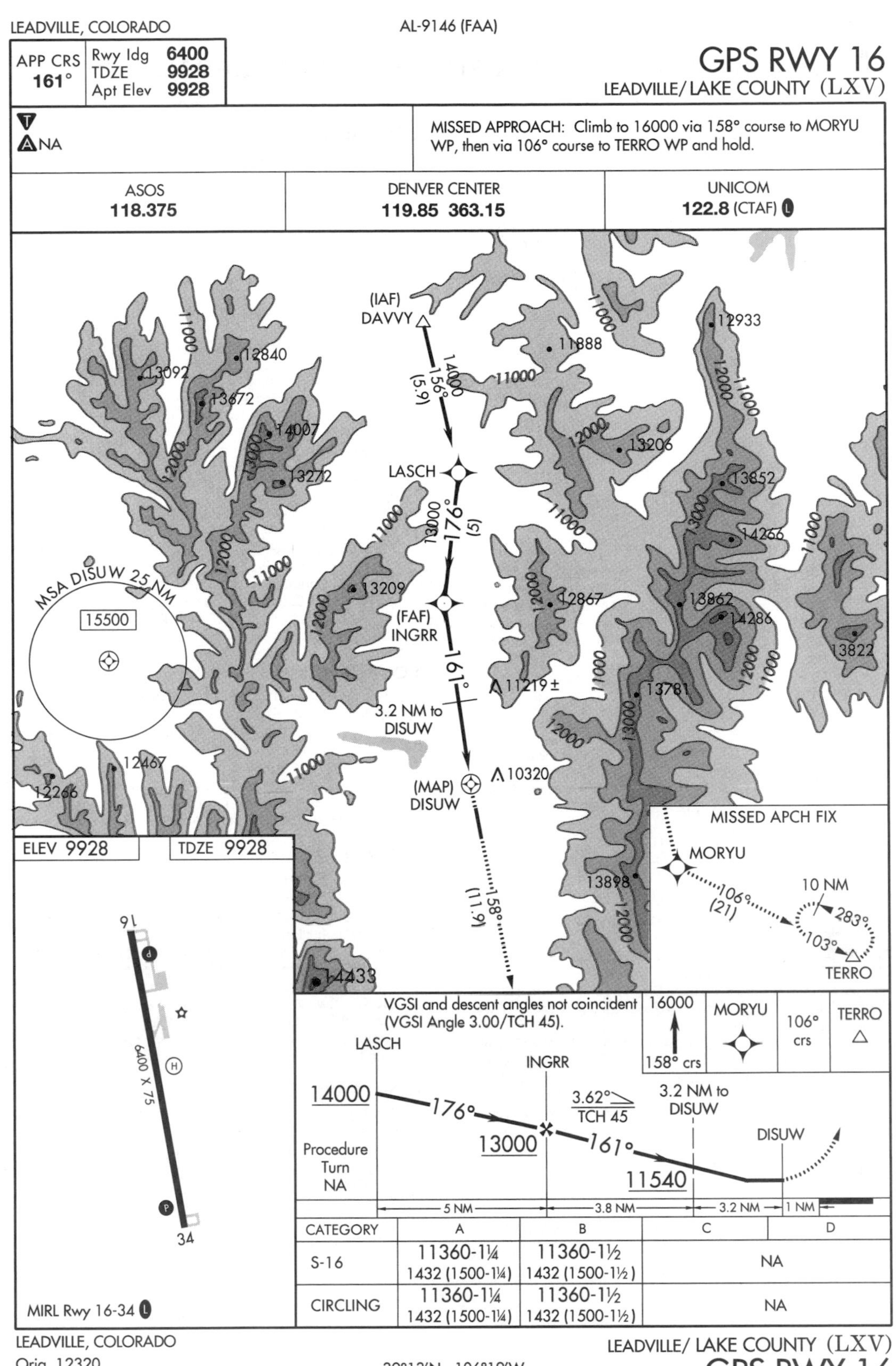

FIGURE 224.—GPS RWY 16 (LXV).

L8

TAKEOFF MINIMUMS AND (OBSTACLE) DEPARTURE PROCEDURES

13262

KREMMLING, CO
MC ELROY AIRFIELD (20V)

TAKEOFF MINIMUMS: **Rwy 9,** 2600-2 or std. with a min. climb of 370' per NM to 12700. **Rwy 27,** 3200-2 or std. with a min. climb of 500' per NM to 12700.

DEPARTURE PROCEDURE: **Rwy 9,** climb runway heading to 10000, then climbing right turn. **Rwy 27,** climb runway heading to 10900, then climbing left turn. **All aircraft** proceed direct RLG VOR/DME. Continue climb to 13,000 in RLG holding pattern (hold SW, left turns, 051° inbound).

LA JUNTA, CO
LA JUNTA MUNI (LHX)
AMDT 3 03191 (FAA)

DEPARTURE PROCEDURE: **Rwy 8,** climb via heading 080°. **Rwy 12,** climb via heading 120°. **Rwy 26,** turn left heading 160°. **Rwy 30,** turn left heading 140°. **All aircraft,** intercept LAA R-238 (V210) to LAA VOR/DME. When at or above 8000 proceed on course.

LAMAR, CO
LAMAR MUNI (LAA)

DEPARTURE PROCEDURE: **Rwys 8,36,** turn left. **Rwy 18,** turn left/right. **Rwy 26,** turn right. Direct LAA VOR/DME. Aircraft departing LAA R-048 CW R-118 climb on course. All others continue climbing in LAA holding pattern (N, right turns, 169° inbound) to 6000 before proceeding on course.

LAS CRUCES, NM
LAS CRUCES INTL (LRU)
AMDT 1 96340 (FAA)

DEPARTURE PROCEDURE: **Rwys 4, 8,** climbing right turn. **Rwy 12,** CAT A,B, climb runway heading CAT C,D, NA. **Rwys 22, 26,** climbing left turn. **Rwy 30,** climbing runway heading to 5100 then climbing left turn.

All aircraft climb direct HAWKE LOM. Continue climb in HAWKE holding pattern (SE, left turns, 304° inbound) to cross HAWKE LOM at or above 10000 before proceeding on course.

LAS VEGAS, NM
LAS VEGAS MUNI (LVS)
AMDT 1 06103 (FAA)

DEPARTURE PROCEDURE: **Rwys 2, 14** turn left/ right. **Rwy 20,** turn left (except via FTI R-215). **Rwy 32,** turn right.

Departures via FTI VORTAC R-001 CW R-215 climb on course. Departures via FTI VORTAC R-216 CW R-360 proceed direct FTI VORTAC. Climb in FTI VORTAC holding pattern (hold north, left turn, 192° inbound) to cross FTI at airway MEA/MCA. (NOTE: climb in hold not authorized for turbojet aircraft).

LEADVILLE, CO
LAKE COUNTY (LXV)
AMDT 2 08101 (FAA)

DEPARTURE PROCEDURE: **Rwy 16,** use LOZUL (RNAV) DEPARTURE. **Rwy 34,** use DAVVY (RNAV) DEPARTURE.

LONGMONT, CO
VANCE BRAND (LMO)
AMDT 1 12040 (FAA)

DEPARTURE PROCEDURE: **Rwy 11,** climbing left turn to intercept GLL VOR/DME R-221 to 7000 . . . **Rwy 29,** climbing right turn to intercept GLL VOR/DME R-221 to 7000 ...

... All aircraft proceed on GLL R-221 to GLL VOR/DME. Cross GLL VOR/DME at or above MEA/MCA for route of flight.

NOTE: **Rwy 11,** trees beginning 130' from DER, 191' right of centerline, up to 80' AGL/5119' MSL. Vehicles on roadway, 449' from DER, 395' left and right of centerline, 17' AGL/5046' MSL. Trees beginning 1383' from DER, 434' left of centerline, up to 80' AGL/5109' MSL. **Rwy 29,** trees beginning 4105' from DER, 220' left of centerline, up to 80' AGL/5189' MSL.

LOS ALAMOS, NM
LOS ALAMOS (LAM)
AMDT 1 12152 (FAA)

TAKEOFF MINIMUMS: **Rwy 27,** NA-obstacles and airport restriction.

DEPARTURE PROCEDURE: **Rwy 9,** climb heading 092° to intercept SAF R-354. Northbound climbing to 11000 on V83. Southbound climbing to 9000 on V83.

NOTE: **Rwy 9,** terrain and trees beginning 101' from DER, 178' left and right of centerline, up to 60' AGL/7139' MSL.

LOVINGTON, NM
LEA COUNTY-ZIP FRANKLIN MEMORIAL (E06)
AMDT 1 99364 (FAA)

DEPARTURE PROCEDURE: **Rwy 3,** climb runway heading to 4700 before turning on course.

NOTE: **Rwy 12,** 35' AGL power line 1250' from DER 150' right of centerline. **Rwy 21,** 40' AGL tower 936' from DER 273' right of centerline. **Rwy 30,** 50' AGL windmill 1800' from DER 50' right of centerline.

MEEKER, CO
MEEKER (EEO)
AMDT 1 08157 (FAA)

TAKEOFF MINIMUMS: **Rwys 3, 21,** 4100-3 for climb in visual conditions.

DEPARTURE PROCEDURE: **Rwys 3, 21,** for climb in visual conditions: cross Meeker Airport at or above 10500 before proceeding on course.

NOTE: **Rwy 21,** multiple trees beginning 843' from DER, 20' left of centerline, up to 100' AGL/7190' MSL. Multiple trees beginning 227' from DER, 187' right of centerline, up to 100' AGL/6862' MSL.

MONTE VISTA, CO
MONTE VISTA MUNI (MVI)
AMDT 3 01025 (FAA)

DEPARTURE PROCEDURE: **Rwy 2,** climbing right turn. **Rwy 20,** climbing left turn. **All aircraft,** climb direct ALS VORTAC, continue climb in ALS holding pattern (SE, right turns, 301° inbound) to cross ALS VORTAC at or above 11000, except V210 westbound 11200 and J102 northeast bound 13700, before proceeding enroute.

13262

TAKEOFF MINIMUMS AND (OBSTACLE) DEPARTURE PROCEDURES

FIGURE 225.—Takeoff Minimums and (Obstacle) Departure Procedures.

LAMAR MUNI (LAA) 3 SW UTC–7(–6DT) N38°04.18´ W102°41.31´ **WICHITA**
3706 B S4 **FUEL** 100LL, JET A OX 1, 3 NOTAM FILE LAA **H–5A, L–10G**
RWY 18–36: H6304X100 (CONC–GRVD) S–45, D–55, 2D–100 MIRL **IAP**
0.4% up S
RWY 18: REIL. VASI(V4L)—GA 3.0° TCH 45´. Road.
RWY 36: REIL. PAPI(P4L)—GA 3.0° TCH 45´. Hill.
RWY 08–26: H5001X60 (ASPH–PFC) S–35, D–50, 2D–95 MIRL
RWY 08: PAPI(P2L)—GA 3.0° TCH 30´. Road.
RWY 26: REIL. PAPI(P2L)—GA 3.0° TCH 31´. Fence.
AIRPORT REMARKS: Attended 1500–0100Z‡. For svc after hrs phone 719–336–7701. Be alert, intensive USAF student training invof Colorado Springs and Pueblo Colorado. Rwy 18–36 now has distance remaining signs. Twr 500´ AGL 4.5 mile SE unlighted. ACTIVATE MIRL Rwy 08–26 and Rwy 18–36—CTAF. NOTE: See Special Notices—Aerobatic Operations in Colorado. USAF 306 FTG Flight Training Areas, Vicinity of Colorado Springs and Pueblo Colorado.
WEATHER DATA SOURCES: ASOS 135.625 (719) 336–3854.
COMMUNICATIONS: CTAF/UNICOM 122.8
DENVER CENTER APP/DEP CON 133.4
RADIO AIDS TO NAVIGATION: NOTAM FILE LAA.
(H) VORW/DME 116.9 LAA Chan 116 N38°11.83´ W102°41.25´ 168° 7.6 NM to fld. 3944/12E.

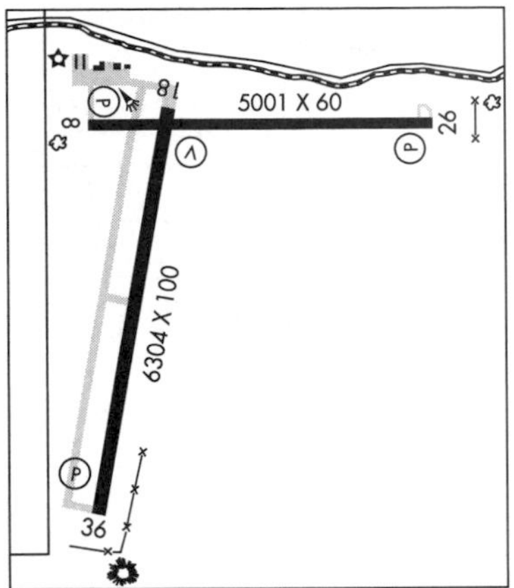

LAS ANIMAS

CITY OF LAS ANIMAS – BENT CO (7V9) 1 S UTC–7(–6DT) N38°03.24´ W103°14.31´ **WICHITA**
3915 S4 NOTAM FILE DEN **L–10F**
RWY 08–26: H3870X40 (ASPH) S–5 HIRL 0.4% up W
RWY 08: REIL. Fence.
RWY 26: REIL. Road.
AIRPORT REMARKS: Attended Mon–Sat 1500–0000Z‡. Be alert, intensive USAF student training invof Colorado Springs and Pueblo Colorado. Rwy 26 has +30´ poles 105´ from thld 210´ left of extd rwy centerline, +15´ tank 321´ from rwy end 270´ right of centerline. Thld lgts NSTD; three lgts each end. Thld lgts OTS indef. Rwy 08 thld lgts 23´ from thld. Rwy 26 thld lgts 12´ from thld. Rwy 08 numbers located 216´ from pavement end, Rwy 08–26 numbers smaller than standard, no centerline markings. ACTIVATE HIRL Rwy 08–26—CTAF. Med ints 5 clicks, high ints 7 clicks. See Special Notices—USAF 306 FTG Flight Training Areas, Vicinity of Colorado Springs and Pueblo Colorado.
COMMUNICATIONS: CTAF 122.9
RADIO AIDS TO NAVIGATION: NOTAM FILE LAA.
LAMAR (H) VORW/DME 116.9 LAA Chan 116 N38°11.83´ W102°41.25´ 240° 27.5 NM to fld. 3944/12E.

LEACH (See CENTER on page 220)

LEADVILLE

LAKE CO (LXV) 2 SW UTC–7(–6DT) N39°13.17´ W106°18.99´ **DENVER**
9934 B **FUEL** 100LL, JET A NOTAM FILE LXV **H–3F, 5A, L–9E**
RWY 16–34: H6400X75 (ASPH) S–20, D–20 MIRL **IAP**
RWY 16: PAPI(P2L)—GA 3.0° TCH 45´. Rgt tfc.
RWY 34: PAPI(P2L)—GA 3.0° TCH 45´.
AIRPORT REMARKS: Attended May–Oct 1430–2330Z‡, Nov–Apr 1500–2330Z‡. For svc after hrs call sheriff dispatch 719–486–1249. PPR for svc after hrs call 719–293–5110. Rwy 34 has +50´ power lines 750´ from right of thld. Twy C and old ramp have potholes and loose aggregate. All twys and new ramp area marked with blue and white reflectors. ACTIVATE MIRL Rwy 16–34 and PAPI Rwy 16 and Rwy 34—CTAF.
WEATHER DATA SOURCES: ASOS 118.375 (719) 486–2735.
COMMUNICATIONS: CTAF/UNICOM 122.8
DENVER CENTER APP/DEP CON 119.85
RADIO AIDS TO NAVIGATION: NOTAM FILE DEN.
RED TABLE (H) VORW/DME 113.0 DBL Chan 77 N39°26.36´ W106°53.68´ 104° 30.0 NM to fld. 11800/12E.

• • • • • • • • • • • • • • • • •

HELIPAD H1: H150X100 (ASPH–CONC)
HELIPORT REMARKS: Rwy H1 has 6–8 inch lip all around edges, concrete has longitudinal and corner cracking. Rwy H1 has 20´ to 30´ trees 130´ east of pad.

FIGURE 226.—Excerpt from Chart Supplement.

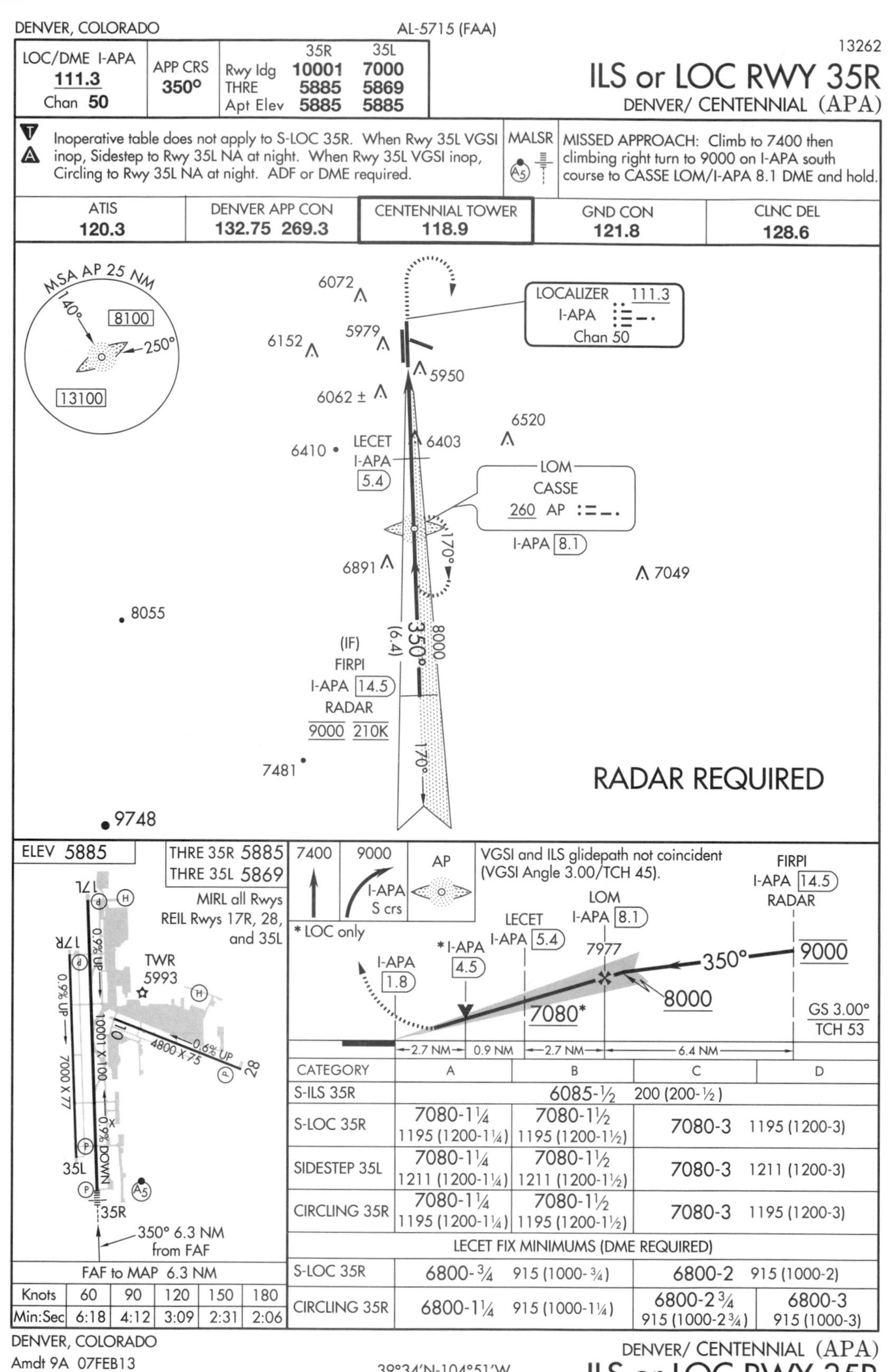

FIGURE 227.—ILS or LOC RWY 35R (APA).

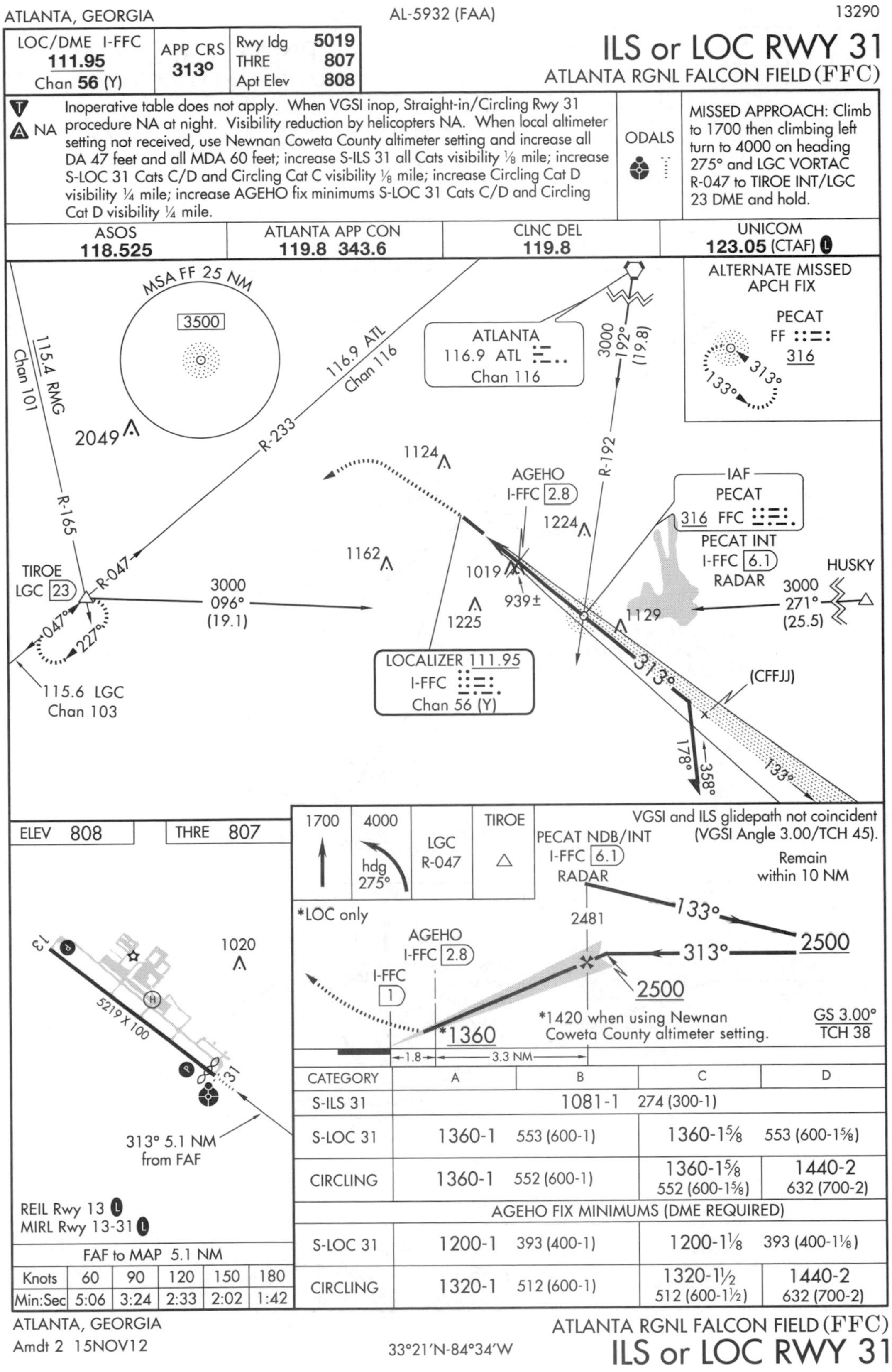

ATLANTA, GEORGIA AL-5932 (FAA) 13290

ILS or LOC RWY 31
ATLANTA RGNL FALCON FIELD (FFC)

LOC/DME I-FFC 111.95 Chan 56 (Y)	APP CRS 313°	Rwy ldg 5019 THRE 807 Apt Elev 808

Inoperative table does not apply. When VGSI inop, Straight-in/Circling Rwy 31 procedure NA at night. Visibility reduction by helicopters NA. When local altimeter setting not received, use Newnan Coweta County altimeter setting and increase all DA 47 feet and all MDA 60 feet; increase S-ILS 31 all Cats visibility ⅛ mile; increase S-LOC 31 Cats C/D and Circling Cat C visibility ⅛ mile; increase Circling Cat D visibility ¼ mile; increase AGEHO fix minimums S-LOC 31 Cats C/D and Circling Cat D visibility ¼ mile.

A NA

ODALS

MISSED APPROACH: Climb to 1700 then climbing left turn to 4000 on heading 275° and LGC VORTAC R-047 to TIROE INT/LGC 23 DME and hold.

ASOS	ATLANTA APP CON	CLNC DEL	UNICOM
118.525	119.8 343.6	119.8	123.05 (CTAF)

MSA FF 25 NM
3500
2049
115.4 RMG Chan 101
116.9 ATL Chan 116
R-233
ATLANTA 116.9 ATL Chan 116
3000 192° (19.8)
R-192
ALTERNATE MISSED APCH FIX
PECAT FF 316
313° 133°
1124
AGEHO I-FFC 2.8
1224
IAF PECAT 316 FFC
PECAT INT I-FFC 6.1 RADAR
HUSKY
3000 271° (25.5)
R-165
1162
1019
939±
1225
1129
TIROE LGC 23
R-047
3000 096° (19.1)
047° 227°
LOCALIZER 111.95 I-FFC Chan 56 (Y)
313°
(CFFJJ)
115.6 LGC Chan 103
178° 358°
133°

ELEV 808 THRE 807

1020
5219 X 100
13 31
313° 5.1 NM from FAF
REIL Rwy 13
MIRL Rwy 13-31

1700 4000 hdg 275° LGC R-047 TIROE

PECAT NDB/INT I-FFC 6.1 RADAR
VGSI and ILS glidepath not coincident (VGSI Angle 3.00/TCH 45).
Remain within 10 NM
*LOC only
AGEHO I-FFC 2.8
I-FFC 1
2481
133°
2500
313°
2500
*1360
*1420 when using Newnan Coweta County altimeter setting.
GS 3.00° TCH 38
1.8 3.3 NM

CATEGORY	A	B	C	D
S-ILS 31	1081-1 274 (300-1)			
S-LOC 31	1360-1 553 (600-1)		1360-1⅝ 553 (600-1⅝)	
CIRCLING	1360-1 552 (600-1)		1360-1⅝ 552 (600-1⅝)	1440-2 632 (700-2)
AGEHO FIX MINIMUMS (DME REQUIRED)				
S-LOC 31	1200-1 393 (400-1)		1200-1⅛ 393 (400-1⅛)	
CIRCLING	1320-1 512 (600-1)		1320-1½ 512 (600-1½)	1440-2 632 (700-2)

FAF to MAP 5.1 NM

Knots	60	90	120	150	180
Min:Sec	5:06	3:24	2:33	2:02	1:42

ATLANTA, GEORGIA
Amdt 2 15NOV12
33°21′N-84°34′W
ATLANTA RGNL FALCON FIELD (FFC)
ILS or LOC RWY 31

FIGURE 228.—ILS or LOC RWY 31 (FFC).

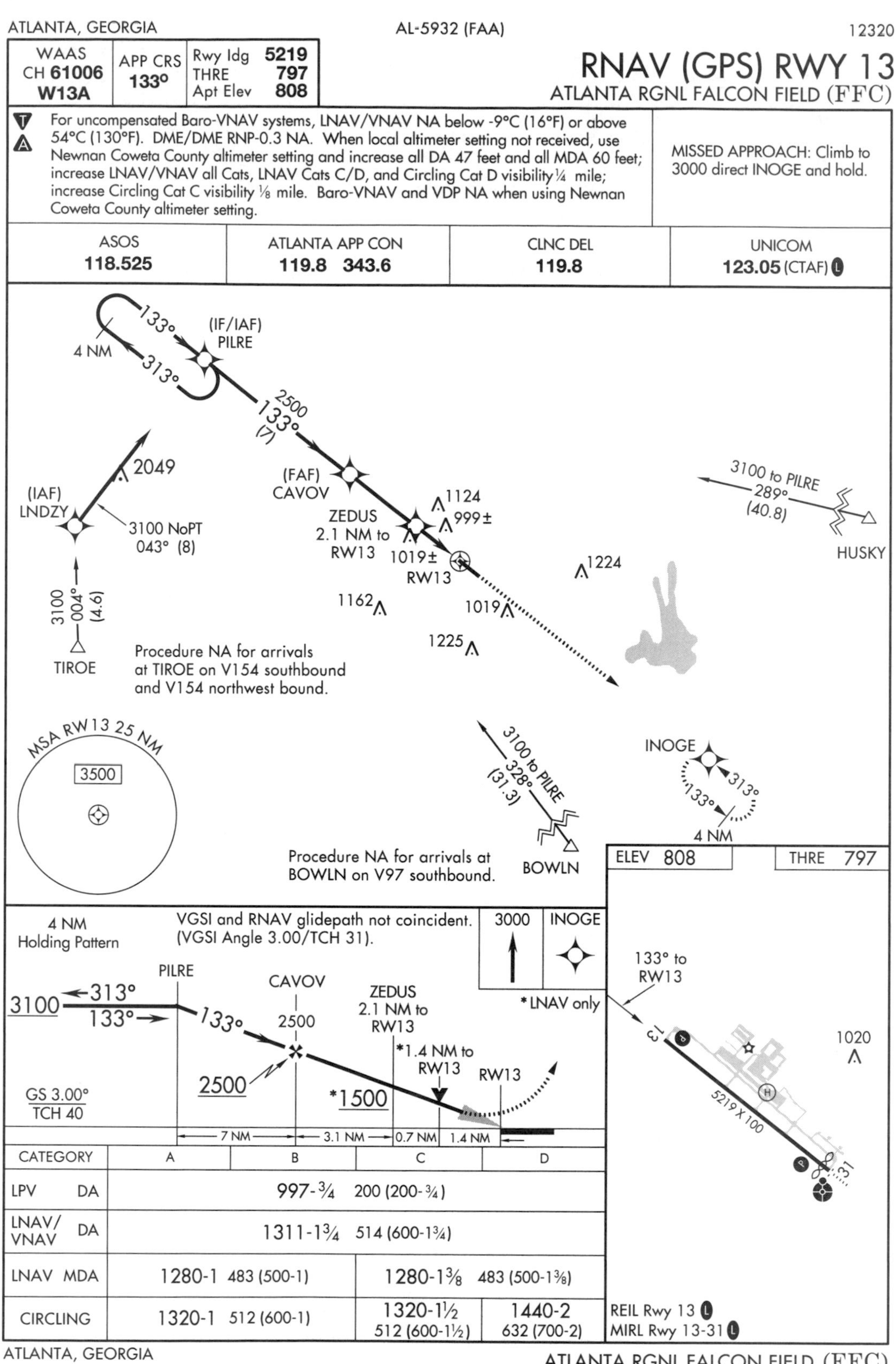

CATEGORY	A	B	C	D
LPV DA	997-¾ 200 (200-¾)			
LNAV/VNAV DA	1311-1¾ 514 (600-1¾)			
LNAV MDA	1280-1 483 (500-1)		1280-1⅜ 483 (500-1⅜)	
CIRCLING	1320-1 512 (600-1)		1320-1½ 512 (600-1½)	1440-2 632 (700-2)

FIGURE 229.—RNAV (GPS) RWY 13 (FFC).

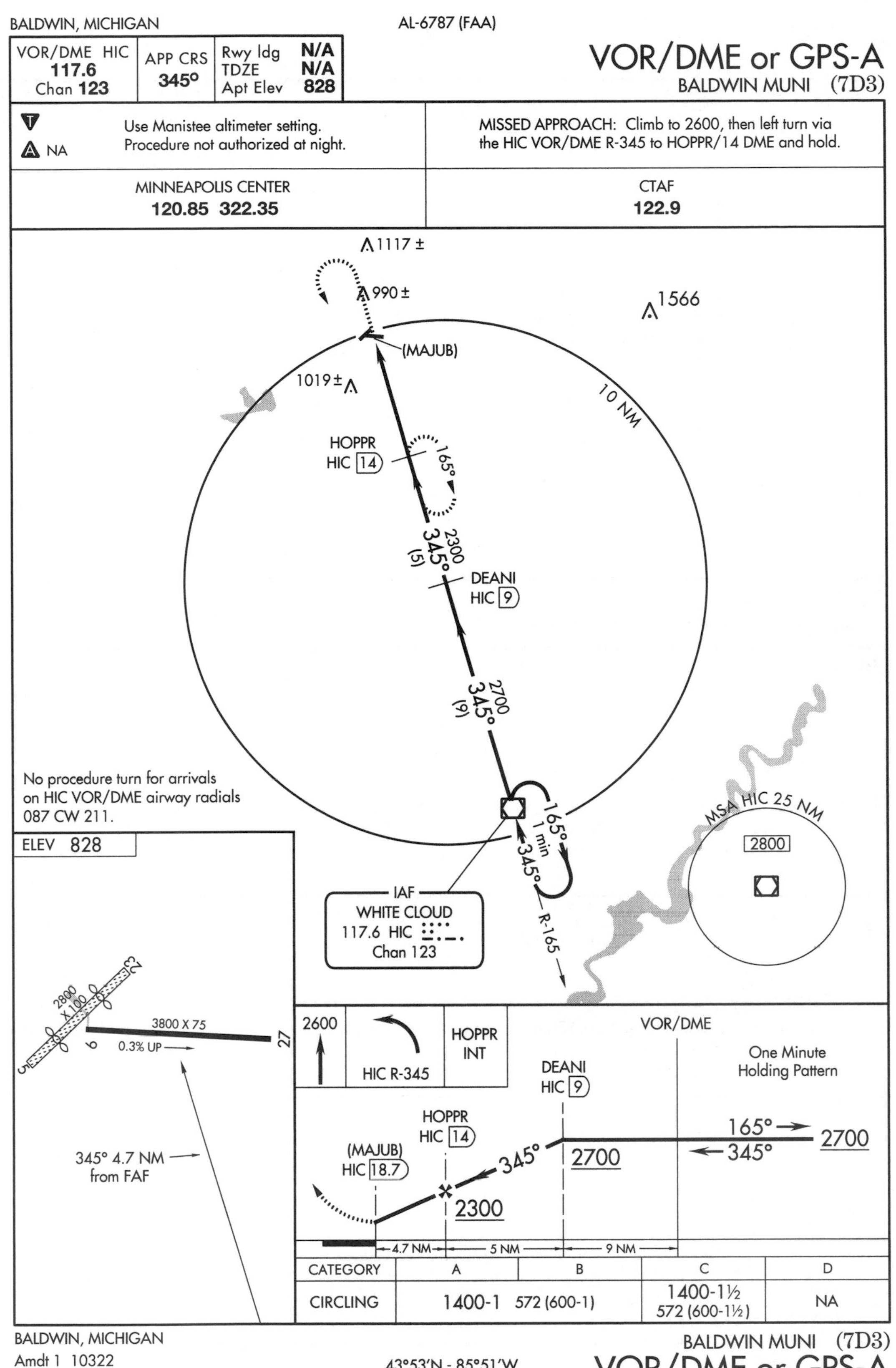

FIGURE 230.—VOR/DME or GPS-A (7D3).

BALDWIN MUNI (7D3) 2 S UTC–5(–4DT) N43°52.53´ W85°50.53´ **CHICAGO L–281 IAP**
828 TPA—1828(1000) NOTAM FILE LAN
RWY 09–27: H3800X75 (ASPH) S–10 0.3% up E
RWY 09: Trees.
RWY 27: Trees.
RWY 05–23: 2800X100 (TURF)
RWY 05: Thld dsplcd 800´. Trees.
RWY 23: Thld dsplcd 800´. Trees.
AIRPORT REMARKS: Unattended. Deer on and invof arpt. Arpt CLOSED Nov thru Apr; no snow removal. Arpt manager cell 231-250-2551. Rwy 09–27 sfc considerable pavement cracking with vegetation growing through cracks. Rwy 05–23 and dsplcd thlds marked with 3´ yellow cones.
COMMUNICATIONS: CTAF 122.9
Ⓡ**MINNEAPOLIS CENTER APP/DEP CON** 120.85
RADIO AIDS TO NAVIGATION: NOTAM FILE LAN.
WHITE CLOUD (L) VOR/DME 117.6 HIC Chan 123 N43°34.49´ W85°42.97´ 344° 18.9 NM to fld. 920/1W.
VOR/DME unusable:
020°–090° byd 30 NM blo 3,000´
DME portion unusable:
270°–290° byd 35 NM blo 3,000´

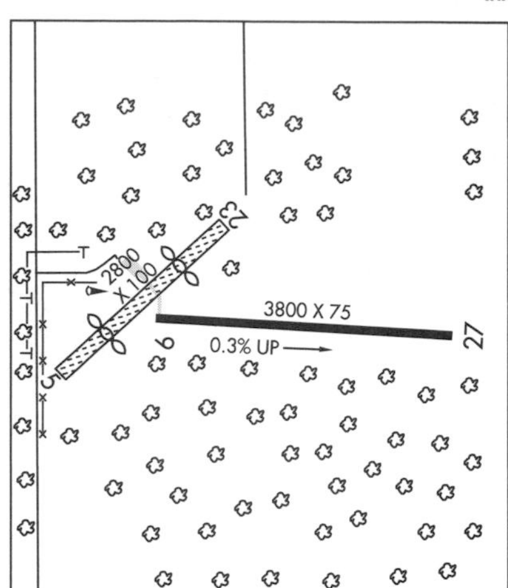

BANGU N45°00.88´ W84°48.49´ NOTAM FILE GLR. **LAKE HURON**
NDB (LOM) 375 GL 097° 4.5 NM to Gaylord Rgnl. Unmonitored.

BANNISTER

SHADY LAWN FLD (4M4) 2 E UTC–5(–4DT) N43°07.72´ W84°22.88´ **CHICAGO**
680 TPA—1680(1000) NOTAM FILE LAN
RWY 09–27: 1850X50 (TURF) LIRL
RWY 09: Bldg.
RWY 27: Trees.
AIRPORT REMARKS: Attended irregularly. Ultralight and AG activity on and invof arpt. Deer and birds on and invof arpt. Crops adjacent to rwy during summer months. NSTD LIRL color and configuration, by prior arrangement. Rwy 09 and Rwy 27 marked by 3´ yellow cones.
COMMUNICATIONS: CTAF 122.9

BARAGA (2P4) 4 W UTC–5(–4DT) N46°47.10´ W88°34.67´ **GREEN BAY**
845 TPA—1845(1000) NOTAM FILE GRB
RWY 09–27: 2200X100 (TURF)
RWY 09: Trees.
RWY 27: Trees.
AIRPORT REMARKS: Unattended. Arpt CLOSED Nov–Apr except to ski equipped acft. 25´ p–line 850´ from thld Rwy 27. Deer and birds on and invof arpt.
COMMUNICATIONS: CTAF 122.9

BATH

UNIVERSITY AIRPARK (41G) 2 NW UTC–5(–4DT) N42°50.42´ W84°28.75´ **DETROIT**
856 B S2 NOTAM FILE LAN
RWY 08–26: 1988X100 (TURF) LIRL
RWY 08: Trees.
RWY 26: Tree.
AIRPORT REMARKS: Attended irregularly. Rwy 08–26 occasionally soft/wet areas E end during spring thaw and after heavy rain. ACTIVATE LIRL Rwy 08–26 and NSTD rotating bcn—122.85. NSTD flashing strobe and alternating white/red bcn. Rwy 08–26 marked with 3´ yellow cones.
COMMUNICATIONS: CTAF 122.9

BATOL N42°21.72´ W85°11.07´ NOTAM FILE BTL. **CHICAGO L–281**
NDB (MHW/LOM) 272 BT 225° 4.4 NM to W K Kellogg.

FIGURE 231.—Excerpt from Chart Supplement.

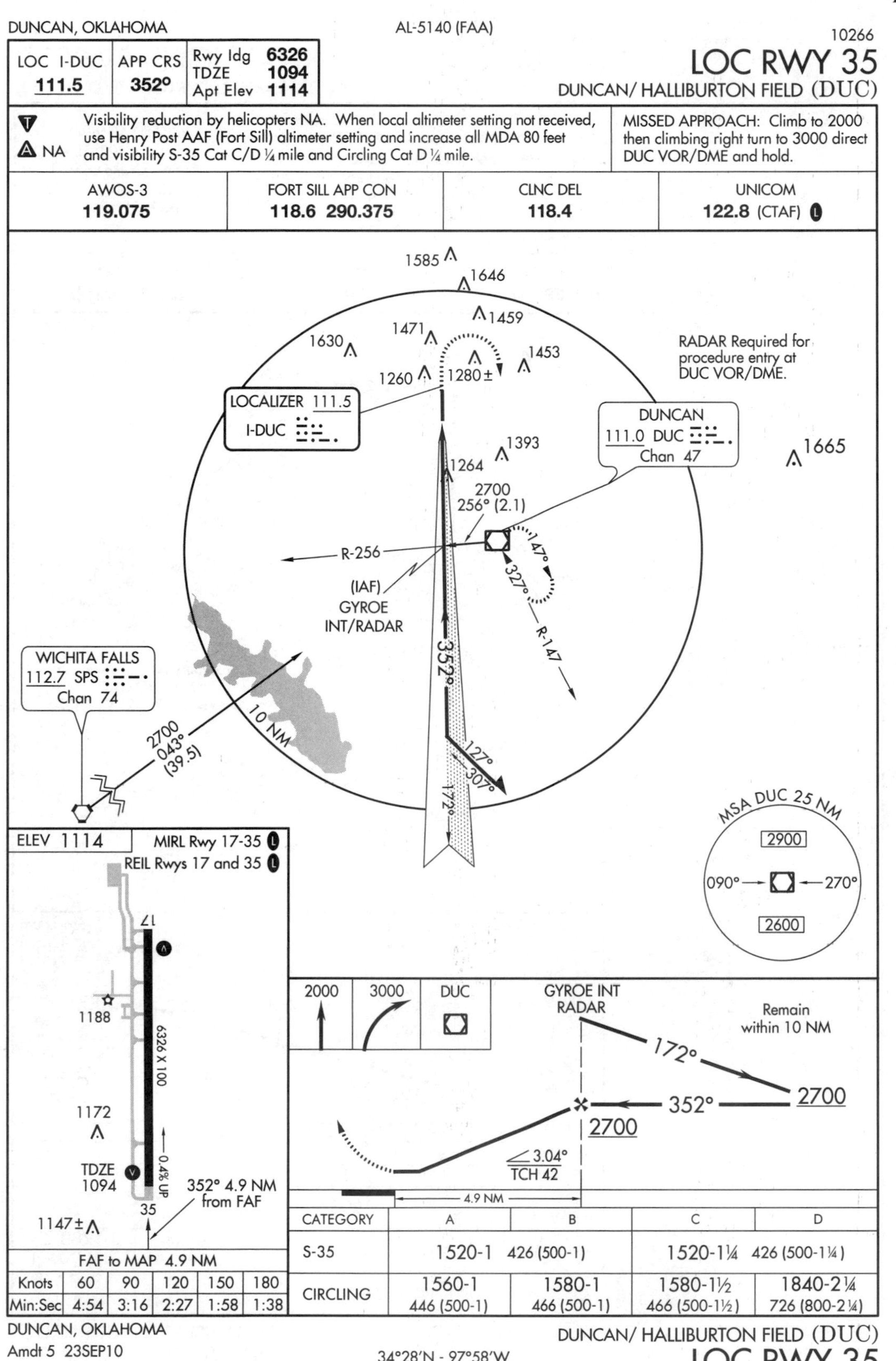

FAF to MAP 4.9 NM					
Knots	60	90	120	150	180
Min:Sec	4:54	3:16	2:27	1:58	1:38

CATEGORY	A	B	C	D
S-35	1520-1 426 (500-1)		1520-1¼ 426 (500-1¼)	
CIRCLING	1560-1 446 (500-1)	1580-1 466 (500-1)	1580-1½ 466 (500-1½)	1840-2¼ 726 (800-2¼)

FIGURE 232.—LOC RWY 35 (DUC).

DUNCAN, OKLAHOMA | AL-5140 (FAA) | 10266

WAAS CH 93619 W17A	APP CRS 172°	Rwy ldg 6326 TDZE 1114 Apt Elev 1114

RNAV (GPS) RWY 17

DUNCAN/ HALLIBURTON FIELD (DUC)

Baro-VNAV NA when using Henry Post AAF, (Fort Sill) altimeter setting. For uncompensated Baro-VNAV systems, LNAV/VNAV NA below -17°C (2°F) or above 46°C (114°F). DME/DME RNP-0.3 NA. Visibility reduction by helicopters NA. When local altimeter setting not received, use Henry Post AAF, (Fort Sill) altimeter setting and increase all DA 67 feet and LPV and LNAV/VNAV visibility ¼ mile all Cats, increase all MDA 80 feet and LNAV Cat B visibility ¼ mile, Cat C and D visibility ½ mile, increase Circling Cat B and D visibility ¼ mile and Cat C visibility ½ mile. VDP NA with Henry Post AAF, (Fort Sill) altimeter setting.

MISSED APPROACH: Climb to 3000 direct JEGMO and on track 140° to DUC VOR/DME and hold.

AWOS-3	FORT SILL APP CON	CLNC DEL	UNICOM
119.075	118.6 290.375	118.4	122.8 (CTAF) L

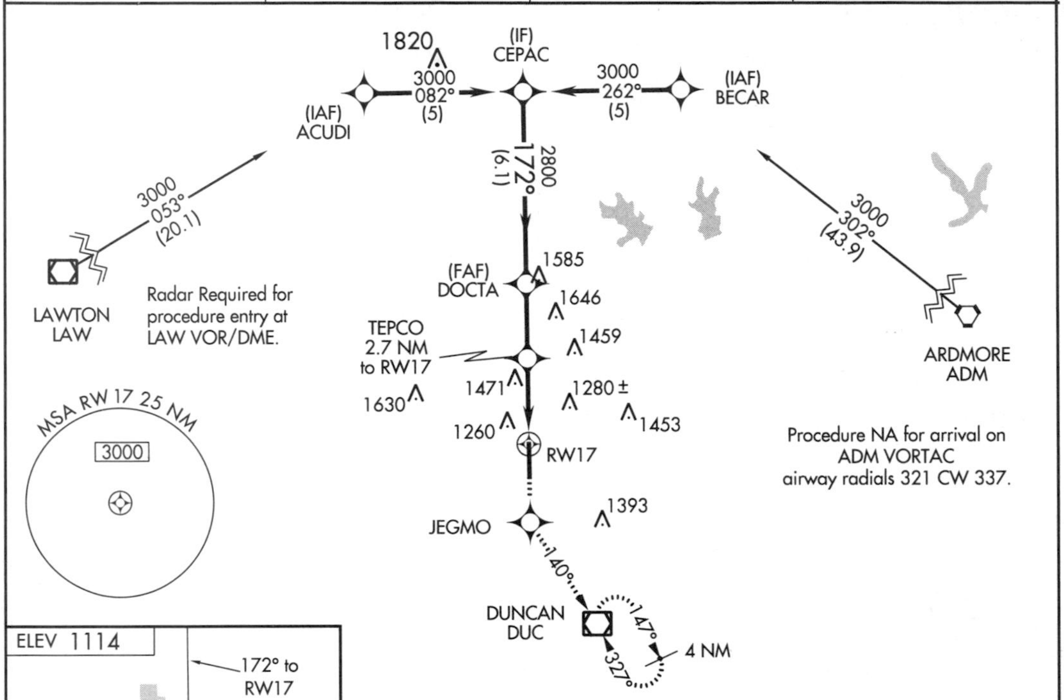

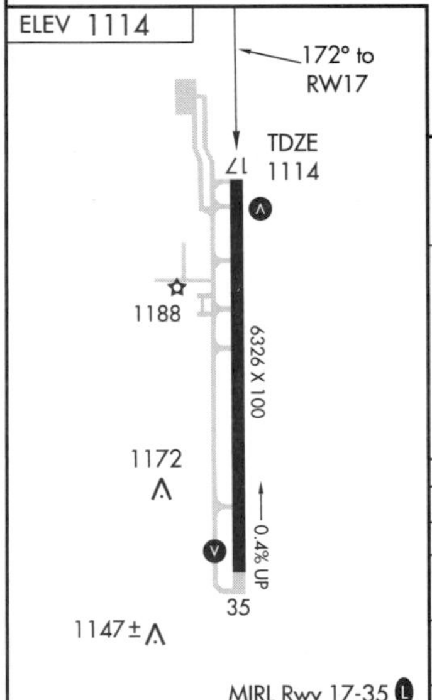

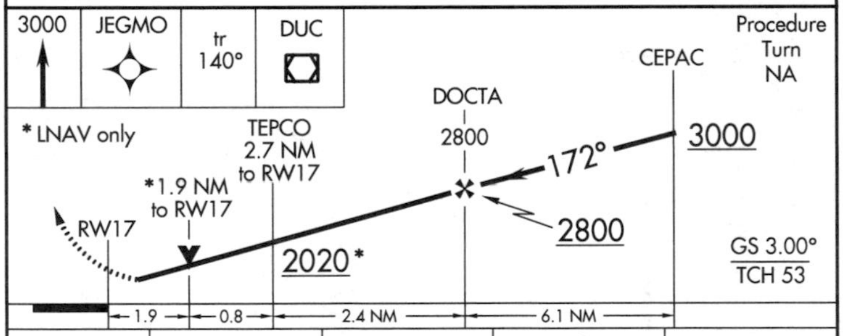

CATEGORY	A	B	C	D
LPV DA	1390-1 276 (300-1)			
LNAV/ VNAV DA	1903-2¾ 789 (800-2¾)			
LNAV MDA	1780-1 666 (700-1)		1780-1¾ 666 (700-1¾)	1780-2 666 (700-2)
CIRCLING	1780-1 666 (700-1)		1780-1¾ 666 (700-1¾)	1840-2¼ 726 (800-2¼)

DUNCAN, OKLAHOMA
Amdt 1 23SEP10

34°28'N - 97°58'W

DUNCAN/ HALLIBURTON FIELD (DUC)
RNAV (GPS) RWY 17

FIGURE 233.—RNAV (GPS) RWY 17 (DUC).

LINCOLN, NEBRASKA — AL-232 (FAA) — 13066

LOC I-OCZ 111.1	APP CRS 174°	Rwy ldg 12901 THRE 1195 Apt Elev 1219

ILS or LOC RWY 18

LINCOLN (LNK)

* RVR 1800 authorized with the use of FD or AP or HUD to DA. When local altimeter setting not received use Beatrice altimeter setting and increase all DA 91 feet and all MDA 100 feet, increase S-LOC 18 Cat C/D/E visibility to 1½, Circling Cat C visibility to 2 and Cat D visibility to 2¼; increase ROROC fix minimums S-LOC 18 Cat C/D/E visibility to 1 ⅜ Circling Cat C visibility to 1¾ and Cat D visibility to 2¼. For inoperative MALSR, increase S-ILS 18 Cat E visibility to RVR 4000, S-LOC 18 Cat E visibility to 1¾, and ROROC fix minimums S-LOC 18 Cat E visibility to 1½. For inoperative MALSR when using Beatrice altimeter setting, increase S-ILS 18 all Cats visibility to RVR 4500, S-LOC 18 Cat E visibility to 2, and ROROC fix minimums S-LOC 18 Cat C/D/E visibility to 1¾.

MALSR

MISSED APPROACH: Climb to 1700 then climbing right turn to 3000 direct LNK VORTAC and hold.

ATIS	LINCOLN APP CON	LINCOLN TOWER ★	GND CON	CLNC DEL	UNICOM
118.05 290.9	124.0 270.3	118.5 (CTAF) 253.5	121.9 275.8	120.7 225.4	122.95

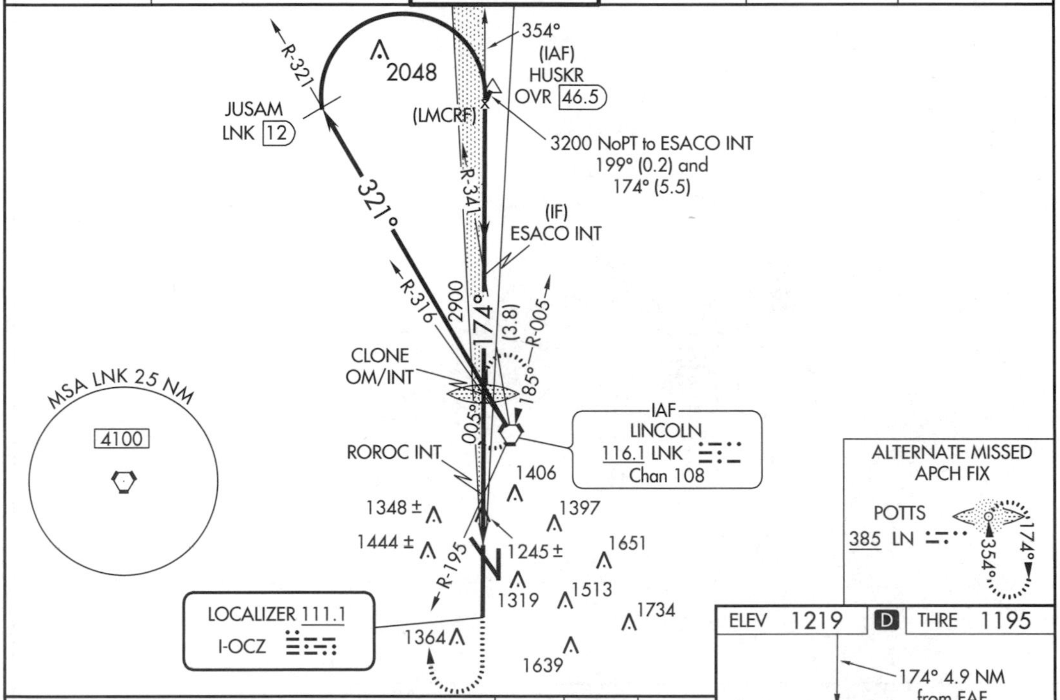

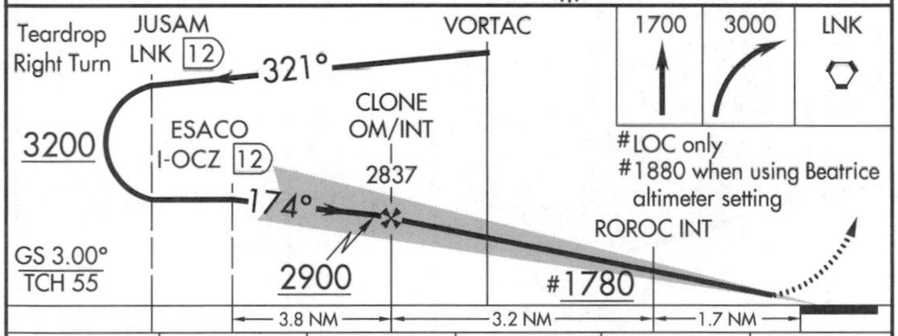

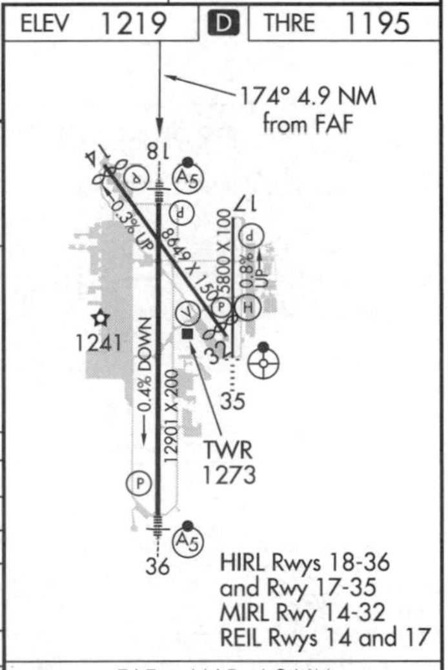

CATEGORY	A	B	C	D	E
S-ILS 18	*1395/24 200 (200-½)				
S-LOC 18	1780/24 585 (600-½)		1780-1¼ 585 (600-1¼)		
CIRCLING	1780-1 561 (600-1)		1780-1¾ 561 (600-1¾)	1820-2 601 (700-2)	2040-3 821 (900-3)
ROROC FIX MINIMUMS (DUAL VOR RECEIVERS REQUIRED)					
S-LOC 18	1720/24 525 (600-½)		1720/55 525 (600-1¼)		
CIRCLING	1720-1 501 (600-1)	1760-1 541 (600-1)	1760-1½ 541 (600-1½)	1820-2 601 (700-2)	2040-3 821 (900-3)

FAF to MAP 4.9 NM

Knots	60	90	120	150	180
Min:Sec	4:54	3:16	2:27	1:58	1:38

LINCOLN, NEBRASKA
Amdt 7 05APR12

40°51'N-96°46'W

LINCOLN (LNK)
ILS or LOC RWY 18

FIGURE 234.—ILS or LOC RWY 18 (LNK).

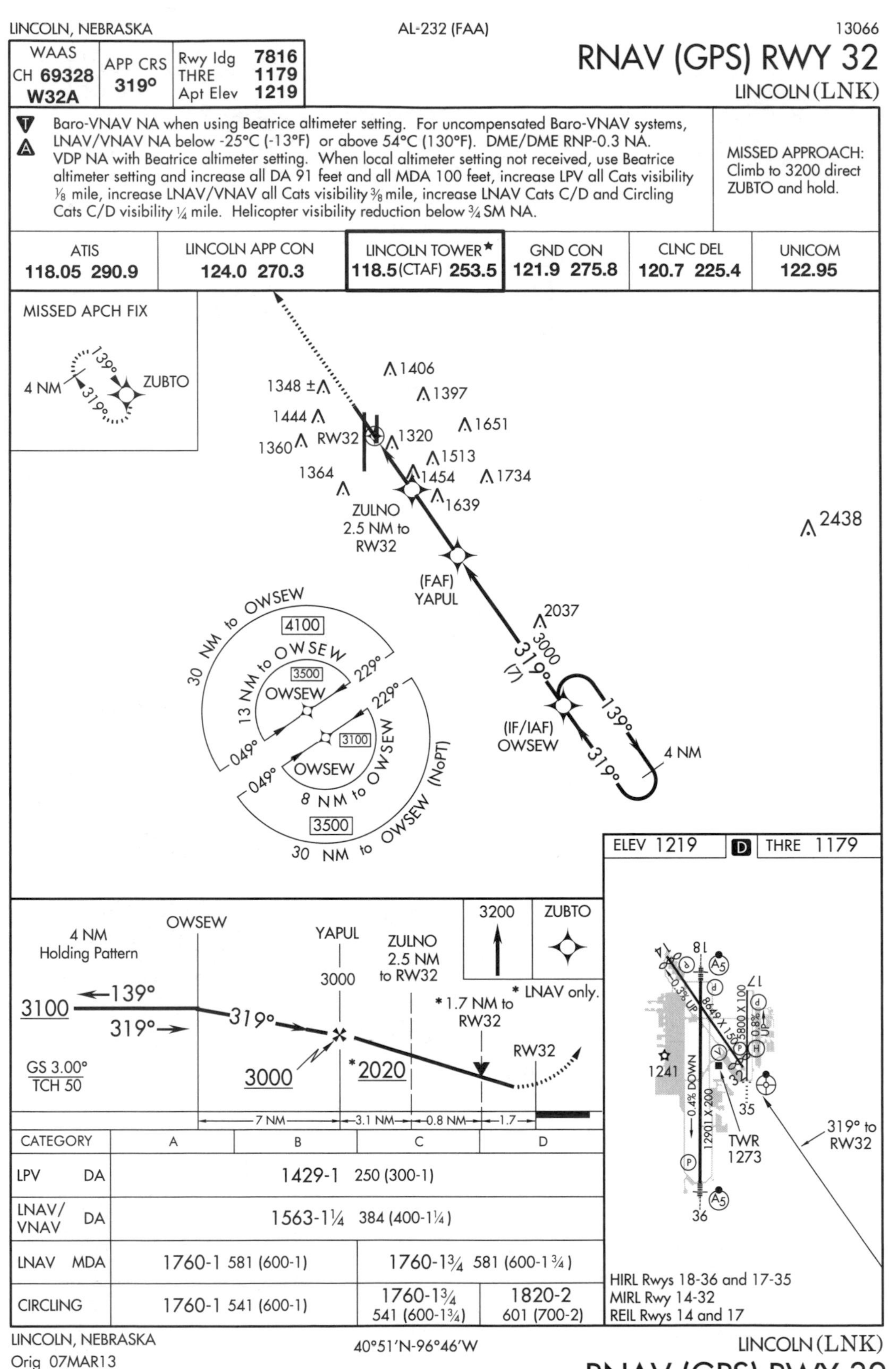

CATEGORY	A	B	C	D
LPV DA	1429-1 250 (300-1)			
LNAV/VNAV DA	1563-1¼ 384 (400-1¼)			
LNAV MDA	1760-1 581 (600-1)		1760-1¾ 581 (600-1¾)	
CIRCLING	1760-1 541 (600-1)		1760-1¾ 541 (600-1¾)	1820-2 601 (700-2)

FIGURE 235.—RNAV (GPS) RWY 32 (LNK).

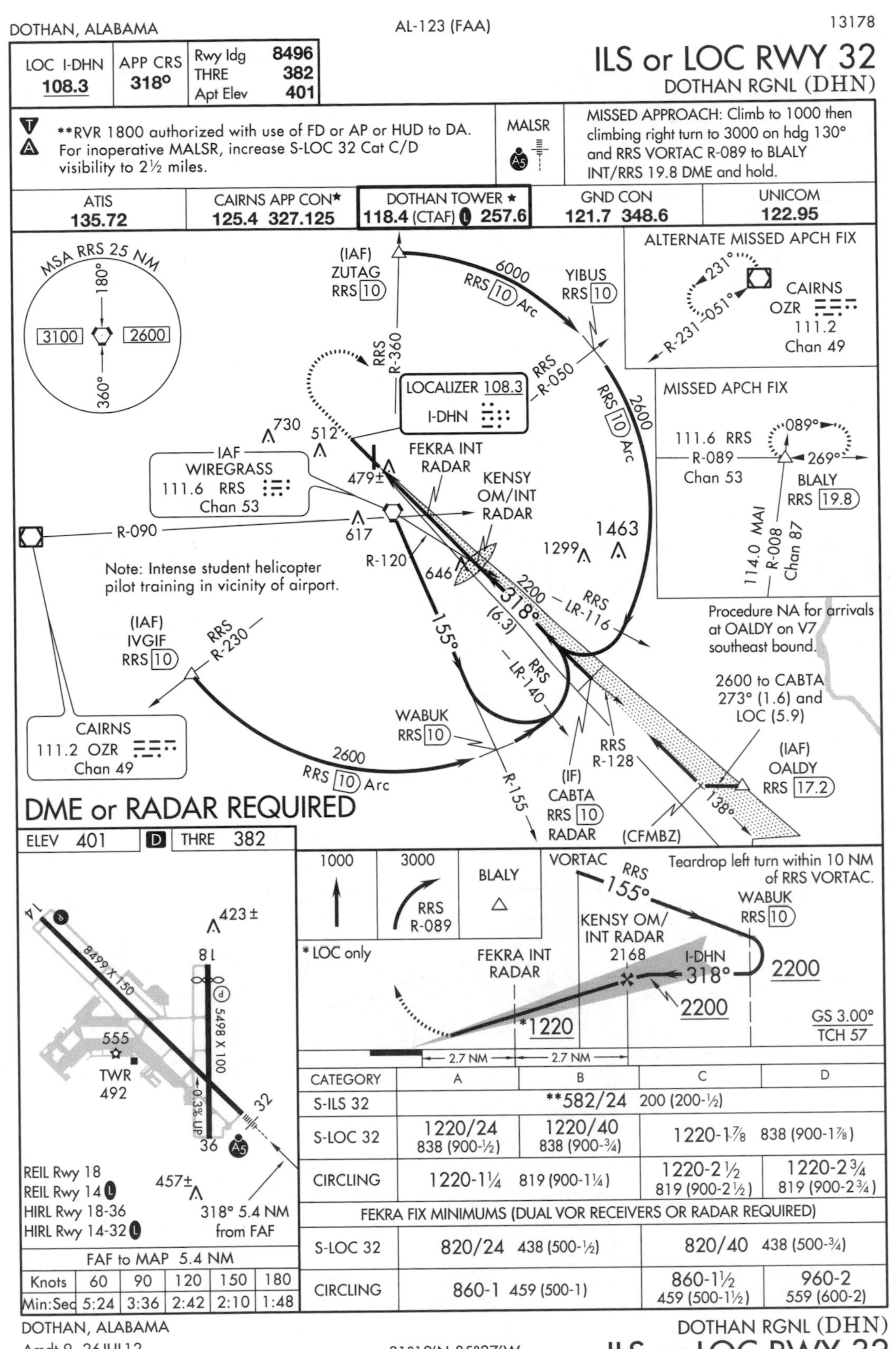

FIGURE 236.—ILS or RWY 32 (DHN).

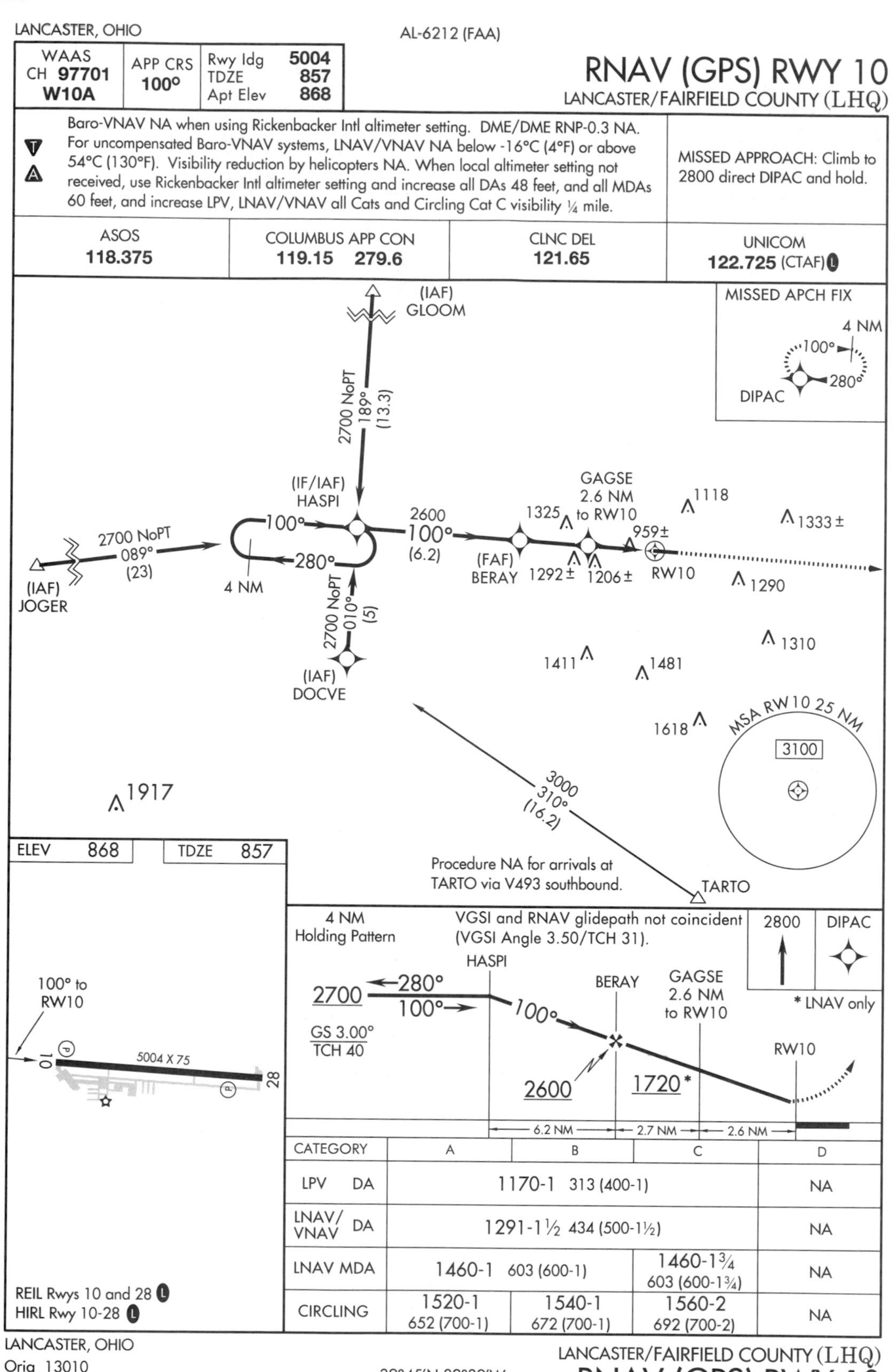

CATEGORY	A	B	C	D
LPV DA	1170-1 313 (400-1)			NA
LNAV/VNAV DA	1291-1½ 434 (500-1½)			NA
LNAV MDA	1460-1 603 (600-1)		1460-1¾ 603 (600-1¾)	NA
CIRCLING	1520-1 652 (700-1)	1540-1 672 (700-1)	1560-2 692 (700-2)	NA

FIGURE 237.—RNAV (GPS) RWY 10 (LHQ).

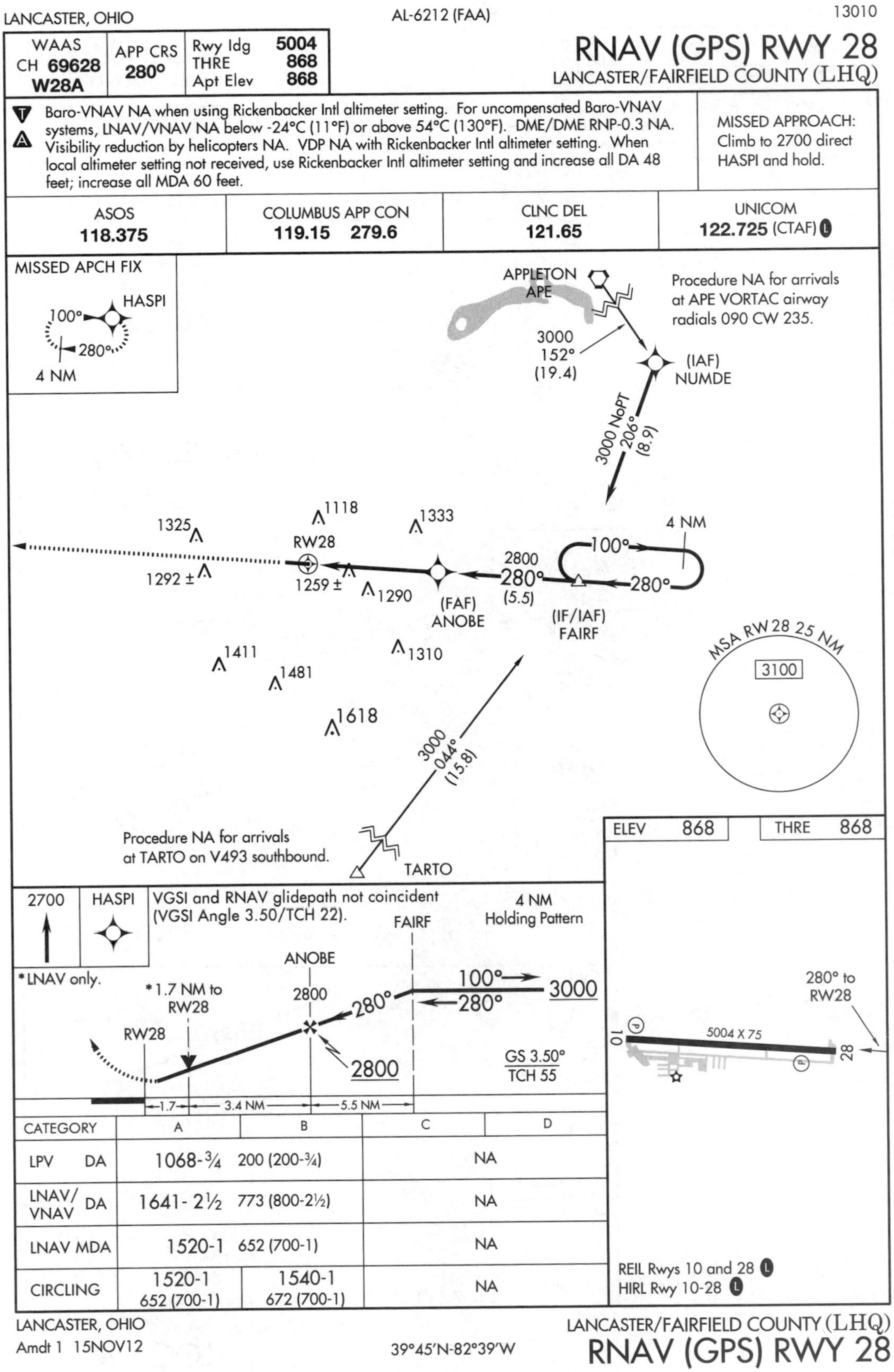

LANCASTER, OHIO

AL-6212 (FAA)

13010

WAAS CH **69628** **W28A**	APP CRS **280°**	Rwy ldg **5004** THRE **868** Apt Elev **868**

RNAV (GPS) RWY 28

LANCASTER/FAIRFIELD COUNTY (LHQ)

Baro-VNAV NA when using Rickenbacker Intl altimeter setting. For uncompensated Baro-VNAV systems, LNAV/VNAV NA below -24°C (11°F) or above 54°C (130°F). DME/DME RNP-0.3 NA. Visibility reduction by helicopters NA. VDP NA with Rickenbacker Intl altimeter setting. When local altimeter setting not received, use Rickenbacker Intl altimeter setting and increase all DA 48 feet; increase all MDA 60 feet.

MISSED APPROACH: Climb to 2700 direct HASPI and hold.

ASOS	COLUMBUS APP CON	CLNC DEL	UNICOM
118.375	**119.15 279.6**	**121.65**	**122.725** (CTAF) L

MISSED APCH FIX

HASPI

100°

280°

4 NM

APPLETON

APE

Procedure NA for arrivals at APE VORTAC airway radials 090 CW 235.

3000

152°

(19.4)

(IAF)

NUMDE

3000 NoPT

206°

(8.9)

1118

1333

1325

RW28

4 NM

100°

2800

280°

(5.5)

280°

1292 ±

1259 ±

1290

(FAF)

ANOBE

(IF/IAF)

FAIRF

MSA RW28 25 NM

3100

1411

1481

1310

1618

3000

044°

(15.8)

Procedure NA for arrivals at TARTO on V493 southbound.

TARTO

ELEV 868

THRE 868

2700

HASPI

VGSI and RNAV glidepath not coincident (VGSI Angle 3.50/TCH 22).

FAIRF

4 NM Holding Pattern

*LNAV only.

ANOBE

2800

100°

3000

280°

280°

*1.7 NM to RW28

RW28

2800

GS 3.50°

TCH 55

1.7 — 3.4 NM — 5.5 NM

280° to RW28

10

5004 X 75

28

CATEGORY	A	B	C	D
LPV DA	1068-¾ 200 (200-¾)		NA	
LNAV/VNAV DA	1641-2½ 773 (800-2½)		NA	
LNAV MDA	1520-1 652 (700-1)		NA	
CIRCLING	1520-1 652 (700-1)	1540-1 672 (700-1)	NA	

REIL Rwys 10 and 28 L

HIRL Rwy 10-28 L

LANCASTER, OHIO

Amdt 1 15NOV12

39°45′N-82°39′W

LANCASTER/FAIRFIELD COUNTY (LHQ)

RNAV (GPS) RWY 28

FIGURE 238.—RNAV (GPS) RWY 28 (LHQ).

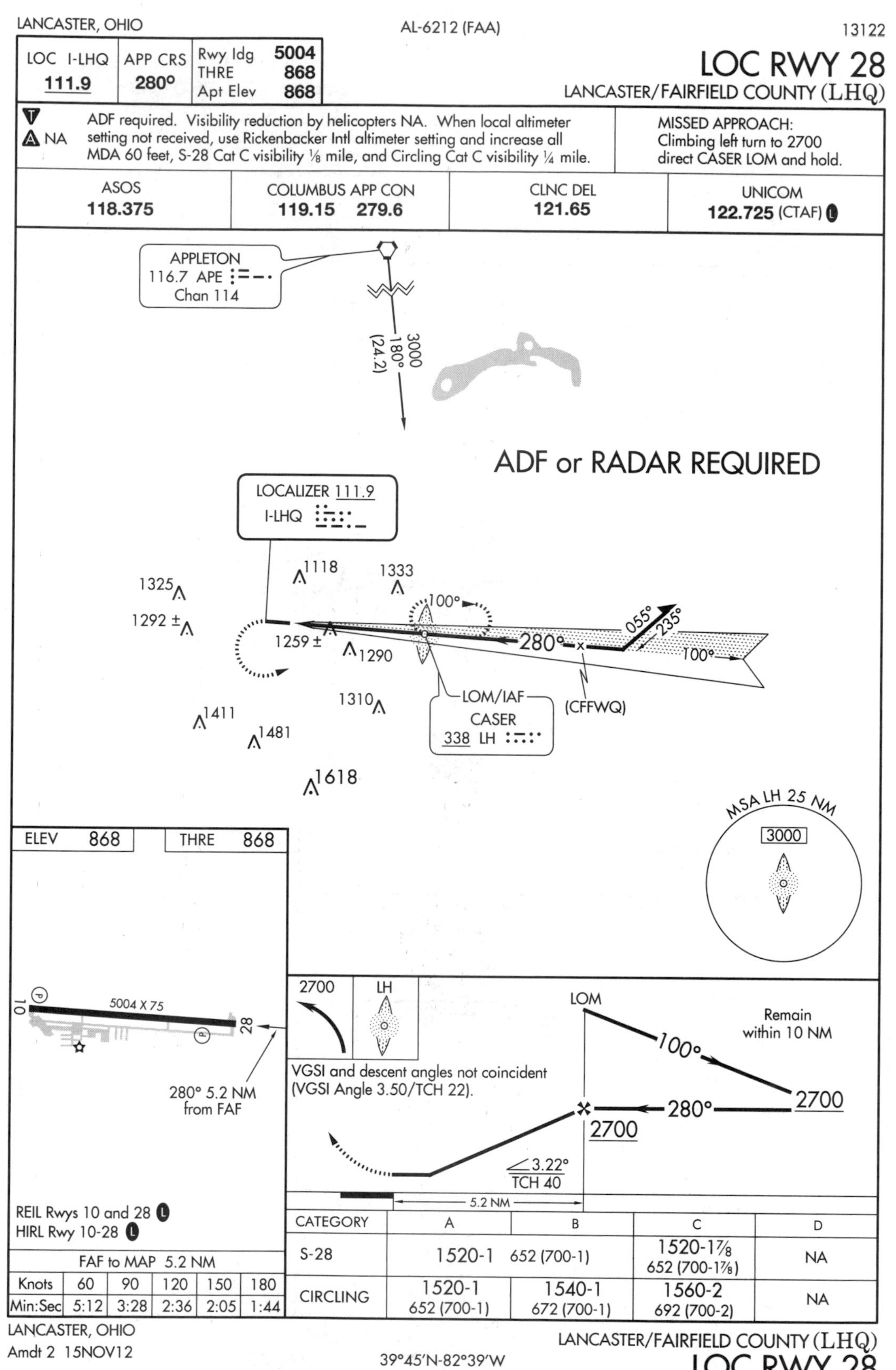

FIGURE 239.—LOC RWY 28 (LHQ).

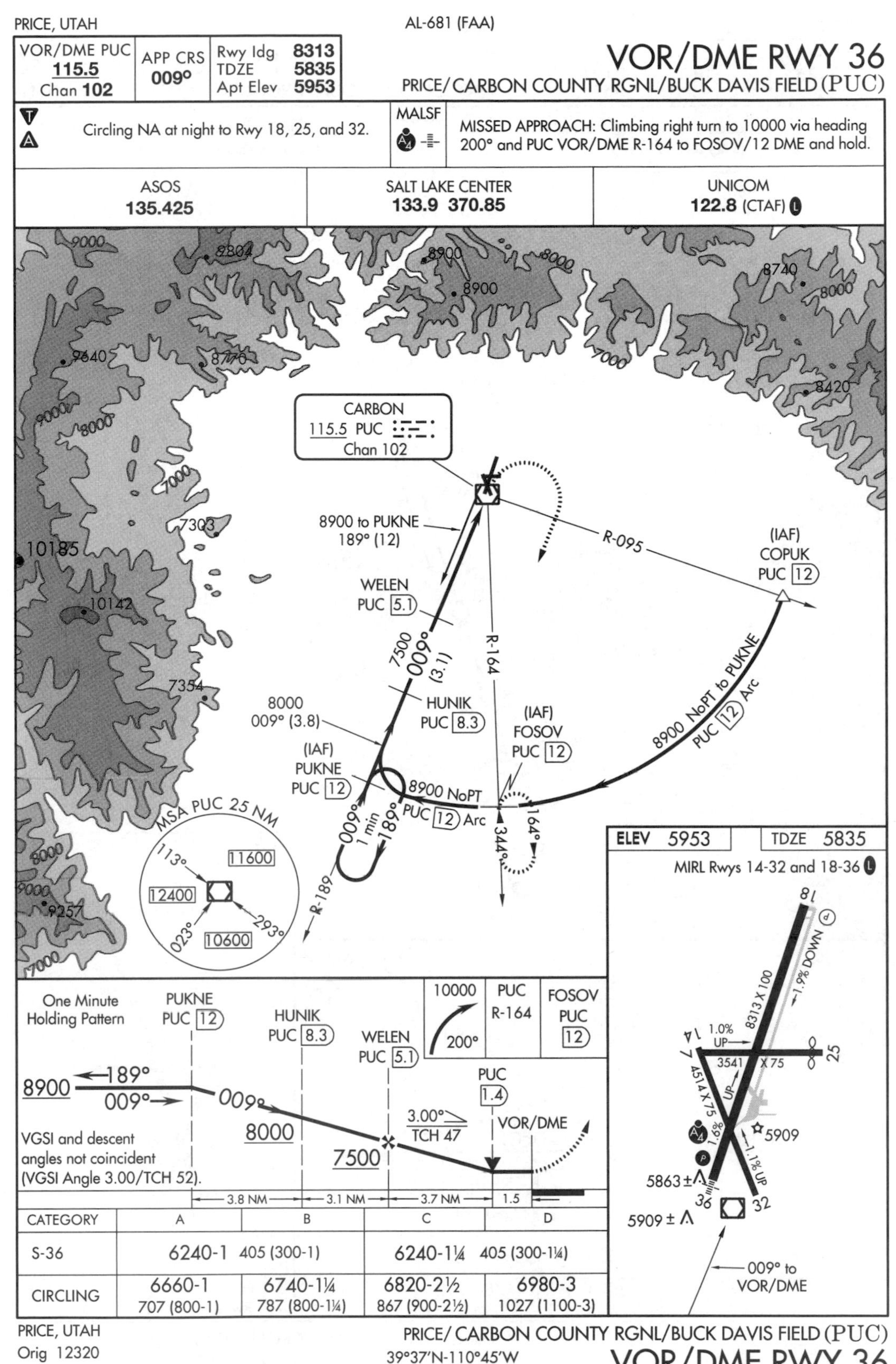

CATEGORY	A	B	C	D
S-36	6240-1 405 (300-1)		6240-1¼ 405 (300-1¼)	
CIRCLING	6660-1 707 (800-1)	6740-1¼ 787 (800-1¼)	6820-2½ 867 (900-2½)	6980-3 1027 (1100-3)

FIGURE 240.—VOR/DME RWY 36 (PUC).

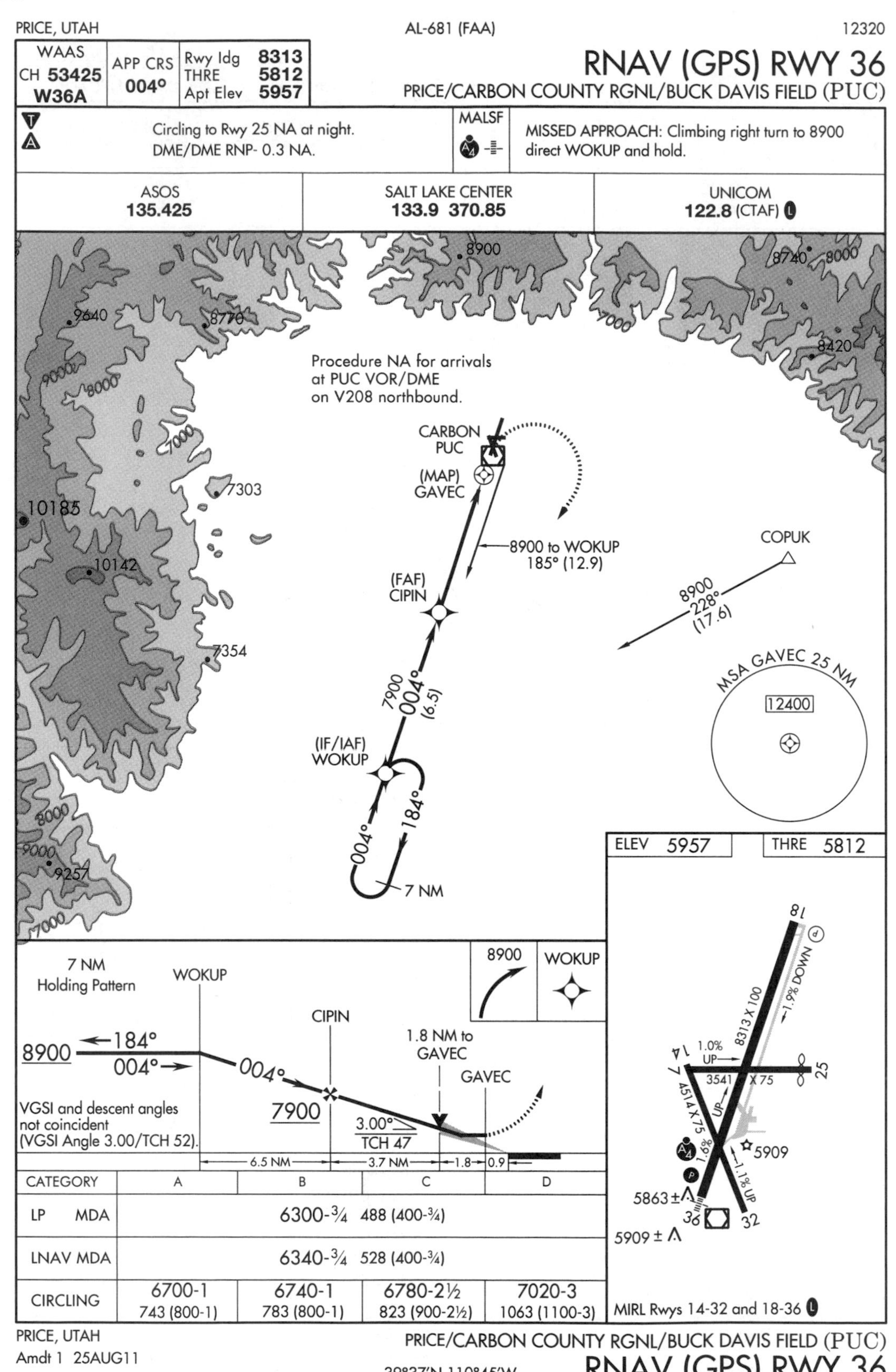

CATEGORY	A	B	C	D
LP MDA	6300-¾ 488 (400-¾)			
LNAV MDA	6340-¾ 528 (400-¾)			
CIRCLING	6700-1 743 (800-1)	6740-1 783 (800-1)	6780-2½ 823 (900-2½)	7020-3 1063 (1100-3)

FIGURE 241.—RNAV (GPS) RWY 36 (PUC).

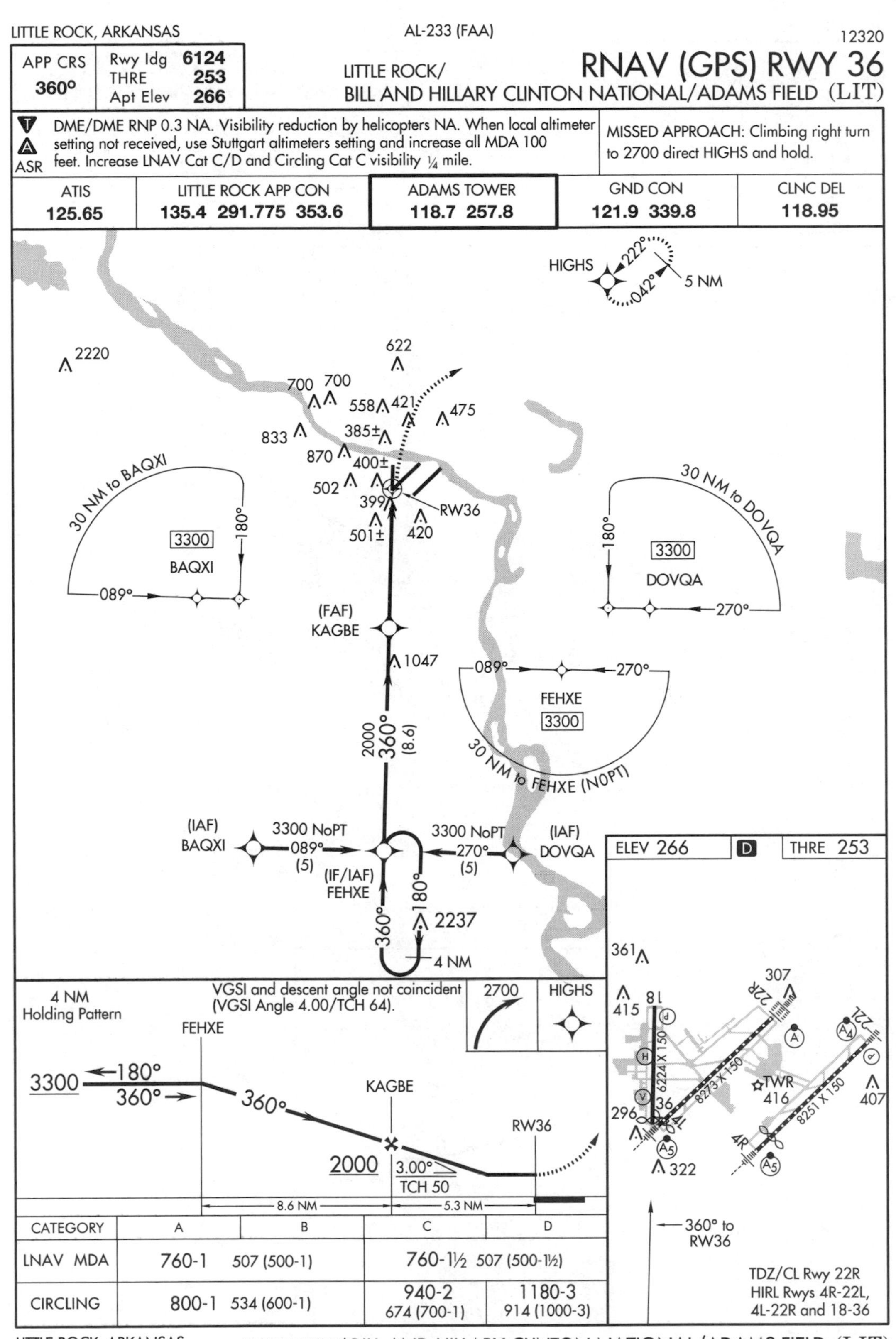

CATEGORY	A	B	C	D
LNAV MDA	760-1 507 (500-1)		760-1½ 507 (500-1½)	
CIRCLING	800-1 534 (600-1)		940-2 674 (700-1)	1180-3 914 (1000-3)

FIGURE 242.—RNAV RWY 36 (LIT).

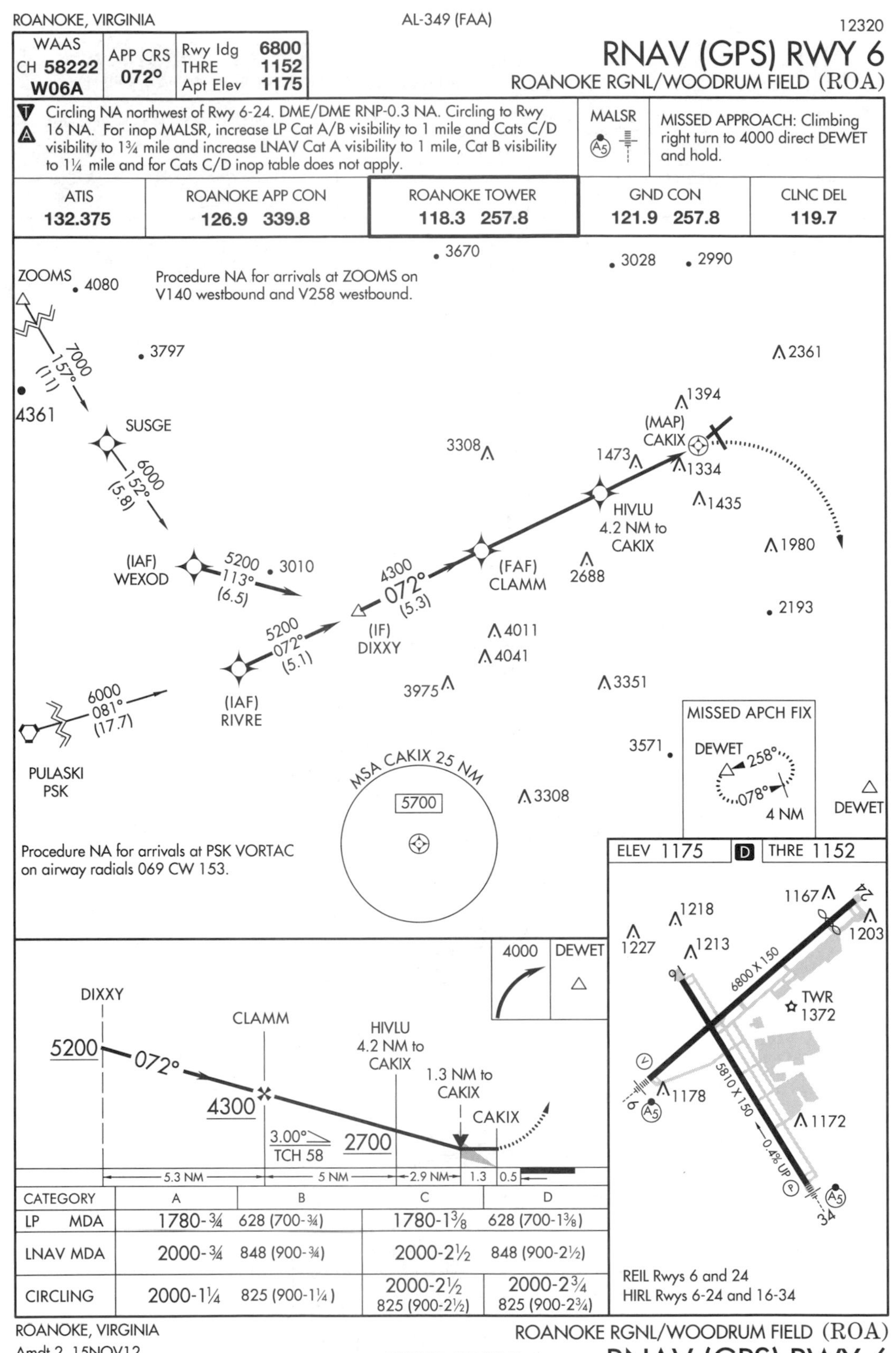

CATEGORY	A	B	C	D
LP MDA	1780-¾ 628 (700-¾)		1780-1⅜ 628 (700-1⅜)	
LNAV MDA	2000-¾ 848 (900-¾)		2000-2½ 848 (900-2½)	
CIRCLING	2000-1¼ 825 (900-1¼)		2000-2½ 825 (900-2½)	2000-2¾ 825 (900-2¾)

FIGURE 243.—RNAV (GPS) RWY 6 (ROA).

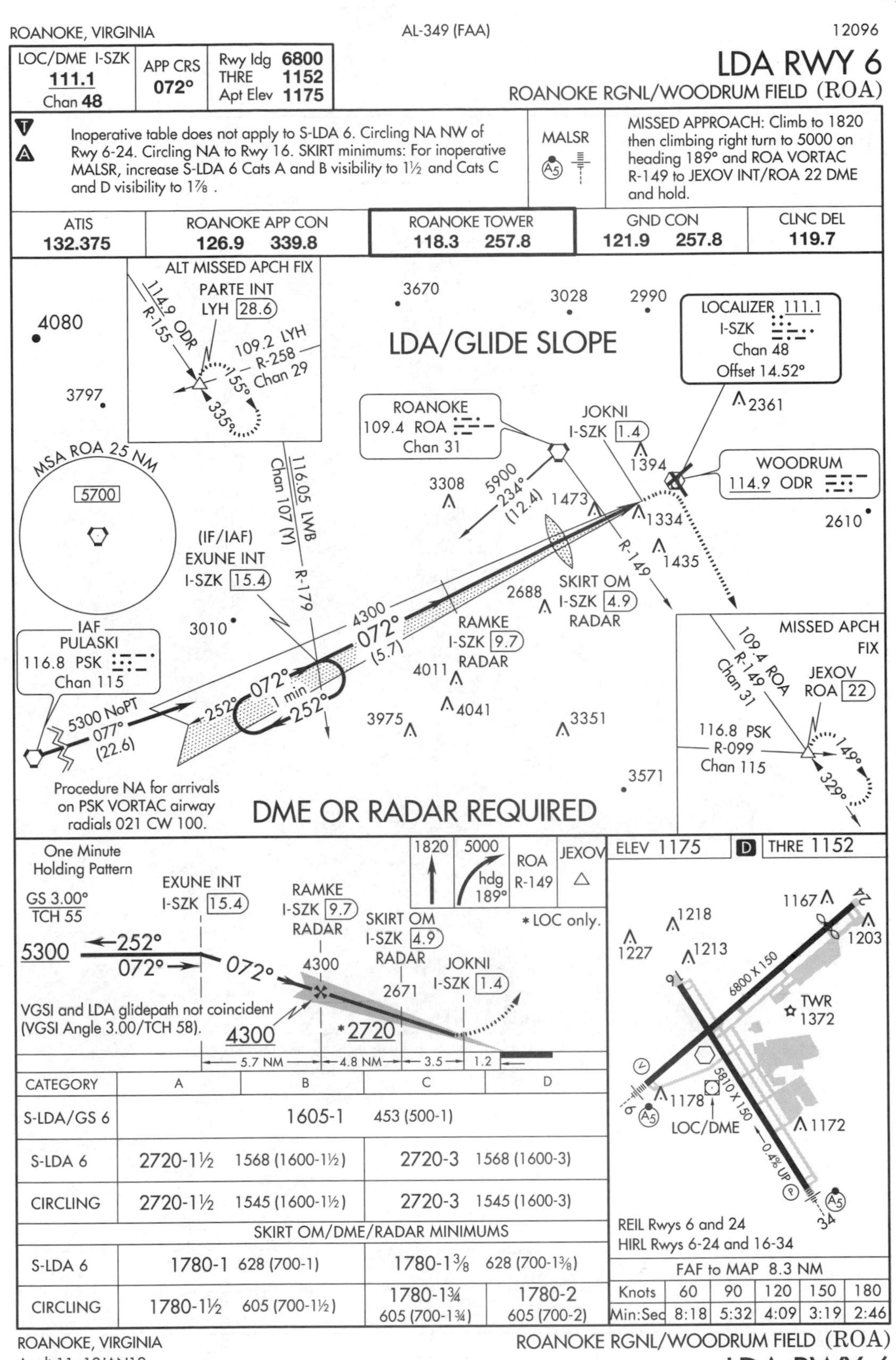

CATEGORY	A	B	C	D
S-LDA/GS 6	1605-1 453 (500-1)			
S-LDA 6	2720-1½ 1568 (1600-1½)		2720-3 1568 (1600-3)	
CIRCLING	2720-1½ 1545 (1600-1½)		2720-3 1545 (1600-3)	
SKIRT OM/DME/RADAR MINIMUMS				
S-LDA 6	1780-1 628 (700-1)		1780-1⅜ 628 (700-1⅜)	
CIRCLING	1780-1½ 605 (700-1½)		1780-1¾ 605 (700-1¾)	1780-2 605 (700-2)

FAF to MAP 8.3 NM					
Knots	60	90	120	150	180
Min:Sec	8:18	5:32	4:09	3:19	2:46

ROANOKE, VIRGINIA
Amdt 11 12JAN12
37°20′N-79°59′W
ROANOKE RGNL/WOODRUM FIELD (ROA)
LDA RWY 6

FIGURE 244.—LDA RWY 6 (ROA).

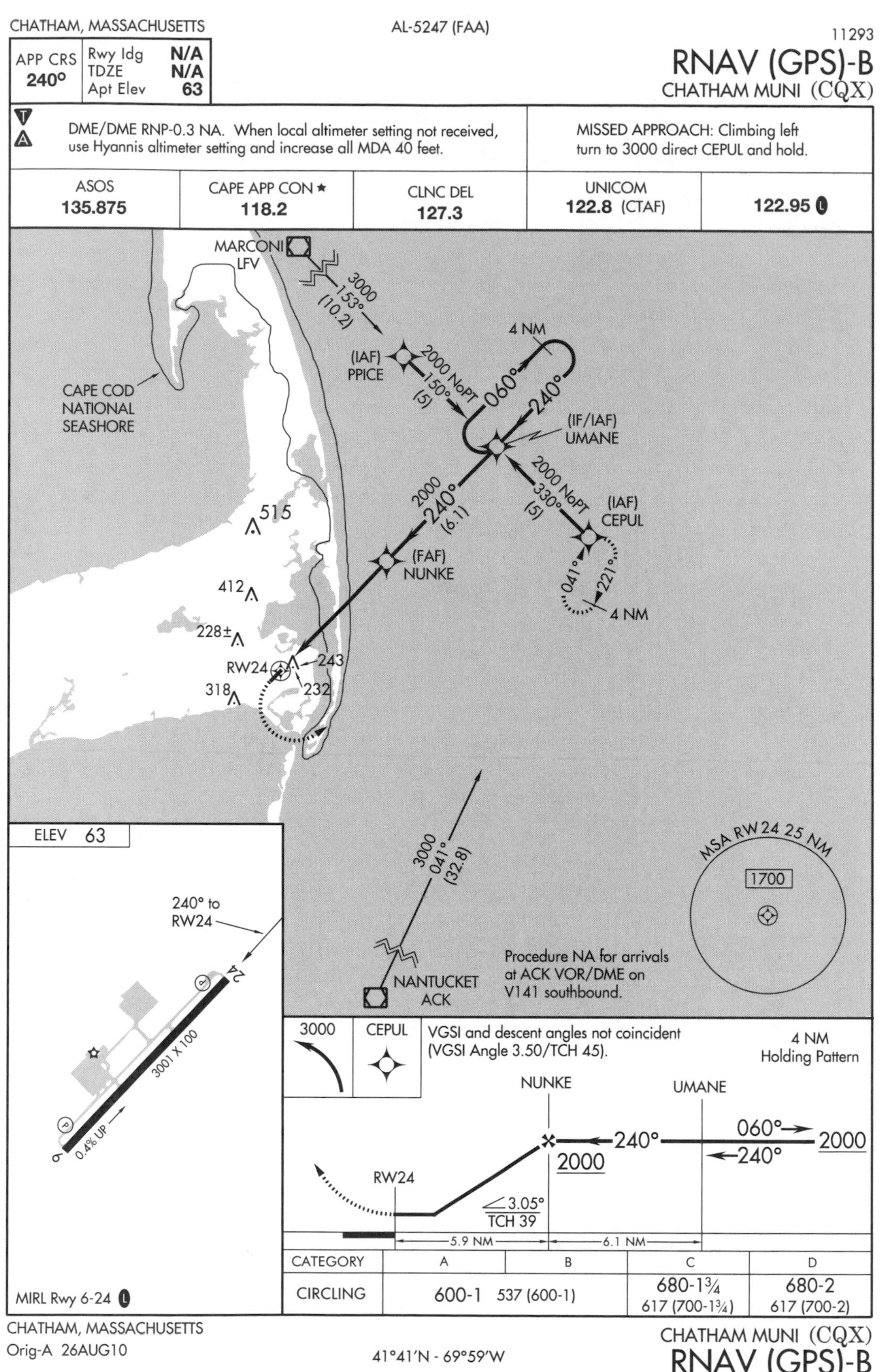

FIGURE 245.—RNAV (GPS)-B (CQX).

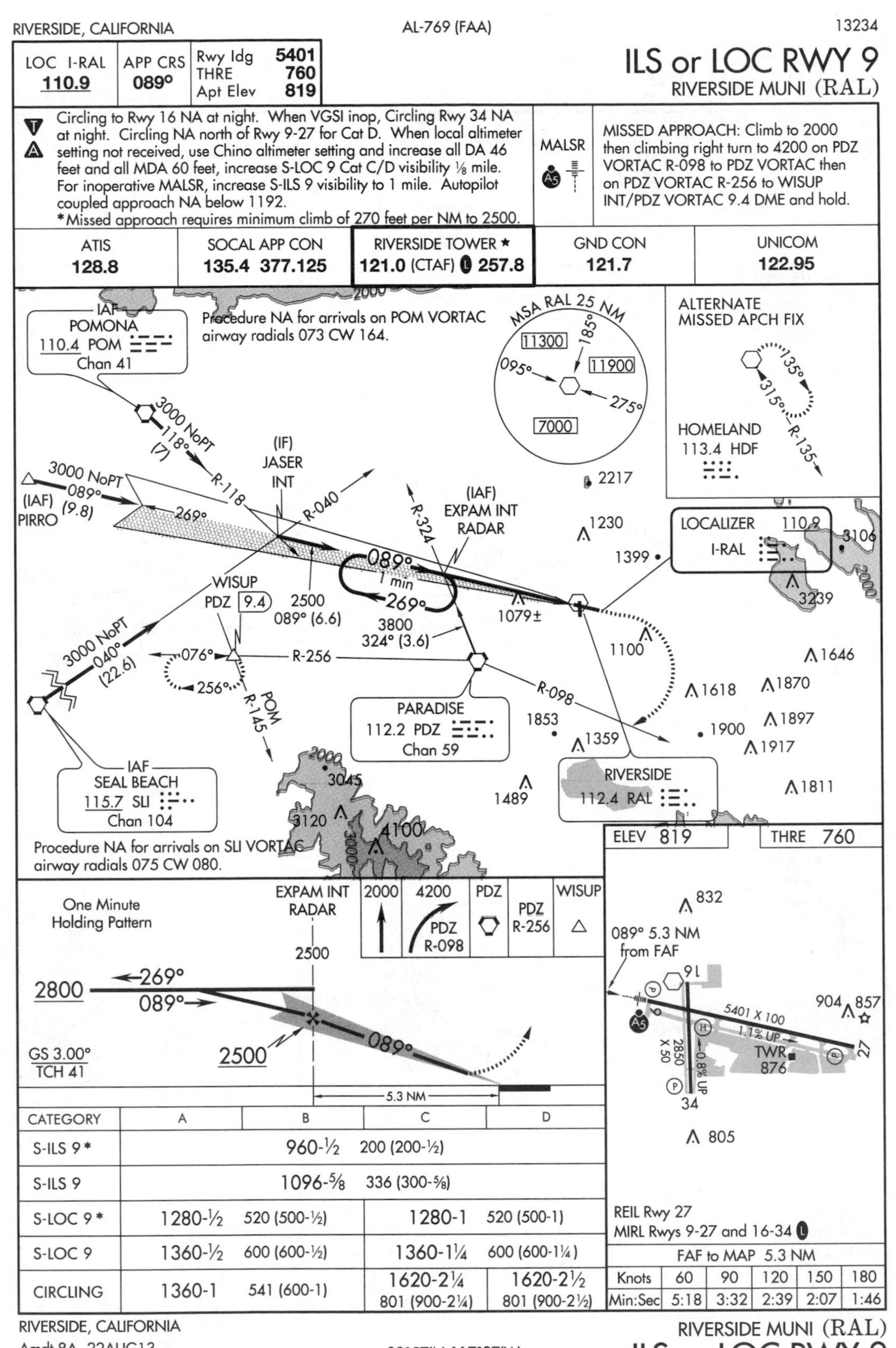

CATEGORY	A	B	C	D
S-ILS 9 *	960-½ 200 (200-½)			
S-ILS 9	1096-⅝ 336 (300-⅝)			
S-LOC 9 *	1280-½ 520 (500-½)		1280-1 520 (500-1)	
S-LOC 9	1360-½ 600 (600-½)		1360-1¼ 600 (600-1¼)	
CIRCLING	1360-1 541 (600-1)		1620-2¼ 801 (900-2¼)	1620-2½ 801 (900-2½)

FAF to MAP 5.3 NM

Knots	60	90	120	150	180
Min:Sec	5:18	3:32	2:39	2:07	1:46

FIGURE 247.—ILS or RWY 9 (RAL).

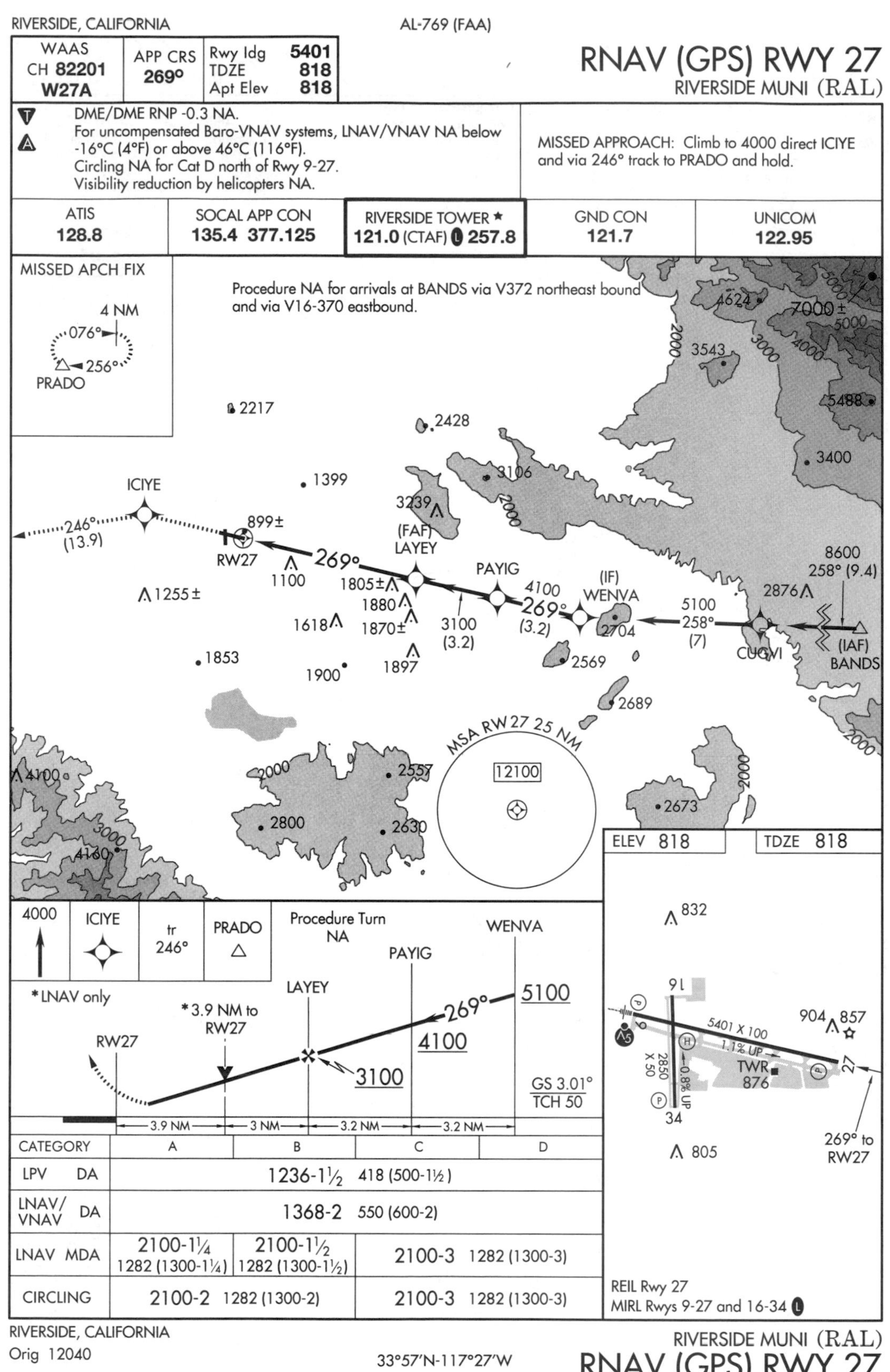

CATEGORY	A	B	C	D
LPV DA	1236-1½ 418 (500-1½)			
LNAV/VNAV DA	1368-2 550 (600-2)			
LNAV MDA	2100-1¼ 1282 (1300-1¼)	2100-1½ 1282 (1300-1½)	2100-3 1282 (1300-3)	
CIRCLING	2100-2 1282 (1300-2)		2100-3 1282 (1300-3)	

FIGURE 248.—RNAV (GPS) RWY 27 (RAL).

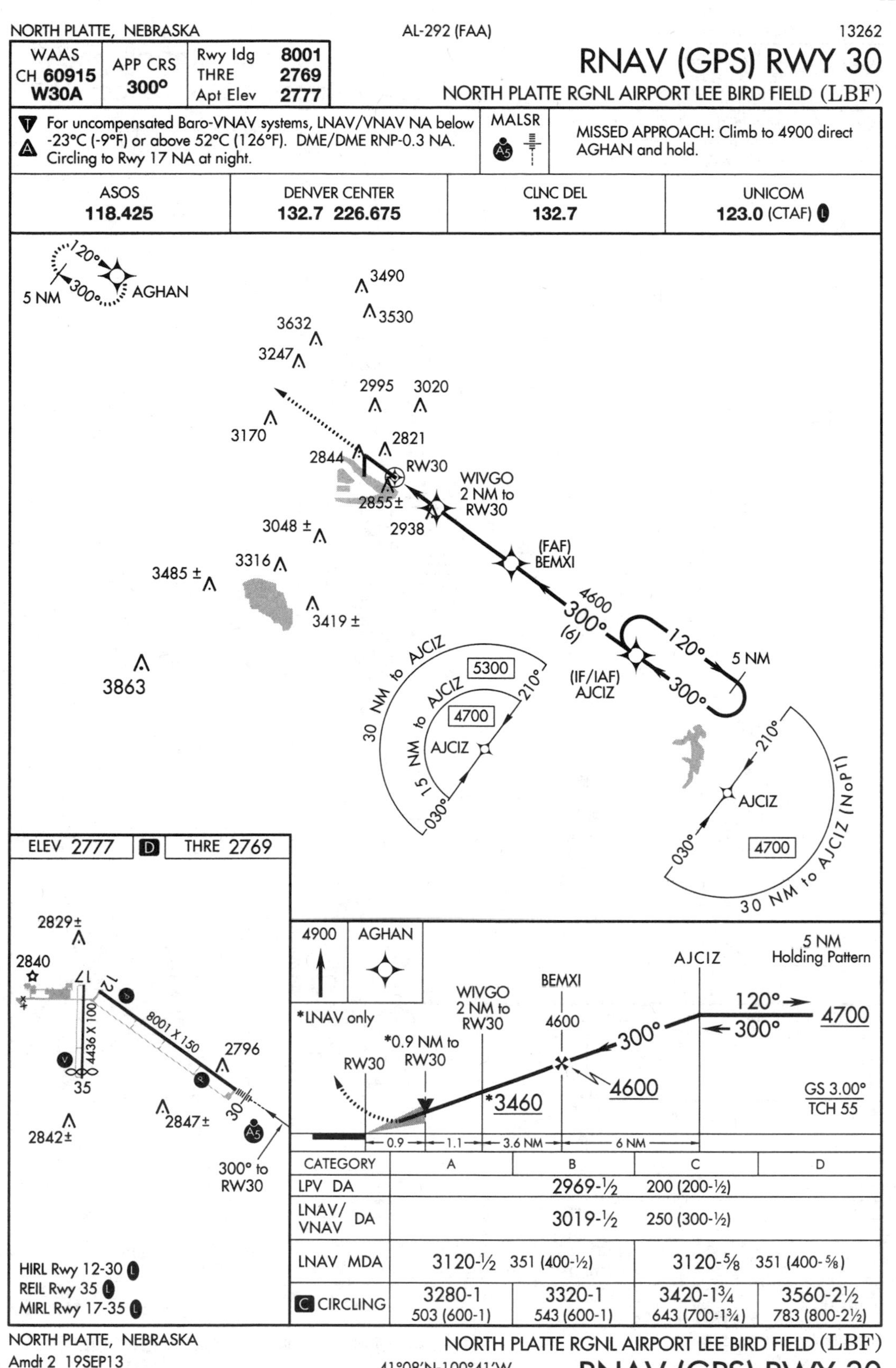

CATEGORY	A	B	C	D
LPV DA		2969-½ 200 (200-½)		
LNAV/VNAV DA		3019-½ 250 (300-½)		
LNAV MDA	3120-½ 351 (400-½)		3120-⅝ 351 (400-⅝)	
CIRCLING	3280-1 503 (600-1)	3320-1 543 (600-1)	3420-1¾ 643 (700-1¾)	3560-2½ 783 (800-2½)

NORTH PLATTE, NEBRASKA
Amdt 2 19SEP13

NORTH PLATTE RGNL AIRPORT LEE BIRD FIELD (LBF)
41°08'N-100°41'W
RNAV (GPS) RWY 30

FIGURE 249.—RNAV (GPS) RWY 30 (LBF).

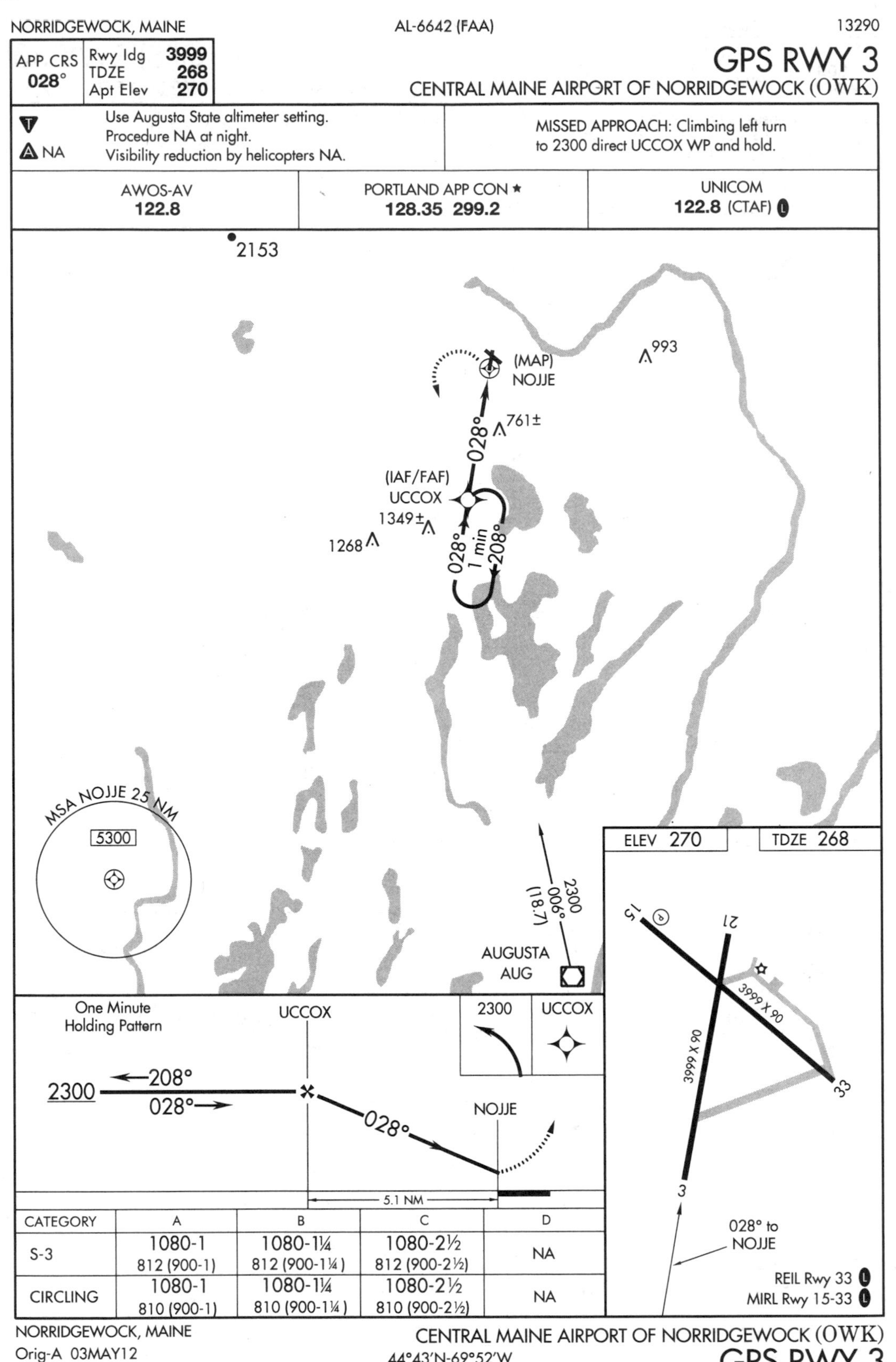

FIGURE 250.—GPS RWY 3 (OWK).

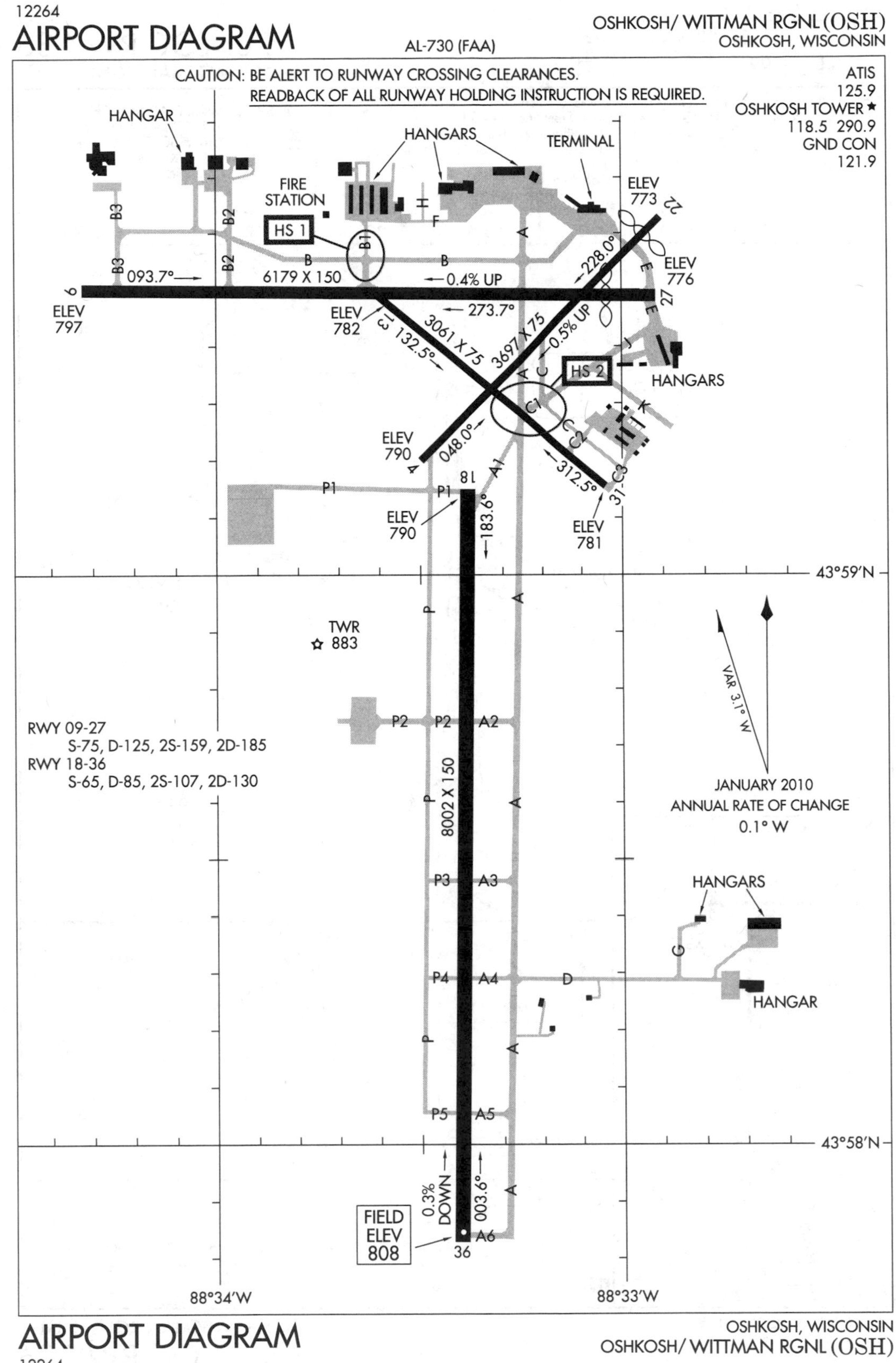

FIGURE 251.—Airport Diagram: Osh Kosh/Wittman Regional (OSH).

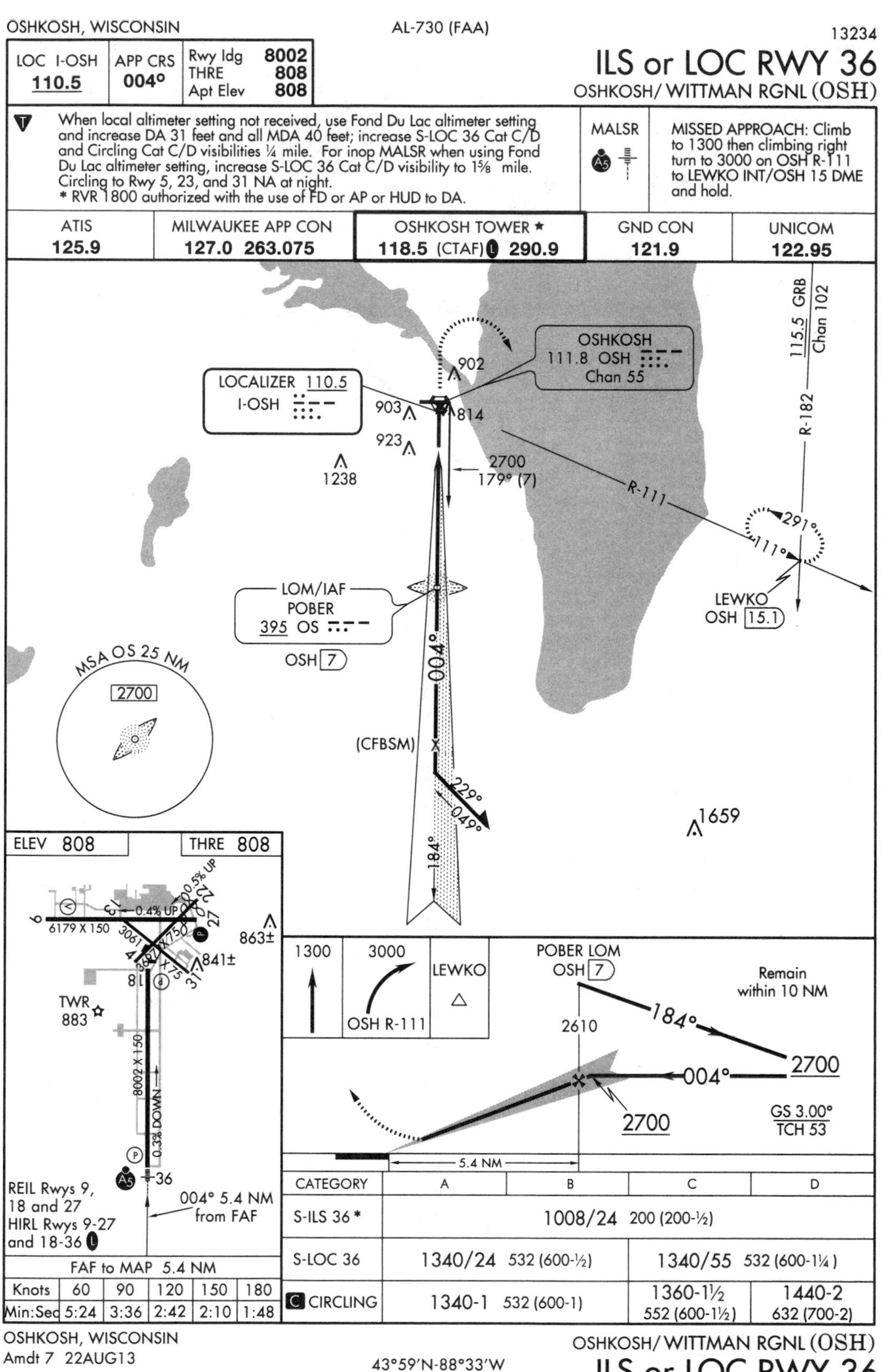

FAF to MAP 5.4 NM					
Knots	60	90	120	150	180
Min:Sec	5:24	3:36	2:42	2:10	1:48

CATEGORY	A	B	C	D
S-ILS 36 *	1008/24 200 (200-½)			
S-LOC 36	1340/24 532 (600-½)		1340/55 532 (600-1¼)	
CIRCLING	1340-1 532 (600-1)		1360-1½ 552 (600-1½)	1440-2 632 (700-2)

FIGURE 252.—ILS or LOC RWY 36 (OSH).

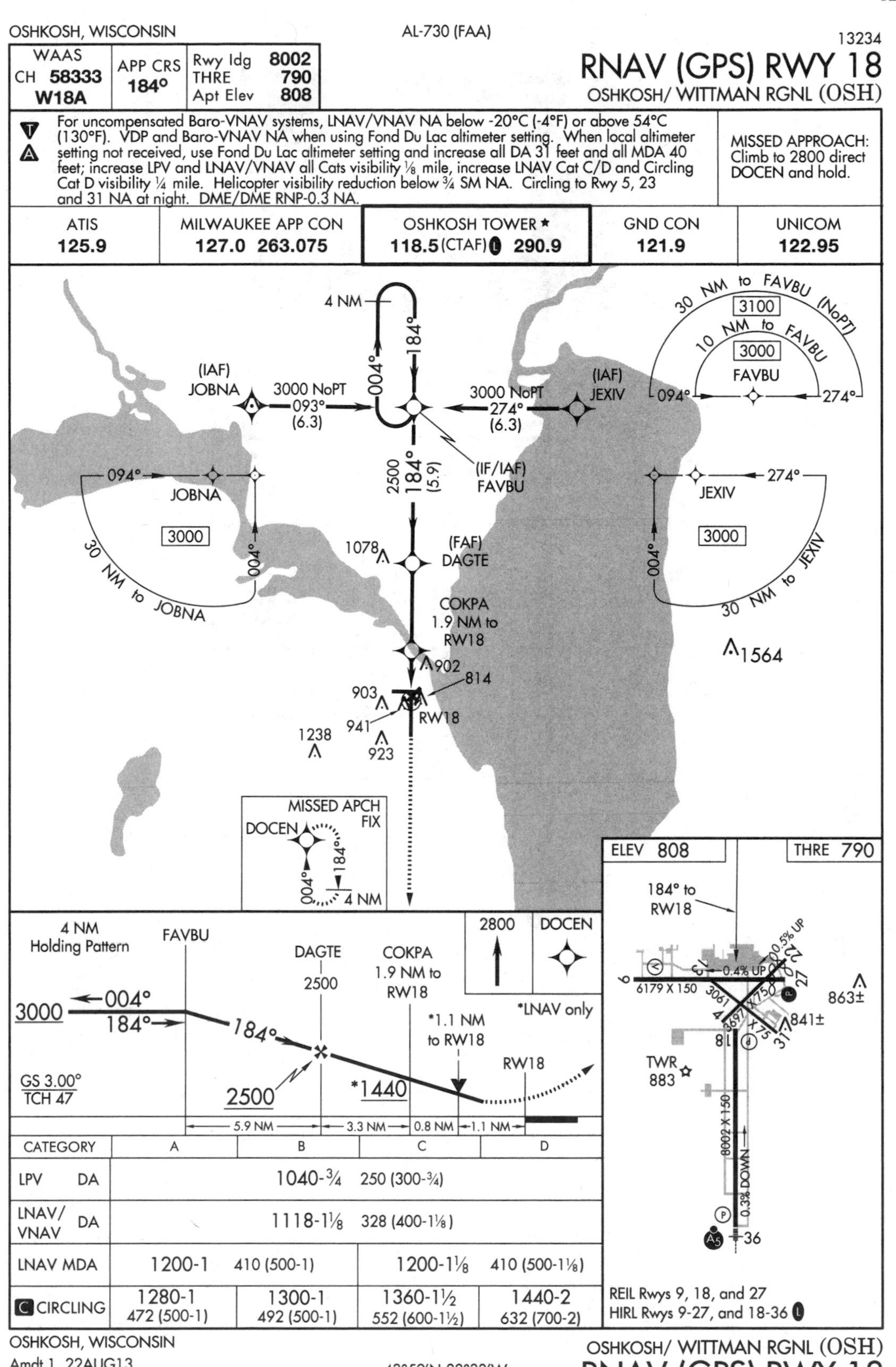

CATEGORY	A	B	C	D
LPV DA	1040-¾ 250 (300-¾)			
LNAV/VNAV DA	1118-1⅛ 328 (400-1⅛)			
LNAV MDA	1200-1 410 (500-1)		1200-1⅛ 410 (500-1⅛)	
CIRCLING	1280-1 472 (500-1)	1300-1 492 (500-1)	1360-1½ 552 (600-1½)	1440-2 632 (700-2)

FIGURE 253.—RNAV (GPS) RWY 18 (OSH).

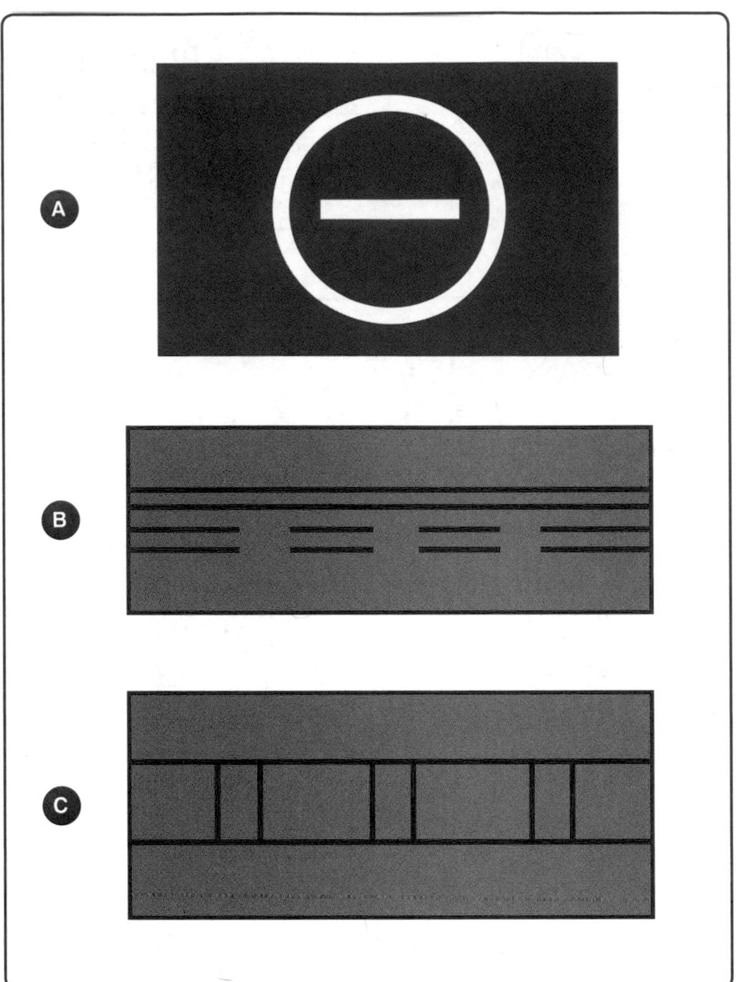

FIGURE 254.—Airport Sign.

FIGURE 255.—Two Signs.

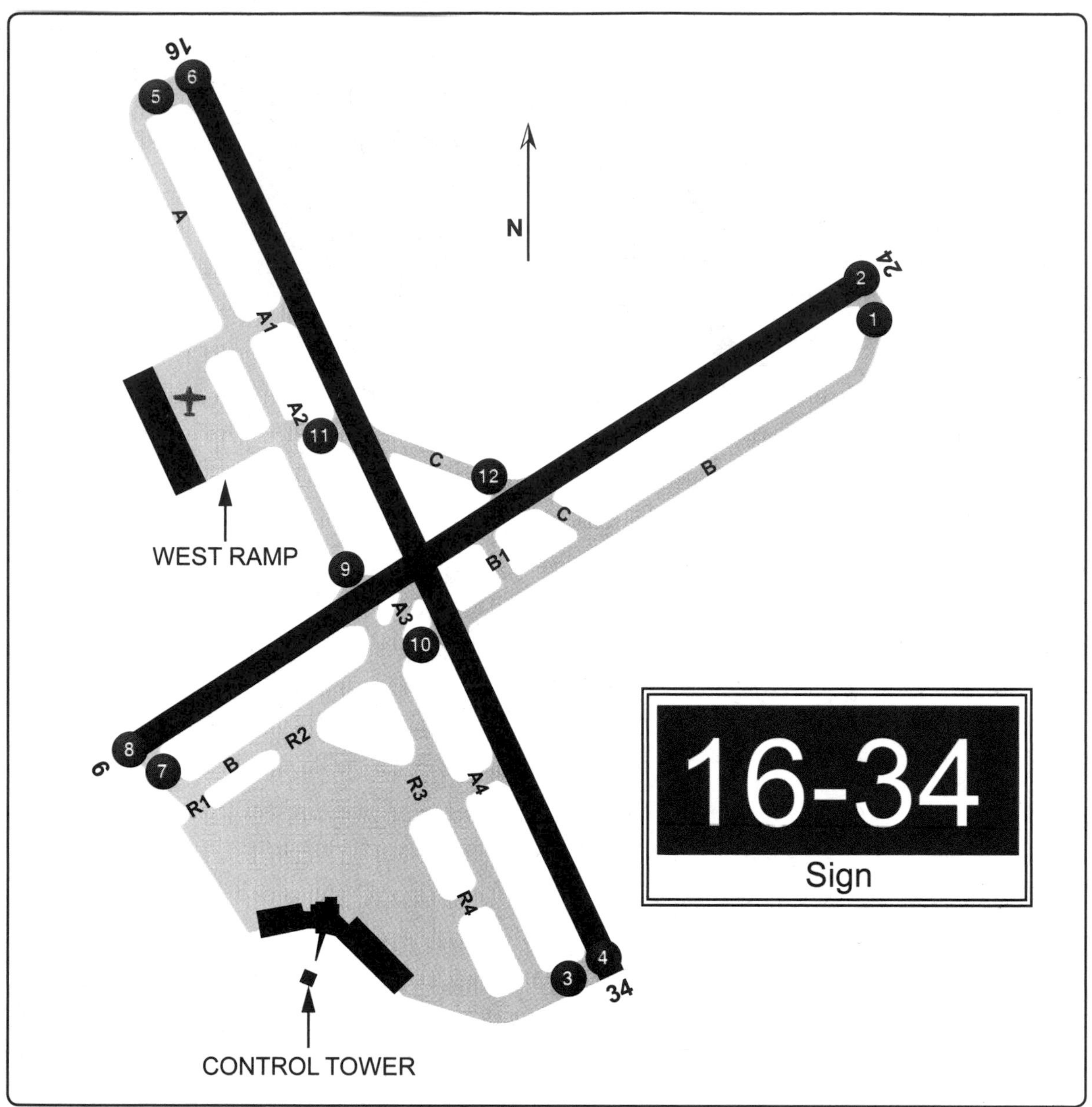

FIGURE 256.—Airport Diagram and Sign.

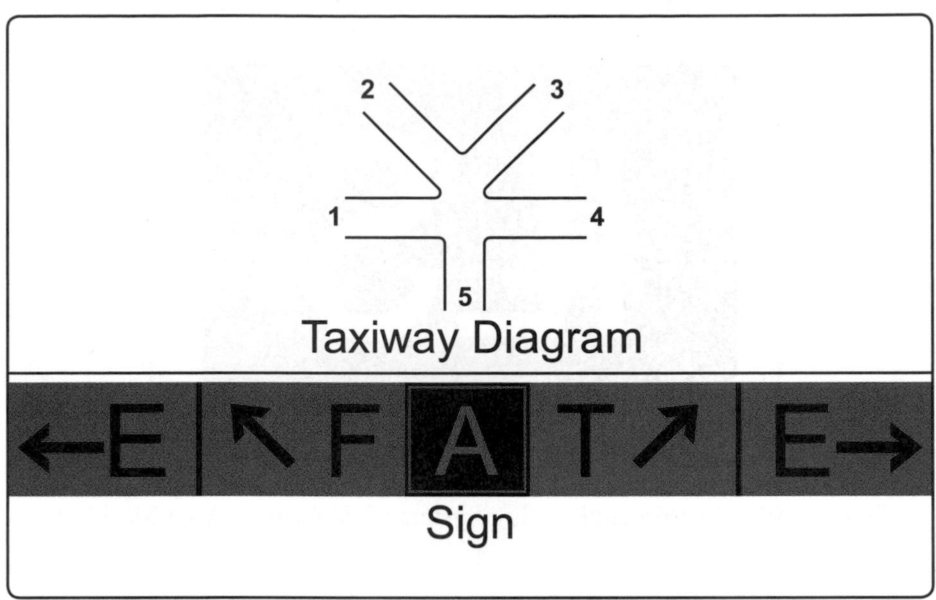

FIGURE 257.—Taxiway Diagram and Sign.

FIGURE 258.—Instrument Landing System (ILS) Critical Area Markings.

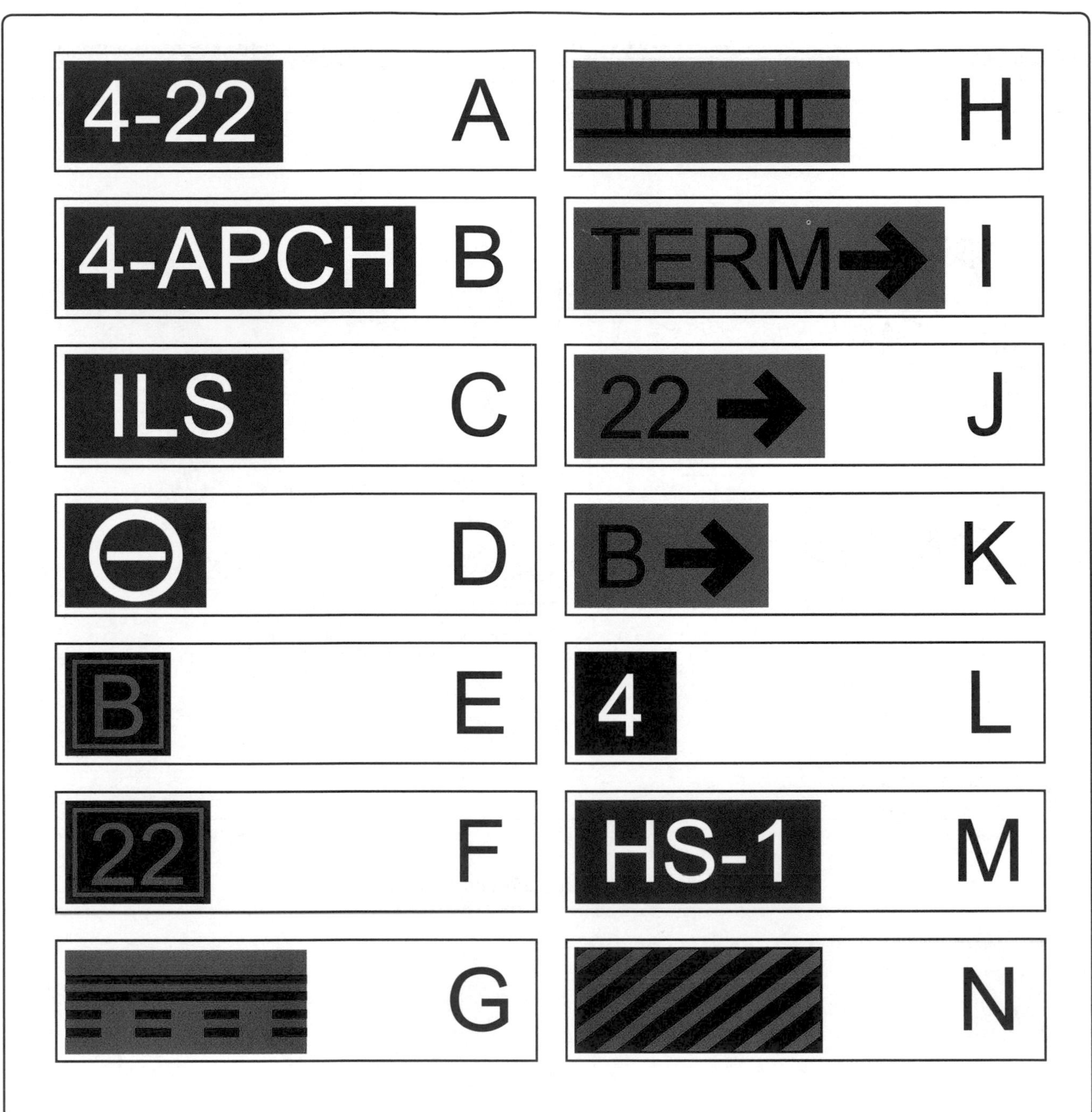

FIGURE 259.—Airport Signs.

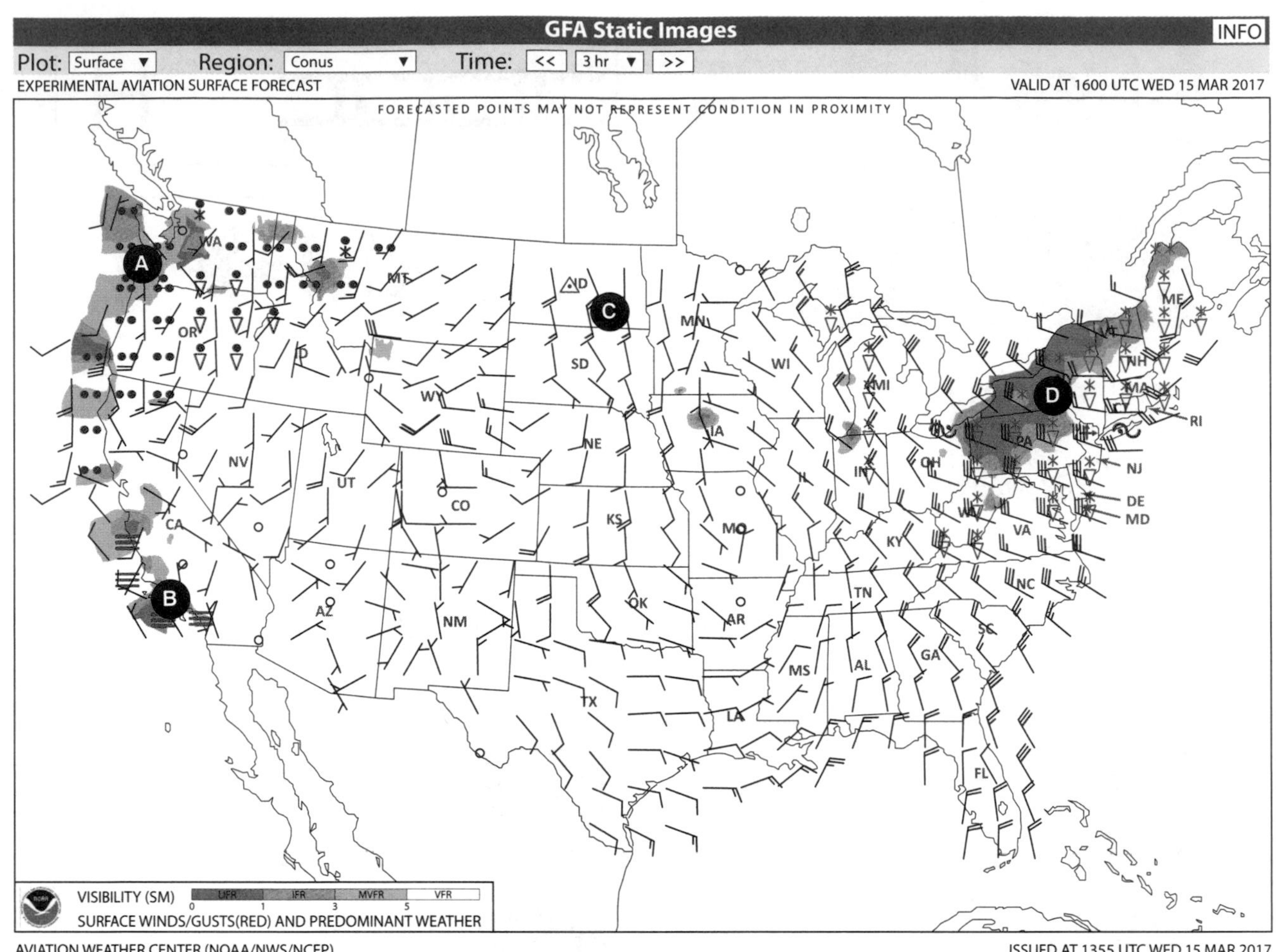

FIGURE 260.—Graphical Forecast for Aviation.

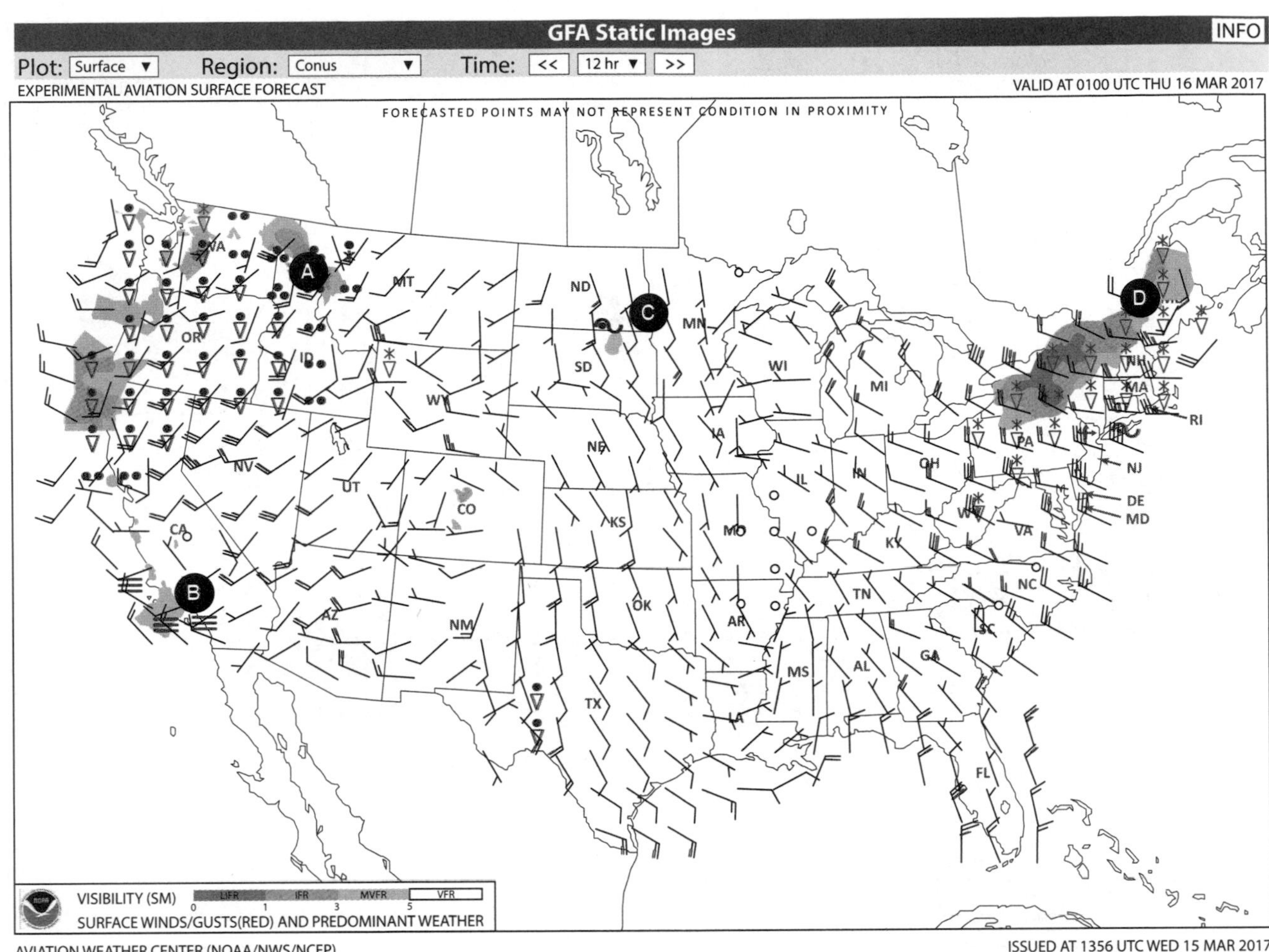

FIGURE 261.—Graphical Forecast for Aviation.

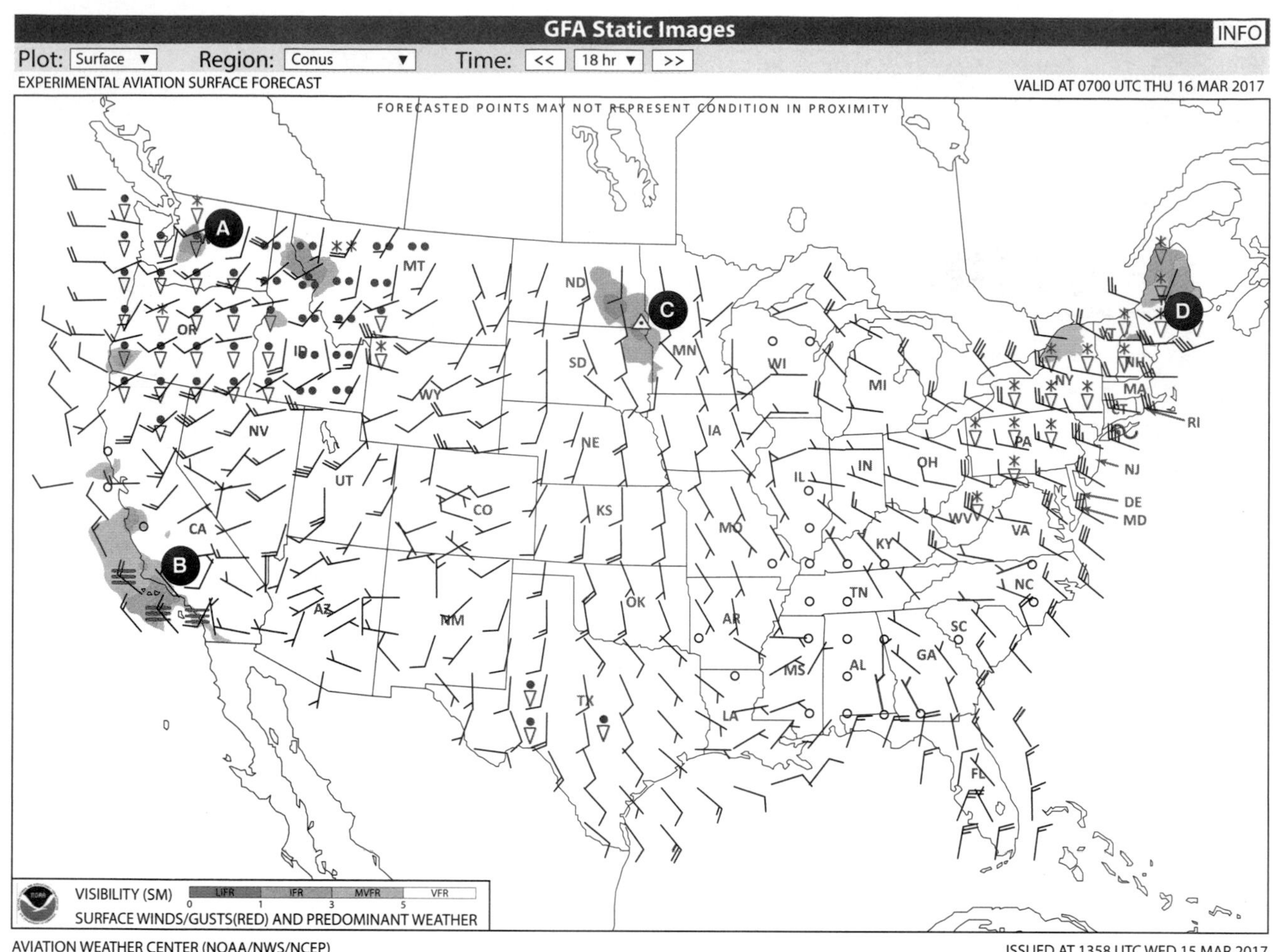

FIGURE 262.—Graphical Forecast for Aviation.

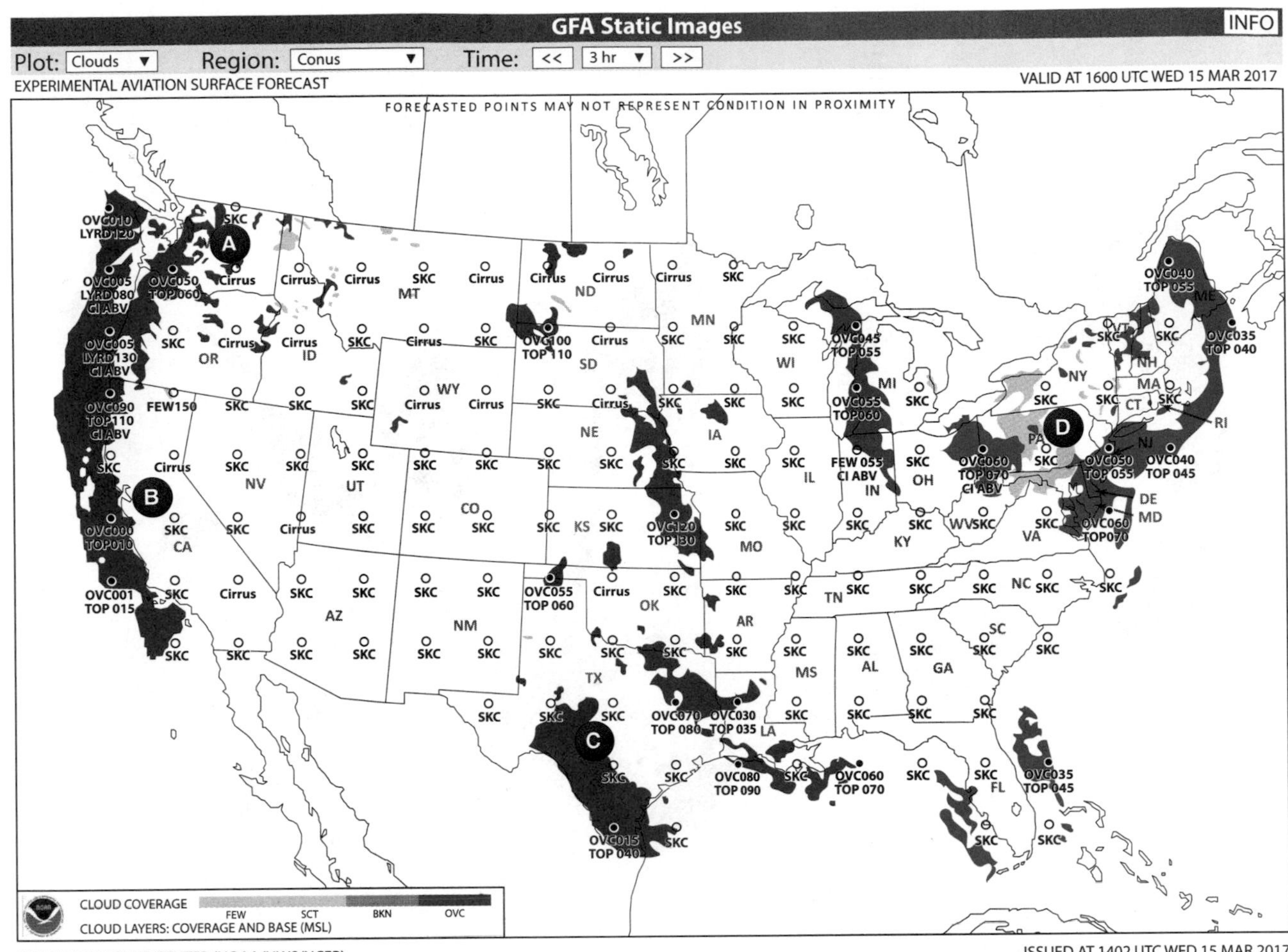

FIGURE 263.—Graphical Forecast for Aviation.

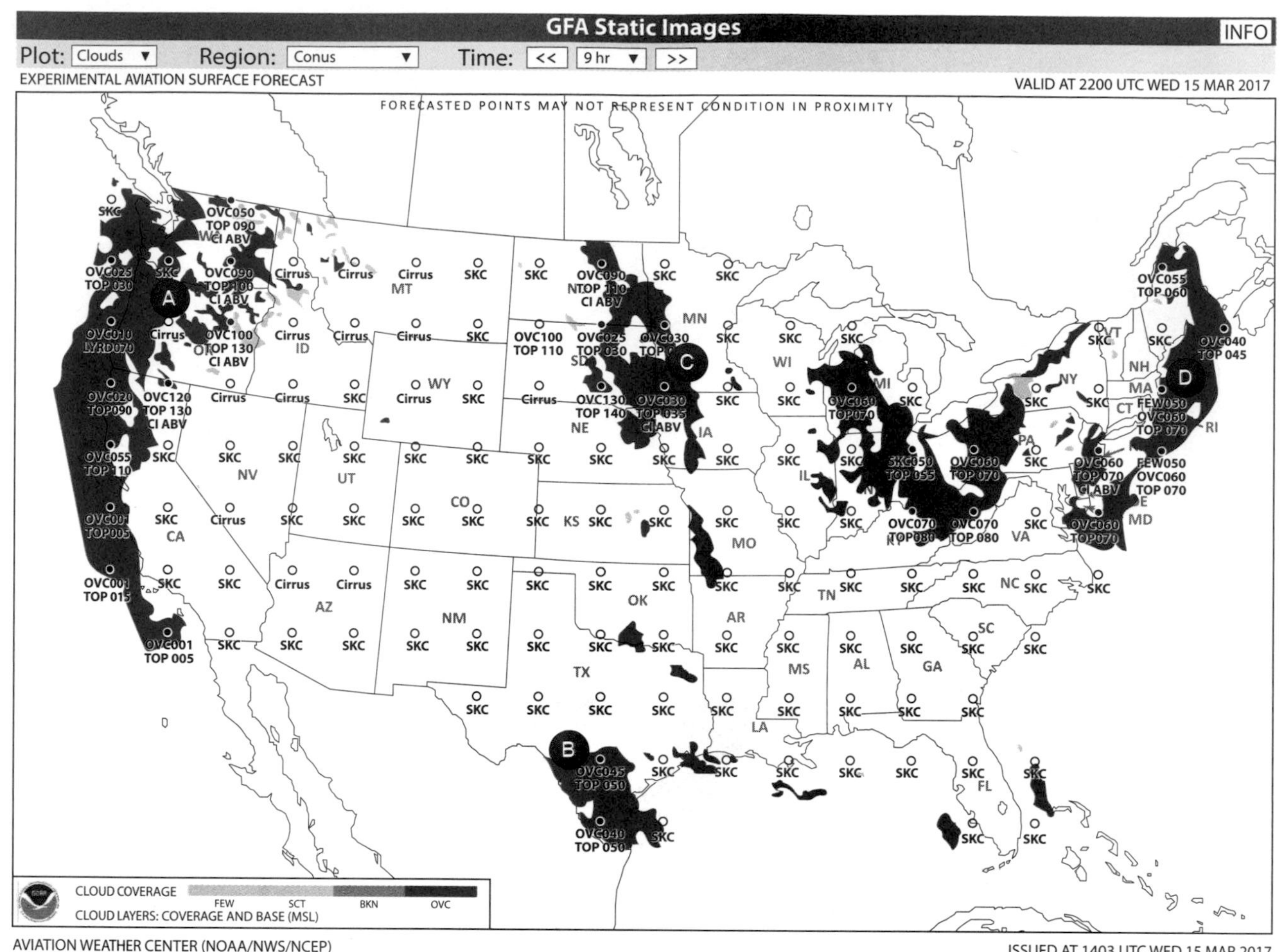

FIGURE 264.—Graphical Forecast for Aviation.

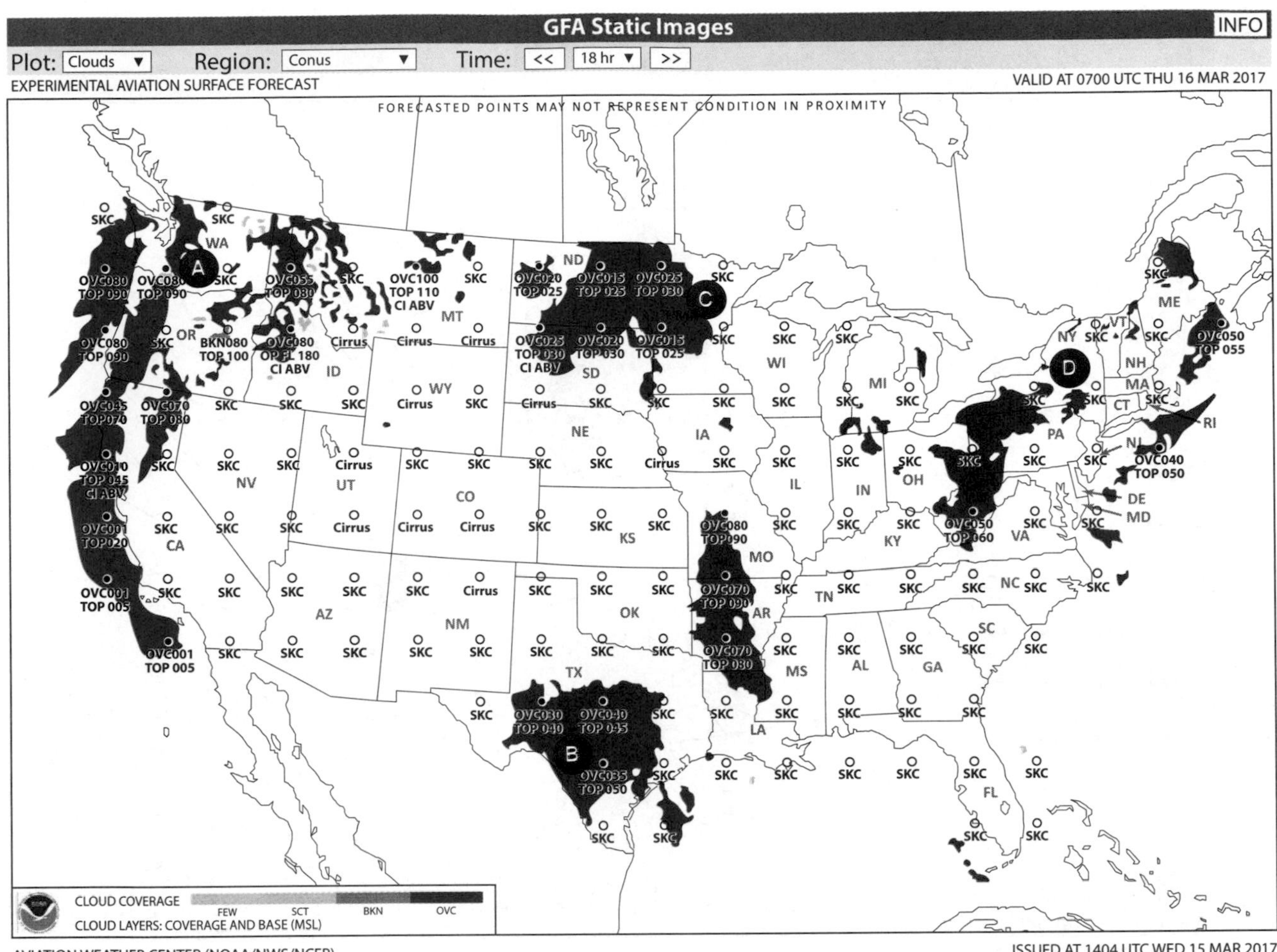

FIGURE 265.—Graphical Forecast for Aviation.

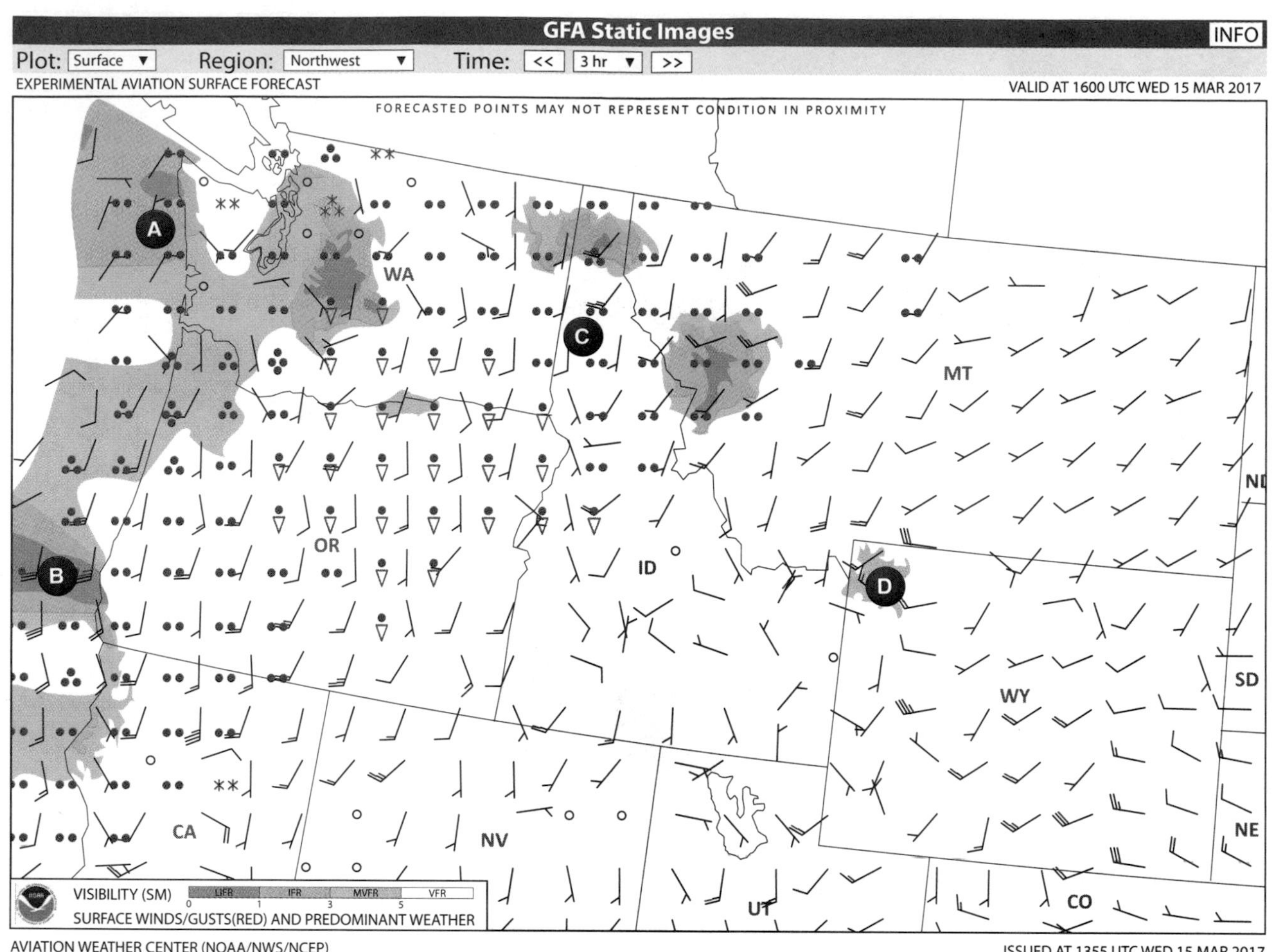

FIGURE 266.—Graphical Forecast for Aviation.

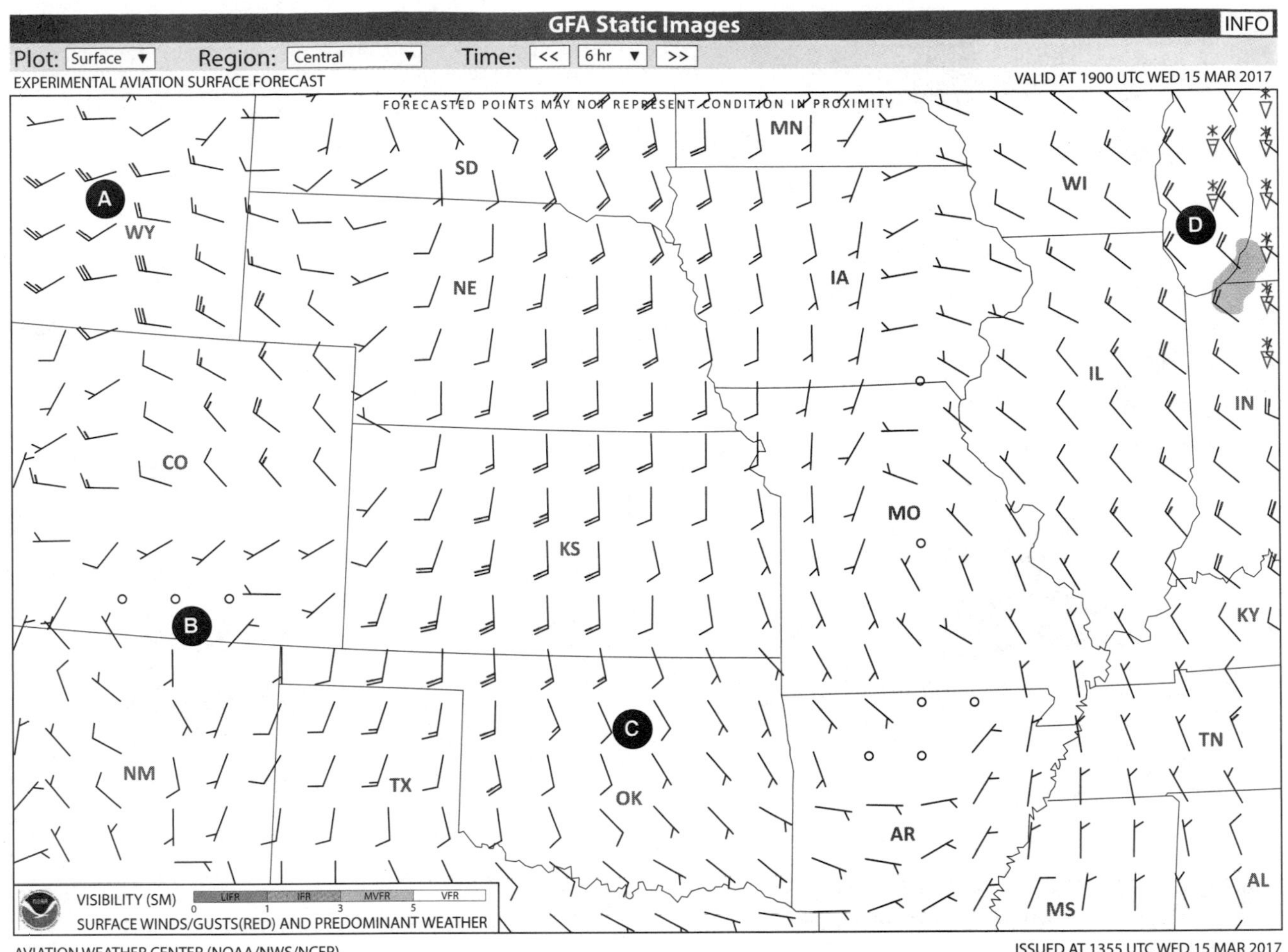

FIGURE 267.—Graphical Forecast for Aviation.

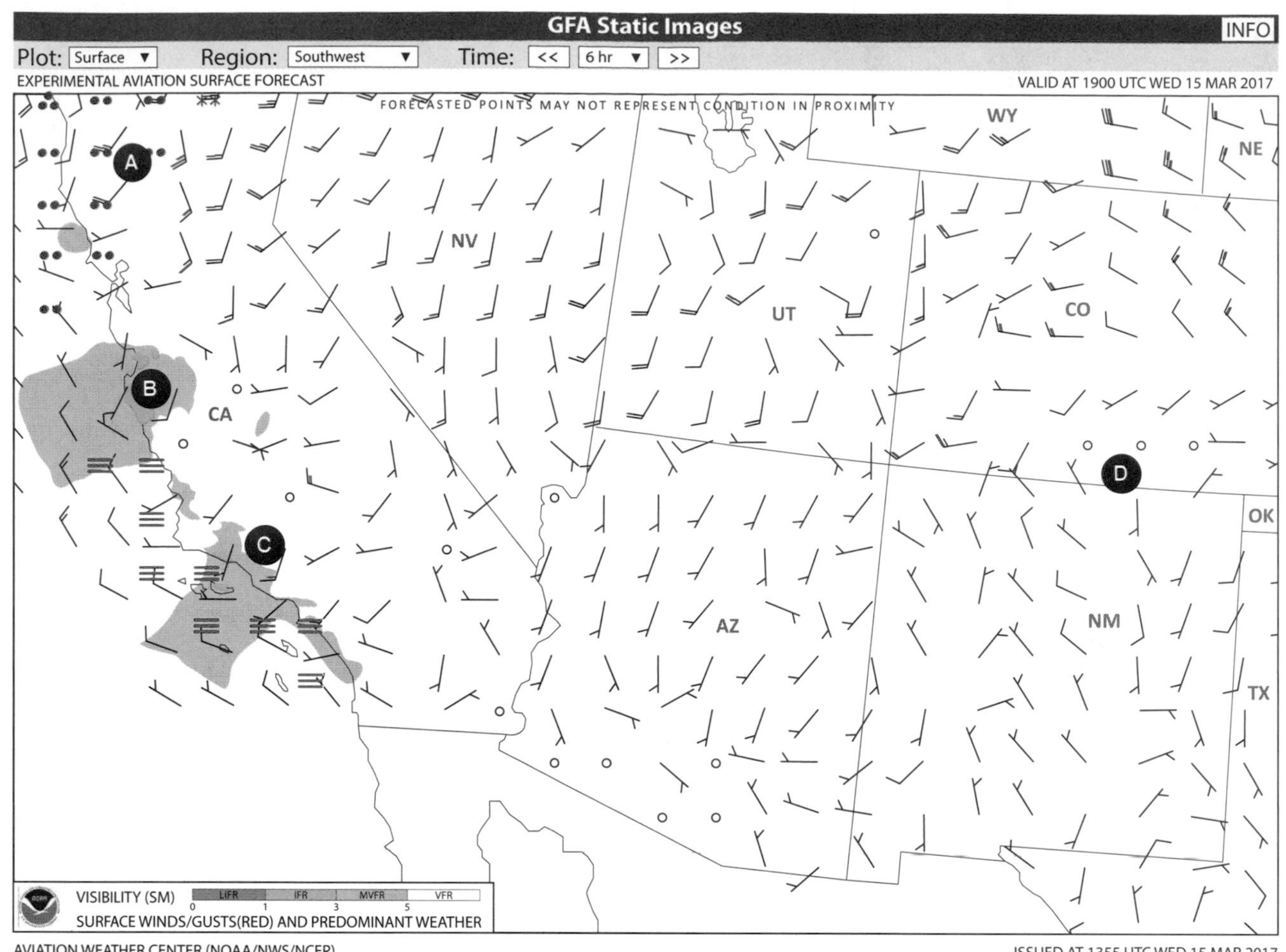

FIGURE 268.—Graphical Forecast for Aviation.

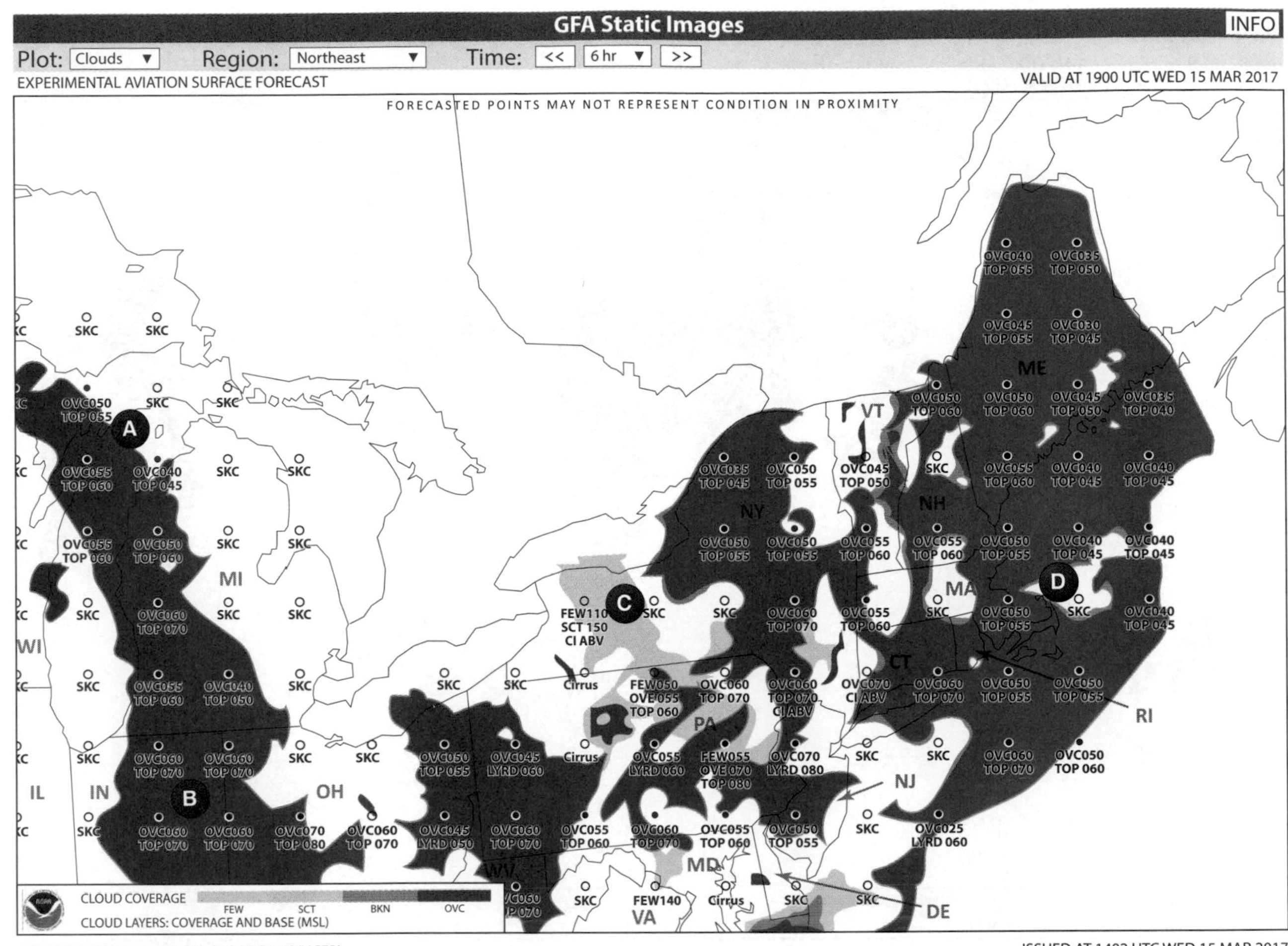

FIGURE 269.—Graphical Forecast for Aviation.

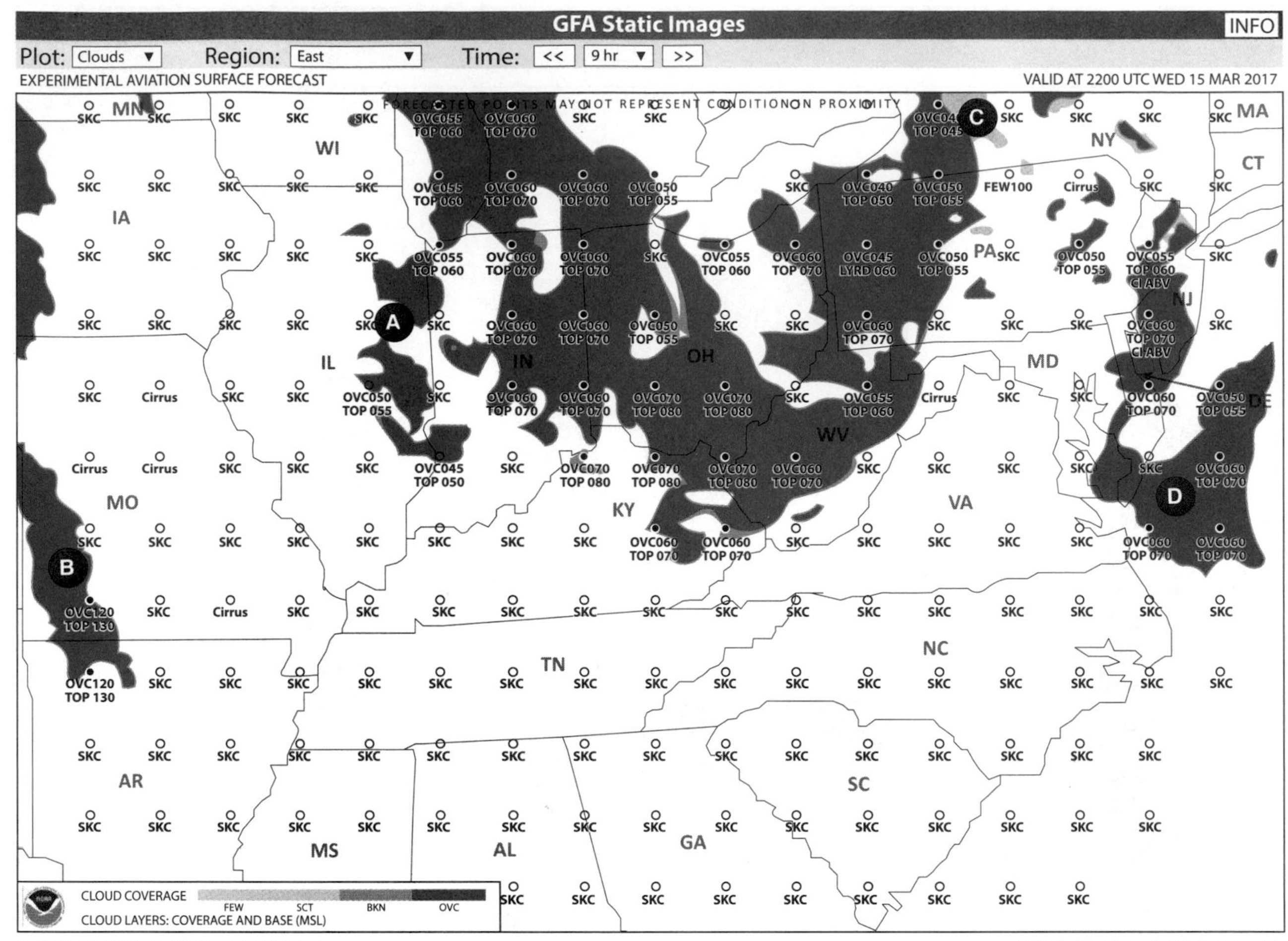

FIGURE 270.—Graphical Forecast for Aviation.

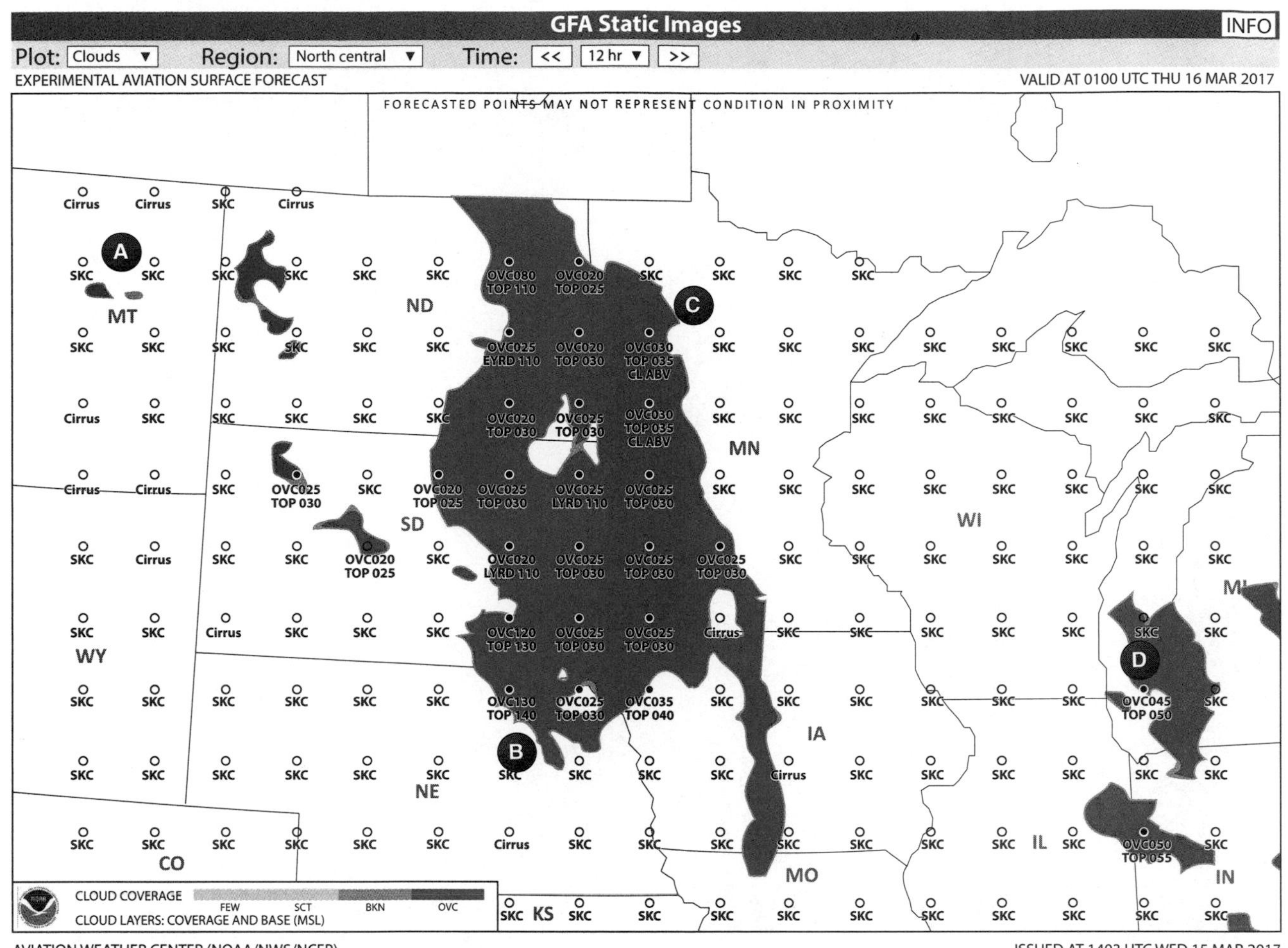

FIGURE 271.—Graphical Forecast for Aviation.